Connect to history

History is more than a chronology of facts. It is an exploration of **big ideas** across time and place. Using the concepts below will help you **understand** and enjoy the study of history by connecting with the **drama** and **meaning** of the human experience.

Explore these concepts to make valuable connections to history.

History

Empire What factors allow empires to rise and cause them to fall?

Cooperation In what ways have groups or countries cooperated over time?

Conflict What issues cause peoples or countries to come into conflict?

Revolution Why have political revolutions occurred?

Nationalism How have people used nationalism as a basis for their actions?

Genocide What factors have led peoples or governments to commit genocide?

Culture

Cultural Diffusion In what ways have migration and trade affected cultures?

Belief Systems What major belief systems have emerged over time?

Science & Technology

Science How has science changed people's lives throughout history?

Technology How has technology affected human development?

Government

Democracy How has democracy developed over time?

Political Systems What types of political systems have societies used to govern and create laws?

Dictatorship How have dictators assumed and maintained power?

Economics

Trade What have been the major trade networks in world history?

Economic Systems What types of economic systems have societies used to produce and distribute goods and services?

Geography

Migration Why do large groups of people move from one place to another?

Geography's Impact How have geographic factors affected the course of history?

People and the Environment What impact have people had on the environment?

Science and technology through time ▶

PRENTICE HALL

WORLD HISTORY
THE MODERN ERA

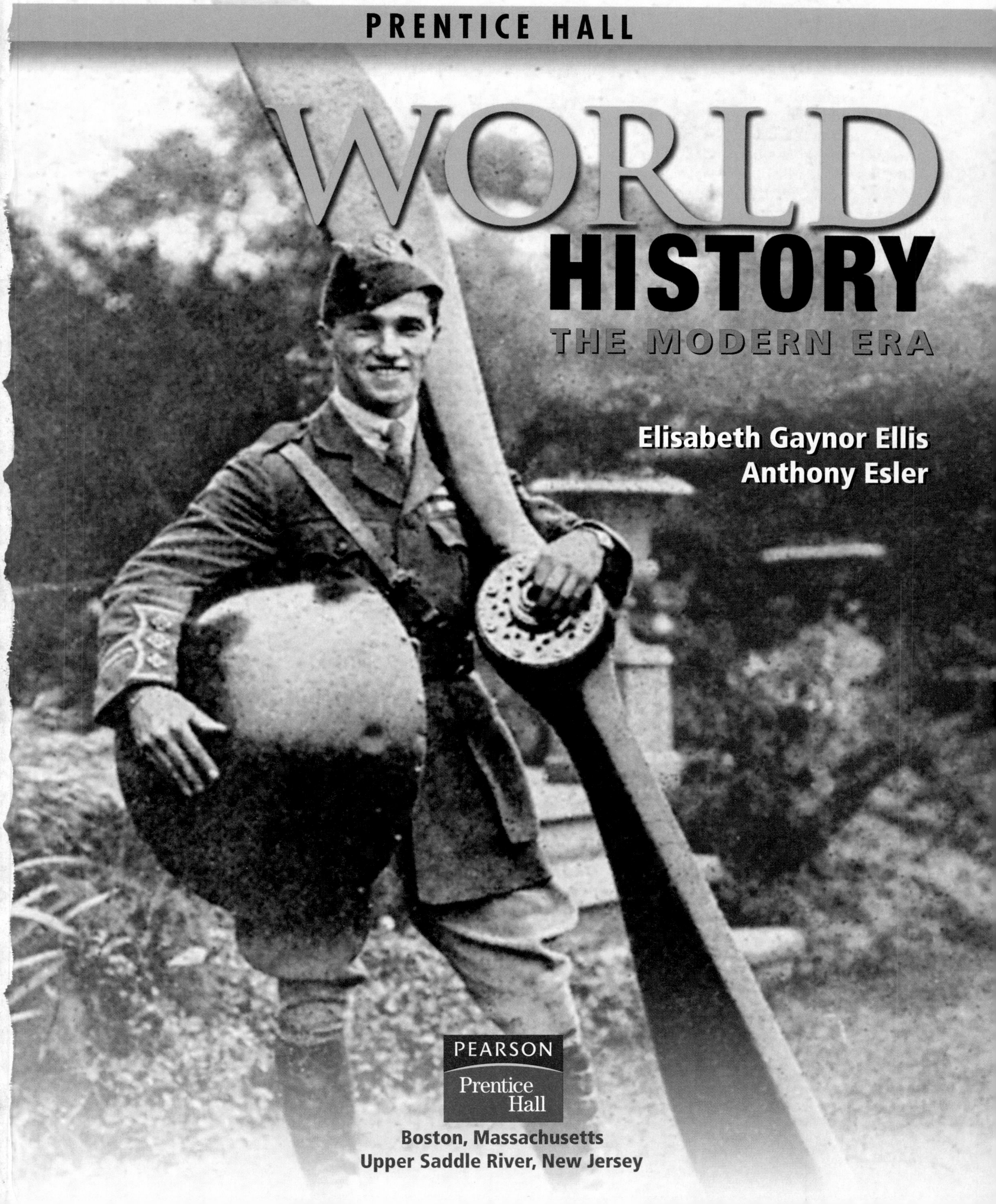

Elisabeth Gaynor Ellis
Anthony Esler

PEARSON
Prentice
Hall

Boston, Massachusetts
Upper Saddle River, New Jersey

Authors

Elisabeth Gaynor Ellis

Elisabeth Gaynor Ellis holds a BS from Smith College and an MA and MS from Columbia University. Before she began writing textbooks, Ms. Ellis taught World Cultures, European History, and Russian Studies in Ardsley, New York. Ms. Ellis co-authored Prentice Hall's *World Cultures: A Global Mosaic*, and *World History: Connections to Today* with Dr. Anthony Esler. Ms. Ellis has also written other social studies materials, including *America's Holidays*, individual state histories, and a variety of Teacher's Edition materials. Ms. Ellis is currently working on a middle grades curriculum on Korea as well as a historical novel.

Anthony Esler

Anthony Esler is an emeritus professor of history at the College of William and Mary in Williamsburg, Virginia. His books include several studies of the conflict of generations in world history, half a dozen historical novels, and two other surveys of world and Western history besides this one. He is a member of the American Historical Association, the World History Association, and the Authors Guild. He has received Fulbright, Social Science Research Council, and other research grants, and is listed in the *Directory of American Scholars*, the *Directory of Poets and Fiction Writers*, and *Who's Who in America*. Books by Dr. Esler include *Bombs, Beards, and Barricades, Forbidden City*, and *The Human Venture*.

Senior Consultant

Burton F. Beers

Burton F. Beers is a retired professor of history from North Carolina State University. He has taught European history, Asian history, and American history. Dr. Beers has published numerous articles in historical journals and several books, including *The Far East: A History of Western Impacts and Eastern Responses*, with Paul H. Clyde, and *World History: Patterns of Civilization*.

Senior Reading Consultants

Kate Kinsella

Kate Kinsella, EdD, a specialist in second-language and adolescent literacy, is a faculty member in the Department of Secondary Education at San Francisco State University. Her teaching addresses language and literacy development across the secondary curricula. Dr. Kinsella earned her MA in TESOL from San Francisco State University, and her EdD in Second Language Acquisition from the University of San Francisco.

Kevin Feldman

Kevin Feldman, EdD, is the Director of Reading and Early Intervention with the Sonoma County Office of Education (SCOE) and an independent educational consultant. At the SCOE, he develops, organizes, and monitors programs related to K–12 literacy. Dr. Feldman has an MA in Special Education, Learning Disabilities and Instructional Design from the University of California, Riverside. He earned his EdD in Curriculum and Instruction from the University of San Francisco.

Cover and title page image: World War I British pilot and fighting ace, Captain Albert Ball, posing with propeller and nose cone, 1917

Acknowledgments appear on page 865, which constitutes an extension of this copyright page.

ISBN 0-13-129973-5

3 4 5 6 7 8 9 10 10 09 08 07

TABLE OF CONTENTS

Before you begin your study of World History, use the pages listed below to help you prepare for success.

▼ A young archaeologist takes measurements

▲ Mali sculpture, *c.* 1300

▼ Goddess Athena supervising a vote

▲ Map of the world, 1560

▲ Thirteen-star flag of the original colonies

► Shuttles used to speed up the weaving process

▲ Chinese Imperial embroidered robe

▼ Mexico's coat of arms (below); sheet music of a patriotic song of World War I (right)

▼ German children greet Berlin airlift plane.

▼ The world's first iron bridge, Shropshire, England

▲ Agricultural development assistance in Zambia, Africa

SPECIAL FEATURES AND MULTIMEDIA

YOUR COURAGE
YOUR CHEERFULNESS
YOUR RESOLUTION
WILL BRING
US VICTORY

Witness History: Janina's War Story

"It was 10:30 in the morning and I was helping my mother and a servant girl with bags and baskets as they set out for the market. . . . Suddenly the high-pitch scream of diving planes caused everyone to freeze. . . . Countless explosions shook our house followed by the *rat-tat-tat* of strafing machine guns. We could only stare at each other in horror. Later reports would confirm that several German Stukas had screamed out of a blue sky and . . . dropped several bombs along the main street—and then returned to strafe the market. The carnage was terrible." ◀)) AUDIO

—Janina Sulkowska,
Krzemieniec, Poland, September 12, 1939

WITNESS HISTORY AUDIO

Primary source audio accounts throughout the text bring the voices and sounds of history to life.*

*Available on Witness History Audio CD and online at PHSchool.com.

WITNESS HISTORY VIDEO

Witness History Discovery School™ videos for each chapter bring the events you read about in the text to life.

History Interactive — Events That Changed the World

Audio, video, and animation-filled features help you explore major turning points in history.

XV

Primary Sources

Full-page excerpts allow you to relive history through eyewitness accounts and documents.

In-text Primary Sources

Gain insights as you read by reading the words of people who were there.

Traveler's Tales

View historic places through the eyes of those who traveled there.

COMPARING VIEWPOINTS

Explore issues by analyzing two opposing viewpoints.

HUMANITIES

Experience great literature and arts from around the world.

BIOGRAPHIES

Meet fascinating history makers.

▼ Marie Curie

INFOGRAPHICS

Photographs, maps, charts, illustrations, audio, and text help you understand the significance of important historical events and developments.

Julius Caesar ▶

Document Based Assessment

Practice the art and science of a historian by analyzing an event through examining multiple historical documents, data, and images.

Cause and Effect

**Diagrams help you see the short- and long-term causes and effects
of history's most important events.**

Charts and Graphs

Diagrams and data help you understand history through visuals.

Charts and Graphs

Maps Geography *Interactive*

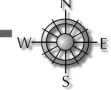

Interactive maps and Audio Guided Tours for each map with a Web code help you understand where history happened.

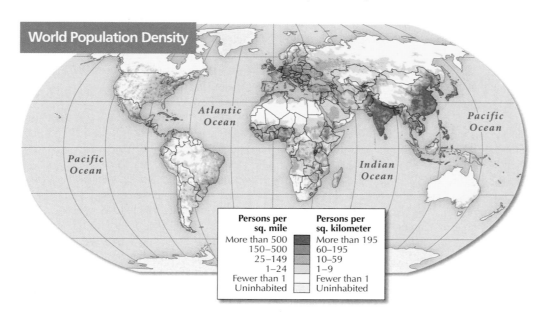

World Population Density

Keys to Unlocking
WORLD HISTORY

Learning about the entire span of World History is no small task. Luckily, your text and its companion Web site—PHSchool.com—come with a number of important tools to make your study of World History easier and more worthwhile.

Experience the Drama of History

WITNESS HISTORY

- **Witness History Audio**
  Throughout your text, you'll notice audio symbols like this
  🔊 AUDIO that indicate sound clips that you can listen to to make the history on the page come alive. These clips are available on the Witness History Audio CD.

- **Witness History Video**
  What did it feel like to fight in the trenches during World War I? **Witness History Discovery School™** video program brings the sights and sounds of times like this to life in every chapter.

History *Interactive*

Some events in history are so dramatic that words alone cannot convey their impact. For these events we've created online interactive Web sites where you'll hear audio clips of people who were there; see photos, maps, and timelines; and view animations to help you experience the full drama of history. Use the Web Codes in your text to go directly to the action.

Go Online at PHSchool.com

History *Interactive*

For: Interactive map, audio, and more
Visit: PHSchool.com
Web Code: nbp-2941
Use the Web Codes that appear throughout this book to access additional information and activities.
1. Go to PHSchool.com.
2. Enter the Web code.
3. Click Go.

Make Connections

Concept Connector

The job of a historian requires more than studying events as they unfolded chronologically. Historians must also look for patterns across time and place. We've created a set of tools to help you do just that. The Concept Connector system was designed to help you connect 18 key concepts across time.

◄ Concept Connector Features
Each of the 18 concepts that you'll be tracking during the course is defined and described in features throughout the text.

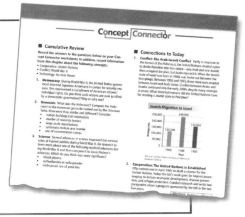

Cumulative Review and Connections to Today ▶
Cumulative Review and Connections to Today appear on the Concept Connector page at the end of each chapter. Cumulative Review questions will help you make connections between chapter events and earlier events. Connections to Today will help you make connections between chapter events and more current events.

◄ Concept Connector Worksheets
Complete these worksheets over the course of the year to help you see patterns across time. There are 18 worksheets in all, one for each of the key concepts listed on this page. You can access and print the Concept Connector Worksheets at PHSchool.com. At the end of each chapter, Cumulative Review questions will direct you to record information on your worksheets. At the end of the course, you can use the completed worksheets to prepare for thematic essays that may appear on your tests.

Concept Connector Handbooks ▶
A series of six handbooks at the end of your text provides you with important reference materials to help you see patterns across time and compare and contrast concepts over time.

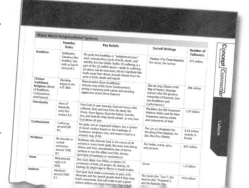

Develop Key Skills

Geography *Interactive*

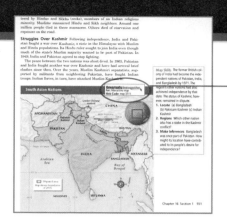

Historical maps are important for understanding where events took place, so we've created easy-to-read maps for your exploration. To make sure you get the most out of each map, we've also provided you with your own historian to take you on an audio-guided tour of each map. You can access these audio tours through the Web Codes provided in your text.

Some of the maps in your text are interactive. Online versions of the map will allow you to see how events shown on the map unfolded over time or will give you additional images and information to make the places shown on the map come alive.

SKILLS
Handbook

The Skills Handbook at the front of this text allows you to brush up on important skills at the beginning of the course or at any time you need help.

- **Reading Informational Texts**

  Reading a text is not the same as reading a novel. Make the most of the time you spend reading your text and improve your reading comprehension by looking at some proven reading strategies to use before you read, while you read, and after you read.

- **Writing Handbook**

  Learning to be a good writer is key to your success in this class, on tests, and in life. Use this part of the Skills Handbook to study models of good writing and to learn hints for writing various types of essays, including expository and persuasive essays.

- **Geography Skills Handbook**

  Maps cover core information in a visual format and expand on concepts taught in the text. Improving your ability to read and understand maps will help you succeed in this course and in other history classes.

- **Critical Thinking About Texts, Visuals, and Media Sources**

  As a practicing historian, you need to train yourself to think critically about everything you read, see, and hear. Is what you're reading accurate? Biased? Use this part of the Skills Handbook to practice your critical thinking skills.

- **Speaking and Listening**

  Speaking is another way to demonstrate what you've learned. Good listening is another key to success in every classroom. Look for key tips on how to prepare a presentation and how to listen actively in this part of the Skills Handbook.

Go Online at PHSchool.com

Geography *Interactive*

For: Audio guided tour
Visit: PHSchool.com
Web Code: nbp-2911
Use the Web Codes that appear throughout this book to access additional information and activities.
1. Go to PHSchool.com.
2. Enter the Web code.
3. Click Go.

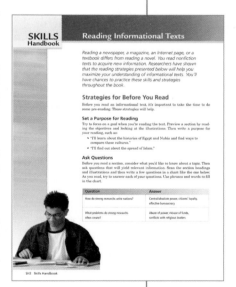

Prepare for Tests

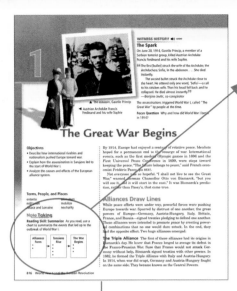

Note Taking

Throughout most of this course, you'll be reading and studying information as it occurred chronologically. In each section of the text, you'll find suggestions for how to take notes using graphic organizers, timelines, and outlines. Complete these graphic organizers in your own notebook, in your Reading and Note Taking Study Guide, or on the Note Taking Worksheets for each section, which you can download at PHSchool.com. If you complete all of the suggested note taking strategies, you'll be able to use your notes to prepare for chapter, midterm, and high stakes end-of-course tests.

Progress Monitoring *Online*

Web Codes at the end of every section take you to an online quiz with multiple-choice questions on section content and vocabulary. At the end of every chapter, you'll find an online self-test on chapter content and a crossword puzzle to test your vocabulary mastery. Both quizzes and tests provide you with instant help to prepare you for in-class exams.

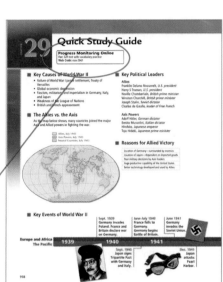

Go Online at PHSchool.com

Progress Monitoring *Online*
For: Self-test with vocabulary practice
Web Code: naa-2961

Quick Study Guide

In addition to the note taking graphics that you create yourself, we've provided some for each chapter on the end-of-chapter Quick Study pages. Use these pages to review for tests and to make sure you've mastered the content in the chapter. The Quick Study pages also include a timeline of key events discussed in the chapter. Interactive versions of these timelines are available online at PHSchool.com.

Document-Based Assessment

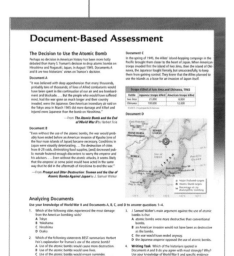

To prepare you for document-based questions on in-class and high-stakes tests, each chapter ends with a page of Document-Based Assessment. Each of these pages contains several documents followed by multiple-choice questions that help you analyze documents and practice your map, graph, visual learning, and critical reading skills. A writing task helps you compare, contrast, and draw conclusions about the various documents.

SKILLS Handbook

Contents

A series of handbooks provide skills instruction to help you read, learn, and demonstrate your knowledge of world history.

Reading Informational Texts

Writing Handbook

Geography Skills Handbook

Critical Thinking About Texts, Visuals, and Media Sources

Speaking and Listening

SKILLS
Handbook

Reading Informational Texts

Reading a newspaper, a magazine, an Internet page, or a textbook differs from reading a novel. You read nonfiction texts to acquire new information. Researchers have shown that the reading strategies presented below will help you maximize your understanding of informational texts. You'll have chances to practice these skills and strategies throughout the book.

Strategies for Before You Read

Before you read an informational text, it's important to take the time to do some pre-reading. These strategies will help.

Set a Purpose for Reading

Try to focus on a goal when you're reading the text. Preview a section by reading the objectives and looking at the illustrations. Then write a purpose for your reading, such as:

- "I'll learn about the histories of Egypt and Nubia and find ways to compare these cultures."
- "I'll find out about the spread of Islam."

Ask Questions

Before you read a section, consider what you'd like to know about a topic. Then ask questions that will yield relevant information. Scan the section headings and illustrations and then write a few questions in a chart like the one below. As you read, try to answer each of your questions. Use phrases and words to fill in the chart.

Question	Answer
How do strong monarchs unite nations?	Central/absolute power, citizens' loyalty, effective bureaucracy
What problems do strong monarchs often create?	Abuse of power, misuse of funds, conflicts with religious leaders

Predict

Engage in the reading process by making predictions about what you are preparing to learn. Scan the section headings and the visuals. Then write a prediction, such as:

- "I will find out what caused feudalism in Europe to develop and later to disappear."

Keep your predictions in mind as you read—do they turn out to be accurate or do you need to revise them?

Use Prior Knowledge

Research shows that if you connect the new information in your reading to your prior knowledge, you'll be more likely to remember the new information. You'll also see the value of studying history if you see how it connects to the present. After previewing a section, create a chart like this one. Complete the chart as you read the section.

What I Know	What I Want to Know	What I Learned
Many people today are Calvinists or Lutherans.	How and when did these religions begin?	John Calvin and Martin Luther led people to start new Protestant churches during the sixteenth-century Reformation.

Strategies for During Reading

It's important to be an active reader. Use these strategies as you read an informational text.

Reread or Read Ahead

If you don't understand a certain passage, reread it to look for connections among the words and sentences. For example, look for cause-and-effect words that link ideas, or sequence words that show when events took place. Or, try reading ahead to see if the ideas are clarified later on. Once you find new clarifying information, return to the confusing text and read it again with the new information in mind.

Paraphrase

To paraphrase is to restate information in your own words, as in the example below. Paraphrasing is a good way to check your understanding of the reading. Think of it this way—if you can explain it to someone else, you understand it.

Original Paragraph	Paraphrase
When Ireland won independence in 1922, Britain retained control of six northern counties where there was a Protestant majority. Faced with widespread discrimination, Catholics demanded civil rights and the reunification of Ireland. Protestants wanted to remain part of Britain.	After Irish independence in 1922, Britain controlled six Protestant-dominated counties in the north. People in these counties divided along religious lines: Catholics called for both civil rights and reunification of the Irish nation; Protestants supported British control.

Summarize

Summarizing—a version of paraphrasing—can also help you confirm your understanding of the text. Summarizing focuses on restating the main ideas of a passage, as you can see in the example below. Include a few important details, such as the time period, to orient yourself or other readers to the text.

Original Paragraph	Summary
Ottoman expansion threatened the crumbling Byzantine empire. After several failed attempts to capture Constantinople, Muhammad II finally succeeded in 1453. Over the next 200 years, the Ottoman empire continued to expand.	The Byzantine empire gave way to the Ottoman empire around 1453, resulting in 200 years of Ottoman rule.

Identify Main Ideas and Details

A main idea is the most important point in a paragraph or section of text. Some main ideas are stated directly, but others are implied. You must determine these yourself by reading carefully. Pause occasionally to make sure you can identify the main idea.

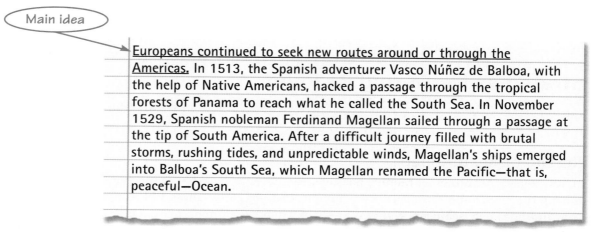

Main idea

Europeans continued to seek new routes around or through the Americas. In 1513, the Spanish adventurer Vasco Núñez de Balboa, with the help of Native Americans, hacked a passage through the tropical forests of Panama to reach what he called the South Sea. In November 1529, Spanish nobleman Ferdinand Magellan sailed through a passage at the tip of South America. After a difficult journey filled with brutal storms, rushing tides, and unpredictable winds, Magellan's ships emerged into Balboa's South Sea, which Magellan renamed the Pacific—that is, peaceful—Ocean.

Main ideas are supported by details. Record main ideas and details in an outline format like the one shown here.

Main idea

Details

European Exploration in the Americas
I. Continued as Europeans sought new routes around or through the Americas
   A. Balboa and Native Americans found a passage across Panama.
   B. Balboa named the South Sea.
   C. Magellan found passage around tip of South America.
   D. Magellan reached the South Sea and renamed it the Pacific Ocean.

Vocabulary

Here are several strategies to help you understand the meaning of a word you do not recognize.

Use Context Clues You can often define an unfamiliar word with clues from the surrounding text. For example, in the sentence "Crusaders fought on and off for more than 200 years, and many died for their cause," the words *fought* and *died* are clues indicating that a Crusader was someone who fought wars. Context clues can be in the same sentence as the unfamiliar word or in nearby sentences or paragraphs.

Analyze Word Parts Use your knowledge of word parts to help you define unfamiliar words. Break the word into its parts—root, prefix, suffix. What do you know about these parts? For example, the suffixes *–ify* and *–ation* mean "make into" and "action or process." The word *desertify* means "turn into a desert." *Desertification* means "the process of turning into a desert."

Recognize Word Origins Another way to figure out the meaning of an unfamiliar word is to understand the word's origins. Use your knowledge of Greek or Latin roots, for example, to build meaning. The words *formation* and *reformation* contain the Latin root *form,* which means "shape." *Formation* is the shape in which something is arranged. *Reformation* is a change in the shape of an idea or institution.

Analyze the Text's Structure

Just as you organize a story about your weekend to highlight the most important parts, authors will organize their writing to stress their key ideas. Analyzing text structure can help you tap into this organization. In a social studies text, the author frequently uses one of the structures listed in the chart at right to organize information. Learn to identify structures in texts and you'll remember text information more effectively.

Analyze the Author's Purpose

Different reading materials are written with different goals, or purposes. For example, this book is written to teach you about world history. The technical manual that accompanies computer software is written to teach readers how to use the product. In a newspaper, some articles will be written to inform readers about news events, while editorials will be written to persuade readers to accept a particular view about those events.

Structures for Organizing Information

Compare and Contrast Here, an author highlights similarities and differences between two or more ideas, cultures, processes, people, etc. Look for clue words such as *on the other hand* or *similarly*.

Sequence Here, an author recounts the order in which events occurred or steps were taken. History is often told in chronological sequence but can also involve flashbacks from later times to earlier times. Look for sequence words such as *initially*, *later*, and *ultimately*.

Cause and Effect Here, an author highlights the impact of one event on another or the effects of key events. Cause and effect is critical to understanding history because events in one time often strongly influence those in later times. Look for clue words such as *because*, *so*, or *as a result*.

An author's purpose influences not only how the material is presented but also how you read it. Thus you must identify the purpose, whether it is stated directly or merely suggested. If it is not directly stated, use clues in the text—such as opinion words in an editorial—to identify the author's purpose.

Distinguish Between Facts and Opinions/Recognize Bias

It's important to read actively, especially when reading informational texts. Decide whether information is factual—which means it can be proven—or if it includes opinions or bias—that is, people's views or evaluations.

Anytime you read material that conveys opinions, such as an editorial, keep an eye out for author bias. This bias might be revealed in the use of emotionally charged words or faulty logic. For example, the newspaper editorial below includes factual statements (in blue) and opinion statements (in red). Underlined words are emotionally charged words—they'll get a rise out of people. Faulty logic (in green) may include circular reasoning that returns to its beginning and either/or arguments that ignore other possibilities.

> ### Editorial
>
> In 1993, the people of Brazil voted to keep their government a republic rather than revert to a monarchy. Voters chose between the two options in a special election. Clearly, anyone who favored monarchy was a reactionary dinosaur who maliciously wanted to undermine Brazil's progress. The republican format allows Brazilians to vote for their leaders directly. As a result, our brilliant leader Fernando Henrique Carlosa spearheaded life-saving reforms to Brazil's dying and antiquated economic system. In a monarchy, this would be impossible.

Identify Evidence

Read critically. Don't accept an author's conclusion automatically. Identify and evaluate the author's evidence. Does it justify the conclusion in quantity and content? An author may present facts to support a claim, but there may be more to the story than facts. For example, what evidence does the writer of the editorial above present to support the claim that a monarch could not help Brazil's economy? Perhaps a monarch would use his or her more centralized authority to achieve more sweeping and rapid reforms.

Evaluate Credibility

After you evaluate evidence, check an author's credentials. Consider his or her level of experience and expertise about the topic. Is he or she likely to be knowledgeable *and* objective about the topic? Evaluating credibility is especially important with sites you may visit on the Internet. Ask the following questions to determine if a site and its author are reliable.

- Who sponsors the Web site? Is it a respected organization, a discussion group of individuals, or a single person?

- What is the source of the Web site's information? Does the site list sources for facts and statements?

- Does the Web site creator include his or her name and credentials?

- Is the information on the Web site balanced and objective or biased to reflect only one point of view?

- Can you verify the Web site's information using two other sources, such as an encyclopedia or news agency?

- Is the information current? Is there a date on the Web site to show when it was created or last updated?

Strategies for After Reading

Evaluate Understanding

Evaluate how well you understand what you've read.

- Go back to the questions you asked yourself before reading. Try to answer each of them.
- Check the predictions you made and revise them if appropriate.
- Draw a conclusion about the author's evidence and credibility.
- Check meanings of unfamiliar words in the dictionary to confirm your definitions.

Recall Information

Before moving on to new material, you should be able to answer the following questions fully:

- What is the text about?
- What is the purpose of the text?
- How is the text structured?

You should also be able to place the new information in the context of your prior knowledge of the topic.

Writing Handbook

Writing is one of the most powerful communication tools you will use for the rest of your life. Research shows that writing about what you read actually helps you learn new information and ideas. A systematic approach to writing—including prewriting, drafting, revising, and proofing—can help you write better, whether you're writing an essay or a research paper.

Narrative Essay

Narrative writing tells a story, often about a personal experience. In social studies, this story might be a narrative essay that recounts how a recent or historical event affected you or your family.

① Prewriting

Choose a topic. The focus of your essay should be an experience of significance to you. Use these ideas as a guide.

- **Look at photos** that show you and/or your family. Perhaps you attended a political rally or visited an important historical monument.
- **Scan the news** in print or through electronic media. Consider how current events relate to you and your family.
- **Brainstorm** with family or friends about recent events. How did you respond to these events? Jot down ideas like the ones below.

> Connections to History This Year
> — trip to art museum: Renaissance painters
> — historical books: World War II Africa
> — mock debate: Vietnam War

Consider audience and purpose.

- Keep your **audience's** knowledge and experience level in mind. Make sure you provide any necessary background information.
- Choose a **purpose** as well. If you want to entertain, include humorous details. To convey how the experience changed you, you might share more serious insights.

Gather details. Collect the facts and details you need to tell your story.

- **Research** any background about the historical event that readers might need to know about.
- **List details** about your own experience as it relates to the event.

❷ Drafting

Identify the climax, or most interesting part of your story. Then logically organize your story into a beginning, middle, and end. Narratives are usually told in chronological order.

Open strongly with an engaging sentence, such as the one below, that will catch your reader's attention.

Use sensory details, such as sights, sounds, or smells, to make the story vivid for readers. Describe people's actions and gestures. Pinpoint and describe locations.

Write a conclusion that sums up the significance of the event or situation you have experienced.

> I never expected to find myself arguing to support America's role in Vietnam. Our recent mock debate on the Vietnam War gave me new insight about this complex time in my nation's history. **Research took me inside the perspective of those who supported the War and its goals.** On the day of the debate, my hands were covered in sweat and my heart pounded as I stood to explain this currently unpopular position.

Strong opening engages the reader.

Insight or significance tells the reader what this event means to you.

Sensory details help the reader envision the experience.

❸ Revising

Add dialogue or description. Dialogue, or conveying a person's thoughts or feelings in his or her own words, can make a narrative more effective. Look for places where the emotions are especially intense. In the model, this might be when the writer's opponents respond to the debate position.

First Draft	Revised Original
At the debate, my hands were wet and my heart beat fast.	On the day of the debate, my hands were covered in sweat and my heart pounded.

Revise word choice. Replace general words with more specific, colorful ones. Choose vivid action verbs, precise adjectives, and specific nouns to convey your meaning. Look at the example above. Notice how much more effective the revised version is at conveying the experience.

Read your draft aloud. Listen for grammatical errors and statements that are unclear. Revise your sentences as necessary.

❹ Publishing and Presenting

Share by reading aloud. Highlight text you want to emphasize and then read your essay aloud to the class. Invite and respond to questions.

Expository Writing

Expository writing explains ideas or information in detail. The strategies on these pages examine each of several expository writing styles.

Prewriting

Choose a topic. In social studies, the focus of your writing might be explaining a historical process, comparing and contrasting cultural trends, explaining causes and effects of current events, or exploring problems societies have faced and the solutions they have sought. These ideas are a guide.

- **Ask questions.** For process writing, consider the question *how*. Think about *how* people in history have accomplished their goals, such as building a giant monument. Identify the steps and procedures involved.

> **Question:** How did great thinkers of the 1600s change people's view of the world?
>
> **Answer:** They developed the scientific method.

- **Create a compare/contrast grab bag.** With a small group, write on separate slips of paper examples from each category: ideas, cultures, or time periods. Mix the slips in a bag and choose two. Compare and contrast the two ideas, cultures, or time periods.
- **Interview** someone who made a major change in lifestyle, such as moving from one culture to another. Find out how and why the person did this. Understanding *why* is the basis of any cause and effect essay.
- **Take a mental walk.** Study a map and envision taking a tour of the region. Think about problems each area you visit might face, such as armed conflict, natural disaster, or governmental change. Choose a problem and suggest solutions for it.

Consider audience and purpose. Consider how much your readers know about the problem, comparison, event, or process you will address. Suit your writing to your audience's knowledge or plan to give explanations of unfamiliar terms and concepts.

Gather details. Collect the facts and details you need to write your essay.

Research the topic. Use books, the Internet, or interviews of local experts. List facts, details, and other evidence related to your topic. Also consider your personal experience. For example, you might know about a process from personal experience or have witnessed the effects of a historic legal decision.

Create a graphic organizer. For cause-and-effect or problem-solution essays, use a two-column chart. Process writing can be listed as a bulleted list of steps. A Venn diagram can help you compare and contrast.

World War I
- new weapons used: machine guns, poison gas, submarines
- 8.5 million military deaths

World War II
- new weapon used: atomic bomb
- 20 million military deaths

- fought by two powerful alliances
- began in Europe, then spread

Identify causes and effects. List possible explanations for events. Remember that many events result from multiple causes. Identify effects both large and small. Note that some events may have effects that in turn cause other events. Look for causes and effects in all your expository essays. For example, in a process explanation, one step often causes the next.

Fine-tune your ideas. For a problem-solution essay, decide what you will suggest as a solution. Keep your solution narrow to be achievable in cost, effort, and timing. Make sure no one has tried it before, or if it has been tried and it failed, address the failure.

❷ Drafting

Match structure to purpose. Typically, process writing and cause-and-effect writing are written in sequence order. Problem-solution essays benefit from block organization, which presents the entire problem and proposes a solution. For compare/contrast essays, you can organize by subject or by point.

> By subject: Discuss the events and outcomes of World War I, and then compare and contrast these with those of World War II.
>
> By point: Introduce a category, such as use of new weapons. Relate both wars to this category, comparing or contrasting them along the way.

Give background. To discuss events from history, first orient the reader to time and place. Choose the important facts but don't overwhelm the reader with detail. If you need to, return to prewriting to narrow your topic further.

Elaborate for interest and emphasis. Give details about each point in your essay. For example, add facts that make the link between events so that a cause-and-effect relationship is clear. Also, readers will support proposed solutions more if your details clearly show how these solutions will solve the stated problem. Use facts and human experiences to make your essay vivid.

Connect to today. Even when you write about historical events, you may find links to today. Explore these links in your essay.

> Mexico's population underwent great change during the mid–twentieth century. Population shifted from rural areas to urban areas. The nation's society went from largely agricultural to largely industrial and urban. Urban populations exploded, with Mexico City alone growing from 1.5 million people in 1940 to nearly 20 million later in the century. These changes resulted from several causes.
>
> First, land reform begun in the 1930s failed. The millions of acres redistributed by then–President Lázaro Cárdenas proved arid and unproductive. Second, the rural population was growing rapidly. This placed increased demands on the land. The land became even more depleted and unproductive. Finally, several Mexican governments in turn shifted their attention from the small rural peasant farmer toward larger scale farming operations.
>
> Mexico's shifting population and changing economic patterns yielded new problems for its leaders by late in the twentieth century.

Identify the topic to orient readers.

Chronological order walks readers through the cause-effect sequence.

Elaboration supports the relationship you are highlighting.

Connection to today tells readers why this matters to them.

③ Revising

Add transition words. Make cause-and-effect relationships clear with words such as *because, as a result,* and *so.* To compare or contrast ideas, use linking words, such as *similarly, both, equally* or *in contrast, instead, yet.* Use words such as *first, second, next,* and *finally* to help readers follow steps in a process. Look at the following examples. In the revised version, a reader knows the correct order in which to perform the steps.

First Draft	Revised
Scientists form an educated guess called a hypothesis. They test that hypothesis with an experiment.	<u>Next,</u> scientists form an educated guess called a hypothesis. <u>Then,</u> they test that hypothesis with an experiment.

Remember purpose. Shape your draft so that it answers the question or thesis you began with. For a problem-solution essay—in which your purpose is to sell your solution—that means anticipating opposing arguments and responding to them. For cause-and-effect, you want to stress the way one event leads to the next. Always tell readers *why* they should care about your topic.

Review organization. Confirm that your ideas flow in a logical order. Write main points on index cards. Reorganize these until you are satisfied that the order best strengthens your essay.

Add details. Make sure you haven't left out any steps in your essay, and don't assume readers will make the connections. For example, you might forget to state explicitly that a process must be repeated in order to produce accurate results. Add more background if necessary for clarity.

Revise sentences and words. Look at your sentence length. Vary it to include both short and long sentences. Then scan for vague words, such as *good.* Replace them with specific and vibrant words, such as *effective.* Use technical terms only when necessary, and then define them.

Peer review. Ask a peer to read your draft. Is it clear? Can he or she follow your ideas? Revise areas of confusion.

④ Publishing and Presenting

Collect in a class manual. Contribute your process explanation to a class manual of *History How-To's.*

Submit to a library. Find a specialized library, such as a presidential library. Mail your essay to the library's publications or public relations department.

Seek publication. If your historical events or issues are local, seek publication in a local historical magazine or contact a historical society. You might speak to their members.

Mail to an advocacy group. Find a local, national, or international organization that is concerned with your topic. Send them your essay and ask for comments on its ideas. Make sure to include a self-addressed stamped envelope and a note explaining your essay and offering thanks for its review.

Research Writing

① Prewriting

Choose a topic. Often, a teacher will assign your research topic. You may have flexibility in choosing your focus or you may have the opportunity to completely define your topic. These ideas are a guide.

- **Catalog scan.** Using a card or electronic catalog, search for topics that interest you. When a title looks promising, find the book on the shelves. Libraries usually use the Dewey Decimal Classification system to group research materials by subject, so you should find other books on similar subjects nearby. You can use them all to decide on your final topic.

- **Notes review.** Review your social studies notes from the last month or so. Jot down topics that you found interesting. Then repeat the process with your other classes. For example, you might find a starting point for research into the Scientific Revolution from a math theorem.

- **Social studies categories game.** With a group, brainstorm categories in social studies. For example, you might list key world leaders or important wars. Within each category, take turns adding subtopics. The chart below looks at different transportation topics.

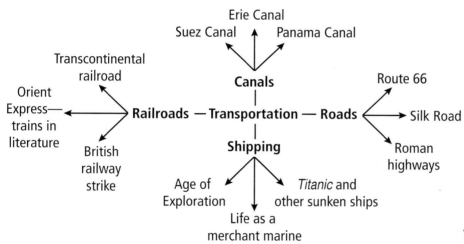

You can use sources such as newspapers to get ideas.

Analyze the audience. Your research and your paper should be strongly influenced by the audience. How much will readers know about this topic and how much will you have to teach them?

Gather details. Collect the facts and details you need to write your paper. Use resources beyond the typical history books. Look at nonfiction books such as memoirs or collections of letters. Also look at magazine and newspaper articles. Consider news magazines, as well as those focused on topics such as history or travel. You may find interviews with experts on your topic or travel articles about a region that interests you. Search the Internet, starting with online encyclopedias, news organizations, and history Web sites.

Organize evidence and ideas. Use note cards to record information and to help you organize your thoughts. Start with a general thesis statement in mind. Then begin reading and taking notes. Write a heading at the top of each note card to group it under a subtopic. Note a number or title to identify the information source. In the examples below, the number 3 is used. Use the same number for an additional source card containing the bibliographic information you will need.

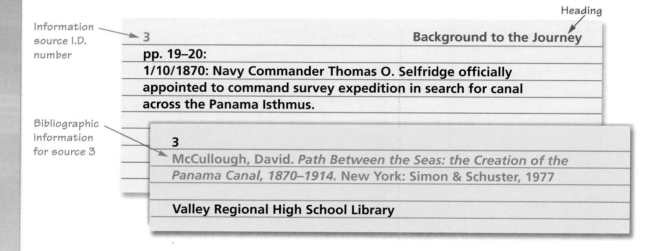

Heading

Information source I.D. number →

3   **Background to the Journey**

pp. 19–20:

1/10/1870: Navy Commander Thomas O. Selfridge officially appointed to command survey expedition in search for canal across the Panama Isthmus.

Bibliographic information for source 3 →

3

McCullough, David. *Path Between the Seas: the Creation of the Panama Canal, 1870–1914.* New York: Simon & Schuster, 1977

Valley Regional High School Library

❷ Drafting

Fine-tune your thesis. Review your notes to find relationships between ideas. Shape a thesis that is supported by the majority of your information, then check that it is narrow enough to address thoroughly in the allotted time and space. Remember, you can fine-tune your thesis further as you draft or even when you revise.

Organize to fit your purpose. Do you want to persuade readers of a particular position about your topic, compare and contrast aspects of the topic, or show a cause-and-effect relationship? Organize appropriately—for example, by looking at parts of a whole to examine events leading to building and completing the Panama Canal.

Make an outline. Create an outline in which you identify each topic and subtopic in a single phrase. You can then turn these phrases into sentences and later into the topic sentences of your draft paragraphs. Study the example at the top of the next page to see how to do this well.

Write by paragraph. Write an introduction, at least three body paragraphs, and a conclusion. Address a subtopic of your main topic in each body paragraph. Support all your statements with the facts and details you gathered.

Building the Panama Canal

Outline

I. Introduction
II. Why the Canal Was Built
III. How the Canal Was Built
  A. Physical Challenges
  B. Medical Challenges
IV. Conclusion

Introduction
Ever since Christopher Columbus first explored the Isthmus of Panama, the Spanish had been looking for a water route through it. They wanted to be able to sail west from Spain to Asia without sailing around South America. However, it was not until 1914 that the dream became a reality.

Conclusion
It took eight years and more than 70,000 workers to build the Panama Canal. It remains one of the greatest engineering feats of modern times.

An outline helps you structure your information.

Each body paragraph looks at a part of the whole topic.

The introduction puts the topic in a context of time and place. The entire paragraph conveys the thesis: Building the Panama Canal was a dream that took centuries to achieve.

The conclusion recaps key points and leaves readers with a final statement to remember.

❸ Revising

Add detail. Mark points where more details would strengthen your statements. Look at the following examples. Notice the added details in the revised version. When adding facts, make certain that they are accurate.

First Draft	Revised
The Navy excursion was a huge undertaking. Supplies were gathered to support the team for many months.	The Navy excursion was a huge undertaking. Supplies were gathered to support the team for many months, including more than 600 pairs of shoes, 100 miles of telegraph wire, 2,500 pounds of coffee, and 10,000 pounds of bread! (McCullough 20).

Make the connection for readers. Help readers find their way through your ideas. First, check that your body paragraphs and the information within them flow in a logical sequence. If they do not, revise to correct this. Then add transition words to link ideas and paragraphs.

Give credit. Check that you have used your own words or given proper credit for borrowed words. You can give credit easily with parenthetical notes. These include the author's last name and the relevant page number from the source. For example, you could cite the note card here as (McCullough 19–20).

❹ Publishing and Presenting

Plan a conference. Gather a group of classmates and present your research projects. You may each wish to create visual materials to accompany your presentations. After you share your papers, hold a question and answer session.

Persuasive Essay

Persuasive writing supports an opinion or position. In social studies, persuasive essays often argue for or against positions on historical or current issues.

❶ Prewriting

Choose a topic. Choose a topic that provokes an argument and has at least two sides. Use these ideas as a guide.

- **Round-table discussion.** Talk with classmates about issues you have studied recently. Outline pro and con positions about these issues.
- **Textbook flip.** Scan the table of contents or flip through the pages of your textbook. Focus on historical issues that engage your feelings.
- **Make connections.** Relate current events to history. Develop a position for or against a situation of importance today using historical evidence.

Narrow your topic.

- **Cover part of the topic** if you find too many pros and cons for a straightforward argument.
- **Use looping.** Write for five minutes on the general topic. Circle the most important idea. Then write for five minutes on that idea. Continue looping until the topic is manageable.

Consider your audience. Choose arguments that will appeal to the audience for your writing and that are likely to persuade them to agree with your views.

Gather evidence. Collect the evidence to support your position convincingly.

- **Identify pros and cons.** Use a graphic organizer like the one below to list points on both sides of the issue.

Position: Education is key to improving life in developing nations.	
Pro ⬅	**Con** ➡
• Education allows people to get higher-paying jobs. • With more money, people can help boost the economy. • With education, people can better handle disease and disaster.	• Building new schools may cost more than the government has available for education. • Some countries have other large problems to handle, such as serious diseases.

- **Interview** adults who have lived or worked in developing nations. What do they think? Ask them for reasons to support their views.
- **Research** to get your facts straight. Read articles or books about life in developing nations.

❷ Drafting

State your thesis. Clearly state your position, as in this example:

> Education is the key to revitalizing developing nations. Once many people are educated, many other problems can be solved.

Use your introduction to provide a context for the issue. Tell your readers when and why the issue arose, and identify the important people involved.

Sequence your arguments. Open or close with your strongest argument. If you close with the strongest argument, open with the second-best argument.

Acknowledge opposition. State, and then refute, opposing arguments.

Use facts and details. Include quotations, statistics, or comparisons to build your case. Include personal experiences or reactions to the topic, such as those a family member might have shared when interviewed.

Write a conclusion that restates your thesis and closes with a strong, compelling argument.

> Many people living in developing nations want to improve life in their countries. They want the people to have everything they need, such as food and clean water, electricity, medicines, and even fun items like televisions and bicycles. Education is the key to revitalizing developing nations. Once many people are educated, many other problems can be solved.
>
> Education allows people to get higher-paying jobs. With more money, people can help boost the economy. As well, education is an added tool people can use to deal with other problems. It's true that building new schools costs a lot. And in some places, people face many other major problems such as serious diseases. But education will only help them handle these issues....

Background orients readers.

Thesis identifies your main argument.

Supporting argument clarifies your thesis.

Opposing argument, noted and refuted, adds to your position.

❸ Revising

Add information. Extra details can generate interest in your topic. For example, add a quotation from a news article that assesses the role of education in a developing nation or a poor area.

Review arguments. Make sure your arguments are logically sound and clearly developed. Avoid faulty logic such as circular reasoning (arguing a point by merely restating it differently). Evidence is the best way to support your points. Look at the following examples. Notice how much more effectively the revised version supports the argument.

First Draft	Revised
Education allows people to make more money, which is helpful.	Education allows people to get higher-paying jobs. With more money, people can help boost the economy.

Use transition words to guide readers through your ideas.

- To show contrast: *however, although, despite*
- To point out a reason: *since, because, if*
- To signal conclusion: *therefore, consequently, so, then*

❹ Publishing and Presenting

Persuasive Speech. Many persuasive essays are delivered orally. Prepare your essay as a speech, highlighting words for emphasis and adding changes in tone, volume, or speed.

Biographical Writing

❶ Prewriting

Choose a topic. Biographical writing tells the story of a real person's life. For social studies, you should focus on the life of an important historical or current figure. The following ideas are a guide.

- **Find a hero.** Think about a person from history whom you admire—for example, a world leader, a great thinker, or an inventor. Remember to choose someone about whom information is easily available.

- **Name game.** On an index card, write the name of a person in the news today. Write a sentence or phrase explaining what makes this person interesting to you, as on the examples below. With a group, shuffle all the cards and then take turns drawing topics. If you like, trade your topic with a friend.

Martin Luther
He thought the Bible—not the pope—should guide a person's actions.

Wangari Maathai
She thinks preserving the environment can improve people's lives.

- **Table of Contents scan.** Your history book lists the short biographies that are included in the text. Scan this listing in the book's Table of Contents for three possible subjects. Read the biography of each subject before you make a final choice.

Focus your approach. Decide how you want to approach your subject. For example, you could emphasize the person's influence on historical events, or you could show how personal experiences affected his or her achievements.

Gather details. Collect the facts and details you need to write your paper. Use the research methods for gathering information explained on page SH14. In particular, check biographical source materials in the reference section of the library.

Isolate episodes. As you learn about your subject, focus on the particular episodes that seem to be most important. Then learn more about the events surrounding these episodes and take notes on them, as in the example below.

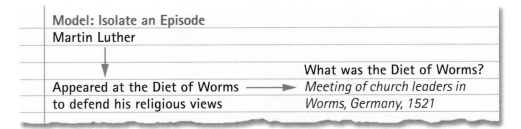

Model: Isolate an Episode
Martin Luther

What was the Diet of Worms?
Appeared at the Diet of Worms ——▶ *Meeting of church leaders in*
to defend his religious views *Worms, Germany, 1521*

Focus your fact-gathering. Your goal is to bring this person's life to readers—to share facts and opinions relating to that life and respond to them with your own conclusions. As you determine the main points you wish to make about this person, find facts to support your assertions. Make sure to give enough factual background for readers to appreciate your points.

② Drafting

Focus your essay. In a single paper, you will probably need to focus on an aspect of your subject's life or on a quick overview of major events in that life.

Organize important events. Choose the events you will discuss, and then order them in a logical way. Biographies are usually organized chronologically.

Reveal your subject. Include direct description of your subject, which allows you to convey information quickly. Balance this with quotations or examples of the person's actions, which lend color and authenticity to your essay.

Open strongly. Get readers' attention immediately with an engaging quotation, an interesting fact about your subject, or an anecdote that sets the tone.

> "Here I stand, I cannot do otherwise." Martin Luther spoke these words at the Diet of Worms in 1521. The Diet, a conference of religious leaders, had summoned Luther to explain his controversial religious views.
>
> Martin Luther was born in 1483 into a German family. Raised a Catholic, Luther entered a monastery after experiencing a religious calling. He became both devout and committed to strict observance. Over time, this approach brought him into conflict with the Church. For example, Luther felt that the Catholic Church should not sell indulgences, or guarantees of good grace after death.
>
> Luther developed new ideas about the Church and its leadership. At the core were his beliefs that people should have a direct relationship to the Bible and that the Church and the pope stood in the way of this. In his 95 Theses, Luther called for widespread reforms in the Catholic Church and later in the German government. Because his views were contrary to accepted beliefs, Luther was called in front of the Diet of Worms. He refused to back down, so the Church expelled him in 1521.

A quote gets the readers attention and quickly establishes the subject's personality.

The biography will focus on this aspect of Luther's life.

Chronological organization helps readers see the development of Luther's ideas.

The conclusion brings the biography back to its initial anecdote.

③ Revising

Examine word choice. Bring your subject to life with vivid adjectives, specific verbs, and precise nouns. Then link your chronological organization with words that show sequence. The draft above uses dates as well as phrases such as *over time* to show the sequence of Luther's life and religious growth.

Make connections for readers. For example, the sentence below connects Luther's life to current times by linking it to the modern Lutheran Church.

> Although Luther himself never called for a new church, today the Protestant branch named for him claims more than 5 million members in America alone.

Give credit. Cite sources for any facts, statistics, or quotations you include. If several pieces of information in a paragraph come from a single source, you may cite the source once at the end of the paragraph. Always check with your teacher for specific bibliographic requirements.

④ Publishing and Presenting

Create a biographical character. Use what you've learned about this person's life to appear as that person. If you wish, wear a costume. Explain who you are and what is most important to you. Ask and answer questions.

Writing for Assessment

Assessment writing differs from all other writing that you do. You have many fewer choices as a writer, and you almost always face a time limit. In social studies, you'll need to write both short answers and extended responses for tests. While these contrast in some ways, they share many requirements.

❶ Prewriting

Choose a topic. Short-answer questions seldom offer a topic choice. For extended response, however, you may have a choice of more than one question. Use the following strategies to help you navigate that choice.

- **Examine the question.** To choose a question you can answer effectively, analyze what each question is asking. Use key words such as those listed below to help you choose topics and respond to short-answer questions in which the topic is given.

Key Words	What You Need in an Answer
Explain	Give a clear, complete account of how something works or why something happened.
Compare/Contrast	Show how two or more things are alike and different.
Define	Give examples to explain meaning.
Argue, Convince, Support, Persuade	Take a position on an issue and present strong reasons to support your side of the issue.
Summarize	Provide the most important elements of a subject.
Evaluate/Judge	Assign a value or explain an opinion.
Interpret	Support a thesis with examples from the text.

Notice in the examples below that the key words are underlined:

Short answer: <u>Describe</u> one way that Chief Joseph showed his <u>military expertise</u>.

Extended response: According to the author of this article, Chief Joseph was both a <u>peace chief</u> and a <u>military genius</u>. Use information from the article to <u>support this conclusion</u>.

- **Plot your answer.** After choosing a question, quickly plot the answer in your mind. Do you have the information to answer this question? If the answer is *no*, try another question.

Measure your time. Your goal is to show the instructor that you've mastered the material. To stay focused on this goal, divide your time: one-quarter on prewriting; half on drafting; one-quarter on revising. For short-answer questions, determine how much of the overall test time you can spend on each question. Don't spend more than that.

Gather details. Organize the facts and details you need to write your answer. For short-answer questions, this usually involves identifying exactly what information is required.

Use a graphic organizer. For extended response, divide your topic into subtopics that fit the type of question. Jot down facts and details for each. For the question on Chief Joseph, the following organizer would be effective:

> Chief Joseph of the Nez Percé
> Peace Chief
> • traded peacefully with white settlers (1)
> • reluctantly went to war (2)
> • famous speech, "I will fight no more forever." (3)
>
> Military Genius
> • won battles with fewer warriors than opposing troops had (a)
> • avoided capture for many months (b)
> • led his people more than 1,000 miles (c)
> • knew when to surrender for the good of his people (c)

❷ Drafting

Choose an organization that fits the question. With a short-answer question, write one to three complete sentences. With extended response, you'll need more elaborate organization. For the question on Chief Joseph, organize your points by importance within each subtopic. For a summary or explanation, use chronological order. For compare/contrast, present similarities first, then differences.

Open and close strongly. Start your answer by restating the question or using its language to state your position. This helps you focus and shows the instructor that you understand the question. Finish with a strong conclusion that restates your position. For short answer, include some language from the question in your response.

> One way that Chief Joseph showed his military expertise was by defeating U.S. Army troops despite having fewer warriors than they had.

Support your ideas. Each paragraph should directly or indirectly support your main idea. Choose facts that build a cohesive argument. The numbered sentences in the draft below show how this writer organized support.

> Chief Joseph was both a peace chief and a military genius.
> He was a peace chief because he traded peacefully with white settlers
> for many years. (1) He went to war reluctantly after the government
> ordered his people to move to a reservation. (2) When he finally
> surrendered, he said in a famous speech, "I will fight no more forever." (3)
> Chief Joseph was also a military genius. He fought off U.S. Army
> forces with fewer warriors than they had, (a) and he avoided capture
> for many months. (b) He led his people more than 1,000 miles
> (c) before he made the decision to surrender. Chief Joseph will long be
> remembered for his dual roles as peace chief and military genius.

The opening restates the question and presents the main idea.

The writer uses information from the graphic organizer, in order of importance.

The writer supports the second subtopic.

The conclusion recaps the main idea and again uses the question's language.

③ Revising

Examine word choice. Replace general words with specific words. Add transitions where these improve clarity. Read the following examples. The revised version shows the relative importance of the writer's supporting evidence.

First Draft	Revised
Chief Joseph was both a peace chief and a military genius. He was a peace chief because he traded peacefully with white settlers for many years. He went to war reluctantly...	Chief Joseph was both a peace chief and a military genius. He was a peace chief for several reasons. First, he traded peacefully with white settlers for many years. Second, he went to war reluctantly...

Check organization. Make sure your introduction includes a main idea and defines subtopics. Review each paragraph for a single main idea. Check that your conclusion summarizes the information you've presented.

④ Publishing and Presenting

Edit and proof. Check spelling, grammar, and mechanics. Make sure that tenses match, that subjects agree with verbs, and that sentences are not too long. Finally, confirm that you have responded to all the questions you were asked to answer.

Writing Rubric

Use this chart, or rubric, to evaluate your writing.

SAT

SCORE OF 6
An essay in this category is **outstanding**, demonstrating **clear and consistent mastery**, although it may have a few minor errors. A typical essay

- effectively and insightfully develops a point of view on the issue and demonstrates outstanding critical thinking, using clearly appropriate examples, reasons, and other evidence to support its position
- is well organized and clearly focused, demonstrating clear coherence and smooth progression of ideas
- exhibits skillful use of language, using a varied, accurate, and apt vocabulary
- demonstrates meaningful variety in sentence structure
- is free of most errors in grammar, usage, and mechanics

SCORE OF 5
An essay in this category is **effective**, demonstrating **reasonably consistent mastery**, although it will have occasional errors or lapses in quality. A typical essay

- effectively develops a point of view on the issue and demonstrates strong critical thinking, generally using appropriate examples, reasons, and other evidence to support its position
- is well organized and focused, demonstrating coherence and progression of ideas
- exhibits facility in the use of language, using appropriate vocabulary
- demonstrates variety in sentence structure
- is generally free of most errors in grammar, usage, and mechanics

SCORE OF 4
An essay in this category is **competent**, demonstrating **adequate mastery**, although it will have lapses in quality. A typical essay

- develops a point of view on the issue and demonstrates competent critical thinking, using adequate examples, reasons, and other evidence to support its position
- is generally organized and focused, demonstrating some coherence and progression of ideas
- exhibits adequate but inconsistent facility in the use of language, using generally appropriate vocabulary
- demonstrates some variety in sentence structure
- has some errors in grammar, usage, and mechanics

SCORE OF 3
An essay in this category is **inadequate**, but demonstrates **developing mastery**, and is marked by **one or more** of the following weaknesses:

- develops a point of view on the issue, demonstrating some critical thinking, but may do so inconsistently or use inadequate examples, reasons, or other evidence to support its position
- is limited in its organization or focus, but may demonstrate some lapses in coherence or progression of ideas
- displays developing facility in the use of language, but sometimes uses weak vocabulary or inappropriate word choice
- lacks variety or demonstrates problems in sentence structure
- contains an accumulation of errors in grammar, usage, and mechanics

SCORE OF 2
An essay in this category is **seriously limited**, demonstrating **little mastery**, and is flawed by **one or more** of the following weaknesses:

- develops a point of view on the issue that is vague or seriously limited, demonstrating weak critical thinking, providing inappropriate or insufficient examples, reasons, or other evidence to support its position
- is poorly organized and/or focused, or demonstrates serious problems with coherence or progression of ideas
- displays very little facility in the use of language, using very limited vocabulary or incorrect word choice
- demonstrates frequent problems in sentence structure
- contains errors in grammar, usage, and mechanics so serious that meaning is somewhat obscured

SCORE OF 1
An essay in this category is **fundamentally lacking**, demonstrating **very little** or **no mastery**, and is severely flawed by one or more of the following weaknesses:

- develops no viable point of view on the issue, or provides little or no evidence to support its position
- is disorganized or unfocused, resulting in a disjointed or incoherent essay
- displays fundamental errors in vocabulary
- demonstrates severe flaws in sentence structure
- contains pervasive errors in grammar, usage, or mechanics that persistently interfere with meaning

SCORE OF 0
Essays not written on the essay assignment will receive a score of zero.

Analyze the Five Themes of Geography

The five themes of geography are tools you can use to analyze geographic information given in photographs, charts, maps, and text.

- **Location** answers the question "Where is it?" The answer might be an absolute location, such as 167 River Lane, or a relative location, such as six miles west of Mill City.

- **Regions** are areas that share at least one common feature. Climate, culture, and government are features that can be used to define a region.

- **Place** identifies natural and human features that make a place different from other places. Landforms, climate, plants, animals, people, culture, and languages are features that can be used to identify a specific place.

- **Movement** answers the question "How do people, goods, and ideas move from place to place?"

- **Human-Environment Interaction** focuses on the relationship between people and the environment. Humans often make changes to the environment, and the environment often affects how humans live.

Use the photograph and steps that follow to analyze the five themes of geography.

The Nile River in Egypt

Read supporting information such as a caption or key. Use this information and your own knowledge of the world to determine location and region.

Analyze the content. Consider the elements of the visual or text to develop ideas about region, place, movement, and human-environment interaction.

Practice and Apply the Skill

Use the photograph above to answer the following questions:

1. How might you describe the relative location of the fields of crops?
2. What is the climate region shown here? How do you know?
3. What elements in the scene identify this specific place?
4. How do you think people, goods, and ideas move to and from this place?
5. How have the people of this area changed their environment?

Understand Latitude and Longitude

Geographers divide the globe along imaginary horizontal lines called parallels of latitude. They measure these parallels in degrees (°) north or south of the Equator, which itself is a line of latitude. Geographers also divide the globe along imaginary vertical lines called meridians of longitude. They measure these meridians in degrees east or west of the Prime Meridian, a line of longitude running through Greenwich, England. All meridians intersect at the North Pole and the South Pole. Together, the lines of latitude and longitude form a grid that gives an absolute location for every place on Earth. Use the globes and the steps that follow to understand latitude and longitude.

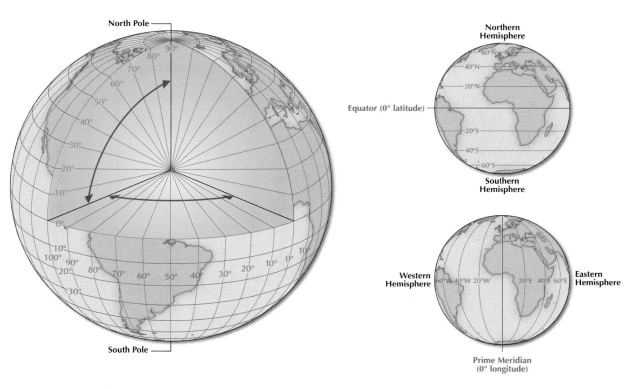

Study purpose. Study the two main globes to understand why geographers divide the globe into parallels and meridians. Study the two smaller globes to understand the role of the Equator and the Prime Meridian as starting points for measuring parallels and meridians.

Read labels and captions. Read the labels and captions to understand how to determine the latitude and longitude of a given location, as well as to identify which hemispheres it sits in.

Identify absolute location. You can use lines of latitude and longitude together to identify the absolute location of any spot on Earth.

Practice and Apply the Skill

Use the text and globes above to answer the following questions:

1. Which part of the location 67° N, 55° E represents the longitude?
2. What line of latitude lies halfway from the Equator to the North Pole?
3. Do lines of latitude ever intersect one another? Explain.
4. If you followed the 70° W line of longitude north to the North Pole and then continued on the same line south, what line of longitude would you be on? (Hint: The globe, like a circle, has a total of 360 degrees.)

Understand Movements of Earth

Earth revolves around the sun in a path called an orbit. One revolution, or complete orbit, takes a year. As Earth revolves, it also rotates on its axis—an invisible line from the North Pole to the South Pole. Every 24 hours, Earth completes one full rotation. As Earth rotates, it is day on the side facing the sun and night on the side away from the sun. Earth's axis is tilted at an angle. Because of this tilt, sunlight strikes different parts of Earth more or less directly at different times of year, creating seasons. Use the diagram below and the steps that follow to understand Earth's movements.

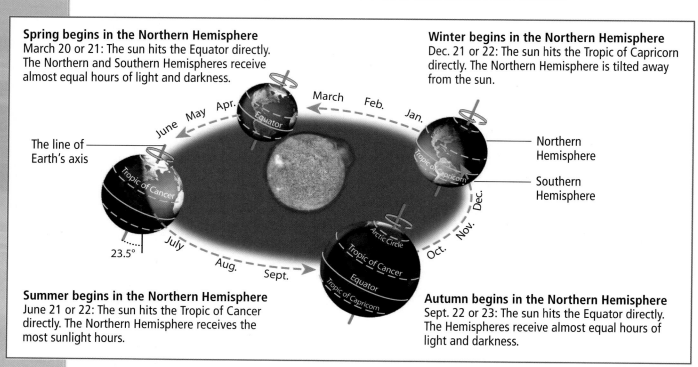

Spring begins in the Northern Hemisphere
March 20 or 21: The sun hits the Equator directly. The Northern and Southern Hemispheres receive almost equal hours of light and darkness.

Winter begins in the Northern Hemisphere
Dec. 21 or 22: The sun hits the Tropic of Capricorn directly. The Northern Hemisphere is tilted away from the sun.

The line of Earth's axis

Northern Hemisphere

Southern Hemisphere

23.5°

Summer begins in the Northern Hemisphere
June 21 or 22: The sun hits the Tropic of Cancer directly. The Northern Hemisphere receives the most sunlight hours.

Autumn begins in the Northern Hemisphere
Sept. 22 or 23: The sun hits the Equator directly. The Hemispheres receive almost equal hours of light and darkness.

Focus on the main ideas. The diagram shows why the seasons change and how seasons differ north and south of the Equator. It also shows how night changes into day. Focus on these ideas one at a time.

Identify the content. Look at each element of the diagram. You see Earth in four different positions around the sun.

Read labels and captions. The caption and labels on each position of Earth describe a different season.

Restate the main points. In your own words, describe to yourself why the seasons change, how seasons differ in the Southern and Northern Hemispheres, and how night changes into day.

Practice and Apply the Skill

Use the diagram above to answer the following questions:

1. At the beginning of winter in the Northern Hemisphere, which of Earth's poles receives more sunlight?

2. How are the Tropic of Capricorn and the Tropic of Cancer related?

3. The term *equinox* means "equal night" and refers to the hours of darkness and sunlight. Which two seasons begin on an equinox?

4. Which hemisphere, Northern or Southern, receives more hours of sunlight on April 1? Explain.

Analyze Map Projections

Because maps are flat, they cannot show the correct size and shape of every feature on Earth's curved surface. Mapmakers must shrink some places and stretch others. Different types of map projections distort Earth's surface in different ways. Mapmakers choose the projection that has the least distortion for the information they are presenting.

Same-shape map projections such as the Mercator projection accurately show the shapes of landmasses. However, they distort sizes and distances. Equal-area map projections show the correct size of landmasses but distort shapes, especially at the edges of a map. The Robinson projection keeps the size and shape relationships of most continents and oceans but distorts the size of the polar regions. Use the maps below and the steps that follow to help you learn how to analyze map projections.

Equal-area projection
The sizes of landmasses are accurate relative to one another.

Mercator projection

The greatest distortion is at the far northern and southern latitudes.

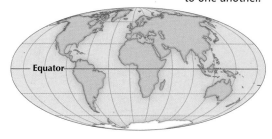

Robinson projection
The entire top edge of the map is the North Pole.

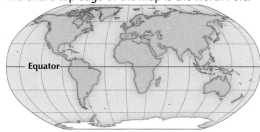

The entire bottom edge of the map is the South Pole.

Identify each projection. Study the appearance of each type of projection.

Read labels and captions. Read the labels and captions to understand the important details of each projection.

Compare the maps. Compare the shape of the maps and then the shapes of landmasses on them. Last, compare the amount of curvature of the lines of latitude and longitude on the maps.

Practice and Apply the Skill

Use the maps above to answer the following questions:

1. If you wanted to plot a course to sail from one port to another on the most direct route, which map projection would work best? Why?

2. Which map shows the most accurate relative size of Antarctica, the white region on each map? Why?

3. How do the grid lines on the Mercator projection vary from a globe's?

4. Why do you think many maps in this book use the Robinson projection?

Read Maps

Mapmakers provide clues to help you read maps, such as a title, compass rose, key, and locator globe. Another helpful feature is a scale bar. Like the two shown here, maps are often drawn to different scales, depending on their purpose. Use the maps below and the steps that follow to learn how to analyze maps.

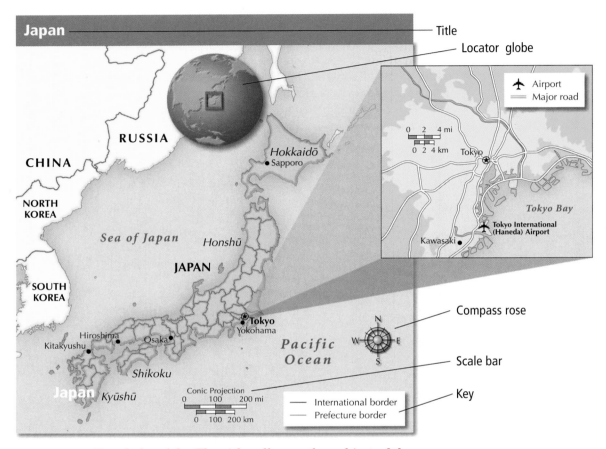

Read the title. The title tells you the subject of the map.

Study the locator globe. The locator globe shows where in the world the area shown on the map is located.

Read the key. The key explains the symbols, lines, and colors on the map.

Use the scale bar and compass rose. Use the scale bar to determine distances between places on the map. Use the compass rose to determine the relative directions of places on the map.

Compare maps of different scale. Since the smaller map zooms in on an area of the main map, it is at a larger scale than the main map. Notice the different features shown on these two maps of different scales.

Practice and Apply the Skill

Use the maps above to answer the following questions:

1. Which body of water borders Japan on the west?
2. On what body of water is Tokyo located?
3. What is the distance between Tokyo and Hiroshima?
4. What is the purpose of the main map? Of the smaller map?
5. Which map could help you get from Tokyo International Airport to downtown Tokyo? How could it help?

Analyze Special-Purpose Maps

Maps can show many different types of information. A physical map represents what a region looks like by showing its major physical features, such as mountains and plains. A political map focuses on elements related to government, such as nations, borders, and cities.

A special-purpose map provides information on a specific subject—for example, land use, population distribution, natural resources, or trade routes. Road maps are special-purpose maps, as are weather maps. These maps often use a variety of colors and symbols to show different pieces of information, so the key is very important. Use the map below and the steps that follow to practice analyzing a special-purpose map.

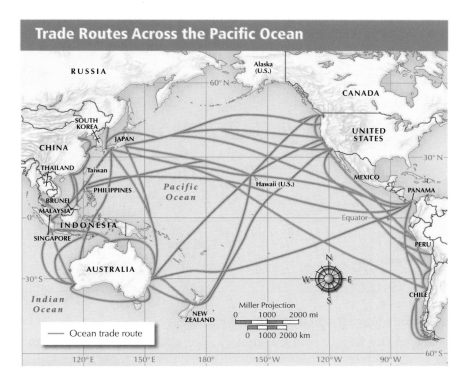

Trade Routes Across the Pacific Ocean

Study the title, locator globe, scale bar, and compass rose. Together, these features tell you the map's context—what part of the world it shows and why.

Read the key. Use the key to learn the specific details shown on the map.

Apply the key and labels to the map. Locate the symbols, lines, or colors from the key on the map. Also read any labels on the map. Then use the information given in the key and labels to understand what the map shows.

Practice and Apply the Skill

Use the map above to answer the following questions:

1. What is the purpose of this map? What part of the world does it show?

2. What do the blue lines on the map represent?

3. How many trade routes go through Panama? Through New Zealand?

4. If trade goods arrive in Hawaii from the northeast, where could they have come from?

5. Name three countries that exchange goods with the continental United States along the trade routes shown on the map.

Critical Thinking

About Texts, Visuals, and Media Sources

Analyze Graphic Data

The study of history requires that you think critically about the text you're reading as well as any visuals or media sources. This section of the Skills Handbook will allow you to practice and apply some important skills for critical thinking.

Graphs show numerical facts in picture form. Bar graphs and line graphs compare things at different times or places, such as changes in school enrollment. Circle graphs show how a whole is divided into parts. To interpret a graph, look closely at its features. Use the graphs below and the steps that follow to practice analyzing graphic data.

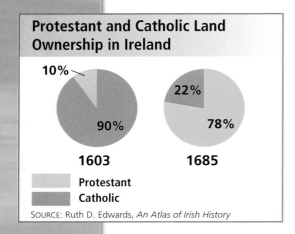

Protestant and Catholic Land Ownership in Ireland

10%
90%
22%
78%
1603
1685
Protestant
Catholic

SOURCE: Ruth D. Edwards, *An Atlas of Irish History*

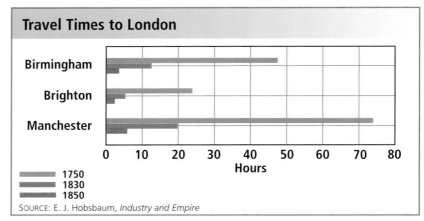

Travel Times to London

Birmingham
Brighton
Manchester
0
10
20
30
40
50
60
70
80
Hours
1750
1830
1850

SOURCE: E. J. Hobsbaum, *Industry and Empire*

Read the title to learn the main topic of the graph.

Use labels and the key to read the data given in the graph. The bar graph is labeled in hours, with intervals of 10 hours. The keys on all three graphs assign different colors to different groups or dates.

Interpret the graph. Look for interesting patterns in the data. Look at changes over time or compare information for different groups.

Practice and Apply the Skill

Use the graphs above to answer the following questions:

1. What is the title of the bar graph? What is its topic?
2. Which cities show the longest travel times to London, and in which years? What does this tell you about changes in transportation?
3. What color on the circle graphs shows Catholic land ownership? How did Irish land ownership change over time? What might explain this change?
4. Could the information in the circle graph be shown as a bar graph? Explain.

Analyze Images

Television, film, the Internet, and print media all carry images that seek to convey information or influence attitudes. To respond, you must develop the ability to understand and interpret visuals. Use the photograph below and the steps that follow to practice analyzing images.

In the 1950s, people everywhere worried about nuclear attack. This 1954 image advertised a bogus "radiation-resistant" blanket.

Identify the content. Look at all parts of the image and determine which are most important.

Note emotions. Study facial expressions and body positions. Consider the emotions they may suggest.

Read captions/credits. Gather information about the image, such as when it was produced.

Study purpose. Consider who might have created this image. Decide if the purpose was to entertain, inform, or persuade.

Consider context. Determine the context in which the image was created— in this case, the Cold War between the United States and the Soviet Union.

Respond. Decide if a visual's impact achieves its purpose—to inform, to entertain, or to persuade.

Practice and Apply the Skill

Use the photograph above to answer the following questions:

1. What are the three main images in this photograph?
2. What feelings are conveyed by the boy's facial expression?
3. What do you think the photograph's purpose is?
4. When was this image produced? How did historical context influence its production?

Analyze Timelines

Timelines show the order in which events occur as well as the amount of time that passes between events. To understand a timeline, study its labels and captions carefully. Use the timeline below and the steps that follow to practice analyzing timelines

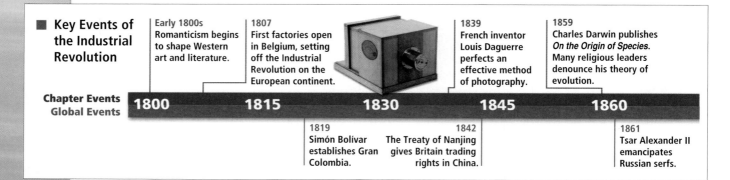

■ **Key Events of the Industrial Revolution**

Early 1800s
Romanticism begins to shape Western art and literature.

1807
First factories open in Belgium, setting off the Industrial Revolution on the European continent.

1839
French inventor Louis Daguerre perfects an effective method of photography.

1859
Charles Darwin publishes *On the Origin of Species.* Many religious leaders denounce his theory of evolution.

Chapter Events
Global Events

1800   **1815**   **1830**   **1845**   **1860**

1819
Simón Bolívar establishes Gran Colombia.

1842
The Treaty of Nanjing gives Britain trading rights in China.

1861
Tsar Alexander II emancipates Russian serfs.

Identify time units. Find the main time units of the timeline. Determine how much time is represented by the entire timeline.

Read each entry. Read each of the entries on the timeline. Connect each entry to the events before and after it.

Look for patterns among the events shown. Determine if any of the entries fall into a common category. Think about whether the events might be causes and/or effects.

Practice and Apply the Skill

Use the timeline above to answer the following questions.

1. What is the most recent event on the timeline? When did it take place?

2. When did the first factories open in Belgium?

3. How many years after the first factories opened did Louis Daguerre perfect his method of photography?

4. What happened in 1859?

Simón Bolívar

Analyze Primary Sources

Primary sources include official documents and firsthand accounts of events or visual evidence such as photographs, paintings, and political cartoons. Such sources provide valuable information about the past. Use the excerpt below and the steps that follow to learn to analyze primary sources.

The following excerpt is a translation from *The Satires*, a series of poems written in Latin by Juvenal about life in Rome in the first century A.D. In this excerpt, Juvenal recounts a friend's reasons for moving away from Rome.

Primary Source

66Since at Rome there is no place for honest pursuits, no profit to be got by honest toil—my fortune is less to-day than it was yesterday. . . .

What shall *I* do at Rome? I can not lie; if a book is bad, I can not praise it and beg a copy. I know not the motions of the stars. . . . no one shall be a thief by my co-operation. . . .

Who, now-a-days, is beloved except the confidant of crime. . .?99

—Juvenal, *The Satires of Juvenal, Persius, Sulpicia, and Lucilius*

Read the headnote, caption, or attribution line. Determine the source's historical context—who wrote it, when, and why.

Read the primary source. Identify and define unfamiliar words. Then look for the writer's main point.

Identify facts and opinions. Facts can be proven. Opinions reflect a person's views or feelings. Use opinion clues to help: exaggeration, phrases such as "I think," or descriptive words such as "gorgeous."

Identify bias and evaluate credibility. Consider whether the author's opinions suggest bias. Evaluate other factors that might lead to author bias, such as his or her previous experiences. Decide if the author knows enough to be credible and was objective enough to be reliable. Determine whether the source might be propaganda, that is, material published to promote a policy, idea, or cause.

Practice and Apply the Skill

Political cartoons reflect an artist's observations about events of the time. They often use symbols to represent things or exaggeration to make a point. Use the cartoon at right to answer the following questions.

1. Who is the author of this primary source?
2. What does the bulldozer represent?
3. What is exaggerated in this cartoon?
4. What opinion is the cartoonist expressing?
5. Do you think the cartoonist's opinion is valid? Why or why not?

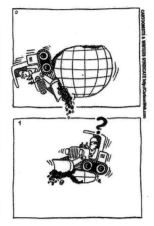

This cartoon by Arcadio Esquivel of Costa Rica comments on environmental destruction.

Compare Viewpoints

A person's viewpoint is shaped by subjective influences such as feelings, prejudices, and past experiences. Two politicians will recommend different policies to address the same problem. Comparing such viewpoints will help you understand issues and form your own views. The excerpts below offer two different views on the purpose of education. Use the excerpts and the steps that follow to learn about comparing viewpoints.

King Henri Christophe of Haiti set up schools for outstanding students. He believed these schools would secure Haiti's new and hard-won freedom. In 1817, he wrote:

Primary Source

66To form good citizens we must educate our children. From our national institutions will proceed a race of men capable of defending by their knowledge and talents those rights so long denied by tyrants. It is from these sources that light will be diffused among the whole mass of the population.99

—Henri Christophe, 1817

Leo Tolstoy, a Russian aristocrat of the late 1800s, became a famous novelist as a young man. As he grew older, he increasingly focused on social issues in his writing. In 1902, he wrote:

Primary Source

66You can take a puppy and feed him, and teach him to carry something, and enjoy the sight of him; but it is not enough to rear and bring up a man, and teach him Greek: he has to be taught to live, that is, to take less from others, and give more.99

—Leo Tolstoy, 1902

Identify the authors. Determine when and where the authors lived.

Examine the viewpoints. Identify the author's main idea and evaluate his or her supporting arguments. Determine whether the arguments are logical and the evidence is sufficient to support the main idea. Confirm that the evidence is valid by doing research if necessary.

Determine the author's frame of reference. Consider how the author's attitudes, beliefs, and past experiences might affect his or her viewpoint.

Recognize facts and opinions. Identify which statements are opinions and which are facts. Opinions represent the author's viewpoint.

Evaluate each viewpoint's validity. Decide whether the viewpoints are based on facts and/or reasonable arguments. Consider whether or not you agree with the viewpoints.

Practice and Apply the Skill

Use the excerpts above to answer the following questions.

1. Who are the authors of these two documents? Where and when did each one live?

2. What is each man's main argument about education? What evidence or supporting arguments does each provide?

3. How might each man's frame of reference affect his viewpoint?

4. How does Tolstoy's phrase "he has to be taught to live" signal an opinion?

5. Are these two viewpoints based on reasonable arguments? Explain.

Synthesize Information

Just as you might ask several friends about a movie before deciding to see it, you can combine information from different sources to develop a fuller understanding of any topic. This process, called synthesizing, will help you become better informed. Study the documents below about developments in the 1400s and 1500s. Then use the steps that follow to learn to synthesize information.

Document A

This caravel helped Europeans sail across and into the wind.

Document B

Improved Technology

Several improvements in technology helped Europeans navigate the vast oceans of the world. Cartographers, or mapmakers, created more accurate maps and sea charts. European sailors learned to use the astrolabe, an instrument developed by the ancient Greeks and perfected by the Arabs, to determine their latitude at sea.

Europeans also designed larger and better ships. The Portuguese developed the caravel, which combined the square sails of European ships with Arab lateen, or triangular, sails. Caravels also adapted the sternpost rudder and numerous masts used on Chinese ships. The new rigging made it easier to sail across or even into the wind.

Document C

Hardships on the Uncharted Sea

In his journal, Italian sailor Antonio Pigafetta detailed the desperate conditions Magellan's sailors experienced as they crossed the Pacific Ocean:

Primary Source

66We remained three months and twenty days without taking in provisions or other refreshments, and we only ate old biscuit reduced to powder, and full of grubs, and stinking from the dirt which the rats had made on it. . . . we drank water that was yellow and stinking. We also ate the ox hides which were under the main-yard [and] were very hard on account of the sun, rain, and wind. . . .99

—Journal of Antonio Pigafetta

Identify thesis statements. Before you can synthesize, you must understand the thesis, or main idea, of each source.

Compare and contrast. Analyze how the information and ideas in the sources are the same or different. When several sources agree, the information is more reliable and thus more significant.

Draw conclusions and generalize. Look at all the information. Use it to draw conclusions that form a single picture of the topic. Make a generalization, or statement that applies to all the sources.

Practice and Apply the Skill

Use the documents above to answer the following questions.

1. What is the main idea of each source?
2. Which sources support the idea that European sailors became better equipped to sail the seas?
3. What view does Antonio Pigafetta contribute to the topic?
4. Draw a conclusion about European ocean exploration in the early 1500s.

Analyze Cause and Effect

One of a historian's main tasks is to understand the causes and effects of the event he or she is studying. Study the facts below, which are listed in random order. Then use the steps that follow to learn how to analyze cause and effect.

In the 1980s and 1990s, the Soviet Union underwent a major change in its economy and government. As a result, the Soviet Union ceased to exist. This list shows key elements in that change.

- Low output of crops and consumer goods
- Soviets want to ensure influence in neighboring Afghanistan, so they invade that nation in 1979
- Soviet Union breaks up into 15 republics after its central government collapses
- Changeover to market economy in Russia
- Ethnic and nationalist movements to achieve independence from Soviet Union
- Cold War with United States leads to high military spending
- Food and fuel shortages
- Rise to power of Mikhail Gorbachev in 1985
- Russian republic approves a new constitution
- Baltic states of Estonia, Latvia, and Lithuania demonstrate for independence
- Cold War ends

Identify the central event. Determine to what event or issue all the facts listed relate.

Locate clue words. Use words such as *because, so,* and *due to* to spot causes and effects.

Identify causes and effects. Causes precede the central event and contribute to its occurrence. Effects come after the central event. They occur or emerge as a result of it.

Consider timeframe. Decide if causes have existed for a long period of time or emerged just prior to the central event. Short-term causes are usually single or narrowly defined events. Long-term causes usually arise from ongoing conditions.

Make recommendations. Use what you've learned to suggest actions or make predictions.

Practice and Apply the Skill

Use the list above to answer the following questions:

1. Which item on the list describes the central event whose causes and effects can be determined?
2. Name three facts that are long-term causes.
3. Name three facts that are probably short-term causes.
4. Name three facts that were most likely effects of the central event.

Problem Solving and Decision Making

You will face many problems in your life, from disputes with friends to how to vote on issues facing your nation. You will be most likely to find solutions if you make decisions in a logical way. Study the situation outlined below. Then use the steps that follow to learn the skills of problem solving and decision making.

A Problem for Japan and China

In the 1800s, Japan and China faced a problem. Industrialized nations had developed machinery and weapons that were superior to those that the Japanese and Chinese had. Some industrialized nations used their new power to demand special trading privileges in Asia.

Options for Japan and China

Option	Advantages	Disadvantages
1. Give in to demands of the industrialized powers.	• Avoid conflict. •	• Native merchants lose profits to foreigners.
2. Give in to demands, but also build modern machines and weapons.	• •	• •
3. Refuse the demands and reject much of the new technology.	• •	• •

The Decisions
- The Japanese government decided to follow option 2.
- The Chinese government decided to follow option 3.

Effects of the Decisions
- Japan quickly became a modern industrial and military power. Although it demilitarized after suffering defeat in World War II, it remains one of the world's leading industrial powers.
- China was weakened by a century of conflict with Great Britain and other major powers, and was invaded and occupied by Japan. Foreign nations gained special privileges in China. Today, China is still struggling to become a leading industrial power.

Identify the problem. You cannot solve a problem until you examine it and understand it.

Gather information and identify options. Most problems have many solutions. Identify as many solution options as possible.

Consider advantages and disadvantages. Analyze each option by predicting benefits and drawbacks.

Decide on and implement the solution. Pick the option with the most desirable benefits and least important drawbacks.

Evaluate the decision. After time, reexamine your solution. If necessary, make a new decision.

Practice and Apply the Skill

Use information from the box above to answer the following questions:

1. What problem did China and Japan face? What caused this problem?
2. Describe an option that Japan or China could have chosen other than those in the list.
3. Identify two advantages and two disadvantages for options 2 and 3.
4. Why do you think China and Japan chose the options they did?

Draw Inferences and Conclusions

Text and artwork may not contain all the facts and ideas you need to understand a topic. You may need to add information from your own experience or knowledge, or use information that is implied but not directly stated in the text or artwork. Study the biography below. Then use the steps that follow to learn how to draw inferences and conclusions.

BIOGRAPHY

James Watt

How did a clever Scottish engineer become the "Father of the Industrial Revolution"? After repairing a Newcomen steam engine, James Watt (1736–1819) had become fascinated with the idea of improving the device. Within a few months, he knew he had a product that would sell. Still, Watt lacked the money needed to produce and market it.

Fortunately, he was able to form a partnership with the shrewd manufacturer Matthew Boulton. They then founded Soho Engineering Works in Birmingham, England, to manufacture steam engines. Watt's version of the steam engine shown here had a separate condensing chamber and was patented in 1769. Eventually, a measure of mechanical and electrical power, the watt, would be named for James Watt. **How might the Industrial Revolution have been different if Watt had not found a business partner?**

Study the facts. Determine what facts and information the text states.

Summarize information. Confirm your understanding of the text by briefly summarizing it.

Ask questions. Use *who, what, when, where, why,* and *how* questions to analyze the text and learn more. For example, you might compare and contrast, or look for causes or effects.

Add your own knowledge. Consider what you know about the topic. Use this knowledge to evaluate the information.

Draw inferences and conclusions. Use what you learned from the text and your own knowledge to draw inferences and conclusions about the topic.

Practice and Apply the Skill

Use the biography above to answer these questions.

1. Who is discussed in the biography? When did he live?
2. Briefly summarize the text.
3. How do Watt's accomplishments still have an impact on our lives today?
4. Why do you think Watt wanted to improve a technology that already existed?

Use the Internet for Research

The Internet is a valuable research tool that provides links to millions of sources of information created by businesses, governments, schools, organizations, and individuals all over the world. Follow the steps to learn how you could use the Internet to research the European Renaissance.

Sample search engine

Begin a search. Use search engines on the Internet to help you find useful Web sites. Type in key words that briefly summarize your topic. Use *and* between words to find documents containing all your keywords. Use *or* between words to find documents containing any one of several keywords.

Find reliable information. Universities, museums, libraries, and government agencies are usually the most reliable and useful for social studies research. The URLs for education sites end in *.edu,* government sites in *.gov,* and not-for-profit organization sites in *.org.* Read each site summary and choose those most likely to be reliable. Click on links to access individual sites.

Evaluate Web sites. Explore each Web site. Note its sponsor and when it was last updated.

Use advanced searches. Try advanced search options. Limit by date or type of site, such as educational institutions. Try new or different key words if you still don't get what you need.

Practice and Apply the Skill

Use a computer connected to the Internet to answer the following questions:

1. What key words might you use to learn about the European Renaissance? Type them into a search engine Web site and see what results you get.

2. Which of the first ten sites that came up in your search is most likely to be reliable? Why?

3. Who is the sponsor of the site you chose? What does this suggest about its quality or its possible bias?

Speaking and listening are forms of communication you use every day. In certain situations, however, specific skills and strategies can increase the effectiveness of your communication. The strategies offered in this section will help you improve both your speaking and listening skills.

Participating in Group Discussions

A group discussion is an informal meeting of people that is used to openly discuss ideas and topics. You can express your views and hear those of others.

Identify Issues

Before you speak, identify the issues and main points you want to address. Incorporate what you already know about these issues into your views. Then find the best words to convey your ideas effectively.

Interact With the Group

As with persuasive writing, in a discussion it helps to accept the validity of opposing views, then argue your position. Always acknowledge the views of others respectfully, but ask questions that challenge the accuracy, logic, or relevance of those views.

Debating

A debate is a formal argument about a specific issue. Explicit rules govern the procedure of a debate, with each debater or team given an allotted time to make arguments and respond to opposing positions. You may also find yourself arguing a position you don't personally hold.

Prepare Your Arguments

If you support a position, use your existing knowledge of it to direct your research. If you personally oppose an assigned position, use that knowledge to identify likely opposing arguments. Generate an outline and then number note cards to highlight key information for each of your main points.

Avoid Common Pitfalls

Stay focused on your arguments. Be aware of words that may reveal bias, such as *unpatriotic*. Speak assertively, but avoid getting overly emotional. Vary the pitch and tone of your voice to keep listeners engaged. Try to speak actively, rather than just reading aloud, and use eye contact and gestures to emphasize your message.

Giving an Oral or Multimedia Presentation

An oral or multimedia presentation provides an audience with information through a variety of media.

Choose Media

If you are limited to speaking only, focus your time on developing a presentation that engages listeners. If you can include other media, consider what kind of information each form of media conveys most effectively.

Maps	Graphs/charts	Pictures	Diagrams	Audio/video
Clarify historical or geographical information	Show complicated information in an accessible format	Illustrate objects, scenes, or other details	Show link between parts and a whole or a process	Brings the subject to life and engages audience

Generate Text

Gather information using library and online sources. Develop your most important ideas in the body of your presentation. Back up assertions with solid facts and use multimedia examples to illustrate key points.

Present With Authority

Practice your presentation to gain comfort with the text and the presentation sequence. Experiment with the timing of how to include multimedia elements. Make sure you have the necessary equipment and know how to use it.

Active Listening

Active listening is a key component of the communication process. Like all communication, it requires your engaged participation.

Focus Your Attention on Ideas

Look at and listen to the speaker. Think about what you hear and see. Which ideas are emphasized or repeated? What gestures or expressions suggest strong feelings? Can you connect the speaker's ideas to your own experiences?

Listen to Fit the Situation

Active listening involves matching your listening to the situation. Listen critically to a speech given by a candidate for office. Listen empathetically to the feelings of a friend. Listen appreciatively to a musical performance.

Ask Questions

Try to think of questions while you're listening. Look at these examples:

Open-ended	Closed	Fact
Why do you think it is so important for young people to vote?	Do you support the current voting age of 18?	How many people aged 18–25 voted in the most recent election?

Connecting With Past Learnings:
From Prehistory to Early Modern Times

Queen Nefertiti

To understand modern world history requires familiarity with the history of ancient and medieval times. Events, concepts, and relationships that began thousands of years ago continue to have an impact on contemporary life.

This unit serves as a review of key developments from prehistory to early modern times. It focuses on major trends and revolutionary ideas of earlier eras—trends and ideas that transformed people and their cultures in new ways. Highlights include the emergence of river valley civilizations, the cultures of Greece and Rome, and the growth of empires and regional civilizations.

Neolithic pottery, *c.* 6000 B.C.

Namib desert, Namibia

Greek hoplite

Benin warrior

PART 1

A Global View: Early Civilizations

How Did the First Civilizations Evolve?

The first humans were wanderers. Wearing animal skins and equipped with crude spears and digging sticks, they followed game animals and searched for ripening fruit, roots, and wild grain from season to season. Over thousands of generations, they learned to chip stone tools, to make fire, and to decorate cave walls with pictures of animals.

Farming Villages

Then, about 10,000 years ago, some human beings abandoned the wandering life of hunter-gatherers. Settling into tiny villages of stone or mud huts, they raised crops and herded or penned up animals. Thanks to these dependable food sources, agricultural villages grew in number. Some of them began to specialize in arts and crafts, trade, and war.

The next step, from scattered farming villages to city-based civilizations, came a little more than 5,000 years ago. Here and there around the world, cities and city-states emerged. Kings, priests, and traders rose to wealth and power. And the invention

of writing symbolized the emergence of a new way of life. We call it civilization.

Ancient Societies

Early civilizations took shape in North Africa, the Middle East, India, and China. Although they emerged in isolation across a widely scattered area, these first civilized societies had much in common.

Politically, the first civilizations turned increasingly to hereditary monarchs for leadership. These rulers depended on priests, officials, aristocrats, or merchants for support. Priests provided divine sanction for royal rule, asserting that the kings of Sumerian city-states were "stewards of the gods" or that Egypt's pharaohs were gods themselves. Royal officials carried out the ruler's decrees, collected taxes, and supervised large-scale public works, including city walls and irrigation projects. Landowning aristocrats dominated agriculture and often served as military officers in royal armies. The merchants of Mesopotamia, India, and elsewhere grew wealthy

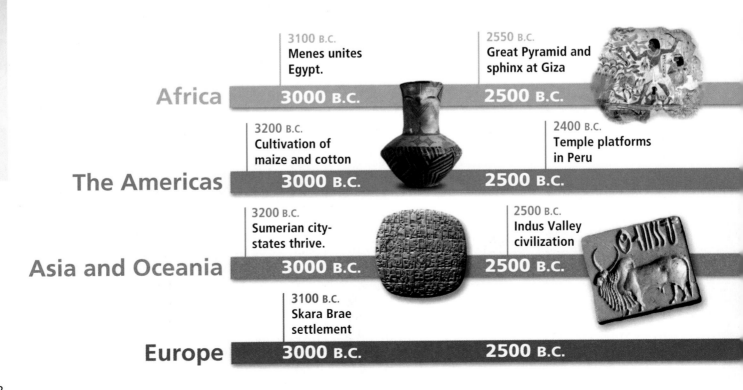

3100 B.C.
Menes unites Egypt.

2550 B.C.
Great Pyramid and sphinx at Giza

Africa   **3000 B.C.**   **2500 B.C.**

3200 B.C.
Cultivation of maize and cotton

2400 B.C.
Temple platforms in Peru

The Americas   **3000 B.C.**   **2500 B.C.**

3200 B.C.
Sumerian city-states thrive.

2500 B.C.
Indus Valley civilization

Asia and Oceania   **3000 B.C.**   **2500 B.C.**

3100 B.C.
Skara Brae settlement

Europe   **3000 B.C.**   **2500 B.C.**

from trade, paid taxes, and strengthened the state economically.

Cities like Mohenjo-Daro or Babylon became the centers of political power and economic development. Most people, however, continued to live in small villages and cultivate the soil. These peasant majorities provided a foundation for the more elaborate lifestyles of their social superiors.

Ancient Cultures

These early civilizations built on the cultural achievements of the simpler societies from which they grew. Architects constructed elaborate royal palaces, temples such as the ziggurats of Mesopotamia, and royal tombs such as the pyramids of Egypt. Sculptors carved beautiful statues of gods, goddesses, and rulers. Painters depicted scenes of everyday life or military victories. The development of writing preserved some of the world's oldest literature, from the Egyptian *Tale of Sinuhe* and Sumerian *Epic of Gilgamesh* to India's *Mahabharata* and ancient China's *Book of Songs*.

Major advances in science and technology may also be traced to ancient times. From metalworking and textiles to mathematics and astronomy, early civilizations contributed greatly to humanity's store of skills. Religions also grew more complex, producing early scriptures, including the Vedas of India. While most ancient societies were polytheistic, the Hebrew people of Mesopotamia introduced monotheism, the worship of one single, all-powerful God.

Looking Ahead

A thousand years before the time of Jesus, civilization was still a rare phenomenon. Most people on all continents still lived in food-gathering bands, in farming villages, or as nomadic herders. But the future belonged to the islands of civilizations that were emerging here and there around the world.

Assessment

Choose two events and two pictures from the timeline below. For each, write a sentence explaining how it relates to the themes expressed in the Global View essay.

2050 B.C.	1472 B.C.	1279–1213 B.C.	730–670 B.C.
Middle Kingdom of Egypt begins.	**Reign of Natshepsut begins.**	**Reign of Ramses II**	**Nubian rule over Egypt**

2000 B.C.   1500 B.C.   1000 B.C.   500 B.C.

2000 B.C.	1500 B.C.	900 B.C.	500 B.C.
Permanent towns in Valley of Mexico	**Rise of Olmec civilization**	**Chavin culture in Peru**	**Adena mounds in Ohio**

2000 B.C.   1500 B.C.   1000 B.C.   500 B.C.

2000 B.C.	1766 B.C.	1100 B.C.	539 B.C.
Development of Chinese writing	**Shang dynasty in China emerges.**	**Assyrians expand power.**	**Persian empire created.**

2000 B.C.   1500 B.C.   1000 B.C.   500 B.C.

2000 B.C.	1600 B.C.	750 B.C.	
Bronze Age in Europe	**Height of Minoan civilization**	**Greeks colonize the Mediterranean.**	

2000 B.C.   1500 B.C.   1000 B.C.   500 B.C.

1 Toward Civilization

(Prehistory–3000 B.C.)

Main Ideas

- About 10,000 years ago, during the Neolithic period, or New Stone Age, people learned to farm.
- By about 5,000 years ago, the advances made by early farming communities led to the rise of civilizations.
- Historians define seven basic features common to most early civilizations: well-organized central governments, complex religions, job specialization, social classes, arts and architecture, public works, and writing.

Ancient Mesopotamian carving of a carpenter at work

Historians call the earliest period of human history the Old Stone Age, or the Paleolithic Period. This long period dates from the time of the first stone toolmakers to about 10,000 B.C. Paleolithic people were **nomads,** moving from place to place to follow game animals and search for edible plants. They lived in small hunting and food-gathering bands of about 20 to 30 people.

Stone Age people learned to adapt to their environment for survival. Men and women made simple tools and weapons such as digging sticks, spears, and axes. They developed spoken language, which let them cooperate as they worked. During the ice ages, people invented clothing made of animal skins and learned to build fires.

The Growth of Farming

About 10,000 years ago, nomadic bands made a dramatic breakthrough. They learned to farm. By producing their own food, they could remain in one place. This change from nomadic to settled farming life ushered in the New Stone Age, or Neolithic Period. Neolithic farmers established permanent villages and developed new skills and tools.

People also learned to tame some of the animals they once hunted. Rather than wait for migrating animals to return each year, the new village dwellers rounded them up and herded the animals or penned them in enclosures. This practice enabled people to have meat, and eventually animal labor, without leaving villages and farms.

Because people could now settle in one place, agriculture led to a growth in population. This growth in population led, in turn, to increased interaction among human communities.

Village life also reshaped the roles of women and men. Heads of families formed a council of elders to make important decisions. Often, a village chief emerged. During times of want, warfare increased. Success in battle enabled some men to gain status as warriors. These warriors had power over both women and other men. The status of women declined, though they did not lose all their influence or rights.

About 5,000 years ago, the advances made by early farming communities led people to a new stage of development—the emergence of civilizations.

Beginnings of Civilization

Historians define eight basic features common to most early civilizations. These features are: (1) cities, (2) well-organized central governments, (3) complex religions, (4) job specialization, (5) social classes, (6) arts and architecture, (7) public works, and (8) writing.

In Africa and Asia, the first cities emerged after farmers began raising crops in fertile lands along river valleys. The nutrient-rich soils and a reliable source of water allowed farmers to produce surplus, or extra, crops. These surpluses provided more food and helped populations to expand. As populations increased, some villages grew into cities.

In these cities, some of the people were able to work at jobs other than farming. This was a radical departure from the traditional economies of the Stone Age. In fact, many aspects of life were dramatically different than they had been before.

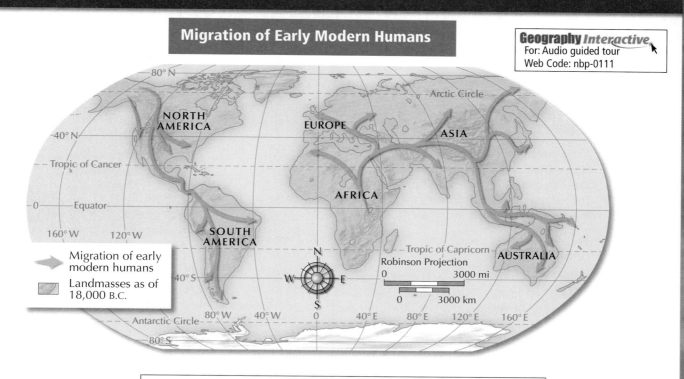

Migration of Early Modern Humans

Geography *Interactive*
For: Audio guided tour
Web Code: nbp-0111

NORTH AMERICA

EUROPE

ASIA

AFRICA

SOUTH AMERICA

AUSTRALIA

→ Migration of early modern humans

Landmasses as of 18,000 B.C.

Robinson Projection
0   3000 mi
0   3000 km

80° N
Arctic Circle
40° N
Tropic of Cancer
0 — Equator
160° W   120° W
40° S
80° W   40° W   0   40° E   80° E   120° E   160° E
Antarctic Circle
80° S
Tropic of Capricorn

Geography and History
Once *Homo sapiens* had emerged, they migrated along the various routes shown above. Many of these routes followed the paths of large herd animals.

Organized Governments The challenge of farming in a river valley contributed to the development of city governments. To control flooding and channel waters to fields, early farmers worked together. Through cooperation, they built dikes, dug canals, and carved out irrigation ditches. Such projects required leadership and well-organized governments. Some city governments grew powerful and complex. Over time, government bureaucracies grew. A **bureaucracy** is a system of managing government through specialized departments run by appointed officials.

Social Classes Social organization also became more complex. People were ranked in social classes according to their jobs. Priests and nobles were usually at the top. Next came wealthy merchants, followed by **artisans,** or skilled craftworkers. Below them stood the vast majority of people, who were peasant farmers. Slaves were at the lowest social level.

A critical new skill emerged—writing. Priests probably developed writing in order to record the amount of grain collected or other information. Early writing was made up of **pictographs,** or simple drawings that represented ideas. As writing grew more complex, specially trained people called scribes learned to read and write.

The First Empires As ancient rulers gained more and more power, they conquered territories beyond the boundaries of their cities. Some were able to conquer many cities and villages, creating empires. An **empire** is a group of states, territories, and peoples ruled by one person. While empire building brought painful defeat for conquered peoples, it also helped limit war and establish connections between neighboring communities.

Assessment

1. **Identify (a)** Old Stone Age **(b)** New Stone Age
2. **Define (a)** nomad **(b)** bureaucracy **(c)** artisan **(d)** pictograph **(e)** empire
3. What dramatic breakthrough allowed nomadic bands to settle in villages for the first time?

2 First Civilizations: Africa and Asia

(3200 B.C.–500 B.C.)

Funeral mask of King Tutankhamen

Main Ideas

- A rich civilization emerged in the valley of the Nile River in Egypt.
- Independent Sumerian city-states developed in Mesopotamia, an area of fertile land between the Tigris and Euphrates rivers.
- The Hebrews developed Judaism, a monotheistic religion based on the worship of one God.

The first civilizations took shape in the river valleys of North Africa, the Middle East, India, and China. Though they grew in isolation in widely scattered areas, they developed complex ways of life and beliefs that continue to affect our world today.

Ancient Kingdoms of the Nile

More than 5,000 years ago, a rich farming civilization grew in the valley of the Nile River in Egypt. To control the Nile's annual floods, village people learned to cooperate. They built dikes, reservoirs, and irrigation ditches to channel the river and store water for the dry season. Eventually, these villages joined together into two kingdoms. About 3100 B.C., King Menes united these kingdoms, creating the world's first unified state along the Nile.

After Menes' reign, the history of ancient Egypt can be divided into three main periods: the Old Kingdom (about 2575 B.C.–2130 B.C.), the Middle Kingdom (about 1938 B.C.–1630 B.C.), and the New Kingdom (about 1539 B.C.–1075 B.C.).

During the Old Kingdom, **pharaohs** (FEHR ohz), or the Egyptian rulers, organized a strong central state. They built majestic pyramids to serve as tombs. During the Middle and New Kingdoms, trade and warfare brought Egypt into contact with other civilizations. New ideas, customs, and technologies spread from one people to another in a process called **cultural diffusion.** Powerful New Kingdom pharaohs such as Queen Hatshepsut and Ramses II established a large empire that eventually reached the Euphrates River. After Ramses II, Egyptian power slowly declined.

Egyptian Civilization

Egyptians worshiped many gods and goddesses. They also built tombs to preserve their bodies for the afterlife and they filled them with items that they would need in their new lives.

Egyptian society was organized into classes. The pharaoh, who was considered both a god and a king, ruled at the top. Next came the nobles, who fought the pharaoh's wars. A tiny class of merchants and artisans developed. Farmers and slaves were at the bottom of society.

City-States of Ancient Sumer

To the northeast of the Nile lies the Fertile Crescent, an arc of soil-rich land. More than 5,000 years ago, the independent city-states of Sumer grew along the Tigris and Euphrates rivers in a part of the Fertile Crescent called Mesopotamia. A **city-state** is a political unit made up of a city and the surrounding lands.

Floods and Irrigation Control of the Tigris and Euphrates rivers was the key to the development of a civilization in the Sumerian city-states. Villagers built dikes and irrigation ditches. Using clay bricks, Sumerians built **ziggurats,** or soaring pyramid-temples.

The city-states of Sumer often fought for control of land and water. War leaders gained importance and eventually became hereditary rulers. A social **hierarchy** (HY ur ahr kee), or system of ranks, emerged. The highest rank included the ruling family, leading officials, and high priests.

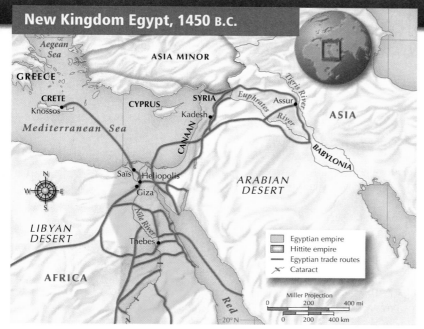

New Kingdom Egypt, 1450 B.C.

Egyptian empire
Hittite empire
— Egyptian trade routes
⤢ Cataract

Miller Projection
0   200   400 mi
0   200   400 km
20° N

Geography *Interactive*
For: Audio guided tour
Web Code: nbp-0231

Geography and History
During the years of the New Kingdom, powerful and ambitious pharaohs created a large empire. At its height, around 1450 B.C., the Egyptian empire reached as far north as Syria and the Euphrates River.

Advances in Learning By 3100 B.C., Sumerians had invented the earliest form of writing, called **cuneiform** (kyoo NEE uh fawrm). **Scribes,** or the specially trained people who knew how to read and write, maintained records for the kingdom.

Invaders, Traders, and Empires

Mesopotamia's location at a geographical crossroads made it tempting to invaders, some of whom built great empires. Sargon, the ruler of Akkad, conquered the city-states of Sumer about 2300 B.C. He built the first empire known to history.

About 1790 B.C., Hammurabi (hah muh RAH bee), king of Babylon, brought much of Mesopotamia under his control. He published a remarkable set of laws, known as the Code of Hammurabi. This code was the first major collection of laws in history. In 539 B.C., Persian armies overthrew Babylon.

Warfare and trade in Mesopotamia spread ideas and technology around the Mediterranean world. Knowledge of ironworking became common throughout the region. An Assyrian king founded one of the first libraries. The Phoenicians created an alphabet and the Persians improved trade by encouraging the use of coins among merchants.

The Roots of Judaism

Among the many peoples who occupied the Fertile Crescent were the Hebrews. According to the Torah, the Hebrews' most sacred text, they once lived in Mesopotamia. About 2000 B.C., they migrated into a region known as Canaan.

The early Hebrews developed Judaism, which is a **monotheistic** religion (based on the belief in one true God). They recorded events and laws, such as the Ten Commandments, in the Torah. **Prophets,** or spiritual leaders, urged the Hebrews to obey God's law. These prophets preached a strong code of **ethics,** or moral standards of behavior. They urged both personal morality and social justice, calling on the rich and powerful to protect the poor and weak.

By 1000 B.C., the Hebrews established the kingdom of Israel. A famous ruler, King Solomon, built a splendid temple dedicated to God, at Jerusalem. Eventually the kingdom split into two parts. A series of invading armies captured the Hebrew kingdoms.

During their captivity, the Hebrews became known as Jews. They lived under foreign rulers until about 2,000 years ago, when many were forced to leave their homeland. This **diaspora** (dy AS pur uh), or scattering of people, sent Jews to different parts of the world. Wherever they settled, they built close-knit communities and kept their traditions. Today, Judaism is considered one of the world's major religions for its unique contribution to religious thought.

Assessment

1. **Identify (a)** Nile River **(b)** Fertile Crescent **(c)** Mesopotamia **(d)** Hebrews
2. **Define (a)** pharaoh **(b)** cultural diffusion **(c)** city-state **(d)** ziggurat **(e)** hierarchy **(f)** cuneiform **(g)** scribe **(h)** monotheistic **(i)** prophet **(j)** ethics **(k)** diaspora
3. Name two geographic locations where early civilizations developed.

3 Early Civilizations in India and China

(2600 B.C.–256 B.C.)

The Hindu god Shiva

Main Ideas

- India's first civilization grew in the Indus River valley.
- The Aryans moved into the Indus Valley and built a new civilization along the Ganges River.
- During the Shang and Zhou dynasties, the ancient Chinese made significant achievements in many areas.

As civilizations took shape in the Nile Valley and Fertile Crescent, people in India and China carved out their own civilizations. These grew along the fertile river valleys of Asia.

Cities of the Indus Valley

India's first civilization emerged in the Indus River valley about 2600 B.C. The people of the Indus flourished there for 1,000 years, building a civilization that covered the largest area of any in ancient times. Its two main cities, Mohenjo-Daro and Harappa, were both carefully planned. Each city was laid out in a grid pattern, with blocks larger than modern city blocks. Houses had complex plumbing systems, with baths, drains, and water chutes that led to underground sewers.

Most Indus people were farmers. Powerful leaders, perhaps priest-kings, made sure the cities had a reliable supply of grain. Merchants and traders sailed with cargoes of cotton cloth, grain, copper, and pearls all the way to the cities of Sumer.

By 1750 B.C., the quality of life in Indus Valley cities was declining. Some scholars think the final blow fell about 1500 B.C. with the arrival of nomadic people from the north. The newcomers were Aryans. With their horse-drawn chariots and superior weapons, they overran the cities and towns of the Indus region.

Kingdoms of the Ganges

The Aryans were Indo-European people who migrated across Europe and Asia seeking water and pasture for their horses and cattle. Over several centuries, waves of Aryan groups moved through the mountain passes into northwestern India. In time, Aryans spread eastward to the forests of the Ganges River basin. They made tools of iron and built walled cities. By 500 B.C., a new Indian civilization had emerged. It consisted of many rival kingdoms, though people shared a common culture.

Most of what we know about the Aryans comes from the Vedas, a collection of prayers, hymns, and other religious teachings. Aryan priests memorized and recited the Vedas for a thousand years before they were written down.

Society The Aryans divided people into social classes by occupation. The three basic groups were the priests; the warriors; and the herders, farmers, artisans, and merchants. Eventually, the Aryans added a fourth group—non-Aryans whom they had conquered. This group was at the lowest level of society. It included farmworkers, servants, and other laborers. Over time, these divisions gave way to a more complex system of castes. **Castes** are social groups into which people are born and which they cannot leave.

Religious Beliefs Aryans were **polytheistic**. That is, they believed in many gods. As society developed and changed, people moved toward the notion of a single spiritual power beyond the many gods of the Vedas. They called this power brahman and believed it lived in all things. Some Aryans became **mystics**, or individuals who devote their lives to seeking spiritual truth.

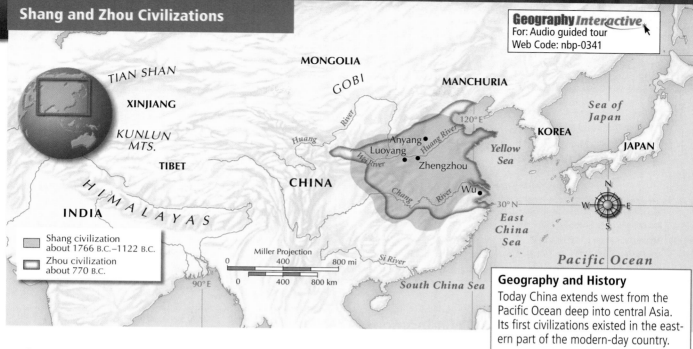

Shang and Zhou Civilizations

Geography Interactive
For: Audio guided tour
Web Code: nbp-0341

Shang civilization about 1766 B.C.–1122 B.C.

Zhou civilization about 770 B.C.

Miller Projection

0   400   800 mi

0   400   800 km

Geography and History
Today China extends west from the Pacific Ocean deep into central Asia. Its first civilizations existed in the eastern part of the modern-day country.

Early Civilizations in China

Long distances and physical barriers separated China from Egypt, the Middle East, and India. This isolation contributed to the Chinese belief that China was at the center of the Earth and the sole source of civilization. This led the ancient Chinese to call their land the Middle Kingdom.

Geography Great barriers blocked the easy movement of the Chinese to the outside world. High mountains, brutal deserts, thick jungles, and the vast Pacific Ocean lay between China and the rest of the world. Still, the people of China found ways to trade with neighboring peoples. In time, Chinese products reached the Middle East and beyond.

Chinese history began in the Huang He valley, where Neolithic people learned to farm. As in other places, the need to control a major river through large water projects probably led to the rise of a strong central government.

The Shang and Zhou Dynasties About 1650 B.C., a Chinese people called the Shang came to power in northern China. In 1027 B.C., the Zhou (joh) people overthrew the Shang. The Zhou dynasty lasted until 256 B.C. A **dynasty** is a ruling family. To justify their rebellion against the Shang, the Zhou dynasty promoted the idea of the Mandate of Heaven, or the divine right to rule. Later, this idea expanded to explain the **dynastic cycle,** or the rise and fall of dynasties. If rulers became corrupt, the Chinese believed that Heaven withdrew its support, or mandate, and the dynasty fell.

Religion By Shang times, the Chinese had developed complex religious beliefs. They prayed to many gods and nature spirits. Over time, Chinese religious practices came to center on respect for ancestors. The Chinese called on the spirits of their ancestors to bring good fortune to the family. The Chinese also believed that the universe reflected a balance between two forces, yin and yang. Yin was linked to the Earth and female forces, while yang stood for Heaven and male forces.

Science and Technology During the Shang and Zhou periods, the Chinese studied the movement of the planets, recorded eclipses, and created an accurate calendar. They developed the technology of bronzemaking and silkmaking. Under the Zhou dynasty, the Chinese made the first books. They bound strips of wood or bamboo together and drew characters on the flat surfaces. By 256 B.C., China was a large, wealthy, and highly developed center of civilization.

Assessment

1. **Identify (a)** Mohenjo-Daro **(b)** Aryans **(c)** Vedas **(d)** Zhou dynasty
2. **Define (a)** caste **(b)** polytheistic **(c)** brahman **(d)** mystic **(e)** dynasty **(f)** dynastic cycle
3. Name the four basic groups, or castes, into which the Aryans divided people.
4. What were some of the religious beliefs of the Chinese during the Shang dynasty?

Quick Study Guide

■ Eras of Civilization

India		China	
Indus civilization	2600 B.C. to 1900 B.C.	Shang dynasty	1766 B.C. to 1122 B.C.
Aryan civilization	1500 B.C. to ?	Zhou dynasty	1122 B.C. to 256 B.C.
Maurya empire	321 B.C. to 185 B.C.	Qin dynasty	221 B.C. to 206 B.C.
Gupta empire	A.D. 320 to A.D. 550	Han dynasty	202 B.C. to A.D. 220

■ Key Stages of Human Development

Old Stone Age
- creation of stone, bone, and wood tools and weapons
- use of fire
- spoken language
- ability to travel across water in boats
- belief in a spiritual world
- creation of cave paintings
- burial of the dead

New Stone Age
- farming and domestication of plants and animals
- settling of permanent villages
- dominance of family, economic, and political life by men
- gaining of prestige by warriors
- appearance of differences in wealth
- creation of first calendars
- more elaborate tools and new technologies

Rise of Civilizations
- production of surpluses of food
- expansion of population
- development of cities, civilizations, and governments
- government oversight of large-scale projects
- belief in polytheistic religions
- job specialization
- development of social classes
- development of arts and architecture
- invention of writing systems
- expansion of some cities into city-states and empires
- cultural diffusion

■ Key Civilizations

Civilization	Time Period	Notable Rulers
Sumer	3200 B.C.–1900 B.C.	
Egypt	Old Kingdom 2575 B.C.–2130 B.C. Middle Kingdom 1938 B.C.–1630 B.C. New Kingdom 1539 B.C.–1075 B.C.	Hatshepsut Thutmose III Ramses II
Akkad	2300 B.C.–2150 B.C.	Sargon
Babylon	Old 1790 B.C.–1595 B.C. New 626 B.C.–539 B.C.	Hammurabi Nebuchadnezzar
Hittite	1650 B.C.–1200 B.C.	
Assyria	1350 B.C.–609 B.C.	Assurbanipal
Israel	1000 B.C.–586 B.C.	David Solomon
Persia	539 B.C.–323 B.C.	Cyrus the Great Darius I

■ Key Innovations

Sumer: social hierarchy; cuneiform writing; advances in astronomy and mathematics

Egypt: bureaucracy; pyramids; peace treaty; mummification; social hierarchy; hieroglyphic, hieratic, and demotic writing; papyrus; advances in medicine, astronomy, and mathematics; 365-day calendar

Babylon: legal code; advances in astronomy and mathematics

Hittites: iron working

Assyrians: legal regulations of royal household; libraries

Israel: monotheistic religion, Judaism

Persians: government organized into provinces with governors; roads; common set of weights and measures; use of coins and money economy; new religion of Zoroaster

Phoenicians: Tyrian purple dye; alphabet

Belief Systems

▲ The Greek god Hermes is shown here as a messenger.

What major belief systems have emerged over time?

Hinduism, Buddhism, Confucianism, and Daoism are all belief systems that originated in ancient India or China and that still attract many followers. Today, thousands of different belief systems exist around the world. Most of them share certain characteristics—for example, belief in the existence of spiritual powers such as gods and respectful worship by followers, often through prayer. Belief systems vary in whether their followers worship gods and if so, how many, as the following examples show:

▲ Many Daoists painted peaceful nature scenes like this one.

Many Gods

The earliest belief systems focused on the idea that a powerful spirit inhabited every element of nature. In later belief systems, followers often worshiped gods associated with natural forces—such as sun, rain, or fire—or forces related to life and death. Of the many Hindu gods, the three most important are a creator, a preserver, and a destroyer. Other belief systems, such as those of the Greeks and Romans, identified each god with human characteristics and behaviors. For example, the Greek god Hermes was known as a trickster and a thief.

One God

Judaism, Christianity, and Islam share the belief that one god created the universe and rules over it. Jews believe that God's law is clear—"You shall have no other gods before me." Jesus, among whose followers Christianity developed, was a Jew. For that reason, much of the Jewish belief system was incorporated into Christianity, including its monotheism. Muslims, or followers of Islam, believe they should serve God by accepting five basic duties. The first is the daily declaration of faith that "there is no God but Allah."

No Gods

Other major belief systems have no gods. Buddhism, Confucianism, and Daoism, for example, all arose in response to the inspiring ideas of wise, human teachers. Siddhartha Gautama, the Buddha, stressed moral principles that would lead people to a state of enlightenment. Confucius offered guidelines about how to live virtuously, his goal being to ensure social order and good government. Laozi, who was believed to be Daoism's founder, taught his followers how to live in harmony with nature.

An Italian artist depicted the Christian God as a father in this painting. ▶

Thinking Critically

1. **Analyze Information** Do you think there is at least one element that all belief systems have in common? If so, what is it?
2. **Connections to Today** Do research to learn more about one of the belief systems described above. Write a summary telling how many people follow this belief system today, and in which countries.

PART 2

A Global View: Empires of the Ancient World

What Characteristics Were Shared by Ancient Empires Around the World?

Empires combining many cities and small countries emerged in various parts of the world in ancient times. Some of the largest of these empires took shape in India, China, Europe, and, later, in the Americas.

These larger political structures had many things in common. Most empires were built by military conquest and ruled by hereditary emperors through appointed governors or lesser kings. Empires everywhere developed powerful centralized bureaucracies like those of China or imposed universal legal codes like Roman law. Emperors protected far-flung trade routes and built large cities, canals, highways, and other public works. They also sponsored the spread of major religions, such as Buddhism in India and Christianity throughout the Roman empire.

Eastern Empires

In India, the Maurya dynasty united the states along the Ganges in about 300 B.C. The Hindu faith continued to flourish, but after 500 B.C., followers of a reformer known as the Buddha converted many Indians to Buddhism.

Shi Huangdi unified the states of eastern China around 200 B.C. After that, for most of China's history, the Han and later dynasties ruled a vast united nation. Philosophers like Confucius, as well as Buddhist missionaries, laid the groundwork for many basic Chinese beliefs.

Classical Civilizations of Europe

The earliest European civilizations emerged among the peoples of two neighboring Mediterranean peninsulas. These people were the Greeks and the Romans. The Greeks built a brilliant civilization centered in independent city-states, while the Romans later constructed a huge empire that spanned three continents.

Two earlier societies—those of the sea-trading Minoans and the warlike Mycenaeans—gave way to the Greek city-states before 500 B.C. Led by Athens and Sparta, the bustling little Greek cities traded with many peoples, Athens also developed an early form of democratic government. Though they often

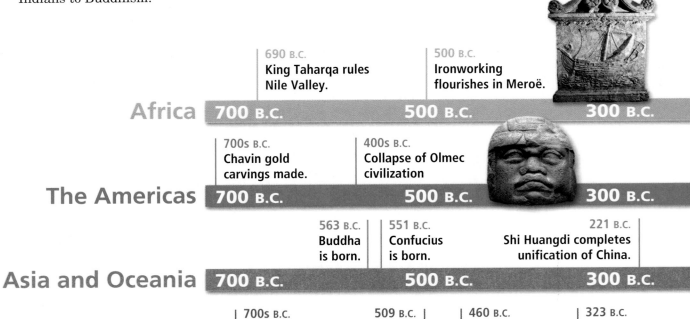

Africa

690 B.C.
King Taharqa rules Nile Valley.

500 B.C.
Ironworking flourishes in Meroë.

700 B.C.   500 B.C.   300 B.C.

The Americas

700s B.C.
Chavin gold carvings made.

400s B.C.
Collapse of Olmec civilization

700 B.C.   500 B.C.   300 B.C.

Asia and Oceania

563 B.C.
Buddha is born.

551 B.C.
Confucius is born.

221 B.C.
Shi Huangdi completes unification of China.

700 B.C.   500 B.C.   300 B.C.

Europe

700s B.C.
Rise of Greek city-states

509 B.C.
Roman republic is established.

460 B.C.
Age of Pericles begins.

323 B.C.
Hellenistic age begins.

700 B.C.   500 B.C.   300 B.C.

fought with one another, the Greeks created a common body of art, science, and philosophy that laid the foundations of Western civilization.

The Romans learned much from the Greeks. Their expanding empire swept around the Mediterranean and then spread northward across Western Europe. Dominated first by its aristocratic Senate, Rome came to be ruled by powerful emperors after the reign of Augustus Caesar.

During the reign of Augustus, Jesus was born in the region of Judea. Christianity spread widely in Roman times. The new religion survived the fall of Rome to become the core of European culture in later centuries.

American Civilizations

Across the Atlantic Ocean, civilizations also emerged in the Americas. Hunters and food-gatherers gradually settled into agricultural villages. In some regions, religious ceremonial centers emerged, then city-states and empires.

In Mexico, the Maya city-states built magnificent temples and mastered complex mathematics. Peru saw a number of regional empires flourish. In the A.D. 1300s and 1400s, the Aztecs established a powerful empire in Mexico, while the Inca built an even larger one in the high Andes of Peru.

Looking Ahead

Some of these mighty empires of Europe, Asia, and the Americas would serve as models for other generations in later centuries. From the Great Wall of China to the Incan royal road through the Andes, these empires left behind impressive monuments. The civilizations of China and India, Greece and Rome, together forged cultural legacies that still influence the world today.

Aztec eagle warrior

Assessment

Choose two events and two pictures from the timeline below. For each, write a sentence explaining how it relates to the themes expressed in the Global View essay.

146 B.C.
Destruction of Carthage

23 B.C.
Roman attack on Nubia fails.

A.D. 350
Axum converts to Christianity.

| 100 B.C. | A.D. 100 | A.D. 300 | A.D. 500 |

A.D. **100s**
Mochica civilization rises.

A.D. **200s**
Hopewell culture flourishes.

A.D. **500s**
Height of Maya civilization

| 100 B.C. | A.D. 100 | A.D. 300 | A.D. 500 |

A.D. **100**
Paper is invented in Han China.

A.D. **370**
Gupta golden age begins.

| 100 B.C. | A.D. 100 | A.D. 300 | A.D. 500 |

27 B.C.
Pax Romana begins.

A.D. 135
Jewish diaspora begins.

A.D. 476
Western Roman empire falls.

| 100 B.C. | A.D. 100 | A.D. 300 | A.D. 500 |

1 Empires of India and China

(600 B.C.–A.D. 550)

Main Ideas

- In ancient India, two major religions developed—Hinduism and Buddhism.
- Under the Maurya and Gupta empires, India grew into a center of trade.
- Shi Huangdi united all of China. Under the Han rulers who followed Shi Huangdi, Chinese civilization made huge advances.

Colossal rock sculpture of Buddha

Between 600 B.C. and A.D. 550, strong, unified empires emerged in India and China. These civilizations established patterns in government, religion, and philosophy that influenced later cultures.

Hinduism and Buddhism

Two major religions, Hinduism and Buddhism, grew in ancient India. Hinduism has no single founder and no single sacred text. It grew from the beliefs of the different groups who settled in India. Even so, all Hindus share certain basic beliefs.

Hindus believe that everything is part of the unchanging, all-powerful spiritual force called brahman. The most important Hindu gods are Brahma, the Creator; Vishnu, the Preserver; and Shiva, the Destroyer. Each can take many forms, human or animal, to represent the various aspects of brahman with which he is associated. The goal of life for Hindus is to achieve union with brahman. **Reincarnation** is the rebirth of the soul in another bodily form. Reincarnation allows people to work toward union with brahman through several lifetimes.

Another major religion, Buddhism, emerged in the 500s B.C. While it shared many Hindu traditions, Buddhism differed from Hinduism. It urged people to seek enlightenment through meditation, rather than through the priests, formal rituals, and many gods of Hinduism.

Buddhism's founder was Siddhartha Gautama. He was known as the Buddha, which means the "Enlightened One." The Buddha taught that desire causes suffering. To overcome suffering, people should rid themselves of desire by following the Eightfold Path. The Buddha describes the Eightfold Path as "right views, right aspirations, right speech, right conduct, right livelihood, right effort, right mindfulness, and right contemplation."

Buddhism's final goal was to achieve **nirvana,** or union with the universe and release from the cycle of rebirth.

Powerful Empires of India

For centuries, northern India was a battleground. Then, in 321 B.C., Chandragupta Maurya (chun druh GUP tuh MOWR yuh) forged the first great Indian empire. The Maurya dynasty eventually conquered much of India.

The most honored Maurya emperor was Chandragupta's grandson, Asoka. Turning his back on violent conquest, Asoka converted to Buddhism. He ruled by moral example. His policies brought peace and wealth. Asoka also paved the way for the spread of Buddhism throughout Asia.

After Asoka's death, rivals battled for power. Despite unrest, India developed into a center of world trade. It established contact with civilizations in Africa, the Middle East, and Central and Southeast Asia. Then, about 500 years after the Mauryas, the Gupta dynasty again united much of India. Under the Guptas, who ruled from A.D. 320 to about A.D. 540, India enjoyed a golden age of peace and achievement.

Maurya and Gupta Empires

Geography *Interactive*
For: Audio guided tour
Web Code: nbp-0331

Bactria

HINDU KUSH

Kabul

Gandhara

Indus River

Brahmaputra River

Tibet

HIMALAYAS

Ganges River

Pataliputra

Nalanda

- - - Tropic of Cancer - - -

Narmada River

Magadha

Ajanta

Arabian Sea

Deccan

Kalinga

Bay of Bengal

15°N

N W E S

Tamil Kingdoms

Sri Lanka

Indian Ocean

Maurya empire about 250 B.C.
Gupta empire about A.D. 400

75°E   90°E

Miller Projection
0   250   500 mi
0   250   500 km

Geography and History
India's diverse people were seldom united. Yet the Maurya and, later, the Guptas were able to unite much of the subcontinent.

Pillars of Indian Life Most Indians of that period were village peasants. Then, as today, the village and the family maintained order in daily life. The caste system also greatly influenced Indian society. Caste rules governed every part of life—including where people lived and how they earned a living. Despite its inequalities, caste created a stable social order.

Philosophy and Religion in China

China's most influential philosopher, Confucius, was born in 551 B.C. A brilliant scholar, Confucius took little interest in religious matters. He was concerned with social order and good government. He taught that harmony resulted when people accepted their place in society. He put **filial piety,** or respect for parents, above all other duties. Confucius' ideas came to influence every area of

Chinese life and eventually spread to neighboring countries.

Another Chinese philosopher, Hanfeizi, introduced ideas that differed sharply from the ideas of Confucius. He insisted that the only way to achieve order in society was to pass strict laws and to impose harsh punishments. Hanfeizi's teachings came to be known as Legalism. Many feudal rulers, including the Qin emperor who united China in 221 B.C., believed Legalism was the most effective way to maintain order.

A third philosophy, Daoism, arose around the same time. Daoists sought to live in harmony with nature, rather than to bring order to human affairs. They viewed government as unnatural and therefore the cause of many problems.

Strong Rulers Unite China

When the Zhou dynasty weakened, a powerful new ruler, Shi Huangdi, rose to unify all of China. He spent 20 years conquering the warring states. He built a strong government and set the stage for China's classical age. His most remarkable and costly achievement was the building of the Great Wall.

After Shi Huangdi died, a new dynasty, the Han, was founded. It lasted from 206 B.C. to A.D. 220. Under Han rulers, the Chinese made huge advances in trade, government, technology, and the arts. The Silk Road, which eventually stretched 4,000 miles, linked China to the Fertile Crescent. The Han empire brought 400 years of unity to China.

Assessment

1. **Identify (a)** Siddhartha Gautama **(b)** Confucius **(c)** Shi Huangdi **(d)** the Han dynasty
2. **Define (a)** reincarnation **(b)** nirvana **(c)** filial piety
3. What are two basic teachings of Hinduism?

15

2 Ancient Greece

(1750 B.C.–133 B.C.)

Main Ideas

- Through trading contacts, Minoan and Mycenaean cultures borrowed many ideas from older civilizations.
- After the Persian Wars, democracy flourished in Athens.
- Guided by a belief in reason, Greek philosophers, writers, and artists used their genius to seek order in the universe.

Interior vase detail of a Greek hoplite warrior

Unlike many other civilizations, Greek civilization did not rise in a fertile river valley. Instead, it grew in a rugged corner of southeastern Europe. Over time, independent Greek city-states created a civilization that set a standard of excellence for later civilizations. Greek ideas about the universe, the individual, and government still live on in the world today.

Early People of the Aegean

The island of Crete in the Aegean Sea was home to the Minoan people, the earliest civilization in the region. The Minoans were traders who set up outposts throughout the Aegean world and on the Greek mainland. Through contact with Egypt and Mesopotamia, this early people gained ideas and technology that they adapted to their own culture. Minoan civilization reached its height between about 1600 B.C. and 1500 B.C. By about 1400 B.C., Minoan civilization had vanished. A natural disaster may have helped destroy these island people.

The Mycenaeans, another civilization of sea traders, soon dominated the Greek mainland and Crete. They flourished between about 1400 B.C. and 1200 B.C. The Mycenaeans, too, absorbed both Egyptian and Mesopotamian ideas, which they passed on to later Greeks. They are best remembered for the Trojan War. The poet Homer described the conflict in his two epic poems, the *Iliad* and the *Odyssey*. These poems reveal much about the values and religion of the ancient Greeks. The heroes display honor and courage. Such ideals greatly influenced Greek culture. Three thousand years later, the epics of Homer and the ideals of the ancient Greeks continue to inspire us.

The Rise of Greek City-States

When Mycenaean civilization declined, the Greeks seemed to step backward. For centuries, Greeks lived in small, isolated farming villages. Eventually, they began to build many small city-states. However, they frequently warred among themselves. Despite their differences, Greeks shared a common culture, including their language, religion, and festivals. They became skilled sailors and traders. Eventually, Greek colonies took root all around the Mediterranean. Greek ideas and culture spread.

As their world expanded after 750 B.C., the Greeks evolved a unique version of the city-state, called the **polis**. Typically, Greeks built cities on two levels. On a hilltop stood the **acropolis** (uh KRAH puh lis), or high city. There, the Greeks dedicated temples to the gods and goddesses. On flatter ground below lay the walled main city with its marketplace, theater, public buildings, and homes.

Governing the City-States At first, the ruler of the polis was a king. A government in which a king or queen exercises central power is a **monarchy**. Slowly, power shifted to a class of noble landowners. The result was an **aristocracy**, or rule by a landholding elite. As trade expanded, a new middle class of wealthy merchants, farmers, and artisans formed in some cities. They challenged the land-owning nobles for power and came to rule some city-states. The result was a form of government called an oligarchy. An **oligarchy** is government by a small, powerful elite, usually from the business class.

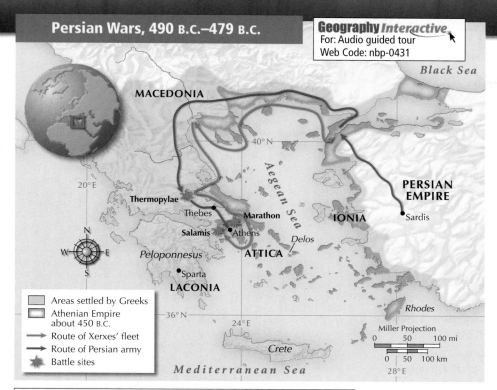

Persian Wars, 490 B.C.–479 B.C.

Geography *Interactive*
For: Audio guided tour
Web Code: nbp-0431

MACEDONIA

Black Sea

40° N

20° E

Aegean Sea

PERSIAN EMPIRE

Thermopylae

Thebes · Marathon

IONIA

Sardis

Salamis · Athens

Delos

Peloponnesus

ATTICA

N
W E
S

· Sparta

LACONIA

36° N

24° E

Rhodes

Miller Projection
0   50   100 mi
0   50   100 km

Crete

28° E

Mediterranean Sea

Legend:
- Areas settled by Greeks
- Athenian Empire about 450 B.C.
- → Route of Xerxes' fleet
- → Route of Persian army
- ✳ Battle sites

Geography and History
When the Persian empire turned its mighty army against Greece, the Greek city-states briefly joined forces to defend their independence.

Sparta and Athens In the Greek city-state of Sparta, a warrior society took root. Spartan boys trained for military service. Because men were occupied with war, some women gained responsibilities such as running their family's estate. The city-state of Athens evolved into a **democracy,** or government by the people. By modern standards, Athenian democracy was quite limited. Only male citizens participated.

Victory and Defeat in the Greek World
When the Persians threatened the Greeks, the city-states briefly joined together to defend themselves. After the Persian Wars, Athens thrived. Under the leadership of Pericles, a Greek statesman who ruled from 460 B.C. to 429 B.C., democracy and culture flourished. Athens developed a **direct democracy.** Under this system, a large number of male citizens took part in the day-to-day affairs of government. Athenian power and influence increased.

The Glory That Was Greece
Greeks had great confidence in the power of the human mind. Many Greek artists, writers, and philosophers denied that events were caused by the gods. Instead, they used observation and reason to find causes for what happened. Philosophers and teachers like Socrates, Plato, and Aristotle developed new ideas about truth, reason, justice, and government. People developed new styles of art and architecture, that reflected those ideas. Philosophers, poets, and dramatists set the standard for what later Europeans called the classic style.

Alexander and the Hellenistic Age
While the Greek city-states warred among themselves, King Philip of neighboring Macedonia built a superb army. Eventually, Philip controlled all of Greece. When he died, his 20-year-old son Alexander took the throne. Over the next 12 years, this confident young man earned the title Alexander the Great. His conquests spread Greek civilization throughout the Mediterranean world and across the Middle East to the outskirts of India.

Alexander's conquests linked a vast area. Greek culture blended with Persian, Egyptian, and Indian cultures to create the Hellenistic civilization. Art, science, mathematics, and philosophy flourished. Even as Greek political power waned, Greek ideas came to dominate the Mediterranean world. This legacy later influenced the civilizations of Rome and Western Europe.

Assessment

1. **Identify (a)** Homer **(b)** Pericles **(c)** Alexander
2. **Define (a)** polis **(b)** acropolis **(c)** monarchy **(d)** aristocracy **(e)** oligarchy **(f)** democracy **(g)** direct democracy
3. What cultural ties united the Greek world?
4. How were Greek city-states governed?
5. Why did many Greek philosophers and writers reject the belief that events were caused by the whims of the gods?

3 Ancient Rome and the Rise of Christianity

(509 B.C.–A.D. 476)

Main Ideas

- Conquest and diplomacy helped the Romans spread their rule from Spain to Egypt.
- During the Pax Romana, Roman emperors brought peace, order, and prosperity to the lands they controlled.
- Christianity, which began in Roman-held lands in the Middle East, spread throughout the Roman empire.

Rome expanded across the Mediterranean and grew into a huge, diverse empire. Rome's 1,000-year history had many lasting effects. Probably none was more important than the spread westward into Europe of key elements of the civilizations of Greece, Egypt, and the Fertile Crescent.

Soldiers and Roman officers of the Praetorian Guard

The Roman World Takes Shape

Rome began as a small city-state in Italy. The Romans were an Indo-European people who settled along the Tiber River in small villages. Their neighbors, the Etruscans, ruled much of central Italy, including Rome. After the Romans threw over the hated Etruscan king in 509 B.C., they resolved never to be ruled by a monarch again. Instead, they set up a **republic,** a government in which officials are chosen by the people. At first, the most powerful people in government were **patricians,** or members of the landholding upper class. Eventually, commoners, or **plebeians,** also gained the right to be elected to the Roman senate.

As Rome's political system changed, its armies expanded Roman power across Italy. By about 270 B.C., Rome occupied all of Italy. Rome's success was due partly to skillful diplomacy and partly to its efficient, well-disciplined army. Furthermore, Rome generally treated its defeated enemies with mercy. By 133 B.C., Roman power reached from Spain to Egypt.

From Republic to Empire

Military victories put the Romans in control of busy trade routes. Incredible riches flooded into Rome from conquered lands. This new wealth, however, had disturbing consequences. Increased corruption and self-interest replaced virtues such as simplicity, hard work, and devotion to duty. Attempts to reform the system led to a backlash. For 100 years, Rome faced a series of civil wars.

Eventually, a powerful Roman general named Octavian restored order. Although he was not called a king, he exercised absolute power. Taking the name Augustus, he ruled from 31 B.C. to A.D. 14, and brought the 500-year-old republic to an end. A new age dawned—the age of the Roman empire.

As Rome's first emperor, Augustus helped the empire recover from the long period of unrest. He laid the foundation for a stable government and undertook economic reforms. The 200-year span that began with Augustus and ended with emperor Marcus Aurelius is known as the Pax Romana, or "Roman Peace." During this time, Roman emperors brought peace, order, unity, and prosperity to the lands under their control. People were able to move easily within the Roman empire, spreading ideas and knowledge.

A fish and the cross, symbols of Christianity

The Roman Achievement

Through war and conquest, Rome spread its civilization to distant lands. Yet, the civilization that developed was not simply Roman. Rather, Rome acted as a bridge between the east and the west by borrowing and transforming Greek and Hellenistic achievements. This blend of cultures became known as Greco-Roman civilization.

The Romans greatly admired Greek culture. They took Greek ideas and adapted them to their own ways. Roman sculptors, for instance, used the Greek idea of realism to reveal an individual's character in each stone portrait. Roman architects improved on design elements such as the arch and the dome. Above all, Romans excelled as engineers. They built roads, bridges, aqueducts, and harbors throughout the empire. Many of these remained standing long after Rome fell.

Probably the greatest legacy of Rome was its commitment to the rule of law and to justice. These ideas still shape Western civilization today. The rule of law fostered unity and stability. Roman law would become the basis for legal systems in Europe and Latin America.

The Rise of Christianity

Early in the Pax Romana, a new religion, Christianity, sprang up in Roman-held lands in the Middle East. Its leading figure was a Jew named Jesus. Jesus was born around 4 B.C. in Bethlehem. He was prophesied to be the **messiah**, or savior sent by God to lead the Jews to freedom. The teachings of Jesus were firmly rooted in the Jewish religion. He believed in one God and accepted the Ten Commandments, a collection of laws that Jews believe God gave them.

At the same time, Jesus preached new beliefs. He called himself the Son of God and taught that his mission was to bring salvation and eternal life to all of God's children—anyone who would believe in him. He extended the Jewish ideas of mercy and sympathy for the poor and helpless to include forgiveness and love for enemies.

To some Jews and Romans, Jesus was a dangerous troublemaker. Eventually, he was executed. But his disciples, or followers, believed that Jesus had risen from the dead, talked with them, and then ascended into heaven. Slowly, a few Jews accepted the teaching that Jesus was the messiah, or the Christ, from the Greek for "the anointed one." These people became the first Christians.

For a while, these first Christians remained a **sect**, or small group, within Judaism. But then Paul, a Jew from Asia Minor, set to work to spread the new faith to non-Jews. At first, Rome persecuted Christians. Nevertheless, Christians organized into a church and grew in strength. Eventually, Christianity reshaped Roman beliefs.

The Long Decline

After the death of the emperor Marcus Aurelius in A.D. 180, turmoil rocked the Roman empire. Eventually, the empire split into two parts, east and west, each with its own ruler. In the west, a corrupt government, poverty and unemployment, and declining moral values contributed to the decline. Germanic peoples along the northern borders began to claim territory from the weakened empire. Then foreign invaders marched into Italy and, in 476, took over Rome itself.

But the Roman empire did not disappear from the map. The eastern Roman empire continued to prosper under the emperor Constantine and other emperors. In time, the eastern Roman empire would become known as the Byzantine empire. It would endure for another 1,000 years.

Assessment

1. **Identify (a)** Augustus **(b)** Pax Romana **(c)** Jesus
2. **Define (a)** republic **(b)** patrician **(c)** plebeian **(d)** messiah **(e)** sect
3. Why did Rome change from a republic to an empire ruled by an emperor?
4. Give an example of a Roman achievement that continues to influence Western civilization today.
5. Describe the relationship between Christianity and Judaism.

4 Civilizations of the Americas

(1400 B.C.–A.D. 1570)

Mesoamerican ball player

Main Ideas

- Between A.D. 300 and A.D. 900, Maya civilization flourished from southern Mexico through Central America. In the 1400s, the Aztecs conquered most of Mexico and built a highly developed civilization.
- By the 1500s, the Inca established a centralized government in Peru.
- Eight culture groups developed in North America. Their diverse ways of life were strongly influenced by geography.

The first American civilization, the Olmecs, began in the tropical forest along the Mexican Gulf Coast. Olmec society lasted from about 1500 B.C. to 500 B.C. Later, other advanced civilizations developed in Mesoamerica and South America, including those of the Maya, Aztecs, and Inca. Diverse groups of people lived in North America.

Civilizations of Middle America

The first settlers in the Americas were nomadic hunters who probably migrated across a land bridge between Siberia and Alaska. Gradually, they populated two vast continents. These early people adapted to a variety of climates and resources. Between 8500 B.C. and 2000 B.C., Neolithic people in Mexico, or perhaps farther south, began to raise a variety of crops, including corn, beans, and squash, and tamed animals.

The Maya Although the Olmec civilization was the first in the Americas, more is known about the Maya city-states of Central America. Maya farmers cleared the rain forests to produce maize, or corn, to feed their cities. Maya society was divided into social classes. Each city-state had its own ruling chief. Priests held great power. Pyramid temples and palaces served as altars and burial places. The Maya developed a hieroglyphic writing system and an accurate calendar. Today, millions of people in Central America speak Maya languages.

The Aztecs Several hundred years after the decline of Maya civilization, the Aztecs conquered most of Mexico. By 1500, the Aztec empire numbered about 30 million people. War brought immense wealth as well as power to the Aztecs. **Tribute,** or payment from conquered peoples, helped the Aztecs turn their capital into a magnificent city.

The Aztecs developed a complex social structure with a single ruler or emperor at the top. A large class of priests performed the various rituals and sacrifices needed to please the many Aztec gods. Conquered peoples often supplied both tribute and human sacrifices for Aztec religious rituals. As a result, the conquered peoples were unhappy and they often rebelled. When armies from Spain later arrived, they found allies among the peoples who were ruled by the Aztecs.

The World of the Inca

In South America, for more than 2,000 years, civilizations rose and fell. Then in the 1400s, the Inca came down from the Andes mountains of Peru. Led by Pachacuti, a skilled warrior and leader, they rapidly conquered an empire that stretched 2,500 miles down the Andes and along the Pacific coast. By the 1500s, the Inca had established a centralized government in Peru, ruled by a god-king and a powerful class of priests.

Inca Government The emperor had absolute power over the Inca empire. He claimed to be divine and lived in splendor. From the capital at Cuzco, he ran an efficient government. His chain of command reached to every village. Specially trained officials kept records on quipus, collections

Anasazi cliff dwelling at Mesa Verde, Colorado

of knotted colored strings, which probably noted dates and events as well as statistics.

Inca Achievements The Inca worked to unite their conquered peoples. They imposed their own language, Quechua (KECH wuh), and religion on the people. They also created one of the great road systems in history. It was even more extensive than the roads that united the Roman empire. The Inca roads wound more than 14,000 miles through mountains and deserts. In the 1500s, civil war broke out in the Inca empire. The fighting weakened the empire at the moment that Spanish invaders were about to arrive.

Peoples of North America

Before 1500, many groups of Native Americans with diverse ways of life lived in North America. Culture groups included societies in the Arctic, Subarctic, Northwest Coast, California, Great Basin, Plateau, Southwest, Plains, Southeast, and Northeast. These societies were strongly influenced by geography.

The Anasazi The best-known society of the desert southwest is that of the Anasazi. These resourceful people built large villages, later called pueblos by the Spanish, of stone and adobe brick. At the center of their village life was the kiva. A **kiva** is a large underground chamber used for religious rituals. In the mid-1100s, the Anasazi began to build housing complexes in the shadow of canyon walls. Cliffs offered protection from raiders. By the late 1200s, drought forced the Anasazi to abandon their cliff dwellings. However, their traditions survive today among the Hopi and other Pueblo Indians.

The Mound Builders Far to the east of the Anasazi, in the Mississippi and Ohio river valleys, other farming cultures emerged as early as 1000 B.C. The Hopewell people left behind giant earthen mounds in many different shapes. Objects found in Hopewell mounds suggest that trade networks stretched from the Gulf of Mexico to the Great Lakes. By about A.D. 800, this culture was replaced by the Mississippians, who grew corn and other crops. They built large towns and ceremonial centers. Their greatest center, Cahokia in present-day Illinois, housed as many as 20,000 people by about 1100.

Variations in climate and resources encouraged the development of different cultures. In the far north, the Inuits adapted to frozen terrain. Along the Northwest Coast, rich food sources encouraged the growth of wealthy societies. In the Northeast, warring farming villages eventually settled their differences and formed the Iroquois League. This was an alliance of five Iroquois groups who were known as the Five Nations. Member nations governed their own villages but met jointly in a council when they needed to address larger issues.

Assessment

1. **Identify (a)** Olmecs **(b)** Maya **(c)** Aztecs **(d)** Inca **(e)** Anasazi **(f)** Mississippians
2. **Define (a)** tribute **(b)** kiva
3. Who ruled the Maya city-states?
4. Describe two steps the Incas took to unite their empire.

Quick Study Guide

Philosophies Founded in China

Confucianism	Daoism
• Founded by Confucius • Focuses on worldly goals of ensuring social order and good government • Stresses accepting one's place in society and behaving correctly • Views government as responsible for setting a good example for people and for being run by well-educated people	• Possibly founded by Laozi • Focuses on living in harmony with nature • Stresses simple ways of nature and the virtue of yielding • Views government as unnatural and as a body that should govern the people as little as possible

Key Greek Political Leaders

Leader	Accomplishments
Solon	Athenian archon who introduced reforms making the government more democratic and the economy more profitable
Pisistratus	Athenian tyrant who gave poor citizens a voice in government and weakened the aristocracy
Cleisthenes	Athenian leader who created the Council of 500 and made the assembly a legislature
Themistocles	Athenian leader who was victorious at the Battle of Marathon
Pericles	Athenian statesman who instituted direct democracy in Athens, increased participation in government, provided salaries for government employees, and encouraged the cultural development of Athens
Philip II	Macedonian king who conquered Greece
Alexander the Great	Macedonian leader who conquered an empire stretching from Greece to India and encouraged the spread of Greek culture throughout his empire

Religions Founded in India

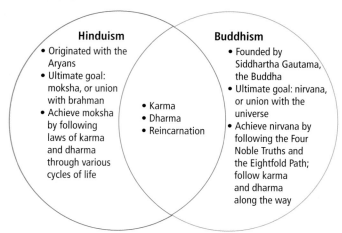

Hinduism
- Originated with the Aryans
- Ultimate goal: moksha, or union with brahman
- Achieve moksha by following laws of karma and dharma through various cycles of life

- Karma
- Dharma
- Reincarnation

Buddhism
- Founded by Siddhartha Gautama, the Buddha
- Ultimate goal: nirvana, or union with the universe
- Achieve nirvana by following the Four Noble Truths and the Eightfold Path; follow karma and dharma along the way

Key Roman Rulers

Ruler	Dates	Key Accomplishments
Julius Caesar	100 B.C.(?)–44 B.C.	• Attempted to make reforms to help save the ailing republic • Made himself absolute ruler
Octavian/Augustus	63 B.C.–A.D. 14	• Declared Exalted One and first citizen by the Senate • First ruler of the Pax Romana
Marcus Aurelius	A.D. 121–A.D. 180	• Last great emperor of the Pax Romana
Diocletian	A.D. 245–A.D. 316	• Divided the empire into two parts, eastern and western
Constantine	A.D. 280 (?)–A.D. 337	• Moved Roman power eastward by building a new capital at Constantinople • Granted toleration to Christians through the Edict of Milan

Cultures of North America

Culture Area	Culture Groups
Arctic	Aleut, Inuit
Subarctic	Beaver, Chipewyan, Cree, Ingalik, Kutchin, Montagnais, Naskapi, Ojibwa, Tanaina
Northwest Coast	Apache, Bella Coola, Chinook, Haida, Kwakiutl, Navajo, Nootka, Tlingit
California	Chumash, Maidu, Miwok, Mojave, Pomo, Paiute, Shastan, Shoshone
Great Basin	Paiute, Shoshone, Ute
Plateau	Nez Percé, Spokan, Sushwap
Southwest	Anasazi, Apache, Hohokam, Navajo, Papago, Pima, Pueblos
Plains	Arapaho, Blackfoot, Cheyenne, Comanche, Cree, Crow, Hidatsa, Kiowa, Mandan, Omaha, Pawnee, Sioux, Wichita
Southeast	Calusa, Catawba, Chickasaw, Choctaw, Creek, Delaware, Iroquois, Mississippians, Natchez, Seminole
Northeast	Adena, Algonquins, Hopewell, Iroquois, Micmac, Winnebago

Empires

Atahuallpa, the last Sapa Inca

What factors allow empires to rise and cause them to fall?

Historically, a key factor in the rise of empires has been success in war. For example, through conquest and alliances, the Inca subdued neighboring groups and established a kingdom based in Cuzco. Leadership, too, is another important factor in empire-building. The Inca used military and diplomatic skills to create an extensive Andean empire. However, controlling a large territory is impossible without an effective system of government. The Inca established a chain of command that reached down to the family level.

Similarly, failures in war, weak leaders, and loss of control of conquered peoples have often caused empires to fall. Civil war among the Inca made them vulnerable to defeat by Spanish invaders. Consider how these other empires rose and fell:

Han Dynasty

Under the Qin dynasty, China was engulfed in disarray as harsh policies provoked rebellions among the military and peasants. One rebel leader emerged victorious, founding a new dynasty—the Han—in 202 B.C. The first Han emperor set up a government aimed at benifiting the Chinese people, relaxing many strict laws and reducing taxes. He sent officials into every province of the empire to maintain the central government's authority. The Han system of government would last into the 1900s, though the dynasty itself would not. Plagued by peasant rebellions and power struggles, the Han empire split apart. The last Han emperor gave up the throne in A.D. 220.

Roman Empire

The Romans established one of the greatest empires of all time. They possessed strong leadership, an army of disciplined and dedicated soldiers, and a talent for absorbing conquered peoples and turning them into loyal citizens. Their established system of law and government brought security and peace to the Mediterranean region. Yet the mighty Roman empire eventually crumpled under the weight of several forces. Foreign invasions, combined with political, economic, and social problems, dissolved the ties that had held the empire together for more than 400 years.

Ottoman Empire

The Ottoman empire began in the early 1300s as a small Muslim state in far-western Asia, bordering the Byzantine empire. The Ottomans' initial success grew out of their location, which allowed them to plunder wealthy Byzantine cities. For 200 years, strong leaders expanded the empire until it extended from Eastern Europe through Southwest Asia and into North Africa. However, starting in the late 1500s, poor leadership, economic problems, and military unrest, as well as the strengthening of its European enemies, led to a slow Ottoman decline. After limping along for many decades, the empire collapsed completely following World War I.

The powerful Ottoman army

Thinking Critically

1. What factor do you think is most important in causing empires to rise? To fall? Explain.
2. **Connections to Today** For each empire described above, research a political or cultural aspect of the world today that represents the lasting impact of that empire.

A Global View: Regional Civilizations

How Did Regional Civilizations Expand the Scope of World History?

During the period of roughly a thousand years from 500 to 1500, sprawling regional civilizations came to dominate much of the world. Extending beyond the borders of any single empire, regional civilizations linked diverse nations within a shared culture.

Shared Cultures

Sometimes regional civilizations were based on a common religion that spread to a number of neighboring countries. Sometimes a powerful empire would influence its neighbors until they all shared a common regional culture. Sometimes geographic features, such as grassy plains or mountains, influenced all the people who lived there, producing a single regional style of civilization.

Important regional civilizations between 500 and 1500 included Christian Europe, the Muslim zone of Eurasia and North Africa, the trading states of Africa south of the Sahara, and the Chinese sphere of influence in East Asia.

Christendom and Islam

Two of the major regional civilizations that took shape during this period were based on a common religion. These were the civilizations of the Christian and Muslim zones.

Within each of these regions, diverse peoples shared powerful religious beliefs. Both Christians and Muslims felt a duty to spread their religions, and the civilizations that went with them, to neighboring peoples. Both of these crusading faiths, therefore, brought cultural unity to many peoples and nations.

Christianity had already spread around the Mediterranean and westward across Europe in Roman times. During the Middle Ages, the Christian religion and related institutions spread across Eastern Europe as well. These influential medieval institutions included feudalism, the manor system, and the medieval Christian churches, which were the Roman Catholic in the West and the Greek Orthodox in the East.

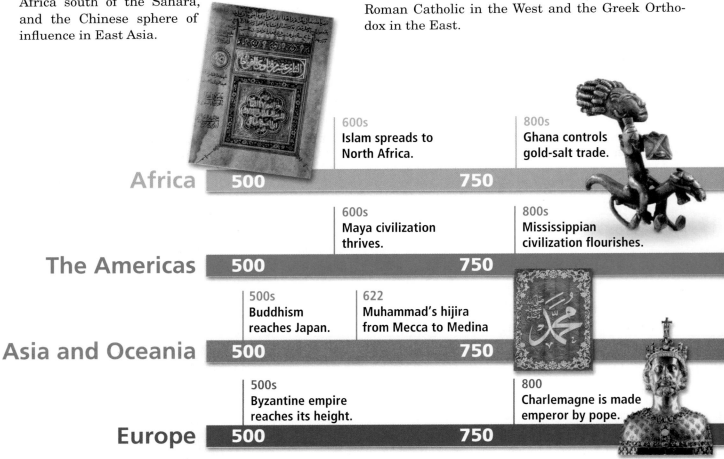

Africa

500 — 750

600s Islam spreads to North Africa.

800s Ghana controls gold-salt trade.

The Americas

500 — 750

600s Maya civilization thrives.

800s Mississippian civilization flourishes.

Asia and Oceania

500 — 750

500s Buddhism reaches Japan.

622 Muhammad's hijira from Mecca to Medina

Europe

500 — 750

500s Byzantine empire reaches its height.

800 Charlemagne is made emperor by pope.

The Prophet Muhammad proclaimed the Muslim faith in the 600s. Believers spread Islam far across North Africa, western Asia, and parts of southern Europe. With the religion came literacy, cities, long-distance trade, and development in philosophy and art. Islam thus shaped the culture of many peoples, from Muhammad's own Arabian neighbors to the Eurasian steppes, from western Africa to India and Southeast Asia.

Africa and Asia

Other regions of Africa and Asia saw the rise of other kinds of regional civilizations during this period. Across Africa, geography and trade linked many peoples, while in East Asia the influence of China imposed a common culture on a wide region.

In West Africa, peoples of the grasslands built a series of similar kingdoms and empires. All profited greatly from their commercial ties to Muslim traders from the north and the gold mines of the Guinea coast to the south. On the other side of the continent, African rulers and Muslim merchants from the north constructed a string of commercial city-states down the East African coast. These coastal trading cities linked India and China to inner Africa and the Mediterranean.

In East Asia, China's looming power continued to influence surrounding states, especially Korea and Japan. From the Chinese empire, the Japanese and Korean people adapted Confucian philosophy, belief in divine emperors, and the Chinese version of Buddhism, among other things. A common civilization, often described as Confucian, thus united this vast region.

Looking Ahead

Regional civilizations were a step beyond kingdoms and empires. They brought common economic and cultural characteristics to regions that were still too large for political unification. Next, regional civilizations headed toward global interdependence. This step would be taken only after European expansion began in 1492.

Assessment

Choose two events and two pictures from the timeline below. For each, write a sentence explaining how it relates to the themes expressed in the Global View essay.

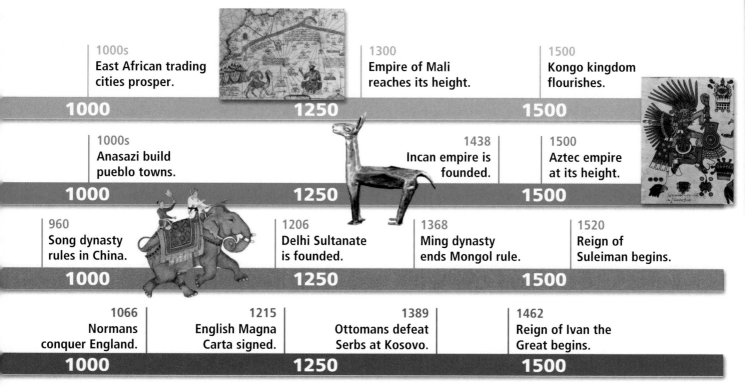

1000s	1300	1500
East African trading cities prosper.	**Empire of Mali reaches its height.**	**Kongo kingdom flourishes.**

1000 — **1250** — **1500**

1000s	1438	1500
Anasazi build pueblo towns.	**Incan empire is founded.**	**Aztec empire at its height.**

1000 — **1250** — **1500**

960	1206	1368	1520
Song dynasty rules in China.	**Delhi Sultanate is founded.**	**Ming dynasty ends Mongol rule.**	**Reign of Suleiman begins.**

1000 — **1250** — **1500**

1066	1215	1389	1462
Normans conquer England.	**English Magna Carta signed.**	**Ottomans defeat Serbs at Kosovo.**	**Reign of Ivan the Great begins.**

1000 — **1250** — **1500**

1 The Rise of Europe

(500–1300)

Main Ideas

- In the 800s, a ruler named Charlemagne temporarily reunited much of Europe. He revived learning and furthered the blending of German, Roman, and Christian traditions.
- Feudalism, the manor economy, and the Roman Catholic Church were dominant forces during the Middle Ages.

A town charter from King John, 1215

When Germanic peoples ended Roman rule in the West, they began to create a new civilization. Their culture differed greatly from that of the Romans. They had no cities and no written laws. Instead, they lived in small communities, ruled by elected kings whose chief role was to lead them in war. Europe became a fragmented, largely isolated region.

The Early Middle Ages

Between 400 and 700, Germanic invaders carved Europe into small kingdoms. Then around 800, Western Europe had a moment of unity when Charlemagne (SHAHR luh mayn), or Charles the Great, built an empire reaching across France, Germany, and part of Italy. He revived learning, extended Christian civilization into northern Europe, and furthered the blending of German, Roman, and Christian traditions. He also set up a strong, efficient government.

After Charlemagne died in 814, his empire crumbled. The resultant power struggle, which lasted almost 30 years, came to an end in 843 when Charlemagne's grandsons divided his empire into three regions. A new wave of raiders overran Europe, plundering and looting. Muslims, Magyars, and Vikings all attacked the fragmented territories held by Charlemagne's heirs. Kings and emperors proved too weak to maintain law and order. People needed to defend their homes and lands. In response to that basic need for protection, a new system, called feudalism, evolved. The rise of feudalism led to new networks linking all levels of European society.

Feudalism and the Manor Economy

Under the system of **feudalism**, powerful local lords divided their large landholdings among the lesser lords. In exchange for land and protection, these lesser lords, or **vassals**, pledged service and loyalty to the greater lord. A lord granted his vassal a **fief** (feef), or estate. It included the peasants who worked the land. Feudalism gave a strict order to medieval society.

Feudal lords battled constantly for power. Many nobles trained from boyhood for a future occupation as a **knight**, or mounted warrior. In the later medieval period, knights adopted a code of conduct called **chivalry**. Chivalry required knights to be brave, loyal, and true to their word. In warfare, knights had to fight fairly and be generous to their enemies. Since warfare often meant seizing lands, lords fortified their homes to withstand attack. Medieval strongholds gradually became sprawling stone castles.

The heart of the medieval economy was the **manor**, or lord's estate. Most manors included one or more villages and surrounding lands. Most of the peasants on a manor were **serfs**, who were bound to the land. Peasants could not be purchased and sold like enslaved people, but they spent their lives working for the lord of the manor. In return, the lord gave them the right to farm some land for themselves, as well as protection from invaders.

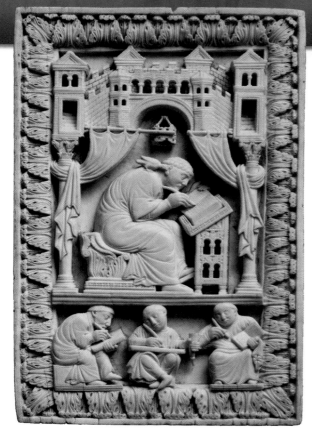

Ivory carving showing monks at work

The Medieval Church After the fall of Rome, the Christian Church split into an eastern and a western church. The western church, headed by the pope, became known as the Roman Catholic Church. As the Church grew stronger and wealthier, it became the most powerful **secular,** or worldly, force in medieval Europe. Some Church leaders, including the pope, ruled over their own territories, like feudal lords. Additionally, Church officials were often appointed to high government positions by the ruling nobility because they were the only educated people. Eventually, the pope claimed to have authority over all secular rulers.

The Church also controlled the spiritual lives of Christians throughout Europe. Christians believed that all people were sinners and that many were doomed to eternal suffering. The only way to avoid hell was to believe in Christ and participate in the sacraments. Because the medieval Church administered the sacraments, it had absolute power in religious matters and significant control over European society.

The very success of the church brought problems. As its wealth and power grew, discipline weakened.

Throughout the Middle Ages, there were calls for reform in the church.

Economic Expansion and Change By the 1000s, advances in agriculture and commerce spurred economic revival throughout Europe. People used new iron plows to improve farming, and windmills to grind grain into flour. The adoption of the three-field system enabled peasants to leave only a third of their land unplanted, and thus expanded crop production. New trade routes and goods also increased wealth. Traders and their customers first did business at local trade fairs. Later, as these markets closed down during the winter, merchants settled in local towns and attracted artisans who made goods for them to sell. Soon, towns became trade and manufacturing centers. Merchant **guilds,** or associations, came to dominate life in medieval towns. In towns, the old social order of nobles, clergy, and peasant gradually changed. By 1000, merchants traders, and artisans formed a new social class —the middle class. By 1300, Western Europe's economic revival was making momentous changes in medieval life.

A monarch knighting a young man on the battlefield

Assessment

1. **Identify (a)** Germanic tribes **(b)** Charlemagne **(c)** Roman Catholic Church
2. **Define (a)** feudalism **(b)** vassal **(c)** fief **(d)** knight **(e)** chivalry **(f)** manor **(g)** serf **(h)** secular **(i)** guild
3. What effect did Charlemagne's rule have on Europe?
4. How was medieval society organized under feudalism?

2 The High and Late Middle Ages

(1050–1450)

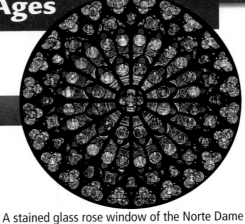

Main Ideas

- During the High Middle Ages, feudal monarchs began to build a framework for the modern nation-state.
- European contacts with the Middle East during the Crusades revived interest in trade and exploration.
- Beginning in the 1300s, famine, plague, and war marked the decline of medieval Europe.

A stained glass rose window of the Norte Dame Cathedral, Paris (above), and a German imperial crown (left)

During the early Middle Ages, hundreds of feudal nobles ruled over territories of varying size. Most were loyal to a king or other overlord, but royal rulers had little power. During the High Middle Ages, feudal monarchs started to increase their power. Slowly, over the next several centuries, these monarchs built the framework for what would become the European nations of today.

Growth of Royal Power in England

When William the Conqueror took the throne of England in 1066, he helped unify England and strengthen the monarchy. William's successors built a system of tax collecting. They also strengthened finances and law. Other English kings broadened the system of royal justice and developed the basis for English **common law**, or law that is based on custom and court rulings. A jury system also developed. A **jury,** or group of men sworn to speak the truth, determined which cases should be brought to trial.

Evolving Traditions As the English kings strengthened the throne, they conflicted with nobles and the Church. Out of those struggles came traditions of government that would influence the modern world. In the early 1200s, a group of nobles checked the growing power of the English kings. They forced King John to sign the Magna Carta, or great charter.

The Magna Carta The Magna Carta contained two basic ideas that in the long run would shape government traditions in England. First, it said that the nobles had certain rights. Over time, the rights that originally had been granted to nobles applied to all English citizens. Second, the Magna Carta made clear that the monarch, like his or her subjects, must obey the law. This included respecting the legal rights of the people. The king also agreed not to raise new taxes without first consulting his Great Council of lords and clergy. Eventually, the Great Council became the Parliament.

The Holy Roman Empire and the Church

The Holy Roman Empire arose from the patchwork of many Germanic states that formed after the death of Charlemagne. When a single ruler united the separate kingdoms, the pope crowned him "emperor." His successors took the title Holy Roman emperor.

During the early Middle Ages, the Church had spread its influence across Europe. By the High Middle Ages, both popes and monarchs were extending their authority. Explosive conflicts erupted. Popes clashed with the Holy Roman emperors who ruled lands from Germany to Italy. Some conflicts arose over who would control appointments to high Church offices. Eventually, some popes claimed the right to remove kings and emperors from the throne. Refusal to obey the Church could possibly result in excommunication. **Excommunication** was a harsh penalty. It meant that someone could not receive the **sacraments,** or sacred rituals of the Church.

In the 1200s, the Roman Catholic Church reached its peak of power. However, after a French king engineered the election of a French pope, the papacy entered a period of decline.

Europeans Look Outward

In 1050, Western Europe was barely emerging from isolation. However, several civilizations in the Middle East and Asia had long been thriving political and economic powers. Muslims, as believers in the Islamic faith are called, had built a great empire and created a major civilization. It reached from Spain across North Africa and the Middle East to India.

The Crusades Begin In the eastern Mediterranean, Byzantine civilization was a rival to Islam. The Byzantines were Christians. In the 1050s, Muslim Turks invaded the Byzantine empire. They also attacked Christian pilgrims to the Holy Land, or Palestine, in the Middle East. The Byzantine emperor asked the pope in Rome for help. Soon, thousands of Christian knights from Europe, as well as armies of ordinary men and women, left for the Holy Land to fight the Muslims. They fought a series of **crusades,** or holy wars.

Effects of the Crusades For 200 years, crusaders marched and fought. For a time, they held parts of Palestine. The Crusades failed in their chief goal—the conquest of the Holy Land. Instead, they left a bitter legacy of religious hatred behind them. However, the Crusades increased European trade, heightened papal power, and increased the power of feudal monarchs. Contacts with the Muslim world also introduced Christians to regions they had never known existed.

Learning, Literature, and the Arts

As economic and political conditions improved in the High Middle Ages, a revival of learning took place. Schools sprang up around the great cathedrals, eventually becoming the first universities. Ideas and texts that had originated in ancient Greece reached the universities through the works of Muslim scholars. New writings began to be

Pope Innocent III (in red) approving the rules of the friars of Saint Francis (kneeling)

produced in the **vernacular,** or everyday languages of ordinary people. Spain's great epic, *Poem of the Cid,* told of conflict with Islam. Famed Italian poet Dante Alighieri (DAHN tay ah leeg YEH ree) wrote the *Divine Comedy,* an imaginary journey into hell and purgatory.

A Time of Crisis

In the late Middle Ages, a series of disasters struck. Bubonic plague raged throughout the world and eventually throughout Europe. Unsanitary conditions aided the spread of the disease, which was called the Black Death. Approximately one in three people died, more than in any war in history.

The plague brought social upheaval and plunged the European economy to a low ebb. Unable to provide sufficient comfort to people, the Church faced opposition and reform efforts. Famine and war added to the turmoil of the period. Western Europe would not fully recover from the effects of the Black Death for 100 years.

Assessment

1. **Identify (a)** Magna Carta **(b)** Holy Roman Empire **(c)** Black Death
2. **Define (a)** common law **(b)** jury **(c)** excommunication **(d)** sacrament **(e)** crusade **(f)** vernacular
3. What principles were established in the Magna Carta?
4. What were the results of the Crusades?

3 The Byzantine Empire and Russia

(330 –1613)

Empress Theodora

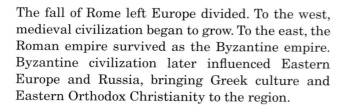

Main Ideas

- After the fall of Rome, Greco-Roman heritage survived in the Byzantine empire.
- Traders and missionaries brought Byzantine culture and Eastern Orthodox Christianity to Russia and Eastern Europe.
- Invasions and migrations created a mix of ethnic and religious groups in Eastern Europe.

The fall of Rome left Europe divided. To the west, medieval civilization began to grow. To the east, the Roman empire survived as the Byzantine empire. Byzantine civilization later influenced Eastern Europe and Russia, bringing Greek culture and Eastern Orthodox Christianity to the region.

The Byzantine Empire

As German invaders pounded the Roman empire in the west, emperors moved their base to the eastern Mediterranean. By 330, the emperor Constantine had rebuilt the Greek city of Byzantium. He renamed it Constantinople. In time, the eastern Roman empire became known as the Byzantine empire. During the Middle Ages, Constantinople thrived, controlling key trade routes that linked Europe and Asia.

Justinian's Code The most famous Byzantine emperor was Justinian, who ruled from 527 to 565. He was aided by his wife, Theodora. Justinian set up a commission to collect and organize the laws of ancient Rome. The result was known as Justinian's Code. By the 1100s, Justinian's Code had reached Western Europe, influencing the laws and principles of the Roman Catholic Church as well as medieval monarchs. The code thus preserved and spread the heritage of Roman law.

Byzantine Christianity As in Western Europe, Christianity was important in the Byzantine empire. But a division grew between Byzantine Christians and Roman Catholics. In the Byzantine empire, the emperor controlled Church affairs, rejecting the pope's claim to authority over all Christians. Further,

Byzantine clergy retained the right to marry. By 1054, a number of such controversies caused a **schism**, or permanent split, between the Eastern (Greek) Orthodox and Roman Catholic churches.

By the time of the schism, the Byzantine empire was declining. In 1453, Constantinople fell to the Ottoman empire. The ancient Christian city, renamed Istanbul, eventually became a great center of Muslim culture.

Byzantine Heritage For 1,000 years, Byzantine civilization had thrived, blending Christian beliefs with Greek science, philosophy, arts, and literature. The Byzantines also expanded upon Roman achievements in engineering and law. When the empire fell in the 1400s, Greek scholars left Constantinople to teach at Italian universities. They took valuable Greek manuscripts to the West. They also brought their knowledge of Greek and Byzantine culture. The work of these scholars contributed to the European cultural flowering known as the Renaissance.

The Rise of Russia

The early history of Russia began in the fertile area of present-day Ukraine. During Roman times, a people called the Slavs moved into southern Russia. Then, in the 700s and 800s, the Vikings began to travel on Russian rivers, trading and collecting tribute from the Slavs. The Vikings also traded with Constantinople. Eventually, the city of Kiev in Ukraine became the center of the first Russian state. Kiev served as a vital trade center.

Growth of Russia, 1300–1584

Geography *Interactive*
For: Audio guided tour
Web Code: nbp-0921

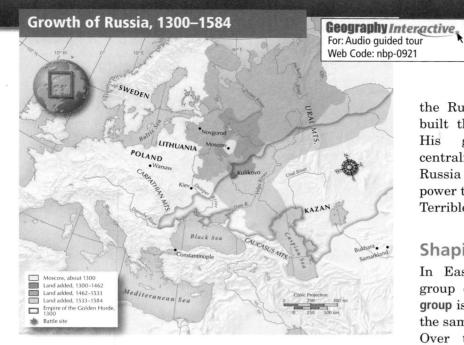

Geography and History
Between 1300 and 1584, the lands ruled by Russian princes and tsars grew from a small area around Moscow to a large area in Asia and Eastern Europe.

Trade brought Kiev into the Byzantine sphere of influence. Constantinople eventually sent missionaries to convert the Slavs to Christianity. About 863, two Greek monks adapted the Greek alphabet so they could translate the Bible into Slavic languages. This alphabet became the written script still used in Russia and Ukraine. A class of educated Russian priests grew. Russians adapted Byzantine art, music, and architecture.

The Mongol Conquest In the early 1200s, the Mongols of central Asia overran land from China to Eastern Europe. Though they were fierce conquerors, the Mongols were generally tolerant rulers. But the absolute power of the Mongols served as a model for later Russian rulers. Mongol rule also cut Russia off from Western Europe at a time when Europeans were making rapid advances in the arts and sciences.

Rise of Moscow Eventually, the princes of Moscow gained power and defeated the Mongols. Between 1462 and 1505, Ivan III, known as Ivan the Great, brought much of northern Russia under his rule. He and his successors took the title **tsar,** the Russian word for Caesar. Ivan III built the framework for absolute rule. His grandson, Ivan IV, further centralized royal power and introduced Russia to a tradition of extreme absolute power that earned him the title "Ivan the Terrible."

Shaping Eastern Europe

In Eastern Europe, no single ethnic group dominated the region. An **ethnic group** is a large group of people who share the same language and cultural heritage.

Over time, many groups settled in Eastern Europe. In the early Middle Ages, the Slavs came from Russia. Waves of Asian peoples moved into the area, among them the Huns, Avars, Bulgars, Khazars, and Magyars. Germanic people added to the mix.

Later, Byzantine missionaries carried Eastern Orthodox Christianity, as well as Byzantine culture, throughout the Balkans. At the same time, German knights and missionaries spread Roman Catholic Christianity to the area. In the late Middle Ages, Eastern Europe was a refuge for many Jewish settlers when Western European Christians persecuted them.

Many kingdoms and small states arose in Eastern Europe. Poland often had to battle Germans, Russians, and Mongols to survive. The Magyars of Hungary controlled parts of present-day Slovakia and Romania. By the late 1100s, the Serbs built a kingdom in the Balkan peninsula. By the 1500s, however, the Ottoman Turks ruled over much of southeastern Europe.

Assessment

1. **Identify (a)** Constantinople **(b)** Justinian **(c)** Kiev **(d)** Ivan III
2. **Define (a)** schism **(b)** tsar **(c)** ethnic group
3. Describe the legacy of Byzantine civilization.
4. What element of Mongol rule continued to influence the tsars, even after they ousted the Mongols from Russia?

4 Muslim Civilizations

(622–1629)

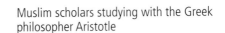

Main Ideas

- The religion of Islam emerged on the Arabian peninsula in the 600s.
- Muslim civilization eventually created cultural ties among diverse peoples across three continents.
- By the 1500s, the Mughals, Ottomans, and Safavids dominated the Muslim world.

Muslim scholars studying with the Greek philosopher Aristotle

In the 600s, a major religion, Islam, emerged in Arabia. Within a few years, Arabs spread Islam across a huge empire. The Arab empire eventually broke apart. Still, Islam continued to spread, creating shared traditions among diverse peoples. Islamic civilization opened routes for the transfer of goods, ideas, and technologies.

Rise of Islam

Muhammad, the prophet of Islam, was born in Mecca in western Arabia about 570. According to Muslim belief, Muhammad was called in a vision to become the messenger of God. He spent the rest of his life spreading Islam. Eventually, thousands of Arabs embraced the new religion.

Like Judaism and Christianity, Islam is monotheistic. Muslims believe in one all-powerful, compassionate God. All Muslims accept five basic duties, known as the Five Pillars of Islam. They include belief in one God, daily prayer, charity to the poor, fasting, and the **hajj,** or pilgrimage to Mecca. Muslims also hold that the Quran contains the sacred word of God and is the final authority on all matters. Over time, Muslim scholars have applied the teachings of the Quran to every aspect of daily life. In this way, Islam is both a religion and a way of life.

Islam Spreads

When Muhammad died in 632, Abu Bakr was elected to be the first **caliph,** or successor to Muhammad. He launched a breathtaking military campaign to conquer territory across the Byzantine and Persian empires. A key reason for the Arabs'

swift and wide-ranging conquests was their belief in the holiness of their faith and certainty of paradise for those who fell in battle.

A series of rulers led the conquests that carried Islam from the Atlantic to the Indus Valley. Eventually, the Abbasid dynasty moved the capital of Islam to Baghdad and ruled until 1258. Under the Abbasids, Baghdad exceeded Constantinople in size and wealth. But as the 1200s drew to a close, the Arab empire had fragmented and fallen. Independent Muslim caliphates and states were scattered across North Africa and the Iberian peninsula in Europe, while Mongol converts to Islam ruled the Muslim Middle East.

Golden Age of Muslim Civilization

The advancing Muslim empire united people from diverse cultures, blending the cultures of Arabs, Persians, Africans, and Europeans. Muslim society was more open than that of medieval Europe. People could advance in society, especially through religious, scholarly, or military achievements. Muslim leaders imposed a tax on non-Muslims but allowed Christians, Jews, and others to practice their own faiths. Many non-Muslims converted to Islam. In later centuries, Turkish and Mongol converts helped spread Islam far across Asia.

Between 750 and 1350, Muslim merchants established a vast trading network. Islamic ideas, products, and technology spread across the Muslim world and beyond. Muslims pioneered the study of algebra and made contributions in the fields of astronomy, philosophy, and literature, as well as advances in medicine. Islamic art reached new heights. Artisans developed elaborate mosaics of

The Arabian Peninsula

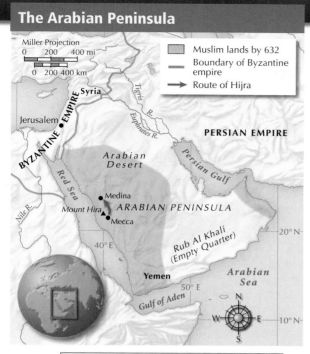

Miller Projection

0   200   400 mi
0   200 400 km

Muslim lands by 632
Boundary of Byzantine empire
Route of Hijra

BYZANTINE EMPIRE
Syria
Jerusalem
Tigris R.
Euphrates R.
PERSIAN EMPIRE
Arabian Desert
Nile R.
Red Sea
Persian Gulf
Medina
Mount Hira
ARABIAN PENINSULA
Mecca
40° E
Rub Al Khali (Empty Quarter)
20° N
Yemen
Arabian Sea
50° E
Gulf of Aden
10° N

Geography Interactive
For: Audio guided tour
Web Code: nbp-0141

Geography and History
Fleeing persecution in Mecca in 622, Muhammad and his followers journeyed to Medina. By the time of his death in 632, thousands had adopted Islam.

abstract and geometric patterns. In the field of architecture, domed **mosques,** or houses of worship, came to dominate Muslim cities. Baghdad became a great Muslim center of learning.

Muslims in India

About 1000, Turkish converts to Islam began making raids into India. A Muslim **sultan,** or ruler, defeated Hindu armies in the late 1100s. He set up a capital in Delhi. His successors founded the Delhi sultanate, which lasted from 1206 to 1526.

Muslims and Hindus Muslim rule brought changes to India. Widespread destruction of Buddhist monasteries contributed to the decline of Buddhism as a major religion in India. Many Hindus were killed. Eventually, Muslim rulers grew more tolerant and Indian Muslims absorbed elements of Hindu culture.

Mughal India In 1526, Turkish and Mongol invaders again poured into India. At their head rode Babur. He swept away the remnants of the Delhi sultanate and set up the Mughal dynasty, which

ruled from 1526 to 1857. In the late 1600s, economic hardship sparked rebellions against the Mughal dynasty. Eventually, European traders began to work against the once-powerful Mughal empire.

The Ottoman and Safavid Empires

While the Mughals ruled India, two other dynasties, the Ottomans and the Safavids dominated the Middle East and parts of Eastern Europe. All three empires owed much of their success to new weapons, including cannons and muskets.

The Ottoman Empire The Ottomans were Turkish-speaking nomadic people who had migrated from Central Asia. In the 1300s, they moved across Asia Minor and into the Balkans. In 1453, they captured Constantinople and renamed it Istanbul. The Ottoman empire was a powerful force for 500 years. Under the sultan Suleiman (soo lay MAHN), who ruled from 1520 to 1566, the Ottoman empire enjoyed its golden age. Ottoman poets adapted Persian and Arab models to produce works in the Turkish language. Painters produced detailed miniatures and illuminated manuscripts. Architects designed hundreds of mosques and palaces. At its height, the empire stretched from Hungary to Arabia and Mesopotamia and across North Africa.

The Safavid Empire By the 1500s, the Safavids (sah FAH vidz), a Turkish-speaking Muslim dynasty, had united a strong empire in present-day Iran. The outstanding Safavid ruler, Shah Abbas the Great, ruled from 1588 to 1629. Abbas revived the glory of ancient Persia. His capital became a center for the international silk trade. In the late 1700s, a new dynasty, the Qajars (kuh JAHRZ) won control of Iran. They ruled until 1925.

Assessment

1. **Identify (a)** Muhammad **(b)** Baghdad **(c)** Mughal dynasty **(d)** Ottoman empire
2. **Define (a)** hajj **(b)** caliph **(c)** mosque **(d)** sultan
3. What are some of the teachings of Islam?
4. How did Islam spread far beyond Arabia so quickly?

5 Kingdoms and Trading States of Africa

(730 B.C.–A.D. 1591)

Main Ideas

- Between 800 and 1600, a series of powerful West African kingdoms controlled the rich Sahara trade route.
- Indian Ocean trade routes led to the growth of wealthy city-states along the East African coast.

Vast migrations of people have contributed to the rich diversity of African cultures. One such series of migrations, called the Bantu migrations, probably occurred because of changes in the environment. Over a period of a thousand years, Bantu-speakers from West Africa moved south and east to populate most of southern Africa. Today, as many as one third of Africans speak a language in the Bantu family.

Bronze plaque of Benin warriors in their battle dress

Early Civilizations of Africa

Long before the Bantu migrations, important civilizations rose and flourished in Africa. While ancient Egyptian civilization developed in Northern Africa, another Nile civilization—called Nubia, or Kush—took shape to the south.

The Kingdom of Nubia For thousands of years, powerful kings and queens reigned over Nubia. From time to time, the Egyptians to the north conquered the land, but Nubians always regained their independence. As a result of conquest and trade, Nubian rulers adopted many Egyptian traditions. By 500 B.C., Nubian rulers moved their capital to Meroë (MEHR oh ay), a thriving trade center. Meroë produced iron for tools and weapons. Finally, about A.D. 350, invading armies from the neighboring African kingdom of Axum overran the kindom of Nubia.

North Africa Unlike Nubia, North Africa and Egypt were ruled, for a time, by the Greeks and then the Romans. Under Roman rule, Christianity spread to the cities of North Africa. Islam eventually replaced Christianity as the main religion of the region. North Africa benefited from the blossoming of Muslim civilization. Linked into a global trade network, North African ports did a busy trade in grain, wine, ivory, and gold.

Kingdoms of West Africa

By A.D. 100, settled farming villages on the western savannas were expanding. Soon trade networks linked the savanna to forest lands in the south and then sent goods across the Sahara.

By A.D. 200, camels, brought to North Africa from Asia, had revolutionized trade across the Sahara. Camel caravans created new, profitable trade networks. Gold and salt were the major products. North Africans sought gold to trade in exchange for European goods. West Africans traded gold to North Africans in exchange for an equally valuable item, salt. People need salt in their diet to stay healthy, especially in hot, tropical areas.

The Kingdom of Ghana By A.D. 800, the rulers of the Soninke people had united many farming villages to form the kingdom of Ghana. The king controlled gold-salt trade routes across West Africa. So great was the flow of gold that Arab writers called Ghana "land of gold." Over time, Muslim merchants established Islam in Ghana.

African Kingdoms and Trading States

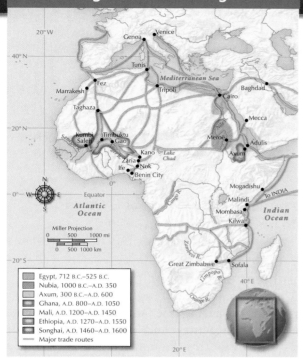

Geography and History

From 1000 B.C. in Nubia to the 1500s in Songhai, Africans built strong kingdoms in East and West Africa. Many of which developed because of profitable trade with other lands.

Muslim art, technology, and philosophy were influential as well. When the empire of Ghana declined in the late 1100s, it was swallowed up by a new rising power, the kingdom of Mali.

The Kingdom of Mali Mali emerged by 1250. It controlled both the gold-mining regions to the south and the salt supplies of the Sahara. The greatest emperor of Mali was Mansa Musa (MAHN sah MOO sah), who came to the throne in 1312. Musa expanded Mali's borders. A convert to Islam, Musa journeyed to Mecca in 1324 to fulfill the hajj. Musa's pilgrimage forged new ties with Muslim states and brought scholars and artists to Mali.

The Kingdom of Songhai As Mali weakened in the 1400s, a new West African kingdom, Songhai (SAWNG hy), arose. Songhai forged the largest state that had ever existed in West Africa. The kingdom controlled trade routes and wealthy cities like Timbuktu, a leading center of learning. Songhai prospered until about 1586. At that time, civil war and invasion weakened and splintered the empire.

Trade Routes of East Africa

By the time the kingdom of Axum conquered Nubia about A.D. 350, Axum had long been an important trading center. Located southeast of Nubia, Axum linked trade routes between Africa, India, and the Mediterranean world. A powerful Axum king converted to Christianity in the 300s. At first, Christianity strengthened Axum's ties to the Mediterranean world. However, in the 600s, Islam came to dominate North Africa, leaving Axum an isolated island of Christianity. Over time the kingdom of Axum slowly declined.

As Axum declined, a string of trading cities gradually rose along the East African coast. Since ancient times, traders had visited this coast. In the 600s, Arab and Persian merchants set up Muslim communities under the protection of local African rulers. By 1000, port cities were thriving from trade across the Indian Ocean.

Societies in Medieval Africa

Factors such as Africa's varied geography, diverse climates, and later migration and trade played major roles in how early societies developed throughout the continent. In some medieval African societies, the **nuclear family** was typical, with parents and children living and working together, while in other communities the family included several generations. Political patterns varied depending in part on the size and culture of the community.

Across Africa, religious beliefs were varied and complex. Some Africans followed traditional beliefs and were polytheistic. By 1000, both Christianity and Islam had spread to many regions of Africa. African societies preserved their values and history through both oral and written literature. In West Africa, **griots** (GREE ohz), or professional storytellers, recited ancient stories as they still do today.

Assessment

1. **Identify (a)** Bantu migrations **(b)** Nubia **(c)** Ghana **(d)** Mansa Musa **(e)** Axum
2. **Define (a)** nuclear family **(b)** griot
3. How did Nubian civilization prosper?
4. How did the gold-salt trade develop between West Africa and North Africa?

6 The Spread of Civilizations in East Asia

(500–1650)

Main Ideas

- China expanded and grew rich under the powerful Tang and Song dynasties.
- During the 1200s and 1300s, the Mongols ruled much of Asia. After the fall of the Mongols, the Ming restored Chinese culture and later imposed a policy of isolation.
- During the 1100s, Japan created a feudal society ruled by powerful military lords.

The Western Market of the Tang dynasty specialized in foreign goods.

After the Han dynasty collapsed in A.D. 220, China remained a divided land for nearly 400 years. Various Chinese dynasties rose and fell. Then in the 500s, China reemerged as a united empire. For a short period, the Sui dynasty ruled. Then a Sui general and his son, Tang Taizong, led a successful revolt and established their own dynasty, the Tang.

Two Golden Ages of China

Under the rule of the Tang dynasty (618–907), China was restored to its earlier glory. Tang armies marched deep into Central Asia and surrounding regions. They forced neighboring lands to become **tributary states.** That is, while these states remained independent, their rulers had to acknowledge Chinese supremacy and send regular tribute to the Tang emperor. Tang emperors restored the bureaucracy. They redistributed land to the peasants. They also completed a system of canals to encourage internal trade and transportation. The Tang dynasty finally collapsed in 907. The Song dynasty soon rose to take its place.

In 960, the Song reunited much of China to rule for 319 years. The Song period was a golden age. Chinese wealth and culture dominated East Asia even when its armies did not. Farming and foreign trade expanded. Paper money came into use. China's cities, which had been mainly centers of government, now prospered as centers of trade. Several cities even had populations over one million.

The first empress of China, Wu Zhao

Government and Society Under the Tang and Song, China was a well-ordered society. Besides the emperor and the aristocratic families, the two main classes were the gentry and the peasantry. The gentry were wealthy landowners who valued scholarship more than physical labor. Most scholar-officials at court came from this class. The peasants farmed on the land. However, even peasants could move up in society through education and government service.

Cultural Achievements A rich economy supported the thriving culture of Tang and Song China. Prose and poetry flourished. Scholars produced works on philosophy, religion, and history. Painting and calligraphy became essential skills for the scholar-gentry.

The Mongol and Ming Empires

In the early 1200s, the Mongols dominated Asia. They invaded China and finally toppled the Song dynasty in 1279. The Mongols established peace and order within their domains. Political stability set the stage for economic growth. Under the protection of the Mongols, trade flourished along the Silk Road and across Eurasia.

Ming Dynasty In 1368, a rebel Chinese army pushed the Mongols back beyond the Great Wall. A new dynasty, the Ming—meaning brilliant—sought to reassert Chinese greatness after years of foreign rule. The Ming restored the civil service exams. Confucian learning again became the road to success. Chinese cities were home to many industries, and the economy thrived.

Exploration Early Ming rulers proudly sent Chinese fleets into distant waters. The Chinese admiral Zheng He (jeng heh) commanded hundreds of vessels carrying 25,000 sailors during a series of expeditions. His goal was to promote trade and collect tribute. Zheng He's fleet explored as far as the coasts of East Africa.

Korea and Its Traditions

As early as Han times, China extended its influence to peoples beyond the Middle Kingdom. To the northeast, the Korean peninsula lay within the Chinese zone of influence. While Korea absorbed many Chinese traditions over the centuries, it also maintained its own identity. Additionally, Koreans improved on a number of Chinese inventions. They advanced Chinese woodblock printing techniques by creating movable metal type to print books. They also created an alphabet for the sounds of their language that was easier to use than Chinese characters. Its use led to an extremely high literacy rate in Korea.

The Emergence of Japan

Like Korea, Japan felt the powerful influence of Chinese civilization early in its history. Even so, the Japanese continued to maintain their own distinct culture. The surrounding seas both protected and isolated Japan. While Japan was close enough to the mainland to learn from China, it was too far away for China to conquer.

By about A.D. 500, Japan's first and only dynasty—the Yamato—dominated Honshu, the largest Japanese island. In the early 600s, the Yamato dynasty sent young Japanese nobles to study in China. They returned to Japan spreading Chinese thought, technology, and arts. For a time, the Japanese modeled much of their society on Chinese culture and government. Eventually, however, the Japanese chose to adopt some Chinese ways while discarding or changing others.

Japan's Feudal Age

In theory, the emperor headed Japanese society. In fact, he was a powerless, though revered, figurehead. Real power lay in the hands of the **shogun,** or supreme military commander. He distributed lands to vassal lords who agreed to support him with their armies in time of need. These great warrior lords were called **daimyo** (DY myoh). They, in turn, granted land to lesser warriors called **samurai,** meaning "those who serve." Samurai were the fighting aristocracy in the constant struggle for power. Japan had evolved into a feudal society.

In 1603, Tokugawa Ieyasu (toh koo gah wah ee AY ah soo) founded the Tokugawa shogunate, which ruled Japan until 1868. The Tokugawas brought peace and stability to Japan. They imposed central government control on all of Japan and created a unified, orderly society. Trade flourished, merchants prospered, and prosperity contributed to a flowering of culture. Still, the shoguns were extremely conservative. They tried to preserve samurai virtues and ancient beliefs. This commitment would bring them into sharp conflict with the foreigners who arrived in the 1500s.

Assessment

1. **Identify (a)** Tang **(b)** Song **(c)** Mongols **(d)** Ming **(e)** Tokugawa
2. **Define (a)** tributary state **(b)** shogun **(c)** daimyo **(d)** samurai
3. How did the Tang and Song dynasties benefit China?
4. Who held the most power in feudal Japan?

Quick Study Guide

■ The Church

Daily Life	Economic Power	Political Power
• Mass • Sacraments • Religious calendar • Aid to needy • Moral guidance	• Owned large tracts of land • People willed riches to Church • Agricultural and commercial activity in monasteries.	• Papal supremacy • Threat of excommunication, interdict • Raised own armies • Clergy served in governments • Moral authority

■ Evolution of English Government

1066	**Norman Conquest** William, Duke of Normandy, defeats King Harold of the Anglo-Saxons at Hastings.
1086	***Domesday Book*** King William uses this census, or survey of people and property, as a basis for taxation.
1160–1180s	**Common Law** Henry II uses accepted customs to lay the foundation for the English legal system.
1215	**Magna Carta** King John approves this document limiting royal power and extending rights to nobles and freemen.
1295	**Model Parliament** King Edward I expands Parliament to include representatives of common people as well as lords and clergy.

■ Power Shifts in the High Middle Ages

England	France	Holy Roman Empire
William the Conqueror consolidates royal power, limiting power of lords.	Hugh Capet is elected king by French nobles who feel he is weak.	Otto is crowned Holy Roman emperor, but nobles and Church officials wield power.
Henry II strengthens royal courts, and tries to make clergy accountable to them.	Capetian kings make throne hereditary, take lands from nobles, build a bureaucracy.	Henry IV is excommunicated by Pope Gregory VII, and then forgiven.
King John approves Magna Carta, limiting monarch's power.	Louis IX improves royal government, ends serfdom, creates strong national feeling.	Henry IV forces Pope Gregory VII into exile.
Parliament develops under Edward I.	After Philip IV clashes with Pope Boniface, French monarchs gain more control over popes.	Frederick Barbarossa and Frederick II try to conquer Italy but fail.
During Hundred Years' War, monarchs ask Parliament for funds, increasing Parliament's power.	During Hundred Years' War, English are expelled from most of France, increasing French national feeling.	Holy Roman Empire remains fragmented.

■ Economic Recovery

Agricultural Revolution	→ Revival of Trade	→ Towns and the Middle Class
• Production increases. • Population grows.	• Warfare decreases. • Travel becomes safer. • Desire for foreign goods increases. • Trade fairs develop. • Towns and cities grow.	• As towns grow, merchants gain power. • Guilds form and become powerful. • Modern business practices develop. • The middle class gains power. • Trade and commerce gain importance.

■ Key Muslim Empires

Empire	Muhammad and First Successors (632–661)	Umayyad (661–750) (756–1031 in Spain)	Abbasid (750–1258)	Mughal (1526–1857)	Ottomans (late 1200s–1924)	Safavids (early 1500s–1722)
Key Leader(s)	• Muhammad • Abu Bakr • Umar • Ali	• Mu'awiyah	• Abu al-Abbas • al-Mansur • Harun al-Rashid	• Babur • Akbar • Jahangir • Shah Jahan • Aurangzeb	• Mehmet II • Suleiman • Selim II	• Shah Abbas
Capital	Mecca	Damascus (Cordóba in Spain)	Baghdad	Delhi, Agra	Istanbul	Isfahan

■ The Byzantine Empire, Eastern Europe and Russia in 1300

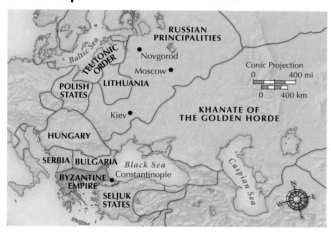

■ Spread of the Arab Empire

Cause and Effect	
Long-Term Causes	**Immediate Causes**
• Weakness of Byzantine and Persian empires • Economic and social changes in Arabia	• Tribes of Arabia unified by Islam around a central message • Wide acceptance of religious message of Islam • Easy acceptance of social ideas of Islam, such as equality among believers

Spread of Islam	
Immediate Effects	**Long-Term Effects**
• Islam spreads from the Atlantic coast to the Indus River valley • Centers of learning flourish in Cairo, Córdoba, and elsewhere	• Muslim civilization emerges • Linking of Europe, Asia, and Africa through Muslim trade network • Arabic becomes shared language of Muslims • Split between Sunni and Shiites

■ Key Political Leaders

Byzantine empire
- Constantine established Constantinople (named for himself) as the capital of the eastern Roman empire; converted to Christianity
- Justinian, emperor during the Byzantine empire's golden age

Russia
- Rurik, Rus prince who ruled Novgorod
- Princess Olga of Kiev, converted to Christianity
- Yaroslav the Wise, presided over golden age in Kiev
- Ivan the Great, expanded Russia and centralized power
- Ivan the Terrible, tsar who established absolute power

Eastern Europe
- Queen Jadwiga, queen of Poland, joint ruler of Poland-Lithuania
- Duke Wladislaw Jagiello, Lithuanian duke, joint ruler of Poland-Lithuania
- Stefan Dusan, ruler of Serbia

Quick Study Guide

Major African Kingdoms and Trading States

Kingdom or State	Date	Location	Religion	Economic Base
Egypt	2575 B.C.–1075 B.C.	North Africa	Local religion	Trade
Nubia	1100 B.C.–A.D. 350	Northeast Africa	Local religion	Trade and iron ore
Ghana	800–1050	West Africa	Islam	Gold
Mali	1235–1400s	West Africa	Local religion and Islam	Gold and salt
Songhai	1460–1591	West Africa	Local religion and Islam	Trade
Benin	1300s–1500s	West Africa	Local religion	Pepper, ivory, and slaves
Axum	350–600s	East Africa	Christianity	Trade
Great Zimbabwe	1300s–1500s	East Africa	Unknown	Trade

Important Ancient and Medieval African Rulers

Ruler	Kingdom	Accomplishment
Piankhi	Nubia	Conquered Egypt and brought it under Nubian control
Sundiata	Mali	Defeated Sumanguru and founded the empire of Mali
Mansa Musa	Mali	Expanded Mali's borders and based justice system on the Quran
Askia Muhammad	Songhai	Expanded Songhai's territory and improved the government by setting up bureaucracies
Amina	Hausa city-states	Gained control of many Saharan trade routes
King Ezana	Axum	Conquered Nubia and made Christianity the official religion
King Lalibela	Ethiopia	Sponsored the building of the Lalibela churches

China's Influence on Its Neighbors

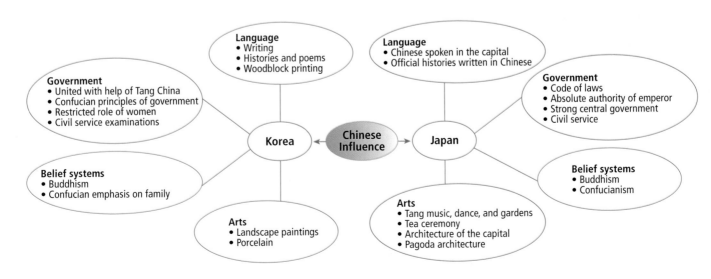

Conflict

What issues cause groups of people or countries to come into conflict?

Conflict has existed throughout history, and has often led to violence. It is so common and widespread that historians have used wars as a framework for telling the story of a civilization. For example, the Crusades and the Hundred Years' War are seen as turning points for medieval Europe. Families, religious and ethnic groups, city-states, and nations have all found reason to take up arms against each other. They have fought over power, territory, natural resources, ideas, beliefs, and a host of other issues. Compare the opponents in and the causes of the following major conflicts.

▲ A father and son watch oil fields burning after the Iraqi occupation of Kuwait.

Conflict and Power: The Wars of the Roses

Rival branches of the royal family, the House of Lancaster and the House of York, fought over the English crown starting in 1455. The trouble began when Richard, Duke of York, tried to seize the throne from Henry VI, head of the House of Lancaster. This led to a series of bloody civil wars lasting 30 years, in what became known as the Wars of the Roses. Both leaders and many of their followers died. Power shifted back and forth between the families until Henry Tudor defeated King Richard III, became King Henry VII, and married Elizabeth of York.

Conflict and Territory: The Russo-Japanese War

A clash between two expansion-minded neighbors, Japan and Russia, led to war in the early 1900s. The prize was China's Liaodong Peninsula and its main city, Port Arthur. Japan, an island nation, saw the peninsula as an entryway to the Asian mainland. Russia saw the port as the perfect home for its Pacific fleet. Russia seized the peninsula in 1898. For six years Japan built up its military. In 1904, it attacked the Russian fleet at Port Arthur and then launched a successful invasion. The Russo-Japanese War ended in 1905, with Japan winning the peninsula.

Conflict and Resources: The Persian Gulf War

In August 1990, Iraqi leader Saddam Hussein ordered his army to cross its southwestern border and invade Kuwait. This small Persian Gulf nation has one important resource: oil. Iraq also has oil reserves, but taking over its neighbor and acquiring Kuwait's large petroleum reserves would greatly increase Iraq's power in the Gulf region and the world. That outcome did not materialize. A coalition of anti-Iraq forces, led by the United States, gathered in nearby Saudi Arabia. In early 1991, they began an offensive that shattered Saddam's army and cleared the Iraqis out of Kuwait.

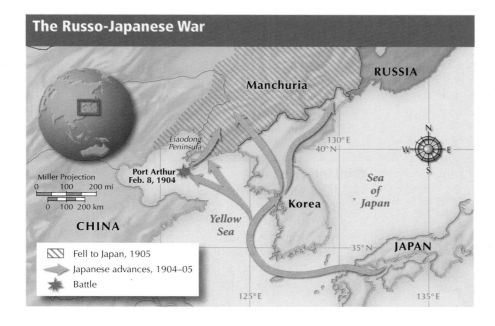

The Russo-Japanese War

Manchuria
RUSSIA
Liaodong Peninsula
Port Arthur
Feb. 8, 1904
130° E
40° N
Sea of Japan
Korea
Yellow Sea
CHINA
35° N
JAPAN
125° E
135° E

Miller Projection
0   100   200 mi
0 100 200 km

▨ Fell to Japan, 1905
➤ Japanese advances, 1904–05
✦ Battle

Thinking Critically

1. **Connect** **(a)** What caused each of the conflicts described above? **(b)** Even though the issues were different, what did the goals and methods of the opponents have in common?
2. Do research to find out more about these and other examples of conflict. Create a chart showing opponents, causes, key events, and results.

In what ways have migration and trade affected cultures?

During their migration, Bantu-speaking peoples from West Africa slowly diffused, or spread, their language over much of the African continent. Today, some 85 million Africans speak one of the many Bantu languages. Throughout history, migrants like the Bantu have carried their language, religion, and other cultural traits with them as they traveled. Merchants, too, have introduced their cultures to people along their trade routes. In these ways migration and trade have often influenced existing cultures. Consider the following examples:

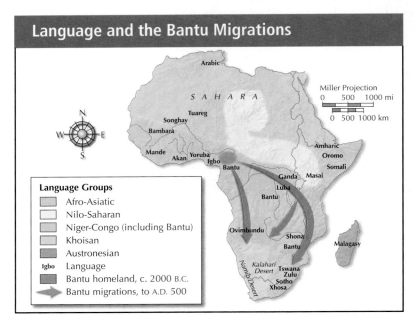

Language and the Bantu Migrations

Language Groups

- Afro-Asiatic
- Nilo-Saharan
- Niger-Congo (including Bantu)
- Khoisan
- Austronesian
- *Igbo* Language
- Bantu homeland, c. 2000 B.C.
- Bantu migrations, to A.D. 500

Miller Projection
0   500   1000 mi
0   500   1000 km

Sports

In the years that followed the Meiji Restoration of 1868, the Japanese looked to Western countries for ideas as they set out to modernize their country. One element of Western culture that they adopted was baseball. A young American transplant, who was teaching history at a Tokyo university, introduced the sport to his students in the early 1870s. Another American professor organized the first official baseball game in Japan. Called *yakkyuu,* or "field ball," the game's popularity grew rapidly. In 1936, Japan's first professional league fielded seven teams, and today its twelve teams compete in two leagues.

Former Tokyo Yomiuri Giants star, Hideki Matsui

Religion

Merchants from India carried Buddhism with them as they traveled along the ancient Silk Road. The oasis towns that served as markets and rest stops catered to the needs of those merchants. They allowed merchants to build monasteries, and they welcomed Buddhist monks. Eventually, the oasis dwellers themselves converted to Buddhism. In this way, by A.D. 100, the religion had reached northern China. For more than 500 years, however, Buddhism remained exclusively a religion of merchants and ruling classes. However, it finally gained popular acceptance in part by blending with traditional Chinese beliefs.

Food

The United States has welcomed immigrants from many cultures, which is reflected in the many styles of food that are now considered "American." Take pizza, for example. Brought to the United States by Italian immigrants, pizza has become a standard American food. So has the hamburger, probably introduced by German immigrants. Bagels, first brought to New York City by Jewish immigrants, can be found in most American supermarkets. Today, the taco, a favorite of Mexican immigrants, is readily available throughout the country.

Mexican meals such as these chicken enchiladas are served throughout the United States.

Thinking Critically

1. Cultural diffusion is not usually a complete replacement of one culture with another, but rather a gradual blending of two cultures in which some new traits are adopted and others are not. Explain why you think this is true.
2. **Connections to Today** Using the map above, compare the modern African language groups with the Bantu migration routes. How do the routes of migration explain the language patterns?

◄ Trade routes were established for valued spices.

What have been the major trade networks in world history?

As trade increased and lands became safe, merchants crossed Asia along the ancient Silk Road. The main trails in this famous network of trade routes ran from China west to the Mediterranean Sea. Connecting routes brought traders from Southeast Asia, India, Persia, Russia, and southern Europe. For more than a thousand years, this network helped shape the tastes and cultures of people over much of Asia and Europe. Other major trade networks around the world had a similar effect. Consider the following examples.

City-to-City Trade

Long before the establishment of the Silk Road, ancient cities traded with one another. A network of overland and water routes connected Bronze Age urban centers such as Mycenae in Greece with Memphis in Egypt, and Ashur in Mesopotamia with Harappa in the Indus Valley. Long-distance trade helped cities obtain resources not available in the local area. Merchants traveled among these ancient cities, carrying copper and tin, stone for making vases, olive oil, grains and other foods, timber, spices, woolen textiles, ivory, and pearls. Meanwhile, the merchants spoke to each other, exchanging ideas about technology, religion, and culture.

Global Trade

Trade involving Europe, Africa, Asia, and the Americas developed between the A.D. 1400s and 1700s. To obtain valued spices such as pepper, nutmeg, and cloves, European powers established routes to the east. Merchants sailed around southernmost Africa and across the Indian Ocean to India, China, and Japan. During the same period, a triangular trade developed in the Atlantic. Europeans traded manufactured goods to Africans for enslaved persons and gold. The enslaved Africans were transported to colonies in the Americas to work on plantations. The sugar, cotton, and tobacco that they produced were shipped to Europe to complete the triangle.

E-Commerce

Toward the end of the twentieth century, a revolutionary kind of trading network took shape. Called electronic commerce, or e-commerce, it combined traditional methods of shipping goods with the efficiency of the Internet. Today, even small businesses can advertise in major markets, show their goods in virtual shops, and sell directly to consumers worldwide. Consumers can also receive some services electronically, such as software updates. E-commerce is also changing the way businesses communicate with each other. More and more companies order supplies and manage transactions via the Internet.

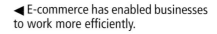

◄ E-commerce has enabled businesses to work more efficiently.

Thinking Critically

1. **(a)** How might a simple trade route grow into a trade network? **(b)** What is revolutionary about the e-commerce trade network?
2. **Connections to Today** Research online to investigate some aspect of global trade today. For example, you might focus on major trade organizations, such as the World Trade Organization, or major trading partners of the United States. Summarize your findings in a brief oral report.

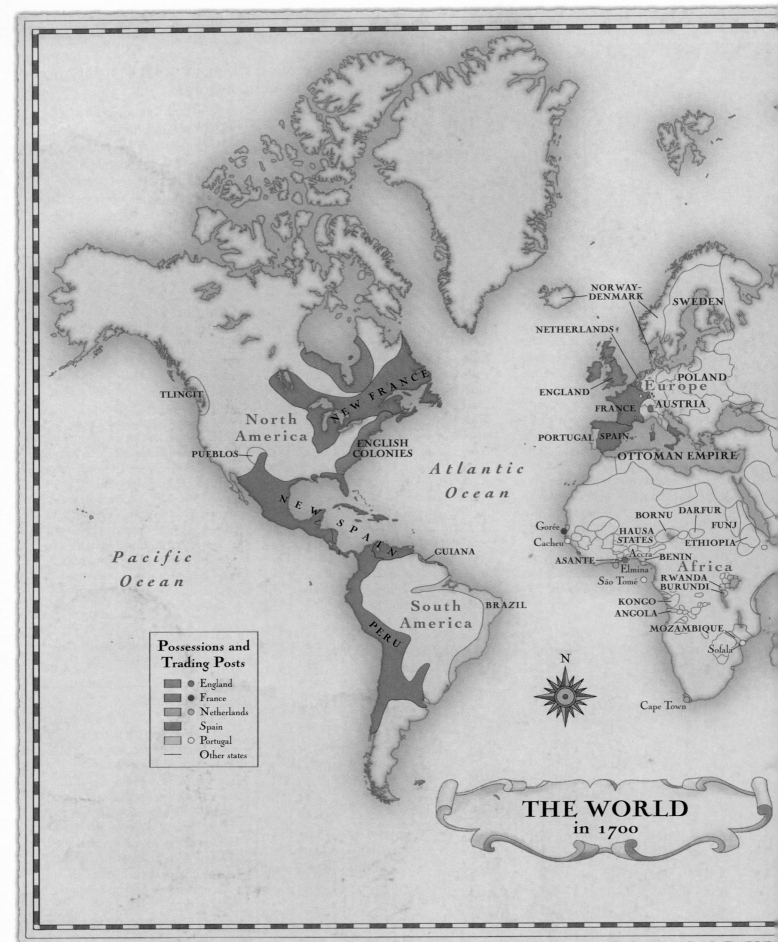

TLINGIT

North America

PUEBLOS

NEW FRANCE

ENGLISH COLONIES

NEW SPAIN

GUIANA

South America

BRAZIL

PERU

Pacific Ocean

Atlantic Ocean

NORWAY-DENMARK

SWEDEN

NETHERLANDS

ENGLAND

FRANCE

PORTUGAL SPAIN

POLAND

Europe

AUSTRIA

OTTOMAN EMPIRE

Gorée
Cacheu

BORNU

DARFUR

HAUSA STATES

FUNJ

ETHIOPIA

ASANTE

Accra

BENIN

Elmina

São Tomé

Africa

RWANDA
BURUNDI

KONGO
ANGOLA

MOZAMBIQUE

Sofala

Cape Town

Possessions and Trading Posts

- ● England
- ● France
- ○ Netherlands
- ● Spain
- ○ Portugal
- — Other states

N

THE WORLD
in 1700

RUSSIAN EMPIRE

Asia

CHINESE
EMPIRE

PERSIAN
EMPIRE

Deshima JAPAN

*Pacific
Ocean*

MUGHAL
EMPIRE   BURMA

Bombay   Macao

Goa   Madras   PHILIPPINE
       SIAM   ISLANDS
Cochin Pondicherry ANNAM

CEYLON

DUTCH EAST INDIES

*Indian
Ocean*   PORTUGUESE
                      TIMOR

Bourbon

Australia

Mercator Projection

0   1,000   2,000 miles

0   1,000   2,000 kilometers
Scale at the Equator

Geography *Interactive*
For: Audio guided tour
Web Code: nbp-3000

The Renaissance and Reformation
1300–1650

Painting a Renaissance Marvel

For four years, painter and sculptor Michelangelo stood on top of a high scaffold, painting the enormous ceiling of the Sistine Chapel in Rome. He hadn't wanted to take the job, but the pope had insisted. Michelangelo wrote a poem about the work:

66My belly is shoved up under my chin . . .
My beard faces skyward and the back of my neck is wedged into my spine . . .
My face is richly carpeted with a thick layer of paint from my brush . . .
I don't want to be here and I'm no painter.99

Listen to the Witness History audio to hear more about Michelangelo's work and how it came to symbolize the great period of cultural rebirth that transformed Europe.

◄An art restorer uses computer technology to restore a portion of the frescoes in the Sistine Chapel.

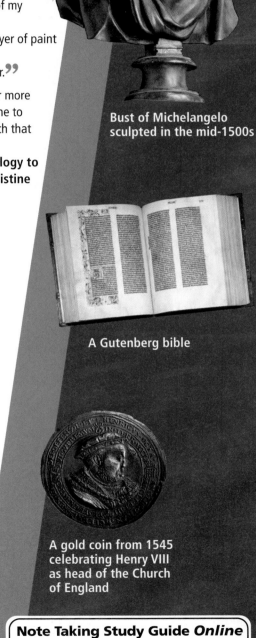

Bust of Michelangelo sculpted in the mid-1500s

A Gutenberg bible

A gold coin from 1545 celebrating Henry VIII as head of the Church of England

Chapter Preview

Chapter Focus Question How did the Renaissance shape European art, thought, and religion?

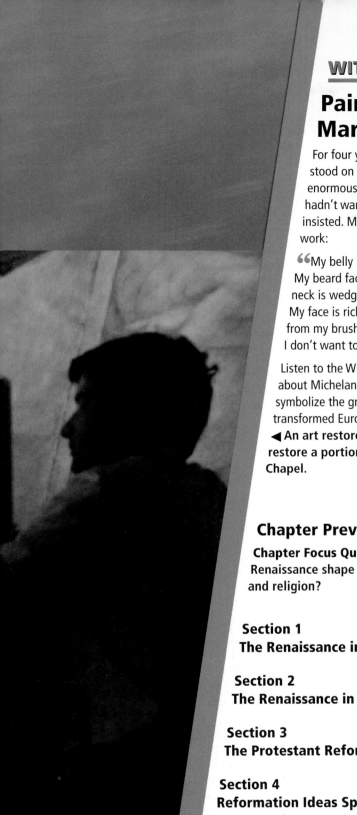

Note Taking Study Guide *Online*
For: Note Taking and Concept Connector worksheets
Web Code: nbd-1301

A detail from the Uffizi

An Artist Becomes a Biographer

In 1546, a young artist named Giorgio Vasari dined at the Cardinal's residence in Rome. The conversation turned to the amazing artistic achievement of Renaissance Italy. Vasari decided to record a tribute to all the important Italian artists who had contributed to this remarkably creative time period. Four years later, Vasari published his book *Lives of the Most Eminent Painters, Sculptors, and Architects.* A true "Renaissance man"— he was an able painter and architect as well as a writer—Vasari also became a biographer and historian of his era.

Focus Question What were the ideals of the Renaissance, and how did Italian artists and writers reflect these ideals?

Vasari designed the Uffizi Gallery in Florence, which houses his self-portrait.

The Renaissance in Italy

Objectives
- Describe the characteristics of the Renaissance and understand why it began in Italy.
- Identify Renaissance artists and explain how new ideas affected the arts of the period.
- Understand how writers of the time addressed Renaissance themes.

Terms, People, and Places

humanism	Leonardo
humanities	Michelangelo
Petrarch	Raphael
Florence	Baldassare Castiglione
patron	Niccolò Machiavelli
perspective	

Note Taking

Reading Skill: Identify Main Ideas As you read, create an outline like the one below to record main ideas about the Italian Renaissance.

> I. What was the Renaissance?
>   A. A changing worldview
>   1.
>   2.
>   B. A spirit of adventure

A new age had dawned in Western Europe, given expression by remarkable artists and thinkers. Europeans called this age the Renaissance, meaning "rebirth." It began in the 1300s and reached its peak around 1500. The Renaissance marked the transition from medieval times to the early modern world.

What Was the Renaissance?

The Renaissance was a time of creativity and great change in many areas—political, social, economic, and cultural. It marked a slow shift from an agricultural to an urban society, in which trade assumed greater importance than in the past. It was also a time when creative thinking and new technology let people <u>comprehend</u> and describe their world more accurately.

A New Worldview Evolves During the Renaissance, creative minds set out to transform their own age. Their era, they felt, was a time of rebirth after what they saw as the disorder and disunity of the medieval world.

Renaissance thinkers had a reawakened interest in the classical learning of Greece and Rome, which medieval scholars had preserved. They continued to use Latin as the language of the Church as well as for scholarship. Yet they produced new attitudes toward culture and learning. Medieval scholars had focused more on religious beliefs and spirituality. In contrast, Renaissance thinkers explored the richness and variety of human experience in the here and now. At the same time, society placed a new emphasis on individual achievement. Indeed, the Renaissance ideal was a person with talents in many fields.

A Spirit of Adventure The Renaissance supported a spirit of adventure and a wide-ranging curiosity that led people to explore new worlds or to reexamine old ones. Navigators who sailed across the ocean, scientists who looked at the universe in new ways, and writers and artists who experimented with new forms and techniques all shared that spirit. In part, that spirit of adventure came from a new view of man himself. As Italian thinker Pico della Mirandola asserted in 1486: "To [man] it is granted to have whatever he chooses, to be whatever he wills."

Expressing Humanism At the heart of the Italian Renaissance was an intellectual movement known as **humanism.** Humanists studied the classical culture of Greece and Rome, but used that study to increase their understanding of their own times. Though most humanists were pious Christians, they focused on worldly subjects rather than on the religious issues that had occupied medieval thinkers. Humanists believed that education should stimulate the individual's creative powers. They emphasized the **humanities**—subjects such as grammar, rhetoric (the study of using language effectively), poetry, and history—that had been taught in ancient Greek and Roman schools.

Francesco **Petrarch** (PEE trahrk), a Florentine who lived in the 1300s, was an early Renaissance humanist, poet, and scholar. He assembled a library of Greek and Roman manuscripts in monasteries and churches. In later years his efforts and those of others encouraged by his example enabled the works of Cicero, Homer, and Virgil to again become known to Western Europeans.

 Checkpoint What were the main characteristics of the Renaissance?

Italy: Cradle of the Renaissance

The Renaissance began in Italy. Over the next hundred years it spread to the rest of Europe, eventually transforming the entire Western world. Italy was the birthplace of the Renaissance for several reasons.

Italy's History and Geography Renaissance thinkers had a new interest in ancient Rome. Since Italy had been the center of the Roman empire, it was a logical place for this reawakening to <u>emerge</u>. Architectural remains, statues, and coins were all available for people to study. Rome was also the seat of the Roman Catholic Church, an important patron of the arts. As the center of Catholicism, Rome also served as an inspiration for religious themes used by artists and writers.

Italy's location encouraged trade with well-developed markets on the eastern Mediterranean and in northern Africa, as well as in northern Europe. Ships carrying a great variety of goods docked at Italy's many ports. Extensive banking, manufacturing, and merchant networks developed to support trade. While trade declined throughout most of Europe during the Middle Ages, it remained strong in Italy. Trade provided the wealth that fueled Italy's Renaissance. Trade routes also carried new ideas, important in shaping the Renaissance.

Michelangelo's *David*
Michelangelo sculpted his masterpiece *David* out of a block of marble left over from another sculpture. Completed in 1504, the statue was commissioned to express the power and strength of Florence.

Vocabulary Builder
<u>comprehend</u>—(kahm pree HEND) *v.* understand; take in
<u>emerge</u>—(ee MURJ) *v.* develop; rise from; become known

Italian Bankers
An illuminated manuscript from the late 1400s depicts a typical scene in an Italian banking house. *How is the wealth of the banker shown in this image?*

Italy's Vibrant City-States Unlike the kingdoms of most of the rest of Europe, Italy was divided into many small city-states. Each Italian city-state was controlled by a powerful family and dominated by a wealthy and powerful merchant class. These merchant families exerted both political and economic leadership, and their interest in art and emphasis on personal achievement helped to shape the Italian Renaissance.

The Medici (MED uh chee) family of **Florence,** for example, ranked among the richest merchants and bankers in Europe. Cosimo de' Medici gained control of the Florentine government in 1434, and the family continued as uncrowned rulers of the city for many years. Cosimo's grandson Lorenzo, known as "the Magnificent," represented the Renaissance ideal. A clever politician, he held Florence together during difficult times in the late 1400s. He was also a generous **patron,** or financial supporter, of the arts. At Lorenzo's invitation, poets and philosophers frequently visited the Medici palace. Artists learned their craft by sketching ancient Roman statues displayed in the Medici gardens.

The Medicis' great wealth and influence transformed Florence. Perhaps more than any other city, it came to symbolize the energy and brilliance of the Italian Renaissance. Like the ancient city of Athens, it produced a dazzling number of gifted poets, artists, architects, scholars, and scientists in a relatively short span of time.

 Checkpoint Why was Italy a favorable setting for the Renaissance?

Renaissance Art Flowers

The Renaissance attained its most glorious expression in its paintings, sculpture, and architecture. Wealthy patrons, popes, and princes played a major role in this artistic flowering. Ordinary people—who were beginning to appreciate human experiences not related to the Church—also played a role.

Reflecting Humanist Thought Renaissance art reflected the ideas of humanism. Like artists of the Middle Ages, Renaissance artists portrayed religious themes. However, they often set religious figures such as Jesus and Mary against classical Greek or Roman backgrounds. Painters also produced portraits of well-known figures of the day, reflecting the humanist interest in individual achievement. Renaissance artists studied ancient Greek and Roman works and revived many classical forms. The sculptor Donatello, for example, created a life-size statue of a soldier on horseback. It was the first such figure done since ancient times.

Using New Artistic Techniques Roman art had been very realistic, but in medieval times art became much more stylized. Renaissance painters returned to the realism of classical times by developing new techniques for representing both humans and landscapes. In particular, the rules of **perspective** allowed Renaissance artists to create realistic art. By making distant objects smaller than those close to the viewer, artists could paint scenes that appeared three-dimensional.

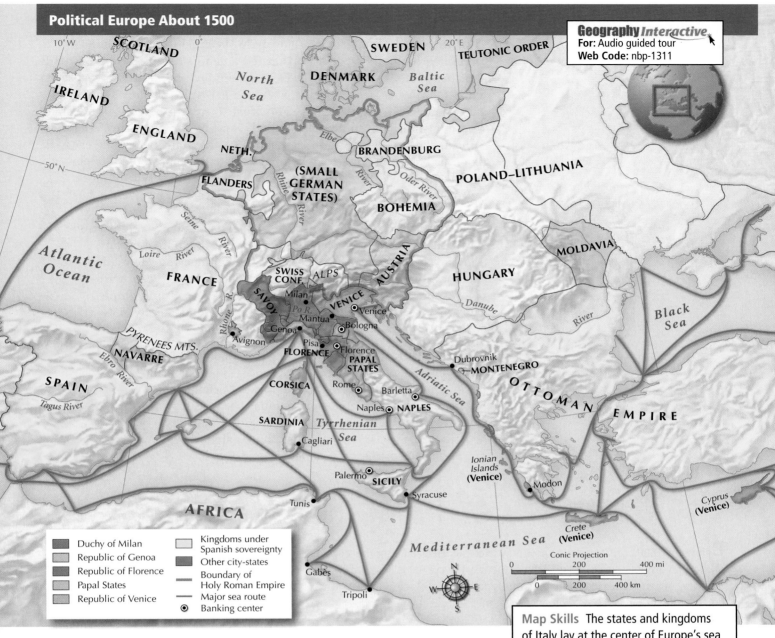

Political Europe About 1500

SCOTLAND
IRELAND
ENGLAND
SWEDEN
TEUTONIC ORDER
DENMARK
North Sea
Baltic Sea
NETH.
BRANDENBURG
FLANDERS
(SMALL GERMAN STATES)
POLAND–LITHUANIA
BOHEMIA
Elbe
Oder River
Rhine River
MOLDAVIA
Atlantic Ocean
FRANCE
Seine River
Loire River
AUSTRIA
HUNGARY
SWISS CONF.
ALPS
Milan
SAVOY
VENICE
Venice
Danube River
Black Sea
Rhone R.
Po R.
Mantua
Bologna
Genoa
OTTOMAN
PYRENEES MTS.
Avignon
Pisa
FLORENCE
Florence
PAPAL STATES
Dubrovnik
MONTENEGRO
NAVARRE
SPAIN
Ebro River
Tagus River
CORSICA
Rome
Barletta
Adriatic Sea
EMPIRE
Naples
NAPLES
SARDINIA
Tyrrhenian Sea
Cagliari
Ionian Islands (Venice)
Modon
Cyprus (Venice)
Palermo
SICILY
Syracuse
AFRICA
Tunis
Crete (Venice)
Gabès
Mediterranean Sea
Tripoli

Legend:
- Duchy of Milan
- Republic of Genoa
- Republic of Florence
- Papal States
- Republic of Venice
- Kingdoms under Spanish sovereignty
- Other city-states
- Boundary of Holy Roman Empire
- Major sea route
- ◉ Banking center

Conic Projection
0   200   400 mi
0   200   400 km
N W E S

Map Skills The states and kingdoms of Italy lay at the center of Europe's sea trade.
1. **Locate** (a) Florence (b) Palermo (c) Crete
2. **Identify** Which republic controlled Crete? Which kingdom controlled Sicily?
3. **Apply Information** Why were so many banking centers located in Italy?

Other techniques enabled Renaissance artists to give their work energy and realism. Renaissance painters used shading to make objects look round and real, and new oil paints to reflect light. Painters and sculptors also studied human anatomy and drew from observing live models. As a result, they were able to portray the human body much more accurately than medieval artists had done.

Architecture: A "Social Art" Architecture was transformed in Renaissance Italy. Architect Leon Alberti described architecture as a "social art," meant to blend beauty with utility and improvement of society. Architects rejected the Gothic style of the late Middle Ages as disorderly. Instead, they adopted the columns, arches, and domes that had been favored by the Greeks and Romans. For the cathedral in Florence, Filippo Brunelleschi (broo nay LAYS kee) created a majestic dome, which he modeled on the dome of the Pantheon in Rome. Like other Renaissance artists, Brunelleschi was multitalented. He studied art and sculpture with Donatello and was an accomplished engineer, inventing many of the machines used to construct his dome.

Leonardo da Vinci Artist **Leonardo** da Vinci (duh VIN chee) (1452–1519) had an endless curiosity that fed a genius for invention. He made sketches of nature and of models in his studio, and dissected corpses to learn how bones and muscles work. As a result, Leonardo's paintings grip people with their realism. The *Mona Lisa* is a portrait of a woman whose mysterious smile has baffled viewers for centuries. *The Last Supper,* showing Jesus and his apostles on the night before the crucifixion, is both a moving religious painting and a masterpiece of perspective. Because Leonardo experimented with a new type of paint, much of *The Last Supper* decayed over the years. However, it has recently been restored.

Leonardo thought of himself as an artist. Yet his talents and accomplishments ranged over many areas, including botany, anatomy, optics, music, architecture, and engineering. He made sketches for flying machines and undersea boats centuries before the first airplane or submarine was actually built. Though most of his paintings are lost today, his many notebooks survive as a testament to his genius and creativity.

Michelangelo Artist **Michelangelo** Buonarroti (1475–1564), like Leonardo, had many talents—he was a sculptor, engineer, painter, architect, and poet. Michelangelo has been called a "melancholy genius" because his work reflects his many life-long spiritual and artistic struggles. In his twenties, he created marble masterpieces such as *David* and the

The Discovery of Perspective

Before the 1400s, artists did not know how to create perspective, or the technique of showing distant objects on flat surfaces the way the eye actually sees them. The discovery of perspective revolutionized art. Using simple geometry, Renaissance artists could for the first time reproduce what their eyes actually saw.

Brunelleschi is credited with inventing perspective. His many studies (left) helped him design Florence's Duomo, completed in 1436. At 185 feet (56 m) high, it was the largest domed structure built since A.D. 125. ▶

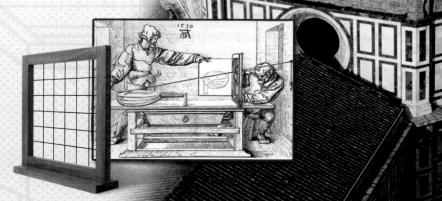

Artist Leon Alberti refined Brunelleschi's ideas. ▶
He wrote books explaining the rules of perspective, and developed the "perspective net" (right).
To show perspective, the artist looks over an eyepiece and through the net at a model (far right).
Then he reproduces the outlines of the model on paper with grids corresponding to those on the net.

Pietà. The *Pietà* captures the sorrow of the Biblical Mary as she cradles her dead son Jesus on her knees. Michelangelo's heroic statue of *David*, the Biblical shepherd who killed the giant Goliath, recalls the harmony and grace of ancient Greek tradition.

One of Michelangelo's greatest projects was painting a series of huge murals to decorate the ceiling of the Sistine Chapel in Rome. The enormous task, which took four years to complete and left the artist partially crippled, depicted the biblical history of the world from the Creation to the Flood. Michelangelo was also a talented architect. His most famous design was for the dome of St. Peter's Cathedral in Rome. It served as a model for many later structures, including the United States Capitol building in Washington, D.C.

Raphael A few years younger than Michelangelo, **Raphael** (rah fah EL) (1483–1520) was widely admired both for his artistic talent and "his sweet and gracious nature." Raphael studied the works of the great masters but developed his own style of painting that blended Christian and classical styles. He is probably best known for his tender portrayals of the Madonna, the mother of Jesus. In *The School of Athens,* Raphael pictured an imaginary gathering of great thinkers and scientists, including Plato, Aristotle, Socrates, and the Arab philosopher Averroës. With typical Renaissance self-confidence, Raphael included the faces of Michelangelo, Leonardo—and himself.

✔ **Checkpoint** How were Renaissance ideals reflected in the arts?

History Interactive
For: Interactive The Last Supper
Visit: www.PHSchool.com
Web Code: nbp-1312

Leonardo eagerly explored perspective in his mural *The Last Supper.* He uses converging lines, like those shown below, to create a vanishing point. This vanishing point draws the viewer's eye to the space above Jesus, and gives the painting the illusion of space and depth. ▶

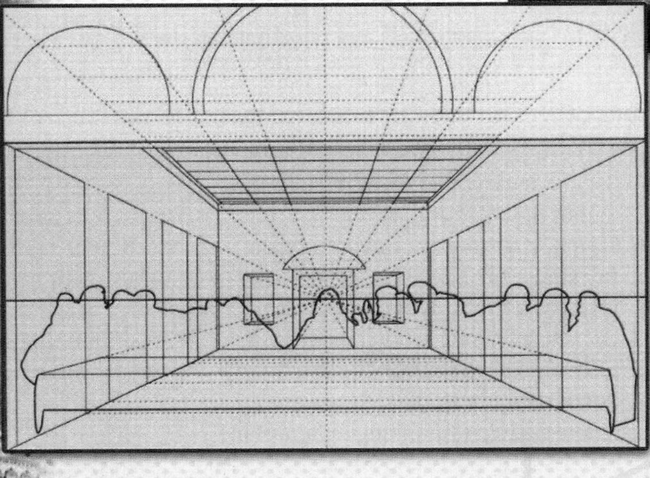

Thinking Critically
1. **Apply Information** Why was the invention of perspective necessary for artists to achieve realism in painting?
2. **Analyze Visuals** What other techniques bring the eye to the central figure of Jesus in *The Last Supper*?

Writing for a New Society

Italian writers reflected the trademark Renaissance curiosity and interest in the humanities. Humanists and historians wrote works of philosophy and scholarship. Other writers developed a literature of guidebooks to help ambitious men and women who wanted to achieve success in the Renaissance world.

In the mid-1500s, Giorgio Vasari wrote a biography of Leonardo da Vinci, whose self-portrait is shown here. Why is Leonardo da Vinci described today as an ideal Renaissan ce man"?

Primary Source

66 Sometimes, in supernatural fashion, beauty, grace, and talent are united beyond measure in one single person. . . . This was seen by all mankind in Leonardo da Vinci . . . so great was his genius, and such its growth, that to whatever difficulties he turned his mind, he solved them with ease. In him was great bodily strength . . . with a spirit and courage ever royal and magnanimous; and the fame of his name so increased, that not only in his lifetime was he held in esteem, but his reputation became even greater among posterity after his death. 99   AUDIO

Castiglione's Ideal Courtier The most widely read of these handbooks was *The Book of the Courtier.* Its author, **Baldassare Castiglione** (kahs teel YOH nay), describes the manners, skills, learning, and virtues that a member of the court should have. Castiglione's ideal courtier was a well-educated, well-mannered aristocrat who mastered many fields, from poetry to music to sports.

Castiglione's ideal differed for men and women. The ideal man, he wrote, is athletic but not overactive. He is good at games, but not a gambler. He plays a musical instrument and knows literature and history but is not arrogant. The ideal woman offers a balance to men. She is graceful and kind, lively but reserved. She is beautiful, "for outer beauty," wrote Castiglione, "is the true sign of inner goodness."

Machiavelli's Successful Prince Niccolò Machiavelli (mahk ee uh VEL ee) wrote a guide for rulers on how to gain and maintain power. Unlike ancient writers such as Plato, Machiavelli did not discuss leadership in terms of high ideals. Instead, his book *The Prince* looked at real rulers in an age of ruthless power politics. Machiavelli stressed that the end justifies the means. He urged rulers to use whatever methods were necessary to achieve their goals.

Machiavelli saw himself as an enemy of oppression and corruption, but critics attacked his cynical advice. (In fact, the term "Machiavellian" came to refer to the use of deceit in politics.) Later students of government, however, argued that Machiavelli provided a realistic look at politics. His work continues to spark debate because it raises important ethical questions about the nature of government and the use of power.

✔ **Checkpoint** How did Renaissance writings express realism?

Progress Monitoring *Online*
For: Self-quiz with vocabulary practice
Web Code: nba-1311

SECTION 1

Assessment

Terms, People, and Places

1. For each term, person, or place listed at the beginning of the section, write a sentence explaining its significance.

Note Taking

2. **Reading Skill: Identify Main Ideas** Use your completed outline to answer the Focus Question: What were the ideals of the Renaissance, and how did Italian artists and writers reflect these ideals?

Comprehension and Critical Thinking

3. **Make Generalizations** How was the Renaissance worldview different from that of the Middle Ages?

4. **Summarize** In what ways did Italian city-states encourage the Renaissance?

5. **Synthesize Information** How did humanism influence Renaissance painting and sculpture?

6. **Recognize Ideologies** Why were nature and human nature important to Renaissance artists and writers?

● Writing About History

Quick Write: Generate Arguments Consider the following thesis statement for a persuasive essay: Renaissance Italy produced some of the greatest writers and thinkers that the world has ever known. Next, generate a number of arguments that support that thesis. Rank your arguments in order of importance.

The Prince by Niccolò Machiavelli

Florentine Niccolò Machiavelli (1469–1527) served in the government as a diplomat for fourteen years before becoming a full-time writer and scholar. In 1513, he used his experience in politics and his studies of ancient Roman history to write a book called *The Prince*. In this book, Machiavelli combined his personal experience of politics with his knowledge of the past to offer a guide to rulers on how to gain and maintain power.

H ere the question arises: is it better to be loved than feared, or vice versa? I don't doubt that every prince would like to be both; but since it is hard to accommodate these qualities, if you have to make a choice, to be feared is much safer than to be loved. For it is a good general rule about men, that they are ungrateful, fickle[1], liars and deceivers, fearful of danger and greedy for gain. While you serve their welfare, they are all yours, offering their blood, their belongings, their lives, and their children's lives, as we noted above—so long as the danger is remote. But when the danger is close at hand, they turn against you. Then, any prince who has relied on their words and has made no other preparations will come to grief; because friendships that are bought at a price, and not with greatness and nobility of soul, may be paid for but they are not acquired, and they cannot be used in time of need. People are less concerned with offending a man who makes himself loved than one who makes himself feared: the reason is that love is a link of obligation which men, because they are rotten, will break any time they think doing so serves their advantage; but fear involves dread of punishment, from which they can never escape.

Still, a prince should make himself feared in such a way that, even if he gets no love, he gets no hate either; because it is perfectly possible to be feared and not hated, and this will be the result if only the prince will keep his hands off the property of his subjects or citizens, and off their women. When he does have to shed blood, he should be sure to have a strong justification and manifest[2] cause; but above all, he should not confiscate[3] people's property, because men are quicker to forget the death of a father than the loss of a patrimony[4]. Besides, pretexts[5] for confiscation are always plentiful; it never fails that a prince who starts living by plunder can find reasons to rob someone else. . . .Returning to the question of being feared or loved, I conclude that since men love at their own inclination but can be made to fear at the inclination of the prince, a shrewd prince will lay his foundations on what is under his own control, not on what is controlled by others.

1. **fickle** (FIK ul) *adj.* changeable
2. **manifest** (MAN uh fest) *adj.* clear; plain to see
3. **confiscate** (KAHN fis kayt) *v.* to seize or take
4. **patrimony** (PA truh moh nee) *n.* property or inheritance
5. **pretexts** (PREE teksts) *n.* excuses; false reasons

A portrait of Niccolò Machiavelli painted in the late 1500s

WITNESS HISTORY VIDEO

Watch *Machiavelli's The Prince* to explore the world of an important "Renaissance man" on the **Witness History Discovery School**™ video program.

Thinking Critically

1. **Summarize Information** Why does Machiavelli believe that it is better for a prince to be feared than to be loved?

2. **Make Comparisons** Reread the section of the text titled Castiglione's Ideal Courtier. Is Machiavelli's description of an ideal prince consistent with that of Castiglione's courtier? Why or why not?

A modern artist depicts Gutenberg and his printing press; at top right is a Bible Gutenberg printed *circa* 1455.

WITNESS HISTORY ◀)) AUDIO

An Expanding World

❝All the world is full of knowing men, of most learned schoolmasters, and vast libraries; and it appears to me as a truth, that neither in Plato's time, nor Cicero's . . . there was ever such conveniency for studying, as we see at this day there is.❞
—François Rabelais, 1532

Scholars and artists throughout northern Europe in the 1500s lived in an exciting time. The newly invented printing press made the world seem smaller. All over Europe, the world of knowledge was expanding in ways that would have been unthinkable in medieval times.

Focus Question How did the Renaissance develop in northern Europe?

The Renaissance in the North

Objectives
- Explain how the printing revolution shaped European society.
- Describe the themes that northern European artists, humanists, and writers explored.

Terms, People, and Places

Johann Gutenberg
Flanders
Albrecht Dürer
engraving
vernacular

Erasmus
Thomas More
utopian
Shakespeare

Note Taking

Reading Strategy: Identify Main Ideas Keep track of the main ideas of the section by creating a chart like the one below. Add boxes to complete the chart.

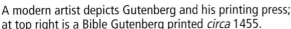

Renaissance in the North		
Printing Revolution	Artists and Writers	Humanists

As the Renaissance began to flower in Italy, northern Europe was still recovering from the ravages of the Black Death. But by the 1400s, the cities of the north began to enjoy the economic growth—and the wealth—needed to develop their own Renaissance.

The Printing Revolution

An astounding invention aided the spread of the Renaissance. In about 1455, **Johann Gutenberg** (GOOT un burg) of Mainz, Germany, printed the first complete edition of the Bible using a printing press with movable type. A printing revolution had begun that would transform Europe. Before the printing press, there were only a few thousand books in all of Europe. These books had been slowly copied out by hand. By 1500, according to some estimates, 15 to 20 million volumes had been produced on printing presses.

The printing revolution brought immense changes. Printed books were cheaper and easier to produce than hand-copied works. With books more readily available, more people learned to read. Readers gained access to a broad range of knowledge, from medicine and law to mining. As printing presses were established in Italy and other parts of Europe, printed books exposed educated Europeans to new ideas and new places.

✓ **Checkpoint** What was the impact of the printing press?

Northern Renaissance Artists

The northern Renaissance began in the <u>prosperous</u> cities of **Flanders,** a region that included parts of present-day northern France, Belgium, and the Netherlands. Flanders was a thriving center of trade for northern Europe. From Flanders, the Renaissance spread to Spain, France, Germany, and England.

Flemish Painters In the 1400s, Jan van Eyck was one of the most important Flemish painters. Van Eyck's portrayals of townspeople as well as religious scenes abound in rich, realistic details. In the 1500s, Flemish painter Pieter Bruegel (BROY gul) used vibrant colors to portray lively scenes of peasant life, earning him the nickname "Peasant Bruegel." Bruegel also addressed religious and classical themes, but he set them against a background of common people.

In the 1600s, Peter Paul Rubens blended the realistic tradition of Flemish painters like Bruegel with the classical themes and artistic freedom of the Italian Renaissance. As a scholar and humanist, Rubens had a wide knowledge of mythology, the Bible, and classical history. Many of his enormous paintings portray these themes.

Dürer: "Leonardo of the North" German painter **Albrecht Dürer** (DYOOR ur) was one of the first northern artists to be profoundly affected by Renaissance Italy. In 1494, he traveled to Italy to study the Italian masters. He soon became a pioneer in spreading Renaissance ideas to northern Europe. At the same time, his own methods influenced artists in Italy. Because of his wide-ranging interests, which extended far beyond art, he is sometimes called the "Leonardo of the North."

Dürer's important innovation was to apply the painting techniques he had learned in Italy to **engraving.** In engraving, an artist etches a design on a metal plate with acid. The artist then uses the plate to make prints. Dürer had studied engraving in his goldsmith father's workshop and perfected the technique. Many of Dürer's engravings and paintings portray religious upheaval, one of the northern Renaissance's most powerful themes.

✓ **Checkpoint** What themes did northern Renaissance artists explore?

Northern Humanists and Writers

Northern European humanists and writers also helped spread Renaissance ideas. Humanist scholars stressed education and classical learning, hoping to bring about religious and moral reform. Though humanist scholars wrote mainly in Latin, other writers began writing in the **vernacular,** or everyday language of ordinary people. This appealed to a new, middle class audience who lived in northern towns and cities.

Erasmus: Making Humanism Popular The Dutch priest and humanist Desiderius **Erasmus** (ih RAZ mus), born in 1466, was one of the most important scholars of the age. He wrote texts on a number of subjects and used his knowledge of classical languages to produce a new Greek edition of the Bible.

Vocabulary Builder

prosperous—(PRAHS pur us) *adj.*
successful; wealthy

Dürer, Artist and Gentleman
In Germany artists were viewed merely as skilled craftsmen, prompting Dürer to comment that "[In Italy] I am a gentleman, at home I am a parasite." He worked hard to change that view, learning languages and court manners to promote himself. Dürer painted this self-portrait in 1498 when he was 26 years old. *Judging from the painting, how did Dürer view his own importance?*

Northern European artists eagerly pursued realism in their art. The new technique of oil painting allowed them to produce strong colors and a hard surface that could survive the centuries. They also used oils to achieve depth and to create realistic details. Artists placed a new emphasis on nature, recording in their art what they actually saw. Landscapes became a major theme, not just the backdrop to human activities.

▲ Pieter Bruegel the Elder is best known for his scenes of daily life. In *Winter Landscape With Skaters and a Bird Trap*, every detail—from the bare trees to the people walking on ice—conveys the white and frozen reality of northern Europe in winter.

Erasmus helped spread Renaissance humanism to a wider public. He called for a translation of the Bible into the vernacular. He scorned those who "... don't want the holy scriptures to be read in translation by the unlearned ... as if the chief strength of the Christian religion lay in people's ignorance of it...." To Erasmus, an individual's chief duties were to be open-minded and to show good will toward others. As a priest, he was disturbed by corruption in the Church and called for reform.

Sir Thomas More's Ideal Society Erasmus's friend, the English humanist Sir Thomas More, also pressed for social reform. In *Utopia,* More describes an ideal society in which men and women live in peace and harmony. No one is idle, all are educated, and justice is used to end crime rather than to eliminate the criminal. Today, the word **utopian** has come to describe any ideal society often with the implication that such a society is ultimately impractical.

Rabelais's Comic Masterpiece The French humanist François Rabelais (rab uh LAY) had a varied career as a monk, physician, Greek scholar, and author. In *Gargantua and Pantagruel,* he chronicles the adventures of two gentle giants. On the surface, the novel is a comic tale of travel and war. But Rabelais uses his characters to offer opinions on religion, education, and other serious subjects. Like More and Erasmus, Rabelais was deeply religious, but had doubts about the organized church.

Shakespeare Writes for All Time The towering figure of Renaissance literature was the English poet and playwright William **Shakespeare.** Between 1590 and 1613, he wrote 37 plays that are still performed around the world. Fellow playwright and poet Ben Jonson correctly predicted at the time that Shakespeare "... was not of an age, but for all time."

◀ Oils made from linseed, walnuts, or poppies were mixed with colored pigments to make oil paint. Oil paints have two qualities that allow them to achieve realism— they can blend together, thus creating more realistic colors, and they reflect light, adding depth and glow.

▲ Jan van Eyck refined and spread the technique of oil painting. In *Portrait of Giovanni Arnolfini and His Wife*, van Eyck layered oil paints to create the shimmering fabrics the couple wore.

▲ Albrecht Dürer kept extensive notebooks on nature. He used his avid curiosity and his keen powers of observation to paint amazingly realistic pictures of plants and animals.

Thinking Critically
1. **Analyze Images** What realistic details appear in van Eyck's painting?
2. **Compare and Contrast** Compare these paintings with the Cranach woodcut in Section 3. How do the artists' intentions differ?

Shakespeare's genius was in expressing universal themes in everyday, realistic settings. His work explores Renaissance ideals such as the complexity of the individual and the importance of the classics. At the same time, his characters speak in language that common people can understand and appreciate. Shakespeare's love of words also vastly enriched the English language. More than 1,700 words appeared for the first time in his works.

✔ **Checkpoint** What Renaissance ideas did Shakespeare's work address?

SECTION 2 Assessment

Progress Monitoring *Online*
For: Self-quiz with vocabulary practice
Web Code: nba-1321

Terms, People, and Places
1. What do the key people listed at the beginning of the section have in common? Explain.

Note Taking
2. **Reading Skill: Identify Main Ideas** Use your completed chart to answer the Focus Question: How did the Renaissance develop in northern Europe?

Comprehension and Critical Thinking
3. **Predict Consequences** What impact would the printing press have on religious reform movements of the 1500s?
4. **Analyze Information** How did northern Renaissance artists blend Italian Renaissance ideas with their own?
5. **Identify Point of View** How did Erasmus's training as a priest sharpen his critique of the Church?
6. **Synthesize Information** What factors encouraged the use of the vernacular in literature in Renaissance society?

● Writing About History
Quick Write: Generate Arguments List a number of arguments that could be used to oppose your thesis in a persuasive essay. For example, reread the thesis statement in the Section 1 Quick Write. Then use the information from Section 2 to generate arguments opposing your thesis. Be sure to cite important northern European artists and technological developments. Organizing your arguments into a pro-and-con chart can be helpful.

Shakespeare's Globe Theatre

In his play *As You Like It,* William Shakespeare wrote that "all the world's a stage." When it came to showcasing his own work, however, the playwright chose the Globe Theatre. In 1599, when the English people were increasingly eager for plays and other sorts of entertainment, Shakespeare and his company of actors built the Globe on the south bank of London's Thames River. The three-story, open-air theater could seat 3,000 people and had a stage more than 40 feet wide. Shakespeare wrote many of his plays—including *Hamlet, Macbeth,* and *Othello*—specifically to be performed at the Globe Theatre. Twenty of Shakespeare's plays were performed there during his lifetime. During a performance of his play *Henry VII* in 1613, onstage cannon fire ignited the theater's thatched roof and destroyed the building.

▲ William Shakespeare

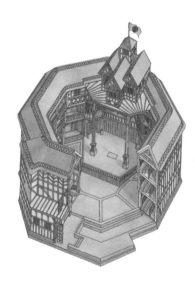

The 1997 reconstruction of the Globe Theatre (below) is faithful to the original. Wealthy theatergoers in the seventeenth century sat in galleries along the theater's walls. Poorer people bought cheap seats on the ground in front of the stage.

The center of the theater was open to the sky. Because the theater had no interior lights, plays were performed in the afternoon to let in as much light as possible.

The theater's round shape meant that the audience surrounded the stage on three sides. The stage was not curtained off, further drawing the audience into the action. ▶

Thinking Critically

1. **Draw Inferences** What are the advantages and disadvantages of staging productions in an open-air theater like the Globe?
2. **Synthesize Information** What about Shakespeare's plays drew people from all social classes to the theater?

Luther is shown tacking his 95 Theses to a church door in Wittenberg. At top right is a print block from a printing press.

WITNESS HISTORY ◀)) AUDIO

A Monk Rebels

❝I have cast the die. . . . I will not reconcile myself to them [the Roman Catholic Church] for all eternity. . . . Let them condemn and burn all that belongs to me; in return I will do as much for them. . . . Now I no longer fear, and I am publishing a book in the German tongue about Christian reform, directed against the pope, in language as violent as if I were addressing the Antichrist.❞
—Martin Luther, 1520

Focus Question How did revolts against the Roman Catholic Church affect northern European society?

The Protestant Reformation

Objectives

- Summarize the factors that encouraged the Protestant Reformation.
- Analyze Martin Luther's role in shaping the Protestant Reformation.
- Explain the teachings and impact of John Calvin.

Terms, People, and Places

indulgences	John Calvin
Martin Luther	predestination
Wittenberg	Geneva
Charles V	theocracy
diet	

N̲o̲te Taking

Reading Skill: Identify Main Ideas Use a concept web like the one below to record main ideas about the Reformation. Add circles as necessary.

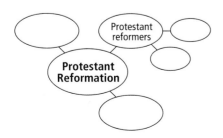

In the 1500s, the Renaissance in northern Europe sparked a religious upheaval that affected Christians at all levels of society. Northern European calls for church reform eventually unleashed forces that would shatter Christian unity. This movement is known as the Protestant Reformation.

Background to the Reformation

Many northern Europeans faced a great deal of uncertainty in their lives. As in Renaissance Italy, most people were poor and life could be violent. Fixed medieval economies were giving way to more uncertain urban, market-based economies, and wealth was distributed unequally. Renaissance humanist ideas found fertile ground in this uncertain society. Spread by the printing press, humanist ideas such as a return to classical education and an emphasis on social reform quickly took root. Many people looked for ways to shape a society that made more sense to them. Increasingly, they used humanist ideas to question a central force in their lives—the Church.

Church Abuses Beginning in the late Middle Ages, the Church had become increasingly caught up in worldly affairs. Popes competed with Italian princes for political power. They fought long wars to protect the Papal States against invasions by secular rulers. They plotted against powerful monarchs who tried to seize control of the Church within their lands. The Church also fought to expand its own interests.

Analyzing Art

Protestant Art German artist Lucas Cranach the Elder expressed his views of Protestantism (left panel) and Catholicism (right panel) in this woodcut made in 1545. He wrote that the work was meant to show the difference between the "true religion" and the "false idolatrous teaching."

A Angels float peacefully in the sky above Luther.

B A preaching Martin Luther is shown as having a direct connection to God above.

C A Catholic clergyman sells indulgences.

D The pope counts bags of money.

1. According to Cranach, which of the religions shown is the "true religion"?
2. Find another detail in the painting that expresses the artist's opinion.

Like other Renaissance rulers, popes led lavish lives, supported the arts, and hired artists to beautify churches. To finance such projects, the Church increased fees for services such as marriages and baptisms. Some clergy also sold **indulgences.** According to Church teaching, an indulgence was a lessening of the time a soul would have to spend in purgatory, a place where souls too impure to enter heaven atoned for sins committed during their lifetimes. In the Middle Ages, the Church had granted indulgences only for good deeds. By the late 1400s, however, indulgences could be bought with money.

Many Christians protested such practices, especially in northern Europe. Christian humanists such as Erasmus urged a return to the simple ways of the early Christian church. They stressed Bible study and rejected what they saw as the worldliness of the Church.

Early Revolts Against the Church Long before the Protestant Reformation, a few thinkers protested against the Church more strongly. In England in the 1300s, John Wycliffe launched a systematic attack against the Church, using sermons and writings to call for change. After his death, his followers met secretly to keep alive the movement he started. Jan Hus, born about 40 years after Wycliffe in what is now the Czech Republic, led a reform movement for which he was executed.

✓ **Checkpoint** What factors set the stage for the Protestant Reformation?

Martin Luther: Catalyst of Change

In 1517, protests against Church abuses erupted into a full-scale revolt. The man who triggered the revolt was a German monk and professor of theology named **Martin Luther.**

As a young man, Luther prayed and fasted and tried to lead a holy life. He once remarked that ". . . if ever a monk got into heaven by monkery, so should I also have gotten there." Still, he found himself growing disillusioned with what he saw as Church corruption and worldliness. At last, an incident in the town of Wittenberg prompted him to take action.

Writing the 95 Theses In 1517, a priest named Johann Tetzel set up a pulpit on the outskirts of **Wittenberg,** in Germany. He offered indulgences to any Christian who contributed money for the rebuilding of the Cathedral of St. Peter in Rome. Tetzel claimed that purchase of these indulgences would assure entry into heaven not only for the purchasers but for their dead relatives as well.

To Luther, Tetzel's actions were the final outrage, because they meant that poor peasants could not get into heaven. He drew up 95 Theses, or arguments, against indulgences. Among other things, he argued that indulgences had no basis in the Bible, that the pope had no authority to release souls from purgatory, and that Christians could be saved only through faith. In accordance with the custom of the time, he may have posted his list on the door of Wittenberg's All Saints Church.

Igniting a Firestorm Almost overnight, copies of Luther's 95 Theses were printed and distributed across Europe, where they stirred furious debate. The Church called on Luther to recant, or give up his views. Luther refused. Instead, he developed even more <u>radical</u> new <u>doctrines</u>. Before long, he was urging Christians to reject the authority of Rome. He wrote that the Church could only be reformed by secular, or non-Church, authorities.

In 1521, Pope Leo X excommunicated Luther. Later that year, the new Holy Roman emperor, **Charles V,** summoned Luther to the **diet** at the city of Worms. The word diet, or assembly of German princes, comes from a Middle English word meaning "a day for a meeting." Luther went, expecting to defend his writings. Instead, the emperor simply ordered him to give them up. Luther again refused to recant.

Charles declared Luther an outlaw, making it a crime for anyone in the empire to give him food or shelter. Still, Luther had many powerful supporters and thousands hailed him as a hero. They accepted his teachings and, following his lead, renounced the authority of the pope.

Vocabulary Builder

<u>radical</u>—(RAD ih kul) *adj.* extreme; calling for change
<u>doctrine</u>—(DAHK trin) *n.* practice; teaching

BIOGRAPHY

Martin Luther

"I am rough, boisterous, stormy, and altogether warlike," concluded Martin Luther (1483–1546). Luther's strong personality allowed him to take on the powerful Catholic Church. As a monk, Luther closely studied the Bible and came to believe that only its words—and not the pope or the Catholic Church—should dictate a person's actions.

When he appeared at the Diet of Worms, Luther (right) was 37 years old. Though depressed and fearful about the confrontation, he is said to have affirmed, "Here I stand, I cannot do otherwise." When he refused to retract his statements, an order was given to destroy his books. Yet his influence grew, leading to a deep division within Christianity and the founding of a new church that took his name. **Why did Luther refuse to retract his statements?**

Comparing Catholicism, Lutheranism, and Calvinism

	Catholicism	Lutheranism	Calvinism
Salvation	Salvation is achieved through faith and good works.	Salvation is achieved through faith.	God alone predetermines who will be saved.
Sacraments	Priests perform seven sacraments, or rituals—baptism, confirmation, marriage, ordination, communion, anointing the sick, and repentance.	Accepts some of the sacraments, but rejects others because rituals cannot erase sin—only God can.	Accepts some of the sacraments, but rejects others because rituals cannot erase sin—only God can.
Head of Church	Pope	Elected councils	Council of elders
Importance of the Bible	Bible is one source of truth; Church tradition is another.	Bible alone is source of truth.	Bible alone is source of truth.
How Belief Is Revealed	Priests interpret the Bible and Church teachings for the people.	People read and interpret the Bible for themselves.	People read and interpret the Bible for themselves.

Chart Skills *Who was the head of the Lutheran church? Why was this an important difference from the organization of the Catholic Church?*

Luther's Teachings At the heart of Luther's teachings were several beliefs, shown in the chart at left. All Christians, he said, have equal access to God through faith and the Bible. Like Erasmus and other humanist scholars, Luther wanted ordinary people to be able to read and study the Bible, so he translated parts of it into German. He also wanted every town to have a school so that all children could learn to read the Bible. Luther wanted to change other church practices. He banned indulgences, confession, pilgrimages, and prayers to saints. He simplified the elaborate ritual of the mass and instead emphasized the sermon. And he permitted the clergy to marry.

Luther's Ideas Spread The new printing presses spread Luther's writings throughout Germany and Scandinavia, prompting him to declare that "Printing was God's highest act of grace." Fiery preachers denounced Church abuses. By 1530, the Lutherans were using a new name, Protestant, for those who "protested" papal authority.

Many clergy saw Luther's reforms as the answer to Church corruption. A number of German princes, however, embraced Lutheran beliefs for more selfish reasons. Some saw Lutheranism as a way to throw off the rule of both the Church and the Holy Roman emperor. Others welcomed a chance to seize Church property in their territories, and use it for their own purposes. Still other Germans supported Luther because of feelings of national loyalty. They were tired of German money going to support churches and clergy in Italy.

The Peasants' Revolt Many peasants also took up Luther's banner. They hoped to gain his support for social and economic change. In 1524, a Peasants' Revolt erupted across Germany. The rebels called for an end to serfdom and demanded other changes in their harsh lives. However, Luther strongly favored social order and respect for political authority. As the Peasants' Revolt grew more violent, Luther denounced it. With his support, nobles suppressed the rebellion, killing tens of thousands of people and leaving thousands more homeless.

The Peace of Augsburg During the 1530s and 1540s, Charles V tried to force Lutheran princes back into the Catholic Church, but with little success. Finally, after a number of brief wars, Charles and the princes reached a settlement. The Peace of Augsburg, signed in 1555, allowed each prince to decide which religion—Catholic or Lutheran—would be followed in his lands. Most northern German states chose Lutheranism. The southern German states remained largely Catholic.

✓ **Checkpoint** How did Luther's teachings affect people and society in northern Europe?

Switzerland's Reformation

Swiss reformers also challenged the Catholic Church. Ulrich Zwingli, a priest and an admirer of Erasmus, lived in the Swiss city of Zurich. Like Luther, he stressed the importance of the Bible and rejected elaborate church rituals. Many of his ideas were adopted by Zurich's city council. The other reformer was **John Calvin,** who would profoundly affect the direction of the Reformation.

Calvin was born in France and trained as a priest and lawyer. In 1536, he published a widely-read book that set forth his religious beliefs and explained how to organize and run a Protestant church. Calvin shared many of Luther's beliefs. But he put forth a number of ideas of his own. He preached **predestination,** the idea that God had long ago determined who would gain salvation. To Calvinists, the world was divided into two kinds of people—saints and sinners. Calvinists tried to live like saints, believing that only those who were saved could live truly Christian lives.

In 1541, Protestants in the Swiss city-state of **Geneva** asked Calvin to lead their community. Calvin set up a **theocracy,** or government run by church leaders. Calvin's followers in Geneva came to see themselves as a new "chosen people" entrusted by God to build a truly Christian society. Calvinists stressed hard work, discipline, thrift, honesty, and morality. Citizens faced fines or other harsher punishments for offenses such as fighting, swearing, laughing in church, or dancing. To many Protestants, Calvinist Geneva seemed like a model community.

Reformers from all over Europe visited Geneva and then returned home to spread Calvin's ideas. By the late 1500s, Calvinism had taken root in Germany, France, the Netherlands, England, and Scotland. This new challenge to the Roman Catholic Church set off bloody wars of religion across Europe. In Germany, Catholics and Lutherans opposed Calvinists. In France, wars raged between French Calvinists and Catholics. Calvinists in the Netherlands avoided persecution by preaching in the remote countryside. In England, some Calvinists sailed to the Americas in the early 1600s to escape persecution at home. In Scotland, a Calvinist preacher named John Knox led a religious rebellion, overthrowing the Catholic queen.

A Calvinist Church, 1564
The Calvinist belief in simplicity is reflected in the design of this church. No images other than scriptures and coats of arms decorate the church, and the preacher's pulpit is the center of focus.

✔ **Checkpoint** How were Calvin's ideas put into practice?

SECTION
3 Assessment

Progress Monitoring *Online*
For: Self-quiz with vocabulary practice
Web Code: nba-1331

Terms, People, and Places

1. For each term, person, or place listed at the beginning of the section, write a sentence explaining its significance.

Note Taking

2. **Reading Skill: Identify Main Ideas** Use your completed concept web to answer the Focus Question: How did revolts against the Roman Catholic Church affect northern European society?

Comprehension and Critical Thinking

3. **Synthesize Information** Why did the sale of indulgences become a critical issue during the Renaissance but not during the Middle Ages?

4. **Compare Points of View** How did Luther's ideas differ from those expressed by the Catholic Church?

5. **Draw Inferences** How might Luther have felt about the Calvinist theocracy in Geneva?

● Writing About History

Quick Write: Choose Strongest Argument Consider this thesis statement: The Reformation was the most important event in European history. List possible arguments for a persuasive essay that supports this thesis. Review each one and choose the strongest. Make sure that factual points in the text support your argument.

Painter Hans Holbein shows Henry VIII as a commanding and regal king. A gold medal (top right) celebrates King Henry as the head of the Church of England.

WITNESS HISTORY 🔊 AUDIO

A King Speaks Out

Henry VIII, the Catholic king of England, was deeply disturbed by Luther's teachings. In 1521 he wrote to the pope to express his displeasure.

❝ . . . we believe that no duty is more incumbent on a Catholic sovereign than to preserve and increase the Catholic faith . . . so when we learned that the pest of Martin Luther's heresy had appeared in Germany and was raging everywhere . . . we bent all our thoughts and energies on uprooting [those heresies] in every possible way. . . . ❞

Just a few years later, Henry would break with the Catholic Church and set England on the path to becoming a Protestant country.

Focus Question How did the Reformation bring about two different religious paths in Europe?

Reformation Ideas Spread

Objectives

- Describe the new ideas that Protestant sects embraced.
- Understand why England formed a new church.
- Analyze how the Catholic Church reformed itself.
- Explain why many groups faced persecution during the Reformation.

Terms, People, and Places

sect	compromise
Henry VIII	Council of Trent
Mary Tudor	Ignatius of Loyola
Thomas Cranmer	Teresa of Avila
Elizabeth	ghetto
canonize	

Note Taking

Reading Skill: Identify Main Ideas As you read about the spread of the Protestant Reformation, record the main ideas in a flowchart like this one below. Add more boxes as necessary.

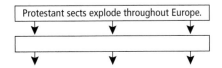

Throughout Europe, Catholic monarchs and the Catholic Church fought back against the Protestant challenge by taking steps to reform the Church and to restore its spiritual leadership of the Christian world. Still, Protestant ideas continued to spread.

An Explosion of Protestant Sects

As the Reformation continued, hundreds of new Protestant **sects,** or religious groups that had broken away from an established church, sprang up. Many of these followed variations on the teachings of Luther, Calvin, and Zwingli. Some sects, however, had ideas that were even more radical—such as rejecting infant baptism. Infants, they argued, are too young to understand what it means to accept the Christian faith. They became known as Anabaptists.

A few Anabaptist sects sought radical social change as well. Some wanted to abolish private property. Others sought to speed up the coming of God's day of judgment by violent means. When radical Anabaptists took over the city of Munster in Germany, even Luther advised his supporters to join Catholics in suppressing the threat to the traditional order. Most Anabaptists, however, were peaceful. They called for religious toleration and separation of church and state. Despite harsh persecution, these groups influenced Protestant thinking in many countries. Today, the Baptists, Mennonites, and Amish all trace their religious ancestry to the Anabaptists.

 Checkpoint Who were the Anabaptists?

The English Reformation

In England, religious leaders like John Wycliffe had called for Church reform as early as the 1300s. By the 1520s, some English clergy were exploring Protestant ideas. The break with the Catholic Church, however, was the work not of religious leaders but of King **Henry VIII.**

Henry VIII Seeks an Annulment At first, Henry VIII stood firmly against the Protestant revolt. The pope even awarded him the title "Defender of the Faith" for a pamphlet that he wrote denouncing Luther.

In 1527, however, an issue arose that set Henry at odds with the Church. After 18 years of marriage, Henry and his Spanish wife, Catherine of Aragon, had only one surviving child, **Mary Tudor.** Henry felt that England's stability depended on his having a male heir. He had already fallen in love with a young noblewoman named Anne Boleyn, who served the Queen. He hoped that if he married her she would bear him a son. Because Catholic law does not permit divorce, he asked the pope to annul, or cancel, his marriage. Popes had annulled royal marriages before. But this pope refused. He did not want to offend the Holy Roman emperor Charles V, Catherine's nephew.

Breaking With the Church Henry was furious. Spurred on by his advisors, many of whom leaned toward Protestantism, he decided to take over the English church. Guided by his chancellor Thomas Cromwell, he had Parliament pass a series of laws. They took the English church from the pope's control and placed it under Henry's rule. At the same time, Henry appointed **Thomas Cranmer** archbishop of the new church. Cranmer annulled the king's marriage, and in 1533 Henry married Anne Boleyn. Soon, Anne gave birth to a daughter, **Elizabeth.**

In 1534, Parliament passed the Act of Supremacy, making Henry "the only supreme head on Earth of the Church of England." Many loyal Catholics refused to accept the Act of Supremacy and were executed for treason. Among them was the great English humanist Sir Thomas More, who served in Henry's government but tried to resign in protest. More was later **canonized,** or recognized as a saint, by the Catholic Church.

Strengthening the Church of England Between 1536 and 1540, royal officials investigated Catholic convents and monasteries. Claiming that they were centers of immorality, Henry ordered them closed. He then confiscated, or seized, their lands and wealth. Henry shrewdly granted some of these lands to nobles and other high-ranking citizens. He thus secured their support for the Anglican Church, as the new Church of England was called. Despite these actions, Henry was not a religious radical. He rejected most Protestant doctrines. Aside from breaking away from Rome and allowing use of the English Bible, he kept most Catholic forms of worship.

Religious Turmoil When Henry died in 1547, he had only one surviving son—despite having married six times. Nine-year-old Edward VI inherited the throne. The young king and his advisors were devout Protestants and took steps to make England a truly Protestant country. Under Edward, Parliament passed new laws bringing Protestant reforms to England. Thomas Cranmer drew up the Protestant *Book of Common Prayer,* which became required reading in all of the country's church services. Though it outlined a moderate form of Protestant service, it sparked uprisings. These uprisings were harshly suppressed.

BIOGRAPHY

Elizabeth I

The life of Elizabeth I (1533–1603) did not start favorably. When she was only two years old her mother, Anne Boleyn, was beheaded so that her father, Henry VIII, could remarry. The young princess grew up in isolation. Still, Henry VIII was affectionate to his daughter and saw to it that she received a rigorous education. Even as a teenager she was well-respected for her sharp mind, fluency in languages, and understanding of philosophy and theology.

Under the reign of her half-sister Mary Tudor, Elizabeth became both a rallying symbol for Protestants and a target for Catholics. Though arrested and imprisoned, she survived her sister to become queen of England at age 25. The well-loved Elizabeth used her talents to unify England, expand its international power, and encourage a period of great artistic flowering. **Why do you think the period under Elizabeth's reign is now called the Elizabethan Age?**

When Edward died in his teens, his half-sister Mary Tudor became queen. She was determined to return England to the Catholic faith. Under Queen Mary hundreds of English Protestants, including Archbishop Cranmer, were burned at the stake for heresy.

The Elizabethan Settlement On Mary's death in 1558, the throne passed to 25-year-old Elizabeth, the daughter of Henry VIII and Anne Boleyn. For years, Elizabeth had survived court intrigues, including the religious swings under Edward and Mary. As queen, Elizabeth had to determine the future of the Church of England. Moving cautiously at first, she slowly enforced a series of reforms that over time came to be called the Elizabethan settlement.

The queen's policies were a **compromise,** or acceptable middle ground, between Protestant and Catholic practices. The Church of England preserved much Catholic ritual, and it kept the hierarchy of bishops and archbishops. Unlike Henry, the queen did not call herself "supreme head" of the church, but she reaffirmed that the monarch was the "supreme governor" over spiritual matters in England. At the same time, Elizabeth restored a version of the *Book of Common Prayer,* accepted moderate Protestant doctrine, and allowed English to replace Latin in church services. Her sensible compromises, which satisfied most Catholics and Protestants, largely ended decades of religious turmoil.

During a long reign, Elizabeth used all her skills to restore unity to England. Even while keeping many Catholic traditions, she made England a firmly Protestant nation. After her death, England faced new religious storms. But it escaped the endless religious wars that tore apart France and many other European states during the 1500s.

✓ **Checkpoint**   Why was the Church of England established?

Major Events of the English Reformation

1521 Henry VIII writes to the pope to condemn Luther's teachings.

King Henry the eyght.

1529 Parliament begins passing laws to make Henry VIII head of the church in England.

1533 Henry VIII divorces Catherine of Aragon and marries Anne Boleyn.

1534 Parliament passes the Act of Supremacy.

The Catholic Reformation

As the Protestant Reformation swept across northern Europe, a vigorous reform movement took hold within the Catholic Church. Led by Pope Paul III, it is known as the Catholic Reformation, or the Counter-Reformation. During the 1530s and 1540s, the pope set out to revive the moral authority of the Church and roll back the Protestant tide. He also appointed reformers to end corruption within the papacy itself. They and their successors led the Catholic Reformation for the rest of the century.

Council of Trent To establish the direction that reform should take, the pope called the Council of Trent in 1545. Led by Italian cardinal Carlo Borromeo, the council met off and on for almost 20 years. The council reaffirmed the traditional Catholic views that Protestants had challenged. It declared that salvation comes through faith and good works. According to the council, the Bible, while a major source of religious truth, is not the only source. The council also took steps to end abuses in the Church. It provided stiff penalties for worldliness and corruption among the clergy. It also established schools to create a better-educated clergy who could challenge Protestant teachings.

Empowering the Inquisition Pope Paul strengthened the Inquisition to fight Protestantism. As you have read, the Inquisition was a Church court set up during the Middle Ages. The Inquisition used secret testimony, torture, and execution to root out heresy. It also prepared the *Index of Forbidden Books*, a list of works considered too immoral or irreligious for Catholics to read. The list included books by Luther and Calvin, as well as earlier works by Petrarch and other humanists.

1547 Henry VIII dies; his son Edward VI becomes king and begins making Protestant reforms.

1553 Edward VI dies; Mary Tudor ▶ becomes queen and restores Catholic doctrines.

1558 Mary Tudor dies; Elizabeth I becomes queen and unifies England with the Elizabethan Settlement.

Analyze Information
Because of Henry VIII's determination to obtain a divorce, Catholic England had become a solidly Protestant nation by 1600. *How long did it take Henry VIII to become head of the Church of England?*

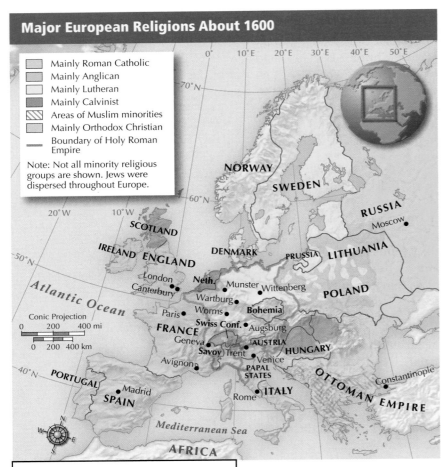

Major European Religions About 1600

Mainly Roman Catholic
Mainly Anglican
Mainly Lutheran
Mainly Calvinist
Areas of Muslim minorities
Mainly Orthodox Christian
Boundary of Holy Roman Empire

Note: Not all minority religious groups are shown. Jews were dispersed throughout Europe.

Map Skills By 1600, the spread of Protestantism had transformed Catholic Europe.

1. **Locate** (a) London (b) Wittenberg (c) Rome
2. **Identify** Identify the religion practiced in each of the locations above.
3. **Understand Main Ideas** Explain why most people in each region were practicing that religion by 1600.

Geography *Interactive*
For: Audio guided tour
Web Code: nbp-1341

Vocabulary Builder
rigorous—(RIG ur us) *adj.* strict; thorough

Founding the Jesuits In 1540, the pope recognized a new religious order, the Society of Jesus, or Jesuits. The order was founded by **Ignatius of Loyola,** a Spanish knight raised in the crusading tradition. After his leg was shattered in battle, he found comfort reading about saints who had overcome mental and physical torture. Vowing to become a "soldier of God," Ignatius drew up a strict program for the Jesuits. It included spiritual and moral discipline, rigorous religious training, and absolute obedience to the Church. Led by Ignatius, the Jesuits embarked on a crusade to defend and spread the Catholic faith worldwide.

To further the Catholic cause, Jesuits became advisors to Catholic rulers, helping them combat heresy in their lands. They set up schools that taught humanist and Catholic beliefs and enforced discipline and obedience. Daring Jesuits slipped into Protestant lands in disguise to minister to Catholics. Jesuit missionaries spread their Catholic faith to distant lands, including Asia, Africa, and the Americas.

Teresa of Avila As the Catholic Reformation spread, many Catholics experienced renewed feelings of intense faith. Teresa of Avila symbolized this renewal. Born into a wealthy Spanish family, Teresa entered a convent in her youth. Finding convent routine not strict enough, she established her own order of nuns. They lived in isolation, eating and sleeping very little and dedicating themselves to prayer and meditation.

Impressed by her spiritual life, her superiors in the Church asked Teresa to reorganize and reform Spanish convents and monasteries. Teresa was widely honored for her work, and after her death the Church canonized her. Her spiritual writings rank among the most important Christian texts of her time, and are still widely read today.

Legacy of the Catholic Reformation By 1600, the majority of Europeans remained Catholic. Tireless Catholic reformers, like Francis de Sales in France, had succeeded in bringing back Protestant converts. Moreover, renewed piety found expression in literature and art. Across Catholic Europe, charity flourished and church abuses were reduced.

Still, Protestantism had gained a major foothold on the continent. The Reformation and the Catholic Reformation stirred up intense feeling and debate. Religious conflict played into heated disagreements about government, which would erupt into war throughout much of Europe. At the end, Europe would remain—and still remains today—divided by differing interpretations of Christianity.

✓ **Checkpoint** What was the outcome of the Catholic Reformation?

Widespread Persecution

During this period of heightened religious passion, persecution was widespread. Both Catholics and Protestants fostered intolerance and persecuted radical sects like the Anabaptists, people they thought were witches, and Jews.

Conducting Witch Hunts Between 1450 and 1750, tens of thousands of women and men died as victims of witch hunts. Those accused of being witches, or agents of the devil, were usually women. Most victims of the witch hunts died in the German states, Switzerland, and France, all centers of religious conflict. When the wars of religion came to an end, the persecution of witches also declined.

Scholars have offered various reasons for this persecution, but most agree that it had to do with people's twin beliefs in Christianity and magic. Most people believed that among them were witches who practiced magical deeds, often with the aid of the devil. Thus witches were seen as anti-Christian. Because witches often behaved in non-traditional ways, many people accused of witchcraft were often social outcasts, such as beggars. Midwives and herbalists were also targeted.

Persecuting Jews For many Jews in Italy, the early Renaissance had been a time of relative prosperity. While Spain had expelled its Jews in 1492, Italy allowed them to remain. Still, pressure remained strong on Jews to convert. In 1516, Venice ordered Jews to live in a separate quarter of the city called the **ghetto.** Other Italian cities soon followed.

During the Reformation, restrictions on Jews increased. At first, Luther hoped that Jews would be converted to his teachings. When they did not convert, he called for them to be expelled from Christian lands and for their synagogues to be burned. In time, some German princes did expel Jews. In the 1550s, Pope Paul IV placed added restrictions on Jews. Even Emperor Charles V, who supported toleration of Jews in the Holy Roman Empire, banned them from Spanish territories and new American colonies. From the early 1500s on, many Jews migrated to the Mediterranean parts of the Ottoman Empire and to the Netherlands.

✓ **Checkpoint** Why were Jews and other people persecuted?

Teresa of Avila wrote a book in 1610 describing her work with reforming Catholic convents and monasteries.

Primary Source

❝ At about this time there came to my notice the harm and havoc that were being wrought in France by these Lutherans and the way in which their unhappy sect was increasing. . . . I wept before the Lord and entreated Him to remedy this great evil. I felt that I would have laid down a thousand lives to save a single one of all the souls that were being lost there. And, seeing that I was a woman, and a sinner . . . I determined to do the little that was in me. . . . ❞

Assessment

Progress Monitoring *Online*
For: Self-quiz with vocabulary practice
Web Code: nba-1341

Terms, People, and Places

1. Place each of the key terms at the beginning of this section into one of the following categories: politics, culture, economy, or geography. Write a sentence for each term explaining your choice.

Note Taking

2. **Reading Skill: Identify Main Ideas** Use your completed flowchart to answer the Focus Question: How did the Reformation bring about two different religious paths in Europe?

Comprehension and Critical Thinking

3. **Identify Point of View** Why were the Anabaptists considered to be radical?

4. **Understand Sequence** How did reforms cause England to become a Protestant country?

5. **Recognize Ideologies** Why might the Catholic Church have found the ideas of Ignatius to be particularly relevant to the Catholic Reformation?

6. **Make Comparisons** Why did witch hunting decline with the end of the religious wars, while persecution of Jews did not?

● **Writing About History**

Quick Write: Decide on an Organizational Strategy Write a thesis statement for a persuasive essay about the spread of the Reformation. List your supporting arguments, from strongest to weakest. Then make an outline that shows where your arguments will appear and how they relate to your thesis statement. You may want to save your strongest argument for the last paragraph of body text before your conclusion.

WITNESS HISTORY 🔊 AUDIO

Mountains on the Moon

In 1609, Italian astronomer Galileo Galilei heard of a new Dutch invention, the telescope. It was designed to help people see distant enemy ships. Galileo was interested for another reason—he wondered what would happen if he trained a telescope on the night sky. So he built his own telescope for this purpose. When he pointed it at the sky, he was amazed. The new telescope allowed him to see mountains on the moon, fiery spots on the sun, and four moons circling the planet Jupiter. "I did discover many particulars in Heaven that had been unseen and unheard of until this our age," he later wrote.

Focus Question How did discoveries in science lead to a new way of thinking for Europeans?

An 1800s artist imagines Galileo at work, peering into the sky. Galileo's telescope is shown at top right.

The Scientific Revolution

Objectives

- Explain how new discoveries in astronomy changed the way people viewed the universe.
- Understand the new scientific method and how it developed.
- Analyze the contributions that Newton and other scientists made to the Scientific Revolution.

Terms, People, and Places

Nicolaus Copernicus	scientific method
heliocentric	hypothesis
Tycho Brahe	Robert Boyle
Johannes Kepler	Isaac Newton
Galileo	gravity
Francis Bacon	calculus
René Descartes	

Note Taking

Reading Skills: Identify Main Ideas Use a table like the one below to record information about important people of the Scientific Revolution.

Thinkers of the Scientific Revolution	
Nicolaus Copernicus	Developed sun-centered universe theory

The Renaissance and the Reformation facilitated the breakdown of the medieval worldview. In the mid-1500s, a profound shift in scientific thinking brought about the final break with Europe's medieval past. Called the Scientific Revolution, this movement pointed toward a future shaped by a new way of thinking about the physical universe. At the heart of the Scientific Revolution was the assumption that mathematical laws governed nature and the universe. The physical world, therefore, could be known, managed, and shaped by people.

Changing Views of the Universe

Until the mid-1500s, Europeans' view of the universe was shaped by the theories of the ancient writers Ptolemy and Aristotle. More than 1,000 years before the Renaissance, they had taught that Earth was the center of the universe. Not only did this view seem to agree with common sense, it was accepted by the Church. In the 1500s and 1600s, however, people began to question this view.

Copernicus Challenges Ancient Astronomy In 1543, Polish scholar **Nicolaus Copernicus** (koh PUR nih kus) published *On the Revolutions of the Heavenly Spheres*. In it, he proposed a **heliocentric,** or sun-centered, model of the universe. The sun, he said, stands at the center of the universe. Earth is just one of several planets that revolve around the sun.

Most experts rejected this revolutionary theory. In Europe at the time, all scientific knowledge and many religious teachings were based on the arguments developed by classical thinkers. If Ptolemy's reasoning about the planets was wrong, people believed, then the whole system of human knowledge might be called into question. But in the late 1500s, the Danish astronomer **Tycho Brahe** (TEE koh BRAH uh) provided evidence that supported Copernicus's theory. Brahe set up an astronomical observatory. Every night for years, he carefully observed the sky, accumulating data about the movement of the heavenly bodies.

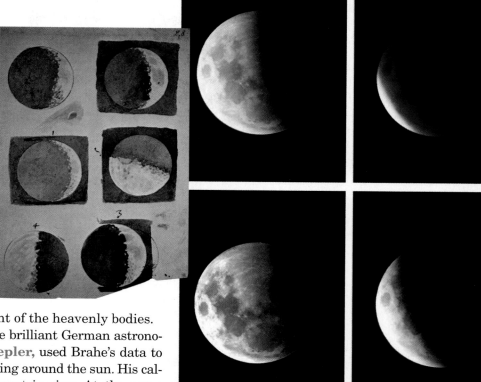

After Brahe's death, his assistant, the brilliant German astronomer and mathematician **Johannes Kepler,** used Brahe's data to calculate the orbits of the planets revolving around the sun. His calculations supported Copernicus's heliocentric view. At the same time, however, they showed that each planet does not move in a perfect circle, as both Ptolemy and Copernicus believed, but in an oval-shaped orbit called an ellipse.

Galileo's "Heresies" Scientists from many different lands built on the foundations laid by Copernicus and Kepler. In Italy, **Galileo** Galilei assembled an astronomical telescope. As you have read, he observed that the four moons of Jupiter move slowly around that planet—exactly, he realized, the way Copernicus said that Earth moves around the sun.

Galileo's discoveries caused an uproar. Other scholars attacked him because his observations <u>contradicted</u> ancient views about the world. The Church condemned him because his ideas challenged the Christian teaching that the heavens were fixed in position to Earth, and perfect.

In 1633, Galileo was tried before the Inquisition, and for a year afterward he was kept under house arrest. Threatened with death unless he withdrew his "heresies," Galileo agreed to state publicly in court that Earth stands motionless at the center of the universe. Legend has it that as he left the court he muttered, "And yet it moves."

✓ **Checkpoint** Why was Copernicus's theory seen as radical?

A New Scientific Method

Despite the opposition of the Church, by the early 1600s a new approach to science had emerged, based upon observation and experimentation. During the Renaissance, the works of the ancient Greek <u>philosopher</u> Plato were rediscovered. Plato taught that man should look beyond simple appearances to learn nature's truths. He believed that mathematics, one of the greatest human achievements, was the key to learning these truths. His teachings were rediscovered by Renaissance scientists and helped shape people's view of the physical world.

Views of the Moon
Galileo sketched the views of the moon he saw through his telescope in 1609 (left). Pictures of the moon taken through a modern telescope (right) look remarkably similar.

Vocabulary Builder
<u>contradict</u>—(kahn truh DIKT) *v.* to go against

Vocabulary Builder
<u>philosopher</u>—(fih LAHS uh fur) *n.* a person who is an expert in the study of knowledge

Bacon and Descartes: Revolutionary Thinkers The new scientific method was really a revolution in thought. Two giants of this revolution were the Englishman **Francis Bacon** and the Frenchman **René Descartes** (day KAHRT). Each devoted himself to understanding how truth is determined. Both Bacon and Descartes, writing in the early 1600s, rejected Aristotle's scientific assumptions. They also challenged the scholarly traditions of the medieval universities that sought to make the physical world fit in with the teachings of the Church. Both argued that truth is not known at the beginning of inquiry but at the end, after a long process of investigation.

Bacon and Descartes differed in their methods, however. Bacon stressed experimentation and observation. He wanted science to make life better for people by leading to practical technologies. Descartes emphasized human reasoning as the best road to understanding. In his *Discourse on Method* (1637), he explains how he decided to discard all traditional authorities and search for provable knowledge. Left only with doubt, he concluded that doubt was the only thing he could not question, and that in order to doubt he had to exist as a rational, thinking being. Therefore he made his famous statement, "I think, therefore I am."

A Step-by-Step Process Over time, a step-by-step process of discovery evolved that became known as the **scientific method.** The scientific method required scientists to collect and accurately measure data. To explain the data, scientists used reasoning to propose a logical **hypothesis,** or possible explanation. They then tested the hypothesis with further observation or experimentation. Mathematical calculations were used to convert the observations and experiments into scientific laws. After reaching a conclusion, scientists repeated their work at least once—and usually many times—to confirm and refine their hypotheses or formulate better ones.

Diagram Skills The scientific method, still used today, is based on careful observation and measurement of data. *Why is Step 7 an important part of the process?*

✓ **Checkpoint** How did Bacon and Descartes each approach the new scientific method?

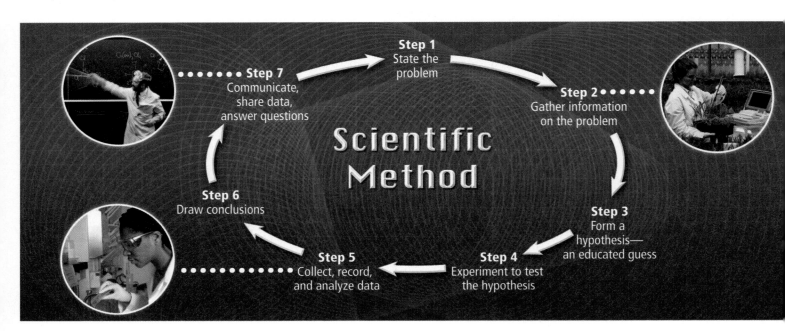

Scientific Method

Step 1
State the problem

Step 2
Gather information on the problem

Step 3
Form a hypothesis— an educated guess

Step 4
Experiment to test the hypothesis

Step 5
Collect, record, and analyze data

Step 6
Draw conclusions

Step 7
Communicate, share data, answer questions

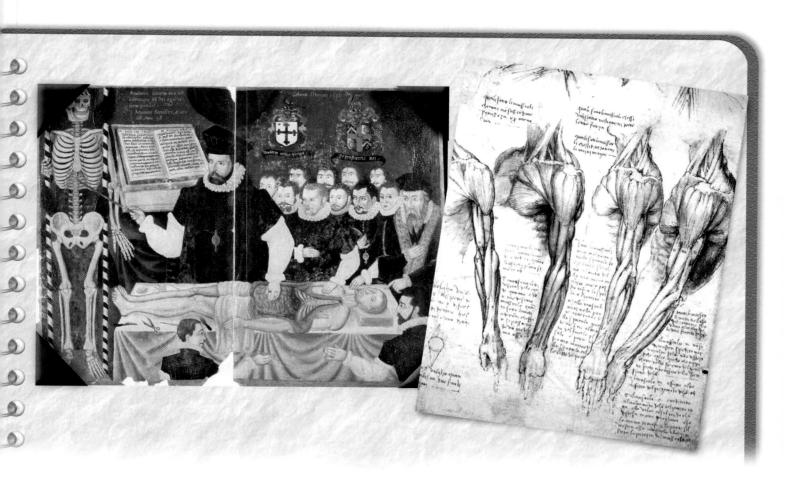

Breakthroughs in Medicine and Chemistry

The 1500s and 1600s saw dramatic changes in many branches of science, especially medicine and chemistry. The rapid changes in science and technology that began in this period still continue to this day.

Exploring the Human Body Medieval physicians relied on the works of the ancient physician Galen. Galen, however, had made many errors, in part because he had limited knowledge of human anatomy. During the Renaissance, physicians made new efforts to study the human body. In 1543, Andreas Vesalius (vuh SAY lee us) published *On the Structure of the Human Body,* the first accurate and detailed study of human anatomy. Vesalius used whatever means he could to increase his knowledge of anatomy. He used friendships with people of influence to get invitations to autopsies. He also autopsied bodies that he himself obtained—counting on friends in the local government to look the other way.

In the early 1540s, French physician Ambroise Paré (pa RAY) developed a new and more effective ointment for preventing infection. He also developed new surgical techniques, introduced the use of artificial limbs, and invented several scientific instruments. Then in the early 1600s, William Harvey, an English scholar, described the circulation of the blood for the first time. He showed how the heart serves as a pump to force blood through veins and arteries. Later in the century, the Dutch inventor Anton van Leeuwenhoek (LAY wun hohk) perfected the microscope and became the first human to see cells and microorganisms. These pioneering scientists opened the way for further discoveries.

Human Anatomy
Renaissance artists and scientists, determined to learn how things really worked, studied nature with great curiosity. In the 1400s, Leonardo drew the muscles of the human arm with amazing accuracy (right). Renaissance doctors learned much about human anatomy from dissections (left). *How does this painting from the 1500s reflect the advances in scientific thinking?*

An English poet wrote the following as an epitaph for Newton's gravestone. What does it suggest about how people of the time viewed Newton's importance?

Primary Source

❝ Nature and Nature's Laws lay hid in night,

God said, Let Newton be! and all was light. ❞

—Alexander Pope, *Epitaphs*

Transforming Chemistry The branch of science now called chemistry was in medieval times called alchemy. Alchemists believed that any substance could be transformed into any other substance, and many of them tried unsuccessfully to turn ordinary metals into gold. With the advances of the Scientific Revolution, the experiments of alchemists were abandoned. However, some of their practices—especially the manipulation of metals and acids—set the stage for modern chemistry.

In the 1600s, English chemist **Robert Boyle** refined the alchemists' view of chemicals as basic building blocks. He explained all matter as being composed of tiny particles that behave in knowable ways. Boyle distinguished between individual elements and chemical compounds, and explained the effect of temperature and pressure on gases. Boyle's work opened the way to modern chemical analysis of the composition of matter.

✔ **Checkpoint** How did Boyle transform the science of chemistry?

Isaac Newton Links the Sciences

As a student in England, **Isaac Newton** devoured the works of the leading scientists of his day. By age 24, he had formed a brilliant theory to explain why the planets moved as they did. According to one story, Newton saw an apple fall from a tree. He wondered whether the force that pulled that apple to Earth might not also control the movements of the planets. In the next 20 years, Newton perfected his theory. Using mathematics, he showed that a single force keeps the planets in their orbits around the sun. He called this force **gravity.**

In 1687, Newton published a book explaining the law of gravity and other workings of the universe. Nature, argued Newton, follows uniform laws. All motion in the universe can be measured and described mathematically. To many, Newton's work seemed to link the sciences just as gravity itself bound the universe together.

For more than 200 years, Newton's laws held fast. In the early 1900s, startling new theories of the universe called some of his ideas into question. Yet his laws of motion and mechanics continue to have many practical uses. For example, **calculus**—a branch of mathematics partially developed by Newton and used to explain his laws—is still applied today.

✔ **Checkpoint** How did Newton use observations of nature to explain the movements of the planets?

SECTION 5 **Assessment**

Progress Monitoring Online
For: Self-quiz with vocabulary practice
Web Code: nba-1351

Terms, People, and Places

1. What do all of the key people listed at the beginning of this section have in common? Explain.

Note Taking

2. **Reading Skill: Identify Main Ideas** Use your completed table to answer the Focus Question: How did discoveries in science lead to a new way of thinking for Europeans?

Comprehension and Critical Thinking

3. **Recognize Ideologies** Why did the theories of Copernicus and Galileo threaten the views of the Church?

4. **Make Generalizations** In what ways did the scientific method differ from earlier approaches to learning?

5. **Recognize Cause and Effect** What impact did Renaissance ideas have on medicine?

6. **Synthesize Information** How did Newton use the ideas of Plato?

● **Writing About History**

Quick Write: Write a Conclusion Write a conclusion to a persuasive essay about the Scientific Revolution. Your conclusion should restate a thesis statement, supported by one or two strong arguments. You may want to end your essay with a quotation. For example, you could use the Pope quotation to support a thesis that Newton's ideas were the most important of the Scientific Revolution.

Science and Technology

How has science changed people's lives throughout history?

Copernicus played a critical role in the Scientific Revolution. His heliocentric theory, supported by the work of Kepler, Galileo, and other scientists, undermined the existing worldview of the Church and of most European scholars. It helped lead to a whole new approach to science, based on observation and experimentation. Despite its revolutionary nature, Copernicus's theory did not directly change people's lives. Yet many of the scientific observations and experiments that followed had important practical effects, as the following medical examples reveal.

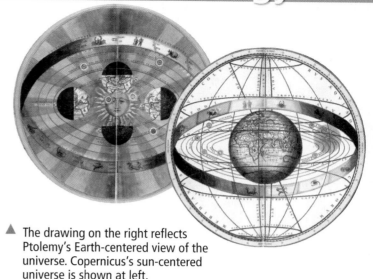

▲ The drawing on the right reflects Ptolemy's Earth-centered view of the universe. Copernicus's sun-centered universe is shown at left.

Organ Transplantation

An organ transplant is the transfer of a living body organ to an ill person in order to restore that person's health. Dr. Joseph Murray performed the first transplant in 1954 when he transferred a kidney from one twin to the other. Since then, the success rate for transplants has grown steadily, thanks to new techniques and new drugs that keep the body from rejecting a donated organ. During 2003, surgeons transplanted more than 25,000 organs, including hearts, lungs, livers, and kidneys.

Vaccination

You probably received your first vaccination as an infant. Vaccination, also called immunization, introduces killed or altered bacteria or viruses into the body. This triggers the body's immune system, enabling it to defend against the disease. In the 1790s, Edward Jenner launched the scientific study of immunization when he discovered a vaccine against smallpox, a disease that had plagued humankind since ancient times. By 1980, vaccination had finally rid the world of smallpox.

Microscope

Anton van Leeuwenhoek had a hobby. In his spare time, he liked to grind lenses and use them to observe worlds formerly hidden from sight. In 1684, using his simple microscope, he became the first person to describe red blood cells accurately. In modern times, the microscope has served as a vital tool for saving lives. Doctors use it to identify the bacteria and other germs causing an illness. Based on their findings, they can tailor their treatment to fight the patient's specific disease.

▲ A greatly enlarged image of tiny bacteria

▲ Alonzo Mourning plays in his first basketball game after receiving a kidney transplant.

▲ This French illustration shows Edward Jenner administering a vaccine.

Thinking Critically

1. How did the Scientific Revolution pave the way for the medical successes described above? How have those successes changed people's lives?
2. **Connections to Today** Do research to find out more about these and other examples of scientific breakthroughs. Choose one breakthrough and write a press release announcing it to the world.

Quick Study Guide

Progress Monitoring *Online*
For: Self-test with vocabulary practice
Web Code: nba-1361

■ Major Themes of the Renaissance

- Importance of classical learning
- Emphasis on the individual
- Adventurous spirit and willingness to experiment
- Focus on realism in art and literature
- Questioning of traditional religious ideas

■ Important Figures of the Scientific Revolution

Person	Achievement	Date
Nicolaus Copernicus	Developed the sun-centered model of the universe	1543
Tycho Brahe and Johannes Kepler	Built astronomical observatory to calculate the planetary orbits; supported Copernicusís views	Late 1500s
Galileo Galilei	Developed telescope to view the planets and confirmed Copernicus's theory	1600
Francis Bacon	Called for new scientific method	Early 1600s
René Descartes	Developed new philosophy of human reasoning	Early 1600s
Isaac Newton	Developed laws of gravity and motion; invented calculus	Late 1600s
Robert Boyle	Identified basic building blocks of matter, opening the way for modern chemistry	Late 1600s

■ Causes and Effects of the Protestant Reformation

Cause and Effect	
Long-Term Causes	**Immediate Causes**
• Roman Catholic Church becomes more worldly. • Humanists urge a return to simple religion. • Shift to more uncertain, urban-based economies causes people to look for society that makes more sense to them. • Monarchs and other leaders question the pope's authority and wealth.	• Johann Tetzel sells indulgences in Wittenberg. • Martin Luther posts 95 Theses. • Luther translates the Bible into German. • The printing press spreads reform ideas. • Calvin and other reformers preach against Roman Catholic traditions.

The Protestant Reformation

Immediate Effects	Long-Term Effects
• Peasants' Revolt • Catholic Reformation • Strengthening of the Inquisition • Luther's calls for Jewish expulsion result in Jewish migration to Eastern Europe	• Religious wars in Europe • Founding of Lutheran, Calvinist, Anglican, Presbyterian, and other Protestant churches • Weakening of Holy Roman Empire • Increased anti-Semitism

■ Key Events of the Renaissance and the Reformation

1300s
The Renaissance begins in the city-states of Italy.

1434
The Medici family gains control of Florence's government.

Chapter Events
World Events

1300 — **1350** — **1400**

1324
Mansa Musa makes hajj.

1368
The Ming dynasty is founded in China.

1450
The kingdom of Songhai emerges in West Africa.

Concept Connector

■ Cumulative Review

Use your Concept Connector worksheets and the text to help answer these questions. In addition, record information from this chapter about the following concepts.

1. **Cultural Diffusion** During the Middle Ages, many European peoples were cut off from each other as trade broke down and disease ravaged populations. With the Renaissance, renewed trade and increased curiosity about the world led to great cultural diffusion. For example, art techniques developed in Italy spread to northern Europe, and vice versa. Compare the cultural diffusion of the Renaissance to the spread of Islam from about 750 to 1200. Consider:
   - cultural achievements
   - trading centers
   - economic growth
   - religious expression

2. **Science** Many people disputed Copernicus's heliocentric view of the universe, because it challenged the belief of the Earth-centered universe that both made sense to them and was taught to them by the Church. Compare the reaction of people to Copernicus's ideas with the reaction of people to the ideas of Isaac Newton. Why were Newton's theories not seen as controversial?

3. **Cultural Diffusion** The European Renaissance ushered in a period of great cultural achievements that would eventually influence people far beyond Europe. Compare the achievements of Europe during the Renaissance with achievements of the Tang and Song dynasties of China. Consider the following: architecture, print technology, literature, and painting.

■ Connections to Today

1. **Technology: The Communications Revolution** During the Renaissance, new technology like the printing press revolutionized life. Consider the various impacts that the printing press had during the Renaissance, in areas ranging from literacy to religion. Then choose a modern technology that has had a comparable effect. Write two paragraphs explaining why the technology you chose is as important in terms of its impact today as the printing press was in Renaissance times.

2. **Science: Controversial Debates** When Galileo invented his telescope and used it to observe the universe, he opened up a firestorm of debate. Galileo's discoveries challenged traditional views and led people to question many of the things that they had held as firm beliefs. Since Galileo's time, scientific theories have continued to spark furious debate. Think of a recent debate caused by a scientific theory, the use of a medical procedure, or the development of a new technology. Identify both sides of the debate, and then list arguments for each.

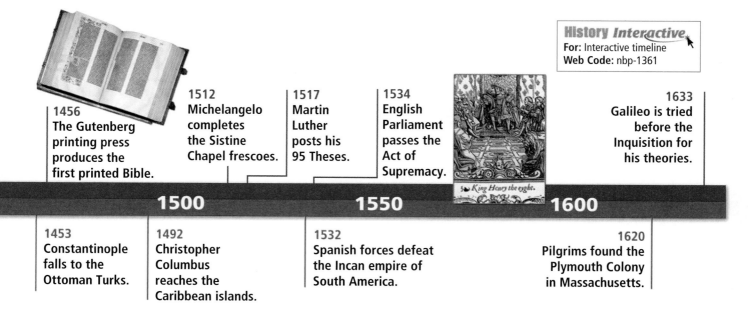

History Interactive
For: Interactive timeline
Web Code: nbp-1361

1456 The Gutenberg printing press produces the first printed Bible.

1512 Michelangelo completes the Sistine Chapel frescoes.

1517 Martin Luther posts his 95 Theses.

1534 English Parliament passes the Act of Supremacy.

1633 Galileo is tried before the Inquisition for his theories.

1500 **1550** **1600**

1453 Constantinople falls to the Ottoman Turks.

1492 Christopher Columbus reaches the Caribbean islands.

1532 Spanish forces defeat the Incan empire of South America.

1620 Pilgrims found the Plymouth Colony in Massachusetts.

Chapter Assessment

Terms, People, and Places

Complete each sentence by choosing the correct answer from the list of terms below. You will not use all of the terms.

patron	indulgence	ghetto
humanism	predestination	heliocentric
vernacular	compromise	hypothesis
utopian		

1. Lorenzo de' Medici was a _____ of the Florentine arts.
2. Rabelais and Shakespeare wrote in the _____ to appeal to the common people.
3. Calvin's belief in _____ set him apart from Catholics.
4. Elizabeth's sensible _____ helped keep England unified in the face of religious conflict.
5. Copernicus's _____ theory of the universe challenged the accepted teachings of the Church.

Main Ideas

Section 1 (pp. 48–54)
6. How did the new Renaissance worldview shape the work of Italian Renaissance artists and writers?

Section 2 (pp. 56–59)
7. What was the role of the printing press in spreading Renaissance ideas?
8. How did northern European artists and writers apply Renaissance ideas in their work?

Section 3 (pp. 61–65)
9. How did the Renaissance open the door to the Protestant Reformation?

Section 4 (pp. 66–71)
10. Why did the Church respond with its Catholic Reformation?

Section 5 (pp. 72–76)
11. How were the scientists of the Scientific Revolution influenced by Renaissance ideas?

Chapter Focus Question
12. How did the Renaissance shape European art, thought, and religion?

Critical Thinking

13. **Geography and History** How did Italy's geography encourage the spread of the Renaissance?
14. **Analyze Information** In what ways was the Renaissance a break with medieval times? In what ways was it a continuation of medieval times?
15. **Predict Consequences** Under what circumstances are religious beliefs likely to inspire anger or violence?
16. **Analyze Visuals** What Renaissance theme does the bas-relief below express?

17. **Test Conclusions** The Renaissance and Scientific Revolution are often described as eras of human progress. Evaluate whether this is an accurate description.
18. **Recognize Cause and Effect** Why did England escape the kinds of religious wars that tore apart other European nations?
19. **Synthesize Information** An English author wrote, "The preaching of sermons is speaking to a few of mankind, but printing books is talking to the whole world." How does this statement suggest a relationship between two of the key events discussed in this chapter?

● Writing About History

Writing a Persuasive Essay European history from 1300 to the 1600s was a time of great change, discovery, and religious upheaval. Write a persuasive essay that presents your position on either the Renaissance, the Reformation, or the Scientific Revolution. Consult page SH16 of the Writing Handbook for additional help.

Prewriting
• Choose a topic and decide what your main position will be.
• Think of arguments that both support and oppose your position, and answer them.
• Gather evidence that supports your position.

Drafting
• State your position in a thesis statement.
• Organize your arguments into a draft outline.
• Write the introduction, body text, and closing arguments. Be sure to support your arguments with a variety of points, including facts, comparisons, and statistics.

Revising
• Use the guidelines for revising your report on page SH17 of the Writing Handbook.

Document-Based Assessment

The Impact of the Printing Press

In a time when new ideas and discoveries were commonplace, the invention of the printing press was no less than astonishing in its impact. Documents A, B, and D describe the spread of printing during the Renaissance. Document C, written by a historian in the 1500s, describes its impact at the time.

Document A

"In 1455 all Europe's printed books could have been carried in a single wagon. Fifty years later, the titles ran to tens of thousands, the individual volumes to millions. Today, books pour off presses at the rate of 10,000 million *a year.* That's some 50 million tons of paper. Add in 8,000 to 9,000 daily newspapers, and the Sundays, and the magazines, and the figure rises to 130 million tons . . . It would make a pile 700 meters [2,297 feet] high—four times the height of the Great Pyramid."

—From ***Gutenberg: How One Man Remade the World with Words*** by John Man

Document B

"Printing spread from Mainz to Strasbourg (1458), Cologne (1465), Augsburg (1468), Nuremberg (1470), Leipzig (1481), and Vienna (1482). German printers, or their pupils, introduced the 'divine' art to Italy in 1467, Switzerland and Bohemia in 1468, France and the Netherlands in 1470, Spain, England, Hungary, and Poland between 1474 and 1476, Denmark and Sweden in 1482–1483. By 1500 the presses had issued about six million books in approximately forty thousand editions, more books, probably, than had been produced in western Europe since the fall of Rome . . . Now individuals could afford to own books, where before they had normally been owned almost exclusively by institutions—monasteries, cathedral chapters, and colleges."

—From ***The Foundation of Early Modern Europe, 1460–1559*** by Eugene F. Rice, Jr.

Document C

"As if to offer proof that God has chosen us to accomplish a special mission, there was invented in our land a marvelous new and subtle art, the art of printing. This opened German eyes even as it is now bringing enlightenment to other countries. Each man became eager for knowledge, not without feeling a sense of amazement at his former blindness."

—From ***Address to the Estates of the Empire*** by Johann Sleidan

Document D

The Spread of Printing in Renaissance Europe

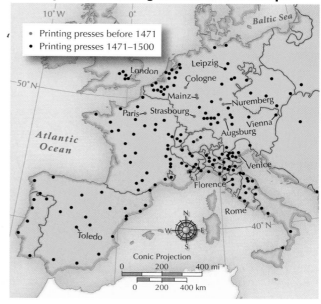

- Printing presses before 1471
- Printing presses 1471–1500

Analyzing Documents

Use your knowledge of the Renaissance and Documents A, B, C, and D to answer questions 1–4.

1. According to Document B, the increased supply and lower cost of books had what effect?
   A More people became teachers.
   B More people became printers.
   C More people bought books.
   D More people bought printing presses.

2. What information about printing can be found only on Document D?
   A specific dates when printing presses were introduced
   B areas where the concentration of printing presses was densest
   C numbers of printing presses introduced into selected cities
   D countries where printing presses were introduced

3. What does German historian Sleidan, in Document C, imply is the *most important* role of the printing press?
   A spreading the Protestant religion
   B teaching German history to other countries
   C making books cheaper
   D giving Germans more knowledge

4. **Writing Task** How did the invention of the printing press affect the spread of the Reformation? Use specific evidence from the documents above, along with information from this chapter, to support your answer.

2

The Beginnings of Our Global Age: Europe, Africa, and Asia

1415–1796

Around the World and Into History

In 1519, a fleet of five Spanish ships with more than 250 crew sailed from Spain. Ferdinand Magellan, the captain, had been commissioned to sail around the Americas to the Spice Islands. Three years later, a single battered ship limped back into a Spanish harbor. On board were just 18 malnourished, skeletal sailors, so weak they could barely walk. Magellan and all but one of the ship's officers had perished. The survivors told an amazing tale. One recorded in his journal:

66From the time we left that bay . . . until the present day, we had sailed 14,460 leagues [nearly 60,000 miles], and furthermore had completed the circumnavigation of the world from east to west.99

Listen to the Witness History audio to hear more about this historic voyage.

◄ A Portuguese painting from 1522 tells the story of the martyrdom of Ursula, a medieval Catholic saint. The religious story and the sailing ships in the background express the themes of the age of exploration.

A pottery dish in the Muslim Spanish style shows a *nao*, a light sailing ship developed in the 1400s.

African statue of a Portuguese soldier

Chapter Preview

Chapter Focus Question How did European voyages of exploration lead to European empires in the Eastern Hemisphere?

Chinese silk robe from the Qing dynasty

Note Taking Study Guide *Online*
For: Note Taking and Concept Connector worksheets
Web Code: nbd-1401

The Search Is On

Cinnamon, pepper, nutmeg, cloves . . . these and other spices were a vital part of the world economy in the 1400s. Because the spice trade was controlled by Arab merchants and traders, Europeans didn't know how to get the spices they desperately wanted. Even when Europeans learned that spice plants could be obtained in Asia, they didn't have a hope of growing them in Europe. As an Indonesian ruler boasted to a European trader,

66 You may be able to take our plants, but you will never be able to take our rain.99

Europeans knew that the only way they could take control of the spice trade would be to establish sea routes to Asia—at any cost.

Focus Question How did the search for spices lead to global exploration?

A French traveler in the 1400s illustrated workers harvesting pepper in southern India; a clove plant is shown at left.

The Search for Spices

Objectives
- Understand European motivations for exploring the seas.
- Analyze early Portuguese and Spanish explorations.
- Describe European searches for a direct route to Asia.

Terms, People, and Places

Moluccas	Line of Demarcation
Prince Henry	Treaty of Tordesillas
cartographer	Ferdinand Magellan
Vasco da Gama	circumnavigate
Christopher Columbus	

Note Taking

Reading Skill: Identify Causes and Effects
Examine the text for clues that signal cause and effect. Then use a flowchart like this one to record major causes and effects of European exploration.

Reasons to Explore	Portugal Leads	
• Control trade	•	•
	•	•

Throughout history, groups of people—from the ancient Greeks to Muslim Arabs and the Vikings of Scandinavia—had explored the seas, trading and migrating over long distances. The European sailors of the 1400s began a dramatic new period of exploration.

Motivations for Exploring the Seas

Europeans traded with Asians long before the Renaissance. The Crusades introduced Europeans to many luxury goods from Asia, carried on complex overland routes through the Mongol empire of the 1200s and 1300s. The Black Death and the breakup of the Mongol empire disrupted that trade. By the 1400s, though, Europe's population was growing, along with its demand for trade goods. The most valued items were spices, used to preserve food, add flavor to meat, and make medicines and perfumes. The chief source of spices was the **Moluccas,** an island chain in present-day Indonesia, which Europeans then called the Spice Islands.

In the 1400s, Arab and Italian merchants controlled most trade between Asia and Europe. Muslim traders brought prized goods to eastern Mediterranean ports, and Italian traders carried them to European markets. Europeans outside Italy knew that it would be more profitable to gain direct access to Asia. They were also driven by Renaissance curiosity to seek new lands.

✓ **Checkpoint** What factors encouraged European exploration?

Map Skills Spain, England, France, and the Netherlands quickly followed Portugal's lead in exploring the world by ship.

1. **Locate** (a) West Indies (b) East Indies (c) Line of Demarcation (d) Strait of Magellan
2. **Describe** Describe the route of Columbus.
3. **Draw Inferences** Why do you think explorers from different countries followed similar routes?

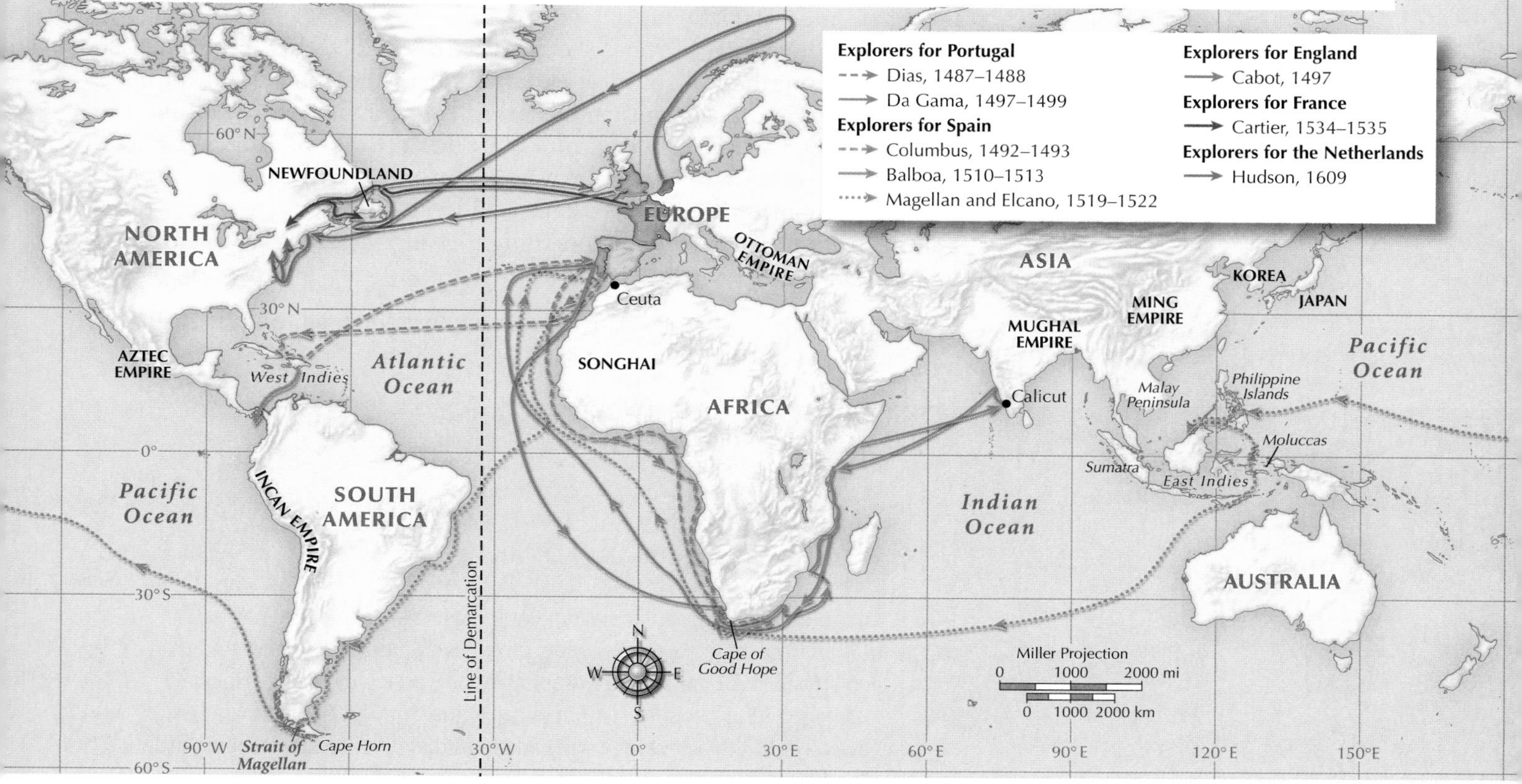

Explorers for Portugal
- - -▸ Dias, 1487–1488
——▸ Da Gama, 1497–1499

Explorers for Spain
- - -▸ Columbus, 1492–1493
——▸ Balboa, 1510–1513
••••▸ Magellan and Elcano, 1519–1522

Explorers for England
——▸ Cabot, 1497

Explorers for France
——▸ Cartier, 1534–1535

Explorers for the Netherlands
——▸ Hudson, 1609

Portugal Sails East

Prince Henry led the way in sponsoring exploration for Portugal, a small nation next to Spain. First, Prince Henry's navigators discovered and claimed the Madeira and Azores islands to the west and southwest of Portugal. By 1415, Portugal had expanded into Muslim North Africa, seizing the port of Ceuta (SYOO tah) on the North African coast.

Mapping the African Coast Prince Henry saw great promise in Africa. The Portuguese could convert the Africans—who practiced either Islam or tribal religions—to Christianity. He also believed that in Africa he would find the sources of riches the Muslim traders controlled.

Finally, Prince Henry hoped to find an easier way to reach Asia, which meant going around Africa. The Portuguese felt that with their expert knowledge and technology, they could accomplish this feat. At Sagres, in southern Portugal, Henry gathered scientists, **cartographers,** or mapmakers, and other experts. They redesigned ships, prepared maps, and trained captains and crews for long voyages. Henry's ships then slowly worked their way south to explore the western coast of Africa.

Henry died in 1460, but the Portuguese continued their quest. In 1488, Bartholomeu Dias rounded the southern tip of Africa. Despite the turbulent seas around it, the tip became known as the Cape of Good Hope because it opened the way for a sea route to Asia.

Seeking India In 1497, Portuguese navigator **Vasco da Gama** followed in Dias's footsteps, leading four ships around the Cape of Good Hope. Da Gama, however, had plans to go farther. After a ten-month voyage, da Gama reached the great spice port of Calicut on the west coast of India. On the long voyage home, the Portuguese lost half their ships, and many sailors died of hunger, thirst, and scurvy, a disease caused by a lack of vitamin C in the diet.

Despite the hard journey, the venture proved highly profitable. In India, da Gama had acquired a cargo of spices that he sold at an enormous profit. He quickly outfitted a new fleet, seeking greater profits. In 1502, he forced a treaty on the ruler of Calicut. Da Gama then left Portuguese merchants there whose job was to buy spices when prices were low and store them until the next fleet could return. Soon, the Portuguese had seized key ports around the Indian Ocean, creating a vast trading empire. Da Gama's voyages confirmed Portugal's status as a world power.

✔ **Checkpoint** How did Portuguese exploration lead to the creation of a trading empire?

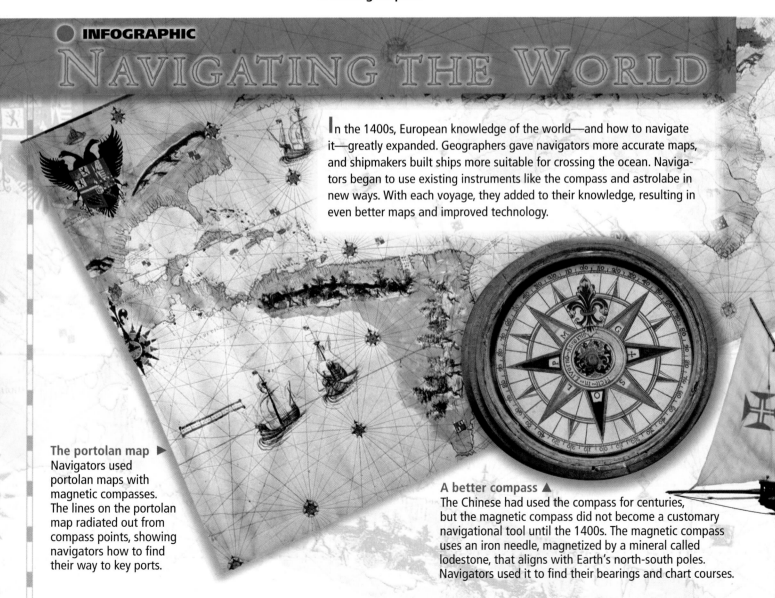

INFOGRAPHIC

NAVIGATING THE WORLD

In the 1400s, European knowledge of the world—and how to navigate it—greatly expanded. Geographers gave navigators more accurate maps, and shipmakers built ships more suitable for crossing the ocean. Navigators began to use existing instruments like the compass and astrolabe in new ways. With each voyage, they added to their knowledge, resulting in even better maps and improved technology.

The portolan map ▶
Navigators used portolan maps with magnetic compasses. The lines on the portolan map radiated out from compass points, showing navigators how to find their way to key ports.

A better compass ▲
The Chinese had used the compass for centuries, but the magnetic compass did not become a customary navigational tool until the 1400s. The magnetic compass uses an iron needle, magnetized by a mineral called lodestone, that aligns with Earth's north-south poles. Navigators used it to find their bearings and chart courses.

Columbus Sails West

News of Portugal's successes spurred other people to look for a sea route to Asia. An Italian navigator from Genoa, named **Christopher Columbus,** wanted to reach the East Indies—a group of islands in Southeast Asia, today part of Indonesia—by sailing west across the Atlantic. Like most educated Europeans, Columbus knew that Earth was a sphere. A few weeks sailing west, he reasoned, would bring a ship to eastern Asia. His plan made sense, but Columbus greatly underestimated Earth's size. And he had no idea that two continents lay in his path.

Reaching Faraway Lands Portugal refused to sponsor him, but Columbus persuaded Ferdinand and Isabella of Spain to finance his voyage. To increase their <u>authority</u>, the Spanish rulers had taken radical measures, including expelling Jews from Spain. They hoped their actions would strengthen Catholicism. However, the loss of some of Spain's most affluent and cultured people weakened the nation. The rulers hoped Columbus's voyage would bring wealth and prestige.

Vocabulary Builder

authority—(uh THAWR uh tee) *n.* the power to give commands and enforce obedience

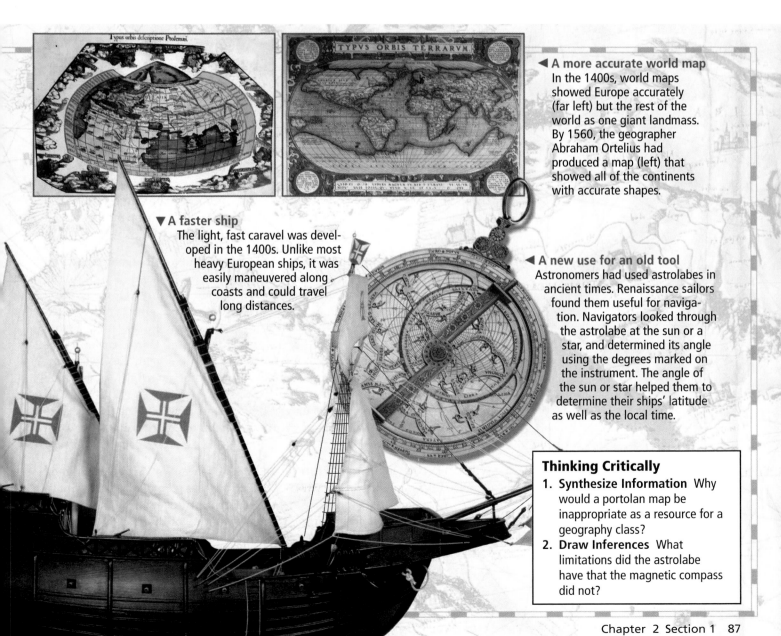

◄ **A more accurate world map** In the 1400s, world maps showed Europe accurately (far left) but the rest of the world as one giant landmass. By 1560, the geographer Abraham Ortelius had produced a map (left) that showed all of the continents with accurate shapes.

▼ **A faster ship** The light, fast caravel was developed in the 1400s. Unlike most heavy European ships, it was easily maneuvered along coasts and could travel long distances.

◄ **A new use for an old tool** Astronomers had used astrolabes in ancient times. Renaissance sailors found them useful for navigation. Navigators looked through the astrolabe at the sun or a star, and determined its angle using the degrees marked on the instrument. The angle of the sun or star helped them to determine their ships' latitude as well as the local time.

Thinking Critically
1. **Synthesize Information** Why would a portolan map be inappropriate as a resource for a geography class?
2. **Draw Inferences** What limitations did the astrolabe have that the magnetic compass did not?

Henry the Navigator

All of the European explorers owed a debt to Prince Henry (1394–1460), whose Christian faith, curiousity, and national pride ushered in the great age of European exploration. The English nicknamed Henry "the Navigator." Yet Henry himself, who sponsored and encouraged navigators, geographers, and merchants, never traveled the seas. Henry's work required financial risks, and his enthusiasm motivated his navigators to take great personal risks. Henry also inspired generations of later explorers. **What characteristics does the artist ascribe to Henry (center figure in black)?**

On August 3, 1492, Columbus sailed west with three small ships, the *Niña*, the *Pinta*, and the *Santa María*. Although the expedition encountered good weather and a favorable wind, no land came into sight for many weeks. Provisions ran low, and the crew became anxious. Finally, on October 12, land was spotted.

Columbus spent several months cruising the islands of the Caribbean. Because he thought he had reached the Indies, he called the people of the region "Indians." In 1493, he returned to Spain to a hero's welcome. In three later voyages, Columbus remained convinced that he had reached the coast of East Asia. Before long, though, other Europeans realized that Columbus had found a route to previously unknown continents.

Dividing the Globe in Half In 1493 Ferdinand and Isabella appealed to the Spanish-born Pope Alexander VI to support their claim to the lands of the new world. The pope set a **Line of Demarcation,** dividing the non-European world into two zones. Spain had trading and exploration rights in any lands west of the line. Portugal had the same rights east of the line. The specific terms of the Line of Demarcation were agreed to in the **Treaty of Tordesillas,** signed between the two countries in 1494. The actual line was unclear, because geography at the time was imprecise. However, the treaty made it obvious to both Spain and Portugal—and to other European nations, eager to defy what they saw as Spain and Portugal's arrogance—that they needed to build their own empires quickly.

Naming the Western Hemisphere An Italian sea captain named Amerigo Vespucci wrote a journal describing his voyage to Brazil. In 1507, a German cartographer named Martin Waldseemüller used Vespucci's descriptions of his voyage to publish a map of the region, which he labeled "America." Over time, the term "Americas" came to be used for both continents of the Western Hemisphere. The islands Columbus had explored in the Caribbean became known as the West Indies.

✓ **Checkpoint** How did Columbus influence the Treaty of Tordesillas?

The Search for a Direct Route Continues

Though Europeans had claimed vast new territories, they had not yet found a direct route to Asia. The English, Dutch, and French explored the coast of North America unsuccessfully for a "northwest passage," or a route from the Atlantic Ocean to the Pacific through the Arctic islands. Meanwhile, in 1513 the Spanish adventurer Vasco Núñez de Balboa, helped by local Indians, hacked a passage westward through the tropical forests of Panama. From a ridge on the west coast, he gazed at a huge body of water. The body of water that he named the South Sea was in fact the Pacific Ocean.

On September 20, 1519, a minor Portuguese nobleman named **Ferdinand Magellan** set out from Spain with five ships to find a way to reach the Pacific. Magellan's ships sailed south and west, through storms and calms and tropical heat. At last, his fleet reached the coast of South America. Carefully, they explored each bay, hoping to find one that would lead to the Pacific. In November 1520, Magellan's ships entered a bay at the southern tip of South America. Amid brutal storms, rushing tides, and unpredictable winds, Magellan found a passage that later became known as the Strait of Magellan. The ships emerged into Balboa's South Sea. Magellan renamed the sea the Pacific, from the Latin word meaning *peaceful*.

Their mission accomplished, most of the crew wanted to return to Spain the way they had come. Magellan, however, insisted that they push on across the Pacific to the East Indies. Magellan underestimated the size of the Pacific. Three more weeks, he thought, would bring them to the Spice Islands. Magellan was wrong. For nearly four months, the ships plowed across the uncharted ocean. Finally, in March 1521, the fleet reached the Philippines, where Magellan was killed. On September 8, 1522, nearly three years after setting out, the survivors— one ship and 18 sailors—reached Spain. The survivors had been the first people to **circumnavigate,** or sail around, the world. Antonio Pigafetta, one of the few survivors of the expedition, observed: "I believe of a certainty that no one will ever again make such a voyage."

✓ **Checkpoint** What was the significance of Balboa's discovery?

SECTION 1
Assessment

Progress Monitoring *Online*
For: Self-quiz with vocabulary practice
Web Code: nba-1411

Terms, People, and Places
1. For each term, person, or place listed at the beginning of the section, write a sentence explaining its significance.

Note Taking
2. **Reading Skill: Identify Causes and Effects** Use your completed flowchart to answer the Focus Question: How did the search for spices lead to global exploration?

Comprehension and Critical Thinking
3. **Recognize Cause and Effect** How did the Renaissance motivate European explorers?
4. **Recognize Ideologies** How did Prince Henry's Christian faith shape his role as a sponsor of exploration?
5. **Identify Alternatives** If Columbus had understood the real geography of the world, would he still have made his voyage? Why or why not?
6. **Predict Consequences** What effect might Magellan's circumnavigation of the world have on English, Dutch, and French explorers?

● Writing About History
Quick Write: Gather Information
Choose one of the following people from this section for a biographical essay: Prince Henry, Christopher Columbus, or Ferdinand Magellan. Gather information about the person you chose. Note events that were both directly and indirectly influenced by this person.

A Benin ivory carving (right) depicts a Portuguese sailor in a ship. Iron weights (top) were used in western Africa to weigh gold.

Great Seabirds Arrive

A Portuguese captain named Alvise Cadamosto reached West Africa in the mid-1400s. He described the reaction of the West Africans to the sight of his ship:

66 It is said that the first time they saw sails . . . they believed they were great seabirds with white wings, which were flying and had come from some strange place. . . . Some thought the ships were fishes, others that they were ghosts that went by night, at which they were terrified.99
—Alvise Cadamosto, 1455

Focus Question What effects did European exploration have on the people of Africa?

Turbulent Centuries in Africa

Objectives
- Describe how the Portuguese established footholds on Africa's coasts.
- Analyze how European actions affected the slave trade and the rise of African states.
- Explain how the European presence in Africa expanded.

Terms, People, and Places

Mombasa
Malindi
plantation
Affonso I
missionary
Asante kingdom

Osei Tutu
monopoly
Oyo empire
Cape Town
Boers

Note Taking

Reading Skill: Identify Effects As you read, record effects of European exploration in Africa in a chart like the one below.

Effects of European Exploration		
European Footholds	Slave Trade	New African States

European encounters with Africa had occurred for hundreds of years. Yet the European explorers who arrived in the 1400s brought great and unforeseen changes to Africa's peoples and cultures.

Portugal Gains Footholds

As you have read, the Portuguese who explored Africa's coasts in the 1400s were looking for a sea route to Asia that bypassed the Mediterranean. They also wanted to buy goods directly from their source, rather than trading through Arab middlemen.

The Portuguese began carrying out their strategy in West Africa, building small forts to collect food and water and to repair their ships. They also established trading posts to trade muskets, tools, and cloth for gold, ivory, hides, and slaves. These were not colonies peopled by settlers. Instead, the Portuguese left just enough men and firepower to defend their forts.

From West Africa, the Portuguese sailed around the continent. They continued to establish forts and trading posts, but they also attacked existing East African coastal cities such as **Mombasa** and **Malindi,** which were hubs of international trade. With cannons blazing, they expelled the Arabs who controlled the East African trade network and took over this thriving commerce for themselves. Each conquest added to their growing trade empire.

Over the next two centuries, some Portuguese explorers managed to reach parts of present-day Congo, Zambia, and Zimbabwe, establishing limited trade. In general, however, the Portuguese did not venture far from the coasts. They knew little about Africa's interior, and they lacked accurate maps or other resources to help them explore there. Furthermore, Africans in the interior, who wanted to control the gold trade, resisted such exploration. As a result of all these factors, when the Portuguese empire declined in the 1600s, the Portuguese did not leave a strong legacy in Africa.

✔ **Checkpoint** Why did the Portuguese establish a presence mainly along the African coast?

The African Slave Trade Explodes

In the 1500s and 1600s, Europeans began to view slaves as the most important item of African trade. Slavery had existed in Africa, as elsewhere around the world, since ancient times. Egyptians, Greeks, Romans, Persians, Indians, and Aztecs often enslaved defeated foes. The English word *slave* comes from the large number of Slavs taken from southern Russia to work as unpaid laborers in Roman times.

The Arab empire also used slave labor, often African captives. In the Middle East, enslaved Africans worked on farming estates or large-scale irrigation projects. Others became artisans, soldiers, or merchants. Some rose to prominence in the Muslim world even though they were slaves.

A Valuable Commodity
Since ancient times, gold was a valuable trade good in western Africa. Beginning in the 1500s, it became an important part of the slave trade. Europeans melted down African gold jewelry like the pieces above to make gold coins.

Europeans Enter the Slave Trade Portuguese traders quickly joined the profitable slave trade, followed by other European traders. Europeans bought large numbers of slaves to perform labor on their **plantations**—large estates run by an owner or an owner's overseer—in the Americas and elsewhere. Europeans also bought slaves as exotic servants for rich households. By the 1500s, European participation had encouraged a much broader Atlantic slave trade.

Europeans seldom went into Africa's interior to take part in slave raids. Instead, they relied on African rulers and traders to seize captives in the interior and bring them to coastal trading posts and forts. There, the captives were exchanged for textiles, metalwork, rum, tobacco, weapons, and gunpowder. Over the next 300 years, the slave trade grew into a huge and profitable business to fill the need for cheap labor. Each year, traders shipped tens of thousands of enslaved Africans across the Atlantic to work on sugar, rice, tobacco, and other plantations in the Americas. These slaves were considered to be property, and they had no hope of bettering their situations.

A Portuguese observer described the first ship of African slaves arriving in Portugal in 1444 from West Africa. Judging from the writer's words, what was his opinion of what he saw?

Primary Source

66 Some kept their heads low and their faces bathed in tears, looking at each other . . . others struck themselves in the face and threw themselves to the ground; and others sang sad songs—although we did not understand their words, the sound told of their great sorrow. . . . The mothers threw themselves flat on the ground. They were beaten but they refused to give up their children. 99
—From *Chronicle of the Discovery and Conquest of Guinea*

 AUDIO

African Leaders Resist Some African leaders tried to slow down or stop the transatlantic slave trade. But in the end, the system that supported the trade was simply too strong for them. An early voice raised against the slave trade was that of **Affonso I,** ruler of Kongo in west-central Africa. As a young man, Affonso had been tutored by Portuguese **missionaries,** who hoped to convert Africans to Christianity.

Major African States About 1700

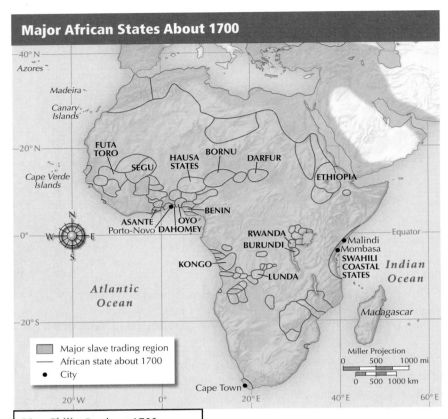

Major African States About 1700

Legend:
- Major slave trading region
- African state about 1700
- City

Atlantic Ocean
Indian Ocean

Labels: Azores, Madeira, Canary Islands, Cape Verde Islands, FUTA TORO, SEGU, HAUSA STATES, BORNU, DARFUR, ETHIOPIA, BENIN, ASANTE, Porto-Novo, OYO, DAHOMEY, RWANDA, BURUNDI, Malindi, Mombasa, SWAHILI COASTAL STATES, KONGO, LUNDA, Madagascar, Cape Town

Miller Projection
0   500   1000 mi
0   500 1000 km

Map Skills By about 1700, many of Africa's states and kingdoms were involved in the slave trade.

1. **Locate** (a) Malindi (b) Kongo (c) Asante (d) Bornu
2. **Describe** Which states were part of a major slave trading region?
3. **Synthesize Information** In general, where were most slave trading regions located? Explain.

Geography *Interactive*
For: Audio guided tour
Web Code: nbp-1421

Vocabulary Builder
dominate—(DAHM uh nayt) *v.* to rule or control by superior power

Vocabulary Builder
unified—(YOO nuh fyd) *v.* combined into one

After becoming king in 1505, he called on the Portuguese to help him develop Kongo as a modern Christian state. But he became alarmed as more and more Portuguese came to Kongo each year to buy slaves. Affonso wanted to maintain contact with Europe but end the slave trade. His appeal failed, and the slave trade continued.

In the late 1700s, another African ruler tried to halt the slave trade in his lands. He was the almany (from the Arabic words meaning "religious leader") of Futa Toro, in present-day Senegal. Since the 1500s, French sea captains had bought slaves from African traders in Futa Toro. In 1788, the almany forbade anyone to transport slaves through Futa Toro for sale abroad. However, the inland slave traders simply worked out a new route to the coast. Sailing to this new market, the French captains easily purchased the slaves that the almany had prevented them from buying in Futa Toro.

✔ **Checkpoint** How did the African slave trade expand?

New African States Arise

The slave trade had major effects on African states in the 1600s and 1700s. In West Africa, for example, the loss of countless numbers of young women and men resulted in some small states disappearing forever. At the same time, there arose new states whose way of life depended on the slave trade. The rulers of these powerful new states waged war against other Africans to dominate the slave trade.

The Asante Kingdom The **Asante kingdom** (uh SAHN teh) emerged in the area occupied by present-day Ghana. In the late 1600s, an able military leader, **Osei Tutu,** won control of the trading city of Kumasi. From there, he conquered neighboring peoples and unified the Asante kingdom. The Asante faced a great challenge in the Denkyera, a powerful neighboring enemy kingdom. Osei Tutu realized that in order to withstand the Denkyera, the people of his kingdom needed to be firmly united. To do this, he claimed that his right to rule came from heaven, and that people in the kingdom were linked by spiritual bonds. This strategy paid off when the Asante defeated the Denkyera in the late 1600s.

Under Osei Tutu, government officials, chosen by merit rather than by birth, supervised an efficient bureaucracy. They managed the royal monopolies on gold mining and the slave trade. A **monopoly** is the exclusive control of a business or industry. The Asante traded with Europeans on the coast, exchanging gold and slaves for firearms. They also played rival Europeans against one another to protect themselves. In this way, they built a wealthy, powerful state.

The Oyo Empire The Oyo empire arose from successive waves of settlement by the Yoruba people of present-day Nigeria. It began as a relatively small forest kingdom. Beginning in the late 1600s, however, its leaders used wealth from the slave trade to build up an impressive army. The Oyo empire used the army to conquer the neighboring kingdom of Dahomey. At the same time, it continued to gain wealth by trading with European merchants at the port city of Porto-Novo.

✓ **Checkpoint** What caused some African states to grow?

The European Presence Expands

Following the Portuguese example, by the 1600s several European powers had established forts along the western coast of Africa. As Portuguese power declined in the region, British, Dutch, and French traders took over their forts. Unlike the Portuguese, they established permanent footholds throughout the continent.

In 1652, Dutch immigrants arrived at the southern tip of the continent. They built **Cape Town,** the first permanent European settlement, to supply ships sailing to or from the East Indies. Dutch farmers, called **Boers,** settled around Cape Town. Over time, they ousted, enslaved, or killed the people who lived there. The Boers held a Calvinist belief that they were the elect, or chosen, of God. They looked on Africans as inferiors and did not respect their claims to their own land. In the 1700s, Boer herders and ivory hunters began to push north from the Cape Colony. Their migrations would eventually lead to battle with several African groups.

By the mid-1600s, the British and French had both reached present-day Senegal. The French established a fort in the region around 1700. In the late 1700s, stories about British explorers' search for the source of the Nile River sparked an interest in Africa among Europeans, especially the French and British. In 1788, the British established the African Association, an organization that sponsored explorers to Africa. Over the next century, European exploration of Africa would explode.

✓ **Checkpoint** How did the European presence in Africa expand?

Elmina Castle
European traders called the places where they held and traded slaves "castles." Built by the Portuguese in 1482, Elmina Castle in present-day Ghana was used as a base for trading slaves, gold, and imported European products.

SECTION 2 **Assessment**

Progress Monitoring *Online*
For: Self-quiz with vocabulary practice
Web Code: nba-1421

Terms, People, and Places
1. What do many of the key terms and people listed at the beginning of the section have in common? Explain.

Note Taking
2. **Reading Skill: Identify Effects** Use your completed chart to answer the Focus Question: What effects did European exploration have on the people of Africa?

Comprehension and Critical Thinking
3. **Determine Relevance** How did the Portuguese strategy of building forts instead of permanent colonies affect Portugal's history in Africa?
4. **Recognize Cause and Effect** How did Europeans change the nature of African slavery?
5. **Analyze Information** Why did the Asante and Oyo need to trade with Europeans to maintain power?
6. **Predict Consequences** Would the Europeans have taken the same course in Africa if the people there had been Christian like themselves?

● **Writing About History**

Quick Write: Write a Thesis Statement Write a thesis statement that will support a biographical essay about either Osei Tutu or Affonso I. Remember that the facts and events you cite in your essay should support your thesis statement. For example, the following thesis statement is not supported by the facts in the text: Affonso I was instrumental in slowing the slave trade in Africa.

King Affonso I:
Letter to King John III of Portugal

In 1490, the Portuguese converted the son of a Kongo king to Christianity and then helped him take his father's throne. The new king, born Nzinga Mbemba, was renamed Affonso. King Affonso soon realized that his relationship with Portugal had extremely negative consequences, as can be seen from his letter to King John III of Portugal in 1526. In this letter, the king of Kongo appeals to the king of Portugal to end the slave trade.

▲ A Congolese brass and wood crucifix dating from the 1500s blends Christian and traditional African symbols.

Sir, Your Highness of Portugal should know how our Kingdom is being lost in so many ways. This is caused by the excessive freedom given by your officials to the men and merchants who are allowed to come to this Kingdom to set up shops with goods and many things which have been prohibited by us. Many of our vassals, whom we had in obedience, do not comply[1] because they have the things in greater abundance than we ourselves. It was with these things that we had them content and subjected under our jurisdiction[2], so it is doing a great harm not only to the service of God, but to the security and peace of our Kingdoms and State as well.

And we cannot reckon how great the damage is, since the mentioned merchants are taking every day our natives, sons of the land and the sons of our noblemen and vassals and our relatives. The thieves and men of bad conscience grab them wishing to have the things and wares of this Kingdom which they are ambitious of; they grab them and get them to be sold. And so great, Sir, is the corruption and licentiousness[3] that our country is being completely depopulated, and your Highness should not agree with this nor accept it as in your service. And to avoid it we need from those your Kingdoms no more than some priests and a few people to teach in schools, and no other goods except wine and flour for the holy sacrament.

That is why we beg of Your Highness to help and assist us in this matter, commanding your factors[4] that they should not send here either merchants or wares, because it is our will that in these kingdoms there should not be any trade of slaves nor outlet for them. Concerning what is referred to above, again we beg of Your Highness to agree with it otherwise we cannot remedy such an obvious damage.

▲ King John III of Portugal

1. **comply** (kum PLY) *v.* agree to a request
2. **jurisdiction** (joor is DIK shun) *n.* area of authority or power
3. **licentiousness** (ly SEN shus nis) *n.* lack of morality
4. **factors** (FAK turs) *n.* agents

Thinking Critically
1. **Identify Causes** What does King Affonso believe has caused his vassals to become disobedient?
2. **Analyze Information** What specifically does King Affonso say he still needs from the Portuguese?

Commander Afonso de Albuquerque (right); a Portuguese rifle (top)

Gunfire Over Malacca

In 1511, a Portuguese fleet commanded by Afonso de Albuquerque (AL buh kur kee) dropped anchor off Malacca, a rich Islamic trading port that controlled the sea route linking India, Southeast Asia, and China. The fleet remained at anchor for several weeks before opening fire. According to a Malaysian account:

66 The cannon balls came like rain. And the noise of the cannon was as the noise of thunder in the heavens and the flashes of fire of their guns were like flashes of lightning in the sky: and the noise of their matchlocks [guns] was like that of groundnuts [peanuts] popping in the frying pan. 99
—From the *Malay Annals*

Focus Question How did European nations build empires in South and Southeast Asia?

European Footholds in South and Southeast Asia

Objectives
- Summarize how Portugal built a trading empire in South and Southeast Asia.
- Analyze the rise of Dutch and Spanish dominance in the region.
- Understand how the decline of Mughal India affected European traders in the region.

Terms, People, and Places

Afonso de Albuquerque	Dutch East India Company
Mughal empire	sovereign
Goa	Philippines
Malacca	sepoys
outpost	

Note Taking

Reading Skill: Identify Causes and Effects As you read this section, fill in a chart like the one below with the causes and effects of European exploration in South and Southeast Asia.

Portugal	Netherlands	Spain	Britain
•	•	•	•
•	•	•	•

Portugal was the first European power to gain a foothold in Asia. The Portuguese ships were small in size and number, but the firepower of their shipboard cannons was unmatched. In time, this superior firepower helped them win control of the rich Indian Ocean spice trade and build a trading empire in Asia.

Portugal Builds an Eastern Empire

After Vasco da Gama's voyage, the Portuguese, under **Afonso de Albuquerque's** command, burst into the Indian Ocean. By that time, Muslim rulers, originally from central Asia, had established the **Mughal empire** throughout much of India. The southern regions of India, however, were still controlled by a patchwork of local princes. The Portuguese won these princes to their side with promises of aid against other Europeans. With these southern footholds, Albuquerque and the Portuguese hoped to end Muslim power and turn the Indian Ocean into a "Portuguese lake."

A Rim of Trading Outposts In 1510, the Portuguese seized the island of **Goa** off the coast of India, making it their major military and commercial base. Albuquerque burned coastal towns and crushed Arab fleets at sea. The Portuguese took the East Indies port of **Malacca** in 1511, massacring the city's Muslims.

In less than 50 years, the Portuguese had built a trading empire with military and merchant **outposts,** or distant areas under their control, rimming the southern seas. They used the cities they had seized on the east coast of Africa to resupply and repair their ships. For most of the 1500s, Portugal controlled the spice trade between Europe and Asia.

A Limited Impact Despite their sea power, the Portuguese lacked resources and faced too much resistance to make great inroads into the region. They made harsher efforts to convert local people to Christianity than they had in Africa, attacking Muslims and destroying Hindu temples. Still, by 1600 the Portuguese had converted fewer than a million people to Christianity. The conversion rate was especially low among Asian Muslims.

✔ **Checkpoint** How did the Portuguese control the spice trade?

Rise of the Dutch

The Dutch were the first Europeans to challenge Portuguese domination of Asian trade. The land we know today as the Netherlands included a group of provinces and prosperous trading cities on the North Sea. In the early 1500s it was part of the Holy Roman Empire, but later the Protestant northern provinces won independence. The independent Netherlands entered vigorously into competition for overseas influence.

Building a Mighty Sea Power In 1599, a Dutch fleet returned to Amsterdam from Asia after more than a year's absence. It carried a cargo of pepper, cloves, and other spices. The success of this voyage led to a frenzy of overseas activity. Soon Dutch warships and trading vessels had made the Netherlands a leader of European commerce. Dutch power set up colonies and trading posts around the world. With their <u>strategic</u> settlement at Cape Town, the Netherlands had a secure foothold in the region.

A Powerful Dutch Company In 1602, a group of wealthy Dutch merchants formed the **Dutch East India Company.** From the beginning, this company had an unusual amount of power. Unlike Portuguese and Spanish traders, whose expeditions, were tightly controlled by government, the Dutch East India Company had full **sovereign** powers. With its power to build armies, wage war, negotiate peace treaties, and govern overseas territory, it came to dominate the region.

Vocabulary Builder

<u>strategic</u>—(struh TEE jik) *adj.* important to carrying out a plan of action

Different Perspectives
A European artist (right) shows the king of Sri Lanka and a Dutch explorer meeting as equals. In the Indian painting to the left, Europeans are shown as vassals bringing gifts to India's ruler. *How did European and Asian artists bring their own perspectives to early encounters?*

Symbols of the Dutch Empire
The Dutch painting *Jacob Mathieusen and His Wife* (*c.* 1650) shows a senior official in the Dutch East India Company overlooking the Dutch fleet in Batavia, Indonesia. A slave holds a parasol, an Asian symbol of power. *How can you tell that the artist was European?*

Asserting Dutch Dominance In 1641, the Dutch captured Malacca from the Portuguese and opened trade with China. Soon they were able to enforce a monopoly in the Spice Islands, controlling shipments to Europe as well as much of the trade within Southeast Asia. Like the Portuguese, the Dutch used military force to further their trading goals. Yet they forged closer ties with local rulers than the Portuguese had. Many Dutch merchants married Asian women.

In the 1700s, the growing power of England and France contributed to the decline of the Dutch trading empire in the East. Still, the Dutch maintained an empire in Indonesia until the 1900s.

 Checkpoint How did the Dutch build up a strong presence in Southeast Asia?

Spain Seizes the Philippines

While the Portuguese and Dutch set up bases on the fringes of Asia, Spain took over the **Philippines.** Magellan had claimed the archipelago for Spain in 1521. Within about 50 years, Spain had conquered and colonized the islands, renaming them for the Spanish king Philip II. Unlike most other peoples of Southeast Asia, the Filipinos were not united. As a result, they could be conquered more easily.

In the spirit of the Catholic Reformation, Spanish priests set out to convert the Filipino people to Christianity. Later, missionaries from the Philippines tried to spread Catholic teachings in China and Japan.

The Philippines became a key link in Spain's overseas trading empire. The Spanish shipped silver mined in Mexico and Peru across the Pacific to the Philippines. From there, they used the silver to buy goods in China. In this way, large quantities of American silver flowed into the economies of East Asian nations.

Checkpoint Why was Spain able to conquer the Philippines easily?

Mughal India and European Traders

For two centuries, the Mughal empire had enjoyed a period of peace, strength, and prosperity. European merchants were dazzled by India's splendid Mughal court and its many luxury goods.

A Center of Valuable Trade Mughal India was the center of the valuable spice trade. It was also the world leader in textile manufacturing, exporting large quantities of silk and cotton cloth. The Mughal empire was larger, richer, and more powerful than any kingdom in Europe. When Europeans sought trading rights, Mughal emperors saw no threat in granting them. The Portuguese—and later the Dutch, English, and French—thus were permitted to build forts and warehouses in Indian coastal towns.

A Great Empire Shatters Over time, the Mughal empire weakened. Conflicts between Hindu and Muslim princes rekindled. Years of civil war drained Mughal resources. Rulers then increased taxes, sparking rebellions. Corruption became widespread, and the central government collapsed. As Mughal power faltered, French and English traders fought for power. Like the Dutch, both the British and the French had established East India companies. These companies made alliances with local officials and independent rajahs, or local chiefs. Each company organized its own army of **sepoys,** or Indian troops.

By the mid-1700s, the British and the French had become locked in a bitter struggle for global power. The fighting involved both nations' lands in Asia and the Americas. In India, the British East India Company used an army of British troops and sepoys to drive out the French. The company then forced the Mughal emperor to recognize its right to collect taxes in the northeast. By the late 1700s, it had used its great wealth to dominate most of India.

✓ **Checkpoint** How did Britain gain control of India?

An Indian Sepoy
An Indian officer in the British army poses with his wife in this Indian painting dating from the 1700s.

SECTION 3 **Assessment**

Progress Monitoring *Online*
For: Self-quiz with vocabulary practice
Web Code: nba-1431

Terms, People, and Places

1. For each term, person, or place listed at the beginning of the section, write a sentence explaining its significance.

Note Taking

2. **Reading Skill: Identify Causes and Effects** Use your completed flowchart to answer the Focus Question: How did European nations build empires in South and Southeast Asia?

Comprehension and Critical Thinking

3. **Draw Inferences** You read that the Portuguese did not attempt to conquer inland territory. What does that tell you about their assessment of the inland empires?

4. **Analyze Information** Why did the leaders of the Netherlands give so much power to the Dutch East India Company?

5. **Identify Central Issues** What about the location of the Philippines made it a valuable asset for Spain?

6. **Identify Assumptions** The Mughal empire gave trading rights to several European countries. What assumptions about the power of those countries does this show?

● **Writing About History**

Quick Write: Present Evidence to Support a Thesis Write a biographical essay about Afonso de Albuquerque. First, think of a thesis statement that describes the main points you want to make. Then write the main body text, referring frequently to your thesis statement. The details in a biographical essay should directly support your main point. For example, if your thesis is that Albuquerque was a violent man, you would include details about his takeover of Malacca.

A Chinese watercolor portrays Matteo Ricci with European objects, including a model of the universe. A geography book that Ricci translated into Chinese is shown at the top.

A Jesuit in China

In 1583, a young Jesuit priest arrived in China. He had studied Chinese and immediately impressed Chinese rulers with his fluency as well as his knowledge of European science. Matteo Ricci recognized that the Chinese would not accept a European religion "unless it be seasoned with an intellectual flavoring." In his nearly 30 years in China, Ricci translated five European books into Chinese. Ricci adopted Chinese dress and established friendships with Confucian scholars. When he died in 1610 at age 58, he was buried near the emperor. Much of Europe's knowledge about China came from Ricci's writings.

Focus Question How were European encounters in East Asia shaped by the worldviews of both Europeans and Asians?

Encounters in East Asia

Objectives

- Describe European contacts with Ming China.
- Understand the Manchu conquest and its impact on European trade.
- Analyze the factors that led Korea to isolate itself from other nations.
- Summarize Japan's attitudes toward foreign trade and how they changed over time.

Terms, People, and Places

Macao	Qing
Guangzhou	Qianlong
Matteo Ricci	Lord Macartney
Manchus	Nagasaki

Note Taking

Reading Skill: Understand Effects Fill in a chart like the one below with effects of European contacts in East Asia.

```
        European Contacts in East Asia
    ┌──────────┬──────────┬──────────┐
   China       Korea       Japan
    • •         • •         • •
```

Portuguese ships first reached China from their base in Malacca in 1514. To the Chinese, the Portuguese, like other foreigners, were barbarians. Europeans, by contrast, wrote enthusiastically about China. In 1590, a visitor described Chinese artisans "cleverly making devices out of gold, silver and other metals," and wrote with approval: "They daily publish huge multitudes of books."

European Contact With Ming China

European interest in China and other parts of East Asia continued to grow. The Ming, however, had no interest in Europe—since, as a Ming document proclaimed, "our empire owns the world."

The Ming Limit Trade The Portuguese wanted Chinese silks and porcelains, but had little to offer in exchange. European textiles and metalwork were inferior to Chinese products. The Chinese therefore demanded payment in gold or silver. The Ming eventually allowed the Portuguese a trading post at **Macao** near Canton, present-day **Guangzhou** (GWAHNG joh). Later, they let Dutch, English, and other Europeans trade with Chinese merchants. Foreigners could trade only at Canton under the supervision of imperial officials. When each year's trading season ended, they had to sail away.

Seeking Converts Portuguese missionaries arrived in China along with the traders. In later years the Jesuits—from Spain, Italy, and Portugal—arrived. Most Jesuits had a broad knowledge of many subjects, and the Chinese welcomed the chance to learn about Renaissance Europe from these scholars. The brilliant Jesuit priest **Matteo Ricci** (mah TAY oh REE chee) made a particularly strong impression on the Chinese. Still, Ricci and other priests had little success spreading their religious beliefs in China. They did, however, become important sources of information for Europeans who knew little about China.

✔ **Checkpoint** Why did Ming China demand that Europeans pay for goods with gold or silver?

The Manchu Conquest

By the early 1600s, the aging Ming dynasty was decaying. Revolts erupted, and Manchu invaders from the north pushed through the Great Wall. The **Manchus** ruled a region in the northeast, Manchuria, that had long been influenced by Chinese civilization. In 1644, victorious Manchu armies seized Beijing and made it their capital.

● **INFOGRAPHIC**

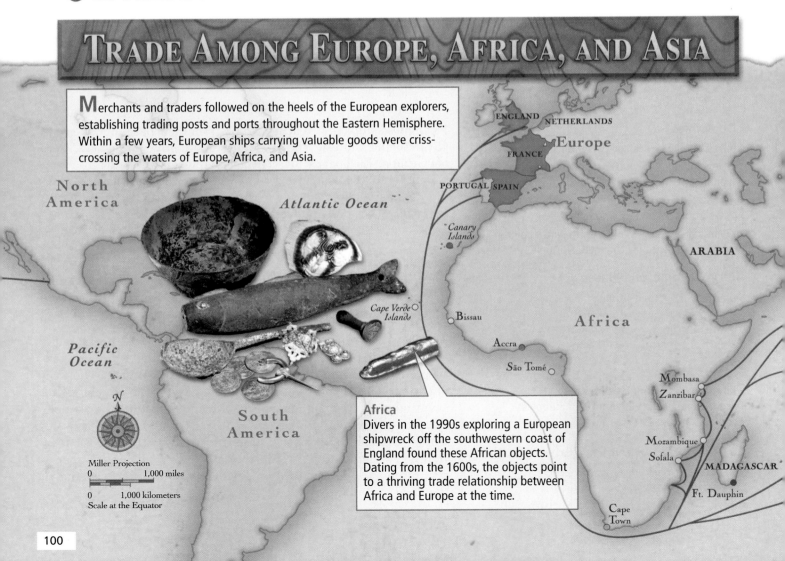

TRADE AMONG EUROPE, AFRICA, AND ASIA

Merchants and traders followed on the heels of the European explorers, establishing trading posts and ports throughout the Eastern Hemisphere. Within a few years, European ships carrying valuable goods were criss-crossing the waters of Europe, Africa, and Asia.

Africa
Divers in the 1990s exploring a European shipwreck off the southwestern coast of England found these African objects. Dating from the 1600s, the objects point to a thriving trade relationship between Africa and Europe at the time.

Miller Projection
0   1,000 miles
0   1,000 kilometers
Scale at the Equator

Founding the Qing Dynasty The Manchus set up a new dynasty called the **Qing** (ching). The Manchus won the support of Chinese scholar-officials because they adopted the Confucian system of government. For each top government position, the Qing chose two people, one Manchu and one Chinese. Local government remained in the hands of the Chinese, but Manchu troops stationed across the empire ensured loyalty.

Two rulers oversaw the most brilliant age of the Qing. Kangxi (kahng shee), who ruled from 1661 to 1722, was an able administrator and military leader. He extended Chinese power into Central Asia and promoted Chinese culture. Kangxi's grandson **Qianlong** (chyahn lung) had an equally successful reign from 1736 to 1796. He expanded China's borders to rule the largest area in the nation's history. Qianlong retired after 60 years because he did not want to rule longer than his grandfather had.

Spreading Peace and Prosperity The Chinese economy expanded under both emperors. New crops from the Americas, such as potatoes and corn, had been introduced into China. These crops boosted farm output, which in turn contributed to a population boom. China's population rose from 140 million in 1740 to over 300 million by 1800. The silk, cotton, and porcelain industries expanded. Internal trade grew, as did the demand for Chinese goods from all over the world.

WITNESS HISTORY VIDEO

Watch *Manchu China and the West* on the **Witness History Discovery School**™ video program to learn more about the interactions between two very different cultures.

DISCOVERY
SCHOOL

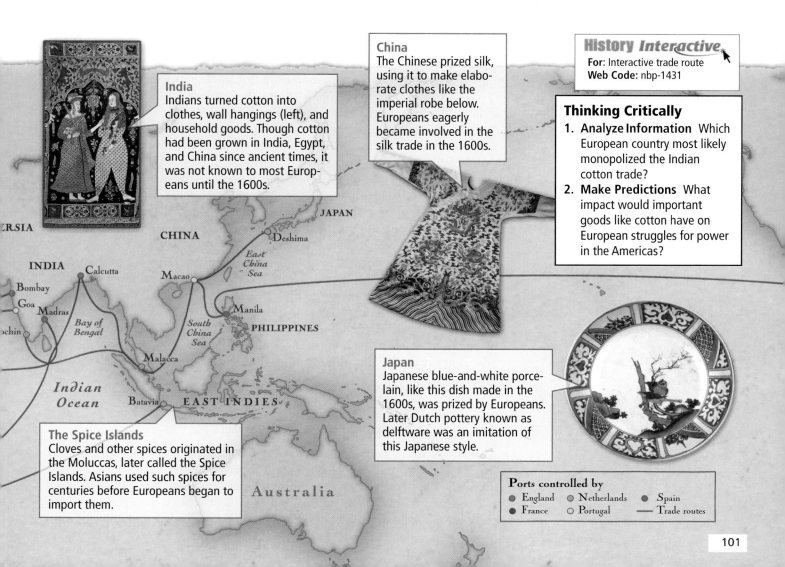

India
Indians turned cotton into clothes, wall hangings (left), and household goods. Though cotton had been grown in India, Egypt, and China since ancient times, it was not known to most Europeans until the 1600s.

China
The Chinese prized silk, using it to make elaborate clothes like the imperial robe below. Europeans eagerly became involved in the silk trade in the 1600s.

History Interactive
For: Interactive trade route
Web Code: nbp-1431

Thinking Critically
1. **Analyze Information** Which European country most likely monopolized the Indian cotton trade?
2. **Make Predictions** What impact would important goods like cotton have on European struggles for power in the Americas?

Japan
Japanese blue-and-white porcelain, like this dish made in the 1600s, was prized by Europeans. Later Dutch pottery known as delftware was an imitation of this Japanese style.

The Spice Islands
Cloves and other spices originated in the Moluccas, later called the Spice Islands. Asians used such spices for centuries before Europeans began to import them.

PERSIA
INDIA
Bombay
Goa
Madras
Cochin
Bay of Bengal
Calcutta
Indian Ocean
Malacca
Batavia
EAST INDIES
Australia
CHINA
Macao
South China Sea
Manila
PHILIPPINES
East China Sea
Deshima
JAPAN

Ports controlled by
● England   ● Netherlands   ● Spain
● France   ○ Portugal   — Trade routes

Emperor Qianlong wrote a letter to King George III denying Britain's request for more trading rights and permanent ambassadors. How does Emperor Qianlong's language express his view that China is superior to Britain?

Primary Source

 As to your entreaty to send one of your nationals . . . to my Celestial Court, this request is contrary to all usage of my dynasty and cannot possibly be entertained. . . .

I have but one aim in view, namely, to maintain a perfect governance and to fulfill the duties of the State: strange and costly objects do not interest me. . . . Our dynasty's majestic virtue has penetrated unto every country under Heaven, and Kings of all nations have offered their costly tribute by land and sea. As your Ambassador can see for himself, we possess all things. I set no value on objects strange or ingenious, and have no use for your country's manufactures.

Rejecting Contact With Europeans The Qing maintained the Ming policy of restricting foreign traders. Still, Europeans kept pressing to expand trade to cities other than Guangzhou. In 1793, **Lord Macartney** arrived in China at the head of a British diplomatic mission. He brought samples of British-made goods to show the Chinese the advantages of trade with Westerners. The Chinese, who looked on the goods as rather crude products, thought they were gifts offered as tribute to the emperor.

Further misunderstandings followed. Macartney insisted on an audience with the emperor. The Chinese told Macartney he would have to perform the traditional kowtow, touching his head to the ground to show respect to the emperor. Macartney refused. He also offended the Chinese by speaking of the natural superiority of the English. The negotiations faltered.

At the time, Qianlong's attitude seemed justified by China's successes. After all, he already ruled the world's greatest empire. Why should he negotiate with a nation as distant as Britain? In the long run, however, his policy proved disastrous. In the 1800s, China would learn that its policy of ignoring Westerners and their technology would have undesired consequences.

✓ **Checkpoint** How did the Qing respond to Britain's diplomatic mission?

Korea Chooses Isolation

Before the 1500s, Korean traders had far-reaching contacts across East Asia. A Korean map from the 1300s accurately outlines lands from Japan to the Mediterranean. Koreans probably acquired this knowledge from Arab traders who came to Korea.

In 1592, and again in 1597, the Japanese invaded Korea. The Japanese were driven out in 1598, but the invasions proved disastrous for Korea. Villages were burned to the ground, famine and disease became widespread, and the population decreased. Then, in 1636, before the country was fully recovered, the Manchus invaded Korea. When the Manchus set up the Qing dynasty in China, Korea became a tributary state. It was run by its own government but forced to acknowledge China's supremacy.

Devastated by the two invasions, Korean rulers adopted a policy of isolation, excluding foreigners except the Chinese and a few Japanese. When European sailors were shipwrecked on Korean shores, they were imprisoned and held as spies. Although Korea had few contacts with much of the world for almost 250 years, Koreans on tribute missions brought back maps as well as books on scientific discoveries. This was also a great age for Korean arts and literature.

✓ **Checkpoint** Why did Korea become isolated?

Foreign Traders in Japan

Unlike the Chinese or Koreans, the Japanese at first welcomed Westerners. In 1543, the Portuguese reached Japan, followed by the Spanish, Dutch, and English. They arrived at a turbulent time, when Japanese daimyo were struggling for power. The daimyo quickly adopted Western firearms which may have helped the Tokugawa shoguns centralize power and impose order.

Jesuits, such as the Spanish priest Francis Xavier, found the Japanese curious about Christianity. A growing number of Japanese adopted the new faith. The Japanese also welcomed the printing press the Jesuits brought. The Tokugawa shoguns, however, grew increasingly hostile toward foreigners. After learning that Spain had seized the Philippines, they may have seen the newcomers as threats. They also worried that Japanese Christians—who may have numbered as many as 300,000—owed their <u>allegiance</u> to the pope, rather than to Japanese leaders. In response, the Tokugawas expelled foreign missionaries. They brutally persecuted Japanese Christians, killing many thousands of people.

By 1638, the Tokugawas had turned against European traders as well. Japan barred all European merchants and forbade Japanese to travel abroad. To further their isolation, they outlawed the building of large ships, thereby ending foreign trade. In order to keep informed about world events, they permitted just one or two Dutch ships each year to trade at a small island in **Nagasaki** harbor.

Japan remained isolated for more than 200 years. Art and literature flourished, and internal trade boomed. Cities grew in size and importance, and some merchant families gained wealth and status. By the early 1700s, Edo (present-day Tokyo) had a million inhabitants, more than either London or Paris.

✔ **Checkpoint** Why did the Tokugawas turn against Europeans?

Bringing Trade and Christianity
This 1600s decorative screen shows Japanese people meeting a Portuguese ship carrying European goods and missionaries. *Did the presence of missionaries help or hurt European-Japanese trade relations?*

Vocabulary Builder
allegiance—(uh LEE juns) *n.* loyalty or devotion to a cause or person

---

SECTION 4 Assessment

Progress Monitoring *Online*
For: Self-quiz with vocabulary practice
Web Code: nba-1441

Terms, People, and Places
1. Place each of the key terms, people, or places listed at the beginning of the section into one of the following categories: politics, culture, government, or geography. Write a sentence for each term explaining your choice.

Note Taking
2. **Reading Skill: Understand Effects** Use your completed chart to answer the Focus Question: How were European encounters in East Asia shaped by the worldviews of both Europeans and Asians?

Comprehension and Critical Thinking
3. **Analyze Credibility** Reread the quotation from the Ming document on page 461. Do you think its characterization of China is credible? Explain.
4. **Draw Inferences** What do Qing China's trade policies with Europeans in the 1700s tell you about the state of the Qing economy?
5. **Make Comparisons** Why did both Japan and Korea respond to increased foreign contact by going into isolation?
6. **Synthesize Information** Why did Japan allow limited contact with the Dutch, but not with the Spanish or Portuguese?

● **Writing About History**
Quick Write: Write a Conclusion Write a sentence to conclude a biographical essay about Matteo Ricci. Read the information about Ricci in this section. Then construct a broad summary sentence that covers the main point you want to make about his life. For example, if your thesis is that Ricci believed Chinese culture to be superior to European culture, you would include that point in your summary sentence.

CHAPTER 2

Quick Study Guide

Progress Monitoring *Online*
For: Self-test with vocabulary practice
Web Code: nba-1451

■ Causes of European Exploration

- Desire for Asian luxury goods such as spices, gold, and silks
- Motivation to spread Christianity
- Strategic need to gain more direct access to trade
- Desire to gain glory for country
- Renaissance curiosity to explore new lands
- Competition with other European countries

■ European Footholds in the Eastern Hemisphere

Country	Date	Foothold	Reason for Interest
Portugal	1502	Calicut, India	Spices
Portugal	1510	Goa, India	Military and commercial base
Portugal	1511	Malacca, Southeast Asia	Center of sea trade
Spain	1521	The Philippines	Center of sea trade
Portugal	1589	Mombasa, East Africa	Hub of international trade
Netherlands	1652	Cape Town, southern Africa	Strategic port for repairing and resupplying ships
Great Britain	1757	Northeastern India	Spices, trade goods

■ Important European Explorers

Explorer	Accomplishment
Vasco da Gama (Portugal)	Sailed around Cape of Good Hope; established ports on Indian Ocean
Christopher Columbus (Spain)	Sailed west across Atlantic Ocean to Caribbean
Vasco Núñez de Balboa (Spain)	Crossed Panama, reaching Pacific Ocean
Ferdinand Magellan (Spain)	Circumnavigated the globe

■ Major Asian Dynasties and Empires

Ruler	Location	Description	European Contact
Mughal empire	India	Major trading empire	After two centuries of peace and prosperity, civil war between Muslim and Hindu princes weakened empire; European powers took control in 1700s
Ming dynasty	China	Prosperous dynasty that had sponsored overseas exploration	Allowed some trade with Europeans and sought out European learning; revolts in the 1600s led to overthrow by the Manchus
Qing dynasty	China	Powerful dynasty that expanded China's borders and promoted Chinese culture	Increasingly restricted European trading rights
Choson dynasty	Korea	Chinese-influenced Confucian state	Had few contacts with the outside world except for China and Japan
Tokugawa shogunate	Japan	Powerful warrior kingdom	Welcomed Europeans at first but then expelled missionaries and most traders

■ Europe, Africa, and Asia 1415–1796

1492
Christopher Columbus reaches the Caribbean.

1498
Portuguese explorer Vasco da Gama rounds Africa and reaches India.

1522
Magellan's expedition circumnavigates the globe.

Chapter Events
Global Events

1450	1500	1550

1453
The Ottoman Turks take Constantinople, ending the Byzantine empire.

1500
The kingdom of Kongo thrives in Africa.

1556
Akbar begins the Mughal reign in India.

Concept Connector

■ Cumulative Review

Record the answers to the questions below on your Concept Connector worksheets. In addition, record information from this chapter about the following concepts:
- Technology: the compass
- Trade: Dutch trading empire; Indian trade in Southeast Asia
- Cultural Diffusion: Indian influence on Southeast Asia

1. **Empire** With the founding of the Qing empire, the Manchus established one of China's most successful dynasties. One reason for the Manchus' success was their adoption of Chinese customs and inclusion of Chinese in their government structure. The Yuan dynasty, established by the Mongols, was another foreign-ruled Chinese dynasty. Compare the Qing and the Yuan dynasties. Consider the following:
   - culture and language
   - approaches to trade
   - involvement of Chinese in the government

2. **Conflict** As the French and British began to establish global empires in the 1600s and 1700s, they frequently came into conflict. This was not the first time that these two nations had opposed each other. List other examples of French-British conflict from European history. Consider the factors that seem to have made them historic enemies.

3. **Trade** In the 1500s and 1600s, Europeans took different approaches to establishing trade in the Eastern Hemisphere. In some regions, Europeans established posts and took over cities without regard to the people who lived there. In other regions, Europeans worked hard to establish legitimate trade relations. Compare these two approaches, using specific examples from the text. Think about the following:
   - the region's geography and European knowledge of it
   - the government of the people in the region
   - European perceptions of the people and their religion
   - the technological achievements of the people

■ Connections to Today

1. **Trade: The Dutch Trading Empire** In the 1500s, the Dutch began establishing an overseas trade empire in Southeast Asia, using the tools of sea power and monopolistic trade policies. Today, the Dutch are not known for their sea power or overseas domination, yet the strong economy of the Netherlands still depends heavily on trade. Research Dutch trade, including its global rank in exports, the number and types of companies owned by the Dutch in the United States, and the role of multinational companies in the economy of the Netherlands. Write two paragraphs summarizing the importance of trade to the Netherlands today.

2. **Technology: The Compass** European exploration would not have been possible without the compass. The compass allowed navigators to find direction accurately, rather than relying on the sun, stars, and moon. Consider the events and discoveries that the compass made possible. Then think of recent technological inventions that have had profound impacts on the world today. Which technology do you consider to be equivalent in its impact to the compass? Why?

1602
The Dutch establish the Dutch East India Company.

1641
The Dutch take Malacca from the Portuguese.

1736
China's emperor Qianlong begins his reign.

History *Interactive*
For: Interactive timeline
Web Code: nbp-1451

1600   **1650**   **1700**   **1750**

1603
The Tokugawas come to power in Japan.

1642
The English Civil War begins.

1756
The Seven Years' War breaks out between Britain and France.

105

Chapter Assessment

Terms, People, and Places

1. Define **cartographer.** How did Prince Henry encourage the work of cartographers?
2. Write a sentence or two that shows why scurvy was a problem for sailors who **circumnavigated** the globe.
3. What was the role of European **plantations** in the growth of slavery?
4. Define **outpost.** Why were European outposts important in the development of overseas empires?
5. Why did European trading companies organize armies of **sepoys** in India?
6. How did the Asante kingdom use **monopolies** to keep its power?

Main Ideas

Section 1 (pp. 84–89)
7. How did the European interest in the spice trade lead to the discovery of new routes and lands?

Section 2 (pp. 90–93)
8. How did new sea routes lead to an expanded European presence in Africa?
9. What impact did Portuguese exploration have on the people of Africa?

Section 3 (pp. 95–98)
10. How did Portugal gain dominance of the spice trade?
11. How did the Dutch use their foothold in Cape Town to develop an overseas trade empire?
12. What effect did European trade have on the Mughal empire?

Section 4 (pp. 99–103)
13. Summarize European attempts to establish trade and missions in East Asia.
14. Why were the Dutch able to maintain a presence in Japan even when other Europeans were kicked out?

Chapter Focus Question
15. How did European voyages of exploration lead to European empires in the Eastern Hemisphere?

Critical Thinking

16. **Predict Consequences** What might have happened if Asian explorers, rather than Europeans, had first reached the Americas?
17. **Geography and History** How did Japan's geography allow the Tokugawas to maintain a long period of isolation?
18. **Draw Conclusions** Did missionaries hurt or help European attempts to establish trade in Asia? Explain your answer.
19. **Analyze Visuals** The woodcut below was made in 1555 by a Swedish geographer. What does it tell you about European knowledge of the world before the age of exploration?

20. **Recognize Cause and Effect** How did competition among European countries affect overseas exploration and conquest?

● Writing About History

Writing a Biographical Essay Many great Europeans, Africans, and Asians shaped the history of our global age. Write about one of the following important people in a biographical essay: Ferdinand Magellan, Affonso I, Afonso de Albuquerque, Emperor Qianlong, or Matteo Ricci. Consult page SH18 of the Writing Handbook for additional help.

Prewriting
• Choose the person who interests you the most. Take notes about this person and his role in shaping the age of global exploration.

• Draw conclusions about the person you have chosen. Think about how you can turn these conclusions into main points for your essay.

Drafting
• Write an introduction and a thesis statement. Your thesis statement should summarize the main point you want to make about the person you chose.
• Write the body text, introducing details and evidence that support your thesis statement. Then write a conclusion.

Revising
• Use the guidelines for revising your essay on page SH19 of the Writing Handbook.

Document-Based Assessment

Why Did Europeans Explore the Seas?

In the 1400s, Europeans began to embark on long and dangerous voyages to unknown destinations. Why did this age of exploration begin? In Documents A and B, a contemporary observer and a modern-day historian describe the impetus behind these early expeditions.

Document A

"The discovery of the new Western World followed, as an incidental consequence, from the long struggle of the nations of Europe for commercial supremacy and control of the traffic with the East. In all these dreams of the politicians and merchants, sailors and geographers, who pushed back the limits of the unknown world, there is the same glitter of gold and precious stones, the same odour of far-fetched spices."

—Sir Walter Raleigh, 1509

Document B

"The starting point for the European expansion out of the Mediterranean and the Atlantic continental shelf had nothing to do with, say, religion or the rise of capitalism—but it had a great deal to do with pepper. . . . . [Pepper] comprised more than half of all the spice imports into Italy over a period of more than a century. No other single spice came within one-tenth of the value of pepper. . . . However, since about 1470 the Turks had been impeding the overland trade routes east from the Mediterranean. As a result the great Portuguese, Italian, and Spanish explorers all sailed west or south in order to reach the Orient. The Americas were discovered as a by-product in the search for pepper."

—From ***Seeds of Change*** by Henry Hobhouse

This page from a sixteenth-century book about navigation depicts England's Queen Elizabeth in the ship at the right. ▶

Document C

◀ This fifteenth-century painting depicts Henry the Navigator, standing at right in round black hat. A Portuguese prince, Henry did much to advance maritime exploration and the fields of navigation and cartography.

Document D

Analyzing Documents

Use your knowledge of European exploration and Documents A, B, C, and D to answer questions 1–4.

1. Documents A and B both make the point that the discovery of new lands was motivated by
   A religious fanaticism.
   B adventurous dreams.
   C wanting to make money.
   D Renaissance ideals.

2. What motivation for exploration is implied in Document C?
   A the search for spices
   B the desire to please king or country
   C the desire to spread Christianity
   D both B and C

3. What does Document D suggest about how European monarchs viewed exploration?
   A They saw it as vitally important to their nations.
   B They viewed exploration as interesting but unnecessary.
   C They saw it as important but not worth spending money on.
   D They had no opinion about exploration.

4. **Writing Task** Using information from the chapter, assess the various motivations for exploration. Are there any that are not shown in these documents? Choose the motivation you think was the most compelling for Europeans. Use specific evidence from the chapter and documents to support your argument.

The Beginnings of Our Global Age: Europe and the Americas

1492–1750

A Heavenly City

By the 1400s, the Aztec city of Tenochtitlán was one of the largest and most well-planned cities in the world. Aztec wealth had provided clean streets, beautiful gardens, and overflowing storehouses. An Aztec poem written in the early 1500s expressed the writer's pride in the great city:

“Proudly stands the city of Mexico— Tenochtitlán.
Here no one fears to die in war . . .
Keep this in mind, oh princes . . .
Who could attack Tenochtitlán?
Who could shake the foundation of heaven?”

Just a few years after this poem was written, Tenochtitlán would fall to an unknown invader from far away. Listen to the Witness History audio to hear more about the end of the Aztec empire.

◀ Contemporary Mexican artist Diego Rivera depicts the Totonacs, Indians who were conquered by the Aztecs and later joined the Spanish.

Aztec feather shield made during the time of Moctezuma

Portuguese colonial carving made from brazilwood

Chapter Preview

Chapter Focus Question How did European colonization of the Americas shape global economies and societies?

Section 1
Conquest in the Americas

Section 2
Spanish and Portuguese Colonies in the Americas

Section 3
Struggle for North America

Section 4
The Atlantic Slave Trade

Section 5
Effects of Global Contact

Canadian powder horn showing fur trading routes

Note Taking Study Guide *Online*
For: Note Taking and Concept Connector worksheets
Web Code: nbd-1501

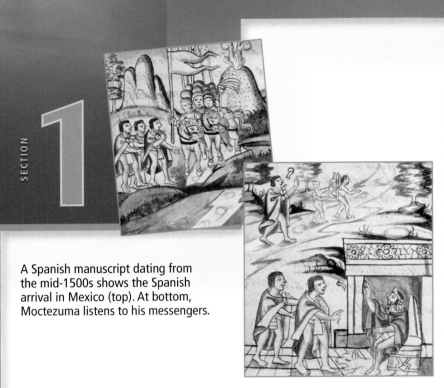

A Spanish manuscript dating from the mid-1500s shows the Spanish arrival in Mexico (top). At bottom, Moctezuma listens to his messengers.

Moctezuma Hears Strange News

In 1519, the Aztec ruler Moctezuma heard an astounding report from his messengers. They described unusual people who had just arrived in the region—people with white skin and yellow hair, clad completely in iron, who rode "deer" as tall as a house and had dogs with burning yellow eyes. According to a Spanish translation of native accounts, "When Moctezuma heard this, he was filled with terror. It was as if his heart grew faint, as it shrank; he was overcome by despair."

Focus Question How did a small number of Spanish conquistadors conquer huge Native American empires?

Conquest in the Americas

Objectives
- Analyze the results of the first encounters between the Spanish and Native Americans.
- Explain how Cortés and Pizarro gained control of the Aztec and Incan empires.
- Understand the short-term and long-term effects of the Spanish on the peoples of the Americas.

Terms, People, and Places

conquistador	alliance
immunity	Moctezuma
Hernán Cortés	Francisco Pizarro
Tenochtitlán	civil war
Malinche	

Note Taking

Reading Skill: Recognize Sequence Keep track of the sequence of events that led to European empires in the Americas by completing a chart like the one below.

Spain Establishes An Empire		
Columbus	**Cortés**	**Pizarro**
• Columbus arrives in the West Indies. •	• •	• •

In 1492, explorer Christopher Columbus landed in the Caribbean islands that are now called the West Indies. The wave of exploration he spurred in the Americas would have drastic, far-reaching consequences for the people who already lived there.

First Encounters in the Americas

Columbus's first meeting with Native Americans began a cycle of encounter, conquest, and death that would be repeated throughout the Western Hemisphere.

Meeting the Taínos When Columbus first arrived in the West Indies, he encountered the Taíno (TY noh) people. The Taínos lived in villages and grew corn, yams, and cotton, which they wove into cloth. They were friendly and open toward the Spanish. Columbus noted that they were "generous with what they have, to such a degree as no one would believe but he who had seen it."

Despite the friendly reception, relations soon soured. The Taínos offended the Spanish when out of ignorance they failed to pay proper respect to Christian symbols. Columbus's actions showed that he felt himself superior to the Taínos and could therefore decide their fate. He claimed their land for Spain, and then took several Taínos as prisoners to take back to the Spanish king.

Columbus's encounter was repeated by a wave of Spanish **conquistadors** (kahn KEES tuh dawrz), or conquerors, who soon arrived in the Americas. They first settled on the islands of Hispaniola (now the Dominican Republic and Haiti), Cuba, and Puerto Rico.

Throughout the region, the conquistadors seized the Native Americans' gold ornaments and then made them pan for more gold. At the same time, the Spanish forced the Native Americans to convert to Christianity.

Guns, Horses, and Disease Although Spanish conquistadors only numbered in the hundreds as compared to millions of Native Americans, they had many advantages. Their guns and cannons were superior to the Native Americans' arrows and spears, and European metal armor provided them with better protection. They also had horses, which not only were useful in battle and in carrying supplies, but also frightened the Native Americans, who had never seen a horse.

Most importantly, an invisible invader—disease—helped the conquistadors take control of the Taínos and other Native Americans. Europeans unknowingly carried diseases such as smallpox, measles, and influenza to which Native Americans had no **immunity,** or resistance. These diseases spread rapidly and wiped out village after village. As a result, the Native American population of the Caribbean islands declined by as much as 90 percent in the 1500s. Millions of Native Americans died from disease as Europeans made their way inland.

✔ **Checkpoint** How did Spanish conquistadors treat the Taínos?

Cortés Conquers Mexico

From the Caribbean, Spanish explorers probed the coasts of the Americas. They spread stories of empires rich in gold, but they also told of fierce fighting people. Attracted by the promise of riches as well as by religious zeal, a flood of adventurers soon followed.

Cortés Advances on the Aztecs Among the earliest conquistadors was Hernán Cortés. Cortés, a landowner in Cuba, heard of Spanish expeditions that had been repelled by Indians. He believed that he could succeed where none had before. In 1519, he landed on the coast of Mexico with about 600 men, 16 horses, and a few cannons. He began an inland trek toward Tenochtitlán (teh nawch tee TLAHN), the capital of the Aztec empire. A young Indian woman named Malinche (mah LEEN chay), called Doña Marina by the Spanish, served as his translator and advisor. Malinche knew both the Maya and Aztec languages, and she learned Spanish quickly.

Malinche told Cortés that the Aztecs had gained power by conquering other groups of people. The Aztecs sacrificed thousands of their captives to the Aztec gods each year. Many conquered peoples hated their Aztec overlords, so Malinche helped Cortés arrange **alliances** with them. They agreed to help Cortés fight the Aztecs.

Moctezuma Faces a Dilemma Meanwhile, messengers brought word about the Spanish to the Aztec emperor Moctezuma (mahk tih ZOO muh). Terrified, he wondered if the leader of the pale-skinned, bearded strangers might be Quetzalcoatl (ket sahl koh AHT el), an Aztec god-king who had long ago vowed to return from the east. Because Moctezuma did not know for sure if Cortés was a god, he did not know how to respond to the news. He sent gifts of turquoise, feathers, and other goods with religious importance, but urged the strangers not to continue to Tenochtitlán.

Cortés, however, had no intention of turning back. He was not interested in the Aztec religious objects, but was extremely interested in the gold and silver ornaments that Moctezuma began sending him.

This passage from a Maya book written in the 1500s describes life before the arrival of the Spanish. What does the writer say was the main effect of Europeans on the Maya?

Primary Source 🔊 AUDIO

❝ There was then no sickness;
They had then no aching bones;
They had then no high fever;
They had then no smallpox;
They had then no burning chest. . .
At that time the course of humanity was orderly.
The foreigners made it otherwise when they arrived here.❞

Malinche Shapes History
Malinche's parents sold her as a slave when she was a child, believing that she was born under an unlucky star. Despite her unfortunate beginning, she left a major mark on the history of the Americas.

Díaz Sets the Record Straight

Bernal Díaz del Castillo was a Spanish soldier who came to Cuba in 1514. In 1519, he accompanied Hernán Cortés on his conquest of the Aztecs. More than 40 years later, Díaz wrote his *True History* because he felt other accounts of the conquest—written by historians who had not been there—were inaccurate. He insisted that as an eyewitness of events he was a better historical source. For example, Díaz was there when Moctezuma took Cortés to the top of the great temple to look at Tenochtitlán, his magnificent capital city on the lake.

Vocabulary Builder

<u>compel</u>—(kum PEL) *v.* to force

Cortés became more determined than ever to reach Tenochtitlán. Fighting and negotiating by turns, Cortés led his forces inland toward the capital. At last, the Spanish arrived in Tenochtitlán, where they were dazzled by the grandeur of the city.

Tenochtitlán Falls to the Spanish Moctezuma welcomed Cortés to his capital. However, relations between the Aztecs and Spaniards soon grew strained. The Spanish scorned the Aztecs' religion and sought to convert them to Christianity. At the same time, as they remained in the city, they saw more of the Aztec treasure. They decided to imprison Moctezuma so they could gain control of the Aztecs and their riches.

Cortés <u>compelled</u> Moctezuma to sign over his land and treasure to the Spanish. In the meantime, a new force of Spanish conquistadors had arrived on the coast to challenge Cortés. In the confusion that followed—with various groups of Spanish, Aztecs, and Native Americans all fighting for control—the Aztecs drove the Spanish from the city. More than half of the Spanish were killed in the fighting, as was Moctezuma.

Cortés retreated to plan an assault. In 1521, in a brutal struggle, Cortés and his Indian allies captured and demolished Tenochtitlán. The Spanish later built Mexico City on the ruins of Tenochtitlán. As in the Caribbean, disease had aided their cause. Smallpox had spread among the Aztecs from the 1519 encounter, decimating the population.

✓ **Checkpoint** What impact did the Aztecs' religious beliefs have on Cortés's approach to Tenochtitlán?

> 66 When we saw so all those cities and villages built in the water, and other great towns on dry land, and that straight and level causeway leading toward [Tenochtitlán], we were astounded. These great towns and [pyramids] and buildings rising from the water, all made of stone, seemed like an enchanted vision… Indeed, some of our soldiers asked whether it was not all a dream…. It was all so wonderful that I do not know how to describe this first glimpse of things never heard of, seen or dreamed of before. 99

> 66 We turned back to the great market and the swarm of people buying and selling. The mere murmur of their voices was loud enough to be heard more than three miles away. Some of our soldiers who had been in many parts of the world, in Constantinople, in Rome, and all over Italy, said that they had never seen a market so well laid out, so large, so orderly, and so filled with people. 99

> — *Bernal Díaz del Castillo*
> from ***The True History of the Conquest of New Spain***

Hernán Cortés ▶

Thinking Critically
1. **Draw Inferences** Why do you think Díaz included the opinions of "some of our soldiers"?
2. **Make a Reasoned Judgment** Do you agree with Díaz that the best historical accounts are written by people who participated in or witnessed the events? Explain your answer.

Pizarro Takes Peru

Cortés's success inspired other adventurers, among them Spaniard **Francisco Pizarro** (pee SAHR oh). Pizarro was interested in Peru's Inca empire, which was reputed to have even more riches than the Aztecs. Pizarro arrived in Peru in 1532, just after the Incan ruler Atahualpa (ah tah WAHL puh) had won the throne from his brother in a bloody **civil war.** A civil war is fought between groups of people in the same nation.

Pizarro's secretary described Atahualpa as

Primary Source

> 66 a man of thirty years, good-looking and poised, somewhat stout, with a wide, handsome, and ferocious face, and the eyes flaming with blood … 99
> —Francisco de Xerez

Atahualpa refused to become a Spanish vassal or convert to Christianity. In response, Pizarro, aided by Indian allies, captured him and slaughtered thousands of Inca. The Spanish demanded a huge ransom for the ruler. The Inca paid it, but the Spanish killed Atahualpa anyway.

Despite continuing resistance, Pizarro and his followers overran the Incan heartland. He had superior weapons, and the Inca were weakened by European diseases. From Peru, Spanish forces surged across Ecuador and Chile. Before long, Spain had added much of South America to its growing empire. Pizarro himself was killed by a rival Spanish faction a few years after he established the city of Lima.

✔ **Checkpoint** What factors encouraged Spanish success in Peru?

Sunken Treasure
Spanish ships sunk in the waters off Cuba's coast hundreds of years ago still yield gold and silver treasure to divers today. A craftsman of mixed Spanish and Native American ancestry made these ceremonial weapons in 1631.

Effects of the Spanish Conquistadors

The Spanish conquistadors accomplished a major victory in the Americas. Within a few decades, a few hundred European soldiers—helped by superior weapons, horses, and especially disease—had conquered millions of Native Americans. The Spanish had seized huge quantities of valuable goods. And they had used Native American labor to establish silver mines in Peru and Mexico to finance their new empire. In the 1500s and early 1600s, treasure fleets sailed each year to Spain or the Spanish Philippines loaded with gold and silver. With this wealth, Spain became Europe's greatest power.

The effect on Native Americans, however, was quite different. Some Native Americans believed that the disasters they suffered marked the world's end. As tens of thousands of Indians died, some of the bewildered and demoralized survivors felt that their gods were less powerful than the god of their conquerors. They therefore stopped resisting. Many Native Americans converted to Christianity in the hopes that their suffering would end.

Yet many Indians continued to resist the Spanish in any way they could. For centuries, the Maya fought Spanish rule in Mexico and Central America. Long after the death of Atahualpa, revolts erupted among the Inca. And throughout the Americas, Indians resisted European influences by preserving aspects of their own culture, including language, religious traditions, and clothing. In time, Native American culture came to influence the culture of Latin America.

The early encounters between the Spanish conquistadors and Native Americans had long-lasting impacts that reached far beyond these two groups. By establishing an empire in the Americas, Spain dramatically changed the pattern of global encounter set in motion with the first European exploration of Africa. For the first time, much of the world was now connected by sea routes, on which traveled ships carrying goods, people, and ideas.

 Checkpoint In what ways did Native Americans resist Europeans?

Progress Monitoring *Online*
For: Self-quiz with vocabulary practice
Web Code: nba-1511

Terms, People, and Places

1. What do each of the key terms listed at the beginning of the section have in common? Explain.

Note Taking

2. **Reading Skill: Recognize Sequence** Use your completed chart to answer the Focus Question: How did a small number of Spanish conquistadors conquer huge Native American empires?

Comprehension and Critical Thinking

3. **Determine Relevance** Which factor was the most important in aiding Spanish success in the Americas?

4. **Summarize Information** How did Cortés gain control of Tenochtitlán?

5. **Recognize Cause and Effect** How did the Incan civil war affect the Spanish outcome in Peru?

6. **Identify Alternatives** How might the history of Europeans in the Americas have been different if the Indians had not been killed by European diseases?

● **Writing About History**

Quick Write: List Things to Compare When you write an expository essay comparing and contrasting two things, you first need to decide which things are useful to compare. List several people, places, or activities from this section to compare. The things you choose should be appropriate for comparison. For example, comparing Malinche and Columbus would not make sense because their roles and purposes were so different from one another.

A 1584 drawing of slaves laboring at the Potosí silver mine, Bolivia

WITNESS HISTORY 🔊 AUDIO

A Missionary Protests

" Everything that has happened since the marvellous discovery of the Americas . . . seems to overshadow all the deeds of famous men past, no matter how heroic, and to silence all talk of other wonders of the world. Prominent amid the aspects of this story which have caught the imagination are the massacres of innocent peoples. . . . **"**
—Friar Bartolomé de Las Casas, 1542

Focus Question How did Spain and Portugal build colonies in the Americas?

Spanish and Portuguese Colonies in the Americas

Objectives
- Explain how Spain ruled its empire in the Americas.
- Analyze the major features of Spanish colonial society and culture.
- Describe how Portugal and other European nations challenged Spanish power.

Terms, People, and Places

viceroy
encomienda
Bartolomé de Las Casas
peon
peninsulare

creole
mestizo
mulatto
privateer

Note Taking

Reading Skill: Recognize Sequence Use a flowchart like this one to keep track of the steps the Spanish took to establish an overseas empire. Add boxes as necessary.

Governing the empire	Catholic Church	Trade
• viceroys	•	•
•	•	•

A flood of Spanish settlers and missionaries followed the conquistadors to Spain's new empire. Wherever they went they established colonies, claiming the land and its people for their king and Church. When there was resistance, the newcomers imposed their will by force. Over time, however, a new culture emerged that reflected European, Native American, and African traditions.

Ruling the Spanish Empire

By the mid-1500s, Spain claimed a vast empire stretching from California to South America. In time, it divided these lands into four provinces, including New Spain (Mexico) and Peru.

Governing the Provinces Spain was determined to maintain strict control over its empire. To achieve this goal, the king set up the Council of the Indies to pass laws for the colonies. He also appointed **viceroys,** or representatives who ruled in his name, in each province. Lesser officials and audiencias (ow dee EN see ahs), or advisory councils of Spanish settlers, helped the viceroy rule. The Council of the Indies in Spain closely monitored these colonial officials to make sure they did not assume too much authority.

Spreading Christianity To Spain, winning souls for Christianity was as important as gaining land. The Catholic Church worked with the government to convert Native Americans to Christianity.

Cultural Blending
Encounters with Native Americans, or stories about such encounters, influenced Spanish and Portuguese artists. This painting dating from the early 1500s places a Biblical story—the adoration of the Magi—in the Americas, with Native American figures.

Vocabulary Builder
drastic—(DRAS tik) *adj.* severe; having a strong effect

Church leaders often served as royal officials and helped to regulate the activities of Spanish settlers. As Spain's American empire expanded, Church authority expanded along with it.

Franciscans, Jesuits, and other missionaries baptized thousands of Native Americans. They built mission churches and worked to turn new converts into loyal subjects of the Catholic king of Spain. They also introduced European clothing, the Spanish language, and new crafts such as carpentry and locksmithing. Where they could, the Spanish missionaries forcibly imposed European culture over Native American culture.

Controlling Trade To make the empire profitable, Spain closely controlled its economic activities, especially trade. The most valuable resources shipped from Spanish America to Spain were silver and gold. Colonists could export raw materials only to Spain and could buy only Spanish manufactured goods. Laws forbade colonists from trading with other European nations or even with other Spanish colonies.

When sugar cane was introduced into the West Indies and elsewhere, it quickly became a profitable resource. The cane was refined into sugar, molasses, and rum. Sugar cane, however, had to be grown on plantations, large estates run by an owner or the owner's overseer. And plantations needed large numbers of workers to be profitable.

Encomienda—A System of Forced Labor At first, Spanish monarchs granted the conquistadors **encomiendas** (en koh mee EN dahs), the right to demand labor or tribute from Native Americans in a particular area. The conquistadors used this system to force Native Americans to work under the most brutal conditions. Those who resisted were hunted down and killed. Disease, starvation, and cruel treatment caused drastic declines in the Native American population.

The encomienda system was used in the mines as well as on plantations. By the 1540s, tons of silver from the Potosí region of Peru and Bolivia filled Spanish treasure ships. Year after year, thousands of Native Americans were forced to extract the rich ore from dangerous shafts deep inside the Andes Mountains. As thousands of Indians died from the terrible conditions, they were replaced by thousands more.

A Spanish Priest Speaks Out A few bold priests, like **Bartolomé de Las Casas** (bahr toh loh MAY deh lahs KAHS ahs), condemned the evils of the encomienda system. In vivid reports to Spain, Las Casas detailed the horrors that Spanish rule had brought to Native Americans and pleaded with the king to end the abuse.

Prodded by Las Casas, Spain passed the New Laws of the Indies in 1542. The laws forbade enslavement and abuse of Native Americans, but Spain was too far away to enforce them. Many Native Americans were forced to become **peons,** workers forced to labor for a landlord in order to pay off a debt. Landlords advanced them food, tools, or seeds, creating debts that workers could never pay off in their lifetime.

Bringing Workers From Africa To fill the labor shortage, Las Casas urged colonists to import workers from Africa. He believed that Africans were immune to tropical diseases and had skills in farming, mining, and metalworking. Las Casas later regretted that advice because it furthered the brutal African slave trade.

The Spanish began bringing Africans to the Americas as slave laborers by the 1530s. As demand for sugar products skyrocketed, the settlers imported millions of Africans as slaves. They were forced to work as field hands, miners, or servants in the houses of wealthy landowners. Others became skilled artists and artisans. Within a few generations, Africans and their American-born descendants greatly outnumbered European settlers throughout the Americas. In the cities, some enslaved Africans earned enough money to buy their freedom. Others resisted slavery by rebelling or running away.

✓ **Checkpoint**   What was the encomienda system?

Colonial Society and Culture

In Spanish America, the mix of diverse peoples gave rise to a new social structure. The blending of Native American, African, and European peoples and traditions resulted in a culture distinct to the Americas.

Cultural Blending   Although Spanish culture was dominant in the cities, the blending of diverse traditions changed people's lives throughout the Americas. Settlers learned Native American styles of building, ate foods native to the Americas, and traveled in Indian-style canoes. Indian artistic styles influenced the newcomers. At the same time, Europeans taught their religion to Native Americans. They also introduced animals, especially the horse, thereby transforming the lives of many Native Americans. Africans contributed to this cultural mix with their farming methods, cooking styles, and crops. African drama, dance, and song heightened Christian services. In Cuba, Haiti, and elsewhere, Africans forged new religions that blended African and Christian beliefs.

A Spanish Cathedral
A group of Tzotzil Maya women gather in front of the Cathedral of San Cristóbal in Chiapas, Mexico. The church was originally built in 1528. *How can you tell that the church is a vital part of life in the town?*

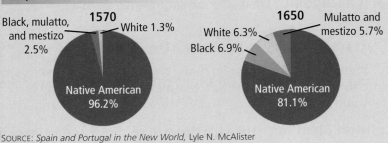

A Changing Population

The population of Spanish America changed dramatically within a century, as the two circle graphs illustrate. Artist Miguel Cabrera showed this diversity in a 1700s painting of a single family made up of a Spanish father, a Native American mother, and a mestizo daughter.

Population of Spanish America

1570
- Black, mulatto, and mestizo 2.5%
- White 1.3%
- Native American 96.2%

1650
- White 6.3%
- Black 6.9%
- Mulatto and mestizo 5.7%
- Native American 81.1%

SOURCE: *Spain and Portugal in the New World*, Lyle N. McAlister

Chart Skills Study the circle graphs. *By what percentage did the black, mulatto, and mestizo population increase from 1570 to 1650?*

A Layered Society Spanish colonial society was made up of distinct social classes. At the top were **peninsulares** (peh neen soo LAH rayz), people born in Spain. (The term *peninsular* referred to the Iberian Peninsula, on which Spain is located.) Peninsulares filled the highest positions in both colonial governments and the Catholic Church. Next came **creoles,** American-born descendants of Spanish settlers. Creoles owned most of the plantations, ranches, and mines.

Lower social groups reflected the mixing of populations. They included **mestizos,** people of Native American and European descent, and **mulattoes,** people of African and European descent. Native Americans and people of African descent formed the lowest social classes.

Lively Towns and Cities Spanish settlers generally lived in towns and cities. The population of Mexico City grew so quickly that by 1550 it was the largest Spanish-speaking city in the world. Colonial cities were centers of government, commerce, and European culture. Around the central plaza, or square, stood government buildings and a Spanish-style church. Broad avenues and public monuments symbolized European power and wealth. Cities were also centers of intellectual and cultural life. Architecture and painting, as well as poetry and the exchange of ideas, flourished in Spanish cities in the Americas.

Note Taking

Compare and Contrast Complete a Venn diagram like this one to compare and contrast the Spanish and Portuguese empires in the Americas.

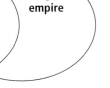

Spanish empire — Portuguese empire

Emphasizing Education To meet the Church's need for educated priests, the colonies built universities. The University of Mexico was established as early as 1551. A dozen Spanish American universities were already educating young men long before Harvard was founded in 1636 as the first college in the 13 English colonies.

Women wishing an education might enter a convent. One such woman was Sor Juana Inés de la Cruz (sawr HWAN uh ee NES deh lah krooz). Refused admission to the University of Mexico because she was female, Juana entered a convent at around the age of 18. There, she devoted herself to study and the writing of poetry. She earned a reputation as one of the greatest poets ever to write in the Spanish language.

✔ **Checkpoint** What was the role of the Church in colonial education?

Beyond the Spanish Empire

A large area of South America remained outside the Spanish empire. By the Treaty of Tordesillas in 1494, Portugal claimed its empire in the east, Brazil.

Settling Brazil As in the Spanish empire, the Native Americans who lived in Brazil—the Tupian Indians—had been largely wiped out by disease. In the 1530s, Portugal began to issue grants of land to Portuguese nobles, who agreed to develop the land and share profits with the crown. Landowners sent settlers to build towns, plantations, and churches.

Unlike Spain's American colonies, Brazil offered no instant wealth from silver or gold. However, early settlers cut and exported brazilwood. The Portuguese named the colony after this wood, which was used to produce a valuable dye. Soon they turned to plantation agriculture and raising cattle. Like the Spanish, the Portuguese forced Indians and Africans to clear land for plantations. As many as four million Africans were sent to Brazil. As in Spanish America, a new culture emerged in Brazil that blended European, Native American, and African elements.

Smuggling Brazilwood
A panel carved from brazilwood in the 1550s shows French privateers illegally cutting Portuguese brazilwood and storing it on their boats.

Challenging Portugal and Spain In the 1500s, the wealth of the Americas helped make Spain the most powerful country in Europe, with Portugal not far behind. The jealous English and Dutch shared the resentment that French king Francis I felt when he declared, "I should like to see Adam's will, wherein he divided the Earth between Spain and Portugal."

To get around those countries' strict control over colonial trade, smugglers traded illegally with Portuguese and Spanish colonists. In the Caribbean and elsewhere, Dutch, English, and French pirates preyed on treasure ships from the Americas. Some pirates, called **privateers,** even operated with the approval of European governments. Other European explorers continued to sail the coasts of the Americas, hunting for gold and other treasure, as well as a northwest passage to Asia.

✔ **Checkpoint** What was Brazil's economy based on?

Progress Monitoring *Online*
For: Self-quiz with vocabulary practice
Web Code: nba-1521

Terms, People, and Places

1. Place each of the key terms at the beginning of the section into one of the following categories: culture, government, or economics. Write a sentence for each term explaining your choice.

2. **Reading Skill: Recognize Sequence** Use your completed flowchart and Venn diagram to answer the Focus Question: How did Spain and Portugal build colonies in the Americas?

Comprehension and Critical Thinking

3. **Identify Alternatives** How might the Spanish have solved the problem of finding a dependable labor supply without the use of slavery?

4. **Analyze Information** How did the mix of peoples in Spanish America result in a new social structure?

5. **Make Comparisons** In what ways were the Spanish and Portuguese empires in the Americas similar? In what ways were they different?

6. **Draw Inferences** Why did some European monarchs support the illegal activities of privateers?

● **Writing About History**

Quick Write: Make a Venn Diagram When you write an essay comparing and contrasting two things, you first need to make clear how they are similar and different. A graphic organizer can help you outline similarities and differences. Choose two people, places, or events from the section. Then create a Venn diagram that you can use to compare and contrast them. Refer to the Venn diagram at the beginning of the section as an example.

A Piece of the Past

In 1867, a Canadian farmer of English descent was cutting logs on his property with his fourteen-year-old son. As they used their oxen to pull away a large log, a piece of turf came up to reveal a round, yellow object. The elaborately engraved object they found, dated 1603, was an astrolabe that had belonged to French explorer Samuel de Champlain. This astrolabe was a piece of the story of the European exploration of Canada and the French-British rivalry that followed.

Focus Question How did European struggles for power shape the North American continent?

A statue of Samuel de Champlain holding up an astrolabe overlooks the Ottawa River in Canada (right). Champlain's astrolabe appears above.

Struggle for North America

Objectives

- Explain why the colony of New France grew slowly.
- Analyze the establishment and growth of the 13 English colonies.
- Understand why Europeans competed for power in North America and how their struggle affected Native Americans.

Terms, People, and Places

New France
revenue
Pilgrims
compact
French and Indian War
Treaty of Paris

Note Taking

Reading Skill: Recognize Sequence Create a timeline like the one below to record the sequence of important events in the struggle for North America.

Cartier explores eastern Canada.

1534   1607

In the 1600s, France, the Netherlands, England, and Sweden joined Spain in settling North America. North America did not yield vast treasure or offer a water passage to Asia, as they had hoped. Before long, though, the English and French were turning large profits. By 1700, France and England controlled large parts of North America. Their colonies differed from each other and from those of Spanish America in terms of language, government, resources, and society.

Building New France

By the early 1500s, French fishing ships were crossing the Atlantic each year to harvest rich catches of cod off Newfoundland, Canada. Within a hundred years, the French had occupied nearly half of North America.

Explorers and Missionaries French claims in Canada—which the French called **New France**—quietly grew while French rulers were distracted by wars at home in Europe. In 1534, Jacques Cartier (zhahk kahr tee AY) began exploring the coastline of eastern Canada, eventually discovering the St. Lawrence River. Traveling inland on the river, he claimed much of present-day eastern Canada for France. Jesuits and other missionaries soon followed the explorers. They advanced into the wilderness, trying with little success to convert the Native Americans they met to Christianity.

Furs, Trapping, and Fishing French explorers and fur traders gradually traveled inland with the help of Native American allies, who sought support against rival Native American groups. Eventually, France's American empire reached from Quebec to the Great Lakes and down the Mississippi River to Louisiana and the Gulf of Mexico.

The population of New France, however, grew slowly. The first permanent French settlement was not established until 1608, when Samuel de Champlain established a colony in Quebec. Wealthy landlords bought huge tracts, or areas of land, along the St. Lawrence River. They sought settlers to farm the land, but the harsh Canadian climate, with its long winters, attracted few French peasants.

Many who went to New France soon abandoned farming in favor of the more profitable fur trapping and trading. They faced a hard life in the wilderness, but the soaring European demand for fur ensured good prices. Fishing was another industry that supported settlers, who exported cod and other fish to Europe.

BIOGRAPHY

Jacques Cartier
In 1534, Jacques Cartier (1491–1557) sailed to North America on behalf of France. His commission was to find spices, gold, and a passage to Asia. Cartier found none of these things, despite several attempts, and ended his career in relative obscurity.

During his own lifetime, no one guessed the impact that Cartier's voyages would have. In his thousand-mile trek into Canada's interior, he staked France's later claim to a huge amount of North American territory. His legacy also lives on in the Canadian place names he coined such as the St. Lawrence River and the name Canada—derived from an Iroquois word meaning "village" or "settlement." **Why were Cartier's discoveries undervalued at the time?**

An Empire Slowly Expands In the late 1600s, the French king Louis XIV set out to strengthen royal power and boost **revenues,** or income, from taxes from his overseas empire. He appointed officials to oversee economic activities in New France. He also sent soldiers and more settlers—including women—to North America. Louis, however, who was Catholic, prohibited Protestants from settling in New France. By the early 1700s, French forts, missions, and trading posts stretched from Quebec to Louisiana, and the population was growing. Yet the population of New France remained small compared to that of the 13 English colonies that were expanding along the Atlantic coast.

✔ **Checkpoint** Why did French settlers abandon farming in favor of fur trapping and trading?

The 13 English Colonies

In 1497, a Venetian navigator known by the English name John Cabot found rich fishing grounds off Newfoundland, which he claimed for England. Later English navigators continued to search for a northwest passage to Asia, with no success. In the 1600s, England concentrated on establishing colonies along the Atlantic seaboard—the coast of the present-day eastern United States.

Establishing the First Colonies The English built their first permanent colony at Jamestown, Virginia, in 1607. Although the colony was meant to bring wealth and profit, in the early years of the colony many settlers died of starvation and disease. The rest survived with the help of friendly Native Americans. The colony finally made headway when the settlers started to grow and export tobacco, a plant that had been cultivated by Native Americans for thousands of years.

In 1620, another group of English settlers landed at Plymouth, Massachusetts. They were **Pilgrims,** or English Protestants who rejected the Church of England. They sought religious freedom rather than commercial profit. Before coming ashore, they signed the Mayflower Compact, in which they set out guidelines for governing their North American colony. A **compact** is an agreement among people. Today, we see this document as an important early step toward self-government.

Many Pilgrims died in the early years of the Plymouth colony. Local Native Americans, however, taught them to grow corn and helped them survive in the new land. Soon, a new wave of English Protestant immigrants arrived to establish the Massachusetts Bay Colony.

The English Colonies Grow In the 1600s and 1700s, the English established a total of 13 colonies. Some, like Virginia and New York, were commercial ventures, organized for profit. Others, like Massachusetts, Pennsylvania, and Maryland, were set up as havens for persecuted religious groups. Still others, like Georgia and South Carolina, were gifts from English kings to loyal supporters.

Settlers in all of the colonies spent the early years just struggling to survive. They quickly abandoned dreams of finding riches like the Spanish gold and silver. However, over time they learned to create wealth by using the resources native to their surroundings. In New England, prosperous fishing, timber, and shipbuilding industries grew. In the middle colonies, farmers grew huge quantities of grain on the abundant land. In the South, colonists found that cash crops such as rice and tobacco grew well in the warm climate. They therefore developed a plantation economy to grow these crops. As in New Spain, the colonists imported African slaves to clear land and work the plantations. In several colonies, especially in the South, enslaved Africans and their descendants would eventually outnumber people of European descent.

Governing the Colonies Like the rulers of Spain and France, English monarchs asserted control over their American colonies. They appointed royal governors to oversee colonial affairs and had Parliament pass laws to regulate colonial trade. Yet, compared with settlers in the Spanish and French colonies, English colonists enjoyed a large degree of self-government. Each colony had its own representative assembly, elected by propertied men, that advised the governor and made decisions on local issues.

The tradition of consulting representative assemblies grew out of the English experience. Beginning in the 1200s, Parliament had begun to play an important role in English affairs. Slowly, too, English citizens had gained certain legal and political rights. England's American colonists expected to enjoy the same rights. When colonists later protested British policies in North America, they viewed themselves as "freeborn Englishmen" who were defending their traditional rights.

✔ **Checkpoint** For what reasons were the 13 English colonies established?

A Fanciful View
An English play promised that "... gold is more plentiful there [Virginia] than copper is with us.... and as for rubies and diamonds, they go forth on holy days and gather them by the seashore." *Does this photo of the re-creation of the Jamestown colony support the playwright's views?*

Geography *Interactive*
For: Audio guided tour
Web Code: nbp-1531

INUIT
KUTCHIN
KASKA
INUIT

NORTH AMERICA
CREE
TLINGIT
OJIBWA
Canada
SIOUX
UTE
NOMADIC PLAINS CULTURES
COMANCHE
PUEBLO
NOMADIC HUNTERS
WOODLAND CULTURES
APACHE
English Colonies

Pacific Ocean

40°N

20°N

Equal-Area Projection
0   500   1000 mi
0   500   1000 km

▲ A Chippewa beadwork bag reflects the influence of the French nuns who taught the Native Americans how to embroider.

▼ Europeans used American gold and silver to make dishes like this Portuguese platter dating from the 1500s.

Viceroyalty of New Spain

Atlantic Ocean

Guiana
CARIBANA
MANOA
SHUAR
NOMADIC HUNTERS
ARUAC
SOUTH AMERICA
Brazil
GÊ
GUARANI

Viceroyalty of Peru

N W E S

0°

▼ A coat of arms from the time the Dutch briefly controlled the colony of New Netherland (New York) shows the importance of the beaver to the colony's trade.

England
France
Spain
Portugal
Netherlands
UTE Native culture

NOMADIC HUNTERS

40°S

140°W   120°W   60°W   40°W

New Encounters
As Europeans explored the Americas, claiming lands for their monarchs, they encountered diverse groups of Native Americans who already lived there. Europeans and Native Americans both relied on the resources of the land they inhabited. Though the groups often clashed, they influenced each other in many ways.

▲ English settlers made chests like this one out of native American oak, using traditional English patterns.

Map Skills Within a hundred years or so, European exploration of the Americas had led to huge land claims by various countries.
1. **Locate** (a) Brazil (b) English colonies (c) Peru (d) New Spain
2. **Describe** What geographical factor do all of the European land claims share? Why is this so?
3. **Draw Conclusions** Why do you think the boundaries of the European land claims end as illustrated on the map?

123

Struggling for Power

By the 1600s, Spain, France, England, and the Netherlands all had colonies in North America. They began to fight—both in the colonies and around the world—to protect and expand their interests.

Vocabulary Builder

prevail—(pree VAYL) *v.* to succeed; to triumph

Living Languages
A sign in British Columbia—written in both English and the local Indian language—shows how Native American influence lingers long after the Americas became British.

Competing for Colonies By the late 1600s, French claims included present-day Canada as well as much of the present-day central United States. The Spanish had moved north, making claims to present-day Texas and Florida. Meanwhile, the English and Dutch maintained colonies along the East Coast. Native Americans throughout the colonies entered the conflict, hoping to play the Europeans against one another. Competition was also fierce in the Caribbean, as European nations fought to acquire the profitable sugar-producing colonies. By the 1700s, the French and English Caribbean islands, worked by enslaved Africans, had surpassed the whole of North America in exports to Europe.

Bitter Rivalry Turns to War During the 1700s, Britain and France emerged as powerful rivals. They clashed in Europe, North America, Africa, and Asia. In North America, war between the two powers erupted in 1754. Called the **French and Indian War,** it raged until 1763. It also turned into a worldwide struggle known as the Seven Years' War, which spread to Europe in 1756 and then to India and Africa.

During the war, British soldiers and colonial troops launched a series of campaigns against the French in Canada and on the Ohio frontier. At first, France won several victories. Then, in 1759, British troops launched an attack on Quebec, the capital of New France. The British scaled steep cliffs along the river and captured the city. Although the war dragged on until 1763, the British had prevailed in Canada.

The 1763 **Treaty of Paris** officially ended the worldwide war and ensured British dominance in North America. France ceded Canada and its lands east of the Mississippi River to Britain, but regained the rich sugar-producing islands in the Caribbean and the slave-trading outposts in Africa that the British had seized during the war. It also retained its territory in the central region of North America.

✓ **Checkpoint** Why was the French and Indian War fought?

SECTION **3** Assessment

Progress Monitoring *Online*
For: Self-quiz with vocabulary practice
Web Code: nba-1531

Terms, People, and Places
1. For each term, person, or place listed at the beginning of the section, write a sentence explaining its significance.

Note Taking
2. **Reading Skill: Recognize Sequence** Use your completed timeline to answer the Focus Question: How did European struggles for power shape the North American continent?

Comprehension and Critical Thinking
3. **Make Comparisons** Why did New France grow slowly compared with Spanish and English colonies?
4. **Identify Central Issues** Why did the English colonies have a large degree of self-government?
5. **Make Generalizations** How did Britain come to dominate North America?
6. **Draw Inferences** Why did Native American groups side with European powers rather than join together to oppose them?

● **Writing About History**
Quick Write: Write a Thesis Statement
Once you have chosen the things you will compare and contrast in your essay, you must write a thesis statement. Your thesis statement should address clearly how the things you are comparing relate similarly or differently to your topic. For example, your thesis statement might focus on how the French and the English took different paths in establishing colonies in the Americas.

This portrait of Olaudah Equiano dates from the 1780s. The iron shackles shown at the right were used to bind slaves during the slave trade.

Forced Into Slavery

❝The first object which saluted my eyes when I arrived on the coast was the sea, and a slave ship which was then riding at anchor and waiting for its cargo. These filled me with astonishment, which was soon converted into terror when I was carried on board.❞

So wrote Olaudah Equiano. In the 1750s, when he was 11 years old, Equiano was seized from his Nigerian village by slave traders. He was then transported as human cargo from West Africa to the Americas.

Focus Question How did the Atlantic slave trade shape the lives and economies of Africans and Europeans?

The Atlantic Slave Trade

Objectives

- Explain how triangular trade worked.
- Understand the nature of the Middle Passage and describe its effects.
- Analyze the impact of the Atlantic slave trade.

Terms, People, and Places

Olaudah Equiano   Middle Passage
triangular trade   mutiny

Note Taking

Reading Skill: Recognize Sequence Use a flowchart like the one below to record the events that led to millions of Africans being shipped to the Americas.

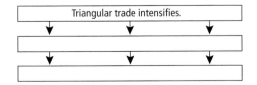

Triangular trade intensifies.

Vocabulary Builder

commodity—(kuh MAHD uh tee) n. anything bought and sold

Enslaved Africans like **Olaudah Equiano** formed part of an international trade network that arose during the 1500s. The Spanish were the first major European partners in the slave trade, buying slaves to labor in Spain's South American empire. As other European powers established colonies in the Americas, the slave trade—and with it the entire international trade network—intensified.

Triangular Trade Across the Atlantic

The Atlantic slave trade formed one part of a three-legged international trade network known as **triangular trade.** This was a triangle-shaped series of Atlantic trade routes linking Europe, Africa, and the Americas.

Shipping People and Goods Triangular trade worked in the following way. On the first leg, merchant ships brought European goods—including guns, cloth, and cash—to Africa. In Africa, the merchants traded these goods for slaves. On the second leg, known as the **Middle Passage,** the slaves were transported to the Americas. There, the enslaved Africans were exchanged for sugar, molasses, and other products manufactured at plantations owned by Europeans.

On the final leg, merchants carried sugar, molasses, cotton, and other American goods such as furs, salt fish, and rum made from molasses. These goods were shipped to Europe, where they were traded at a profit for the European commodities that merchants needed to return to Africa.

WITNESS HISTORY VIDEO

Watch *The Atlantic Slave Trade* on the **Witness History Discovery School**™ video program to experience the Middle Passage.

Discovery
SCHOOL

Industries and Cities Thrive Triangular trade was immensely profitable for many people. Merchants grew wealthy. Even though there were risks such as losing ships at sea, the money to be made from valuable cargoes usually outweighed the risks. Certain industries that supported trade thrived. For example, a shipbuilding industry in New England grew to support the shipping industry. Other colonial industries, such as fishing, raising tobacco, and processing sugar, became hugely successful.

Thriving trade led to successful port cities. European cities such as Nantes, France, and Bristol, England, grew prosperous because of triangular trade. In North America, even newly settled towns such as Salem, Massachusetts, and Newport, Rhode Island, quickly grew into thriving cities. Even though few slaves were imported directly to the northern cities, the success of the port cities there was made possible by the Atlantic slave trade.

✓ **Checkpoint** How did triangular trade affect colonial economies?

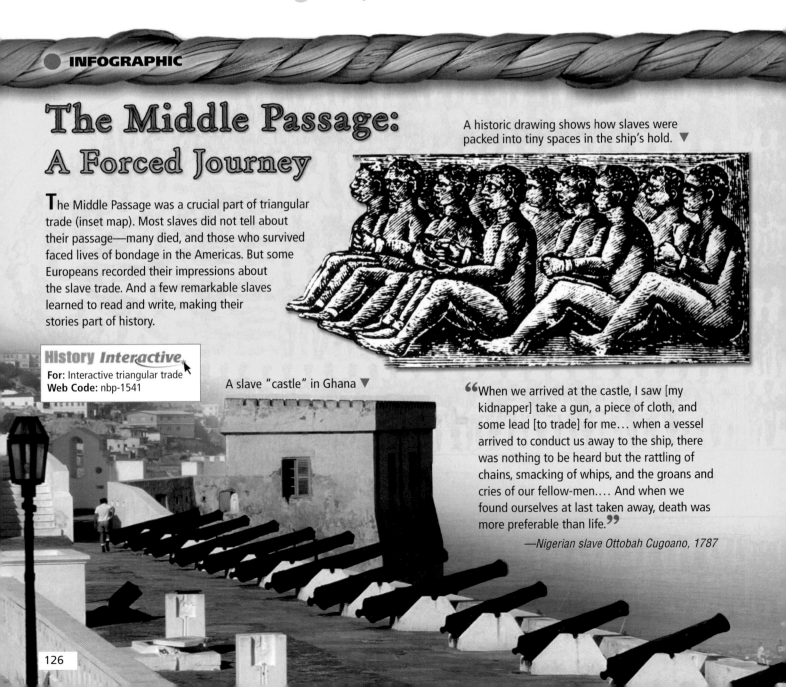

● **INFOGRAPHIC**

The Middle Passage: A Forced Journey

The Middle Passage was a crucial part of triangular trade (inset map). Most slaves did not tell about their passage—many died, and those who survived faced lives of bondage in the Americas. But some Europeans recorded their impressions about the slave trade. And a few remarkable slaves learned to read and write, making their stories part of history.

History Interactive
For: Interactive triangular trade
Web Code: nbp-1541

A historic drawing shows how slaves were packed into tiny spaces in the ship's hold. ▼

A slave "castle" in Ghana ▼

❝When we arrived at the castle, I saw [my kidnapper] take a gun, a piece of cloth, and some lead [to trade] for me… when a vessel arrived to conduct us away to the ship, there was nothing to be heard but the rattling of chains, smacking of whips, and the groans and cries of our fellow-men.… And when we found ourselves at last taken away, death was more preferable than life.❞

—*Nigerian slave Ottobah Cugoano, 1787*

Horrors of the Middle Passage

To merchants, the Middle Passage was just one leg of triangular trade. For enslaved Africans, the Middle Passage was a horror.

The Trek to the Ships The terrible journey began before the slave ships set sail. Most Africans were taken from inland villages. After they were enslaved, they were forced to march to coastal ports. Men, women, and children were bound with ropes and chains, often to one another, and forced to walk distances as long as a thousand miles. They might be forced to carry heavy loads, and often the men's necks were encircled with thick iron bands.

Many captives died along the way. Others tried to escape, and were often quickly recaptured and brutally punished. Those who survived the march were <u>restrained</u> in coastal holding pens and warehouses in slave shipping ports such as Elmina, Ghana, or Gorée, Senegal. They were held there until European traders arrived by ship.

Vocabulary Builder

<u>restrain</u>—(rih STRAYN) *v.* to keep under control; to keep from action

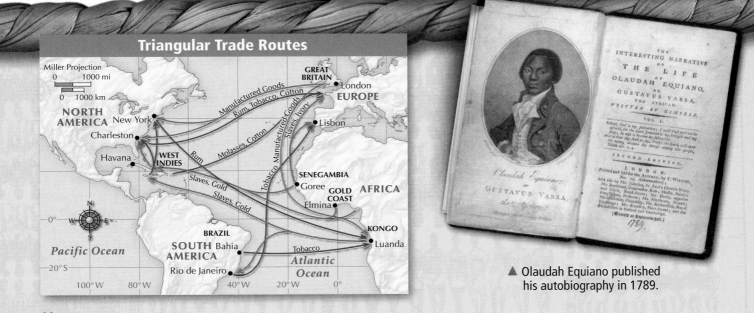

Triangular Trade Routes

▲ Olaudah Equiano published his autobiography in 1789.

❝This work is so hard that any slave, newly put to it, in the course of a month becomes so weak that often he is totally unfit for labour. If he falls back behind the rest, the driver keeps forcing him up with the whip.❞

—*Ashton Warner, early 1800s*

An 1823 painting shows slaves ▶ laboring on the island of Antigua.

Thinking Critically

1. **Map Skills** What were slaves exchanged for in the West Indies?
2. **Draw Inferences** Why are there so few first-person slave narratives?

Just Imported in the Ship GRANBY, JOSEPH BLEWER,
Master,
Seventy *Gold-Coast* SLAVES
of various ages, and both sexes,
To be sold on board said ship at Mr. Plumsted's wharf, by
WILLING and *MORRIS,*
And a part of them are intended to be sent in a few days to Dook
Creek, there to be sold, by Mr. Thomas Mudock for cash or
country produce.
SLAVERY ADVERTISEMENT.

William Cowper wrote the following poem in the 1700s. How does he use irony to express his disapproval of the slave trade?

Primary Source

❝I own I am shocked at the purchase
    of slaves,
And fear those who buy them and
    sell them are knaves;
What I hear of their hardships, their
    tortures and groans,
Is almost enough to draw pity
    from stones.
I pity them greatly, but I must
    be mum,
For how could we do without sugar
    and rum?❞

Aboard the "Floating Coffins" Once purchased, Africans were packed below the decks of slave ships, usually in chains. Hundreds of men, women, and children were crammed into a single vessel for voyages that lasted from three weeks to three months. The ships faced many perils, including storms at sea, raids by pirate ships, and **mutinies,** or revolts, by the captives.

Disease was the biggest threat to the lives of the captives and the profit of the merchants. Of the slaves who died, most died of dysentery. Many died of smallpox. Many others died from apparently no disease at all. Whatever the cause, slave ships became "floating coffins" on which up to half the Africans on board died from disease or brutal mistreatment.

Some enslaved Africans resisted, and others tried to seize control of the ship and return to Africa. Suicide, however, was more common than mutiny. Many Africans believed that in death they would be returned to their home countries. So they hanged themselves, starved themselves, or leapt overboard.

✔ **Checkpoint**   How did enslaved Africans resist captivity?

Impact of the Atlantic Slave Trade

The slave trade brought enormous wealth to merchants and traders, and provided the labor that helped profitable colonial economies grow. Yet the impact on Africans was devastating. African states and societies were torn apart. The lives of individual Africans were either cut short or forever brutalized.

Historians still debate the number of Africans who were directly involved in the Atlantic slave trade. In the 1500s, they estimate about 2,000 enslaved Africans were sent to the Americas each year. In the 1780s, when the slave trade was at its peak, that number approached 80,000 a year. By the mid-1800s, when the overseas slave trade was finally stopped, an estimated 11 million enslaved Africans had reached the Americas. Another 2 million probably died under the brutal conditions of the Middle Passage between Africa and the Americas.

✔ **Checkpoint**   How did the slave trade affect Africans?

SECTION 4 **Assessment**

Progress Monitoring *Online*
For: Self-quiz with vocabulary practice
Web Code: nba-1541

Terms, People, and Places

1. What do each of the key terms and people listed at the beginning of the section have in common? Explain.

Note Taking

2. **Reading Skill: Recognize Sequence** Use your completed flowchart to answer the Focus Question: How did the Atlantic slave trade shape the lives and economies of Africans and Europeans?

Comprehension and Critical Thinking

3. **Synthesize Information** What role did each of the following play in triangular trade: a New England merchant, an African slave, and a Southern plantation owner?

4. **Recognize Assumptions** What European assumptions about Africans does the Atlantic slave trade show?

5. **Predict Consequences** Would the growth of the American colonies have been different if there had been no Atlantic slave trade? Explain.

● **Writing About History**

Quick Write: Gather Evidence to Support a Thesis Statement Once you have written your thesis statement, gather specific evidence—facts and quotes—that support it. For example, assume for this section that your thesis statement concludes that the African slave trade was the most influential event of the age of exploration. Gather specific evidence from the section that supports this statement.

A trading post in the West Indies thrives in the mid-1500s; a powder horn is inscribed with North American fur trading routes.

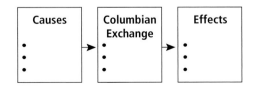

WITNESS HISTORY 🔊 AUDIO

Uniting the World

❝ The discovery of America, and that of a passage to the East Indies by the Cape of Good Hope, are the two greatest and most important events recorded in the history of mankind. By uniting, in some measure, the most distant parts of the world, by enabling them to relieve one another's wants, to increase one another's enjoyments, and to encourage one another's industry, their general tendency would seem to be beneficial.❞
—Adam Smith, *The Wealth of Nations,* 1776

Focus Question How did the voyages of European explorers lead to new economic systems in Europe and its colonies?

Effects of Global Contact

Objectives
- Explain how European exploration led to the Columbian Exchange.
- Analyze the commercial revolution.
- Understand the impact that mercantilism had on European and colonial economies.

Terms, People, and Places

Columbian Exchange	entrepreneur
inflation	mercantilism
price revolution	tariff
capitalism	

Note Taking

Reading Skill: Recognize Sequence Create a flowchart like the one below to keep track of the events that resulted from global exchange in the 1500s and 1600s.

Causes	Columbian Exchange	Effects
• • •	• • •	• • •

The voyages of exploration in the 1500s and 1600s marked the beginning of what would become European domination of the globe. By the 1700s, European exploration had brought major changes to the people of Europe, Asia, Africa, and the Americas.

The Columbian Exchange

When Columbus returned to Spain in March 1493, he brought with him plants and animals that he had found in the Americas. Later that year, Columbus returned to the Americas with some 1,200 settlers and a collection of European animals and plants. In this way, Columbus began a vast global exchange that would profoundly affect the world. Because this exchange began with Columbus, we call it the **Columbian Exchange.**

New Foods and Animals In the Americas, Europeans found a variety of foods that were new to them, including tomatoes, pumpkins, peppers. They eagerly transported these to Europe. Two of these new foods, corn and potatoes, became important foods in the Old World. Easy to grow and store, potatoes helped feed Europe's rapidly growing population. Corn spread all across Europe and to Africa and Asia, becoming one of the world's most important cereal crops.

Europeans also carried a wide variety of plants and animals to the Americas, including wheat and grapes from Europe and bananas and sugar cane from Africa and Asia. Cattle, pigs, goats, and chickens, unknown before the European encounter, joined the Native American diet. Horses and donkeys transported people and goods quickly. Horses also provided the nomadic peoples of western North America with a new, more effective way to hunt buffalo.

Horses Transform a Continent
The Spanish brought horses to the Americas by ship (below). A Spanish saying went "After God, we owe the victory to the horses." Horses also dramatically affected Native American life. An artist painted this scene of Plains Indians in 1830. *How does the artist show the importance of the horse to Native American life and culture?*

The Global Population Explodes The transfer of food crops from continent to continent took time. By the 1700s, however, corn, potatoes, manioc, beans, and tomatoes were contributing to population growth around the world. While other factors help account for the population explosion that began at this time, the <u>dispersal</u> of new food crops from the Americas was certainly a key cause.

The Columbian Exchange also sparked the migration of millions of people. Each year shiploads of European settlers sailed to the Americas, lured by the promise of a new life in a land of opportunities. Europeans also settled on the fringes of Africa and Asia, places made known to them because of exploration. In addition, as you have read, the Atlantic slave trade forcibly brought millions of Africans to the Americas.

In some parts of the world, populations declined as a result of increased global contact. The transfer of European diseases, such as smallpox and measles, decimated many Native American populations. Other populations were wiped out as a result of conflicts.

✓ **Checkpoint** Why did the global population explode?

A Commercial Revolution

The opening of direct links with Asia, Africa, and the Americas had far-reaching economic consequences for Europeans and their colonies.

The Price Revolution Strikes In the 1500s, prices began to rise in many parts of Europe. At the same time, there was much more money in circulation. A rise in prices that is linked to a sharp increase in the amount of money available is called **inflation.** The period in European history when inflation rose rapidly is known as the **price revolution.** Inflation was fueled by the enormous amount of silver and gold flowing into Europe from the Americas by the mid-1500s.

Capitalism Emerges Expanded trade, an increased money supply, and the push for overseas empires spurred the growth of European **capitalism,** or an economic system in which most businesses are owned privately. **Entrepreneurs,** or people who take on financial risk to make profits, were key to the success of capitalism. Entrepreneurs organized, managed, and assumed the risks of doing business. They hired workers and paid for raw materials, transport, and other costs of production.

As trade increased, entrepreneurs sought to expand into overseas ventures. Capitalists, because of their resources, were more willing to take risks. Thus, the price revolution of the early modern age gave a boost to capitalism. Entrepreneurs and capitalists made up a new business class devoted to the goal of making profits. Together, they helped change local European economies into an international trading system.

Exploring New Business Methods Early European capitalists discovered new ways to create wealth. From the Arabs, they adapted methods of bookkeeping to show profits and losses from their ventures. During the late Middle Ages, as you have read, banks increased in importance, allowing wealthy merchants to lend money at interest. Joint stock companies, also developed in late medieval times, grew in importance. They allowed people to pool large amounts of capital needed for overseas ventures. Individuals who invested in these companies could join in any profits that the company made. If the company lost money, individuals would only lose their initial investments.

Note Taking

Recognize Sequence Use a flowchart like this one to keep track of the sequence of events that led to new global economic systems.

Causes	New Economic Systems	Effects
• • •	• Capitalism •	• • •

TULIPMANIA
The Boom of the 1630s

In the 1630s, frenzy over a single good—the tulip—took hold in the Netherlands. People made and lost fortunes as the price of tulips rose from a handful of change to over a million dollars, only to abruptly crash. At the height of the mania, it was actually cheaper to purchase a painting of tulips by a Dutch master than to buy one tulip bulb.

Prices in Holland, 1630s

150 guilders	Average annual income
5,000 guilders	Price for a still-life painting of tulips by a Dutch master
10,000 guilders	Cost of a luxurious Amsterdam estate house

(Note: 100 guilders = approx. $12,500 in U.S. dollars today)

△ Joannes Busschaert painted *Still Life of Tulips, Roses, Fruit, and Shells* in the early 1600s. A tulip bulb with its flower is shown at right.

Price of a Single Tulip Bulb

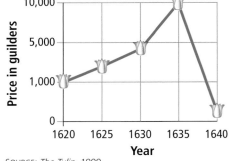

SOURCE: *The Tulip*, 1999

Who Loses in a Trade War?

In the 1990s, a trade war over bananas broke out between the United States and the European Union. The European Union wanted to buy bananas from small banana growers in its former colonies in Africa and the Caribbean. The United States, wanting to assist large South and Central American banana growers, responded by heavily taxing common European imports. In 2001, an agreement was reached that ended the trade war. **Critical Thinking** *In a trade war, who are the winners and losers?*

Everyone Wins

"The discrimination of the current illegal system is eliminated because all applicants will be treated equally and each applicant gains market access in the same proportion . . . . Dole believes that this system will benefit those banana exporters that invest in the jobs, people, countries and infrastructure that it takes to grow markets, open trade and compete. . . ."

—Dole Food Company press release, 2001

The Less Powerful Lose

"St. Lucia continues to be concerned that the thrust towards allowing market forces to totally determine the scope, structure and outcomes of economic activity, is not being counterbalanced by mechanisms to fairly distribute welfare gains and to protect the more vulnerable, small states like Saint Lucia, from the consequences of market failure. . . ."

—Earl Huntley, ambassador of Saint Lucia, in a statement to the UN, 2001

Bypassing the Guilds The growing demand for goods led merchants to find ways to increase production. Traditionally, guilds controlled the manufacture of goods. But guild masters often ran small-scale businesses without the capital to produce for large markets. They also had strict rules regulating quality, prices, and working conditions.

Enterprising capitalists devised a way to bypass the guilds called the "putting-out" system. It was first used to produce textiles but later spread to other industries. Under this system, for example, a merchant capitalist distributed raw wool to peasant cottages. Cottagers spun the wool into thread and then wove it into cloth. Merchants bought the wool cloth from the peasants and sent it to the city for finishing and dyeing. Finally, the merchants sold the finished product for a profit.

The "putting-out" system, also known by the term "cottage industry," separated capital and labor for the first time. In the 1700s, this system would lead to the capitalist-owned factories of the Industrial Revolution.

✓ **Checkpoint** How did the "putting-out" system work?

Mercantilism Arises

European monarchs enjoyed the benefits of the commercial revolution. In the fierce competition for trade and empire, they adopted a new economic policy, known as **mercantilism,** aimed at strengthening their national economies. Mercantilists believed that a nation's real wealth was measured in its gold and silver treasure. To build its supply of gold and silver, they said, a nation must export more goods than it imported.

The Role of Colonies To mercantilists, overseas colonies existed for the benefit of the parent country. They provided resources and raw materials not available in Europe. In turn, they enriched a parent country by serving as a market for its manufactured goods. To achieve these goals, European powers passed strict laws regulating trade with their colonies. Colonists could not set up their own industries to manufacture goods. They were also forbidden to buy goods from a foreign country. In addition, only ships from the parent country or the colonies themselves could be used to send goods in or out of the colonies.

Increasing National Wealth Mercantilists urged rulers to adopt policies that they believed would increase national wealth and government revenues. To boost production, governments exploited mineral and timber resources, built roads, and backed new industries. They imposed national currencies and established standard weights and measures.

Governments also sold monopolies to large producers in certain industries as well as to big overseas trading companies. Finally, they imposed **tariffs,** or taxes on imported goods. Tariffs were designed to protect local industries from foreign competition by increasing the price of imported goods. All of these measures led to the rise of national economies, in which national governments had a lot of control over their economies. However, modern economists debate whether mercantilist measures actually made nations wealthier.

Impact on European Society By the 1700s, European societies were still divided into distinct social classes. Merchants who invested in overseas ventures acquired wealth, while the price revolution hurt nobles, whose wealth was in land. Economic changes took generations, even centuries, to be felt by the majority of Europeans, who were still peasants. The merchants and skilled workers of Europe's growing cities thrived. Middle-class families enjoyed a comfortable life. In contrast, hired laborers and those who served the middle and upper classes often lived in crowded quarters on the edge of poverty.

✓ **Checkpoint** How did economic changes affect different Europeans?

A Dutch Merchant Family
Dutch artist Adriaen van Ostade painted this scene of a Dutch family in the mid-1600s. With the Netherlands' trading wealth, even middle-class families could afford fine clothes, luxury goods, and paintings.

Progress Monitoring *Online*
For: Self-quiz with vocabulary practice
Web Code: nba-1551

SECTION 5 Assessment

Terms, People, and Places
1. For each term, person, or place listed at the beginning of the section, write a sentence explaining its significance.

Note Taking
2. **Reading Skill: Recognize Sequence** Use your completed flowcharts to answer the Focus Question: How did the voyages of European explorers lead to new economic systems in Europe and its colonies?

Comprehension and Critical Thinking
3. **Identify Point of View** How might a Native American assess the impact—both positive and negative—of the Columbian Exchange?
4. **Draw Inferences** What characteristics must a society have in order for capitalism to be possible?
5. **Identify Assumptions** What basic assumption did mercantilists hold about their colonies?
6. **Synthesize Information** Why did the economic changes of the time have little impact on many Europeans?

● **Writing About History**
Quick Write: Write the Body and Conclusion The body of a compare-and-contrast essay should include specific evidence to support your thesis. Suppose that you are comparing the effects of global contact on European merchants and European peasants. Find evidence in this section that you can use to make this comparison.

Transforming the World:
The Columbian Exchange

Christopher Columbus's landing in the Americas in 1492, and his later voyages, revolutionized the world. European ships—heading both to and from the Americas—carried animals, food plants, and diseases that transformed lives and ways of life around the world. Hundreds of years after the Columbian Exchange began, the patterns of people's lives still reflect the influence of those early European voyages of exploration.

NORTH AMERICA

Atlantic Ocean

SOUTH AMERICA

Barley, a grain cultivated by the ancient Egyptians, is widely used in the Americas to feed livestock. ▼

From the Western Hemisphere
Corn
Potatoes
Sweet potatoes
Beans
Peanuts
Squash
Pumpkins
Chili peppers
Turkeys
Pineapples
Tomatoes
Cocoa
Cassava/Manioc
Silver
Quinine
Sunflowers

Originally from India, chickens and their eggs shaped diets worldwide—adding nutrition that boosted population growth. ▼

A Cuban man plows a field with oxen, work animals brought to the Americas from Africa and Asia. ▼

▲ Native to Asia, goats provide milk and wool to people throughout both hemispheres.

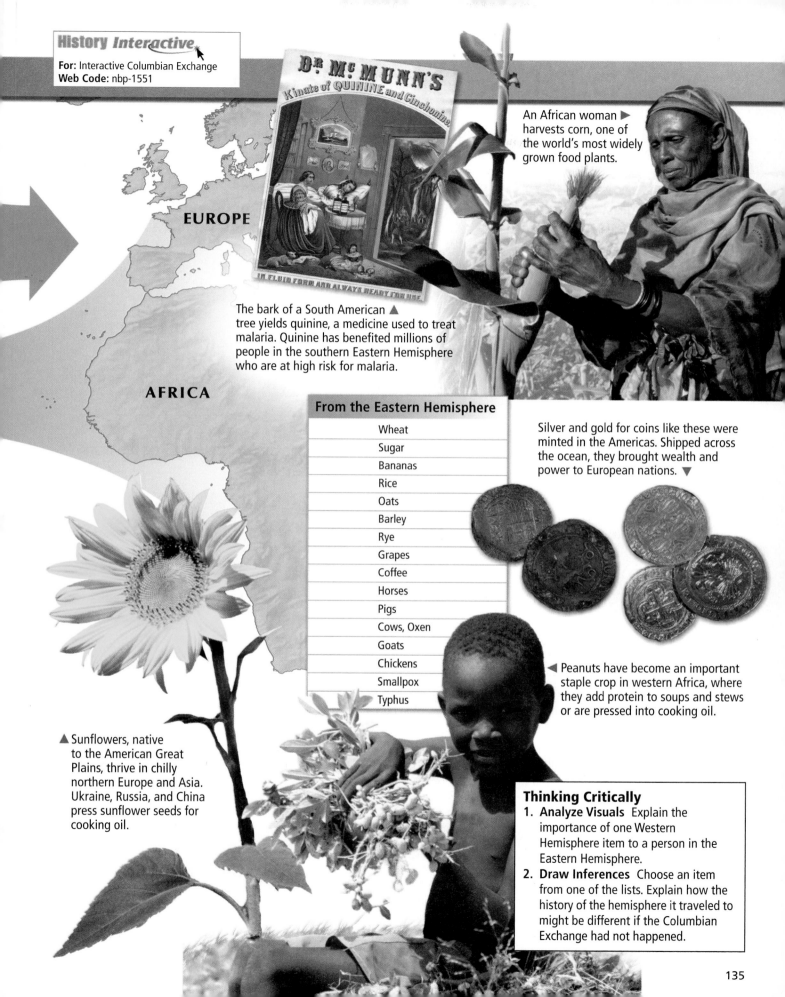

DR. McMUNN'S
Kinate of QUININE and Cinchonine

IN FLUID FORM AND ALWAYS READY FOR USE

EUROPE

AFRICA

The bark of a South American ▲
tree yields quinine, a medicine used to treat
malaria. Quinine has benefited millions of
people in the southern Eastern Hemisphere
who are at high risk for malaria.

An African woman ▶
harvests corn, one of
the world's most widely
grown food plants.

From the Eastern Hemisphere
Wheat
Sugar
Bananas
Rice
Oats
Barley
Rye
Grapes
Coffee
Horses
Pigs
Cows, Oxen
Goats
Chickens
Smallpox
Typhus

Silver and gold for coins like these were
minted in the Americas. Shipped across
the ocean, they brought wealth and
power to European nations. ▼

◀ Peanuts have become an important
staple crop in western Africa, where
they add protein to soups and stews
or are pressed into cooking oil.

▲ Sunflowers, native
to the American Great
Plains, thrive in chilly
northern Europe and Asia.
Ukraine, Russia, and China
press sunflower seeds for
cooking oil.

Thinking Critically
1. **Analyze Visuals** Explain the
   importance of one Western
   Hemisphere item to a person in the
   Eastern Hemisphere.
2. **Draw Inferences** Choose an item
   from one of the lists. Explain how the
   history of the hemisphere it traveled to
   might be different if the Columbian
   Exchange had not happened.

135

Quick Study Guide

CHAPTER 3

Progress Monitoring *Online*
For: Self-test with vocabulary practice
Web Code: nba-1561

■ Key Elements of Europe's Commercial Revolution

- **Columbian Exchange** Foods, ideas, and technologies are exchanged between the hemispheres, resulting in population growth.
- **Inflation** Rising prices occur along with an increase in the money supply.
- **Price Revolution** Rising prices are coupled with inflation.
- **Capitalism** People invest money to make a profit.
- **Mercantilism** European countries adopt mercantilist policies—such as establishing colonies, increasing exports, and limiting imports—to compete for trade and empire.

■ Major European Settlements/ Colonies in the Americas

Date	Region Settled	Country	Purpose
1520s	Mexico	Spain	Find gold
1530s	Peru	Spain	Find gold
1530s	Brazil	Portugal	Establish settlements and plantations
Early 1500s	New France (eastern Canada)	France	Take part in fur trade and fishing
Early 1600s	13 colonies (present-day eastern United States)	England	Various reasons including establishing settlements and escaping religious persecution

■ Triangular Trade Routes

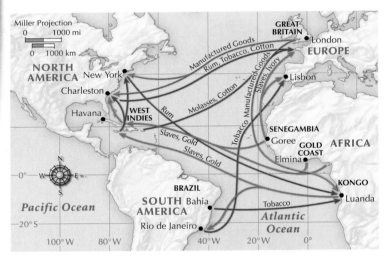

■ The Native American Population Declines

Native American Population of Central Mexico

SOURCE: Nicolás Sánchez-Albornoz, *The Population of Latin America*

■ Europe and the Americas, 1492–1750

1492 Columbus lands in the Americas.

1521 Cortés completes conquest of the Aztecs.

1530s Cartier explores the St. Lawrence River, claiming eastern Canada for France.

1607 British colonists found Jamestown, Virginia.

Chapter Events
Global Events

1500   1550   1600

1498 Portuguese explorer da Gama rounds Africa and reaches India.

1526 The Mughal dynasty is founded in India.

136

Concept | Connector

■ Cumulative Review

Record the answers to the questions below on your Concept Connector worksheets. In addition, record information from this chapter about the following concept:

• Genocide: Native Americans

1. **Empire** Compare the establishment of the Spanish empire in the Americas with the establishment of the Roman empire. How were they similar and different? Think about the role of
   • imperialism
   • technology
   • disease
   • methods of rule
   • religion

2. **Trade** The slave trade reached its height after the age of exploration, when overseas colonies established by Europeans required huge numbers of laborers to grow cash crops. However, the slave trade had existed long before this time period. Think about the early slave trade that occurred in ancient Egypt, Greece, and Rome, as well as in the Muslim world. Compare those examples with the Atlantic slave trade of the 1700s and 1800s.

3. **Economic Systems** In the 1700s, European nations adopted the economic policy of mercantilism in order to gain wealth and build empires. Mercantilism depended heavily on the establishment of overseas colonies. How did mercantilism differ from the manorialism practiced in medieval times? Consider the following:
   • the roles of colonists and serfs
   • the purposes of self-sufficiency and profit-making
   • the global impact

■ Connections to Today

1. **Cultural Diffusion** During the Columbian Exchange, people were exposed to goods, ideas, and diseases that changed their lives forever. Many of these exchanges were positive, such as the introduction of the horse to the Americas. Some were negative, such as the introduction of European diseases to the Americas. Think about similar exchanges that have happened in recent times. Research and write about a positive exchange and a negative exchange. To direct your research, consider topics such as disease, new technology, the introduction of fish or animals into non-native regions, and the availability of new foods.

2. **Trade** Throughout history, people and governments have worked to establish profitable trade methods. Some very successful trade methods have had terrible consequences for other people. Consider how Europe's commercial revolution was achieved in large part because of the Atlantic slave trade. Then think about trade practices today that, though profitable, might hurt some people. Write two to three paragraphs describing the pros and cons of modern trade practices. Consider the following:
   • trade pacts like NAFTA
   • voluntary labeling of products such as Fair Trade
   • practices such as child labor

1619
First cargo of African slaves arrives in Virginia.

1750s
Olaudah Equiano writes a book about his experiences during the Atlantic slave trade.

1763
The Treaty of Paris is signed, ending the French and Indian War.

1650

1700

1750

1630s
Japan bars foreign merchants from the country.

1687
Englishman Isaac Newton publishes his book explaining the laws of gravity.

1735
The reign of Chinese emperor Qianlong begins.

History *Interactive*
For: Interactive timeline
Web Code: nbp-1561

Chapter Assessment

Terms, People, and Places

Match the following terms with the definitions listed below.

immunity	inflation
revenue	encomienda
privateer	mutiny

1. the right to demand labor from Native Americans
2. income from taxes
3. rise in prices linked to an increase in the money supply
4. pirate operating under government approval
5. resistance to disease
6. revolt

Main Ideas

Section 1 (pp. 110–114)

7. How did the explorations of conquistadors such as Hernán Cortés and Francisco Pizarro contribute to the Spanish empire in the Americas?
8. What effect did European exploration have on Native American populations?

Section 2 (pp. 115–119)

9. How did Spain structure its American empire?
10. Write a sentence or two explaining the role of each of the following in Spanish colonial society: peon, peninsulare, creole, mulatto, and mestizo.

Section 3 (pp. 120–124)

11. Why did the Pilgrims make a compact when they arrived in North America?
12. What was the result of the British and French struggle in North America?

Section 4 (pp. 125–128)

13. How did triangular trade affect Africans?
14. How did the slave trade benefit Europeans?

Section 5 (pp. 129–133)

15. What impact did American gold and silver have on European economies?
16. How did the policy of mercantilism affect global economies?

Chapter Focus Question

17. How did European colonization of the Americas shape global economies and societies?

Critical Thinking

18. **Compare Points of View** You read that many Native Americans saw the Spanish takeover as a sign that their gods were less powerful than those of the Spanish. How did the Spanish likely interpret their victory?
19. **Predict Consequences** How would society in the United States today be affected if mysterious diseases wiped out 90 percent or more of the population?
20. **Analyzing Visuals** The painting below, titled *First Landing of Columbus*, was painted in 1803. Consider what you have learned in this chapter. Do you think this painting accurately shows that event? Explain your answer.

● Writing About History

Writing a Compare and Contrast Essay The European nations that settled the Americas all wanted wealth and empire—but went about getting them in different ways. Write a compare and contrast essay that discusses two of the European powers involved in settling the Americas. Consult page SH10 of the Writing Handbook for additional help.

Prewriting

- Choose a topic that lends itself to comparison and contrast. Possibilities include important leaders, economic goals, interactions with Native Americans, or religious goals.

- Create graphic organizers, such as tables or Venn diagrams, to help you see similarities and differences.

Drafting

- Write an introduction and a thesis statement. Your thesis statement should summarize the main points you want to make about the things you are comparing.
- Write the body text, introducing details and evidence that support your thesis statement. Organize your text by subject or by point. Then write a conclusion.

Revising

- Use the guidelines for revising your essay on page SH12 of the Writing Handbook.

Document-Based Assessment

The Impact of Piracy

In 1580, Admiral Francis Drake returned to England after circumnavigating the globe. A delighted Queen Elizabeth I knighted the commander when she visited his ship, the *Golden Hind*, in 1581. The British queen had good reason to be grateful. Drake's voyage brought huge revenues to the royal treasury and dealt a blow to her enemy, King Philip II of Spain. The documents below give different views of Drake's activities.

Document A

"Passing the Straits of Magellan, untraversed as yet by any Englishman, [Drake] swept the unguarded coast of [Chile] and Peru, loaded his bark with the gold-dust and silver-ingots of Potosí, and with the pearls, emeralds, and diamonds which formed the cargo of the great galleon that sailed once a year from Lima to Cadiz. With spoils of above half-a-million in value the daring adventurer steered undauntedly for the Moluccas, rounded the Cape of Good Hope, and after completing the circuit of the globe dropped anchor again in Plymouth harbour. . . . The welcome he received from Elizabeth on his return was accepted by Philip as an outrage which could only be expiated [atoned for] by war. . . . She met a request for Drake's surrender by knighting the freebooter, and by wearing in her crown the jewels he had offered her as a present."

—From ***A Short History of the English People*** by J.R. Green

Document B

"[The Ambassador urged his king] . . . that no foreign ship be spared, in . . . the . . . Indies, but that every one should be sent to the bottom, and not a soul on board of them allowed to live. This will be the only way to prevent the English and French from going to these parts to plunder, for at present there is hardly an Englishman who is not talking of undertaking the voyage, so encouraged are they by Drake's return."

—Don Bernardino de Mendoza,
Philip II's ambassador to London, around 1580

Document C

"To Lima we came the 13th of February; and, being entered the haven, we found there about twelve sail of ships lying fast moored at an anchor, having all their sails carried on shore; for the masters and merchants were here most secure, having never been assaulted by enemies, and at this time feared the approach of none such as we were. Our general rifled these ships, and found in one of them a chest full of reals of plate, and good store of silks and linen cloth. . . . In which ship he had news of another ship called the *Cacafuego*, which was gone toward Payta, and that the same ship was laden with treasure. Whereupon we stayed no longer here, but cutting all the cables of the ships in the haven, we let them drive whither they would, either to sea or to the shore; and with all speed we followed the *Cacafuego* which was gone toward Payta. . . ."

—From ***Sir Francis Drake's Famous Voyage
Round the World, 1580*** by Francis Pretty

Document D

Analyzing Documents

Use your knowledge of American colonial history and Documents A, B, C, and D to answer questions 1–4.

1. According to Document A, Drake's exploits in Chile and Peru
   A were not commercially successful.
   B were done impulsively, without Queen Elizabeth's consent or approval.
   C gave King Philip II a reason to start a war against England.
   D met with outrage and anger from Queen Elizabeth and the English-speaking world.

2. According to Document B, what was Don Bernardino de Mendoza's main concern regarding Drake?
   A that Drake would return to the West Indies soon
   B that other seamen would copy Drake's exploits
   C that Spanish seamen would join future Drake expeditions
   D that other nations would join with England against Spain

3. Document D shows Queen Elizabeth I with Francis Drake. Which of the other documents does this one support?
   A Document A
   B Document B
   C Document C
   D Documents A, B, and C

4. **Writing Task** Write a news article about Drake's exploits that might have appeared in a Spanish newspaper around 1580. Use the documents along with information from the chapter to support your article.

A Child Becomes King

In 1643, the five-year-old heir to the French crown, Louis XIV, made his first public appearance. The tiny monarch climbed the throne and sat for hours as officials conducted the ceremony announcing the new reign. Louis XIV had been orphaned as a baby, and was a sickly, shy child. As a child, he would often bring a cat to government councils, stroking the fur as he sat in silence. Despite this quiet beginning, Louis XIV proved to be a strong, able ruler who came to symbolize the period of absolute monarchy we now call the "Age of Absolutism." Listen to the Witness History audio to hear more about this powerful king.

◄ Louis XIV receives foreign ambassadors at his Versailles court in 1678.

A French bishop's official seal

Chapter Preview

Chapter Focus Question What events led to the rise of absolute monarchies and the development of centralized nation-states in Europe?

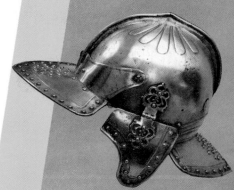

Oliver Cromwell's battle helmet

Section 1
Spanish Power Grows

Section 2
France Under Louis XIV

Section 3
Parliament Triumphs in England

Section 4
Rise of Austria and Prussia

Section 5
Absolute Monarchy in Russia

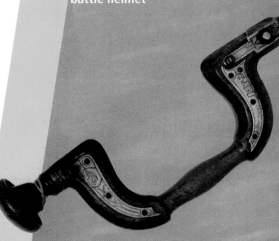

Carpentry tool owned by Peter the Great

> **Note Taking Study Guide *Online***
> **For:** Note Taking and Concept Connector worksheets
> **Web Code:** nbd-1601

Philip II wears royal dress. In the background, his Armada heads to England.

A late 1500s Spanish coin commemorates Philip's rule.

WITNESS HISTORY 🔊 AUDIO

A Working Monarch

"It is best to keep an eye on everything," Philip II of Spain often said—and he meant it. As king of the most powerful nation in Europe, he gave little time to pleasure. Instead, he plowed through a mountain of paperwork each day, making notes on even the most trivial matters. But Philip's determination to "keep an eye on everything" extended far beyond trivia. It helped him build Spain into a strong centralized state. By the late 1500s, he had concentrated all power in his own hands. Over the next 200 years, other European monarchs would pursue similar goals.

Focus Question How did Philip II extend Spain's power and help establish a golden age?

Spanish Power Grows

Objectives

- Describe the empire that Charles V inherited.
- Analyze how Spanish power increased under Philip II.
- Explain how the arts flourished during Spain's golden age.

Terms, People, and Places

Hapsburg empire	divine right
Charles V	armada
Philip II	El Greco
absolute monarch	Miguel de Cervantes

Note Taking

Reading Skill: Identify Main Ideas and Supporting Details As you read about how Philip II extended Spanish power, create an outline to record details that support the main ideas in this section. This example will help you get started.

I. Charles V Inherits Two Crowns
  A. Ruling the Hapsburg Empire
    1. Spain
    2. Holy Roman Empire and Netherlands
  B. Charles V abdicates

By the 1500s, Spain had shaken off its feudal past and emerged as the first modern European power. Queen Isabella and King Ferdinand had unified the country, enforced religious unity, and commanded the Spanish conquest of the Americas.

Charles V Inherits Two Crowns

In 1516, Ferdinand and Isabella's grandson, Charles I, became king of Spain, and thereby ruler of the Spanish colonies in the Americas as well.

Ruling the Hapsburg Empire When his other grandfather died in 1519, Charles I also became heir to the sprawling **Hapsburg empire,** which included the Holy Roman Empire and the Netherlands. As ruler of this empire, Charles took the name **Charles V.** Historians now usually refer to him by this title.

Ruling two empires involved Charles in constant warfare. As a devout Catholic, he fought to suppress Protestantism in the German states. After years of religious conflict, however, Charles was forced to allow the German princes to choose their own religion.

Charles also faced the Muslim Ottoman empire, which was based in Turkey but stretched across the Balkans. Under Suleiman, Ottoman forces advanced across central Europe to the walls surrounding Vienna, Austria. Although Austria held firm during the siege, the Ottomans occupied much of Hungary following their crushing victory at the Battle of Mohács. Ottoman naval forces also continued to challenge Spanish power in the Mediterranean.

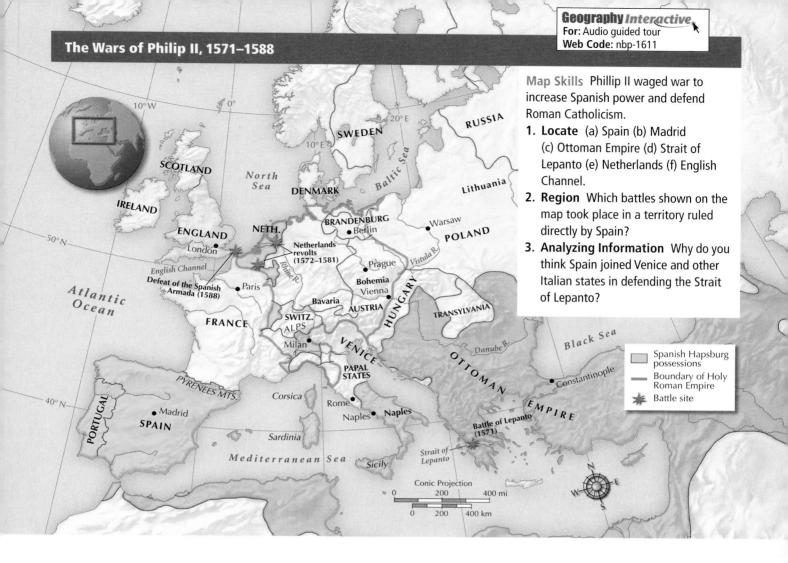

The Wars of Philip II, 1571–1588

Geography *Interactive*
For: Audio guided tour
Web Code: nbp-1611

Map Skills Phillip II waged war to increase Spanish power and defend Roman Catholicism.

1. **Locate** (a) Spain (b) Madrid (c) Ottoman Empire (d) Strait of Lepanto (e) Netherlands (f) English Channel.
2. **Region** Which battles shown on the map took place in a territory ruled directly by Spain?
3. **Analyzing Information** Why do you think Spain joined Venice and other Italian states in defending the Strait of Lepanto?

Legend:
- Spanish Hapsburg possessions
- Boundary of Holy Roman Empire
- Battle site

Charles V Abdicates The Hapsburg empire proved to be too scattered and <u>cumbersome</u> for any one person to rule effectively. Exhausted and disillusioned, Charles V gave up his titles and entered a monastery in 1556. He divided his empire, leaving the Hapsburg lands in central Europe to his brother Ferdinand, who became Holy Roman emperor. He gave Spain, the Netherlands, some southern Italian states, and Spain's overseas empire to his 29-year-old son Philip, who became Philip II.

✔ **Checkpoint** Why did Charles V divide the Hapsburg Empire?

Philip II Solidifies Power

During his 42-year reign, **Philip II** expanded Spanish influence, strengthened the Catholic Church, and made his own power absolute. Thanks in part to silver from Spanish colonies in the Americas, he made Spain the foremost power in Europe.

Centralizing Power Like his father, Philip II was hard working, devout, and ambitious. Unlike many other monarchs, Philip devoted most of his time to government work. He seldom hunted, never jousted, and lived as simply as a monk. The King's isolated, somber palace outside Madrid, known as the Escorial (es kohr YAHL), reflected his character. It served as a church, a residence, and a tomb for the royal family.

Vocabulary Builder

<u>cumbersome</u>—(KUM bur sum) *adj.* hard to handle because of size, weight, or many parts

PHILIP II AND THE RISE OF SPAIN

Philip II's Marriages

Maria	Mary Tudor	Elizabeth Valois	Anna
Alliance: Portugal	Alliance: England	Alliance: France	Alliance: Austria

In his pursuit of building and extending Spanish power, Philip II had many tools in his arsenal. Marriage was one. To build important alliances—and to pacify potential enemies—he married a total of four times, gaining power and in some cases additional territory. Yet because alliances lasted only as long as the marriage, and Renaissance women often did not live long, Philip needed other ways to expand Spain's power. War was another useful strategy, it gained him the kingdom of Portugal and established him as the defender of the Roman Catholic Church. Wealth was perhaps his most important tool. Silver and gold from his colonies in the Americas fueled the Spanish economy and ensured Spanish power.

Philip's marriage to Mary Tudor in 1554 created an alliance with England until Mary's death four years later. ▼

The Spanish melted down Native American gold ornaments like this one to make Spanish coins like those above. ▲

Philip's victory against the Turks in the Battle of Lepanto assured his role as defender of the Catholic Church. ▼

Thinking Critically
1. **Apply Information** What various purposes could royal marriages serve during the age of absolutism?
2. **Understand Cause and Effect** How did Philip's colonies in the Americas affect his goals for Spain?

Philip surpassed Ferdinand and Isabella in making every part of the government responsible to him. He reigned as an **absolute monarch,** a ruler with complete authority over the government and the lives of the people. Like other European rulers, Philip asserted that he ruled by **divine right.** That is, he believed that his authority to rule came directly from God. Philip therefore saw himself as the guardian of the Roman Catholic Church. The great undertaking of his life was to defend the Catholic Reformation and turn back the rising Protestant tide in Europe. Within his empire, Philip enforced religious unity, turning the Inquisition against Protestants and other people thought to be heretics.

Battles in the Mediterranean and the Netherlands Philip fought many wars as he attempted to advance Spanish Catholic power. In the Mediterranean, the Ottoman empire continued to pose a threat to European control of the region. At the Battle of Lepanto in 1571, Spain and its Italian allies soundly defeated an Ottoman fleet off the coast of Greece. Although the Ottoman Empire would remain a major power in the Mediterranean region for three more centuries, Christians still hailed the battle as a great victory and a demonstration of Spain's power.

During the last half of his reign, Philip battled rebels in the Netherlands. At the time, the region included 17 provinces that are today Belgium, the Netherlands, and Luxembourg. It was the richest part of Philip's empire. Protestants in the region resisted Philip's efforts to crush their faith. Protestants and Catholics alike opposed high taxes and autocratic Spanish rule, which threatened local traditions of self-government.

In the 1560s, riots against the Inquisition sparked a general uprising in the Netherlands. Savage fighting raged for decades. In 1581, the northern, largely Protestant provinces declared their independence from Spain and became known as the Dutch Netherlands. They did not gain official recognition, however, until 1648. The southern, mostly Catholic provinces of the Netherlands remained part of the Spanish Empire.

The Armada Sails Against England By the 1580s, Philip saw England's Queen Elizabeth I as his chief Protestant enemy. First secretly, then openly, Elizabeth had supported the Dutch against Spain. She encouraged English captains such as Francis Drake, known as sea dogs, to plunder Spanish treasure ships and loot Spanish cities in the Americas. To Philip's dismay, Elizabeth made the pirate Drake a knight.

To end English attacks and subdue the Dutch, Philip prepared a huge **armada,** or fleet, to carry a Spanish invasion force to England. In 1588, the Spanish Armada sailed with more than 130 ships, 20,000 men, and 2,400 pieces of artillery. The Spanish were confident of victory. "When we meet the English," predicted one Spanish commander, "God will surely arrange matters so that we can grapple and board them, either by sending some strange freak of weather or, more likely, just by depriving the English of their wits."

This prediction did not come to pass. In the English Channel, lumbering Spanish ships were outmaneuvered by the lighter, faster English ships. Strong winds favored the English, scattering the Armada. After further disasters at sea, the tattered remnants limped home in defeat.

An Empire Declines The defeat of the Armada marked the beginning of the end of Spanish power. Throughout the 1600s, Spain's strength and prosperity decreased. One reason for this decline was that Philip II's successors ruled far less ably than he had.

Spain Loses Territory
The Treaty of Munster, signed in 1648, recognized the independence of the Netherlands' Protestant provinces.

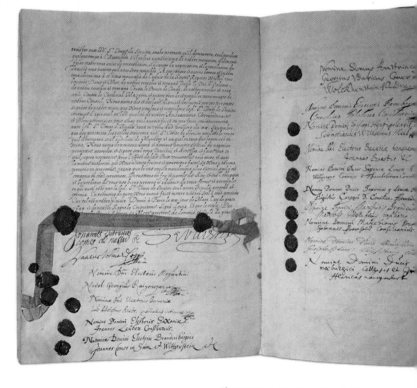

View of Toledo
El Greco's painting shows the Spanish city of Toledo, where he lived for 40 years. This is El Greco's only landscape painting. *How does El Greco express religious themes in this painting?*

Economic problems were also to blame. Costly overseas wars drained wealth out of Spain almost as fast as it came in. Treasure from the Americas led Spain to neglect farming and commerce. The government heavily taxed the small middle class, weakening a group that in other European nations supported royal power. The expulsion of Muslims and Jews from Spain deprived the economy of many skilled artisans and merchants. Finally, the influx of American gold and silver led to soaring inflation.

As Spain's power dwindled in the 1600s and 1700s, Dutch, English, and French fleets challenged—and eventually surpassed—Spanish power both in Europe and around the world.

✓ **Checkpoint** What were Philip II's motivations for waging war?

Spain's Golden Age

The century from 1550 to 1650 is often referred to as Spain's *Siglo de Oro* (SEEG loh day OHR oh), or "golden century," for the brilliance of its arts and literature. Philip II was an enthusiastic patron of the arts and also founded academies of science and mathematics.

Among the famous painters of this period was a man called **El Greco,** meaning "the Greek." Though not Spanish by birth, El Greco is considered to be a master of Spanish painting. Born on the Greek island of Crete, El Greco had studied in Italy before settling in Spain. He produced haunting religious pictures and striking portraits of Spanish nobles. El Greco's use of vibrant colors influenced the work of Diego Velázquez (vuh LAHS kes), court painter to King Philip IV. Velázquez is perhaps best known for his vivid portraits of Spanish royalty.

Spain's golden century produced several outstanding writers. Lope de Vega (LOH pay duh VAY guh), a peasant by birth, wrote more than 1,500 plays, including witty comedies and action-packed romances. **Miguel de Cervantes** (sur VAN teez) was the most important writer of Spain's golden age. His *Don Quixote*, which pokes fun at medieval tales of chivalry, is considered to be Europe's first modern novel. Although *Don Quixote* mocks the traditions of Spain's feudal past, Cervantes depicts with affection both the foolish but heroic idealism of Don Quixote and the unromantic, earthy realism of his sidekick, Sancho Panza.

✓ **Checkpoint** What was the *Siglo de Oro?*

SECTION 1 Assessment

Progress Monitoring *Online*
For: Self-quiz with vocabulary practice
Web Code: nba-1611

Terms, People, and Places

1. For each term, person, or place listed at the beginning of the section, write a sentence explaining its significance.

Note Taking

2. **Reading Skill: Identify Main Ideas and Supporting Details** Use your completed outline to answer the Focus Question: How did Philip II extend Spain's power and help establish a golden age?

Comprehension and Critical Thinking

3. **Compare and Contrast** How were Charles V and Philip II alike and different in their goals of ensuring absolute power and strengthening Catholicism?

4. **Synthesize Information** Why did Spanish power and prosperity decline?

5. **Summarize** Why is the period from 1550 to 1650 considered Spain's golden age?

● **Writing About History**

Quick Write: Generate Arguments
Choose a topic from this section that could be the subject of a persuasive essay—for example, whether England was really a threat to Spain. Then write two thesis statements, one arguing each side of your topic. Make sure that the arguments clearly explain opposite or differing opinions on the topic.

Don Quixote by Miguel de Cervantes

Although the age of chivalry had long passed, stories about knights-errant were still popular in the early 1600s. The heroes of these stories were brave knights who traveled far and wide performing noble deeds. Miguel de Cervantes's novel *Don Quixote* satirizes such romances. His hero, the elderly Don Quixote, has read too many tales of chivalry. Imagining himself a knight-errant, he sets out across the Spanish countryside with his practical servant, Sancho Panza. In this famous excerpt, Don Quixote's noble motives give dignity to his foolish battle with the windmills.

▲ Miguel de Cervantes

▼ An illustration from *Don Quixote* shows Sancho Panza shouting after his master, who is battling windmills.

Just then they came in sight of thirty or forty windmills that rise from that plain, and no sooner did Don Quixote see them than he said to his squire: "Fortune is guiding our affairs better than we ourselves could have wished. Do you see over yonder, friend Sancho, thirty or forty hulking giants? I intend to do battle with them and slay them. With the spoils we shall begin to be rich, for this is a righteous war. . . ."

"What giants?" asked Sancho Panza.

"Those you see over there," replied his master, "with the long arms; some of them have them well-nigh[1] two leagues in length."

"Take care, sir," cried Sancho. "Those over there are not giants but windmills, and those things that seem to be armed are their sails, which when they are whirled around by the wind turn the millstone."

"It is clear," replied Don Quixote, "that you are not experienced in adventures. Those are giants, and if you are afraid, turn aside and pray whilst I enter into fierce and unequal battle with them."

Uttering these words, he clapped spurs to Rozinante, his steed, without heeding the cries of his squire, Sancho, who warned him that he was not going to attack giants, but windmills. But so convinced was he that they were giants that he neither heard his squire's shouts nor did he notice what they were, though he was very near them. Instead, he rushed on, shouting in a loud voice: "Fly not, cowards and vile caitliffs[2]; one knight alone attacks you!" At that moment a slight breeze arose and the great sails began to move. . . .

He ran his lance into the sail, but the wind twisted it with such violence that it shivered the lance in pieces and dragged both rider and horse after it, rolling them over and over on the ground, sorely damaged.

Thinking Critically

1. **Synthesize Information** What values of chivalry motivate Don Quixote's attack on the windmills?
2. **Analyze Literature** How does Cervantes show both sides of Don Quixote—the noble and the foolish—in this excerpt?

1. **well-nigh** (wel ny) *adv.* nearly
2. **caitliff** (KAYT lif) *n.* cowardly person

Louis XIV rides a powerful horse, displaying his strength and abilities.

A delicate, beaded shoe from Louis's era

Life at Versailles

At Versailles, the palace court of Louis XIV, life revolved around the king. Nobles waited days or weeks for the honor of attending the king while he dressed or bathed. Every evening the king was at the center of a lavish entertainment, followed by a supper of dozens of rich dishes. The elaborate and extravagant rituals that governed life at court masked a very serious purpose—they were a way for Louis XIV to control every aspect of court life and ensure his absolute authority.

Focus Question How did France become the leading power of Europe under the absolute rule of Louis XIV?

France Under Louis XIV

Objectives

- Understand how Henry IV rebuilt France after the wars of religion.
- Explain how Louis XIV became an absolute monarch.
- Describe how Versailles was a symbol of royal power.
- Identify Louis XIV's successes and failures.

Terms, People, and Places

Huguenots	intendant
Henry IV	Jean-Baptiste Colbert
Edict of Nantes	Versailles
Cardinal Richelieu	*levée*
Louis XIV	balance of power

N̲o̲te Taking

Reading Skill: Identify Supporting Details As you read about the rule of Louis XIV and how he strengthened the monarchy, use a concept web like the one below to record details that support the main ideas in this section. Add as many circles as you need.

In the last half of the fifteenth century, France enjoyed a period of peace. After driving out the English, the French kings were able to solidify their power within their own realm. But in the 1500s, rivalry with Charles V of Spain and then religious conflict plunged the kingdom into turmoil.

Henry IV Restores Order

In the late 1500s France was torn apart by turbulent wars of religion. A century later, France was a strong, unified nation-state ruled by the most powerful monarch in Europe.

Religious Strife From the 1560s to the 1590s, religious wars between the Catholic majority and French Protestants, called **Huguenots** (HYOO guh nahts), tore France apart. Leaders on both sides used the strife to further their own ambitions.

The worst incident began on St. Bartholomew's Day (a Catholic holiday), August 24, 1572. While Huguenot and Catholic nobles were gathered for a royal wedding, a plot by Catholic royals led to the massacre of 3,000 Huguenots. In the next few days, thousands more were slaughtered. For many, the St. Bartholomew's Day Massacre symbolized the complete breakdown of order in France.

Bringing Peace to a Shattered Land In 1589, a Huguenot prince inherited the French throne as **Henry IV.** For four years Henry fought against fierce Catholic opposition to gain control of France. Finally, to end the conflict, he converted to Catholicism. "Paris is well worth a Mass," he is supposed to have said. To protect Protestants, however, in 1598 he issued the **Edict of Nantes** granting the Huguenots religious toleration and other freedoms.

Henry IV then set out to repair France. His goal, he said, was not the victory of one sect over another, but "a chicken in every pot"—a good Sunday dinner for every peasant. Under Henry, the government reached into every area of French life. Royal officials administered justice, improved roads, built bridges, and revived agriculture. By building the royal bureaucracy and reducing the influence of nobles, Henry IV laid the foundations on which future French monarchs would build absolute power.

Cardinal Richelieu Strengthens Royal Authority When Henry IV was killed by an assassin in 1610, his nine-year-old son, Louis XIII, inherited the throne. For a time, nobles reasserted their power. Then, in 1624, Louis appointed Cardinal Richelieu (ree shul YOO) as his chief minister. This cunning, capable leader devoted the next 18 years to strengthening the central government.

Richelieu sought to destroy the power of the Huguenots and nobles—two groups that did not bow to royal authority. Although he allowed the Huguenots to practice their religion, he smashed their walled cities and outlawed their armies. Likewise, he defeated the private armies of the nobles and destroyed their fortified castles. While reducing their independence, Richelieu tied the nobles to the king by giving them high posts at court or in the royal army.

Richelieu also handpicked his able successor, Cardinal Mazarin (ma za RAN). When five-year-old Louis XIV inherited the throne in 1643, the year after Richelieu's death, Mazarin was in place to serve as chief minister. Like Richelieu, Mazarin worked tirelessly to extend royal power.

✔ **Checkpoint** What rights did the Edict of Nantes extend to Huguenots?

An Absolute Monarch Rises

Soon after Louis XIV became king, disorder again swept France. In an uprising called the *Fronde*, nobles, merchants, peasants, and the urban poor each rebelled in order to protest royal power or preserve their own. On one occasion, rioters drove the boy king from his palace. It was an experience Louis would never forget. When Mazarin died in 1661, the 23-year-old Louis resolved to take complete control over the government himself. "I have been pleased to entrust the government of my affairs to the late Cardinal," he declared. "It is now time that I govern them myself."

"I Am the State" Like his great-grandfather Philip II of Spain, Louis XIV firmly believed in his divine right to rule. He took the sun as the symbol of his absolute power. Just as the sun stands at the center of the solar system, he argued, so the Sun King stands at the center of the nation. Louis is often quoted as saying, *"L'état, c'est moi"* (lay TAH seh MWAH), which in English translates as "I am the state."

During his reign, Louis did not once call a meeting of the Estates General, the medieval council made up of representatives of all French social classes. In fact, the Estates General did not meet between 1614 and 1789. Thus, the Estates General played no role in checking royal power.

● BIOGRAPHY

Cardinal Richelieu
Armand Richelieu's (1585–1642) parents expected great things from him. They even invited the king of France to attend Armand's christening, promising that someday he would be a leader of France.

The young boy also aspired to greatness as he was growing up. At first, he received training to become a disciplined and authoritative military officer. Then, at his family's request, he switched direction. At age 17, he began training to become a bishop in the Catholic Church. The path was different but the purpose was the same: to become a leader and to serve the monarch.

Over the next 40 years, Armand Richelieu rose to the highest levels of authority in both religious and political circles. He became the true power behind the throne of King Louis XIII. **What characteristics of Richelieu does the artist portray in this painting?**

Louis XIV Strengthens Royal Power Louis spent many hours each day attending to government affairs. To strengthen the state, he followed the policies of Richelieu. He expanded the bureaucracy and appointed **intendants,** royal officials who collected taxes, recruited soldiers, and carried out his policies in the provinces. These and other government jobs often went to wealthy middle-class men. In this way Louis cemented his ties with the middle class, thus checking the power of the nobles and the Church. The king also built the French army into the strongest in Europe. The state paid, fed, trained, and supplied up to 300,000 soldiers. Louis used this highly disciplined army to enforce his policies at home and abroad.

Colbert Builds France's Finances Louis's brilliant finance minister, **Jean-Baptiste Colbert** (kohl behr), imposed mercantilist policies to bolster the economy. He had new lands cleared for farming, encouraged mining and other basic industries, and built up luxury trades such as lacemaking. To protect French manufacturers, Colbert put high tariffs on imported goods. He also fostered overseas colonies, such as New France in North America, and regulated trade with the colonies to enrich the royal treasury. Colbert's policies helped make France the wealthiest state in Europe. Yet not even the financial genius of Colbert could produce enough income to support the huge costs of Louis's court and his many foreign wars.

 Checkpoint Why did Louis XIV choose the sun as his symbol?

Versailles: Symbol of Royal Power

In the countryside near Paris, Louis XIV turned a royal hunting lodge into the immense palace of **Versailles** (ver SY). He spared no expense to make it the most magnificent building in Europe. Its halls and salons displayed the finest paintings and statues, and they glittered with chandeliers and mirrors. In the royal gardens, millions of flowers, trees, and fountains were set out in precise geometric patterns. Versailles became the perfect symbol of the Sun King's wealth and power. As both the king's home and the seat of government, it housed nobles, officials, and servants.

Conducting Court Ceremonies Louis XIV perfected elaborate ceremonies that emphasized his own importance. Each day began in the king's bedroom with a major ritual known as the *levée* (luh VAY), or rising. High-ranking nobles competed for the honor of holding the royal washbasin or handing the king his diamond-buckled shoes. At night, the ceremony was repeated in reverse. Wives of nobles vied to attend upon women of the royal family.

Rituals such as the *levée* served a serious purpose. French nobles were descendants of the feudal lords who held power in medieval times. At liberty on their estates, these nobles were a threat to the power of the monarchy. By luring nobles to Versailles, Louis turned them into courtiers angling for privileges rather than rival warriors battling for power. His tactic worked because he carefully protected their prestige and left them exempt from paying taxes.

The Sun King developed his philosophy of absolutism with the help of a brilliant bishop named Jacques Bénigne Bossuet (1627–1704). In his writings, Bossuet argued that the Bible shows that a monarch rules by the will of God. Therefore, opposition to the monarch is a sin. Bossuet also believed that, although the monarch should rule absolutely, it was God's will that he or she act only in the best interest of the nation. **According to Bossuet, what is the role of a king?**

Primary Source

66 The royal power is absolute. . . . The prince need render account of his acts to no one. . . . Without this absolute authority [he] could neither do good nor repress evil. It is necessary that his power be such that no one can hope to escape him. . . . The prince . . . is not regarded as a private person: he is a public personage, all the state is in him; the will of all the people is included in his. As all perfection and all strength are united in God, so all the power of individuals is united in the person of the prince.99

—Bishop Jacques Bénigne Bossuet, "Politics Drawn from the Very Words of Scripture," 1679

Separate Classes
LIFE IN FRANCE IN THE 1600s

It is no surprise that the life of Louis XIV is central to French history. Historians and social observers wrote volumes about this larger-than-life king, and buildings like Versailles survive as testaments to his legacy. Yet the vast majority of French people were not nobles, and never set foot in Versailles. They performed various jobs, from artisan, to soldier, to merchant. Rather than fancy balls, they enjoyed street plays and cockfights. Many were peasants, living hard and simple lives in the countryside. All of these people paid heavy taxes that supported the nobles' lavish lifestyles.

▲ A noblewoman is dressed in the romantic style of the time. French monarchs used Versailles' Hall of Mirrors, in the background above, for political and social ceremonies. In the foreground is a richly embroidered bag that a noble may have owned.

Women in the lower classes, like the woman below, might have been field workers, street vendors, or maids for noble families. In the background, French villagers tend livestock and wash clothes. ▼

"In France, nine-tenths of the people die of hunger, one-tenth of indigestion."

—Italian ambassador to Louis's court

Thinking Critically
1. **Draw Inferences** Read the quotation. Judging from the quotation, what is the speaker's view of the differences between nobles and commoners?
2. **Draw Conclusions** Why are the lives of nobles and royalty better documented than those of commoners?

Patronizing the Arts The king and his court supported a "splendid century" of the arts. The age of Louis XIV came to be known as the classical age of French drama. In painting, music, architecture, and decorative arts, French styles became the model for all Europe. A new form of dance drama, ballet, gained its first great popularity at the French court. As a leading patron of culture, Louis sponsored the French Academies, which set high standards for both the arts and the sciences.

✔ **Checkpoint** How did Louis XIV secure support from the nobility?

A Strong State Declines

Louis XIV ruled France for 72 years—far longer than any other monarch. At the end of Louis's reign, France was the strongest state in Europe. However, some of Louis's decisions eventually caused France's prosperity to erode.

Vocabulary Builder

erode—(ee ROHD) v. wear away or disintegrate

Waging Costly Wars Louis XIV poured vast resources into wars meant to expand French borders. However, rival rulers joined forces to check these ambitions. Led by the Dutch or the English, these alliances fought to maintain the **balance of power.** The goal was to maintain a distribution of military and economic power among European nations to prevent any one country from dominating the region.

In 1700, Louis's grandson Philip V inherited the throne of Spain. To maintain the balance of power, neighboring nations led by England fought to prevent the union of France and Spain. The War of the Spanish Succession dragged on until 1713, when an exhausted France signed the Treaty of Utrecht (YOO trekt). Philip remained on the Spanish throne, but France agreed never to unite the two crowns.

Persecuting Huguenots Louis saw France's Protestant minority as a threat to religious and political unity. In 1685, he revoked the Edict of Nantes. More than 100,000 Huguenots fled France, settling mainly in England, the Netherlands, Germany, Poland, and the Americas. The Huguenots had been among the hardest working and most prosperous of Louis's subjects. Their loss was a serious blow to the French economy, just as the expulsion of Spanish Muslims and Jews had hurt Spain.

✔ **Checkpoint** How did Louis's actions weaken France's economy?

SECTION 2 Assessment

Progress Monitoring Online
For: Self-quiz with vocabulary practice
Web Code: nba-1621

Terms, People, and Places
1. What do each of the key terms, people, and places listed at the beginning of the section have in common? Explain.

Note Taking
2. **Reading Skill: Identify Supporting Details** Use your completed concept web to answer the Focus Question: How did France become the leading power of Europe under the absolute rule of Louis XIV?

Comprehension and Critical Thinking
3. **Draw Inferences** How did Henry IV's conversion to Catholicism help France unite?
4. **Identify Central Issues** What was the purpose of Louis XIV's extravagant palace and daily rituals?
5. **Recognize Ideologies** Why did other European nations form alliances to oppose France's plans to expand?

● **Writing About History**

Quick Write: Support Opinions With Evidence Choose a topic from the section, such as whether or not you think Louis XIV's reign was good for France. Make a list of evidence from the text that supports your opinion.

Political Systems

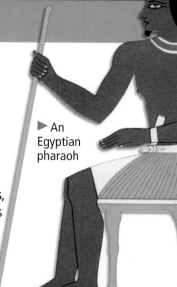

► An Egyptian pharaoh

How have societies chosen to govern themselves?

A society is a complex network of relationships among individuals and groups whose goals may clash. To avoid chaos, societies create governments to make decisions in the common interest. They also create governments to defend themselves from attack. Throughout history those governments, or political systems, have taken many forms, depending on historical circumstances. The ancient Greeks designated three types of government: rule by one (monarchy, autocracy); rule by the few (aristocracy, oligarchy); and rule by the many (democracy). Consider the following historical examples:

▲ A present-day artist recreates a meeting of the Roman Senate.

Rule by One

1. The ancient Egyptians needed an efficient government to manage activities related to the annual flooding of the Nile. At the head of the government stood an absolute monarch, the pharaoh. The pharaoh relied on his vizier, or chief minister, to handle the country's affairs. The vizier directed a large government bureaucracy. Most Egyptians had no say in how they were governed.

2. As chairman of the Communist Party, Mao Zedong ruled China from 1949 until his death in 1976. In reality, he stood above the party as an autocrat with dictatorial powers. At will, he purged party members and military leaders who crossed him. Through the party, he maintained tight control over the government, economy, and most other aspects of Chinese society.

Rule by the Few

1. Ancient Sparta, a military society, had two kings, a council of elders, and a group of officials who ran the day-to-day affairs. They were all members of the aristocracy, Sparta's governing class of nobles and soldiers. For the Greeks, *aristocracy* meant government by those best suited to rule. Unlike neighboring Athens, Sparta never experienced tyranny.

2. After the fall of the Roman Empire, the political system known as feudalism arose in Europe. In this system, the power lay with a military elite. The Greeks might have preferred to call it an *oligarchy*—government based on private interests rather than the interests of the whole society. Nobles traded land and labor for political and military service. Warfare dominated people's lives.

Rule by the Many

1. In 1789, the French Revolution abolished the monarchy and established a republic. This democracy, however, was unstable. France went through periods of empire, republic, and monarchy until the constitution of 1958 established the Fifth Republic. Today the government has a two-house parliament and a strong president who is directly elected. All citizens 18 and older, except for certain criminals, can vote.

2. In 1961, South Africa left the British Commonwealth to become an independent republic. The movement to end apartheid, or racial separation, resulted in a new constitution in 1997. All citizens over age 18 can vote to elect members to a two-house Parliament. The lower house then elects a president as the nation's head of state and chief executive.

▼ A black South African votes in his country's first open election since the end of apartheid.

Thinking Critically

1. **Connect** (a) Which of these three forms of government strikes you as the fairest? Why? (b) Which do you think is most capable of defending a society from attack? Why?
2. Conduct Internet or library research to find out more about these and other examples of political systems. Write a paragraph expressing your thoughts about one political system.

A portrait of King James of England painted around 1619 gives no hint of the monarch's frequent clashes with Parliament.

WITNESS HISTORY 🔊 AUDIO

Charting a Collision Course

In 1603 James I, a monarch with strong ideas about his role, took the English throne. In 1610 the king made a speech to Parliament that would have quite the opposite effect of what he intended:

66 The state of Monarchy is the supremest thing upon earth; for kings are not only God's lieutenants upon earth and sit upon God's throne, but even by God himself they are called gods. . . . Kings are justly called gods for that they exercise a manner or resemblance of Divine power upon earth. . . . And to the King is due both the affection of the soul and the service of the body of his subjects. . . . 99
—James I

Focus Question How did the British Parliament assert its rights against royal claims to absolute power in the 1600s?

Parliament Triumphs in England

Objectives
- Describe the Tudor monarchs' relations with Parliament.
- Analyze how clashes between the Stuarts and Parliament ushered in a century of revolution.
- Understand how the English Civil War and the development of the Commonwealth led to the Glorious Revolution.
- Explain the development of English constitutional government.

Terms, People, and Places

James I	limited monarchy
dissenter	constitutional
Puritans	government
Charles I	cabinet
Oliver Cromwell	oligarchy
English Bill of Rights	

Note Taking

Reading Skill: Identify Supporting Details As you read the section, use a flowchart to record details about the evolution of the English Parliament. One has been started for you.

> Tudors consult with and control Parliament.

↓   ↓   ↓

In the 1600s, while Louis XIV perfected royal absolutism in France, political power in England took a different path. Despite attempts by English monarchs to increase royal authority, Parliament steadily expanded its own influence.

The Tudors Work With Parliament

From 1485 to 1603, England was ruled by Tudor monarchs. Although the Tudors believed in divine right, they shrewdly recognized the value of good relations with Parliament. As you have read, when Henry VIII broke with the Roman Catholic Church, he turned to Parliament to legalize his actions. Parliament approved the Act of Supremacy, making the monarch head of the Church of England.

A constant need for money also led Henry to consult Parliament frequently. Although he had inherited a bulging treasury, he quickly used up his funds fighting overseas wars. To levy new taxes, the king had to seek the approval of Parliament. Members of Parliament tended to vote as Henry's agents instructed. Still, they became accustomed to being consulted on important matters.

When Elizabeth I gained the throne, she too both consulted and controlled Parliament. Her advisors conveyed the queen's wishes to Parliament and forbade discussion of certain subjects, such as foreign policy or the queen's marriage. Her skill in handling Parliament helped make "Good Queen Bess" a popular and successful ruler.

✔ **Checkpoint** Why did Henry VIII work with Parliament?

A Century of Revolution Begins

Elizabeth died childless in 1603. Her heir was her relative James Stuart, the ruling king of Scotland. The Stuarts were neither as popular as the Tudors nor as skillful in dealing with Parliament. They also inherited problems that Henry and Elizabeth had long <u>suppressed</u>. The result was a "century of revolution" that pitted the Stuart monarchs against Parliament.

The Stuarts Issue a Challenge The first Stuart monarch, **James I,** had agreed to rule according to English laws and customs. Soon, however, he was lecturing Parliament about divine right. "I will not be content that my power be disputed upon," he declared. Leaders in the House of Commons fiercely resisted the king's claim to absolute power.

James repeatedly clashed with Parliament over money and foreign policy. He needed funds to finance his lavish court and wage wars. When members wanted to discuss foreign policy before voting funds, James dissolved Parliament and collected taxes on his own.

James also clashed with **dissenters,** Protestants who differed with the Church of England. One group, called **Puritans,** sought to "purify" the church of Catholic practices. Puritans called for simpler services and a more democratic church without bishops. James rejected their demands, vowing to "harry them out of this land or else do worse."

Parliament Responds In 1625, **Charles I** inherited the throne. Like his father, Charles behaved like an absolute monarch. He imprisoned his foes without trial and squeezed the nation for money. By 1628, however, his need to raise taxes forced Charles to summon Parliament. Before voting any funds, Parliament insisted that Charles sign the Petition of Right. This document prohibited the king from raising taxes without Parliament's consent or from jailing anyone without legal justification.

Charles did sign the Petition, but he then dissolved Parliament in 1629. For 11 years, he ignored the Petition and ruled the nation without Parliament. During that time, he created bitter enemies, especially among Puritans. His Archbishop of Canterbury, William Laud, tried to force all clergy to follow strict Anglican rules, dismissing or imprisoning dissenters. Many people felt that the archbishop was trying to revive Catholic practices.

In 1637, Charles and Laud tried to impose the Anglican prayer book on Scotland. The Calvinist Scots revolted. To get funds to suppress the Scottish rebellion, Charles once again had to summon Parliament in 1640. When it met, however, Parliament launched its own revolt.

The Long Parliament Begins The 1640 Parliament became known as the Long Parliament because it lasted on and off until 1653. Its actions triggered the greatest political revolution in English history. In a mounting struggle with Charles I, Parliament tried and executed his chief ministers, including Archbishop Laud. It called for the abolition of bishops and declared that the Parliament could not be dissolved without its own consent.

Vocabulary Builder

<u>suppressed</u>—(suh PRESD) *v.* kept from being revealed; put down by force

A Voice for Absolutism

In 1651, two years after the English Civil War ended, English political philosopher Thomas Hobbes published *Leviathan*. In this book, he explained why he favored an absolute monarchy. How might people who supported Parliament over the monarch have argued against Hobbes's view?

Primary Source

66 During the time men live without a common power to keep them all in awe, they are in that condition which is called war. . . . In such condition, there is no place for industry. . . . no arts; no letters; no society; and, which is worst of all, continual fear and danger of violent death. And the life of man [is] solitary, poor, nasty, brutish, and short. 99

—Thomas Hobbes, *Leviathan* AUDIO

ENGLAND DIVIDED:
PARLIAMENT AND THE MONARCHY FIGHT FOR POWER

1485–1603
The Tudors rule England.
The Tudor monarchs, especially Henry VIII and Elizabeth I, ❶ control Parliament tactfully, recognizing and respecting its role in government.

1603–1625
Stuart king James I rules.
James I becomes king and immediately clashes with Parliament. In 1621, James scolds Parliament for usurping royal power, and Parliament responds with a declaration of its own rights. In the last Parliament of his reign, the aging James gives in to Parliament.

1625–1649
Stuart king Charles I rules.
Charles dissolves Parliament when it tries to expand powers to deal with an economic crisis. The Parliament of 1628 produces the Petition of Right, and later Parliaments ❷ clash with Charles over what they charge are violations of the document. Charles dissolves Parliament again.

1640–1653
The Long Parliament meets.
Faced with economic problems and invasions by Scotland, Charles is forced to call Parliament. The Long Parliament, as it became known, works to steadily expand its powers. Eventually Charles strikes back, adopting the motto "Give Caesar his Due."

Charles lashed back. In 1642, he led troops into the House of Commons to arrest its most radical leaders. They escaped through a back door and soon raised their own army. The clash now moved to the battlefield.

✔ **Checkpoint** What was the Petition of Right?

Fighting a Civil War

The civil war that followed lasted from 1642 to 1651. Like the *Fronde* that occurred about the same time in France, the English Civil War posed a major challenge to absolutism. But while the forces of royal power won in France, in England the forces of revolution triumphed.

Cavaliers and Roundheads At first, the odds seemed to favor the supporters of Charles I, called Cavaliers. Many Cavaliers were wealthy nobles, proud of their plumed hats and fashionably long hair. Well trained in dueling and warfare, the Cavaliers expected a quick victory. But their foes proved to be tough fighters with the courage of their convictions. The forces of Parliament were composed of country gentry, town-dwelling manufacturers, and Puritan clergy. They were called Roundheads because their hair was cut close around their heads.

The Roundheads found a leader of genius in **Oliver Cromwell.** A Puritan member of the lesser gentry, Cromwell proved himself to be a skilled general. He organized a "New Model Army" for Parliament, made up of officers selected for skill rather than social class, into a disciplined fighting force.

Warrant to Execute King Charles the First. AD 1648.

1642–1649
The English Civil War rages.
War breaks out ③ between Parliament's Roundheads (right) and Charles I's Cavaliers (left). The parliamentary forces, led by Oliver Cromwell, eventually win. In 1649, Charles is executed. ④

1649–1660
The English Commonwealth begins and ends.
Abolishing the monarchy and House of Lords, Parliament rules as a commonwealth with Cromwell as leader. ⑤ Problems plague the nation, and the Commonwealth falls apart upon Cromwell's death in 1658. Groups in favor of monarchy begin to gain power.

1660–1685
The monarchy is restored.
Charles II works with Parliament to repair the shattered nation, but clashes with Parliament when he works to restore Catholicism. In 1678, Charles dissolves Parliament and builds the monarchy's power. His successor, James II, continues to push for Catholic power, and incites a backlash. James II flees England in 1688.

1688
The Glorious Revolution assures Parliament's power.
William and Mary become England's monarchs ⑥ with Parliament's blessing— provided that they agree to very limited powers under Parliament's domination.

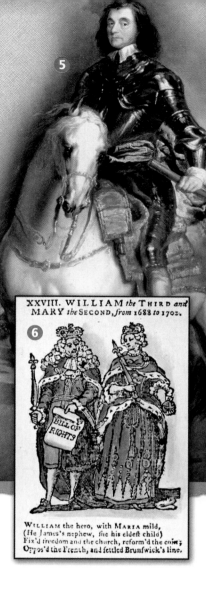

XXVIII. WILLIAM the THIRD and MARY the SECOND, from 1688 to 1702.

WILLIAM the hero, with MARIA mild,
(He James's nephew, she his eldest child)
Fix'd freedom and the church, reform'd the coin;
Oppos'd the French, and settled Brunswick's line.

Thinking Critically
1. **Recognize Point of View** What does Charles I's usage of the phrase "Give Caesar his Due" tell you about his view of royal power?
2. **Recognize Ideologies** How did the religious beliefs of key people on this timeline shape political outcomes?

Cromwell's army defeated the Cavaliers in a series of decisive battles. By 1647, the king was in the hands of parliamentary forces.

A King Is Executed Eventually, Parliament set up a court to put the king on trial. It condemned him to death as "a tyrant, traitor, murderer, and public enemy." On a cold January day in 1649, Charles I stood on a scaffold surrounded by his foes. "I am a martyr of the people," he declared. Showing no fear, the king told the executioner that he himself would give the sign for him to strike. After a brief prayer, Charles knelt and placed his neck on the block. On the agreed signal, the executioner severed the king's neck with a single stroke.

The execution sent shock waves throughout Europe. In the past, a king had occasionally been assassinated or killed in battle. But for the first time, a ruling monarch had been tried and executed by his own people. The parliamentary forces had sent a clear message that, in England, no ruler could claim absolute power and ignore the rule of law.

✓ **Checkpoint** What was the result of the English Civil War?

Cromwell and the Commonwealth
After the execution of Charles I, the House of Commons abolished the monarchy, the House of Lords, and the established Church of England. It declared England a republic, known as the Commonwealth, under the leadership of Oliver Cromwell.

Cromwell's Armor
Oliver Cromwell wore this helmet and sword when he led the English forces into Ireland.

Vocabulary Builder
tolerate—(TAHL er ayt) *v.* to respect other's beliefs without sharing them

Challenging the Commonwealth The new government faced many threats. Supporters of Charles II, the uncrowned heir to the throne, attacked England by way of Ireland and Scotland. Cromwell led forces into Ireland and brutally crushed the uprising. He then took harsh measures against the Irish Catholic majority that are still vividly remembered in that nation today. In 1652, Parliament passed a law exiling most Catholics to barren land in the west of Ireland. Any Catholic found disobeying this order could be killed on sight.

Squabbles also splintered forces within the Commonwealth. One group, called Levellers, thought that poor men should have as much say in government as the gentry, lawyers, and other leading citizens. "The poorest he that is in England hath a life to live as the greatest he," wrote one Leveller. In addition, female Levellers asserted their right to petition Parliament. These ideas horrified the gentry, who dominated Parliament. Cromwell suppressed the Levellers, as well as more radical groups who threatened ownership of private property. In 1653, as the challenges to order grew, Cromwell took the title Lord Protector. From then on, he ruled as a virtual dictator through the army.

Puritans: A Sobering Influence Under the Commonwealth, Puritans—with their goal of rooting out godlessness—gained a new voice in society. The English Civil War thus ushered in a social revolution as well as a political one.

Parliament enacted a series of laws designed to make sure that Sunday was set aside for religious observance. Anyone over the age of 14 who was caught "profaning the Lord's Day" could be fined. To the Puritans, theaters were frivolous. So, like John Calvin in Geneva, Cromwell closed all theaters. Puritans also frowned on taverns, gambling, and dancing.

Puritans felt that every Christian, rich and poor, must be able to read the Bible. To spread religious knowledge, they encouraged education for all people. By mid-century, families from all classes were sending their children to school, girls as well as boys. Puritans also pushed for changes in marriage to ensure greater fidelity. In addition to marriages based on business interests, they encouraged marriages based on love. Still, as in the past, women were seen mainly as caretakers of the family, subordinate to men.

Although Cromwell did not <u>tolerate</u> open worship by Roman Catholics, he believed in religious freedom for other Protestant groups. He even welcomed Jews back to England after more than 350 years of exile.

The Commonwealth Ends Oliver Cromwell died in 1658. Soon after, the Puritans lost their grip on England. Many people were tired of military rule and strict Puritan ways. In 1660, a newly elected Parliament invited Charles II to return to England from exile.

England's "kingless decade" ended with the Restoration, or return of the monarchy. Yet Puritan ideas about morality, equality, government, and education endured. In the following century, these ideas would play an important role in shaping the future of Britain's colonies in the Americas.

✔ **Checkpoint** What was the Commonwealth?

From Restoration to Glorious Revolution

In late May 1660, cheering crowds welcomed Charles II back to London. John Evelyn, a supporter and diarist whose writings are an important source of information about English political and social history, wrote:

" This day came in his Majesties Charles the Second to London after a sad, and long Exile . . . with a Triumph of above 20,000 horse and [soldiers], brandishing their swords, and shouting with unexpressible joy; the [ways strewn] with flowers, the bells ringing, the streetes hung with [tapestry]. "
—John Evelyn, *Diary*

Charles II With his charm and flashing wit, young Charles II was a popular ruler. He reopened theaters and taverns and presided over a lively court in the manner of Louis XIV. Charles reestablished the Church of England but encouraged toleration of other Protestants such as Presbyterians, Quakers, and Baptists.

Although Charles accepted the Petition of Right, he shared his father's belief in absolute monarchy and secretly had Catholic sympathies. Still, he shrewdly avoided his father's mistakes in dealing with Parliament.

James II is Forced to Flee Charles's brother, James II, inherited the throne in 1685. Unlike Charles, James practiced his Catholic faith openly. He angered his subjects by suspending laws on a whim and appointing Catholics to high office. Many English Protestants feared that James would restore the Roman Catholic Church.

In 1688, alarmed parliamentary leaders invited James's Protestant daughter, Mary, and her Dutch Protestant husband, William III of Orange, to become rulers of England. When William and Mary landed with their army late in 1688, James II fled to France. This bloodless overthrow of the king became known as the Glorious Revolution.

The English Bill of Rights Before they could be crowned, William and Mary had to accept several acts passed by Parliament in 1689 that became known as the **English Bill of Rights.** The Bill of Rights ensured the superiority of Parliament over the monarchy. It required the monarch to summon Parliament regularly and gave the House of Commons the "power of the purse," or control over spending. A king or queen could no longer interfere in parliamentary debates or suspend laws. The Bill of Rights also barred any Roman Catholic from sitting on the throne.

The Bill of Rights also restated the traditional rights of English citizens, such as trial by jury. It abolished excessive fines and cruel or unjust punishment. It affirmed the principle of *habeas corpus.* That is, no person could be held in prison without first being charged with a specific crime.

In addition, a separate Toleration Act, also of 1689, granted limited religious freedom to Puritans, Quakers, and other dissenters. Still, only members of the Church of England could hold public office. And Catholics were allowed no religious freedom.

Puritan girls spent hours working on embroidered samplers like this one. Such work was considered part of their education. ▼

Our Puritan Heritage

Decades before the Puritans gained power in England, Puritans living in the Massachusetts Bay colony worked to put into action their own ideas about religion and government. The Puritans knew that to assure survival of their beliefs and culture, they would have to educate their children to read and write. As soon as they were able, the Puritans began to set up schools, starting with the Boston Latin School in 1635 and then Harvard College (below) in 1636.

Eventually, the colonies became the United States. Over time, the rest of the country adopted the Puritan tradition of establishing public schools to help train children to become good citizens of their community. A literate, well-informed citizenry has continued to be a major aim of American schools to this day. **What other institutions help to train American children to be good citizens?**

A Limited Monarchy The Glorious Revolution created not a democracy, but a type of government called **limited monarchy,** in which a constitution or legislative body limits the monarch's powers. English rulers still had much power, but they had to obey the law and govern in partnership with Parliament. In the age of absolute monarchy elsewhere in Europe, the limited monarchy in England was quite radical.

The Glorious Revolution also greatly influenced important political thinkers of the time, such as John Locke. Locke's ideas were later used by leaders of the American Revolution as the basis for their struggle, and are found in documents such as the Declaration of Independence.

✓ **Checkpoint** What was the Glorious Revolution?

Constitutional Government Evolves

In the century following the Glorious Revolution, three new political institutions arose in Britain: political parties, the cabinet, and the office of prime minister. The appearance of these institutions was part of the evolution of Britain's **constitutional government**—that is, a government whose power is defined and limited by law.

Political Parties Emerge In the late 1600s, political parties emerged in England as a powerful force in politics. At first, there were just two political parties—Tories and Whigs. Tories were generally aristocrats who sought to preserve older traditions. They supported broad royal powers and a dominant Anglican Church. Whigs backed the policies of the Glorious Revolution. They were more likely to reflect urban business interests, support religious toleration, and favor Parliament over the crown.

The Cabinet System The cabinet, another new feature of government, evolved in the 1700s after the British throne passed to a German prince. George I spoke no English and relied on the leaders in Parliament to help him rule. Under George I and his German-born son George II, a handful of parliamentary advisors set policy. They came to be referred to as the **cabinet** because of the small room, or "cabinet," where they met. In time, the cabinet gained official status.

The Prime Minister Leads the Cabinet Over time, the head of the cabinet came to be known as the prime minister. This person was always the leader of the majority party in the House of Commons. Eventually, the prime minister became the chief official of the British government. From 1721 to 1742, the able Whig leader Robert Walpole molded the cabinet into a unified body by requiring all members to agree on major issues.

Influence of the Glorious Revolution

Outcome in England

English Bill of Rights	Writings of John Locke	Constitutional Government
• People elect representatives to Parliament, which is supreme over monarch. • All citizens have natural rights.	• People have natural rights such as life, liberty, and property. • There is a social contract between people and government.	• Government is limited and defined by law. • Political parties, the cabinet, and the office of prime minister arise.

↓ ↓ ↓

Impact on the United States

Colonists believed that they too had rights, including the right to elect people to represent them.	Locke's ideas shaped the American Revolution and the writing of the Declaration of Independence and the Constitution.	The new American nation formed a constitutional government with two parties and a cabinet; the American system included even more provisions for the separation of powers.

Chart Skills A common protest during the American Revolution was "no taxation without representation." *Which English outcome of the Glorious Revolution influenced that idea?*

Although the title was not yet in use, Walpole is often called Britain's first prime minister. In time, the power of the prime minister would exceed that of the monarch. Other countries later adopted and adapted the cabinet system, including the United States.

✓ **Checkpoint** **What three political institutions contributed to the evolution of Britain's constitutional government?**

A Society Still Ruled by the Few

The decades that Walpole headed the cabinet were a time of peace and prosperity. But even as Parliament and the cabinet assumed new powers, British government was far from democratic. Rather, it was an **oligarchy**—a government in which the ruling power belongs to a few people.

In Britain, landowning aristocrats were believed to be the "natural" ruling class. The highest nobles held seats in the House of Lords. Other wealthy landowners and rich business leaders in the cities controlled elections to the House of Commons. The right to vote was limited to a relatively few male property owners.

Most Britons had neither the wealth nor the privileges of the upper class and lived very differently, making a meager living from the land. In the 1700s, even that poor existence was threatened. Wealthy landowners, attempting to increase agricultural production, bought up farms and took over common lands, evicting tenant farmers and small landowners. Because they controlled Parliament, they easily passed laws ensuring that their actions were legal. As a result many landless families drifted into towns, where they faced a harsh existence.

However, a relatively strong middle class—including merchants, craftspeople, and manufacturers—was growing. These prosperous and often wealthy people controlled affairs in the towns and cities. Some improved their social standing by marrying into the landed gentry. The middle class also produced talented inventors and entrepreneurs who would soon help usher in the Industrial Revolution.

✓ **Checkpoint** **How did British society remain divided?**

 SECTION **3** Assessment

Progress Monitoring *Online*
For: Self-quiz with vocabulary practice
Web Code: nba-1631

Terms, People, and Places

1. Place each of the key terms at the beginning of the section into one of the following categories: politics, culture, or government. Write a sentence for each explaining your choice.

Note Taking

2. **Reading Skill: Identify Supporting Details** Use your completed flowchart to answer the Focus Question: How did the British Parliament assert its rights against royal claims to absolute power in the 1600s?

Comprehension and Critical Thinking

3. **Contrast** How did the Stuarts differ from the Tudors in their approach to Parliament?

4. **Identify Central Issues** In less than 100 years, England changed from a monarchy to a commonwealth and back to a monarchy. What central issue caused this political upheaval?

5. **Draw Conclusions** What were two results of the Glorious Revolution?

6. **Summarize** How did constitutional government evolve in England in the 1700s?

● **Writing About History**

Quick Write: Answer Opposing Arguments To write a strong persuasive essay you need to address arguments that could be raised to refute your own position. Choose a topic from this section—for example, whether Parliament had the right to replace James II—and list the arguments for and against your position.

The English Bill of Rights

When the Catholic James II was forced from the English throne in 1688, Parliament offered the crown to his Protestant daughter Mary and her husband, William of Orange. But Parliament insisted that William and Mary submit to a Bill of Rights. This document, reflecting the long-standing struggle between monarch and Parliament, sums up the powers that Parliament had been seeking since the Petition of Right in 1628. This document ensured the superiority of Parliament over the monarchy and spelled out basic rights.

An engraving made in 1689 shows the new English rulers, William and Mary.

The original English Bill of Rights, now more than 300 years old, is carefully preserved in a museum in London, England.

Whereas, the late King James II . . . did endeavor to subvert[1] and extirpate[2] the Protestant religion and the laws and liberties of this kingdom . . . and whereas the said late King James II having abdicated the government, and the throne being vacant . . . the said lords [Parliament] . . . being now assembled in a full and free representative [body] of this nation . . . do in the first place . . . declare:

1. That the pretended power of suspending of laws or the execution of laws by regal authority without consent of Parliament is illegal. . . .

4. That levying money for or to the use of the crown by pretense of prerogative[3] without grant of Parliament . . . is illegal;

5. That it is the right of the subjects to petition the king, and all commitments and prosecutions for such petitioning are illegal.

6. That . . . raising or keeping a standing army within the kingdom in time of peace, unless it be with consent of Parliament, is against law. . . .

8. That election of members of Parliament ought to be free. . . .

9. That the freedom of speech and debates or proceedings in Parliament ought not to be challenged or questioned in any court or place out of Parliament. . . .

10. That excessive bail ought not to be required, nor excessive fines imposed, nor cruel and unusual punishments inflicted. . . .

13. And that, for redress of all grievances and for the amending, strengthening, and preserving of the laws, Parliaments ought to be held frequently. . . .

Thinking Critically
1. **Synthesize Information** What is the meaning of item 6, and why do you think it was included in the Bill of Rights?
2. **Draw Inferences** Why do you think the members of Parliament included item 9? Why do you think this item might have been important?

1. **subvert** (sub VURT) *v.* to destroy, overthrow, or undermine

2. **extirpate** (EKS tur payt) *v.* to eliminate

3. **prerogative** (pree RAHG uh tiv) *n.* a right

This silver flask held musket powder in the Thirty Years' War.

Flemish artist Pieter Snayers painted several battles during the Thirty Years' War, including this one fought near Prague in 1620.

WITNESS HISTORY 🔊 AUDIO

War Rages in Germany

The conflict known as the Thirty Years' War ravaged the German states of central Europe for much of the first half of the seventeenth century. A German family Bible contained this entry describing the war's end:

❝ They say that the terrible war is now over. But there is still no sign of a peace. Everywhere there is envy, hatred, and greed: that's what the war has taught us. . . . We live like animals, eating bark and grass. No one could have imagined that anything like this would happen to us. Many people say that there is no God.❞

Focus Question How did the two great empires of Austria and Prussia emerge from the Thirty Years' War and subsequent events?

Rise of Austria and Prussia

Objectives
- Outline causes and results of the Thirty Years' War.
- Understand how Austria and Prussia emerged as great powers.
- Describe how European nations tried to maintain a balance of power.

Terms, People, and Places

elector	War of the Austrian
Ferdinand	Succession
mercenary	Prussia
depopulation	Frederick William I
Peace of Westphalia	Frederick II
Maria Theresa	

Note Taking

Reading Skill: Identify Supporting Details As you read this section, use a table like the one below to record details about the emergence of Austria and Prussia as European powers.

Rise of Austria	Rise of Prussia
• Austrian ruler keeps title of Holy Roman Emperor.	• Hohenzollern rulers take over German states.
•	•

The Thirty Years' War took a terrible toll on the people of the German states. Finally, two great German-speaking powers, Austria and Prussia, rose out of the ashes. Like Louis XIV in France, their rulers perfected skills as absolute monarchs.

The Thirty Years' War Ravages Europe

By early modern times, as the French philosopher Voltaire later observed, the Holy Roman Empire was neither holy, nor Roman, nor an empire. Instead, by the seventeenth century it had become a patchwork of several hundred small, separate states. In theory, these states were ruled by the Holy Roman emperor, who was chosen by seven leading German princes called **electors.** In practice, the emperor had little power over the many rival princes. This power vacuum contributed to the outbreak of the Thirty Years' War. Religion further divided the German states. The north had become largely Protestant, while the south remained Catholic.

A Brutal War Begins The Thirty Years' War was actually a series of wars. It began in Bohemia, the present-day Czech Republic. **Ferdinand,** the Catholic Hapsburg king of Bohemia, sought to suppress Protestants and to assert royal power over nobles. In May 1618, a few rebellious Protestant noblemen tossed two royal officials out of a castle window in Prague. This act, known as the Defenestration of Prague, sparked a general revolt, which Ferdinand moved to suppress. As both sides sought allies, what began as a local conflict widened into a general European war.

Europe After the Thirty Years' War (1648)

Geography *Interactive*
For: Audio guided tour
Web Code: nbp-1641

Legend:
- Controlled by Spanish Hapsburgs
- Controlled by Austrian Hapsburgs
- Italian city-states
- Controlled by Prussian Hohenzollerns
- Boundary of Holy Roman Empire

NORWAY
SCOTLAND
SWEDEN
North Sea
DENMARK
IRELAND ENGLAND
Dutch Neth.
London
Spanish Neth.
WESTPHALIA
Berlin
BRANDENBURG
PRUSSIA
Baltic Sea
POLAND
RUSSIA
SAXONY
Silesia
Prague
Bohemia
Atlantic Ocean
Paris
Lorraine
Alsace
Vienna
TRANSYLVANIA
BAVARIA
SWISS FED.
AUSTRIA
HUNGARY
FRANCE
Milan
Black Sea
Papal States
OTTOMAN EMPIRE
Corsica
Rome
Naples
PORTUGAL
Madrid
SPAIN
Sardinia
Mediterranean Sea
Sicily

Conic Projection
0   200   400 mi
0   200   400 km

Map Skills After the Thirty Years' War, the Peace of Westphalia redrew the map of Europe.

1. **Locate** (a) Poland (b) Sweden (c) Spanish Netherlands (d) Westphalia
2. **Regions** (a) Who controlled Bohemia in 1648? (b) What lands did the Spanish Hapsburgs control?
3. **Drawing Conclusions** How can you tell from the maps that the Holy Roman Empire was not a strong, unified state?

European Nation-States, 1700

SWEDEN
Stockholm
Moscow
North Sea
Baltic Sea
ENGLAND
PRUSSIA
Berlin
Warsaw
POLAND
Dnieper R.
RUSSIA
London
Atlantic Ocean
Paris
Prague
Rhine R.
Vistula R.
Vienna
FRANCE
ALPS
AUSTRIA
Black Sea
PYRENEES MTS.
Danube R.
Rome
Madrid
SPAIN
Mediterranean Sea

Conic Projection
0   200   400 mi
0   200   400 km

👑 Major European monarchy

The following year, Ferdinand was elected Holy Roman Emperor. With the support of Spain, Poland, and other Catholic states, he tried to roll back the Reformation by force. In the early stages of the war, he defeated the Bohemians (who had rebelled when he became emperor) and their Protestant allies. Alarmed, Protestant powers like the Netherlands and Sweden sent troops into Germany. Before long, political motives outweighed religious issues. Catholic and Protestant rulers shifted alliances to suit their own interests. At one point, Catholic France joined Lutheran Sweden against the Catholic Hapsburgs.

A Terrible Loss of Life The fighting took a terrible toll. Roving armies of **mercenaries,** or soldiers for hire, burned villages, destroyed crops, and killed without mercy. Murder and torture were followed by famine and disease. Wolves, not seen in settled areas since the Middle Ages, stalked the deserted streets of once-bustling villages. The war led to a severe **depopulation,** or reduction in population. Exact statistics do not exist, but historians estimate that as many as one third of the people in the German states may have died as a result of the war.

Peace at Last Finally, in 1648, the exhausted combatants accepted a series of treaties, known as the **Peace of Westphalia.** Because so many powers had been involved in the conflict, the treaties <u>aspired</u> both to bring about a general European peace and to settle other international problems. Among the combatants France emerged a clear winner, gaining territory on both its Spanish and German frontiers. The Hapsburgs were not so fortunate. They had to accept the almost total independence of all the princes of the Holy Roman Empire. In addition, the Netherlands and the Swiss Federation (present-day Switzerland) won recognition as independent states.

The Thirty Years' War left German lands divided into more than 360 separate states—"one for every day of the year." These states still acknowledged the rule of the Holy Roman emperor. Yet each state had its own government, currency, church, armed forces, and foreign policy. The German states, potentially the most powerful nation in Europe if they could be unified, thus remained fragmented for another 223 years.

✓ **Checkpoint** What were some effects of the Peace of Westphalia?

Vocabulary Builder
<u>aspired</u>—(uh SPY urd) v. aimed; sought

Hapsburg Austria Changes its Focus

Though weakened by war, the Hapsburgs still wanted to create a strong united state. They kept the title "Holy Roman emperor," but focused their attention on expanding their own lands. To Austria, they would soon add Bohemia, Hungary, and, later, parts of Poland and some Italian states.

Challenges to Unity Uniting these lands proved difficult. Not only were they divided by geography, they included a number of diverse peoples and cultures as well. By the 1700s, the Hapsburg Empire included Germans, Magyars, Slavs, and others. In many parts of the empire, people had their own languages, laws, political assemblies, and customs.

The Hapsburgs did exert some control over these diverse peoples. They sent German-speaking officials to Bohemia and Hungary and settled Austrians on lands they had seized in these provinces. They also put down revolts in Bohemia and Hungary. Still, the Hapsburgs never developed a centralized governmental system like that of France.

Maria Theresa

When Maria Theresa (1717–1780) became Hapsburg empress at the age of 23, her chances of remaining in power seemed very slim. She later said, "I found myself all at once without money, without troops, and without advice." A decade after her crowning she wrote, "I do not think anyone would deny that history hardly knows of a crowned head who started his rule under circumstances more grievous than those attending my accession."

But the determined empress survived. She appointed superb advisors and was able to maintain control of her empire. During her 40-year reign, Vienna became a center for music and the arts.

Maria Theresa had one thing in common with most women of her day—being a mother. She gave birth to a total of 16 children—11 girls and 5 boys. Among them were future emperors Joseph II and Leopold II and Queen Marie Antoinette of France. **What traits did Maria Theresa need to stay in power?**

A Woman Emperor Takes the Throne In the early 1700s, a new challenge threatened Hapsburg Austria. Emperor Charles VI had no male heir. His daughter, **Maria Theresa,** was intelligent and capable, but no woman had yet ruled Hapsburg lands in her own name. Charles persuaded other European rulers to recognize his daughter's right to succeed him. When he died, however, many ignored their pledge.

The War of the Austrian Succession Shortly after Charles's death in 1740, Frederick II of Prussia seized the rich Hapsburg province of Silesia. This action sparked the eight-year **War of the Austrian Succession.** Maria Theresa set off for Hungary to appeal for military help from her Hungarian subjects. The Hungarians were ordinarily unfriendly to the Hapsburgs. But she made a dramatic plea before an assembly of Hungarian nobles. According to one account, the nobles rose to their feet and shouted, "Our lives and blood for your Majesty!" She eventually got further help from Britain and Russia, who did not want Prussia to upset the balance of power by gaining new lands.

Maria Theresa never succeeded in forcing Frederick out of Silesia. Still, she did preserve her empire and win the support of most of her people. Equally important, she strengthened Hapsburg power by reorganizing the bureaucracy and improving tax collection. She even forced nobles and clergy to pay taxes and tried to ease the burden of taxes and labor services on peasants. As you will read, her son and successor, Joseph II, later extended many of her reforms.

✓ **Checkpoint** What caused the War of the Austrian Succession?

Hohenzollern Prussia

While Austria was molding a strong Catholic state, a region called **Prussia** emerged as a new Protestant power. In the 1600s, the Hohenzollern (HOH un tsahl urn) family ruled scattered lands across north Germany. In the century following the Peace of Westphalia, ambitious Hohenzollern rulers united their holdings, creating Prussia.

Creating a Bureaucracy Hohenzollerns rulers set up an efficient central bureaucracy. **Frederick William I** was a Prussian ruler who came to power upon the death of his father in 1713. He cleverly gained the loyalty of the Prussian nobles, called *Junkers* (YOON kerz), by giving them positions in the army and government. His tactic reduced the nobles' independence and increased his own control. Frederick also placed great emphasis on military values and forged one of the best-trained armies in Europe. One Prussian military leader boasted, "Prussia is not a state which possesses an army, but an army which possesses a state." By 1740, Prussia was strong enough to challenge its rival Austria.

A Crown Prince Learns the Art of War Frederick William made sure that, from an early age, his son Frederick was trained in the art of war. He wrote,

Primary Source

 His tutor must take the greatest pains to imbue my son with a sincere love for the soldier's profession and to impress upon him that nothing else in the world can confer upon a prince such fame and honor as the sword. **"**

In fact, young **Frederick II** preferred playing the flute and writing poetry. His father despised these pursuits and treated the young prince so badly that he tried to flee the country. Discovering these plans, Frederick William put his son in solitary confinement. Then he forced the 18-year-old prince to watch as the friend who had helped him was beheaded.

Frederick's harsh military training had an effect. After becoming king in 1740, Frederick II lost no time in using his army. As you have read, he boldly seized Silesia from Austria, sparking the War of the Austrian Succession. In several later wars, Frederick continued to brilliantly use his disciplined army, forcing all to recognize Prussia as a great power. His exploits earned him the name Frederick the Great.

✔ **Checkpoint** How did Frederick William increase his power?

The Rivalry of Great Powers

By 1750, the great European powers included Austria, Prussia, France, Britain, and Russia. These nations formed various alliances to maintain the balance of power. Though nations sometimes switched partners, two basic rivalries persisted. Prussia battled Austria for control of the German states, while Britain and France competed to develop their overseas empires.

On occasion, these rivalries resulted in worldwide conflict. The Seven Years' War, which lasted from 1756 until 1763, was fought on four continents. Prussia, Austria, Russia, France, and Britain battled in Europe. Britain and France also fought in India and Africa. In North America, where the conflict is known as the French and Indian War, Native American groups took sides with the French or the British. The Treaty of Paris ending these wars gave Britain a huge empire, thus changing Europe's balance of power for the next hundred years.

✔ **Checkpoint** What were the two main rivalries after 1750?

Petitioning a King
Frederick the Great, strolling in his gardens, receives a petition from a common person. *What characteristics of Frederick does the artist hint at in the painting?*

SECTION 4 Assessment

Progress Monitoring *Online*
For: Self-quiz with vocabulary practice
Web Code: nba-1641

Terms, People, and Places

1. For each term, person, or place listed at the beginning of the section, write a sentence explaining its significance.

Note Taking

2. **Reading Skill: Identify Supporting Details** Use your completed table to answer the Focus Question: How did the two great empires of Austria and Prussia emerge from the Thirty Years' War and subsequent events?

Comprehension and Critical Thinking

3. **Recognize Cause and Effect** What impact did the Thirty Years' War have on the German states?

4. **Compare** What two major powers emerged in Europe at the end of the Thirty Years' War? How were the goals of these two nations similar?

5. **Make Generalizations** How did European nations maintain a balance of power?

● **Writing About History**
Quick Write: Write a Thesis Statement Select a topic from the section that you might use as the subject of a persuasive essay—for example, whether Austria or Prussia was more successful at developing a strong nation-state. Then write a thesis statement that summarizes your opinion on this topic.

The palace (left) of Catherine the Great (far left) reflects both European and traditional Russian architectural styles.

WITNESS HISTORY 🔊 AUDIO

A Foreign Princess Takes the Throne

For twenty years, the German princess Catherine lived at the Russian court, enduring an unhappy marriage to the Russian heir apparent, who was widely considered to be insane. She filled her time reading, studying French philosophy, building alliances behind the scenes, and biding her time. When her husband became emperor in 1762, she called on her allies to act. Within a few months he had been deposed and Catherine proclaimed empress of Russia. Like Peter the Great before her, Catherine would rule with intelligence, a firm hand, and a mind set on modernization.

Focus Question How did Peter the Great and Catherine the Great strengthen Russia and expand its territory?

Absolute Monarchy in Russia

Objectives

- Explain how Peter the Great tried to make Russia into a modern state.
- Identify the steps Peter took to expand Russia's borders.
- Describe how Catherine the Great strengthened Russia.

Terms, People, and Places

Peter the Great	warm-water port
westernization	St. Petersburg
autocratic	Catherine the Great
boyar	partition

Note Taking

Reading Skill: Identify Main Ideas As you read this section, make a Venn diagram like the one below to compare events in the reigns of Peter the Great and Catherine the Great.

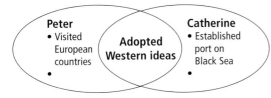

In the early 1600s, Russia was still a medieval state, untouched by the Renaissance or Reformation and largely isolated from Western Europe. As you have read, the "Time of Troubles" had plunged the country into a period of disorder and foreign invasions. The reign of the first Romanov tsar in 1613 restored a measure of order. Not until the end of the century, however, did a tsar emerge who was strong enough to regain the absolute power of earlier tsars. **Peter the Great,** as he came to be called, used his power to put Russia on the road to becoming a great modern power.

Peter the Great Modernizes Russia

Peter, just 10 years old when he took the throne in 1682, did not take control of the government until 1689. Although he was not well educated, the young tsar was immensely curious. He spent hours in the "German quarter," the Moscow neighborhood where many Dutch, Scottish, English, and other foreign artisans and soldiers lived. There, he heard of the new technology that was helping Western European monarchs forge powerful empires.

Journey to the West In 1697, Peter set out to learn about Western ways for himself. He spent hours walking the streets of European cities, noting the manners and homes of the people. He visited factories and art galleries, learned anatomy from a doctor, and even had a dentist teach him how to pull teeth. In England, Peter was impressed by Parliament. "It is good," he said, "to hear subjects speaking truthfully and openly to their king."

Peter brought to Russia a group of technical experts, teachers, and soldiers he had recruited in Europe. He then embarked on a policy of **westernization,** that is, the adoption of Western ideas, technology, and culture. But persuading fellow Russians to change their way of life proved difficult. To impose his will, Peter became the most **autocratic** of Europe's absolute monarchs, meaning that he ruled with unlimited authority.

Controlling the Church and the Nobles

Peter pursued several related goals. He wanted to strengthen the military, expand Russian borders, and centralize royal power. To achieve his ends, he brought all Russian institutions under his control, including the Russian Orthodox Church. He also forced the haughty **boyars,** or landowning nobles, to serve the state in civilian or military positions.

Some changes had a symbolic meaning. For example, after returning from the West, Peter <u>stipulated</u> that boyars shave their beards. He also forced them to replace their old-fashioned robes with Western-style clothes. To end the practice of secluding upper-class women in separate quarters, he held grand parties at which women and men were expected to dance together. Russian nobles opposed this radical mixing of the sexes in public, but they had to comply.

Peter knew that nobles would serve the state only if their own interests were protected. Therefore, he passed laws ensuring that nobles retained control over their lands, including the serfs on those lands. In doing so, Peter strengthened serfdom. Under his rule serfdom spread in Russia, long after it had died out in Western Europe. Further, he forced some serfs to become soldiers or to work as laborers on roads, canals, and other government projects.

Modernizing With Force

Using autocratic methods, Peter pushed through social and economic reforms. He imported Western technology, improved education, simplified the Russian alphabet, and set up academies for the study of mathematics, science, and engineering. To pay for his sweeping reforms, Peter adopted mercantilist policies, such as encouraging exports. He improved waterways and canals, developed mining and textile manufacturing, and backed new trading companies.

Peter had no mercy for any who resisted the new order. When elite palace guards revolted, he had more than 1,000 of the rebels tortured and executed. Then, as an example of his power, he left their rotting corpses outside the palace walls for months.

✓ **Checkpoint** What rewards and punishments did Peter use to solidify his control over the nobles?

Peter Expands Russia's Borders

From his earliest days as tsar, Peter worked to build Russia's military power. He created the largest standing army in Europe, built a world-class navy from scratch, and set out to extend Russian borders to the west and south.

Seeking a Warm-Water Port

Russian seaports, located along the Arctic Ocean, were frozen over during the winter. To increase Russia's ability to trade with the West, Peter desperately wanted a **warm-water port**—one that would be free of ice all year round.

Vocabulary Builder

<u>stipulated</u>—(STIP yuh layt ed) *v.* made a specific demand

A Russian cartoon shows Peter the Great personally cutting off the beard of a boyar.

169

The nearest warm-water coast was located along the Black Sea. To gain control of this territory, Peter had to push through the powerful Ottoman Empire. In the end, Peter was unable to defeat the Ottomans and gain his warm-water port, but the later Russian monarch Catherine the Great would achieve that goal before the century ended.

The Great Northern War In 1700, Peter began a long war against the kingdom of Sweden, which at the time, dominated the Baltic region. Early on, Russia suffered humiliating defeats. A Swedish force of only 8,000 men

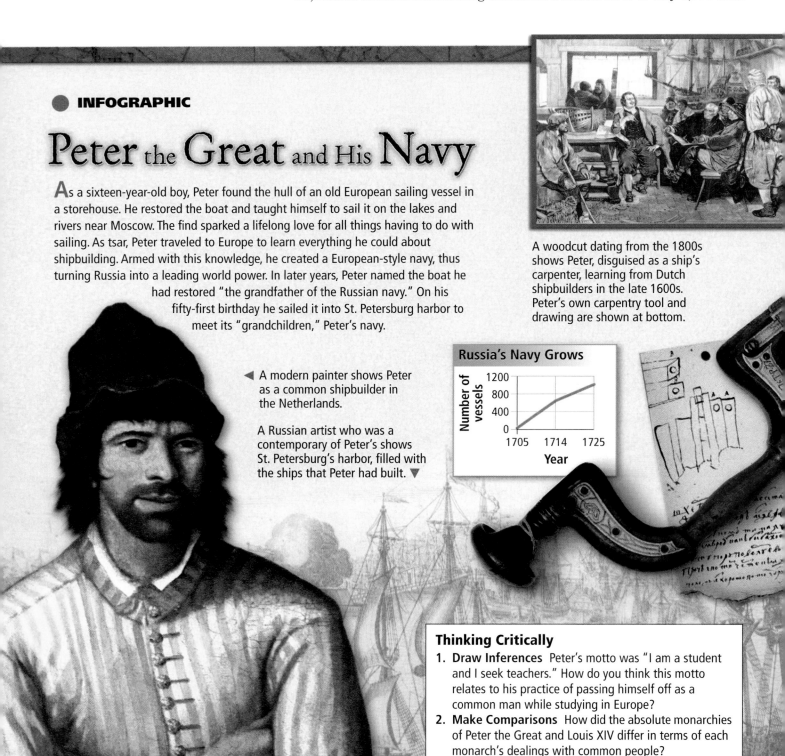

● **INFOGRAPHIC**

Peter the Great and His Navy

As a sixteen-year-old boy, Peter found the hull of an old European sailing vessel in a storehouse. He restored the boat and taught himself to sail it on the lakes and rivers near Moscow. The find sparked a lifelong love for all things having to do with sailing. As tsar, Peter traveled to Europe to learn everything he could about shipbuilding. Armed with this knowledge, he created a European-style navy, thus turning Russia into a leading world power. In later years, Peter named the boat he had restored "the grandfather of the Russian navy." On his fifty-first birthday he sailed it into St. Petersburg harbor to meet its "grandchildren," Peter's navy.

A woodcut dating from the 1800s shows Peter, disguised as a ship's carpenter, learning from Dutch shipbuilders in the late 1600s. Peter's own carpentry tool and drawing are shown at bottom.

◄ A modern painter shows Peter as a common shipbuilder in the Netherlands.

A Russian artist who was a contemporary of Peter's shows St. Petersburg's harbor, filled with the ships that Peter had built. ▼

Russia's Navy Grows

Number of vessels

1200
800
400
0

1705   1714   1725

Year

Thinking Critically

1. **Draw Inferences** Peter's motto was "I am a student and I seek teachers." How do you think this motto relates to his practice of passing himself off as a common man while studying in Europe?

2. **Make Comparisons** How did the absolute monarchies of Peter the Great and Louis XIV differ in terms of each monarch's dealings with common people?

defeated a Russian army five times its size. Undaunted, Peter rebuilt his army, modeling it after European armies. Finally, in 1709, he defeated the Swedes and won territory along the Baltic Sea.

Building St. Petersburg On this land won from Sweden, Peter built a magnificent new capital city, **St. Petersburg.** Seeking to open a "window on the West," he located the city on the Baltic coast along the swampy shores of the Neva River. He forced tens of thousands of serfs to drain the swamps. Many thousands died, but Peter's plan for the city succeeded. He then invited Italian architects and artisans to design great palaces in Western style. Peter even planned the city's parks and boulevards himself. Just as Versailles became a monument to French absolutism, St. Petersburg became a great symbol of Peter's effort to forge a modern Russia.

Blazing Trails to the Pacific Russian traders and raiders also crossed the plains and rivers of Siberia, forging new trails westward. Under Peter, Russia signed a treaty with Qing China that defined their common border in the east. The treaty recognized Russia's right to lands north of Manchuria.

In the early 1700s, Peter hired the Danish navigator Vitus Bering to explore what became known as the Bering Strait between Siberia and Alaska (see map on next page). After Peter's death, Russian traders built outposts in Alaska and northern California. Few Russians moved east of the Ural Mountains at this time, but the expansion made Russia the largest country in the world. It still is today, nearly 300 years later.

Peter the Great's Legacy When Peter died in 1725, he left a mixed legacy. He had expanded Russian territory, gained ports on the Baltic Sea, and created a mighty army. He had also ended Russia's long period of isolation. From the 1700s on, Russia would be increasingly involved in the affairs of Western Europe. Yet many of Peter's ambitious reforms died with him. Nobles, for example, soon ignored his policy of service to the state.

Like earlier tsars, Peter the Great had used terror to enforce his absolute power. His policies contributed to the growth of serfdom, which served only to widen the gap between Russia and the West that Peter had sought to narrow.

✔ **Checkpoint** What impact did Peter's defeat of Sweden have on Russia's expansion?

Catherine the Great Follows Peter's Lead

Peter died without an heir and without naming a successor. This set off a power struggle within the Romanov family, from whom all the tsars had come since the early 1600s. Under a series of ineffective rulers, Russian nobles reasserted their independence. Then, a new monarch took the reins of power firmly in hand. She became known to history as **Catherine the Great.**

WITNESS HISTORY VIDEO

Watch *Peter the Great* on the **Witness History Discovery School**™ video program to learn more about this larger-than-life tsar.

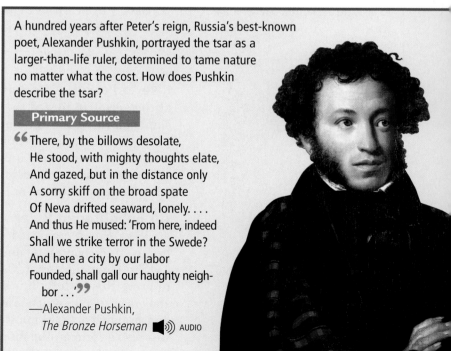

A hundred years after Peter's reign, Russia's best-known poet, Alexander Pushkin, portrayed the tsar as a larger-than-life ruler, determined to tame nature no matter what the cost. How does Pushkin describe the tsar?

Primary Source

66 There, by the billows desolate,
He stood, with mighty thoughts elate,
And gazed, but in the distance only
A sorry skiff on the broad spate
Of Neva drifted seaward, lonely. . . .
And thus He mused: 'From here, indeed
Shall we strike terror in the Swede?
And here a city by our labor
Founded, shall gall our haughty neighbor . . .'99
—Alexander Pushkin,
The Bronze Horseman 🔊 AUDIO

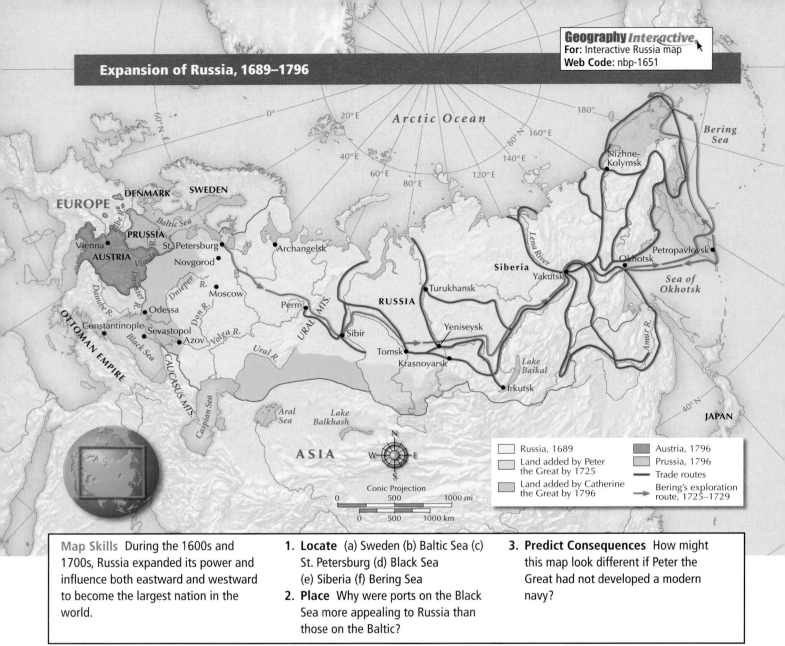

Expansion of Russia, 1689–1796

Geography *Interactive*
For: Interactive Russia map
Web Code: nbp-1651

Legend:
- Russia, 1689
- Land added by Peter the Great by 1725
- Land added by Catherine the Great by 1796
- Austria, 1796
- Prussia, 1796
- Trade routes
- Bering's exploration route, 1725–1729

Conic Projection
0   500   1000 mi
0   500   1000 km

Map Skills During the 1600s and 1700s, Russia expanded its power and influence both eastward and westward to become the largest nation in the world.

1. **Locate** (a) Sweden (b) Baltic Sea (c) St. Petersburg (d) Black Sea (e) Siberia (f) Bering Sea
2. **Place** Why were ports on the Black Sea more appealing to Russia than those on the Baltic?
3. **Predict Consequences** How might this map look different if Peter the Great had not developed a modern navy?

Rise to Power A German princess by birth, Catherine came to Russia at the age of 15 to wed the heir to the Russian throne. She learned Russian, embraced the Russian Orthodox faith, and won the loyalty of the people. In 1762, a group of Russian army officers loyal to her deposed and murdered her mentally unstable husband, Tsar Peter III. Whether or not Catherine was involved in the assassination is uncertain. In any case, with the support of the military, she ascended the Russian throne.

An Enlightened Ruler Catherine proved to be an efficient, energetic empress. She reorganized the provincial government, codified laws, and began state-sponsored education for both boys and girls.

Like Peter the Great, Catherine embraced Western ideas and worked to bring Russia fully into European cultural and political life. At court, she encouraged French language and customs, wrote histories and plays, and organized performances. As you will read in the next chapter, she was also a serious student of the French thinkers who led the intellectual movement known as the Enlightenment.

A Ruthless Absolute Monarch Catherine was also an absolute monarch, like other European rulers of the time, and often she was among the most ruthless. She granted a charter to the boyars outlining important rights, such as exemption from taxes. She also allowed them to increase their stranglehold on the peasants. When peasants rebelled against the harsh burdens of serfdom, Catherine took firm action to repress them. As a result, conditions grew worse for Russian peasants. Under Catherine, even more peasants were forced into serfdom.

Like Peter the Great, Catherine was determined to expand Russia's borders. Waging the Russo-Turkish war against the Ottoman Empire gained her a warm-water port on the Black Sea in 1774. She also took steps to seize territory from neighboring Poland.

The Partitions of Poland In the 1770s, Catherine, King Frederick II of Prussia, and Emperor Joseph II of Austria hungrily eyed Poland. As you have read, the Polish-Lithuanian Commonwealth had once been a great European power. However, its rulers were unable to centralize their power or diminish the influence of the Polish nobility. The divided Polish government was ill-prepared to stand up to the increasing might of its neighbors, Russia, Prussia, and Austria.

To avoid fighting one another, the three monarchs agreed in 1772 to **partition,** or divide up, Poland. Catherine took part of eastern Poland, where many Russians and Ukrainians lived. Frederick and Joseph took control of Polish territory in the west. Poland was further partitioned in 1793. Then in 1795, Austria, Prussia, and Russia each took their final slices and the independent country of Poland vanished from the map. Not until 1919 would a free Polish state reappear.

✓ **Checkpoint** How were Catherine's goals similar to those of Peter?

Looking Ahead

By the mid-1700s, absolute monarchs ruled four of the five leading countries in Europe. Britain, with its strong Parliament, was the only exception. As these five nations competed with one another, they often ended up fighting to maintain a balance of power. At the same time, new ideas were in the air. Radical changes would soon shatter the French monarchy, upset the balance of power, and revolutionize European societies.

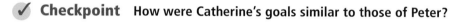

SECTION 5 Assessment

Progress Monitoring *Online*
For: Self-quiz with vocabulary practice
Web Code: nba-1651

Terms, People, and Places

1. For each term, person, or place listed in the beginning of the section, write a sentence explaining its significance.

Note Taking

2. **Reading Skill: Identify Main Ideas** Use your completed Venn diagram to answer the Focus Question: How did Peter the Great and Catherine the Great strengthen Russia and expand its territory?

Comprehension and Critical Thinking

3. **Identify Central Issues** What were three goals of Peter the Great and what was one step that he undertook to achieve each goal?

4. **Analyze Information** Why was obtaining a warm-water port a major priority for Peter?

5. **Compare Points of View** How did Peter and Catherine envision Russia's future?

● **Writing About History**

Quick Write: Write the Text Body
Choose a topic from the section on which you might write a persuasive essay—for example: Was Peter the Great really "great"? Write the body of your text, using a list of points you have made to guide you. Remember to open and close the body of the text with particularly strong arguments.

Quick Study Guide

Progress Monitoring *Online*
For: Self-test with vocabulary practice
Web Code: nba-1652

■ Key Rulers

Spain: Charles V (Charles I of Spain); Philip II
France: Henry IV; Louis XIV
Britain: Henry VIII; Elizabeth I; James I; Charles I; Oliver Cromwell; Charles II; James II; William and Mary
Austria: Ferdinand; Charles VI; Maria Theresa
Prussia: Frederick William; Frederick the Great
Russia: Peter the Great; Catherine the Great

■ Key Events

- **Battle of Lepanto, 1571**—Spain and allies against Ottoman Empire
- **Netherlands rebellions, 1560s–1580s**—political and religious revolts against Spain
- **Spanish Armada attacks England, 1588**
- **St. Bartholomew's Day Massacre, 1572**—slaughter of French Huguenots
- **Thirty Years' War, 1618–1648**
- **English Civil War, 1642–1648**
- **The *Fronde*, 1648–1653**—uprising of various groups in France
- **Glorious Revolution, 1688**—bloodless change of monarchs in England
- **War of the Spanish Succession, 1700–1713**
- **Great Northern War, 1700–1721**—Russia and allies against Sweden
- **War of the Austrian Succession, 1740–1748**
- **Seven Years' War, 1756–1763**
- **Russo-Turkish War, 1768–1774**—Russia against the Ottoman Empire
- **Partitions of Poland, 1772, 1793, 1795**

■ Partitions of Poland, 1701–1795

1701
RUSSIA
Moscow
Baltic Sea
Berlin
PRUSSIA
Vistula R.
Warsaw
POLAND
Kiev
Dnieper R.
Vienna
AUSTRIA
Danube
Black Sea

1772
St. Petersburg
Baltic Sea
to Prussia
to Russia
Moscow
PRUSSIA
Berlin
POLAND
Warsaw
RUSSIA
Kiev
Dnieper R.
to Austria
Vienna
AUSTRIA
Danube
Black Sea

1795
St. Petersburg
Baltic Sea
Moscow
PRUSSIA
Berlin
to Prussia
Warsaw
to Austria
to Russia
RUSSIA
Kiev
Dnieper R.
Vienna
AUSTRIA
Danube R.
Black Sea

N W E S

Conic Projection
0   200   400 mi
0   200   400 km

■ Key Events in the Age of Absolutism

1556
Philip II becomes king of Spain.

1618
The Thirty Years' War begins.

1642
The English Civil War begins.

Chapter Events
Global Events

1550　　　**1600**　　　**1650**

1556
Akbar the Great becomes emperor of Mughal India.

1607
British colonists found Jamestown.

Concept Connector

■ Cumulative Review

Record the answers to the questions below in your Concept Connector worksheets.

1. **Revolution** In England, the Glorious Revolution of 1688 was celebrated as a bloodless transfer of power—ordained by the people embodied by the Parliament—from one ruler to another. This was a radical event for its time, because the transfer of power had never been accomplished by Parliament in this way before, nor with so little violence. Read about how power was transferred from one English ruler to another between 1377 and 1688 and create an annotated timeline of these events. Think about the following:
   - the cause of each transfer of power
   - the fate of each ruler
   - the level of conflict related to each transfer of power

2. **Political Systems** Compare the absolute monarchy in France under Louis XIV to imperial rule in ancient Rome. How were these two systems similar, and how were they different? Create a chart to compare and contrast the two systems in the following categories. Consider the following aspects:
   - theoretical basis
   - ruler's level of power
   - symbols
   - status of democratic institutions

3. **Democracy** The Magna Carta of 1215 was a landmark legal development because it limited the power of the English monarch and protected some civil rights. Read about the rights and protections it granted as well as the limits it established on the monarchy. Compare these with the rights and protections ensured by the English Bill of Rights of 1688. Write one or two paragraphs that summarize how the later document increased democracy in England from what it was under Magna Carta and further limited the powers of the monarchy.

■ Connections to Today

1. **Conflict** The Age of Absolutism was also an "age of religious conflicts." Many of these conflicts, primarily between Catholics and Protestants, were long lasting and extremely violent. Several caused major wars. Find and read a newspaper or Internet article about a country or region where religious conflict is still a concern today—for example, Bosnia, India, Iraq, Israel, or Northern Ireland. Write a two- or three-paragraph summary of what you learn.

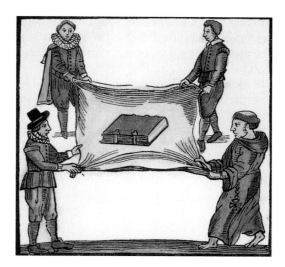

2. **Democracy** The English Bill of Rights is one of the source documents for ideas included in the American Declaration of Independence and the United States Constitution. Review the excerpt from the English Bill of Rights on page 524. Write a three-paragraph essay that summarizes how aspects of the English Bill of Rights are still present in American ideas of democracy today.

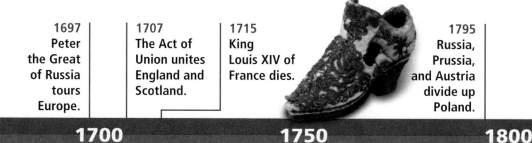

1697 Peter the Great of Russia tours Europe.

1707 The Act of Union unites England and Scotland.

1715 King Louis XIV of France dies.

1795 Russia, Prussia, and Austria divide up Poland.

1700

1750

1800

History *Interactive*
For: Interactive timeline
Web Code: nbp-1652

1680s The Asante kingdom is organized in West Africa.

1736 Qianlong begins reign as emperor of China.

1754 The French and Indian War erupts in North America.

1793 The emperor of China rejects British trade.

175

Chapter Assessment

Terms, People, and Places

Complete each sentence by choosing the correct answer from the list of terms below. You will not use all the terms.

absolute monarch	constitutional monarchy
divine right	limited monarchy
balance of power	oligarchy
westernization	partition
habeas corpus	

1. After the Glorious Revolution, several new institutions marked the transition of England's government to a _____.
2. The theory of _____ states that monarchs rule by the will of God.
3. The English Bill of Rights sets out the principle of _____.
4. Peter the Great pursued a policy of _____ to make Russia more modern.
5. The _____ of Poland occurred in the 1700s when the rulers of Austria, Russia, and Prussia agreed to split that country among themselves.
6. In this period, nearly every major European nation was ruled by a(n) _____.

Main Ideas

Section 1 (pp. 142–146)
7. How did resources from the Spanish colonies in the Americas contribute to the decline of Spain?
8. What was the Spanish Armada?

Section 2 (pp. 148–152)
9. What were two symbols of the reign of Louis XIV and what was their significance?

Section 3 (pp. 154–161)
10. (a) What were the immediate causes of the English Civil War? (b) What were some important results?
11. How did the Glorious Revolution limit royal power in England?

Section 4 (pp. 163–167)
12. What events led to the start of the Thirty Years' War?

Section 5 (pp. 168–173)
13. What reforms did Peter the Great carry out?
14. What was one long-term goal of the Russian monarchs and how was it finally achieved?

Chapter Focus Question
15. What events led to the rise of absolute monarchies and the development of centralized nation-states in Europe?

Critical Thinking

16. **Draw Conclusions** Based on the material in the chapter, how effective do you think the policy of maintaining a balance of power was among European nations?
17. **Analyze Information** Explain what Louis XIV meant when he said, "I am the state."
18. **Test Conclusions** Based on what you have learned about the Glorious Revolution, do you think the name for that event is accurate? Why or why not?
19. **Compare** Compare the goals and policies of Peter the Great with those of one of the following monarchs: (a) Louis XIV (b) Frederick II (c) Maria Theresa.
20. **Synthesize Information** What was the historical significance of the execution of Charles I of England?
21. **Understand Effects** What was the general impact of the Thirty Years' War on Europe?

● Writing About History

Writing a Persuasive Essay During the Age of Absolutism, strong monarchs created centralized nation-states whose governments they ruled with complete authority. Write a persuasive essay in which you argue a position on one aspect of this age. Consider topics such as: Was absolute monarchy an effective system? Was the divine right of kings a valid basis for rule? Consult page SH16 of the Writing Handbook for additional help.

Prewriting
• Choose a listed topic or another one that interests you, one that provokes an argument and has at least two sides. Then choose a side of the argument.
• Collect evidence, using a graphic organizer to list points on both sides of the issue.

• Research Internet or print sources to find materials that analyze your position from both sides. Take notes on relevant details, events, and people.

Drafting
• Clearly state the position that you will argue in a thesis statement. Use the rest of your introduction to provide readers necessary context about the issue.
• Make an outline to organize your argument and supporting details. Then choose information from your research that supports each part of your outline.

Revising
• Use the guidelines for revising your essay on page SH17 of the Writing Handbook.

Document-Based Assessment

The Rise of Parliament

The struggle between English monarchs and Parliament raged through the seventeenth century, and was fought on battlefields and legal fronts. The documents below illustrate the points of view of a monarch, Parliament, and a well-known philosopher.

Document A

"THE KINGS THEREAFTER in Scotland were before any estates or ranks of men within the same, before any Parliaments were holden or laws made; and by them was the land distributed (which at first was wholly theirs), states erected and decerned, and forms of government devised and established. And it follows of necessity that the Kings were the authors and makers of the laws and not the laws of the Kings."

—From *True Law of Free Monarchies,* 1598

Document B

"The Petition exhibited to his Majesty by the lords Spiritual and Temporal, and Commons, in this present Parliament assembled, concerning divers Rights and Liberties of the Subjects, with the King's Majesty's royal answer thereunto in full Parliament.
. . . Your subjects have inherited this freedom, that they should not be compelled to contribute to any tax, tallage, aid, or other like charge not set by common consent, in parliament.
. . . No man, of what estate or condition that he be, should be put out of his land or tenements, nor taken, nor imprisoned, nor disinherited nor put to death without being brought to answer by due process of law."

—From *The Petition of Right, 1628*

Document C

"Men, being, as has been said, by nature all free, equal, and independent, no one can be . . . subjected to the political power of another without his own consent. The only way whereby anyone divests himself of his natural liberty, and puts on the bonds of civil society is by agreeing with other men to join and unite into a community. . . .
It is evident, that *absolute monarchy,* which by some men is counted the only government in the world, is indeed *inconsistent with civil society.*"

—From *Two Treatises on Government* by John Locke, 1690.

Document D

A mid-1600s engraving depicts Charles I as a political and religious martyr.

Analyzing Documents

Use your knowledge of the age of absolutism and Documents A, B, C, and D to answer questions 1–4.

1. What is the main point of Document A?
   A Kings are subject only to laws of parliament.
   B Kings make laws but are not subject to them.
   C Kings no longer have the power of life and death over subjects.
   D Parliament now has the power of life and death over subjects.

2. Document B is a declaration of whose rights?
   A the king's rights
   B Parliament's rights
   C subjects' rights
   D the landed aristocracy's rights

3. Document C
   A supports Document A.
   B supports Document B.
   C supports both Document A and Document B.
   D supports Document A and Document D.

4. **Writing Task** Would you describe the rise of Parliament in England as an evolution or a revolution? Use documents from this page along with information from the chapter in your response.

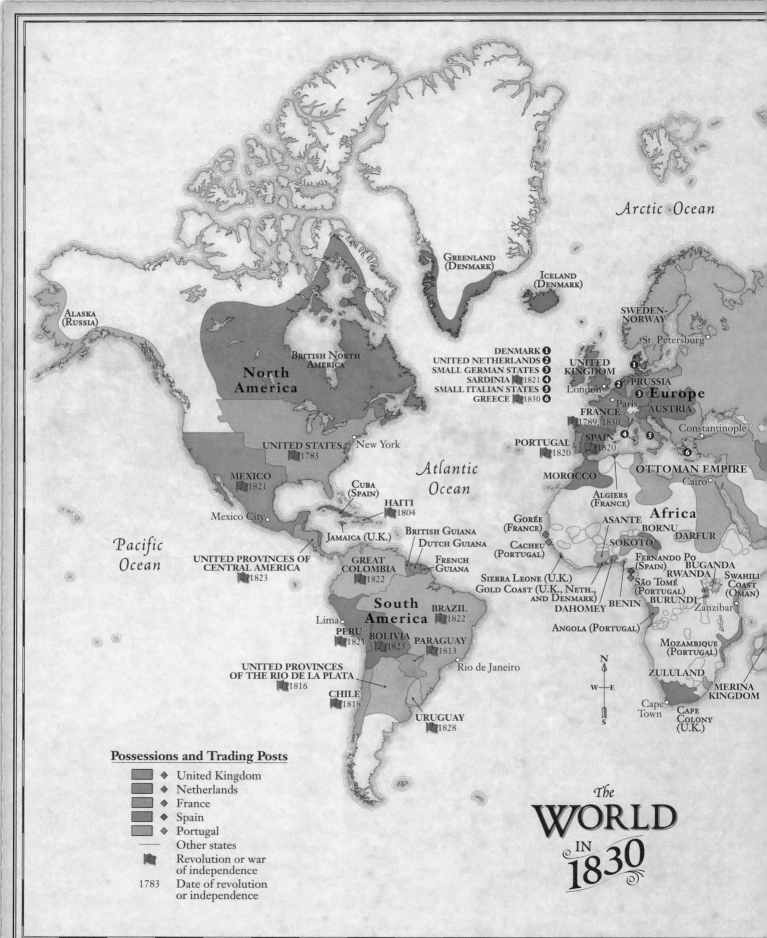

Arctic Ocean

GREENLAND (DENMARK)

ICELAND (DENMARK)

ALASKA (RUSSIA)

BRITISH NORTH AMERICA

North America

SWEDEN-NORWAY

St. Petersburg

DENMARK ❶
UNITED NETHERLANDS ❷
SMALL GERMAN STATES ❸
SARDINIA 🚩 1821 ❹
SMALL ITALIAN STATES ❺
GREECE 🚩 1830 ❻

UNITED KINGDOM
London
❶ PRUSSIA
❷
❸ **Europe**
Paris
FRANCE (1789, 1830) AUSTRIA
❹ ❺ Constantinople
PORTUGAL 🚩 1820
SPAIN 🚩 1820
❻

UNITED STATES 🚩 1783

New York

Atlantic Ocean

OTTOMAN EMPIRE
Cairo

MEXICO 🚩 1821

CUBA (SPAIN)

HAITI 🚩 1804

Mexico City

MOROCCO

ALGIERS (FRANCE)

ASANTE **Africa**

JAMAICA (U.K.)

GORÉE (FRANCE)

BORNU DARFUR

Pacific Ocean

UNITED PROVINCES OF CENTRAL AMERICA 🚩 1823

BRITISH GUIANA
DUTCH GUIANA

GREAT COLOMBIA 🚩 1822

FRENCH GUIANA

CACHEU (PORTUGAL)

SOKOTO

FERNANDO PO (SPAIN)
SÃO TOMÉ (PORTUGAL)

BUGANDA
RWANDA
SWAHILI COAST (OMAN)

SIERRA LEONE (U.K.)
GOLD COAST (U.K., NETH., AND DENMARK)

BENIN BURUNDI
DAHOMEY

South America

BRAZIL 🚩 1822

Zanzibar

ANGOLA (PORTUGAL)

Lima
PERU 🚩 1821
BOLIVIA 🚩 1825
PARAGUAY 🚩 1813

Rio de Janeiro

MOZAMBIQUE (PORTUGAL)

UNITED PROVINCES OF THE RIO DE LA PLATA 🚩 1816

N
W   E
S

ZULULAND

CHILE 🚩 1818

URUGUAY 🚩 1828

Cape Town
CAPE COLONY (U.K.)

MERINA KINGDOM

Possessions and Trading Posts

◆ United Kingdom
◆ Netherlands
◆ France
◆ Spain
◆ Portugal
— Other states
🚩 Revolution or war of independence
1783 Date of revolution or independence

The **WORLD** IN **1830**

RUSSIAN EMPIRE

Asia

CENTRAL
ASIAN
STATES
PERSIA   SIKH
          KINGDOM
          NEPAL
AFGHAN-   BHUTAN
ISTAN
          Delhi

OMAN   INDIA
Bombay   (U.K.)   BURMA
GOA   Calcutta
(PORTUGAL)
          Bangkok   SIAM
PONDICHERRY
(FRANCE)
CEYLON (U.K.)   MALAY
                  STATES
Tenasserim (U.K.)

Indian
Ocean   SINGAPORE (U.K.)

          Batavia   DUTCH EAST INDIES

          PORTUGUESE TIMOR

MAURITIUS (U.K.)

RÉUNION (FRANCE)

CHINA   Beijing

          KOREA   JAPAN
          (CHINA)
                   Edo (Tokyo)
          DESHIMA (NETHERLANDS)

          MACAO (PORTUGAL)
SOUTHEAST ASIAN STATES
          PHILIPPINES
          (SPAIN)

Pacific
Ocean

Australia

WESTERN AUSTRALIA   NEW SOUTH WALES
(U.K.)   (U.K.)
                      Sydney

TASMANIA (U.K.)

MERCATOR PROJECTION
SCALE IN MILES
0   1000   2000   3000

0   1000   2000   3000
SCALE IN KILOMETERS
SCALE AT THE EQUATOR

Geography *Interactive*
For: Audio guided tour
Web Code: nbp-4000

UNIT

2

Enlightenment and Revolution

1700–1850

CHAPTER 5
The Enlightenment and the American Revolution (1700–1800)

CHAPTER 6
The French Revolution and Napoleon (1789–1815)

CHAPTER 7
The Industrial Revolution Begins (1750–1850)

CHAPTER 8
Revolutions in Europe and Latin America (1790–1848)

The Enlightenment and the American Revolution

1700–1800

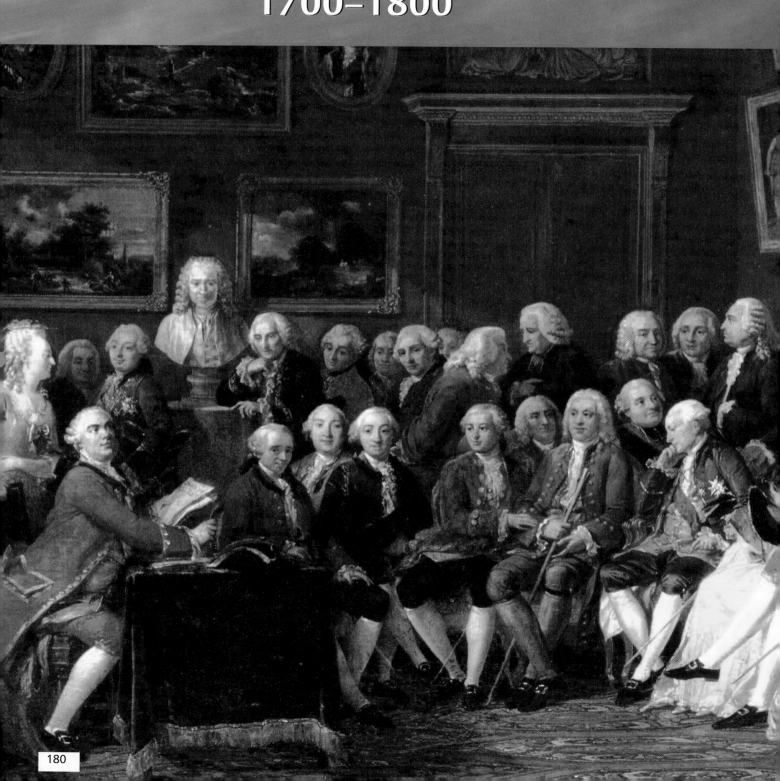

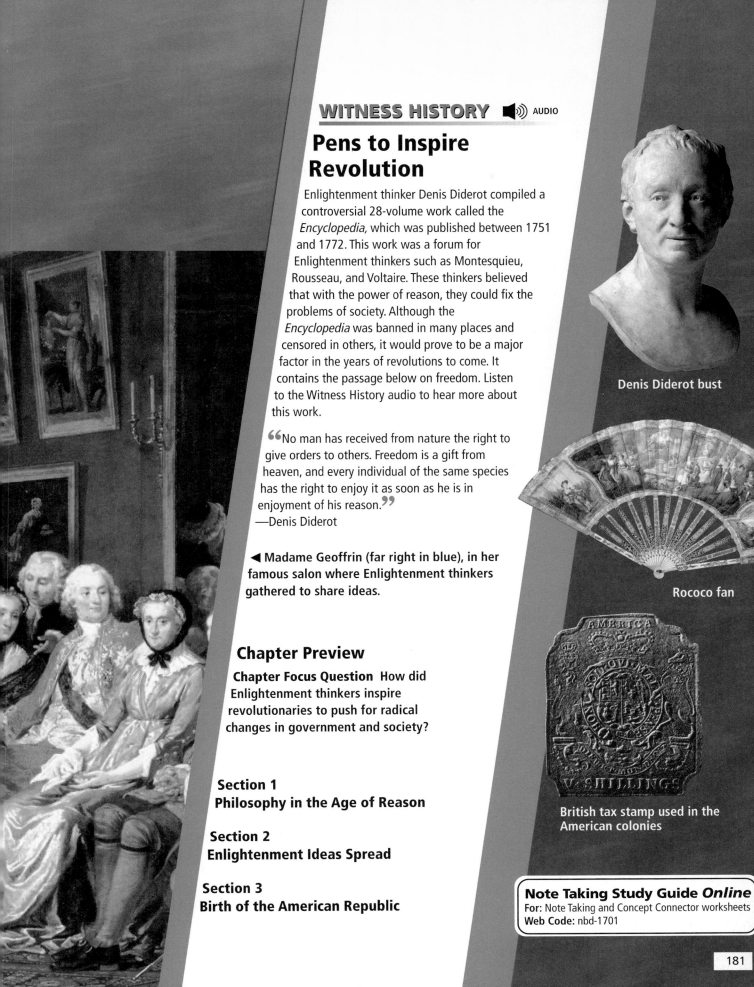

Pens to Inspire Revolution

Enlightenment thinker Denis Diderot compiled a controversial 28-volume work called the *Encyclopedia,* which was published between 1751 and 1772. This work was a forum for Enlightenment thinkers such as Montesquieu, Rousseau, and Voltaire. These thinkers believed that with the power of reason, they could fix the problems of society. Although the *Encyclopedia* was banned in many places and censored in others, it would prove to be a major factor in the years of revolutions to come. It contains the passage below on freedom. Listen to the Witness History audio to hear more about this work.

❝No man has received from nature the right to give orders to others. Freedom is a gift from heaven, and every individual of the same species has the right to enjoy it as soon as he is in enjoyment of his reason.❞
—Denis Diderot

◀ Madame Geoffrin (far right in blue), in her famous salon where Enlightenment thinkers gathered to share ideas.

Denis Diderot bust

Rococo fan

British tax stamp used in the American colonies

Chapter Preview

Chapter Focus Question How did Enlightenment thinkers inspire revolutionaries to push for radical changes in government and society?

Section 1
Philosophy in the Age of Reason

Section 2
Enlightenment Ideas Spread

Section 3
Birth of the American Republic

Jean-Jacques Rousseau and quill pen

Rousseau Stirs Things Up

In Jean-Jacques Rousseau's most important work, *The Social Contract,* he argued that in order to be free, people should do what is best for their community. Rousseau had many supporters who were inspired by his passionate writings. European monarchs, on the other hand, were angry that Rousseau was questioning authority. As a result, Rousseau worried about persecution for much of his life. The "chains" below represent the social institutions that confined society.

66 Man is born free, and everywhere he is in chains. 99
—Rousseau, *The Social Contract*

Focus Question What effects did Enlightenment philosophers have on government and society?

Philosophy in the Age of Reason

Objectives
- Explain how science led to the Enlightenment.
- Compare the ideas of Hobbes and Locke.
- Identify the beliefs and contributions of the *philosophes.*
- Summarize how economic thinking changed during this time.

Terms, People, and Places

natural law	Montesquieu
Thomas Hobbes	Voltaire
John Locke	Diderot
social contract	Rousseau
natural right	laissez faire
philosophe	Adam Smith

Note Taking

Reading Skill: Summarize Draw a table like the one shown here. As you read the section, summarize each thinker's works and ideas.

Thinkers' Works and Ideas	
Hobbes	*Leviathan,* social contract
Locke	
Montesquieu	

By the early 1700s, European thinkers felt that nothing was beyond the reach of the human mind. Through the use of reason, insisted these thinkers, people and governments could solve every social, political, and economic problem. In essence, these writers, scholars, and philosophers felt they could change the world.

Scientific Revolution Sparks the Enlightenment

The Scientific Revolution of the 1500s and 1600s had transformed the way people in Europe looked at the world. In the 1700s, other scientists expanded European knowledge. For example, Edward Jenner developed a vaccine against smallpox, a disease whose path of death spanned the centuries.

Scientific successes convinced educated Europeans of the power of human reason. **Natural law,** or rules discoverable by reason, govern scientific forces such as gravity and magnetism. Why not, then, use natural law to better understand social, economic, and political problems? Using the methods of the new science, reformers thus set out to study human behavior and solve the problems of society. In this way, the Scientific Revolution led to another revolution in thinking, known as the Enlightenment. Immanuel Kant, a German philosopher best known for his work *The Critique of Pure Reason,* was one of the first to describe this era with the word "Enlightenment." Despite Kant's skepticism about the power of reason, he was enthusiastic about the Enlightenment and believed, like many European philosophers, that natural law could help explain aspects of humanity.

✓ **Checkpoint** What convinced educated Europeans to accept the power of reason?

Hobbes and Locke Have Conflicting Views

Thomas Hobbes and **John Locke,** two seventeenth-century English thinkers, set forth ideas that were to become key to the Enlightenment. Both men lived through the upheavals of the English Civil War. Yet they came to very different conclusions about human nature and the role of government.

Hobbes Believes in Powerful Government Thomas Hobbes outlined his ideas in a work titled *Leviathan.* In it, he argued that people were naturally cruel, greedy, and selfish. If not strictly controlled, they would fight, rob, and oppress one another. Life in the "state of nature"—without laws or other control—would be "solitary, poor, nasty, brutish, and short."

To escape that "brutish" life, said Hobbes, people entered into a **social contract,** an agreement by which they gave up their freedom for an organized society. Hobbes believed that only a powerful government could ensure an orderly society. For him, such a government was an absolute monarchy, which could impose order and compel obedience.

Locke Advocates Natural Rights John Locke had a more optimistic view of human nature. He thought people were basically reasonable and moral. Further, they had certain **natural rights,** or rights that belonged to all humans from birth. These included the right to life, liberty, and property.

In *Two Treatises of Government,* Locke argued that people formed governments to protect their natural rights. The best kind of government, he said, had limited power and was accepted by all citizens. Thus, unlike Hobbes, Locke rejected absolute monarchy. England during this time experienced a shift in political power known as the Glorious Revolution. James II, an unpopular absolute monarch, left the throne and fled England in 1688. Locke later wrote that he thought James II deserved to be dethroned for violating the rights of the English.

Locke proposed a radical idea about this time. A government, he said, has an obligation to the people it governs. If a government fails its obligations or violates people's natural rights, the people have the right to overthrow that government. Locke's idea would one day influence leaders of the American Revolution, such as Benjamin Franklin, Thomas Jefferson, and James Madison. Locke's idea of the right of revolution would also echo across Europe and Latin America in the centuries that followed.

✓ **Checkpoint** How did Hobbes and Locke differ in their views on the role of government?

Hobbes Writes the *Leviathan*
The title page from *Leviathan* (1651) by Hobbes demonstrates his belief in a powerful ruler. The monarch here represents the Leviathan who rises above all of society.

Voltaire

François-Marie Arouet, known as Voltaire (1694–1778) was an impassioned poet, historian, essayist, and philosopher who wrote with cutting sarcasm and sharp wit. Voltaire was sent to the Bastille prison twice due to his criticism of French authorities and was eventually banned from Paris. When he was able to return to France, he wrote about political and religious freedom. Voltaire spent his life fighting enemies of freedom, such as ignorance, superstition, and intolerance. **What did Voltaire attack in his writings?**

Montesquieu

Born to wealth, Charles Louis de Secondat (1689–1755) inherited the title Baron de Montesquieu from his uncle. Like many other reformers, he did not let his privileged status keep him from becoming a voice for democracy. His first book titled *Persian Letters* ridiculed the French government and social classes. In his work published in 1748, *The Spirit of the Laws,* he advanced the idea of separation of powers—a foundation of modern democracy. **What did Montesquieu think was necessary to protect liberty?**

The *Philosophes*

In the 1700s, there was a flowering of Enlightenment thought. This was when a group of Enlightenment thinkers in France applied the methods of science to understand and improve society. They believed that the use of reason could lead to reforms of government, law, and society. These thinkers were called *philosophes* (fee loh ZOHFS), which means "philosophers." Their ideas soon spread beyond France and even beyond Europe.

Montesquieu Advances the Idea of Separation of Powers An early and influential thinker was Baron de **Montesquieu** (MAHN tus kyoo). Montesquieu studied the governments of Europe, from Italy to England. He read about ancient and medieval Europe, and learned about Chinese and Native American cultures. His sharp criticism of absolute monarchy would open doors for later debate.

In 1748, Montesquieu published *The Spirit of the Laws*, in which he discussed governments throughout history. Montesquieu felt that the best way to protect liberty was to divide the various functions and powers of government among three branches: the legislative, executive, and judicial. He also felt that each branch of government should be able to serve as a check on the other two, an idea that we call checks and balances. Montesquieu's beliefs would soon profoundly affect the Framers of the United States Constitution.

Voltaire Defends Freedom of Thought Probably the most famous of the *philosophes* was François-Marie Arouet, who took the name **Voltaire.** "My trade," said Voltaire, "is to say what I think," and he did so throughout his long, controversial life. Voltaire used biting wit as a weapon to expose the abuses of his day. He targeted corrupt officials and idle aristocrats. With his pen, he battled inequality, injustice, and superstition. He detested the slave trade and deplored religious prejudice.

Voltaire's outspoken attacks offended both the French government and the Catholic Church. He was imprisoned and forced into exile. Even as he saw his books outlawed and even burned, he continued to defend the principle of freedom of speech.

Diderot Edits the *Encyclopedia* Denis **Diderot** (DEE duh roh) worked for years to produce a 28-volume set of books called the *Encyclopedia*. As the editor, Diderot did more than just compile articles.

His purpose was "to change the general way of thinking" by explaining ideas on topics such as government, <u>philosophy</u>, and religion. Diderot's *Encyclopedia* included articles by leading thinkers of the day, including Montesquieu and Voltaire. In these articles, the *philosophes* denounced slavery, praised freedom of expression, and urged education for all. They attacked divine-right theory and traditional religions. Critics raised an outcry. The French government argued that the *Encyclopedia* was an attack on public morals, and the pope threatened to excommunicate Roman Catholics who bought or read the volumes.

Despite these and other efforts to ban the *Encyclopedia,* more than 4,000 copies were printed between 1751 and 1789. When translated into other languages, the *Encyclopedia* helped spread Enlightenment ideas throughout Europe and across the Atlantic Ocean to the Americas.

Rousseau Promotes *The Social Contract*

Jean-Jacques **Rousseau** (roo SOH), believed that people in their natural state were basically good. This natural innocence, he felt, was corrupted by the evils of society, especially the unequal distribution of property. Many reformers and revolutionaries later adopted this view. Among them were Thomas Paine and Marquis de Lafayette, who were leading figures of the American and French Revolutions.

In 1762, Rousseau set forth his ideas about government and society in *The Social Contract.* Rousseau felt that society placed too many limitations on people's behavior. He believed that some controls were necessary, but that they should be minimal. Additionally, only governments that had been freely elected should impose these controls.

Rousseau put his faith in the "general will," or the best conscience of the people. The good of the community as a whole, he said, should be placed above individual interests. Rousseau has influenced political and social thinkers for more than 200 years. Woven through his work is a hatred of all forms of political and economic oppression. His bold ideas would help fan the flames of revolt in years to come.

Women Challenge the *Philosophes*

The Enlightenment slogan "free and equal" did not apply to women. Though the *philosophes* said women had natural rights, their rights were limited to the areas of home and family.

By the mid- to late-1700s, a small but growing number of women protested this view. Germaine de Staël in France and Catharine Macaulay and Mary Wollstonecraft in Britain argued that women were being excluded from the social contract itself. Their arguments, however, were ridiculed and often sharply condemned.

Wollstonecraft was a well-known British social critic. She accepted that a woman's first duty was to be a good mother but felt that a woman should be able to decide what was in her own interest without depending on her husband. In 1792, Wollstonecraft published *A Vindication of the Rights of Woman.* In it, she called for equal education for girls and boys. Only education, she argued, could give women the tools they needed to participate equally with men in public life.

✓ **Checkpoint** What topics were addressed by the *philosophes* in their *Encyclopedia* articles?

Vocabulary Builder

<u>philosophy</u>—(fih LAHS uh fee) *n.* love of, or the search for, wisdom or knowledge

Heated Debate
Rousseau (left) and Voltaire (right) are pictured here in the midst of an argument. Even though the *philosophes* were reform-minded, they disagreed about some issues. *Compare the beliefs of Rousseau and Voltaire.*

New Economic Thinking

French thinkers known as physiocrats focused on economic reforms. Like the *philosophes,* physiocrats based their thinking on natural laws. The physiocrats claimed that their rational economic system was based on the natural laws of economics.

Laissez Faire Replaces Mercantilism Physiocrats rejected mercantilism, which required government regulation of the economy to achieve a favorable balance of trade. Instead, they urged a policy of **laissez faire** (les ay FEHR), allowing business to operate with little or no government interference. Physiocrats also supported free trade and opposed tariffs.

Smith Argues for a Free Market Scottish economist **Adam Smith** greatly admired the physiocrats. In his influential work *The Wealth of Nations,* he argued that the free market should be allowed to regulate business activity. Smith tried to show how manufacturing, trade, wages, profits, and economic growth were all linked to the market forces of supply and demand. Wherever there was a demand for goods or services, he said, suppliers would seek to meet that demand in order to gain profits. Smith was a strong supporter of laissez faire. However, he felt that government had a duty to protect society, administer justice, and provide public works. Adam Smith's ideas would help to shape productive economies in the 1800s and 1900s.

✔ **Checkpoint** Why did Smith support laissez faire?

Investors in Paris, France, 1720

Progress Monitoring *Online*
For: Self-quiz with vocabulary practice
Web Code: nba-1711

SECTION 1
Assessment

Terms, People, and Places

1. For each term, person, or place listed at the beginning of the section, write a sentence explaining its significance.

Note Taking

2. **Reading Skill: Summarize** Use your completed tables to answer the Focus Question: What effects did Enlightenment philosophers have on government and society?

Comprehension and Critical Thinking

3. **Summarize** How did the achievements of the Scientific Revolution contribute to the Enlightenment?

4. **Recognize Cause and Effect** What did the *philosophes* do to better understand and improve society?

5. **Synthesize Information** Explain the connection between the policy of laissez faire and natural economic laws.

● Writing About History

Quick Write: Explore a Topic On some essay tests, you may have a choice of topic. You should choose one that you feel most knowledgeable about. Choose from the following, and draft a single sentence that identifies the main idea:
(a) social contracts (b) freedom of speech (c) women in the mid-1700s

John Locke:
Two Treatises of Government

English philosopher John Locke (1632–1704) published *Two Treatises of Government* in 1690. Locke believed that all people had the same natural rights of life, liberty, and property. In this essay, Locke states that the primary purpose of government is to protect these natural rights. He also states that governments hold their power only with the consent of the people. Locke's ideas greatly influenced revolutions in America and France.

John Locke and a book of his writings

But though men, when they enter into society give up the equality, liberty, and executive power they had in the state of Nature into the hands of society . . . the power of the society or legislative constituted by them can never be supposed to extend farther than the common good. . . . Whoever has the legislative or supreme power of any commonwealth, is bound to govern by established standing laws, promulgated[1] and known to the people, and not by extemporary[2] decrees, by indifferent and upright judges, who are to decide controversies by those laws; and to employ the force of the community at home only in the execution of such laws, or abroad to prevent or redress foreign injuries and secure the community from inroads[3] and invasion. And all this to be directed to no other end but the peace, safety, and public good of the people. . . .

The reason why men enter into society is the preservation of their property; and the end while they choose and authorize a legislative is that there may be laws made, and rules set, as guards and fences to the properties of all the society, . . .

Whensoever, therefore, the legislative [power] shall transgress[4] this fundamental rule of society, and either by ambition, fear, folly, or corruption, endeavor to grasp themselves, or put into the hands of any other, an absolute power over the lives, liberties, and estates of the people, by this breach of trust they forfeit the power the people had put into their hands for quite contrary ends, and it devolves[5] to the people; who have a right to resume their original liberty, and by the establishment of a new legislative (such as they shall think fit), provide for their own safety and security. . . .

1. **promulgated** (PRAHM ul gayt id) *vt.* published or made known.
2. **extemporary** (ek STEM puh rehr ee) *adj.* without any preparation.
3. **inroads** (IN rohdz) *n.* advances at the expense of someone.
4. **transgress** (trans GRES) *vt.* go beyond; break.
5. **devolves** (dih VAHLVZ) *vt.* passes.

Thinking Critically
1. **Draw Inferences** According to Locke, how should a land be governed? Why do you think this is the case?
2. **Identify Central Issues** What does Locke say can happen if a government fails to protect the rights of its people?

Mozart and a sheet of his music

WITNESS HISTORY 🔊 AUDIO

Mozart, the Musical Genius

As a young boy, Wolfgang Amadeus Mozart astonished royalty with his musical talent. Although his life was relatively short, he composed more than 600 pieces of music. Many pieces embraced the spirit of the Enlightenment.

> 66 Few have captured the spirit of the Enlightenment, its intellectual and social agenda, as has Mozart in his opera, *The Magic Flute,* . . . [It] is a series of variations on the triumph of light over darkness, of sun over moon, of day over night, of reason, tolerance, and love over passion, hate, and revenge. 99
>
> —Isaac Kramnick, historian

Focus Question As Enlightenment ideas spread across Europe, what cultural and political changes took place?

Enlightenment Ideas Spread

Objectives

- Identify the roles that censorship and salons played in the spread of new ideas.
- Describe how the Enlightenment affected the arts and literature.
- Understand how *philosophes* influenced enlightened despots.
- Explain why Enlightenment ideas were slow to reach most Europeans.

Terms, People, and Places

censorship	enlightened despot
salons	Frederick the Great
baroque	Catherine the Great
rococo	Joseph II

Note Taking

Reading Skill: Categorize On a sheet of paper, draw a concept web to help you record information from this section.

Paris, France, the heart of the Enlightenment, drew many intellectuals and others eager to debate new ideas. Reforms proposed one evening became the talk of the town the next day. Enlightenment ideas flowed from France, across Europe, and beyond. Everywhere, thinkers examined traditional beliefs and customs in the light of reason and found them flawed. Even some absolute monarchs experimented with Enlightenment ideas, although they drew back when changes threatened the established way of doing things.

New Ideas Challenge Society

Enlightenment ideas spread quickly through many levels of society. Educated people all over Europe eagerly read not only Diderot's *Encyclopedia* but also the small, inexpensive pamphlets that printers churned out on a broad range of issues. More and more, people saw that reform was necessary in order to achieve a just society.

During the Middle Ages, most Europeans had accepted without question a society based on divine-right rule, a strict class system, and a belief in heavenly reward for earthly suffering. In the Age of Reason, such ideas seemed unscientific and irrational. A just society, Enlightenment thinkers taught, should ensure social justice and happiness in this world. Not everyone agreed with this idea of replacing the values that existed, however.

Writers Face Censorship Most, but not all, government and church authorities felt they had a sacred duty to defend the old order. They believed that God had set up the old order. To protect against the attacks of the Enlightenment, they waged a war of **censorship,** or restricting access to ideas and information. They banned and burned books and imprisoned writers.

To avoid censorship, *philosophes* and writers like Montesquieu and Voltaire sometimes disguised their ideas in works of fiction. In the *Persian Letters,* Montesquieu used two fictional Persian travelers, named Usbek and Rica, to mock French society. The hero of Voltaire's satirical novel *Candide,* published in 1759, travels across Europe and even to the Americas and the Middle East in search of "the best of all possible worlds." Voltaire slyly uses the tale to expose the corruption and hypocrisy of European society.

Ideas Spread in Salons New literature, the arts, science, and philosophy were regular topics of discussion in **salons,** or informal social gatherings at which writers, artists, *philosophes,* and others exchanged ideas. The salon originated in the 1600s, when a group of noblewomen in Paris began inviting a few friends to their homes for poetry readings. By the 1700s, some middle-class women began holding salons. Here middle-class citizens could meet with the nobility on an equal footing to discuss and spread Enlightenment ideas.

Madame Geoffrin (zhoh FRAN) ran one of the most respected salons. In her home on the Rue St. Honoré (roo sant ahn ur AY), she brought together the brightest and most talented people of her day. The young musical genius Wolfgang Amadeus Mozart played for her guests, and Diderot was a regular at her weekly dinners for philosophers and poets.

✓ **Checkpoint** What did those opposed to Enlightenment ideas do to stop the spread of information?

Arts and Literature Reflect New Ideas

In the 1600s and 1700s, the arts evolved to meet changing tastes. As in earlier periods, artists and composers had to please their patrons, the men and women who commissioned works from them or gave them jobs.

From Grandeur to Charm In the age of Louis XIV, courtly art and architecture were either in the Greek and Roman tradition or in a grand, ornate style known as **baroque.** Baroque paintings were huge, colorful, and full of excitement. They glorified historic battles or the lives of saints. Such works matched the grandeur of European courts at that time.

Louis XV and his court led a much less formal lifestyle than Louis XIV. Architects and designers reflected this change by developing the **rococo** style. Rococo art moved away from religion and, unlike the heavy splendor of the baroque, was lighter, elegant, and charming. Rococo art in salons was believed to encourage the imagination. Furniture and tapestries featured delicate shells and flowers, and more pastel colors were used. Portrait painters showed noble subjects in charming rural settings, surrounded by happy servants and pets. Although this style was criticized by the *philosophes* for its superficiality, it had a vast audience in the upper class and with the growing middle class as well.

Satire by Swift
Jonathan Swift published the satirical *Gulliver's Travels* in 1726. Here, an illustration from the book depicts a bound Gulliver and the Lilliputians, who are six-inch-tall, bloodthirsty characters. Although *Gulliver's Travels* satirizes political life in eighteenth-century England, it is still a classic today. *Why did writers hide their feelings about society?*

Vocabulary Builder

evolved—(ee VAHLVD) *v.* developed gradually over time

The Enlightenment Inspires Composers The new Enlightenment ideals led composers and musicians to develop new forms of music. There was a transition in music, as well as art, from the baroque style to rococo. An elegant style of music known as "classical" followed. Ballets and opera—plays set to music—were performed at royal courts, and opera houses sprang up from Italy to England. Before this era, only the social elite could afford to commission musicians to play for them. In the early to mid-1700s, however, the growing middle class could afford to pay for concerts to be performed publicly.

Among the towering musical figures of the era was Johann Sebastian Bach. A devout German Lutheran, Bach wrote beautiful religious works for organ and choirs. He also wrote sonatas for violin and harpsichord. Another German-born composer, George Frideric Handel, spent much of his life in England. There, he wrote *Water Music* and other pieces for King George I, as well as more than 30 operas. His most celebrated work, the *Messiah,* combines instruments and voices and is often performed at Christmas and Easter.

Composer Franz Joseph Haydn was one of the most important figures in the development of classical music. He helped develop forms for the string quartet and the symphony. Haydn had a close friendship with another famous composer, Wolfgang Amadeus Mozart. Mozart was a child prodigy who gained instant celebrity status as a composer and performer. His brilliant operas, graceful symphonies, and moving religious music helped define the new style of composition. Although he died in poverty at age 35, he produced an enormous amount of music during his lifetime. Mozart's musical legacy thrives today.

● **INFOGRAPHIC**

ROCOCO REACTION

In the eighteenth century, France experienced an aesthetic shift in art, clothing, music, and architecture. Curving lines, pastel colors, elegant music, and paintings depicting delightful love scenes replaced the formal lines and dark colors of the baroque style. The rise of this new style, referred to as rococo, reflected changes in French society that were brought about by the Enlightenment. As the French elite became more involved in the salons of the day (numbering about 800 in Paris), they competed with each other for the most fashionable home in which to host their intellectual discussions.

Composers adopted the graceful rococo style in their works of music. They wrote pieces for an instrument called the harpsichord (above) that reflected this new style. ◀)) AUDIO

The Novel Takes Shape By the 1700s, literature developed new forms and a wider audience. Middle-class readers, for example, liked stories about their own times told in straightforward prose. One result was an outpouring of novels, or long works of prose fiction. English novelists wrote many popular stories. Daniel Defoe wrote *Robinson Crusoe,* an exciting tale about a sailor shipwrecked on a tropical island. This novel is still well known today. In a novel called *Pamela,* Samuel Richardson used a series of letters to tell a story about a servant girl. This technique was adopted by other authors of the period.

✓ **Checkpoint** How did the arts and literature change as Enlightenment ideas spread?

Enlightened Despots Embrace New Ideas

The courts of Europe became enlivened as *philosophes* tried to persuade rulers to adopt their ideas. The *philosophes* hoped to convince the ruling classes that reform was necessary. Some monarchs did accept Enlightenment ideas. Others still practiced absolutism, a political doctrine in which a monarch had seemingly unlimited power. Those that did accept these new ideas became **enlightened despots,** or absolute rulers who used their power to bring about political and social change.

Frederick II Attempts Reform Frederick II, known as **Frederick the Great,** exerted extremely tight control over his subjects during his reign as king of Prussia from 1740 to 1786. Still, he saw himself as the "first servant of the state," with a duty to work for the common good.

Ornate Artifacts
In the examples of the rococo style shown here, notice the elegance of the delicate lace and floral patterns, as well as the charming paintings depicting the pleasures of everyday life.

Thinking Critically
1. **Make Generalizations** Based on what you see in the collection of images here, describe what you think it would have been like to live during this time period.
2. **Draw Inferences** Why might the *philosophes* have disliked the rococo style?

191

Enlightened Rulers in the Eighteenth Century

Geography *Interactive.*
For: Audio guided tour
Web Code: nbp-1721

Catherine the Great

Emperor Joseph II

Frederick the Great

Map Skills Although the center of the Enlightenment was in France, the ideas of reform spread to the rulers of Austria, Prussia, and Russia.

1. **Locate** (a) Paris (b) Prussia (c) Austria
2. **Location** Which enlightened despot ruled farthest from Paris?
3. **Draw Conclusions** According to the map, what regions of Europe were affected by enlightened despots?

Frederick openly praised Voltaire's work and invited several of the French intellectuals of the age to Prussia. Some of his first acts as king were to reduce the use of torture and allow a free press. Most of Frederick's reforms were directed at making the Prussian government more efficient. To do this, he reorganized the government's civil service and simplified laws. Frederick also tolerated religious differences, welcoming victims of religious persecution. "In my kingdom," he said, "everyone can go to heaven in his own fashion." His religious tolerance and also his disdain for torture showed Frederick's genuine belief in enlightened reform. In the end, however, Frederick desired a stronger monarchy and more power for himself.

Catherine the Great Studies *Philosophes'* Works
Catherine II, or **Catherine the Great,** empress of Russia, read the works of the *philosophes* and exchanged letters with Voltaire and Diderot. She praised Voltaire as someone who had "fought the united enemies of humankind: superstition, fanaticism, ignorance, trickery." Catherine believed in the Enlightenment ideas of equality and liberty.

Catherine, who became empress in 1762, toyed with implementing Enlightenment ideas. Early in her reign, she made some limited reforms in law and government. Catherine abolished torture and established religious tolerance in her lands. She granted nobles a charter of rights and criticized the institution of serfdom. Still, like Frederick in Prussia, Catherine did not intend to give up power. In the end, her main political contribution to Russia proved to be an expanded empire.

Joseph II Continues Reform In Austria, Hapsburg empress Maria Theresa ruled as an absolute monarch. Although she did not push for reforms, she is considered to be an enlightened despot by some historians because she worked to improve peasants' way of life. The most radical of the enlightened despots was her son and successor, **Joseph II.** Joseph was an eager student of the Enlightenment, and he traveled in disguise among his subjects to learn of their problems.

Joseph continued the work of Maria Theresa, who had begun to modernize Austria's government. Despite opposition, Joseph supported religious equality for Protestants and Jews in his Catholic empire. He ended censorship by allowing a free press and attempted to bring the Catholic Church under royal control. He sold the property of many monasteries that were not involved in education or care of the sick and used the proceeds to support those that were. Joseph even abolished serfdom. Like many of his other reforms, however, this measure was canceled after his death.

 Checkpoint Why were the *philosophes* interested in sharing their beliefs with European rulers?

Lives of the Majority Change Slowly

Most Europeans were untouched by either courtly or middle-class culture. They remained what they had always been—peasants living in small rural villages. Echoes of serfdom still remained throughout Europe despite advances in Western Europe. Their culture, based on centuries-old traditions, changed slowly.

By the late 1700s, however, radical ideas about equality and social justice finally seeped into peasant villages. While some peasants eagerly sought to topple the old order, others resisted efforts to bring about change. In the 1800s, war and political upheaval, as well as changing economic conditions, would transform peasant life in Europe.

 Checkpoint During this time, why did change occur slowly for most Europeans?

Progress Monitoring *Online*
For: Self-quiz with vocabulary practice
Web Code: nba-1721

SECTION 2 **Assessment**

Terms, People, and Places

1. For each term, person, or place listed at the beginning of the section, write a sentence explaining its significance.

Note Taking

2. **Reading Skill: Categorize** Use your completed concept webs to answer the Focus Question: As Enlightenment ideas spread across Europe, what cultural and political changes took place?

Comprehension and Critical Thinking

3. **Draw Conclusions** How did ideas of a "just society" change during the Age of Reason?

4. **Summarize** Explain the differences between baroque and rococo, and how these styles were reflected in art.

5. **Analyze Information** What did Frederick the Great mean when he said, "In my kingdom, everyone can go to heaven in his own fashion"?

6. **Predict Consequences** What actions might peasants take as they learn more about ideas such as equality?

● **Writing About History**

Quick Write: Narrowing Your Response In the essay prompt below, identify and list the key words. Then write a brief outline of the main ideas to help you form the best response. In your own words, explain what is being asked of you in the instructions.

• Think of the various effects of the Enlightenment. Identify which effect you think most contributed to society, both short-term and long-term. Explain your response.

Note Taking

Reading Skill: Summarize Fill in a concept web like the one below with information about the enlightened despots and their contributions.

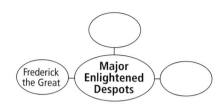

View of La Scala in Milan, mid-1800s ▼

Opera

Operas originated in Florence, Italy, in the seventeenth century. First called *drama per musica*, or drama through music, these musical performances typically involve large casts and elaborate sets and costumes. When Italian operas were performed in France, they emphasized glory and love, and included ballet and lavish stage settings to please the French court. Handel, Mozart, Verdi, Wagner, and Puccini composed some of the world's most famous operas. AUDIO

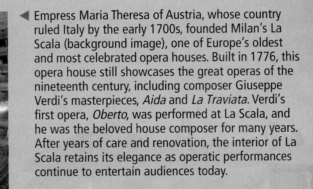

◄ Empress Maria Theresa of Austria, whose country ruled Italy by the early 1700s, founded Milan's La Scala (background image), one of Europe's oldest and most celebrated opera houses. Built in 1776, this opera house still showcases the great operas of the nineteenth century, including composer Giuseppe Verdi's masterpieces, *Aida* and *La Traviata*. Verdi's first opera, *Oberto*, was performed at La Scala, and he was the beloved house composer for many years. After years of care and renovation, the interior of La Scala retains its elegance as operatic performances continue to entertain audiences today.

◄ The "Three Tenors" (from left), Placido Domingo, José Carreras, and Luciano Pavarotti, are some of the best-known opera singers of the modern era. In the hierarchy of the opera stage, the tenor is the highest male voice and usually plays the part of the hero. The female lead is typically sung by a soprano, which is the highest female voice. Singers in the lower ranges (mezzo-soprano and alto for women, baritone and bass for men) generally play villainous or comic roles.

Thinking Critically

1. **Draw Inferences** How do you think composing an opera is different from composing a symphony?
2. **Determine Relevance** Why did operas appeal to composers and musicians during the Enlightenment?

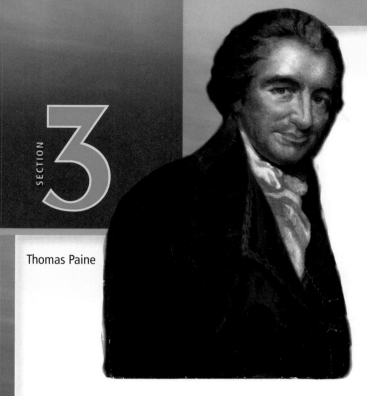

Thomas Paine

Paine's *Common Sense*

Early in 1776, English colonists in North America eagerly read the newly published *Common Sense,* by Thomas Paine. This pamphlet called on them to declare their independence from Britain and echoed the themes of the Enlightenment.

66 'Tis repugnant to reason, to the universal order of things, to all examples from former ages, to suppose that this Continent can long remain subject to any external power.99
—Thomas Paine, *Common Sense*

Focus Question How did ideas of the Enlightenment lead to the independence and founding of the United States of America?

Birth of the American Republic

Objectives

- Describe characteristics of Britain and the 13 English colonies in the mid-1700s.
- Outline the events that led to the American Revolution.
- Summarize the events and significance of the American Revolution.
- Analyze how the new Constitution reflected the ideas of the Enlightenment.

Terms, People, and Places

George III	Yorktown, Virginia
Stamp Act	Treaty of Paris
George Washington	James Madison
Thomas Jefferson	Benjamin Franklin
popular sovereignty	federal republic

Note Taking

Reading Skill: Recognize Sequence As you read, complete a timeline like the one below with important dates that led up to the formation of the United States government.

French and Indian War ends.

1763

On the eve of the American Revolution, Britain was a formidable foe whose power stretched throughout the world. In addition, an ambitious new ruler sought to expand the powers of the monarchy.

Britain Becomes a Global Power

There are several key reasons for Britain's rise to global prominence:

- Location placed England in a position to control trade. In the 1500s and 1600s, English merchants sent ships across the world's oceans and planted outposts in the West Indies, North America, and India. From these tiny settlements, England would build a global empire.
- England offered a climate favorable to business and commerce and put fewer restrictions on trade than some of its neighbors.
- In the 1700s, Britain was generally on the winning side in European conflicts. With the Treaty of Utrecht, France gave Nova Scotia and Newfoundland to Britain. In 1763, the end of the French and Indian War and the Seven Years' War brought Britain all of French Canada. The British also monopolized the slave trade in Spanish America, which brought enormous wealth to British merchants.
- England's territory expanded closer to home as well. In 1707, England and Wales were united with Scotland to become the United Kingdom of Great Britain. Free trade with Scotland created a larger market for farmers and manufacturers. Ireland had come under English control during the 1600s. It was formally united with Great Britain in 1801.

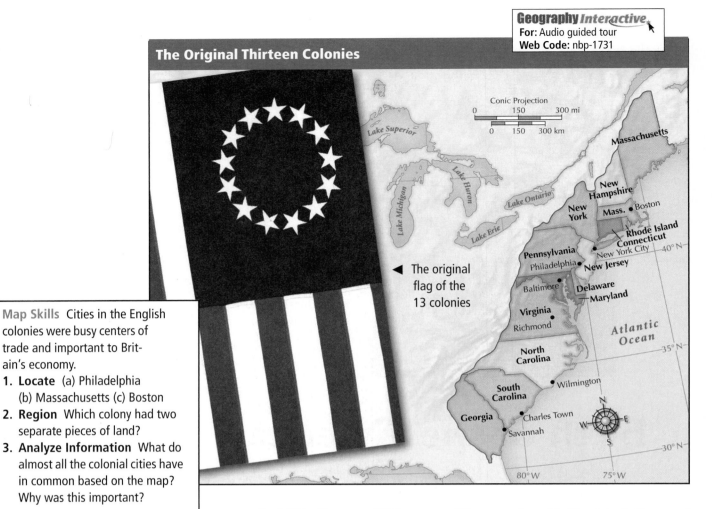

The Original Thirteen Colonies

Geography *Interactive*
For: Audio guided tour
Web Code: nbp-1731

Conic Projection

◀ The original flag of the 13 colonies

Map Skills Cities in the English colonies were busy centers of trade and important to Britain's economy.

1. **Locate** (a) Philadelphia (b) Massachusetts (c) Boston
2. **Region** Which colony had two separate pieces of land?
3. **Analyze Information** What do almost all the colonial cities have in common based on the map? Why was this important?

Vocabulary Builder

<u>assert</u>—(uh SURT) *vt.* to insist on being recognized

In 1760, George III began a 60-year reign. Unlike his father and grandfather, the new king was born in England. He spoke English and loved Britain. But George was eager to recover the powers the crown had lost. Following his mother's advice, "George, be a king!" he set out to reassert royal power. He wanted to end Whig domination, choose his own ministers, dissolve the cabinet system, and make Parliament follow his will. Gradually, George found seats in Parliament for "the king's friends." Then, with their help, he began to <u>assert</u> his leadership. Many of his policies, however, would prove disastrous.

✓ **Checkpoint** What led to Britain's rise to global prominence in the mid-1700s?

The 13 Colonies in the Mid-1700s

By 1750, a string of 13 prosperous colonies stretched along the eastern coast of North America. They were part of Britain's growing empire. Colonial cities such as Boston, New York, and Philadelphia were busy commercial centers that linked North America to the West Indies, Africa, and Europe. Colonial shipyards produced many vessels for this trade.

Britain applied mercantilist policies to its colonies in an attempt to strengthen its own economy by exporting more than it imported. To this end, in the 1600s, Parliament had passed the Navigation Acts to regulate colonial trade and manufacturing. For the most part, however, these acts were not rigorously enforced. Therefore, activities like smuggling were common and not considered crimes by the colonists.

By the mid-1700s, the colonies were home to diverse religious and ethnic groups. Social distinctions were more blurred than in Europe, although wealthy landowners and merchants dominated government and society. In politics, as in much else, there was a good deal of free discussion. Colonists felt entitled to the rights of English citizens, and their colonial assemblies exercised much control over local affairs. Many also had an increasing sense of their own destiny separate from Britain.

✓ **Checkpoint** In what ways were the colonies already developing independence from Britain?

Colonists Express Discontent

The Seven Years' War and the French and Indian War in North America had drained the British treasury. King George III and his advisors thought that the colonists should help pay for these wars. To increase taxes paid by colonists, Parliament passed the Sugar Act in 1764, which imposed import taxes, and the **Stamp Act** in 1765, which imposed taxes on items such as newspapers and pamphlets. "No taxation without representation," the colonists protested. They believed that because they had no representatives in Parliament, they should not be taxed. Parliament repealed the Stamp Act in 1766, but then passed a Declaratory Act that said it had complete authority over the colonists.

Colonists Rebel Against Britain A series of violent clashes intensified the colonists' anger. In March 1770, British soldiers in Boston opened fire on a crowd that was pelting them with stones and snowballs. Colonists called the death of five protesters the Boston Massacre. Then in December 1773, a handful of colonists hurled a cargo of recently arrived British tea into the harbor to protest a tax on tea. The incident became known as the Boston Tea Party. When Parliament passed harsh laws to punish Massachusetts for the destruction of the tea, other colonies rallied to oppose the British response.

As tensions increased, fighting spread. Finally, representatives from each colony gathered in Philadelphia and met in a Continental Congress to decide what action to take. Among the participants were the radical yet fair-minded Massachusetts lawyer John Adams, who had defended the British soldiers involved in the Boston Massacre in their trial; Virginia planter and soldier **George Washington;** and political and social leaders from all 13 colonies.

Colonists Declare Independence In April 1775, the ongoing tension between the colonists and the British exploded into war in Lexington and Concord, Massachusetts. This war is known as the Revolutionary War, or the American Revolution. The Congress met soon after and set up a Continental Army, with George Washington in command. Although many battles ended in British victories, the colonists were determined to fight at any cost. In 1776, the

Drafting the Declaration
Benjamin Franklin, John Adams, and Thomas Jefferson (from left to right)

The Declaration of Independence stands as one of the most important documents in all of history. It still serves as inspiration for people around the world. Where did some of the ideas of the Declaration originate?

Primary Source

❝We hold these truths to be self-evident, that all men are created equal, that they are endowed by their Creator with certain unalienable Rights, that among these are Life, Liberty and the pursuit of Happiness. That to secure these rights, Governments are instituted among Men, deriving their just powers from the consent of the governed; That whenever any Form of Government becomes destructive of these ends it is the Right of the People to alter or to abolish it, and to institute new Government, laying its foundation on such principles and organizing its powers in such form, as to them shall seem most likely to effect their Safety and Happiness.❞
—*Declaration of Independence,* July 4, 1776 🔊 AUDIO

George Washington

When George Washington (1732–1799) was chosen to lead the American army, the British thought he would be a failure. Washington indeed faced many challenges, including an army that did not have weapons, uniforms, or bedding. He struggled to incorporate order and discipline and to instill pride and loyalty in his soldiers. Washington persevered to American victory. His success as a leader continued when he became the nation's first President. **How did Washington hold the army together through difficult times?**

James Madison

James Madison (1751–1836) arrived at the Constitutional Convention in Philadelphia in May 1787 with his thick notebooks on history and government. Madison chose a seat in front of the president's chair and kept detailed notes of the debates. Madison was greatly respected and quickly became the Convention's floor leader. His notebooks remained unpublished for more than 50 years, but they are now our main source of information about the birth of the Constitution. **What did the Framers of the Constitution have in common?**

Benjamin Franklin

Benjamin Franklin (1706–1790) was a philosopher, scientist, publisher, legislator, and diplomat. Sent by Congress to France in 1776 to seek financial and military support for the war, he soon became popular in France because of his intellect and wit. Those who admired America's goal of attaining freedom also admired Franklin. When Franklin returned to America after nine years, he served as a delegate to the Constitutional Convention as the eldest of the delegates. **Why was Franklin admired in France?**

Second Continental Congress took a momentous step, voting to declare independence from Britain. **Thomas Jefferson** of Virginia was the principal author of the Declaration of Independence, a document that reflects John Locke's ideas of the government's obligation to protect the people's natural rights to "life, liberty, and property."

The Declaration included another of Locke's ideas: people had the right "to alter or to abolish" unjust governments—a right to revolt. The principle of **popular sovereignty,** which states that all government power comes from the people, is also an important point in the Declaration. Jefferson carefully detailed the colonists' grievances against Britain. Because the king had trampled colonists' natural rights, he argued, the colonists had the right to rebel and set up a new government that would protect them. Aware of the risks involved, on July 4, 1776, American leaders adopted the Declaration, pledging "our lives, our fortunes, and our sacred honor" to creating and protecting the new United States of America.

✔ **Checkpoint** What Enlightenment ideas are reflected in the Declaration of Independence?

The American Revolution Continues

At first, the American cause looked bleak. The British had a large number of trained soldiers, a huge fleet, and greater resources. About one third of the American colonists were Loyalists, or those who supported Britain. Many others refused to fight for either side. The Americans lacked military resources, had little money to pay soldiers, and did not have a strategic plan.

Still, colonists had some advantages. One was the geography of the diverse continent. Since colonists were fighting on their own soil, they were familiar with its thick woods and inadequate roads. Other advantages were their strong leader, George Washington, and their fierce determination to fight for their ideals of liberty.

To counteract these advantages, the British worked to create alliances within the colonies. A number of Native American groups sided with the British, while others saw potential advantages in supporting the colonists' cause. Additionally, the British offered freedom to any enslaved people who were willing to fight the colonists.

France Provides Support The first turning point in the war came in 1777, when the Americans triumphed over the British at the Battle of Saratoga. This victory persuaded France to join the Americans against its old rival, Britain. The alliance brought the Americans desperately needed supplies, trained soldiers, and French warships. Spurred by the French example, the Netherlands and Spain added their support.

Hard times continued, however. In the brutal winter of 1777–1778, Continental troops at Valley Forge suffered from cold, hunger, and disease. Throughout this crisis and others, Washington was patient, courageous, and determined. He held the ragged army together.

Fearless Leader
George Washington directs his troops on the battlefield. *What traits did Washington possess that helped lead Americans to victory?*

The Roots of American Democracy

The Framers of the United States Constitution were well educated and widely read. They were familiar with governments of ancient Greece and Rome and those of contemporary Great Britain and Europe. Political writings such as Montesquieu's *The Spirit of the Laws*, Rousseau's *Social Contract*, and Locke's *Two Treatises of Government* contained principles that greatly influenced the Framers in the development of the Constitution. Centuries later, these fundamental democratic principles of American government—popular sovereignty, limited government, separation of powers, and checks and balances—are still in place. The diagram here shows checks and balances, one of Montesquieu's ideas, which ensures that one branch does not accumulate too much power.

We the People

Checks and Balances

Judicial Branch

Legislative Branch

Executive Branch

Congress may impeach judges; Senate may reject appointment of judges.

Courts may declare acts of Congress unconstitutional.

Courts may declare executive actions unconstitutional.

President appoints judges.

President may veto legislation.

Congress may impeach the President and may override veto; Senate approves or rejects treaties and appointments.

History *Interactive*
For: Interactive diagram
Web Code: nbp-1732

Thinking Critically
1. **Draw Conclusions** What additional ideas might the Framers have learned from the political writings of the Enlightenment thinkers?
2. **Summarize** Explain how the basic principle of checks and balances works.

Treaty of Paris Ends the War In 1781, the French fleet blockaded the Chesapeake Bay, which enabled Washington to force the surrender of a British army at **Yorktown, Virginia.** With that defeat, the British war effort crumbled. Two years later, American, British, and French diplomats signed the **Treaty of Paris,** ending the war. In that treaty, Britain recognized the independence of the United States of America. The Americans' victory can be attributed to their resilient dedication to attaining independence.

✔ **Checkpoint** What advantages did the colonists have in battling Britain for their independence?

A New Constitution

The Articles of Confederation was the nation's first constitution. It proved to be too weak to rule the new United States effectively. To address this problem, the nation's leaders gathered once more in Philadelphia. Among them were George Washington, **James Madison,** and **Benjamin Franklin.**

During the hot summer of 1787, they met in secret to redraft the articles of the new constitution. The result was a document that established a government run by the people, for the people.

Enlightenment Ideas Have Great Impact The Framers of the Constitution had studied history and absorbed the ideas of Locke, Montesquieu, and Rousseau. They saw government in terms of a social contract into which "We the People of the United States" entered. They provided not only for an elective legislature but also for an elected president rather than a hereditary monarch. For the first President, voters would choose George Washington.

The Constitution created a **federal republic,** with power divided between the federal, or national, government and the states. A central feature of the new federal government was the separation of powers among the legislative, executive, and judicial branches, an idea borrowed directly from Montesquieu. Within that structure, each branch of government was provided with checks and balances on the other branches.

The Bill of Rights, the first ten amendments to the Constitution, was important to the passage of the Constitution. It recognized the idea that people had basic rights that the government must protect, such as freedom of religion, speech, and the press. The Bill of Rights, like the Constitution, put the *philosophes'* Enlightenment ideas into practice. In 1789, the Constitution became the supreme law of the land, which means it became the nation's fundamental law. This remarkable document has endured for more than 200 years.

Symbol of Freedom The Constitution of the United States created the most progressive government of its day. From the start, the new republic was a symbol of freedom to European countries and reformers in Latin America. Its constitution would be copied or adapted by many lands throughout the world. The Enlightenment ideals that had inspired American colonists brought changes in Europe too. In 1789, a revolution in France toppled the monarchy in the name of liberty and equality. Before long, other Europeans would take up the cry for freedom as well.

✓ **Checkpoint** Explain the influence of Enlightenment ideas on the United States Constitution and Bill of Rights.

The U.S. Bill of Rights

1st: Guarantees freedom of religion, speech, press, assembly, and petition

2nd: Right to bear arms

3rd: Prohibits quartering of troops in private homes

4th: Protects from unreasonable searches and seizures

5th: No punishment without due process of law

6th: Right to a speedy and public trial in the state where the offense was committed

7th: Right to jury trial for civil cases if over $20

8th: Prohibits excessive bail and cruel and unusual punishments

9th: Civil rights are not restricted to those specified by these amendments.

10th: Powers not granted to the national government belong to the states and to the people.

Chart Skills The first ten amendments to the United States Constitution are known as the Bill of Rights. *What is the significance of the 10th Amendment?*

SECTION 3 Assessment

Progress Monitoring *Online*
For: Self-quiz with vocabulary practice
Web Code: nba-1731

Terms, People, and Places

1. For each term, person, or place listed at the beginning of the section, write a sentence explaining its significance.

Note Taking

2. **Reading Skill: Recognize Sequence** Use your completed timeline to answer the Focus Question: How did ideas of the Enlightenment lead to the independence and founding of the United States of America?

Comprehension and Critical Thinking

3. **Make Generalizations** Describe society and politics in the 13 English colonies during the mid-1700s.

4. **Express Problems Clearly** Explain why conflict between the colonists and Britain increased after 1763.

5. **Identify Point of View** What reasons might a Loyalist have for opposing the American Revolution?

6. **Determine Relevance** Give two examples of why the Bill of Rights is important to you.

● **Writing About History**

Quick Write: Providing Elaboration To prove that you fully understand a subject, you need to include specific details. You should use facts, dates, names, examples, explanations, or quotes to support your answer. Write a paragraph to describe the events that led to the American Revolution. Then read through your response and add specific details where you can.

SPREADING THE WORD OF REVOLUTION

While Enlightenment thinkers had a profound impact on the leaders of the American Revolution, newspapers made a great impact on the colonists. Colonists depended on newspapers for information about the war and the economy. News about the war was the first great news event to report in America. Would the colonists be free? Or would English control continue? As demand increased, newspapers began publishing several times a week instead of weekly. The number of newspapers increased from 29 to 48 from 1770 to 1775. During this time, the American newspaper changed from a weak form of communication to a propaganda machine that included controversial political cartoons and essays.

Trouble for newspapers came in 1765 when the British government passed the Stamp Act. Newspapers were forced to pay the tax imposed by the Stamp Act or face heavy penalties. Colonists already felt they had no representation so they became even more discontented. Many newspapers strongly opposed the Stamp Act and showed their resentment in their pages with cartoons, editorial content, and typographical devices. The *Maryland Gazette*, for example, set a skull and crossbones on its front page where the tax stamp belonged (facing page). Others ceased publication. The strength of the press was evident when the British government was forced to repeal the Stamp Act. Newspapers had voiced protest effectively and would continue to be a powerful medium of communication for years to come.

The BLOODY MASSACRE perpetrated in King — Street BOSTON on March 5th 1770 by a party of the 29th REG.t

Engrav'd Printed & Sold by PAUL REVERE BOSTON

Unhappy Boston! see thy Sons deplore,
Thy hallow'd Walks besmear'd with guiltless Gore:
While faithless P—n and his savage Bands,
With murd'rous Rancour stretch their bloody Hands;
Like fierce Barbarians grinning o'er their Prey,
Approve the Carnage and enjoy the Day.

If scalding drops from Rage from Anguish Wrung
If speechless Sorrows lab'ring for a Tongue,
Or if a weeping World can ought appease
The plaintive Ghosts of Victims such as these;
The Patriot's copious Tears for each are shed,
A glorious Tribute which embalms the Dead.

But know Fate summons to that awful Goal.
Where Justice strips the Murd'rer of his Soul:
Should venal C—ts the scandal of the Land,
Snatch the relentless Villain from her Hand,
Keen Execrations on this Plate inscrib'd,
Shall reach a Judge who never can be brib'd.

The unhappy Sufferers were Mess.rs Sam.l Gray Sam.l Maverick, Jam.s Caldwell, Crispus Attucks & Pat.k Carr
Killed. Six wounded; two of them (Christ.r Monk & John Clark) Mortally

◀ Engraving by Paul Revere of the 1770 Boston Massacre. Revere exaggerated the event to incite anger among the colonists against the British.

▼ Engraving of the Battle of Lexington, the first battle of the American Revolution. Demand for exciting news of the war led to the creation of more newspapers.

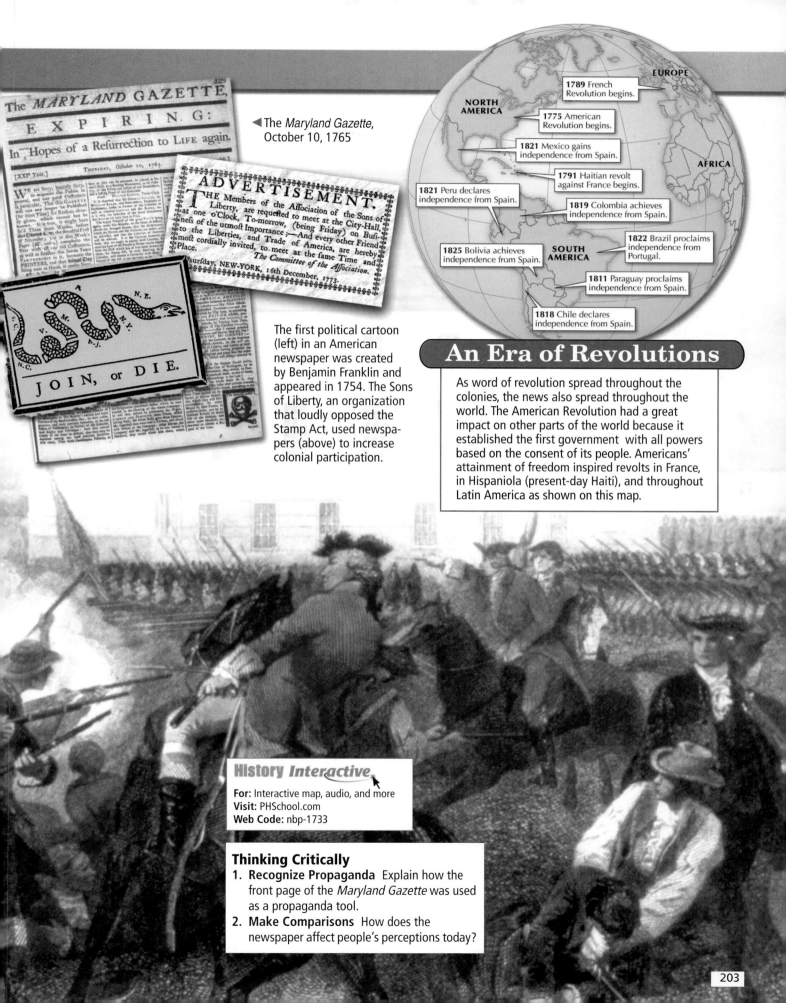

The *Maryland Gazette*, October 10, 1765

The first political cartoon (left) in an American newspaper was created by Benjamin Franklin and appeared in 1754. The Sons of Liberty, an organization that loudly opposed the Stamp Act, used newspapers (above) to increase colonial participation.

1789 French Revolution begins.

1775 American Revolution begins.

1821 Mexico gains independence from Spain.

1791 Haitian revolt against France begins.

1821 Peru declares independence from Spain.

1819 Colombia achieves independence from Spain.

1822 Brazil proclaims independence from Portugal.

1825 Bolivia achieves independence from Spain.

1811 Paraguay proclaims independence from Spain.

1818 Chile declares independence from Spain.

EUROPE
NORTH AMERICA
AFRICA
SOUTH AMERICA

An Era of Revolutions

As word of revolution spread throughout the colonies, the news also spread throughout the world. The American Revolution had a great impact on other parts of the world because it established the first government with all powers based on the consent of its people. Americans' attainment of freedom inspired revolts in France, in Hispaniola (present-day Haiti), and throughout Latin America as shown on this map.

History Interactive

For: Interactive map, audio, and more
Visit: PHSchool.com
Web Code: nbp-1733

Thinking Critically
1. **Recognize Propaganda** Explain how the front page of the *Maryland Gazette* was used as a propaganda tool.
2. **Make Comparisons** How does the newspaper affect people's perceptions today?

Quick Study Guide

> **Progress Monitoring *Online***
> **For:** Self-test with vocabulary practice
> **Web Code:** nba-1741

■ Enlightenment Thinkers

- **Thomas Hobbes:** social contract in which people give power to the government for an organized society
- **John Locke:** natural rights—life, liberty, and property
- **Baron de Montesquieu:** separation of powers; checks and balances
- **Voltaire:** battled corruption, injustice, and inequality; defended freedom of speech
- **Denis Diderot:** *Encyclopedia*
- **Jean-Jacques Rousseau:** social contract in which people follow the "general will" for true liberty
- **Adam Smith:** free market; laissez faire

■ Enlightenment Ideas Influence Democracy

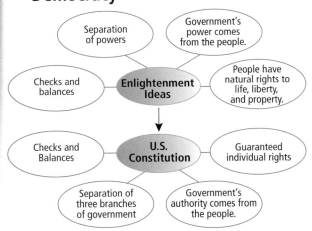

■ American Declaration of Independence: Main Ideas

Declaration of Independence: Main Ideas
• All men are created equal and have natural rights to life, liberty, and the pursuit of happiness.
• It is the government's obligation to protect these rights.
• If a government fails to protect these rights, the people can revolt and set up a new government.

■ The U.S. Bill of Rights

The U.S. Bill of Rights
1st: Guarantees freedom of religion, speech, press, assembly, and petition
2nd: Right to bear arms
3rd: Prohibits quartering of troops in private homes
4th: Protects from unreasonable searches and seizures
5th: No punishment without due process of law
6th: Right to a speedy and public trial in the state where the offense was committed
7th: Right to jury trial for civil cases if over $20
8th: Prohibits excessive bail and cruel and unusual punishments
9th: Civil rights are not restricted to those specified by these amendments.
10th: Powers not granted to the national government belong to the states and to the people.

■ Key Events From 1700–1789

1700s
France sees flowering of Enlightenment thought.

1721
Johann Sebastian Bach publishes his Brandenburg Concertos.

1740
Frederick II begins his reign in Prussia.

Chapter Events
Global Events

1720   **1730**   **1740**

1735
China's Emperor Qianlong begins his long reign.

Concept Connector

■ Cumulative Review

Record the answers to the questions below on your Concept Connector worksheets. In addition, record information from this chapter about the following concepts:
- Political Systems: federal government
- Democracy: The American Declaration of Independence

1. **Cooperation** Throughout time, people have used cooperation to reach common goals. As you have read in this chapter, colonists in America joined together to fight for their independence from Britain and were ultimately successful. Without cooperation, change would be difficult to achieve. Think of another time in history when groups of people cooperated for a mutual benefit. How might the outcome have changed had they not cooperated? Read to learn more about the:
   - development of trade routes in medieval Europe
   - Glorious Revolution

2. **Conflict** There are many different causes for the conflicts that have occurred throughout history. There have been conflicts about religion, land, and power, for example. The Thirty Years War in the early 1600s had both religious and politi cal causes. Compare the American Revolution to the Thirty Years' War. How were they similar and different? Think about the:
   - cause(s) of conflict
   - scope of conflict
   - groups involved
   - goals or strategic plans
   - results

3. **Culture** Enlightenment thinkers found inspiration not only in the cultures of other lands, but also in the cultures of other times. The relatively new science of archaeology gave thinkers more access to the knowledge of past civilizations. During the early 1700s, archaeologists discovered the ruins of the ancient Roman cities of Herculaneum and Pompeii, buried under volcanic debris for many centuries. How do you think Enlightenment thinkers may have benefited from this discovery?

■ Connections To Today

1. **Democracy: Still Strong Today** As you have read, the Framers of the United States Constitution were inspired by Montesquieu, Rousseau, and Locke. Democratic revolutions around the world were inspired by the same Enlightenment ideas that had inspired American colonists. Even today, nations seeking a model for democratic government often turn to the Constitution of the United States. Research and write a newspaper article about one of these nations.

2. **Culture: Modern Salons** Salons provided a way for people to gather and share ideas, especially during the Enlightenment. Today, we know that many people do this without ever meeting in person—through the Internet. People are able to join chat rooms and newsgroups to share their thoughts. Many discussions on the Internet lack the serious-minded tone of a salon conversation and the benefit of face-to-face conversation. The Internet does, however, provide a sense of community, where people can gather to discuss ideas, even if it is a "virtual" living room. Compare salons of the Enlightenment and Internet chat rooms. Explain which you think is the better forum for sharing ideas, and why.

1751 Diderot publishes Encyclopedia.	1759 Voltaire publishes Candide.	1762 Rousseau publishes *The Social Contract*.	1776 American leaders sign the Declaration of Independence.	**History Interactive** For: Interactive timeline Web Code: nbp-1701

1750   **1760**   **1770**   **1780**

1754 French and Indian War begins.	1763 Treaty of Paris gives Britain control of Canada.	1789 The French Revolution begins.

Chapter Assessment

Terms, People, and Places

Complete each sentence by choosing the correct answer from the list of terms below. You will not use all of the terms.

natural rights	Montesquieu
John Locke	federal republic
laissez faire	Yorktown, Virginia
rococo	Frederick the Great
baroque	Treaty of Paris
Joseph II	Rousseau

1. In a _____, power is divided between the federal government and the states.
2. _____ advanced the idea of separation of powers.
3. The _____ style influenced by the Enlightenment was personal, elegant, and charming.
4. The enlightened despot who ended censorship was _____.
5. The American Revolution ended when George Washington forced the surrender of the British at _____.
6. _____ believed in _____, which are the rights to life, liberty, and property.

Main Ideas

Section 1 (pp. 182–186)
7. What idea did John Locke advocate for the role of a government?
8. Explain the economic policy of laissez faire.

Section 2 (pp. 188–193)
9. How did the Enlightenment affect some rulers in Europe, and what are these rulers known as?

Section 3 (pp. 195–201)
10. How did taxation create tensions between the American colonies and the British government?

11. How does the Bill of Rights reflect a key Enlightenment idea?

Chapter Focus Question
12. How did Enlightenment thinkers inspire revolutionaries to push for radical changes in government and society?

Critical Thinking

13. **Synthesize Information** Choose one *philosophe* from this chapter and describe how he or she might respond to a human rights issue that has been in the news recently.
14. **Predict Consequences** Given the impact the Enlightenment thinkers had on the American Revolution, what can you predict will happen in other areas of the world? Explain why you predicted what you did.
15. **Analyzing Visuals** Identify the style of this painting and describe its characteristics.

16. **Make Comparisons** Compare Britain and the 13 colonies in the mid-1700s.
17. **Analyze Information** What ideas about government do you think English settlers brought with them to the Americas?

● Writing About History

Writing for Assessment Select either a philosopher from the Enlightenment or an important figure from the American Revolution. Explain how his or her actions, beliefs, and/or works contributed to improving society. Provide specific examples.

Prewriting
- Consider what you know about the people in this chapter and choose one who interests you.
- Develop a focus or main idea. Write a single sentence identifying the main idea you will develop.
- As you prepare to write your essay, make sure you understand the instructions. Circle verbs, nouns, or important phrases in the question.

Drafting
- Develop a thesis statement that identifies the focus of your essay.
- Make an outline for your essay and fill in facts and examples.
- Write an introduction to explain your thesis, a body to provide evidence for your thesis, and a conclusion.

Revising
- Even though time is limited on essay tests, you should still leave time to check your writing for accuracy and clarity.
- Use the guidelines for revising your essay on page SH22 of the Writing Handbook.

Enlightenment Thought

Enlightenment thinkers believed in the possibility of social, political, and economic change. Often critical of society during this time, they were driven by the power of human reason and progress.

Diderot and Catherine the Great

"Common sense is not so common."

—From ***Philosophical Dictionary*** by Voltaire

"A prince ought not to deem it beneath his dignity to state that he considers it his duty not to dictate anything to his subjects in religious matters, but to leave them complete freedom."

—From ***What Is Enlightenment?*** by Immanuel Kant

"A strange consequence that necessarily follows from the use of torture is that the innocent person is placed in a condition worse than that of the guilty, for if both are tortured, the circumstances are all against the former. Either he confesses the crime and is condemned, or he is declared innocent and has suffered a punishment he did not deserve."

—From ***On Crimes and Punishments*** by Marchese di Beccaria

Selected Enlightenment Thinkers			
Thinker	**Lifespan**	**Nationality**	**Key Work**
Jean D'Alembert	1717–1783	French	*Encyclopedia*
Jeremy Bentham	1748–1832	English	*The Principles of Morals and Legislation*
Cesare Beccaria	1738–1794	Italian	*Crimes and Punishment*
Denis Diderot	1713–1784	French	*Encyclopedia*
David Hume	1711–1776	Scottish	*Treatise of Human Nature*
Immanuel Kant	1724–1804	E. Prussian	*Critique of Pure Reason*
John Locke	1632–1704	English	*Essay Concerning Human Understanding*
Charles Montesquieu	1689–1755	French	*The Spirit of the Laws*
Jean-Jacques Rousseau	1712–1778	French	*The Social Contract*
Adam Smith	1723–1790	English	*The Wealth of Nations*
Voltaire	1694–1778	French	*Philosophical Dictionary*

The French Revolution and Napoleon

1789–1815

The Loss of Blood Begins

On July 14, 1789, after a daylong hunting expedition, King Louis XVI returned to his palace in Versailles. Hours earlier, armed Parisians had attacked the Bastille. They had cut the chains of the prison drawbridge, crushing a member of the crowd, and poured into the courtyard. Chaos ensued as shots rang out, blood was spattered, and heads were paraded down the streets on spikes. When Louis heard the news, he exclaimed, "Then it's a revolt?" "No, sire," replied the duke bearing the news, "it's a revolution!" The French Revolution had begun. Listen to the Witness History audio to hear more about the fall of the Bastille.

Plate declaring "Live Free or Die"

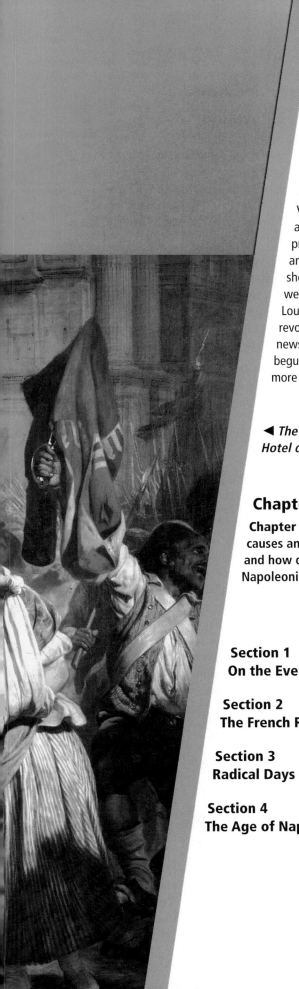

◀ *The Conquerors of the Bastille before the Hotel de Ville,* painted by Paul Delaroche.

Chapter Preview

Chapter Focus Question What were the causes and effects of the French Revolution, and how did the revolution lead to the Napoleonic era?

Drum from the French revolutionary period

Section 1
On the Eve of Revolution

Section 2
The French Revolution Unfolds

Section 3
Radical Days of the Revolution

Section 4
The Age of Napoleon

Bust of Napoleon Bonaparte

Note Taking Study Guide *Online*
For: Note Taking and Concept Connector worksheets
Web Code: nbd-1801

Camille Desmoulins and French Revolution banner

LIBERTÉ · ÉGALITÉ

WITNESS HISTORY ◀)) AUDIO

Inciting Revolution

Camille Desmoulins was a French revolutionary leader and journalist who wrote pamphlets and journals to express his views on the revolution. He also spoke to Parisian crowds and his stirring speeches in 1789 were a cause of the storming of the Bastille prison on July 14, 1789. This excerpt is from one of his speeches, "Better to Die than not Live Free":

❝ In a democracy, tho the people may be deceived, yet they at least love virtue. It is merit which they believe they put in power as substitutes for the rascals who are the very essence of monarchies. The vices, conceal-ments, and crimes which are the diseases of republics are the very health and existence of monarchies. ❞

Focus Question What led to the storming of the Bastille, and therefore, to the start of the French Revolution?

On the Eve of Revolution

Objectives

- Describe the social divisions of France's old order.
- List reasons for France's economic troubles in 1789.
- Explain why Louis XVI called the Estates-General and summarize what resulted.
- Understand why Parisians stormed the Bastille.

Terms, People, and Places

ancien régime	Jacques Necker
estate	Estates-General
bourgeoisie	cahier
deficit spending	Tennis Court Oath
Louis XVI	Bastille

Note Taking

Reading Skill: Recognize Multiple Causes
Create a chart to identify causes of the French Revolution. Add as many boxes as you need.

Causes of the French Revolution

Inequalities among classes

On April 28, 1789, unrest exploded at a Paris wallpaper factory. A rumor had spread that the factory owner was planning to cut wages even though bread prices were soaring. Enraged workers vandalized the owner's home.

Riots like these did not worry most nobles. They knew that France faced a severe economic crisis but thought financial reforms would ease the problem. The nobles were wrong. The crisis went deeper than government finances. Reform would not be enough. By July, the hungry, unemployed, and poorly paid people of Paris had taken up arms. Their actions would push events further and faster than anyone could have foreseen.

French Society Divided

In 1789, France, like the rest of Europe, still clung to an outdated social system that had emerged in the Middle Ages. Under this **ancien régime,** or old order, everyone in France was divided into one of three social classes, or **estates.** The First Estate was made up of the clergy; the Second Estate was made up of the nobility; and the Third Estate comprised the vast majority of the population.

The Clergy Enjoy Wealth During the Middle Ages, the Church had exerted great influence throughout Christian Europe. In 1789, the French clergy still enjoyed enormous wealth and privilege. The Church owned about 10 percent of the land, collected tithes, and paid no direct taxes to the state. High Church leaders such as bishops and abbots were usually nobles who lived very well. Parish priests, however, often came from humble origins and might be as poor as their peasant congregations.

The First Estate did provide some social services. Nuns, monks, and priests ran schools, hospitals, and orphanages. But during the Enlightenment, *philosophes* targeted the Church for reform. They criticized the idleness of some clergy, the Church's interference in politics, and its intolerance of dissent. In response, many clergy condemned the Enlightenment for undermining religion and moral order.

Nobles Hold Top Government Jobs The Second Estate was the titled nobility of French society. In the Middle Ages, noble knights had defended the land. In the 1600s, Richelieu and Louis XIV had crushed the nobles' military power but had given them other rights—under strict royal control. Those rights included top jobs in government, the army, the courts, and the Church.

At Versailles, ambitious nobles competed for royal appointments while idle courtiers enjoyed endless entertainments. Many nobles, however, lived far from the center of power. Though they owned land, they received little financial income. As a result, they felt the pinch of trying to maintain their status in a period of rising prices.

Many nobles hated absolutism and resented the royal bureaucracy that employed middle-class men in positions that once had been reserved for them. They feared losing their traditional privileges, especially their freedom from paying taxes.

Third Estate Is Vastly Diverse The Third Estate was the most diverse social class. At the top sat the **bourgeoisie** (boor zhwah ZEE), or middle class. The bourgeoisie included prosperous bankers, merchants, and manufacturers, as well as lawyers, doctors, journalists, and professors. The bulk of the Third Estate, however, consisted of rural peasants.

REVEIL DU TIERS ETAT

Analyzing Political Cartoons

The Old Regime This cartoon represents the social order in France before the French Revolution. While a member of the Third Estate is beginning to express anger and rise up, a nobleman representing the Second Estate and a priest, representing the First Estate, recoil in surprise and fear.

1. How does the cartoonist portray the Third Estate? Explain why.
2. What were the differences among the social classes in pre-revolutionary France?

Some were prosperous landowners who hired laborers to work for them. Others were tenant farmers or day laborers.

The poorest members of the Third Estate were <u>urban</u> workers. They included apprentices, journeymen, and others who worked in industries such as printing or cloth making. Many women and men earned a meager living as servants, stable hands, construction workers, or street sellers of everything from food to pots and pans. A large number of the urban poor were unemployed. To survive, some turned to begging or crime.

From rich to poor, members of the Third Estate resented the privileges enjoyed by their social "betters." Wealthy bourgeois families in the Third Estate could buy political office and even titles, but the best jobs were still reserved for nobles. Urban workers earned miserable wages. Even the smallest rise in the price of bread, their main food, brought the threat of greater hunger or even starvation.

Because of traditional privileges, the First and Second Estates paid almost no taxes. Peasants were burdened by taxes on everything from land to soap to salt. Though they were technically free, many owed fees and services that dated back to medieval times, such as the corvée (kawr VAY), which was unpaid labor to repair roads and bridges. Peasants were

● INFOGRAPHIC

What Is the Third Estate?

❝1. What is the Third Estate? *Everything.*
2. What has it been until now in the political order? *Nothing.*
3. What does it want to be? *Something.***❞**
—Abbé Emmanuel Sieyès

Sieyès, a clergyman before the revolution, captured the spirit of the Third Estate with these words in a pamphlet published in January 1789. The vast Third Estate—peasants, dentists, laborers, and more—comprising more than 95 percent of France, was ready to fight for equality.

▲ Ceramic bottle depicting dentist and patient

▲ *Woman of the French Revolution,* painting of a peasant woman by Jacques-Louis David

▼ Eighteenth-century French street traders

Thinking Critically
1. **Identify Point of View** According to the quote by Sieyès, why was the Third Estate ready to revolt?
2. **Make Generalizations** Why did Sieyès say the Third Estate was "nothing"?

also incensed when nobles, hurt by rising prices, tried to reimpose old manor dues.

In towns and cities, Enlightenment ideas led people to question the inequalities of the old regime. Why, people demanded, should the first two estates have such great privileges at the expense of the majority? Throughout France, the Third Estate called for the privileged classes to pay their share.

✔ **Checkpoint** What was the social structure of the old regime in France?

Financial Troubles

Economic woes in France added to the social unrest and heightened tensions. One of the causes of the economic troubles was a mushrooming financial crisis that was due in part to years of **deficit spending.** This occurs when a government spends more money than it takes in.

National Debt Soars Louis XIV had left France deeply in debt. The Seven Years' War and the American Revolution strained the treasury even further. Costs generally had risen in the 1700s, and the lavish court soaked up millions. To bridge the gap between income and expenses, the government borrowed more and more money. By 1789, half of the government's income from taxes went to paying the interest on this enormous debt. Also, in the late 1780s, bad harvests sent food prices soaring and brought hunger to poorer peasants and city dwellers.

To solve the financial crisis, the government would have to increase taxes, reduce expenses, or both. However, the nobles and clergy fiercely resisted any attempt to end their exemption from taxes.

Economic Reform Fails The heirs of Louis XIV were not the right men to solve the economic crisis that afflicted France. Louis XV, who ruled from 1715 to 1774, pursued pleasure before serious business and ran up more debts. **Louis XVI** was well-meaning but weak and indecisive. He did, however, wisely choose **Jacques Necker,** a financial expert, as an advisor. Necker urged the king to reduce extravagant court spending, reform government, and abolish burdensome tariffs on internal trade. When Necker proposed taxing the First and Second Estates, however, the nobles and high clergy forced the king to dismiss him.

As the crisis deepened, the pressure for reform mounted. The wealthy and powerful classes demanded, however, that the king summon the **Estates-General,** the legislative body consisting of representatives of the three estates, before making any changes. A French king had not called the Estates-General for 175 years, fearing that nobles would use it to recover the feudal powers they had lost under absolute rule. To reform-minded nobles, the Estates-General seemed to offer a chance of carrying out changes like those that had come with the Glorious Revolution in England. They hoped that they could bring the absolute monarch under the control of the nobles and guarantee their own privileges.

✔ **Checkpoint** What economic troubles did France face in 1789, and how did they lead to further unrest?

Poorer peasants and city dwellers in France were faced with great hunger as bad harvests sent food prices soaring. People began to riot to demand bread. In the countryside, peasants began to attack the manor houses of the nobles. Arthur Young, an English visitor to France, witnessed these riots and disturbances. Why did the poor attack the nobles' homes?

Primary Source

66 Everything conspires to render the present period in France critical: the [lack] of bread is terrible: accounts arrive every moment from the provinces of riots and disturbances, and calling in the military, to preserve the peace of the markets. 99
—Arthur Young, *Travels in France During the Years 1787–1789*

Louis XVI Calls the Estates-General

As 1788 came to a close, France tottered on the verge of bankruptcy. Bread riots were spreading, and nobles, fearful of taxes, were denouncing royal tyranny. A baffled Louis XVI finally summoned the Estates-General to meet at Versailles the following year.

Estates Prepare Grievance Notebooks In preparation, Louis had all three estates prepare **cahiers** (kah YAYZ), or notebooks, listing their grievances. Many cahiers called for reforms such as fairer taxes, freedom of the press, or regular meetings of the Estates-General. In one town, shoemakers denounced regulations that made leather so expensive they could not afford to make shoes. Servant girls in the city of Toulouse demanded the right to leave service when they wanted and that "after a girl has served her master for many years, she receive some reward for her service."

The cahiers testified to boiling class resentments. One called tax collectors "bloodsuckers of the nation who drink the tears of the unfortunate from goblets of gold." Another one of the cahiers condemned the courts of nobles as "vampires pumping the last drop of blood" from the people. Another complained that "20 million must live on half the wealth of France while the clergy . . . devour the other half."

Delegates Take the Tennis Court Oath Delegates to the Estates-General from the Third Estate were elected, though only propertied men could vote. Thus, the delegates were mostly lawyers, middle-class officials, and writers. They were familiar with the writings of Voltaire, Rousseau, and other *philosophes*. They went to Versailles not only to solve the financial crisis but also to insist on reform.

The Estates-General convened in May 1789. From the start, the delegates were deadlocked over the issue of voting. Traditionally, each estate had met and voted separately. Each group had one vote. Under this system, the First and Second Estates always outvoted the Third Estate two to one. This time, the Third Estate wanted all three estates to meet in a single body, with votes counted "by head."

After weeks of stalemate, delegates of the Third Estate took a daring step. In June 1789, claiming to represent the people of France, they declared themselves to be the National Assembly. A few days later, the National Assembly found its meeting hall locked and guarded. Fearing that the king planned to dismiss them, the delegates moved to a nearby indoor tennis court. As curious spectators looked on, the delegates took their famous **Tennis Court Oath.** They swore "never to separate

The Oath Is Taken
Delegates of the Third Estate declare themselves to be the National Assembly, representing the people of France. They take the Tennis Court Oath (bottom), vowing to create a constitution. The National Assembly later issues the assignat (top) as currency to help pay the government's debts. *What was the significance of the Tennis Court Oath?*

and to meet wherever the circumstances might require until we have established a sound and just constitution."

When reform-minded clergy and nobles joined the Assembly, Louis XVI grudgingly accepted it. But royal troops gathered around Paris, and rumors spread that the king planned to dissolve the Assembly.

✓ **Checkpoint** What actions did delegates of the Third Estate take when the Estates-General met in 1789?

Parisians Storm the Bastille

On July 14, 1789, the city of Paris seized the spotlight from the National Assembly meeting in Versailles. The streets buzzed with rumors that royal troops were going to occupy the capital. More than 800 Parisians assembled outside the **Bastille,** a grim medieval fortress used as a prison for political and other prisoners. The crowd demanded weapons and gunpowder believed to be stored there.

The commander of the Bastille refused to open the gates and opened fire on the crowd. In the battle that followed, many people were killed. Finally, the enraged mob broke through the defenses. They killed the commander and five guards and released the handful of prisoners who were being held there, but found no weapons.

The Bastille was a symbol to the people of France representing years of abuse by the monarchy. The storming of and subsequent fall of the Bastille was a wake-up call to Louis XVI. Unlike any other riot or short-lived protest, this event posed a challenge to the sheer existence of the regime. Since 1880, the French have celebrated Bastille Day annually as their national independence day.

✓ **Checkpoint** What was the significance of the storming of the Bastille?

Parisians storm the Bastille on July 14, 1789.

Progress Monitoring *Online*
For: Self-quiz with vocabulary practice
Web Code: nba-1811

SECTION 1
Assessment

Terms, People, and Places

1. What do many of the key terms, people, and places listed at the beginning of the section have in common? Explain.

Note Taking

2. **Reading Skill: Recognize Multiple Causes** Use your completed chart to answer the Focus Question: What led to the storming of the Bastille, and therefore, to the start of the French Revolution?

Comprehension and Critical Thinking

3. **Compare Point of View** How did the views of society differ between the nobles and peasants in 1789 France?

4. **Identify Point of View** Suppose that you are Jacques Necker. Write a paragraph that explains how your economic reform program will benefit France.

5. **Express Problems Clearly** What issues arose when Louis XVI called the Estates-General in 1789?

● Writing About History

Quick Write: Make a Cause-and-Effect Organizer Choose a specific event from this section and write it in the center of a piece of paper. List causes above it and effects below it. This will give you the details to include in your cause-and-effect essay. You may need to do additional research to gather more details.

Women march to the palace.

WITNESS HISTORY 🔊 AUDIO

Parisian Women Storm Versailles

On October 5, 1789, anger turned to action as thousands of women marched from Paris to Versailles. They wanted the king to stop ignoring their suffering. They also wanted the queen. French women were particularly angry with the Austrian-born queen, Marie Antoinette. They could not feed their children, yet she lived extravagantly. The women yelled as they looked for her in the palace:

66 Death to the Austrian! We'll wring her neck! We'll tear her heart out!**99**
—mob of women at Versailles, October 6, 1789

Focus Question What political and social reforms did the National Assembly institute in the first stage of the French Revolution?

The French Revolution Unfolds

Objectives
- Explain how the political crisis of 1789 led to popular revolts.
- Summarize the moderate reforms enacted by the National Assembly in August 1789.
- Identify additional actions taken by the National Assembly as it pressed onward.
- Analyze why there was a mixed reaction around Europe to the events unfolding in France.

Terms, People, and Places

faction	émigré
Marquis de Lafayette	sans-culotte
Olympe de Gouges	republic
Marie Antoinette	Jacobins

Note Taking

Reading Skill: Identify Supporting Details As you read this section, prepare an outline like the one shown below. Remember to use numbers for supporting details.

> I. Political crisis leads to revolt
>   A. The Great Fear
>   1. Inflamed by famine and rumors
>   2.
>   B.

Excitement, wonder, and fear engulfed France as the revolution unfolded at home and spread abroad. Historians divide this revolutionary era into different phases. The moderate phase of the National Assembly (1789–1791) turned France into a constitutional monarchy. A radical phase (1792–1794) of escalating violence led to the end of the monarchy and a Reign of Terror. There followed a period of reaction against extremism, known as the Directory (1795–1799). Finally, the Age of Napoleon (1799–1815) consolidated many revolutionary changes. In this section, you will read about the moderate phase of the French Revolution.

Political Crisis Leads to Revolt

The political crisis of 1789 coincided with the worst famine in memory. Starving peasants roamed the countryside or flocked to towns, where they swelled the ranks of the unemployed. As grain prices soared, even people with jobs had to spend as much as 80 percent of their income on bread.

Rumors Create the "Great Fear" In such desperate times, rumors ran wild and set off what was later called the "Great Fear." Tales of attacks on villages and towns spread panic. Other rumors asserted that government troops were seizing peasant crops.

Inflamed by famine and fear, peasants unleashed their fury on nobles who were trying to reimpose medieval dues. Defiant peasants set fire to old manor records and stole grain from storehouses. The attacks died down after a period of time, but they clearly demonstrated peasant anger with an unjust regime.

Paris Commune Comes to Power Paris, too, was in turmoil. As the capital and chief city of France, it was the revolutionary center. A variety of **factions,** or dissenting groups of people, competed to gain power. Moderates looked to the **Marquis de Lafayette,** the aristocratic "hero of two worlds" who fought alongside George Washington in the American Revolution. Lafayette headed the National Guard, a largely middle-class militia organized in response to the arrival of royal troops in Paris. The Guard was the first group to don the tricolor—a red, white, and blue badge that was eventually adopted as the national flag of France.

A more radical group, the Paris Commune, replaced the royalist government of the city. It could mobilize whole neighborhoods for protests or violent action to further the revolution. Newspapers and political clubs—many even more radical than the Commune—blossomed everywhere. Some demanded an end to the monarchy and spread scandalous stories about the royal family and members of the court.

✓ **Checkpoint** What caused French peasants to revolt against nobles?

The National Assembly Acts

Peasant uprisings and the storming of the Bastille stampeded the National Assembly into action. On August 4, in a combative all-night meeting, nobles in the National Assembly voted to end their own privileges. They agreed to give up their old manorial dues, exclusive hunting rights, special legal status, and exemption from taxes.

Special Privilege Ends "Feudalism is abolished," announced the proud and weary delegates at 2 A.M. As the president of the Assembly later observed, "We may view this moment as the dawn of a new revolution, when all the burdens weighing on the people were abolished, and France was truly reborn."

Were nobles sacrificing much with their votes on the night of August 4? Both contemporary observers and modern historians note that the nobles gave up nothing that they had not already lost. Nevertheless, in the months ahead, the National Assembly turned the reforms of August 4 into law, meeting a key Enlightenment goal—the equality of all male citizens before the law.

Declaration of the Rights of Man In late August, as a first step toward writing a constitution, the Assembly issued the Declaration of the Rights of Man and the Citizen. The document was modeled in part on the American Declaration of Independence, written 13 years earlier. All men, the French declaration announced, were "born and remain free and equal in rights." They enjoyed natural rights to "liberty, property, security, and resistance to oppression." Like the writings of Locke and the *philosophes,* the constitution insisted that governments exist to protect the natural rights of citizens.

The declaration further <u>proclaimed</u> that all male citizens were equal before the law. Every Frenchman had an equal right to hold public office "with no distinction other than that of their virtues and talents." In addition, the declaration asserted freedom of religion and called for taxes to

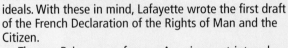

French Reaction to the American Revolution

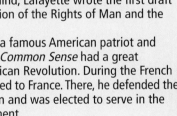

The Marquis de Lafayette (honored on ribbon at right) and Thomas Paine were leading figures in both the American and French revolutions. Lafayette, a French nobleman and military commander, helped the Americans defeat the British at Yorktown. He admired the American Declaration of Independence and American democratic ideals. With these in mind, Lafayette wrote the first draft of the French Declaration of the Rights of Man and the Citizen.

Thomas Paine was a famous American patriot and writer whose ideas in *Common Sense* had a great influence on the American Revolution. During the French Revolution, Paine moved to France. There, he defended the ideals of the revolution and was elected to serve in the revolutionary government.

Identify Central Issues How did the American Revolution influence the French Revolution?

Vocabulary Builder

<u>proclaimed</u>—(proh KLAYMD) *vt.* announced officially

be levied according to ability to pay. Its principles were captured in the enduring slogan of the French Revolution, "Liberty, Equality, Fraternity."

Many women were disappointed that the Declaration of the Rights of Man did not grant equal citizenship to them. In 1791, **Olympe de Gouges** (oh LAMP duh GOOZH), a journalist, demanded equal rights in her Declaration of the Rights of Woman and the Female Citizen. "Woman is born free," she proclaimed, "and her rights are the same as those of man." Therefore, Gouges reasoned, "all citizens, be they men or women, being equal in the state's eyes, must be equally eligible for all public offices, positions, and jobs." Later in the revolution, women met resistance for expressing their views in public, and many, including Gouges, were imprisoned and executed.

The Declaration of the Rights of Man met resistance as well. Uncertain and hesitant, Louis XVI did not want to accept the reforms of the National Assembly. Nobles continued to enjoy gala banquets while people were starving. By autumn, anger again turned to action.

Women March on Versailles On October 5, about six thousand women marched 13 miles in the pouring rain from Paris to Versailles. "Bread!" they shouted. They demanded to see the king.

Much of the crowd's anger was directed at the Austrian-born queen, **Marie Antoinette** (daughter of Maria Theresa and brother of Joseph II). The queen lived a life of great pleasure and extravagance, and this led to further public unrest. Although compassionate to the poor, her small acts went largely unnoticed because her lifestyle overshadowed them. She was against reforms and bored with the French court. She often retreated to the Petit Trianon, a small chateau on the palace grounds at Versailles where she lived her own life of amusement.

The women refused to leave Versailles until the king met their most important demand—to return to Paris. Not too happily, the king agreed. The next morning, the crowd, with the king and his family in tow, set out for the city. At the head of the procession rode women perched on the barrels of seized cannons. They told bewildered spectators that they were bringing Louis XVI, Marie Antoinette, and their son back to Paris. "Now

Playing Dress-Up
Marie Antoinette spent millions on her clothing and jewels and set fashion trends throughout France and Europe. This painting (top) was painted by her friend and portraitist, Elisabeth Vigée-Lebrun. Queens traditionally did not own property, but Marie Antoinette had her own small royal mansion and amusement village, or hamlet (bottom), where she played as milkmaid and shepherdess. *Why did the French common people resent Marie Antoinette?*

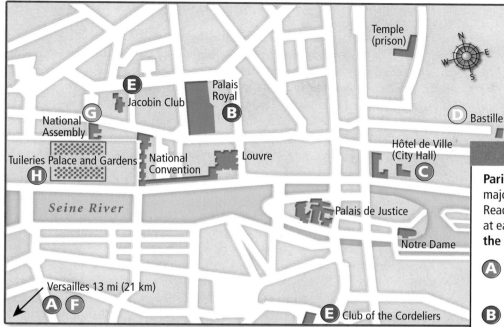

Analyzing Visuals

Paris in Revolution This map shows major landmarks of the French Revolution. Read below about the events that occurred at each landmark. **Why was Paris the revolutionary center in France?**

(A) **June 5, 1789** Delegates of the Third Estate take the Tennis Court Oath in Versailles.

(B) **July 12, 1789** Desmoulins incites a crowd at the Palais Royal, a famous meeting place.

(C) **July 14, 1789** Crowd meets at City Hall, the traditional protest place, before storming the Bastille.

(D) **July 14, 1789** Parisians storm the Bastille.

(E) **Oct. 1789** Political clubs (Cordeliers and Jacobins) established in Paris.

(F) **Oct. 5, 1789** Women march from Paris to Versailles.

(G) **Sept. 3, 1791** National Assembly produces the Constitution of 1791.

(H) **Aug. 10, 1792** Mob invades the Tuileries palace after meeting at City Hall.

we won't have to go so far when we want to see our king," they sang. Crowds along the way cheered the king, who now wore the tricolor. In Paris, the royal family moved into the Tuileries (TWEE luh reez) palace. For the next three years, Louis was a virtual prisoner.

✔ **Checkpoint** How did the National Assembly react to peasant uprisings?

The National Assembly Presses Onward

The National Assembly soon followed the king to Paris. Its largely bourgeois members worked to draft a constitution and to solve the continuing financial crisis. To pay off the huge government debt—much of it owed to the bourgeoisie—the Assembly voted to take over and sell Church lands.

The Church Is Placed Under State Control In an even more radical move, the National Assembly put the French Catholic Church under state control. Under the Civil Constitution of the Clergy, issued in 1790, bishops and priests became elected, salaried officials. The Civil Constitution ended papal authority over the French Church and dissolved convents and monasteries.

Reaction was swift and angry. Many bishops and priests refused to accept the Civil Constitution. The pope condemned it. Large numbers of French peasants, who were conservative concerning religion, also rejected the changes. When the government punished clergy who refused to support the Civil Constitution, a huge gulf opened between revolutionaries in Paris and the peasantry in the provinces.

The Constitution of 1791 Establishes a New Government The National Assembly completed its main task by producing a constitution. The Constitution of 1791 set up a limited monarchy in place of the absolute monarchy that had ruled France for centuries. A new Legislative Assembly had the power to make laws, collect taxes, and decide on issues of war and peace. Lawmakers would be elected by tax-paying male citizens over age 25.

To make government more efficient, the constitution replaced the old provinces with 83 departments of roughly equal size. It abolished the old provincial courts, and it reformed laws.

To moderate reformers, the Constitution of 1791 seemed to complete the revolution. Reflecting Enlightenment goals, it ensured equality before the law for all male citizens and ended Church interference in government. At the same time, it put power in the hands of men with the means and leisure to serve in government.

Louis's Escape Fails Meanwhile, Marie Antoinette and others had been urging the king to escape their humiliating situation. Louis finally gave in. One night in June 1791, a coach rolled north from Paris toward the border. Inside sat the king disguised as a servant, the queen dressed as a governess, and the royal children.

The attempted escape failed. In a town along the way, Louis's disguise was uncovered by someone who held up a piece of currency with the king's face on it. A company of soldiers escorted the royal family back to Paris, as onlooking crowds hurled insults at the king. To many, Louis's dash to the border showed that he was a traitor to the revolution.

✔ **Checkpoint** What were the provisions of the Constitution of 1791?

Radicals Take Over

Events in France stirred debate all over Europe. Supporters of the Enlightenment applauded the reforms of the National Assembly. They saw the French experiment as the dawn of a new age for justice and equality. European rulers and nobles, however, denounced the French Revolution.

Rulers Fear Spread of Revolution European rulers increased border patrols to stop the spread of the "French plague." Fueling those fears were the horror stories that were told by **émigrés** (EM ih grayz)—nobles, clergy, and others who had fled France and its revolutionary forces. Émigrés reported attacks on their privileges, their property, their religion, and even their lives. Even "enlightened" rulers turned against France. Catherine the Great of Russia burned Voltaire's letters and locked up her critics.

Edmund Burke, a British writer and statesman who earlier had defended the American Revolution, bitterly condemned revolutionaries in Paris. He predicted all too accurately that the revolution would become more violent. "Plots and assassinations," he wrote, "will be anticipated by preventive murder and preventive confiscation." Burke warned: "When ancient opinions and rules of life are taken away . . . we have no compass to govern us."

Threats Come From Abroad The failed escape of Louis XVI brought further hostile rumblings from abroad. In August 1791, the king of Prussia and the

emperor of Austria—who was Marie Antoinette's brother—issued the Declaration of Pilnitz. In this document, the two monarchs threatened to intervene to protect the French monarchy. The declaration may have been mostly a bluff, but revolutionaries in France took the threat seriously and prepared for war. The revolution was about to enter a new, more radical phase of change and conflict.

Radicals Fight for Power and Declare War In October 1791, the newly elected Legislative Assembly took office. Faced with crises at home and abroad, it survived for less than a year. Economic problems fed renewed turmoil. Assignats (AS ig nats), the revolutionary currency, dropped in value, causing prices to rise rapidly. Uncertainty about prices led to hoarding and caused additional food shortages.

In Paris and other cities, working-class men and women, called **sans-culottes** (sanz koo LAHTS), pushed the revolution into more radical action. They were called sans-culottes, which means "without breeches," because they wore long trousers instead of the fancy knee breeches that upper-class men wore. By 1791, many sans-culottes demanded a **republic,** or government ruled by elected representatives instead of a monarch.

Within the Legislative Assembly, several hostile factions competed for power. The sans-culottes found support among radicals in the Legislative Assembly, especially the Jacobins. A revolutionary political club, the **Jacobins** were mostly middle-class lawyers or intellectuals. They used pamphleteers and sympathetic newspaper editors to advance the republican cause. Opposing the radicals were moderate reformers and political officials who wanted no more reforms at all.

The National Assembly Declares War on Tyranny The radicals soon held the upper hand in the Legislative Assembly. In April 1792, the war of words between French revolutionaries and European monarchs moved onto the battlefield. Eager to spread the revolution and destroy tyranny abroad, the Legislative Assembly declared war first on Austria and then on Prussia, Britain, and other states. The great powers expected to win an easy victory against France, a land divided by revolution. In fact, however, the fighting that began in 1792 lasted on and off until 1815.

Sans-culotte, 1792

✔️ **Checkpoint**   How did the rest of Europe react to the French Revolution?

SECTION 2 Assessment

Progress Monitoring Online
For: Self-quiz with vocabulary practice
Web Code: nba-1821

Terms, People, and Places

1. For each term, person, or place listed at the beginning of the section, write a sentence explaining its significance.

Note Taking

2. **Reading Skill: Identify Supporting Details** Use your completed outline to answer the Focus Question: What political and social reforms did the National Assembly institute in the first stage of the French Revolution?

Comprehension and Critical Thinking

3. **Make Comparisons** How was the French Declaration of the Rights of Man and the Citizen similar to the American Declaration of Independence?

4. **Summarize** What did the Constitution of 1791 do, and how did it reflect Enlightenment ideas?

5. **Draw Inferences** Describe what happened to France's constitutional monarchy because of the French Revolution.

● **Writing About History**

Quick Write: Create a Flowchart As you prepare to write a cause-and-effect essay, you need to decide how to organize it. To do this, create a flowchart that shows the effects of the French Revolution on other countries. Do you want to write about the events in chronological order? By the importance of each event?

Declaration of the Rights of Man and the Citizen

Painting of the declaration

The National Assembly issued this document in 1789 after having overthrown the established government in the early stages of the French Revolution. The document was modeled in part on the English Bill of Rights and on the American Declaration of Independence. The basic principles of the French declaration were those that inspired the revolution, such as the freedom and equality of all male citizens before the law. The Articles below identify additional principles.

Therefore the National Assembly recognizes and proclaims, in the presence and under the auspices[1] of the Supreme Being, the following rights of man and of the citizen:

1. Men are born and remain free and equal in rights. Social distinctions may be founded only upon the general good.
2. The aim of all political association is the preservation of the natural and imprescriptible[2] rights of man. These rights are liberty, property, security, and resistance to oppression. . . .
4. Liberty consists in the freedom to do everything which injures no one else. . . .
5. Law can only prohibit such actions as are hurtful to society. . . .
6. Law is the expression of the general will. Every citizen has a right to participate personally, or through his representative, in its formation. It must be the same for all, whether it protects or punishes. All citizens, being equal in the eyes of the law, are equally eligible to all dignities and to all public positions and occupations, according to their abilities, and without distinction except that of their virtues and talents.
7. No person shall be accused, arrested, or imprisoned except in the cases and according to the forms prescribed by law. . . .
11. The free communication of ideas and opinions is one of the most precious of the rights of man. Every citizen may, accordingly, speak, write, and print with freedom. . . .
13. A common contribution is essential for the maintenance of the public [military] forces and for the cost of administration. This should be equitably distributed among all the citizens in proportion to their means.

Thinking Critically

1. **Summarize** Summarize article 6. Why is this article especially significant?
2. **Identify Central Issues** What central idea does this declaration share with the American Declaration of Independence?

1. **auspices** (AWS puh siz) *n.* approval and support
2. **imprescriptible** (im prih SKRIP tuh bul) *adj.* that which cannot be rightfully taken away

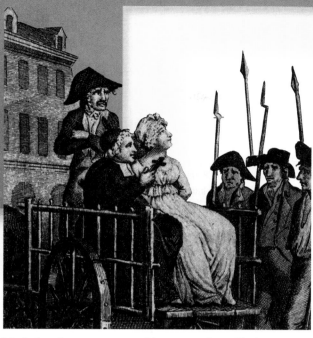

Marie Antoinette transported by cart to the guillotine

WITNESS HISTORY 🔊 AUDIO

The Engine of Terror

A new execution device called the guillotine was introduced during this phase of the revolution. With its large, diagonal blade that came crashing down from a great height, it cut off heads swiftly and accurately. Thousands of people were sent to the guillotine and executed without trial. In his novel *A Tale of Two Cities*, Charles Dickens describes daily life during the Reign of Terror:

❝ Along the Paris streets, the death-carts rumble, hollow and harsh. Six tumbrils [carts that carried condemned persons to the guillotine] carry the day's wine to La Guillotine. ❞

Focus Question What events occurred during the radical phase of the French Revolution?

Radical Days of the Revolution

Objectives

- Understand how and why radicals abolished the monarchy.
- Explain why the Committee of Public Safety was created and why the Reign of Terror resulted.
- Summarize how the excesses of the Convention led to the formation of the Directory.
- Analyze how the French people were affected by the changes brought about by the revolution.

Terms, People, and Places

suffrage	Napoleon
Robespierre	nationalism
Reign of Terror	Marseilles
guillotine	

Note Taking

Reading Skill: Recognize Sequence Make a timeline like the one shown here. Add dates and important events as you read this section.

Aug. 1792
Mob invades
royal palace.

Sept.	Jan.	July
1792	1793	1794

In 1793, the revolution entered a radical phase. For a year, France experienced one of the bloodiest regimes in its long history as determined leaders sought to extend and preserve the revolution.

The Monarchy Is Abolished

As the revolution continued, dismal news about the war abroad heightened tensions. Well-trained Prussian forces were cutting down raw French recruits. In addition, royalist officers were deserting the French army, joining émigrés and others hoping to restore the king's power.

Tensions Lead to Violence Battle disasters quickly inflamed revolutionaries who thought the king was in league with the enemies. On August 10, 1792, a crowd of Parisians stormed the royal palace of the Tuileries and slaughtered the king's guards. The royal family fled to the Legislative Assembly, escaping before the mob arrived.

A month later, citizens attacked prisons that held nobles and priests accused of political offenses. About 1,200 prisoners were killed; among them were many ordinary criminals. Historians disagree about the people who carried out the "September massacres." Some call them bloodthirsty mobs. Others describe them as patriots defending France from its enemies. In fact, most were ordinary citizens fired to fury by real and imagined grievances.

Radicals Take Control and Execute the King Backed by Paris crowds, radicals then took control of the Assembly. Radicals

Vocabulary Builder

radical—(RAD ih kul) *adj.* extreme; departure from the usual or traditional

called for the election of a new legislative body called the National Convention. **Suffrage,** the right to vote, was to be extended to all male citizens, not just to property owners.

The Convention that met in September 1792 was a more radical body than earlier assemblies. It voted to abolish the monarchy and establish a republic—the French Republic. Deputies then drew up a new constitution for France. The Jacobins, who controlled the Convention, set out to erase all traces of the old order. They seized lands of nobles and abolished titles of nobility.

During the early months of the Republic, the Convention also put Louis XVI on trial as a traitor to France. The king was convicted by a single vote and sentenced to death. On a foggy morning in January 1793, Louis mounted a scaffold in a public square in Paris. He started to speak, "Frenchmen, I die innocent. I pardon the authors of my death. I pray God that the blood about to be spilt will never fall upon the head of France. . . ." Then a roll of drums drowned out his words. Moments later, the king was beheaded. The executioner lifted the king's head by its hair and held it before the crowd.

In October, Marie Antoinette was also executed. The popular press celebrated her death. The queen, however, showed great dignity as she went to her death.

✓ **Checkpoint** What occurred after radicals took control of the Assembly?

■ **COMPARING VIEWPOINTS**

On the Execution of a King

On January 21, 1793, King Louis XVI of France was executed by order of the National Convention. Reaction to this event was both loud and varied throughout Europe. The excerpts below present two different views on this event. **Critical Thinking** *Which of the two viewpoints makes a better case for or against the execution of King Louis XVI? Cite examples from both statements to support your argument.*

For the Execution

The crimes of Louis XVI are unhappily all too real; they are consistent; they are notorious. Do we even have to ask the question of whether a nation has the right to judge, and execute, its highest ranking public official . . . when, to more securely plot against the nation, he concealed himself behind a mask of hypocrisy? Or when, instead of using the authority confided to him to protect his countrymen, he used it to oppress them? Or when he turned the laws into an instrument of violence to crush the supporters of the Revolution? Or when he robbed the citizens of their gold in order to subsidize their foes, and robbed them of their subsistence in order to feed the barbarian hordes who came to slaughter them? Or when he created monopolies in order to create famine by drying up the sources of abundance so that the people might die in misery and hunger? . . .

—Jean-Paul Marat

Against the Execution

The Republican tyrants of France have now carried their bloody purposes to the uttermost diabolical stretch of savage cruelty. They have murdered their King without even the shadow of justice, and of course they cannot expect friendship nor intercourse with any civilized part of the world. The vengeance of Europe will now rapidly fall on them; and, in process of time, make them the veriest wretches on the face of the earth. The name of Frenchman will be considered as the appellation of savage, and their presence shunned as a poison, deadly destructive to the peace and happiness of Mankind. It appears evident, that the majority of the National Convention, and the Executive Government of that truly despotic country, are comprised of the most execrable villains upon the face of the earth. . . .

—*London Times*, January 25, 1793

Terror and Danger Grip France

By early 1793, danger threatened France on all sides. The country was at war with much of Europe, including Britain, the Netherlands, Spain, and Prussia. In the Vendée (vahn DAY) region of France, royalists and priests led peasants in rebellion against the government. In Paris, the sans-culottes demanded relief from food shortages and inflation. The Convention itself was bitterly divided between Jacobins and a rival group, the Girondins.

The Convention Creates a New Committee To deal with the threats to France, the Convention created the Committee of Public Safety. The 12-member committee had almost absolute power as it battled to save the revolution. The Committee prepared France for all-out war, issuing a *levée en masse,* or mass levy (tax) that required all citizens to contribute to the war effort. In addition, the 12 members of the Committee were in charge of trials and executions.

Spurred by revolutionary fervor, French recruits marched off to defend the republic. Young officers developed effective new tactics to win battles with masses of ill-trained but patriotic forces. Soon, French armies overran the Netherlands. They later invaded Italy. At home, they crushed peasant revolts. European monarchs shuddered as the revolutionaries carried "freedom fever" into conquered lands.

Robespierre "the Incorruptible" At home, the government battled counterrevolutionaries under the guiding hand of Maximilien **Robespierre** (ROHBZ pyehr). Robespierre, a shrewd lawyer and politician, quickly rose to the leadership of the Committee of Public Safety. Among Jacobins, his selfless dedication to the revolution earned him the nickname "the incorruptible." The enemies of Robespierre called him a tyrant.

Robespierre had embraced Rousseau's idea of the general will as the source of all legitimate law. He promoted religious toleration and wanted to abolish slavery. Though cold and humorless, he was popular with the sans-culottes, who hated the old regime as much as he did. He believed that France could achieve a "republic of virtue" only through the use of terror, which he coolly defined as nothing more than "prompt, severe, inflexible justice." "Liberty cannot be secured," Robespierre cried, "unless criminals lose their heads."

The Guillotine Defines the Reign of Terror Robespierre was one of the chief architects of the **Reign of Terror,** which lasted from September 1793 to July 1794. Revolutionary courts conducted hasty trials. Spectators greeted death sentences with cries of "Hail the Republic!" or "Death to the traitors!"

In a speech given on February 5, 1794, Robespierre explained why the terror was necessary to achieve the goals of the revolution:

Primary Source

66 It is necessary to stifle the domestic and foreign enemies of the Republic or perish with them. . . . The first maxim of our politics ought to be to lead the people by means of reason and the enemies of the people by terror. . . . If the basis of popular government in time of peace is virtue, the basis of popular government in time of revolution is both virtue and terror. 99
—Maximilien Robespierre, quoted in *Pageant of Europe* (Stearns)

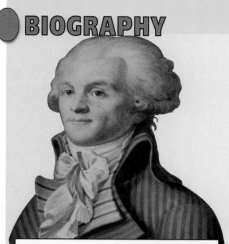

BIOGRAPHY

Robespierre

Maximilien Robespierre (1758–1794) did not have an easy childhood. His mother died when he was only 6 years old. Two years later, his father abandoned him and his three siblings. The children's aunts and grandfather then raised them. Because of this, Robespierre assumed responsibilities at an early age. Eventually, he went to study law at the University of Paris. His performance was so noteworthy that he was chosen to deliver a speech to Louis XVI on the occasion of the king's coronation. But young Robespierre was snubbed. After listening to the address in a pouring rainstorm, the king and queen left without acknowledging Robespierre in any way. Years later, in 1789, Robespierre was elected to the Estates-General, where his career as a revolutionary began. **How do you think Robespierre's early life might have influenced his political ideas?**

Suspect were those who resisted the revolution. About 300,000 were arrested during the Reign of Terror. Seventeen thousand were executed. Many were victims of mistaken identity or were falsely accused by their neighbors. Many more were packed into hideous prisons, where deaths from disease were common.

The engine of the Terror was the **guillotine** (GIL uh teen). Its fast-falling blade extinguished life instantly. A member of the legislature, Dr. Joseph Guillotin (gee oh TAN), had introduced it as a more humane method of beheading than the uncertain ax. But the guillotine quickly became a symbol of horror.

Within a year, the Terror consumed those who initiated it. Weary of bloodshed and fearing for their own lives, members of the Convention turned on the Committee of Public Safety. On the night of July 27, 1794, Robespierre was arrested. The next day he was executed. After the heads of Robespierre and other radicals fell, executions slowed dramatically.

✓ **Checkpoint** Why did Robespierre think the Terror was necessary to achieve the goals of the revolution?

The Revolution Enters Its Third Stage

In reaction to the Terror, the revolution entered a third stage. Moving away from the excesses of the Convention, moderates produced another constitution, the third since 1789. The Constitution of 1795 set up a five-

● **INFOGRAPHIC**

THE REIGN OF TERROR

From autumn 1793 to midsummer 1794, the revolution in France was overshadowed by a time of terror as the Committee of Public Safety rounded up "suspected persons" all over France. Only about 15 percent of those sentenced to death by guillotine (model at left) were of the nobility and clergy. Most were artisans and peasants of the Third Estate. Prisons in Paris—which included places such as former mansions and palaces, religious premises, and colleges—became more and more crowded as the number of suspects increased. Once sentenced to death, the condemned might travel an hour to the guillotine by cart as onlookers threw mud at them.

Thieves stole ▲ items such as silver as émigrés fled the country due to the Terror.

◀ Interrogation of aristocratic prisoners at L'Abbaye prison

man Directory and a two-house legislature elected by male citizens of property. The middle class and professional people of the bourgeoisie were the dominant force during this stage of the French Revolution. The Directory held power from 1795 to 1799.

Weak but dictatorial, the Directory faced growing discontent. Peace was made with Prussia and Spain, but war with Austria and Great Britain continued. Corrupt leaders lined their own pockets but failed to solve pressing problems. When rising bread prices stirred hungry sans-culottes to riot, the Directory quickly suppressed them. Another threat to the Directory was the revival of royalist feeling. Many émigrés were returning to France, and devout Catholics, who resented measures that had been taken against the Church, were welcoming them. In the election of 1797, supporters of a constitutional monarchy won the majority of seats in the legislature.

As chaos threatened, politicians turned to **Napoleon** Bonaparte, a popular military hero who had won a series of brilliant victories against the Austrians in Italy. The politicians planned to use him to advance their own goals. To their dismay, however, before long Napoleon would outwit them all to become ruler of France.

✔ **Checkpoint** What changes occurred after the Reign of Terror came to an end?

History Interactive
For: Interactive French Revolution
Web Code: nbp-1821

◄ People never knew if friends or family might appear on a list of guillotine victims. There is some debate on the humaneness of death by guillotine. Some authorities claim that even after the head has been severed, the victim could remain conscious for up to 30 seconds.

Georges Danton, ► a Revolutionary leader, challenged the Terror and was guillotined.

◄ This engraving depicts Robespierre's execution by guillotine. His was not the last. "Twenty minutes later, [those condemned for the day] were in front of the scaffold.... Pale, tense, shivering... several of them lowered their heads or shut their eyes.... The third [victim] was...the Princess of Monaco.... On the platform, her youthful beauty shone in the dazzling July light." The executioners then tossed the bodies and heads into large baskets near the scaffold.

Thinking Critically
1. **Identify Point of View** What were the goals of the Committee of Public Safety?
2. **Predict Consequences** How do you think life in France changed after the Terror came to an end?

Revolution Brings Change

By 1799, the 10-year-old French Revolution had dramatically changed France. It had dislodged the old social order, overthrown the monarchy, and brought the Church under state control.

New symbols such as the red "liberty caps" and the tricolor confirmed the liberty and equality of all male citizens. The new title "citizen" applied to people of all social classes. All other titles were eliminated. Before he was executed, Louis XVI was called Citizen Capet, from the name of the dynasty that had ruled France in the Middle Ages. Elaborate fashions and powdered wigs gave way to the practical clothes and simple haircuts of the sans-culottes.

Nationalism Spreads Revolution and war gave the French people a strong sense of national identity. In earlier times, people had felt loyalty to local authorities. As monarchs centralized power, loyalty shifted to the king or queen. Now, the government rallied sons and daughters of the revolution to defend the nation itself. **Nationalism,** a strong feeling of pride in and devotion to one's country, spread throughout France. The French people attended civic festivals that celebrated the nation and the revolution. A variety of dances and songs on themes of the revolution became immensely popular.

By 1793, France was a nation in arms. From the port city of **Marseilles** (mahr say), troops marched to a rousing new song. It urged the "children of the fatherland" to march against the "bloody banner of tyranny." This song, "La Marseillaise" (mahr say ez), would later become the French national anthem.

Revolutionaries Push For Social Reform Revolutionaries pushed for social reform and religious toleration. They set up state schools to replace religious ones and organized systems to help the poor, old soldiers, and war widows. With a major slave revolt raging in the colony of St. Domingue (Haiti), the government also abolished slavery in France's Caribbean colonies.

French Nationalism
"La Marseillaise" (top) and a revolutionary-period drum (bottom) helped rally the French people.

✔ **Checkpoint** What changes occurred in France because of the French Revolution?

SECTION **3** Assessment

Progress Monitoring *Online*
For: Self-quiz with vocabulary practice
Web Code: nba-1831

Terms, People, and Places

1. Place each of the key terms at the beginning of the section into one of the following categories: politics, culture, geography, or technology. Write a sentence for each term explaining your choice.

Note Taking

2. **Reading Skill: Recognize Sequence** Use your completed timeline to answer the Focus Question: What events occurred during the radical phase of the French Revolution?

Comprehension and Critical Thinking

3. **Summarize** Summarize the goals and actions of the Jacobins.
4. **Identify Central Issues** Why was the Committee of Public Safety created?
5. **Recognize Cause and Effect** How did the Reign of Terror cause the National Convention to be replaced by the Directory?
6. **Predict Consequences** How do you think French nationalism affected the war between France and the powers of Europe?

● Writing About History

Quick Write: Provide Elaboration To illustrate each cause and effect of your essay, you should have supporting details, facts, and examples. Choose one of the events below and list as many specific details as possible. Then write a paragraph using the details you listed to explain what caused the event.
- Reign of Terror
- Execution of King Louis XVI
- Creation of the Committee of Public Safety

Art of Revolution

Revolutions have visual chronicles as well as written ones, and in the days before photography, these depictions were often rendered with paint. The French artist Jacques-Louis David (ZHAHK loo EE dah VEED) and the Spanish artist Francisco Goya both portrayed aspects of revolution on canvas, but they had differing viewpoints. David supported the early French Revolution and embraced the revolutionary spirit in his work. Goya, however, was a realist who showed human suffering and the horrors of war in his paintings.

▲ *Napoleon Crossing Mont Saint Bernard,* **Jacques-Louis David, 1801**
Imprisoned after moderates turned against the Reign of Terror, David barely escaped with his life. When Napoleon rose to power, David deftly switched his political allegiance to the new Emperor of France and became one of Bonaparte's chief portraitists. Notice the names carved into the rocks. David included these names of great past rulers to show Napoleon's level of greatness. David's depictions of Napoleon helped cement him as a strong and heroic leader.

▲ *The Third of May, 1808,* **Francisco José de Goya y Lucientes, 1814**
One of the consequences of the French Revolution and Napoleon's rise was that France soon found itself at war with the rest of Europe. Francisco Goya saw firsthand the impact of these wars. Born in northern Spain, he rose to become the official painter of the Spanish court. When Napoleon invaded Spain and deposed its king, Goya chronicled the horrors of the resulting guerrilla warfare.

Thinking Critically
1. **Compare Points of View** What elements in each painting express the viewpoint of the artist? How are the elements different?
2. **Recognize Ideologies** How do you think the ideology of the French Revolution led to the scene Goya portrays here?

Enter Napoleon Bonaparte

After the execution of King Louis XVI, France entered a state of confusion and chaos without a single leader. Meanwhile, Napoleon Bonaparte, a brilliant and ambitious captain in the French army, was rapidly rising in the military ranks. Soon enough, Napoleon would come to rule almost all of Europe. One of his earliest victories in Lodi, Italy, convinced him that he was only just beginning his successful rise to power:

❝ From that moment, I foresaw what I might be. Already I felt the earth flee from beneath me, as if I were being carried into the sky. **❞**
—Napoleon Bonaparte

Unfinished portrait of Napoleon by Jacques-Louis David and Napoleon's signature

Focus Question Explain Napoleon's rise to power in Europe, his subsequent defeat, and how the outcome still affects Europe today.

The Age of Napoleon

Objectives

- Understand Napoleon's rise to power and why the French strongly supported him.
- Explain how Napoleon built an empire and what challenges the empire faced.
- Analyze the events that led to Napoleon's downfall.
- Outline how the Congress of Vienna tried to create a lasting peace.

Terms, People, and Places

plebiscite	scorched-earth policy
Napoleonic Code	abdicate
annex	Congress of Vienna
Continental System	legitimacy
guerrilla warfare	Concert of Europe

Note Taking

Reading Skill: Identify Main Ideas As you read the section, use a flowchart to list the important events that led from Napoleon's rise to power to his defeat. Add boxes as you need them.

```
┌─────────────────────────────────────────────┐
│ Napoleon quickly advances through military ranks. │
└─────────────────────────────────────────────┘
        ▼           ▼           ▼
┌─────────────────────────────────────────────┐
│                                             │
└─────────────────────────────────────────────┘
```

From 1799 to 1815, Napoleon Bonaparte would dominate France and Europe. A hero to some, an evil force to others, he gave his name to the final phase of the revolution—the Age of Napoleon.

Napoleon Rises to Power

Napoleon was born in Corsica, a French-ruled island in the Mediterranean. At age nine, he was sent to France to be trained for a military career. When the revolution broke out, he was an ambitious 20-year-old lieutenant, eager to make a name for himself.

Napoleon favored the Jacobins and republican rule. However, he found the conflicting ideas and personalities of the French Revolution confusing. He wrote to his brother in 1793: "Since one must take sides, one might as well choose the side that is victorious, the side which devastates, loots, and burns. Considering the alternative, it is better to eat than be eaten."

Victories Cloud Losses During the turmoil of the revolution, Napoleon rose quickly in the army. In December 1793, he drove British forces out of the French port of Toulon (too LOHN). He then went on to win several dazzling victories against the Austrians, capturing most of northern Italy and forcing the Hapsburg emperor to make peace. Hoping to disrupt British trade with India, he led an expedition to Egypt in 1798. The Egyptian campaign proved to be a disaster, but Napoleon managed to hide stories of the worst losses from his admirers in France. He did so by establishing a network of spies and censoring the press.

Success fueled Napoleon's ambition. By 1799, he moved from victorious general to political leader. That year, he helped overthrow the weak Directory and set up a three-man governing board known as the Consulate. Another constitution was drawn up, but Napoleon soon took the title First Consul. In 1802, he had himself named consul for life.

Napoleon Crowns Himself Emperor Two years later, Napoleon had acquired enough power to assume the title Emperor of the French. He invited the pope to preside over his coronation in Paris. During the ceremony, however, Napoleon took the crown from the pope's hands and placed it on his own head. By this action, Napoleon meant to show that he owed his throne to no one but himself.

At each step on his rise to power, Napoleon had held a **plebiscite** (PLEB uh syt), or popular vote by ballot. Each time, the French strongly supported him. As you will read, although the people theoretically had a say in government through their votes, Napoleon still held absolute power. This is sometimes called democratic despotism. To understand why people supported him, we must look at his policies.

✔ **Checkpoint** How did Napoleon rise to power so quickly in France?

Napoleon Reforms France

During the Consulate and empire, Napoleon consolidated his power by strengthening the central government. Order, security, and efficiency replaced liberty, equality, and fraternity as the slogans of the new regime.

To restore economic prosperity, Napoleon controlled prices, encouraged new industry, and built roads and canals. He set up a system of public schools under strict government control to ensure well-trained officials and military officers. At the same time, Napoleon backed off from some of the revolution's social reforms. He made peace with the Catholic Church in the Concordat of 1801. The Concordat kept the Church under state control but recognized religious freedom for Catholics. Revolutionaries who opposed the Church denounced the agreement, but Catholics welcomed it.

Napoleon won support across class lines. He encouraged émigrés to return, provided they take an oath of loyalty. Peasants were relieved when he recognized their right to lands they had bought from the Church and nobles during the revolution. The middle class, who had benefited most from the revolution, approved of Napoleon's economic reforms and the restoration of order after years of chaos. Napoleon also opened jobs to all, based on talent, a popular policy among those who remembered the old aristocratic monopoly of power.

Among Napoleon's most lasting reforms was a new code of laws, popularly called the **Napoleonic Code.** It embodied Enlightenment principles such as the equality of all citizens before the law, religious toleration, and the abolition of feudalism.

The Egyptian Campaign
The Battle of the Pyramids, July 21, 1798, painted by Louis-Francois Lejeune. *How did Napoleon hide the fact that the Egyptian campaign was a disaster?*

But the Napoleonic Code undid some reforms of the French Revolution. Women, for example, lost most of their newly gained rights and could not exercise the rights of citizenship. Male heads of households regained complete authority over their wives and children. Again, Napoleon valued order and authority over individual rights.

 Checkpoint What reforms did Napoleon introduce during his rise to power?

Napoleon Builds an Empire

From 1804 to 1812, Napoleon furthered his reputation on the battlefield. He successfully battled the combined forces of the greatest European powers. He took great risks and even suffered huge losses. "I grew up on the field of battle," he once said, "and a man such as I am cares little for the life of a million men." By 1812, his Grand Empire reached its greatest extent.

As a military leader, Napoleon valued rapid movements and made effective use of his large armies. He developed a new plan for each battle so opposing generals could never <u>anticipate</u> what he would do next. His enemies paid tribute to his leadership. Napoleon's presence on the battlefield, said one, was "worth 40,000 troops."

Vocabulary Builder
<u>anticipate</u>—(an TIS uh payt) *vt.* to foresee or expect

The Map of Europe Is Redrawn As Napoleon created a vast French empire, he redrew the map of Europe. He **annexed,** or incorporated into his empire, the Netherlands, Belgium, and parts of Italy and Germany. He also abolished the tottering Holy Roman Empire and created a 38-member Confederation of the Rhine under French protection. He cut Prussian territory in half, turning part of old Poland into the Grand Duchy of Warsaw.

Napoleon controlled much of Europe through forceful diplomacy. One tactic was placing friends and relatives on the thrones of Europe. For example, after unseating the king of Spain, he placed his own brother, Joseph Bonaparte, on the throne. He also forced alliances on European powers from Madrid to Moscow. At various times, the rulers of Austria, Prussia, and Russia reluctantly signed treaties with the "Corsican ogre," as the monarchs he overthrew called him.

In France, Napoleon's successes boosted the spirit of nationalism. Great victory parades filled the streets of Paris with cheering crowds. The people celebrated the glory and grandeur that Napoleon had gained for France.

Napoleon Strikes Britain Britain alone, of all the major European powers, remained outside Napoleon's European empire. With only a small army, Britain relied on its sea power to stop Napoleon's drive to rule the continent. In 1805, Napoleon prepared to invade England. But at the Battle of Trafalgar, fought off the southwest coast of Spain, British Admiral Horatio Nelson smashed the French fleet.

With an invasion ruled out, Napoleon struck at Britain's lifeblood, its commerce. He waged economic warfare through the **Continental System,** which closed European ports to British goods. Britain responded with its own blockade of European ports. A blockade involves shutting off ports to keep people or supplies from moving in or out. During their long struggle, both Britain and France seized neutral ships suspected of trading with the other side. British attacks on American ships sparked anger in the United States and eventually triggered the War of 1812.

Geography *Interactive*
For: Audio guided tour
Web Code: nbp-1841

Map Legend

- Empire of France
- States dependent on Napoleon
- States allied with Napoleon
- States against Napoleon
- Battle sites, 1800–1815
- Route of Napoleon's invasion of Russia

10° W
0°
20° E
60° N
50° N
40° N
30° N

KINGDOM OF NORWAY AND DENMARK
SWEDEN
North Sea
Baltic Sea
Borodino • Moscow
Smolensk
UNITED KINGDOM OF GREAT BRITAIN AND IRELAND
London •
PRUSSIA
Friedland
RUSSIAN EMPIRE
• Berlin
Warsaw •
GRAND DUCHY OF WARSAW
Jena
Leipzig
Waterloo
Paris •
CONFEDERATION OF THE RHINE
Versailles •
Austerlitz
Wagram
Atlantic Ocean
FRENCH EMPIRE
Ulm
• Vienna
SWITZ.
AUSTRIAN EMPIRE
KINGDOM OF ITALY
Marengo
Illyrian Provinces
Black Sea
PORTUGAL
Elba
Corsica
Rome •
MONTENEGRO
Adriatic Sea
OTTOMAN EMPIRE
• Madrid
SPAIN
SARDINIA
KINGDOM OF NAPLES
Cape Trafalgar
Balearic Islands
Mediterranean Sea
SICILY
AFRICA

Conic Projection
0   200   400 mi
0   200   400 km

Europe Today

Conic Projection
0   200   400 mi
0   200 400 km

NORWAY
SWEDEN
FINLAND
North Sea
ESTONIA
LATVIA
RUSSIA
IRELAND
UNITED KINGDOM
DENMARK
Baltic Sea
LITH.
RUSSIA
BELARUS
NETH.
GERMANY
POLAND
UKRAINE
BELG.
Atlantic Ocean
LUX.
CZECH REP.
SLOVAKIA
MOLDOVA
FRANCE
SWITZ.
AUSTRIA
HUNGARY
ROMANIA
Black Sea
SLOVENIA
CROATIA
SERB. & MONT.
BULGARIA
PORTUGAL
ITALY
BOS. & HERZ.
TURKEY
SPAIN
Corsica
Sardinia
ALBANIA
MACEDONIA
GREECE
Balearic Is.
Mediterranean Sea
Sicily
Crete
CYPRUS
MALTA

Bust of Napoleon Bonaparte

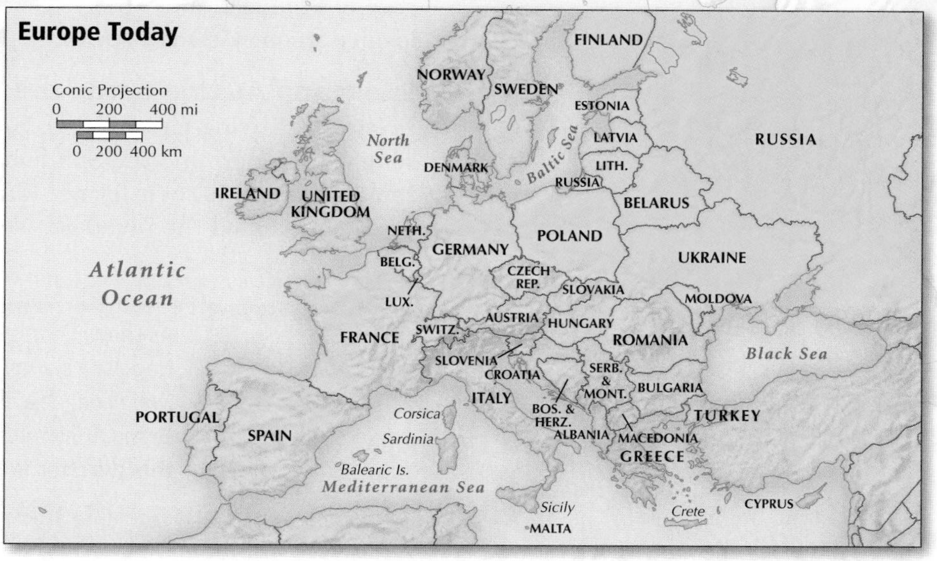

Map Skills Napoleon's empire reached its greatest extent in 1812. Most of the countries in Europe today have different names and borders.

1. **Locate:** (a) French empire, (b) Russian empire, (c) Germany
2. **Region** Locate the Confederation of the Rhine. What is this area called today?
3. **Make Comparisons** Compare Europe of Napoleon's empire to Europe of today on the maps above. How has Europe changed?

In the end, Napoleon's Continental System failed to bring Britain to its knees. Although British exports declined, Britain's powerful navy kept vital trade routes open to the Americas and India. Meanwhile, trade restrictions created a scarcity of goods in Europe, sent prices soaring, and intensified resentment against French power.

French armies under Napoleon spread ideas of the revolution across Europe. They backed liberal reforms in the lands they conquered. In some places, they helped install revolutionary governments that abolished titles of nobility, ended Church privileges, opened careers to men of talent, and ended serfdom and manorial dues. The Napoleonic Code, too, influenced countries in continental Europe and Latin America.

✓ **Checkpoint**   **How did Napoleon come to dominate most of Europe by 1812?**

Napoleon's Empire Faces Challenges

In 1812, Napoleon continued his pursuit of world domination and invaded Russia. This campaign began a chain of events that eventually led to his downfall. Napoleon's final defeat brought an end to the era of the French Revolution.

Nationalism Works Against Napoleon Napoleon's successes contained seeds of defeat. Although nationalism spurred French armies to success, it worked against them too. Many Europeans who had welcomed the ideas of the French Revolution nevertheless saw Napoleon and his armies as foreign oppressors. They resented the Continental System and Napoleon's effort to impose French culture on them.

From Rome to Madrid to the Netherlands, nationalism unleashed revolts against France. In the German states, leaders encouraged national loyalty among German-speaking people to counter French influence.

Spain and Austria Battle the French Resistance to foreign rule bled French-occupying forces dry in Spain. Napoleon introduced reforms that sought to undermine the Spanish Catholic Church. But many Spaniards remained loyal to their former king and devoted to the Church. When the Spanish resisted the invaders, well-armed French forces responded with

As shown in this painting, the Russian winter took its toll on Napoleon's army. Philippe Paul de Ségur, an aide to Napoleon, describes the grim scene as the remnants of the Grand Army returned home. **What were the effects of this disaster in Russia?**

Primary Source

❝ In Napoleon's wake [was] a mob of tattered ghosts draped in . . . odd pieces of carpet, or greatcoats burned full of holes, their feet wrapped in all sorts of rags. . . . [We] stared in horror as those skeletons of soldiers went by, their gaunt, gray faces covered with disfiguring beards, without weapons . . . with lowered heads, eyes on the ground, in absolute silence. ❞
—*Memoirs of Philippe Paul de Ségur*

brutal repression. Far from crushing resistance, however, the French response further inflamed Spanish nationalism. Efforts to drive out the French intensified.

Spanish patriots conducted a campaign of **guerrilla warfare,** or hit-and-run raids, against the French. (In Spanish, *guerrilla* means "little war.") Small bands of guerrillas ambushed French supply trains or troops before retreating into the countryside. These attacks kept large numbers of French soldiers tied down in Spain when Napoleon needed them elsewhere.

Spanish resistance encouraged Austria to resume hostilities against the French. In 1805, at the Battle of Austerlitz, Napoleon had won a crushing victory against an Austro-Russian army of superior numbers. Now, in 1809, the Austrians sought revenge. But once again, Napoleon triumphed—this time at the Battle of Wagram. By the peace agreement that followed, Austria surrendered lands populated by more than three million subjects.

The Russian Winter Stops the Grand Army Tsar Alexander I of Russia was once an ally of Napoleon. The tsar and Napoleon planned to divide Europe if Alexander helped Napoleon in his Continental System. Many countries objected to this system, and Russia became unhappy with the economic effects of the system as well. Yet another cause for concern was that Napoleon had enlarged the Grand Duchy of Warsaw that bordered Russia on the west. These and other issues led the tsar to withdraw his support from the Continental System. Napoleon responded to the tsar's action by assembling an army with soldiers from 20 nations, known as the Grand Army.

In 1812, with about 600,000 soldiers and 50,000 horses, Napoleon invaded Russia. To avoid battles with Napoleon, the Russians retreated eastward, burning crops and villages as they went. This **scorched-earth policy** left the French hungry and cold as winter came. Napoleon entered Moscow in September. He realized, though, that he would not be able to feed and supply his army through the long Russian winter. In October, he turned homeward.

The 1,000-mile retreat from Moscow turned into a desperate battle for survival. Russian attacks and the brutal Russian winter took a terrible toll. Fewer than 20,000 soldiers of the once-proud Grand Army survived. Many died. Others deserted. French general Michel Ney sadly concluded: "General Famine and General Winter, rather than Russian bullets, have conquered the Grand Army." Napoleon rushed to Paris to raise a new force to defend France. His reputation for success had been shattered.

✓ **Checkpoint** What challenges threatened Napoleon's empire and what led to the disaster in Russia?

Napoleon Falls From Power
A defeated Napoleon after his abdication on April 6, 1814, in a painting by Paul Delaroche

WITNESS HISTORY VIDEO

Watch *Napoleon's Lost Army* on the **Witness History Discovery School**™ video program to learn about Napoleon's invasion of Russia in 1812.

Napoleon Falls From Power

The disaster in Russia brought a new alliance of Russia, Britain, Austria, and Prussia against a weakened France. In 1813, they defeated Napoleon in the Battle of the Nations at Leipzig.

Napoleon Abdicates Briefly The next year, Napoleon **abdicated,** or stepped down from power. The victors exiled him to Elba, an island in the Mediterranean. They then recognized Louis XVIII, brother of Louis XVI, as king of France.

The restoration of Louis XVIII did not go smoothly. He agreed to accept the Napoleonic Code and honor the land settlements made during the revolution. However, many émigrés rushed back to France bent on revenge. An economic depression and the fear of a return to the old regime helped rekindle loyalty to Napoleon.

As the victorious allies gathered in Vienna for a general peace conference, Napoleon escaped his island exile and returned to France. Soldiers flocked to his banner. As citizens cheered Napoleon's advance, Louis XVIII fled. In March 1815, Napoleon entered Paris in triumph.

Crushed at the Battle of Waterloo Napoleon's triumph was short-lived. His star soared for only 100 days, while the allies reassembled their forces. On June 18, 1815, the opposing armies met near the town of Waterloo in Belgium. British forces under the Duke of Wellington and a Prussian army commanded by General Blücher crushed the French in an agonizing day-long battle. Once again, Napoleon was forced to abdicate and to go into exile on St. Helena, a lonely island in the South Atlantic. This time, he would not return.

Napoleon's Legacy Napoleon died in 1821, but his legend lived on in France and around the world. His contemporaries as well as historians today have long debated his legacy. Was he "the revolution on horseback," as he claimed? Or was he a traitor to the revolution?

No one, however, questions Napoleon's impact on France and on Europe. The Napoleonic Code consolidated many changes of the revolution. The France of Napoleon was a centralized state with a constitution. Elections were held with expanded, though limited, suffrage. Many more citizens had rights to property and access to education than under the old regime. Still, French citizens lost many rights promised so fervently by republicans during the Convention.

On the world stage, Napoleon's conquests spread the ideas of the revolution. He failed to make Europe into a French empire. Instead, he sparked nationalist feelings across Europe. The abolition of the Holy Roman Empire would eventually help in creating a new Germany. Napoleon's impact also reached across the

BIOGRAPHY

Prince Clemens von Metternich

As Austria's foreign minister, Metternich (1773–1859) used a variety of means to achieve his goals. In 1809, when Napoleon seemed vulnerable, Metternich favored war against France. In 1810, after France had crushed Austria, he supported alliance with France. When the French army was in desperate retreat from Russia, Metternich became the "prime minister of the coalition" that defeated Napoleon. At the Congress of Vienna, Metternich helped create a new European order and made sure that Austria had a key role in it. He would skillfully defend that new order for more than 30 years. **Why did Metternich's policies toward France change?**

Europe After the Congress of Vienna, 1815

Geography *Interactive*
For: Audio guided tour
Web Code: nbp-1842

Map Skills At the Congress of Vienna, European leaders redrew the map of Europe in order to contain France and keep a balance of power.

1. **Locate** (a) German Confederation, (b) Netherlands, (c) Vienna
2. **Region** Name three states that were in the German Confederation.
3. **Recognize Cause and Effect** Why did the Congress enlarge some of the countries around France?

Boundary of the German Confederation

Quadruple Alliance, 1815
- Great Britain
- Prussia
- Austrian Empire
- Russian Empire

Atlantic. In 1803, his decision to sell France's vast Louisiana Territory to the American government doubled the size of the United States and ushered in an age of American expansion.

✔ **Checkpoint** How did Napoleon impact Europe and the rest of the world?

Leaders Meet at the Congress of Vienna

After Waterloo, diplomats and heads of state again sat down at the **Congress of Vienna.** They faced the monumental task of restoring stability and order in Europe after years of war. The Congress met for 10 months, from September 1814 to June 1815. It was a brilliant gathering of European leaders. Diplomats and royalty dined and danced, attended concerts and ballets, and enjoyed parties arranged by their host, Emperor Francis I of Austria. The work fell to Prince Clemens von Metternich of Austria, Tsar Alexander I of Russia, and Lord Robert Castlereagh of Britain. Defeated France was represented by Prince Charles Maurice de Talleyrand.

Congress Strives For Peace The chief goal of the Vienna decision makers was to create a lasting peace by establishing a balance of power and protecting the system of monarchy. Each of the leaders also pursued his own goals. Metternich, the dominant figure at the Congress, wanted to restore things the way they were in 1792. Alexander I urged a "holy alliance" of Christian monarchs to suppress future revolutions. Lord Castlereagh was determined to prevent a revival of French military power. The aged diplomat Talleyrand shrewdly played the other leaders against one another so France would be accepted as an equal partner.

The peacemakers also redrew the map of Europe. To contain French ambitions, they ringed France with strong countries. In the north, they added Belgium and Luxembourg to Holland to create the kingdom of the Netherlands. To prevent French expansion eastward, they gave Prussia lands along the Rhine River. They also allowed Austria to reassert control over northern Italy.

To turn back the clock to 1792, the architects of the peace promoted the principle of **legitimacy,** restoring hereditary monarchies that the French Revolution or Napoleon had unseated. Even before the Congress began, they had put Louis XVIII on the French throne. Later, they restored "legitimate" monarchs in Portugal, Spain, and the Italian states.

Congress Fails to See Traps Ahead To protect the new order, Austria, Russia, Prussia, and Great Britain extended their wartime alliance into the postwar era. In the Quadruple Alliance, the four nations pledged to act together to maintain the balance of power and to suppress revolutionary uprisings, especially in France. Another result of the Congress was a system known as the **Concert of Europe,** in which the powers met periodically to discuss any problems affecting the peace of Europe.

The Vienna statesmen achieved their immediate goals in creating a lasting peace. Their decisions influenced European politics for the next 100 years. Europe would not see war on a Napoleonic scale until 1914. They failed, however, to foresee how powerful new forces such as nationalism would shake the foundations of Europe and Latin America in the next decades.

✔ **Checkpoint** Explain the chief goal and outcome of the Congress of Vienna.

Portrait of Louis XVIII

SECTION 4 **Assessment**

Progress Monitoring Online
For: Self-quiz with vocabulary practice
Web Code: nba-1841

Terms, People, and Places

1. For each term, person, or place listed at the beginning of the section, write a sentence explaining its significance.

Note Taking

2. **Reading Skill: Identify Main Ideas** Use your completed flowchart to answer the Focus Question: Explain Napoleon's rise to power in Europe, his subsequent defeat, and how the outcome still affects Europe today.

Comprehension and Critical Thinking

3. **Demonstrate Reasoned Judgment** If you were a French voter in 1803, how would you have voted on the plebiscite to make Napoleon emperor? Explain.

4. **Synthesize Information** Describe the resistance Napoleon encountered as countries grew to resent him.

5. **Make Comparisons** How does the peacekeeping solution adopted by the Congress of Vienna compare to today's peacekeeping missions?

● **Writing About History**

Quick Write: Clarify When you write a rough draft of a cause-and-effect essay, you should highlight the causes and effects. Use two highlighters, one to show causes, and the other to show effects. Eliminate causes or effects that do not support your main point, and add transitional phrases as needed. Write a paragraph about Napoleon's downfall. Highlight the causes and effects to evaluate the effectiveness of your paragraph.

Geography's Impact

How have geographic factors affected the course of history?

Geography played a critical role in Napoleon's disastrous invasion of Russia in 1812. Russia's severe winter weather helped destroy his Grand Army. In this way, geography affected the course of history by helping end Napoleon's quest to control all of Europe. Geography has also had more subtle—but still powerful—effects on history. The first civilizations arose in river valleys, where rich soil helped farmers feed growing populations. Humans continue to settle near rivers and along coastlines to have access to food, transportation, and trade. Consider the additional examples below that show the role of geography in history.

Silk was traded between China and Europe.

German soldiers in Russia, World War II

Landforms and Defense

People throughout history have taken advantage of local landforms to defend themselves. For example, settlements located on high ground made enemies' attacks more difficult as they had to climb as they fought. It also made it easier to spy an enemy. With this type of defense in mind, Greeks built the Acropolis of Athens on a steep hill thousands of years ago. *Acropolis* means "city at the top." In Paris, France, the founders used a different approach. They built their town on an island in the middle of the Seine River. Medieval castles often reflected all these strategies: positioned on a hill, beside a river, and encircled by a moat.

Resources and Trade Routes

Ancient overland trade routes were really just beaten paths. Merchants traveled far and wide for resources that were not available at home. Towns grew up along the trade routes to serve the merchants' needs for food and shelter. A famous trade route named the Silk Road was a set of caravan trails that led from China all the way to the Mediterranean Sea. Europeans willingly paid great sums for silk, porcelain, and other products that only China, with its particular set of resources, could provide.

The Acropolis, built on a hill for defense

Climate and Military Outcomes

Napoleon could rightfully blame his defeat on Russia's harsh climate. But he was not the only general who has cursed the forces of nature. Throughout history, climate has affected the outcome of military campaigns. It has helped turn back invaders or otherwise brought misery to foreign armies. In the late 1200s, Japan twice avoided becoming a province of Mongol China because a typhoon destroyed the invading Mongol fleet. The Japanese refer to this climatic savior as *kamikaze,* or "divine wind." In 1941, Hitler moved to take over the Soviet Union. Hitler's forces, much like Napoleon's, were not prepared for Russia's harsh winter. Thousands of Germans froze to death.

Thinking Critically

1. How have landforms and climate affected where people live? Explain your answer.

2. **Connections to Today** Research online to find information on the tsunami that occurred in South Asia in 2004. Summarize the impact of geography.

Quick Study Guide

Progress Monitoring *Online*
For: Self-test with vocabulary practice
Web Code: nba-1851

■ What Inspired the French Revolution?

- **Social:** Enlightenment ideas such as equality and justice
- **Political:** Ideas from the American Revolution
- **Economic:** Inequalities among classes; unrest due to extravagant monarchy

■ Reforms of the National Assembly

Political
• Proclaimed all male citizens equal before the law.
• Limited the power of the monarchy.
• Established the Legislative Assembly to make laws.
• Granted all tax-paying male citizens the right to elect members of the Legislative Assembly.
Social and Economic
• Abolished special privileges of the nobility.
• Announced an end to feudalism.
• Called for taxes to be levied according to ability to pay.
• Abolished guilds and forbade labor unions.
• Compensated nobles for lands seized by peasants.
Religious
• Declared freedom of religion.
• Took over and sold Church lands.
• Placed the French Catholic Church under control of the state.
• Provided that bishops and priests be elected and receive government salaries.

■ Causes and Effects of the French Revolution

Cause and Effect	
Long-Term Causes	**Immediate Causes**
• Corrupt and inconsistent leadership • Prosperous members of Third Estate resent privileges of First and Second Estates. • Spread of Enlightenment ideas	• Huge government debt • Poor harvests and rising price of bread • Failure of Louis XVI to accept financial reforms • Formation of National Assembly • Storming of Bastille

The French Revolution

Immediate Effects	**Long-Term Effects**
• Declaration of the Rights of Man and the Citizen adopted. • France adopts its first written constitution. • Revolutionary France fights coalition of European powers. • Monarchy abolished; execution of king and queen. • Reign of Terror	• Napoleon gains power. • Napoleonic Code established. • French public schools set up. • French conquests spread nationalism. • Congress of Vienna convenes to restore stability to Europe. • Revolutions occur elsewhere in Europe and in Latin America.

Connections to Today
• French law reflects Napoleonic Code.   • France eventually became a democratic republic.

■ Key Events From 1789–1815

	1789 **Parisians storm the Bastille on July 14, starting the French Revolution.**	1793 **Radicals execute the king and queen, which leads to the Reign of Terror.**	1799 **Napoleon overthrows the Directory.**
Chapter Events **Global Events**	**1790**	**1795**	**1800**
	1789 **The United States Constitution is ratified.**	1793 **China rejects British trade offer.**	

Concept | Connector

◼ Cumulative Review

Record the answers to the questions below on your Concept Connector worksheets. In addition, record information from this chapter about the following concepts:

- Cooperation: Coalitions against Napoleon

1. **Democracy** The First and Second Estates had power and wealth at the expense of the Third Estate. These class differences in France caused revolt and revolution, as you have learned in this chapter. Thus began the fight for democracy as members of the Third Estate demanded equal say in government. Compare the Assembly's Declaration of the Rights of Man and the Citizen to the American Declaration of Independence. What principles of democracy are included in both documents? Consider these influencing factors:
   - the early governments in Greece and Rome
   - England's political system
   - Enlightenment thinkers

2. **Nationalism** The French Revolution brought about waves of nationalism that spread throughout France. Under Napoleon, nationalism spurred French armies to success. The tricolor flag, the song *La Marseillaise,* and the words Liberty, Equality, and Fraternity all helped unite the French people in a cause to defend their nation. What spurred nationalism in the American Revolution? Think about the following:
   - symbols
   - common goals

3. **Revolution** In the French Revolution, the Third Estate revolted to topple the Old Regime. The Protestant Reformation caused a similar upheaval when peasants revolted for an end to serfdom. Research the Peasants' Revolt that erupted in Germany in 1524. How does it compare to the French Revolution? Think about the following:
   - causes
   - effects
   - goals

◼ Connections To Today

1. **Geography's Impact: Wars in the Middle East** Geography played an important role in Napoleon's defeat in Russia. Napoleon's Grand Army, once nearly 500,000 soldiers strong, shrank to about 20,000 due to the brutal Russian winter. Research newspaper and magazine articles to find how geography has impacted wars in the Middle East. Compile your research and write a script for your local newscast. Consider the following:
   - location
   - landforms
   - climate

   Burning oil pipeline, September 14, 2004, caused by sabotage in the Middle East

2. **Cooperation: United Nations** Diplomats and heads of states from the powers that defeated Napoleon—Austria, Russia, Prussia, and Great Britain—gathered at the Congress of Vienna in 1814. Their main goal was to restore peace after the French Revolution and Napoleonic era. Today, U.N. peacekeeping operations take place around the globe with the same goal of keeping or restoring peace. Research to find more information on the Congress of Vienna and U.N. peacekeeping operations. Draw a table to write facts about each in individual columns. Think about the following:
   - history and purpose of the organizations
   - definitions of "peacekeeping"

1804	1812	1814	1815
Napoleon crowns himself emperor of France.	**Napoleon invades Russia.**	**Congress of Vienna meets.**	**Napoleon is defeated at Waterloo.**

1805 **1810** **1815**

1804	1812	
Haiti declares independence from France.	**The United States declares war on Britain.**	**History Interactive** **For:** Interactive timeline **Web Code:** nbp-1801

Chapter Assessment

Terms, People, and Places

Match the following terms with the definitions below.

sans-culotte
bourgeoisie
Napoleonic Code
abdicate
Estates-General

Olympe de Gouges
plebiscite
deficit spending
Maximilien Robespierre
nationalism

1. a meeting of the representatives of the three estates
2. situation in which a government spends more money than it takes in
3. strong feeling of devotion to one's country
4. the middle class
5. journalist who demanded equal rights for women
6. leader of the Committee of Public Safety
7. ballot in which voters have a direct say on an issue
8. working-class men and women in France; means "without breeches"
9. law code that embodied Enlightenment principles such as equality
10. step down from power

Main Ideas

Section 1 (pp. 208–213)
11. What caused discontent in the old French regime?
12. When the Estates-General convened in May 1789, what actions did members of the Third Estate take and why?

Section 2 (pp. 214–220)
13. Describe one reform that the National Assembly enacted through each of the following documents: **(a)** the Declaration of the Rights of Man and the Citizen, **(b)** the Civil Constitution of the Clergy, **(c)** the Constitution of 1791.

Section 3 (pp. 221–227)
14. What was the Reign of Terror?

Section 4 (pp. 228–237)
15. List the reforms that Napoleon made as leader of France.
16. How did the Congress of Vienna try to restore the balance of power in Europe?

Chapter Focus Question
17. What were the causes and effects of the French Revolution, and how did the revolution lead to the Napoleonic era?

Critical Thinking

18. **Draw Conclusions** What impact did Enlightenment ideas have on the French Revolution?
19. **Recognize Cause and Effect** Explain the events that led to the end of the monarchy.
20. **Geography and History** How did the geography of the Russian empire work against Napoleon's Grand Army?
21. **Analyzing Cartoons** In the cartoon shown here, the figure on the left represents the British, and the other figure represents Napoleon. What are the figures carving, and why?

Writing About History

Expository Essay: Cause and Effect There were many key events in the French Revolution and Napoleonic era that affected France and the rest of the world. Write an essay that explains the causes of one of the following events and discuss what resulted: Parisians storming the Bastille; Women marching on Versailles; Napoleon crowning himself emperor of the French. Consult page SH10 of the Writing Handbook for additional help.

Prewriting
• Consider what you know about these events and choose one that you think best shows cause and effect.

• Take time to research facts, descriptions, and examples, to clearly illustrate the causes and effects in your essay.

Drafting
• Choose one of the following to organize the causes and effects in your essay: show the chronological order of events, or order the events from the least important to the most important.
• As you draft your essay, illustrate each cause and effect with supporting facts and details.

Revising
• Review your entire draft to ensure you show a clear relationship between the causes and effects.
• Analyze each paragraph to check that you have provided a thorough set of facts and details.

Document-Based Assessment

Storming the Bastille

One of the most famous and dramatic moments of the French Revolution was the storming of the Bastille. This prison fortress with 90-foot-high walls symbolized the injustices of absolute monarchy. The following documents describe the event from different viewpoints.

Document A

"Shouts of 'Give us the Bastille' were heard, and nine hundred had pressed into the undefended outer courtyard, becoming angrier by the minute. . . . At about half past three in the afternoon the crowd was reinforced by companies of *gardes françaises* [French guards] and by defecting soldiers, including a number who were veterans of the American campaign. Two in particular, Second-Lieutenant Jacob Elie, the standard-bearer of the Infantry of the Queen, and Pierre-Augustin Hulin, the director of the Queen's laundry, were crucial in turning the incoherent assault into an organized siege."

—From ***Citizens: A Chronicle of the French Revolution,*** (1989) by Simon Schama

Document B

"How much the greatest event it is that ever happened in the world! and how much the best!"

—**Letter, July 30, 1789,** by Charles James Fox (1749–1806), British politician, on the fall of the Bastille

Document C

"The mob came closer and the governor declared his willingness to capitulate [give up]. . . The streets and houses, even the roofs were filled with people abusing and cursing me. Daggers, bayonets, pistols were constantly pointed at me. I did not know how I would be killed but was sure my last hour had come. Those who had no arms were throwing stones at me, the women wrenched their teeth and threatened me with their fists. Two soldiers behind me had already been killed by the furious mob and I am convinced I could not have reached City Hall had not one officer . . . escorted me."

—**"Reports of the Taking of the Bastille, July 14, 1789, by One of Its Defenders"** (1834) by Ludwig von der Fluhe (Swiss officer)

Document D

≥ *Demolition of the Bastille, 1789*

Analyzing Documents

Use your knowledge of the storming of the Bastille and Documents A, B, C, and D to answer questions 1–4.

1. In Document B, Charles James Fox was mostly likely enthusiastic about the fall of the Bastille because
   A he had a personal grudge against prison guards.
   B the people stood up to authority.
   C he supported King Louis XVI.
   D he was anxious to see what the people of France would do next.

2. Which document attempts to give an objective view of the storming of the Bastille?
   A Document B
   B Document A
   C Document C
   D Document D

3. In Document C, which words best indicate which side the author is on?
   A the governor declared his willingness to capitulate
   B daggers, bayonets, pistols
   C even the roofs were filled with people
   D furious mob

4. **Writing Task** Compare the four documents. Which lasting document best conveys the significance of the event? Use your knowledge of this event and specific evidence from the documents to support your opinion.

7

The Industrial Revolution Begins

1750–1850

A Different Kind of Revolution

While the American Revolution and the French Revolution were being fought in the late 1700s, another kind of revolution took hold in Britain. Though not political, this revolution—known as the Industrial Revolution—brought about just as many changes to society. Paul Johnson, historian, describes this time period as "the age, above all in history, of matchless opportunities for penniless men with powerful brains and imaginations." Listen to the Witness History audio to hear more about the start of the Industrial Revolution.

Train ticket, 1830

◄ **On September 27, 1825, the Stockton and Darlington Railway in England became the world's first steam railway to offer passenger and freight service.**

James Watt

Chapter Preview

Chapter Focus Question What technological, social, economic, and cultural changes occurred as the Industrial Revolution took hold?

Section 1
Dawn of the Industrial Age

Section 2
Britain Leads the Way

Section 3
Social Impact of the Industrial Revolution

Section 4
New Ways of Thinking

Socialist leaflet

Note Taking Study Guide *Online*
For: Note Taking and Concept Connector worksheets
Web Code: nbd-1901

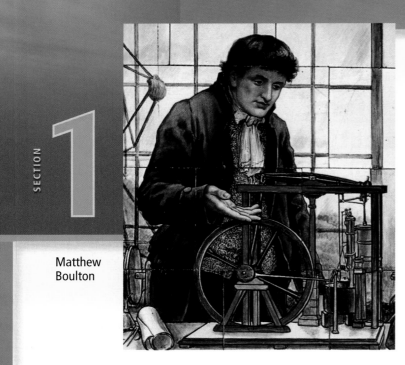

Matthew
Boulton

WITNESS HISTORY 🔊 AUDIO

From Hand Power to Steam Power

For centuries, people used their own energy to provide the power for their work. While the idea of using steam power came about in the seventeenth century, it was not until engineer James Watt improved the steam engine that it could be applied to machinery. His financial partner Matthew Boulton, a successful manufacturer, proclaimed:

❝I have at my disposal what the whole world demands, something which will uplift civilization more than ever by relieving man of all undignified drudgery. I have *steam power.*❞

Focus Question What events helped bring about the Industrial Revolution?

Dawn of the Industrial Age

Objectives
- Analyze why life changed as industry spread.
- Summarize how an agricultural revolution led to the growth of industry.
- Outline the new technologies that helped trigger the Industrial Revolution.

Terms, People, and Places

anesthetic
enclosure
James Watt
smelt

Note Taking

Reading Skill: Recognize Multiple Causes
Several key events led to the Industrial Revolution. As you read the section, create a flowchart of these causes. Add categories as needed.

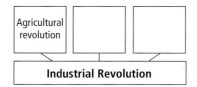

For thousands of years following the rise of civilization, most people lived and worked in small farming villages. However, a chain of events set in motion in the mid-1700s changed that way of life for all time. Today, we call this period of change the Industrial Revolution.

The Industrial Revolution started in Britain. The economic changes that Britain experienced affected people's lives as much as previous political changes and revolutions had. In contrast with most political revolutions, it was neither sudden nor swift. Instead, it was a long, slow, uneven process in which production shifted from simple hand tools to complex machines. From its beginnings in Britain, the Industrial Revolution has spread to the rest of Europe, North America, and around the globe.

Life Changes as Industry Spreads

In 1750, most people worked the land, using handmade tools. They lived in simple cottages lit by firelight and candles. They made their own clothing and grew their own food. In nearby towns, they might exchange goods at a weekly outdoor market.

Like their ancestors, these people knew little of the world that existed beyond their village. The few who left home traveled only as far as their feet or a horse-drawn cart could take them. Those bold adventurers who dared to cross the seas were at the mercy of the winds and tides.

With the onset of the Industrial Revolution, the rural way of life began to disappear. By the 1850s, many country villages had grown into industrial towns and cities. Those who lived there were able to buy clothing and food that someone else produced.

Industrial-age travelers moved rapidly between countries and continents by train or steamship. Urgent messages flew along telegraph wires. New inventions and scientific "firsts" poured out each year. Between 1830 and 1855, for example, an American dentist first used an **anesthetic,** or drug that prevents pain during surgery; an American inventor patented the first sewing machine; a French physicist measured the speed of light; and a Hungarian doctor introduced antiseptic methods to reduce the risk of women dying in childbirth.

Still more stunning changes occurred in the next century, which created our familiar world of skyscraper cities and carefully tended suburbs. How and why did these great changes occur? Historians point to a series of interrelated causes that helped trigger the industrialization of the West. The "West" referred originally to the industrialized countries in Europe but today includes many more.

✓ **Checkpoint** Why was the Industrial Revolution a turning point in world history?

Agriculture Spurs Industry

Oddly enough, the Industrial Revolution was made possible in part by a change in the farming fields of Western Europe. From the first agricultural revolution some 11,000 years ago, when people learned to farm and domesticate animals, until about 300 years ago, farming had remained pretty much the same. Then, a second agricultural revolution took place that greatly improved the quality and quantity of farm products.

Farming Methods Improve The Dutch led the way in this new agricultural revolution. They built earthen walls known as dikes to reclaim land from the sea. They also combined smaller fields into larger ones to make better use of the land and used fertilizer from livestock to renew the soil.

In the 1700s, British farmers expanded on Dutch agricultural experiments. Educated farmers exchanged news of experiments through farm journals. Some farmers mixed different kinds of soils to get higher crop yields. Others tried out new methods of crop rotation. Lord Charles Townshend urged farmers to grow turnips, which restored exhausted soil. Jethro Tull invented a new mechanical device, the seed drill, to aid farmers. It deposited seeds in rows rather than scattering them wastefully over the land.

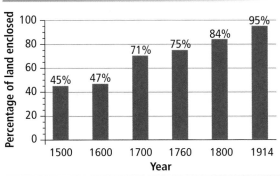

Land Enclosures in England, 1500–1914

Percentage of land enclosed

Year	
1500	45%
1600	47%
1700	71%
1760	75%
1800	84%
1914	95%

Graph Skills According to the graph, between which years was the largest percentage of land enclosed? What was the result of these land enclosures?

SOURCE: *Oxford Atlas of World History,* 1999

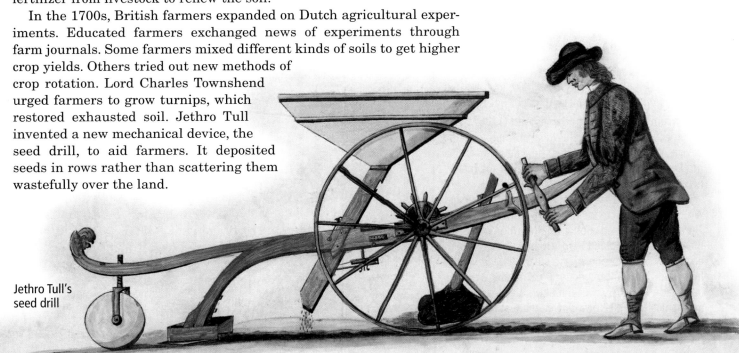

Jethro Tull's seed drill

Enclosure Increases Output but Causes Migration Meanwhile, rich landowners pushed ahead with **enclosure,** the process of taking over and consolidating land formerly shared by peasant farmers. In the 1500s, landowners had enclosed land to gain more pastures for sheep to increase wool output. By the 1700s, they wanted to create larger fields that could be cultivated more efficiently. The British Parliament facilitated enclosures through legislation.

As millions of acres were enclosed, farm output rose. Profits also rose because large fields needed fewer workers. But such progress had a large human cost. Many farm laborers were thrown out of work, and small farmers were forced off their land because they could not compete with large landholders. Villages shrank as cottagers left in search of work. In time, jobless farm workers migrated to towns and cities. There, they formed a growing labor force that would soon tend the machines of the Industrial Revolution.

Population Multiplies The agricultural revolution contributed to a rapid growth of population. Precise population <u>statistics</u> for the 1700s are rare, but those that do exist are striking. Britain's population, for example, soared from about 5 million in 1700 to almost 9 million in 1800. The population of Europe as a whole shot up from roughly 120 million to about 180 million during the same period. Such growth had never before been seen.

Why did this population increase occur? First, the agricultural revolution reduced the risk of death from famine because it created a surplus of food. Since people ate better, they were healthier. Also, better hygiene and sanitation, along with improved medical care, further slowed deaths from disease.

✓ **Checkpoint** How did an agricultural revolution contribute to population growth?

Vocabulary Builder

<u>statistics</u>—(stuh TIS tiks) *pl.n.* data that are gathered and tabulated to present information

BIOGRAPHY

James Watt

How did a clever Scottish engineer become the "Father of the Industrial Revolution"? After repairing a Newcomen steam engine, James Watt (1736–1819) became fascinated with the idea of improving the device. Within a few months, he knew he had a product that would sell. Still, Watt lacked the money needed to produce and market it.

Fortunately, he was able to form a partnership with the shrewd manufacturer Matthew Boulton. They then founded Soho Engineering Works in Birmingham, England, to manufacture steam engines. Watt's version of the steam engine shown here had a separate condensing chamber and was patented in 1769. Eventually, a measure of mechanical and electrical power, the watt, would be named for James Watt. **How might the Industrial Revolution have been different if Watt had not found a business partner?**

New Technology Becomes Key

Another factor that helped trigger the Industrial Revolution was the development of new technology. Aided by new sources of energy and new materials, these new technologies enabled business owners to change the ways work was done.

An Energy Revolution During the 1700s, people began to harness new sources of energy. One vital power source was coal, used to develop the steam engine. In 1712, British inventor Thomas Newcomen had developed a steam engine powered by coal to pump water out of mines. Scottish engineer **James Watt** looked at Newcomen's invention in 1764 and set out to make improvements on the engine in order to make it more efficient. Watt's engine, after several years of work, would become a key power source of the Industrial Revolution. The steam engine opened the door not only to operating machinery but eventually to powering locomotives and steamships.

The Quality of Iron Improves Coal was also a vital source of fuel in the production of iron, a material needed for the construction of machines and steam engines. The Darby family of Coalbrookdale pioneered new methods of producing iron. In 1709, Abraham Darby used coal instead of charcoal to smelt iron, or separate iron from its ore.

Darby's experiments led him to produce less expensive and better-quality iron, which was used to produce parts for the steam engines. Both his son and grandson continued to improve on his methods. In fact, Abraham Darby III built the world's first iron bridge. In the decades that followed, high-quality iron was used more and more widely, especially after the world turned to building railroads.

✔ **Checkpoint** What new technologies helped trigger the Industrial Revolution?

Abraham Darby III completed the world's first iron bridge in 1779. The bridge still stands today.

Assessment

Progress Monitoring *Online*
For: Self-quiz with vocabulary practice
Web Code: nba-1911

Terms, People, and Places

1. For each term, person, or place listed at the beginning of the section, write a sentence explaining its significance.

Note Taking

2. **Reading Skill: Recognize Multiple Causes** Use your completed flowchart to answer the Focus Question: What events helped bring about the Industrial Revolution?

Comprehension and Critical Thinking

3. **Recognize Cause and Effect** What were the immediate and long-term effects of the agricultural revolution that occurred in the 1700s?

4. **Predict Consequences** How do you think population growth contributed to the Industrial Revolution?

5. **Summarize** Explain how new sources of energy, specifically coal, contributed to the Industrial Revolution.

● **Writing About History**

Quick Write: Give Background To explain a historical process, you should first orient the reader to time and place. Ask yourself when and where the process occurred. Practice by explaining in one or two sentences how an agricultural revolution led to the Industrial Revolution.

Train passengers
in Britain

WITNESS HISTORY 🔊 AUDIO

Riding the Railway

One of the most important developments of the Industrial Revolution was the creation of a countrywide railway network. The world's first major rail line went from Liverpool to Manchester in England. Fanny Kemble, the most famous actress of the day, was one of the first passengers:

❝ We were introduced to the little engine which was to drag us along the rails. . . This snorting little animal, . . . started at about ten miles an hour. . . . You can't imagine how strange it seemed to be journeying on thus, without any visible cause of progress other than the magical machine . . .❞

Focus Question What key factors allowed Britain to lead the way in the Industrial Revolution?

Britain Leads the Way

Objectives
- Understand why Britain was the starting point for the Industrial Revolution.
- Describe the changes that transformed the textile industry.
- Explain the significance of the transportation revolution.

Terms, People, and Places

capital	Eli Whitney
enterprise	turnpike
entrepreneur	Liverpool
putting-out system	Manchester

Note Taking

Reading Skill: Identify Causes and Effects Fill in the circles of a concept web like the one below with the key factors that helped Britain take an early lead in industrialization. In a separate concept web, fill in the effects of Britain's early lead.

Resources

Britain Takes the Lead

When agricultural practices changed in the eighteenth century, more food was able to be produced, which in turn fueled population growth in Britain. The agricultural changes also left many farmers homeless and jobless. These two factors led to a population boom in the cities as people migrated from rural England into towns and cities. This population increase, in turn, created a ready supply of labor to mine the coal, build the factories, and run the machines. The start of the Industrial Revolution in Britain can be attributed to many factors. Population growth was just one of them.

Why Britain?

What characteristics of eighteenth-century Britain made it ripe for industrialization? Historians cite several reasons for Britain's lead.

Natural Resources Abound Britain had the advantage of plentiful natural resources such as natural ports and navigable rivers. Rivers supplied water power and allowed for the construction of canals. These canals increased accessibility for trade and were instrumental in bringing goods to market. In addition, Britain was able to establish communications and transport relatively cheaply due to its easy accessibility to the sea from all points. Britain's plentiful supply of coal was fundamental to its industrialization and was used to power steam engines. Vast supplies of iron were available to be used to build the new machines.

The Effects of Demand and Capital In the 1700s, Britain had plenty of skilled mechanics who were eager to meet the growing demand for new, practical inventions. This ready workforce, along with the population explosion, boosted demand for goods. In order to increase the production of goods to meet the demand, however, another key ingredient was needed. Money was necessary to start businesses.

From the mid-1600s to 1700s, trade from a growing overseas empire helped the British economy prosper. Beginning with the slave trade, the business class accumulated **capital,** or money used to invest in enterprises. An **enterprise** is a business organization in an area such as shipping, mining, railroads, or factories. Many businessmen were ready to risk their capital in new ventures due to the healthy economy.

In addition to the advantages already cited, Britain had a stable government that supported economic growth. While other countries in Europe faced river tolls and other barriers, Britain did not. The government built a strong navy that protected its empire, shipping, and overseas trade. Although the upper class tended to look down on business people, it did not reject the wealth produced by the new entrepreneurs. These **entrepreneurs** were those who managed and assumed the financial risks of starting new businesses.

✔ **Checkpoint** What conditions in Britain paved the way for the Industrial Revolution?

Shuttle used to speed up weaving process

Geography *Interactive*
For: Audio guided tour
Web Code: nbp-1921

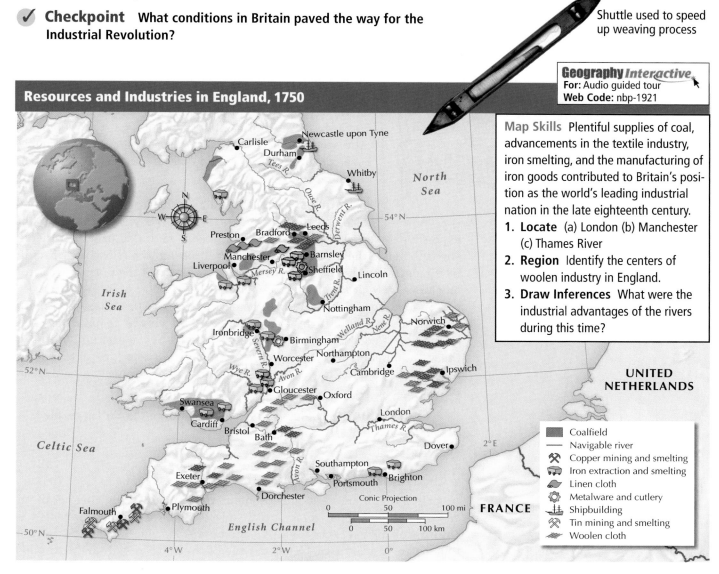

Resources and Industries in England, 1750

Map Skills Plentiful supplies of coal, advancements in the textile industry, iron smelting, and the manufacturing of iron goods contributed to Britain's position as the world's leading industrial nation in the late eighteenth century.
1. **Locate** (a) London (b) Manchester (c) Thames River
2. **Region** Identify the centers of woolen industry in England.
3. **Draw Inferences** What were the industrial advantages of the rivers during this time?

Legend:
- Coalfield
- Navigable river
- Copper mining and smelting
- Iron extraction and smelting
- Linen cloth
- Metalware and cutlery
- Shipbuilding
- Tin mining and smelting
- Woolen cloth

These textile machines were constructed to increase cotton production. The flying shuttle sped up weaving, while the spinning jenny and the water frame increased the speed of spinning thread. How did these inventions change the textile industry?

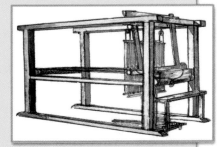

John Kay's flying shuttle, 1733 ▶

◀ James Hargreaves' spinning jenny, 1764

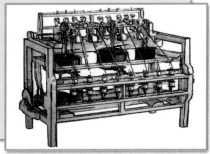

Richard Arkwright's water frame, 1769 ▶

The Textile Industry Advances

The Industrial Revolution first took hold in Britain's largest industry—textiles. In the 1600s, cotton cloth imported from India had become popular. British merchants tried to organize a cotton cloth industry at home. They developed the **putting-out system,** also known as cottage industry, in which raw cotton was distributed to peasant families who spun it into thread and then wove the thread into cloth in their own homes. Skilled artisans in the towns then finished and dyed the cloth.

Inventions Speed Production Under the putting-out system, production was slow. As the demand for cloth grew, inventors came up with a string of remarkable devices that revolutionized the British textile industry. For example, John Kay's flying shuttle enabled weavers to work so fast that they soon outpaced spinners. James Hargreaves solved that problem by producing the spinning jenny in 1764, which spun many threads at the same time. A few years later, in 1769, Richard Arkwright patented the water frame, which was a spinning machine that could be powered by water.

Meanwhile, in America, these faster spinning and weaving machines presented a challenge—how to produce enough cotton to keep up with England. Raw cotton grown in the South had to be cleaned of dirt and seeds by hand, a time-consuming task. To solve this, **Eli Whitney** invented a machine called the cotton gin that separated the seeds from the raw cotton at a fast rate. He finished the cotton gin in 1793, and cotton production increased exponentially.

Factories Are Born in Britain The new machines doomed the putting-out system. They were too large and expensive to be operated at home. Instead, manufacturers built long sheds to house the machines. At first, they located the sheds near rapidly moving streams, harnessing the water power to run the machines. Later, machines were powered by steam engines.

Spinners and weavers now came each day to work in these first factories, which brought together workers and machines to produce large quantities of goods. Early observers were awed at the size and output of these establishments. One onlooker noted: "The same [amount] of labor is now performed in one of these structures which formerly occupied the industry of an entire district."

 Checkpoint **What led to the advancement of the British textile industry?**

The Transportation Revolution

As production increased, entrepreneurs needed faster and cheaper methods of moving goods from place to place. Some capitalists invested in **turnpikes,** private roads built by entrepreneurs who charged travelers a toll, or fee, to use them. Goods traveled faster as a result, and turnpikes soon linked every part of Britain. Other entrepreneurs had canals dug to connect rivers together or to connect inland towns with coastal ports. Engineers also built stronger bridges and upgraded harbors to help the expanding overseas trade.

Canals Boom During the late 1700s and early 1800s, factories needed an efficient, inexpensive way to receive coal and raw materials and then to ship finished goods to market. In 1763, when the Bridgewater canal opened, it not only made a profit from tolls, but it cut in half the price of coal in Manchester. The success of this canal set off a canal-building frenzy. Entrepreneurs formed companies to construct canals for profit. Not all the canals that were built had enough traffic to support them, however, and bankruptcy often resulted. Then, beginning in the 1830s, canals lost their importance as steam locomotives made railroads the new preferred form of transportation.

Welcome the Steam Locomotive It was the invention of the steam locomotive that made the growth of railroads possible. In the early 1800s, pioneers like George Stephenson developed steam-powered locomotives to pull carriages along iron rails. The railroad did not have to follow the course of a river. This meant that tracks could go places where rivers did not, allowing factory owners and merchants to ship goods swiftly and cheaply over land. The world's first major rail line, from **Liverpool** to **Manchester,** opened in England in 1830. In the following decades, railroad travel became faster and railroad building boomed. By 1870, rail lines crisscrossed Britain, Europe, and North America.

One Thing Leads to Another As the Industrial Revolution got under way, it triggered a chain reaction. Once inventors developed machines that could produce large quantities of goods more efficiently, prices fell. Lower prices made goods more affordable and thus created more consumers who further fed the demand for goods. This new cycle caused a wave of economic and social changes that dramatically affected the way people lived.

 Checkpoint Why was the development of railroads important to industrialization?

Vocabulary Builder

decades—(DEK aydz) *n.* ten-year periods

SECTION 2 Assessment

Progress Monitoring Online
For: Self-quiz with vocabulary practice
Web Code: nba-1921

Terms, People, and Places

1. For each term, person, or place listed at the beginning of the section, write a sentence explaining its significance.

Note Taking

2. **Reading Skill: Identify Causes and Effects** Use your completed concept webs to answer the Focus Question: What key factors allowed Britain to lead the way in the Industrial Revolution?

Comprehension and Critical Thinking

3. **Analyze Information** Explain how each of the following helped contribute to demand for consumer goods in Britain: **(a)** population explosion, **(b)** general economic prosperity.

4. **Determine Relevance** What was the significance of new machines to the textile industry?

5. **Summarize** Explain how advances in transportation contributed to Britain's global trade.

● **Writing About History**

Quick Write: Create a Flowchart Flowcharts are useful tools to help you write an explanatory essay. Create a flowchart to show the changes that occurred in the textile industry. Be sure that the sequence of events is clear.

Monmouth Street, London

WITNESS HISTORY ◀)) AUDIO

Stench and Sickness

As more and more people moved to the cities to work, they had little choice about where to live. There was no public water supply, waste lined the unpaved streets, and disease spread rapidly in these unsanitary conditions. Dr. Southwood-Smith worked in two districts of London and wrote:

❝ Uncovered sewers, stagnant ditches and ponds, gutters always full of putrefying matter . . . It is not possible for any language to convey an adequate conception of the poisonous condition in which large portions of both these districts always remain, . . . from the masses of putrefying matter which are allowed to accumulate.❞

Focus Question What were the social effects of the Industrial Revolution?

Social Impact of the Industrial Revolution

Objectives

- Explain what caused urbanization and what life was like in the new industrial cities.
- Compare and contrast the industrial working class and the new middle class.
- Understand how the factory system and mines changed the way people worked.
- Analyze the benefits and challenges of industrialization.

Terms, People, and Places

urbanization
tenement
labor union

Note Taking

Reading Skill: Understand Effects As you read the section, complete a table that lists benefits and challenges of industrialization.

Industrialization	
Benefits	Challenges
• Created jobs	• Crowded cities
•	•

The Industrial Revolution brought great riches to most of the entrepreneurs who helped set it in motion. For the millions of workers who crowded into the new factories, however, the industrial age brought poverty and harsh living conditions.

In time, reforms would curb many of the worst abuses of the early industrial age in Europe and the Americas. As standards of living increased, people at all levels of society would benefit from industrialization. Until then, working people would suffer with dangerous working conditions; unsafe, unsanitary, and overcrowded housing; and unrelenting poverty.

People Move to New Industrial Cities

The Industrial Revolution brought rapid **urbanization,** or the movement of people to cities. Changes in farming, soaring population growth, and an ever-increasing demand for workers led masses of people to migrate from farms to cities. Almost overnight, small towns around coal or iron mines mushroomed into cities. Other cities grew up around the factories that entrepreneurs built in once-quiet market towns.

The British market town of Manchester numbered 17,000 people in the 1750s. Within a few years, it exploded into a center of the textile industry. Its population soared to 40,000 by 1780 and 70,000 by 1801. Visitors described the "cloud of coal vapor" that polluted

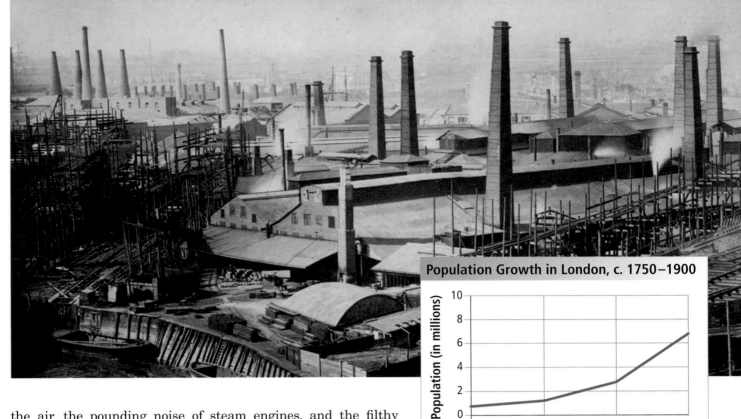

Population Growth in London, c. 1750–1900

Graph Skills Population increased dramatically as factories sprung up in cities such as London (pictured here). How many more people were in London in 1900 than in 1750 according to the line graph?

SOURCE: *International Historical Statistics, Europe 1750–1993*, 1998

the air, the pounding noise of steam engines, and the filthy stench of its river. This growth of industry and rapid population growth dramatically changed the location and distribution of two resources—labor and people.

✓ **Checkpoint** What led to the massive migration of people from farms to cities?

New Social Classes Emerge

The Industrial Revolution created a new middle class along with the working class. Those in the middle class owned and operated the new factories, mines, and railroads, among other industries. Their lifestyle was much more comfortable than that of the industrial working class.

When farm families moved to the new industrial cities, they became workers in mines or factories. Many felt lost and bewildered. They faced tough working conditions in uncomfortable environments. In time, though, factory and mine workers developed their own sense of community despite the terrible working conditions.

The Industrial Middle Class Those who benefited most from the Industrial Revolution were the entrepreneurs who set it in motion. The Industrial Revolution created this new middle class, or bourgeoisie (boor zhwah ZEE), whose members came from a variety of backgrounds. Some were merchants who invested their growing profits in factories. Others were inventors or skilled artisans who developed new technologies. Some rose from "rags to riches," a pattern that the age greatly admired.

Middle-class families lived in well-furnished, spacious homes on paved streets and had a ready supply of water. They wore fancy clothing and ate well. The new middle class took pride in their hard work and their determination to "get ahead." Only a few had sympathy for the poor. Women of the middle class did not leave the home to work but instead focused their energy on raising their children. This contrasted with the

Vocabulary Builder

contaminated—(kun TAM uh nayt id)
adj. unclean and impure; polluted

wealthy, who had maidservants to look after their children, and the working class, whose children were a part of the workforce.

The Industrial Working Class While the wealthy and the middle class lived in pleasant neighborhoods, vast numbers of poor struggled to survive in foul-smelling slums. They packed into tiny rooms in **tenements,** or multistory buildings divided into apartments. These tenements had no running water, only community pumps. There was no sewage or sanitation system, so wastes and garbage rotted in the streets. Sewage was also dumped into rivers, which created an overwhelming stench and contaminated drinking water. This led to the spread of diseases such as cholera.

Workers Stage Futile Protests Although **labor unions,** or workers' organizations, were illegal at this time, secret unions did exist among frustrated British workers. They wished to initiate worker reforms, such as increases in pay, but had no political power to effect change. Sometimes their frustration led to violence. The first instances of industrial riots occurred in England from 1811 to 1813. Groups of textile workers known as the Luddites (LUD yts) resisted the labor-saving machines that were costing them their jobs. Some of them smashed textile machines with sledgehammers and burned factories. They usually wore masks and operated at night. There was widespread support among the working class for these Luddite groups.

Vocabulary Builder

stressed—(stresd) *vt.* emphasized

Workers Find Comfort in Religion Many working-class people found comfort in a religious movement called Methodism. This movement was influenced by the Industrial Revolution as people moved to cities and lost connections with their old churches. John Wesley had founded the Methodist movement in the mid-1700s. Wesley stressed the need for a personal sense of faith. He encouraged his followers to improve themselves by adopting sober, moral ways.

Methodist meetings featured hymns and sermons promising forgiveness of sin and a better life to come. Methodist preachers took this message of salvation into the slums. There, they tried to rekindle hope among the working poor. They set up Sunday schools where followers not only studied the Bible but also learned to read and write. Methodists helped channel workers' anger away from revolution and toward reform.

 Checkpoint How did members of the working class react to their new experiences in industrial cities?

Life in the Factories and Mines

The heart of the new industrial city was the factory. There, the technology of the machine age and the rapid pace of industrialization imposed a harsh new way of life on workers.

Factory Workers Face Harsh Conditions Working in a factory system differed greatly from working on a farm. In rural villages, people worked hard, but their work varied according to the season. Life was also hard for poor rural workers who were part of the putting-out system, but at least they worked at their own pace. In the grim factories of industrial towns, workers faced a rigid schedule set by the factory whistle.

WITNESS HISTORY VIDEO

Watch *In Old New York* on the **Witness History Discovery School**™ video program to learn about life during the Industrial Age.

Discovery
SCHOOL

Working hours were long, with shifts lasting from 12 to 16 hours, six or seven days a week. Workers could only take breaks when the factory owners gave permission. Exhausted workers suffered accidents from machines that had no safety devices. They might lose a finger, a limb, or even their lives. In textile mills, workers constantly breathed air filled with lint, which damaged their lungs. Those workers who became sick or injured lost their jobs.

The majority of early factory workers were women rather than men. Employers often preferred to hire women workers because they thought women could adapt more easily to machines and were easier to manage. In addition, employers generally paid women half what they paid men.

Factory work created a double burden for women. Their new jobs took them out of their homes for 12 hours or more a day. They then returned to their tenements, which might consist of one damp room with a single bed. They had to feed and clothe their families, clean, and cope with such problems as sickness and injury.

Miners Face Worse Conditions The Industrial Revolution increased the demand for iron and coal, which in turn increased the need for miners. Although miners were paid more, working conditions in the mines were even worse than in the factories. They worked in darkness, and the coal dust destroyed their lungs. There were always the dangers of explosions, flooding, and collapsing tunnels. Women and children carted heavy loads of coal, sometimes on all fours in low passages. They also climbed ladders carrying heavy baskets of coal several times a day.

Children Have Dangerous Jobs Factories and mines also hired many boys and girls. These children often started working at age seven or eight, a few as young as five. Nimble-fingered and quick-moving, they changed spools in the hot and humid textile mills where sometimes they could not see because of all the dust. They also crawled under machinery to repair broken threads in the mills. Conditions were even worse for children who worked in the mines. Some sat all day in the dark, opening

Even children as young as five years old worked in the mines. James Kay-Shuttleworth worked as a physician among the different classes of the Industrial Revolution in Manchester. His profession allowed him to see the working conditions of poor in the cities. How was work in factories and mines different from work on the farm?

> **Primary Source**
>
> 66 Whilst the engine runs, people must work—men, women, and children are yoked together with iron and steam. The animal machine is chained fast to the iron machine, which knows no suffering and weariness. 99
> —James Kay-Shuttleworth, 1832

and closing air vents. Others hauled coal carts in the extreme heat. Because children had helped with work on the farm, parents accepted the idea of child labor. The wages the children earned were needed to keep their families from starving.

Child labor reform laws called "factory acts" were passed in the early 1800s. These laws were passed to reduce a child's workday to twelve hours and also to remove children under the age of eight or nine from the cotton mills. Because the laws were generally not enforced, British lawmakers formed teams of inspectors to ensure that factories and mines obeyed the laws in the 1830s and 1840s. More laws were then passed to shorten the workday for women and require that child workers be educated.

✔ **Checkpoint** How did the Industrial Revolution affect the lives of men, women, and children?

Families could afford to take trips to such places as the zoo as wages increased.

The Results of Industrialization

Since the 1800s, people have debated whether the Industrial Revolution was a blessing or a curse. The early industrial age brought terrible hardships. In time, however, reformers pressed for laws to improve working conditions. Labor unions won the right to bargain with employers for better wages, hours, and working conditions. Eventually working-class men gained the right to vote, which gave them political power.

Despite the social problems created by the Industrial Revolution—low pay, dismal living conditions—the Industrial Age did have some positive effects. As demand for mass-produced goods grew, new factories opened, which in turn created more jobs. Wages rose so that workers had enough left after paying rent and buying food to buy a newspaper or visit a music hall. As the cost of railroad travel fell, people could visit family in other towns. Horizons widened and opportunities increased.

✔ **Checkpoint** Why was the Industrial Revolution seen as both a blessing and a curse?

SECTION 3 Assessment

Progress Monitoring *Online*
For: Self-quiz with vocabulary practice
Web Code: nba-1931

Terms, People, and Places

1. What do each of the key terms listed at the beginning of the section have in common? Explain.

Note Taking

2. **Reading Skill: Understand Effects**
   Use your completed table to answer the Focus Question: What were the social effects of the Industrial Revolution?

Comprehension and Critical Thinking

3. **Analyze Information** How did the Industrial Revolution affect (a) cities and (b) population distribution?

4. **Synthesize Information** Explain how the Industrial Revolution changed the living conditions for both the middle class and the working class.

5. **Demonstrate Reasoned Judgment** Do you think increases in wages justify harsh working conditions? Why or why not?

● **Writing About History**

Quick Write: Gather Details When writing an explanatory essay, you should include facts, examples, and descriptions that help explain your topic. Make a list of details to help explain what life was like when people moved from rural areas to the new industrial cities.

Friedrich Engels: *The Condition of the Working Class in England in 1844*

In *The Condition of the Working Class in England in 1844*, Friedrich Engels recorded his observations of the wretched living conditions in poor areas of nineteenth-century England. In this excerpt, Engels describes working-class districts in Manchester. He depicts the misery and filth typical of the living areas of industrial workers.

Friedrich Engels, 1845

The houses are packed very closely together and since the bank of the river is very steep it is possible to see a part of every house. All of them have been blackened by soot, all of them are crumbling with age and all have broken window-panes and window-frames. In the background there are old factory buildings which look like barracks. On the opposite, low-lying bank of the river, one sees a long row of houses and factories. The second house is a roofless ruin, filled with refuse, and the third is built in such a low situation that the ground floor is uninhabitable and has neither doors nor windows. In the background one sees the paupers'[1] cemetery, and the stations of the railways to Liverpool and Leeds. . . .

The recently constructed extension of the Leeds railway which crosses the Irk at this point has swept away some of these courts and alleys, but it has thrown open to public gaze some of the others. So it comes about that there is to be found immediately under the railway bridge a court which is even filthier and more revolting than all the others. This is simply because it was formerly so hidden and secluded that it could only be reached with considerable difficulty [but is now exposed to the human eye]. I thought I knew this district well, but even I would never have found it had not the railway viaduct [elevated roadway] made a breach[2] in the slums at this point. One walks along a very rough path on the river bank, in between clothesposts and washing lines, to reach a chaotic group of little, one-storied, one-roomed cabins. Most of them have earth floors, and working, living and sleeping all take place in the one room. In such a hole, barely six feet long and five feet wide, I saw two beds—and what beds and bedding!—which filled the room, except for the fireplace and the doorstep. Several of these huts, as far as I could see, were completely empty, although the door was open and the inhabitants were leaning against the door posts. In front of the doors filth and garbage abounded. I could not see the pavement, but from time to time I felt it was there because my feet scraped it. . . .

1. **pauper** (PAW pur) *n.* poor person
2. **breach** (breech) *n.* break

Thinking Critically
1. **Draw Inferences (a)** How did the development of the railways affect the working-class districts? **(b)** How does Engels feel about the living conditions he observes?
2. **Make Generalizations** What seems to be Engels' general attitude toward the Industrial Revolution?

Workers on break, London

WITNESS HISTORY 🔊 AUDIO

The Struggle of the Working Class

Karl Marx and Friedrich Engels give their view on how the Industrial Revolution affected workers:

❝Owing to the extensive use of machinery and to division of labor, the work of the proletarians has lost all individual character, and, consequently, all charm for the workman. He becomes [a limb] of the machine, and it is only the most simple, most monotonous, and most easily acquired knack, that is required of him. . . .❞
—From *The Communist Manifesto*

Focus Question What new ideas about economics and society were fostered as a result of the Industrial Revolution?

New Ways of Thinking

Objectives

- Understand laissez-faire economics and the beliefs of those who supported it.
- Describe the doctrine of utilitarianism.
- Summarize the theories of socialism.
- Explain Marx's views of the working class and the response to Marxism.

Terms, People, and Places

Thomas Malthus	Robert Owen
Jeremy Bentham	Karl Marx
utilitarianism	communism
socialism	proletariat
means of production	social democracy

N̲o̲te Taking

Reading Skill: Identify Main Ideas Write an outline like the one here to show the new economic and social theories.

> I. Laissez-faire economics
>   A. Adam Smith and free enterprise
>   1.
>   2.
> II. Malthus on population
>   A.

Everywhere in Britain, British economist **Thomas Malthus** saw the effects of the population explosion—crowded slums, hungry families, unemployment, and widespread misery. After careful study, in 1798 he published *An Essay on the Principle of Population*. He concluded that poverty was unavoidable because the population was increasing faster than the food supply. Malthus wrote: "The power of population is [far] greater than the power of the Earth to produce subsistence for man."

Malthus was one of many thinkers who tried to understand the staggering changes taking place in the early Industrial Age. As heirs to the Enlightenment, these thinkers looked for natural laws that governed the world of business and economics.

Laissez-Faire Economics

During the Enlightenment, physiocrats argued that natural laws should be allowed to operate without interference. As part of this philosophy, they believed that government should not interfere in the free operation of the economy. In the early 1800s, middle-class business leaders embraced this laissez-faire, or "hands-off," approach.

As you have learned, the main proponent of laissez-faire economics was Adam Smith, author of bestseller *The Wealth of Nations*. Smith asserted that a free market—the unregulated exchange of goods and services—would come to help everyone, not just the rich. The free market, Smith said, would produce more goods at lower prices, making them affordable to everyone. A growing economy would also encourage capitalists to reinvest profits in new ventures. Supporters of this free-enterprise capitalism pointed to the successes of the Industrial Age, in which government had played no part.

Malthus Holds Bleak View Also a laissez-faire economist, Thomas Malthus predicted that population would outpace the food supply. The only checks on population growth, he said, were nature's "natural" methods of war, disease, and famine. As long as population kept increasing, he went on, the poor would suffer. He thus urged families to have fewer children and discouraged charitable handouts and vaccinations.

During the early 1800s, many people accepted Malthus's bleak view as the factory system changed people's lifestyles for the worse. His view was proved wrong, however. Although the population boom did continue, the food supply grew even faster. As the century progressed, living conditions for the Western world slowly improved—and then people began having fewer children. By the 1900s, population growth was no longer a problem in the West, but it did continue to afflict many nations elsewhere.

Ricardo Shares View Another influential British laissez-faire economist, David Ricardo, dedicated himself to economic studies after reading Smith's *The Wealth of Nations*. Like Malthus, Ricardo did not hold out hope for the working class to escape poverty. Because of such gloomy predictions, economics became known as the "dismal science." In his "Iron Law of Wages," Ricardo pointed out that wage increases were futile because increases would only cover the cost of necessities. This was because when wages were high, families often had more children instead of raising the family's current standard of living.

Both Malthus and Ricardo opposed any government help for the poor. In their view, the best cure for poverty was not government relief but the unrestricted "laws of the free market." They felt that individuals should be left to improve their lot through thrift, hard work, and limiting the size of their families.

✓ **Checkpoint** Explain the response to laissez-faire economics during the nineteenth century.

Population Theory
Thomas Malthus believed poor families should have fewer children to preserve the food supply. *What were the advantages of families with many children?*

Utilitarians For Limited Government

Other thinkers sought to modify laissez-faire doctrines to justify some government intervention. By 1800, British philosopher and economist **Jeremy Bentham** was advocating **utilitarianism,** or the idea that the goal of society should be "the greatest happiness for the greatest number" of its citizens. To Bentham, all laws or actions should be judged by their "utility." In other words, did they provide more pleasure or happiness than pain? Bentham strongly supported individual freedom, which he believed guaranteed happiness. Still, he saw the need for government to become involved under certain circumstances.

Bentham's ideas influenced the British philosopher and economist John Stuart Mill. Although he believed strongly in individual freedom, Mill wanted the government to step in to improve the hard lives of the working class. "The only purpose for which power can be rightfully exercised over any member of a civilized community, against his will," Mill wrote, "is to prevent harm to others." Therefore, while middle-class business and factory owners were entitled to increase their own happiness, the government should prevent them from doing so in a manner that would harm workers.

Mill further called for giving the vote to workers and women. These groups could then use their political power to win reforms. Most middle-class people rejected Mill's ideas. Only in the later 1800s were his views

INFOGRAPHIC

"The population… is crowded into one dense mass of cottages. …This is an atmosphere loaded with the exhalation of a large manufacturing city."
—J.P. Kay

Owen's Utopia

The poverty and filth of the Industrial Age did not sit well with Robert Owen, a British social reformer. Like other Utopians, he believed there was a way he could change society for the better. To prove his point, he set up his cotton mill in New Lanark, Scotland, as a model village. He insisted that the conditions in which people lived shaped their character. Owen reduced working hours, built homes for workers, started a school for children, and opened a company store where workers could buy food and clothes. He showed that an employer could offer decent living and working conditions and still run a profitable business. Between 1815 and 1825, about 20,000 people visited New Lanark to study Owen's reforms. The complex eventually fell into decline but visitors can still wander the village today.

▲ The Industrial Age brought harsh living conditions and poverty as people crowded into cities.

Thinking Critically

1. **Make Generalizations** Based on the images, how did life for children at New Lanark differ from those who lived in industrial cities?

2. **Recognize Ideologies** Do you think Utopianism was an effective solution for the challenges of the Industrial Age? Why or why not?

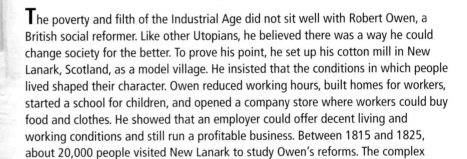

"…[I have never seen] so much order, good government, tranquility, and rational happiness prevail."
—Visitor to New Lanark

▲ Children attended geography classes and dance lessons at the school in New Lanark.

History *Interactive*
For: Interactive Village
Web Code: nbp-1941

slowly accepted. Today's democratic governments, however, have absorbed many ideas from Mill and the other utilitarians.

 Checkpoint What did John Stuart Mill see as the proper role of government?

Socialist Thought Emerges

While the champions of laissez-faire economics praised individual rights, other thinkers focused on the good of society in general. They condemned the evils of industrial capitalism, which they believed had created a gulf between rich and poor. To end poverty and injustice, they offered a radical solution—**socialism.** Under socialism, the people as a whole rather than private individuals would own and operate the **means of production**— the farms, factories, railways, and other large businesses that produced and distributed goods. Socialism grew out of the Enlightenment faith in progress, its belief in the basic goodness of human nature, and its concern for social justice.

Are Utopians Dreamers? A number of early socialists established communities in which all work was shared and all property was owned in common. When there was no difference between rich and poor, they said, fighting between people would disappear. These early socialists were called Utopians. The name implied that they were impractical dreamers. The Utopian **Robert Owen** set up a model community in New Lanark, Scotland, to put his own ideas into practice.

Owen Establishes a Utopia A poor Welsh boy, Owen became a successful mill owner. Unlike most industrialists at the time, he refused to use child labor. He campaigned vigorously for laws that limited child labor and encouraged the organization of labor unions.

 Checkpoint What did early socialists believe?

Karl Marx Explains Class Struggles

In the 1840s, **Karl Marx,** a German philosopher, condemned the ideas of the Utopians as unrealistic idealism. He <u>formulated</u> a new theory, "scientific socialism," which he claimed was based on a scientific study of history. He teamed up with another German socialist, Friedrich Engels, whose father owned a textile factory in England.

Marx and Engels wrote a pamphlet, *The Communist Manifesto*, which they published in 1848. "A spectre [ghost] is haunting Europe," it began, "the spectre of communism." **Communism** is a form of socialism advocated by Marx, in which an inevitable struggle between social classes would lead to the creation of a classless society where all means of production would be owned by the community.

In *The Communist Manifesto*, Marx theorized that economics was the driving force in history. He argued that there was "the history of class struggles" between the "haves" and the "have-nots." The "haves" had always owned the means of production and thus controlled society and all its wealth. In industrialized Europe, Marx said, the "haves" were the bourgeoisie. The "have-nots" were the **proletariat,** or working class.

According to Marx, the modern class struggle pitted the bourgeoisie against the proletariat. In the end, he predicted, the proletariat would be

Vocabulary Builder

<u>formulated</u>—(FAWR myoo layt id) *vt.* devised or developed, as in a theory or plan

triumphant. Workers would then take control of the means of production and set up a classless, communist society. Such a society would mark the end of the struggles people had endured throughout history, because wealth and power would be equally shared. Marx despised capitalism. He believed it created prosperity for only a few and poverty for many. He called for an international struggle to bring about its downfall. "Workers of all countries," he urged, "unite!"

✓ **Checkpoint** What did Marx predict was the future of the proletariat?

Marxism in the Future

At first, Marxism gained popularity with many people around the world. Leaders of a number of reform movements adopted the idea that power should be held by workers rather than by business owners. Marx's ideas, however, would never be practiced exactly as he imagined.

Marxism Briefly Flourishes In the 1860s, Germany adapted Marx's beliefs to form a social democracy, a political ideology in which there is a gradual transition from capitalism to socialism instead of a sudden violent overthrow of the system. In the late 1800s, Russian socialists embraced Marxism, and the Russian Revolution of 1917 set up a communist-inspired government. For much of the 1900s, revolutionaries around the world would adapt Marxist ideas to their own situations and needs. Independence leaders in Asia, Latin America, and Africa would turn to Marxism.

Marxism Loses Appeal As time passed, however, the failures of Marxist governments would illustrate the flaws in Marx's arguments. He predicted that workers would unite across national borders to wage class warfare. Instead, nationalism won out over working-class loyalty. In general, people felt stronger ties to their own countries than to the international communist movement. By the end of the twentieth century, few nations remained with communist governments, while nearly every economy included elements of free-market capitalism.

✓ **Checkpoint** How accurate did Marx's predictions about social classes prove to be?

Workers of the World
An 1895 leaflet urges that "Workers of the World Unite," the slogan of the socialist movement of Marx (above) and Engels.

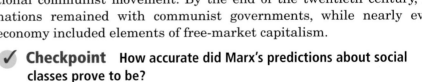

SECTION 4 Assessment

Progress Monitoring Online
For: Self-quiz with vocabulary practice
Web Code: nba-1941

Terms, People, and Places

1. For each term, person, or place listed at the beginning of the section, write a sentence explaining its significance.

Note Taking

2. **Reading Skill: Identify Main Ideas** Use your completed outline to answer the Focus Question: What new ideas about economics and society were fostered as a result of the Industrial Revolution?

Comprehension and Critical Thinking

3. **Identify Points of View** What were the views of laissez-faire economists (a) Adam Smith, (b) Thomas Malthus, and (c) David Ricardo?

4. **Compare Points of View** Contrast the approaches of utilitarians and socialists to solving economic problems.

5. **Synthesize Information** How might workplace reforms have altered Marxist predictions of world revolution?

● **Writing About History**

Quick Write: Write a Thesis Statement As in other types of essays, it is important to clearly state your thesis, or main idea, when writing an explanatory essay. Write a thesis statement followed by a short paragraph on one of the theories discussed in this section.

Economic Systems

What types of economic systems have societies used to produce and distribute goods and services?

When Adam Smith wrote *The Wealth of Nations* in 1776, traditional agriculture formed the heart of nearly all world economies. In the 1800s, industry began to dominate, especially in Europe and the United States. Industrialists wanted to control their own businesses. Using Smith's laissez-faire ideas, they pushed for free markets and an end to government interference. The resulting market economy is one of the basic economic systems in the modern world. Other systems followed. These systems can be differentiated by those who make the following key economic decisions: (1) What will be produced? (2) How will it be produced? (3) To whom will the product be distributed?

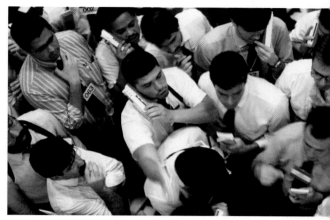

Brazilian market economy

Market Economy

In a market economy, the key economic decisions emerge from the interaction of buyers and sellers in a market. A market allows individuals to exchange, or trade, things. The market economy is also called the free market, the free enterprise system, or capitalism. One key element of this economic system is supply and demand. Producers make, or supply, only what consumers want, or demand. Another element is self-interest, where producers and consumers consider only their own personal gain when making decisions. A third element is competition. Here, producers compete for consumers' money by lowering prices or introducing new products.

Centrally Planned Economy

In a centrally planned economy, the central government, rather than individual producers and consumers in markets, makes the key economic decisions. The centrally planned economy is also called a command economy, a socialist economy, or communism. In a typical communist country, the government sets goals for production and manages nearly all aspects of production and distribution. Everything in a command economy is produced according to a rigid plan. This discourages new ideas and new products that could stimulate economic growth. The result is often poor quality goods, serious shortages, and falling production.

Mixed Economy

A mixed economy is one that has both free enterprise and socialist characteristics. Economic equality, socialists argue, is possible only if the public—in the form of the government—controls the centers of economic power. Although socialist nations may be democracies, socialism requires a high degree of central planning to achieve economic equality. In mixed economies, government plays a significant role in making the key economic decisions. In modern times, the number of mixed economies has grown. Market systems have benefited from some government intervention, and centrally planned systems have benefited from some free enterprise.

Thinking Critically

1. (a) What legitimate role might government have in what is otherwise a market economy? (b) Why might a centrally planned economy begin encouraging some free enterprise?
2. **Connections to Today** Locate a newspaper article about China's economy. Write a one-paragraph summary of the article and try to relate the content of the article to the information about economic systems described above.

A Cuban government poster seeks to inspire productivity.

Quick Study Guide

Progress Monitoring *Online*
For: Self-test with vocabulary practice
Web Code: nba-1951

■ New Inventions and Ideas

Inventors and Thinkers	Inventions and Ideas
Jethro Tull	Seed drill
Thomas Newcomen	Steam engine
James Watt	Improved steam engine
John Kay	Flying shuttle
James Hargreaves	Spinning jenny
Richard Arkwright	Water frame
Eli Whitney	Cotton gin
George Stephenson	Steam-powered locomotive
John Wesley	Methodism
Adam Smith	Laissez-faire economics
Thomas Malthus	Population growth could outpace food supply.
Jeremy Bentham	Utilitarianism
Robert Owen	Utopian communities
Karl Marx	Communism, Marxism

■ Effects of the Industrial Revolution

Industrial Revolution

↓

- Population growth
- Rural to urban migration
- Growth of cities

↓

- Poor working conditions in factories
- Low wages
- Overcrowding in cities

↓

- Laissez-faire economics
- Utilitarianism
- Socialism
- Marxism

■ Why Britain Industrialized First

Industrial Revolution in Britain
Plentiful natural resources
Ready workforce
Prosperous economy
Availability of capital and demand
Stable government

■ Responses to the Industrial Revolution

- Bentham/Mill: utilitarianism
- Socialism
- Owen: utopianism
- Marx/Engels: communism

■ Events From 1750–1850

Early Industrial Revolution Events
Global Events

1750

1775

1760s
Watt improves the steam engine.

1764
The spinning jenny is invented.

1762
Catherine the Great comes to power in Russia.

1770
Cook claims Australia for Britain.

1788
Futa Toro outlaws slave trade.

Concept | Connector

■ Cumulative Review

Record the answers to the questions below on your Concept Connector worksheets. In addition, record information from this chapter about the following concepts:

- Economic Systems: market economy
- Economic Systems: centrally planned economy
- Economic Systems: mixed economy

1. **Economic Systems** What is socialism? Compare socialism to mercantilism, another economic system. Research to learn how they are similar and different. Think about these factors:
   - who supported each system
   - main theories
   - existence today

2. **Technology** Once James Watt made improvements to Thomas Newcomen's steam engine, it became a key power source of the Industrial Revolution. Research to learn why steam power made such an impact and then compare it to the impact of the printing press. Think about the following:
   - who benefited from the use of the invention
   - what preceded the invention
   - why the invention was so important

3. **Trade** The development of the railway network in the 1800s led to increased trade as people and goods were able to travel faster and farther. Research the Silk Road, the ancient trade route that started in China and stretched to Asia Minor and India. How was railroad travel of the Industrial Revolution both similar to and different from travel on the Silk Road? Think about the following:
   - speed of transport
   - multiple uses
   - advantages and disadvantages

■ Connections To Today

1. **Migration: Twentieth Century Global Migrations** During the Industrial Revolution, rural workers migrated to urban areas to live and work. Today, people still migrate in various parts of the world. Do online and library research to find information on rural-to-urban migration in a country located in Asia or Africa. Write a brief newspaper article in which you compare the experiences of those who migrated then and now.

Strawberry pickers at work, South Africa

2. **People and the Environment: Population Growth** The population growth that occurred during the Industrial Revolution often created filth and unsanitary conditions as people crowded into tenements. The growth also caused an increase in the demand for products, which led to the opening of more factories. Do online and library research to find the history of population growth in the town or state in which you live. What are the patterns and results?

| 1800 Owen begins social reforms at New Lanark. | 1807 Fulton develops the first successful steamboat, the *Clermont*. | 1830 The Liverpool-Manchester Railroad opens. | 1848 Marx and Engels publish *The Communist Manifesto*. | **History Interactive** For: Interactive timeline Web Code: nbp-1901 |

1800   1825   1850

| 1804 Napoleon becomes the emperor of France. | 1814 Congress of Vienna meets to restore stability in Europe. | 1819 Bolívar captures Bogotá. | 1848 Revolutions sweep Europe. |

Chapter Assessment

Terms, People, and Places

Complete each sentence by choosing the correct answer from the list of terms below. You will not use all of the terms.

smelt	James Watt
urbanization	Manchester
Thomas Malthus	tenement
proletariat	socialism
enterprise	utilitarianism

1. _____ predicted that population would outpace the food supply.
2. A member of the _____ most likely lived in a small, crowded building called a _____.
3. Investors in Britain were ready to risk their capital to invest in _____.
4. Those who advocated _____ believed that the goal of society was to bring about the greatest happiness for the greatest number.
5. To _____ involves separating iron from its ore.
6. _____ improved the efficiency and design of Newcomen's steam engine.

Main Ideas

Section 1 (pp. 246–249)
7. How did the enclosure movement affect farmers?
8. Identify three causes of the population explosion that occurred in the 1700s.

Section 2 (pp. 250–253)
9. Describe four factors that helped bring about the Industrial Revolution in England.

10. How did the Industrial Revolution transform the textile industry?

Section 3 (pp. 254–258)
11. (a) What were the main characteristics of factory work? (b) What challenges did factory work create for women?

Section 4 (pp. 260–264)
12. List the government reforms sought by John Stuart Mill.
13. (a) Describe Karl Marx's view of history. (b) How have events challenged that view?

Chapter Focus Question
14. What technological, social, economic, and cultural changes occurred as the Industrial Revolution took hold?

Critical Thinking

15. **Synthesize Information** What were the impacts of each of the following technologies: (a) steam power, (b) improved methods for smelting iron, (c) railroad?
16. **Geography and History** Explain the link between Britain's natural resources and its rise as an industrial nation.
17. **Analyze Information** Describe how the Industrial Revolution affected each of the following: (a) size of population, (b) cities, (c) working and living conditions, (d) women and children.
18. **Predict Consequences** If more people had supported utilitarianism, how do you think it would have influenced society?
19. **Recognize Ideologies** Explain the major differences between Adam Smith's free market ideas and Karl Marx's socialist ideas.

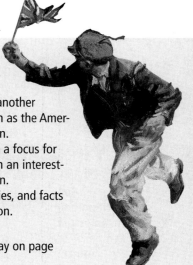

● Writing About History

Expository: Explanatory Essay During the late 1700s, the Industrial Revolution began to transform Britain. An agricultural revolution triggered a chain of events, and Britain sped ahead of the rest of the world to become the first industrial nation. But why is the Industrial Revolution considered to be a "revolution"? Write an explanatory essay to answer this question.

Prewriting
• Ask yourself what you need to know in order to write an effective explanation. Think about what you already know about revolutions.
• Do research to gather facts, descriptions, examples, and other details to clearly illustrate your point.

Drafting
• Create a Venn diagram to compare aspects of the Industrial Revolution to another revolution you have learned about, such as the American Revolution or the French Revolution.
• Write a thesis statement once you have a focus for your essay. Begin your introduction with an interesting lead-in to get your reader's attention.
• Be sure to include comparisons, analogies, and facts in your essay to support your explanation.

Revising
• Use the guidelines for revising your essay on page SH12 of the Writing Handbook.

Document-Based Assessment

New Economic and Social Theories

Various thinkers of the day attempted to understand and interpret the dramatic changes brought about by the Industrial Revolution. They responded with a wide range of explanations and solutions, as the documents below illustrate.

Document A

"As every individual, therefore, endeavours as much as he can both to employ his capital in the support of domestic industry, and so to direct that industry that its produce may be of the greatest value; every individual necessarily labours to render the annual revenue of the society as great as he can. . . . By preferring the support of domestic to that of foreign industry, he intends only his own security; and by directing that industry in such a manner as its produce may be of the greatest value, he intends only his own gain, and he is in this, as in many other cases, led by an invisible hand to promote an end which was no part of his intention. . . . every individual it is evident, can, in his local situation, judge much better than any statesman or law-giver can do for him."

—From **The Wealth of Nations** by Adam Smith, 1776

Document B

"In those characters which now exhibit crime, the fault is obviously not in the individual, but the defects proceed from the system in which the individual was trained. Withdraw those circumstances which tend to create crime in the human character, and crime will not be created. Replace them with such as are calculated to form habits of order, regularity, temperance, industry; and these qualities will be formed. . . . Proceed systematically on principles of undeviating persevering kindness, yet retaining and using, with the least possible severity, the means of restraining crime from immediately injuring society, and by degrees even the crimes now existing in adults will also gradually disappear. . . ."

—From **A New View of Society** by Robert Owen, 1816

Document C
New Lanark Mills, Scotland

Document D

". . . the power of population is indefinitely greater than the power in the earth to produce subsistence for man. Population, when unchecked, increased in a geometrical ratio. Subsistence increases only in an arithmetical ratio. A slight acquaintance with numbers will show the immensity of the first power in comparison of the second. . . . No fancied equality, no agrarian regulations in their utmost extent, could remove the pressure of it even for a single century. And it appears, therefore, to be decisive against the possible existence of a society, all the members of which should live in ease, happiness, and comparative leisure; and feel no anxiety about providing the means of subsistence for themselves and families. Consequently, if the premises are just, the argument is conclusive against the perfectibility of the mass of mankind."

—From **An Essay on the Principle of Population 1798**
by Thomas Malthus

Analyzing Documents

Use your knowledge of the new economic and social theories and Documents A, B, C, and D to answer the questions below.

1. According to Adam Smith in Document A, individuals promote the good of society because of
   A high ideals.
   B self-interest.
   C government pressure.
   D religion.

2. How did Robert Owen explain the fact that some people become criminals?
   A the invisible hand of fate
   B struggles between the ruling class and the oppressed
   C the influence of problems in society
   D the power of population over production

3. Thomas Malthus argued that a society where all individuals enjoy happiness, comfort, and pleasure is
   A only possible with increased agricultural output.
   B impossible because of the base nature of human greed.
   C impossible because of the pressures of population.
   D possible when people are treated decently and fairly.

4. **Writing Task** Suppose you were working in Britain in the year 1840. Which of the above economic philosophies would you support? Remember to identify your occupation and social class. Use your knowledge of the Industrial Revolution and the documents above to support your opinion.

Revolutions in Europe and Latin America

1790–1848

Freedom From Tyranny

Several revolutions erupted in Europe between 1815 and 1829, and the spread of revolutionary ideals would ignite new uprisings in 1830 and 1848. Also occurring during this time were the wars of independence in Latin America. These revolts began in the late 1700s and early 1800s and were inspired by the success of the American Revolution and the ideals of the French Revolution. Simón Bolívar was one of the great heroes in the fight for independence in Spanish South America. He helped win independence for Bolivia, Colombia, Ecuador, Peru, and Venezuela. Listen to the Witness History audio to learn more about revolutions in Europe and Latin America.

Simón Bolívar's crown

66A state too extensive in itself, or by virtue of its dependencies, ultimately falls into decay; its free government is transformed into a tyranny; it disregards the principles which it should preserve, and finally degenerates into despotism. The distinguishing characteristic of small republics is stability. . . .99
—Simón Bolívar

◀ Bolívar fights Spanish troops in his endeavor to free South America.

French tricolor flag

Chapter Preview

Chapter Focus Question How did revolutionary ideals in Europe and Latin America ignite uprisings in the first half of the nineteenth century?

Section 1
An Age of Ideologies

Section 2
Revolutions of 1830 and 1848

Section 3
Revolts in Latin America

José de San Martín

Note Taking Study Guide *Online*
For: Note Taking and Concept Connector worksheets
Web Code: nbd-2001

SECTION 1

Hungarian revolutionary
Lajos Kossuth

WITNESS HISTORY ◀)) AUDIO

A "Revolutionary Seed"

Prince Clemens von Metternich warned that a seed had been planted in Europe that threatened Europe's monarchs and undermined its basic social values. This seed was nourished with the ideas spread by the French Revolution and Napoleon Bonaparte.

66 Passions are let loose . . . to overthrow everything that society respects as the basis of its existence: religion, public morality, laws, customs, rights, and duties, all are attacked, confounded [defeated], overthrown, or called in question. 99

Focus Question What events proved that Metternich was correct in his fears?

An Age of Ideologies

Objectives

- Understand the goals of the conservatives.
- Explain how liberals and nationalists challenged the old order.
- Summarize the early challenges to the old order in Europe.

Terms, People, and Places

ideology
universal manhood suffrage
autonomy

Note Taking

Reading Skill: Identify Main Ideas As you read the section, fill in a table like the one below with main ideas about conservatism, liberalism, and nationalism.

Conservatism	Liberalism	Nationalism
•	•	•
•	•	•

At the Congress of Vienna, the powers of Europe tried to uproot the "revolutionary seed" and suppress nationalist fervor. Others, however, challenged the order imposed in 1815. The clash of people with opposing **ideologies,** or systems of thought and belief, plunged Europe into more than 30 years of turmoil.

Conservatives Prefer the Old Order

The Congress of Vienna was a victory for the conservative forces, which included monarchs and their officials, noble landowners, and church leaders. Conservatives agreed to work together—in an agreement called the Concert of Europe—to support the political and social order that had existed before Napoleon and the French Revolution. Conservative ideas also appealed to peasants, who wanted to preserve traditional ways.

Conservatives of the early 1800s wanted to return to the way things had been before 1789. After all, they had benefited under the old order. They wanted to restore royal families to the thrones they had lost when Napoleon swept across Europe. They supported a social hierarchy in which lower classes respected and obeyed their social superiors. Conservatives also backed an established church—Catholic in Austria and southern Europe, Protestant in northern Europe, and Eastern Orthodox in eastern Europe.

Conservatives believed that talk about natural rights and constitutional government could lead only to chaos, as in France in 1789. If change had to come, they argued, it must come slowly. Conservatives felt that they benefited all people by defending peace and stability. Conservative leaders like Metternich sought to suppress revolutionary ideas. Metternich urged monarchs to oppose freedom of the press, crush protests in their own countries, and send troops to douse the flames of rebellion in neighboring lands.

✓ **Checkpoint** What was the goal of the conservatives in the Concert of Europe?

Liberals and Nationalists Seek Change

Inspired by the Enlightenment and the French Revolution, liberals and nationalists challenged the conservatives at every turn. Liberalism and nationalism ignited a number of revolts against established rule.

Liberals Promise Freedom Because liberals spoke mostly for the bourgeoisie, or middle class, their ideas are sometimes called "bourgeois liberalism." Liberals included business owners, bankers, and lawyers, as well as politicians, newspaper editors, writers, and others who helped to shape public opinion.

Liberals wanted governments to be based on written constitutions and separation of powers. Liberals spoke out against divine-right monarchy, the old aristocracy, and established churches. They defended the natural rights of individuals to liberty, equality, and property. They called for rulers elected by the people and responsible to them. Thus, most liberals favored a republican form of government over a monarchy, or at least wanted the monarch to be limited by a constitution.

The liberals of the early 1800s saw the role of government as limited to protecting basic rights such as freedom of thought, speech, and religion. They believed that only male property owners or others with a financial stake in society should have the right to vote. Only later in the century did liberals support the principle of **universal manhood suffrage,** giving all adult men the right to vote.

Liberals also strongly supported the laissez-faire economics of Adam Smith and David Ricardo. They saw the free market as an opportunity for capitalist entrepreneurs to succeed. As capitalists (and often employers), liberals had different goals from those of workers laboring in factories, mines, and other enterprises of the early Industrial Revolution.

Nationalists Strive for Unity For centuries, European rulers had gained or lost lands through wars, marriages, and treaties. They exchanged territories and the people in them like pieces in a game. As a result, by 1815 Europe had several empires that included many nationalities. The Austrian, Russian, and Ottoman empires, for example, each included diverse peoples.

Analyzing Political Cartoons

Conflicting Ideologies This cartoon shows Prince Metternich standing resolute against the angry crowd behind him who are pushing for reform. Metternich represented the conservative order and opposed revolutionary ideals such as freedom and progress.
1. How does the cartoonist portray those in the crowd? What does the crowd support?
2. What did Metternich do to suppress revolutionary ideas?

273

In the 1800s, national groups who shared a common heritage set out to win their own states. Within the diverse Austrian empire, for example, various nationalist leaders tried to unite and win independence for each particular group. Nationalism gave people with a common heritage a sense of identity and the goal of creating their own homeland. At the same time, however, nationalism often bred intolerance and led to persecution of other ethnic or national groups.

✓ **Checkpoint** How did the liberalism of the early 1800s reflect Enlightenment ideals?

Central Europe Challenges the Old Order

Spurred by the ideas of liberalism and nationalism, revolutionaries fought against the old order. During the early 1800s, rebellions erupted in the Balkan Peninsula and elsewhere along the southern fringe of Europe. The Balkans, in southeastern Europe, were inhabited by people of various religions and ethnic groups. These peoples had lived under Ottoman rule for more than 300 years.

Serbia Seeks Independence The first Balkan people to revolt were the Serbs. From 1804 to 1813, the Serb leader Karageorge (ka rah JAWR juh) led a guerrilla war against the Ottomans. The intense struggle was unsuccessful, but it fostered a sense of Serbian identity. A revival of Serbian literature and culture added to the sense of nationhood.

In 1815, Milos Obrenovic (oh BRAY noh vich) led the Serbs in a second, more successful rebellion. One reason for the success was that Obrenovic turned to Russia for assistance. Like the Serbs, the Russian people were Slavic in language and Christian Orthodox in religion. By 1830, Russian support helped the Serbs win **autonomy,** or self-rule, within the

Serbs in Battle
Serb leader Karageorge (below left) leads the Serbs against the Ottomans at the Battle of Misar during the first Serbian rebellion. *(a) Why would this battle and others like it help lead to a sense of Serbian national identity? (b) Why was this sense of nationalism important for the Serbs?*

Ottoman empire. The Ottoman sultan later agreed to formal independence. In the future, Russia would continue to defend Serbian interests and affect events in the Balkans.

Greece Revolts to End Ottoman Rule

In 1821, the Greeks revolted, seeking to end centuries of Ottoman rule. At first, the Greeks were badly divided. But years of suffering in long, bloody wars of independence helped shape a national identity. Leaders of the rebellion justified their struggle as "a national war, a holy war, a war the object of which is to reconquer the rights of individual liberty." The Greeks had the support of romantic writers such as English poet Lord Byron, who went to Greece to aid the fight for independence.

Admirers of Greece in Europe backed the Greek rebels. In the late 1820s, Britain, France, and Russia forced the Ottomans to grant independence to some Greek provinces. By 1830, Greece was independent. The European powers, however, pressured the Greeks to accept a German king, a move meant to show that they did not support the nationalism that brought about the revolution.

More Challenges Erupt

Several other challenges to the Vienna peace settlement erupted in the 1820s. Revolts occurred along the southern fringe of Europe. In Spain, Portugal, and various states in the Italian peninsula, rebels struggled to gain constitutional governments.

Metternich urged conservative rulers to act decisively and crush the dangerous uprisings. In response, a French army marched over the Pyrenees to suppress a revolt in Spain. Austrian forces crossed the Alps to smash rebellious outbreaks in Italy.

Troops dampened the fires of liberalism and nationalism, but could not smother them. In the next decades, sparks would flare anew. Added to liberal and nationalist demands were the goals of the new industrial working class. By the mid-1800s, social reformers and agitators were urging workers to support socialism or other ways of reorganizing property ownership.

 Checkpoint Why would a monarch order his army to suppress an uprising in another country?

Note Taking

Reading Skill: Identify Supporting Details As you read, fill in a table like the one below with supporting details about revolts in Serbia, Greece, and other countries during the early 1800s.

Serbia	Greece	Other Revolts
•	•	•
•	•	•

Vocabulary Builder

agitator—(AJ ih tayt ur) *n.* someone who attempts to arouse feeling for or against something, especially a political cause

SECTION 1 Assessment

Progress Monitoring *Online*
For: Self-quiz with vocabulary practice
Web Code: nba-2011

Terms, People, and Places

1. For each term, person, or place listed at the beginning of the section, write a sentence explaining its significance.

Note Taking

2. **Reading Skill: Identify Main Ideas** Use your completed charts to answer the Focus Question: What events proved that Metternich was correct in his fears?

Comprehension and Critical Thinking

3. **Identify Point of View** What were the goals of conservative leaders?
4. **Compare Points of View** (a) How did the political goals of liberals differ from those of conservatives? (b) How did nationalists threaten the borders set up by European monarchs?
5. **Recognize Cause and Effect** (a) Why did the Serbs and Greeks revolt? (b) Why were there uprisings in Spain, Portugal, and the Italian states?

● Writing About History

Quick Write: Choose a Topic To write an effective persuasive essay, you should begin with a clearly stated opinion or argument on an issue that has more than one side. Look back over Section 1, jotting down issues that have two or more sides. Then choose an issue and write a well-constructed sentence that states your opinion or argument against it.

Alexis de Tocqueville

French tricolor flag

WITNESS HISTORY 🔊 AUDIO

More Revolution in the Wind

Alexis de Tocqueville was a liberal French leader who closely observed the widespread support for revolutionary ideas. He knew that the revolutions of the 1820s were not over.

❝ We are sleeping on a volcano . . . Do you not see that the Earth trembles anew? A wind of revolution blows, the storm is on the horizon. ❞
—Alexis de Tocqueville

Focus Question What were the causes and effects of the revolutions in Europe in 1830 and 1848?

Revolutions of 1830 and 1848

Objectives
- Describe how French rebels won some reforms in 1830.
- Analyze how the spirit of reform spread in 1830.
- Explain the revolutions that surged through France and throughout the rest of Europe in 1848.

Terms, People, and Places

radicals
Louis Philippe
recession
Napoleon III
Louis Kossuth

Note Taking

Reading Skill: Identify Main Ideas As you read the section, fill in a table like the one below with a country, date, and a main idea about the revolutions of 1830 and 1848. Add rows as needed.

Revolutions of 1830 and 1848		
France	1830	Radicals force king to abdicate.

The quick suppression of liberal and nationalist uprisings in the 1820s did not end Europe's age of revolutions. In 1830 and 1848, Europeans saw street protests explode into full-scale revolts. As in 1789, the upheavals began in Paris and radiated out across the continent.

French Rebels Win in 1830

When the Congress of Vienna restored Louis XVIII to the French throne, he wisely issued a constitution, the Charter of French Liberties. It created a two-house legislature and allowed limited freedom of the press. Still, the king retained much power.

Citizens Lead the July Revolution When Louis XVIII died in 1824, his younger brother, Charles X, inherited the throne. Charles, a strong believer in absolutism, rejected the very idea of the charter. In July 1830, he suspended the legislature, limited the right to vote, and restricted the press.

Liberals and **radicals**—those who favor extreme change—responded forcefully to the king's challenge. In Paris, angry citizens threw up barricades across the narrow streets. From behind them, they fired on the soldiers and pelted them with stones and roof tiles. Within days, rebels controlled Paris. The revolutionary tricolor flew from the towers of Notre Dame cathedral. A frightened Charles X abdicated and fled to England.

The "Citizen King" Rules France With the king gone, radicals wanted to set up a republic. Moderate liberals, however, insisted on a constitutional monarchy and chose **Louis Philippe** as king. Louis Philippe was a cousin of Charles X and in his youth had supported the revolution of 1789.

The French called Louis Philippe the "citizen king" because he owed his throne to the people. Louis got along well with the liberal bourgeoisie. He dressed like them in a frock coat and top hat. Sometimes he strolled the streets, shaking hands with well-wishers. Liberal politicians filled his government.

Under Louis Philippe, the upper bourgeoisie prospered. Louis extended suffrage, but only to France's wealthier citizens. The vast majority of the people still could not vote. The king's other policies also favored the middle class at the expense of the workers.

 Checkpoint What actions did Charles X take in 1830, and how did French rebels respond?

The Spirit of Reform Spreads

The revolts in Paris inspired the outbreak of uprisings elsewhere in Europe. As Metternich said, "When France sneezes, Europe catches cold." Most of the uprisings were suppressed by military force. But some rebels did win changes. Even when they failed, revolutions frightened rulers badly enough to encourage reform.

Belgium Wins Independence The one notable success in 1830 took place in Belgium. In 1815, the Congress of Vienna had united the Austrian Netherlands (present-day Belgium) and the Kingdom of Holland under the Dutch king. The Congress had wanted to create a strong barrier to help prevent French expansion in the future.

The Belgians resented the new arrangement. They and the Dutch had different languages. The Belgians were Catholic, while the Dutch were Protestant. The Belgian economy was based on manufacturing; the Dutch, on trade.

In 1830, news of the Paris uprising ignited a revolutionary spark in Belgium. Students and workers threw up barricades in Brussels, the

To the Barricades!

In 1830 and again in 1848, French rebels erected barricades in the streets using mattresses, wagons, furniture, and whatever else they could find that might offer protection during the fighting with government soldiers. *How does Hugo describe the barricades in his famous novel* Les Misérables?

Primary Source

❝You saw there, in a chaos full of despair, rafters from roofs, patches from garrets with their wall paper, window sashes with all their glass planted in the rubbish, awaiting artillery, chimneys torn down, wardrobes, tables, benches, a howling topsy-turvy, . . . which contain at once fury and nothingness.❞
—Victor Hugo

WITNESS HISTORY VIDEO

Watch *Revolutionary France:* Les Misérables on the **Witness History Discovery School**™ video program to learn more about the 1830 revolution in France.

capital. Britain and France believed that they would benefit from the separation of Belgium and Holland and supported Belgian demands for independence. As a result, in 1831, Belgium became an independent state with a liberal constitution.

Rebels Fail in Poland Nationalists in Poland also staged an uprising in 1830. But, unlike the Belgians, the Poles failed to win independence for their country.

In the late 1700s, Russia, Austria, and Prussia had divided up Poland. Poles had hoped that the Congress of Vienna would restore their homeland in 1815. Instead, the great powers handed most of Poland to Russia.

In 1830, Polish students, army officers, and landowners rose in revolt. The rebels failed to gain widespread support, however, and were brutally crushed by Russian forces. Some survivors fled to Western Europe and the United States, where they kept alive the dream of freedom.

✓ **Checkpoint**   How did the Belgian and Polish revolutions in 1830 end differently?

The French Revolt Again in 1848

In the 1840s, discontent began to grow in France once again. Radicals formed secret societies to work for a French republic. Utopian socialists called for an end to private ownership of property. Even liberals <u>denounced</u> Louis Philippe's government for corruption and called for expanded suffrage.

Near the end of the decade, discontent was heightened by a **recession,** or period of reduced economic activity. Factories shut down and people lost their jobs. Poor harvests caused bread prices to rise. Newspapers blamed government officials for some of the problems. With conditions much like those in 1789, Paris was again ripe for revolution.

Vocabulary Builder

<u>denounce</u>—(dee NOWNS) *vt.* to express harsh criticism of something or somebody, usually in public

1848: The Year of Hope and Despair

Revolution in Europe spread like wildfire in the days and months of 1848. Although an outbreak in January occurred in Italy, France's successful February Revolution was the spark for other revolts throughout Europe. As shown on the map here, revolutions were not confined to one city or country. They engulfed the continent of Europe and numbered almost fifty in the first four months of the year alone. Despite the failures of the revolutions, Europe was transformed as governments and the rising middle class began to cooperate with one another.

Gained independence, 1830–1831
Repression of revolutions in 1848
Revolutions of 1848

Turmoil Spreads During "February Days"

In February 1848, when the government took steps to silence critics and prevent public meetings, angry crowds took to the streets. During the "February Days," overturned carts, paving stones, and toppled trees again blocked the streets of Paris. Church bells rang alarms, while women and men on the barricades sang the revolutionary anthem "La Marseillaise." A number of demonstrators clashed with royal troops and were killed.

As the turmoil spread, Louis Philippe abdicated. A group of liberal, radical, and socialist leaders proclaimed the Second Republic. (The First Republic had lasted from 1792 until 1804, when Napoleon became emperor.)

From the start, deep differences divided the new government. Middle-class liberals wanted moderate political reforms. Socialists wanted far-reaching social and economic change and forced the government to set up national workshops to provide jobs for the unemployed.

The Working Class Loses Out During "June Days"

By June, however, upper- and middle-class interests had won control of the government. They saw the national workshops as a waste of money and shut them down.

Furious, workers again took to the streets of Paris. This time, however, bourgeois liberals turned violently against the protesters. Peasants, who feared that socialists might take their land, also attacked the rioting workers. At least 1,500 people were killed before the government crushed the rebellion.

The fighting of the "June Days" left a bitter legacy. The middle class both feared and distrusted the socialists, while the working class harbored a deep hatred for the bourgeoisie.

A New Napoleon Comes to Power

By the end of 1848, the National Assembly, now dominated by members who wanted to restore order,

FEBRUARY

Opposition grew as Louis Philippe refused to listen to the middle class, workers, or peasants. In February, crowds revolted in the streets. As the turmoil of the "February Days" spread, Louis Philippe abdicated and a group of liberal, radical, and socialist leaders proclaimed the Second Republic.

MARCH

News of France's successful February revolution spread throughout the German states. In March, demonstrations broke out in the streets of Berlin, and the king agreed to an all-German constitution. When troops randomly fired two shots into the crowd, the demonstrations turned into eight hours of bitter violence.

JUNE

"June Days" in France again saw Paris streets crowded with angry protestors when the workshops for the unemployed were closed. Before this worker revolt ended, about 1,500 died in the first two days, while as many as 3,000 more were executed for their participation in the uprising.

Thinking Critically

1. **Make Comparisons** How were the "February Days" and the "June Days" similar and different?
2. **Recognize Ideologies** What ideals survived despite how quickly most rebellions throughout Europe were crushed?

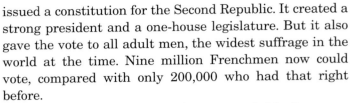

Cause and Effect

Long-Term Causes
- Spread of Enlightenment ideas
- Growth of nationalism and liberalism
- Poverty caused by the Industrial Revolution

Immediate Causes
- Uprisings in Paris
- Economic recession
- Poor harvests
- Corrupt governments

The Revolutions of 1848

Immediate Effects
- A new republic in France
- Fall of Metternich
- Promises of reform in Austria, Italy, and Prussia

Long-Term Effects
- A new empire in France
- Successes for liberalism, nationalism, and socialism
- Germany and Italy united
- Labor unions
- Increased voting rights for men

Connections to Today

- Ongoing efforts to ensure basic rights for all citizens
- Ongoing efforts to ensure limited government and popular sovereignty worldwide

Analyze Cause and Effect The revolutions of 1848 were the result of new ways of thinking and hard times for workers. *Could one of these factors by itself have caused such widespread rebellion? Why or Why not?*

Italian revolutionary flag

issued a constitution for the Second Republic. It created a strong president and a one-house legislature. But it also gave the vote to all adult men, the widest suffrage in the world at the time. Nine million Frenchmen now could vote, compared with only 200,000 who had that right before.

When elections for president were held, the overwhelming winner was Louis Napoleon, nephew of Napoleon Bonaparte. The "new" Napoleon attracted the working classes by presenting himself as a man who cared about social issues such as poverty. At the same time, his famous name, linked with order and past French glory, helped him with conservatives.

Once in office, Louis Napoleon used his position as a stepping-stone to greater power. By 1852, he had proclaimed himself emperor, taking the title **Napoleon III.** Thus ended the short-lived Second Republic.

Like his celebrated uncle, Napoleon III used a plebiscite to win public approval for his seizure of power. A stunning 90 percent of voters supported his move to set up the Second Empire. Many thought that a monarchy was more stable than a republic or hoped that Napoleon III would restore the glory days of Napoleon Bonaparte.

Napoleon III, like Louis Philippe, ruled at a time of rapid economic growth. For the bourgeoisie, the early days of the Second Empire brought prosperity and contentment. In time, however, Napoleon III would embark on foreign adventures that would bring down his empire and end French leadership in Europe.

 Checkpoint How did the French revolutions of 1830 and 1848 differ?

Revolution Surges Through Europe

In 1848, revolts in Paris again unleashed a tidal wave of revolution across Europe. For opponents of the old order, it was a time of such hope that they called it the "springtime of the peoples." Although events in France touched off the revolts, grievances had been piling up for years. Middle-class liberals wanted a greater share of political power for themselves, as well as protections for the basic rights of all male citizens. Workers demanded relief from the miseries of the Industrial Revolution. And nationalists of all classes ached to throw off foreign rule.

Change in the Austrian Empire In the Austrian empire, revolts broke out in the major cities. Even though Metternich censored the press, books were smuggled to universities throughout the empire. Students demanded change. When workers joined the students on the streets of Vienna, Metternich resigned and fled in disguise.

Revolution continued to spread. In Budapest, Hungarian nationalists led by journalist **Louis Kossuth** demanded an independent government, an end to serfdom, and a written constitution to protect basic rights. In Prague, the Czechs made similar demands. Overwhelmed by events, the Austrian government agreed to the reforms. The gains were temporary, however.

Austrian troops soon regained control of Vienna and Prague and smashed the rebels in Budapest.

Revolts in Italy Uprisings also erupted in the Italian states. Nationalists wanted to end Hapsburg domination and set up a constitutional government. From Venice in the north to Naples in the south, Italians set up independent republics. Revolutionaries even expelled the pope from Rome and installed a nationalist government. Before long, the forces of reaction surged back here, too. Austrian troops ousted the new governments in northern Italy. A French army restored the pope to power in Rome. In Naples, local rulers canceled the reforms they had reluctantly accepted.

Rebellion in the German States In the German states, university students demanded national unity and liberal reforms. Economic hard times and a potato famine brought peasants and workers into the struggle. In Prussia, liberals forced King Frederick William IV to agree to a constitution written by an elected assembly. Within a year, though, he dissolved the assembly.

Throughout 1848, delegates from German states met in the Frankfurt Assembly. Divisions soon <u>emerged</u> over whether Germany should be a republic or a monarchy and whether to include Austria in a united German state. Finally, the assembly offered Prussia's Frederick William IV the crown of a united Germany. To their dismay, the conservative king rejected the offer because it came not from the German princes but from the people—"from the gutter," as he described it.

By 1850, rebellion faded, ending the age of liberal revolution that had begun in 1789. Why did the uprisings fail? The rulers' use of military force was just one reason. Another was that revolutionaries did not have mass support, and in many instances, constitutions that represented their principles were withdrawn or replaced. In the decades ahead, liberalism, nationalism, and socialism would win successes not through revolution, but through political activity.

Analyzing Political Cartoons

A Year of Revolution This English cartoonist comments on the revolutions of 1848 and the reaction of European rulers. Based on the cartoon,
1. What ideal led to the revolutions of 1848?
2. How did the revolutions affect Europe's monarchs?

Vocabulary Builder

emerge—(ee MURJ) *v.* to arise, appear, or come out of

✓ **Checkpoint** What was the outcome of most of the revolutions outside France in 1848?

SECTION 2 Assessment

Progress Monitoring *Online*
For: Self-quiz with vocabulary practice
Web Code: nba-2021

Terms, People, and Places
1. For each term, person, or place listed at the beginning of the section, write a sentence explaining its significance.

Note Taking
2. **Reading Skill: Identify Causes and Effects** Use your completed chart to answer the Focus Question: What were the causes and effects of revolutions in Europe in 1830 and 1848?

Comprehension and Critical Thinking
3. **Draw Conclusions** What were the conditions under which the people of France lived that led to revolution rather than peace?
4. **Analyze Information** (a) Where did revolution spread in 1830? (b) Were these revolutions successful? Explain.
5. **Make Generalizations** Why did most of the revolutions of 1848 fail to achieve their goals?

● **Writing About History**
Quick Write: Gather and Organize Evidence In order to write a well-organized persuasive essay, you need to gather evidence to support your position. Gather evidence from the section to support an essay on whether workers were justified in taking to the streets in 1830 and 1848. Then create a chart that lists both sides of the issue.

Revolution

Fighting at the Hôtel de Ville, July 28, 1830

Why have political revolutions occurred?

The wave of revolution that swept Europe in the early 1800s mainly involved a clash between liberal and conservative political ideas. Conservatives wanted to ensure stability and preserve their own power and wealth by restoring traditional social and political structures. Liberals wanted more power for the people in the form of written constitutions and republican governments. Liberal ideas also crossed the Atlantic to Latin America, where they fueled revolutionary movements for independence. Consider these other examples of political revolutions.

Glorious Revolution

For centuries, England's kings struggled with Parliament for power. The Revolution of 1688 resolved this long-standing dispute in favor of Parliament. King James II wanted to restore Roman Catholicism, but Parliament supported the Church of England. When the queen gave birth to a boy, members of Parliament feared that it was the start of a Catholic monarchy. They invited James's daughter Mary and her husband, William III of Orange, to rule England, and James II fled the country. Parliament emerged with increased powers. The revolution was called "glorious" because it was bloodless.

Meiji Restoration

Military dictators known as shoguns governed Japan for some 600 years, well into the 1800s. Emperors ruled in name only during this time. By the mid-1800s, industrialization and the growth of trade had created new groups of wealthy Japanese who challenged the traditional class structure. In addition, Western powers threatened Japan's self-imposed isolation from outside "barbarians." In 1858, the shogun—against the emperor's wishes—gave in to American demands and signed a treaty giving the United States trading rights. The resulting anti-foreign uprising swept the shogun from power in 1868 and restored direct rule to the emperor, in what is called the Meiji Restoration.

Islamic Revolution

In 1953, the United States helped restore the shah of Iran, Muhammad Reza Pahlavi, to the ruling position that he had lost during World War II. In the next 25 years, as an American ally in the Cold War, the shah increased his power. Favoring Western culture, he modernized Iran and tried to undercut the power of the Muslim clergy, who held fast to traditional religious ways. Meanwhile, the shah's secret police tortured and executed many of his critics. Widespread discontent led to huge anti-shah and anti-Western demonstrations, eventually causing the shah to flee. An exiled Muslim religious leader, the Ayatollah Ruhollah Khomeini, returned to Iran. In 1979, he and his supporters proclaimed Iran an Islamic republic.

William and Mary

Thinking Critically

1. Identify the revolution, or huge political change, that took place in each of the examples presented above. What factors led to the revolution in each case?
2. **Connection to Today** Research online to find a news article on a recent revolution. Summarize the article in one or two paragraphs.

Crown awarded to Bolívar

Simón Bolívar

WITNESS HISTORY 🔊 AUDIO

A Revolutionary Is Born

Like many wealthy Latin Americans, young Simón Bolívar was sent to Europe to complete his education. In Europe he became a strong admirer of the ideals of the Enlightenment and the French Revolution. One day while speaking with his Italian tutor about freedom and individual rights, he fell on his knees and swore an oath:

❝ I swear before God and by my honor never to allow my hands to be idle nor my soul to rest until I have broken the chains that bind us to Spain. **❞**

Focus Question Who were the key revolutionaries that led the movements for independence in Latin America, and what were their accomplishments?

Revolts in Latin America

Objectives
- Explain the causes of discontent in Latin America.
- Describe Haiti's fight for freedom.
- Summarize the revolts in Mexico and Central America.
- Understand how revolutions ignited South America.

Terms, People, and Places

peninsulare	Toussaint L'Ouverture
creole	Father Miguel Hidalgo
mestizo	Father José Morelos
mulatto	José de San Martín
Simón Bolívar	Dom Pedro

Note Taking

Reading Skill: Identify Main Ideas As you read the section, fill in a table like the one below with a country, a date, and a main idea about revolts in Latin America. Add rows as needed.

Revolts in Latin America		
Haiti	1791	Toussaint L'Ouverture

Liberal ideas were spreading to Latin America with explosive results. From Mexico to the tip of South America, revolutionary movements arose to overthrow the reigning European powers. By 1825, most of Latin America was freed from colonial rule.

Discontent Fans the Fires

By the late 1700s, the revolutionary fever that gripped Western Europe had spread to Latin America. There, discontent was rooted in the social, racial, and political system that had emerged during 300 years of Spanish rule.

Social and Ethnic Structures Cause Resentment Spanish-born *peninsulares,* members of the highest social class, dominated Latin American political and social life. Only they could hold top jobs in government and the Church. Many **creoles**—the European-descended Latin Americans who owned the haciendas, ranches, and mines—bitterly resented their second-class status. Merchants fretted under mercantilist policies that tied the colonies to Spain.

Meanwhile, a growing population of **mestizos,** people of Native American and European descent, and **mulattoes,** people of African and European descent, were angry at being denied the status, wealth, and power that were available to whites. Native Americans suffered economic misery under the Spanish, who had conquered the lands of their ancestors. In the Caribbean region and parts of South America, masses of enslaved Africans who worked on plantations longed for freedom.

Portrait of Joseph Bonaparte,
King of Spain, 1808

The Enlightenment Inspires Latin Americans In the 1700s, educated creoles read the works of Enlightenment thinkers. They watched colonists in North America throw off British rule. Translations of the Declaration of Independence and the Constitution of the United States circulated among the creole elite.

During the French Revolution, young creoles like **Simón Bolívar** (boh LEE vahr) traveled in Europe and were inspired by the ideals of "liberty, equality, and fraternity." Yet despite their admiration for Enlightenment ideas and revolutions in other lands, most creoles were reluctant to act.

Napoleon Invades Spain The spark that finally ignited widespread rebellion in Latin America was Napoleon's invasion of Spain in 1808. Napoleon ousted the Spanish king and placed his brother Joseph on the Spanish throne. In Latin America, leaders saw Spain's weakness as an opportunity to reject foreign domination and demand independence from colonial rule.

✔ **Checkpoint** Where did creoles get many of their revolutionary ideas?

Slaves Win Freedom for Haiti

Even before Spanish colonists hoisted the flag of freedom, revolution had erupted in a French-ruled colony on the island of Hispaniola. In Haiti, as the island is now called, French planters owned very profitable sugar plantations worked by nearly a half million enslaved Africans. Sugar plantations were labor-intensive. The slaves were overworked and underfed.

Toussaint L'Ouverture Leads a Slave Revolt Embittered by suffering and inspired by the talk of liberty and equality, the island's slaves rose up in revolt in 1791. The rebels were fortunate to find an intelligent and skillful leader in **Toussaint L'Ouverture** (too SAN loo vehr TOOR), a self-educated former slave. Although untrained, Toussaint was a brilliant general and inspiring commander.

Toussaint's army of former slaves faced many enemies. Some mulattoes joined French planters against the rebels. France, Spain, and Britain all sent armies against them. The fighting took more lives than any other revolution in the Americas. But by 1798, the rebels had achieved their goal: slavery was abolished, and Toussaint's forces controlled most of the island.

Haiti Wins Independence In 1802, Napoleon Bonaparte sent a large army to reconquer the former colony. Toussaint urged his countrymen to take up arms once again to resist the invaders. In April 1802 the French agreed to a truce, but then they captured Toussaint and carried him in chains to France. He died there in a cold mountain prison a year later.

The struggle for freedom continued, however, and late in 1803, with yellow fever destroying their army, the French surrendered. In January 1804, the island declared itself an independent country under the name Haiti. In the following years, rival Haitian leaders fought for power. Finally, in 1820, Haiti became a republic.

✔ **Checkpoint** How were slaves instrumental in achieving Haiti's independence?

Liberty!
Toussaint L'Ouverture and his army of former slaves battle for independence from France and an end to slavery. Although Toussaint achieved his goal of ending slavery, Haiti (see inset) did not become independent until after his death. *Why do you think Toussaint and his army were willing to risk death to achieve their goals?*

Mexico and Central America Revolt

The slave revolt in Haiti frightened creoles in Spanish America. Although they wanted power themselves, most had no desire for economic or social changes that might threaten their way of life. In 1810, however, a creole priest in Mexico, **Father Miguel Hidalgo** (hee DAL goh), raised his voice for freedom.

Father Hidalgo Cries Out for Freedom Father Hidalgo presided over the poor rural parish of Dolores. On September 15, 1810, he rang the church bells summoning the people to prayer. When they gathered, he startled them with an urgent appeal, "My children, will you be free?" Father Hidalgo's speech became known as "el Grito de Dolores"—the cry of Dolores. It called Mexicans to fight for independence.

A ragged army of poor mestizos and Native Americans rallied to Father Hidalgo and marched to the outskirts of Mexico City. At first, some creoles supported the revolt. However, they soon rejected Hidalgo's call for an end to slavery and his plea for reforms to improve conditions for Native Americans. They felt that these policies would cost them power.

After some early successes, the rebels faced growing opposition. Less than a year after he issued the "Grito," Hidalgo was captured and executed, and his followers scattered.

José Morelos Continues the Fight Another priest picked up the banner of revolution. **Father José Morelos** was a mestizo who called for wide-ranging social and political reform. He wanted to improve conditions for the majority of Mexicans, abolish slavery, and give the vote to all men. For four years, Morelos led rebel forces before he, too, was captured and shot in 1815.

Spanish forces, backed by conservative creoles, hunted down the surviving guerrillas. They had almost succeeded in ending the rebel movement when events in Spain had unexpected effects.

Mexico Wins Independence In Spain in 1820, liberals forced the king to issue a constitution. This move alarmed Agustín de Iturbide (ee toor BEE day), a conservative creole in Mexico. He feared that the new Spanish government might impose liberal reforms on the colonies as well.

Iturbide had spent years fighting Mexican revolutionaries. Suddenly, in 1821, he reached out to them. Backed by creoles, mestizos, and Native Americans, he overthrew the Spanish viceroy. Mexico was independent at last. Iturbide took the title Emperor Agustín I. Soon, however, liberal Mexicans toppled the would-be monarch and set up the Republic of Mexico.

New Republics Emerge in Central America Spanish-ruled lands in Central America declared independence in the early 1820s. Iturbide tried to add these areas to his Mexican empire. After his overthrow, local leaders set up a republic called the United Provinces of Central America. The union soon fragmented into the separate republics of Guatemala, Nicaragua, Honduras, El Salvador, and Costa Rica.

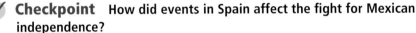 **Checkpoint** How did events in Spain affect the fight for Mexican independence?

Revolution Ignites South America

In South America, Native Americans had rebelled against Spanish rule as early as the 1700s, though with limited results. It was not until the 1800s that discontent among the creoles sparked a widespread drive for independence.

Bolívar Begins the Fight In the early 1800s, discontent spread across South America. Educated creoles like Simón Bolívar admired the French and American revolutions. They dreamed of winning their own independence from Spain.

In 1808, when Napoleon Bonaparte occupied Spain, Bolívar and his friends saw the occupation as a signal to act. In 1810, Bolívar led an uprising that established a republic in his native Venezuela. Bolívar's new republic was quickly toppled by conservative forces, however. For years, civil war raged in Venezuela. The revolutionaries suffered many setbacks. Twice Bolívar was forced into exile on the island of Haiti.

Then, Bolívar conceived a daring plan. He would march his army across the Andes and attack the Spanish at Bogotá, the capital of the viceroyalty of New Granada (present-day Colombia). First, he cemented an alliance with the hard-riding llañeros, or Venezuelan cowboys. Then, in a grueling campaign, he led an army through swampy lowlands and over the snowcapped Andes. Finally, in August 1819, he swooped down to take Bogotá from the surprised Spanish.

Other victories followed. By 1821, Bolívar had succeeded in freeing Caracas, Venezuela. "The Liberator," as he was now called, then moved south into Ecuador, Peru, and Bolivia. There, he joined forces with another great leader, **José de San Martín.**

LATIN AMERICAN INDEPENDENCE

LATIN AMERICA, 1844

Independent nations with dates of independence

*United Provinces of Central America had dissolved by 1844.

**Gran Colombia had dissolved by 1830.

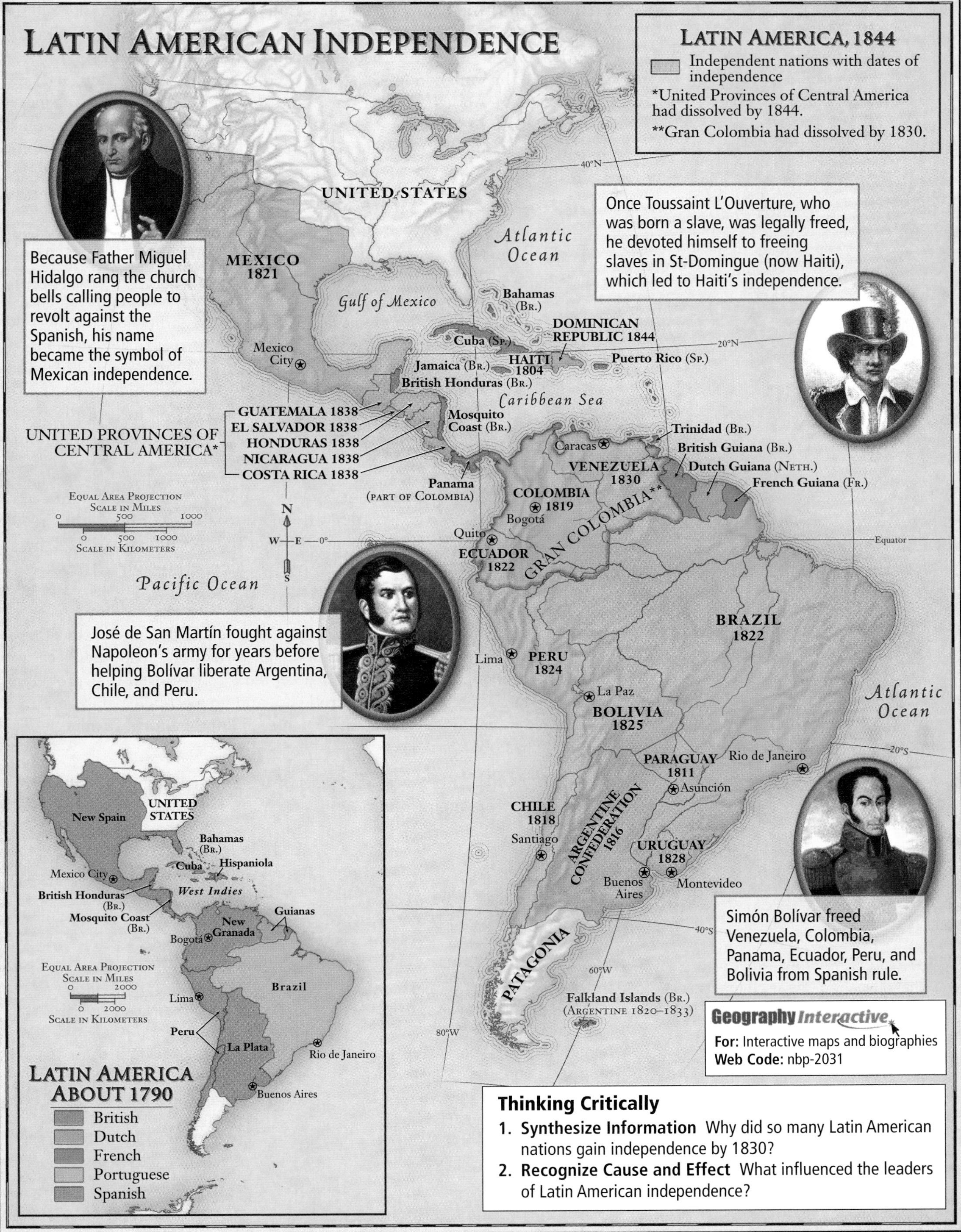

Because Father Miguel Hidalgo rang the church bells calling people to revolt against the Spanish, his name became the symbol of Mexican independence.

Once Toussaint L'Ouverture, who was born a slave, was legally freed, he devoted himself to freeing slaves in St-Domingue (now Haiti), which led to Haiti's independence.

UNITED STATES

Atlantic Ocean

MEXICO 1821

Gulf of Mexico

Mexico City

Bahamas (Br.)

Cuba (Sp.)

DOMINICAN REPUBLIC 1844

HAITI 1804

Puerto Rico (Sp.)

40°N

20°N

Jamaica (Br.)

British Honduras (Br.)

Caribbean Sea

UNITED PROVINCES OF CENTRAL AMERICA*

GUATEMALA 1838
EL SALVADOR 1838
HONDURAS 1838
NICARAGUA 1838
COSTA RICA 1838

Mosquito Coast (Br.)

Trinidad (Br.)

British Guiana (Br.)

Dutch Guiana (Neth.)

French Guiana (Fr.)

Caracas

VENEZUELA 1830

Panama (part of Colombia)

COLOMBIA 1819

GRAN COLOMBIA**

Bogotá

EQUAL AREA PROJECTION
SCALE IN MILES
0   500   1000

0   500   1000
SCALE IN KILOMETERS

Quito

ECUADOR 1822

Equator

N
W — E — 0°
S

Pacific Ocean

BRAZIL 1822

Atlantic Ocean

José de San Martín fought against Napoleon's army for years before helping Bolívar liberate Argentina, Chile, and Peru.

Lima

PERU 1824

La Paz

BOLIVIA 1825

20°S

PARAGUAY 1811

Rio de Janeiro

Asunción

New Spain

UNITED STATES

Bahamas (Br.)

Cuba   Hispaniola

Mexico City

West Indies

British Honduras (Br.)

Mosquito Coast (Br.)

Bogotá

New Granada

Guianas

CHILE 1818

ARGENTINE CONFEDERATION 1816

Santiago

URUGUAY 1828

Buenos Aires

Montevideo

Simón Bolívar freed Venezuela, Colombia, Panama, Ecuador, Peru, and Bolivia from Spanish rule.

EQUAL AREA PROJECTION
SCALE IN MILES
0   2000

0   2000
SCALE IN KILOMETERS

Lima

Brazil

Peru

La Plata

Rio de Janeiro

40°S

60°W

PATAGONIA

Falkland Islands (Br.)
(Argentine 1820–1833)

80°W

Buenos Aires

LATIN AMERICA ABOUT 1790

British
Dutch
French
Portuguese
Spanish

Geography *Interactive*

For: Interactive maps and biographies
Web Code: nbp-2031

Thinking Critically

1. **Synthesize Information** Why did so many Latin American nations gain independence by 1830?

2. **Recognize Cause and Effect** What influenced the leaders of Latin American independence?

Dom Pedro, Emperor of Brazil

San Martín Joins the Fight Like Bolívar, San Martín was a creole. He was born in Argentina but went to Europe for military training. In 1816, this gifted general helped Argentina win freedom from Spain. He then joined the independence struggle in other areas. He, too, led an army across the Andes, from Argentina into Chile. He defeated the Spanish in Chile before moving into Peru to strike further blows against colonial rule. San Martín turned his command over to Bolívar in 1822, allowing Bolívar's forces to win the final victories against Spain.

Freedom Leads to Power Struggles The wars of independence ended by 1824. Bolívar then worked tirelessly to unite the lands he had liberated into a single nation, called Gran Colombia. Bitter rivalries, however, made that dream impossible. Before long, Gran Colombia split into four independent countries: Colombia, Panama, Venezuela, and Ecuador.

Bolívar faced another disappointment as power struggles among rival leaders triggered destructive civil wars. Before his death in 1830, a discouraged Bolívar wrote, "We have achieved our independence at the expense of everything else." Contrary to his dreams, South America's common people had simply changed one set of masters for another.

Brazil Gains Independence When Napoleon's armies conquered Portugal, the Portuguese royal family fled to Brazil. When the king returned to Portugal, he left his son **Dom Pedro** to rule Brazil. "If Brazil demands independence," the king advised Pedro, "proclaim it yourself and put the crown on your own head."

In 1822, Pedro followed his father's advice. A revolution had brought new leaders to Portugal who planned to abolish reforms and demanded that Dom Pedro return. Dom Pedro refused to leave Brazil. Instead, he became emperor of an independent Brazil. He accepted a constitution that provided for freedom of the press, freedom of religion, and an elected legislature. Brazil remained a monarchy until 1889, when social and political turmoil led it to become a republic.

✔ **Checkpoint** How were the goals of the South American revolutions different from their results?

Vocabulary Builder

proclaim—(proh KLAYM) *vt.* to announce publicly or formally

SECTION **3** Assessment

Progress Monitoring *Online*
For: Self-quiz with vocabulary practice
Web Code: nba-2031

Terms, People, and Places

1. What do many of the key terms listed at the beginning of the section have in common? Explain.

Note Taking

2. **Reading Skill: Identify Supporting Details** Use your completed chart to answer the Focus Question: Who were the key revolutionaries that led the movements for independence in Latin America, and what were their accomplishments?

Comprehension and Critical Thinking

3. **Draw Conclusions** How did social structure contribute to discontent in Latin America?

4. **Analyze Information** **(a)** What was the first step on Haiti's road to independence? **(b)** Why did creoles refuse to support Hidalgo or Morelos?

5. **Identify Central Issues** Why did Bolívar admire the American and French revolutions?

● **Writing About History**

Quick Write: Use Effective Language Most effective persuasive essays contain memorable and convincing details and vivid, persuasive language. Suppose you were one of the revolutionary leaders mentioned in the section. Write notes for a speech in which you persuade others to join your cause. Include at least three compelling reasons why people should follow you.

Simón Bolívar: *Address to the Congress of Venezuela*

Encouraged by the revolutions in British North America and France, colonists in Spanish South America soon began to create a force for independence. Simón Bolívar was one of the leaders of this movement. The excerpt below is from Bolívar's Address to the Second National Congress of Venezuela, given in 1819. In this speech, Bolívar offers advice on what type of government to set up in Venezuela.

Statue of Bolívar as the Liberator, Mexico City

Subject to the threefold yoke of ignorance, tyranny, and vice, the American people have been unable to acquire knowledge, power, or [civic] virtue. The lessons we received and the models we studied, as pupils of such pernicious[1] teachers, were most destructive. . . .

If a people, perverted by their training, succeed in achieving their liberty, they will soon lose it, for it would be of no avail to endeavor to explain to them that happiness consists in the practice of virtue; that the rule of law is more powerful than the rule of tyrants, because, as the laws are more inflexible everyone should submit to their beneficent austerity; that proper morals, and not force, are the bases of law; and that to practice justice is to practice liberty.

Therefore, Legislators, your work is so much the more arduous[2], inasmuch as you have to reeducate men who have been corrupted by erroneous[3] illusions and false incentives[4]. Liberty, says Rousseau, is a succulent[5] morsel, but one difficult to digest. . . .

Legislators, meditate well before you choose. Forget not that you are to lay the political foundation for a newly born nation which can rise to the heights of greatness that Nature has marked out for it if you but proportion this foundation in keeping with the high plane that it aspires to attain. Unless your choice is based upon the peculiar . . . experience of Venezuelan people—a factor that should guide you in determining the nature and form of government you are about to adopt for the well-being of the people . . . the result of our reforms will again be slavery.

1. **pernicious** (pur NISH us) *adj.* harmful, injurious
2. **arduous** (AHR joo us) *adj.* difficult
3. **erroneous** (eh ROH nee us) *adj.* mistaken, wrong
4. **incentive** (in SEN tiv) *n.* reason for doing something
5. **succulent** (SUK yoo lunt) *adj.* juicy, tasty

Thinking Critically
1. **Analyze Literature** How did Bolívar feel the people of Latin America were prepared for new government?
2. **Draw Inferences** Do you think Bolívar was practical or idealistic? Use examples from the excerpt to defend your opinion.

Quick Study Guide

Progress Monitoring *Online*
For: Self-test with vocabulary practice
Web Code: nba-2041

■ Revolutions in Europe

Successful	Unsuccessful
Serbia (autonomy 1830)	Poland (1830)
Greece (1830)	Austria (1848)
Belgium (1830)	Italy (1848)
	Germany (1848)

■ Events in France

July 1830	**1840**	**February 1848**
• Rebels take control of Paris. • Constitutional monarchy proclaimed. • Louis Philippe becomes king.	• Recession heightens discontent.	• Rebels take to the streets. • Second Republic is proclaimed. • Louis Philippe abdicates.

June 1848	**1850**	**1852**
• Bourgeois liberals crush workers' rebellion.	• Louis Napoleon is voted president of the Second Republic.	• Louis Napoleon becomes emperor of the Second Empire.

■ Independence Movements in Latin America

Cause and Effect

Long-Term Causes	Immediate Causes
• European domination • Spread of Enlightenment ideas • American and French Revolutions • Growth of nationalism	• Social injustices • Revolutionary leaders emerge. • Napoleon invades Spain.

Independence Movements

Immediate Effects	Long-Term Effects
• Toussaint L'Ouverture leads slave revolt in Haiti. • Bolívar, San Martin, and others lead successful revolts. • Colonial rule ends in much of Latin America.	• Numerous independent nations in Latin America • Continuing efforts to achieve stable democratic governments and to gain economic independence

■ Age of Revolution

1804
Haiti declares independence from France.

1810
Father Miguel Hidalgo urges Mexicans to fight for independence from Spain.

1819
Simón Bolívar seizes Bogotá from the Spanish.

1821
Simón Bolívar liberates Caracas, Venezuela.

Chapter Events
Global Events

1800   **1810**   **1820**

1803
United States buys Louisiana from France.

1814
Napoleon is banished to Elba.

1819
The United States acquires Spanish Florida.

1823
U.S. President James Monroe issues the Monroe Doctrine.

Concept Connector

■ Cumulative Review

Record the answers to the questions below on your Concept Connector worksheets. In addition, record information from this chapter about the following concepts:
- Conflict: European revolutionaries in 1830 and 1848
- Revolution: Latin American revolutions against European rulers

1. **Empire** Colonists in Latin America in the early 1800s had much in common with colonists in North America in the mid-1700s. In each case, the colonies were part of an empire whose capital was thousands of miles away. How did the empires use their colonies for their own gain? What did the colonists have in common? Think about the following:
   - nationalism
   - the role of geography in empires
   - economic exploitation by empires

2. **Nationalism** How was Latin American nationalism in the early 1800s similar to, or different from, French nationalism in 1789? Think about the following:
   - leaders of each revolution
   - targets of each revolution

3. **Democracy** After the American Revolution, a new nation was formed under a written constitution. This did not happen in Latin America. How were the results of the American Revolution different from the revolutions in Latin America? Think about the following:
   - groups that had power afterwards
   - the relationship between land ownership and power

■ Connections to Today

1. **Independence: Mexican Independence Day** Today, the people of Mexico remember Father Hidalgo's speech as "el Grito de Dolores." Every September 15, the anniversary of the speech, the president of Mexico rings a bell—suggestive of the church bell in Dolores. The president then honors the Grito de Dolores by repeating the speech. The next day, September 16, marks the anniversary of the beginning of the fight against the Spanish. It is celebrated as Mexican Independence Day, a national holiday. Schools and businesses shut down, and people throw huge parties. Fireworks light the night sky. Why is the ringing of bells an important custom of Mexican Independence Day?

2. **Conflict: Chechnya and Russia** There are many struggles for independence in the world today. Certain Basques in Spain, Tibetans in China, and Chechens in Russia are all seeking their independence. In some cases, such as in Chechnya, revolutionaries resort to terrorism to fight for their goals. Conduct research and write a one-page report about Chechnya and why its revolutionaries seek independence from Russia.

1830
French revolutionaries battle the king's troops in the streets of Paris.

1848
Revolutions break out across much of Europe.

History *Interactive*
For: Interactive timeline
Web Code: nbp-2001

1830   **1840**   **1850**

1839
China and Britain clash in the Opium War.

1850
Taiping Rebellion begins in China.

Chapter Assessment

Terms, People, and Places

Match the following terms with the definitions below.

creole
autonomy
Louis Philippe
recession

peninsulare
ideology
mestizo
José de San Martín

1. system of thought and belief
2. self-rule
3. person in Spain's colonies in the Americas who was an American-born descendant of Spanish settlers
4. period of reduced economic activity
5. person in Spain's colonies in the Americas who was of Native American and European descent
6. known as the "citizen king"
7. fought for freedom in South America
8. member of the highest class in Spain's colonies in the Americas

Main Ideas

Section 1 (pp. 272–275)
9. In the early 1800s, what were the main goals of **(a)** conservatives, **(b)** liberals, and **(c)** nationalists?

Section 2 (pp. 276–281)
10. What were the causes of the French revolution of 1830?
11. Describe the outcomes of the 1848 rebellions in Europe.

Section 3 (pp. 283–288)
12. **(a)** How did Mexico gain independence from Spain? **(b)** How did Mexico's independence change the lives of its people?
13. Why is Simón Bolívar known as "The Liberator"?

Chapter Focus Question
14. How did revolutionary ideals in Europe and Latin America ignite uprisings in the first half of the nineteenth century?

Critical Thinking

15. **Recognize Cause and Effect** How did the clash of conservatism, liberalism, and nationalism contribute to unrest in Europe in the 1800s?
16. **Draw Conclusions** Why do you think liberals of the early 1800s supported limited voting rights?
17. **Synthesize Information** In the 1820s, Britain, France, and Russia supported the Greek struggle for independence. **(a)** Why did these European powers support the Greeks? **(b)** Did the European powers usually respond to revolution in this way? Explain.
18. **Analyze Information** You have read Metternich's comment: "When France sneezes, Europe catches cold." **(a)** What did he mean by these words? **(b)** Was Metternich correct?
19. **Geography and History** Review the map in Section 3. How does the map show that Bolívar failed to achieve one of his dreams?
20. **Analyzing Visuals** The scene below is part of a famous mural by José Clemente Orozco. How do you think Orozco feels about Father Hidalgo?

21. **Geography and History** **(a)** How did climatic conditions help Haitians defeat the French? **(b)** Do you think the distance between Europe and Latin America affected the Latin American wars for independence? Explain.

● Writing About History

Writing a Persuasive Essay The early 1800s were a time of revolution across Europe. Liberals and nationalists attempted to organize revolts that might overthrow Europe's colonial rule. Write a persuasive essay that a liberal or nationalist might have published in a local newspaper in an attempt to persuade people to join a revolution.

Prewriting
• Take notes about the ideas that motivated revolutionaries in the early 1800s.
• Generate arguments that a liberal or nationalist might make.

Drafting
• Using a convincing thesis, or main argument, make an outline that organizes the essay.
• Write an attention-grabbing introduction, a body, and a conclusion.
• Open and close with your strongest argument.

Revising
• Make sure your arguments are logical and clearly explained. Provide additional evidence where needed.
• Use the guidelines for revising your report on page SH17 of the Writing Handbook.

Document-Based Assessment

The Revolutions of 1848: The Aftermath

The revolutions of 1848 began spontaneously in February 1848 on the streets of Paris. Reformers won short-lived success with the abdication of Louis Philippe. Uprisings spread across Europe to Austria, Hungary, Germany, and Italy, among others. These rebellions were quelled in short order, as the documents below illustrate, but some reverberations were more lasting.

Document A

"[O]n June 23rd, 1848 . . . the proletarians of Paris were defeated, decimated [killed off so that a large part of the population was removed], crushed with such an effect that even now they have not yet recovered from the blow. And immediately, all over Europe, the new and old Conservatives and Counter-Revolutionists raised their heads with an effrontery [boldness] that showed how well they understood the importance of the event. The Press was everywhere attacked, the rights of meeting and association were interfered with, every little event in every small provincial town was taken profit of to disarm the people to declare a state of siege, to drill the troops in the new maneuvers and artifices [clever tricks] that Cavaignac [French general known for his harsh treatment of Parisian rebels] had taught them."

—From ***The Paris Rising—Frankfort Assembly*** by Frederich Engels (February, 1852)

Document B

"[German] factory workers failed to win any lasting class advantages in 1848–1849 . . . Many artisans exerted themselves for the revolution; in October 1849 the magazine of the cigar workers estimated that three hundred in this industry alone had been forced to flee to Switzerland. . . . For German democrats— whether workers or from the middle class—the revolution left little immediate consolation. In a few states democrats retained large representation in the parliaments, but reactionary changes in the suffrage systems soon ended that. . . . But the long-range results of the revolution were not altogether negative. To be sure, those who worked for democracy after 1849 knew better than to try to create a republic. They also knew the futility of resorting to revolutionary violence. But their effort did not cease."

—From ***The Democratic Movement in Germany, 1789–1914*** by John L. Snell

Document C

Metternich Flees Austria

Document D

"The rising of 1848 was a spontaneous expression of national feeling but completely uncoordinated and therefore defeated in detail. After it, once more patrolled by Austria, Italy sank back into inaction. . . . From the wreck of Italian political institutions in 1849 there was only one survival, the constitution granted by [King] Charles Albert in Piedmont [kingdom in northwestern Italy]. It provided for a Premier or President of the Council, who, like the Senate, was nominated by the King, and a Chamber of Deputies numbering two hundred and four, elected on a narrow franchise [vote]."

—From ***The Evolution of Modern Italy*** by Arthur James Whyte

Analyzing Documents

Use your knowledge of the revolutions of 1848 and Documents A, B, C, and D to answer questions 1–4.

1. Which words describe the attitude of the author of Document A toward the counter-revolutionaries?
   A admiration and pride
   B understanding and sympathy
   C hatred and disapproval
   D respect and sympathy

2. According to Document B, what strategies did the democrats of Germany follow after the revolution was put down?
   A revolutionary plots
   B voter-registration drives
   C underground efforts
   D parliamentary politics

3. In Document C, Prince Clemens von Metternich is
   A proud to resign.
   B continuing Austrian governance.
   C expressing nationalism.
   D unpopular and defeated.

4. **Writing Task** Describe the aftermath of the revolutions of 1848. If you had lived in 1849, would you have seen causes for optimism or pessimism? How would your answer be different from the viewpoint of the twenty-first century?

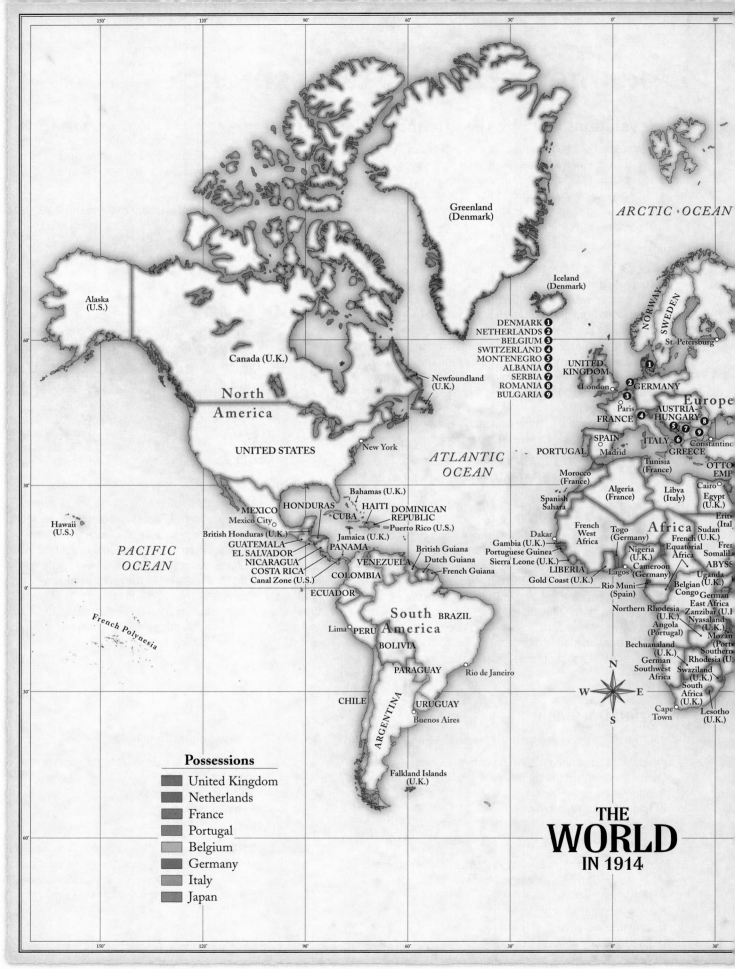

THE
WORLD
IN 1914

Possessions
- United Kingdom
- Netherlands
- France
- Portugal
- Belgium
- Germany
- Italy
- Japan

DENMARK ❶
NETHERLANDS ❷
BELGIUM ❸
SWITZERLAND ❹
MONTENEGRO ❺
ALBANIA ❻
SERBIA ❼
ROMANIA ❽
BULGARIA ❾

RUSSIAN EMPIRE

MONGOLIA

Asia

AFGHANISTAN

Beijing

Korea (Japan)

JAPAN

PACIFIC OCEAN

CHINA

Tehran

PERSIA

Persian Gulf
Protectorates
(U.K.)

Delhi

TIBET

NEPAL

BHUTAN

Tokyo

Macao (Portugal)

Taiwan (Japan)

Oman (U.K.)

India (U.K.)

Calcutta

Hong Kong (U.K.)

Aden and South
Arabia (U.K.)

Bombay

SIAM

French Indochina

Guam (U.S.)

German Pacific
Possessions

Marshall
Islands

Bangkok

Philippines
(U.S.)

Caroline Islands

British Somaliland

Malaya
(U.K.)

Saigon

Brunei
(U.K.)

Italian
Somaliland

Ceylon
(U.K.)

Sarawak
(U.K.)

British North Borneo

Kaiser
Wilhelm's
Land
(Germany)

Bismarck
Archipelago

Singapore

INDIAN
OCEAN

Batavia

Dutch East Indies

Papua
(U.K.)

Solomon
Islands
(U.K.)

Portuguese Timor

Madagascar
(France)

Mauritius (U.K.)

Réunion (France)

New
Caledonia
(France)

Fiji (U.K.)

Australia (U.K.)

Sydney

New
Zealand
(U.K.)

Scale in Miles
0   1000   2000   3000

0   1000   2000   3000
Scale in Kilometers
Scale at the Equator
Mercator Projection

Geography *Interactive*
For: Audio guided tour
Web Code: nbp-5000

CHAPTER 9

Life in the Industrial Age

1800–1914

Factory Life

In 1888, Nell Cusack, a reporter for the Chicago *Times*, worked undercover to write a series of newspaper articles about the conditions under which factory girls worked:

66 . . . The place was noisy with flying shuttles, clicking needles, and the whizzing wheels of the roaring machinery. . . . The clatter of the machines was deafening. . . . The room was low . . . and clouds of lint seemed floating about in space. Add to that poor light, bad ventilation, the exhalations of so many people, [and] the smell of dye from the cloth . . . and you have material for the make-up of [the] shop. All afternoon we sewed; sewed incessantly without uttering a syllable or resting a moment. **99**

Listen to the Witness History audio to learn more about factory life.

◄ **Spinner at a cotton mill in Whitnel, North Carolina, 1908**

German labor union poster

Banner from the National Union of Women's Suffrage Societies

Chapter Preview

Chapter Focus Question What were the technological, social, and economic effects of the Industrial Revolution?

The first commercially successful typewriter, 1875

Note Taking Study Guide *Online*
For: Note Taking and Concept Connector worksheets
Web Code: nbd-2101

Painting of a nineteenth-century steel mill

WITNESS HISTORY ◀)) AUDIO

The Steelmaking Process

By the 1880s, steel had replaced steam as the great symbol of the Industrial Revolution. In huge steel mills, visitors watched with awe as tons of molten metal were poured into giant mixers:

66 At night the scene is indescribably wild and beautiful. The flashing fireworks, the terrific gusts of heat, the gaping, glowing mouth of the giant chest, the quivering light from the liquid iron, the roar of a near-by converter . . . combine to produce an effect on the mind that no words can translate. 99
—J. H. Bridge, *The Inside History of the Carnegie Steel Company*

Focus Question How did science, technology, and big business promote industrial growth?

The Industrial Revolution Spreads

Objectives

- List the industrial powers that emerged in the 1800s.
- Describe the impact of new technology on industry, transportation, and communication.
- Understand how big business emerged in the late 1800s.

Terms, People, and Places

Henry Bessemer
Alfred Nobel
Michael Faraday
dynamo
Thomas Edison
interchangeable parts

assembly line
Orville and Wilbur Wright
Guglielmo Marconi
stock
corporation
cartel

Note Taking

Reading Skill: Identify Main Ideas Fill in a chart like this one with the major developments of the Industrial Revolution.

The Second Industrial Revolution		
New Powers	**Industry/Business**	**Transportation/ Communication**
•	•	•
•	•	•

The first phase of industrialization had largely been forged from iron, powered by steam engines, and driven by the British textile industry. By the mid-1800s, the Industrial Revolution entered a second phase. New industrial powers emerged. Factories powered by electricity used innovative processes to turn out new products. Changes in business organization contributed to the rise of giant companies. As the twentieth century dawned, this second Industrial Revolution transformed the economies of the Western world.

New Industrial Powers Emerge

During the early Industrial Revolution, Britain stood alone as the world's industrial giant. To protect its head start, Britain tried to enforce strict rules against exporting inventions.

For a while, the rules worked. Then, in 1807, British mechanic William Cockerill opened factories in Belgium to manufacture spinning and weaving machines. Belgium became the first European nation after Britain to industrialize. By the mid-1800s, other nations had joined the race, and several newcomers were challenging Britain's industrial supremacy.

Nations Race to Industrialize How were other nations able to catch up with Britain so quickly? First, nations such as Germany, France, and the United States had more abundant supplies of coal, iron, and other resources than did Britain. Also, they had the advantage of being able to follow Britain's lead. Like Belgium,

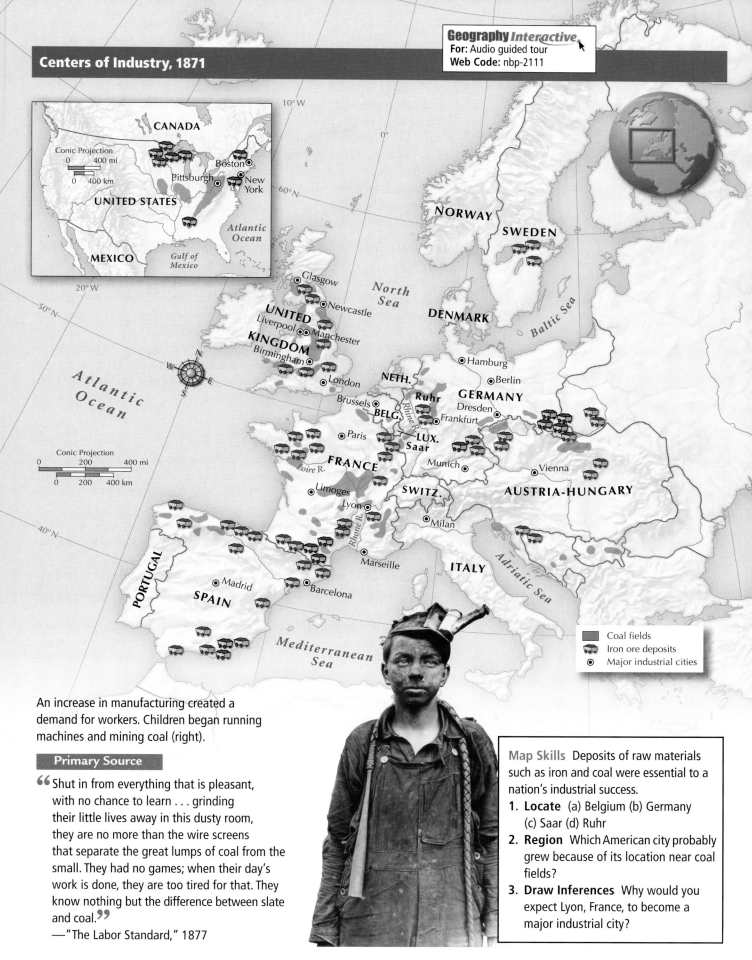

Centers of Industry, 1871

Geography *Interactive*
For: Audio guided tour
Web Code: nbp-2111

CANADA

Conic Projection
0   400 mi
0   400 km

Boston
Pittsburgh
New York

UNITED STATES

Atlantic Ocean

MEXICO

Gulf of Mexico

Atlantic Ocean

Conic Projection
0   200   400 mi
0   200   400 km

Glasgow
Newcastle

UNITED KINGDOM
Liverpool Manchester
Birmingham
London

NETH.

NORWAY

SWEDEN

North Sea

DENMARK

Baltic Sea

Hamburg
Berlin
Ruhr
GERMANY
Dresden
Frankfurt

Brussels
BELG.
LUX.
Saar

Paris
FRANCE
Loire R.

Limoges
Lyon

SWITZ.

Munich

Milan

Vienna

AUSTRIA-HUNGARY

Rhone R.

Marseille

ITALY

Adriatic Sea

PORTUGAL

Madrid
Barcelona

SPAIN

Mediterranean Sea

Coal fields
Iron ore deposits
Major industrial cities

An increase in manufacturing created a demand for workers. Children began running machines and mining coal (right).

Primary Source

66 Shut in from everything that is pleasant, with no chance to learn . . . grinding their little lives away in this dusty room, they are no more than the wire screens that separate the great lumps of coal from the small. They had no games; when their day's work is done, they are too tired for that. They know nothing but the difference between slate and coal. 99
—"The Labor Standard," 1877

Map Skills Deposits of raw materials such as iron and coal were essential to a nation's industrial success.
1. **Locate** (a) Belgium (b) Germany (c) Saar (d) Ruhr
2. **Region** Which American city probably grew because of its location near coal fields?
3. **Draw Inferences** Why would you expect Lyon, France, to become a major industrial city?

latecomers often borrowed British experts or technology. The first American textile factory was built in Pawtucket, Rhode Island, with plans smuggled out of Britain. American inventor Robert Fulton powered his steamboat with one of James Watt's steam engines.

Two countries in particular—Germany and the United States—thrust their way to industrial leadership. Germany united into a powerful nation in 1871. Within a few decades, it became Europe's leading industrial power. Across the Atlantic, the United States advanced even more rapidly, especially after the Civil War. By 1900, the United States was manufacturing about 30 percent of the world's industrial goods, surpassing Britain as the leading industrial nation.

Uneven Development Other nations industrialized more slowly, particularly those in eastern and southern Europe. These nations often lacked natural resources or the capital to invest in industry. Although Russia did have resources, social and political conditions slowed its economic development. Only in the late 1800s, more than 100 years after Britain, did Russia lumber toward industrialization.

In East Asia, however, Japan offered a remarkable success story. Although Japan lacked many basic resources, it industrialized rapidly after 1868 because of a political revolution that made modernization a priority. Canada, Australia, and New Zealand also built thriving industries during this time.

Effects of Industrialization Like Britain, the new industrial nations underwent social changes, such as rapid urbanization. Men, women, and children worked long hours in difficult and dangerous conditions. As you will read, by 1900, these conditions had begun to improve in many industrialized nations.

The factory system produced huge quantities of new goods at lower prices than ever before. In time, ordinary workers were buying goods that in earlier days only the wealthy could afford. The demand for goods created jobs, as did the building of cities, railroads, and factories. Politics changed, too, as leaders had to meet the demands of an industrial society.

Globally, industrial nations competed fiercely, altering patterns of world trade. Because of their technological and economic advantage, the Western powers came to <u>dominate</u> the world more than ever before.

✔ **Checkpoint** What factors led to the industrialization of other nations after Britain?

Technology Sparks Industrial Growth

During the early Industrial Revolution, inventions such as the steam engine were generally the work of gifted tinkerers. They experimented with simple machines to make them better. By the 1880s, the pace of change quickened as companies hired professional chemists and engineers to create new products and machinery. The union of science, technology, and industry spurred economic growth.

Steel Production and the Bessemer Process American inventor William Kelly and British engineer **Henry Bessemer** independently developed a new process for making steel from iron. In 1856, Bessemer

---

Vocabulary Builder

<u>dominate</u>—(DAHM uh nayt) v. to rule or control by power or influence

Steel Production, 1880–1910

Graph Skills By the late 1800s, steel was the major material used in manufacturing tools, such as the sheep shears (above). The graph shows the amount of steel produced by the United States, Germany, and Great Britain. *Between 1890 and 1910, which nation had the greatest increase in steel production? The smallest?*

SOURCES: *European Historical Statistics, 1750–1970; Historical Statistics of the United States*

patented this process. Steel was lighter, harder, and more durable than iron, so it could be produced very cheaply. Steel quickly became the major material used in tools, bridges, and railroads.

As steel production soared, industrialized countries measured their success in steel output. In 1880, for example, the average German steel mill produced less than 5 million metric tons of steel a year. By 1910, that figure reached nearly 15 million metric tons.

Innovations in Chemistry Chemists created hundreds of new products, from medicines such as aspirin to perfumes and soaps. Newly developed chemical fertilizers played a key role in increasing food production.

In 1866, the Swedish chemist **Alfred Nobel** invented dynamite, an explosive much safer than others used at the time. It was widely used in construction and, to Nobel's dismay, in warfare. Dynamite earned Nobel a huge fortune, which he willed to fund the famous Nobel prizes that are still awarded today.

Electric Power Replaces Steam In the late 1800s, a new power source—electricity—replaced steam as the dominant source of industrial power. Scientists like Benjamin Franklin had tinkered with electricity a century earlier. The Italian scientist Alessandro Volta developed the first battery around 1800. Later, the English chemist **Michael Faraday** created the first simple electric motor and the first **dynamo,** a machine that generates electricity. Today, all electrical generators and transformers work on the principle of Faraday's dynamo.

In the 1870s, the American inventor **Thomas Edison** made the first electric light bulb. Soon, Edison's "incandescent lamps" illuminated whole cities. The pace of city life quickened, and factories could continue to operate after dark. By the 1890s, cables carried electrical power from dynamos to factories.

New Methods of Production The basic features of the factory system remained the same during the 1800s. Factories still used large numbers of workers and power-driven machines to mass-produce goods. To improve efficiency, however, manufacturers designed products with **interchangeable parts,** identical components that could be used in place of one another. Interchangeable parts simplified both the assembly and repair of products.

By the early 1900s, manufacturers had introduced another new method of production, the **assembly line.** Workers on an assembly line add parts to a product that moves along a belt from one work station to the next. A different person performs each task along the assembly line. This division of labor in an assembly line, like interchangeable parts, made production faster and cheaper, lowering the price of goods. Although dividing labor into separate tasks proved to be more efficient, it took much of the joy out of the work itself.

Electricity Lights Up Cities
This early dynamo (above) generated enough electricity to power lights in factories. Electricity changed life outdoors as well. *Judging from this print, how did electricity make life easier for people in the city?*

✓ **Checkpoint** What was the dynamo's impact on the Industrial Revolution?

The Modern Office

The Bessemer process prepared the way for the use of steel in building construction. Before steel, frameworks consisted of heavy iron. Steel provided a much lighter framework and enabled the construction of taller buildings. The first skyscrapers were between 10 and 20 stories high. They were built in the United States in the 1880s to house large corporations.

Elevators made it practical for buildings to have more than five or six stories.

Offices could be illuminated with **electric lights** both night and day.

Telephones allowed workers to send and receive messages faster than the telegraph.

Typewriters enabled workers to type information faster than they could write it by hand.

Automobiles and subway systems permitted rapid transit to and from cities.

ILLUSTRATION NOT TO SCALE

Thinking Critically

1. **Draw Inferences** Why did industrialization create a need for skyscrapers?
2. **Synthesize Information** What invention do you think had the most impact on offices? Explain.

Transportation and Communication Advances

During the Industrial Revolution, transportation and communications were transformed by technology. Steamships replaced sailing ships, and railroad building took off. In Europe and North America, rail lines connected inland cities and seaports, mining regions and industrial centers. In the United States, a transcontinental railroad provided rail service from the Atlantic to the Pacific. In the same way, Russians built the Trans-Siberian Railroad, linking Moscow in European Russia to Vladivostok on the Pacific. Railroad tunnels and bridges crossed the Alps in Europe and the Andes in South America. Passengers and goods rode on rails in India, China, Egypt, and South Africa.

The Automobile Age Begins The transportation revolution took a new turn when a German engineer, Nikolaus Otto, invented a gasoline-powered internal combustion engine. In 1886, Karl Benz received a patent for the first automobile, which had three wheels. A year later, Gottlieb Daimler (DYM lur) introduced the first four-wheeled automobile. People laughed at the "horseless carriages," but they quickly transformed transportation.

The French nosed out the Germans as early automakers. Then the American Henry Ford started making models that reached the breathtaking speed of 25 miles per hour. In the early 1900s, Ford began using the assembly line to mass-produce cars, making the United States a leader in the automobile industry.

Airplanes Take Flight The internal combustion engine powered more than cars. Motorized threshers and reapers boosted farm production. Even more dramatically, the internal combustion engine made possible sustained, pilot-controlled flight. In 1903, American bicycle makers **Orville and Wilbur Wright** designed and flew a flimsy airplane at Kitty Hawk, North Carolina. Although their flying machine stayed aloft for only a few seconds, it ushered in the air age.

Soon, daredevil pilots were flying airplanes across the English Channel and over the Alps. Commercial passenger travel, however, would not begin until the 1920s.

Rapid Communication A revolution in communications also made the world smaller. An American inventor, Samuel F. B. Morse, developed

In 1901, Guglielmo Marconi (left) was in Newfoundland to receive the first overseas radio transmission from his assistant in England. Did Marconi's prediction come true? Explain.

Primary Source

66 Shortly before mid-day I placed the single earphone to my ear and started listening. . . . I heard, faintly but distinctly, *pip-pip-pip*. . . . I now felt for the first time absolutely certain that the day would come when mankind would be able to send messages without wires not only across the Atlantic, but between the farthermost ends of the earth. 99

the telegraph, which could send coded messages over wires by means of electricity. His first telegraph line went into service between Washington, D.C. and Baltimore, in 1844. By the 1860s, an undersea cable was relaying messages between Europe and North America. This trans-Atlantic cable was an amazing engineering accomplishment for its day.

Communication soon became even faster. In 1876, the Scottish-born American inventor Alexander Graham Bell patented the telephone. By the 1890s, the Italian pioneer **Guglielmo Marconi** had invented the radio. In 1901, Marconi received a radio message, using Morse code, sent from Britain to Canada. Radio would become a cornerstone of today's global communications network.

✔ **Checkpoint** How did technological advances in transportation and communications affect the Industrial Revolution?

Business Takes a New Direction

By the late 1800s, what we call "big business" came to dominate industry. Big business refers to an establishment that is run by entrepreneurs who finance, manufacture, and distribute goods. As time passed, some big businesses came to control entire industries.

Rise of Big Business New technologies required the investment of large amounts of money, or capital. To get the needed capital, owners sold **stock,** or shares in their companies, to investors. Each stockholder became owner of a tiny part of a company. Large-scale companies, such as steel foundries, needed so much capital that they sold hundreds of thousands of shares. These businesses formed giant **corporations,** businesses that are owned by many investors who buy shares of stock. With large amounts of capital, corporations could expand into many areas.

Move Toward Monopolies Powerful business leaders created monopolies and trusts, huge corporate structures that controlled entire industries or areas of the economy. In Germany, Alfred Krupp inherited a steelmaking business from his father. He bought up coal and iron mines as well as ore deposits—supply lines or raw materials that fed the steel business. Later, he and his son acquired plants that made tools, railroad cars, and weapons. In the United States, John D. Rockefeller built Standard Oil Company into an empire. By gaining control of oil wells, oil refineries, and oil pipelines, he dominated the American petroleum industry.

Analyzing Political Cartoons

One View of Big Business To some critics, the growth of monopolies had a dangerous effect on society. This 1899 American cartoon shows a monopoly as an octopus-like monster. *Do you think this cartoonist favored or opposed government regulation of business? Explain.*

In their pursuit of profit, ruthless business leaders destroyed competing companies. With the competition gone, they were free to raise prices. Sometimes, a group of corporations would join forces and form a **cartel,** an association to fix prices, set production quotas, or control markets. In Germany, a single cartel fixed prices for 170 coal mines.

Move Toward Regulation The rise of big business and the creation of such great wealth sparked a stormy debate. Some people saw the Krupps and Rockefellers as "captains of industry" and praised their vision and skills. They pointed out that capitalists invested their wealth in worldwide ventures, such as railroad building, that employed thousands of workers and added to the general prosperity.

To others, the aggressive magnates were "robber barons." Destroying competition, critics argued, damaged the free-enterprise system, or the laissez-faire economy. Reformers called for laws to prevent monopolies and regulate large corporations. Despite questionable business practices, big business found support from many government leaders. By the early 1900s, some governments did move against monopolies. However, the political and economic power of business leaders often hindered efforts at regulation.

✓ **Checkpoint** Why were big business leaders "captains of industry" to some, but "robber barons" to others?

Progress Monitoring Online
For: Self-quiz with vocabulary practice
Web Code: nba-2111

Terms, People, and Places

1. For each term, person, or place listed at the beginning of the section, write a sentence explaining its significance.

Note Taking

2. **Reading Skill: Identify Main Ideas** Use your completed chart to answer the Focus Question: How did science, technology, and big business promote industrial growth?

Comprehension and Critical Thinking

3. **Summarize** How did the Industrial Revolution spread in the 1800s?
4. **Draw Conclusions** How did technology help industry expand?
5. **Recognize Cause and Effect** How did the need for capital lead to new business organizations and methods?
6. **Predict** How might government change as a result of industrialization?

● **Writing About History**

Quick Write: Define a Problem Choose one topic from this section that you could use to write a problem-and-solution essay. For example, you could write about the impact of powerful monopolies. Make a list of details, facts, and examples that define the problems that monopolies pose to a free market.

Charles Dickens with an illustration from one of his serialized novels

London Fog

Between 1850 and 1900, London's population more than doubled, rising from about 2.6 million people to more than 6.5 million people. With the rapid population growth came increased pollution and health problems:

❝ It was a foggy day in London, and the fog was heavy and dark. Animate [living] London, with smarting eyes and irritated lungs, was blinking, wheezing, and choking; inanimate [nonliving] London was a sooty spectre, divided in purpose between being visible and invisible, and so being wholly neither.❞
—Charles Dickens, *Our Mutual Friend*

Focus Question How did the Industrial Revolution change life in the cities?

The Rise of the Cities

Objectives
- Summarize the impact of medical advances in the late 1800s.
- Describe how cities had changed by 1900.
- Explain how working-class struggles led to improved conditions for workers.

Terms, People, and Places

germ theory	Joseph Lister
Louis Pasteur	urban renewal
Robert Koch	mutual-aid society
Florence Nightingale	standard of living

Note Taking

Reading Skill: Identify Supporting Details As you read, look for the main ideas and supporting details and how they relate to each other. Use the format below to create an outline of the section.

> I. Medicine and the population explosion
>   A. The fight against disease
>   1.
>   2.
>   B.
> II.

The population explosion that had begun during the 1700s continued through the 1800s. Cities grew as rural people streamed into urban areas. By the end of the century, European and American cities had begun to take on many of the features of cities today.

Medicine Contributes to the Population Explosion

Between 1800 and 1900, the population of Europe more than doubled. This rapid growth was not due to larger families. In fact, families in most industrializing countries had fewer children. Instead, populations soared because the death rate fell. Nutrition improved, thanks in part to improved methods of farming, food storage, and distribution. Medical advances and improvements in public sanitation also slowed death rates.

The Fight Against Disease Since the 1600s, scientists had known of microscopic organisms, or microbes. Some scientists speculated that certain microbes might cause specific infectious diseases. Yet most doctors scoffed at this **germ theory.** Not until 1870 did French chemist **Louis Pasteur** (pas TUR) clearly show the link between microbes and disease. Pasteur went on to make other major contributions to medicine, including the development of vaccines against rabies and anthrax. He also discovered a process called pasteurization that killed disease-carrying microbes in milk.

Florence Nightingale

When Florence Nightingale (1820–1910) arrived at a British military hospital in the Crimea in 1854, she was horrified by what she saw. The sick and wounded lay on bare ground. With no sanitation and a shortage of food, some 60 percent of all patients died. But Nightingale was a fighter. Bullying the military and medical staff, she soon had every available person cleaning barracks, digging latrines, doing laundry, and caring for the wounded. Six months later, the death rate had dropped to 2 percent.

Back in England, Nightingale was hailed as a saint. Ballads were even written about her. She took advantage of her popularity and connections to pressure the government for reforms. **How did Nightingale achieve reforms in British army hospitals?**

In the 1880s, the German doctor **Robert Koch** identified the bacterium that caused tuberculosis, a respiratory disease that claimed about 30 million human lives in the 1800s. The search for a tuberculosis cure, however, took half a century. By 1914, yellow fever and malaria had been traced to microbes carried by mosquitoes.

As people understood how germs caused disease, they bathed and changed their clothes more often. In European cities, better hygiene helped decrease the rate of disease.

Hospital Care Improves In the early 1840s, anesthesia was first used to relieve pain during surgery. The use of anesthetics allowed doctors to experiment with operations that had never before been possible.

Yet, throughout the century, hospitals could be dangerous places. Surgery was performed with dirty instruments in dank rooms. Often, a patient would survive an operation, only to die days later of infection. For the poor, being admitted to a hospital was often a death sentence. Wealthy or middle-class patients insisted on treatment in their own homes.

"The very first requirement in a hospital," said British nurse **Florence Nightingale,** "is that it should do the sick no harm." As an army nurse during the Crimean War, Nightingale insisted on better hygiene in field hospitals. After the war, she worked to introduce sanitary measures in British hospitals. She also founded the world's first school of nursing.

The English surgeon **Joseph Lister** discovered how antiseptics prevented infection. He insisted that surgeons sterilize their instruments and wash their hands before operating. Eventually, the use of antiseptics drastically reduced deaths from infection.

 Checkpoint Which factors caused population rates to soar between 1800 and 1900?

WITNESS HISTORY VIDEO

Watch *The Jungle: A View of Industrial America* on the **Witness History Discovery School**™ video program to learn more about city life during the industrial age.

Discovery SCHOOL

City Life Changes

As industrialization progressed, cities came to dominate the West. City life, as old as civilization itself, underwent dramatic changes in Europe and the United States.

City Landscapes Change Growing wealth and industrialization altered the basic layout of European cities. City planners created spacious new squares and boulevards. They lined these avenues with government buildings, offices, department stores, and theaters.

The most extensive **urban renewal,** or rebuilding of the poor areas of a city, took place in Paris in the 1850s. Georges Haussmann, chief planner for Napoleon III, destroyed many tangled medieval streets full of tenement housing. In their place, he built wide boulevards and splendid public buildings. The project put many people to work, decreasing the threat of social unrest. The wide boulevards also made it harder for rebels to put up barricades and easier for troops to reach any part of the city.

Gradually, settlement patterns shifted. In most American cities, the rich lived in pleasant neighborhoods on the outskirts of the city. The poor crowded into slums near the city center, within reach of factories. Trolley lines made it possible to live in one part of the city and work in another.

Sidewalks, Sewers, and Skyscrapers Paved streets made urban areas much more livable. First gas lamps, and then electric street lights <u>illuminated</u> the night, increasing safety. Cities organized police forces and expanded fire protection.

Beneath the streets, sewage systems made cities much healthier places to live. City planners knew that clean water supplies and better sanitation methods were needed to combat epidemics of cholera and tuberculosis. In Paris, sewer lines expanded from 87 miles (139 kilometers) in 1852 to more than 750 miles (1200 kilometers) by 1911. The massive new sewer systems of London and Paris were costly, but they cut death rates dramatically.

By 1900, architects were using steel to construct soaring buildings. American architects like Louis Sullivan pioneered a new structure, the skyscraper. In large cities, single-family middle-class homes gave way to multistory apartment buildings.

Slum Conditions Despite efforts to improve cities, urban life remained harsh for the poor. Some working-class families could afford better clothing, newspapers, or tickets to a music hall. But they went home to small, cramped row houses or tenements in overcrowded neighborhoods.

In the worst tenements, whole families were often crammed into a single room. Unemployment or illness meant lost wages that could ruin a family. High rates of crime and alcoholism were a constant curse. Conditions had improved somewhat from the early Industrial Revolution, but slums remained a fact of city life.

Vocabulary Builder

illuminate—(ih LOO muh nayt) *v.* to light up; to give light to

Jacob Riis, a police reporter, photographer, and social activist in New York City published *How the Other Half Lives* in 1890 in an effort to expose the horrible living conditions of the city slums and tenements. Conditions among the urban working class in Britain (right) were similar to those in New York described by Riis:

Primary Source

❝ Look into any of these houses, everywhere the same . . . . Here is a "flat" or "parlor" and two pitch-dark coops called bedrooms. . . . One, two, three beds are there, if the old boxes and heaps of foul straw can be called by that name; a broken stove with crazy pipe from which the smoke leaks at every joint, a table of rough boards propped up on boxes, piles of rubbish in the corner. The closeness and smell are appalling. How many people sleep here? The woman with the red bandanna shakes her head sullenly, but the bare-legged girl with the bright face counts on her fingers. . . "Six, sir!"❞

Cause and Effect

Causes

- Increased agricultural productivity
- Growing population
- New sources of energy, such as steam and coal
- Growing demand for mass-produced goods
- Improved technology
- Available natural resources, labor, and money
- Strong, stable governments

Industrial Revolution

Immediate Effects

- Rise of factories
- Changes in transportation and communication
- Urbanization
- New methods of production
- Rise of urban working class
- Growth of reform movements

Long-Term Effects

- Growth of labor unions
- Inexpensive new products
- Increased pollution
- Rise of big business
- Expansion of public education
- Expansion of middle class
- Competition for world trade
- Progress in medical care

Connections to Today

- Improvements in world health
- Growth in population
- Industrialization in developing nations
- New energy sources, such as oil and nuclear power
- Environmental pollution
- Efforts to regulate world trade

Analyze Cause and Effect The long-term effects of the Industrial Revolution touched nearly every aspect of life. *Identify two social and two economic effects of the Industrial Revolution.*

The Lure of the City Despite their drawbacks, cities attracted millions. New residents were drawn as much by the excitement as by the promise of work. For tourists, too, cities were centers of action.

Music halls, opera houses, and theaters provided entertainment for every taste. Museums and libraries offered educational opportunities. Sports, from tennis to bare-knuckle boxing, drew citizens of all classes. Few of these enjoyments were available in country villages.

 Checkpoint How did industrialization change the face of cities?

The Working Class Advances

Workers tried to improve the harsh conditions of industrial life. They protested low wages, long hours, unsafe conditions, and the constant threat of unemployment. At first, business owners and governments tried to silence protesters. By midcentury, however, workers began to make progress.

Labor Unions Begin to Grow Workers formed **mutual-aid societies,** self-help groups to aid sick or injured workers. Men and women joined socialist parties or organized unions. The revolutions of 1830 and 1848 left vivid images of worker discontent, which governments could not ignore.

By the late 1800s, most Western countries had granted all men the vote. Workers also won the right to organize unions to bargain on their behalf. Germany legalized labor unions in 1869. Britain, Austria, and France followed. By 1900, Britain had about three million union members, and Germany had about two million. In France, membership grew from 140,000 in 1890 to over a million in 1912.

The main tactic of unions was the strike, or work stoppage. Workers used strikes to demand better working conditions, wage increases, or other benefits from their employers. Violence was often a result of strikes, particularly if employers tried to continue operating their businesses without the striking workers. Employers often called in the police to stop strikes.

Pressured by unions, reformers, and working-class voters, governments passed laws to regulate working conditions. Early laws forbade employers to hire children under the age of ten. Later, laws were passed outlawing child labor entirely and banning the employment of women in mines. Other laws limited work hours and improved safety. By 1909, British coal miners had won an eight-hour day, setting a standard for workers in other countries. In Germany, and then elsewhere, Western governments established old-age pensions, as well as disability insurance for workers who were hurt or became ill. These programs protected workers from poverty once they were no longer able to work.

Family Life and Leisure
With standards of living rising, families could pursue activities such as going to the movies. This 1896 French poster (left) advertises the Cinématographe Lumière (loom YEHR), the most successful motion-picture camera and projector of its day. *What does the clothing of the people in the poster suggest about their social rank?*

Standards of Living Rise Wages varied throughout the industrialized world, with unskilled laborers earning less than skilled workers. Women received less than half the pay of men doing the same work. Farm laborers barely scraped by during the economic slump of the late 1800s. Periods of unemployment brought desperate hardships to industrial workers and helped boost union membership.

Overall, though, standards of living for workers did rise. The standard of living measures the quality and availability of necessities and comforts in a society. Families ate more varied diets, lived in better homes, and dressed in inexpensive, mass-produced clothing. Advances in medicine improved health. Some workers moved to the suburbs, traveling to work on subways and trolleys. Still, the gap between workers and the middle class widened.

✔ **Checkpoint** How did workers try to improve their living and working conditions?

SECTION 2 Assessment

Progress Monitoring *Online*
For: Self-quiz with vocabulary practice
Web Code: nba-2121

Terms, People, and Places
1. For each term, person, or place listed at the beginning of the section, write a sentence explaining its significance.

Note Taking
2. **Reading Skill: Identify Supporting Details** Use your completed outline to answer the Focus Question: How did the Industrial Revolution change life in the cities?

Comprehension and Critical Thinking
3. **Recognize Cause and Effect** Why did the rate of population growth increase in the late 1800s?
4. **Summarize** What are three ways that city life changed in the 1800s?
5. **Analyze Information** What laws helped workers in the late 1800s?
6. **Synthesize Information** How did the rise of the cities challenge the economic and social order of the time?

● **Writing About History**
Quick Write: Brainstorm Possible Solutions Choose one topic from this section, such as the hardships of city life, about which you could write a problem-solution essay. Use the text and your own knowledge to create a list of possible solutions to the problem that you've chosen to write about. Next, organize your list to rank the solutions from most effective to least effective.

Electricity's Impact on Daily Life

Few technologies have transformed daily life as dramatically as electrification. Electric power lit up city streets, helped to improve workplace productivity, revolutionized life at home, and modernized rural farms and businesses. Although electrification began in urban areas of Europe and the United States in the 1880s, it took several decades to spread to rural areas. Electrification remains an ongoing process in developing nations today.

Installing insulators on an electric pole in 1940

Electricity Customers in England and Wales

Year	Customers in Millions
1920	0.9
1930	3.5
1940	9.6
1950	12.0
1960	15.5
1970	18.3
1980	20.3

SOURCE: Department of Trade and Industry, United Kingdom

Advertisement for household electrical appliances

An electric streetcar in England, around 1900

Poster celebrating the use of hydroelectric power in the former Soviet Union

CЛАВА ВЕЛИКОМУ ОКТЯБРЮ!

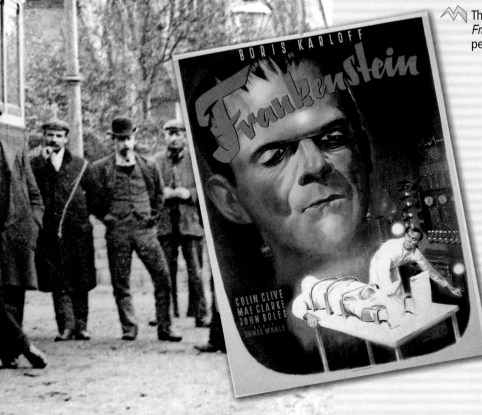

Although only two percent of Japanese homes had electric power in 1907, nearly 90% had electric lighting by 1927. Above, the first electric streetlight in Tokyo's Ginza district draws a crowd.

Electric Generation Stations

Country	Year	Number of Stations
Russia	1913	220
Germany	1913	4,040
Great Britain	1912	568
Sweden	NA*	440
United States	1912	5,221

*NA Not available
SOURCE: *The Electrification of Russia, 1880–1926*

American electric mixer

The 1931 horror film *Frankenstein* exploited people's fear of electricity.

Thinking Critically

1. **Chart Skills** Which country had the fewest number of electric generation stations by 1913? Which country had the largest number? Why was there such a large difference between the two countries?
2. **Draw Conclusions** How did electricity change daily life?

BORIS KARLOFF
Frankenstein

COLIN CLIVE
MAE CLARKE
JOHN BOLES

Women's suffrage banner

Suffragette arrested in London, 1914

WITNESS HISTORY ◀)) AUDIO

Votes for Women

After years of peacefully protesting the British government's refusal to allow women to vote, some activists turned to confrontation:

❝We have been driven to the conclusion that only through legislation can any improvement be effected, and that that legislation can never be effected until we have the same power as men have to bring pressure to bear upon our representatives and upon Governments to give us the necessary legislation. . . . We are here not because we are law-breakers; we are here in our efforts to become law-makers.❞
—Emmeline Pankhurst, October 21, 1908

Focus Question How did the Industrial Revolution change the old social order and long-held traditions in the Western world?

Changing Attitudes and Values

Objectives
- Explain what values shaped the new social order.
- Understand how women and educators sought change.
- Learn how science challenged existing beliefs.

Terms, People, and Places

cult of domesticity	John Dalton
temperance movement	Charles Darwin
Elizabeth Cady Stanton	racism
women's suffrage	social gospel
Sojourner Truth	

Note Taking

Reading Skill: Identify Supporting Details As you read, create a table listing new attitudes and values in the left-hand column. List the supporting details in the right-hand column.

Changes in Social Order and Values	
Issue	**Change**
• New social order	•
• Rights for women	•
•	•

Demand for women's rights was one of many issues that challenged the traditional social order in the late 1800s. By then, in many countries, the middle class—aspiring to upper-class wealth and privilege—increasingly came to dominate society.

A New Social Order Arises

The Industrial Revolution slowly changed the social order in the Western world. For centuries, the two main classes were nobles and peasants. Their roles were defined by their relationship to the land. While middle-class merchants, artisans, and lawyers played important roles, they still had a secondary position in society. With the spread of industry, a more complex social structure emerged.

Three Social Classes Emerge By the late 1800s, Western Europe's new upper class included very rich business families. Wealthy entrepreneurs married into aristocratic families, gaining the status of noble titles. Nobles needed the money brought by the industrial rich to support their lands and lifestyle.

Below this tiny elite, a growing middle class was pushing its way up the social ladder. Its highest rungs were filled with mid-level business people and professionals such as doctors and scientists. With comfortable incomes, they enjoyed a wide range of material goods. Next came the lower middle class, which included teachers and office workers. They struggled to keep up with their "betters."

Workers and peasants were at the base of the social ladder. In highly industrialized Britain, workers made up more than 30 percent of the population in 1900. In Western Europe and the United States, the number of farmworkers dropped, but many families still worked the land. The rural population was higher in eastern and southern Europe, where industrialization was more limited.

Middle-Class Tastes and Values By mid-century, the modern middle class had developed its own way of life. A strict code of etiquette governed social behavior. Rules dictated how to dress for every occasion, how to give a dinner party, how to pay a social call, when to write letters, and how long to mourn for dead relatives.

Parents strictly supervised their children, who were expected to be "seen but not heard." A child who misbehaved was considered to reflect badly on the entire family. Servants, too, were seen as a reflection of their employers. Even a small middle-class household was expected to have at least a cook and a housemaid.

The Ideal Home Within the family, the division of labor between wife and husband changed. Earlier, middle-class women had helped run family businesses out of the home. By the later 1800s, most middle-class husbands went to work in an office or shop. A successful husband was one who earned enough to keep his wife at home. Women spent their time raising children, directing servants, and doing religious or charitable service.

Books, magazines, and popular songs supported a **cult of domesticity** that idealized women and the home. Sayings like "home, sweet home" were stitched into needlework and hung on parlor walls. The ideal woman was seen as a tender, self-sacrificing caregiver who provided a nest for her children and a peaceful refuge for her husband to escape from the hardships of the working world.

This ideal rarely applied to the lower classes. Working-class women labored for low pay in garment factories or worked as domestic servants. Young women might leave domestic service after they married, but often had to seek other employment. Despite long days working for wages, they were still expected to take full responsibility for child care and homemaking.

✔ **Checkpoint** How had the social order changed by the late 1800s?

Tin toys (at right and below), about 1890

Domestic Life in the 1800s

During the Industrial Age, the middle-class nuclear family lived in a large house with a parlor like the one above, or perhaps in one of the new apartment houses. Rooms were crammed with large overstuffed furniture, and paintings and photographs lined the walls. Clothing reflected middle-class tastes for luxury and respectability. For the first time, women began spending more time buying household items than producing them. Women shopped at stores and through mail-order catalogs (below) that were geared toward attracting their business.

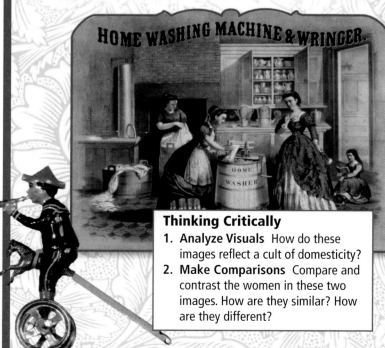

Thinking Critically
1. **Analyze Visuals** How do these images reflect a cult of domesticity?
2. **Make Comparisons** Compare and contrast the women in these two images. How are they similar? How are they different?

313

Women Work for Rights

Some individual women and women's groups protested restrictions on women. They sought a broad range of rights. Across Europe and the United States, politically active women campaigned for fairness in marriage, divorce, and property laws. Women's groups also supported the **temperance movement,** a campaign to limit or ban the use of alcoholic beverages. Temperance leaders argued not only that drinking threatened family life, but that banning it was important for a productive and efficient workforce.

These reformers faced many obstacles. In Europe and the United States, women could not vote. They were barred from most schools and had little, if any, protection under the law. A woman's husband or father controlled all of her property.

Early Voices Before 1850, some women—mostly from the middle class—had campaigned for the abolition of slavery. In the process, they realized the severe restrictions on their own lives. In the United States, Lucretia Mott, **Elizabeth Cady Stanton,** and Susan B. Anthony crusaded against slavery before organizing a movement for women's rights.

Many women broke the barriers that kept them out of universities and professions. By the late 1800s, a few women trained as doctors or lawyers. Others became explorers, researchers, or inventors, often without recognition. For example, Julia Brainerd Hall worked with her brother to develop an aluminum-producing process. Their company became hugely successful, but Charles Hall received almost all of the credit.

The Suffrage Struggle By the late 1800s, married women in some countries had won the right to control their own property. The struggle for political rights proved far more difficult. In the United States, the Seneca Falls Convention of 1848 demanded that women be granted the right to vote. In Europe, groups dedicated to **women's suffrage,** or women's right to vote, emerged in the later 1800s.

Among men, some liberals and socialists supported women's suffrage. In general, though, suffragists faced intense opposition. Some critics claimed that women were too emotional to be allowed to vote. Others argued that women needed to be "protected" from grubby politics or that a woman's place was in the home, not in government. To such claims, **Sojourner Truth,** an African American suffragist, is believed to have replied, "Nobody ever helps me into carriages, or over mudpuddles, or gives me any best place! And ain't I a woman?"

On the edges of the Western world, women made faster strides. In New Zealand, Australia, and some western territories of the United States, women won the vote by the early 1900s. There, women who had "tamed the frontier" alongside men were not dismissed as weak and helpless. In the United States, Wyoming became the first state to grant women the right to vote. In Europe and most of the United States, however, the suffrage struggle succeeded only after World War I.

✓ **Checkpoint**   What were the arguments against women's suffrage?

African American suffragist Sojourner Truth

Growth of Public Education

By the late 1800s, reformers persuaded many governments to set up public schools and require basic education for all children. Teaching "the three Rs"—reading, writing, and 'rithmetic—was thought to produce better citizens. In addition, industrialized societies recognized the need for a literate workforce. Schools taught punctuality, obedience to authority, disciplined work habits, and patriotism. In European schools, children also received basic religious education.

Public Education Improves At first, elementary schools were primitive. Many teachers had little schooling themselves. In rural areas, students attended class only during the times when they were not needed on the farm or in their parents' shops.

By the late 1800s, more and more children were in school, and the quality of elementary education improved. Teachers received training at Normal Schools, where the latest "norms and standards" of educational practices were taught. Beginning in 1879, schools to train teachers were established in France. In England, schooling girls and boys between the ages of five and ten became compulsory after 1881. Also, governments began to expand secondary schools, known as high schools in the United States. In secondary schools, students learned the "classical languages," Latin and Greek, along with history and mathematics.

In general, only middle-class families could afford to have their sons attend these schools, which trained students for more serious study or for government jobs. Middle-class girls were sent to school primarily in the hope that they might marry well and become better wives and mothers. Education for girls did not include subjects such as science, mathematics, or physical education because they were not seen as necessary subjects for girls to learn.

Higher Education Expands Colleges and universities expanded in this period, too. Most university students were the sons of middle- or upper-class families. The university curriculum emphasized ancient history and languages, philosophy, religion, and law. By the late 1800s, universities added courses in the sciences, especially in chemistry and physics. At the same time, engineering schools trained students who would have the knowledge and skills to build the new industrial society.

Some women sought greater educational opportunities. By the 1840s, a few small colleges for women opened, including Bedford College in England and Mount Holyoke in the United States. In 1863, the British reformer Emily Davies campaigned for female students to be allowed to take the entrance examinations for Cambridge University. She succeeded, but as late as 1897, male Cambridge students rioted against granting degrees to women.

✓ **Checkpoint** Why did more children attend school in the late 1800s than before?

Public Education
Before 1870, the only formal education available for British children was in religious schools or "ragged schools," which taught poor children basic skills, such as reading. The Industrial Revolution changed that as it created a growing need for people to be better educated. *How does this 1908 photo of a science class in London illustrate the changes that had taken place in the British educational system?*

Science Takes New Directions

Science in the service of industry brought great changes in the later 1800s. At the same time, researchers advanced startling theories about the natural world. Their new ideas challenged long-held beliefs.

Atomic Theory Develops A crucial breakthrough in chemistry came in the early 1800s when the English Quaker schoolteacher **John Dalton** developed modern atomic theory. The ancient Greeks had <u>speculated</u> that all matter was made of tiny particles called atoms. Dalton showed that each element has its own kind of atoms. Earlier theories put forth the idea that all atoms were basically alike. Dalton also showed how different kinds of atoms combine to make all chemical substances. In 1869, the Russian chemist Dmitri Mendeleyev (men duh LAY ef) drew up a table that grouped elements according to their atomic weights. His table became the basis for the periodic table of elements used today.

Debating the Earth's Age The new science of geology opened avenues of debate. In *Principles of Geology*, Charles Lyell offered evidence to

Vocabulary Builder

<u>speculate</u>—(SPEK yuh layt) *v.* to think about

● **INFOGRAPHIC**

In 1831, the HMS *Beagle* sailed from England on a five-year voyage around the world to survey and chart the oceans. Aboard was 22-year-old Charles Darwin, whose role was to observe, record, and collect samples of rocks, plants, animals, insects, and fossils. Some of the animals that he studied are pictured on the map. The specimens Darwin collected and studied helped him develop his theory of evolution. Controversy over Darwin's theory continues today.

► Clockwise from upper right: blue common Morpho butterfly, bottlenose dolphin, jaguar, Galápagos tortoise

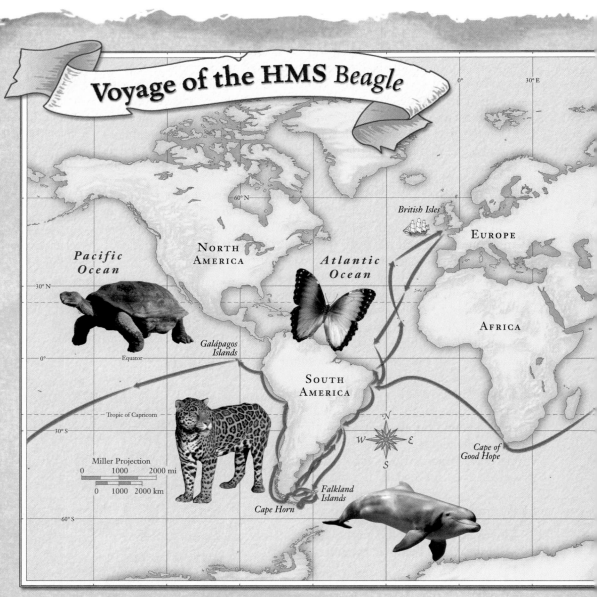

Voyage of the HMS *Beagle*

show that Earth had formed over millions of years. His successors concluded that Earth was at least two billion years old and that life had not appeared until long after Earth was formed. These ideas did not seem to agree with biblical accounts of creation.

Archaeology added other pieces to an emerging debate about the origins of life on Earth. In 1856, workers in Germany accidentally uncovered fossilized Neanderthal bones. Later scholars found fossils of other early modern humans. These archaeologists had limited evidence and often drew mistaken conclusions. But as more discoveries were made, scholars developed new ideas about early humans and their ancestors.

Darwin's Theory of Natural Selection The most controversial new idea came from the British naturalist **Charles Darwin.** In 1859, after years of research, he published *On the Origin of Species*. Darwin argued that all forms of life, including human beings, had evolved into their present state over millions of years. To explain the long, slow process of evolution, he put forward his theory of natural selection.

Darwin adopted Thomas Malthus's idea that all plants and animals produced more offspring than the food supply could support. As a result,

Vocabulary Builder

controversial—(kahn truh VUR shul) *adj.* that is or can be argued about or debated

These four species of finches from the Galápagos Islands have different beaks and eating habits. Darwin (above) theorized that isolation, plus time, and adapting to local conditions, leads to new species.

1. Geospiza magnirostris.
2. Geospiza fortis.
3. Geospiza parvula.
4. Certhidea olivacea.

◄ From top to bottom: black-browed albatross, pink cockatoo, flying fish

History Interactive
For: Interactive map, audio, and more
Web Code: nba-4174

Thinking Critically
1. **Draw Conclusions** How did Darwin's voyage help him develop his theory of natural selection?
2. **Synthesize Information** Why would the isolation of Galápagos Islands attract scientists such as Darwin?

he said, members of each species constantly competed to survive. Natural forces "selected" those with physical traits best adapted to their environment to survive and to pass the trait on to their offspring. This process of natural selection came to be known as "survival of the fittest."

Social Darwinism and Racism Although Darwin himself never promoted any social ideas, some thinkers used his theories to support their own beliefs about society. Applying the idea of survival of the fittest to war and economic competition came to be known as Social Darwinism. Industrial tycoons, argued Social Darwinists, were more "fit" than those they put out of business. War brought progress by weeding out weak nations. Victory was seen as proof of superiority.

Social Darwinism encouraged **racism,** the unscientific belief that one racial group is superior to another. By the late 1800s, many Europeans and Americans claimed that the success of Western civilization was due to the supremacy of the white race. As you will read, such powerful ideas would have a long-lasting impact on world history.

✓ **Checkpoint** How did science begin to challenge existing beliefs in the late 1800s?

Religion in an Urban Age

Despite the challenge of new scientific ideas, religion continued to be a major force in Western society. Christian churches and Jewish synagogues remained at the center of communities. Religious leaders influenced political, social, and educational developments.

The grim realities of industrial life stimulated feelings of compassion and charity. Christian labor unions and political parties pushed for reforms. Individuals, church groups, and Jewish organizations all tried to help the working poor. Catholic priests and nuns set up schools and hospitals in urban slums. Many Protestant churches backed the **social gospel,** a movement that urged Christians to social service. They campaigned for reforms in housing, healthcare, and education.

✓ **Checkpoint** How did religious groups respond to the challenges of industrialization?

The Salvation Army
By 1878, William and Catherine Booth had set up the Salvation Army in London to spread Christian teachings and provide social services. Their daughter, Evangeline (below), stands in front of one the kettles used to gather funds for the needy. *What services did religious organizations provide?*

Progress Monitoring *Online*
For: Self-quiz with vocabulary practice
Web Code: nba-2131

SECTION 3 **Assessment**

Terms, People, and Places

1. For each term, person, or place listed at the beginning of the section, write a sentence explaining its significance.

Note Taking

2. **Reading Skill: Identify Supporting Details** Use your completed table to answer the Focus Question: How did the Industrial Revolution change the old social order and long-held traditions in the Western world?

Comprehension and Critical Thinking

3. **Describe** What are three values associated with the middle class?
4. **Draw Conclusions** Why did the women's movement face strong opposition?
5. **Draw Inferences** Why do you think reformers pushed for free public education?
6. **Synthesize Information** Why did the ideas of Charles Darwin cause controversy?

● **Writing About History**

Quick Write: Write a Thesis Statement
Imagine that you are writing a problem-solution essay on the unequal treatment of women in the 1800s. Based on what you have read in this section, write a thesis statement, or the main idea, for your problem-solution essay.

Albert Bierstadt, *Hetch Hetchy Canyon,* 1875

SECTION

4

WITNESS HISTORY 🔊 AUDIO

Sunset

In the 1800s, many writers turned away from the harsh realities of industrial life to celebrate nature. The English poet William Wordsworth described the peace and beauty of sunset:

❝ It is a beauteous evening, calm and free,
The holy time is quiet as a Nun
Breathless with adoration; the broad sun
Is sinking down in its tranquillity. ❞
—William Wordsworth,
Complete Poetical Works

Focus Question What artistic movements emerged in reaction to the Industrial Revolution?

Arts in the Industrial Age

Objectives

- Understand what themes shaped romantic art, literature, and music.
- Explain how realists responded to the industrialized, urban world.
- Describe how the visual arts changed.

Terms, People, and Places

William Wordsworth	realism
William Blake	Charles Dickens
romanticism	Gustave Courbet
Lord Byron	Louis Daguerre
Victor Hugo	impressionism
Ludwig van Beethoven	Claude Monet
	Vincent van Gogh

Note Taking

Reading Skill: Identify Supporting Details Fill in a table like the one below with details about the artistic movements in the 1800s.

Major Artistic Movements of the 1800s		
Movement	**Goals/ Characteristics**	**Major Figures**
Romanticism	• Rebellion against reason	• Wordsworth
Realism	•	•
Impressionism	•	•

William Wordsworth, along with **William Blake,** Samuel Taylor Coleridge, and Percy Bysshe Shelley among others, was part of a cultural movement called romanticism. From about 1750 to 1850, romanticism shaped Western literature and arts.

The Romantic Revolt Against Reason

Romanticism does not refer to romance in the sense of an affectionate relationship, but rather to an artistic style emphasizing imagination, freedom, and emotion. Romanticism was a reaction to the neoclassical writers of the Enlightenment, who had turned to classical Greek and Roman literature and ideals that stressed order, harmony, reason, and emotional restraint. In contrast to Enlightenment literature, the works of romantic writers included simple, direct language, intense feelings, and a glorification of nature. Artists, composers, and architects were also followers of the movement.

The Romantic Hero Romantic writers created a new kind of hero—a mysterious, melancholy figure who felt out of step with society. "My joys, my grief, my passions, and my powers, / Made me a stranger," wrote Britain's George Gordon, **Lord Byron.** He himself was a larger-than-life figure equal to those he created. After a rebellious, wandering life, he joined Greek forces battling for freedom. When he died of a fever there, his legend bloomed. In fact, public interest in his poetry and adventures was so great that moody, isolated romantic heroes came to be described as "Byronic."

Ludwig van Beethoven

An accomplished musician by age 12, composer Ludwig van Beethoven (1770–1827) agonized over every note of every composition. The result was stunning music that expresses intense emotion. The famous opening of his Fifth Symphony conveys the sense of fate knocking at the door. His Sixth Symphony captures a joyful day in the countryside, interrupted by a violent thunderstorm.

Beethoven's career was haunted by perhaps the greatest tragedy a musician can face. In 1798, he began to lose his hearing. Still, he continued to compose music he could hear only in his mind. **How did Beethoven's music reflect romanticism?**

 AUDIO

The romantic hero often hid a guilty secret and faced a grim destiny. German writer Johann Wolfgang von Goethe (GUR tuh) wrote the dramatic poem *Faust*. The aging scholar Faust makes a pact with the devil, exchanging his soul for youth. After much agony, Faust wins salvation by accepting his duty to help others. In *Jane Eyre,* British novelist Charlotte Brontë weaves a tale about a quiet governess and her brooding, Byronic employer, whose large mansion conceals a terrifying secret.

Inspired by the Past Romantic writers combined history, legend, and folklore. Sir Walter Scott's novels and ballads evoked the turbulent history of Scottish clans or medieval knights. Alexandre Dumas (doo MAH) and **Victor Hugo** re-created France's past in novels like *The Three Musketeers* and *The Hunchback of Notre Dame.*

Architects, too, were inspired by old styles and forms. Churches and other buildings, including the British Parliament, were modeled on medieval Gothic styles. To people living in the 1800s, medieval towers and lacy stonework conjured up images of a glorious past.

Music Stirs Emotions Romantic composers also tried to stir deep emotions. Audiences were moved to laughter or tears at Hungarian Franz Liszt's piano playing. The passionate music of German composer **Ludwig van Beethoven** combined classical forms with a stirring range of sound. He was the first composer to take full advantage of the broad range of instruments in the modern orchestra. In all, Beethoven produced nine symphonies, five piano concertos, a violin concerto, an opera, two masses, and dozens of shorter pieces. To many, he is considered the greatest composer of his day.

Other romantic composers wove traditional folk melodies into their works to glorify their nations' pasts. In his piano works, Frederic Chopin (shoh PAN) used Polish peasant dances to convey the sorrows and joys of people living under foreign occupation.

Romanticism in Art Painters, too, broke free from the discipline and strict rules of the Enlightenment. Landscape painters like J.M.W. Turner sought to capture the beauty and power of nature. Using bold brush strokes and colors, Turner often showed tiny human figures struggling against sea and storm.

Romantics painted many subjects, from simple peasant life to medieval knights to current events. Bright colors conveyed violent energy and emotion. The French painter Eugène Delacroix (deh luh KRWAH) filled his canvases with dramatic action. In *Liberty Leading the People,* the Goddess of Liberty carries the revolutionary tricolor as French citizens rally to the cause.

✔ **Checkpoint** How did romantic writers, musicians, and artists respond to the Enlightenment?

The Call to Realism

By the mid-1800s, a new artistic movement, **realism,** took hold in the West. Realism was an attempt to represent the world as it was, without the sentiment associated with romanticism. Realists often focused their work on the harsh side of life in cities or villages. Many writers and artists were committed to improving the lot of the unfortunates whose lives they depicted.

Novels Depict Grim Reality The English novelist **Charles Dickens** vividly portrayed the lives of slum dwellers and factory workers, including children. In *Oliver Twist,* Dickens tells the story of a nine-year-old orphan raised in a grim poorhouse. In response to a request for more food, Oliver is smacked on the head and sent away to work. Later, he runs away to London. There he is taken in by Fagin, a villain who trains homeless children to become pickpockets. The book shocked many middle-class readers with its picture of poverty, mistreatment of children, and urban crime. Yet Dickens's humor and colorful characters made him one of the most popular novelists in the world.

French novelists also portrayed the ills of their time. Victor Hugo, who moved from romantic to realistic novels, revealed how hunger drove a good man to crime and how the law hounded him ever after in *Les Misérables* (lay miz ehr AHB). The novels of Émile Zola painted an even grimmer picture. In *Germinal*, Zola exposed class warfare in the French mining industry. To Zola's characters, neither the Enlightenment's faith in reason nor the romantic movement's feelings mattered at all.

Realism in Drama Norwegian dramatist Henrik Ibsen brought realism to the stage. His plays attacked the hypocrisy he observed around him. *A Doll's House* shows a woman caught in a straitjacket of social rules. In *An Enemy of the People,* a doctor discovers that the water in a local spa is polluted. Because the town's economy depends on its spa, the citizens denounce the doctor and suppress the truth. Ibsen's realistic dramas had a wide influence in Europe and the United States.

Arts Reject Romantic Ideas Painters also represented the realities of their time. Rejecting the romantic <u>emphasis</u> on imagination, they focused on ordinary subjects, especially working-class men and women. "I cannot paint an angel," said the French realist **Gustave Courbet** (koor BAY) "because I have never seen one." Instead, he painted works such as *The Stone Breakers,* which shows two rough laborers on a country road. Later in the century, *The Gross Clinic,* by American painter Thomas Eakins, shocked viewers with its realistic depiction of an autopsy conducted in a medical classroom.

✔️ **Checkpoint** How did the realism movement differ from the romantic movement?

Realism in the Arts

A Thomas Eakins's 1875 painting *The Gross Clinic* depicts the realism of medical school where students learn by performing autopsies. The artist included many realistic elements such as the surgical tools in the foreground and the reaction of the spectator at the far left.

B Edvard Munch's 1898 painting shows an impression of Henrik Ibsen filled with psychological realism, similar to that found in Ibsen's plays.

C This 1896 portrait of Ibsen shows photographic realism in the playwright's appearance and expression.

D Victor Hugo's 1862 novel *Les Misérables* describes the reality of poverty, hunger, and corruption among the poor in Paris. This 1886 poster depicts the novel's main characters: the convict Jean Valjean at the center, and Cosette, the girl he adopts, at the right.

Vocabulary Builder

<u>emphasis</u>—(EM fuh sis) *n.* special attention given to something to make it stand out

The Visual Arts Take New Directions

By the 1840s, a new art form, photography, was emerging. **Louis Daguerre** (dah GEHR) in France and William Fox Talbot in England had improved on earlier technologies to produce successful photographs. At first, many photos were stiff, posed portraits of middle-class families or prominent people. Other photographs reflected the romantics' fascination with faraway places.

In time, photographers used the camera to present the grim realities of life. During the American Civil War, Mathew B. Brady preserved a vivid, realistic record of the corpse-strewn battlefields. Other photographers showed the harsh conditions in industrial factories or slums.

The Impressionists Photography posed a challenge to painters. Why try for realism, some artists asked, when a camera could do the same thing better? By the 1870s, a group of painters took art in a new direction, seeking to capture the first fleeting impression made by a scene or object on the viewer's eye. The new movement, known as **impressionism,** took root in Paris, capital of the Western art world.

Since the Renaissance, painters had carefully finished their paintings so that no brush strokes showed. But impressionists like **Claude Monet** (moh NAY) and Edgar Degas (day GAH) brushed strokes of color side by side without any blending. According to new scientific studies of optics, the human eye would mix these patches of color.

By concentrating on visual impressions rather than realism, artists achieved a fresh view of familiar subjects. Monet, for example, painted the cathedral at Rouen (roo AHN), France, dozens of times from the same angle, capturing how it looked in different lights at different times of day.

The Postimpressionists Later painters, called postimpressionists, developed a variety of styles. Georges Seurat (suh RAH) arranged small dots of color to define the shapes of objects. **Vincent van Gogh** experimented with sharp brush lines and bright colors. His unique brushwork lent a dreamlike quality to everyday subjects. Paul Gauguin (goh GAN) also developed a bold, personal style. In his paintings, people look flat, as in "primitive" folk art. But his brooding colors and black outlining of shapes convey <u>intense</u> feelings and images.

 Checkpoint How did photography influence the development of painting?

Postimpressionism
This self-portrait of Dutch painter Vincent van Gogh shows his bandaged ear, which he cut off in a state of depression. *What postimpressionist features are demonstrated in Van Gogh's self-portrait?*

Vocabulary Builder
intense—(in TENS) *adj.* very strong or deep

SECTION **4** Assessment

Progress Monitoring *Online*
For: Self-quiz with vocabulary practice
Web Code: nba-2141

Terms, People, and Places

1. For each term, person, or place listed at the beginning of the section, write a sentence explaining its significance.

Note Taking

2. **Reading Skill: Identify Supporting Details** Use your completed table to answer the Focus Question: What artistic movements emerged in reaction to the Industrial Revolution?

Comprehension and Critical Thinking

3. **Summarize** What are three subjects romantics favored?

4. **Draw Conclusions** What did Courbet mean when he said, "I cannot paint an angel because I have never seen one"? Do you agree with his attitude? Explain.

5. **Recognize Cause and Effect** In what ways were the new artistic styles of the 1800s a reaction to changes in society?

● **Writing About History**

Quick Write: Support a Solution Based on what you've read, list supporting information, such as details, data, and facts, for the following thesis statement of a problem-solution essay: Artists in the 1800s portrayed subjects realistically to make the public more aware of some of the grim problems of life in industrialized nations.

Impressionism

Impressionism was one of the most important art movements of the 1800s. It marked a departure from tradition, both in subject matter and painting technique. Artists sought to depict the human eye's first perception of a scene. Characterized by the use of unmixed primary colors and small, visible brush strokes, impressionism attempted to show the effects of direct or reflected light. Impressionist artists often painted outdoors for maximum effect.

▲ Claude Monet, *Impression: Sunrise*, 1872
In the 1800s, "The Salon," an annual exhibition that accepted only traditional paintings, dominated the Parisian art scene. In 1874, a group of artists held their own exhibition at a local photographer's studio. Claude Monet's *Impression: Sunrise* was one of the works displayed. Monet's painting demonstrates several characteristics of impressionist work, including short, visible brush strokes and an idealized depiction of a landscape.

▲ Edgar Degas, *The Dancing Class*, c. 1873–1875
This painting by Edgar Degas shows the influence of the newly invented camera. Impressionists' paintings moved away from the traditional placement of subjects in favor of off-center compositions. Figures were also painted on the outermost parts of the canvas. Much like photographs, impressionist paintings were often snapshots of life rather than elaborate portraits.

▲ Berthe Morisot, *Eugène Manet and His Daughter at Bougival*, c. 1881
French impressionist painter Berthe Morisot also participated in the first impressionist exhibit in 1874. Morisot's delicate, subtle paintings often portrayed her family and friends—as this one of her husband and daughter.

Thinking Critically
1. **Summarize** How did impressionism depart from tradition?
2. **Draw Conclusions** What are the advantages and disadvantages of painting outdoors?

Quick Study Guide

■ Key People

Inventors/Developers
Henry Bessemer—steel processing
Michael Faraday—dynamo
Thomas Edison—electric light bulb
Gottlieb Daimler—automobile
Samuel F.B. Morse—telegraph
Alexander Graham Bell—telephone
Guglielmo Marconi—radio

Scientists
Louis Pasteur—vaccinations, pasteurization
Joseph Lister—antiseptics
John Dalton—modern atomic theory
Charles Darwin—theory of natural selection

Reformers
Florence Nightingale—sanitary measures in hospitals
Elizabeth Cady Stanton—women's rights
Susan B. Anthony—women's rights
William and Catherine Booth—Salvation Army

Artists, Writers, and Composers
William Wordsworth—romantic writer
Lord Byron—romantic writer
Ludwig van Beethoven—romantic composer
Charles Dickens—realist writer
Émile Zola—realist writer
Gustave Courbet—realist painter
Claude Monet—impressionist painter
Edgar Degas—impressionist painter
Vincent van Gogh—postimpressionist painter

■ Life Expectancy in the Industrial Age

Average Life Expectancy in Selected Industrial Areas, 1850–1910		
Year	Male	Female
1850	40.3 years	42.8 years
1870	42.3 years	44.7 years
1890	45.8 years	48.5 years
1910	52.7 years	56.0 years

SOURCE: E.A. Wrigley, *Population and History* (based on data for parts of Western Europe and the United States)

■ Impact of the Industrial Revolution

Key Effects of the Industrial Revolution		
Industrialization	**Urbanization**	**Social Structure**
• Germany, France, and the U.S. join Great Britain as industrial powers. • Rise of factories; new production methods • Advances in transportation and communication • Rise of big business • Growth of labor unions	• Advances in medicine and science • Population growth due to falling death rates • Higher standard of living	• Three social classes emerge • Middle class expands • Rise of urban working class • Reform movements grow • Public education expands

■ Key Events of the Industrial Revolution

Early 1800s
Romanticism begins to shape Western art and literature.

1807
First factories open in Belgium, setting off the Industrial Revolution on the European continent.

1839
French inventor Louis Daguerre perfects an effective method of photography.

Chapter Events
Global Events

| 1800 | 1815 | 1830 | 1845 |

1819
Simón Bolívar establishes Gran Colombia.

1842
The Treaty of Nanjing gives Britain trading rights in China.

Concept Connector

■ Cumulative Review

Record the answers to the questions below on your Concept Connector worksheets.

1. **Science** Compare the changes that took place during the Scientific Revolution of the 1500s and 1600s to the scientific ideas of the late 1800s. Think about the following:
   - how new discoveries changed the way that people viewed the world during each period
   - how religious leaders responded during each period

2. **Technology** During the High Middle Ages, an agricultural revolution brought about great change. Create a chart comparing the technological changes that took place from about 1000 to 1300 to the changes that took place during the Industrial Revolution. Think about the following:
   - the introduction of new technology
   - how new technology sparked economic growth
   - how new technology changed people's lives

3. **Technology** How did the second phase of the Industrial Revolution during the late 1800s differ from the first phase during the early 1800s? Create a chart comparing the two phases in terms of these factors:
   - countries involved
   - changes in transportation
   - changes in communication
   - sources of energy/power
   - major inventions

4. **Economic Systems** The revival of trade during the High Middle Ages resulted in a commercial revolution. Hundreds of years later, the Industrial Revolution brought about changes in business. In what ways were the changes during the two periods similar? Think about the following:
   - new business practices
   - role of guilds and labor unions

■ Connections to Today

1. **Technology: Power Outage** In August 2003, people in Canada and the northeastern part of the United States found out just how much their lives depend on electricity. When an energy plant unexpectedly shut down, it led to the largest power outage in North America's history—more than 50 million people were left in the dark.

   Lights and elevators stopped working in skyscrapers, and workers had to carefully make their way down darkened stairways. Others were trapped on trains or stuck in traffic jams caused by inoperable traffic lights. Airports experienced extended delays. Business slowed because Internet servers were not functioning properly, phone systems crashed, computerized cash registers could not ring up sales, and ATMs went down. With today's linked power grids, the possibility of more massive blackouts that disrupt the lives of millions of people across county, state, and international lines is very real. What economic effects might a power outage have?

2. **Belief Systems: Social Darwinism** British philosopher and Social Darwinist Herbert Spencer coined the phrase "survival of the fittest," meaning that the strong grow in power and influence over the weaker members of society. Social Darwinists promoted the beliefs that the group was more important than the individual, and that privileged, powerful people had the right to make decisions about those whom they believed were inferior.

   These ideas had horrific consequences for people of color throughout the world. For example, they led to unethical medical experimentation, abuse of the mentally ill, and countless acts of violence toward people of "different" religions, races, and ethnicities. To what degree do you think Social Darwinism is still a part of our culture today?

| 1859 **Charles Darwin publishes On the Origin of Species. Many religious leaders denounce his theory of evolution.** | 1869 **Germany legalizes labor unions.** | | 1903 **Wilbur and Orville Wright conduct tests of their airplane at Kitty Hawk, North Carolina.** | **History Interactive** For: Interactive timeline Web Code: nbp-2151 |

| **1860** | **1875** | **1890** | **1905** |

| 1861 **Tsar Alexander II emancipates Russian serfs.** | 1884 **European nations carve up Africa at the Berlin Conference.** | 1898 **Spanish-American War is fought.** | 1914 **The Panama Canal opens.** |

Chapter Assessment

Terms, People, and Places

Choose the italicized term in parentheses that best completes each sentence.

1. A *(dynamo/cartel)* is a machine that generates electricity.
2. Business owners sell *(corporations/stock),* or shares in their companies, to investors.
3. *(Racism/Germ theory)* is the belief that one racial group is superior to another.
4. The *(cult of domesticity/standard of living)* measures the quality and availability of necessities and comforts in a society.
5. A self-help group to aid sick or injured workers is called a *(social gospel/mutual-aid society).*
6. *(Impressionism/Realism)* attempted to represent the world as it was.

Main Ideas

Section 1 (pp. 298–304)

7. Describe the impact of new technology on industry, transportation, and communication.
8. Why did big businesses emerge during the Industrial Revolution?

Section 2 (pp. 305–309)

9. How did the Industrial Revolution improve city life? How did it make city life worse?

Section 3 (pp. 312–318)

10. How did the Industrial Revolution influence the class structure of Western Europe?
11. What existing beliefs did new scientific theories challenge?

Section 4 (pp. 319–322)

12. How did artists, composers, writers, and others respond to industrialization?

Chapter Focus Question

13. What were the technological, social, and economic effects of the Industrial Revolution?

Critical Thinking

14. **Geography and History** How did technology affect the movement of people and goods in the 1800s and in the early 1900s?
15. **Identify Point of View** How might each of the following have viewed the Industrial Revolution: (a) an inventor, (b) an entrepreneur, (c) a worker?
16. **Draw Conclusions** Do you think women's lives improved as a result of the Industrial Revolution? Why or why not?
17. **Draw Inferences** Referring to *Oliver Twist,* Dickens wrote that "to show [criminals] as they really are, for ever skulking uneasily through the dirtiest paths of life . . . would be a service to society." How does his claim reflect the goals of realism?
18. **Summarize** How would you describe Victorian middle-class values?
19. **Demonstrate Reasoned Judgment** Some historians have suggested that we are now in a third phase of the Industrial Revolution, characterized by information technology and computers. Do you agree or disagree? Explain the reasons for your answer.
20. **Analyzing Visuals** Which artistic movement of the 1800s does *Cathedral of Rouen, Afternoon* (right) by Claude Monet reflect: romanticism, realism, or impressionism? Explain your reasoning.

● Writing About History

Writing a Problem-Solution Essay The second Industrial Revolution ushered in a period of great change to the modern world. But it brought with it problems that people had not experienced before, such as hardships in cities and powerful monopolies controlling big business. Write a problem-solution essay about one of these topics or choose your own topic relating to the content in this chapter.

Prewriting

• Choose the topic that interests you most. If you have a personal interest in a problem and its solution, your essay will be easier to develop.

• Narrow your topic.
• Make a list of details, facts, and examples that proves there is a problem. Then, identify the specific parts of your solution.

Drafting

• Develop a working thesis and choose information to support it.
• Organize the paragraphs in a logical order so that readers can understand the solution you propose.

Revising

• Use the guidelines for revising your essay on page SH12 of the Writing Handbook.

Document-Based Assessment

Birth of the Modern City

The birth of the modern city helped to define the Industrial Age. The documents below show that the modern city represented progress, but not without costs.

Document A

"The first shock of a great earthquake had, just at that period, rent the whole neighborhood to its center. Traces of its course were visible on every side. Houses were knocked down; streets broken through and stopped; deep pits and trenches dug in the ground; enormous heaps of earth and clay thrown up; buildings that were undermined and shaking, propped by great beams of wood. . . . In short, the yet unfinished and unopened Railroad was in progress; and, from the very core of all this dire disorder, trailed smoothly away, upon its mighty course of civilization and improvement."

—from ***Dombey and Son*** by Charles Dickens

Document B

Selected Inventions, 1824–1911	
Cement	1824
Locomotive	1830
Dynamite	1866
Telephone	1876
Cash register	1879
Electric trolley car	1884–1887
Steel alloy	1891
Self-starting auto	1911

SOURCE: *The World Almanac*, 2004

Document C

Population of Major Cities		
City	1850	1900
Berlin, Germany	419,000	1,889,000
London, England	2,685,000	6,586,000
Moscow, Russia	365,000	989,000
New York, United States	696,000	3,437,000
Paris, France	1,053,000	2,714,000

SOURCE: *International Historical Statistics*

Document D

Brooklyn Bridge, 1883

Analyzing Documents

Use your knowledge of the industrial age and Documents A, B, C, and D to answer questions 1–4.

1. The cause of the earthquake described in Document A was
   A an underground fault in London.
   B poorly constructed tall buildings.
   C construction of a railroad.
   D deep pits and trenches in the ground.

2. Which inventions from Document B had the most impact on New York City at the time Document D was created?
   A trolley cars, steel alloy, cash registers
   B dynamite, telephones, cash registers
   C cement, locomotives, telephones
   D cement, locomotives, dynamite

3. Which trend does Document C illustrate?
   A the shift in population from Europe to the United States
   B the shift in population from East Coast to West Coast
   C the increase in population of cities
   D the decrease in rural population

4. **Writing Task** What were the most significant features of the modern city? Why? Use the information from Documents A through D, as well as what you've learned in this chapter, to support your opinion.

The Price of Nationalism

The last half of the 1800s can be called the Age of Nationalism. By harnessing national feeling, European leaders fought ruthlessly to create strong, unified nations. Under Otto von Bismarck, Germany emerged as Europe's most powerful empire—but at a considerable cost. In his 1870 diary, Crown Prince Friedrich wrote:

66 [Germany had once been admired as a] nation of thinkers and philosophers, poets and artists, idealists and enthusiasts . . . [but now the world saw Germany as] a nation of conquerors and destroyers, to which no pledged word, no treaty, is sacred. . . . We are neither loved nor respected, but only feared. 99

Listen to the Witness History audio to learn more about nationalism.

◄ Otto von Bismarck (center), chancellor of Germany, meets with European and Turkish leaders at the Congress of Berlin.

Helmet from the Franco-Prussian war era

Chapter Preview

Chapter Focus Question What effects did nationalism and the demand for reform have in Europe?

UNIONE . FORZA E LIBERTA !!

Flag of Italy, 1833

Section 1
Building a German Nation

Section 2
Germany Strengthens

Section 3
Unifying Italy

Section 4
Nationalism Threatens Old Empires

Soviet stamp commemorating the Decembrist Revolt

Section 5
Russia: Reform and Reaction

Note Taking Study Guide *Online*
For: Note Taking and Concept Connector worksheets
Web Code: nbd-2201

Otto von Bismarck

Franco-Prussian war era helmet

WITNESS HISTORY ◀))) AUDIO

Blood and Iron

Prussian legislators waited restlessly for Otto von Bismarck to speak. He wanted them to vote for more money to build up the army. Liberal members opposed the move. Bismarck rose and dismissed their concerns:

❝ Germany does not look to Prussia's liberalism, but to her power. . . . The great questions of the day are not to be decided by speeches and majority resolutions—that was the mistake of 1848 and 1849—but by blood and iron! ❞
—Otto von Bismarck, 1862

Focus Question How did Otto von Bismarck, the chancellor of Prussia, lead the drive for German unity?

Building a German Nation

Objectives
- Identify several events that promoted German unity during the early 1800s.
- Explain how Bismarck unified Germany.
- Analyze the basic political organization of the new German empire.

Terms, People, and Places

Otto von Bismarck   annex
chancellor   kaiser
Realpolitik   Reich

Note Taking

Reading Skill: Recognize Sequence Keep track of the sequence of events that led to German unification by completing a chart like the one below. Add more boxes as needed.

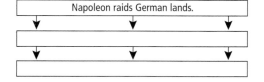

Napoleon raids German lands.

Otto von Bismarck delivered his "blood and iron" speech in 1862. It set the tone for his future policies. Bismarck was determined to build a strong, unified German state, with Prussia at its head.

Taking Initial Steps Toward Unity

In the early 1800s, German-speaking people lived in a number of small and medium-sized states as well as in Prussia and the Austrian Hapsburg empire. Napoleon's invasions unleashed new forces in these territories.

Napoleon Raids German Lands Between 1806 and 1812, Napoleon made important territorial changes in German-speaking lands. He annexed lands along the Rhine River for France. He dissolved the Holy Roman Empire by forcing the emperor of Austria to agree to the lesser title of king. He also organized a number of German states into the Rhine Confederation.

At first, some Germans welcomed the French emperor as a hero with enlightened, modern policies. He encouraged freeing the serfs, made trade easier, and abolished laws against Jews. However, not all Germans appreciated Napoleon and his changes. As people fought to free their lands from French rule, they began to demand a unified German state.

Napoleon's defeat did not resolve the issue. At the Congress of Vienna, Metternich pointed out that a united Germany would require dismantling the government of each German state. Instead, the peacemakers created the German Confederation, a weak alliance headed by Austria.

Economic Changes Promote Unity In the 1830s, Prussia created an economic union called the *Zollverein* (TSAWL fur yn). It dismantled tariff barriers between many German states. Still, Germany remained politically fragmented.

In 1848, liberals meeting in the Frankfurt Assembly again demanded German political unity. They offered the throne of a united German state to Frederick William IV of Prussia. The Prussian ruler, however, rejected the notion of a throne offered by "the people."

✓ **Checkpoint** What was the German Confederation?

Bismarck Unites Germany

Otto von Bismarck succeeded where others had failed. Bismarck came from Prussia's Junker (YOONG kur) class, made up of conservative landowning nobles. Bismarck first served Prussia as a diplomat in Russia and France. In 1862, King William I made him prime minister. Within a decade, the new prime minister had become **chancellor,** or the highest official of a monarch, and had used his policy of "blood and iron" to unite the German states under Prussian rule.

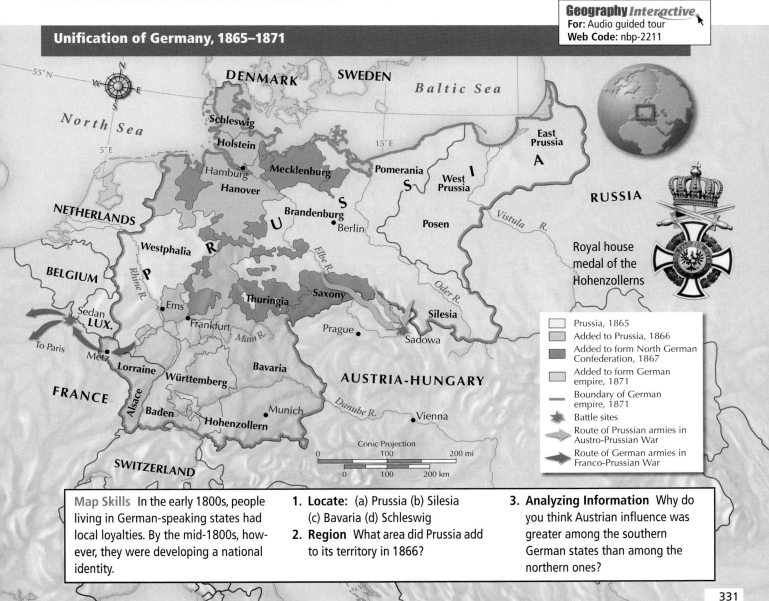

Geography *Interactive*
For: Audio guided tour
Web Code: nbp-2211

Unification of Germany, 1865–1871

Royal house medal of the Hohenzollerns

Prussia, 1865
Added to Prussia, 1866
Added to form North German Confederation, 1867
Added to form German empire, 1871
Boundary of German empire, 1871
★ Battle sites
Route of Prussian armies in Austro-Prussian War
Route of German armies in Franco-Prussian War

Map Skills In the early 1800s, people living in German-speaking states had local loyalties. By the mid-1800s, however, they were developing a national identity.

1. **Locate:** (a) Prussia (b) Silesia (c) Bavaria (d) Schleswig
2. **Region** What area did Prussia add to its territory in 1866?
3. **Analyzing Information** Why do you think Austrian influence was greater among the southern German states than among the northern ones?

Master of Realpolitik Bismarck's success was due in part to his strong will. He was a master of **Realpolitik** (ray AHL poh lee teek), or realistic politics based on the needs of the state. In the case of Realpolitik, power was more important than principles.

Although Bismarck was the architect of German unity, he was not really a German nationalist. His primary loyalty was to the Hohenzollerns (hoh un TSAWL urnz), the ruling dynasty of Prussia, who represented a powerful, traditional monarchy. Through unification, he hoped to bring more power to the Hohenzollerns.

Strengthening the Army As Prussia's prime minister, Bismarck first moved to build up the Prussian army. Despite his "blood and iron" speech, the liberal legislature refused to vote for funds for the military. In response, Bismarck strengthened the army with money that had been collected for other purposes. With a powerful, well-equipped military, he was then ready to pursue an aggressive foreign policy. Over the next decade, Bismarck led Prussia into three wars. Each war increased Prussian prestige and power and paved the way for German unity.

Prussia Declares War With Denmark and Austria Bismarck's first maneuver was to form an alliance in 1864 with Austria. Prussia and Austria then seized the provinces of Schleswig and Holstein from Denmark. After a brief war, Prussia and Austria "liberated" the two provinces and divided up the spoils. Austria was to administer Holstein and Prussia was to administer Schleswig.

In 1866, Bismarck invented an excuse to attack Austria. The Austro-Prussian War lasted just seven weeks and ended in a decisive Prussian victory. Prussia then **annexed,** or took control of, several other north German states.

Bismarck dissolved the Austrian-led German Confederation and created a new confederation dominated by Prussia. Austria and four other southern German states remained independent. Bismarck's motives, as always, were strictly practical. Attempting to conquer Austria might have meant a long and risky war for Prussia.

War and Power

In 1866, Field Marshal Helmuth von Moltke analyzed the importance of Prussia's war against Austria. Why, according to von Moltke, did Prussia go to war against Austria?

Primary Source

66 The war of 1866 was entered on not because the existence of Prussia was threatened, nor was it caused by public opinion and the voice of the people; it was a struggle, long foreseen and calmly prepared for, recognized as a necessity by the Cabinet, not for territorial expansion, for an extension of our domain, or for material advantage, but for an ideal end—the establishment of power. Not a foot of land was exacted from Austria. . . . Its center of gravity lay out of Germany; Prussia's lay within it. Prussia felt itself called upon and strong enough to assume the leadership of the German races. 99

Austro-Prussian War painting (above) and a medal of victory (left)

France Declares War on Prussia In France, the Prussian victory over Austria angered Napoleon III. A growing rivalry between the two nations led to the Franco-Prussian War of 1870.

Germans recalled only too well the invasions of Napoleon I some 60 years earlier. Bismarck played up the image of the French menace to spur German nationalism. For his part, Napoleon III did little to avoid war, hoping to mask problems at home with military glory.

Bismarck furthered the crisis by rewriting and then releasing to the press a telegram that reported on a meeting between King William I and the French ambassador. Bismarck's editing of the "Ems dispatch" made it seem that William I had insulted the Frenchman. Furious, Napoleon III declared war on Prussia, as Bismarck had hoped.

A superior Prussian force, supported by troops from other German states, smashed the badly organized and poorly supplied French soldiers. Napoleon III, old and ill, surrendered within a few weeks. France had to accept a humiliating peace.

✔ **Checkpoint**   What techniques did Bismarck use to unify the German states?

Vocabulary Builder

edit—(ED it) *v.* to make additions, deletions, or other changes to a piece of writing

Birth of the German Empire

Delighted by the victory over France, princes from the southern German states and the North German Confederation persuaded William I of Prussia to take the title **kaiser** (KY zur), or emperor. In January 1871, German nationalists celebrated the birth of the second **Reich,** or empire. They called it that because they considered it heir to the Holy Roman Empire.

A constitution drafted by Bismarck set up a two-house legislature. The Bundesrat (BOON dus raht), or upper house, was appointed by the rulers of the German states. The Reichstag (RYKS tahg), or lower house, was elected by universal male suffrage. Because the Bundesrat could veto any decisions of the Reichstag, real power remained in the hands of the emperor and his chancellor.

✔ **Checkpoint**   How was the new German government, drafted by Bismarck, structured?

SECTION 1 Assessment

Progress Monitoring *Online*
For: Self-quiz with vocabulary practice
Web Code: nba-2211

Terms, People, and Places

1. For each term, person, or place listed at the beginning of the section, write a sentence explaining its significance.

Note Taking

2. **Reading Skill: Recognize Sequence** Use your completed chart to answer the Focus Question: How did Otto von Bismarck, the chancellor of Prussia, lead the drive for German unity?

Comprehension and Critical Thinking

3. **Summarize** What territorial and economic changes promoted German unity?

4. **Analyze Information** Identify three examples of Bismarck's use of Realpolitik.

5. **Draw Conclusions** How did the emperor and his chancellor retain power in the new German government?

● **Writing About History**

Quick Write: Generate Arguments Choose one topic from this section that you could use to write a persuasive essay. For example, you could write about whether Germany's war against Austria was justifiable. Make sure that the topic you choose to write about has at least two sides that could provoke an argument.

French bayonet

WITNESS HISTORY 🔊 AUDIO

The New German Empire

In 1870, German historian Heinrich von Treitschke (vawn TRYCH kuh) wrote a newspaper article demanding the annexation of Alsace and Lorraine from France. A year later, annexation became a condition of the peace settlement in the Franco-Prussian War:

66 The sense of justice to Germany demands the lessening of France. . . . These territories are ours by the right of the sword, and . . . [by] virtue of a higher right—the right of the German nation, which will not permit its lost children to remain strangers to the German Empire. 99

Focus Question How did Germany increase its power after unifying in 1871?

Prussian soldiers at Versailles

Germany Strengthens

Objectives

- Describe how Germany became an industrial giant.
- Explain why Bismarck was called the Iron Chancellor.
- List the policies of Kaiser William II.

Terms, People, and Places

Kulturkampf
William II
social welfare

Note Taking

Reading Skill: Recognize Sequence Keep track of the sequence of events described in this section by completing a chart like the one below. List the causes that led to a strong German nation.

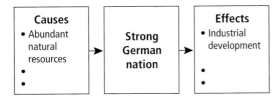

Causes		Effects
• Abundant natural resources	Strong German nation	• Industrial development
•		•
•		•

In January 1871, German princes gathered in the glittering Hall of Mirrors at the French palace of Versailles. They had just defeated Napoleon III in the Franco-Prussian War. Once home to French kings, the palace seemed the perfect place to proclaim the new German empire. To the winners as well as to the losers, the symbolism was clear: French domination of Europe had ended. Germany was now the dominant power in Europe.

Germany Becomes an Industrial Giant

In the aftermath of unification, the German empire emerged as the industrial giant of the European continent. By the late 1800s, German chemical and electrical industries were setting the standard worldwide. Among the European powers, German shipping was second only to Britain's.

Making Economic Progress Germany, like Great Britain, possessed several of the factors that made industrialization possible. Germany's spectacular growth was due in part to ample iron and coal resources, the basic ingredients for industrial development. A disciplined and educated workforce also helped the economy. The German middle class and educated professionals helped to create a productive and efficient society that prided itself on its sense of responsibility and deference to authority. Germany's rapidly growing population—from 41 million in 1871 to 67 million by 1914—also provided a huge home market along with a larger supply of industrial workers.

The new nation also benefited from earlier progress. During the 1850s and 1860s, Germans had founded large companies and built many railroads. The house of Krupp (kroop) boomed after 1871, becoming an enormous industrial complex that produced steel and weapons for a world market. Between 1871 and 1914, the business tycoon August Thyssen (TEES un) built a small steel factory of 70 workers into a giant empire with 50,000 employees. Optics was another important industry. German industrialist and inventor Carl Zeiss built a company that became known for its telescopes, microscopes, and other optical equipment.

Promoting Scientific and Economic Development German industrialists were the first to see the value of applied science in developing new products such as <u>synthetic</u> chemicals and dyes. Industrialists, as well as the government, supported research and development in the universities and hired trained scientists to solve technological problems in their factories.

The German government also promoted economic development. After 1871, it issued a single currency for Germany, reorganized the banking system, and <u>coordinated</u> railroads built by the various German states. When a worldwide depression hit in the late 1800s, Germany raised tariffs to protect home industries from foreign competition. The leaders of the new German empire were determined to maintain economic strength as well as military power.

Vocabulary Builder

<u>synthetic</u>—(sin THET ik) *adj.* prepared or made artificially

Vocabulary Builder

<u>coordinate</u>—(koh AWR dih nate) *v.* to design or adjust so as to have harmonious action

✓ **Checkpoint** What factors did Germany possess that made industrialization possible there?

The Iron Chancellor

As chancellor of the new German empire, Bismarck pursued several foreign-policy goals. He wanted to keep France weak and isolated while building strong links with Austria and Russia. He respected British naval power but did not seek to compete in that arena. "Water rats," he said, "do not fight with land rats." Later, however, he would take a more aggressive stand against Britain as the two nations competed for overseas colonies.

BIOGRAPHY

Otto von Bismarck

Otto von Bismarck (1815–1898) spent his early years on his father's country estate. He worked briefly as a civil servant, but found the work boring. At 24, Bismarck resigned his post as a bureaucrat. "My ambition strives more to command than to obey," the independent-minded young man explained.

The resignation did not end his career in government. While he was a delegate to a United Diet that was called by Prussian King Frederick William IV, Bismarck's conservative views and passionate speeches in defense of government policies won him the support of the king. He then served as a diplomat to the German Federation. He became chancellor of the German empire in 1871, a position he held for 19 years. **What path did Bismarck take to win political power?**

A Political Game of Chess This political cartoon shows Otto von Bismarck and Pope Pius IX trying to checkmate each other in a game of chess.

1. How does this cartoon reflect the relationship between Bismarck and the Catholic Church?
2. How did the conflict between church and state affect German politics in the 1870s?

On the domestic front, Bismarck applied the same ruthless methods he had used to achieve unification. The Iron Chancellor, as he was called, sought to erase local loyalties and crush all opposition to the imperial state. He targeted two groups—the Catholic Church and the Socialists. In his view, both posed a threat to the new German state.

Campaign Against the Church After unification, Catholics made up about a third of the German population. Bismarck, who was Lutheran, distrusted Catholics—especially the clergy—whose first loyalty, he believed, was to the pope instead of to Germany.

In response to what he saw as the Catholic threat, Bismarck launched the *Kulturkampf* (kool TOOR kahmpf), or "battle for civilization," which lasted from 1871 to 1878. His goal was to make Catholics put loyalty to the state above allegiance to the Church. The chancellor had laws passed that gave the state the right to supervise Catholic education and approve the appointment of priests. Other laws closed some religious orders, expelled the Jesuits from Prussia, and made it compulsory for couples to be married by civil authority.

Bismarck's moves against the Catholic Church backfired. The faithful rallied behind the Church, and the Catholic Center party gained strength in the Reichstag. A realist, Bismarck saw his mistake and worked to make peace with the Church.

Campaign Against the Socialists Bismarck also saw a threat to the new German empire in the growing power of socialism. By the late 1870s, German Marxists had organized the Social Democratic party, which called for parliamentary democracy and laws to improve conditions for the working class. Bismarck feared that socialists would undermine the loyalty of German workers and turn them toward revolution. Following a failed assassination plot against the kaiser, Bismarck had laws passed that dissolved socialist groups, shut down their newspapers, and banned their meetings. Once again, repression backfired. Workers were unified in support of the socialist cause.

Bismarck then changed course. He set out to woo workers away from socialism by sponsoring laws to protect them. By the 1890s, Germans had health and accident insurance as well as old-age insurance to provide retirement benefits. Thus, under Bismarck, Germany was a pioneer in social reform. Its system of economic safeguards became the model for other European nations.

Although workers benefited from Bismarck's plan, they did not abandon socialism. In fact, the Social Democratic party continued to grow in strength. By 1912, it held more seats in the Reichstag than any other party. Yet Bismarck's program showed that conditions for workers could be improved without the upheaval of a revolution. Later, Germany and other European nations would build on Bismarck's social policies, greatly increasing government's role in providing for the needs of its citizens.

✔ **Checkpoint** Why did Bismarck try to crush the Catholic Church and the Socialists?

Kaiser William II

In 1888, **William II** succeeded his grandfather as kaiser. The new emperor was supremely confident in his abilities and wished to put his own stamp on Germany. In 1890, he shocked Europe by asking the dominating Bismarck to resign. "There is only one master in the Reich," he said, "and that is I."

William II seriously believed that his right to rule came from God. He expressed this view when he said:

Primary Source

66 My grandfather considered that the office of king was a task that God had assigned to him. . . . That which he thought I also think. . . . Those who wish to aid me in that task . . . I welcome with all my heart; those who oppose me in this work I shall crush.99
—William II

Not surprisingly, William resisted efforts to introduce democratic reforms. At the same time, however, his government provided programs for **social welfare,** or programs to help certain groups of people. His government also provided services such as cheap transportation and electricity. An excellent system of public schools, which had flourished under Bismarck, taught students obedience to the emperor along with reading, writing, and mathematics.

Like his grandfather, William II lavished funds on the German military machine, already the most powerful in Europe. He also launched an ambitious campaign to expand the German navy and win an overseas empire to rival those of Britain and France. William's nationalism and aggressive military stance helped increase tensions on the eve of World War I.

✓ **Checkpoint** Why did William II ask Bismarck to resign in 1890?

Social Reform
Under Bismarck's leadership, Germany pioneered social reform. By 1884, Germans had health and accident insurance. By 1889, they had disability and old-age insurance. *Why did Bismarck introduce these social reforms?*

Progress Monitoring Online
For: Self-quiz with vocabulary practice
Web Code: nba-2222

Terms, People, and Places

1. For each term, person, or place listed at the beginning of the section, write a sentence explaining its significance.

Note Taking

2. **Reading Skill: Recognize Sequence** Use your completed chart to answer the Focus Question: How did Germany increase its power after unifying in 1871?

Comprehension and Critical Thinking

3. **Summarize** How did Germany become an industrial giant in the late 1800s?

4. **Demonstrate Reasoned Judgment** Do you think Bismarck's methods were justified by his social reforms? Explain.

5. **Draw Conclusions** Do you think the supporters of a democratic government in Germany in the late 1800s had hope of success? Explain.

● **Writing About History**

Quick Write: Answer Opposing Arguments To write a strong persuasive essay, you need to address arguments that can be used to contradict your position. Choose a topic from the section. For example, think about whether a government should guarantee that its citizens have adequate healthcare. List the arguments for and against your position on a piece of paper.

Giuseppe Mazzini, around 1865

Flag of Italy, 1833

UNIONE, FORZA E LIBERTA !!

WITNESS HISTORY 🔊 AUDIO

Stirrings of Nationalism

After a failed revolution against Austrian rule in northern Italy, many rebels, fearing retribution, begged for funds to pay for safe passage to Spain. Giuseppe Mazzini (mat SEE nee), still a boy, described his reaction to the situation:

❝ He (a rebel) held out a white handkerchief, merely saying, For the refugees of Italy.' My mother . . . dropped some money into the handkerchief. . . . That day was the first in which a confused idea presented itself to my mind . . . an idea that we Italians could and therefore ought to struggle for the liberty of our country. . . . ❞
—Giuseppe Mazzini, *Life and Writings*

Focus Question How did influential leaders help to create a unified Italy?

Unifying Italy

Objectives

- List the key obstacles to Italian unity.
- Understand what roles Count Camillo Cavour and Giuseppe Garibaldi played in the struggle for Italy.
- Describe the challenges that faced the new nation of Italy.

Terms, People, and Places

Camillo Cavour
Giuseppe Garibaldi
anarchist
emigration

Note Taking

Reading Skill: Recognize Sequence As you read, create a timeline showing the sequence of events from 1831 to 1871 that led to Italian unification.

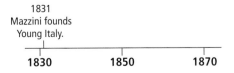

1831
Mazzini founds
Young Italy.

1830   1850   1870

Although the people of the Italian peninsula spoke the same language, they had not experienced political unity since Roman times. By the early 1800s, though, Italian patriots—including Mazzini, who would become a revolutionary—were determined to build a new, united Italy. As in Germany, unification was brought about by the efforts of a strong state and furthered by a shrewd, ruthless politician—Count **Camillo Cavour** (kah VOOR).

Obstacles to Italian Unity

For centuries, Italy had been a battleground for ambitious foreign and local princes. Frequent warfare and foreign rule had led people to identify with local regions. The people of Florence considered themselves Tuscans, those of Venice Venetians, those of Naples Neapolitans, and so on. But as in Germany, the invasions of Napoleon had sparked dreams of national unity.

The Congress of Vienna, however, ignored the nationalists who hoped to end centuries of foreign rule and achieve unity. To Prince Metternich of Austria, the idea of a unified Italy was laughable. At Vienna, Austria took control of much of northern Italy, while Hapsburg monarchs ruled various other Italian states. In the south, a French Bourbon ruler was put in charge of Naples and Sicily.

In response, nationalists organized secret patriotic societies and focused their efforts on expelling Austrian forces from northern Italy. Between 1820 and 1848, nationalist revolts exploded across the region. Each time, Austria sent in troops to crush the rebels.

Mazzini Establishes Young Italy In the 1830s, the nationalist leader Giuseppe Mazzini founded Young Italy. The goal of this secret society was "to <u>constitute</u> Italy, one, free, independent, republican nation." In 1849, Mazzini helped set up a revolutionary republic in Rome, but French forces soon toppled it. Like many other nationalists, Mazzini spent much of his life in exile, plotting and dreaming of a united Italy.

Nationalism Takes Root "Ideas grow quickly," Mazzini once said, "when watered by the blood of martyrs." Although revolution had failed, nationalist agitation had planted seeds for future harvests.

To nationalists like Mazzini, a united Italy made sense not only because of geography, but also because of a common language and history. Nationalists reminded Italians of the glories of ancient Rome and the medieval papacy. To others, unity made practical economic sense. It would end trade barriers among the Italian states and stimulate industry.

✓ Checkpoint What forces hindered Italian unity?

The Struggle for Italy

After 1848, leadership of the Risorgimento (ree sawr jee MEN toh), or Italian nationalist movement, passed to the kingdom of Sardinia, which included Piedmont, Nice, and Savoy as well as the island of Sardinia. Its constitutional monarch, Victor Emmanuel II, hoped to join other states to his own, thereby increasing his power.

Cavour Becomes Prime Minister In 1852, Victor Emmanuel made Count Camillo Cavour his prime minister. Cavour came from a noble family but favored liberal goals. He was a flexible, practical, crafty politician, willing to use almost any means to achieve his goals. Like Bismarck in Prussia, Cavour was a monarchist who believed in Realpolitik.

Once in office, Cavour moved first to reform Sardinia's economy. He improved agriculture, had railroads built, and encouraged commerce by supporting free trade. Cavour's long-term goal, however, was to end Austrian power in Italy and annex the provinces of Lombardy and Venetia.

Vocabulary Builder
<u>constitute</u>—(KAHN stuh toot) *v.* to set up; establish

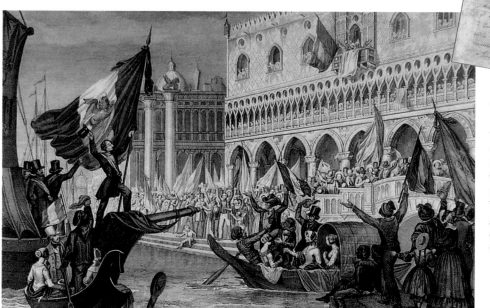

Opposing Austrian Rule
In March 1848, nationalists in Venice took over the city's arsenal and declared the establishment of the Republic of Venice (left). Their success was short lived, however, as the republic was soon disbanded and Venice again fell under the rule of Austria in 1849. The image above is a draft of a speech written by Camillo Cavour in 1861.

Intrigue With France In 1855, Sardinia, led by Cavour, joined Britain and France against Russia in the Crimean War. Sardinia did not win territory, but it did have a voice at the peace conference. Sardinia also gained the attention of Napoleon III.

In 1858, Cavour negotiated a secret deal with Napoleon, who promised to aid Sardinia in case it faced a war with Austria. A year later, the shrewd Cavour provoked that war. With help from France, Sardinia defeated Austria and annexed Lombardy. Meanwhile, nationalist groups overthrew Austrian-backed rulers in several other northern Italian states. These states then joined with Sardinia.

Garibaldi's "Red Shirts" Next, attention shifted to the Kingdom of the Two Sicilies in southern Italy. There, Giuseppe Garibaldi (gah ree BAHL dee), a longtime nationalist and an ally of Mazzini, was ready for action. Like Mazzini, Garibaldi wanted to create an Italian republic. He did not hesitate, however, to accept aid from the monarchist Cavour. By 1860, Garibaldi had recruited a force of 1,000 red-shirted volunteers. Cavour provided weapons and allowed two ships to take Garibaldi and his "Red Shirts" south to Sicily. With surprising speed, Garibaldi's forces won control of Sicily, crossed to the mainland, and marched triumphantly north to Naples.

Unity at Last Garibaldi's success alarmed Cavour, who feared that the nationalist hero would set up his own republic in the south. To prevent this, Cavour urged Victor Emmanuel to send Sardinian troops to deal with Garibaldi. Instead, the Sardinians overran the Papal States and linked up with Garibaldi and his forces in Naples.

In a patriotic move, Garibaldi turned over Naples and Sicily to Victor Emmanuel. Shortly afterward, southern Italy voted to approve the move, and in 1861, Victor Emmanuel II was crowned king of Italy.

Two areas remained outside the new Italian nation: Rome and Venetia. Cavour died in 1861, but his <u>successors</u> completed his dream. In a deal negotiated with Bismarck after the Austro-Prussian War, Italy acquired Venetia. Then, during the Franco-Prussian War in 1870, France was forced to withdraw its troops from Rome. For the first time since the fall of the Roman empire, Italy was a united land.

✓ **Checkpoint** What steps did Camillo Cavour take to promote Italian unity?

Challenges Facing the New Nation

Italy faced a host of problems. Like the German empire that Bismarck cemented together out of many states, Italy had no tradition of unity. Few Italians felt ties to the new nation. Strong regional rivalries left Italy unable to solve critical national issues.

Divisions The greatest regional differences were between the north and the south. The north was richer and had more cities than the south. For centuries, northern Italian cities had flourished as centers of business and culture. The south, on the other hand, was rural and poor. Its population was booming, but illiterate peasants could extract only a meager existence from the exhausted farmland.

Hostility between Italy and the Roman Catholic Church further divided the nation. Popes bitterly resented the seizure of the Papal

Vocabulary Builder

<u>successor</u>—(suk SES ur) *n.* a person who succeeds another to an office or rank

Unifying Italy

The Italian peninsula had been divided into small independent states since the fall of the Roman empire in 476. Political unification seemed impossible. However, rebellion, nationalism, and unity slowly took hold with the help of four individuals: a revolutionary, a statesman, a soldier, and a king.

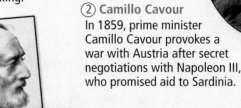

② Camillo Cavour
In 1859, prime minister Camillo Cavour provokes a war with Austria after secret negotiations with Napoleon III, who promised aid to Sardinia.

① Giuseppe Mazzini
Giuseppe Mazzini, founder of Young Italy, helps set up a revolutionary republic in Rome in 1849. French troops soon topple it.

③ Nationalist Revolts
Italian nationalists overthrow Austrian-backed rulers in several northern states.

④ Giuseppe Garibaldi
In 1860, Cavour provides weapons to Giuseppe Garibaldi, who invades Sicily with 1,000 Red Shirt volunteers (below). Garibaldi then captures Naples.

SWITZERLAND
AUSTRIA-HUNGARY
LOMBARDY
VENETIA
Venice
Trieste
SAVOY (To France)
Turin
Milan
PIEDMONT
Genoa
PARMA
MODENA
SAN MARINO
NICE (To France)
Florence
TUSCANY
PAPAL STATES
Adriatic Sea
CORSICA (France)
N
W—E
S
Rome
KINGDOM OF THE TWO SICILIES
SARDINIA
Naples
Tyrrhenian Sea
Mediterranean Sea
Palermo
SICILY
MILLER PROJECTION
SCALE IN MILES
0   100   200
0   100   200
SCALE IN KILOMETERS

⑤ Victor Emmanuel II
In a patriotic move, Garibaldi turns over Naples and Sicily to Victor Emmanuel, who is crowned king. In 1870, Italians conquer Rome, which becomes the capital city of a unified Italy.

☐ Kingdom of Sardinia, 1858
☐ Added to Sardinia, 1859 and 1860
☐ Added to Italy, 1866
☐ Added to Italy, 1870
→ Route of Garibaldi's expedition, 1860

Thinking Critically
1. **Map Skills** What route did Garibaldi's expedition take?
2. **Draw Conclusions** Why was Italian unification difficult to achieve?

History *Interactive*
For: Interactive timeline
Web Code: nbp-2232

States and of Rome. The government granted the papacy limited rights and control over church properties. Popes, however, saw themselves as "prisoners" and urged Italian Catholics—almost all Italians—not to cooperate with their new government.

Turmoil Under Victor Emmanuel, Italy was a constitutional monarchy with a two-house legislature. The king appointed members to the upper house, which could veto bills passed by the lower house. Although the lower house consisted of elected representatives, only a small number of men had the right to vote.

In the late 1800s, unrest increased as radicals on the left struggled against a conservative government. Socialists organized strikes while **anarchists,** people who want to abolish all government, turned to sabotage and violence. Slowly, the government extended suffrage to more men and passed laws to improve social conditions. Still, the turmoil continued. To distract attention from troubles at home, the government set out to win an overseas empire in Ethiopia.

Economic Progress Despite its problems, Italy did develop economically, especially after 1900. Although the nation lacked important natural resources such as coal, industries did sprout up in northern regions. Industrialization, of course, brought urbanization as peasants flocked to the cities to find jobs in factories. As in other countries, reformers campaigned to improve education and working conditions.

The population explosion of this period created tensions. One important safety valve for many people was **emigration,** or movement away from their homeland. Many Italians left for the United States, Canada, and Latin American nations. By 1914, the country was significantly better off than it had been in 1861. But, it was hardly prepared for the great war that broke out in that year.

Italian Emigration
Emigrants crowd the port of Naples (above). *Why did Italians immigrate to other countries in the early 1900s?*

✔ **Checkpoint** What problems did Italians experience after unification?

Progress Monitoring *Online*
For: Self-quiz with vocabulary practice
Web Code: nba-2233

SECTION 3 **Assessment**

Terms, People, and Places

1. For each term, person, or place listed at the beginning of the section, write a sentence explaining its significance.

Note Taking

2. **Reading Skill: Recognize Sequence** Use your completed timeline to answer the Focus Question: How did influential leaders help to create a unified Italy?

Comprehension and Critical Thinking

3. **Summarize** (a) What obstacles to unity did Italian nationalists face? (b) What conditions favored unity?

4. **Analyze Information** (a) What was the source of conflict between Garibaldi and Cavour? (b) How was the conflict resolved?

5. **Express Problems Clearly** What challenges did Italians face after unification?

● **Writing About History**

Quick Write: Decide on an Organizational Strategy Using clear organization to present a logical argument is a good way to keep the reader's attention in a persuasive essay. Choose an issue from the section about which you could make an argument. Then write an outline showing how you would organize a persuasive essay.

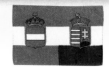

Hungarian parliament passes legislation funding an army to fight against the Hapsburg empire, 1848

WITNESS HISTORY 🔊 AUDIO

Balkan Nationalism

❝How is it that they [European powers] cannot understand that less and less is it possible . . . to direct the destinies of the Balkans from the outside? We are growing up, gaining confidence, and becoming independent . . .❞
—Bulgarian statesman on the first Balkan War and the European powers

Focus Question How did the desire for national independence among ethnic groups weaken and ultimately destroy the Austrian and Ottoman empires?

Nationalism Threatens Old Empires

Objectives

- Describe how nationalism contributed to the decline of the Hapsburg empire.
- List the main characteristics of the Dual Monarchy.
- Understand how the growth of nationalism affected the Ottoman empire.

Terms, People, and Places

Francis Joseph
Ferenc Deák
Dual Monarchy

Note Taking

Reading Skill: Recognize Sequence Complete a table like the one below to keep track of the sequence of events that led Austria into the Dual Monarchy. Look for dates and other clues to sequence in the text.

Events in Austrian History	
1840	
1848	
1859	
1866	
1867	

Napoleon had dissolved the Holy Roman Empire, which the Hapsburgs had led for nearly 400 years. Austria's center of power had shifted to Central Europe. Additional wars resulted in continued loss of territory to Germany and Italy. Why did nationalism bring new strength to some countries and weaken others?

In Eastern and Central Europe, the Austrian Hapsburgs and the Ottoman Turks ruled lands that included diverse ethnic groups. Nationalist feelings among these subject peoples contributed to tensions building across Europe.

The Hapsburg Empire Declines

In 1800, the Hapsburgs were the oldest ruling house in Europe. In addition to their homeland of Austria, over the centuries they had acquired the territories of Bohemia and Hungary, as well as parts of Romania, Poland, Ukraine, and northern Italy.

Austria Faces Change Since the Congress of Vienna, the Austrian emperor Francis I and his foreign minister Metternich had upheld conservative goals against liberal forces. "Rule and change nothing," the emperor told his son. Under Francis and Metternich, newspapers could not even use the word *constitution,* much less discuss this key demand of liberals. The government also tried to limit industrial development, which would threaten traditional ways of life.

Austria, however, could not hold back the changes that were engulfing the rest of Europe. By the 1840s, factories were springing up. Soon, the Hapsburgs found themselves facing the problems of industrial life that had long been familiar in Britain—the growth of cities, worker discontent, and the stirrings of socialism.

A Multinational Empire Equally disturbing to the old order were the urgent demands of nationalists. The Hapsburgs presided over a multinational empire. Of its 50 million people at mid-century, fewer than a quarter were German-speaking Austrians. Almost half belonged to different Slavic groups, including Czechs, Slovaks, Poles, Ukrainians, Serbs, Croats, and Slovenes. Often, rival groups shared the same region. The empire also included large numbers of Hungarians and Italians. The Hapsburgs ignored nationalist demands as long as they could. When nationalist revolts broke out in 1848, the government crushed them.

Francis Joseph Grants Limited Reforms Amid the turmoil, 18-year-old Francis Joseph inherited the Hapsburg throne. He would rule until 1916, presiding over the empire during its fading days into World War I.

An early challenge came when Austria suffered its humiliating defeat at the hands of France and Sardinia in 1859. Francis Joseph realized he needed to strengthen the empire at home. Accordingly, he made some limited reforms. He granted a new constitution that set up a legislature. This body, however, was dominated by German-speaking Austrians. The reforms thus satisfied none of the other national groups that populated the empire. The Hungarians, especially, were determined to settle for nothing less than total self-government.

 Checkpoint What actions did Francis Joseph take to maintain power?

Formation of the Dual Monarchy

Austria's disastrous defeat in the 1866 war with Prussia brought renewed pressure for change from Hungarians within the empire. One year later, Ferenc Deák (DEH ahk), a moderate Hungarian leader, helped work out a compromise that created a new political power known as the Dual Monarchy of Austria-Hungary.

The Austria-Hungary Government Under the agreement, Austria and Hungary were separate states. Each had its own constitution and parliament. Francis Joseph ruled both, as emperor of Austria and king of Hungary. The two states also shared ministries of finance, defense, and foreign affairs, but were independent of each other in all other areas.

Nationalist Unrest Increases Although Hungarians welcomed the compromise, other subject peoples resented it. Restlessness increased among various Slavic groups, especially the Czechs in Bohemia. Some nationalist leaders called on Slavs to unite, insisting that "only through liberty, equality, and fraternal solidarity" could Slavic peoples fulfill their "great mission in the history of mankind." By the early 1900s, nationalist unrest often left the government paralyzed in the face of pressing political and social problems.

 Checkpoint How did Hungarians and Slavic groups respond to the Dual Monarchy?

Vocabulary Builder
fraternal—(fruh TUR nul) adj. brotherly

Geography *Interactive*

For: Audio guided tour
Web Code: nbp-2243

WHITE RUSSIANS

GREAT RUSSIANS

GERMANY

POLES

UKRAINIANS

UKRAINIANS

CZECHS

POLES

SLOVAKS

FRANCE

ROMANIANS

SWITZ.

GERMANS

HUNGARIANS

ROMANIANS

ITALIANS

SLOVENES

ROMANIANS

GREAT RUSSIANS

ITALIANS

CROATS

ROMANIA

ROMANIANS

SERBIANS

Black Sea

ITALY

Adriatic Sea

BOSNIAKS

SERBIA

MONTENEGRINS

BULGARIANS

N W E S

30° E

40° N

MONT.

ALBANIANS

10° E

MACEDONIANS

Mediterranean Sea

TURKS

GREEKS

Aegean Sea

Conic Projection
0   200   400 mi
0   200   400 km

GREECE

The Balkans, 1878

RUSSIA

AUSTRIA-HUNGARY

Bosnia-Herzegovina (occupied by Austria)

ROMANIA

Danube R.

Black Sea

ITALY

Adriatic Sea

SERBIA

Bulgaria (autonomous)

N W E S

MONTENEGRO

Eastern Rumelia (semi-autonomous)

★ Constantinople

40° N

Aegean Sea

Conic Projection
0   300 mi
0   300 km

GREECE

Independent Balkan states

Ottoman Empire

Mediterranean Sea

20° E

30° E

Crete

Colors reflect the major languages spoken in Eastern Europe, 1800 to 1914.

Map Skills In the late 1800s, the Balkans had become a center of conflict, as various peoples and empires competed for power.

1. **Locate** (a) Black Sea (b) Ottoman empire (c) Serbia (d) Greece (e) Austria-Hungary
2. **Place** Which four large seas border the Balkan Peninsula?
3. **Identify Central Issues** Why do you think competing interests in the Balkans led the region to be called a powder keg?

The Ottoman Empire Collapses

Like the Hapsburgs, the Ottomans ruled a multinational empire. It stretched from Eastern Europe and the Balkans to North Africa and the Middle East. There, as in Austria, nationalist demands tore at the fabric of the empire.

Balkan Nationalism Erupts In the Balkans, Serbia won autonomy in 1830, and southern Greece won independence during the 1830s. But many Serbs and Greeks still lived in the Balkans under Ottoman rule. The Ottoman empire was also home to other national groups, such as Bulgarians and Romanians. During the 1800s, various subject peoples staged revolts against the Ottomans, hoping to set up their own independent states.

European Powers Divide Up the Ottoman Empire Such nationalist stirrings became mixed up with the ambitions of the great European powers. In the mid-1800s, Europeans came to see the Ottoman empire as "the sick man of Europe." Eagerly, they scrambled to divide up Ottoman lands. Russia pushed south toward the Black Sea and Istanbul, which Russians still called Constantinople. Austria-Hungary took control of the provinces of Bosnia and Herzegovina. This action angered the Serbs, who also had hoped to expand into that area. Meanwhile, Britain and France set their sights on other Ottoman lands in the Middle East and North Africa.

War in the Balkans In the end, a complex web of competing interests contributed to a series of crises and wars in the Balkans. Russia fought several wars against the Ottomans. France and Britain sometimes joined the Russians and sometimes the Ottomans. Germany supported Austrian authority over the discontented national groups. But Germany also encouraged the Ottomans because of their strategic location in the eastern Mediterranean. In between, the subject peoples revolted and then fought among themselves. By the early 1900s, observers were referring to the region as the "Balkan powder keg." The explosion that came in 1914 helped set off World War I.

✔ **Checkpoint** How did the European powers divide up Ottoman lands?

"The Sick Man of Europe"
Turkey's Abdul Hamid II (right) reacts to Bulgarian and Austrian rulers claiming parts of the Ottoman empire. *How does this cartoon show the Ottoman empire as "the sick man of Europe"?*

SECTION **4** Assessment

Progress Monitoring *Online*
For: Self-quiz with vocabulary practice
Web Code: nba-2244

Terms, People, and Places
1. For each term, person, or place listed at the beginning of the section, write a sentence explaining its significance.

Note Taking
2. **Reading Skill: Recognize Sequence** Use your completed table to answer the Focus Question: How did the desire for national independence among ethnic groups weaken and ultimately destroy the Austrian and Ottoman empires?

Comprehension and Critical Thinking
3. **Identify Alternatives** What alternatives did Francis Joseph have in responding to nationalist demands? How might Austrian history have been different if he had chosen a different course of action?
4. **Draw Conclusions** Why did the Dual Monarchy fail to end nationalist demands?
5. **Identify Central Issues** How did Balkan nationalism contribute to the decline of the Ottoman empire?

● **Writing About History**
Quick Write: Draft an Opening Paragraph In a persuasive essay, you want to grab the reader's attention by opening with a strong example, and then convincingly stating your views. Choose a topic from the section, such as whether the Hapsburgs or the Ottoman Turks could have built a modern, unified nation from their multinational empires. Then draft an opening paragraph.

Nationalism

How have people used nationalism as a basis for their actions?

Starting in the late 1700s, a spirit of nationalism swept across Europe and the Americas. Nationalism is a powerful force characterized by strong feelings of pride in and devotion to one's nation. It gives people a sense of identity beyond their family and local area. Nationalism can compel people to fight to establish their own nation, through revolution. It can move people to volunteer to defend their country from outside attack. It can even cause people to attack another country in order to acquire more territory for the homeland. Consider the following examples:

Three Sarajevan girls run through "Sniper Alley" in Sarajevo.

Revolution

The American Revolution may have been the first major eruption of nationalism. Americans sought liberty and equality. This search, prevented by Britain's efforts to maintain control, helped unify the diverse American colonies. Americans already spoke the same language and followed the same basic religion. Faced with Britain's tyranny, nationalist feelings arose in the form of patriotism. Those feelings gained full expression in the Declaration of Independence of July 4, 1776.

Defense

In June 1940, the British expected an invasion. Their nation stood alone against the German military machine, which was ready to strike as soon as Britain's defenses weakened. They never weakened. Prime Minister Winston Churchill set the tone when he urged the nation to stand up to Hitler. The British responded with courage and devotion to the cause of freedom. Despite a bombing blitz that devastated London, British morale remained high, and Hitler gave up his plans.

Aggression

Yugoslavia has been an ethnic powder keg since its creation in 1918. Nationalist tensions broke up this federation of six republics after the fall of communism. Four republics declared their independence, but the republic of Serbia aggressively tried to keep the nation together. It supported Serbian nationalists in civil wars and used "ethnic cleansing" to clear regions of non-Serbs in hopes of absorbing those regions into a "Greater Serbia." Intervention by NATO finally ended this practice and restored an uneasy peace in 1999.

Queen Elizabeth and King George VI of Great Britain visit a London neighborhood that had been bombed by Germany in 1941.

Thinking Critically

1. **(a)** Is nationalism a positive force? Explain your answer. **(b)** What event or events in recent years brought out nationalistic feelings among Americans? Why?
2. **Connections to Today** Do library research to identify an example of nationalism today.

Russian peasant women clearing stones from a field

Plight of the Serfs

Although serfdom had almost disappeared in Western Europe by the 1700s, it survived in Russia. Masters exercised almost total power over their serfs. A noble turned revolutionary described the treatment of the serfs:

❝ I heard . . . stories of men and women torn from their families and their villages, and sold, or lost in gambling, or exchanged for a couple of hunting dogs, and then transported to some remote part of Russia to create a [master's] new estate; of children taken from their parents and sold to cruel . . . masters. ❞
—Peter Kropotkin, *Memoirs of a Revolutionist*

Focus Question Why did industrialization and reform come more slowly to Russia than to Western Europe?

Russia: Reform and Reaction

Objectives

- Describe major obstacles to progress in Russia.
- Explain why tsars followed a cycle of absolutism, reform, and reaction.
- Understand why the problems of industrialization contributed to the outbreak of revolution.

Terms, People, and Places

colossus	pogrom
Alexander II	refugees
Crimean War	Duma
emancipation	Peter Stolypin
zemstvo	

Note Taking

Reading Skill: Recognize Sequence Create a timeline of Russian events like the one below to keep track of the sequence of events that led to the revolution of 1905. Look for dates and other clues to sequence in the text.

```
    1801
 Alexander I
inherits throne.
    |
    |_____
    |        |        |        |
  1800     1850     1900     1950
```

Reformers hoped to free Russia from autocratic rule, economic backwardness, and social injustice. But efforts to modernize Russia had little success, as tsars imprisoned critics or sent them into exile.

Conditions in Russia

By 1815, Russia was not only the largest, most populous nation in Europe but also a great world power. Since the 1600s, explorers had pushed the Russian frontier eastward across Siberia to the Pacific. Peter the Great and Catherine the Great had added lands on the Baltic and Black seas, and tsars in the 1800s had expanded into Central Asia. Russia had thus acquired a huge multinational empire, part European and part Asian.

Other European nations looked on the Russian **colossus,** or giant, with a mixture of wonder and misgiving. Russia had immense natural resources. Its vast size gave it global interests and influence. But Western Europeans disliked its autocratic government and feared its expansionist aims. Despite efforts by Peter and Catherine to westernize Russia, it remained economically undeveloped. By the 1800s, tsars saw the need to modernize but resisted reforms that would undermine their absolute rule.

Russia's Social Structure A great obstacle to progress was the rigid social structure. Landowning nobles dominated society and rejected any change that would threaten their privileges. The middle class was too small to have much influence. The majority of Russians were serfs, or laborers bound to the land and to masters who controlled their fates.

Most serfs were peasants. Others were servants, artisans, or soldiers forced into the tsar's army. As industry expanded, some masters sent serfs to work in factories but took much of their pay.

Many enlightened Russians knew that serfdom was inefficient. As long as most people had to serve the whim of their masters, Russia's economy would remain backward. However, landowning nobles had no reason to improve agriculture and took little interest in industry.

Ruling With Absolute Power For centuries, tsars had ruled with absolute power, imposing their will on their subjects. On occasion, the tsars made limited attempts at liberal reform, such as easing censorship or making legal and economic reforms to improve the lives of serfs. However, in each instance the tsars drew back from their reforms when they began to fear losing the support of nobles. In short, the liberal and nationalist changes brought about by the Enlightenment and the French Revolution had almost no effect on Russian autocracy.

✔ **Checkpoint** Describe the social structure that existed in Russia during the 1800s.

Emancipation and Stirrings of Revolution

Alexander II came to the throne in 1855 during the **Crimean War.** His reign represents the pattern of reform and repression used by his father and grandfather, Alexander I and Nicholas I. The Crimean War had broken out after Russia tried to seize Ottoman lands along the Danube River. Britain and France stepped in to help the Ottoman Turks, invading the Crimean peninsula that juts into the Black Sea. The war, which ended in a Russian defeat, revealed the country's backwardness. Russia had only a few miles of railroads, and the military bureaucracy was hopelessly inefficient. Many felt that dramatic changes were needed.

Freeing the Serfs A widespread popular reaction followed. Liberals demanded changes, and students demonstrated, seeking reform. Pressed from all sides, Alexander II finally agreed to reforms. In 1861, he issued a royal decree that required **emancipation,** or freeing of the serfs.

Freedom brought problems. Former serfs had to buy the land they had worked, but many were too poor to do so. Also, the lands allotted to peasants were often too small to farm efficiently or to support a family. Peasants remained poor, and discontent festered.

Still, emancipation was a turning point. Many peasants moved to the cities, taking jobs in factories and building Russian industries. Equally important, freeing the serfs boosted the drive for further reform.

Introducing Other Reforms Along with emancipation, Alexander II set up a system of local government. Elected assemblies, called **zemstvos,** were made responsible for matters such as road repair, schools, and agriculture. Through this system, Russians gained some experience of self-government at the local level.

The Decembrist Revolt
In 1825, army officers led an uprising known as the Decembrist Revolt (below). They had picked up liberal ideas while fighting in Western Europe and demanded reforms and a constitution. Tsar Nicholas I repressed the revolt. This stamp (inset) commemorates the 125th anniversary of the revolt. *How did the revolt symbolize Russia in the 1800s?*

The tsar also introduced legal reforms based on ideas like trial by jury, and he eased censorship. Military service terms were reduced, and brutal discipline was limited. Alexander also encouraged the growth of industry in Russia, which still relied heavily on agriculture.

Revolutionary Currents Alexander's reforms failed to satisfy many Russians. Peasants had freedom but not land. Liberals wanted a constitution and an elected legislature. <u>Radicals</u>, who had adopted socialist ideas from the West, demanded even more revolutionary changes. The tsar, meantime, moved away from reform and toward repression.

In the 1870s, some socialists went to live and work among peasants, preaching reform and rebellion. They had little success. The peasants scarcely understood them and sometimes turned them over to the police. The failure of this movement, combined with renewed government repression, sparked anger among radicals. Some turned to terrorism. On March 13, 1881, terrorists assassinated Alexander II.

Crackdown Alexander III responded to his father's assassination by reviving the harsh methods of Nicholas I. To wipe out liberals and revolutionaries, he increased the power of the secret police, restored strict censorship, and exiled critics to Siberia. The tsar also launched a program of Russification aimed at suppressing the cultures of non-Russian peoples within the empire. Alexander insisted on one language, Russian,

Vocabulary Builder
<u>radical</u>—(RAD ih kul) *n.* a person who favors great changes or reforms

INFOGRAPHIC

Tug of War: Reform and Repression by the Russian Tsars

The five tsars that ruled Russia from 1801 to 1917 all followed a similar pattern of autocratic rule: at times they appeared open to liberal ideas and enacted reforms to satisfy the groups demanding change. In every case, however, the tsars pulled back on these reforms and launched a battery of repressive measures designed to preserve their absolute power and the support of the nobles.

The Tsars Resist: Repression and Crackdown
- Secret police, arrests, executions
- Strict censorship of liberal ideas
- Exiling liberals
- Bolstering Russian Orthodox Church
- Insisting on the absolute power of the state
- Persecuting non-Russian groups within empire

◀ **Tsars**
Alexander I,
Nicholas I, Alexander II,
Alexander III, Nicholas II

▲ Jewish men survey damage done to sacred Torah scrolls during an 1881 pogrom in Russia.

and one church, the Russian Orthodox Church. Poles, Ukrainians, Finns, Armenians, Muslims, Jews, and many others suffered persecution.

Persecution and Pogroms Russia had acquired a large Jewish population when it carved up Poland and expanded into Ukraine. Under Alexander III, persecution of Jewish people in Russia increased. The tsar limited the number of Jewish people who were allowed to study in universities and practice certain professions. He also forced them to live in restricted areas.

Official persecution encouraged **pogroms,** or violent mob attacks on Jewish people. Gangs beat and killed Jewish people and looted and burned their homes and stores. Faced with savage persecution, many left Russia. They became **refugees,** or people who flee their homeland to seek safety elsewhere. Large numbers of Russian Jews went to the United States.

 Checkpoint How did Alexander III respond to the murder of his father?

The Drive to Industrialize

Russia finally entered the industrial age under Alexander III and his son Nicholas II. In the 1890s, Nicholas' government

▲ Russian peasants in a rural village around 1900

The Tsars Give In:
Concessions and Reforms
• Easing censorship
• Revising law code
• Limiting the power of landowners
• Freeing serfs (1861)
• Creating local self-government, or zemstovs
• Creating national legislature, or Duma
• Land reforms

Opposing the Tsars ▶
Liberals, socialists, nationalists, army officers, workers

Thinking Critically
1. **Identify Main Ideas** What factors brought about so much opposition to the tsars?
2. **Draw Conclusions** Why do you think the tsars swung back and forth between repression and reform?

WITNESS HISTORY VIDEO

Watch *Crisis and Revolution in Russia* on the **Witness History Discovery School**™ video program to examine the discontent in tsarist Russia.

focused on economic development. It encouraged the building of railroads to connect iron and coal mines with factories and to transport goods across Russia. It also secured foreign capital to invest in industry and transportation systems, such as the Trans-Siberian Railroad, which linked European Russia to the Pacific Ocean.

Political and social problems increased as a result of industrialization. Government officials and business leaders applauded economic growth. Nobles and peasants opposed it, fearing the changes it brought. Industrialization also created new social ills as peasants flocked to cities to work in factories. Instead of a better life, they found long hours and low pay in dangerous conditions. In the slums around the factories, poverty, disease, and discontent multiplied. Radicals sought supporters among the new industrial workers. At factory gates, Socialists often handed out pamphlets that preached the revolutionary ideas of Karl Marx.

✔ **Checkpoint** How did Russia industrialize?

Turning Point: Crisis and Revolution

When war broke out between Russia and Japan in 1904, Nicholas II called on his people to fight for "the Faith, the Tsar, and the Fatherland." Despite all of their efforts, the Russians suffered one humiliating defeat after another.

Bloody Sunday

An artist's depiction shows the execution of workers in front of the Winter Palace in Saint Petersburg, January 9, 1905 (below). The magazine cover (inset) shows "Le Tzar Rouge," or "The Red Tsar." *Compare and contrast these images of Bloody Sunday.*

Bloody Sunday News of the military disasters unleashed pent-up discontent created by years of oppression. Protesters poured into the streets. Workers went on strike, demanding shorter hours and better wages. Liberals called for a constitution and reforms to overhaul the government.

As the crisis deepened, a young Orthodox priest organized a peaceful march for Sunday, January 22, 1905. Marchers flowed through the streets of St. Petersburg toward the tsar's Winter Palace. Chanting prayers and singing hymns, workers carried holy icons and pictures of the tsar. They also brought a petition for justice and freedom.

Fearing the marchers, the tsar had fled the palace and called in soldiers. As the people approached, they saw troops lined up across the square. Suddenly, gunfire rang out. Hundreds of men and women fell dead or wounded in the snow. One woman stumbling away from the scene moaned: "The tsar has deserted us! They shot away the orthodox faith." Indeed, the slaughter marked a turning point for Russians. "Bloody Sunday" killed the people's faith and trust in the tsar.

The Revolution of 1905 In the months that followed Bloody Sunday, discontent exploded across Russia. Strikes multiplied. In some cities, workers took over local government. In the countryside, peasants revolted and demanded land. Minority nationalities called for autonomy from Russia. Terrorists targeted officials, and some assassins were cheered as heroes by discontented Russians.

At last, the clamor grew so great that Nicholas was forced to announce sweeping reforms. In the October Manifesto, he promised "freedom of person, conscience, speech, assembly, and union." He agreed to summon a **Duma,** or elected national legislature. No law, he declared, would go into effect without approval by the Duma.

Results of the Revolution The manifesto won over moderates, leaving Socialists isolated. These divisions helped the tsar, who had no intention of letting strikers, revolutionaries, and rebellious peasants challenge him.

In 1906, the first Duma met, but the tsar quickly dissolved it when leaders criticized the government. Nicholas then appointed a new prime minister, **Peter Stolypin** (stuh LIP yin). Arrests, pogroms, and executions followed as the conservative Stolypin sought to restore order.

Stolypin soon realized that Russia needed reform, not just repression. To regain peasant support, he introduced moderate land reforms. He strengthened the zemstvos and improved education. Unfortunately, these reforms were too limited to meet the broad needs of most Russians, and dissatisfaction still simmered. Stolypin was assassinated in 1911. Several more Dumas met during this period, but new voting laws made sure they were conservative. By 1914, Russia was still an autocracy, but one simmering with unrest.

 Checkpoint Why was Bloody Sunday a turning point for the Russians?

SECTION 5 Assessment

Progress Monitoring *Online*
For: Self-quiz with vocabulary practice
Web Code: nba-2255

Terms, People, and Places

1. For each term, person, or place listed at the beginning of the section, write a sentence explaining its significance.

Note Taking

2. **Reading Skill: Recognize Sequence** Use your completed timeline to answer the Focus Question: Why did industrialization and reform come more slowly to Russia than to Western Europe?

Comprehension and Critical Thinking

3. **Summarize** What conditions in Russia challenged progress during the early 1800s?

4. **Draw Conclusions** How did Russian tsars typically react to change?

5. **Draw Inferences** What does Bloody Sunday suggest about the relationship between the tsar and the Russian people?

● **Writing About History**

Quick Write: Gather Evidence to Support Thesis Statement Choose a topic from the section, such as whether you think emancipation helped or hurt Russian serfs. Make a list of evidence from the section that supports your view.

Quick Study Guide

■ Effects of Nationalism

Nationalism by Region				
Germany	**Italy**	**Austria**	**Balkans**	**Russia**
• German states unite under William I. • Empire takes leading role in Europe. • Bismarck becomes known as the Iron Chancellor.	• Mazzini founds Young Italy. • Garibaldi leads Red Shirts. • Victor Emmanuel II makes Cavour prime minister of Sardinia. • Italian states become unified by 1871.	• Francis I and Metternich uphold conservative goals. • Dual Monarchy with Hungary is set up. • Nationalist groups grow restless. • Empire becomes weakened.	• Serbians achieve autonomy in 1830. • Greeks achieve independence in the 1830s. • European nations divide up Ottoman lands. • "Balkan powder keg" helps set off World War I.	• Serfs are freed in 1861. • Alexander III encourages persecution and pogroms. • Russia enters the industrial age late. • Bloody Sunday leads to revolution in 1905. • Duma has limited power.

■ Unification in Europe, 1873

As the map below shows, nationalist movements led to the creation of several new nations across Europe.

■ Key Leaders

Germany
Otto von Bismarck, *chancellor*
William I, *Prussian king, German kaiser*
William II, *kaiser*

Italy
Giuseppe Mazzini, *founder of Young Italy*
Victor Emmanuel II, *king*
Count Camillo Cavour, *prime minister*
Giuseppe Garibaldi, *leader of Red Shirts*

Austria-Hungary
Ferenc Deák, *Hungarian politician*
Francis Joseph, *Austrian emperor, Hungarian king*

Russia
Alexander II, *tsar of Russia*
Alexander III, *tsar of Russia*
Nicholas II, *tsar of Russia*

■ Key Events of Nationalism

Early 1800s Nationalism rises in Germany.

1814 The Congress of Vienna redraws the map of Europe after Napoleon's defeat.

1830s Giuseppe Mazzini founds Young Italy to encourage Italian unification.

Chapter Events
Global Events

1800 — **1825** — **1850**

1804 Haiti declares independence from France.

1848 Revolutions take place throughout Europe.

Concept | Connector

■ Cumulative Review

Record the answers to the questions below on your Concept Connector worksheets.

1. **Empire** In 1871, German nationalists celebrated the birth of the second Reich, or empire. They called it that because they considered Germany heir to the Holy Roman Empire. Compare the second Reich to the Holy Roman Empire. How were they similar? How were they different? Think about the following:
   - structure of government
   - power of the kaiser and emperor
   - the rule of William II and Otto I
   - who had voting rights
   - who held the real power

2. **Nationalism** During the early 1800s, nationalist rebellions erupted in the Balkans and elsewhere along the southern fringe of Europe. Between 1820 and 1848, nationalist revolts exploded across Italy. Compare and contrast Greece's unification and nationalism to Italy's. Think about the following:
   - the empires they revolted against
   - which countries they turned to for help
   - the structure of their governments

3. **Nationalism** During the 1800s, various subject peoples in the Balkans revolted against the Ottoman empire, hoping to set up independent states of their own. A complicated series of crises and wars soon followed. Take notes on the situation in the Balkans between 1800 and the early 1900s. Why did competing interests in the Balkans lead the region to be called a powder keg?

■ Connections To Today

1. **Nationalism: The State of Nationalism Today** You've read how nationalism was a strong enough force in the 1800s to help unify nations, such as Italy and Germany, but threatened to destroy the Austrian and Ottoman empires. Do you think that nationalism is still a force in the world today? Conduct research to learn more about current nationalist issues. You may want to focus your research on Kurdistan, Northern Ireland, the former Yugoslavia, or Russia. Write two paragraphs on nationalism today, citing examples from current events to support your answer.

2. **Economic Systems: Social Welfare Programs** Under Otto von Bismarck, Germany was a pioneer in social reform, providing several social welfare programs to its citizens. By the 1890s, Germans had health and accident insurance as well as retirement benefits. Social welfare programs soon spread to other European nations. Conduct research to learn more about social welfare programs today. Compare social welfare programs in one country in Europe with those in the United States. How are they similar? How are they different?

History Interactive
For: Interactive timeline
Web Code: nbp-2264

1861
Tsar Alexander II frees the serfs.

1870
Bismarck provokes Franco-Prussian War to create a unified German empire.

1905
Revolution breaks out in St. Petersburg after Bloody Sunday massacre.

1875　　　　　　　　　　　**1900**　　　　　　　　　　　**1925**

1861
The Civil War begins in the United States.

1898
The Philippines declares independence from Spain.

1914
World War I begins.

Chapter Assessment

Terms, People, and Places

Match the following definitions with the terms listed below.

chancellor	emigration
Realpolitik	emancipation
kaiser	pogrom
social welfare	Duma
anarchist	

1. someone who wants to abolish all government
2. elected national legislature in Russia
3. emperor of Germany
4. granting of freedom to serfs
5. the highest official of a monarch
6. violent attack on a Jewish community
7. movement away from one's homeland
8. realistic politics based on the needs of the state
9. programs to help people in need

Main Ideas

Section 1 (pp. 330–333)
10. What was Chancellor Otto von Bismarck's main goal? What policies did he follow to meet that goal?

Section 2 (pp. 334–337)
11. How did Germany increase its power in the late 1800s?

Section 3 (pp. 338–342)
12. Summarize the process by which Italy unified. Include information on the leaders who helped unify Italy.

Section 4 (pp. 343–346)
13. How did nationalism contribute to the decline of the Hapsburg and Ottoman empires?

Section 5 (pp. 348–353)
14. Why was Russia slow to industrialize?

Chapter Focus Question
15. What effects did nationalism and the demand for reform have in Europe?

Critical Thinking

16. **Make Comparisons** How did the nationalism represented by Bismarck differ from that embraced by liberals in the early 1800s?
17. **Make Comparisons** Compare and contrast the goals and methods of Cavour in Italy and Bismarck in Germany.
18. **Analyze Information** Tsar Alexander II declared that it is "better to abolish serfdom from above than to wait until it will be abolished by a movement from below." Explain his statement.
19. **Geography and History** How did regional differences contribute to continued divisions in Italy after unification?
20. **Analyzing Cartoons** How does this French cartoonist view Bismarck? Explain.
21. **Predict Consequences** Based on your reading of the chapter, predict the consequences of the following: (a) defeat of France in the Franco-Prussian War, (b) growth of German nationalism and militarism in the late 1800s, (c) failure to satisfy nationalist ambitions in Austria-Hungary, and (d) weakening of the Ottoman empire.

LE GRAND ÔGRE ALLEMAND.

● **Writing About History**

Writing a Persuasive Essay Some people define nationalism as excessive, narrow, or jingoist patriotism. A nationalist might be described as someone who boasts of his patriotism and favors aggressive or warlike policies. The rise of nationalism in Europe led to both division and unification. For example, it unified Germany, but it led Russian tsars to suppress the cultures of national minorities within the country. Nationalism remains a powerful force to this day for unifying countries and for sparking rivalries, conflicts, and bloodshed. Write a persuasive essay in which you support or oppose the idea that nationalism is an excessive form of patriotism.

Prewriting
• Collect the examples and evidence that you need to support your position convincingly.
• Use a graphic organizer to list points on both sides of the issue.

Drafting
• Focus on a thesis statement. Clearly state the position that you will prove. Use the rest of your introduction to provide readers with the necessary context about the issue.
• Acknowledge the opposition by stating, and then refuting, opposing arguments.

Revising
• Use the guidelines for revising your essay on page SH17 of the Writing Handbook.

Document-Based Assessment

On the Crimean Front

In 1853, the British, the French, and their allies took on the vast Russian empire in the Crimean War. Called a "perfectly useless modern war," it was fought in the Black Sea region, although major campaigns took place well beyond that area. Like all wars, it was grim. More than 500,000 people died during the conflict.

Document A

"[The Crimean War] was one of the last times that the massed formations of cavalry and infantry were employed—the thin red line was to disappear forever. Henceforward, armies would rely on open, flexible formations and on trench warfare. For the British, it was the end of an era: never again would their soldiers fight in full-dress uniform. Never again would the colors be carried into the fray and the infantry would no longer march into battle to the stirring tunes of regimental bands. The Crimean War ushered in the age of the percussion cap rifle. The new Minie rifle was the decisive weapon, replacing the clumsy . . . musket. The weapon fired a cartridge, not a ball, with accuracy far superior to the old firelocks. . . ."

—From ***The Road to Balaklava,*** by Alexis S. Troubetzkoy

Document B

"I see men in hundreds rushing from the Mamelon [bastion] to the Malakoff [tower]. . . . with all its bristling guns. Under what a storm of fire they advance, supported by that impenetrable red line, which marks our own infantry! The fire from the Malakoff is tremendous—terrible. . . . Presently the twilight deepens, and the light of rocket, mortar, and shell falls over the town."

—From ***Journal kept during the Russian War: From the Departure of the Army from England in April 1854, to the Fall of Sebastopol,*** by Mrs. Henry Duberly, an army wife

Document C

"Men sent in there [French hospital] with fevers and other disorders were frequently attacked with the cholera in its worst form, and died with unusual rapidity, in spite of all that could be done to save them. I visited the hospital, and observed that a long train of . . . carts, filled with sick soldiers, were drawn up by the walls. . . . the quiet that prevailed was only broken now and then by the moans and cries of pain of the poor sufferers in the carts."

—From ***The British Expedition to the Crimea*** by W. H. Russell, ***Times*** correspondent

Document D

Treating Cholera

Analyzing Documents

Use your knowledge of the Crimean War and Documents A, B, C, and D to answer questions 1–4.

1. According to Document A, the Crimean War marked the end of
   A private soldiers in war.
   B most small wars in Europe.
   C old ways of fighting.
   D soldiers dying of diseases in military hospitals.

2. With what purpose did the author write Document B?
   A to help people understand the dangers of fighting with new weapons
   B to criticize inadequate technology
   C to describe the state of mind of the soldiers
   D to make the British public understand how quickly the war was progressing

3. With what purpose did the artist create Document D?
   A to help the British public understand the dangers of fighting with new weapons
   B to criticize the inadequate state of army hospitals
   C to describe the dangers of soldiering and soldiers' valor
   D to make the British public understand the toll that disease was taking on soldiers

4. **Writing Task** Suppose you are a surgeon working near the war front. Write a brief letter home describing your impressions. Use the four documents along with information from the chapter to write your letter.

The People Demand Reform

A series of political reforms during the 1800s and early 1900s transformed Great Britain from a monarchy and aristocracy into a democracy. While some British politicians opposed the reforms, most sided in favor of reforming Parliament to make it more representative of the nation's growing industrial population.

❝No doubt, at that very early period, the House of Commons did represent the people of England but. . . . the House of Commons, as it presently subsists, does not represent the people of England. . . . The people called loudly for reform, saying that whatever good existed in the constitution of this House—whatever confidence was placed in it by the people, was completely gone.❞
—Lord John Russell, March 1, 1831

Listen to the Witness History audio to learn more about democratic developments in Britain.

◀ **Parliamentary Election of 1836**
Though most were unable to vote, many townspeople gathered in the marketplace to cheer or harass the candidates.

Queen Victoria of Great Britain and Ireland

Badge commemorating a union strike in Britain, 1888

Advertisement for transportation to California during the Gold Rush

Note Taking Study Guide *Online*
For: Note Taking and Concept Connector worksheets
Web Code: nbd-2345

Fashions of the rich (above right), and poverty on the streets of London, circa 1877 (above)

WITNESS HISTORY 🔊 AUDIO

Two Nations

One day a wealthy Englishman named Charles Egremont boasted to strangers that Victoria, the queen of England, "reigns over the greatest nation that ever existed."

"Which nation?" asks one of the strangers, "for she reigns over two. . . . Two nations; between whom there is no [communication] and no sympathy; who are as ignorant of each other's habits, thoughts, and feelings, as if they were . . . inhabitants of different planets."
What are these "two nations," Egremont asks. "THE RICH AND THE POOR," the stranger replies.
—Benjamin Disraeli, *Sybil*

Focus Question How did political reform gradually expand suffrage and make the British Parliament more democratic during the 1800s?

Democratic Reform in Britain

Objectives

- Describe how reformers worked to change Parliament in the 1800s.
- Understand the values that Queen Victoria represented.
- Summarize how the Liberal and Conservative parties helped bring a new era to British politics.

Terms, People, and Places

rotten borough	Benjamin Disraeli
electorate	William Gladstone
secret ballot	parliamentary democracy
Queen Victoria	

Note Taking

Reading Skill: Identify Main Ideas As you read this section, complete an outline of the contents.

> I. Reforming Parliament
>   A. Reformers press for change
>   1.
>   2.

In the 1800s, Benjamin Disraeli and other political leaders slowly worked to bridge Britain's "two nations" and extend democratic rights. Unlike some of its neighbors in Europe, Britain generally achieved change through reform rather than revolution.

Reforming Parliament

In 1815, Britain was a constitutional monarchy with a parliament and two political parties. Still, it was far from democratic. Although members of the House of Commons were elected, less than five percent of the people had the right to vote. Wealthy nobles and squires, or country landowners, dominated politics and heavily influenced voters. In addition, the House of Lords—made up of hereditary nobles and high-ranking clergy—could veto any bill passed by the House of Commons.

Reformers Press for Change Long-standing laws kept many people from voting. Catholics and non-Anglican Protestants, for example, could not vote or serve in Parliament. In the 1820s, reformers pushed to end religious restrictions. After fierce debate, Parliament finally granted Catholics and non-Anglican Protestants equal political rights.

An even greater battle soon erupted over making Parliament more representative. During the Industrial Revolution, centers of population shifted. Some rural towns lost so many people that they had few or no voters. Yet local landowners in these **rotten boroughs** still sent members to Parliament. At the same time, populous new industrial cities like Manchester and Birmingham had no seats <u>allocated</u> in Parliament because they had not existed as population centers in earlier times.

Vocabulary Builder

<u>allocate</u>—(AL oh kayt) *vt.* to distribute according to a plan

Reform Act of 1832 By 1830, Whigs and Tories were battling over a bill to reform Parliament. The Whig Party largely represented middle-class and business interests. The Tory Party spoke for nobles, landowners, and others whose interests and income were rooted in agriculture. In the streets, supporters of reform chanted, "The Bill, the whole Bill, and nothing but the Bill!" Their shouts seemed to echo the cries of revolutionaries on the continent.

Parliament finally passed the Great Reform Act in 1832. It redistributed seats in the House of Commons, giving representation to large towns and cities and eliminating rotten boroughs. It also enlarged the **electorate,** the body of people allowed to vote, by granting suffrage to more men. The Act did, however, keep a property requirement for voting.

The Reform Act of 1832 did not bring full democracy, but it did give a greater political voice to middle-class men. Landowning nobles, however, remained a powerful force in the government and in the economy.

The Chartist Movement The reform bill did not help rural or urban workers. Some of them demanded more radical change. In the 1830s, protesters known as Chartists drew up the People's Charter. This petition demanded universal male suffrage, annual parliamentary elections, and salaries for members of Parliament. Another key demand was for a **secret ballot,** which would allow people to cast their votes without announcing them publicly.

Meeting of the Unions on Newhall Hill, Birmingham
The Birmingham Political Union's enormous rallies (above) and calls for reform are credited with the final passage of the Great Reform Bill of 1832. As one politician said of the BPU, "To this body, more than to any other, is confessedly due the triumph (such as it was) of the Reform Bill. Its well-ordered proceedings, extended organisation, and immense assemblages of people, at critical periods of its progress, rendered the measure irresistible."

Twice the Chartists presented petitions with over a million signatures to Parliament. Both petitions were ignored. In 1848, as revolutions swept Europe, the Chartists prepared a third petition and organized a march on Parliament. Fearing violence, the government moved to suppress the march. Soon after, the unsuccessful Chartist movement declined. In time, however, Parliament would pass most of the major reforms proposed by the Chartists.

 **Checkpoint** How was the British Parliament reformed during the early 1800s?

The Victorian Age

From 1837 to 1901, the great symbol in British life was **Queen Victoria.** Her reign was the longest in British history. Although she exercised little real political power, she set the tone for what is now called the Victorian age.

Symbol of a Nation's Values As queen, Victoria came to embody the values of her age. These Victorian ideals included duty, thrift, honesty, hard work, and above all respectability. Victoria herself embraced a strict code of morals and manners. As a young woman, she married a German prince, Albert, and they raised a large family.

A Confident Age Under Victoria, the British middle class—and growing numbers of the working class—felt great confidence in the future. That confidence grew as Britain expanded its already huge empire.

From Monarchy to Democracy in Britain

In the early 1800s, Britain's government was a monarchy and an aristocracy under the rule of Queen Victoria ① and the aristocrats and landowners in the House of Lords. ② A series of reforms during the 1800s and early 1900s transformed Britain's government into a democracy. The first of these reforms was the Great Reform Act of 1832, by which seats in the Parliament were redistributed to give more representation to growing industrial areas. The act also expanded the vote to include about one in five adult men. The Second Reform Act in 1867 was spearheaded by Benjamin Disraeli, ④ a Conservative leader who hoped to defeat his liberal rival William Gladstone ③ and

Victoria, the empress of India and ruler of some 300 million subjects around the world, became a revered symbol of British might.

During her reign, Victoria witnessed growing agitation for social reform. The queen herself commented that the lower classes "earn their bread and riches so deservedly that they cannot and ought not to be kept back." As the Victorian era went on, reformers continued the push toward greater social and economic justice.

✔ **Checkpoint** What values did Queen Victoria represent and how did these values relate to economic reform?

A New Era in British Politics

In the 1860s, a new era dawned in British politics. The old political parties regrouped under new leadership. **Benjamin Disraeli** forged the Tories into the modern Conservative Party. The Whigs, led by **William Gladstone,** evolved into the Liberal Party. Between 1868 and 1880, as the majority in Parliament swung between the two parties, Gladstone and Disraeli alternated as prime minister. Both fought for important reforms.

Expanding Suffrage Disraeli and the Conservative Party pushed through the Reform Bill of 1867. By giving the vote to many working-class men, the new law almost doubled the size of the electorate.

In the 1880s, it was the turn of Gladstone and the Liberal Party to extend suffrage. Their reforms gave the vote to farmworkers and most other men. By century's end, almost-universal male suffrage, the secret ballot, and other Chartist ambitions had been achieved. Britain had truly transformed itself from a constitutional monarchy to a **parliamentary democracy,** a form of government in which the executive leaders (usually

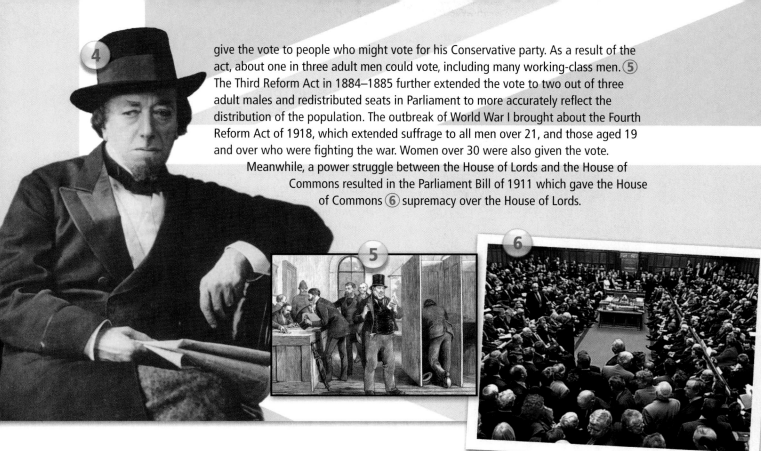

give the vote to people who might vote for his Conservative party. As a result of the act, about one in three adult men could vote, including many working-class men. ⑤ The Third Reform Act in 1884–1885 further extended the vote to two out of three adult males and redistributed seats in Parliament to more accurately reflect the distribution of the population. The outbreak of World War I brought about the Fourth Reform Act of 1918, which extended suffrage to all men over 21, and those aged 19 and over who were fighting the war. Women over 30 were also given the vote.

Meanwhile, a power struggle between the House of Lords and the House of Commons resulted in the Parliament Bill of 1911 which gave the House of Commons ⑥ supremacy over the House of Lords.

a prime minister and cabinet) are chosen by and responsible to the legislature (parliament), and are also members of it.

Limiting the Lords In the early 1900s, many bills passed by the House of Commons met defeat in the House of Lords. In 1911, a Liberal government passed measures to restrict the power of the Lords, including their power to veto tax bills. The Lords resisted. Finally, the government threatened to create enough new lords to approve the law, and the Lords backed down. People hailed the change as a victory for democracy. In time, the House of Lords would become a largely ceremonial body with little power. The elected House of Commons would reign supreme.

✔ **Checkpoint** How was Parliament reformed during the late 1800s and early 1900s?

Thinking Critically
1. **Recognize Ideologies** Which group in the early 1800s do you think most feared the "democratization" of Britain? Why?
2. **Identify Central Issues** How did the Parliament Bill in 1911 reflect the same trends occurring as a result of the reform acts?

SECTION 1 **Assessment**

Progress Monitoring *Online*
For: Self-quiz with vocabulary practice
Web Code: nba-2312

Terms, People, and Places
1. What do each of the key terms listed at the beginning of the section have in common? Explain.

Note Taking
2. **Reading Skill: Identify Main Ideas** Use your completed outline to answer the Focus Question: How did political reform gradually expand suffrage and make the British Parliament more democratic during the 1800s?

Comprehension and Critical Thinking
3. **Summarize** How did the Reform Act of 1832 change Parliament?
4. **Categorize** What middle-class values are associated with the Victorian age?
5. **Identify Central Issues** What reforms did the Liberal and Conservative parties achieve?
6. **Draw Conclusions** Why do you think the Chartists demanded (a) a secret ballot, (b) salaries for members of Parliament?

● **Writing About History**
Quick Write: Gather Information If you were assigned to write a biographical essay on Queen Victoria, Benjamin Disraeli, or William Gladstone, what questions about these individuals would you want to answer in your essay? Choose one of these people and create a list of such questions about that person.

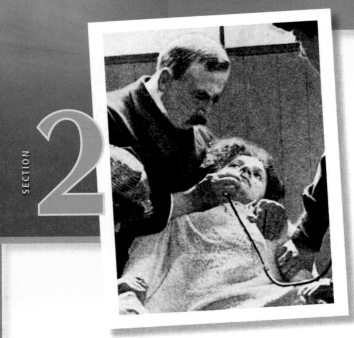

Forced feeding of English suffragist, 1912

WITNESS HISTORY 🔊 AUDIO

No Surrender

Lady Constance Lytton had been arrested for taking part in a women's suffrage protest. Once arrested, she refused to eat. Her hunger strike, she vowed, would go on until the British government granted the vote to women. Lytton later recalled:

66 I was visited again by the Senior Medical Officer, who asked me how long I had been without food. I said I had eaten . . . on Friday at about midnight. He said, Oh, then, this is the fourth day; that is too long, I shall feed you, I must feed you at once.'99
—Constance Lytton, *Prisons and Prisoners*

In the end, the doctor force-fed Lytton through a tube. Yet the painful ordeal failed to weaken her resolve. "No surrender," she whispered. "No surrender."

Focus Question What social and economic reforms were passed by the British Parliament during the 1800s and early 1900s?

Social and Economic Reform in Britain

Objectives
- Identify the social and economic reforms benefiting British workers and others.
- Describe how British women worked to win the right to vote.
- Understand the causes of conflict between the British and the Irish nationalists.

Terms, People, and Places

free trade	penal colony
repeal	absentee landlord
abolition movement	home rule
capital offense	

Note Taking

Reading Skill: Categorize Complete a chart like this one listing the reforms in Britain during the 1800s and early 1900s.

Reforms in Britain		
Economic	Social	Political
•	•	•
•	•	•

Lytton's 1910 hunger strike was part of the long struggle for women's suffrage in Britain. Suffragists were not the only people to fight for change. Between 1815 and 1914, Parliament responded to widespread discontent with a series of social and economic reforms. At the same time, the question of British control over Ireland was becoming a dominant and divisive political issue.

A Series of Reforms

During the early and mid-1800s, Parliament passed a wide variety of important new laws. One of the most controversial measures involved the issue of **free trade**, or trade between countries without quotas, tariffs, or other restrictions.

Free Trade and the Corn Laws In the early 1800s, Britain, like other European nations, taxed foreign imports in order to protect local economies. But supporters of free trade demanded an end to such protective tariffs. Free traders, usually middle-class business leaders, agreed with Adam Smith that a policy of laissez faire would increase prosperity for all. If tariffs were abolished, merchants everywhere would have larger markets in which to sell their goods, and consumers would benefit from open competition.

Some British tariffs were repealed in the 1820s. However, fierce debate erupted over the Corn Laws, which imposed high tariffs on imported grain. (In Britain, "corn" refers to all cereal grains, such as wheat, barley, and oats.) Farmers and wealthy landowners supported the Corn Laws because they kept the price of British grain high. Free traders, however, wanted Parliament to **repeal,** or cancel, the Corn Laws. They argued that repeal of these laws would lower the price of grain, make bread cheaper for workers, and open up trade in general.

Parliament finally repealed the Corn Laws in 1846, after widespread crop failures swept many parts of Europe. Liberals hailed the repeal as a victory for free trade and laissez-faire capitalism. However, in the late 1800s, economic hard times led Britain and other European countries to impose protective tariffs on many goods again.

Campaign Against Slavery During the 1700s, Enlightenment thinkers had turned the spotlight on the evils of the slave trade. At the time, British ships were carrying more Africans to the Americas than any other European country. Under pressure from middle-class reformers in Britain, France, and the United States, the **abolition movement,** or the campaign against slavery and the slave trade, slowly took off. In 1807, Britain became the first European power to abolish the slave trade.

Banning the slave trade did not end slavery. Although the Congress of Vienna had condemned slavery, it had taken no action. In Britain, liberals preached the immorality of slavery. Finally, in 1833, Parliament passed a law banning slavery in all British colonies.

Crime and Punishment Other reforms were aimed at the criminal justice system. In the early 1800s, more than 200 crimes were punishable by death. Such **capital offenses** included not only murder but also shoplifting, sheep stealing, and impersonating an army veteran. In practice, some juries refused to convict criminals, because the punishments were so harsh. Executions were public occasions, and the hanging of a well-known murderer might attract thousands of curious spectators. Afterward, instead of receiving a proper burial, the criminal's body might be given to a medical college for dissection.

Reformers began to reduce the number of capital offenses. By 1850, the death penalty was reserved for murder, piracy, treason, and arson. Many petty criminals were instead transported to **penal colonies,** or settlements for convicts, in the new British territory of Australia. In 1868, Parliament ended public hangings. Additional reforms improved prison conditions and outlawed imprisonment due to debt.

✓ **Checkpoint** How did abolition and criminal justice reform reflect Victorian values?

Victories for the Working Class

"Four [ghosts] haunt the Poor: Old Age, Accident, Sickness and Unemployment," declared Liberal politician David Lloyd George in 1905. "We are going to [expel] them." Parliament had begun passing laws aimed at improving social conditions as early as the 1840s. During the early 1900s, it passed a series of additional reforms designed to help the men, women, and children whose labor supported the new industrial society.

Improving Working Conditions As you have read, working conditions in the early industrial age were grim and often dangerous. Gradually, Parliament passed laws to regulate conditions in factories and mines. In 1842, for example, mineowners were forbidden to employ

Abolitionist Poster
Abolitionists hoped that ending the slave trade would also bring about the end of slavery. As this poster shows, even ending slavery did not end the economic mistreatment of people of African descent.

women or children under age 10. An 1847 law limited women and children to a 10-hour day. Later in the 1800s, the government regulated many safety conditions in factories and mines—and sent inspectors to see that the laws were enforced. Other laws set minimum wages and maximum hours of work.

The Growth of Labor Unions Early in the Industrial Revolution, labor unions were outlawed. Under pressure, government and business leaders slowly accepted worker organizations. Trade unions were made legal in 1825 but it remained illegal to go on strike until later in the century.

Despite restrictions, unions spread, and gradually they won additional rights. Between 1890 and 1914, union membership soared. Besides winning higher wages and shorter hours for workers, unions pressed for other laws to improve the lives of the working class.

Later Reforms During the late 1800s and early 1900s, both political parties enacted social reforms to benefit the working class. Disraeli sponsored laws to improve public health and housing for workers in cities. Under Gladstone, an education act called for free elementary education for all children. Gladstone also pushed to open up government jobs based on merit rather than on birth or wealth.

Another force for reform was the Fabian Society, a socialist organization founded in 1883. The Fabians promoted gradual change through legal means rather than by violence. Though small in number, the Fabians had a strong influence on British politics.

In 1900, socialists and union members backed the formation of a new political party, which became the Labour Party. ("Labour" is the British spelling of "labor.") The Labour Party would quickly grow in power and membership until, by the 1920s, it surpassed the Liberal Party and became one of Britain's two major parties.

▼ **Riots in Hyde Park, London**
An 1866 meeting of the Reform League in London dissolved into rioting. Riots such as these helped bring about the Second Reform Bill in 1867.

In the early 1900s, Britain began to pass social welfare laws to protect the well-being of the poor and disadvantaged. These laws were modeled on those Bismarck had introduced in Germany. They protected workers with accident, health, and unemployment insurance as well as old-age pensions. One result of such reforms was that Marxism gained only limited support among the British working class. The middle class hailed reforms as proof that democracy was working.

✔ **Checkpoint** Describe several social welfare reforms during the 1800s and early 1900s.

The Struggle to Win Votes for Women

In Britain, as elsewhere, women struggled against strong opposition for the right to vote. Women themselves were divided on the issue. Some women opposed suffrage altogether. Queen Victoria, for example, called the suffrage struggle "mad, wicked folly." Even women in favor of suffrage disagreed about how best to achieve it.

Suffragists Revolt By the early 1900s, Emmeline Pankhurst, a leading suffragist, had become convinced that only aggressive tactics would bring victory. Pankhurst and other radical suffragists interrupted speakers in Parliament, shouting, "Votes for women!" until they were carried away. They collected petitions and organized huge public demonstrations. When mass meetings and other peaceful efforts brought no results, some women turned to more drastic, violent protest. They smashed windows or even burned buildings. Pankhurst justified such tactics as necessary to achieve victory. "There is something that governments care far more for than human life," she declared, "and that is the security of property, so it is through property that we shall strike the enemy." As you have read, some suffragists went on hunger strikes, risking their lives to achieve their goals.

Victory at Last Even middle-class women who disapproved of such radical and violent actions increasingly demanded votes for women. Still, Parliament refused to grant women's suffrage. Not until 1918 did Parliament finally grant suffrage to women over age 30. Younger women did not win the right to vote for another decade.

✔ **Checkpoint** Why do you think women disagreed about how best to gain suffrage?

Instability in Ireland

Throughout the 1800s, Britain faced the ever-present "Irish question." The English had begun conquering Ireland in the 1100s. In the 1600s, English and Scottish settlers colonized Ireland, taking possession of much of the best farmland.

The Irish never accepted English rule. They bitterly resented settlers, especially **absentee landlords** who owned large estates but did not live on them. Many Irish peasants lived in desperate poverty, while paying high rents to landlords living in England. In addition, the Irish, most of whom were Catholic, had to pay tithes to support the Church of England. Under these conditions, resistance and rebellion were common.

▲ A pin from the British Trades Union Conference (above) and a Liberal Party poster from 1911

Vocabulary Builder

drastic—(DRAS tik) *adj.* severe, harsh, extreme

The Irish Potato Famine

Under British rule, three quarters of Irish farmland was used to grow crops that were exported. The potato was the main source of food for most of the Irish people. In 1845, disaster struck. A blight, or disease, destroyed the potato crop. Other crops, such as wheat and oats, were not affected. Yet British landowners continued to ship these crops outside Ireland, leaving little for the Irish except the blighted potatoes. The result was a terrible famine that the Irish called the "Great Hunger." In four years, about one million Irish men, women, and children died of starvation or disease. Many more emigrated to the United States and Canada. The Great Hunger left a legacy of Irish bitterness toward the English. ◀)) AUDIO

"Tumbled" Houses and Eviction ▶
Unable to grow potatoes to sell or eat, thousands of penniless tenants were evicted from their homes by landlords who needed the rent to pay their taxes. The roofs of the peasants' homes were "tumbled," or removed, to prevent the tenants from returning.

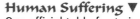

Number of Overseas Emigrants from Ireland, 1851–1921*	
1851–1860	1,216,219
1861–1870	818,582
1871–1880	542,703
1881–1890	734,475
1891–1900	461,282
1901–1910	485,461
1911–1921	355,295
Total 1851–1921	**4,614,017**

*Primarily to the United States, Canada, Australia, and New Zealand
SOURCE: Commission on Emigration and Other Population Problems, Dublin, 1954

Human Suffering ▼
One official told of entering what he thought was a deserted village. In one home, he saw "six famished and ghastly skeletons, to all appearances dead…" huddled in a corner on some filthy straw. "I approached with horror and found by a low moaning they were alive—they were in a fever, four children, a woman and what had once been a man…."

Limited Relief Measures ▲
Charles Trevelyan, the senior British official in charge of Irish relief efforts, held ruthless views of the Irish, insisting that they learn to "depend upon themselves…instead of…the assistance of the Government on every occasion."

Thinking Critically
1. **Graph Skills** Which decade saw the greatest number of emigrants from Ireland?
2. **Draw Conclusions** Do you think the Irish famine was more accurately described as a natural disaster or a human-made disaster? Why?

Irish Nationalism Like the national minorities in the Austrian empire, Irish nationalists campaigned vigorously for freedom and justice in the 1800s. Nationalist leader Daniel O'Connell, nicknamed "the Liberator," organized an Irish Catholic League and held mass meetings to demand repeal of unfair laws. "My first object," declared O'Connell, "is to get Ireland for the Irish."

Under pressure from O'Connell and other Irish nationalists, Britain slowly moved to improve conditions in Ireland. In 1829, Parliament passed the Catholic Emancipation Act, which allowed Irish Catholics to vote and hold political office. Yet many injustices remained. Absentee landlords could evict tenants almost at will. Other British laws forbade the teaching and speaking of the Irish language.

Struggle for Home Rule The famine in Ireland (see facing page) left the Irish with a legacy of bitterness and distrust toward Britain. In the 1850s, some Irish militants organized the Fenian Brotherhood. Its goal was to liberate Ireland from British rule by force. In the 1870s, moderate Irish nationalists found a rousing leader in Charles Stewart Parnell. He rallied Irish members of Parliament to press for **home rule,** or local self-government. The debate dragged on for decades.

The "Irish question" disrupted English politics. At times, political parties were so deeply split over the Irish question that they could not take care of other business. As prime minister, Gladstone pushed for reforms in Ireland. He ended the use of Irish tithe money to support the Anglican church and tried to ease the hardships of Irish tenant farmers. New laws prevented landlords from charging unfair rents and protected the rights of tenants to the land they worked.

Finally, in 1914, Parliament passed a home rule bill. But it delayed putting the new law into effect when World War I broke out that year. As you will read, the southern counties of Ireland finally became independent in 1921.

 Checkpoint How did English policies toward Ireland affect the cause of Irish Nationalism?

SECTION **2** Assessment

Terms, People, and Places

1. Place each of the key terms at the beginning of the section into these two categories: economic or political. Write a sentence for each term explaining your choice.

Note Taking

2. **Reading Skill: Categorize** Use your chart to answer the Focus Question: What social and economic reforms were passed by the British Parliament during the 1800s and early 1900s?

Comprehension and Critical Thinking

3. **Summarize** Describe three reforms that helped the British working class.

4. **Compare Points of View** What actions did women suffragists take to achieve their goals? How did the views of women differ regarding tactics?

5. **Identify Central Issues** (a) Why did Irish nationalists oppose British rule? (b) Describe two reforms that improved conditions in Ireland.

● **Writing About History**

Quick Write: Write a Thesis Statement Write the thesis statement for an editorial written by an Irish nationalist of the late 1800s or early 1900s. First, decide whether your main goal is to win support for your cause from the Irish or to persuade members of the British Parliament.

Migration

What factors cause large groups of people to move from one place to another?

In the 1800s, famine drove more than a million Irish to leave their homeland. In later years, millions more Europeans would migrate to North and South America, mainly seeking economic opportunity. Like most emigrants, they left behind their homes and cultures for a future that was uncertain at best. What drives people to take such a bold step? Motivators include poverty and unemployment, civil unrest, and natural disasters such as famine and drought. These "push factors" sometimes, but not always, combine with a common "pull factor": the promise of a better life in the new location. Consider the following causes and historical examples of migration:

◀ Migration of refugees during the 1947 partition of India and Pakistan.

Aggression

Migration played a major role in the fall of the Roman empire. It all started with the Mongols, aggressive warriors from central Asia, who attacked the Huns in the A.D. 200s. Over time, the Huns migrated westward. They pushed the Goths, a Germanic group, out of the Russian steppe and toward Roman lands. The Goths, in turn, displaced another Germanic people, the Vandals. This chain reaction or "bumper car" migration continued, sending wave after wave of invaders into the western Roman empire, which eventually collapsed.

Forced Migration

European traders imposed the forced migration of some 12 million enslaved Africans from the 1500s to the 1800s. More than a million Africans died during the brutal passage across the Atlantic to the Americas. Another involuntary migration took place in the Soviet Union during the 1930s. Joseph Stalin sent millions of peasants and political opponents to forced-labor camps in Siberia and other remote areas. Many of them died or were killed in the camps.

Persecution

In 1948, the British granted India independence, splitting it along religious lines into India (Hindu) and Pakistan (Muslim). Hundreds of thousands died in the violence that followed. More than 7 million Muslims fled from India to Pakistan to escape persecution. More than 7 million Hindus and Sikhs migrated in the opposite direction for the same reason.

▼ Immigrants arriving in New York City.

Thinking Critically

1. (a) What were some possible "pull" factors for Irish emigrants? (b) How do the "push" and "pull" factors for voluntary migration differ from those for involuntary migration?
2. **Connections to Today** Use news sources to read about an example of recent migration. Write a one paragraph summary of the migration including explanations of push and/ or pull factors influencing the migration.

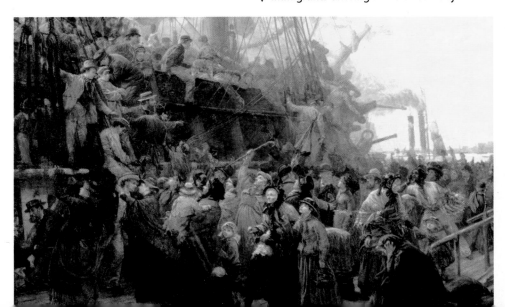

Following Napoleon III's surrender (above), Georges Clemenceau (above right) rallied the people of Paris to defend their city.

SECTION
3

Vive la France!

The news sent shock waves through Paris. Napoleon III had surrendered to the Prussians and Prussian forces were now about to advance on Paris. Could the city survive? Georges Clemenceau (kleh mahn soh), a young French politician, rallied the people of Paris to defend their homeland:

66 Citizens, must France destroy herself and disappear, or shall she resume her old place in the vanguard of nations? . . . Each of us knows his duty. We are children of the Revolution. Let us seek inspiration in the example of our forefathers in 1792, and like them we shall conquer. *Vive la France!* (Long Live France!)99

Focus Question What democratic reforms were made in France during the Third Republic?

Division and Democracy in France

Objectives
- List the domestic and foreign policies of Napoleon III.
- Analyze the impact of the Dreyfus affair and other challenges of the Third Republic.
- Describe the French government's steps toward reform in the early 1900s.

Terms, People, and Places

Napoleon III	coalition
Suez Canal	Dreyfus affair
provisional	libel
premier	Zionism

Note Taking

Reading Skill: Recognize Sequence Draw a timeline and label the main events described in this section.

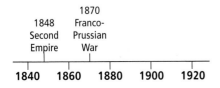

For four months, Paris resisted the German onslaught. But finally, in January 1871, the French government at Versailles was forced to accept Prussian surrender terms.

The Franco-Prussian War ended a long period of French domination of Europe that had begun under Louis XIV. Yet a Third Republic rose from the ashes of the Second Empire of Napoleon III. Economic growth, democratic reforms, and the fierce nationalism expressed by Clemenceau all played a part in shaping modern France.

France Under Napoleon III

After the revolution of 1848, **Napoleon III,** nephew of Napoleon Bonaparte, rose to power and set up the Second Empire. His appeal cut across lines of class and ideology. The bourgeoisie saw him as a strong leader who would restore order. His promise to end poverty gave hope to the lower classes. People of all classes were attracted by his name, a reminder of the days when France had towered over Europe. Unlike his famous uncle, however, Napoleon III would bring France neither glory nor an empire.

Limits on Liberty On the surface, the Second Empire looked like a constitutional monarchy. In fact, Napoleon III ruled almost as a dictator, with the power to appoint his cabinet, the upper house of the legislature, and many officials. Although the assembly was elected by universal male suffrage, appointed officials "managed" elections so that supporters of the emperor would win. Debate was limited, and newspapers faced strict censorship.

In the 1860s, the emperor began to ease controls. He lifted some censorship and gave the legislature more power. On the eve of his disastrous war with Prussia, Napoleon III even issued a new constitution that extended democratic rights.

Promoting Economic Growth Like much of Europe, France prospered at mid-century. Napoleon III promoted investment in industry and large-scale ventures such as railroad building and the urban renewal of Paris. During this period, a French entrepreneur, Ferdinand de Lesseps (duh lay seps), organized the building of the **Suez Canal** in Egypt to link the Mediterranean with the Red Sea and the Indian Ocean.

Workers enjoyed some benefits of economic growth. Napoleon legalized labor unions, extended public education to girls, and created a small public health program. Still, in France, as in other industrial nations, many people lived in great poverty.

Foreign Adventures Napoleon's worst failures were in foreign affairs. In the 1860s, he tried to place Maximilian, an Austrian Hapsburg prince, on the throne of Mexico. Through Maximilian, Napoleon hoped to turn Mexico into a French satellite. But after a large commitment of troops and money, the adventure failed. Mexican patriots resisted fiercely, and the United States protested. After four years, France withdrew its troops. Maximilian was overthrown and shot by Mexican patriots.

Napoleon's successes were almost as costly as his failures. He helped Italian nationalists defeat Austria, and in return, the regions of Nice (nees) and Savoy were ceded to France. But this victory soon backfired when a united Italy emerged as a rival on France's border. And, though

● **INFOGRAPHIC**

The Siege of Paris

For over four months beginning in September 1870, Prussian troops surrounded Paris. The city was almost completely cut off from the rest of the country except for messages that could be carried out on perilous balloon flights (far right top), by carrier pigeon, or by small capsules floated down the Seine River (far right bottom). Despite the large amounts of food that had been amassed prior to the siege, food was in short supply. Parisians searched for horses, rats (right), and even zoo and circus animals were consumed in the face of hunger. In the end, the French surrendered and agreed to disband their army and pay a war indemnity. Nearly 2,000 French troops were killed and thousands of Parisians died of diseases worsened by malnutrition and the cold weather.

Victorious Prussian troops pose in front of the ruins of the French Fort Issy near Paris.

France and Britain won the Crimean War, France had little to show for its terrible losses except a small foothold in the Middle East.

A Disastrous War With Prussia At this same time, France was growing increasingly concerned about the rise of a great rival, Prussia. The Prussian leader Otto von Bismarck shrewdly manipulated the French and lured Napoleon into war in 1870.

As you have read, the Franco-Prussian War was a disaster for France. Following the capture of Napoleon III, German forces advanced toward Paris and encircled the city. After four months of siege by Prussian troops, starving Parisians were reduced to catching rats and killing circus animals for food.

✔ **Checkpoint** What were some of the successes and failures of Napoleon III's Second Empire?

Challenges of the Third Republic

At the news of Napoleon's capture, republicans in Paris declared an end to the Second Empire. They set up a **provisional,** or temporary, government that shortly evolved into France's Third Republic. In 1871, the newly elected National Assembly accepted a harsh peace with Germany. France had to surrender the provinces of Alsace and Lorraine and pay a huge sum to Germany. The French were eager to avenge their loss.

The Paris Commune In 1871, an uprising broke out in Paris. Rebels set up the Paris Commune. Like the radical government during the French Revolution, its goal was to save the Republic from royalists. Communards,

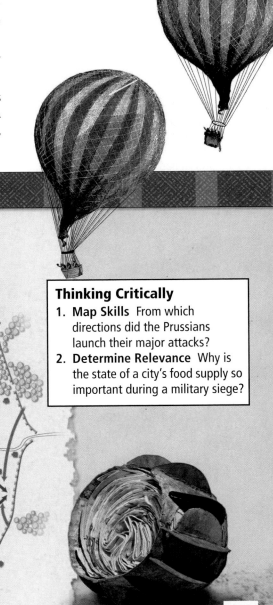

Paris Under Seige

Key:
- ⌐⌐⌐ Prussian siege line
- ✇ Prussian batteries
- → Prussian attacks
- ⌐⌐⌐ French defensive line
- ⬠ French forts
- → French attacks
- ∿∿∿ City walls

Seine River

PARIS

Seine River

Marne River

VERSAILLES

Scale in Miles
0 1 2 3 4

Scale in Kilometers
0 1 2 3 4

Thinking Critically
1. **Map Skills** From which directions did the Prussians launch their major attacks?
2. **Determine Relevance** Why is the state of a city's food supply so important during a military siege?

373

as the rebels were called, included workers and socialists as well as bourgeois republicans. As patriots, they rejected the harsh peace that the National Assembly had signed with Germany. Radicals dreamed of creating a new socialist order.

The National Assembly ordered the Paris Commune to disband. When the Communards refused, the government sent troops to retake Paris. For weeks, civil war raged. As government troops advanced, the rebels set fire to several government buildings, toppled a monument commemorating Napoleon I, and slaughtered a number of hostages. Finally, government forces butchered some 20,000 Communards. The suppression of the Paris Commune left bitter memories that deepened social divisions within France.

Government Structure Despite its shaky beginnings, the Third Republic remained in place for 70 years. The new republic had a two-house legislature. The powerful lower house, or Chamber of Deputies, was elected by universal male suffrage. Together with the Senate, it elected the president of the republic. However, he had little power and served mostly as a figurehead. Real power was in the hands of the **premier** (prih MIR), or prime minister.

Unlike Britain, with its two-party system, France had many parties, reflecting the wide splits within the country. Among them were royalists, constitutional monarchists, moderate republicans, and radicals. With so many parties, no single party could win a majority in the legislature. In order to govern, politicians had to form **coalitions,** or alliances of various parties. Once a coalition controlled enough votes, it could then name a premier and form a cabinet.

Multiparty systems and coalition governments are common in Europe. Such alliances allow citizens to vote for a party that most nearly matches their own beliefs. Coalition governments, however, are often unstable. If one party deserts a coalition, the government might lose its majority in the legislature. The government then falls, and new elections must be held. In the first 10 years of the Third Republic, 50 different coalition governments were formed and fell.

Political Scandals Despite frequent changes of governments, France made economic progress. It paid Germany the huge sum required by the peace treaty and expanded its overseas empire. But in the 1880s and 1890s, a series of political scandals shook public trust in the government.

One crisis erupted when a popular minister of war, General Georges Boulanger (boo lahn zhay), rallied royalists and ultranationalists eager for revenge on Germany. Accused of plotting to overthrow the republic, Boulanger fled to Belgium. In another scandal, a nephew of the president was caught selling nominations for the Legion of Honor, France's highest award. The president was forced to resign.

✔ **Checkpoint** What challenges did the Third Republic face during its 70 years in power?

Anti-Semitism and the Dreyfus Affair

The most serious and divisive scandal began in 1894. A high-ranking army officer, Alfred Dreyfus, was accused of spying for Germany. However, at his military trial, neither Dreyfus nor his lawyer was allowed to

The French Tricolor
The Third Republic eventually adopted the tricolor, a symbol of the French Revolution, as the official flag of France.

see the evidence against him. The injustice was rooted in anti-Semitism. The military elite detested Dreyfus, the first Jewish person to reach such a high position in the army. Although Dreyfus proclaimed his innocence, he was convicted and condemned to life imprisonment on Devil's Island, a desolate penal colony off the coast of South America. By 1896, new evidence pointed to another officer, Ferdinand Esterhazy, as the spy. Still, the army refused to grant Dreyfus a new trial.

Deep Divisions The **Dreyfus affair,** as it was called, scarred French politics and society for decades. Royalists, ultranationalists, and Church officials charged Dreyfus supporters, or "Dreyfusards," with undermining France. Paris echoed with cries of "Long live the army!" and "Death to traitors!" Dreyfusards, mostly liberals and republicans, upheld ideals of justice and equality in the face of massive public anger. In 1898, French novelist Émile Zola joined the battle. In an article headlined *J'Accuse!* (I Accuse!), he charged the army and government with suppressing the truth. As a result, Zola was convicted of **libel,** or the knowing publication of false and damaging statements. He fled into exile.

Slowly, though, the Dreyfusards made progress and eventually the evidence against Dreyfus was shown to be forged. In 1906, a French court finally cleared Dreyfus of all charges and restored his honors. That was a victory for justice, but the political scars of the Dreyfus affair took longer to heal.

Calls for a Jewish State The Dreyfus case reflected the rise of anti-Semitism in Europe. The Enlightenment and the French Revolution had spread ideas about religious toleration. In Western Europe, some Jews had gained jobs in government, universities, and other areas of life. Others had achieved success in banking and business, but most struggled to survive in the ghettos of Eastern Europe or the slums of Western Europe.

By the late 1800s, however, anti-Semitism was again on the rise. Anti-Semites were often members of the lower middle class who felt insecure in their social and economic position. Steeped in the new nationalist fervor, they adopted an aggressive intolerance for outsiders and a violent hatred of Jews.

The Dreyfus case and the pogroms in Russia stirred Theodor Herzl (HURT sul), a Hungarian Jewish journalist living in France. He called for Jews to form their own separate state, where they would have rights that were otherwise denied to them in European countries. Herzl helped launch modern **Zionism,** a movement devoted to rebuilding a Jewish state in Palestine. Many Jews had kept this dream alive since the destruction of the temple in Jerusalem by the Romans. In 1897, Herzl organized the First Zionist Congress in Basel, Switzerland.

✓ **Checkpoint** In what ways was the Zionist movement a reaction to the Dreyfus case?

Reforms in France

Although shaken by the Dreyfus affair, France achieved serious reforms in the early 1900s. Like Britain, France passed laws regulating wages, hours, and safety conditions for workers. It set up a system of free public elementary schools. Creating public

Dreyfus Affair Caricature
This 1899 caricature, *The Traitor*, portrays Alfred Dreyfus as a lindworm, a mythical dragon with no wings in many German legends. In protest of Dreyfus's conviction, French novelist Émile Zola published a letter in 1898 in which he accused the army and government of suppressing the truth in the Dreyfus trial. "The truth is on the march, and nothing shall stop it," Zola wrote.

Penmanship Lesson
One of the many reforms of the early 1900s in France was the establishment of free public elementary schools.

Vocabulary Builder
repress—(ree PRES) *vt.* to put down, subdue

schools was also part of a campaign to reduce the power of the Roman Catholic Church, which controlled education.

Separating Church and State Like Germany, France tried to repress Church involvement in government. Republicans viewed the Church as a conservative force that opposed progressive policies. In the Dreyfus affair, it had backed the army and ultranationalists.

The government closed Church schools, along with many convents and monasteries. In 1905, it passed a law to separate church and state and stopped paying the salaries of the clergy. Catholics, Protestants, and Jews were all to enjoy freedom of worship, but none would have any special treatment from the government.

Women's Rights Under the Napoleonic Code, French women had few rights. By the 1890s, a growing women's rights movement sought legal reforms. It made some gains, such as an 1896 law giving married women the right to their own earnings. In 1909, Jeanne-Elizabeth Schmahl founded the French Union for Women's Suffrage. Rejecting the radical tactics used in Britain, Schmahl favored legal protests. Yet even liberal men were reluctant to grant women suffrage. They feared that women would vote for Church and conservative causes. In the end, French women did not win the vote until after World War II.

✓ **Checkpoint** Describe two social reforms during the late 1800s and early 1900s in France.

Looking Ahead

By 1914, France was the largest democratic country in Europe, with a constitution that protected basic rights. France's economy was generally prosperous, and its overseas empire was second only to that of Britain.

Yet the outlook was not all smooth. Coalition governments rose and fell at the slightest pressure. To the east loomed the industrial might of Germany. Many French citizens were itching for a chance to avenge the defeat in the Franco-Prussian War and liberate the "lost provinces" of Alsace and Lorraine. That chance came in 1914, when all of Europe exploded into World War I.

SECTION **3** Assessment

Progress Monitoring *Online*
For: Section quiz with vocabulary practice
Web Code: nba-2334

Terms, People, and Places
1. For each term, person, or place listed at the beginning of the section, write a sentence explaining its significance.

Note Taking
2. **Reading Skill: Recognize Sequence** Use your completed timeline to answer the Focus Question: What democratic reforms were made in France during the Third Republic?

Comprehension and Critical Thinking
3. **Summarize** Describe the government of France during the Second Empire.
4. **Draw Inferences** How did the Paris Commune and the Dreyfus affair heighten divisions in France?
5. **Summarize** Describe two reforms enacted in France in the early 1900s.
6. **Express Problems Clearly** (a) What solution did Zionists propose for the problem of widespread anti-Semitism? (b) Why do you think they felt it was the best solution?

● **Writing About History**
Quick Write: Write a Conclusion Do additional research to learn more about Ferdinand de Lesseps, the Frenchman who orchestrated the construction of the Suez Canal. Write a one-paragraph conclusion that could be used at the end of a biographical essay on de Lesseps.

The Statue of Liberty ▶

WITNESS HISTORY 🔊 AUDIO

America!

For many Irish families fleeing hunger, Russian Jews escaping pogroms, or poor Italian farmers seeking economic opportunity, the answer was the same—America! A poem inscribed on the base of the Statue of Liberty expressed the welcome and promise of freedom that millions of immigrants dreamed of:

❝Give me your tired, your poor,
  Your huddled masses yearning to breathe free,
  The wretched refuse of your teeming shore.
  Send these, the homeless, tempest-tossed to me.
  I lift my lamp beside the golden door.❞
  —Emma Lazarus, "The New Colossus"

Focus Question How did the United States develop during the 1800s?

Expansion of the United States

Objectives
- Describe how the territory of the United States changed during the 1800s.
- Summarize how American democracy grew before and after the Civil War.
- Analyze the impact of economic growth and social reform on the United States.

Terms, People, and Places

expansionism
Louisiana Purchase
Manifest Destiny
secede
segregation

Note Taking

Reading Skill: Categorize Create a chart like the one below. As you read this section, list key events under the appropriate columns.

Civil War	
Before	**After**
• Western expansion	• Fifteenth Amendment
•	•
•	•

In the 1800s, the United States was a beacon of hope for many people. The American economy was growing rapidly, offering jobs to newcomers. The Constitution and Bill of Rights held out the hope of political and religious freedom. Not everyone shared in the prosperity or the ideals of democracy. Still, by the turn of the nineteenth century, important reforms were being made.

Territorial Expansion

From the earliest years of its history, the United States followed a policy of **expansionism,** or extending the nation's boundaries. At first, the United States stretched only from the Atlantic coast to the Mississippi River. In 1803, President Thomas Jefferson bought the Louisiana territory from France. In one stroke, the **Louisiana Purchase** virtually doubled the size of the nation.

By 1846, the United States had expanded to include Florida, Oregon, and the Republic of Texas. The Mexican War (1846–1848) added California and the Southwest. With growing pride and confidence, Americans claimed that their nation was destined to spread across the entire continent, from sea to sea. This idea became known as **Manifest Destiny.** Some expansionists even hoped to absorb Canada and Mexico. In fact, the United States did go far afield. In 1867, it bought Alaska from Russia and in 1898 annexed the Hawaiian Islands.

✓ **Checkpoint** Describe the United States' physical expansion during the 1800s.

Lewis and Clark Reach the Pacific Ocean

In 1803, Thomas Jefferson appointed Meriwether Lewis to lead an expedition from the Missouri River to the Pacific Ocean. Lewis invited William Clark to share the leadership. The expedition set out from St. Louis in May 1804 and returned in September 1806. Along the way, both Lewis and Clark kept extensive journals (background), which included detailed maps, drawings (below), and descriptions of the land, people, and animals they encountered. The entry here describes the events surrounding what he believed was the group's first view of the Pacific Ocean (above).

❝November 7th, 1805—A cloudy foggy morning some rain. …Two canoes of Indians met and returned with us to their village…. They gave us to eat some fish, and sold us, fish, wappato roots, three dogs, and 2 otter skins for which we gave fishhooks principally, of which they were very fond….

After delaying at this village one hour and a half we set out piloted by an Indian…. Rain continued moderately all day…our small canoe which got separated in the fog this morning joined us this evening….

Great joy in camp we are in view of the Ocean, …this great Pacific Ocean which we [have] been so long anxious to see. And the roaring or noise made by the waves breaking on the rocky shores (as I suppose) may be heard distinctly.❞

—*Captain William Clark, from* **The Journals of the Lewis and Clark Expedition**

Thinking Critically

1. **Summarize** According to Clark's entry, what was the land like in this area?
2. **Draw Conclusions** What conclusions can you draw about William Clark's character from this journal entry?

Expanding Democracy

In 1800, the United States had the most liberal suffrage in the world, but still only white men who owned property could vote. States slowly chipped away at requirements. By the 1830s, most white men had the right to vote. Democracy was still far from complete, however.

By mid-century, reformers were campaigning for many changes. Some demanded a ban on the sale of alcoholic beverages. Others called for better treatment of the mentally ill or pushed for free elementary schools. But two crusades stood out above all others because they highlighted the limits of American democracy—the abolition movement and the women's rights movement.

Calls for Abolition In the early 1800s, a few Americans began to call for an immediate and complete end to slavery. One of these abolitionists was William Lloyd Garrison, who pressed the antislavery cause through his newspaper, the *Liberator*. Another was Frederick Douglass. He had been born into slavery and escaped, and he spoke eloquently in the North about the evils of the system.

By the 1850s, the battle over slavery had intensified. As each new state entered the union, proslavery and antislavery forces met in violent confrontations to decide whether slavery would be legal in the new state. Harriet Beecher Stowe's novel *Uncle Tom's Cabin* helped convince many northerners that slavery was a great social evil.

Women's Rights Movement Women worked hard in the antislavery movement. Lucretia Mott and Elizabeth Cady Stanton traveled to London for the World Antislavery Convention—only to find they were forbidden to speak because they were women. Gradually, American women began to protest the laws and customs that limited their lives.

In 1848, in Seneca Falls, New York, Mott and Stanton organized the first women's rights convention. The convention passed a resolution, based on the Declaration of Independence. It began, "We hold these truths to be self evident: that all men and women are created equal." The women's rights movement set as its goal equality before the law, in the workplace, and in education. Some women also demanded the vote.

✔ **Checkpoint** How did the abolition movement and the women's rights movement highlight the limits of American democracy?

The Civil War and Its Aftermath

Economic differences, as well as the slavery issue, drove the Northern and Southern regions of the United States apart. The division reached a crisis in 1860 when Abraham Lincoln was elected president. Lincoln opposed extending slavery into new territories. Southerners feared that he would eventually abolish slavery altogether and that the federal government would infringe on their states' rights.

North Versus South Soon after Lincoln's election, most southern states seceded, or withdrew, from the Union and formed the Confederate States of America. This action sparked the Civil War, which lasted from 1861 to 1865.

The South had fewer resources, fewer people, and less industry than the North. Still, Southerners fought fiercely to defend their cause. The Confederacy finally surrendered in 1865. The struggle cost more than 600,000 lives—the largest casualty figures of any American war.

Challenges for African Americans During the war, Lincoln issued the Emancipation Proclamation, by which enslaved African Americans in the South were declared free. After the war, three amendments to the Constitution banned slavery throughout the country and granted political rights to African Americans. Under the Fifteenth Amendment, African American men won the right to vote.

Still, African Americans faced many restrictions. In the South, state laws imposed segregation, or legal separation of the races, in hospitals, schools, and other public places. Other state laws imposed conditions for voter eligibility that, despite the Fifteenth Amendment, prevented African Americans from voting.

✔ **Checkpoint** What changes did the Civil War bring about for African Americans?

The American Civil War, 1861–1865
During the American Civil War, Union forces from the North fought against the Confederate Army of the South. This scene shows the black 54th Massachusetts Regiment of the Union army attacking Fort Wagner in South Carolina.

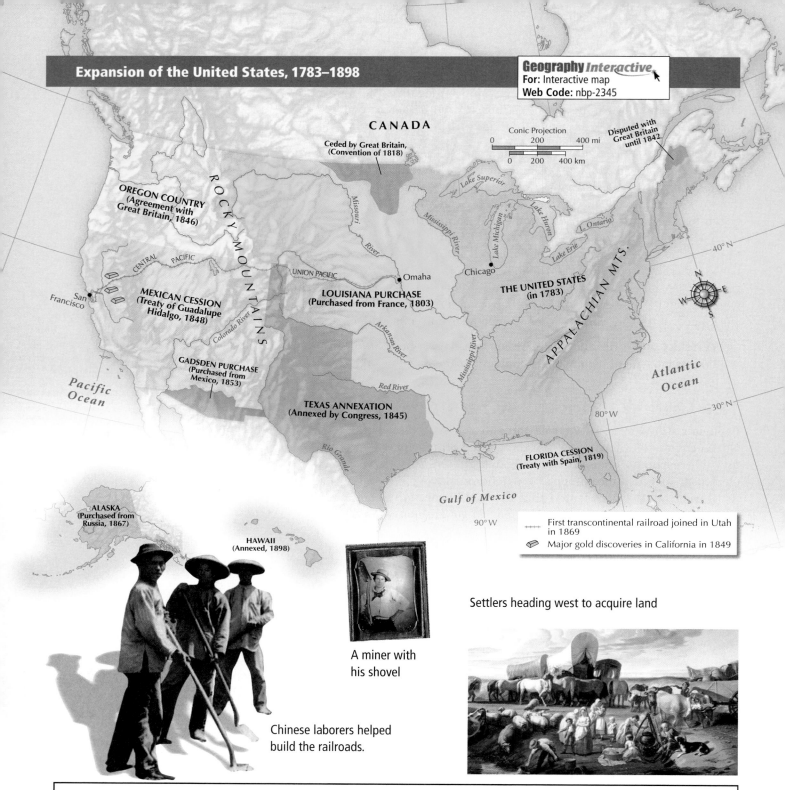

Expansion of the United States, 1783–1898

Geography *Interactive*
For: Interactive map
Web Code: nbp-2345

CANADA

Ceded by Great Britain, (Convention of 1818)

Disputed with Great Britain until 1842

Conic Projection
0   200   400 mi
0   200   400 km

OREGON COUNTRY (Agreement with Great Britain, 1846)

ROCKY MOUNTAINS

Lake Superior

Missouri River

Mississippi River

Lake Michigan

Lake Huron

L. Ontario

Lake Erie

CENTRAL PACIFIC

UNION PACIFIC

Omaha

Chicago

THE UNITED STATES (in 1783)

APPALACHIAN MTS.

40° N

San Francisco

MEXICAN CESSION (Treaty of Guadalupe Hidalgo, 1848)

Colorado River

LOUISIANA PURCHASE (Purchased from France, 1803)

Arkansas River

Atlantic Ocean

GADSDEN PURCHASE (Purchased from Mexico, 1853)

Red River

Mississippi River

80° W

30° N

Pacific Ocean

TEXAS ANNEXATION (Annexed by Congress, 1845)

Rio Grande

FLORIDA CESSION (Treaty with Spain, 1819)

Gulf of Mexico

90° W

ALASKA (Purchased from Russia, 1867)

HAWAII (Annexed, 1898)

First transcontinental railroad joined in Utah in 1869
Major gold discoveries in California in 1849

A miner with his shovel

Settlers heading west to acquire land

Chinese laborers helped build the railroads.

Map Skills Through wars and treaties, the United States expanded its borders to its present size. During the 1800s, settlers flocked to newly acquired lands. The discovery of gold in California drew a flood of easterners. Other people, like the Mormons, sought a place to practice their religion freely. Still others headed west in the spirit of adventure. Some Native American nations resisted the invaders, but they were outgunned and outnumbered. By the 1890s, most surviving Native Americans had been driven onto reservations.

1. **Locate** (a) Louisiana Purchase (b) Florida (c) Texas (d) Alaska (e) Hawaii
2. **Place** Identify three countries that sold territories to the United States.
3. **Make Comparisons** Compare this map to a map of the present-day United States. How did the area where you live become part of the United States?

Economic Growth and Social Reform

After the Civil War, the United States grew to lead the world in industrial and agricultural production. A special combination of factors made this possible including political stability, private property rights, a free enterprise system, and an inexpensive supply of land and labor—supplied mostly by immigrants. Finally, a growing network of transportation and communications technologies aided businesses in transporting resources and finished products.

Business and Labor By 1900, giant monopolies controlled whole industries. Scottish-born Andrew Carnegie built the nation's largest steel company, while John D. Rockefeller's Standard Oil Company dominated the world's petroleum industry. Big business enjoyed tremendous profits.

But the growing prosperity was not shared by all. In factories, wages were low and conditions were often brutal. To defend their interests, American workers organized labor unions such as the American Federation of Labor. Unions sought better wages, hours, and working conditions. Struggles with management sometimes erupted into violent confrontations. Slowly, however, workers made gains.

Populists and Progressives In the economic hard times of the late 1800s, farmers also organized themselves to defend their interests. In the 1890s, they joined city workers to support the new Populist party. The Populists never became a major party, but their platform of reforms, such as an eight-hour workday, eventually became law.

By 1900, reformers known as Progressives also pressed for change. They sought laws to ban child labor, limit working hours, regulate monopolies, and give voters more power. Another major goal of the Progressives was obtaining voting rights for women. After a long struggle, American suffragists finally won the vote in 1920, when the Nineteenth Amendment went into effect.

✔ **Checkpoint** Describe the factors that helped the United States become an industrial and agricultural leader.

Vocabulary Builder

dominate—(DAHM un nayt) *vt.* to rule or control by superior power or influence

---

SECTION 4 Assessment

Progress Monitoring Online
For: Self-quiz with vocabulary practice
Web Code: nba-2346

Terms, People, and Places

1. Place each of the key terms at the beginning of the section into one of these two categories: geography or politics. Explain your choices.

Note Taking

2. **Reading Skill: Categorize** Use your completed chart to answer the Focus Question: How did the United States develop during the 1800s?

Comprehension and Critical Thinking

3. **Summarize** Describe how the United States grew in each of these areas in the 1800s: (a) territory, (b) population, (c) economy.

4. **Identify Central Issues** Describe two ways that democracy expanded.

5. **Draw Conclusions** (a) How did immigrants benefit from economic growth in the United States after the Civil War? (b) What problems did workers face?

● Writing About History

Quick Write: Write a Thesis Statement Conduct research to learn more about American entrepreneur, Andrew Carnegie. While some historians have portrayed Carnegie and others like him as philanthropists and captains of industry, others have portrayed him as a "robber baron." Write a thesis statement for a biographical essay on Carnegie in which you summarize your views of the man and his achievements.

Quick Study Guide

Progress Monitoring *Online*
For: Self-test with vocabulary practice
Web Code: nba-2307

■ Democratic Reforms in Britain 1800s–Early 1900s

- Redistribution of seats in the House of Commons from rural towns to growing cities (1832)
- Expansion of suffrage for men with property (1832)
- Expansion of suffrage for many working-class men (1867)
- Expansion of suffrage to farm workers and most men
- Introduction of secret ballot
- Power of the House of Lords restricted (1911)

■ Social and Economic Reforms in Britain 1800s–Early 1900s

- Slave trade prohibited (1807)
- Slavery in all British colonies abolished (1833)
- Repeal of high tariffs on grains (1846)
- Women and children under ten forbidden to work in mines (1842)
- Women and children limited to 10-hour workday (1847)
- Improvements in public health and housing
- Free elementary education
- Accident, health, and unemployment insurance
- Old-age pensions
- Suffrage extended to women over 30 (1918)

■ Key Events in France, 1800s–Early 1900s

1852 Napoleon III sets up Second Empire.
1856 France and Britain defeat Russia in Crimean War.
1863 Napoleon III sends troops and Archduke Maximilian to Mexico.
1860 France gains Nice and Savoy by helping Italian nationalists defeat Austria.
1870 Napoleon III captured in Franco-Prussian war; Four-month siege of Paris by Prussians; France defeated and Alsace Lorraine ceded to Germany; Republicans in Paris establish the Third Republic.
1871 Paris Commune uprising
1894 Dreyfus affair
1905 Separation of church and state established by law.

■ Key Events in the United States 1800s–Early 1900s

1803	Louisiana Purchase
1846–1848	Mexican War
1849	California Gold Rush
1861–1865	Civil War
1867	Purchase of Alaska
1869	Completion of Transcontinental Railroad
1882	Formation of Standard Oil Trust
1898	Spanish-American War; Hawaiian islands annexed
1908	Development of Henry Ford's Model T

■ Key Events in the Growth of Western Democracies

Europe and North America World Events	**1832** Great Reform Act gives more British men suffrage and redistributes seats in House of Commons.	**1845** Potato famine in Ireland begins.	**1861–1865** American Civil War ends slavery in the United States.
1815	**1835**		**1855**
	1821 Mexico wins independence from Spain.		**1858** Britain begins rule of India.

382

Concept Connector

■ Cumulative Review

Record the answers to the questions below on your Concept Connector worksheets. In addition, record information from this chapter about the following concept:

• **Migration:** Westward Movement in the United States

1. **Cooperation** Do research to learn more about various abolitionist groups, including the Society of Friends (or Quakers), the Society for the Abolition of the Slave Trade, the British Antislavery Society, or the American Anti-Slavery Society. What tactics did these groups use in their efforts to abolish slavery?

2. **Migration** Compare the "push and pull" factors that caused Europeans to emigrate to the Americas during the nineteenth and early twentieth century to the factors influencing earlier migrations of Europeans to the Americas during the seventeenth and eighteenth centuries. Think about the following:
   • Religious factors, such as religious intolerance
   • Economic factors, such as the availability of land and other resources
   • Political factors, such as racial or ethnic discrimination

3. **Democracy** Do you think John Locke's ideas about natural rights contributed to the expansion of suffrage to include working class men and all women? Explain your answer.

■ Connections to Today

1. **Trade: Free Trade and Tariffs** The British Corn laws imposed high, protective tariffs on imported grains and kept the price of British grown grain high. Do library research to learn more about a current protective tariff that is opposed by those who favor free trade. Which country has imposed this tariff on imports? What goods are affected? Which groups oppose the tariff and why?

2. **Conflict: Northern Ireland** The southern counties of Ireland gained independence from Britain in 1922, but Northern Ireland remained under British rule. Conflict ensued between minority Catholics in Northern Ireland, who demanded the reunification of Ireland, and majority Protestants, who favored a continued union with Britain. In 1998, the main political parties signed a peace accord that would eventually bring self-rule to Northern Ireland. Do research to learn more about the status of peace in Northern Ireland.

3. **Conflict: Native Americans** The expansion of the United States proved to be devastating for most Native American groups in North America. By the 1890s, most surviving Native Americans had been driven onto reservations. Conduct library research to learn more about the status of Native Americans living in the United States today. Write a paragraph summarizing the information you find.

History *Interactive*
For: Interactive timeline
Web Code: nbp-2308

1870	1897	1900s
France defeated in the Franco-Prussian War; Third Republic established.	Theodor Herzl organizes the First Zionist Congress for the purpose of found-ing a Jewish state.	The women's suffrage movement grows in Britain and the United States.

1875   1895   1915

1869	1889	1893	1910
The French-built Suez Canal opens in Egypt.	Brazil becomes a republic.	New Zealand is the first nation to give women the vote.	The Union of South Africa is formed.

Chapter Assessment

Terms, People, and Places

1. How did the Great Reform Act of 1832 correct the problem of **rotten boroughs?**
2. What group of people was added to the British **electorate** in 1918?
3. Why did members of the Chartist movement demand the use of **secret ballots?**
4. Why did the opponents of the Corn Laws in Britain favor **free trade?**
5. Why did French politicians need to form **coalitions?**
6. Where did Britain establish **penal colonies?**
7. What is **segregation?**
8. What is a **provisional** government?

Main Ideas

Section 1 (pp. 360–363)
9. What were the effects of the Great Reform Act of 1832?

Section 2 (pp. 364–369)
10. How did British policy toward slavery change in 1833?

Section 3 (pp. 371–376)
11. How did the party system in France's Third Republic differ from the British party system?
12. What was the main goal of the Zionist movement?

Section 4 (pp. 377–381)
13. List two goals of the Progressives in the United States in the early 1900s.

Chapter Focus Question

14. How did Britain, France, and the United States slowly extend democratic rights during the 1800s and early 1900s?

Critical Thinking

15. **Analyzing Cartoons** What views of suffrage does this cartoon reflect?

16. **Draw Conclusions** Britain and France faced many similar political and social problems in the 1800s. Why do you think Britain was able to avoid the upheavals that plagued France?

17. **Recognize Cause and Effect** (a) List two long-term causes and two immediate causes of the Great Hunger; (b) list two immediate effects. (c) Why do you think the famine sparked lasting feelings of bitterness against Britain?

18. **Synthesize Information** Describe how each of the following was related to nationalism: (a) the prestige of Queen Victoria, (b) the revolt of the Paris Commune, (c) the rise of Zionism.

19. **Geography and History** How did the geography of the United States encourage the American government to achieve its goal of Manifest Destiny?

● Writing About History

Writing a Compare and Contrast Expository Essay Conduct research and write a compare and contrast essay on the careers and accomplishments of Benjamin Disraeli and William Gladstone (left). How were the two alike? How were they different?

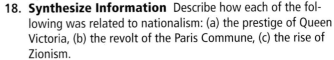

Prewriting
- Identify points of comparison and contrast for your essay. For example, you may want to compare and contrast the two men in terms of their background, political views, specific accomplishments, and impact on British politics. These categories will help you organize details in your essay.
  - Create a Venn Diagram showing differences between the two men in the outside circles and similarities in the overlapping center.
  - Collect the facts you need to write your essay.

Drafting
- Start with an engaging opening that defines the comparison/contrast and grabs readers' interest. This could be a quotation, surprising detail or statistic, or a question.
- Give details about each point of comparison to make it more accessible to readers. For example, you might give the years during which each man served as prime minister.
- Discuss the points about each man in the same order. You might even use similar sentence structure to emphasize this.

Revising
- Use the guidelines for revising your essay on page SH12 of the Writing Handbook.

Document-Based Assessment

The Dreyfus Affair

On December 22, 1894, a French military court convicted an innocent Jewish man, Captain Alfred Dreyfus, of selling state secrets to Germany. Dreyfus was imprisoned on Devil's Island off of South America and his conviction was reversed only after nearly twelve years. The Dreyfus affair caused a great division between conservatives, who still disliked the outcome of the French Revolution and held strong anti-Semitic beliefs, and liberals, who viewed the case as a gross abuse of individual rights.

Document A

". . . if my voice ceased to be heard, it would mean that it had been extinguished forever, for if I have survived, it has been in order to insist on my honor—my property and the patrimony of our children—and in order to do my duty, as I have done it everywhere and always, and as it must always be done, when right and justice are on one's side, without ever fearing anything or anyone."

—From a letter to his wife Lucie, by Alfred Dreyfus, September 1898, published in **Cinq Années**

Document B

"I accuse the offices of War of having conducted in the press, particularly in L'Eclair and in L'Echo de Paris, an abominable campaign designed to mislead public opinion and to conceal their wrongdoing."

"Finally, I accuse the first Court Martial of having violated the law in convicting a defendant on the basis of a document kept secret, and I accuse the second Court Martial of having covered up . . . [and] knowingly acquitting a guilty man."

—From **"J'Accuse"** a letter to the President of the Republic by Émile Zola

Document C

UN DINER EN FAMILLE

"Un Diner En Famille"
   Translation: "It is agreed that there should be no talk of the affair! But they did talk about it . . ."

—From **Le Figaro** by Caran d'Ache, February, 1898

Analyzing Documents

Use your knowledge of the Dreyfus affair and Documents A, B, and C to answer questions 1–4.

1. In Document A, Dreyfus suggests that his wish to prove his innocence helped to—
   A keep him close to his family.
   B keep him alive.
   C make the Army take illegal actions.
   D make anti-Semitic groups angry.

2. Which statement best summarizes Zola's letter in Document B?
   A Although the French military convicted the wrong man, they attempted to carry out a fair trial.
   B The French military was fooled by handwriting experts, who tried to convict the wrong man.
   C The French military knowingly and illegally convicted an innocent man.
   D The French military showed that the army was anti-Semitic at the highest levels.

3. Document C illustrates—
   A why many French families believed Dreyfus was guilty.
   B why Dreyfus was convicted unfairly of treason.
   C how the Dreyfus case divided France.
   D how anti-Semitism was a factor in the Dreyfus case.

4. **Writing Task** On July 21, 1906, a French general knighted Alfred Dreyfus a member of the Legion of Honor. Well wishers attended the ceremony in the courtyard of the École Militaire. Some shouted "Long live Dreyfus." Suppose you were reporting on the event for an American newspaper. Write a news story, using the documents on this page along with information from the chapter.

WITNESS HISTORY 🔊 AUDIO

Empire Builders

Lord Frederick Lugard, a British empire builder, tried to justify imperialism in Africa with these words:

❝There are some who say we have no *right* to Africa at all, that 'it belongs to the natives.' I hold that our right is the necessity that is upon us to provide for our ever-growing population—either by opening new fields for emigration, or by providing work and employment . . . and to stimulate trade by finding new markets.❞

Listen to the Witness History audio to learn more about imperialism.

◄ One of several journalists in South Africa, British writer Rudyard Kipling (bottom right) considered imperialism to be beneficial to Africans.

British East India Company coat of arms

Ivory carving of Africans carrying a European

Chapter Preview

Chapter Focus Question How did Western industrial powers gain global empires?

Section 1
Building Overseas Empires

Section 2
The Partition of Africa

Section 3
European Claims in Muslim Regions

Section 4
The British Take Over India

Section 5
China and the New Imperialism

Lamp from a mosque

Note Taking Study Guide *Online*
For: Note Taking and Concept Connector worksheets
Web Code: nbd-2401

Missionary prayer book in Korean

English writer
Rudyard Kipling

WITNESS HISTORY 🔊 AUDIO

The White Man's Burden

Born in India, English writer Rudyard Kipling witnessed British imperialism firsthand. His 1899 poem "The White Man's Burden" summarizes his view of the duties of imperial nations:

❝ Take up the White Man's burden—
  In patience to abide,
To veil the threat of terror
  And check the show of pride;
By open speech and simple,
  An hundred times made plain,
To seek another's profit,
  And work another's gain. **❞**

Focus Question How did Western nations come to dominate much of the world in the late 1800s?

Building Overseas Empires

Objectives
- Analyze the causes of the "new imperialism."
- Explain why Western imperialism spread so rapidly.
- Describe how imperial governments ruled their empires.

Terms, People, and Places

imperialism
protectorate
sphere of influence

Note Taking

Reading Skill: Recognize Multiple Causes As you read the section, make a chart like the one below showing the multiple causes of imperialism in the 1800s.

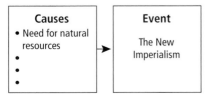

Causes	Event
• Need for natural resources • • •	The New Imperialism

Like Great Britain, other Western countries built overseas empires in the late 1800s. The Industrial Revolution had transformed the West. Advances in science and technology, industry, transportation, and communication provided Western nations with many advantages. Armed with new economic and political power, Western nations set out to dominate the world.

Motives Driving the New Imperialism

European imperialism did not begin in the 1800s. **Imperialism** is the domination by one country of the political, economic, or cultural life of another country or region. As you have learned, European states won empires in the Americas after 1492, established colonies in South Asia, and gained toeholds on the coasts of Africa and China. Despite these gains, between 1500 and 1800, Europe had little influence on the lives of the peoples of China, India, or Africa.

By the 1800s, however, Europe had gained considerable power. Strong, centrally governed nation-states had emerged, and the Industrial Revolution had greatly enriched European economies. Encouraged by their new economic and military strength, Europeans embarked on a path of aggressive expansion that today's historians call the "new imperialism." In just a few decades, beginning in the 1870s, Europeans brought much of the world under their influence and control. Like other key developments in world history, the new imperialism exploded out of a combination of causes.

Economic Interests Spur Expansion The Industrial Revolution created needs and desires that spurred overseas expansion. Manufacturers wanted access to natural resources such as rubber, petroleum, manganese for steel, and palm oil for machinery. They also hoped for new markets of consumers to whom they could sell their factory goods. Bankers sought ventures to invest their profits. In addition, colonies offered a valuable outlet for Europe's growing population.

Political and Military Motives Political and military issues were closely linked to economic motives. Steam-powered merchant ships and naval vessels needed bases around the world to take on coal and supplies. Industrial powers seized islands or harbors to satisfy these needs.

Nationalism played an important role, too. When France, for example, moved into West Africa, rival nations like Britain and Germany seized lands nearby to halt further French expansion. Western leaders claimed that colonies were needed for national security. They also felt that ruling a global empire increased a nation's <u>prestige</u> around the world.

Vocabulary Builder

<u>prestige</u>—(pres TEEZH) *n.* the power to impress or influence because of success or wealth

Humanitarian and Religious Goals Many Westerners felt a genuine concern for their "little brothers" beyond the seas. Missionaries, doctors, and colonial officials believed they had a duty to spread what they saw as the blessings of Western civilization, including its medicine, law, and Christian religion.

Applying Social Darwinism Behind the idea of the West's civilizing mission was a growing sense of racial superiority. Many Westerners had embraced the ideas of Social Darwinism. They applied Darwin's ideas about natural selection and survival of the fittest to human societies. European races, they argued, were superior to all others, and imperial domination of weaker races was simply nature's way of improving the human species. As a result, millions of non-Westerners were robbed of their cultural heritage.

✔ **Checkpoint** What factors contributed to European imperialism in the 1800s?

JUNGLES TO-DAY ARE GOLD MINES TO-MORROW.

TROPICAL AFRICAN COLONIES
= IN ACCOUNT WITH =
THE HOME COUNTRY

GOODS WE SOLD	GOODS WE RECEIVED
1895 - £ 2,250,000	1895 - £ 2,000,000
1905 - £ 4,500,000	1905 - £ 3,000,000
1910 - £ 8,750,000	1910 - £ 5,250,000
1915 - £ 9,500,000	1915 - £ 10,500,000
1925 - £ 24,000,000	1925 - £ 20,250,000

GROWING MARKETS FOR OUR GOODS

A Market for Goods
A driving force behind imperialism was the desire for access to new markets in which to sell goods. This British propaganda poster boasts that Africa would become a gold mine for British-made products. Britain's sense of national pride and aggressive foreign policy during this period came to be known as jingoism. *What does this poster show about the British attitude toward Africa?*

European Conquest of Africa

The excerpts below present two different views on the partition of Africa by European nations in the 1800s. **Critical Thinking** *What is Cecil Rhodes's argument for imperialism? What is Chief Kabongo's argument against it?*

Favoring Imperialism

"I contend that we are the first race in the world and that the more of the world we inhabit the better it is for the human race. I contend that every acre added to our territory provides for the birth of more of the English race, who otherwise would not be brought into existence . . . . I believe it to be my duty to God, my Queen and my country to paint the whole map of Africa red, red from the Cape to Cairo. That is my creed, my dream and my mission."

—*Cecil Rhodes*

Opposing Imperialism

"A Pink Cheek man came one day to our Council . . . and he told us of the King of the Pink Cheek who . . . lived in a land over the seas. 'This great king is now your king,' he said. This was strange news. For this land was ours. . . . We had no king, we elected our Councils and they made our laws. With patience, our leading Elders tried to tell this to the Pink Cheek. . . . But at the end he said, 'This we know, but in spite of this what I have told you is a fact. You have now a king . . . and his laws are your laws.'"

—*Chief Kabongo of the Kikuyu in Kenya*

The Rapid Spread of Western Imperialism

From about 1870 to 1914, imperialist nations gained control over much of the world. Leading the way were soldiers, merchants, settlers, missionaries, and explorers. In Europe, imperial expansion found favor with all classes, from bankers and manufacturers to workers. Western imperialism expanded rapidly for a number of reasons.

Weakness of Non-Western States While European nations had grown stronger in the 1800s, several older civilizations were in decline, especially the Ottoman Middle East, Mughal (MOO gul) India, and Qing (ching) China. In West Africa, wars among African peoples and the damaging effect of the slave trade had undermined established empires, kingdoms, and city-states. Newer African states were not strong enough to resist the Western onslaught.

The Maxim Gun
Sir Hiram Maxim with his invention, the Maxim machine gun. *Why were European armies often able to defeat African or Asian forces?*

Western Advantages European powers had the advantages of strong economies, well-organized governments, and powerful armies and navies. Superior technology, including riverboats and the telegraph, as well as improved medical knowledge also played a role. Quinine and other new medicines helped Europeans survive deadly tropical diseases. And, of course, advances such as Maxim machine guns, repeating rifles, and steam-driven warships were very strong arguments in persuading Africans and Asians to accept Western control.

Resisting Imperialism Africans and Asians strongly resisted Western expansion into their lands. Some people fought the invaders, even though they had no weapons to equal the Maxim gun. Ruling groups in certain areas tried to strengthen their societies against outsiders by reforming their own Muslim, Hindu, or Confucian traditions. Finally, many

Western-educated Africans and Asians organized nationalist movements to expel the imperialists from their lands.

Facing Criticism at Home In the West itself, a small group of anti-imperialists emerged. Some argued that colonialism was a tool of the rich. Others said it was immoral. Westerners, they pointed out, were moving toward greater democracy at home but were imposing undemocratic rule on other peoples.

✔ **Checkpoint** How did Western imperialism spread through Africa and Asia so quickly?

Forms of Imperial Rule

The leading imperial powers developed several kinds of colonial rule. The French practiced direct rule, sending officials and soldiers from France to administer their colonies. Their goal was to impose French culture on their colonies and turn them into French provinces.

The British, by contrast, relied on a system of indirect rule. To govern their colonies, they used sultans, chiefs, or other local rulers. They then encouraged the children of the local ruling class to get an education in Britain. In that way, they groomed a new "Westernized" generation of leaders to continue indirect imperial rule and to spread British civilization. Like France and other imperialist nations, however, Britain could still resort to military force if its control over a colony was threatened.

In a **protectorate,** local rulers were left in place but were expected to follow the advice of European advisors on issues such as trade or missionary activity. A protectorate cost less to run than a colony did, and usually did not require a large commitment of military forces.

A third form of Western control was the **sphere of influence,** an area in which an outside power claimed exclusive investment or trading privileges. Europeans carved out these spheres in China and elsewhere to prevent conflicts among themselves.

✔ **Checkpoint** Compare and contrast how Britain and France ruled their colonies.

Indian princes and British army officers play polo in 1880.

SECTION **1** Assessment

Progress Monitoring *Online*
For: Self-quiz with vocabulary practice
Web Code: nba-2411

Terms, People, and Places

1. What do each of the key terms listed at the beginning of the section have in common? Explain.

Note Taking

2. **Reading Skill: Recognize Multiple Causes** Use your completed chart to answer the Focus Question: How did Western nations come to dominate much of the world in the late 1800s?

Comprehension and Critical Thinking

3. **Explain** (a) What were three reasons for the rapid spread of Western imperialism? (b) How did people oppose it?

4. **Recognize Bias** Western colonial officials and missionaries thought that they had a duty to spread the "blessings of Western civilization" to their African and Asian "little brothers." How was this a biased viewpoint?

● **Writing About History**

Quick Write: Write a Thesis Statement Suppose that you are writing a persuasive essay using the point of view of an anti-imperialist from a Western nation trying to persuade the public that imperialism is wrong. Based on what you have read in this section, write a thesis statement for your essay.

African soldiers in German uniforms

WITNESS HISTORY ◀)) AUDIO

Resisting Imperialism

In 1890, Chief Machemba (mah CHEM bah) of the Yao (YAH oh) people in East Africa wrote in Swahili to a German officer:

❝ If it be friendship that you desire, then I am ready for it . . . but to be your subject, that I cannot be. . . . I do not fall at your feet, for you are God's creature just as I am.**❞**
—Chief Machemba, Letter to Herman von Wissman

Focus Question How did imperialist European powers claim control over most of Africa by the end of the 1800s?

The Partition of Africa

Objectives

- Analyze the forces that shaped Africa.
- Explain why European contact with Africa increased during the 1800s.
- Understand how Leopold II started a scramble for colonies.
- Describe how Africans resisted imperialism.

Terms, People, and Places

Usman dan Fodio
Shaka
paternalistic
David Livingstone
Henry Stanley
King Leopold II
Boer War
Samori Touré
Yaa Asantewaa
Nehanda
Menelik II
elite

Note Taking

Reading Skill: Identify Causes and Effects As you read the section, fill in the chart with information about the causes and effects of the partition of Africa by European nations.

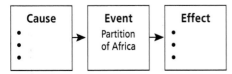

In the late 1800s, Britain, France, Germany, and other European powers began a scramble for African territories. Within about 20 years, the Europeans had carved up the continent and dominated millions of Africans. Although the Yao and others resisted, they could not prevent European conquest.

Africa in the Early 1800s

To understand the impact of European domination, we must look at Africa in the early 1800s, before the scramble for colonies began. Africa is a huge continent, nearly three times the size of Europe. Across its many regions, people spoke hundreds of languages and had developed varied governments. Some people lived in large centralized states, while others lived in village communities.

North Africa North Africa includes the enormous Sahara and the fertile land along the Mediterranean. Since long before 1800, the region was a part of the Muslim world. In the early 1800s, much of North Africa remained under the rule of the declining Ottoman empire.

Islamic Crusades in West Africa By the early 1800s, an Islamic revival spread across West Africa. It began among the Fulani people in northern Nigeria. The scholar and preacher **Usman dan Fodio** (oo SMAHN dahn foh DEE oh) denounced the corruption of the local Hausa rulers. He called for social and religious reforms based on the sharia, or Islamic law. Usman inspired Fulani herders and Hausa townspeople to rise up against their European rulers.

Usman and his successors set up a powerful Islamic state in northern Nigeria. Under their rule, literacy increased, local wars quieted, and trade improved. Their success inspired other Muslim reform movements in West Africa. Between about 1780 and 1880, more than a dozen Islamic leaders rose to power, replacing old rulers or founding new states in the western Sudan.

In the forest regions, strong states like the Asante (uh SAHN teh) kingdom had arisen. The Asante traded with Europeans and Muslims and controlled several smaller states. However, these tributary states were ready to turn to Europeans or others who might help them defeat their Asante rulers.

East Africa Islam had long influenced the east coast of Africa, where port cities like Mombasa (mahm BAH suh) and Kilwa (KEEL wah) carried on profitable trade. The cargoes were often slaves. Captives were marched from the interior to the coast to be shipped as slaves to the Middle East. Ivory and copper from Central Africa were also exchanged for goods such as cloth and firearms from India.

Southern Africa In the early 1800s, the Zulus emerged as a major force in southern Africa under a ruthless and brilliant leader, **Shaka.** Between 1818 and 1828, Shaka waged relentless war and conquered many nearby peoples. He absorbed their young men and women into Zulu regiments. By encouraging rival groups to forget their differences, he cemented a growing pride in the Zulu kingdom.

His conquests, however, set off mass migrations and wars, creating chaos across much of the region. Groups driven from their homelands by the Zulus then migrated north, conquering still other peoples and creating their own powerful states. By the 1830s, the Zulus faced a new threat, the arrival of well-armed, mounted Boers, descendants of Dutch farmers who were migrating north from the Cape Colony. In 1814, the Cape Colony had passed from the Dutch to the British. Many Boers resented British laws that abolished slavery and otherwise interfered with their way of life. To escape British rule, they loaded their goods into covered wagons and started north. Several thousand Boer families joined this "Great Trek."

As the migrating Boers came into contact with Zulus, fighting quickly broke out. At first, Zulu regiments held their own. But in the end, Zulu spears could not defeat Boer guns. The struggle for control of the land would rage until the end of the century.

Impact of the Slave Trade In the early 1800s, European nations began to outlaw the transatlantic slave trade, though it took years to end. Meanwhile, the East African slave trade continued to Asia.

Some people helped freed slaves resettle in Africa. In 1787, the British organized Sierra Leone in West Africa as a colony for former slaves. Later, some free blacks from the United States settled in nearby Liberia. By 1847, Liberia had become an independent republic.

✔ **Checkpoint** What factors shaped each of the main regions of Africa during the early 1800s?

Zulu King Cetshwayo
A nephew of Shaka, Cetshwayo (kech WY oh) was the last of the great Zulu kings. He ruled a disciplined army of about 40,000 men until the British defeated him in 1879. *Why was Cetshwayo considered a threat to British colonial interests?*

European Contact Increases

From the 1500s through the 1700s, Europeans traded along the African coast. Africans wanted trade with Europeans but did not want to "house them." Resistance by Africans, difficult geography, and diseases all kept Europeans from moving into the interior regions of the continent. Medical advances and river steamships changed all that in the 1800s.

Explorers Advance Into Africa's Interior In the early 1800s, European explorers began pushing into the interior of Africa. Explorers like Mungo Park and Richard Burton set out to map the course and sources of the great African rivers such as the Niger, the Nile, and the Congo. They were fascinated by African geography, but they had little understanding of the peoples they met. All, however, endured great hardships while exploring Africa.

Missionaries Follow Explorers Catholic and Protestant missionaries followed the explorers. All across Africa, they sought to win people to Christianity. The missionaries were sincere in their desire to help Africans. They built schools and medical clinics alongside churches. They also focused attention on the evils of the slave trade. Still, missionaries, like most Westerners, took a **paternalistic** view of Africans, meaning they saw them as children in need of guidance. To them, African cultures and religions were "degraded." They urged Africans to reject their own traditions in favor of Western civilization.

Livingstone Blazes a Trail The best-known explorer and missionary was **Dr. David Livingstone.** For 30 years, he crisscrossed Africa. He wrote about the many peoples he met with more sympathy and less bias than did most Europeans. He relentlessly opposed the slave trade, which remained a profitable business for some African rulers and foreign traders. The only way to end this cruel traffic, he believed, was to open up the interior of Africa to Christianity and trade.

Livingstone blazed a trail that others soon followed. In 1869, the journalist **Henry Stanley** trekked into Central Africa to find Livingstone, who had not been heard from for years. He finally tracked him down in 1871 in what is today Tanzania, greeting him with the now-legendary phrase "Dr. Livingstone, I presume?"

✔ **Checkpoint** How did European contact with Africa increase in the late 1800s?

A Scramble for Colonies

Shortly afterward, **King Leopold II** of Belgium hired Stanley to explore the Congo River basin and arrange trade treaties with African leaders. Publicly, Leopold spoke of a civilizing mission to carry the light "that for millions of men still plunged in barbarism will be the dawn of a better era." Privately, he dreamed of conquest and profit. Leopold's activities in the Congo set off a scramble by other nations. Before long, Britain, France, and Germany were pressing rival claims to the region.

Berlin Conference To avoid bloodshed, European powers met at an international conference in 1884. It took place not in Africa but in Berlin, Germany. No Africans were invited to the conference.

Missionaries at Work
Missionaries conduct a baptism ceremony in the Lower Congo in 1907. Others performed communion with chalices and patens, or ceremonial plates, like those above. *Why did missionaries seek to convert people to Christianity?*

WITNESS HISTORY VIDEO

Watch *The Scramble for African Colonies* on the **Witness History Discovery School**™ video program to learn more about the partition of Africa.

Discovery
SCHOOL

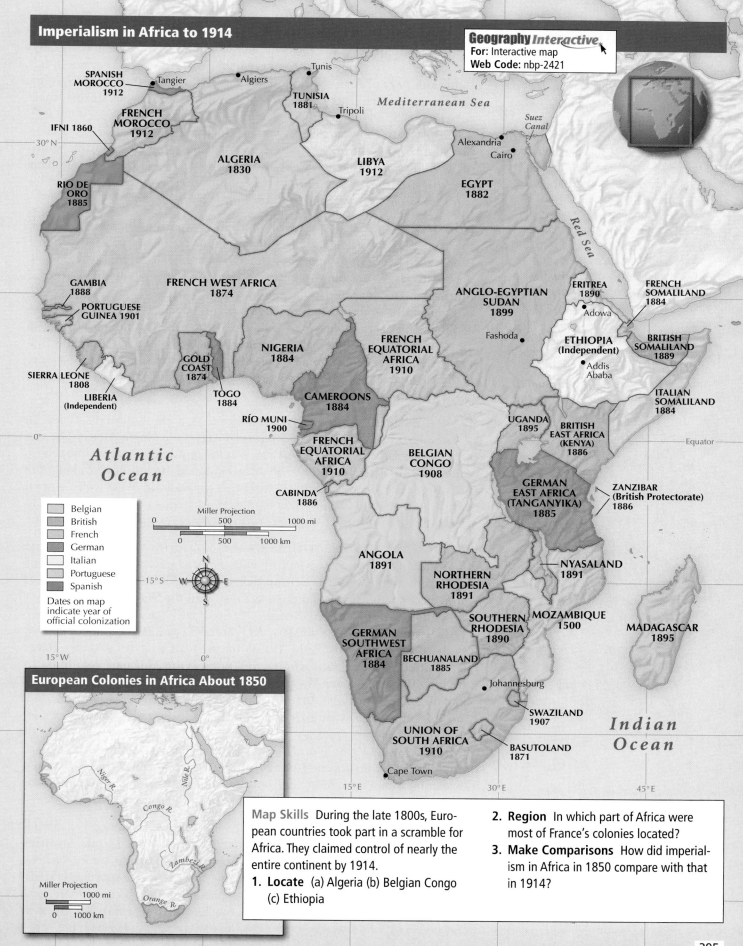

Imperialism in Africa to 1914

Geography *Interactive*
For: Interactive map
Web Code: nbp-2421

SPANISH MOROCCO 1912 • Tangier

• Algiers

• Tunis

TUNISIA 1881

Mediterranean Sea

• Tripoli

Suez Canal

IFNI 1860

FRENCH MOROCCO 1912

30° N

ALGERIA 1830

LIBYA 1912

Alexandria • Cairo •

RIO DE ORO 1885

EGYPT 1882

Red Sea

GAMBIA 1888

FRENCH WEST AFRICA 1874

ANGLO-EGYPTIAN SUDAN 1899

ERITREA 1890

FRENCH SOMALILAND 1884

PORTUGUESE GUINEA 1901

• Adowa

Fashoda •

ETHIOPIA (Independent)

BRITISH SOMALILAND 1889

SIERRA LEONE 1808

NIGERIA 1884

FRENCH EQUATORIAL AFRICA 1910

• Addis Ababa

LIBERIA (Independent)

GOLD COAST 1874

TOGO 1884

CAMEROONS 1884

ITALIAN SOMALILAND 1884

RÍO MUNI 1900

FRENCH EQUATORIAL AFRICA 1910

UGANDA 1895

BRITISH EAST AFRICA (KENYA) 1886

0°

Atlantic Ocean

CABINDA 1886

BELGIAN CONGO 1908

GERMAN EAST AFRICA (TANGANYIKA) 1885

ZANZIBAR (British Protectorate) 1886

Equator

Belgian
British
French
German
Italian
Portuguese
Spanish

Dates on map indicate year of official colonization

Miller Projection
0   500   1000 mi
0   500   1000 km

N
W — E
S

ANGOLA 1891

NYASALAND 1891

15° S

NORTHERN RHODESIA 1891

MOZAMBIQUE 1500

MADAGASCAR 1895

SOUTHERN RHODESIA 1890

15° W

0°

GERMAN SOUTHWEST AFRICA 1884

BECHUANALAND 1885

• Johannesburg

SWAZILAND 1907

Indian Ocean

UNION OF SOUTH AFRICA 1910

BASUTOLAND 1871

• Cape Town

15° E   30° E   45° E

European Colonies in Africa About 1850

Niger R.

Nile R.

Congo R.

Zambezi R.

Miller Projection
0   1000 mi
0   1000 km

Orange R.

Map Skills During the late 1800s, European countries took part in a scramble for Africa. They claimed control of nearly the entire continent by 1914.

1. **Locate** (a) Algeria (b) Belgian Congo (c) Ethiopia

2. **Region** In which part of Africa were most of France's colonies located?

3. **Make Comparisons** How did imperialism in Africa in 1850 compare with that in 1914?

Cecil Rhodes

Cecil Rhodes (1853–1902) arrived in South Africa at age 17, determined to make his fortune. He got off to a slow start. His first venture, a cotton-farming project, failed. Then, Rhodes turned to diamond and gold mining. By the age of 40, he had become one of the richest men in the world.

However, money was not his real interest. "For its own sake I do not care for money," he once wrote. "I want the power." Rhodes strongly supported British imperialism in Africa. He helped Britain extend its African empire by 1,000,000 square miles and had an entire British colony named after himself—Rhodesia (now Zimbabwe). Rhodes also helped promote the policy of the separation of races in southern Africa. **How was Cecil Rhodes' desire for power illustrated by his actions?**

At the Berlin Conference, European powers recognized Leopold's private claims to the Congo Free State but called for free trade on the Congo and Niger rivers. They further agreed that a European power could not claim any part of Africa unless it had set up a government office there. This principle led Europeans to send officials who would exert their power over local rulers and peoples.

The rush to colonize Africa was on. In the 20 years after the Berlin Conference, the European powers partitioned almost the entire continent. As Europeans carved out their claims, they established new borders and frontiers. They redrew the map of Africa with little regard for traditional patterns of settlement or ethnic boundaries.

Horrors in the Congo Leopold and other wealthy Belgians exploited the riches of the Congo, including its copper, rubber, and ivory. Soon, there were horrifying reports of Belgian overseers brutalizing villagers. Forced to work for almost nothing, laborers were savagely beaten or mutilated. The overall population declined drastically.

Eventually, international outrage forced Leopold to turn over his personal colony to the Belgian government. It became the Belgian Congo in 1908. Under Belgian rule, the worst abuses were ended. Still, the Belgians regarded the Congo as a possession to be exploited. Africans were given little or no role in the government, and the wealth of their mines went out of the country to Europe.

France Extends Its Influence France took a giant share of Africa. In the 1830s, it had invaded and conquered Algeria in North Africa. The victory cost tens of thousands of French lives and killed many times more Algerians. In the late 1800s, France extended its influence along the Mediterranean into Tunisia. It also won colonies in West and Central Africa. At its height, the French empire in Africa was as large as the continental United States.

Britain Takes Its Share Britain's share of Africa was more scattered than that of France. However, it included more heavily populated regions with many rich resources. Britain took chunks of West and East Africa. It gained control of Egypt and pushed south into the Sudan.

In southern Africa, Britain clashed with the Boers, who were descendants of Dutch settlers. As you have read, Britain had acquired the Cape Colony from the Dutch in 1814. At that time, many Boers fled British rule, migrating north and setting up their own republics. In the late 1800s, however, the discovery of gold and diamonds in the Boer lands led to conflict with Britain. The **Boer War,** which lasted from 1899 to 1902, involved bitter guerrilla fighting. The British won in the end, but at great cost.

In 1910, the British united the Cape Colony and the former Boer republics into the Union of South Africa. The new constitution set up a government run by whites and laid the foundation for a system of complete racial segregation that would remain in force until 1993.

Others Join the Scramble Other European powers joined the scramble for colonies, in part to bolster their national image, while also furthering their economic growth and influence. The Portuguese carved out large colonies in Angola and Mozambique. Italy reached across the Mediterranean to occupy Libya and then pushed into the "horn" of Africa, at the southern end of the Red Sea. The newly united German empire took lands in eastern and southwestern Africa, including Cameroons and Togo. A German politician, trying to ease the worries of European rivals, explained, "We do not want to put anyone in the shade, but we also demand our place in the sun."

✔ **Checkpoint** How did King Leopold II set off a scramble for colonies in Africa?

Africans Resist Imperialism

Europeans met armed resistance across the continent. The Algerians battled the French for years. **Samori Touré** (sah MAWR ee too RAY) fought French forces in West Africa, where he was building his own empire. The British battled the Zulus in southern Africa and the Asante in West Africa. When their king was exiled, the Asante put themselves under the command of their queen, **Yaa Asantewaa** (YA uh ah sahn TAY wuh). She led the fight against the British in the last Asante war. Another woman who became a military leader was **Nehanda** (neh HAHN duh), of the Shona in Zimbabwe. Although a clever tactician, Nehanda was captured and executed. However, the memory of her achievements inspired later generations to fight for freedom.

In East Africa, the Germans fought wars against the Yao and Herero (huh REHR oh). Fighting was especially fierce in the Maji-Maji Rebellion of 1905. The Germans triumphed only after burning acres and acres of farmland, leaving thousands of local people to die of starvation.

Ethiopia Survives One ancient Christian kingdom in East Africa, Ethiopia, managed to resist European colonization and maintain its independence. Like feudal Europe, Ethiopia had been divided up among a number of rival princes who ruled their own <u>domains</u>. In the late 1800s, however, a reforming ruler, **Menelik II,** began to modernize his country. He hired European experts to plan modern roads and bridges and set up a Western school system. He imported the latest weapons and European officers to help train his army. Thus, when Italy invaded Ethiopia in 1896, Menelik was prepared. At the battle of Adowa (AH duh wuh), the Ethiopians smashed the Italian invaders. Ethiopia was the only African nation, aside from Liberia, to preserve its independence.

Vocabulary Builder

<u>domain</u>—(doh MAYN) *n.* territory over which rule or control is exercised

BIOGRAPHY

Menelik II

Before becoming emperor of Ethiopia, Menelik II (1844–1913) ruled the Shoa region in central Ethiopia. He ensured that he would succeed John IV as emperor by marrying his daughter to John's son. After John died in 1889, Menelik took the throne.

Menelik used profits from ivory sales to buy modern weapons. He then hired European advisors to teach his soldiers how to use the new guns. Menelik's army conquered neighboring lands and won a stunning victory over the Italians at Adowa. European nations rushed to establish diplomatic ties with Ethiopia. Around the world, people of African descent hailed Menelik's victory over European imperialism. **How did Menelik preserve Ethiopian independence?**

An Asante King
A king of the Asante people in Ghana (center) sits surrounded by his people. *What do the clothes of the man to the left of the king suggest about his social rank?*

A New African Elite Emerges During the Age of Imperialism, a Western-educated African **elite,** or upper class, emerged. Some middle-class Africans admired Western ways and rejected their own culture. Others valued their African traditions and condemned Western societies that upheld liberty and equality for whites only. By the early 1900s, African leaders were forging nationalist movements to pursue self-determination and independence.

✓ **Checkpoint**   How did Ethiopians resist imperialism?

SECTION 2 Assessment

Progress Monitoring *Online*
For: Self-quiz with vocabulary practice
Web Code: nba-2421

Terms, People, and Places

1. For each term, person, or place listed at the beginning of the section, write a sentence explaining its significance.

Note Taking

2. **Reading Skill: Identify Causes and Effects** Use your completed chart to answer the Focus Question: How did imperialist European powers claim control over most of Africa by the end of the 1800s?

Comprehension and Critical Thinking

3. **Describe** Name one development in each region of Africa in the early 1800s.
4. **Analyze Information** What impact did explorers and missionaries have on Africa?
5. **Draw Inferences** (a) Why do you think the Europeans did not invite Africans to the Berlin Conference? (b) What might be the effect of this exclusion upon later African leaders?
6. **Summarize** How did Africans resist European imperialism?

● **Writing About History**

Quick Write: Generate Arguments One way to approach a persuasive essay is to create a list of arguments that you can include to persuade your audience. For practice, create a list of three arguments that could be used in a persuasive essay either in favor of or opposed to the European colonization of Africa.

On Trial for My Country
by Stanlake Samkange

European imperialists gained control over much of Africa by signing treaties with local rulers. In most cases, the chiefs did not understand what rights they were signing away. Cecil Rhodes used this tactic with King Lobengula, who thought that he was allowing the British only to dig on his land. Rhodes, however, took control of the kingdom, eventually naming it Rhodesia. The novel *On Trial for My Country* is a fictional account of a conversation between King Lobengula and his father.

"Why did you not stand up to Rhodes and prevent him from taking your country by strength? Why did you not fight?"

"I thought that if I appealed to the white men's sense of justice and fair play, reminding them how good I had been to them since I had never killed or ill-treated a white man, they might hear my word and return to their homes. . . ."

"I . . . told them that I had not given them the road to Mashonaland."

"Yes, and they replied and told you that they had been given the road by their Queen and would only return on the orders of their Queen. What did you do then?"

"I mobilized[1] the army and told them to wait for my word."

"Did you give that word?"

"No."

"Were the soldiers keen to fight?"

"Yes, they were dying to fight."

"Why did you not let them fight?"

"I wanted to avoid bloodshed and war. . . ."

"And you allowed them to flout[2] your word as king of the Amandebele? You let them have their way. . . . Is that right? . . . .Why did you not . . . seek their protection and declare your country a British protectorate?"

". . . I knew that if I fought the white men I would be beaten. If I sought the white man's friendship and protection, there would be opposition to me or civil war. So I decided to pretend to the white men that if they came into the country I would fight, and hoped that they would be afraid and not come. . . . [T]hey called my bluff and came . . ."

"Was there no other way out of your dilemma?"

"I did consider marrying the Queen, but even though I hinted at this several times no one followed it up."

"I see!"

▲ King Lobengula of the Matabele nation in present-day Zimbabwe

1. **mobilize** (MOH buh lyz) *v.* to assemble for war
2. **flout** (flowt) *v.* to mock

Thinking Critically
1. **Synthesize Information** Why did King Lobengula want to avoid fighting the British?
2. **Analyze Literature** How does Samkange show that Lobengula's father disagreed with his son's decision?

Poster of Napoleon in Egypt

WITNESS HISTORY 🔊 AUDIO

The Egyptian Campaign

By 1797, Napoleon Bonaparte felt that Europe offered too few chances for glory. Setting his sights toward Africa in 1798, he invaded Egypt, a province of the Ottoman empire.

66 Europe is a molehill. . . . We must go to the East. . . .
All great glory has been acquired there. 99

Focus Question How did European nations extend their power into Muslim regions of the world?

Lamp from a mosque

European Claims in Muslim Regions

Objectives
- Analyze the sources of stress in Muslim regions.
- Explain the problems the Ottoman empire faced.
- Describe how Egypt sought to modernize.
- Understand European interest in Persia.

Terms, People, and Places

Muhammad Ahmad
Mahdi
pasha
sultan

genocide
Muhammad Ali
concession

Note Taking

Reading Skill: Understand Effects As you read, fill in a concept web like the one below with the effects of European imperialism in Muslim regions of the world.

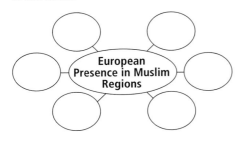

European Presence in Muslim Regions

Napoleon's Egyptian campaign highlighted Ottoman decline and opened a new era of European contact with Muslim regions of the world. European countries were just nibbling at the edges of Muslim countries. Before long, they would strike at their heartland.

Stresses in Muslim Regions

Muslim lands extended from western Africa to Southeast Asia. In the 1500s, three giant Muslim empires ruled much of this world—the Ottomans in the Middle East, the Safavids (sah FAH vidz) in Persia, and the Mughals in India.

Empires in Decline By the 1700s, all three Muslim empires were in decline. The decay had many causes. Central governments had lost control over powerful groups such as landowning nobles, military elites, and urban craft guilds. Corruption was widespread. In some places, Muslim scholars and religious leaders were allied with the state. In other areas, they helped to stir discontent against the government.

Rise of Muslim Reform Movements In the 1700s and 1800s, reform movements sprang up across various Muslim regions of Africa and Asia. Most stressed religious piety and strict rules of behavior. Usman dan Fodio led the struggle to reform Muslim practices in northern Africa. In the Sudan, **Muhammad Ahmad** (AHK mud) announced that he was the **Mahdi** (mahk DEE), the long-awaited savior of the faith. The Mahdi and his followers fiercely resisted British expansion into the region.

Another Islamic reform movement, the Wahhabi (wah HAHB ee) movement in Arabia, rejected the schools of theology and law that had emerged in the Ottoman empire. In their place, they wanted to recapture the purity and simplicity of Muhammad's original teachings. Although the revolt was put down, the Wahhabi movement survived. Its teachings remain influential in the kingdom of Saudi Arabia today.

European Imperialism In addition to internal decay and stress, the three Muslim empires faced powerful threats from Western imperialists. Through diplomacy and military threats, European powers won treaties giving them favorable trading terms. They then demanded special rights for Europeans residing in Muslim lands. At times, European powers protected those rights by intervening in local affairs.

✔ **Checkpoint** How was Western imperialism a source of stress in Muslim regions of the world?

Problems for the Ottoman Empire

At its height, the Ottoman empire had extended across North Africa, Southeastern Europe, and the Middle East. By the early 1800s, however, it faced serious challenges. Ambitious **pashas,** or provincial rulers, had increased their power. Economic problems and corruption added to Ottoman decay.

Nationalist Revolts Break Out As ideas of nationalism spread from Western Europe, internal revolts weakened the multiethnic Ottoman empire. Subject peoples in North Africa, Eastern Europe, and the Middle East threatened to break away. In the Balkans, Greeks, Serbs, Bulgarians, and Romanians gained their independence. Revolts against Ottoman rule also erupted in Arabia, Lebanon, and Armenia. The Ottomans suppressed these uprisings, but Egypt slipped out of their control.

European Pressure Increases European states sought to benefit from the slow crumbling of the Ottoman empire. After seizing Algeria in the 1830s, France hoped to gain more Ottoman territory. Russia schemed to gain control of the Bosporus (BAHS puh rus) and the Dardanelles. Control of these straits would give the Russians access to the Mediterranean Sea. Britain tried to thwart Russia's ambitions, which it saw as a threat to its own power in the Mediterranean and beyond to India. And in 1898, the new German empire hoped to increase its influence in the region by building a Berlin-to-Baghdad railway.

Efforts to Westernize Since the late 1700s, several Ottoman rulers had seen the need for reform and looked to the West for ideas. They reorganized the <u>bureaucracy</u> and system of tax collection. They built railroads, improved education, and hired Europeans to train a modern military. Young men were sent to the West to study science and technology. Many returned with Western political ideas about democracy and equality.

The reforms also brought improved medical care and revitalized farming. These improvements,

Vocabulary Builder

<u>bureaucracy</u> (bur OK re see) *n.* government staffed by administrators and officials who follow rigid rules.

General Ismail Pasha (center) fought for the British army in the Crimean War.

however, created a different set of problems. Better healthcare resulted in a population explosion that increased the already intense competition for the best land and led to unrest.

The adoption of Western ideas also increased tension. Many officials objected to changes that were inspired by a foreign culture. For their part, repressive **sultans,** rulers of the Ottoman Turkish empire, rejected reform and tried to rebuild the autocratic power enjoyed by earlier rulers.

Young Turks Demand Reform In the 1890s, a group of liberals formed a movement called the Young Turks. They insisted that reform was the only way to save the empire. In 1908, the Young Turks overthrew the sultan. Before they could achieve their planned reforms, however, the Ottoman empire was plunged into the world war that erupted in 1914.

Armenian Genocide Traditionally, the Ottomans had let minority nationalities live in their own communities and practice their own religions. By the 1890s, however, nationalism was igniting new tensions, especially between Turkish nationalists and minority peoples who sought their own states. These tensions triggered a brutal genocide of the Armenians, a Christian people concentrated in the eastern mountains of the empire. **Genocide** is a deliberate attempt to destroy a racial, political, or cultural group.

The Muslim Turks accused Christian Armenians of supporting Russian plans against the Ottoman empire. When Armenians protested repressive Ottoman policies, the sultan had tens of thousands of them slaughtered. Over the next 25 years, between 600,000 and 1.5 million Armenians were killed or died from disease and starvation.

✓ **Checkpoint** How were efforts to Westernize problematic for the Ottoman empire?

Egypt Seeks to Modernize

In the early 1800s, Egypt was a semi-independent province of the Ottoman empire, making great strides toward reform. Its success was due to **Muhammad Ali,** an ambitious soldier appointed governor of Egypt by the Ottomans. Ali used the opportunity created by Napoleon's invasion and the civil war that followed to seize power in 1805.

Muhammad Ali Introduces Reforms Muhammad Ali is sometimes called the "father of modern Egypt." He introduced a number of political and economic reforms, including improving tax collection, reorganizing the landholding system, and backing large irrigation projects to increase farm output. By expanding cotton production and encouraging the development of many local industries, Ali increased Egyptian participation in world trade.

Muhammad Ali also brought Western military experts to Egypt to help him build a well-trained, modern army. He conquered the neighboring lands of Arabia, Syria, and Sudan. Before he died in 1849, he had set Egypt on the road to becoming a major Middle Eastern power.

Building the Suez Canal Muhammad Ali's successors lacked his skills, and Egypt came increasingly under foreign control. In 1858, a French entrepreneur, Ferdinand de Lesseps (LAY seps), organized a company to build the Suez Canal. European nations gained power over the Ottomans by extending loans at high interest rates. In 1875, the ruler of

Suez Canal

Geography *Interactive*
For: Audio guided tour
Web Code: nbp-2431

The Suez Canal is a waterway in Egypt that stretches for more than 100 miles (160 kilometers). It connects the Mediterranean and Red seas, shortening the travel distance from Western Europe to ports in East Africa and Asia. After it opened in 1869, European ships no longer had to sail around the southern tip of Africa. The canal reduced the trip from London, England, to Bombay, India, by 5,150 miles (8,280 kilometers). The canal averaged between one and two ships per day (below) in its first year of operation and travel time averaged about 40 hours. Today, oil tankers and cargo ships make up most of the canal's traffic with a travel time of about 14 hours.

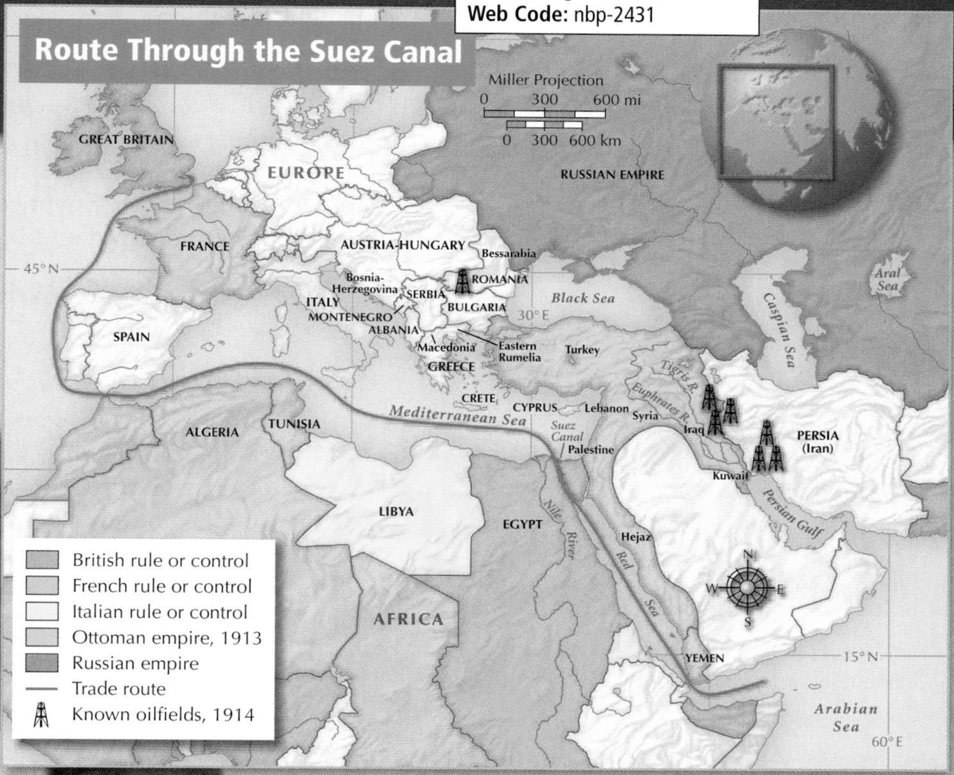

Route Through the Suez Canal

Miller Projection

0 300 600 mi
0 300 600 km

GREAT BRITAIN
EUROPE
RUSSIAN EMPIRE
45° N
FRANCE
AUSTRIA-HUNGARY
Bessarabia
Bosnia-Herzegovina
ROMANIA
Black Sea
ITALY
SERBIA
MONTENEGRO
BULGARIA
30° E
ALBANIA
SPAIN
Macedonia
Eastern Rumelia
Turkey
GREECE
Caspian Sea
CRETE
Aral Sea
CYPRUS
Lebanon
Syria
Euphrates R.
Tigris R.
Iraq
PERSIA (Iran)
Mediterranean Sea
Suez Canal
Palestine
ALGERIA
TUNISIA
Kuwait
Persian Gulf
LIBYA
EGYPT
Nile River
Hejaz
AFRICA
Red Sea
YEMEN
15° N
Arabian Sea
60° E

■ British rule or control
■ French rule or control
■ Italian rule or control
■ Ottoman empire, 1913
■ Russian empire
— Trade route
⚒ Known oilfields, 1914

▲ Construction of the Suez Canal began in 1859 and took workers 10 years to complete. Although digging was first done by hand, laborers later used dredgers and steam shovels to remove sediment.

Thinking Critically

1. **Draw Conclusions** Why was the Suez Canal an important waterway?
2. **Map Skills** Which countries benefited the most from the Suez Canal? Explain.

Oil flows out of one of the first oil wells to be drilled in Persia, around 1910.

Egypt was unable to repay loans he had contracted for the canal and other projects. To pay his debts, he sold his shares in the canal. The British bought the shares, gaining a controlling interest in the canal.

Becoming a British Protectorate When Egyptian nationalists revolted against foreign influence in 1882, Britain made Egypt a protectorate. In theory, the governor of Egypt was still an official of the Ottoman government. In fact, he followed policies dictated by Britain. Under British influence, Egypt continued to modernize. However, nationalist discontent simmered and flared into protests and riots.

✓ **Checkpoint**   How did Egypt fall under British control?

Persia and the European Powers

Like the Ottoman empire, Persia faced major challenges in the 1800s. The Qajar (kah JAHR) shahs, who ruled Persia from 1794 to 1925, exercised absolute power. Still, they did take steps to introduce reforms. The government helped build telegraph lines and railroads and experimented with a liberal constitution. Reform, however, did not save Persia from Western imperialism. Russia wanted to protect its southern frontier and expand into Central Asia. Britain wanted to protect its interests in India.

For a time, each nation set up its own sphere of influence in Persia. The discovery of oil in the early 1900s heightened foreign interest in the region. Both Russia and Britain plotted for control of Persian oil fields. They persuaded the Persian government to grant them **concessions,** or special rights given to foreign powers. To protect their interests, they sent troops into Persia. Persian nationalists were outraged. The nationalists included two very different groups. Some Persians wanted to move swiftly to adopt Western ways. Others, led by Muslim religious leaders, condemned the Persian government and Western influences.

✓ **Checkpoint**   How did Persia attract foreign interest in the early 1900s?

Progress Monitoring *Online*
For: Self-quiz with vocabulary practice
Web Code: nba-2431

SECTION 3 Assessment

Terms, People, and Places

1. For each term, person, or place listed at the beginning of the section, write a sentence explaining its significance.

Note Taking

2. **Reading Skill: Understand Effects** Use your completed concept web to answer the Focus Question: How did European nations extend their power into Muslim regions of the world?

Comprehension and Critical Thinking

3. **Draw Conclusions** How did European nations take advantage of stresses in the Muslim world?

4. **Summarize** Describe two problems that contributed to Ottoman decline.

5. **Synthesize Information** How did Muhammad Ali modernize Egypt?

6. **Identify Central Issues** Why did Russia and Britain compete for power in Persia?

● **Writing About History**

Quick Write: Answer Opposing Arguments Suppose that you are writing a persuasive essay on whether the Suez Canal was a positive or negative development for Egypt. An effective way to make your arguments convincing is to address both sides of the topic. Create a chart noting facts and ideas that support your position on one side and arguments that might be used against your position on the other.

WITNESS HISTORY 🔊 AUDIO

Critical of British Rule

In 1871, Indian nationalist Dadabhai Naoroji (DAH dah by now ROH jee) criticized British rule in India:

    ❝ [Indians] call the British system 'Sakar ki Churi' (SA kur kee CHOO ree), the knife of sugar. That is to say, there is no oppression, it is all smooth and sweet, but it is the knife notwithstanding. **❞**

Focus Question How did Britain gradually extend its control over most of India, despite opposition?

Queen Victoria writes letters as her Indian servant waits for his orders.

British East India Company's coat of arms

The British Take Over India

Objectives

- Understand the causes and effects of the Sepoy Rebellion.
- Explain how British rule affected India.
- Describe how Indians viewed Western culture.
- Identify the origins of Indian nationalism.

Terms, People, and Places

sati   deforestation
sepoy   Ram Mohun Roy
viceroy   purdah

Note Taking

Reading Skill: Identify Causes and Effects As you read this section, make a flowchart to show the causes and effects of British rule in India.

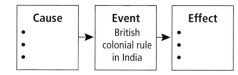

Cause	Event	Effect
• • •	British colonial rule in India	• • •

For more than 200 years, Mughal rulers governed a powerful empire in India. By the mid-1700s, however, the Mughal empire was collapsing from a lack of strong rulers. Britain then turned its commercial interests in the region into political ones.

East India Company and Rebellion

In the early 1600s, the British East India Company won trading rights on the fringe of the Mughal empire. As Mughal power declined, the company's influence grew. By the mid-1800s, it controlled three fifths of India.

Exploiting Indian Diversity The British were able to conquer India by exploiting its diversity. Even when Mughal power was at its height, India was home to many people and cultures. As Mughal power crumbled, India became fragmented. Indians with different traditions and dozens of different languages were not able to unite against the newcomers. The British took advantage of Indian divisions by encouraging competition and disunity among rival princes. Where diplomacy or intrigue did not work, the British used their superior weapons to overpower local rulers.

Implementing British Policies The East India Company's main goal in India was to make money, and leading officials often grew rich. At the same time, the company did work to improve roads, preserve peace, and reduce banditry.

THE SEPOY REBELLION

In 1857, the British issued new rifles to the sepoys. Troops were told to bite off the tips of cartridges before loading them into the rifles (right). Sepoys believed the cartridges (below) were greased with animal fat—from cows, which Hindus considered sacred, and from pigs, which were forbidden to Muslims. When sepoys (right) refused to load the guns, they were imprisoned. Angry sepoys rebelled against British officers, sparking a massacre of British troops, as well as women and children.

◄ A Sepoy rebels against British forces.

By the early 1800s, British officials introduced Western education and legal procedures. Missionaries tried to convert Indians to Christianity, which they felt was superior to Indian religions. The British also pressed for social change. They worked to end slavery and the caste system and to improve the position of women within the family. One law banned **sati** (SUH tee), a Hindu custom practiced mainly by the upper classes. It called for a widow to join her husband in death by throwing herself on his funeral fire.

Growing Discontent In the 1850s, the East India Company made several unpopular moves. First, it required **sepoys** (SEE poyz), or Indian soldiers in its service, to serve anywhere, either in India or overseas. For high-caste Hindus, however, overseas travel was an offense against their religion. Second, the East India Company passed a law that allowed Hindu widows to remarry. Hindus viewed both moves as a Christian conspiracy to undermine their beliefs.

Then, in 1857, the British issued new rifles to the sepoys. Troops were told to bite off the tips of cartridges before loading them into the rifles. The cartridges, however, were greased with animal fat—either from cows, which Hindus considered sacred, or from pigs, which were forbidden to Muslims. When the troops refused the order to "load rifles," they were imprisoned.

Rebellion and Aftermath Angry sepoys rose up against their British officers. The Sepoy Rebellion swept across northern and central India. Several sepoy regiments marched off to Delhi, the old Mughal capital. There, they hailed the last Mughal ruler as their leader.

In some places, the sepoys brutally massacred British men, women, and children. But the British soon rallied and crushed the revolt. They then took terrible revenge for their earlier losses, torching villages and slaughtering thousands of unarmed Indians.

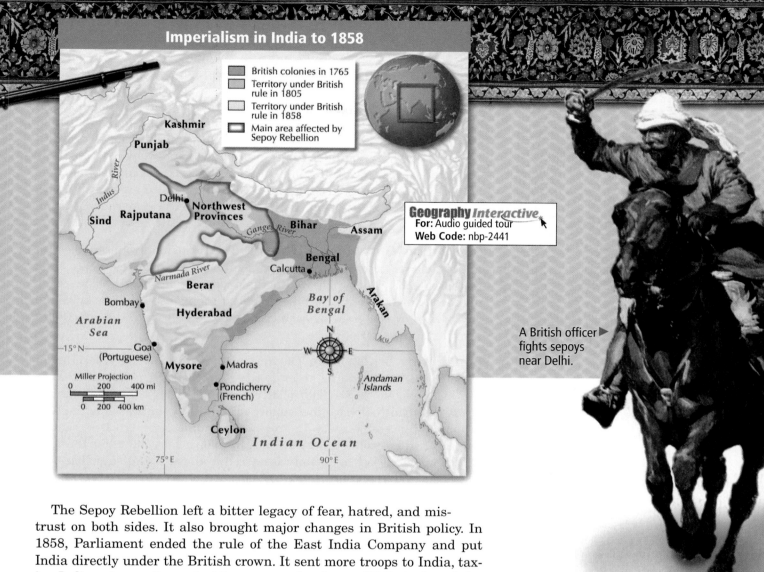

Imperialism in India to 1858

British colonies in 1765
Territory under British rule in 1805
Territory under British rule in 1858
Main area affected by Sepoy Rebellion

Kashmir
Punjab
Indus River
Delhi
Sind
Rajputana
Northwest Provinces
Ganges River
Bihar
Assam
Bengal
Calcutta
Narmada River
Berar
Bombay
Hyderabad
Bay of Bengal
Arakan
Arabian Sea
—15°N—
Goa (Portuguese)
Mysore
Madras
Miller Projection
0   200   400 mi
0   200 400 km
Pondicherry (French)
Andaman Islands
Ceylon
Indian Ocean
75°E
90°E

Geography *Interactive*
For: Audio guided tour
Web Code: nbp-2441

A British officer ► fights sepoys near Delhi.

The Sepoy Rebellion left a bitter legacy of fear, hatred, and mistrust on both sides. It also brought major changes in British policy. In 1858, Parliament ended the rule of the East India Company and put India directly under the British crown. It sent more troops to India, taxing Indians to pay the cost of these occupying forces. While it slowed the "reforms" that had angered Hindus and Muslims, it continued to develop India for Britain's own economic benefit.

✓ **Checkpoint** What were the causes of the Sepoy Rebellion in northern and central India?

Impact of British Colonial Rule

After 1858, Parliament set up a system of colonial rule in India called the British Raj. A British **viceroy** in India governed in the name of the queen, and British officials held the top positions in the civil service and army. Indians filled most other jobs. With their cooperation, the British made India the "brightest jewel" in the crown of their empire.

British policies were designed to incorporate India into the <u>overall</u> British economy. At the same time, British officials felt they were helping India to modernize. In their terms, modernizing meant adopting not only Western technology but also Western culture.

An Unequal Partnership Britain saw India both as a market and as a source of raw materials. To this end, the British built roads and an impressive railroad network. Improved transportation let the British sell

Thinking Critically
1. **Draw Conclusions** How was the Sepoy Rebellion a clash of cultures?
2. **Map Skills** Which regions were most affected by the Sepoy Rebellion?

Vocabulary Builder
<u>overall</u>—(OH vur awl) *adj.* total

their factory-made goods across the subcontinent and carry Indian cotton, jute, and coal to coastal ports for transport to factories in England. New methods of communication, such as the telegraph, also gave Britain better control of India. After the Suez Canal opened in 1869, British trade with India soared. But it remained an unequal partnership, favoring the British. The British flooded India with inexpensive, machine-made textiles, ruining India's once-prosperous hand-weaving industry.

Britain also transformed Indian agriculture. It encouraged nomadic herders to settle into farming and pushed farmers to grow cash crops, such as cotton and jute, that could be sold on the world market. Clearing new farmlands led to massive **deforestation,** or cutting of trees.

Population Growth and Famine The British introduced medical improvements and new farming methods. Better healthcare and increased food production led to rapid population growth. The rising numbers, however, put a strain on the food supply, especially as farmland was turned over to growing cash crops instead of food. In the late 1800s, terrible famines swept India.

Benefits of British Rule On the positive side, British rule brought some degree of peace and order to the countryside. The British revised the legal system to promote justice for Indians regardless of class or caste. Railroads helped Indians move around the country, while the telegraph and postal system improved communication. Greater contact helped bridge regional differences and develop a sense of national unity.

The upper classes, especially, benefited from some British policies. They sent their sons to British schools, where they were trained for posts in the civil service and military. Indian landowners and princes, who still ruled their own territories, grew rich from exporting cash crops.

✓ Checkpoint How did British colonial rule affect Indian agriculture?

Different Views on Culture

Some educated Indians were impressed by British power and technology and urged India to follow a Western model of progress. These mostly upper-class Indians learned English and adopted Western ways. Other Indians felt that the answer to change lay with their own Hindu or Muslim cultures.

Indian Attitudes In the early 1800s, **Ram Mohun Roy** combined both views. A great scholar, he knew Sanskrit, Persian, and Arabic classics, as well as English, Greek, and Latin works. Roy felt that India could learn from the West. He was a founder of Hindu College in Calcutta, which provided an English-style education to Indians. Many of its graduates went on to establish English schools all over the region. While Roy saw the value of Western education, he also wanted to reform traditional Indian culture.

Roy condemned some traditions, such as rigid caste distinctions, child marriage, sati, and **purdah** (PUR duh), the isolation of women in separate quarters. But he also set up educational societies that helped revive pride in Indian culture. Because of his influence on later leaders, he is often hailed today as the founder of Indian nationalism.

Railroads and Trade
By building thousands of miles of railroads, the British opened up India's vast interior to trade. The British also encouraged Indians to grow tea (top photo) and jute (bottom photo). Today, tea is one of India's biggest crops. *What were some of the benefits of British rule?*

Western Attitudes The British disagreed among themselves about India. A few admired Indian theology and philosophy. As Western scholars translated Indian classics, they acquired respect for India's ancient heritage. Western writers and philosophers borrowed ideas from Hinduism and Buddhism.

However, most British people knew little about Indian achievements and dismissed Indian culture with contempt. In an essay on whether Indians should be taught in English or their own languages, British historian Thomas Macaulay arrogantly wrote that "a single shelf of a good European library is worth the whole native literature of India and Arabia."

✔ **Checkpoint** How did Indians and British view each other's culture in the 1800s?

Indian Nationalism Grows

During the years of British rule, a class of Western-educated Indians emerged. In the view of Macaulay and others, this elite class would bolster British power. As it turned out, exposure to European ideas had the opposite effect. By the late 1800s, Western-educated Indians were spearheading a nationalist movement. Schooled in Western ideals such as democracy and equality, they dreamed of ending imperial rule.

Indian National Congress In 1885, nationalist leaders organized the Indian National Congress, which became known as the Congress party. Its members believed in peaceful protest to gain their ends. They called for greater democracy, which they felt would bring more power to Indians like themselves. The Indian National Congress looked forward to eventual self-rule, but supported Western-style modernization.

Muslim League At first, Muslims and Hindus worked together for self-rule. In time, however, Muslims grew to resent Hindu domination of the Congress party. They also worried that a Hindu-run government would oppress Muslims. In 1906, Muslims formed the Muslim League to pursue their own goals. Soon, they were talking of a separate Muslim state.

✔ **Checkpoint** How are the origins of Indian nationalism linked to British rule?

SECTION 4 **Assessment**

Progress Monitoring Online
For: Self-quiz with vocabulary practice
Web Code: nba-2441

Terms, People, and Places

1. What do the key terms listed at the beginning of the section have in common?

Note Taking

2. **Reading Skill: Identify Causes and Effects** Use your completed flowchart to answer the Focus Question: How did Britain gradually extend its control over most of India, despite opposition?

Comprehension and Critical Thinking

3. **Recognize Cause and Effect** What were the causes and effects of the Sepoy Rebellion?

4. **Draw Conclusions** What were the positive and negative effects of British rule on Indians?

5. **Analyze Information** How did British rule lead to growing Indian nationalism?

● **Writing About History**

Quick Write: Draft an Opening Paragraph Write an opening paragraph for a persuasive essay on whether the British were right to pass laws that tried to reform the caste system. Remember that the first few sentences of your draft are your chance to build interest in your topic. Add details that will help grab the reader's attention.

Technology

How has technology changed the way people live and work?

The British colonized India to extract its natural resources and to sell British-made products. To serve these ends, Britain made sure that the Suez Canal, its shipping "lifeline" to India, remained open. Britain also built a massive railway system to carry finished goods into India and raw materials out. The introduction of railway technology changed India and encouraged a spirit of nationalism. As the following examples demonstrate, advances in transportation technology always have the potential of changing society.

Container Ships

By the early 1900s, diesel ships replaced the sailing and steam-powered ships that had carried British goods to India years before. Some shippers had begun putting cargo in sealed, standard-sized containers for easier handling. By the 1960s, specially designed container ships could transport hundreds of the locked and sealed cargo boxes. Shippers developed automated equipment to unload and store the containers quickly. These containers fit perfectly onto truck trailers and railroad flatcars. The new technology greatly increased the efficiency of shipping goods, while reducing the cost.

Automobiles

Like the first machine-powered ships, the earliest automobiles ran on steam power. That changed, however, after the invention of the internal-combustion gasoline engine in 1878. Until the early 1900s, cars served mainly as recreational vehicles for the rich. Then Henry Ford mass produced his inexpensive Model T. By 1930, more than 25 million cars were on the road in the United States alone. The rise of the automobile changed industrialized societies. Networks of roads and highways grew. Suburbs blossomed. More people traveled than ever before.

Airplanes

Decades after the Wright brothers made their first successful flight in 1903, only the most adventurous people traveled by air. In 1940, airliners began to have pressurized cabins that allowed them to fly above turbulence. Other technological innovations, including radar, made airplanes safer. By 1960, more Americans traveled from city to city on planes than on trains and buses, and air travel had replaced ships as the leading way to cross the Atlantic. Today, airlines throughout the world carry millions of passengers each year.

Freight Transport Billion tkm*			
	Road	Rail	Sea
European Union	1,516	358	1,254
United States	1,534	2,183	414
Japan	313	22	244
China	597	1,362	NA
Russia	22	1,434	93

* Tons per kilometer
NA Not available
SOURCE: EUROPA Statistical Pocketbook Online, 2004

Thinking Critically

1. How did each of these transportation technologies affect people's lives?
2. **Connections to Today** Learn more about a present-day advance in transportation technology. Write a summary of how this innovation may change the way people live or work.

Lin Zexu,
Chinese official

WITNESS HISTORY 🔊 AUDIO

Trading Opium for Tea

By the 1830s, British merchant ships were arriving in China loaded with opium to trade with the Chinese for tea. In 1839, Chinese government official Lin Zexu (lin DZUH shoo) wrote a letter to Britain's Queen Victoria condemning the practice:

❝ We have heard that in your own country opium is prohibited with the utmost strictness and severity—this is strong proof that you know full well how hurtful it is. . . . Since . . . you do not permit it to injure your own country, you ought not to have the injurious drug transferred to another country. ❞

Britain's Union Jack

Focus Question How did Western powers use diplomacy and war to gain power in Qing China?

China and the New Imperialism

Objectives
- Describe what trade rights Westerners sought in China.
- Explain the internal problems Chinese reformers tried to solve.
- Understand how the Qing dynasty fell.

Terms, People, and Places

balance of trade	Taiping Rebellion
trade surplus	Sino-Japanese War
trade deficit	Open Door Policy
Opium War	Guang Xu
indemnity	Boxer Uprising
extraterritoriality	Sun Yixian

Note Taking

Reading Skill: Recognize Multiple Causes As you read, create a flowchart like the one below in which you can record key events and developments that led to the decline of Qing China.

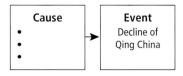

Cause	Event
• • •	Decline of Qing China

For centuries, Chinese regulations had ensured that China had a favorable **balance of trade** with other nations. A nation's balance of trade refers to the difference between how much a country imports and how much it exports. By the 1800s, however, Western nations were using their growing power to tilt the balance of trade with East Asia in their favor.

Trade Between Britain and China

Prior to the 1800s, Chinese rulers placed strict limits on foreign traders. European merchants were restricted to a small area in southern China. China sold them silk, porcelain, and tea in exchange for gold and silver. Under this arrangement, China enjoyed a **trade surplus,** or exported more than it imported. Westerners, on the other hand, had a **trade deficit** with China, buying more from the Chinese than they sold to them.

By the late 1700s, two developments were underway that would transform China's relations with the Western world. First, China entered a period of decline. Second, the Industrial Revolution created a need for expanded markets for European goods. At the same time, it gave the West superior military power.

The Opium War During the late 1700s, British merchants began making huge profits by trading opium grown in India for Chinese tea, which was popular in Britain. Soon, many Chinese had become addicted to the drug. Silver flowed out of China in payment for the drug, disrupting the economy.

The Chinese government outlawed opium and executed Chinese drug dealers. They called on Britain to stop the trade. The British refused, insisting on the right of free trade.

In 1839, Chinese warships clashed with British merchants, triggering the **Opium War.** British gunboats, equipped with the latest in firepower, bombarded Chinese coastal and river ports. With outdated weapons and fighting methods, the Chinese were easily defeated.

Unequal Treaties In 1842, Britain made China accept the Treaty of Nanjing (NAHN jing). Britain received a huge **indemnity,** or payment for losses in the war. The British also gained the island of Hong Kong. China had to open five ports to foreign trade and grant British citizens in China **extraterritoriality,** the right to live under their own laws and be tried in their own courts.

The treaty was the first of a series of "unequal treaties" that forced China to make concessions to Western powers. A second war, lasting from 1856 to 1858, ended with France, Russia, and the United States pressuring China to sign treaties <u>stipulating</u> the opening of more ports to foreign trade and letting Christian missionaries preach in China.

✔ **Checkpoint** How did British trade with China trigger the Opium Wars?

The Taiping Rebellion Weakens China

By the 1800s, the Qing dynasty was in decline. Irrigation systems and canals were poorly maintained, leading to massive flooding of the Huang valley. The population explosion that had begun a century earlier created hardship

Vocabulary Builder

<u>stipulate</u>—(STIP yuh layt) *v.* to specifically demand something in an agreement

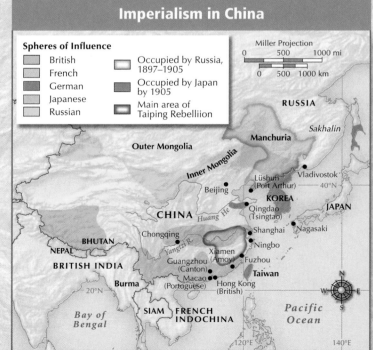

● **INFOGRAPHIC**

Taiping Rebellion

Taiping Rebellion leader Hong Xiuquan (at right), was a village schoolteacher. Inspired by religious visions and Christian missionaries, he wanted to establish a "Heavenly Kingdom of Peace"—the Taiping. Hong endorsed ideas that Chinese leaders considered radical, including community ownership of property and the equality of women and men.

◄ Chinese coins *c.*1850

Imperialism in China

Spheres of Influence
- British
- French
- German
- Japanese
- Russian
- Occupied by Russia, 1897–1905
- Occupied by Japan by 1905
- Main area of Taiping Rebelliion

Miller Projection

0   500   1000 mi
0   500   1000 km

RUSSIA
Sakhalin
Manchuria
Outer Mongolia
Inner Mongolia
Lüshun (Port Arthur)   Vladivostok   40°N
Beijing
KOREA   JAPAN
CHINA   Huang He   Qingdao (Tsingtao)
Chongqing   Shanghai   Nagasaki
BHUTAN   Yangzi R.   Ningbo
NEPAL   Xiamen (Amoy)   Fuzhou
BRITISH INDIA   Guangzhou (Canton)   Taiwan
Burma   Macao (Portuguese)   Hong Kong (British)
20°N
Bay of Bengal   SIAM   FRENCH INDOCHINA   Pacific Ocean
120°E   140°E

for China's peasants. An extravagant imperial court, tax evasion by the rich, and widespread official corruption added to the peasants' burden. As poverty and misery increased, peasants rebelled. The **Taiping Rebellion** (TY ping), which lasted from 1850 to 1864, was probably the most devastating peasant revolt in history. The leader, Hong Xiuquan (hong shyoo CHWAHN), called for an end to the hated Qing dynasty. The Taiping rebels won control of large parts of China and held out for 14 years. However, with the help of loyal regional governors and generals, the government crushed the rebellion.

The Taiping Rebellion almost toppled the Qing dynasty. It is estimated to have caused the deaths of between 20 million and 30 million Chinese. The Qing government survived, but it had to share power with regional commanders. During the rebellion, Europeans kept up pressure on China, and Russia seized lands in the north.

✔ **Checkpoint** How did the Taiping Rebellion and other internal problems weaken the Qing dynasty?

Launching Reform Efforts

By the mid-1800s, educated Chinese were divided over the need to adopt Western ways. Most saw no reason for new industries because China's wealth and taxes came from land. Although Chinese merchants were allowed to do business, they were not seen as a source of prosperity.

Scholar-officials also disapproved of the ideas of Western missionaries, whose emphasis on individual choice challenged the Confucian order. They saw Western technology as dangerous, too, because it threatened Confucian ways that had served China successfully for so long.

Geography *Interactive*
For: Audio guided tour
Web Code: nbp-2451

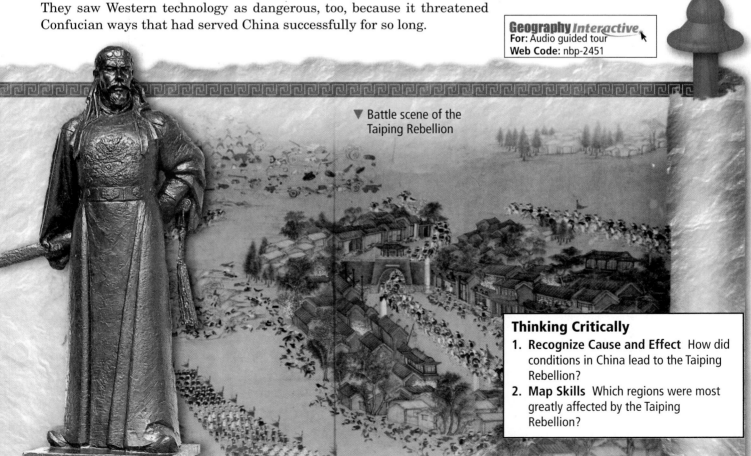

▼ Battle scene of the Taiping Rebellion

Thinking Critically
1. **Recognize Cause and Effect** How did conditions in China lead to the Taiping Rebellion?
2. **Map Skills** Which regions were most greatly affected by the Taiping Rebellion?

By the late 1800s, the empress Ci Xi (tsih shih) had gained power. A strong-willed ruler, she surrounded herself with advisors who were deeply committed to Confucian traditions.

Self-Strengthening Movement In the 1860s, reformers launched the "self-strengthening movement." They imported Western technology, setting up factories to make modern weapons. They developed shipyards, railroads, mining, and light industry. The Chinese translated Western works on science, government, and the economy. However, the movement made limited progress because the government did not rally behind it.

War With Japan Meanwhile, the Western powers and nearby Japan moved rapidly ahead. Japan began to modernize after 1868. It then joined the Western imperialists in the competition for a global empire.

In 1894, Japanese pressure on China led to the **Sino-Japanese War.** It ended in disaster for China, with Japan gaining the island of Taiwan.

Carving Spheres of Influence The crushing defeat revealed China's weakness. Western powers moved swiftly to carve out spheres of influence along the Chinese coast. The British took the Chang River valley. The French acquired the territory near their colony of Indochina. Germany and Russia gained territory in northern China.

The United States, a longtime trader with the Chinese, did not take part in the carving up of China. It feared that European powers might shut out American merchants. A few years later, in 1899, it called for a policy to keep Chinese trade open to everyone on an equal basis. The imperial powers accepted the idea of an **Open Door Policy,** as it came to be called. No one, however, consulted the Chinese.

Hundred Days of Reform Defeated by Japan and humiliated by Westerners, Chinese reformers blamed conservative officials for not modernizing China. They urged conservative leaders to stop looking back at China's past and to modernize as Japan had.

In 1898, a young emperor, **Guang Xu** (gwahng shoo), launched the Hundred Days of Reform. New laws set out to modernize the civil service exams, streamline government, and encourage new industries. Reforms affected schools, the military, and the bureaucracy. Conservatives soon rallied against the reform effort. The emperor was imprisoned, and the aging empress Ci Xi reasserted control. Reformers fled for their lives.

✓ **Checkpoint** How did reformers try to solve China's internal problems?

The Qing Dynasty Falls

As the century ended, China was in turmoil. Anger grew against Christian missionaries who threatened traditional Chinese Confucianism. The presence of foreign troops was another source of discontent. Protected by extraterritoriality, foreigners ignored Chinese laws and lived in their own communities.

Boxer Uprising Anti-foreign feeling finally exploded in the **Boxer Uprising.** In 1899, a group of Chinese had formed a secret society, the Righteous Harmonious Fists. Westerners watching them

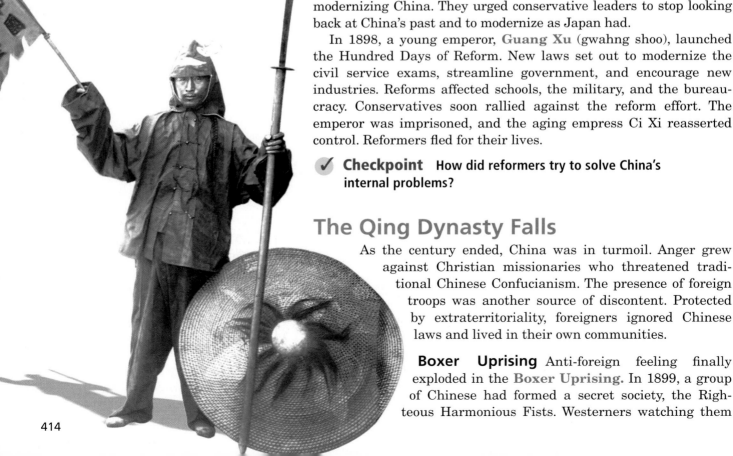

The Boxer Rebellion
Suffering from the effects of floods and famine, poverty, and foreign aggression, Boxers (below) participated in an anti-foreign movement. In 1900, some 140,000 Boxers attempted to drive Westerners out of China. An international force eventually put down the uprising. *Why were Westerners and Western influences a source of discontent for the Boxers?*

train in the martial arts dubbed them Boxers. Their goal was to drive out the "foreign devils" who were polluting the land with their un-Chinese ways, strange buildings, machines, and telegraph lines.

In 1900, the Boxers attacked foreigners across China. In response, the Western powers and Japan organized a multinational force. This force crushed the Boxers and rescued foreigners besieged in Beijing. The empress Ci Xi had at first supported the Boxers but reversed her policy as they retreated.

Aftermath of the Uprising China once again had to make concessions to foreigners. The defeat, however, forced even Chinese conservatives to support Westernization. In a rush of reforms, China admitted women to schools and stressed science and mathematics in place of Confucian thought. More students were sent abroad to study.

China also expanded economically. Mining, shipping, railroads, banking, and exports of cash crops grew. Small-scale Chinese industry developed with the help of foreign capital. A Chinese business class emerged, and a new urban working class began to press for rights.

Three Principles of the People Although the Boxer Uprising failed, the flames of Chinese nationalism spread. Reformers wanted to strengthen China's government. By the early 1900s, they had introduced a constitutional monarchy. Some reformers called for a republic.

A passionate spokesman for a Chinese republic was Sun Yixian (soon yee SHYAHN), also known as Sun Yat-sen. In the early 1900s, he organized the Revolutionary Alliance to rebuild China on "Three Principles of the People." The first principle was nationalism, or freeing China from foreign domination. The second was democracy, or representative government. The third was livelihood, or economic security for all Chinese.

Birth of a Republic When Ci Xi died in 1908 and a two-year-old boy inherited the throne, China slipped into chaos. In 1911, uprisings in the provinces swiftly spread. Peasants, students, local warlords, and even court politicians helped topple the Qing dynasty.

In December 1911, Sun Yixian was named president of the new Chinese republic. The republic faced overwhelming problems and was almost constantly at war with itself or foreign invaders.

✓ **Checkpoint** What caused the Qing dynasty to fall?

BIOGRAPHY

Sun Yixian

Sun Yixian (1866–1925) was not born to power. His parents were poor farmers. Sun's preparation for leadership came from his travels, education, and personal ambitions. In his teen years, he lived with his brother in Hawaii and attended British and American schools. Later on, he earned a medical degree.

Sun left his career in medicine to struggle against the Qing government. After a failed uprising in 1895, he went into exile. Sun visited many nations, seeking support against the Qing dynasty. When revolution erupted in China, Sun was in Denver, Colorado. He returned to China to begin his leading role in the new republic. **How did Sun's background prepare him to lead?**

SECTION 5 Assessment

Progress Monitoring *Online*
For: Self-quiz with vocabulary practice
Web Code: nba-2451

Terms, People, and Places
1. For each term, person, or place listed at the beginning of the section, write a sentence explaining its significance.

Note Taking
2. **Reading Skill: Recognize Multiple Causes** Use your completed flowchart to answer the Focus Question: How did Western powers use diplomacy and war to gain power in Qing China?

Comprehension and Critical Thinking
3. **Draw Conclusions** How did Western powers gain greater trading rights in China?
4. **Summarize** (a) What internal problems threatened the Qing dynasty? (b) What were the goals of Chinese reformers?
5. **Synthesize Information** How was the Qing dynasty replaced by a republic?

● **Writing About History**
Quick Write: Write a Conclusion Before writing a persuasive essay, make a list of your arguments. In organizing the essay, it's often a good idea to save your strongest argument for last. For practice, write a concluding paragraph for a persuasive essay that either supports or opposes internal reform efforts to Westernize China in the 1800s.

Quick Study Guide

Progress Monitoring *Online*
For: Self-test with vocabulary practice
Web Code: nba-2461

■ Western Imperialism

Africa	Muslim Regions	India	China
• Berlin Conference • Raw materials exploited • Boer War • Racial segregation in South Africa • Western-educated African elite • Nationalism grows	• Islamic reform movements • Internal revolts • Armenian genocide • Egypt modernizes	• British East India Company • Changes to legal and caste systems • Sepoy Rebellion • Indians forced to raise cash crops • Population growth and famine • Indian National Congress • Muslim League	• Opium War • Unequal trade treaties • Self-strengthening movement • Sino-Japanese War • Boxer Uprising

■ Imports from Africa and Asia about 1870

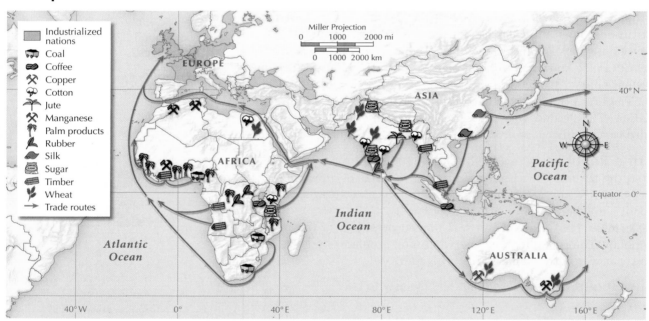

Legend:
- Industrialized nations
- Coal
- Coffee
- Copper
- Cotton
- Jute
- Manganese
- Palm products
- Rubber
- Silk
- Sugar
- Timber
- Wheat
- → Trade routes

Miller Projection
0   1000   2000 mi
0   1000 2000 km

EUROPE
ASIA
AFRICA
Atlantic Ocean
Indian Ocean
Pacific Ocean
AUSTRALIA
Equator—0°
40° N
40° W   0°   40° E   80° E   120° E   160° E

■ Key Events of the New Imperialism

1805 Muhammad Ali is named governor of Egypt.

1830 France begins efforts to conquer Algeria in North Africa.

1857 The Sepoy Rebellion breaks out in India.

Chapter Events
Global Events

1800   **1825**   **1850**

1807 In the United States, Robert Fulton uses a steam engine to power a ship.

1848 Revolutions break out throughout much of Europe.

■ Cumulative Review

Record the answers to the questions below on your Concept Connector worksheets. In addition, record information from this chapter about the following concepts:
- Nationalism: English nationalism
- Nationalism: American nationalism

1. **Belief Systems** In the late 1800s, many missionaries believed that they had a duty to spread the ideas of Western civilization, including its medicine, law, and Christian religion. Do research to learn more about the positive and negative impact of missionaries during this time period. Is there any evidence of the blending of Christian and native religions? How many Christian followers are there in Africa today?

2. **Empire** European imperialism began long before the 1800s. European states had overseas empires as early as the 1400s and 1500s. Do research to learn more about the Spanish empire of the 1500s and then compare it to the British empire of the late 1800s. How were they similar? How were they different? Think about the following:
   - economic motives
   - religious motives
   - political and military motives

3. **Empire** As you have read, there were small groups of people in the West who were against imperialism for both political and moral reasons. Some anti-imperialists believed that colonialism was a tool of the wealthy. Others believed that it was immoral to impose undemocratic rule on other peoples. Do research to learn more about the arguments against imperialism in the late 1800s and early 1900s. Summarize your findings in two or three paragraphs.

■ Connections to Today

1. **Economics: Trade and the Suez Canal** Reread the information in Section 3 on the Suez Canal. How did the opening of the Suez Canal in 1869 transform world trade? Then, find a recent newspaper or magazine article on the Suez Canal today. Do you think the canal is more or less important today than it was in 1869? Write two paragraphs on trade and the Suez Canal today, citing examples from current events to support your answer.

Suez Canal Traffic		
Year	Number of Ships	Net Tons
1975	5,579	50,441,000
1985	19,791	352,579,000
1995	15,051	360,372,000
2003	15,667	549,381,000

SOURCE: Leth Suez Transit Online, 2004

2. **People and the Environment: Famine** You have read how disaster struck Ireland in October 1845 when a deadly plant disease ruined the potato crop. In the late 1800s, famines also swept through India. What were the major causes of these famines? What was the effect of growing cash crops instead of food? Conduct research to learn more about the causes of hunger and malnutrition in the world today.

| 1884 European officials meet at the Berlin Conference to settle rival land claims in Africa. |  | 1899 Boer War erupts in South Africa. | 1911 Sun Yixian becomes president of Chinese republic. |

History *Interactive*
For: Interactive timeline
Web Code: nbp-2462

1875   **1900**   **1925**

Mid-1880s
German engineers develop the first automobile.

1914
World War I begins in Europe.

Chapter Assessment

Terms, People, and Places

Match the following definitions with the terms listed below. You will not use all of the terms.

genocide	trade surplus
imperialism	trade deficit
indemnity	Menelik II
Sino-Japanese War	Muhammad Ali
pasha	Taiping Rebellion
viceroy	Boxer Uprising

1. the domination by one country of the political, economic, or cultural life of another country or region
2. war between China and Japan where Japan gained Taiwan
3. provincial ruler in the Ottoman empire
4. situation in which a country imports more than it exports
5. governor of Egypt, sometimes called the "father of modern Egypt"
6. peasant revolt in China from 1850–1864
7. a deliberate attempt to destroy an entire religious or ethnic group
8. payment for losses in war

Main Ideas

Section 1 (pp. 386–389)
9. Describe the four main motives of the new imperialists.
10. Why did Western imperialism spread so rapidly?

Section 2 (pp. 390–397)
11. How did European contact with Africa increase during the 1800s?
12. How did the scramble for African colonies begin?

Section 3 (pp. 398–402)
13. What problems faced the Ottoman empire in the 1800s?
14. How did the modernization of Egypt lead to British rule?

Section 4 (pp. 403–408)
15. Explain the impact of British colonial rule on India.
16. Describe the origins of Indian nationalism.

Section 5 (pp. 409–413)
17. How did westerners gain trading rights in China during the 1800s?
18. Why did the Qing dynasty come to an end?

Chapter Focus Question
19. How did Western industrial powers gain global empires?

Critical Thinking

20. **Geography and History** Why were the natural resources of Africa and Asia important to Europeans in the 1800s?
21. **Analyzing Cartoons** The political cartoon below shows a French soldier (left) and a British soldier (right) ripping apart a map. How do you think the situation depicted in the cartoon affected relations between Britain and France?

22. **Summarize** How did the Ottoman empire try to westernize?
23. **Predict Consequences** How do you think rivalries between religious groups affected anti-imperialism efforts in India? Explain your answer.
24. **Analyze Information** Why did Western industrial nations establish spheres of influence in China rather than colonies as they did in Africa and India?

● Writing About History

Writing a Persuasive Essay During the 1800s, European powers embarked on a period of expansion known as the Age of Imperialism. Despite resistance, these powers brought much of the world under their control between 1870 and 1914. Write a persuasive essay from the point of view of a Chinese government official in which the official tries to persuade the British that the Treaty of Nanjing is too harsh and will lead to dangerous anti-foreign feelings. Consult page SH16 of the Writing Handbook for additional help.

Prewriting
• Make a list of what you believe to be the strongest arguments of the Chinese official.

• Organize the arguments on your list from weakest to strongest.

Drafting
• Clearly state the position that you will prove in the thesis statement.
• Sequence your arguments so that you open or close with your strongest one.
• Write a conclusion that restates your thesis and closes with a strong argument.

Revising
• Review your arguments to make sure that you have explained them logically and clearly.

Document-Based Assessment

The Forgotten Genocide

The Armenian massacre has been called the "forgotten genocide." It refers to the destruction, between 1895 and 1923, of the Christian Armenians of Turkey under the Muslim Ottoman government. More than 2 million Armenians lived in Turkey before the genocide. Estimates of those killed vary from 600,000 to 1.5 million. The rest were driven from their ancestral home. Most perpetrators were freed, despite pledges by the Allies to punish them after World War I.

Document A

"As it got worse, all of us, and all the people, began gathering in our school. The word came around that the Turks were going on the streets and killing all the Armenians and leaving them on the streets. I, myself, was in school already, so I simply stayed there. Then orders came from the school that we, too, should run away. But where? All the buildings were on fire! The Turks were burning everything. There was a whole group of us running away from the school."

—Annalin, a survivor from Smyrna on events of 1922

Document B

"The massacre of Armenian subjects in the Ottoman Empire in 1896 . . . was amateur and ineffective compared with the largely successful attempt to exterminate [them] during the First World War in 1915. . . . [This] genocide was carried out under the cloak of legality by cold-blooded governmental action. These were not mass-murders committed spontaneously by mobs of private people. . . ."

—Arnold Toynbee, British historian, cited in *Experiences*

Document C

"The 1,000 Armenian houses are being emptied of furniture by the police one after the other. The furniture, bedding and everything of value is being stored in large buildings about the city. . . . The goods are piled in without any attempt at labeling or systematic storage. A crowd of Turkish women and children follow the police about like a lot of vultures and seize anything they can lay their hands on and when the more valuable things are carried out of the house by the police they rush in and take the balance. . . . I suppose it will take several weeks to empty all the houses and then the Armenian shops and stores will be cleared out."

—From a report to the American embassy by Oscar S. Heizer, American consul in Tebizond, July 1915

Document D

"The proportion of Armenians killed by the Turks in World War I out of the general number of Armenians in the Ottoman Empire was no less than that of the Jewish victims [during the Holocaust] out of the total Jewish population in Europe. Nor are the methods of killing unique. . . . The type of murder committed by the Germans in the USSR—mass machine-gunning—was the traditional method of mass murder in our century, and the death marches of Jews in the closing stages of the war had their precedent in the Armenian case as well. Nor is the fact that in the case of the Holocaust it was a state machine and a bureaucracy that was responsible for the murder unique, because there, too, the Young Turks had preceded the German Nazis in planning the execution of a population with such means as were modern at the time."

—From *Remembrance and Denial* by Richard G. Hovannisian

Analyzing Documents

Use your knowledge of the Armenian massacre and Documents A, B, C, and D to answer questions 1–4.

1. According to Document B, the 1915 massacre of Armenians
   A went unpunished.
   B was ineffective and unsuccessful.
   C was not as well documented as the 1896 massacre.
   D was committed with the knowledge of the Turkish government.

2. Document C shows that the Turkish police
   A tried to protect the property of Armenian citizens, despite their government's orders.
   B tried to help Armenian citizens as best they could.
   C took part in stealing the property of Armenian citizens.
   D protested to the American embassy to try to help their friends.

3. According to Document D, the Armenian Massacre and the Holocaust
   A were committed by the same people.
   B were carried out in a similar way.
   C had very few similarities, except for the large number of murders.
   D both took place in Germany.

4. **Writing Task** Ismayale Kemal Pasha, a governor in Marash, was described by one survivor as kind and justice-loving. He tried saving Armenian citizens, despite orders from his superiors to carry out the genocide without remorse. Suppose Ismayale Kemal Pasha explained his decision to help in a memoir. Write a brief explanation from his point of view. Use these documents along with information from the chapter in your writing.

13

New Global Patterns
1800–1914

A New Pattern

Japan's response to the threat of Western imperialism was different from that of many other countries. In 1871, a delegation of Japanese officials journeyed to the United States with the goal of learning as much as possible about Western culture and technology.

66 We expect and intend to reform and improve so as to stand upon a similar footing with the most enlightened nations. . . . It is our purpose to select from the various institutions prevailing among enlightened nations such as are the best suited to our present condition and adopt them, in gradual reforms and improvements of our policy and customs. . . . 99
—Japanese emperor Meiji in a letter to the American president introducing the delegation

Listen to the Witness History audio to hear more about Japan's drive to modernize.

◀ **Japanese women mingle with Europeans in Yokohama's trading compound in this woodcut print created by a Japanese artist in 1861.**

A New Zealand postage stamp featuring the British empire's Queen Victoria

An Australian Aborigine boomerang

Chapter Preview

Chapter Focus Question How did political and economic imperialism influence nations around the world?

Section 1
Japan Modernizes

Section 2
Imperialism in Southeast Asia and the Pacific

Section 3
Self-Rule for Canada, Australia, and New Zealand

Section 4
Economic Imperialism in Latin America

A bottle of quinine, which was used to fight malaria in Panama

---

Note Taking Study Guide *Online*
For: Note Taking and Concept Connector worksheets
Web Code: nbd-2501

A traditional Japanese fan

Emperor Meiji

WITNESS HISTORY 🔊 AUDIO

Changes for Japan

The emperor Meiji wrote a poem to provide inspiration for Japan's efforts to become a modern country in the late 1800s:

66 May our country,
   Taking what is good,
   and rejecting what is bad,
   Be not inferior
   To any other.99

Focus Question How did Japan become a modern industrial power, and what did it do with its new strength?

Japan Modernizes

Objectives

- Explain how problems in Japanese society and the opening of Japan to other countries led to the Meiji Restoration.
- Describe the main reforms under the Meiji government.
- Analyze the factors contributing to Japan's drive for empire.

Terms, People, and Places

Matthew Perry	zaibatsu
Tokyo	homogeneous society
Meiji Restoration	First Sino-Japanese War
Diet	Russo-Japanese War

N̲o̲te Taking

Reading Skill: Identify Causes and Effects
As you read this section, identify the causes and effects of the Meiji Restoration in a chart like the one below.

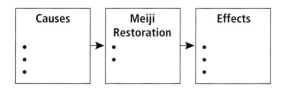

In 1853, the United States displayed its new military might, sending a naval force to make Japan open its ports to trade. Japanese leaders debated how to respond. While some resisted giving up their 215-year-old policy of seclusion, others felt that it would be wiser for Japan to learn from the foreigners.

In the end, Japan chose to abandon its centuries of isolation. The country swiftly transformed itself into a modern industrial power and then set out on its own imperialist path.

Discontent in Tokugawa Japan

In the early 1600s, Japan was still ruled by shoguns, or supreme military dictators. Although emperors still lived in the ceremonial capital of Kyoto, the shoguns held the real power in Edo. Daimyo, or landholding warrior lords, helped the shoguns control Japan. In 1603, a new family, the Tokugawas, seized power. The Tokugawa shoguns reimposed centralized feudalism, closed Japan to foreigners, and forbade Japanese people to travel overseas. The nation's only window on the world was through Nagasaki, where the Dutch were allowed very limited trade.

For more than 200 years, Japan developed in isolation. Internal commerce expanded, agricultural production grew, and bustling cities sprang up. However, these economic changes strained Japanese society. Many daimyo suffered financial hardship. They needed money in a commercial economy, but a daimyo's wealth was in land rather than cash. Lesser samurai were unhappy, too, because they lacked the money to live as well as urban merchants.

Merchants in turn resented their place at the bottom of the social ladder. No matter how rich they were, they had no political power. Peasants, meanwhile, suffered under heavy taxes.

The government responded by trying to revive old ways, <u>emphasizing</u> farming over commerce and praising traditional values. These efforts had scant success. By the 1800s, shoguns were no longer strong leaders, and corruption was common. Discontent simmered throughout Japan.

✔ **Checkpoint** By the mid-1800s, why did so many groups of people in Japan feel discontented?

Vocabulary Builder

emphasizing—(EM fuh syz ing) *vt.* stressing

Japan Opens Up

While the shoguns faced troubles at home, disturbing news of the British victory over China in the Opium War and the way in which imperialists had forced China to sign unequal treaties reached Japan. Surely, Japanese officials reasoned, it would not be long before Western powers turned towards Japan.

External Pressure and Internal Revolt The officials' fears were correct. In July 1853, a fleet of well-armed American ships commanded by Commodore **Matthew Perry** sailed into lower Tokyo Bay. Perry carried a letter from Millard Fillmore, the President of the United States. The letter demanded that Japan open its ports to diplomatic and commercial exchange.

The shogun's advisors debated what to do. Japan did not have the ability to defend itself against the powerful United States Navy. In the Treaty of Kanagawa in 1854, the shogun Iesada agreed to open two Japanese ports to American ships, though not for trade.

The United States soon won trading and other rights, including extraterritoriality and low taxes on American imports. European nations demanded and won similar rights. Like the Chinese, the Japanese felt humiliated by the terms of these unequal treaties. Some bitterly criticized the shogun for not taking a strong stand against the foreigners.

In the Japanese woodblock print below, Japanese boats go out to meet one of Commodore Matthew Perry's ships in Tokyo Bay. In response to Perry's expedition, the Japanese statesman Lord Ii considered Japan's strategy toward contact with foreign powers:

Primary Source

66 There is a saying that when one is besieged in a castle, to raise the drawbridge is to imprison oneself. . . . Even though the Shogun's ancestors set up seclusion laws, they left the Dutch and Chinese to act as a bridge. . . . Might this bridge not now be of advantage to us in handling foreign affairs, providing us with the means whereby we may for a time avert the outbreak of hostilities and then, after some time has elapsed, gain a complete victory? 99

Japanese Diplomat
Fukuzawa Yukichi Visits America

In 1860, writer and educator Fukuzawa Yukichi (1835–1901) joined the first Japanese diplomatic mission to the United States. When he returned home, he wrote articles and books explaining Western customs and practices to the Japanese. In this selection from his autobiography, Fukuzawa recalls his early impressions of San Francisco and discusses some of the differences between American and Japanese cultures and attitudes.

Foreign pressure deepened the social and economic unrest. In 1867, discontented daimyo and samurai led a revolt that unseated the shogun and "restored" the 15-year-old emperor Mutsuhito to power. When he was crowned emperor, Mutsuhito took the name Meiji (MAY jee), which means "enlightened rule." He moved from the old imperial capital in Kyoto to the shogun's palace in Edo, which was renamed **Tokyo,** or "eastern capital."

The Meiji Restoration The young emperor began a long reign known as the **Meiji Restoration.** This period, which lasted from 1868 to 1912, was a major turning point in Japanese history. The Meiji reformers, who ruled in the emperor's name, were determined to strengthen Japan. Their goal was summarized in their motto, "A rich country, a strong military." The emperor supported and embodied the reforms.

The new leaders set out to study Western ways, adapt them to Japanese needs, and thereby keep Japan from having to give in to Western demands. In 1871, members of the government traveled overseas to learn about Western governments, economies, technology, and customs. The government brought experts from Western countries to Japan and sent young samurai to study abroad, furthering Japan's knowledge of Western industrial techniques.

Vocabulary Builder

thereby—(THEHR by) *adv.* by that means, because of that

✓ **Checkpoint** How did Japan react when it was forced to accept unequal treaties?

"All of us wore the usual pair of swords at our sides and the [rope] sandals. So attired, we were taken to the modern hotel. There we noticed, covering the interior, the valuable carpets which in Japan only the more wealthy could buy from importers' shops at so much a square inch to make purses and tobacco pouches with. Here the carpet was laid over an entire room—something quite astounding—[and] upon this costly fabric walked our hosts wearing the shoes with which they had come in from the streets!"

"One evening our hosts said that some ladies and gentlemen were having a dancing party and that they would be glad to have us attend it. We went. To our dismay we could not make out what they were doing. The ladies and gentlemen seemed to be hopping about the room together. As funny as it was, we knew it would be rude to laugh, and we controlled our expressions with difficulty as the dancing went on. These were but a few of the instances of our bewilderment at the strange customs of American society."

From *The Autobiography of Fukuzawa Yukichi*

◀ Fukuzawa Yukichi

▲ Calligraphy by Fukuzawa, which means "a spirit of independence and self-respect"

◀ An American scene by a Japanese artist

Thinking Critically
1. **Make Inferences** Why is Fukuzawa amazed that people in America walk on carpeting with their shoes on?
2. **Identify Point of View** What opinion do you think Fukuzawa has of American culture?

The Meiji Transformation

The Meiji reformers faced an enormous task. They were committed to replacing the rigid feudal order with a completely new political and social system and to building a modern industrial economy. Change did not come easily. In the end, however, Japan adapted foreign ideas with great speed and success.

A Modern Government The reformers wanted to create a strong central government, equal to those of Western powers. After studying various European governments, they adapted the German model. In 1889, the emperor issued the Meiji constitution. It set forth the principle that all citizens were equal before the law. Like the German system, however, it gave the emperor autocratic, or absolute, power. A legislature, or **Diet,** was formed, made up of one elected house and one house appointed by the emperor. Additionally, voting rights were sharply limited.

Japan then established a Western-style bureaucracy with separate departments to supervise finance, the army, the navy, and education. To strengthen the military, it turned to Western technology and ended the special privilege of samurai. In the past, samurai alone were warriors. In modern Japan, as in the West, all men were subject to military service.

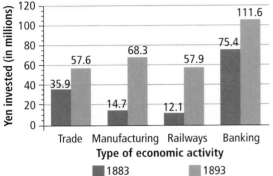

Investment in Meiji Japan

Yen invested (in millions)

Type of economic activity	1883	1893
Trade	35.9	57.6
Manufacturing	14.7	68.3
Railways	12.1	57.9
Banking	75.4	111.6

Chart Skills Japanese women (above) work in a silk manufacturing factory in the 1890s. *How does the graph reflect the Meiji reformers' drive to industrialize Japan?*

SOURCE: S. Uyehara, *The Industry and Trade of Japan*

Industrialization Meiji leaders made the economy a major priority. They encouraged Japan's businesses to adopt Western methods. They set up a modern banking system, built railroads, improved ports, and organized a telegraph and postal system.

To get industries started, the government typically built factories and then sold them to wealthy business families who developed them further. With such support, business dynasties like the Kawasaki family soon ruled over industrial empires. These powerful banking and industrial families were known as **zaibatsu** (zy baht soo).

By the 1890s, industry was booming. With modern machines, silk manufacturing soared. Shipyards, copper and coal mining, and steel making also helped make Japan an industrial powerhouse. As in other industrial countries, the population grew rapidly, and many peasants flocked to the growing cities for work.

Changes in Society The constitution ended legal distinctions between classes, thus allowing more people to become involved in nation building. The government set up schools and a university. It hired Westerners to teach the new generation how to use modern technology.

Despite the reforms, class distinctions survived in Japan as they did in the West. Also, although literacy increased and some women gained an education, women in general were still assigned a secondary role in society. The reform of the Japanese family system, and women's position in it, became the topic of major debates in the 1870s. Although the government agreed to some increases in education for women, it dealt harshly with other attempts at change. After 1898, Japanese women were forbidden any political participation and legally were lumped together with minors.

An Amazing Success Japan modernized with amazing speed during the Meiji period. Its success was due to a number of causes. Japan had a strong sense of identity, partly because it had a **homogeneous society**— that is, its people shared a common culture and language. Economic growth during Tokugawa times had set Japan on the road to development. Japan also had experience in learning and adapting ideas from foreign nations, such as China.

The Japanese were determined to resist foreign rule. By the 1890s, Japan was strong enough to force Western powers to revise the unequal treaties. By then, it was already acquiring its own overseas empire.

✓ **Checkpoint** What changes did the reforms of the Meiji Restoration bring about in Japan?

Japan's Growing Military Strength

As in Western industrial nations, Japan's economic needs fed its imperialist desires. As a small island nation, Japan lacked many basic resources that were essential for industrial growth. It depended on other countries to obtain raw materials. Spurred by this dependency and a strong ambition to equal the West, Japan sought to build an empire. With its modern army and navy, it maneuvered for power in East Asia.

Korea in the Middle Imperialist rivalries put the spotlight on Korea. Located at a crossroads of East Asia, the Korean peninsula was a focus of competition among Russia, China, and Japan. Korea had been a tributary state to China for many years. A tributary state is a state that is independent but acknowledges the supremacy of a stronger state. Although influenced by China, Korea had its own traditions and government. Korea had also shut its doors to foreigners. It did, however, maintain relations with China and sometimes with Japan.

By the 1800s, Korea faced pressure from outsiders. As Chinese power declined, Russia expanded into East Asia. Then, as Japan industrialized, it too eyed Korea. In 1876, Japan used its superior power to force Korea to open its ports to Japanese trade. Faced with similar demands from Western powers, the "Hermit Kingdom" had to accept unequal treaties.

Japan Gains Power As Japan extended its influence in Korea, it came into conflict with China. In 1894, competition between Japan and China in Korea led to the **First Sino-Japanese War.** ("Sino" means "Chinese.") Although China had greater resources, Japan had benefited from modernization. To the surprise of China and the West, Japan won easily. It used its victory to gain treaty ports in China and control over the island of Taiwan, thus joining the West in the race for empire.

Japan Rising
In this political cartoon, Japan is depicted marching over Korea on its way to Russia. *Why would Russia feel threatened by Japan's aggression in Korea?*

■ COMPARING VIEWPOINTS

Colonization in Korea

The excerpts below present two different views of the effect of Japan's control of Korea in the early 1900s. **Critical Thinking** *How do the two views on the results of colonization in Korea differ?*

Positive Effects	Negative Effects
Mining, fishery, and manufacturing have advanced. The bald mountains have been covered with young trees. Trade has increased by leaps and bounds.... Study what we are doing in Korea.... Japan is a steward on whom devolves [falls] the gigantic task of uplifting the Far East.	The result of annexation, brought about without any conference with the Korean people, is that the Japanese ... by a false set of figures show a profit and loss account between us two peoples most untrue, digging a trench of everlasting resentment deeper and deeper....
—*Japanese academic Nitobe Inazo*	—*From the Declaration of Korean Independence, 1919*

Ten years later, Japan successfully challenged Russia, its other rival for power in Korea and Manchuria. During the **Russo-Japanese War,** Japan's armies defeated Russian troops in Manchuria, and its navy destroyed almost an entire Russian fleet. For the first time in modern history, an Asian power humbled a European nation. In the 1905 Treaty of Portsmouth, Japan gained control of Korea as well as rights in parts of Manchuria.

Japan Rules Korea Japan made Korea a protectorate. In 1910, it annexed Korea outright, absorbing the kingdom into the Japanese empire. Japan ruled Korea for 35 years. Like Western imperialists, the Japanese set out to modernize their newly acquired territory. They built factories, railroads, and communications systems. Development, however, generally benefited Japan. Under Japanese rule, Koreans produced more rice than ever before, but most of it went to Japan.

The Japanese were as unpopular in Korea as Western imperialists were elsewhere. They imposed harsh rule on their colony and deliberately set out to erase the Korean language and identity. Repression bred resentment. And resentment, in turn, nourished a Korean nationalist movement.

Nine years after annexation, a nonviolent protest against the Japanese began on March 1, 1919, and soon spread throughout Korea. The Japanese crushed the uprising and massacred many Koreans. The violence did not discourage people who worked to end Japanese rule. Instead, the March First Movement became a rallying symbol for Korean nationalists.

The Koreans would have to wait many years for freedom. Japan continued to expand in East Asia during the years that followed, seeking natural resources and territory. By the early 1900s, Japan was the strongest power in Asia.

✔ **Checkpoint** How did industrialization help start Japan on an imperialist course?

The Japanese in Korea
In this illustration, Japanese soldiers march into Seoul, Korea's capital city. Japan controlled Korea from 1905 until 1945.

SECTION 1 **Assessment**

Progress Monitoring Online
For: Self-quiz with vocabulary practice
Web Code: nba-2511

Terms, People, and Places
1. Place each of the terms listed at the beginning of the section into one of the following categories: politics, culture, or economics. Write a sentence for each term explaining your choice.

Note Taking
2. **Reading Strategy: Identify Causes and Effects** Use your completed chart to answer the section Focus Question: How did Japan become a modern industrial power, and what did it do with its new strength?

Comprehension and Critical Thinking
3. **Identify Central Issues** What problems weakened shogun rule in Japan in the mid-1800s?
4. **Recognize Causes** What caused Japan to end over 200 years of seclusion?
5. **Draw Conclusions** List three ways in which Japan modernized. Explain how each of these actions helped strengthen Japan so it could resist Western pressure.
6. **Connect to Geography** Why was control of Korea desirable to both China and Japan?

● **Writing About History**
Quick Write: Choose a Topic When you write for assessment, you may occasionally be given a choice of topics. In that case, quickly jot down notes you could use to answer each prompt. Then, choose the prompt you know the most about. Practice this process using the two sample prompts below. Jot down notes about each prompt, choose one, and then write a sentence explaining why you chose that prompt.
• Explain how Japan modernized under the Meiji reformers.
• Summarize how and why Korea became a Japanese colony.

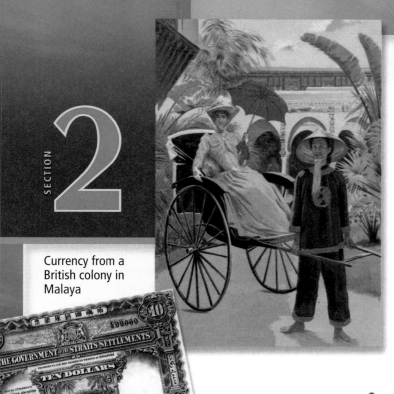

A European woman being transported in a rickshaw in French Indochina

WITNESS HISTORY 🔊 AUDIO

A Patriot's Dilemma

In 1867, Phan Thanh Gian, a Vietnamese official, faced a dilemma. The French were threatening to invade. As a patriot, Phan Thanh Gian wanted to resist. But as a devoted follower of Confucius, he was obliged "to live in obedience to reason." And based on the power of the French military, he concluded that the only reasonable course was to surrender:

66 The French have immense warships, filled with soldiers and armed with huge cannons. No one can resist them. They go where they want, the strongest [walls] fall before them.99

Focus Question How did industrialized powers divide up Southeast Asia and the Pacific, and how did the colonized peoples react?

Currency from a British colony in Malaya

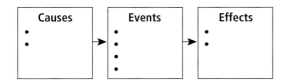

Imperialism in Southeast Asia and the Pacific

Objectives

- Outline how Europeans colonized Southeast Asia and how Siam avoided colonial rule.
- Explain how the United States gained control over the Philippines.
- Describe how imperialism spread to the Pacific islands.

Terms, People, and Places

French Indochina   Spanish-American War
Mongkut   Liliuokalani

Note Taking

Reading Skill: Identify Causes and Effects As you read, fill in a flowchart similar to the one below to record the causes, events, and effects of imperialism in Southeast Asia and the Pacific.

Causes	Events	Effects
•	•	•
	•	•
	•	
	•	

Leaders throughout Southeast Asia faced the same dilemma as Phan Thanh Gian did in 1867. As they had in Africa, Western industrial powers divided up the region in search of raw materials, new markets, and Christian converts.

Europeans Colonize Southeast Asia

Southeast Asia commands the sea lanes between India and China. The region had been influenced by both civilizations. From the 1500s through the 1700s, European merchants gained footholds in Southeast Asia, but most of the area remained independent. This changed in the 1800s. Westerners—notably the Dutch, British, and French—manipulated local rivalries and used modern armies and technology to colonize much of Southeast Asia.

The Dutch East Indies Established During the early 1600s, the Dutch East India Company established bases on the island of Java and in the Moluccas, or Spice Islands. From there, the Dutch slowly expanded to dominate the rest of the Dutch East Indies (now Indonesia). The Dutch expected their Southeast Asian colonies to produce profitable crops of coffee, indigo, and spices.

The British in Burma and Malaya In the early 1800s, rulers of Burma (present-day Myanmar) clashed with the British, who were expanding eastward from India. The Burmese suffered disastrous defeats in several wars. They continued to resist British rule, however, even after Britain annexed Burma in 1886.

At the same time, the British expanded their influence in Malaya. The busy port of Singapore grew up at the southern tip of the peninsula. Soon, natural resources and profits from Asian trade flowed through Singapore to enrich Britain.

French Indochina Seized The French, meanwhile, were building an empire on the Southeast Asian mainland. In the 1500s, Portuguese traders had set up a trading center in what today is Vietnam. Christian missionaries from France and other European countries moved into Vietnam and won some converts. Threatened by growing Western influence, Vietnamese officials tried to suppress Christianity by killing converts and missionary priests. Partly in response, France invaded Vietnam in 1858. The French also wanted more influence and markets in Southeast Asia.

The Vietnamese fought fiercely but could not withstand superior European firepower. By the early 1860s, France had seized a portion of southern Vietnam. Over the next decades, the French took over the rest of Vietnam and all of Laos and Cambodia. The French and other Westerners referred to these holdings as **French Indochina.** (Mainland Southeast Asia was known during this period as "Indochina.")

Siam Survives The kingdom of Siam (present-day Thailand) lay between British-ruled Burma and French Indochina. The king of Siam, **Mongkut** (mahng KOOT), who ruled from 1851 to 1868, did not underestimate Western power. He studied foreign languages and read widely on modern science and mathematics. He used this knowledge to negotiate with the Western powers and satisfy their goals in Siam by making agreements in unequal treaties. In this way, Siam escaped becoming a European colony.

Mongkut and his son, Chulalongkorn, (CHOO lah lawng kawrn) set Siam on the road to modernization. They reformed the government, modernized the army, and hired Western experts to teach Thais how to use the new technology. They abolished slavery and gave women some choice in marriage. As Siam modernized, Chulalongkorn bargained to remove the unequal treaties.

Colonial Southeast Asia During this period, many Chinese people migrated to Southeast Asia to take advantage of the economic opportunities there. They left China to escape hardship and turmoil. Despite local resentment, these communities formed vital networks in trade, banking, and other economic activities.

By the 1890s, Europeans controlled most of Southeast Asia. They introduced modern technology and expanded commerce and industry. Europeans directed the mining of tin, the harvesting of rubber, and the building of harbors and railroads. But these changes benefited the European colonizers far more than they did the Southeast Asians.

✔ **Checkpoint** How did the Burmese and the Vietnamese respond to attempts to colonize them?

Two Paths in Southeast Asia
King Mongkut of Siam managed to keep his kingdom out of European control. In other parts of Southeast Asia, colonized peoples labored to produce export crops for their colonial rulers. Below, workers process sugar cane in the Philippines in the early 1900s.

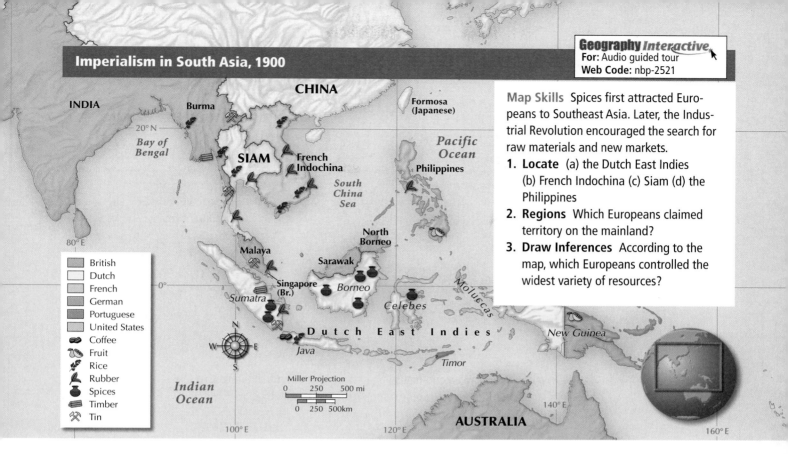

Geography *Interactive*
For: Audio guided tour
Web Code: nbp-2521

Map Skills Spices first attracted Europeans to Southeast Asia. Later, the Industrial Revolution encouraged the search for raw materials and new markets.

1. **Locate** (a) the Dutch East Indies (b) French Indochina (c) Siam (d) the Philippines
2. **Regions** Which Europeans claimed territory on the mainland?
3. **Draw Inferences** According to the map, which Europeans controlled the widest variety of resources?

Map labels: INDIA, CHINA, Burma, Formosa (Japanese), Bay of Bengal, SIAM, French Indochina, Pacific Ocean, Philippines, South China Sea, North Borneo, Malaya, Sarawak, Singapore (Br.), Borneo, Sumatra, Celebes, Moluccas, New Guinea, Dutch East Indies, Java, Timor, Indian Ocean, AUSTRALIA

Legend: British, Dutch, French, German, Portuguese, United States, Coffee, Fruit, Rice, Rubber, Spices, Timber, Tin

Miller Projection
0   250   500 mi
0   250 500km

The United States and the Philippines

In the 1500s, Spain had seized the Philippines. Catholic missionaries spread Christianity among the Filipinos. As the Catholic Church gained enormous power and wealth, many Filipinos accused the Church of abusing its position. By the late 1800s, their anger fueled strong resistance to Spanish rule.

The opening of the Suez Canal in 1860 helped the economy of the Philippines by making trade with European countries easier. Some upper class Filipinos gained access to better education. Leaders such as José Rizal inspired Filipinos to work to gain better treatment from Spain.

The **Spanish-American War** broke out in 1898 between Spain and the United States over Cuba's attempts to win independence from Spain. During the war, American battleships destroyed the Spanish fleet, which was stationed in the Philippines. Encouraged by American naval officers, Filipino rebel leaders declared independence from Spain. Rebel soldiers threw their support into the fight against Spanish troops.

In return for their help, the Filipino rebels expected the Americans to recognize their independence. Instead, in the treaty that ended the war with Spain, the United States agreed to give Spain $20 million in return for control of the Philippines. Within the United States, debate raged over the treaty's ratification. American imperialists wanted to join the European competition for territory. Anti-imperialists wanted the United States to steer clear of foreign entanglements. The United States Senate ratified the treaty by only one vote over the required two-thirds majority.

Bitterly disappointed, Filipino nationalists renewed their struggle. From 1899 to 1901, Filipinos led by Emilio Aguinaldo (ah gee NAHL doh) battled American forces. Thousands of Americans and hundreds of thousands of Filipinos died. In the end, the Americans crushed the rebellion.

THE EFFECTS OF IMPERIALISM

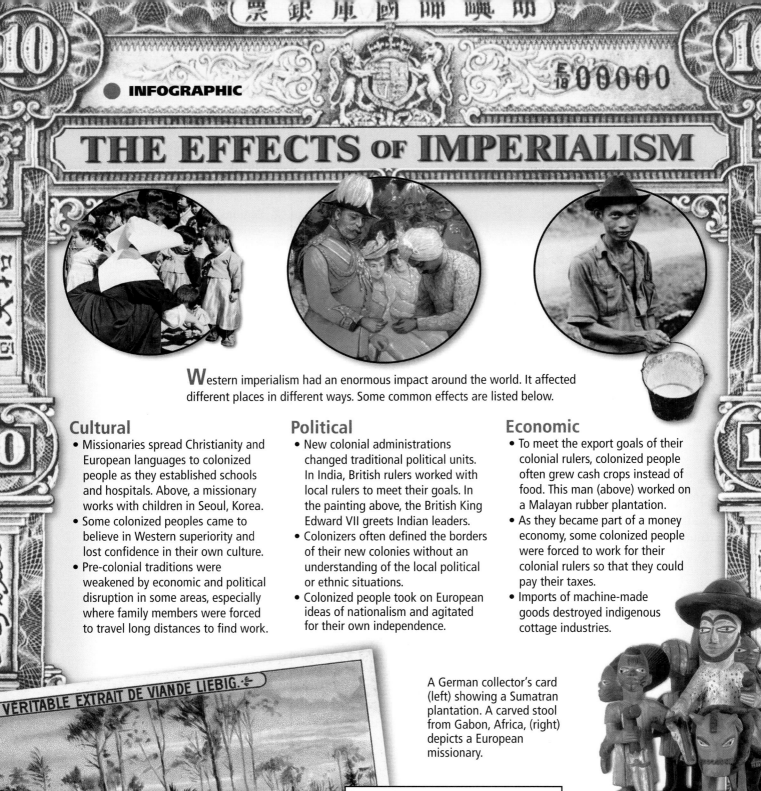

Western imperialism had an enormous impact around the world. It affected different places in different ways. Some common effects are listed below.

Cultural

- Missionaries spread Christianity and European languages to colonized people as they established schools and hospitals. Above, a missionary works with children in Seoul, Korea.
- Some colonized peoples came to believe in Western superiority and lost confidence in their own culture.
- Pre-colonial traditions were weakened by economic and political disruption in some areas, especially where family members were forced to travel long distances to find work.

Political

- New colonial administrations changed traditional political units. In India, British rulers worked with local rulers to meet their goals. In the painting above, the British King Edward VII greets Indian leaders.
- Colonizers often defined the borders of their new colonies without an understanding of the local political or ethnic situations.
- Colonized people took on European ideas of nationalism and agitated for their own independence.

Economic

- To meet the export goals of their colonial rulers, colonized people often grew cash crops instead of food. This man (above) worked on a Malayan rubber plantation.
- As they became part of a money economy, some colonized people were forced to work for their colonial rulers so that they could pay their taxes.
- Imports of machine-made goods destroyed indigenous cottage industries.

VERITABLE EXTRAIT DE VIANDE LIEBIG.

A German collector's card (left) showing a Sumatran plantation. A carved stool from Gabon, Africa, (right) depicts a European missionary.

Culture du tabac à Sumatra.
Voir au verso.

Thinking Critically

1. **Categorize** How is migrating to find work a cultural as well as an economic effect of imperialism?
2. **Predict Consequences** How might grouping several rival ethnic groups into one political unit cause friction when that region gains independence?

History Interactive
For: Interactive content
Web Code: nbp-2522

The United States set out to modernize the Philippines through education, improved health care, and economic reforms. The United States also built dams, roads, railways, and ports. In addition, the United States promised Filipinos a gradual <u>transition</u> to self-rule some time in the future.

Vocabulary Builder

<u>transition</u>—(tran ZISH un) *n.* passage from one way to another

✓ **Checkpoint**   How did the United States gain control of the Philippines?

Western Powers Seize the Pacific Islands

In the 1800s, the industrialized powers also began to take an interest in the islands of the Pacific. The thousands of islands splashed across the Pacific include the three regions of Melanesia, Micronesia, and Polynesia.

At first, American, French, and British whaling and sealing ships looked for bases to take on supplies in the Pacific. Missionaries, too, moved into the region and opened the way for political involvement.

In 1878, the United States secured an unequal treaty from Samoa, a group of islands in the South Pacific. The United States gained rights such as extraterritoriality and a naval station. Other nations gained similar agreements. As their rivalry increased, the United States, Germany, and Britain agreed to a triple protectorate over Samoa.

Beginning in the mid-1800s, American sugar growers pressed for power in the Hawaiian Islands. When the Hawaiian queen **Liliuokalani** (lih lee uh oh kuh LAH nee) tried to reduce foreign influence, American planters overthrew her in 1893. They then asked the United States to annex Hawaii, which it finally did in 1898. Supporters of annexation argued that if the United States did not take Hawaii, Britain or Japan might do so. By 1900, the United States, Britain, France, and Germany had claimed nearly every island in the Pacific.

✓ **Checkpoint**   Why did some Americans think the United States should control Hawaii?

SECTION 2 **Assessment**

Progress Monitoring *Online*
For: Self-quiz with vocabulary practice
Web Code: nba-2521

Terms, People, and Places

1. For each term, person, or place listed at the beginning of the section, write a sentence explaining its significance.

Note Taking

2. **Reading Strategy: Identify Causes and Effects** Use your completed chart to answer the Focus Question: How did industrialized powers divide up Southeast Asia and the Pacific, and how did the colonized peoples react?

Comprehension and Critical Thinking

3. **Summarize** What steps did Siam take to preserve its independence?
4. **Draw Conclusions** Why were Filipino rebels disappointed when the United States took control of the Philippines?
5. **Synthesize Information** How did Hawaii become part of the United States?
6. **Make Comparisons** Compare the partition of Southeast Asia to the partition of Africa. How was it similar? How was it different?

● **Writing About History**

Quick Write: Examine the Question To answer a short answer or extended-response question effectively, first examine the question. Look for key words like *explain, compare,* or *persuade,* which will tell you what type of answer to provide. Then look for words that signal the topic. Identifying key words will help you focus and organize your response. Copy the prompt below and underline its key words.
• Compare Siam's relationship with imperial powers to that of Vietnam.

WITNESS HISTORY 🔊 AUDIO

O Canada!

In the early 1860s, the separate colonies of British North America considered whether they should join together to create one powerful confederation—Canada. George Brown, an influential politician who helped bring about the confederation, shared his dream for Canada:

> 66 Sir, it may be that some among us will live to see the day when, as the result of [the confederation], a great and powerful people may have grown up in these lands—when the boundless forests all around us shall have given way to smiling fields and thriving towns—and when one united government, under the British flag, shall extend from shore to shore. 99

Focus Question How were the British colonies of Canada, Australia, and New Zealand settled, and how did they win self-rule?

Settler's Log House (above) was painted in 1856 by a Dutch immigrant to Canada, Cornelius Krieghoff. The maple leaf (above right) is an emblem of Canada.

Self-Rule for Canada, Australia, and New Zealand

Objectives
- Describe how Canada achieved self-rule.
- Analyze how European settlement changed the course of Australian history.
- Summarize how New Zealand was settled and how it emerged as an independent nation.

Terms, People, and Places

confederation	indigenous
dominion	penal colony
métis	Maori

Note Taking

Reading Skill: Identify Cause and Effects As you read, record the causes and effects of the events you read about in a chart like this one.

Cause	Event	Effect
Loyalist Americans flee to Canada.	Up to 30,000 loyalists settle in Canada.	Ethnic tensions arise between English- and French-speaking Canadians.

Canada, Australia, and New Zealand won independence faster and easier than other British colonies in Africa or Asia. The language and cultural roots they shared with Britain helped. Racial attitudes also played a part. Imperialists in nations like Britain felt that whites, unlike non-whites, were capable of governing themselves.

Canada Achieves Self-Rule

When France lost Canada to Britain in 1763, thousands of French-speaking Catholic settlers remained. After the American Revolution, about 30,000 British loyalists fled to Canada. They were English-speaking Protestants. In addition, in the 1790s, several groups of Native American peoples still lived in eastern Canada. Others, in the west and the north, had not yet come into contact with European settlers.

Unrest in the Two Canadas To ease ethnic tensions, Britain passed the Constitutional Act of 1791. The act created two provinces: English-speaking Upper Canada (now Ontario) and French-speaking Lower Canada (now Quebec). French traditions and the Catholic Church were protected in Lower Canada. English traditions and laws guided Upper Canada.

During the early 1800s, unrest grew in both colonies. The people of Upper Canada resented the power held by a small group of elites who controlled the government. Lower Canada had similar problems. In 1837, discontent flared into rebellion in both places. Louis Joseph Papineau, the head of the French Canadian Reform party, led the rebellion in Lower Canada. William Lyon Mackenzie led the revolt in Upper Canada, crying, "Put down the villains who oppress and enslave our country!"

Britain Responds The British had learned from the American Revolution. While they hurried to put down the disorder, they sent an able politician, Lord Durham, to <u>compile</u> a report on the causes of the unrest. In 1840, Parliament acted on some of Durham's recommendations by passing the Act of Union. The act joined the two Canadas into one province. It also gave them an elected legislature that determined some domestic policies. Britain still controlled foreign policy and trade.

Canada Becomes a Dominion In the mid-1800s, thousands of English, Scottish, and Irish people immigrated to Canada. As the country grew, two Canadians, John Macdonald and George Étienne Cartier, urged **confederation,** or unification, of Britain's North American colonies. These colonies included Nova Scotia, New Brunswick, Prince Edward Island, and British Columbia, as well as the united Upper and Lower Canadas. The two leaders felt that confederation would strengthen the new nation against American ambitions and help its economic development.

Britain finally agreed, passing the British North America Act of 1867. The act created the Dominion of Canada. A **dominion** is a self-governing nation. As a dominion, Canada had its own parliament, modeled on that

Vocabulary Builder

<u>compile</u>—(kum PYL) *vt.* to put together from several sources

Geography *Interactive*
For: Audio guided tour
Web Code: nbp-2531

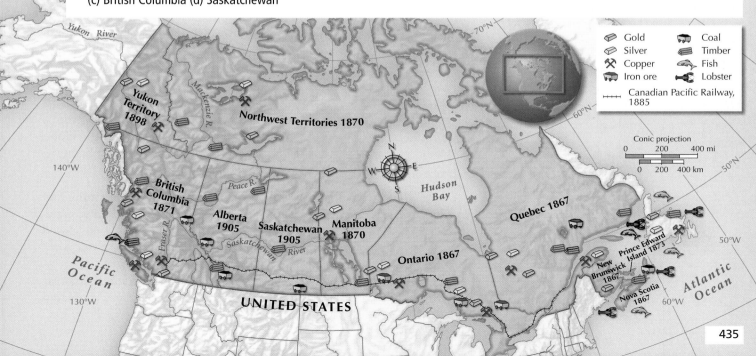

Canada, 1867–1914

Map Skills Canada grew throughout the latter half of the 1800s.
1. **Locate:** (a) Quebec (b) Ontario (c) British Columbia (d) Saskatchewan

2. **Movement** Why did British Columbia become a part of Canada before Alberta and Saskatchewan?

3. **Make Comparisons** Compare Nova Scotia's natural resources to those of Manitoba.

Gold   Coal
Silver   Timber
Copper   Fish
Iron ore   Lobster
———— Canadian Pacific Railway, 1885

Conic projection
0   200   400 mi
0   200   400 km

Yukon River

Yukon Territory 1898

Mackenzie R.

Northwest Territories 1870

British Columbia 1871

Peace R.

Fraser R.

Alberta 1905

Saskatchewan River

Saskatchewan 1905

Manitoba 1870

Hudson Bay

Quebec 1867

Ontario 1867

Pacific Ocean

140°W

130°W

UNITED STATES

70°N

60°N

50°N

50°W

60°W

Prince Edward Island 1873

New Brunswick 1867

Nova Scotia 1867

Atlantic Ocean

of Britain. By 1900, Canada also had some control over its own foreign policy. Still, Canada maintained close ties with Britain.

Canada Grows Like the United States, Canada expanded westward in the 1800s. In 1885, the Canadian Pacific Railway opened, linking eastern and western Canada. Wherever the railroad went, settlers followed. It moved people and products, such as timber and manufactured goods across the country. In the late 1800s and early 1900s, more immigrants flooded into Canada from Germany, Italy, Poland, Russia, Ukraine, China, and Japan. They enriched Canada's economy and culture.

As in the United States, westward expansion destroyed the way of life of Native Americans in Canada. Most were forced to sign treaties giving up their lands. Some resisted. In central Canada, Louis Riel led a revolt of the **métis,** people of mixed Native American and French Canadian descent, in 1869 and again in 1885. Many métis were French-speaking Catholics who believed that the government was trying to take their land and destroy their language and religion. Government troops put down both uprisings. Riel was executed in 1885.

By 1914, Canada was a flourishing nation. Still, French-speaking Canadians were determined to preserve their separate heritage, making it hard for Canadians to create a single national identity. Also, the cultural and economic influence of the United States threatened to dominate Canada. Both issues continue to affect Canada today.

✔ **Checkpoint** How did the British respond to the Canadians' desire for self-rule?

Europeans in Australia

The Dutch in the 1600s were the first Europeans to reach Australia. In 1770, Captain James Cook claimed Australia for Britain. For a time, however, Australia remained too distant to attract European settlers.

The First Settlers Like most regions claimed by imperialist powers, Australia had long been inhabited by other people. The first settlers had reached Australia perhaps 40,000 years earlier, probably from Southeast Asia, and spread across the continent. These **indigenous,** or original, people were called Aborigines, a word used by Europeans to denote the earliest people to live in a place. Today, many Australian Aborigines call themselves Kooris. Isolated from the larger world, the Aborigines lived in small hunting and food-gathering bands, much as their Stone Age ancestors had. Aboriginal groups spoke as many as 250 distinct languages. When white settlers arrived in Australia, the indigenous population suffered disastrously.

A Penal Colony During the 1700s, Britain had sent convicts to its North American colonies, especially to Georgia. The American Revolution closed that outlet. Prisons in London and other cities were jammed.

To fill the need for prisons, Britain made Australia into a **penal colony,** or a place where convicted

Life in Australia
Australian Aborigines used boomerangs, like this one decorated with traditional motifs, to hunt and in battles. The first British settlers in Australia were convicted criminals. The convicts in the illustration below are being forced to carry heavy loads of shingles as part of their hard labor. *What happened to Aborigines as British settlement spread?*

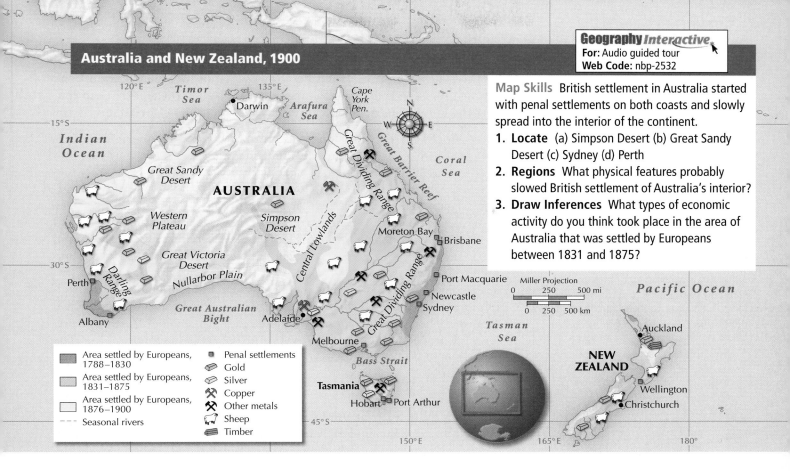

Australia and New Zealand, 1900

Map Skills British settlement in Australia started with penal settlements on both coasts and slowly spread into the interior of the continent.

1. **Locate** (a) Simpson Desert (b) Great Sandy Desert (c) Sydney (d) Perth
2. **Regions** What physical features probably slowed British settlement of Australia's interior?
3. **Draw Inferences** What types of economic activity do you think took place in the area of Australia that was settled by Europeans between 1831 and 1875?

Legend:
- Area settled by Europeans, 1788–1830
- Area settled by Europeans, 1831–1875
- Area settled by Europeans, 1876–1900
- Seasonal rivers
- Penal settlements
- Gold
- Silver
- Copper
- Other metals
- Sheep
- Timber

criminals are sent to be punished. The first British ships, carrying about 700 convicts, arrived in Botany Bay, Australia, in 1788. The people who survived the grueling eight-month voyage faced more hardships on shore. Many were city dwellers with no farming skills. Under the brutal discipline of soldiers, work gangs cleared land for settlement.

The Colonies Grow In the early 1800s, Britain encouraged free citizens to emigrate to Australia by offering them land and tools. A prosperous wool industry grew up as settlers found that the land and climate suited sheepherding. In 1851, a gold rush in eastern Australia brought a population boom. Many gold hunters stayed on to become ranchers and farmers. They pushed into the rugged interior known as the Outback, carving out huge sheep ranches and wheat farms. As the newcomers settled in, they thrust aside or killed the Aborigines.

Achieving Self-Government Like Canada, Australia was made up of separate colonies scattered around the continent. Britain worried about interference from other European powers. To counter this threat and to boost development, it responded to Australian demands for self-rule. In 1901, Britain helped the colonies unite into the independent Commonwealth of Australia. The new country kept its ties to Britain by recognizing the British monarch as its head of state.

The Australian constitution drew on both British and American models. Unlike Britain and the United States, Australia quickly granted women the right to vote. In 1856, it also became the first nation to introduce the secret ballot.

✔ **Checkpoint** What effect did colonization have on Australia's indigenous population?

WITNESS HISTORY VIDEO

Watch *Australia: The Story of a Penal Colony* on the **Witness History Discovery School**™ video program to learn more about life in an Australian penal colony.

Discovery
SCHOOL

New Zealand's Story

To the southeast of Australia lies New Zealand. In 1769, Captain Cook claimed its islands for Britain. Missionaries landed there in 1814 to convert the indigenous people, the **Maori** (MAH oh ree), to Christianity.

The Maori Struggle Unlike Australia, where the Aborigines were spread thinly across a large continent, the Maori were concentrated in a smaller area. They were descended from seafaring people who had reached New Zealand from Polynesia in the 1200s. The Maori were settled farmers. They were also determined to defend their land.

White settlers, who were attracted by New Zealand's mild climate and good soil, followed the missionaries. These settlers introduced sheep and cattle and were soon exporting wool, mutton, and beef. In 1840, Britain annexed New Zealand.

As colonists poured in, they took over more and more of the land, leading to fierce wars with the Maori. Many Maori died in the struggle. Still more perished from disease, alcoholism, and other misfortunes that followed European colonization. By the 1870s, resistance crumbled. The Maori population had fallen drastically, from about 200,000 to less than 45,000 in 1896. Only recently has the Maori population started to grow once more.

Settlers Win Self-Government Like settlers in Australia and Canada, white New Zealanders sought self-rule. In 1907, they won independence, with their own parliament, prime minister, and elected legislature. They, too, preserved close ties to the British empire.

✔ **Checkpoint** Compare and contrast the European settlement of Australia and New Zealand.

Maori Traditions
The portrait below shows a Maori leader in 1882. Many Maori men of high social standing commissioned tattoos on their faces. Maori war canoes, like the one below, often carried distinctive carving.

Progress Monitoring *Online*
For: Self-quiz with vocabulary practice
Web Code: nba-2531

Terms, People, and Places

1. For each term, person, or place listed at the beginning of the section, write a sentence explaining its significance.

Note Taking

2. **Reading Skill: Identify Causes and Effects** Use your completed chart to answer the Focus Question: How were the British colonies of Canada, Australia, and New Zealand settled, and how did they win self-rule?

Comprehension and Critical Thinking

3. **Sequence** What steps led to Canadian self-rule?
4. **Compare** Compare the European settlement of Australia with that of Canada.
5. **Identify Causes** Why did the Maori fight colonists in New Zealand?
6. **Synthesize Information** What ethnic tensions did Australia, Canada, and New Zealand face?

● **Writing About History**

Quick Write: Focus Your Time To stay focused as you respond to a short answer or extended-response question on a test, plan to spend a quarter of the allotted time on prewriting, half on drafting, and the remaining quarter on revising. Write a short answer response to the following prompt using a 20-minute time limit. Time yourself to practice staying within the appropriate time limit during each stage.

• Compare how Canada and Australia gained self-rule.

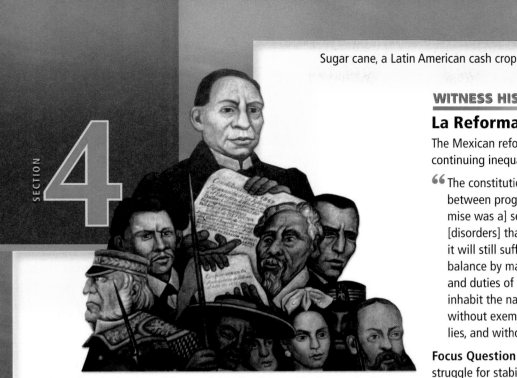

Sugar cane, a Latin American cash crop

SECTION 4

Benito Juárez is the central figure of this detail from Mexican artist Diego Rivera's mural *Sunday Afternoon in Alameda Park.*

WITNESS HISTORY ◀》 AUDIO

La Reforma

The Mexican reformer Benito Juárez criticized the continuing inequality in Mexico:

❝ The constitution of 1824 was a compromise between progress and reaction, and [that compromise was a] seedbed of the incessant convulsions [disorders] that the Republic has suffered, and that it will still suffer while society does not recover its balance by making effective the equality of rights and duties of all citizens and of all persons who inhabit the national territory, without privileges, without exemptions [exceptions], without monopolies, and without odious distinctions . . . .❞

Focus Question How did Latin American nations struggle for stability, and how did industrialized nations affect them?

Economic Imperialism in Latin America

Objectives

- Describe the political problems faced by Mexico and other new Latin American nations.
- List the ways industrialized nations affected Latin America.

Terms, People, and Places

regionalism
caudillo
Benito Juárez
La Reforma

peonage
Monroe Doctrine
Panama Canal

Note Taking

Reading Skill: Recognize Multiple Causes As you read, record the causes of instability in Latin America in a chart similar to this one. Then give an example of how each cause affected Mexico.

Instability in Latin America	
Causes	Mexican Example

Despite bright hopes, democracy failed to take root in most of the newly independent nations of Latin America in the 1800s. Instead, wealth and power remained in the hands of the few. At the same time, new technology such as refrigerated ships helped to intertwine the economies of nations that were thousands of miles apart. Latin American economies became increasingly dependent upon those of more developed countries. Britain, and later the United States, invested heavily in Latin America.

Lingering Political Problems

Simón Bolívar had hoped to create strong ties among the nations of Latin America. But feuds among leaders, geographic barriers, and local nationalism shattered that dream of unity. In the end, 20 separate nations emerged.

These new nations wrote constitutions modeled on that of the United States. They set up republics with elected legislatures. However, true democracy failed to take hold. During the 1800s, many succumbed to revolts, civil war, and dictatorships.

The Colonial Legacy Many of the problems in the new nations had their origins in colonial rule. The existing social and political hierarchy barely changed. Creoles simply replaced *peninsulares* as the ruling class. The Roman Catholic Church kept its privileged position and still controlled huge amounts of land.

For most people—mestizos, mulattoes, blacks, and Indians—life did not improve after independence. The new constitutions guaranteed equality before the law, but deep-rooted inequalities remained. Voting rights were limited. Many people felt the effects of racial prejudice. Small groups of people held most of the land. Owners of haciendas ruled their great estates, and the peasants who worked them, like medieval European lords.

The Search for Stability With few roads and no tradition of unity, **regionalism,** or loyalty to a local area, weakened the new nations. Local strongmen, called *caudillos* (kaw DEE yohs), assembled private armies to resist the central government. At times, popular caudillos, occasionally former military leaders, gained national power. They looted the treasury and ruled as dictators. Power struggles led to frequent revolts that changed little except the name of the leader. In the long run, power remained in the hands of a privileged few who had no desire to share it.

As in Europe, the ruling elite in Latin America were divided between conservatives and liberals. Conservatives defended the traditional social order, favored press censorship, and strongly supported the Catholic Church. Liberals backed laissez-faire economics, religious toleration, greater access to education, and freedom of the press. Liberals saw themselves as <u>enlightened</u> supporters of progress but often showed little concern for the needs of the majority of the people.

✓ **Checkpoint** What factors undermined democracy in post-independence Latin America?

Mexico's Struggle for Stability

During the 1800s, each Latin American nation followed its own course. Mexico provides an example of the challenges facing many Latin American nations. Large landowners, army leaders, and the Catholic Church dominated Mexican politics. However, bitter battles between conservatives and liberals led to revolts and the rise of dictators. Deep social divisions separated wealthy creoles from mestizos and Indians who lived in poverty.

Santa Anna and War With the United States Between 1833 and 1855, an ambitious and cunning *caudillo,* Antonio López de Santa Anna, gained and lost power many times. At first, he posed as a liberal reformer.

Life on a Hacienda
Peasant women process a crop grown on a hacienda in Mexico in the 1800s.

Soon, however, he reversed his stand and crushed efforts at reform.

In Mexico's northern territory of Texas, discontent grew. In 1835, settlers who had moved to Texas from the United States and other places revolted. After a brief struggle with Santa Anna's forces, the settlers gained independence from Mexico. They quickly set up an independent republic. Then in 1845 the United States annexed Texas. Mexicans saw this act as a declaration of war. In the fighting that followed, the United States invaded and defeated Mexico. In the Treaty of Guadalupe-Hidalgo, which ended the war, Mexico lost almost half its territory. The embarrassing defeat triggered new violence between conservatives and liberals.

La Reforma Changes Mexico In 1855, Benito Juárez (WAHR ez), a liberal reformer of Zapotec Indian heritage, and other liberals gained power and opened an era of reform known as **La Reforma.** Juárez offered hope to the oppressed people of Mexico. He and his fellow reformers revised the Mexican constitution to strip the military of power and end the special privileges of the Church. They ordered the Church to sell unused lands to peasants.

Conservatives resisted La Reforma and began a civil war. Still, Juárez was elected president in 1861 and expanded his reforms. His opponents turned to Europe for help. In 1863, Napoleon III sent troops to Mexico and set up Austrian archduke Maximilian as emperor.

For four years, Juárez's forces battled the combined conservative and French forces. When France withdrew its troops, Maximilian was captured and shot. In 1867, Juárez returned to power and tried to renew reform, but opponents resisted. Juárez died in office in 1872, never achieving all the reforms he envisioned. He did, however, help unite Mexico, bring mestizos into politics, and separate church and state.

Growth and Oppression Under Díaz After Juárez died, General Porfirio Díaz, a hero of the war against the French, staged a military coup and gained power. From 1876 to 1880 and 1884 to 1911, he ruled as a dictator. In the name of "Order and Progress," he strengthened the army, local police, and central government. He crushed opposition.

Under his harsh rule, Mexico made <u>tangible</u> economic advances. Railroads were built, foreign trade increased, some industry developed, and mining expanded. Growth, however, had a high cost. Capital for development came from foreign investors, to whom Díaz granted special rights. He also let wealthy landowners buy up Indian lands.

The rich prospered, but most Mexicans remained poor. Many Indians and mestizos fell into **peonage** to their employers. In the peonage system, hacienda owners would give workers advances on their wages and require them to stay on the hacienda until they had paid back what they owed. Wages remained low, and workers were rarely able to repay the hacienda owner. Many children died in infancy. Other children worked 12-hour days and never learned to read or write.

✔ **Checkpoint** What struggles did Mexico go through as it tried to find stability in the 1800s?

Remember the Alamo!
Mexican President Antonio López de Santa Anna (above) is well-known for his ruthless decision to give no quarter to the Texan defenders of the Alamo, a fort in San Antonio, Texas, during the Texas Revolution. The illustration above shows Texan defenders of the Alamo bravely fighting against overwhelming odds. *In what light does this illustration present the defenders of the Alamo?*

Vocabulary Builder
<u>tangible</u>—(TAN juh bul) *adj.* real or concrete

Note Taking

Reading Skill: Identify Effects Use a chart like the one below to record how foreign influence, including that of the United States, affected Latin America.

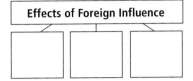

Effects of Foreign Influence

The Economics of Dependence

Under colonial rule, mercantilist policies made Latin America economically dependent on Spain and Portugal. Colonies sent raw materials such as cash crops or precious metals to the parent country and had to buy manufactured goods from them. Strict laws kept colonists from trading with other countries and possibly obtaining goods at a lower price. In addition, laws prohibited the building of local industries that would have competed with the parent country. In short, the policies prevented the colonies from developing their own economies.

The Cycle of Economic Dependence After independence, this pattern changed very little. The new Latin American republics did adopt free trade, welcoming all comers. Britain and the United States rushed into the new markets, replacing Spain as Latin America's chief trading partners. But the region remained as economically dependent as before.

Foreign Influence Mounts In the 1800s, foreign goods flooded Latin America, creating large profits for foreigners and for a handful of local business people. Foreign investment, which could yield enormous profits, was often accompanied by local interference. Investors from Britain, the United States, and other nations pressured their own governments to take action if political events or reform movements in a Latin American country seemed to threaten their interests.

Some Economic Growth After 1850, some Latin American economies did grow. With foreign capital, they were able to develop mining and agriculture. Chile exported copper and nitrates, and Argentina expanded

Geography *Interactive*
For: Audio guided tour
Web Code: nbp-2541

Imperialism in Latin America, 1898–1917

Map Skills In the early 1900s, European powers held possessions in Latin America. The United States often intervened to protect business interests there.

1. **Locate** (a) Cuba (b) Canal Zone (c) British Guiana (d) Honduras
2. **Location** Why did the United States have a particularly strong interest in Latin American affairs?
3. **Identify Point of View** What natural resources did the Dutch exploit in Dutch Guiana?

its livestock and wheat production. Brazil exported the cash crops coffee and sugar, as well as rubber. By the early 1900s, both Venezuela and Mexico were developing important and lucrative oil industries.

Throughout the region, foreigners invested in modern ports and railroads to carry goods from the interior to coastal cities. European immigrants poured into Latin America. The newcomers helped to promote economic activity, and a small middle class emerged.

Thanks to trade, investment, technology, and migration, Latin American nations moved into the world economy. Yet internal development was limited. The tiny elite at the top benefited from the economic upturn, but very little trickled down to the masses of people at the bottom. The poor earned too little to buy consumer goods. Without a strong demand, many industries failed to develop.

 Checkpoint How did foreign influence and investment affect Latin America?

The Influence of the United States

As nations like Mexico tried to build stable governments, a neighboring republic, the United States, expanded across North America. Latin American nations began to feel threatened by the "Colossus of the North," the giant power that cast its shadow over the entire hemisphere.

The Monroe Doctrine In the 1820s, Spain plotted to recover its American colonies. Britain opposed any move that might close the door to trade with Latin America. British leaders asked American President James Monroe to join them in a statement opposing any new colonization of the Americas.

Monroe, however, wanted to avoid any "entangling alliance" with Britain. Acting alone, he issued the **Monroe Doctrine** in 1823. "The American continents," it declared, "are henceforth not to be considered as subjects for future colonization by any European powers." The United States lacked the military power to enforce the doctrine. But with the support of Britain's strong navy, the doctrine discouraged European interference. For more than a century, the Monroe Doctrine would be the key to United States policy in the Americas.

The United States Expands Into Latin America As a result of the war with Mexico, in 1848 the United States acquired the thinly populated regions of northern Mexico, gaining all or part of the present-day states of California, Arizona, New Mexico, Nevada, Utah, and Colorado. The victory fed dreams of future expansion. Before the century had ended, the United States controlled much of North America and was becoming involved in overseas conflicts.

For decades, Cuban patriots had battled to free their island from Spanish rule. As they began to make headway, the United States joined their cause, declaring war on Spain in 1898. The brief Spanish-American War ended in a crushing defeat for Spain. At the war's end, Cuba was granted independence. But in 1901, the United States forced Cubans to add the Platt Amendment to their constitution. The amendment gave the United States naval bases in Cuba and the right to intervene in Cuban affairs.

AN EPIC UNDERTAKING: PANAMA CANAL

The Panama Canal was a massive undertaking. The sheer scale of the project astounded engineers, politicians, and tourists. Building the canal cost the American government $352 million (about $7 billion in today's money). Workers excavated about 232 million cubic yards of dirt, rocks, and debris from the Canal Zone—enough debris to create a pyramid seven times the height of the Washington Monument, as one newspaper writer noted. Nearly six thousand workers died from industrial accidents or disease in the ten years it took to build the canal.

Despite many challenges, the builders would not give up. They completed the canal in 1914. The beginning of World War I in the summer of 1914, however, overshadowed what was to be its grand opening.

UNITED STATES
San Francisco
New York City
6,100 MILES
9,820 KILOMETERS
15,100 MILES
24,200 KILOMETERS
Atlantic Ocean
PANAMA CANAL
Pacific Ocean

Haut Obispo (Higher Obispo)—Showing one of the old French steam scoops now being used by Americans, and the height of bank it excavates.

Dump Train—Pedro Miguel. The greatest problem on the Isthmus is not to dig the Canal, but to get rid of the great mass of excavated dirt.

Steam Sho... pathway, lifting five scoops ...utes and loading ten cars in thirty minutes.

▲ Playing cards featuring scenes from the canal's construction (above) helped to feed Americans' fascination with the canal.

◄ Two men (below) stand inside one of the canal lock's enormous gates. The gates allow water to flow in and out of the lock, raising or lowering ships to different levels.

▼ The tropical diseases malaria and yellow fever killed many workers. Quinine (below right) was used to treat some cases of malaria. The canal builders' massive efforts to kill disease-carrying mosquitoes, using methods, such as spraying swampy areas with oil (below left), were more effective.

Quinine G...

Thinking Critically

1. **Draw Conclusions** Based on the map, why did Americans want to build a canal in Panama?
2. **Draw Inferences** Why was it important to control disease during the building of the canal?

The United States Interferes American investments in Latin America grew in the early 1900s. Citing the need to protect those investments, in 1904 the United States issued the Roosevelt Corollary to the Monroe Doctrine. Under this policy, the United States claimed "international police power" in the Western Hemisphere. When the Dominican Republic failed to pay its foreign debts, the United States sent in troops. Americans collected customs duties, paid off the debts, and remained for years.

Under the Roosevelt Corollary and then President William Howard Taft's policy of Dollar Diplomacy, American companies continued to invest in the countries of Latin America. To protect those investments, the United States sent troops to Cuba, Haiti, Mexico, Honduras, Nicaragua, and other countries in Central America and the Caribbean. As a result, like European powers in Africa and Asia, the United States became the target of increasing resentment and rebellion.

Building the Panama Canal From the late 1800s, the United States had wanted to build a canal across Central America. Panama was a proposed site. However, Panama belonged to Colombia, which refused to sell the United States land for the canal. In 1903, the United States backed a revolt by Panamanians against Colombia. The Panamanians quickly won independence and gave the United States control of the land to build the canal.

Construction began in 1904. Engineers solved many difficult problems in the course of building the canal. The **Panama Canal** opened in 1914. The canal cut the distance of a sea journey between such cities as New York and San Francisco by thousands of miles. It was an engineering marvel that boosted trade and shipping worldwide.

To people in Latin America, however, the canal was another example of "Yankee imperialism." Nationalist feeling in the hemisphere was often expressed as anti-Americanism. Panama did not gain complete control over the canal until 2000. It now forms a vital part of the Panamanian economy.

 Checkpoint How did the United States act as an imperialist power in Latin America?

SECTION 4 Assessment

Progress Monitoring Online
For: Self-quiz with vocabulary practice
Web Code: nba-2541

Terms, People, and Places

1. For each term, person, or place listed at the beginning of the section, write a sentence explaining its significance.

Note Taking

2. **Reading Skill: Recognize Multiple Causes** Use your completed charts to answer the Focus Question: How did Latin American nations struggle for stability, and how did industrialized nations affect them?

Critical Thinking and Comprehension

3. **Express Problems Clearly** What problems faced new nations in Latin America?

4. **Recognize Cause and Effect** How did the cycle of economic dependence continue after independence?

5. **Synthesize Information** Describe two ways the United States influenced Latin America.

6. **Draw Conclusions** Why might developing nations encourage foreign investment? Do you think foreign investors should have the right to intervene in another nation's affairs to protect their investments? Explain.

● **Writing About History**

Quick Write: Support Your Ideas As you respond to a short-answer or extended-response question on a test, keep in mind that each sentence or paragraph should support your main idea. Omit information, no matter how interesting, that is not central to your argument. To practice, write an outline of an argument responding to the following extended-response prompt.

• Explain how American interference led to the building of the Panama Canal.

Quick Study Guide

Progress Monitoring *Online*
For: Self-test with vocabulary practice
Web Code: nba-2551

■ Imperialism in Japan and Southeast Asia and the Pacific

Japan	Southeast Asia and the Pacific
• United States opens by show of force. • Meiji restoration begins modernization. • Japan becomes an imperialist power itself.	• European powers expand footholds. • Some countries resist, but succumb to European force. • Europeans gain resources and trade networks at expense of indigenous people.

■ Three British Colonies: Canada, Australia, and New Zealand

British Colony	Settled by	Impact on Indigenous People	Gained Self-Rule From Britain
Canada	First France, then Britain	Native Americans forced to give up lands	1867
Australia	Britain, as penal colony	Aborigines suffered disastrously	1901
New Zealand	Britain, attracted by climate	Maori fought against settlers, population reduced drastically	1907

■ The Cycle of Economic Dependence in Latin America

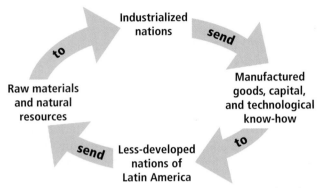

The relationship is unequal because the stronger, more developed nations control prices and terms of trade.

■ Key Events in Worldwide Imperialism

Southeast Asia, the Pacific, and Japan
British Colonies and Latin America

1835

1853 American ships commanded by Commodore Perry arrive in Japan.

1858 France invades Vietnam.

1850

1868 Meiji Restoration begins in Japan.

1865

1840 Britain annexes New Zealand.

1855 La Reforma begins in Mexico.

1867 Britain grants Canada self-rule.

Concept Connector

■ Cumulative Review

Record the answers to the question below on your Concept Connector worksheets.

1. **Genocide** Read about what happened to the indigenous peoples of North America when Europeans colonized Mexico, the United States, and Canada. Then learn more about the effects of colonization on the Aborigines in Australia and the Maori in New Zealand. Compare the experiences of these indigenous groups. Consider the following:
   - population and way of life prior to and after colonization
   - effects of disease
   - attitudes towards land ownership
   - treatment today

2. **Geography's Impact** Location links the fate of Latin America with that of the United States. In the 1800s, ideas about independence springing from the American Revolution inspired independence leaders in Latin America, such as Simón Bolívar. However, in the late 1800s, the United States began to interfere more aggressively in the affairs of Latin American countries. Create a timeline tracking the relationship between the United States and Latin America from 1800 through 1914. Include a brief description of the significance of each event on the timeline.

3. **Trade** One of the strengths of the British empire was its commercial trading network, which touched almost every continent. As you have read, the Dutch were also far-flung traders, even maintaining ties with Japan when traders from other countries were forbidden. Learn more about the Dutch trading empire, beginning in the 1600s. Compare the two trading empires in terms of the following:
   - areas controlled
   - types of colonies
   - duration
   - relations with other industrialized countries

■ Connections To Today

1. **Conflict: Unrest in Quebec** Although French-Canadian leaders agreed to confederation with the rest of Canada in 1867, the French-English question was never truly put to rest. Many French-Canadians continued to feel that the English-speaking majority in Canada threatened their unique French culture. In the late 1900s, a movement for an independent Quebec arose. Research the path of this movement and create a bulleted list of significant events that occurred within the last fifty years.

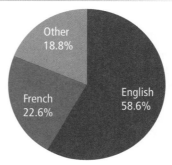

Languages Spoken in Canada Today

Other 18.8%
French 22.6%
English 58.6%

SOURCE: Statistics Canada, 2001 Census

2. **Cooperation: Japan as a World Power** After its rapid modernization in the late 1800s, Japan took its place among the leading powers of the world. It asserted that power throughout the 1900s, with varying results. Today, Japan's economy is second in size only to that of the United States. Conduct research on Japan and write a paragraph describing its role in international affairs today.

1886 Britain annexes Burma.

1898 The Philippines declares independence from Spain.

1910 Japan annexes Korea.

History Interactive
For: Interactive timeline
Web Code: nbp-2562

1880　　　　**1895**　　　　**1910**　　　　**1925**

1885 The Canadian Pacific Railway opens.

1904 The United States issues the Roosevelt Corollary.

1914 The Panama Canal opens.

Chapter Assessment

Terms, People, and Places

1. In what ways did **Matthew Perry's** opening of Japan lead to the **Meiji Restoration?**
2. How did the **Sino-Japanese** and **Russo-Japanese wars** spring out of Japan's new strength as a modernized nation?
3. What steps did **King Mongkut** take to help Siam avoid the fate of **French Indochina?**
4. How did Canada become a **dominion?**
5. Describe how the **Spanish-American War** affected both the Philippines and Cuba.
6. How did **regionalism** and *caudillos* weaken the stability of Latin American countries in the 1800s?

Main Ideas

Section 1 (pp. 422–428)
7. How did Japan change course in the late 1800s?

Section 2 (pp. 429–433)
8. Why were imperialist nations drawn to Southeast Asia and the Pacific?
9. How did the colonized peoples of Southeast Asia react to Western attempts to dominate the region?

Section 3 (pp. 434–438)
10. Describe settlement in Canada, Australia, and New Zealand.
11. How did these colonies gain independence?

Section 4 (pp. 439–445)
12. What factors caused instability in Latin America after independence?
13. How did the United States influence Latin America?

Chapter Focus question:
14. How did political and economic imperialism influence nations around the world?

Critical Thinking

15. **Compare** Compare Japan's response to Western imperialism to that of China. How were the two responses similar? How were they different?
16. **Identify Causes** In the image below, a Japanese woman wears Western clothing. What role did westernization play in helping both Japan and Siam avoid colonization by European nations?

17. **Connect to Geography** How did the creation of the Dominion of Canada encourage expansion?
18. **Synthesize Information** What principle did the United States express in the Monroe Doctrine? How did the Roosevelt Corollary alter the Monroe Doctrine?
19. **Draw Conclusions** List the benefits and disadvantages brought about by colonial rule. Do you think subject people were better or worse off as a result of the Age of Imperialism? Explain.

● Writing About History

Writing for Assessment The effects of imperialism are still being felt around the world today. Write an answer to one of the following extended response essay prompts. Spend only 40 minutes on the writing process. Consult page SH20 of the Writing Handbook for additional help.

- Analyze the effects of Japanese imperialism in Korea.
- Analyze the effects of American intervention in Latin America.

Prewriting
- Read both prompts and determine what you know about each. Choose the one whose topic you recall the most information about.

- Look for key words that will tell you what kind of answer to provide, such as *"explain."*

Drafting
- Focus your time by allowing 10 minutes for prewriting, 20 minutes for drafting, and 10 minutes for revising your response.
- Develop a thesis for your essay and make sure each piece of information supports it.

Revising
- Check that you open and close your response strongly, that each point supports your main idea, and that you've answered all aspects of the question.

Document-Based Assessment

The Imperialism Debate and the Philippines

After defeating Spain in Manila Bay in May 1898, American forces remained in the Philippines. In February 1899, the United States Senate voted to annex the Philippines. The Philippines were one aspect of the United States' efforts to compete with Europe in the scramble for new foreign markets, investment opportunities and raw materials. A great debate took place in the United States over the issue of imperialism, as the documents below show.

Document A

"I have been criticized a good deal about the Philippines, but don't deserve it. The truth is I didn't want the Philippines, and when they came to us, as a gift from the gods, I did not know what to do with them. . . . And one night late it came to me this way—I don't know how it was, but it came: (1) That we could not give them back to Spain—that would be cowardly and dishonorable; (2) that we could not turn them over to France and Germany—our commercial rivals in the Orient—that would be bad business and discreditable; (3) that we could not leave them to themselves—they were unfit for self-government—and they would soon have anarchy and misrule over there worse than Spain's was; and (4) that there was nothing left for us to do but to take them all, and to educate the Filipinos, and uplift and civilize and Christianize them . . ."

—From remarks to a visiting delegation of Methodist church leaders made by President William McKinley on November 21, 1899

Document B

"We hold that the policy known as imperialism is hostile to liberty and tends toward militarism, an evil from which it has been our glory to be free. . . . We maintain that governments derive their just powers from the consent of the governed. We insist that the subjugation of any people is "criminal aggression" and open disloyalty to the distinctive principles of our government.

We earnestly condemn the policy of the present National Administration in the Philippines. It seeks to extinguish the spirit of 1776 in those islands. . . . We denounce the slaughter of the Filipinos as a needless horror."

—From the Platform of the American Anti-Imperialist League, 1899

Document C

"Isn't Every American proud of the part that American soldiers bore in the relief of Pekin [i.e., Beijing, where some U.S. citizens were held hostage by the Boxers]? But that would have been impossible if our flag had not been in the Philippines.

Gen. Chaffee led two infantry regiments, the Ninth and the Fourteen, and one battery of the Fifth Artillery to Pekin. They did not come direct from the United States; there was not time. . . . But for these men and the marines from Manilla barracks, Minister Conger and his American comrades in the besieged legation would not have seen their country's flag, and would OWE THEIR RELIEF TO BRITISH, JAPANESE AND RUSSIANS.

When Mr. Bryan [Democratic candidate for president] tells you that the Philippines are worth nothing to America, you tell him to 'REMEMBER PEKIN!'"

—From a leaflet of the Republican Club of Massachusetts, 1900

Analyzing Documents

Use your knowledge of this chapter and Documents A, B, and C to answer questions 1–4.

1. In Document A, which of McKinley's four reasons for the takeover of the Philippines explained that important business interests were at stake?
   A 1
   B 2
   C 3
   D 4

2. In Document B, what is the meaning of "It seeks to extinguish the spirit of 1776 in those islands"?
   A The U.S. vowed never to give the Philippines its freedom.
   B The U.S. is undermining an independence movement that is like the American Revolution.
   C Self-government in the Philippines is inevitable.
   D The U.S. has the ability and the duty to educate Filipinos about self-government.

3. According to Document C, the Philippines are necessary to the United States as a(n)
   A source for raw materials.
   B outpost for Christian missionaries.
   C base for military actions.
   D market for U.S. goods.

4. William Jennings Bryan considered imperialism which he opposed, to be the top issue in the 1900 presidential campaign. Who would have received your vote, the Democratic candidate, Bryan, or the Republican, William McKinley? Give your reasons, using these documents and information from the chapter.

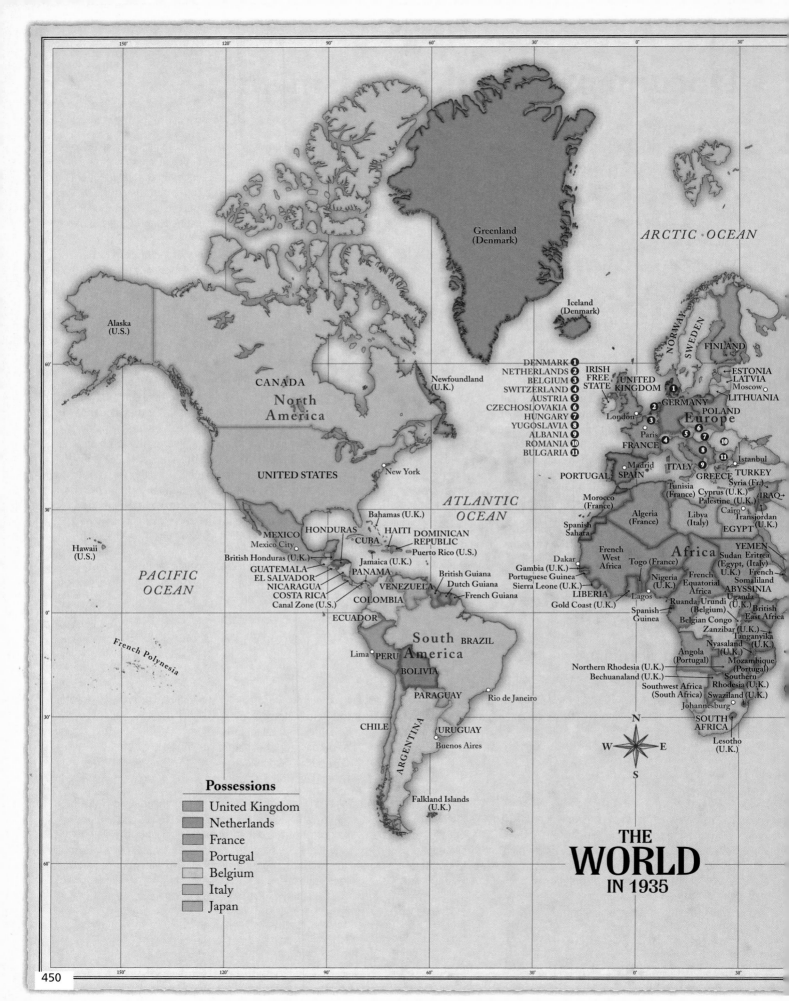

THE
WORLD
IN 1935

Possessions

- United Kingdom
- Netherlands
- France
- Portugal
- Belgium
- Italy
- Japan

Map labels

SOVIET UNION

TANNU-TUVA

MONGOLIA

Manchukuo (Japan)

Asia

AFGHANISTAN

Beijing

JAPAN

Korea (Japan)

Tehran
PERSIA

CHINA

Tokyo

Persian Gulf
Protectorates
(U.K.)

TIBET   BHUTAN

NEPAL

Delhi

Macao (Portugal)

*PACIFIC
OCEAN*

Oman (U.K.)

India (U.K.)

Calcutta

Taiwan (Japan)

Hong Kong (U.K.)

SAUDI
ARABIA

Bombay

Guam (U.S.)

Japanese Pacific
Possessions

Aden and South
Arabia (U.K.)

SIAM   French
Indochina

*Marshall
Islands*

British Somaliland

Bangkok

Philippines (U.S.)

Italian
Somaliland

Malaya (U.K.)

Saigon

Brunei (U.K.)

Caroline Islands

Ceylon (U.K.)

Sarawak (U.K.)

British North Borneo

Singapore

New Guinea
Territory
(Australia)

*Bismarck
Archipelago*

Solomon
Islands
(U:K.)

*INDIAN
OCEAN*

Dutch East Indies

Batavia

Papua
(Australia)

Fiji
(U.K.)

Madagascar (France)

Portuguese Timor

New
Caledonia
(France)

Mauritius (U.K.)

Réunion (France)

AUSTRALIA

Sydney

NEW
ZEALAND

Scale in Miles
0   1000   2000   3000

0   1000 2000 3000
Scale in Kilometers
Scale at the Equator
Mercator Projection

Geography *Interactive*
For: Audio guided tour
Web Code: nbp-6000

14
World War I and the Russian Revolution
1914–1924

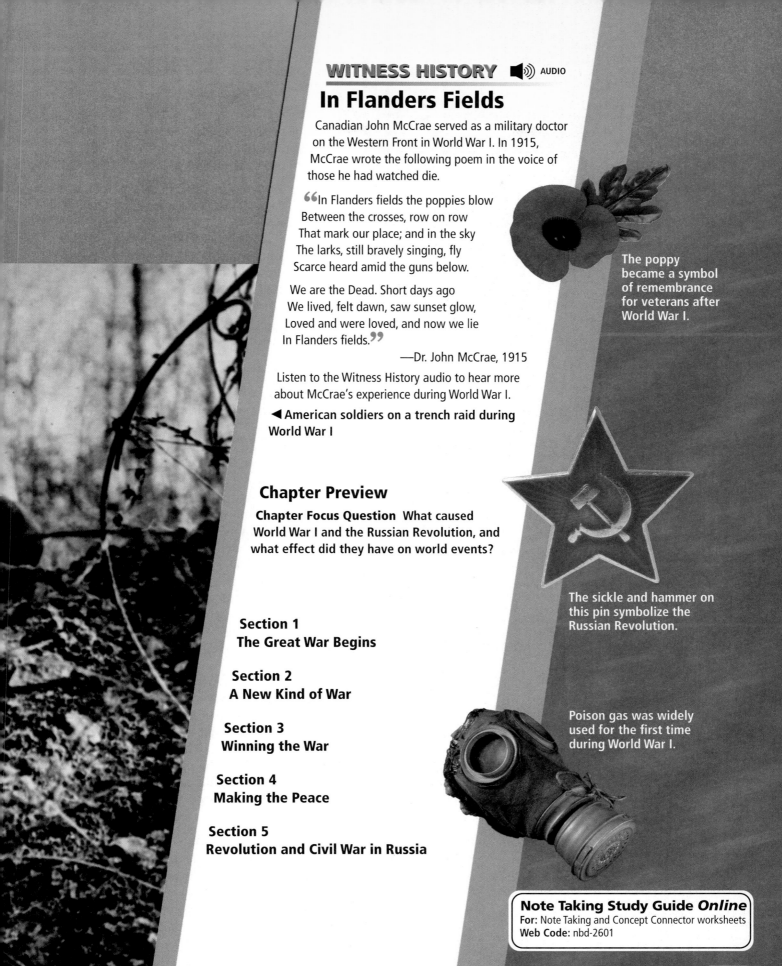

In Flanders Fields

Canadian John McCrae served as a military doctor on the Western Front in World War I. In 1915, McCrae wrote the following poem in the voice of those he had watched die.

❝In Flanders fields the poppies blow
Between the crosses, row on row
That mark our place; and in the sky
The larks, still bravely singing, fly
Scarce heard amid the guns below.

We are the Dead. Short days ago
We lived, felt dawn, saw sunset glow,
Loved and were loved, and now we lie
In Flanders fields.**❞**

—Dr. John McCrae, 1915

Listen to the Witness History audio to hear more about McCrae's experience during World War I.

◀ American soldiers on a trench raid during World War I

The poppy became a symbol of remembrance for veterans after World War I.

Chapter Preview

Chapter Focus Question What caused World War I and the Russian Revolution, and what effect did they have on world events?

The sickle and hammer on this pin symbolize the Russian Revolution.

Poison gas was widely used for the first time during World War I.

Note Taking Study Guide *Online*
For: Note Taking and Concept Connector worksheets
Web Code: nbd-2601

The Spark

On June 28, 1914, Gavrilo Princip, a member of a Serbian terrorist group, killed Austrian Archduke Francis Ferdinand and his wife Sophie.

66 The first [bullet] struck the wife of the Archduke, the Archduchess Sofia, in the abdomen. . . . She died instantly.

The second bullet struck the Archduke close to the heart. He uttered only one word, 'Sofia'—a call to his stricken wife. Then his head fell back and he collapsed. He died almost instantly.99
—Borijove Jevtic, co-conspirator

▲ The assassin, Gavrilo Princip

◄ Austrian Archduke Francis Ferdinand and his wife Sophie

The assassinations triggered World War I, called "The Great War" by people at the time.

Focus Question Why and how did World War I begin in 1914?

The Great War Begins

Objectives

- Describe how international rivalries and nationalism pushed Europe toward war.
- Explain how the assassination in Sarajevo led to the start of World War I.
- Analyze the causes and effects of the European alliance system.

Terms, People, and Places

entente	ultimatum
militarism	mobilize
Alsace and Lorraine	neutrality

Note Taking

Reading Skill: Summarize As you read, use a chart to summarize the events that led up to the outbreak of World War I.

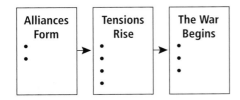

By 1914, Europe had enjoyed a century of relative peace. Idealists hoped for a permanent end to the scourge of war. International events, such as the first modern Olympic games in 1896 and the First Universal Peace Conference in 1899, were steps toward keeping the peace. "The future belongs to peace," said French economist Frédéric Passy (pa SEE).

Not everyone was so hopeful. "I shall not live to see the Great War," warned German Chancellor Otto von Bismarck, "but you will see it, and it will start in the east." It was Bismarck's prediction, rather than Passy's, that came true.

Alliances Draw Lines

While peace efforts were under way, powerful forces were pushing Europe towards war. Spurred by distrust of one another, the great powers of Europe—Germany, Austria-Hungary, Italy, Britain, France, and Russia—signed treaties pledging to defend one another. These alliances were intended to promote peace by creating powerful combinations that no one would dare attack. In the end, they had the opposite effect. Two huge alliances emerged.

The Triple Alliance The first of these alliances had its origins in Bismarck's day. He knew that France longed to avenge its defeat in the Franco-Prussian War. Sure that France would not attack Germany without help, Bismarck signed treaties with other powers. In 1882, he formed the Triple Alliance with Italy and Austria-Hungary. In 1914, when war did erupt, Germany and Austria-Hungary fought on the same side. They became known as the Central Powers.

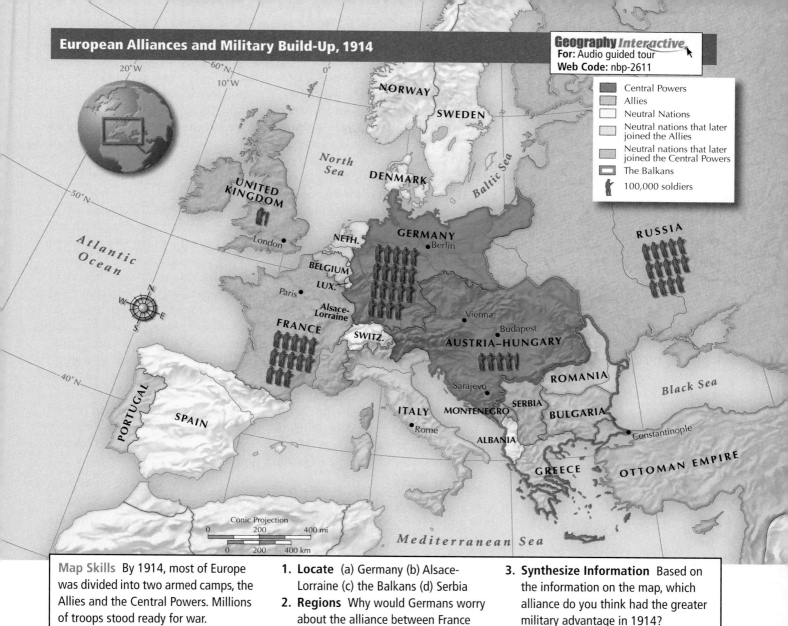

European Alliances and Military Build-Up, 1914

Geography *Interactive*
For: Audio guided tour
Web Code: nbp-2611

Legend:
- Central Powers
- Allies
- Neutral Nations
- Neutral nations that later joined the Allies
- Neutral nations that later joined the Central Powers
- The Balkans
- 100,000 soldiers

Map Skills By 1914, most of Europe was divided into two armed camps, the Allies and the Central Powers. Millions of troops stood ready for war.

1. **Locate** (a) Germany (b) Alsace-Lorraine (c) the Balkans (d) Serbia
2. **Regions** Why would Germans worry about the alliance between France and Russia?
3. **Synthesize Information** Based on the information on the map, which alliance do you think had the greater military advantage in 1914?

The Triple Entente A rival bloc took shape in 1893, when France and Russia formed an alliance. In 1904, France and Britain signed an **entente** (ahn TAHNT), a nonbinding agreement to follow common policies. Though not as formal as a treaty, the entente led to close military and diplomatic ties. Britain later signed a similar agreement with Russia. When war began, these powers became known as the Allies.

Other alliances also formed. Germany signed a treaty with the Ottoman empire. Britain drew close to Japan.

✔ **Checkpoint** What two large alliances took shape before the beginning of World War I?

Rivalries and Nationalism Increase Tension

The European powers jealously guarded their <u>status</u>. They competed for position in many areas. Two old empires, Austria-Hungary and Ottoman Turkey, struggled to survive in an age of nationalism.

Vocabulary Builder

status—(STAT us) *n.* high standing, rank, or prestige

Competition Economic rivalries helped sour the international atmosphere. Germany, the newest of the great powers, was growing into an economic and military powerhouse. Britain felt threatened by its rapid economic growth. Germany, in turn, thought the other great powers did not give it enough respect. Germany also feared that when Russia caught up to other industrialized nations, its huge population and vast supply of natural resources would make it an unbeatable competitor.

Overseas rivalries also divided European nations. In 1905 and again in 1911, competition for colonies brought France and Germany to the brink of war in Morocco, then under France's influence. Although diplomats kept the peace, Germany did gain some territory in central Africa. As a result of the two Moroccan crises, Britain and France strengthened their ties against Germany.

With international tensions on the rise, the great powers began to build up their armies and navies. The fiercest competition was the naval rivalry between Britain and Germany. To protect its vast overseas empire, Britain had built the world's most respected navy. As Germany began acquiring overseas colonies, it began to build up its own navy. Suspicious of Germany's motives, Britain in turn increased naval spending. Sensational journalism dramatized the arms race and stirred national public opinion against rival countries.

The rise of **militarism,** or the glorification of the military, also helped to feed the arms race. The militarist tradition painted war in romantic colors. Young men dreamed of blaring trumpets and dashing cavalry charges—not at all the sort of conflict they would soon face.

Nationalism Aggressive nationalism also caused tension. Nationalism was strong in both Germany and France. Germans were proud of their new empire's military power and industrial leadership. The French were bitter about their 1871 defeat in the Franco-Prussian War and yearned to recover the lost border province of **Alsace and Lorraine.**

In Eastern Europe, Russia sponsored a powerful form of nationalism called Pan-Slavism. It held that all Slavic peoples shared a common nationality. As the largest Slavic country, Russia felt that it had a duty to lead and defend all Slavs. By 1914, it stood ready to support Serbia, a proud young nation that dreamed of creating a South Slav state.

Germany's Glorious Military
Eager crowds watch a cavalry regiment, or group of troops serving on horseback, ride through Berlin in August 1914. Germany's army was known to be highly trained and well disciplined, making it a formidable fighting force. *How are the people pictured showing pride in their military?*

Two old multinational empires particularly feared rising nationalism. Austria-Hungary worried that nationalism might foster rebellion among the many minority populations within its empire. Ottoman Turkey felt threatened by nearby new nations, such as Serbia. If realized, Serbia's dream of a South Slav state could take territory away from both Austria-Hungary and Turkey.

In 1912, several Balkan states attacked Turkey and succeeded in taking a large area of land away from Turkish control. The next year, the Balkan states fought among themselves over the spoils of war. These brief but bloody Balkan wars raised tensions to a fever pitch. By 1914, the Balkans were called the "powder keg of Europe"—a barrel of gunpowder that a tiny spark might cause to explode.

✓ **Checkpoint** How did international competition and nationalism increase tensions in Europe?

The Powder Keg Ignites

As Bismarck had predicted, the Great War began in Eastern Europe. A regional conflict between tiny Serbia and the huge empire of Austria-Hungary grew rapidly into a general war.

Assassination in Sarajevo The crisis began when Archduke Francis Ferdinand of Austria-Hungary announced that he would visit Sarajevo (sa ruh YAY voh), the capital of Bosnia. Francis Ferdinand was the nephew and heir of the aging Austrian emperor, Francis Joseph. At the time of his visit, Bosnia was under the rule of Austria-Hungary. But it was also the home of many Serbs and other Slavs. News of the royal visit angered many Serbian nationalists. They viewed the Austrians as foreign oppressors. Some members of Unity or Death, a Serbian terrorist group commonly known as the Black Hand, vowed to take action.

The archduke ignored warnings of anti-Austrian unrest in Sarajevo. On June 28, 1914, he and his wife, Sophie, rode through Sarajevo in an open car. As the car passed by, a conspirator named Gavrilo Princip (GAV ree loh PREEN tseep) seized his chance and fired twice into the car. Moments later, the archduke and his wife were dead.

Austria Strikes Back The news of the assassination shocked Francis Joseph. Still, he was reluctant to go to war. The government in Vienna, however, saw the incident as an excuse to crush Serbia. In Berlin, Kaiser William II was horrified at the assassination of his ally's heir. He wrote to Francis Joseph, advising him to take a firm stand toward Serbia. Instead of urging restraint, Germany gave Austria a "blank check," or a promise of unconditional support no matter what the cost.

Austria sent Serbia a sweeping **ultimatum,** or final set of demands. To avoid war, said the ultimatum, Serbia must end all anti-Austrian agitation and punish any Serbian official involved in the murder plot. It must even let Austria join in the investigation. Serbia agreed to most, but not all, of the terms of Austria's ultimatum. This partial refusal gave Austria the opportunity it was seeking. On July 28, 1914, Austria declared war on Serbia.

✓ **Checkpoint** What happened because of the assassination of Francis Ferdinand and his wife?

Reasons for Entering the War, July–August 1914

Country	Allied With	Reasons for Entering War
Austria-Hungary	Germany	Wanted to punish Serbia for encouraging terrorism
Germany	Austria-Hungary	Stood by its one dependable ally, Austria-Hungary
Serbia	Russia	Attacked by Austria-Hungary after assassination of Archduke
Russia	Serbia, France, Britain	Wanted to defend Slavic peoples in Serbia
France	Russia and Britain	Wanted to avoid facing Germany alone at a later date
Belgium	Neutral	Invaded by Germany
Britain	France and Russia	Outraged by invasion of Belgium

Chart Skills Who started the war? During the war, each side blamed the other. Afterward, the victorious Allies placed all blame on Germany, because it invaded Belgium. Today, historians still debate who should bear the blame for a catastrophe nobody wanted. **Using information from the chart, describe why Russians might feel that Germany started the war.**

Alliances Kick In

The war between Austria and Serbia might have been another "summer war," like most European wars of the previous century. However, the carefully planned alliances soon drew the great powers deeper into conflict.

Russia and France Back Serbia After Austria's declaration of war, Serbia turned to its ally, Russia, the champion of Slavic nations. From St. Petersburg, Nicholas II telegraphed William II. The tsar asked the kaiser to urge Austria to soften its demands. When this plea failed, Russia began to **mobilize,** or prepare its military forces for war. On August 1, Germany responded by declaring war on Russia.

Russia, in turn, appealed to its ally France. In Paris, nationalists saw a chance to avenge France's defeat in the Franco-Prussian War. Though French leaders had some doubts, they gave Russia the same kind of backing Germany offered to Austria. When Germany demanded that France keep out of the conflict, France refused. Germany then declared war on France.

Germany Invades Belgium By early August, the battle lines were hardening. Italy and Britain still remained uncommitted. Italy chose to stay neutral for the time being. **Neutrality** is a policy of supporting neither side in a war. Britain had to decide quickly whether or not to support its ally France. Then, Germany's war plans suddenly made the decision for Britain.

A cornerstone of Germany's military policy was a plan developed years earlier by General Alfred von Schlieffen (SHLEE fun). Germany's location presented the possibility of a two-front war—against France in the west and Russia to the east. The Schlieffen Plan was designed to avoid this problem. Schlieffen reasoned that Germany should move against France first because Russia's lumbering military would be slow to mobilize.

However, Germany had to defeat France quickly so that its armies could then turn around and fight Russia.

To ensure a swift victory in the west, the Schlieffen Plan required German armies to march through neutral Belgium and then swing south behind French lines. The goal was to encircle and crush France's army. The Germans embarked on the plan by invading Belgium on August 3. However, Britain and other European powers had signed a treaty guaranteeing Belgian neutrality. Outraged by the invasion of Belgium, Britain declared war on Germany on August 4.

Once the machinery of war was set in motion, it seemed impossible to stop. Military leaders insisted that they must mobilize their forces immediately to accomplish their military goals. These military timetables made it impossible for political leaders to negotiate instead of fight.

✓ **Checkpoint** How did the alliance system deepen the original conflict between Austria-Hungary and Serbia into a general war?

Reaction to the War

Before the war, many countries were troubled by domestic problems. For example, Britain struggled with labor unrest and the issue of home rule in Ireland. Russia wrestled with problems stirred up by the Revolution of 1905. The outbreak of war brought a temporary relief from these internal divisions. A renewed sense of patriotism united countries. Governments on both sides emphasized that their countries were fighting for justice and a better world. Young men rushed to enlist, cheered on by women and their elders. Now that war had come at last, it seemed an exciting adventure.

British diplomat Edward Grey was less optimistic. As armies began to move, he predicted, "The lamps are going out all over Europe. We shall not see them lit again in our lifetime."

✓ **Checkpoint** Why were young men on both sides eager to fight when World War I started?

War Enthusiasm
People cheered as soldiers marched off to war. In this photograph, a woman is giving a soldier an apple to eat on his journey.

Progress Monitoring *Online*
For: Self-quiz with vocabulary practice
Web Code: nba-2611

Terms, People, and Places

1. For each term or place listed at the beginning of the section, write a sentence explaining its significance.

Note Taking

2. **Reading Skill: Summarize** Use your completed chart to answer the Focus Question: Why and how did World War I begin in 1914?

Comprehension and Critical Thinking

3. **Analyze Information** Why did European nations form alliances?

4. **Identify Central Issues** Why might the Balkans be called the "powder keg of Europe"?

5. **Recognize Causes** How did Austria's government react to the assassination of Archduke Francis Ferdinand?

6. **Determine Relevance** What role did geography play in the outbreak of World War I?

● **Writing About History**

Quick Write: Identify Causes and Effects Choose a specific event from the section and identify one cause and one effect of the event. Ask yourself the following questions:

• Why did this event happen? (cause)
• What happened as a result of this event? (effect)

Record your ideas in a chart that shows their cause-and-effect relationships.

▼ A wounded German soldier in 1915

WITNESS HISTORY ◀ AUDIO

A Soldier on the Western Front

❝ The blue French cloth mingled with the German grey upon the ground, and in some places the bodies were piled so high that one could take cover from shell-fire behind them. The noise was so terrific that orders had to be shouted by each man into the ear of the next. And whenever there was a momentary lull in the tumult of battle and the groans of the wounded, one heard, high up in the blue sky, the joyful song of birds! Birds singing just as they do at home in spring-time! It was enough to tear the heart out of one's body! ❞
—German soldier Richard Schmieder, writing from the trenches in France

Focus Question How and where was World War I fought?

World War I artillery shell ▶

A New Kind of War

Objectives

- Understand why a stalemate developed on the Western Front.
- Describe how technology made World War I different from earlier wars.
- Outline the course of the war on the Eastern Front, in other parts of Europe, in Turkey, and in the Middle East.
- Summarize how colonies fought in the war.

Terms, People, and Places

stalemate	convoy
zeppelin	Dardanelles
U-boat	T. E. Lawrence

Note Taking

Reading Skill: Identify Supporting Details Record important details about the various battlefronts of World War I in a flowchart.

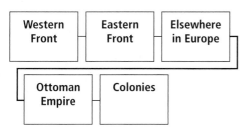

The Great War was the largest conflict in history up to that time. The French mobilized almost 8.5 million men, the British nearly 9 million, the Russians 12 million, and the Germans 11 million. "One out of every four men who went out to the World War did not come back again," recalled a survivor, "and of those who came back, many are maimed and blind and some are mad."

Stalemate on the Western Front

As the war began, German forces fought their way through Belgium toward Paris. The Belgians resisted more than German generals had expected, but the German forces prevailed. However, Germany's plans for a quick defeat of France soon faltered.

The Germans' Schlieffen Plan failed for several reasons. First, Russia mobilized more quickly than expected. After a few small Russian victories, German generals hastily shifted some troops to the east, weakening their forces in the west. Then, in September 1914, British and French troops pushed back the German drive along the Marne River. The first battle of the Marne ended Germany's hopes for a quick victory on the Western Front.

Both sides then began to dig deep trenches to protect their armies from fierce enemy fire. They did not know that the conflict would turn into a long, deadly **stalemate,** a deadlock in which neither side is able to defeat the other. Battle lines in France would remain almost unchanged for four years.

✓ **Checkpoint** How did the Allies stop the Germans from executing the Schlieffen Plan?

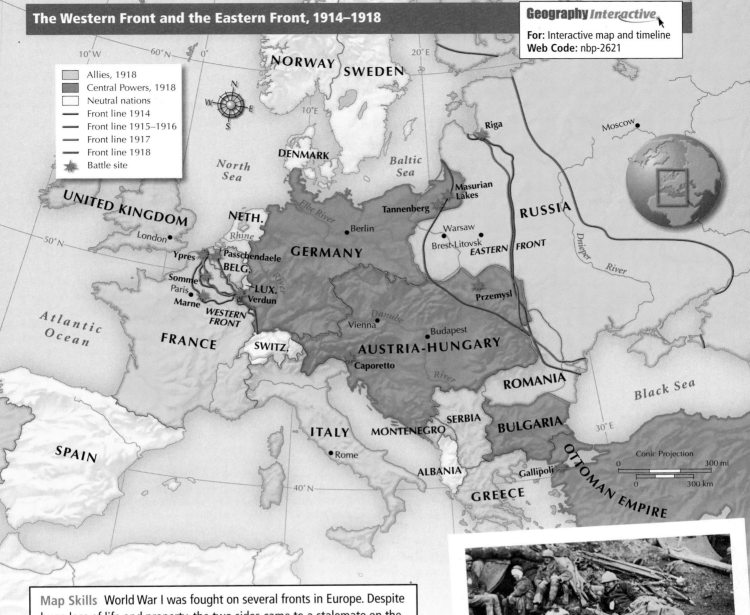

The Western Front and the Eastern Front, 1914–1918

Geography *Interactive*
For: Interactive map and timeline
Web Code: nbp-2621

Legend:
- Allies, 1918
- Central Powers, 1918
- Neutral nations
- Front line 1914
- Front line 1915–1916
- Front line 1917
- Front line 1918
- ✷ Battle site

NORWAY SWEDEN Riga Moscow
DENMARK Baltic Sea Masurian Lakes
North Sea Tannenberg RUSSIA
UNITED KINGDOM NETH. Berlin Warsaw Dnieper River
London Rhine Elbe River GERMANY Brest-Litovsk EASTERN FRONT
Ypres Passchendaele BELG. Przemysl
Somme LUX. Verdun
Paris Marne WESTERN FRONT Danube
Atlantic Ocean FRANCE Vienna Budapest
SWITZ. AUSTRIA-HUNGARY
Caporetto River ROMANIA Black Sea
SPAIN ITALY MONTENEGRO SERBIA BULGARIA
Rome ALBANIA Gallipoli OTTOMAN EMPIRE
GREECE

Conic Projection
0 300 mi
0 300 km

Map Skills World War I was fought on several fronts in Europe. Despite huge loss of life and property, the two sides came to a stalemate on the Western and Eastern fronts in 1915 and 1916.

1. **Locate** (a) Paris (b) Battle of the Marne (c) Verdun (d) Tannenberg
2. **Movement** Using the scale, describe how the battle lines moved on the Western Front from 1914 to 1918.
3. **Draw Inferences** Based on this map, why do you think many Russians were demoralized by the progress of the war?

▲ Wounded soldiers on stretchers in Verdun in 1916

WITNESS HISTORY VIDEO

Watch *World War I: A New Kind of War* on the **Witness History Discovery School**™ video program to learn more about trench warfare.

Discovery SCHOOL

The Human Cost To break the stalemate on the Western Front, both the Allies and the Central Powers launched massive offensives in 1916. German forces tried to overwhelm the French at Verdun (vur DUN). The French defenders held firm, sending up the battle cry "They shall not pass." The 11-month struggle cost more than a half a million casualties, or soldiers killed, wounded, or missing, on both sides.

An Allied offensive at the Somme River (sum) was even more costly. In a single grisly day, nearly 60,000 British soldiers were killed or wounded. In the five-month battle, more than one million soldiers were killed, without either side winning an advantage.

Note Taking

Reading Skill: Summarize Review the information under the heading "Technology of Modern Warfare." Summarize key points using a concept web like the one below. Add circles as needed.

Technology of Modern Warfare

The enormous casualties suffered on the Western Front proved the destructive power of modern weapons. Two significant new or improved weapons were the rapid-fire machine gun and the long-range artillery gun. Machine guns mowed down waves of soldiers. The shrapnel, or flying debris from artillery shells, killed or wounded even more soldiers than the guns. Artillery allowed troops to shell the enemy from more than 10 miles away.

Poison Gas In 1915, first Germany and then the Allies began using another new weapon—poison gas. Poison gas blinded or choked its victims or caused agonizing burns and blisters. It could be fatal. Though soldiers were eventually given gas masks, poison gas remained one of the most dreaded hazards of the war. One British soldier recalled the effects of being gassed:

> **Primary Source**
>
> 66 I suppose I resembled a kind of fish with my mouth open gasping for air. It seemed as if my lungs were gradually shutting up and my heart pounded away in my ears like the beat of a drum. . . . To get air into my lungs was real agony. 99
> —William Pressey, quoted in *People at War 1914–1918*

Poison gas was an uncertain weapon. Shifting winds could blow the gas back on the soldiers who launched it.

● INFOGRAPHIC

Trench Warfare

From the end of 1914 through 1918, the warring armies on the Western Front faced each other from a vast system of deep trenches. There, millions of soldiers lived out in the open, sharing their food with rats and their beds with lice. Between the opposing trench lines lay "no man's land." In this tract of land pocked with shell holes, every house and tree had long since been destroyed. Sooner or later, soldiers would go "over the top," charging into this manmade desert. With luck, the attackers might overrun a few enemy trenches. In time, the enemy would launch a counterattack, with similar results. The struggle continued, back and forth, over a few hundred yards of territory.

Soldiers peered over the edges of their trenches, watching for the next attack.

► Soldiers ate, slept, and fought in trenches. Tea tins (above) supplied to British soldiers in World War I, contained 200 tablets of compressed tea.

Tanks, Airplanes, and Submarines During World War I, advances in technology, such as the gasoline-powered engine, led the opposing forces to use tanks, airplanes, and submarines against each other. In 1916, Britain introduced the first armored tank. Mounted with machine guns, the tanks were designed to move across no man's land. Still, the first tanks broke down often. They failed to break the stalemate.

Both sides also used aircraft. At first, planes were <u>utilized</u> simply to observe enemy troop movements. In 1915, Germany used **zeppelins** (ZEP uh linz), large gas-filled balloons, to bomb the English coast. Later, both sides equipped airplanes with machine guns. Pilots known as "flying aces" <u>confronted</u> each other in the skies. These "dogfights" were spectacular, but had little effect on the course of the war on the ground.

Submarines proved much more important. German **U-boats,** nicknamed from the German word for submarine, *Unterseeboot,* did tremendous damage to the Allied side, sinking merchant ships carrying vital supplies to Britain. To defend against the submarines, the Allies organized **convoys,** or groups of merchant ships protected by warships.

Vocabulary Builder

<u>utilized</u>—(YOOT il yzd) *vt.* put to practical use
<u>confronted</u>—(kun FRUNT id) *vt.* faced in opposition

✔ **Checkpoint** What made World War I much more deadly than previous wars?

Battle on Other European Fronts

On Europe's Eastern Front, battle lines shifted back and forth, sometimes over large areas. Even though the armies were not mired in trench warfare, casualties rose even higher than on the Western Front. The results were just as indecisive.

Messenger dogs, trained to leap over barbed wire, carried vital information to the front lines. ▼

◄ **Trench Design**

Front line trenches were dug in a zigzag pattern to prevent the enemy from firing down the line.

Communications trenches, perpendicular to the front line trenches, served as routes for mail, food, supplies, reinforcements, and the transport of wounded soldiers.

Tanks, developed during the ► war, rolled on sturdy tracks, which allowed them to navigate through barbed wire and over the rough terrain of no man's land.

Thinking Critically

1. **Determine Relevance** How did technological advances in machine guns and tanks affect soldiers in the trenches?
2. **Make Inferences** What effect do you think that trench warfare had on soldiers' morale?

Russian Losses on the Eastern Front In August 1914, Russian armies pushed into eastern Germany. Then, the Russians suffered a disastrous defeat at Tannenberg, causing them to retreat back into Russia. As the least industrialized of the great powers, Russia was poorly equipped to fight a modern war. Some troops even lacked rifles. Still, Russian commanders continued to send masses of soldiers into combat.

New Combatants in the Balkans and Southern Europe The Balkans were another battleground. In 1915, Bulgaria joined the Central Powers and helped defeat its old Balkan rival Serbia. Romania, hoping to gain some land in Hungary, joined the Allies in 1916, only to be crushed by the Central Powers.

Also in 1915, Italy declared war on Austria-Hungary and later on Germany. The Allies had agreed in a secret treaty to give Italy some Austrian-ruled lands inhabited by Italians. Over the next two years, the Italians and Austrians fought eleven battles along the Isonzo river, with few major breakthroughs. In October 1917, the Austrians and Germans launched a major offensive against the Italian position at Caporetto, also on the Isonzo. The Italians retreated in disarray. British and French forces later helped stop the Central Powers' advance into Italy. Still, Caporetto proved as disastrous for Italy as Tannenberg had been for Russia.

✔ **Checkpoint** In what way was the Eastern Front different from the Western Front?

Geography *Interactive*
For: Audio guided tour
Web Code: nbp-2622

The Ottoman Empire, 1914–1918

Ottoman Empire, 1913
Area of Arab Revolt, 1916–1918
Allied forces under T.E. Lawrence
Battle site

Miller Projection
0   400 mi
0   400 km

RUSSIA
Black Sea
30°E
Constantinople
Gallipoli
Tigris R.
Euphrates R.
Mediterranean Sea
Megiddo
Jerusalem
Baghdad
PERSIA
KUWAIT
Persian Gulf
EGYPT
NEJD
Red Sea
HEJAZ
20°N
ANGLO-EGYPTIAN SUDAN
BRITISH ARABIAN PROTECTORATES
ERITREA
Arabian Sea
50°E
ETHIOPIA
60°E

Map Skills From 1914 to 1918, the Ottoman empire struggled against enemies on multiple fronts.

Location Given that Britain controlled Egypt at this time, describe how the Ottoman empire's location affected what happened to it during World War I.

War Around the World

Though most of the fighting took place in Europe, World War I was a global conflict. Japan, allied with Britain, used the war as an excuse to seize German outposts in China and islands in the Pacific.

The Ottoman Empire Joins the Central Powers Because of its strategic location, the Ottoman empire was a desirable ally. If the Ottoman Turks had joined the Allies, the Central Powers would have been almost completely encircled. However, the Turks joined the Central Powers in late October 1914. The Turks then cut off crucial Allied supply lines to Russia through the **Dardanelles,** a vital strait connecting the Black Sea and the Mediterranean.

In 1915, the Allies sent a massive force of British, Indian, Australian, and New Zealander troops to attempt to open up the strait. At the battle of Gallipoli (guh LIP uh lee), Turkish troops trapped the Allies on the beaches of the Gallipoli peninsula. In January 1916, after 10 months and more than 200,000 casualties, the Allies finally withdrew from the Dardanelles.

Meanwhile, Turkey was fighting Russia in the Caucasus mountains on Turkey's northern border. This region was home to ethnic Armenians, some of whom lived under Ottoman rule and some of whom lived under Russian rule. As Christians, the Armenians were a minority in the Ottoman empire and did not have the same rights as Muslims. As the Russians advanced in 1914, some

Turkish Armenians joined or helped the Russian army against the Turks. The Ottoman government used this cooperation as a reason to deport the entire Armenian population south to Syria and Mesopotamia. During the deportation, between 600,000 and 1.5 million Armenians died. Many were killed by planned massacres; others starved as they were forced to march with no food. Many Armenians fled to other countries, including the United States, leaving almost no Armenians in the historic Armenian homeland in Turkey.

On a third front, the Turks were hard hit in the Middle East. The Ottoman empire included vast areas of Arab land. In 1916, Arab nationalists led by Husayn ibn Ali (HOO sayn IB un AH lee) declared a revolt against Ottoman rule. The British government sent Colonel **T. E. Lawrence**—later known as Lawrence of Arabia—to support the Arab revolt. Lawrence led guerrilla raids against the Turks, dynamiting bridges and supply trains. Eventually, the Ottoman empire lost a great deal of territory to the Arabs, including the key city of Baghdad.

Armenian Refugees
A group of Armenian refugees wait for their daily rations from Near East Relief, an American organization founded to help the surviving Turkish Armenians. Public opinion, especially in the United States, was sympathetic to the Armenians during and after World War I. However, the Allies' attempts to protect the Armenians through the treaty that ended the war with Turkey ultimately failed.

War and the Colonies European colonies were also drawn into the struggle. The Allies overran scattered German colonies in Africa and Asia. They also turned to their own colonies and dominions for troops, laborers, and supplies. Colonial recruits from British India and French West Africa fought on European battlefields. Canada, Australia, and New Zealand sent troops to Britain's aid.

People in the colonies had mixed feelings about serving. Some were reluctant to serve rulers who did not treat them fairly. Other colonial troops volunteered eagerly. They expected that their service would be a step toward citizenship or independence. As you will read, such hopes would be dashed after the war.

✔ **Checkpoint** How did World War I affect the Ottoman empire and European colonies and dominions?

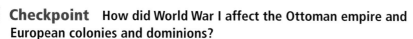

SECTION 2 Assessment

Progress Monitoring Online
For: Self-quiz with vocabulary practice
Web Code: nba-2621

Terms, People, and Places
1. For each term, person, or place listed at the beginning of the section, write a sentence explaining its significance.

Note Taking
2. **Reading Skill: Identify Supporting Details** Use your chart and concept web to answer the Focus Question: How and where was World War I fought?

Comprehension and Critical Thinking
3. **Draw Conclusions** Why did a stalemate develop on the Western Front?

4. **Synthesize Information** Describe three ways in which technology affected the war.
5. **Predict Consequences** Governments on both sides of World War I tried to keep full casualty figures and other bad news from reaching the public. What effect do you think news about disastrous defeats such as Tannenberg and Caporetto would have had on the attitudes of people back home?
6. **Recognize Causes** How did nationalism within the Ottoman Empire come into play during the war?

● **Writing About History**
Quick Write: Write a Thesis Statement Suppose that you are writing an essay on the effects of Ottoman Turkey's decision to join the Central Powers during World War I. Answer the questions below. Use your answers to create a thesis statement for the essay.
• Why were the Dardanelles important to the Allies?
• Who won the Battle of Gallipoli?
• What impact do you think Gallipoli had on the Russian war effort?

Erich Maria Remarque: *All Quiet on the Western Front*

Erich Maria Remarque (1898–1970) was wounded five times while serving in the German army during World War I. In 1929, he published *All Quiet on the Western Front,* which is often considered the greatest novel about World War I.

It follows the narrator, Paul Baumer, from eager recruit to disillusioned veteran. In this passage, Paul is trapped for hours in a foxhole with a French soldier he has just killed.

▲ This painting is titled *Notre-Dame de Lorette—A Soldier Walks Through the Flooded Trenches.* It was painted by François Flameng, a French artist who was given access to the front lines by the French government.

In the afternoon, about three, he is dead.

I breathe freely again. But only for a short time. Soon the silence is more unbearable than the groans. I wish the gurgling were there again, gasping hoarse, now whistling softly and again hoarse and loud.

It is mad, what I do. But I must do something. I prop the dead man up again so that he lies comfortably, although he feels nothing any more. I close his eyes. They are brown, his hair is black and a bit curly at the sides. . . .

The silence spreads. I talk and must talk. So I speak to him and say to him: "Comrade, I did not want to kill you. If you jumped in here again, I would not do it, if you would be sensible too. But you were only an idea to me before, an abstraction[1] that lived in my mind and called forth its appropriate response. It was that abstraction I stabbed. But now, for the first time, I see you are a man like me. I thought of your hand-grenades, of your bayonet[2], of your rifle; now I see your wife and your face and our fellowship. Forgive me, comrade. We always see it too late. Why do they never tell us that you are poor devils like us, that your mothers are just as anxious as ours, and that we have the same fear of death, and the same dying and the same agony—Forgive me, comrade; how could you be my enemy? If we threw away these rifles and this uniform you could be my brother just like Kat and Albert. Take twenty years of my life, comrade, and stand up—take more, for I do not know what I can even attempt to do with it now."

It is quiet, the front is still except for the crackle of rifle fire. The bullets rain over, they are not fired haphazard, but shrewdly aimed from all sides. I cannot get out.

---

1. **abstraction** (ab STRAK shun) *n.* an idea or term that is developed from a concrete reality

2. **bayonet** (bay oh NET) *n.* a blade attached to an end of a rifle for stabbing in hand-to-hand combat

---

Thinking Critically

1. **Recognize Point of View** Why does Paul speak to the dead French soldier?
2. **Synthesize Information** What does Paul mean by "We always see it too late"?

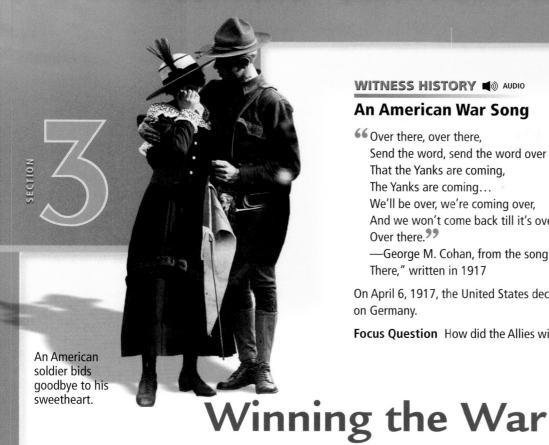

An American soldier bids goodbye to his sweetheart.

WITNESS HISTORY 🔊 AUDIO

An American War Song

❝ Over there, over there,
Send the word, send the word over there,
That the Yanks are coming,
The Yanks are coming…
We'll be over, we're coming over,
And we won't come back till it's over
Over there. ❞
—George M. Cohan, from the song "Over There," written in 1917

On April 6, 1917, the United States declared war on Germany.

Focus Question How did the Allies win World War I?

Sheet music for the patriotic song "Over There"

Winning the War

Objectives
- Describe how World War I became a total war.
- Explain the effect that years of warfare had on morale.
- Analyze the causes and effects of American entry into the war.
- Summarize events that led to the end of the war.

Terms, People, and Places

total war	atrocity
conscription	Fourteen Points
contraband	self-determination
Lusitania	armistice
propaganda	

Note Taking

Reading Skill: Summarize As you read, use an outline to summarize the events in this section.

> I. Waging total war
> A. Economies committed to war production
>   1. Conscription
>   2. Rationing
>   3. Price controls
> B. Economic warfare

By 1917, European societies were cracking under the strain of war. Casualties on the fronts and shortages at home sapped morale. The stalemate dragged on, seemingly without end. Soon, however, the departure of one country from the war and the entry of another would tip the balance and end the stalemate.

Waging Total War

As the struggle wore on, nations realized that a modern, mechanized war required the channeling of a nation's entire resources into the war effort, or **total war.** To achieve total war, governments began to take a stronger role in directing the economic and cultural lives of their people.

Economies Committed to War Production Early on, both sides set up systems to recruit, arm, transport, and supply armies that numbered in the millions. All of the warring nations except Britain immediately imposed universal military **conscription,** or "the draft," which required all young men to be ready for military or other service. Britain, too, instituted conscription in 1916. Germany set up a system of forced civilian labor as well.

Governments raised taxes and borrowed huge amounts of money to pay the costs of war. They rationed food and other products, from boots to gasoline. In addition, they introduced other economic controls, such as setting prices and forbidding strikes.

Economic Warfare At the start of the war, Britain's navy formed a blockade in the North Sea to keep ships from carrying supplies in and out of Germany. International law allowed wartime blockades to confiscate **contraband,** or military supplies and raw materials needed to make military supplies, but not items such as food and clothing. In spite of international law, the British blockade stopped both types of goods from reaching Germany. As the war progressed, it became harder and harder to feed the German and Austrian people. In Germany, the winter of 1916 and 1917 was remembered as "the turnip winter," because the potato crop failed and people ate turnips instead.

To retaliate, Germany used U-boats to create its own blockade. In 1915, Germany declared that it would sink all ships carrying goods to Britain. In May 1915, a German submarine torpedoed the British liner *Lusitania* off the coast of Ireland. Almost 1,200 passengers were killed, including 128 Americans. Germany justified the attack, arguing that the *Lusitania* was carrying weapons. When American President Woodrow Wilson threatened to cut off diplomatic relations with Germany, though, Germany agreed to restrict its submarine campaign. Before attacking any ship, U-boats would surface and give warning, allowing neutral passengers to escape to lifeboats. Unrestricted submarine warfare stopped— for the moment.

Propaganda War Total war also meant controlling public opinion. Even in democratic countries, special boards censored the press. Their aim was to keep complete casualty figures and other discouraging news from reaching the public. Government censors also restricted popular literature, historical writings, motion pictures, and the arts.

Both sides waged a propaganda war. **Propaganda** is the spreading of ideas to promote a cause or to damage an opposing cause. Governments used propaganda to motivate military mobilization, especially in Britain before conscription started in 1916. In France and Germany, propaganda urged civilians to loan money to the government. Later in the war, Allied propaganda played up the brutality of Germany's invasion of Belgium. The British and French press circulated tales of **atrocities,** horrible acts

A German Submarine Sinks the *Lusitania*
The sinking of the British line *Lusitania* in 1915, illustrated below, was part of Germany's policy of unrestricted submarine warfare. The incident was featured in propaganda posters as evidence of German brutality. *How does the poster below use emotion to encourage men to enlist?*

committed against innocent people. Although some atrocities did occur, often the stories were distorted by exaggerations or completely made up.

Women Join the War Effort Women played a critical role in total war. As millions of men left to fight, women took over their jobs and kept national economies going. Many women worked in war industries, manufacturing weapons and supplies. Others joined women's branches of the armed forces. When food shortages threatened Britain, volunteers in the Women's Land Army went to the fields to grow their nation's food.

Nurses shared the dangers of the men whose wounds they tended. At aid stations close to the front lines, nurses often worked around the clock, especially after a big "push" brought a flood of casualties. In her diary, English nurse Vera Brittain describes sweating through 90-degree days in France, "stopping hemorrhages, replacing intestines, and draining and reinserting innumerable rubber tubes" with "gruesome human remnants heaped on the floor."

War work gave women a new sense of pride and confidence. After the war, most women had to give up their jobs to men returning home. Still, they had challenged the idea that women could not handle demanding and dangerous jobs. In many countries, including Britain, Germany, and the United States, women's support for the war effort helped them finally win the right to vote, after decades of struggle.

 Checkpoint Why was it important for both sides to keep civilian morale high during the war?

Morale Collapses

Despite inspiring propaganda, by 1917 the morale of troops and civilians had plunged. Germany was sending 15-year-old recruits to the front. Britain was on the brink of bankruptcy.

War Fatigue Long casualty lists, food shortages, and the failure of generals to win promised victories led to calls for peace. Instead of praising the glorious deeds of heroes, war poets began denouncing the leaders whose errors wasted so many lives. British poet and soldier Siegfried Sassoon captured the bitter mood:

Primary Source

> "You smug-faced crowds with kindling eye
> Who cheer when soldier lads march by,
> Sneak home and pray you'll never know
> The hell where youth and laughter go."
> —Siegfried Sassoon, "Suicide in the Trenches"

As morale collapsed, troops in some French units mutinied. In Italy, many soldiers deserted during the retreat at Caporetto. In Russia, soldiers left the front to join in a full-scale revolution back home.

Revolution in Russia Three years of war had hit Russia especially hard. Stories of incompetent generals and corruption <u>eroded</u> public confidence. In March 1917, bread riots in St. Petersburg erupted into a revolution that brought down the Russian monarchy. (You'll read more about the causes and effects of the Russian Revolution in Section 5.)

At first, the Allies welcomed the overthrow of the tsar. They hoped Russia would institute a democratic government and become a stronger

BIOGRAPHY

Edith Cavell

Like most ordinary people caught up in war, Edith Cavell (1865–1915) did not plan on becoming a hero. An English nurse, she was in charge of a hospital in Belgium. After the German invasion, Cavell cared for wounded soldiers on both sides. She also helped Allied soldiers escape to the Netherlands.

In 1915, the Germans arrested Cavell for spying. As she faced a firing squad, her last reported words were, "Standing as I do in view of God and Eternity, I realize that patriotism is not enough. I must have no hatred or bitterness toward anyone." **Why do you think the British government spread the story of Edith Cavell?**

Vocabulary Builder

<u>eroded</u> (ee ROHD id)—*vt.* ate into or wore away

ally. But later that year V. I. Lenin came to power with a promise to pull Russian troops out of the war. Early in 1918, Lenin signed the Treaty of Brest-Litovsk (brest lih TAWFSK) with Germany. The treaty ended Russian participation in World War I.

Russia's withdrawal had an immediate impact on the war. With Russia out of the struggle, Germany could concentrate its forces on the Western Front. In the spring of 1918, the Central Powers stood ready to achieve the great breakthrough they had sought for so long.

✓ **Checkpoint** How did Russia's loss of morale affect the strategic position of the Allies in World War I?

The United States Declares War

Soon after the Russian Revolution began, however, another event altered the balance of forces. The United States declared war on Germany. Many factors contributed to the decision of the United States to exchange neutrality for war in 1917.

Why Join the Allies? Many Americans supported the Allies because of cultural ties. The United States shared a cultural history and language with Britain and sympathized with France as another democracy. On the other hand, some German Americans favored the Central Powers. So did many Irish Americans, who resented British rule of Ireland, and Russian Jewish immigrants, who did not want to be allied with the tsar.

Germany had ceased submarine attacks in 1915 after pressure from President Wilson. However, in early 1917, Germany was desperate to break the stalemate. On February 1, the German government announced that it would resume unrestricted submarine warfare. Wilson angrily denounced Germany.

Also, in early 1917, the British intercepted a message from the German foreign minister, Arthur Zimmermann, to his ambassador in Mexico. In the note, Zimmermann authorized his ambassador to propose that Germany would help Mexico "to reconquer the lost territory in New Mexico, Texas, and Arizona" in return for Mexican support against the United States. Britain revealed the Zimmermann note to the American government. When the note became public, anti-German feeling intensified in the United States.

Declaring War In April 1917, Wilson asked Congress to declare war on Germany. "We have no selfish ends to serve," he stated. Instead, he painted the conflict idealistically as a war "to make the world safe for democracy" and later as a "war to end war."

The United States needed months to recruit, train, supply, and transport a modern army across the Atlantic. But by 1918, about two million American soldiers had joined the war-weary Allied troops fighting on the Western Front. Although relatively few American troops engaged in combat, their arrival gave Allied troops a much-needed morale boost. Just as important to the debt-ridden Allies was American financial aid.

American Troops "Over There"
The arrival of fresh American troops in Europe throughout 1918 helped turn the tide of the war in favor of the Allies. Recruitment posters, like the one above, inspired soldiers to enlist. *How was the experience of American soldiers different from that of other Allied soldiers?*

The Fourteen Points Though he had failed to maintain American neutrality, Wilson still hoped to be a peacemaker. In January 1918, he issued the **Fourteen Points,** a list of his terms for resolving this and future wars. He called for freedom of the seas, free trade, large-scale reductions of arms, and an end to secret treaties. For Eastern Europe, Wilson favored **self-determination,** the right of people to choose their own form of government. Finally, Wilson urged the creation of a "general association of nations" to keep the peace in the future.

✓ **Checkpoint** What are three factors that led the United States to enter the war?

Victory at Last

A final showdown on the Western Front began in early 1918. The Germans badly wanted to achieve a major victory before eager American troops arrived in Europe. In March, the Germans launched a huge offensive that by July had pushed the Allies back 40 miles. These efforts exhausted the Germans, however, and by then American troops were arriving by the thousands. The Allies then launched a counterattack, slowly driving German forces back across France and Belgium. In September, German generals told the kaiser that the war could not be won.

Uprisings exploded among hungry city dwellers across Germany. German commanders advised the kaiser to step down. William II did so in early November, fleeing into exile in the Netherlands.

By autumn, Austria-Hungary was also reeling toward collapse. As the government in Vienna tottered, the subject nationalities revolted, splintering the empire of the Hapsburgs. Bulgaria and the Ottoman empire also asked for peace.

The new German government sought an **armistice,** or agreement to end fighting, with the Allies. At 11 A.M. on November 11, 1918, the Great War at last came to an end.

✓ **Checkpoint** Why did Germany ask the Allies for an armistice in November 1918?

Celebrating the Armistice
Around the globe, crowds celebrated the end of the war. Here, British and American soldiers and civilians wave the American and French flags in relief and jubilation.

SECTION 3 **Assessment**

Progress Monitoring Online
For: Self-quiz with vocabulary practice
Web Code: nba-2631

Terms, People, and Places

1. For each term, person, or place listed at the beginning of the section, write a sentence explaining its significance.

Note Taking

2. **Reading Skill: Summarize** Use your completed outline to answer the Focus Question: How did the Allies win World War I?

Comprehension and Critical Thinking

3. **Summarize** What measures did wartime governments take to control national economies and public opinion?

4. **Recognize Effects** What impact did wartime failures have on Russia?

5. **Draw Conclusions** Describe how the entry of United States into the war was a turning point.

6. **Analyze Information** Reread the poem by Siegfried Sassoon. What does it suggest about the effects of trench warfare?

● **Writing About History**

Quick Write: Gather Evidence to Support Thesis Statement Suppose you are writing an essay with the following thesis statement "Women played a critical role in World War I." Write three questions like the two below that would help you gather evidence to support this thesis.
- What types of things did women do during the war?
- Why was this work important?

Lloyd George, Clemenceau, and Wilson (left to right) at the Paris Peace Conference. Above right, a medal sold to raise funds for wounded soldiers.

WITNESS HISTORY 🔊 AUDIO

Worth the Cost?

Vera Brittain, a British nurse, lost her brother Edward and her fiancé Roland on the battlefield.

66 Although they would no doubt have welcomed the idea of a League of Nations, Roland and Edward certainly had not died in order that Clemenceau should outwit Lloyd George, and both of them bamboozle President Wilson, and all three combine to make the beaten, block-aded enemy pay the cost of the War.**99**
—Vera Brittain, *Testament of Youth*

Focus Question What factors influenced the peace treaties that ended World War I, and how did people react to the treaties?

Making the Peace

Objectives

- Analyze the costs of World War I.
- Describe the issues faced by the delegates to the Paris Peace Conference.
- Explain why many people were dissatisfied with the Treaty of Versailles and other peace settlements.

Terms, People, and Places

pandemic
reparations

radicals
collective security
mandate

Note Taking

Reading Skill: Summarize As you read, summarize the main points of the text under the heading "The Costs of War" in a concept web like the one below.

Just weeks after the war ended, President Wilson boarded a steamship bound for France. He had decided to go in person to Paris, where Allied leaders would make the peace. Wilson was certain that he could solve the problems of old Europe. "Tell me what is right," Wilson urged his advisors, "and I'll fight for it." Sadly, it would not be that easy. Europe was a shattered continent. Its problems, and those of the world, would not be solved at the Paris Peace Conference, or for many years afterward.

The Costs of War

The human and material costs of the war were staggering. Millions of soldiers were dead, and even more wounded. The devastation was made even worse in 1918 by a deadly **pandemic** of influenza. A pandemic is the spread of a disease across a large area—in this case, the whole world. In just a few months, the flu killed more than 20 million people worldwide.

The Financial Toll In battle zones from France to Russia, homes, farms, factories, roads, and churches had been shelled into rubble. People had fled these areas as refugees. Now they had to return and start to rebuild. The costs of reconstruction and paying off huge war debts would burden an already battered world.

Shaken and disillusioned, people everywhere felt bitter about the war. The Allies blamed the conflict on their defeated foes and insisted that the losers make **reparations,** or payments for war damage. The stunned Central Powers, who had viewed the armistice as a cease-fire rather than a surrender, looked for scapegoats on whom they could blame their defeat.

Political Turmoil Under the stress of war, governments had collapsed in Russia, Germany, Austria-Hungary, and the Ottoman empire. Political **radicals,** or people who wanted to make extreme changes, dreamed of building a new social order from the chaos. Conservatives warned against the spread of bolshevism, or communism, as it was soon called.

Unrest also swept through Europe's colonial empires. African and Asian soldiers had discovered that the imperial powers were not as invincible as they seemed. Colonial troops returned home with a more cynical view of Europeans and renewed hopes for independence.

✓ **Checkpoint** What were some of the human, economic, and political costs of the war?

● **INFOGRAPHIC**

The Costs of World War I

The war ended in 1918, but its effects would be felt for decades to come. More than 8.5 million men had died in battle. Twice that number had been wounded, many of them disabled for life. Historians estimate that from 6 to 13 million civilians also lost their lives as a result of the war. Many of the combatant nations had thrown all of their resources into the fight, leaving them little with which to rebuild. Below an American nurse tends to soldiers in France in 1918.

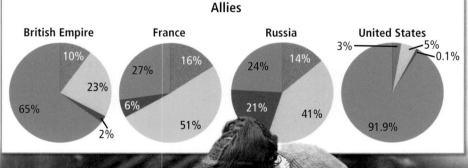

Financial Costs of the War*

British empire	$ $ $ $ $ $
France	$ $ $ $ $
Russia	$ $ $
United States	$ $ $
Germany	$ $ $ $ $ $
Austria-Hungary	$ $ $

$ Represents $10 billion

SOURCE: *The Harper Encyclopedia of Military History*, R. Ernest Dupuy and Trevor N. Dupuy
* Includes war expenditures, property losses, and shipping losses

Casualties of Mobilized Soldiers

■ Died ■ Taken prisoner
□ Wounded and missing ■ Unharmed

Central Powers

Germany
16%
36%
10%
38%

Austria-Hungary
11% 15%
28%
46%

Allies

British Empire
10%
23%
65%
2%

France
16%
27%
6%
51%

Russia
14%
24%
21%
41%

United States
3% 5%
0.1%
91.9%

SOURCE: *Encyclopædia Britannica*, 2004

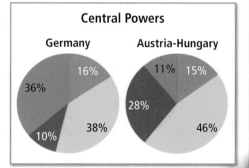

Thinking Critically

1. **Draw Conclusions** Which two nations suffered the highest proportion of soldier deaths? Why were American casualties relatively low?

2. **Predict Consequences** What long-term impact might the number of casualties have on a country like France?

473

Reading Skill: Categorize One way to summarize information is to divide it into categories. In the table below, the left-hand column lists issues the world faced after World War I. As you read, categorize the information in the text in one of the second two columns.

Issue	Treaty Settlement	Problems
War Debt		
Fear of German Strength		
Nationalism		
Colonies and Other Non-European Territories		
League of Nations		

The Paris Peace Conference

The victorious Allies met at the Paris Peace Conference to discuss the fate of Europe, the former Ottoman empire, and various colonies around the world. The Central Powers and Russia were not allowed to take part in the negotiations.

Conflicting Goals Wilson was one of three strong leaders who dominated the Paris Peace Conference. He was a dedicated reformer and at times was so stubbornly convinced that he was right that he could be hard to work with. Wilson urged for "peace without victory" based on the Fourteen Points.

Two other Allied leaders at the peace conference had different aims. British prime minister David Lloyd George had promised to build a postwar Britain "fit for heroes"—a goal that would cost money. The chief goal of the French leader, Georges Clemenceau (KLEM un soh), was to weaken Germany so that it could never again threaten France. "Mr. Wilson bores me with his Fourteen Points," complained Clemenceau. "Why, God Almighty has only ten!"

Problems With the Peace Crowds of other representatives circled around the "Big Three" with their own demands and interests. The Italian prime minister, Vittorio Orlando (awr LAN doh), insisted that the Allies honor their secret agreement to give former Austro-Hungarian lands to Italy. Such secret agreements violated the principle of self-determination.

Self-determination posed other problems. Many people who had been ruled by Russia, Austria-Hungary, or the Ottoman empire now demanded national states of their own. The territories claimed by these peoples often overlapped, so it was impossible to satisfy them all. Some ethnic groups became unwanted minorities in newly created states.

Wilson had to compromise on his Fourteen Points. However, he stood firm on his goal of creating an international League of Nations. The League would be based on the idea of **collective security,** a system in which a group of nations acts as one to preserve the peace of all. Wilson felt sure that the League could correct any mistakes made in Paris.

 Checkpoint How did the goals of the Big Three leaders conflict at the Paris Peace Conference?

The Treaty of Versailles

In June 1919, the Allies ordered representatives of the new German Republic to sign the treaty they had drawn up at the palace of Versailles (vur SY) outside Paris. The German delegates were horrified. The treaty forced Germany to assume full blame for causing the war. It also imposed huge reparations that would burden an already damaged German economy. The reparations covered not only the destruction caused by the war, but also pensions for millions of Allied soldiers or their widows and families. The total cost of German reparations would later be calculated at $30 billion (the equivalent of about $2.7 trillion today).

Other parts of the treaty were aimed at weakening Germany. The treaty severely limited the size of the once-feared German military. It returned Alsace and Lorraine to France, removed hundreds of square miles of territory from western and eastern Germany, and stripped Germany of its overseas colonies. The treaty compelled many Germans to

Europe, 1914

Europe, 1920

Geography *Interactive*
For: Audio guided tour
Web Code: nbp-2641

Map Skills The peace treaties that ended World War I redrew the map of Europe.
1. **Locate** (a) Lithuania (b) Czechoslovakia (c) Yugoslavia (c) Poland (d) Danzig
2. **Regions** Which countries lost territory in Eastern Europe?
3. **Draw Conclusions** Why might the distribution of territory after World War I leave behind widespread dissatisfaction?

---

leave the homes they had made in Russia, Poland, Alsace-Lorraine, and the German colonies to return to Germany or Austria.

The Germans signed because they had no choice. However, German resentment of the Treaty of Versailles would poison the international climate for 20 years. It would help spark an even deadlier world war in the years to come.

✔ **Checkpoint** Why were the German delegates surprised when they read the treaty?

Outcome of the Peace Settlements

The Allies drew up separate treaties with the other Central Powers. Like the Treaty of Versailles, these treaties left <u>widespread</u> dissatisfaction. Discontented nations waited for a chance to revise the peace settlements in their favor.

Self-Determination in Eastern Europe Where the German, Austrian, and Russian empires had once ruled, a band of new nations emerged. Poland became an independent nation after more than 100 years of foreign rule. The Baltic states of Latvia, Lithuania, and Estonia fought for and achieved independence.

Three new republics—Czechoslovakia, Austria, and Hungary—rose in the old Hapsburg heartland. In the Balkans, the peacemakers created a new South Slav state, Yugoslavia, dominated by Serbia.

The Mandate System European colonies in Africa, Asia, and the Pacific had looked to the Paris Peace Conference with high hopes. Colonial leaders expected that the peace would bring new respect and an end to imperial rule. However, the leaders at Paris applied self-determination only to parts of Europe. Outside Europe, the victorious Allies added to

Vocabulary Builder

<u>widespread</u>—(wyd SPRED) *adj.* occurring in many places

COME, ALONG, GENTS, DINNER'S READY.

Analyzing Political Cartoons

This cartoon portrays one view of the peace treaties that ended World War I.

(A) The turkey symbolizes Germany.

(B) Britain holds a carving knife and fork, ready to carve the turkey.

(C) Other Allies await the feast.

1. What does carving up the turkey symbolize?
2. What attitude do you think that the cartoonist has towards the treaties?

their overseas empires. The treaties created a system of **mandates,** territories administered by Western powers. Britain and France gained mandates over German colonies in Africa. Japan and Australia were given mandates over some Pacific islands. The treaties handled lands that used to be part of the Ottoman empire as if they were colonies, too.

In theory, mandates were to be held until they were able to stand alone. In practice, they became European colonies. From Africa to the Middle East and across Asia, people felt betrayed by the peacemakers.

The League of Nations Offers Hope The Paris Peace Conference did offer one beacon of hope with the establishment of the League of Nations. More than 40 nations joined the League. They agreed to negotiate disputes rather than resort to war and to take common action against any aggressor state.

Wilson's dream had become a reality, or so he thought. On his return from Paris, Wilson faced resistance from his own Senate. Some Republican senators, led by Henry Cabot Lodge, wanted to restrict the treaty so that the United States would not be obligated to fight in future wars. Lodge's reservations echoed the feelings of many Americans. Wilson would not accept Lodge's compromises. In the end, the Senate refused to ratify the treaty, and the United States never joined the League.

The loss of the United States weakened the League's power. In addition, the League had no power outside of its member states. As time soon revealed, the League could not prevent war. Still, it was a first step toward something genuinely new—an international organization dedicated to maintaining peace and advancing the interests of all peoples.

✓ **Checkpoint** Why did the League of Nations fail to accomplish Wilson's dreams?

SECTION 4 Assessment

Progress Monitoring Online
For: Self-quiz with vocabulary practice
Web Code: nba-2641

Terms, People, and Places

1. For each term, person, or place listed at the beginning of the section, write a sentence explaining its significance.

Note Taking

2. **Reading Skill: Summarize** Use your completed concept web and table to answer the Focus Question: What factors influenced the peace treaties that ended World War I, and how did people react to the treaties?

Comprehension and Critical Thinking

3. **Make Generalizations** Describe conditions in Europe after World War I.
4. **Draw Conclusions** How did the peace treaties both follow and violate the principle of self-determination?
5. **Draw Inferences** Wilson's closest advisor wrote of the Paris Peace Conference, "there is much to approve and much to regret." What do you think he might have approved? What might he have regretted?

● Writing About History

Quick Write: Choose an Organization Use an organizational strategy that suits the topic of your essay. For instance, if you are writing about one event with many causes, you might write one paragraph about each cause, followed by a paragraph that sums up the effects. If you are writing about a series of events, you might order your paragraphs chronologically.

Choose two topics from this section, one that suits the first type of organization and on that suits the second. Then write a brief outline for an essay about each.

SECTION 5

A pin showing the Soviet hammer and sickle (left). A propaganda poster asks Russians to choose sides in the Russian Civil War (right).

WITNESS HISTORY 🔊 AUDIO

Voices From the Front

❝ Mr. War Minister!

We, soldiers from various regiments,... ask you to end the war and its bloodshed at any cost.... If this is not done, then believe us when we say that we will take our weapons and head out for our own hearths to save our fathers, mothers, wives, and children from death by starvation (which is nigh). And if we cannot save them, then we'd rather die with them in our native lands then be killed, poisoned, or frozen to death somewhere and cast into the earth like a dog. ❞

—Letter from the front, 1917

The voices from the front joined voices at home, calling for change in Russia.

Focus Question How did two revolutions and a civil war bring about Communist control of Russia?

Revolution and Civil War in Russia

Objectives
- Explain the causes of the March Revolution.
- Describe the goals of Lenin and the Bolsheviks in the November Revolution.
- Outline how the Communists defeated their opponents in Russia's civil war.
- Analyze how the Communist state developed under Lenin.

Terms, People, and Places

proletariat	Cheka
soviet	commissar

Note Taking

Reading Skill: Summarize Copy the timeline below and fill it in as you read this section. When you finish, write two sentences that summarize the information in your timeline.

Russia enters World War I.

1914   1916   1918   1920

The year 1913 marked the 300th anniversary of the Romanov dynasty. Everywhere, Russians honored the tsar and his family. Tsarina Alexandra felt confident that the people loved Nicholas too much to ever threaten him. "They are constantly frightening the emperor with threats of revolution," she told a friend, "and here,—you see it yourself—we need merely to show ourselves and at once their hearts are ours."

Appearances were deceiving. In March 1917, the first of two revolutions would topple the Romanov dynasty and pave the way for even more radical changes.

The March Revolution Ends Tsarism

In 1914, the huge Russian empire stretched from Eastern Europe east to the Pacific Ocean. Unlike Western Europe, Russia was slow to industrialize despite its huge potential. Landowning nobles, priests, and an autocratic tsar controlled the government and economy. Much of the majority peasant population endured stark poverty. As Russia began to industrialize, a small middle class and an urban working class emerged.

Unrest Deepens After the Revolution of 1905, Nicholas had failed to solve Russia's basic political, economic, and social problems. The elected Duma set up after the revolution had no real power. Moderates pressed for a constitution and social change. But Nicholas II, a weak and ineffective leader, blocked attempts to limit his authority. Like past tsars, he relied on his secret police and other enforcers to impose his will. A corrupt bureaucracy and an overburdened court system added to the government's problems.

Revolutionaries hatched radical plots. Some hoped to lead discontented peasants to overthrow the tsarist regime. Marxists tried to ignite revolution among the **proletariat**—the growing class of factory and railroad workers, miners, and urban wage earners. A revolution, they believed, would occur when the time was ripe.

Impact of World War I The outbreak of war in 1914 fueled national pride and united Russians. Armies dashed to battle with enthusiasm. But like the Crimean and Russo-Japanese wars, World War I quickly strained Russian resources. Factories could not turn out enough supplies. The transportation system broke down, delivering only a trickle of <u>crucial</u> materials to the front. By 1915, many soldiers had no rifles and no ammunition. Badly equipped and poorly led, they died in staggering numbers. In 1915 alone, Russian casualties reached two million.

In a patriotic gesture, Nicholas II went to the front to take personal charge. The decision proved a disastrous blunder. The tsar was no more competent than many of his generals. Worse, he left domestic affairs to the tsarina, Alexandra. In Nicholas' absence, Alexandra relied on the advice of Gregory Rasputin, an illiterate peasant and self-proclaimed "holy man." The tsarina came to believe that Rasputin had miraculous powers after he helped her son, who suffered from hemophilia, a disorder in which any injury can result in uncontrollable bleeding.

By 1916, Rasputin's influence over Alexandra had reached new heights and weakened confidence in the government. Fearing for the monarchy, a group of Russian nobles killed Rasputin on December 29, 1916.

The Tsar Steps Down By March 1917, disasters on the battlefield, combined with food and fuel shortages on the home front, brought the monarchy to collapse. In St. Petersburg (renamed Petrograd during the war), workers were going on strike. Marchers, mostly women, surged through the streets, shouting, "Bread! Bread!" Troops refused to fire on the demonstrators, leaving the government helpless. Finally, on the advice of military and political leaders, the tsar abdicated.

Duma politicians then set up a provisional, or temporary, government. Middle-class liberals in the government began preparing a constitution for a new Russian republic. At the same time, they continued the war against Germany.

Outside the provisional government, revolutionary socialists plotted their own course. In Petrograd and other cities, they set up **soviets,** or councils of workers and soldiers. At first, the soviets worked democratically within the government. Before long, though, the Bolsheviks, a radical socialist group, took charge. The leader of the Bolsheviks was a determined revolutionary, V. I. Lenin.

The revolutions of March and November 1917 are known to Russians as the February and October revolutions. In 1917, Russia still used an old calendar, which was 13 days behind the one used in Western Europe. Russia adopted the Western calendar in 1918.

✔ **Checkpoint** What provoked the March Revolution?

Vocabulary Builder

<u>crucial</u>—(KROO shul) *adj.* of vital importance

The Tsar's Downfall
Tsarina Alexandra's reliance on the "mad monk" Gregory Rasputin (below left) to help her govern proved fatal for Rasputin, and ultimately for Alexandra. A lavish Fabergé egg (below right) details three centuries of Romanov tsars. *How do both images show the gulf between Russia's rulers and its people?*

Lenin and the Bolsheviks

Vladimir Ilyich Ulyanov (ool YAHN uf) was born in 1870 to a middle-class family. He adopted the name Lenin when he became a revolutionary. When he was 17, his older brother was arrested and hanged for plotting to kill the tsar. The execution branded his family as a threat to the state and made the young Vladimir hate the tsarist government.

A Brilliant Revolutionary As a young man, Lenin read the works of Karl Marx and participated in student demonstrations. He spread Marxist ideas among factory workers along with other socialists, including Nadezhda Krupskaya (nah DYEZ duh kroop SKY uh), the daughter of a poor noble family. In 1895, Lenin and Krupskaya were arrested and sent to Siberia. During their imprisonment, they were married. After their release, they went into exile in Switzerland. There they worked tirelessly to spread revolutionary ideas.

Lenin's View of Marx Lenin adapted Marxist ideas to fit Russian conditions. Marx had predicted that the industrial working class would rise spontaneously to overthrow capitalism. But Russia did not have a large urban proletariat. Instead, Lenin called for an elite group to lead the revolution and set up a "dictatorship of the proletariat." Though this elite revolutionary party represented a small percentage of socialists, Lenin gave them the name Bolsheviks, meaning "majority."

In Western Europe, many leading socialists had come to think that socialism could be achieved through gradual and moderate reforms such as higher wages, increased suffrage, and social welfare programs. A group of socialists in Russia, the Mensheviks, favored this approach. The Bolsheviks rejected it. To Lenin, reforms of this nature were merely capitalist tricks to repress the masses. Only revolution, he said, could bring about needed changes.

In March 1917, Lenin was still in exile. As Russia stumbled into revolution, Germany saw a chance to weaken its enemy by helping Lenin return home. Lenin rushed across Germany to the Russian frontier in a special train. He greeted a crowd of fellow exiles and activists with this cry: "Long live the worldwide Socialist revolution!"

✔ **Checkpoint** Why did Germany want Lenin to return to Russia in 1917?

The November Revolution Brings the Bolsheviks to Power

Lenin threw himself into the work of furthering the revolution. Another dynamic Marxist revolutionary, Leon Trotsky, helped lead the fight. To the hungry, war-weary Russian people, Lenin and the Bolsheviks promised "Peace, Land, and Bread."

The Provisional Government's Mistakes Meanwhile, the provisional government, led by Alexander Kerensky, continued the war effort and failed to deal with land reform. Those decisions proved fatal. Most Russians were tired of war. Troops at the front were deserting in droves. Peasants wanted land, while city workers demanded an end to the desperate shortages.

In July 1917, the government launched the disastrous Kerensky offensive against Germany. By November, according to one official report, the army was "a huge crowd of tired, poorly clad, poorly fed, embittered men." Growing numbers of troops mutinied. Peasants seized land and drove off fearful landlords.

The Bolshevik Takeover Conditions were ripe for the Bolsheviks to make their move. In November 1917, squads of Red Guards—armed factory workers—joined mutinous sailors from the Russian fleet in attacking the provisional government. In just a matter of days, Lenin's forces overthrew the provisional government without a struggle.

The Bolsheviks quickly seized power in other cities. In Moscow, it took a week of fighting to blast the local government out of the walled Kremlin, the former tsarist center of government. Moscow became the Bolsheviks' capital, and the Kremlin their headquarters.

"We shall now occupy ourselves in Russia in building up a proletarian socialist state," declared Lenin. The Bolsheviks ended private ownership of land and distributed land to peasants. Workers were given control of the factories and mines. A new red flag with an entwined hammer and sickle symbolized union between workers and peasants. Throughout the land, millions thought they had at last gained control over their own lives. In fact, the Bolsheviks—renamed Communists—would soon become their new masters.

✔ **Checkpoint**   How were the Bolsheviks able to seize power from the provisional government?

RUSSIA
1914 WAR AND 1920
REVOLUTION

1914
July
Russia enters
World War I.

August
Germans defeat
Russians at the Battle
of Tannenberg.

1915
June–September
Russians retreat from
German-Austrian
offensive.

1917
March
The March Revolution forces Tsar
Nicholas to abdicate. The Duma
sets up a provisional government.

April
Lenin returns to Russia
to instigate revolution. ▶

November
The provisional government fails
to end the war and resolve internal
problems. The November Revolution
brings Bolsheviks to power.

Tsar Nicholas II (left), preoccupied by war, neglected unrest at home. Revolts erupted in March 1917 in response to poor leadership and equipment on the front, and lack of food at home. ▶

Russia Plunges Into Civil War

After the Bolshevik Revolution, Lenin quickly sought peace with Germany. Russia signed the Treaty of Brest-Litovsk in March 1918, giving up a huge chunk of its territory and its population. The cost of peace was extremely high, but the Communist leaders knew that they needed all their energy to defeat a collection of enemies at home. Russia's <u>withdrawal</u> affected the hopes of both the Allies and the Central Powers, as you read in Section 3.

Opposing Forces For three years, civil war raged between the "Reds," as the Communists were known, and the counterrevolutionary "Whites." The "White" armies were made up of tsarist imperial officers, Mensheviks, democrats, and others, all of whom were united only by their desire to defeat the Bolsheviks. Nationalist groups from many of the former empire's non-Russian regions joined them in their fight. Poland, Estonia, Latvia, and Lithuania broke free, but nationalists in Ukraine, the Caucasus, and Central Asia were eventually subdued.

The Allies intervened in the civil war. They hoped that the Whites might overthrow the Communists and support the fight against Germany. Britain, France, and the United States sent forces to help the Whites. Japan seized land in East Asia that tsarist Russia had once claimed. The Allied presence, however, did little to help the Whites. The Reds appealed to nationalism and urged Russians to drive out the foreigners. In the long run, the Allied invasion fed Communist distrust of the West.

Vocabulary Builder

withdrawal—(with DRAW ul) *n.* the act of leaving

▲ The victorious Reds' symbol of worker and farmer unity—the hammer and sickle—comes to represent the new regime.

1918

March
Bolsheviks sign Treaty of Brest-Litovsk.

June–July
Civil war erupts between the Reds (Bolsheviks) and the Whites; the Reds execute the tsar and his family.

November
Allies sign armistice with Germany.

1920

November
Communist (Red) government wins civil war, after years of bloody fighting.

Thinking Critically

1. **Identify Central Issues** Describe Russia's performance in World War I.
2. **Draw Conclusions** How did involvement in World War I affect events within Russia?

Brutality was common in the civil war. Counterrevolutionary forces slaughtered captured Communists and tried to assassinate Lenin. The Communists shot the former tsar and tsarina and their five children in July 1918 to keep them from becoming a rallying symbol for counterrevolutionary forces.

WITNESS HISTORY VIDEO

Watch *The Fall of the Tsar* on the **Witness History Discovery School**™ video program to learn more about the end of the tsarist rule in Russia.

Discovery
SCHOOL

War Under Communism The Communists used terror not only against the Whites, but also to control their own people. They organized the **Cheka,** a secret police force much like the tsar's. The Cheka executed ordinary citizens, even if they were only suspected of taking action against the revolution. The Communists also set up a network of forced-labor camps in 1919—which grew under Stalin into the dreaded Gulag.

The Communists adopted a policy known as "war communism." They took over banks, mines, factories, and railroads. Peasants in the country-side were forced to deliver almost all of their crops to feed the army and hungry people in the cities. Peasant laborers were drafted into the military or forced to work in factories.

Meanwhile, Trotsky turned the Red Army into an effective fighting force. He used former tsarist officers under the close watch of **commissars,** Communist party officials assigned to the army to teach party principles and ensure party loyalty. Trotsky's passionate speeches roused soldiers to fight. So did the order to shoot every tenth man if a unit performed poorly.

The Reds' position in the center of Russia gave them a strategic advantage. The White armies were forced to attack separately from all sides. They were never able to cooperate effectively with one another. By 1921, the Communists had managed to defeat their scattered foes.

 Checkpoint How did the Red army defeat the White army to end the civil war?

Building the Communist Soviet Union

Russia was in chaos. Millions of people had died since the beginning of World War I. Millions more perished from famine and disease. Lenin faced the enormous problem of rebuilding a shattered state and economy.

New Government, Same Problems In 1922, Lenin's Communist government united much of the old Russian empire into the Union of Soviet Socialist Republics (USSR), or Soviet Union. The Communists produced a constitution that seemed both democratic and socialist. It set up an elected legislature, later called the Supreme Soviet, and gave all citizens over 18 the right to vote. All political power, resources, and means of production would belong to workers and peasants. The Soviet Union was a multinational state made up of European and Asian peoples. In theory, all the member republics shared certain equal rights.

Reality, however, differed greatly from theory. The Communist party, not the people, reigned supreme. Just as the Russian tsars had, the party used the army and secret police to enforce its will. Russia, which was the largest republic, dominated the other republics.

Lenin's New Economic Policy On the economic front, Lenin retreated from his policy of "war communism," which had brought the economy to near collapse. Under party control, factory and mine output had fallen. Peasants stopped producing grain, knowing the government would only seize it.

In 1921, Lenin adopted the New Economic Policy, or NEP. It allowed some capitalist ventures. Although the state kept control of banks, foreign trade, and large industries, small businesses were allowed to reopen for private profit. The government also stopped squeezing peasants for grain. Under the NEP, peasants held on to small plots of land and freely sold their surplus crops.

Lenin's compromise with capitalism helped the Soviet economy recover and ended armed resistance to the new government. By 1928, food and industrial production climbed back to prewar levels. The standard of living improved, too. But Lenin always saw the NEP as just a temporary retreat from communism. His successor would soon return the Soviet Union to "pure" communism.

Stalin Takes Over Lenin died in 1924 at the age of 54. His death set off a power struggle among Communist leaders. The chief contenders were Trotsky and Joseph Stalin. Trotsky was a brilliant Marxist thinker, a skillful speaker, and an architect of the Bolshevik Revolution. Stalin, by contrast, was neither a scholar nor an orator. He was, however, a shrewd political operator and behind-the-scenes organizer. Trotsky and Stalin differed on the future of communism. Trotsky urged support for a worldwide revolution against capitalism. Stalin, more cautious, wanted to concentrate on building socialism at home first.

Eventually, Stalin isolated Trotsky within the party and stripped him of party membership. Trotsky fled the country in 1929, but continued to criticize Stalin. In 1940, a Stalinist agent murdered Trotsky in Mexico.

In 1922, Lenin had expressed grave doubts about Stalin's ambitious nature: "Comrade Stalin . . . has concentrated an enormous power in his hands; and I am not sure that he always knows how to use that power with sufficient caution." Just as Lenin had warned, in the years that followed, Stalin used ruthless measures to win dictatorial power.

Famine in Russia
Years of war took its toll on Russian people, like these starving families in the Volga region. An American journalist, accompanying an international relief team in Russia, described the horrible desolation. In village after village, he noted, "no one stirred from the little wooden house…where Russian families were hibernating and waiting for death."

✓ **Checkpoint** How did the government and the economy under Lenin differ from "pure" communism?

Progress Monitoring *Online*
For: Self-quiz with vocabulary practice
Web Code: nba-2651

SECTION 5 **Assessment**

Terms, People, and Places
1. For each term, person, or place listed at the beginning of the section, write a sentence explaining its significance.

Note Taking
2. **Reading Skill: Summarize** Use your completed timeline to answer the Focus Question: How did two revolutions and a civil war bring about Communist control of Russia?

Comprehension and Critical Thinking
3. **Draw Conclusions** What were the causes of the March Revolution?
4. **Recognize Ideologies** How did Lenin adapt Marxism to conditions in Russia?
5. **Recognize Cause and Effect** What were the causes and effects of the civil war in Russia?
6. **Recognize Effects** Why did Lenin compromise between the ideas of capitalism and communism in creating the NEP?

● **Writing About History**
Quick Write: Clarify Cause-and-Effect Transitions Writing clear transitions can help strengthen your points in a cause-and-effect essay. Connecting words like *since, as soon as, because* and *until* introduce causes. *Therefore, consequently, as a result,* and *then* introduce effects. Rewrite the sentence below to include a clear transition.
• Tsar Nicholas' government collapsed. He did not solve key problems.

Quick Study Guide

■ Causes and Effects of World War I

Cause and Effect	
Long-Term Causes	**Immediate Causes**
• Rivalries among European powers • European alliance system • Militarism and arms race • Nationalist tensions in the Balkans	• Austria-Hungary's annexation of Bosnia and Herzegovina • Fighting in the Balkans • Assassination of Archduke Francis Ferdinand • Russian mobilization • German invasion of Belgium

↓

World War I	

↓

Immediate Effects	**Long-Term Effects**
• Enormous cost in lives and property • Revolution in Russia • Creation of new nations in Eastern Europe • German reparations • German loss of overseas colonies • Balfour Declaration • League of Nations	• Economic impact of war debts on Europe • Stronger central governments • Emergence of United States and Japan as important powers • Growth of nationalism in colonies • Rise of fascism • Increased anti-Semitism in Germany • World War II

■ The Allies Fight the Central Powers

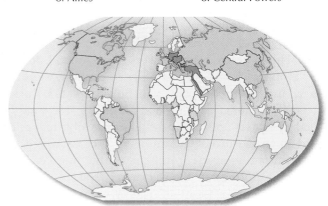

☐ Allies
☐ Colonial possessions of Allies
☐ Central Powers
☐ Colonial possessions of Central Powers

■ Key Events in the Russian Revolution

1914–1917 World War I pressures Russia.
March 1917 March Revolution causes tsar to abdicate; the provisional government takes power.
November 1917 Bolsheviks under Lenin topple provisional government (November Revolution).

■ Key Events of World War I

June 1914
Archduke Francis Ferdinand and his wife are assassinated in Sarajevo.

1916
More than two million soldiers are killed in the battle of Verdun and the battle of the Somme.

Chapter Events
Global Events

1914   **1915**   **1916**

August 1914
The Panama Canal opens.

January 1915
Japan tries to establish a protectorate over China with the Twenty-One Demands.

Concept Connector

■ Cumulative Review

Record the answers to the questions below in your Concept Connector worksheets.

1. **Conflict** Read about the 1814–1815 Congress of Vienna, which met to decide the fate of Europe after the Napoleonic wars. Write one paragraph comparing this meeting to the Paris Peace Conference of 1919 at the end of World War I. Think about the following:
   - key negotiators
   - goals
   - treatment of the defeated country or countries
   - outcomes

2. **Revolution** Compare the Russian Revolution and the French Revolution. How were they similar and different? Create a chart comparing the two revolutions in the following categories:
   - causes
   - duration/phases
   - leaders
   - world reaction
   - results

3. **Cooperation** The League of Nations, established after World War I, was an important step towards a new type of international cooperation. It was intented to maintain peace so that a conflict like World War I would never happen again. Conduct research on the League of Nations and write a paragraph summarizing your findings. Consider the following:
   - factors that contributed to its establishment
   - key goals
   - significant accomplishments
   - reasons for its ultimate failure

■ Connections To Today

1. **Conflict: The Balkan Powder Keg** The formation of Yugoslavia after World War I fulfilled the dream of a South Slav state in the Balkans. Yet unrest continued, erupting as recently as 1999. Conduct research and create a timeline of major events in the Balkans from 1918 to 2000.

The Balkans, 2004

2. **Genocide: Memory and the Armenian Genocide** The Republic of Turkey still maintains that the deportation of the Turkish Armenian population during World War I was a result of civil unrest, not a genocide. Armenian advocacy groups disagree and wage an ongoing campaign for recognition of the Armenians' experience as a planned genocide. Find out where the campaign stands now. Summarize your findings in an essay.

April 1917 The United States joins the Allies.

November 1918 Armistice with Germany ends the war.

April–May 1919 Delegates to the Paris Peace Conference draft the Treaty of Versailles.

1917 1918 1919

1918–1919 A deadly influenza pandemic sweeps across the world, killing more than 20 million people.

February 1919 The first Pan-African Congress meets in Paris.

History Interactive
For: Interactive timeline
Web Code: nbp-2662

Chapter Assessment

Terms, People, and Places

Choose the italicized term in parentheses that best completes each sentence.

1. The Allies tried to regain access to (*Alsace and Lorraine/the Dardanelles*) in the Battle of Gallipoli.
2. After the first battle of the Marne, the war on the Western Front turned into a/an (*entente/stalemate*) until 1918.
3. The British blockade kept both (*contraband/conscription*) and goods like food and clothing from reaching Germany.
4. Both sides used (*reparations/propaganda*) to influence public opinion as a part of total war.
5. After World War I, parts of the Middle East became (*soviets/mandates*) of Britain and France.
6. Lenin wanted to set up a "dictatorship of the (*Fourteen Points/proletariat*)" in Russia.

Main Ideas

Section 1 (pp. 454–459)

7. How did the alliance system that developed in the early 1900s help cause World War I?

Section 2 (pp. 460–465)

8. Describe trench warfare.
9. How did technology affect the way the war was fought?

Section 3 (pp. 467–471)

10. What nation joined the Allied war effort in 1917? What nation dropped out of the war in 1918? How did these two changes affect the war?

Section 4 (pp. 472–476)

11. How did the Treaty of Versailles punish Germany?

Section 5 (pp. 477–483)

12. How did World War I contribute to the collapse of the Russian monarchy?
13. How did the Bolsheviks take power in Russia?

Chapter Focus Question

14. What caused World War I and the Russian Revolution, and what effect did they have on world events?

Critical Thinking

15. **Geography and History** What role did geography play in Germany's war plans?
16. **Synthesize Information** Describe how World War I was a global war.

17. **Analyze Visuals** How did the poster above appeal to the emotions of its intended audience?
18. **Draw Inferences** What do you think Woodrow Wilson meant by "peace without victory"? Why do you think the European Allies were unwilling to accept this idea?
19. **Make Comparisons** In what ways did Soviet communism conform to the teachings of Marx? In what ways did it differ?

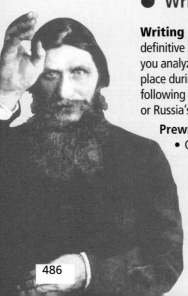

● Writing About History

Writing a Cause-and-Effect Essay World War I was a definitive event of the 1900s. Write an essay in which you analyze the causes and effects of an event that took place during the World War I era. Consider using one of the following topics: Archduke Francis Ferdinand's assassination or Russia's March Revolution.

Prewriting
- Choose the topic listed above that interests you most, or choose another topic that appeals to you.
- Consider multiple causes and immediate and long-term effects of the event you've chosen. Create a cause-and-effect chart to identify your essay's most important points.

Drafting
- Develop a thesis and find information to support it.
- Choose an organizational structure for your essay.
- Write an introduction, several body paragraphs, and a conclusion. State the cause-and-effect relationship you are focusing on clearly in your introduction, and follow up your points in the conclusion.

Revising
- As you review your essay, make sure that each body paragraph supports or develops the cause-and-effect relationship you laid out in your thesis statement.
- Use the guidelines for revising your essay on page SH12 of the Writing Handbook.

Document-Based Assessment

The United States Enters the War

The entry of the United States into the war in April 1917 was a turning point in World War I. The documents below describe different ways that the United States affected the war.

Document A

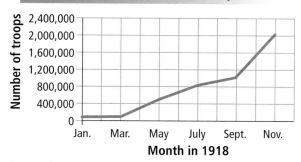

American Soldiers Arrive in Europe, 1918

SOURCE: *The First World War: An Eyewitness History*, Joe H. Kirchberger

Document B

"British shipping losses, especially since the declaration of unrestricted submarine warfare, had risen dangerously. . . . But the entry of the United States into the war made the German submarine warfare an evident failure, because thereafter the number of ships convoyed and the number of ships protecting the convoys was increased steadily. Convoys of ships transporting food, war materials, and troops arrived safely in Britain, and the rate of shipping construction soon exceeded the rate of loss."

—From ***The End of the European Era, 1890 to the Present,***
by Felix Gilbert and David Clay Large

Document C

Winston Churchill, who served in Britain's navy and army during World War I, wrote about the effect American troops had on their tired Allies.

"The impression made upon the hard-pressed French by this seemingly inexhaustible flood of gleaming youth in its first maturity of health and vigour was prodigious [amazing]. None were under twenty, and few were over thirty . . . the French Headquarters were thrilled with the impulse of new life. . . . Half trained, half organized, with only their courage, their numbers and their magnificent youth behind their weapons, they were to buy their experience at a bitter price. But this they were quite ready to do."

Document D

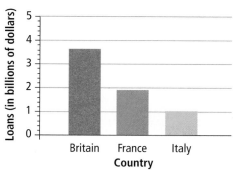

Loans From the United States to Allies

SOURCE: *The End of the European Era, 1890 to the Present,* Felix Gilbert and David Clay Large

Analyzing Documents

Use your knowledge of World War I and Documents A, B, C, and D to answer questions 1–4.

1. How would you describe the arrival of American troops in Europe in 1918?
   - **A** slow at first, but rapid after March
   - **B** steady throughout the year
   - **C** rapid at first, but slow after March
   - **D** No American troops arrived in Europe in 1918.

2. How did the United States navy help break Germany's submarine blockade of Britain?
   - **A** by completely destroying the German submarine fleet
   - **B** by finding new routes around the German submarine fleet
   - **C** by strengthening the convoys
   - **D** by sending supplies to France rather than Britain

3. Based on Document C, how did Churchill feel about American soldiers?
   - **A** They were experienced, but had a poor attitude towards the war.
   - **B** They were energetic and willing to fight, although not experienced.
   - **C** They were well-trained and energetic.
   - **D** They were neither energetic nor experienced.

4. **Writing Task** How did the United States help bring about the Allied victory in 1918? Use your knowledge of World War I and specific evidence from the documents to support your points.

WITNESS HISTORY 🔊 AUDIO

Revolution in Mexico

This Mexican peasants' song from the early 1900s reflected many Mexican's desire for change under the rule of the dictator Porfirio Díaz:

66Our homes and humble dwellings
always full of sadness
living like animals
in the midst of riches.
On the other hand, the haciendados,
owners of lives and lands,
appear disinterested
and don't listen to our complaints.99

Listen to the Witness History audio to learn more about the Mexican Revolution.

◀ **General Carranza with some of his rebel forces during the Mexican Revolution**

Chapter Preview

Chapter Focus Question How did nationalism and the desire for change shape world events in the early 1900s?

Section 1
Struggle in Latin America

Section 2
Nationalism in Africa and the Middle East

Section 3
India Seeks Self-Rule

Section 4
Upheavals in China

Section 5
Conflicting Forces in Japan

Mexico's Coat of Arms

Beaded elephant mask from Africa

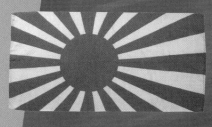

Japan's naval flag

Note Taking Study Guide *Online*
For: Note Taking and Concept Connector worksheets
Web Code: nbd-2701

Mexican peasant revolutionaries

Coffee beans, one of Latin America's major export crops

WITNESS HISTORY ◀)) AUDIO

Fighting for an Ideal

Zeferino Diego Ferreira, a peasant soldier at the time of the Mexican Revolution, describes his feelings on fighting with the rebel leaders Pancho Villa and Emiliano Zapata:

❝I am glad to have fought in the same cause with Zapata . . . and so many of my dear revolutionary friends who were left behind in the hills, their bones eaten by animals. I wasn't afraid. Just the opposite, I was *glad*. It's a *beautiful* thing to fight to realize an ideal.❞

Mexico's revolution was a dramatic fight for reform, with mixed results.

Focus Question How did Latin Americans struggle for change in the early 1900s?

Struggle in Latin America

Objectives
- Identify the causes and effects of the Mexican Revolution.
- Describe the Institutional Revolutionary Party (PRI) and the reforms it introduced in Mexico after the revolution.
- Analyze the effects of nationalism in Latin America in the 1920s and 1930s.

Terms, People, and Places

haciendas	cultural nationalism
nationalization	Good Neighbor Policy
economic nationalism	

Note Taking

Reading Skill: Identify Causes and Effects As you read, note the causes and effects of the Mexican Revolution in a chart like the one below.

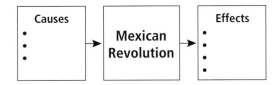

In the early 1900s, Latin America's economy was booming because of exports. Latin Americans sold their plentiful natural resources and cash crops to industrialized countries. In return, they bought products made in those countries. Meanwhile, foreign investors controlled many of Latin America's natural resources.

Stable governments helped to keep the region's economy on a good footing. Some Latin American nations, such as Argentina and Uruguay, had democratic constitutions. However, military dictators or small groups of wealthy landowners held the real power. The tiny ruling class kept the economic benefits of the booming economy for themselves. The growing middle class and the lower classes—workers and peasants—had no say in their own government. These inequalities troubled many Latin American countries, but in Mexico the situation led to an explosive revolution.

The Mexican Revolution

By 1910, the dictator Porfirio Díaz had ruled Mexico for almost 35 years, winning reelection as president again and again. On the surface, Mexico enjoyed peace and economic growth. Díaz welcomed foreign investors who developed mines, built railroads, and drilled for oil. However, underneath the surface, discontent rippled through Mexico. The country's prosperity benefited only a small group. Most Mexicans were mestizos or Indian peasants who lived in desperate poverty. Most of these peasants worked on **haciendas,** or large plantations, controlled by the landowning elite. Some peasants earned meager wages in factories and mines in Mexico's cities. Meanwhile, the growing urban middle class wanted democracy and the elite resented the power of foreign companies. All of these groups opposed the Díaz dictatorship.

The unrest boiled over in 1910 when Francisco Madero, a liberal reformer from an elite family, demanded free elections. Faced with rebellion in several parts of the country, Díaz resigned in 1911. Soon a bloody, complex struggle engulfed Mexico. (See below.)

✓ **Checkpoint** What political and economic factors helped to cause the Mexican Revolution?

THE MEXICAN REVOLUTION

Fighting raged across Mexico for over a decade. Peasants, small farmers, ranchers, and urban workers were drawn into the violent struggle. Women soldiers called *soldaderas* cooked, tended the wounded, and fought alongside the men. The struggle took a terrible toll. When it ended, the Mexican economy was in shambles and more than one million people were dead.

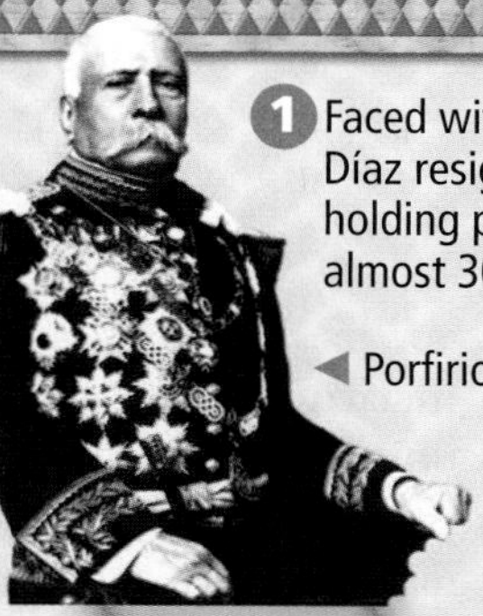

1 Faced with rebellion, Díaz resigned after holding power for almost 30 years.

◀ Porfirio Díaz

2 Madero, a liberal reformer, was democratically elected in 1911. But within two years he was assassinated by one of his generals, Victoriano Huerta.

Francisco Madero ▶

Victoriano Huerta

3 Huerta lost no time setting up his own dictatorship.

Francisco "Pancho" Villa ▼

Emiliano Zapata ▼

4 Villa, Zapata, and Carranza formed an uneasy coalition against Huerta. Villa and Zapata, peasants themselves, wanted to make broad changes to improve peasants' lives. Carranza, a rich landowner, disagreed. After defeating Huerta, Carranza turned on Villa and Zapata and defeated them.

◀ Venustiano Carranza

Venustiano ▶ Carranza

5 Carranza became president of Mexico in 1917. A new constitution passed, but reforms were slow to materialize.

Thinking Critically
1. **Sequence** Describe the events of the Mexican Revolution.
2. **Draw Inferences** Why might Carranza feel that it was in his best interests to eliminate Zapata and Villa?

Revolution Leads to Change

In 1917, voters elected Venustiano Carranza president of Mexico. That year, Carranza reluctantly approved a new constitution that included land and labor reform. With amendments, it is still in force today.

The Constitution of 1917 The Constitution of 1917 addressed three major issues: land, religion, and labor. The constitution strengthened government control over the economy. It permitted the breakup of large estates, placed restrictions on foreigners owning land, and allowed **nationalization,** or government takeover, of natural resources. Church land was made "the property of the nation." The constitution set a minimum wage and protected workers' right to strike.

Although the constitution gave suffrage only to men, it did give women some rights. Women doing the same job as men were entitled to the same pay. In response to women activists, Carranza also passed laws allowing married women to draw up contracts, take part in legal suits, and have equal authority with men in spending family funds.

The PRI Controls Mexico Fighting continued on a smaller scale throughout the 1920s, including Carranza's overthrow in 1920. In 1929, the government organized what later became the Institutional Revolutionary Party (PRI). The PRI managed to accommodate many groups in Mexican society, including business and military leaders, peasants, and workers. The PRI did this by adopting some of the goals of these groups, while keeping real power in its own hands. It suppressed opposition and dissent. Using all of these tactics, the PRI brought stability to Mexico and over time carried out many desired reforms. The PRI dominated Mexican politics from the 1930s until the free election of 2000.

Reforms Materialize At first, the Constitution of 1917 was just a set of goals to be achieved in the future. But in the 1920s and 1930s, as the government finally restored order, it began to carry out reforms.

In the 1920s, the government helped some Indian communities regain lands that had been taken from them. In the 1930s, under President Lázaro Cárdenas, millions of acres of land were redistributed to peasants

A President of the People

Mexican President Lázaro Cárdenas greets people at a train station in the 1930s (below). Between 1915 and 1940, nearly 75 million acres of land was distributed to Mexico's people, fulfilling one of the goals of the Mexican Revolution. *Which president distributed the most land?*

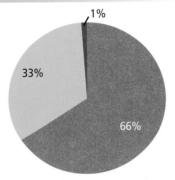

Land Distribution in Mexico by President, 1915–1940

- 1%
- 33%
- 66%

■ Lázaro Cárdenas, 1934–1940
■ Five presidents, 1920–1934
■ Venustiano Carranza, 1915–1920

SOURCE: Michael C. Meyer and William L. Sherman, *The Course of Mexican History*

under a communal land program. The government supported labor unions and launched a massive effort to combat illiteracy. Schools and libraries were set up. Dedicated teachers, often young women, worked for low pay. While they taught basic skills, they spread ideas of nationalism that began to bridge the gulf between the regions and the central government. As the revolutionary era ended, Mexico became the first Latin American nation to pursue real social and economic reforms for the majority of its people.

The government also took a strong role in directing the economy. In 1938, labor disputes broke out between Mexican workers and the management of some foreign-owned petroleum companies. In response, President Cárdenas decreed that the Mexican government would nationalize Mexico's oil resources. American and British oil companies resisted Cárdenas's decision, but eventually accepted compensation for their losses. Mexicans felt that they had at last gained economic independence from foreign influence.

✔ **Checkpoint** How did the Constitution of 1917 try to resolve some of the problems that started the revolution?

Nationalism at Work in Latin America

Mexico's move to reclaim its oil fields from foreign investors reflected a growing spirit of nationalism throughout Latin America. This spirit focused in part on ending economic dependence on the industrial powers, especially the United States, but it echoed throughout political and cultural life as well.

Economic Nationalism During the 1920s and 1930s, world events affected Latin American economies. After World War I, trade with Europe fell off. The Great Depression that struck the United States in 1929 spread around the world in the 1930s. Prices for Latin American exports plunged as demand dried up. At the same time, the cost of imported consumer goods rose. Latin America's economies, dependent on export trade, declined rapidly.

A tide of **economic nationalism,** or emphasis on home control of the economy, swept Latin American countries. They were determined to develop their own industries so they would not have to buy so many products from other countries. Local entrepreneurs set up factories to produce goods. Governments raised tariffs, or taxes on imports, to protect the new industries. Governments also invested directly in new businesses. Following Mexico's lead, some nations took over foreign-owned assets. The drive to create domestic industries was not wholly successful. Unequal distribution of wealth held back economic development.

Political Nationalism The Great Depression also triggered political changes in Latin America. The economic crisis caused people to lose faith in the ruling oligarchies and the ideas of liberal government. Liberalism, a belief in the individual and in limited government, was a European theory. People began to feel that it did not work in Latin America. However, ideas about what form a new type of government should take varied.

In the midst of economic crisis, stronger, authoritarian governments of different types rose in Latin American countries. People hoped that these governments could control, direct, and protect each country's economy more effectively.

Analyzing Political Cartoons

Nationalizing Oil In 1938, Mexican President Cárdenas nationalized foreign-owned oil companies. In response, some nations boycotted Mexican oil.
1. Why is Cárdenas shown standing on a pile of oil barrels?
2. Do you think the cartoonist is Mexican? Why or why not?

Vocabulary Builder

assets—(AS ets) *n.* things of value

Note Taking

Identify Effects As you read, identify the effects of nationalism in Latin America and record them a chart like the one below.

Effects of Latin American Nationalism		
Economic	**Political**	**Cultural**
•	•	•
•	•	•

Mexico's Heritage
This stained glass image shows one variation of the Mexican coat of arms that appears on Mexico's flag today. An ancient prophecy dictated that the Aztec capital should be founded where scouts saw an eagle perched on a cactus growing out of a rock surrounded by water, holding a snake in its beak. Accordingly, the founders of Tenochtitlán were believed to have seen this sign in 1325 at the site of present-day Mexico City. The symbol is an emblem of Mexican nationalism. *Why do you think that an Aztec symbol is included on the Mexican flag?*

Vocabulary Builder
intervening—(in tur VEEN ing) *vi.* coming between two arguing factions

Cultural Nationalism By the 1920s, Latin American writers, artists, and thinkers began to reject European influences in culture as well. Instead, they took pride in their own culture, with its blend of Western and native traditions.

In Mexico, **cultural nationalism,** or pride in one's own culture, was reflected in the revival of mural painting, a major art form of the Aztecs and Maya. In the 1920s and 1930s, Diego Rivera, José Clemente Orozco (oh ROHS koh), David Alfaro Siqueiros (see KEH rohs), and other muralists created magnificent works. On the walls of public buildings, they portrayed the struggles of the Mexican people for liberty. The murals have been a great source of national pride ever since.

The Good Neighbor Policy During and after World War I, investments by the United States in the nations of Latin America soared. British influence declined. The United States continued to play the role of international policeman, <u>intervening</u> to restore order when it felt its interests were threatened.

During the Mexican Revolution, the United States stepped in to support the leaders who favored American interests. In 1914, the United States attacked the port of Veracruz to punish Mexico for imprisoning several American sailors. In 1916, the U.S. army invaded Mexico after Pancho Villa killed more than a dozen Americans in New Mexico. This interference stirred up anti-American feelings, which increased throughout Latin America during the 1920s. For example, in Nicaragua, Augusto César Sandino led a guerrilla movement against United States forces occupying his country.

In the 1930s, President Franklin Roosevelt took a new approach to Latin America and pledged to follow "the policy of the good neighbor." Under the **Good Neighbor Policy,** the United States pledged to lessen its interference in the affairs of Latin American nations. The United States withdrew troops stationed in Haiti and Nicaragua. It lifted the Platt Amendment, which had limited Cuban independence. Roosevelt also supported Mexico's nationalization of its oil companies. The Good Neighbor policy strengthened Latin American nationalism and improved relations between Latin America and the United States.

✓ **Checkpoint** Describe how economic and political nationalism in Latin America were related.

SECTION 1 Assessment

Progress Monitoring *Online*
For: Self-quiz with vocabulary practice
Web Code: nba-2711

Terms, People, and Places
1. What do each of the key terms listed at the beginning of the section, except "haciendas," have in common? Explain.

Note Taking
2. **Reading Skill: Identify Causes and Effects** Use your completed flow-charts to answer the Focus Question: How did Latin Americans struggle for change in the early 1900s?

Comprehension and Critical Thinking
3. **Recognize Causes** Describe three causes of the Mexican Revolution.
4. **Analyze Credibility** How did the PRI fulfill some goals of the revolution but not others?
5. **Identify Central Issues** How did nationalism affect Latin America?
6. **Summarize** How did Franklin Roosevelt change the policy of the United States toward Latin America?

● **Writing About History**
Quick Write: Write a Thesis Statement A persuasive essay seeks to convince its reader to accept the writer's position on a topic. To be effective, the thesis statement must state a position that provokes valid arguments. Write an effective thesis statement on the topic of economic nationalism in Latin America.

Mexican Murals

Diego Rivera ▶

During the 1920s and 1930s, the Mexican government commissioned artists to paint beautiful murals about revolutionary themes on the walls of public buildings. The murals were meant to help all Mexicans, even those who couldn't read, learn about the ideals of the Revolution.

The most famous Mexican muralist was Diego Rivera. The panel to the right is part of a huge work on Mexican history that Rivera painted on the stairway of the National Palace in Mexico City.

Zapata, Villa, and other revolutionaries appear at the top of the panel, holding a banner that reads "Tierra y Libertad" ("Land and Liberty")—Zapata's slogan.

The center of the composition shows an eagle sitting on a cactus. The eagle is part of a national symbol of Mexico. A variation of it appears on the current Mexican flag. However, here, the eagle holds the Aztec war symbol in its beak rather than the traditional serpent.

The bottom segment shows the conquest of Mexico by Hernán Cortés. Cortés's armies battle the native Aztecs.

Thinking Critically

1. **Make Inferences** Why do you think Diego Rivera has the Mexican eagle holding the Aztec war symbol rather than the serpent?
2. **Draw Conclusions** What do Rivera's murals reveal about how he viewed Mexican history?

An African Protests Colonialism

❝ If you woke up one morning and found that somebody had come to your house, and had declared that house belonged to him, you would naturally be surprised, and you would like to know by what arrangement. Many Africans at that time found that, on land that had been in the possession of their ancestors from time immemorial, they were now working as squatters or as laborers. ❞
—Jomo Kenyatta, Kenyan independence leader

A woman (right) carries a load of wood in the British colony of Kenya. A French poster (above) urges Europeans to visit Africa.

Focus Question How did nationalism contribute to changes in Africa and the Middle East following World War I?

Nationalism in Africa and the Middle East

Objectives

- Describe how Africans resisted colonial rule.
- Analyze how nationalism grew in Africa.
- Explain how Turkey and Persia modernized.
- Summarize how European mandates contributed to the growth of Arab nationalism.
- Understand the roots of conflict between Jews and Arabs in the Palestinian mandate.

Terms, People, and Places

apartheid	Asia Minor
Pan-Africanism	Pan-Arabism
négritude movement	Balfour Declaration

Note Taking

Reading Skill: Identify Causes and Effects
Record reasons for the rise of nationalism in Africa and the Middle East and its effects in a chart like the one below.

Rise of Nationalism		
Region	Reasons for Rise	Effects
Africa		
Turkey and Persia		
Middle East		

Jomo Kenyatta, quoted above, was a leader in Kenya's struggle for independence from British rule. During the 1920s and 1930s, a new generation of leaders, proud of their unique heritage, struggled to stop imperialism and restore Africa for Africans.

Africans Resist Colonial Rule

During the early 1900s, almost every part of Africa was a European colony. Agricultural improvements in some areas caused a boom in export crops. However, the colonizers exploited the boom solely for their own benefit.

Some Africans were forced to work on plantations or in mines run by Europeans. The money they earned went to pay taxes to the colonial government. In Kenya and Rhodesia, white settlers forced Africans off the best land. The few who kept their land were forbidden to grow the most profitable crops. Only Europeans could grow these. Also in Kenya, the British made all Africans carry identification cards, imposed a tax, and restricted where they could live or travel. In other parts of Africa, farmers kept their land but had to grow cash crops, like cotton, instead of food. This led to famines in some regions.

During World War I, more than one million Africans had fought on behalf of their colonial rulers. Many had hoped that their service would lead to more rights and opportunities. Instead, the situation remained mostly the same or even worsened.

Opposing Imperialism Many Western-educated Africans criticized the injustice of imperial rule. Although they had trained for professional careers, the best jobs went to Europeans. Inspired by President Woodrow Wilson's call for self-determination, Africans condemned the colonial system. In Africa, as in other regions around the world, socialism found a growing audience. Protests and opposition to imperialism multiplied.

Racial Segregation and Nationalism in South Africa Between 1910 and 1940, whites strengthened their grip on South Africa. They imposed a system of racial segregation. Their goal was to ensure white economic, political, and social supremacy. New laws, for example, restricted better-paying jobs in mines to whites only. Blacks were pushed into low-paid, less-skilled work. As in Kenya, South African blacks had to carry passes at all times. They were evicted from the best land, which was set aside for whites, and forced to live on crowded "reserves," which were located in dry, infertile areas.

Other laws chipped away at the rights of blacks. In one South African province, educated blacks who owned property had been allowed to vote in local elections. In 1936, the government abolished that right. The system of segregation set up at this time would become even stricter after 1948, when **apartheid** (uh PAHR tayt), a policy of rigid segregation, became law.

Yet South Africa was also home to a vital nationalist movement. African Christian churches and African-run newspapers demanded rights for black South Africans. They formed a political party, later known as the African National Congress (ANC), to protest unfair laws. Their efforts, however, had no effect on South Africa's white government. Still, the ANC did build a framework for political action in later years.

✔️ **Checkpoint** In what ways did colonial powers try to control African life?

Nationalism and an "Africa for Africans"

In the 1920s, a movement known as **Pan-Africanism** began to nourish the nationalist spirit and strengthen resistance. Pan-Africanism emphasized the unity of Africans and people of African descent worldwide. Among its most inspiring leaders was Jamaica-born Marcus Garvey. He preached a forceful, appealing message of "Africa for Africans" and

Segregation in South Africa
In the early 1900s, white people in South Africa began to force urban Africans to move to camps outside of the larger cities, such as this settlement outside of Cape Town. *Why do you think that the white people have forced the African people behind a barbed wire fence?*

497

African Resistance

Opposition to imperialism grew among Africans in the 1920s and 1930s. Resistance took many forms. Those who had lost their lands to Europeans sometimes squatted, or settled illegally, on European-owned plantations. In cities, workers began to form labor unions, even though they were illegal under colonial law codes. Africans formed associations and political parties to express their opposition to the colonial system. Although large-scale revolts were rare, protests were common.

Nigeria

In 1929, Ibo market women in Nigeria denounced British policies. They demanded a voice in decisions that affected their markets (below). The "Women's War," as it was called, soon became a full-fledged revolt.

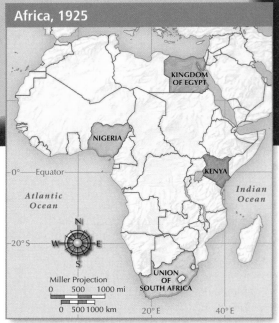

Africa, 1925

KINGDOM OF EGYPT

NIGERIA

0° Equator

Atlantic Ocean

KENYA

Indian Ocean

20°S

Miller Projection
0   500   1000 mi

0   500 1000 km

UNION OF SOUTH AFRICA

20°E   40°E

South Africa

In 1912, educated Africans organized a political party that later became the African National Congress (ANC). Its members worked through legal means, protesting laws that restricted the freedom of black Africans. One ANC member (left) gave a speaking tour in England to raise support for his cause.

demanded an end to colonial rule. Garvey's ideas influenced a new generation of African leaders.

Pan-African Congress Forges Ties African American scholar and activist W.E.B. DuBois (doo BOYS) organized the first Pan-African Congress in 1919. It met in Paris, where the Allies were holding their peace conference. Delegates from African colonies, the West Indies, and the United States called on the Paris peacemakers to approve a charter of rights for Africans. Although the Western powers ignored their demands, the Pan-African Congress established cooperation among African and African American leaders.

The Négritude Movement Shows Pride French-speaking writers in West Africa and the Caribbean further awakened self-confidence among Africans through the **négritude movement.** In the négritude movement, writers expressed pride in their African roots and protested colonial rule. Best known among them was the Senegalese poet Léopold Senghor, who celebrated Africa's rich cultural heritage. He fostered African pride by rejecting the negative views of Africa spread by colonial rulers. Later, Senghor would take an active role in Senegal's drive to independence, and he would serve as its first president.

Egypt Gains Independence African nationalism brought little political change, except to Egypt. Egyptians had suffered during World War I. After the war, protests, strikes, and riots forced Britain to grant Egypt independence in 1922. However, Britain still controlled Egypt's monarchy.

Egypt

Simmering resistance to British rule in Egypt flared as World War I ended. Peasants, landowners, Christians, Muslims and Western-educated officials united behind the Wafd party, which launched strikes and protests (right). In 1922, the British finally agreed to declare Egypt independent. In fact, however, British troops stayed in Egypt to guard the Suez Canal, and Britain remained the real power behind Egypt's King Faud.

Kenya

Members of the Kikuyu ethnic group formed the Kikuyu Central Association in 1924. The Association protested the Kikuyu's loss of land, forced labor, heavy taxes, and the hated identification cards. The British jailed Harry Thuku (right) and other Kikuyu leaders, but protests continued.

Thinking Critically
1. **Make Comparisons** How did the methods of the ANC in South Africa differ from the Wafd party in Egypt?
2. **Determine Relevance** Why is it important to learn about early protest movements in Africa, despite the fact that most colonies did not gain independence until after World War II?

Displeased with this state of affairs, during the 1930s many young Egyptians joined an organization called the Muslim Brotherhood. This group fostered a broad Islamic nationalism that rejected Western culture and denounced corruption in the Egyptian government.

✓ **Checkpoint** What significance does the phrase "Africa for Africans" have?

Turkey and Persia Modernize

Nationalist movements brought immense changes to the Middle East in the aftermath of World War I. The defeated Ottoman empire was near collapse in 1918. Its Arab lands, as you have read, were divided between Britain and France. However, in **Asia Minor**, the Turkish peninsula between the Black Sea and the Mediterranean Sea, Turks resisted Western control and fought to build a modern nation.

Atatürk Sets Goals In 1920, the Ottoman sultan reluctantly signed the Treaty of Sèvres, in which the empire lost its Arab and North African lands. The sultan also had to give up some land in Asia Minor to a number of Allied countries, including Greece. A Greek force landed in the city of Smyrna (now Izmir) to <u>assert</u> Greece's claims. Turkish nationalists, led by the determined and energetic Mustafa Kemal, overthrew the sultan, defeated the Greeks, and declared Turkey a republic. Kemal negotiated a new treaty. Among other provisions, the treaty called for about 1.3 million Greeks to leave Turkey, while some 400,000 Turks left Greece.

Vocabulary Builder

<u>assert</u>—(uh SURT) *vt.* maintain or defend

Atatürk (1881–1938)

"Atatürk" is the name that Mustafa Kemal gave himself when he ordered all Turkish people to take on surnames, or last names. It means "Father of the Turks." In 1920, he led Turkish nationalists in the fight against Greek forces trying to enforce the Treaty of Sèvres, establishing the borders of the modern Republic of Turkey. Once in power, he passed many reforms to modernize, Westernize, and secularize Turkey. Atatürk is still honored throughout Turkey today—his portrait appears on postage and all currency. **Why is Atatürk considered the "Father of the Turks"?**

Atatürk's Reforms in Turkey

- Replaced Islamic law with European model
- Replaced Muslim calendar with Western (Christian) calendar
- Moved day of rest from Friday to Sunday
- Closed religious schools and opened state schools
- Forced people to wear Western-style clothes
- Replaced Arabic alphabet with Latin alphabet
- Gave women the right to vote and to work outside the home.

Kemal later took the name Atatürk (ah tah TURK), meaning "father of the Turks." Between 1923 and his death in 1938, Atatürk forced through an ambitious program of radical reforms. His goals were to modernize Turkey along Western lines and to separate religion from government. To achieve these goals, Atatürk mandated that Islamic traditions in several fields be replaced with Western alternatives (see Biography).

Westernization Transforms Turkey Atatürk's government encouraged industrial expansion. The government built railroads, set up factories, and hired westerners to advise on how to make Turkey economically independent.

To achieve his reforms, Atatürk ruled with an iron hand. To many Turks, he was a hero who was transforming Turkey into a strong, modern power. Others questioned Atatürk's dictatorial powers and complete rejection of religion in laws and government. They believed that Islam could play a constructive role in a modern, civil state.

Nationalism and Reform at Work in Persia The success of Atatürk's reforms inspired nationalists in neighboring Persia (present-day Iran). Persian nationalists greatly resented the British and Russians, who had won spheres of influence over Persia in 1907. In 1925, an ambitious army officer, Reza Khan, overthrew the shah. He set up his own dynasty, with himself as shah.

Like Atatürk, Reza Khan rushed to modernize Persia and make it fully independent. He built factories, roads, and railroads and strengthened the army. He forced Persians to wear Western clothing and set up modern, secular schools. In addition, he moved to replace Islamic law with secular law and encouraged women to take part in public life. Muslim religious leaders fiercely condemned Reza Khan's efforts to introduce Western ways to the nation.

Reza Khan also persuaded the British company that controlled Persia's oil industry to give Persia a larger share of the profits and insisted that Persian workers be hired at all levels of the company. In the decades ahead, oil would become a major factor in Persia's economy and foreign policy.

✔ **Checkpoint** What did the reforms of Atatürk and Reza Khan have in common?

Arab Nationalism in the Middle East

Oil became a major factor throughout the Middle East during this period. The use of gasoline-powered engines in various vehicles during World War I showed that oil was the fuel of the future. Foreign companies began to move into the Middle East to exploit its large oil reserves.

Pan-Arabism Grows Partly in response to foreign influence, Arab nationalism grew after World War I and gave rise to **Pan-Arabism.** This nationalist movement was built on the shared heritage of Arabs who lived in lands from the Arabian Peninsula to North Africa. Today, this

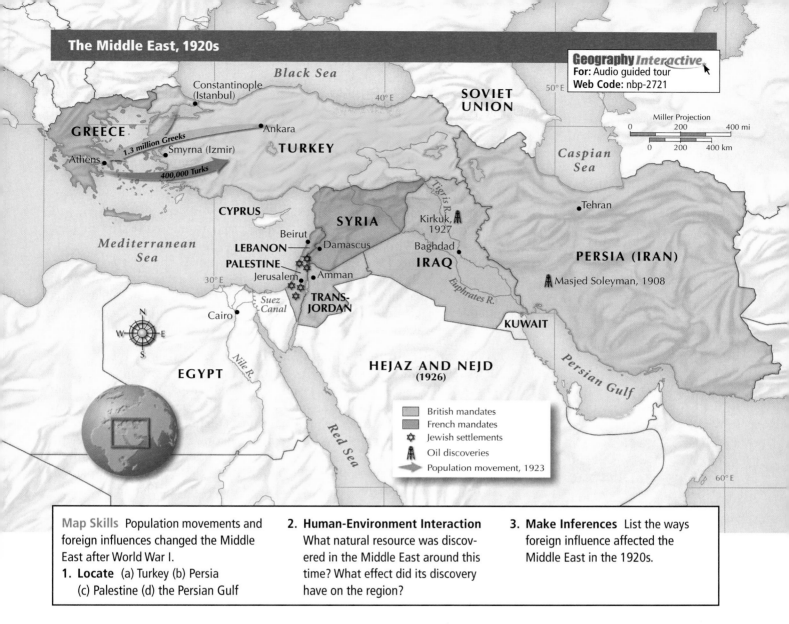

The Middle East, 1920s

Geography *Interactive*
For: Audio guided tour
Web Code: nbp-2721

Black Sea

Constantinople
(Istanbul)

SOVIET
UNION

40° E

50° E

GREECE

Ankara

1.3 million Greeks

Athens

Smyrna (Izmir)

TURKEY

Caspian
Sea

Tehran

400,000 Turks

Miller Projection
0   200   400 mi
0   200   400 km

CYPRUS

Mediterranean
Sea

Beirut

LEBANON

SYRIA

Damascus

Kirkuk,
1927

Baghdad

Tigris R.

PERSIA (IRAN)

PALESTINE

30° E

Jerusalem

Amman

IRAQ

Masjed Soleyman, 1908

TRANS-
JORDAN

Euphrates R.

Suez
Canal

Cairo

KUWAIT

N
W   E
S

EGYPT

Nile R.

HEJAZ AND NEJD
(1926)

Persian Gulf

60° E

Red Sea

British mandates
French mandates
Jewish settlements
Oil discoveries
Population movement, 1923

Map Skills Population movements and foreign influences changed the Middle East after World War I.

1. Locate (a) Turkey (b) Persia (c) Palestine (d) the Persian Gulf

2. Human-Environment Interaction What natural resource was discovered in the Middle East around this time? What effect did its discovery have on the region?

3. Make Inferences List the ways foreign influence affected the Middle East in the 1920s.

area includes Syria, Jordan, Iraq, Egypt, Algeria, and Morocco. Pan-Arabism emphasized the common history and language of Arabs and recalled the golden age of Arab civilization. The movement sought to free Arabs from foreign domination and unite them in their own state.

Betrayal at the Peace Conference Arabs were outraged by the European-controlled mandates set up at the Paris Peace Conference. During World War I, Arabs had helped the Allies against the Central Powers, especially the Ottoman empire. In return for their help, the Allies led the Arabs to believe that they would gain independence after the war. Instead, the Allies carved up the Ottoman lands, giving France mandates in Syria and Lebanon and Britain mandates in Palestine and Iraq. Later, Britain gave a large part of the Palestinian mandate, Trans-Jordan, to Abdullah for a kingdom.

Arabs felt betrayed by the West—a feeling that has endured to this day. During the 1920s and 1930s, their anger erupted in frequent protests and revolts against Western imperialism. A major center of turmoil was the British mandate of Palestine. There, Arab nationalists and Jewish nationalists, known as Zionists, increasingly clashed.

Two Views of One Place
Posters encouraged visitors and settlers to go to Palestine. At the same time, Palestinian Arabs tried to limit Jewish settlement in the area.

Promises in Palestine Since Roman times, Jews had dreamed of returning to the land of Judea, or Israel. In 1897, Theodor Herzl (HURT sul) responded to growing anti-Semitism, or prejudice against Jewish people, in Europe by founding the modern Zionist movement. His goal was to rebuild a Jewish state in Palestine. Among other things, violent pogroms against Jews in Russia prompted thousands of them to migrate to Palestine. They joined the small Jewish community that had lived there since biblical times.

During World War I, the Allies made two conflicting sets of promises. First, they promised Arabs their own kingdoms in former Ottoman lands, including Palestine. Then, in 1917, the British attempted to win the support of European Jews by issuing the **Balfour Declaration.** In it, the British advocated the idea of setting up "a national home for the Jewish people" in Palestine. The declaration noted, however, that "nothing shall be done which may prejudice the civil and religious rights of existing non-Jewish communities in Palestine." Those communities were Arab. The stage was thus set for conflict between Arab and Jewish nationalists.

A Bitter Struggle Begins From 1919 to 1940, tens of thousands of Jews immigrated to Palestine due to the Zionist movement and the effects of anti-Semitism in Europe. Despite great hardships, Jewish settlers set up factories, built new towns, and established farming communities. At the same time, the Arab population almost doubled. Many were immigrants from nearby lands. As a result, Palestine's population included a changing mix of newcomers. The Jewish population, which was less than 60,000 in 1919, grew to about 400,000 in 1936, while the Muslim population increased from about 568,000 in 1919 to about 1 million in 1940.

At first, some Arabs welcomed the money and modern technical skills that the newcomers brought with them. But as more Jews moved to Palestine, tensions between the two groups developed. Jewish organizations tried to purchase as much land as they could, while Arabs sought to slow down or stop Jewish immigration. Religious differences between Jews and Arabs heightened tensions. Arabs attacked Jewish settlements, hoping to discourage settlers. The Jewish settlers established their own military defense force. For the rest of the century, Arab and Jews fought over the land that Arabs called Palestine and Jews called Israel.

✔ **Checkpoint** Why did Palestine become a center of conflict after World War I?

SECTION 2 **Assessment**

Progress Monitoring *Online*
For: Self-quiz with vocabulary practice
Web Code: nba-2721

Terms, People, and Places
1. For each term, person, or place listed at the beginning of the section, write a sentence explaining its significance.

Note Taking
2. **Reading Skill: Identify Causes and Effects** Use your completed chart to answer the Focus Question: How did nationalism contribute to changes in Africa and the Middle East following World War I?

Comprehension and Critical Thinking
3. **Identify Central Issues** How did Africans resist colonial rule?
4. **Summarize** What are three examples of the rise of nationalism in Africa?
5. **Identify Central Issues** Why might Muslim religious leaders object to reforms in Turkey and Persia?
6. **Draw Conclusions** How did the Balfour Declaration affect the Middle East?

● **Writing About History**
Quick Write: Generate Arguments
When you write a persuasive essay, you want to support your thesis statement with valid, convincing arguments. You'll need to read about your topic in order to formulate your list of arguments. Write down ideas for three arguments supporting the following thesis: The ANC was a valuable political party even though it did not affect the white-run government of South Africa for many years.

A Hindu servant serves tea to his mistress in colonial India.

WITNESS HISTORY 🔊 AUDIO

Indian Frustration

In the early 1900s, many Indians were dissatisfied with British rule. An early leader of the Indian National Congress party expressed his frustration with an unpopular policy to divide the province of Bengal into smaller sections:

    66 The scheme [to divide Bengal] . . . will always stand as a complete illustration of the worst features of the present system of bureaucratic rule—its utter contempt for public opinion, its arrogant pretensions to superior wisdom, its reckless disregard of the most cherished feelings of the people, the mockery of an appeal to its sense of justice, [and] its cool preference of [British civil service workers'] interests to those of the governed.99
    —Gopal Krishna Gokhale, 1905

Focus Question How did Gandhi and the Congress party work for independence in India?

India Seeks Self-Rule

Objectives

- Explain what motivated the Indian independence movement after World War I.
- Analyze how Mohandas Gandhi influenced the independence movement.
- Describe the impact of the Salt March on the course of the Indian independence movement.

Terms, People, and Places

Amritsar massacre   untouchables
ahimsa   boycott
civil disobedience

Note Taking

Reading Skill: Identify Causes and Effects
Recognizing causes and effects can help you understand the significance of certain events. In a chart like the one below, record the causes and effects of Gandhi's leadership of India's independence movement.

Tensions were running high in Amritsar, a city in northern India. Protests against British rule had sparked riots and attacks on British residents. On April 13, 1919, a large but peaceful crowd of Indians jammed into an enclosed field. The British commander, General Reginald Dyer, had banned public meetings, but the crowd either ignored or had not heard the order. As Indian leaders spoke, Dyer and 50 soldiers opened fire on the unarmed crowd, killing nearly 400 people and wounding more than 1,100. The **Amritsar massacre** was a turning point for many Indians. It convinced them that India needed to govern itself.

Calls for Independence

The tragedy at Amritsar was linked to broader Indian frustrations after World War I. During the war, more than a million Indians had served overseas. Under pressure from Indian nationalists, the British promised Indians greater self-government. But when the fighting ended, Britain proposed only a few minor reforms.

Since 1885, the Indian National Congress party, called the Congress party, had pressed for self-rule within the British empire. After Amritsar, it began to call for full independence. But party members were mostly middle-class, Western-educated elite who had little in common with the masses of Indian peasants. In the 1920s, a new leader named Mohandas Gandhi emerged and united Indians across class lines.

Gandhi came from a middle-class Hindu family. At age 19, he went to England to study law. Then, like many Indians, Gandhi

The Salt March
Gandhi's march to the sea to collect forbidden salt started out with Gandhi and 78 followers, but gathered strength as it progressed. As he picked up the first lump of salt, he declared, "With this, I am shaking the foundations of the British empire." *How do you think people in other countries would have reacted to British authorities using violence against this group?*

Vocabulary Builder
discriminated—(dih SKRIM ih nayt ed) *vi.* treated differently because of a prejudice

went to South Africa. For 20 years, Gandhi fought laws that <u>discriminated</u> against Indians in South Africa. In 1914, Gandhi returned to India. Soon, he became the leader of the Congress party.

✔ **Checkpoint** Why did Indians call for independence after World War I?

The Power of Nonviolence

Gandhi's ideas inspired Indians of all religious and ethnic backgrounds. His nonviolent protests caught the attention of the British government and the world.

Gandhi's Ideas Gandhi's theories embraced Hindu traditions. He preached the ancient doctrine of **ahimsa** (uh HIM sah), or nonviolence and reverence for all life. By using the power of love, he believed, people could convert even the worst wrongdoer to the right course of action. To fight against injustice, he advocated the use of nonviolent resistance.

Gandhi's philosophy reflected Western as well as Indian influences. He admired Christian teachings about love. He believed in the American philosopher Henry David Thoreau's ideas about **civil disobedience,** the refusal to obey unjust laws. Gandhi was also influenced by Western ideas of democracy and nationalism. He urged equal rights for all Indians, women as well as men. He fought hard to end the harsh treatment of **untouchables,** who were members of the lowest caste, or class.

Gandhi Sets an Example During the 1920s and 1930s, Gandhi launched a series of nonviolent actions against British rule. He called for Indians to **boycott,** or refuse to buy, British goods, especially cotton textiles. He worked to restore pride in India's traditional industries, making the spinning wheel a symbol of the nationalist movement. Gandhi's campaigns of civil disobedience attracted wide support.

✔ **Checkpoint** What methods did Indians under Gandhi use to resist British rule?

Gandhi Takes a Stand: The Salt March

To mobilize mass support, Gandhi decided to take a stand against the British salt monopoly, which he saw as a symbol of British oppression. Natural salt was available in the sea, but the British government required Indians to buy only salt sold by the monopoly.

Breaking the Law On March 12, 1930, Gandhi set out with 78 followers on a 240-mile march to the sea. As the tiny band passed through villages, crowds responded to Gandhi's message. By the time they reached the sea, the marchers numbered in the thousands. On April 6, Gandhi waded into the surf and picked up a lump of sea salt. He was soon arrested and jailed. Still, Indians followed his lead. Coastal villages started collecting salt. Indians sold salt on city streets. As Gandhi's campaign gained force, tens of thousands of Indians were imprisoned.

Steps Toward Freedom All around the world, newspapers criticized Britain's harsh reaction to the protests. Stories revealed how police brutally clubbed peaceful marchers who tried to occupy a government saltworks. Slowly, Gandhi's campaign forced Britain to hand over some power to Indians. Britain also agreed to meet other demands of the Congress party.

 Checkpoint What did the Salt March symbolize?

Looking Ahead

In 1939, a new world war exploded. Britain outraged Indian leaders by postponing independence and bringing Indians into the war without consulting them. Angry nationalists launched a campaign of noncooperation and were jailed. Millions of Indians, however, did help Britain during World War II.

When the war ended in 1945, India's independence could no longer be delayed. As it neared, Muslim fears of the Hindu majority increased. Conflict between Hindus and Muslims would trouble the new nation in the years to come.

SECTION 3 Assessment

Progress Monitoring *Online*
For: Self-quiz with vocabulary practice
Web Code: nba-2731

Terms, People, and Places

1. Place each of the key terms listed at the beginning of the section into one of the following categories: politics, culture, or economy. Write a sentence for each term explaining your choice.

Note Taking

2. **Reading Skill: Identify Causes and Effects** Use your completed chart to answer the Focus Question: How did Gandhi and the Congress party work for independence in India?

Comprehension and Critical Thinking

3. **Identify Point of View** How did the Amritsar massacre affect the movement for Indian independence?

4. **Recognize Cause and Effect** Why do you think Gandhi was able to unite Indians when earlier attempts had not succeeded?

5. **Analyze Information** How did the Salt March force Britain to respond to Indian demands?

● **Writing About History**

Quick Write: Use Valid Logic In a persuasive essay, you must back up your conclusions with valid logic. One common pattern of weak logic is circular reasoning, where a writer simply restates ideas instead of defending them. Bring in an example of weak logic from recent editorials in your local paper. Include a paragraph explaining the problems with the author's logic.

Mohandas Gandhi: *Hind Swaraj*

Mohandas Gandhi led a successful, peaceful revolution in India against British rule. In the following excerpt from his book *Hind Swaraj (Indian Home Rule),* Gandhi explains the ideas behind his nonviolent method of passive resistance in the form of an imaginary conversation between an editor and a reader. *Hind Swaraj* was first published in 1909 in South Africa, but was banned in India.

Mohandas Gandhi

Editor: Passive resistance is a method of securing rights by personal suffering; it is the reverse of resistance by arms. When I refuse to do a thing that is repugnant [offensive] to my conscience, I use soul-force. For instance, the Government of the day has passed a law which is applicable to me. I do not like it. If by using violence I force the Government to repeal the law, I am employing what may be termed body-force. If I do not obey the law and accept the penalty for its breach, I use soul-force. It involves sacrifice of self.

Everybody admits that sacrifice of self is infinitely superior to sacrifice of others. Moreover, if this kind of force is used in a cause that is unjust, only the person using it suffers. He does not make others suffer for his mistakes. Men have before now done many things which were subsequently found to have been wrong. No man can claim that he is absolutely in the right or that a particular thing is wrong because he thinks so, but it is wrong for him so long as that is his deliberate judgment. It is therefore meet [proper] that he should not do that which he knows to be wrong, and suffer the consequence whatever it may be. This is the key to the use of soul-force.

Reader: You would then disregard laws—this is rank disloyalty. We have always been considered a law-abiding nation. You seem to be going even beyond the extremists. They say that we must obey the laws that have been passed, but that if the laws be bad, we must drive out the lawgivers even by force.

Editor: Whether I go beyond them or whether I do not is a matter of no consequence to either of us. We simply want to find out what is right and to act accordingly. The real meaning of the statement that we are a law-abiding nation is that we are passive resisters. When we do not like certain laws, we do not break the heads of law-givers but we suffer and do not submit to the laws.

Thinking Critically

1. **Identify Central Issues** What is the goal of passive resistance?
2. **Draw Conclusions** According to Gandhi, could soul-force ever be used to support an unjust cause? What does Gandhi mean when he says that a person using soul-force "does not make others suffer for his mistakes"?

A family of refugees (right) flee a conflict between warlords in 1926.

Chinese currency showing Jiang Jieshi, the next leader of Sun Yixian's Guomindang party.

WITNESS HISTORY ◀)) AUDIO

Change in China

Sun Yixian, "father" of modern China, painted a grim picture of China after the end of the Qing dynasty.

66 But the Chinese people have only family and clan solidarity; they do not have national spirit. Therefore, even though we have four hundred million people gathered together in one China, in reality they are just a heap of loose sand. Today we are the poorest and weakest nation in the world and occupy the lowest position in international affairs. Other men are the carving knife and serving dish, we are the fish and the meat.99

As Sun emphasized, China needed to change, but how and in what direction?

Focus Question How did China cope with internal division and foreign invasion in the early 1900s?

Upheavals in China

Objectives

- Explain the key challenges faced by the Chinese republic in the early 1900s.
- Analyze the struggle between two rival parties as they fought to control China.
- Describe how invasion by Japan affected China.

Terms, People, and Places

Twenty-One Demands   Guomindang
May Fourth Movement   Long March
vanguard

Note Taking

Reading Skill: Recognize Multiple Causes
Use a chart like the one below to record the causes of upheaval in the Chinese Republic.

Causes of Upheaval

As the new Chinese republic took shape, nationalists like Sun Yixian (soon yee SHYAHN) set the goal of "catching up and surpassing the powers, east and west." But that goal would remain a distant dream as China suffered the turmoil of civil war and foreign invasion.

The Chinese Republic in Trouble

As you have read, China's Qing dynasty collapsed in 1911. The president of China's new republic, Sun Yixian (also called Sun Yat-sen) hoped to rebuild China on the Three Principles of the People—nationalism, democracy, and economic security for everyone. But he made little progress. China quickly fell into chaos in the face of the "twin evils" of warlord uprisings and foreign imperialism.

The Warlord Problem In 1912, Sun Yixian stepped down as president in favor of Yuan Shikai (yoo AHN shih KY), a powerful general. Sun hoped that Yuan would create a strong central government, but instead, the ambitious general tried to set up a new dynasty. The military, however, did not support Yuan, and opposition divided the nation. When Yuan died in 1916, China plunged into still greater disorder.

In the provinces, local warlords seized power. As rival armies battled for control, the economy collapsed and millions of peasants suffered terrible hardships. Famine and attacks by bandits added to their misery.

Reading Skill: Sequence Use a chart like the one below to sequence the fighting that went on among the Guomindang, the warlords, the Chinese Communists, and the Japanese from 1921 through 1937.

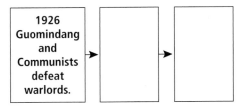

Vocabulary Builder

intellectual—(in teh LEK choo ul) *adj.* involving the ability to reason or think clearly

Foreign Imperialism During this period of upheaval, foreign powers increased their influence over Chinese affairs. Foreign merchants, missionaries, and soldiers dominated the ports China had opened to trade.

During World War I, Japanese officials presented Yuan Shikai with the **Twenty-One Demands,** a list of demands that sought to make China a Japanese protectorate. With China too weak to resist, Yuan gave in to some of the demands. Then, in 1919, at the Paris Peace Conference, the Allies gave Japan control over some former German possessions in China. That news infuriated Chinese Nationalists.

May Fourth Movement In response, student protests erupted in Beijing on May 4, 1919, and later spread to cities across China. The protests set off a cultural and <u>intellectual</u> ferment known as the **May Fourth Movement.** Its goal was to strengthen China. Reformers sought to improve China's position by rejecting Confucian traditions and learning from the West. As in Meiji Japan, they hoped to use their new knowledge to end foreign domination.

Women played a key role in the May Fourth Movement. They joined marches and campaigned to end a number of traditional practices, including footbinding. Their work helped open doors for women in education and the economy.

The Appeal of Marxism Some Chinese turned to the revolutionary ideas of Marx and Lenin. The Soviet Union was more than willing to train Chinese students and military officers to become the **vanguard,** or elite leaders, of a communist revolution. By the 1920s, a small group of Chinese Communists had formed their own political party.

✔ **Checkpoint** How did warlord uprisings and foreign imperialism lead to the May Fourth movement?

Struggle for a New China

In 1921, Sun Yixian and his **Guomindang** (gwoh meen DAWNG) or Nationalist party, established a government in south China. Sun planned to raise an army, defeat the warlords, and spread his government's rule over all of China. When Western democracies refused to help, Sun accepted aid from the Soviet Union and joined forces with the small group of Chinese Communists. However, he still believed that China's future should be based on his Three Principles of the People.

Jiang Jieshi, Leader of the Guomindang
Jiang Jieshi headed the Guomindang (Nationalist) government in China from the late 1920s until 1949.

Jiang Jieshi Leads the Nationalists After Sun's death in 1925, an energetic young army officer, Jiang Jieshi (jahng jeh shur), took over the Guomindang. Jiang Jieshi (also called Chiang Kai-Shek) was determined to smash the power of the warlords and reunite China, but he had little interest in either democracy or communism.

In 1926, Jiang Jieshi began the Northern Expedition in cooperation with the Chinese Communists. In the Northern Expedition, Jiang led the combined forces into northern China, crushing or winning over local warlords as he advanced and capturing Beijing. Jiang would go on to take control of a new government led by the Guomindang—without the Communists.

Who Should Lead the New China?

The excerpts below present the views of China's two most influential leaders on who should direct the future of China. **Critical Thinking** *Who does each person think should lead China?*

One Strong Leader	Peasant Masses
The most important point of fascism is absolute trust in a sagely able leader. Aside from complete trust in one person, there is no other leader or ism. Therefore, with the organization, although there are cadre, council members, and executives, there is no conflict among them, there is only the trust in the one leader. The leader has final decision in all matters. —Jiang Jieshi, 1933	The broad peasant masses have risen to fulfill their historic mission . . . the democratic forces in the rural areas have risen to overthrow the rural feudal power. . . . To overthrow this feudal power is the real objective of the national revolution. What Dr. Sun Yat-sen [Yixian] wanted to do . . . but failed to accomplish, the peasants have accomplished in a few months. —Mao Zedong, 1927

In mid-campaign, Jiang seized the chance to strike at the Chinese Communist Party, which he saw as a threat to his power. The Communists were winning converts among the small proletariat in cities like Shanghai. Early in 1927, on orders from Jiang, Guomindang troops slaughtered Communist Party members and the workers who supported them. In Shanghai and elsewhere, thousands of people were killed. This massacre marked the beginning of a bitter civil war between the Communists and the Guomindang that lasted for 22 years.

Mao Zedong and the Communists Among the Communists who escaped Jiang's attack was a young revolutionary of peasant origins, Mao Zedong (mow dzuh doong) (also called Mao Tse-tung). Unlike earlier Chinese Communists, Mao believed that the Communists should seek support not among the small urban working class but among the large peasant masses.

Although the Communists were pursued at every turn by Guomindang forces, Mao was optimistic about eventual success. In southeastern China, Mao and the Communists redistributed land to peasants and promised other reforms.

The Long March Jiang Jieshi, however, was determined to destroy the "Red bandits," as he called the Communists. He led the Guomindang in a series of "extermination campaigns" against them. The Guomindang harassed Mao's retreating army throughout the **Long March** from 1934 to 1935. Mao's forces used guerrilla, or irregular hit-and-run, tactics to fight back. At the end of the Long March, the Communists set up a new base in a remote region of northern China. There, Mao rebuilt his forces and plotted new strategies for fighting the Guomindang.

During the march, the Communists enforced strict discipline. Soldiers were told to treat peasants politely, pay for goods they wanted, and avoid damaging crops. Such behavior made Mao's forces welcome among peasants, many of whom had suffered greatly at the hands of the Guomindang.

Mao Zedong, Leader of the Communists
Mao Zedong led the Chinese Communists through some of their darkest times, including the Long March.

✓ **Checkpoint** How did the Communists manage to survive Jiang's "extermination campaigns"?

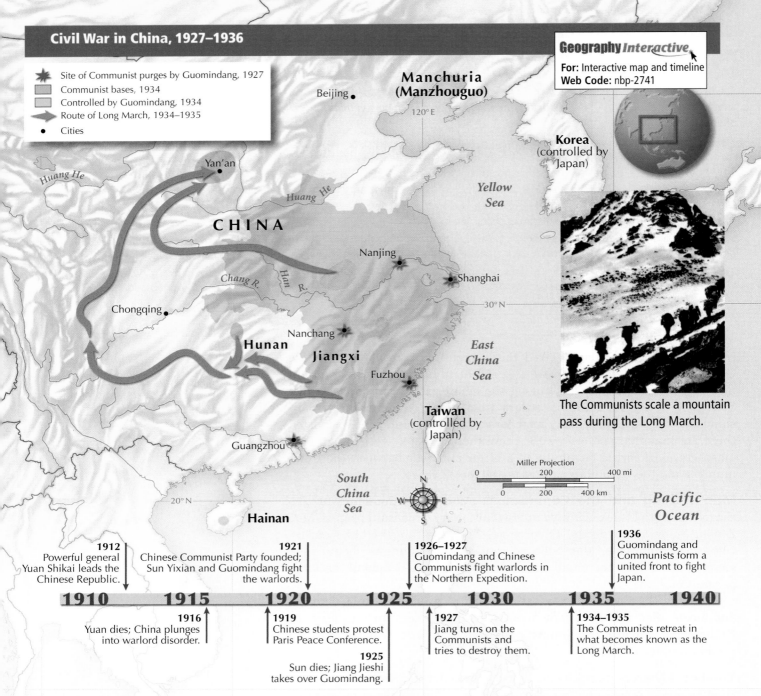

Civil War in China, 1927–1936

* Site of Communist purges by Guomindang, 1927
■ Communist bases, 1934
□ Controlled by Guomindang, 1934
➤ Route of Long March, 1934–1935
• Cities

Geography *Interactive*

For: Interactive map and timeline
Web Code: nbp-2741

Manchuria (Manzhouguo)

Beijing

120° E

Korea (controlled by Japan)

Huang He

Yan'an

CHINA

Huang He

Yellow Sea

Nanjing

Shanghai

30° N

Chang R.

Han R.

Chongqing

Nanchang

East China Sea

Hunan

Jiangxi

Fuzhou

Taiwan (controlled by Japan)

Guangzhou

Miller Projection

0   200   400 mi

0   200   400 km

South China Sea

Pacific Ocean

20° N

Hainan

The Communists scale a mountain pass during the Long March.

1912 Powerful general Yuan Shikai leads the Chinese Republic.

1921 Chinese Communist Party founded; Sun Yixian and Guomindang fight the warlords.

1926–1927 Guomindang and Chinese Communists fight warlords in the Northern Expedition.

1936 Guomindang and Communists form a united front to fight Japan.

1910   1915   1920   1925   1930   1935   1940

1916 Yuan dies; China plunges into warlord disorder.

1919 Chinese students protest Paris Peace Conference.

1925 Sun dies; Jiang Jieshi takes over Guomindang.

1927 Jiang turns on the Communists and tries to destroy them.

1934–1935 The Communists retreat in what becomes known as the Long March.

Map Skills The Guomindang and the Communists waged a long and bitter war for control of China.

1. **Locate:** (a) Beijing (b) Shanghai (c) Jiangxi (d) Yan'an
2. **Movement** What natural features made the Long March difficult?
3. **Synthesize Information** Based on the map and timeline, describe the relationship between the Guomindang and the Communists.

One of the most dramatic events in the conflict between the Guomindang and the Communists was the epic retreat known as the Long March. During the Long March, Mao and about 100,000 of his followers fled the Guomindang. In the next year, they trekked more than 6,000 miles, facing daily attacks as they crossed rugged mountains and mighty rivers. Only about 8,000 marchers survived the ordeal. For decades, the Long March stood as a symbol of communist heroism and inspired new recruits to follow Mao. He claimed the great retreat as a victory. As he observed:

Primary Source

66 The Long March is also a seeding-machine. It has sown many seeds in eleven provinces, which will sprout, grow leaves, blossom into flowers, bear fruit, and yield a crop. 99
—Mao Zedong, "On the Tactics of Fighting Japanese Imperialism"

Japanese Invasion

While Jiang was pursuing the Communists across China, the country faced another danger. In 1931, Japan invaded Manchuria in northeastern China, adding it to the growing Japanese empire. As Japanese aggression increased, a <u>faction</u> within the Guomindang forced Jiang to form a united front with the Communists against Japan.

In 1937, the Japanese struck again, starting what became the Second Sino-Japanese War. Airplanes bombed Chinese cities, and Japanese troops overran eastern China, including Beijing and Guangzhou. Jiang Jieshi and his government retreated to the interior and set up a new capital at Chongqing (chawng CHING).

After a lengthy siege, Japanese troops marched into the city of Nanjing (nahn jing) on December 13. Nanjing was an important cultural center and had been the Guomindang capital before Chongqing. After the city's surrender, the Japanese killed hundreds of thousands of soldiers and civilians and brutalized still more. The cruelty and destruction became known around the world as the "rape of Nanjing."

The united Chinese fought back against the Japanese. The Soviet Union sent advisors and equipment to help. Great Britain, France, and the United States gave economic aid. The Guomindang and the Communists still clashed occasionally, but the united front stayed intact until the end of the war with Japan.

Vocabulary Builder

<u>faction</u>—(FAK shun) *n.* a group within a larger group

✔ **Checkpoint**   How did the Japanese invasion help unify the Chinese temporarily?

Looking Ahead

The bombing of Pearl Harbor in 1941 brought the United States into the war against Japan and into an alliance with the Chinese. By the end of World War II, Jiang and the Guomindang controlled China's central government, but Mao's Communist Party controlled much of northern and central China. The Communists had organized hundreds of thousands of Chinese peasants at the village level, spreading their political ideas. Meanwhile, corruption grew in Jiang's government. Soon, the Communists would triumph, and Mao would impose revolutionary change on China.

SECTION 4 Assessment

Progress Monitoring *Online*
For: Self-quiz with vocabulary practice
Web Code: nba-2741

Terms, People, and Places

1. What do many of the key terms listed at the beginning of the section have in common? Explain.

Note Taking

2. **Reading Skill: Recognize Multiple Causes** Use your completed charts to answer the Focus Question: How did China cope with internal division and foreign invasion in the early 1900s?

Comprehension and Critical Thinking

3. **Identify Central Issues** Why did the new republic of China fall into chaos after 1912?
4. **Identify Point of View** Do you think that the retreating Communists' policy to pay for goods they wanted during the Long March was a good idea? Why or why not?
5. **Predict Consequences** How do you think the "rape of Nanjing" affected Japan's reputation around the world?

● Writing About History

Quick Write: Answer Opposing Arguments Every persuasive essay should present arguments that support the thesis *and* refute arguments that oppose the thesis. Your thesis for a persuasive essay is "The Long March ultimately helped the Chinese Communists' cause." Think of the strongest argument against this thesis, and then write a paragraph to refute that argument.

Japanese soldiers occupying a Chinese city in 1938

Japan in the Midst of Change

Groups with conflicting ideologies fought for control of Japan in the 1930s.

66 Look straight at the present state of your father-land, Japan! Where, we dare ask, can you find the genuine manifestation of the godliness of the Imperial Country of Japan? Political parties are blind in their pursuit of power and egoistic gains. Large enterprises are firmly in collusion with politicians as they suck the sweat and blood of the common people . . . Diplomacy is weak-kneed. Education is rotten to the core. Now is the time to carry out drastic, revolutionary change. Rise, and take action now! 99
—A Japanese ultranationalist criticizing the government, 1932

Focus Question How did Japan change in the 1920s and 1930s?

Conflicting Forces in Japan

Objectives
- Explain the effects of liberal changes in Japan during the 1920s.
- Analyze how nationalists reacted to Japan's problems during the Great Depression.
- Describe how the militarists used their power in the 1930s.

Terms, People, and Places
Hirohito
ultranationalist
Manchuria

Note Taking

Reading Skill: Understand Effects As you read this section, fill in the effects of two opposing outlooks in Japan in the 1920s and 1930s in a table like the one below.

Conflicting Forces in Japan	
Liberalism in the 1920s	Militarism in the 1930s
•	•
•	•
•	•

Solemn ceremonies marked the start of Emperor Hirohito's reign. In the Secret Purple Hall, the new emperor sat on the ancient throne of Japan. Beside him was his wife, the empress Nagako. Calling on the spirits of his ancestors, he pledged "to preserve world peace and benefit the welfare of the human race."

In fact, **Hirohito** reigned from 1926 to 1989—an astonishing 63 years. During those decades, Japan experienced remarkable successes and appalling tragedies. In this section, we will focus on the 1920s and 1930s, when the pressures of extreme nationalism and economic upheaval set Japan on a militaristic and expansionist path that would engulf all of Asia.

Japan on the Rise in the 1920s

In the 1920s, Japan moved toward greater prosperity and democracy. To strengthen its relationship with other countries, Japan drew back from some of its imperial goals in the 1920s. The country grew in international prestige. However, conflicts lurked beneath the surface. The economic crisis of the Great Depression in the 1930s would bring them to light.

Growth and Expansion After World War I During World War I, the Japanese economy enjoyed remarkable growth. Its exports to Allied nations soared. Heavy industrial production grew, making Japan a true industrial power.

While Western powers battled in Europe, Japan expanded its influence throughout East Asia. Japan had already annexed Korea as a colony in 1910. During the war, Japan also sought further rights in China with the Twenty-One Demands. After the war, Japan took over former German possessions in East Asia, including the Shandong province in China.

Liberal Changes in the 1920s During the 1920s, Japan moved toward more widespread democracy. Political parties grew stronger. Elected members of the Diet—the Japanese parliament—exercised their power. In 1925, all adult men, regardless of class, won the right to vote. In addition, Western ideas about women's rights brought some changes. Overall, however, the status of Japanese women remained below that of men. They would not win suffrage, or the right to vote, until 1945.

Despite leaning toward greater democracy, political parties were manipulated by the zaibatsu (zy baht soo), Japan's powerful business leaders. The zaibatsu influenced the government through donations to political parties. They pushed for policies that favored international trade and their own interests.

Japan's aggressive expansion began to affect its economic relationship with the Western powers. To protect relations, moderate Japanese politicians decided to slow down foreign expansion. In 1922, Japan signed an agreement to limit the size of its navy with the United States, Britain, and France. It also agreed to leave Shandong. The government reduced military spending.

Problems Below the Surface Behind this well-being, Japan faced some grave problems. Rural peasants did not share in the nation's prosperity. They were still very poor. In the cities, factory workers earned low wages. Their poverty drew them to the socialist ideas of Marx and Lenin.

In the cities, members of the younger generation were also in revolt against tradition. They adopted Western fads and fashions. Also, they rejected family authority for the Western ideal of individual freedom, shocking their elders.

During the 1920s, tensions between the government and the military simmered not far below the surface. Conservatives, especially military officers, blasted government corruption, including payoffs by powerful zaibatsu. They also condemned Western influences for undermining basic Japanese values of obedience and respect for authority.

Although the economy grew throughout the 1920s, it experienced many highs and lows. One low point occurred when a devastating earthquake, one of the most destructive quakes in history, struck the Tokyo area in 1923. The earthquake and the widespread fires it caused resulted in the deaths of over 100,000 people and damaged more than 650,000 buildings. As many as 45 percent of surviving workers lost their jobs because so many businesses were destroyed. With help from the government, the Tokyo area gradually recovered—just as Japan faced a worldwide economic crisis.

Vocabulary Builder

manipulated—(muh NIP yoo layt id) vt. influenced skillfully, often unfairly

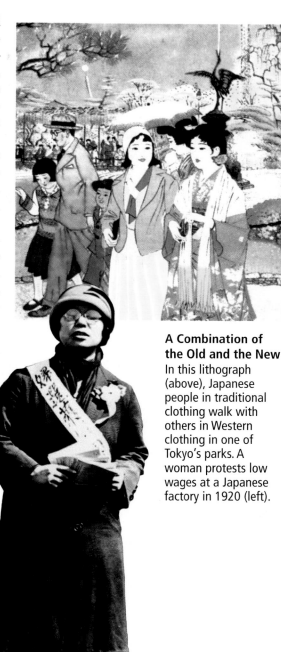

A Combination of the Old and the New In this lithograph (above), Japanese people in traditional clothing walk with others in Western clothing in one of Tokyo's parks. A woman protests low wages at a Japanese factory in 1920 (left).

✔ **Checkpoint** How did democratic participation in Japan both grow and stagnate in the 1920s?

Geography *Interactive*
For: Audio guided tour
Web Code: nbp-2751

Miller Projection
0   200   400 mi
0   200   400 km

SOVIET UNION

MONGOLIA

Manchuria
(Manzhouguo)

Vladivostok

Beijing

Port
Arthur   **Korea**

Yellow
Sea

CHINA

Shanghai

Sakhalin

50° N

Sea of
Japan

40° N

Tokyo

Osaka

JAPAN

30° N

East
China
Sea

Pacific
Ocean

Taiwan

20° N

Hong Kong
(Britain)

140° E

South
China
Sea

PHILIPPINES

10° N

120° E   130° E

	Japan, 1890
	Territory added by 1918
	Territory added by 1934
	Main manufacturing areas
	Bauxite
	Coal
	Copper
	Gold
	Iron ore
	Petroleum

Map Skills Japan expanded its territory in Asia between 1918 and 1934. From their conquered lands, the Japanese acquired natural resources to fuel their industries.

1. **Locate:** (a) Japan (b) Korea (c) Manchuria (d) Taiwan
2. **Region** Where were Japan's main manufacturing areas located?
3. **Draw Conclusions** What natural resource does Korea lack but Manchuria have?

The Nationalist Reaction

In 1929, the Great Depression rippled across the Pacific, striking Japan with devastating force. Trade suffered as foreign buyers could no longer afford to purchase Japanese silks and other exports. Unemployment in the cities soared, while rural peasants were only a mouthful from starvation.

Unrest Grows Economic disaster fed the discontent of the leading military officials and extreme nationalists, or **ultranationalists.** They condemned politicians for agreeing to Western demands to stop overseas expansion. Western industrial powers, they pointed out, had long ago grabbed huge empires. By comparison, Japan's empire was tiny.

Japanese nationalists were further outraged by racial policies in the United States, Canada, and Australia that shut out Japanese immigrants. The Japanese took great pride in their industrial achievements. They bitterly resented being treated as second-class citizens in other parts of the world.

As the economic crisis worsened, nationalists demanded renewed expansion. An empire in Asia, they argued, would provide much-needed raw materials as well as an outlet for Japan's rapidly growing population. They set their sights on the northern Chinese province of **Manchuria.** This region was rich in natural resources, and Japanese businesses had already invested heavily there.

The Manchurian Incident In 1931, a group of Japanese army officers provoked an incident that provided an excuse to seize Manchuria. They set explosives and blew up tracks on a Japanese-owned railroad line. Then, they claimed that the Chinese had committed the act. Claiming self-defense, the army attacked Chinese forces. Without consulting their own government, the Japanese military forces conquered all of Manchuria and set up a puppet state there that they called Manzhouguo (man choo KWOO). They brought in Puyi, the last Chinese emperor, to head the puppet state. When politicians in Tokyo objected to the army's highhanded actions, public opinion sided with the military.

When the League of Nations condemned Japanese aggression against China, Japan simply withdrew itself from the League. Soon, the Japanese government nullified the agreements limiting naval armament that it had signed with the Western democracies in the 1920s. The League's member states failed to take military action against Japanese aggression.

 Checkpoint How did the Great Depression lead to calls for renewed expansion?

Militarists in Power

In the early 1930s, ultranationalists were winning support from the people for foreign conquests and a tough stand against the Western powers. Members of extreme nationalist societies assassinated a number of politicians and business leaders who opposed expansion. Military leaders plotted to overthrow the government and, in 1936, briefly occupied the center of Tokyo.

Traditional Values Revived Civilian government survived, but the unrest forced the government to accept military domination in 1937. To please the ultranationalists, the government cracked down on socialists and suppressed most democratic freedoms. It revived ancient warrior values and built a cult around Emperor Hirohito, whom many believed was descended from the sun goddess. To spread its nationalist message, the government used schools to teach students absolute obedience to the emperor and service to the state.

More Expansion in China During the 1930s, Japan took advantage of China's civil war to increase its influence there. Japan expected to complete its conquest of China within a few years. But in 1939, while the two nations were locked in deadly combat, World War II broke out in Europe. That conflict swiftly spread to Asia.

In 1936, Japan allied with two aggressive European powers, Germany and Italy. These three powers signed the Tripartite Pact in September 1940, cementing the alliance known as the Axis Powers. That alliance, combined with renewed Japanese conquests, would turn World War II into a brutal, wide-ranging conflict waged not only across the continent of Europe but across Asia and the islands of the Pacific as well.

✔ **Checkpoint** What changes did militarists make when they came to power?

● **BIOGRAPHY**

Hirohito
Hirohito (1901–1989) became emperor of Japan in 1926. As emperor, according to Japanese tradition, he was the nation's supreme authority and a living god—no one could look at his face or even mention his name. In practice, however, he merely approved the policies that his ministers formulated.

Hirohito was a private man who preferred marine biology to power politics. As a result, his role in Japan's move toward aggression is unclear. Some historians believe that Hirohito did not encourage Japanese military leaders. Others assert that he was actively involved in expansionist policies. **Why was Hirohito given great respect?**

SECTION 5 Assessment

● **Progress Monitoring Online**
For: Self-quiz with vocabulary practice
Web Code: nba-2751

Terms, People, and Places

1. For each term, person, or place listed at the beginning of the section, write a sentence explaining its significance.

Note Taking

2. **Reading Skill: Understand Effects** Use your completed chart to answer the Focus Question: How did Japan change in the 1920s and 1930s?

Comprehension and Critical Thinking

3. **Summarize** What changes occurred in Japan in the 1920s?

4. **Recognize Effects** How did nationalists respond to the Great Depression?

5. **Geography and History** What role did geography play in Japan's desire to expand its empire?

6. **Predict Consequences** Why might a nation turn to military leaders and extreme nationalists during a crisis?

● **Writing About History**

Quick Write: Decide on an Organizational Strategy Most persuasive essays follow this organization:
 I. Introduction, including thesis statement
 II. Second-strongest argument
 III. Answer to opposing arguments
 IV. Strongest argument
 V. Conclusion
Write a thesis statement based on the content of this section, and write an outline showing how you would organize your arguments.

Quick Study Guide

> **Progress Monitoring *Online***
> For: Self-test with vocabulary practice
> **Web Code:** nba-2761

■ Nationalism Around the World 1910–1939

Location	Goals	Expression
Mexico	To reject foreign influence	Nationalizing foreign companies; emphasizing Latin American culture
Africa	To fight for rights under colonial system	Organizing resistance, including protests, boycotts, strikes, squatting; founding of associations and political parties
Turkey and Persia	To strengthen countries by modernizing and westernizing	Secularizing daily life; adopting Western ways; building industry
The Middle East	To create a Pan-Arab state	Resisting mandate system; ongoing friction between Jewish settlers and Palestinians
India	To gain independence from British	Protesting British rule using nonviolent methods, under Gandhi's leadership
China	To lessen foreign domination of China	Resisting Japanese encroachment; attempting to strengthen China
Japan	To build an empire	Issuing the Twenty-One Demands; invading China multiple times

■ Key Leaders

Emiliano Zapata—Mexican land reformer
Venustiano Carranza—conservative Mexican president
Atatürk—father of modern Turkey
Reza Khan—modernizing Shah of Persia
Gandhi—Congress Party leader (led self-rule protest movement)
Jiang Jieshi—leader of Guomindang (Chinese Nationalists)
Mao Zedong—leader of Chinese Communist Party

■ Effects of World War I on World Events

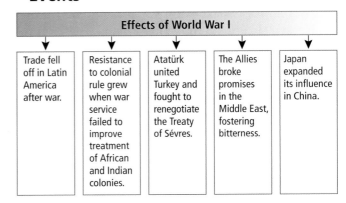

Effects of World War I				
Trade fell off in Latin America after war.	Resistance to colonial rule grew when war service failed to improve treatment of African and Indian colonies.	Atatürk united Turkey and fought to renegotiate the Treaty of Sévres.	The Allies broke promises in the Middle East, fostering bitterness.	Japan expanded its influence in China.

■ Key Events in Latin America, Africa, and Asia

Latin America and Africa

Asia

1910 Mexican Revolution begins.

1912 Black South Africans form a political party, which later becomes the African National Congress (ANC).

1917 A new Mexican constitution is passed, but fighting continues.

1910 — **1915** — **1920**

1911 Sun Yixian and the Guomindang establish the Republic of China.

1923 Atatürk founds modern Turkey.

Concept Connector

Cumulative Review

Record the answers to the questions below on your Concept Connector worksheets.

1. **Conflict** The Chinese Communists and the Guomindang (Nationalists) battled each other off and on for control of China from the 1920s through the 1940s. The Communists ultimately triumphed. Compare this conflict to the Russian Revolution of 1917. Consider the following:
   - causes
   - nature and duration of fighting
   - role of foreign interference
   - role of communist ideology
   - effect on economy and daily life

2. **Nationalism** Compare Pan-Arab nationalism in the Middle East to Pan-Slav nationalism in the Balkans. How were the aims, goals, and results of the two movements similar? How did they differ? Answer these questions in an essay.

3. **Nationalism** By the early 1900s, Japan was an industrial power and wanted to build an empire similar to those of other industrialized powers. Throughout the 1800s, the United States had expanded its hold on North America, while several European nations had built large empires. However, these nations sought to limit Japanese expansion. Read more about expansion in Japan, the United States, and Britain, and create a chart comparing the three countries. Include the following in your chart:
   - reasons for expansion
   - expansionist goals
   - international reaction to expansion

Connections to Today

1. **Conflict: The Zapatista Army of National Liberation** Although Emiliano Zapata was assassinated in 1919, the spirit of his movement has lived on. In the early 1990s, poverty-stricken Indian peasants in the southern state of Chiapas formed a revolutionary group named the Zapatista Army of National Liberation, after Zapata. Conduct research on the issues behind the Zapatista movement, and then create a chart comparing issues from the Mexican Revolution era to those of the Zapatistas today.

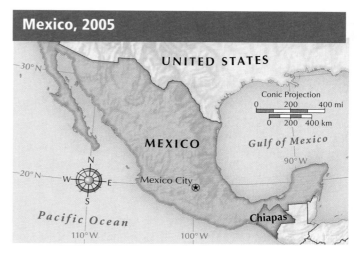

Mexico, 2005

2. **Conflict: Soweto, Then and Now** Soweto, a poor suburb of Johannesburg, South Africa, was a harsh symbol of apartheid. Soweto has changed since apartheid began to end in 1990, but poverty is still widespread. Conduct research and write two paragraphs about life in Soweto today.

1929
Ibo women protest British policies in Nigeria.

1938
Mexico nationalizes foreign-owned oil companies.

History Interactive
For: Interactive timeline
Web Code: nbp-2762

1925

1930

1935

1940

1925
Jiang Jieshi becomes the leader of the Guomindang in China.

1930
Thousands of Indians join Gandhi in the Salt March.

1937
The Japanese army captures Nanjing.

Chapter Assessment

Terms, People, and Places

1. Define **economic nationalism.** How did this movement bring change to Latin America in the early 1900s?
2. What was the **Balfour Declaration**? Did it further or hinder the aims of **Pan-Arabism**? Explain.
3. Define **ahimsa** and **civil disobedience**. How did Gandhi use both in his campaign for self-rule in India?
4. What were the **Twenty-One Demands**? How were they an example of foreign imperialism in China?
5. Define **Manchuria** and **ultranationalist**. Describe how what happened in Manchuria was a result of ultranationalist aims in Japan.

Main Ideas

Section 1 (pp. 490–494)
6. What caused the Mexican Revolution?
7. How did nationalism affect Latin America in the early 1900s?

Section 2 (pp. 496–502)
8. How did African nationalism grow in the early 1900s?
9. What changes took place in the Middle East?

Section 3 (pp. 503–505)
10. How did Mohandas Gandhi help Indians work to gain self-rule?

Section 4 (pp. 507–511)
11. Describe the two phases of civil war in China.
12. How did Japan interfere in China in the 1930s?

Section 5 (pp. 512–515)
13. Describe how ultranationalists in Japan sought to solve Japan's economic problems during the Great Depression.

Chapter Focus Question
14. How did nationalism and the desire for change shape world events in the early 1900s?

Critical Thinking

15. **Draw Conclusions** How did the Good Neighbor Policy change the relationship between the United States and Latin America?
16. **Draw Inferences** How did Pan-Africanism affect people around the world?
17. **Recognize Cause and Effect** How did World War I affect relations between India and Britain?

18. **Analyzing Visuals** In the photo above, Mexican *soldaderas* stand with some male soldiers. How does this image embody some of the goals of the Mexican Revolution?
19. **Identify Central Issues** What three-sided struggle took place in China from 1937 to 1945?
20. **Predict Consequences** How were liberal changes in 1920s Japan reversed by ultranationalists in the 1930s?

● Writing About History

Writing a Persuasive Essay In this chapter, you learned about how people in many different regions of the world struggled to change their lives in the early 1900s. Pick a major issue from one of these regions, choose a stance on it, and then write an essay that persuades the reader to believe in your point of view.

Prewriting
- Choose a topic that provokes a valid argument, not a topic on which most people would agree or disagree.
- Gather information about your topic to help you generate arguments.

Drafting
- Develop a thesis and arguments that support your position.
- Use an organizational structure to help build your argument.
- Write an introduction outlining your position and arguments on the topic, a body, and a conclusion.

Revising
- As you review your essay, look for and eliminate weak logic.
- Use the guidelines for revising your essay on page SH17 of the Writing Handbook.

Document-Based Assessment

A Fistful of Salt

Mohandas Gandhi's campaign of nonviolent resistance was a potent weapon in the Indian struggle for independence from Britain. The documents below describe one hard-fought battle: the Salt March of 1930.

Document A

"Wherever possible, civil disobedience of the salt laws should be started. These laws can be violated in three ways. It is an offense to manufacture salt wherever there are facilities for doing so. The possession and sale of contraband salt, which includes natural salt or salt earth, [is] also an offense. The purchasers of such salt will be equally guilty. To carry away the natural salt deposits on the seashore is likewise violation of the law. So is the hawking of such salt. In short, you may choose any one or all of these devices to break the salt monopoly."

—Gandhi on the Salt March

Document B

"The Salt Satyagraha started with a dramatic long march by Gandhi and a group of picked companions from Sabarmati to the coast at Dandi, 240 miles away, where he proceeded to make salt illegally by boiling sea water. The march was a publicity enterprise of great power as the press followed the party's progress . . . As he journeyed . . ., deliberately challenging established authority, village headmen began to resign in large numbers . . . in April, [India's Viceroy, Lord] Irwin reported to London that in Gujarat 'the personal influence of Gandhi threatens to create a position of real embarrassment to the administration . . . as in some areas he has already achieved a considerable measure of success in undermining the authority of Government.'"

—From ***Modern India: The Origins of Asian Democracy***
by Judith M. Brown

Document C

"Suddenly, at a word of command, scores of native policemen rushed upon the advancing marchers and rained blows on their heads with their steel-shod *lathis*. Not one of the marchers even raised an arm to fend off the blows. They went down like ten-pins. . . . The survivors, without breaking ranks, silently and doggedly marched on until struck down."

—Webb Miller, a British journalist reporting on a march to the salt deposits at Dharsana

Document D

Gandhi picking up salt at the coastal village of Dandi in India, April 6, 1930

Analyzing Documents

Use your knowledge of India's struggle for self-rule and Documents A, B, C, and D to answer questions 1–4.

1. In Document A, Gandhi was mainly addressing
   A British authorities.
   B journalists around the world.
   C the British people.
   D the Indian people.

2. In Document B, the historian describes the effect of the Salt March on
   A the supply of salt.
   B the authority of the British government.
   C protesters in other countries.
   D Gandhi's health.

3. Which words from Document C reflect the attitude of the reporter toward the marchers?
   A suddenly, command
   B steel-shod *lathis*, ten-pins
   C fend, blows
   D silently, doggedly

4. **Writing Task** How was the Salt March a turning point in India's struggle for independence? Use what you have learned from these documents and the chapter in your response.

Nazi Germany

Martin Niemöller, a Lutheran minister, preached against ruthless Nazi policies and was ultimately jailed. He later observed:

❝[The Nazis] came first for the Communists, and I didn't speak up because I wasn't a Communist. Then they came for the Jews, and I didn't speak up because I wasn't a Jew. Then they came for the Catholics, and I didn't speak up because I was a Protestant. Then they came for me, and by that time there was no one left to speak up.**❞**
—Martin Niemöller, quoted in *Time* magazine

Listen to the Witness History audio to learn more about totalitarian states in Europe.

◀ **Adolf Hitler surrounded by supporters at a Nazi party rally in 1934**

A toy replica of a Nazi storm trooper

Chapter Preview

Chapter Focus Question What political and economic challenges did the Western world face in the 1920s and 1930s, and how did various countries react to these challenges?

A magazine cover showing a Jazz Age flapper

A mug shot from a Soviet secret police file

Notetaking Study Guide *Online*
For: Notetaking and Concept Connector worksheets
Web Code: nbd-2801

Jazz musician
Louis Armstrong

WITNESS HISTORY 🔊 AUDIO

The Jazz Age

Many young people reacted to the trauma of World War I by rejecting the values of their parents. During the Jazz Age, this rebellion was exemplified by a new type of young woman—the flapper.

❝ The Flapper awoke from her lethargy [tiredness] . . . bobbed her hair, put on her choicest pair of earrings and a great deal of audacity [boldness] and rouge, and went into the battle. She flirted because it was fun to flirt and . . . refused to be bored chiefly because she wasn't boring. . . . Mothers disapproved of their sons taking the Flapper to dances, to teas, to swim, and most of all to heart. ❞
—Zelda Fitzgerald, flapper and wife of author F. Scott Fitzgerald

Focus Question What changes did Western society and culture experience after World War I?

Postwar Social Changes

Objectives

- Analyze how Western society changed after World War I.
- Describe the literary and artistic trends that emerged in the 1920s.
- List several advances in modern scientific thought.

Terms, People, and Places

flapper   psychoanalysis
Prohibition   abstract
speakeasies   dada
Harlem Renaissance   surrealism

Note Taking

Reading Skill: Identify Supporting Details Use a concept web like the one below to record details related to the main ideas of this section.

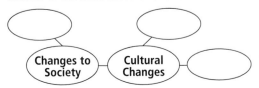

Changes to Society   Cultural Changes

The catastrophe of World War I shattered the sense of optimism that had grown in the West since the Enlightenment. Despair gripped survivors on both sides as they added up the staggering costs of the war. It seemed as though a whole generation of young men had been lost on the battlefields. In reaction, the society and culture of Europe, the United States, and many other parts of the world experienced rapid changes.

Changes in Society After World War I

During the 1920s, new technologies helped create a mass culture shared by millions in the world's developed countries. Affordable cars, improved telephones, and new forms of media such as motion pictures and radio brought people around the world closer together than ever before.

The Roaring Twenties In the 1920s, many radios tuned into the new sounds of jazz. In fact, the 1920s are often called the Jazz Age. African American musicians combined Western harmonies with African rhythms to create jazz. Jazz musicians, like trumpeter Louis Armstrong and pianist Duke Ellington, took simple melodies and improvised endless subtle variations in rhythm and beat. They produced original music, and people loved it. Much of today's popular music has been influenced by jazz.

While Europe recovered from the war, the United States experienced a boom time. Europeans embraced American popular culture, with its greater freedom and willingness to experiment. The nightclub and the sounds of jazz were symbols of that freedom.

After the war, rebellious young people, disillusioned by the war, rejected the moral values and rules of the Victorian Age and chased after excitement. One symbol of rebellious Jazz Age youth was the liberated young woman called the **flapper.** The first flappers were American, but their European sisters soon adopted the fashion. Flappers rejected old ways in favor of new, exciting freedom.

Women's Lives

Flappers were highly visible, but they were a small minority. Most women saw limited progress in the postwar period. During the war, women had held a wide range of jobs. Although most women left those jobs when the war ended, their war work helped them win the vote in many Western countries. A few women were elected to public office, such as Texas governor Miriam Ferguson or Lady Nancy Astor, the first woman to serve in the British Parliament.

By the 1920s, labor-saving devices had become common in middle-class homes. Washing machines, vacuum cleaners, and canned foods lightened the burden of household chores. Some women then sought work outside the home or did volunteer work to help the less fortunate.

In the new atmosphere of <u>emancipation</u>, women pursued careers in many areas—from sports to the arts. Women golfers, tennis players, swimmers, and pilots set new records. Women worked as newspaper reporters, published bestselling novels, and won recognition as artists. Most professions, though, were still dominated by men.

Reactions to the Jazz Age

Not everyone approved of the freewheeling lifestyle of the Jazz Age. For example, many Americans supported **Prohibition,** a ban on the manufacture and sale of alcoholic beverages. For almost 90 years, social activists had waged an intense campaign against the abuse of alcohol. Finally, they gained enough support to get the Eighteenth, or Prohibition, Amendment ratified in 1919. Prohibition was meant to keep people from the negative effects of drinking. Instead, it caused an explosion of organized crime and **speakeasies,** or illegal bars. The Amendment was repealed in 1933.

In the United States in the early 1900s, a Christian fundamentalist movement swept rural areas. Fundamentalists support traditional Christian ideas about Jesus and believe that all of the events described in the Bible are literally true. Popular fundamentalist preachers traveled around the country holding inspirational revival meetings. Some used the new technology of radio to spread their message.

In 1925, a biology teacher in Tennessee named John T. Scopes was tried for teaching evolution in his classroom. His action broke a law that barred any teaching that went against the Bible's version of creation. The teacher was found guilty in the well-publicized Scopes trial, but many fundamentalists believed that the proceedings had hurt their cause.

✔ **Checkpoint** Describe the Jazz Age and some of the reactions to it.

Vocabulary Builder

<u>emancipation</u>—(ee man suh PAY shun) *n.* freedom from restrictions

Life Under Prohibition

A well-dressed couple waits to enter an illicit speakeasy (below right). Members of the United States Prohibition Service wore badges (below left) when they raided speakeasies and breweries and fought bootleggers such as Al Capone. *What does the clothing the couple is wearing tell you about who could afford to go to speakeasies?*

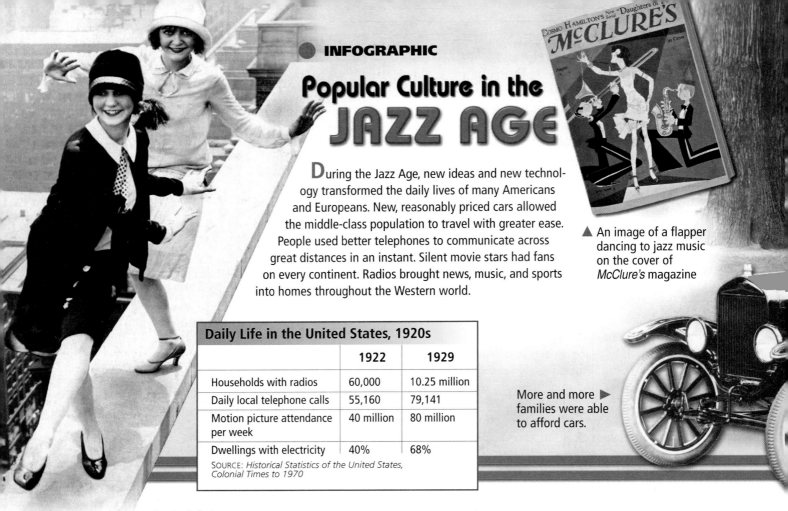

Popular Culture in the JAZZ AGE

During the Jazz Age, new ideas and new technology transformed the daily lives of many Americans and Europeans. New, reasonably priced cars allowed the middle-class population to travel with greater ease. People used better telephones to communicate across great distances in an instant. Silent movie stars had fans on every continent. Radios brought news, music, and sports into homes throughout the Western world.

▲ An image of a flapper dancing to jazz music on the cover of *McClure's* magazine

Daily Life in the United States, 1920s		
	1922	**1929**
Households with radios	60,000	10.25 million
Daily local telephone calls	55,160	79,141
Motion picture attendance per week	40 million	80 million
Dwellings with electricity	40%	68%

SOURCE: *Historical Statistics of the United States, Colonial Times to 1970*

More and more ▶ families were able to afford cars.

▲ Jazz Age flappers shocked their elders by bobbing, or cutting short, their hair and wearing skirts far shorter than those of prewar fashions. They went out on dates unchaperoned, enjoyed wild new dance fads such as the Charleston, smoked cigarettes, and drank in nightclubs.

The New Literature

In the 1920s, war novels, poetry, plays, and memoirs flowed off the presses. *All Quiet on the Western Front* by German novelist Erich Remarque, and other works like it, exposed the grim horrors of modern warfare. These works reflected a powerful disgust with war.

A Loss of Faith To many postwar writers, the war symbolized the moral breakdown of Western civilization. In 1922, the English poet T. S. Eliot published *The Waste Land*. This long poem portrays the modern world as spiritually empty and barren. In *The Sun Also Rises*, the American novelist Ernest Hemingway shows the rootless wanderings of young people who lack deep convictions. "I did not care what it was all about," says the narrator. "All I wanted to know was how to live in it." Many of these authors, including Hemingway and F. Scott Fitzgerald, left the United States and moved to Paris. Gertrude Stein, an American writer living in Paris, called them the "lost generation." Her label caught on. It referred to Stein's literary friends, and their generation as a whole.

In 1921, the Irish poet William Butler Yeats summed up the mood of many in postwar Europe and the United States:

Primary Source

❝ Things fall apart; the centre cannot hold;
Mere anarchy is loosed upon the world,
The blood-dimmed tide is loosed, and everywhere
The ceremony of innocence is drowned. ❞
—William Butler Yeats, "The Second Coming"

Literature of the Inner Mind Some writers experimented with stream of consciousness. In this technique, a writer appears to present a character's random thoughts and feelings without imposing any logic or order. In the novel *Mrs. Dalloway*, British novelist Virginia Woolf used stream of consciousness to explore the thoughts of people going through the

Listening to the ▶
radio was a
family activity.
🔊 AUDIO

History *Interactive*
For: For Interactive Audio and Visuals
Web Code: nbp-2811

Thinking Critically
1. **Draw Inferences** Why do you think the flapper is considered the symbol of the Jazz Age?
2. **Draw Conclusions** How did technology affect daily life in the United States during the Jazz Age?

Silent movie ▲
star Charlie Chaplin

ordinary actions of their everyday lives. In *Finnegans Wake,* the Irish novelist James Joyce explored the inner mind of a hero who remains sound asleep throughout the novel.

The Harlem Renaissance Also during the 1920s, an African American cultural awakening called the Harlem Renaissance began in Harlem, a neighborhood in New York City that was home to many African Americans. African American writers and artists expressed their pride in their unique culture. James Weldon Johnson, Jean Toomer, and Zora Neale Hurston explored the African American experience in their novels and essays. The poets Claude McKay and Langston Hughes experimented with new styles, while Countee Cullen adapted traditional poetic forms to new content.

✓ **Checkpoint** How did postwar authors show disillusionment with prewar institutions?

New Scientific Theories

It was not only the war that fostered a sense of uncertainty. New scientific discoveries challenged long-held ideas about the nature of the world. Discoveries made in the late 1800s and early 1900s showed that the atom was more complex than anyone suspected.

Marie Curie and Radioactivity In the early 1900s, the Polish-born French scientist Marie Curie and others found that the atoms of certain elements, such as radium and uranium, <u>spontaneously</u> release charged particles. As scientists studied radioactivity further, they discovered that

Vocabulary Builder

<u>spontaneously</u>—(spahn TAY nee us lee) *adv.* caused by inner forces, self-generated

Marie Curie

Marie Curie (1867–1934) won two Nobel prizes, one in physics and one in chemistry. Still, like many other women, she struggled to balance her work with home duties. "I have a great deal of work," she said, "what with the housekeeping, the children, the teaching, and the laboratory, and I don't know how I shall manage it all."

Curie won worldwide fame for her groundbreaking research on radioactivity. But she paid a high price for knowledge. Although she shrugged off the health dangers, she died from radiation poisoning. **Why do you think Marie Curie's achievements were unique for her time?**

it can change atoms of one element into atoms of another. Such findings proved that atoms are not solid and indivisible.

Einstein's Theory of Relativity In 1905 and 1916, the German-born physicist Albert Einstein introduced his theories of relativity. Einstein argued that measurements of space and time are not absolute but are determined by the relative position of the observer. Einstein's ideas raised questions about Newtonian science, which compared the universe to a machine operating according to absolute laws.

In 1934, building on Curie's and Einstein's theories, Italian physicist Enrico Fermi and other scientists around the world discovered atomic fission, or the splitting of the nuclei of atoms in two. This splitting produces a huge burst of energy. In the 1940s, Fermi (now an American), along with fellow American physicists J. Robert Oppenheimer and Edward Teller, would use this discovery to create the devastating atomic bomb.

In the postwar years, many scientists came to accept the theories of relativity. To the general public, however, Einstein's ideas were difficult to understand. They seemed to further reinforce the unsettling sense of a universe whirling beyond the understanding of human reason.

Fleming Discovers Penicillin In 1928, the Scottish scientist Alexander Fleming made a different type of scientific discovery. He accidentally discovered a type of nontoxic mold that kills bacteria, which he called "penicillin." Later, other scientists used Fleming's work to develop antibiotics, which are now used all over the world to treat infections.

Freud Probes the Mind The Austrian physician Sigmund Freud (froyd) also challenged faith in reason. He suggested that the subconscious mind drives much of human behavior. Freud said that learned social values such as morality and reason help people to repress, or check, powerful urges. But an individual feels constant tension between repressed drives and social training. This tension, argued Freud, may cause psychological or physical illness. Freud pioneered **psychoanalysis,** a method of studying how the mind works and treating mental disorders. Although many of his theories have been discredited, Freud's ideas have had an extraordinary impact far beyond medicine.

✓ **Checkpoint** How did scientific discoveries in the 1920s change people's views of the world?

Modern Art and Architecture

In the early 1900s, many Western artists rejected traditional styles. Instead of trying to reproduce the real world, they explored other dimensions of color, line, and shape. Painters like Henri Matisse (ma TEES) utilized bold, wild strokes of color and odd distortions to produce works of strong emotion. He and fellow artists outraged the public and were dubbed *fauves* (fohv), or wild beasts, by critics.

New Directions in Painting While Matisse continued in the fauvist style, other artists explored styles based on new ideas. Before World War I, the Spanish artist Pablo Picasso and the French artist Georges Braque (brak) created a revolutionary new style called cubism. Cubists painted three-dimensional objects as complex patterns of angles and planes, as if they were composed of fragmented parts.

Later, the Russian Vasily Kandinsky and the Swiss Paul Klee moved even further away from representing reality. Their artwork was **abstract,** composed only of lines, colors, and shapes, sometimes with no recognizable subject matter at all.

During and after the war, the **dada** movement burst onto the art world. Dadaists rejected all traditional conventions and believed that there was no sense or truth in the world. Paintings and sculptures by Jean Arp and Max Ernst were intended to shock and disturb viewers. Other dadaist artists created collages, photomontages, or sculptures made of objects they found abandoned or thrown away.

Cubism and dada both helped to inspire **surrealism,** a movement that attempted to portray the workings of the unconscious mind. Surrealism rejected rational thought, which had produced the horrors of World War I, in favor of irrational or unconscious ideas. The Spanish surrealist Salvador Dali used images of melting clocks and burning giraffes to suggest the chaotic dream state described by Freud.

New Styles of Architecture Architects, too, rejected classical traditions and developed new styles to match a new world. The famous Bauhaus school in Germany influenced architecture by blending science and technology with design. Bauhaus buildings feature glass, steel, and concrete but have little ornamentation. The American architect Frank Lloyd Wright held that the function of a building should determine its form. He used materials and forms that fit a building's environment.

✓ **Checkpoint** What effect did World War I have on art movements in the 1920s?

Abstract Art
Vasily Kandinsky painted *Swinging* (above) in 1925. He used geometrical shapes to convey the feeling of movement that the title suggests. **Analyzing Art** *How does* Swinging *show the abstract style of art that Kandinsky pioneered?*

Looking Ahead

Stunned by the trauma of World War I, many people sought to change the way they thought and acted during the turbulent 1920s. As nations recovered from the war, people began to feel hope rising out of their disillusionment. But soon, the "lost generation" would face a new crisis—this one economic—that would revive many old problems and spark new conflicts.

 SECTION 1 Assessment

Progress Monitoring *Online*
For: Self-quiz with vocabulary practice
Web Code: nba-2811

Terms, People, and Places

1. What do many of the key terms listed at the beginning of the section have in common? Explain.

Note Taking

2. **Reading Skill: Identify Supporting Details** Use your completed concept web to answer the Focus Question: What changes did Western society and culture experience after World War I?

Comprehension and Critical Thinking

3. **Determine Relevance** How did flappers symbolize changes in Western society during the 1920s?

4. **Identify Point of View** How did the ideas of Einstein and Freud contribute to a sense of uncertainty?

5. **Synthesize Information** Choose one postwar writer and one postwar artist. Explain how the work of each reflected a new view of the world.

● **Writing About History**

Quick Write: Choose a Topic The topic of a compare-and-contrast essay must involve two things that are neither nearly identical nor extremely different. Think of a topic from this section that would be a good candidate for a compare-and-contrast essay. Show why it would be a good topic by listing categories in which the two items could be compared and contrasted.

Pablo Picasso

The painter Pablo Picasso was one of the most important artists of the last century. Picasso and his friend Georges Braque together developed the art movement known as Cubism. The movement began around 1907 and continued through the First World War into the 1920s. Picasso's work continued to develop until his death in 1973 at the age of 91. Here are some of his best known artworks.

Picasso in his studio working on a sculpture

Still Life With Violin, 1912. In this Cubist still life, the objects, which include a violin, are fragmented into so many views that they are barely distinguishable.

Mother and Child, 1901. The years 1901 to 1904 are known as Picasso's Blue Period. Following the death of a close friend, Picasso used the color blue in many paintings to express his sadness.

Hands With Flowers, 1958. This lithograph, done after Picasso's Cubist period, is a simple image of a hand holding flowers.

Thinking Critically
1. **Compare** Describe the differences between *Mother and Child* and *Still Life With Violin.*
2. **Synthesize Information** Describe how Picasso's style changed over time, based on the artworks shown here.

Tin cup

WITNESS HISTORY 🔊 AUDIO

Brother, Can You Spare a Dime?

In the early 1930s, a worldwide economic depression threw thousands out of work and into lives of poverty. The song below summed up the mood of the time:

❝ They used to tell me I was building a dream
With peace and glory ahead—
Why should I be standing in line,
Just waiting for bread?

Once I built a railroad, I made it run,
Made it race against time.
Once I built a railroad, now it's done—
Brother, can you spare a dime?❞
— from the song "Brother, Can You Spare a Dime?," lyrics by E.Y. "Yip" Harburg & Jay Gorney. Published by Glocca Morra Music (ASCAP) & Gorney Music (ASCAP). Administered by Next Decade Entertainment, Inc. All rights reserved. Used by permission.

Focus Question What political and economic challenges did the leading democracies face in the 1920s and 1930s?

Men eating at a soup kitchen during the Great Depression

The Western Democracies Stumble

Objectives

- Summarize the domestic and foreign policy issues Europe faced after World War I.
- Compare the postwar economic situations in Britain, France, and the United States.
- Describe how the Great Depression began and spread and how Britain, France, and the United States tried to address it.

Terms, People, and Places

Maginot Line	finance
Kellogg-Briand Pact	Federal Reserve
disarmament	Great Depression
general strike	Franklin D. Roosevelt
overproduction	New Deal

Note Taking

Reading Skill: Identify Main Ideas Record main ideas from the first part of this section in a table like the one below.

Postwar Issues			
Country	Politics	Foreign Policy	Economics

In 1919, the three Western democracies—Britain, France, and the United States—appeared powerful. They had ruled the Paris Peace Conference and boosted hopes for democracy among the new nations of Eastern Europe. Beneath the surface, however, postwar Europe faced grave problems. To make matters worse, many members of the younger generation who might have become the next great leaders had been killed in the war.

Politics in the Postwar World

At first, the most pressing issues were finding jobs for returning veterans and rebuilding war-ravaged lands. Economic problems fed social unrest and made radical ideas more popular.

Party Struggles in Britain In Britain during the 1920s, the Labour party surpassed the Liberal party in strength. The Labour party gained support among workers by promoting a gradual move toward socialism. The Liberal party passed some social legislation, but it traditionally represented middle-class business interests. As the Liberal party faltered, the middle class began to back the Conservative party, joining the upper class, professionals, and farmers. With this support, the Conservative party held power during much of 1920s. After a massive strike of over three million workers in 1926, Conservatives passed legislation limiting the power of workers to strike.

The Irish Resist

Members of the Irish Republican Army prepare to resist the British occupation of Dublin in 1921 by erecting a barbed wire barricade. The Irish Free State, established in 1922, was a compromise between the opposing sides, but peace was short-lived.

Vocabulary Builder

suppressed—(suh PRESD) *vt.* put down by force, subdued

Irish Independence at Last Britain still faced the "Irish question." In 1914, Parliament passed a home-rule bill that was shelved when the war began. On Easter 1916, a small group of militant Irish nationalists launched a revolt against British rule. Although the Easter Rising was quickly suppressed, it stirred wider support for the Irish cause. When Parliament again failed to grant home rule in 1919, members of the Irish Republican Army (IRA) began a guerrilla war against British forces and their supporters. In 1922, moderates in Ireland and Britain reached an agreement. Most of Ireland became the self-governing Irish Free State. The largely Protestant northern counties remained under British rule. However, the IRA and others fought for decades against the division.

France's Troubled Peace Like Britain, France emerged from World War I both a victor and a loser. Political divisions and financial scandals plagued the government of the Third Republic. Several parties—from conservatives to communists—competed for power. The parties differed on many issues, including how to get reparations payments from Germany. A series of quickly changing coalition governments ruled France.

"The Red Scare" and Isolationism in the United States In contrast, the United States emerged from World War I in good shape. A late entrant into the war, it had suffered relatively few casualties and little loss of property. However, the United States did experience some domestic unrest. Fear of radicals and the Bolshevik Revolution in Russia set off a "Red Scare" in 1919 and 1920. Police rounded up suspected foreign-born radicals, and a number were expelled from the United States.

The "Red Scare" fed growing demands to limit immigration. Millions of immigrants from southern and eastern Europe had poured into the United States between 1890 and 1914. Some native-born Americans sought to exclude these newcomers, whose cultures differed from those of earlier settlers from northern Europe. In response, Congress passed laws limiting immigration from Europe. Earlier laws had already excluded or limited Chinese and Japanese immigration.

✓ **Checkpoint** What political issues did each of the three democracies face after World War I?

Postwar Foreign Policy

In addition to problems at home, the three democracies faced a difficult international situation. The peace settlements caused friction, especially in Germany and among some ethnic groups in Eastern Europe.

Arguing Allies France's chief concern after the war was securing its borders against Germany. The French remembered the German invasions of 1870 and 1914. To prevent a third invasion, France built massive fortifications called the **Maginot Line** (ma zhee NOH) along its border with Germany. However, the line would not be enough to stop another German invasion in 1940.

In its quest for security, France also strengthened its military and sought alliances with other countries, including the Soviet Union. It insisted on strict enforcement of the Versailles treaty and complete payment of reparations. France's goal was to keep the German economy weak.

Britain disagreed with this aim. Almost from the signing of the Treaty of Versailles, British leaders wanted to relax the treaty's harsh treatment of Germany. They feared that if Germany became too weak, the Soviet Union and France would become too powerful.

The Search for Peace Despite disagreements, many people worked for peace in the 1920s. Hopes soared in 1925 when representatives from seven European nations signed a series of treaties at Locarno, Switzerland. These treaties settled Germany's disputed borders with France, Belgium, Czechoslovakia, and Poland. The Locarno treaties became the symbol of a new era of peace.

The **Kellogg-Briand Pact,** which was sponsored by the United States in 1928, echoed the hopeful "spirit of Locarno." Almost every independent nation signed this agreement, promising to "renounce war as an instrument of national policy." In this optimistic spirit, the great powers pursued **disarmament,** the reduction of armed forces and weapons. The United States, Britain, France, Japan, and other nations signed treaties to reduce the size of their navies. However, they failed to agree on limiting the size of their armies.

From its headquarters in Geneva, Switzerland, the League of Nations encouraged cooperation and tried to get members to make a commitment to stop aggression. In 1926, after signing the Locarno agreements, Germany joined the League. Later, the Soviet Union was also admitted.

The League's Weakness The peace was fragile. Although the Kellogg-Briand Pact outlawed war, it provided no way of enforcing the ban. The League of Nations, too, was powerless to stop aggression. In 1931, the League vigorously condemned Japan's invasion of Manchuria, but did not take military action to stop it. Ambitious dictators in Europe noted the League's weakness and began to pursue aggressive foreign policies.

✓ **Checkpoint** How did the Treaty of Versailles affect the relationship between France and Britain?

Analyzing Political Cartoons

An End to War? The Kellogg-Briand Pact raised hopes for an end to war. But not everyone was so optimistic, as this 1929 American cartoon shows.

Ⓐ Kellogg-Briand Pact framed as a fire insurance policy

Ⓑ Adequate navy as a fire extinguisher

Ⓒ Uncle Sam looking at both

1. Do you think that the cartoonist feels that a fire insurance policy is enough to prevent a fire?
2. What point do you think the cartoonist is making about the Kellogg-Briand Pact?

HAVING AN INSURANCE POLICY DOESN'T MEAN YOU CAN DO WITHOUT FIRE PREVENTION

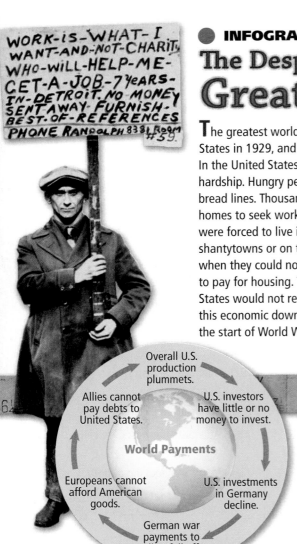

WORK-IS-WHAT-I-WANT-AND-NOT-CHARITY-WHO-WILL-HELP-ME-GET-A-JOB-7-YEARS-IN-DETROIT. NO MONEY SENT-AWAY-FURNISH-BEST-OF-REFERENCES
PHONE RANDOLPH 8331 Room #59.

The Despair of the Great Depression

The greatest worldwide depression in history began in the United States in 1929, and soon spread to touch most parts of the world. In the United States alone, millions lost their jobs and endured great hardship. Hungry people visited soup kitchens or waited in long bread lines. Thousands of people left their homes to seek work in cities. Some were forced to live in makeshift shantytowns or on the streets when they could no longer afford to pay for housing. The United States would not recover from this economic downturn until the start of World War II.

Unemployment led people to visit soup kitchens like the one below in Berlin. In New York and other cities, bread lines spanned multiple city blocks (below right), and many people became homeless (far right).

World Payments

Overall U.S. production plummets. → U.S. investors have little or no money to invest. → U.S. investments in Germany decline. → German war payments to Allies fall off. → Europeans cannot afford American goods. → Allies cannot pay debts to United States. →

.NEW.YORK.STOCK.EXCHANGE.OCT
29.1929...   SHO   500 .10.   NKPPR   3.107.   NSC   3.

▲ A man tries to find work (above). The cycle of war payments helped spread the Great Depression to Europe.

Postwar Economics

The war affected economies all over the world, hurting some and helping others. Britain and France both owed huge war debts to the United States. Both relied on reparation payments from Germany to pay back their loans. Meanwhile, the crushing reparations and other conditions hurt Germany's economy.

Britain and France Recover Britain faced serious economic problems in the 1920s. It was deeply in debt, and its factories were out of date. Unemployment was severe. Wages remained low, leading to worker unrest and frequent strikes. In 1926, a **general strike,** or strike by workers in many different industries at the same time, lasted nine days and involved some three million workers.

In comparison, the French economy recovered fairly rapidly. Financial reparations and territories gained from Germany helped. Still, economic swings did occur, adding to an unstable political scene.

Despite these problems, Europe made a shaky recovery during the 1920s. Economies returned to peacetime manufacturing and trade. Veterans gradually found jobs, although unemployment never ceased to be a problem. Middle-class families enjoyed a rising standard of living.

Vocabulary Builder
affluent—(AF loo unt) *adj.* rich, wealthy

The United States Booms In contrast, the United States emerged from the war as the world's leading economic power. In the affluent 1920s, middle-class Americans enjoyed the benefits of capitalism. American loans and investments backed the recovery in Europe. As long as the American economy prospered, the global economy remained stable.

✔ **Checkpoint** How did the war and its peace treaties affect the international economy?

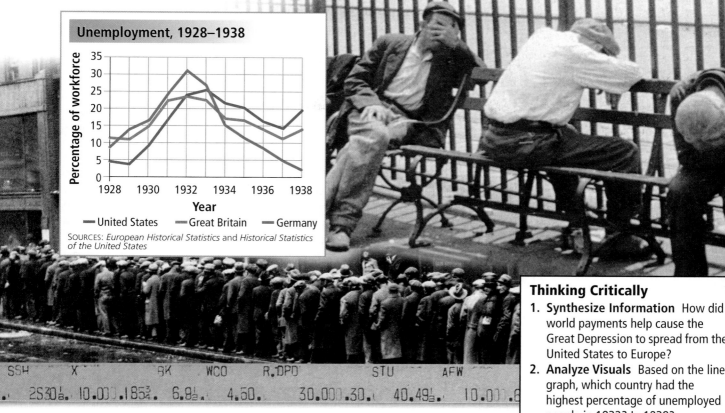

Unemployment, 1928–1938

Percentage of workforce (y-axis: 0, 5, 10, 15, 20, 25, 30, 35)
Year (x-axis: 1928, 1930, 1932, 1934, 1936, 1938)

— United States — Great Britain — Germany

SOURCES: *European Historical Statistics* and *Historical Statistics of the United States*

SSH X BK WCO R.DPD STU AFW NA
.| 2S30⅛. 10.0⅜.185¾. 6.8⅛.| 4.50.| 30.0⅜.30.| 40.49⅜.| 10.0⅜.6 1.3⅛

Thinking Critically

1. **Synthesize Information** How did world payments help cause the Great Depression to spread from the United States to Europe?
2. **Analyze Visuals** Based on the line graph, which country had the highest percentage of unemployed people in 1932? In 1938?

The Great Depression

This prosperity did not last. At the end of the 1920s, an economic crisis began in the United States and spread to the rest of the world, leaving almost no corner untouched.

Falling Demand and Overproduction The wealth created during the 1920s in the United States was not shared evenly. Farmers and unskilled workers were on the losing end. Though demand for raw materials and agricultural products had skyrocketed during the war, demand dwindled and prices fell after the war. Farmers, miners and other suppliers of raw materials suffered. Because they earned less, they bought less. At the same time, better technology allowed factories to make more products faster. This led to **overproduction,** a condition in which the production of goods exceeds the demand for them. As demand slowed, factories cut back on production and workers lost their jobs.

Crash and Collapse Meanwhile, a crisis in finance—the management of money matters, including the circulation of money, loans, investments, and banking—was brewing. Few saw the danger. Prices on the New York Stock Exchange were at an all-time high. Eager investors acquired stocks through risky methods. To slow the run on the stock market, the **Federal Reserve,** the central banking system of the United States, which regulates banks, raised interest rates in 1928 and again 1929. It didn't work. Instead, the higher interest rates made people nervous about borrowing money and investing, thereby hurting demand.

In the autumn of 1929, jitters about the economy caused many people to sell their stocks at once. Financial panic set in. Stock prices crashed, wiping out the fortunes of many investors. The **Great Depression,** a painful time of global economic collapse, had begun quietly in the

Note Taking

Reading Skill: Identify Main Ideas To help you to remember what you've read, use a chart like the one below to record the main ideas of the next two subsections.

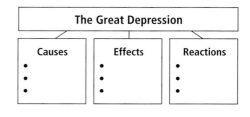

The Great Depression

Causes	Effects	Reactions
•	•	•
•	•	•
•	•	•

summer of 1929 with decreasing production. The October stock market crash aggravated the economic decline.

In 1931, the Federal Reserve again increased the interest rate, with an even more disastrous effect. As people bought and invested less, businesses closed and banks failed, throwing millions out of work. The cycle spiraled steadily downward. The jobless could not afford to buy goods, so more factories had to close, which in turn increased unemployment. People slept on park benches and lined up to eat in soup kitchens.

The Depression Spreads The economic problems quickly spread around the world. American banks stopped making loans abroad and demanded repayment of foreign loans. Without support from the United States, Germany suffered. It could not make its reparations payments. France and Britain were not able to make their loan payments.

Desperate governments tried to protect their economies from foreign competition. The United States imposed the highest tariffs in its history. The policy backfired when other nations retaliated by raising their tariffs. In 1932 and 1933, global world trade sank to its 1900 level. As you have read, the Great Depression spread misery from the industrial world to Latin America, Africa, and Asia.

✓ **Checkpoint** How did the Federal Reserve's policies affect the Great Depression?

The Democracies React to the Depression

The governments of Britain, France, and the United States, like others around the world, tried to find ways to lift the Depression. None of their methods provided a quick fix, but they did alleviate some of the suffering.

Britain and France Search for Solutions In response to the Depression, Britain set up a coalition government made up of leaders from all three of its major political parties. The government provided some unemployment benefits but failed to take decisive action to improve the economy. By 1931, one in every four workers was unemployed.

The Great Depression took longer to hurt France than some other countries. However, by the mid-1930s, France was feeling the pinch of decreased production and unemployment. In response, several leftist parties united behind the socialist leader Leon Blum. His Popular Front government tried to solve labor problems and passed some social legislation. But it could not satisfy more radical leftists. Strikes soon brought down Blum's government. Democracy survived, but the country lacked strong leadership able to respond to the clamor for change.

The Dust Bowl
In Dorothea Lange's famous 1936 photo *Migrant Mother, Nipomo, California,* a mother looks into the future with despair. She migrated to escape scenes like the one below, where huge dust storms buried farm equipment in Dallas, Texas. *How did geography help aggravate the depression in the United States?*

Roosevelt Offers the United States a New Deal Meanwhile, in the United States, President Herbert Hoover firmly believed that the government should not intervene in private business matters. Even so, he did try a variety of limited measures to solve the crisis. Nothing seemed to work. In 1932, Americans elected a new President, **Franklin D. Roosevelt.** "FDR" argued that the government had to take an active role in combating the Great Depression. He introduced the **New Deal,** a massive package of economic and social programs.

Under the New Deal, the federal government became more directly involved in people's everyday lives than ever before. New laws regulated the stock market and protected bank deposits. Government programs created jobs and gave aid to farmers. A new Social Security system provided pensions for the elderly and other benefits.

As the New Deal programs were being put into effect, a natural disaster in 1934 hit several central states. After years of drought and over-farming, huge winds blew across the plains. The winds picked up and carried away the topsoil exposed by erosion, creating the Dust Bowl. The storms destroyed crops, land, and equipment. Thousands of farmers lost their land. Many migrated to the cities of the West Coast in search of work and a new life.

The New Deal failed to end the Great Depression, although it did ease the suffering for many. Still, some critics fiercely condemned FDR's expansion of the role of government. The debate about the size and role of the federal government continues to this day.

Loss of Faith in Democracy As the Depression wore on, many people lost faith in the ability of democratic governments to solve the problems of the modern world. Postwar disillusionment, soothed by the few good years of the 1920s, turned into despair in Europe. Misery and hopelessness created fertile ground for extremists who promised radical solutions.

✔ **Checkpoint** How did the government of the United States react to the Depression?

Economic Theories and the Great Depression

According to classical economists, free market economies naturally regulate their own highs and lows. The government should interfere as little as possible. The economist John Maynard Keynes argued that during a depression, the government should step in and spend more to bring the economy back up to its full productive capacity.

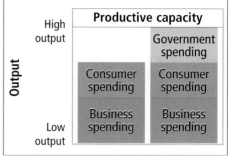

Diagram Skills *What role did Keynes envision for government in the economy?*

Progress Monitoring Online
For: Self-quiz with vocabulary practice
Web Code: nba-2821

SECTION 2 Assessment

Terms, People, and Places

1. For each term, person, or place listed at the beginning of the section, write a sentence explaining its significance.

Note Taking

2. **Reading Skill: Identify Main Ideas** Use your completed table and chart to answer the Focus Question: What political and economic challenges did the leading democracies face in the 1920s and 1930s?

Comprehension and Critical Thinking

3. **Synthesize Information** How did Britain and France emerge from World War I as both victors and losers?

4. **Predict Consequences** What steps did the major powers take to protect the peace? Why did these moves have limited effects?

5. **Recognize Cause and Effect** Explain how each of the following contributed to the outbreak or spread of the Great Depression: (a) falling demand, (b) Federal Reserve Board, and (c) financial crisis.

6. **Identify Central Issues** How did the Great Depression affect political developments in the United States?

● **Writing About History**

Quick Write: Make a Venn Diagram A useful way to gather details for a compare-and-contrast essay is to use a Venn diagram. Place similarities between two ideas in the overlapping part of the circles; place differences in the parts that don't overlap. Create a Venn diagram for an essay on the following thesis statement: The United States was in better shape than Britain and France after World War I.

An image from a magazine of Benito Mussolini leading his nation to war ▶

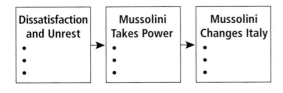

◀ Italian national flag during Mussolini's rule

WITNESS HISTORY ◀)) AUDIO

A New Leader: Mussolini

In the early 1920s, a new leader named Benito Mussolini arose in Italy. The Italian people were inspired by Mussolini's promises to bring stability and glory to Italy.

66 [Only joy at finding such a leader] can explain the enthusiasm [Mussolini] evoked at gathering after gathering, where his mere presence drew the people from all sides to greet him with frenzied acclamations. Even the men who at first came out of mere curiosity and with indifferent or even hostile feelings gradually felt themselves fired by his personal magnetic influence. . . . 99
—Margherita G. Sarfatti, *The Life of Benito Mussolini* (tr. Frederic Whyte)

Focus Question How and why did fascism rise in Italy?

Fascism in Italy

Objectives

- Describe how conditions in Italy favored the rise of Mussolini.
- Summarize how Mussolini changed Italy.
- Understand the values and goals of fascist ideology.
- Compare and contrast fascism and communism.

Terms, People, and Places

Benito Mussolini
Black Shirts
March on Rome
totalitarian state
fascism

Note Taking

Reading Skill: Identify Main Ideas Find the main points of the text under the first two headings and record them in a flowchart like the one below.

Dissatisfaction and Unrest	Mussolini Takes Power	Mussolini Changes Italy
•	•	•
•	•	•
•	•	•

"I hated politics and politicians," said Italo Balbo. Like many Italian veterans of World War I, he had come home to a land of economic chaos and political corruption. Italy's constitutional government, he felt, "had betrayed the hopes of soldiers, reducing Italy to a shameful peace." Disgusted and angry, Balbo rallied behind a fiercely nationalist leader, Benito Mussolini. Mussolini's rise to power in the 1920s served as a model for ambitious strongmen elsewhere in Europe.

Mussolini's Rise to Power

When Italy agreed to join the Allies in 1915, France and Britain secretly promised to give Italy certain Austro-Hungarian territories. When the Allies won, Italy received some of the promised territories, but others became part of the new Yugoslavia. The broken promises outraged Italian nationalists.

Disorders within Italy multiplied. Inspired in part by the revolution in Russia, peasants seized land, and workers went on strike or seized factories. Amid the chaos, returning veterans faced unemployment. Trade declined and taxes rose. The government, split into feuding factions, seemed powerless to end the crisis.

A Leader Emerges Into this turmoil stepped **Benito Mussolini.** The son of a socialist blacksmith and a teacher, Mussolini had been a socialist in his youth. During the war, however, he rejected socialism for intense nationalism. In 1919, he organized veterans and other discontented Italians into the Fascist party. They took the name from the Latin *fasces,* a bundle of sticks wrapped around an ax. In ancient Rome, the fasces symbolized unity and authority.

Mussolini was a fiery and charismatic speaker. He promised to end corruption and replace turmoil with order. He also spoke of reviving Roman greatness, pledging to turn the Mediterranean into a "Roman lake" once again.

Mussolini Gains Control Mussolini organized his supporters into "combat squads." The squads wore black shirts to emulate an earlier nationalist revolt. These **Black Shirts,** or party militants, rejected the democratic process in favor of violent action. They broke up socialist rallies, smashed leftist presses, and attacked farmers' cooperatives. Fascist gangs used intimidation and terror to oust elected officials in northern Italy. Many Italians accepted these actions because they, too, had lost faith in constitutional government.

In 1922, the Fascists made a bid for power. At a rally in Naples, they announced their intention to go to Rome to demand that the government make changes. In the **March on Rome,** tens of thousands of Fascists swarmed towards the capital. Fearing civil war, King Victor Emmanuel III asked Mussolini to form a government as prime minister. Mussolini entered the city triumphantly on October 30, 1922. He thus obtained a nominally legal, constitutional appointment from the king to lead Italy.

✓ **Checkpoint** How did postwar disillusionment contribute to Mussolini's rise?

Mussolini's Rule

At first, Fascists held only a few cabinet posts in the new government. By 1925, though, Mussolini had assumed more power and taken the title Il Duce (eel DOO chay), "The Leader." He suppressed rival parties, muzzled the press, rigged elections, and replaced elected officials with Fascist supporters. In 1929, Mussolini received support from Pope Pius XI in return for recognizing Vatican City as an independent state, although the pope continued to disagree with some of Mussolini's goals. In theory, Italy remained a parliamentary monarchy. In fact, it was a dictatorship upheld by terror. Critics were thrown into prison, forced into exile, or murdered. Secret police and propaganda bolstered the regime.

State Control of the Economy To spur economic growth and end conflicts between owners and workers, Mussolini brought the economy under state control. However, he preserved capitalism. Under Mussolini's corporate state, representatives of business, labor, government, and the Fascist

Mussolini and the People
An excited crowd of women and children greets the Italian leader in 1940.

party controlled industry, agriculture, and trade. Mussolini's system favored the upper classes and industrial leaders. Although production increased, success came at the expense of workers. They were forbidden to strike, and their wages were kept low.

The Individual and the State In Mussolini's new system, loyalty to the state replaced conflicting individual goals. To Fascists, the glorious state was all-important, and the individual was unimportant except as a member of the state. Men, women, and children were bombarded with slogans glorifying the state and Mussolini. "Believe! Obey! Fight!" loudspeakers blared and posters <u>proclaimed</u>. Men were urged to be ruthless, selfless warriors fighting for the glory of Italy. Women were pushed out of paying jobs. Instead, Mussolini called on women to "win the battle of motherhood." Those who bore more than 14 children were given a medal by Il Duce himself.

Shaping the young was a major Fascist goal. Fascist youth groups toughened children and taught them to obey strict military discipline. Boys and girls learned about the glories of ancient Rome. Young Fascists marched in torchlight parades, singing patriotic hymns and chanting, "Mussolini is always right." By the 1930s, a generation of young soldiers stood ready to back Il Duce's drive to expand Italian power.

✔ **Checkpoint** How did the Fascist party transform Italy's government and economy?

Vocabulary Builder
<u>proclaimed</u>—(proh KLAYMD) *vt.* announced officially

● **INFOGRAPHIC**

The Makings of a *Totalitarian* State

As part of a propaganda drive, German mothers received medals for bearing several children. ▶

In totalitarian Italy, Mussolini's government tried to dominate every part of the lives of Italians. Mussolini's totalitarian state became a model for others, although his rule in Italy was not as absolute as that of Stalin in the Soviet Union or Adolf Hitler in Germany. Still, all three governments shared the following basic features: (1) a single-party dictatorship with blind obedience to a single leader, (2) state control of the economy, (3) use of police spies and terror to enforce the will of the state, (4) government control of the media to indoctrinate and mobilize citizens through propaganda, (5) use of schools and youth organizations to spread ideology to children, and (6) strict censorship of artists and intellectuals with dissenting opinions.

◀ The dictators built cults of personality around themselves. At left, a statue of Stalin in a heroic pose, and (inset) Mussolini depicted working alongside Italian builders.

A photo from the Soviet secret police file on Osip Mandelstam, who was sent to the Gulag for writing poems unsympathetic to Stalin. ▶

93145 МАНДЕЛЬШТАМ О.Э

538

The Nature of Fascism

Mussolini built the first **totalitarian state.** In this form of government, a one-party dictatorship attempts to regulate every aspect of the lives of its citizens. Other dictators, notably Stalin and Hitler, followed Mussolini's lead. Mussolini's rule was fascist in nature, as was Hitler's, but totalitarian governments rise under other kinds of ideology as well, such as communism in Stalin's Soviet Union.

What is Fascism? Historians still debate the real nature of Mussolini's fascist <u>ideology</u>. Mussolini coined the term, but fascists had no unifying theory as Marxists did. Today, we generally use the term **fascism** to describe any centralized, authoritarian government that is not communist whose policies glorify the state over the individual and are destructive to basic human rights. In the 1920s and 1930s, though, fascism meant different things in different countries.

All forms of fascism, however, shared some basic features. They were rooted in extreme nationalism. Fascists glorified action, violence, discipline, and, above all, blind loyalty to the state. Fascists also pursued aggressive foreign expansion. Echoing the idea of "survival of the fittest," Fascist leaders glorified warfare as a noble struggle for survival.

Fascists were also antidemocratic. They rejected faith in reason and the concepts of equality and liberty. To them, democracy led to corruption and weakness and put individual or class interests above national goals. Instead, fascists emphasized emotion and the supremacy of the state.

Note Taking

Reading Skill: Identify Main Ideas Use a table like the one below to record information about fascism.

What is Fascism?	
Values	
Characteristics	
Differences From Communism	
Similarities to Communism	

Vocabulary Builder

<u>ideology</u>—(ih dee AHL uh jee) *n.* a system of ideas that guides an individual, movement, or political program

▼ Huge numbers of people turned out for Nazi Party rallies.

▼ Mussolini spread his ideal of Italian military supremacy to Italian children through the Young Fascists.

Thinking Critically

1. **Draw Inferences** Why did totalitarian governments try to win the loyalty of their nations' young people?
2. **Recognize Ideologies** Why did leaders honor women for having many children?

A Fascist Childhood
Children were required to use notebooks that featured fascist drawings and quotes from Mussolini.

The Appeal of Fascism Given its restrictions on individual freedom, why did fascism appeal to many Italians? First, it promised a strong, stable government and an end to the political feuding that had paralyzed democracy in Italy. Mussolini projected a sense of power and confidence at a time of disorder and despair. Mussolini's intense nationalism also revived national pride.

At first, newspapers in Britain, France, and North America applauded the discipline and order of Mussolini's government. "He got the trains running on time," admirers said. Only later, when Mussolini embarked on a course of foreign conquest, did Western democracies protest.

Fascism Compared to Communism Fascists were the sworn enemies of socialists and communists. While communists worked for international change, fascists pursued nationalist goals. Fascists supported a society with defined classes. They found allies among business leaders, wealthy landowners, and the lower middle class. Communists touted a classless society. They won support among both urban and agricultural workers.

Despite such differences, the products of these two ideologies had much in common. Both drew their power by inspiring a blind devotion to the state, or a charismatic leader as the embodiment of the state. Both used terror to guard their power. Both flourished during economic hard times by promoting extreme programs of social change. In both, a party elite claimed to rule in the name of the national interest.

 Checkpoint   Describe the similarities between fascism and communism.

Looking Ahead

Three systems of government competed for influence in postwar Europe. Democracy endured in Britain and France but faced an uphill struggle in hard times. Communism emerged in Russia and won support elsewhere. In Italy, fascism offered a different option. As the Great Depression spread, other nations—most notably Germany—looked to fascist leaders.

SECTION **3** Assessment

Progress Monitoring *Online*
For: Self-quiz with vocabulary practice
Web Code: nba-2831

Terms, People, and Places

1. For each term listed at the beginning of the section, write a sentence explaining its significance.

Note Taking

2. **Reading Skill: Identify Main Ideas** Use your completed flowchart and table to answer the section Focus Question: How and why did fascism rise in Italy?

Comprehension and Critical Thinking

3. **Recognize Cause and Effect** What problems did Italy face after World War I? How did these problems help Mussolini win power?

4. **Summarize** Describe one of Mussolini's economic or social goals, and explain the actions he took to achieve it.

5. **Compare and Contrast** List two similarities and two differences between fascism and communism.

6. **Identify Point of View** Mussolini said, "Machines and women are the two main causes of unemployment." (a) What do you think he meant? (b) How did Mussolini's policies reflect his attitude toward women?

● **Writing About History**

Quick Write: Write a Thesis Statement A compare-and-contrast thesis statement should introduce the items you are comparing and the point you intend to make. Which of the following thesis statements would work best for a compare-and-contrast essay?

• Fascism and communism are very different ideologies, but they both led to the imposition of totalitarian governments.

• Fascism led to a totalitarian government in Italy.

Dictatorship

◀ Francisco Franco in 1948

How have dictators assumed and maintained power?

One easy way to compare forms of government is to divide them into two categories: democracies and dictatorships. In democracies the people tell the leaders what to do, and in dictatorships the leaders tell the people what to do. Not all dictators are fascist, like Mussolini was. However, Mussolini, like Stalin and Hitler, was a classic dictator. Each took all political power for himself and used brutal police or military forces to maintain that power. None was held responsible to the will of the people. Consider these other examples of dictators, ancient and modern:

▲ Julius Caesar on a Roman coin, c. 44 B.C.

Julius Caesar, Ancient Rome

During the Roman Republic, the Roman Senate would appoint a dictator to serve as Rome's top official in times of civil strife. Dictators had broad powers, but usually served for only six months. Some Roman rulers, including Julius Caesar, found the law too restrictive. In 49 B.C., Caesar and his army crossed the Rubicon River and marched on Rome. As a result of the civil war that followed, Caesar took control of Rome and declared himself dictator. By 44 B.C., he had gained enough power to have himself made dictator for life. He had also gained enemies in the Senate, many of whom joined in a successful scheme to assassinate him.

Francisco Franco, Spain

Civil war raged in Spain during the 1930s. Loyalists fought to preserve Spain's republican government. They fought against the conservative Nationalists, who were made up largely of military groups, led by General Francisco Franco.

During the war, Franco accepted military help from Hitler and Mussolini. After his victory, Franco created a dictatorship based on fascism. One of his first actions was to kill or imprison thousands of former Loyalists. He remained in power into the 1970s by limiting dissent and by satisfying the varied factions on whom he relied for support.

Fidel Castro, Cuba

In 1952, an army revolt brought Fulgencio Batista to power in Cuba. Batista promised to end government corruption. Instead, he looted the treasury, threw his opponents in jail, and stifled the press. In 1956, Fidel Castro and a small group of rebels began a guerrilla war against the Batista regime. In 1959, Batista fled and Castro took control. However, Castro did not restore political and civil rights, as he had promised. Instead, he began a communist dictatorship. His regime killed political opponents and jailed anyone suspected of disloyalty. The Soviet Union supported Castro by giving Cuba economic and military aid.

◀ Fidel Castro visiting a school in 1961

Thinking Critically

1. Why is it difficult for political opponents to succeed against a dictator?
2. **Connect to Today** Do research at a local library or on the Internet to find out more about these and other dictators. Write a biographical sketch of a fictional modern-day dictator. Give your leader characteristics of several real dictators.

In this propaganda image, children surround a gentle Stalin.

WITNESS HISTORY ◀)) AUDIO

The Heart of the Party

On the occasion of Stalin's sixtieth birthday, the Communist party newspaper, *Pravda,* or "Truth," printed this praise of Stalin:

66 There is no similar name on the planet like the name of Stalin. It shines like a bright torch of freedom, it flies like a battle standard for millions of laborers around the world. . . . Stalin is today's Lenin! Stalin is the brain and heart of the party! Stalin is the banner of millions of people in their fight for a better life. 99

Far from helping people fight for a better life, Stalin's ruthless policies brought suffering and death to millions of Soviets.

Focus Question How did Stalin transform the Soviet Union into a totalitarian state?

The Soviet Union Under Stalin

Objectives

- Describe the effects of Stalin's five-year plans.
- Explain how Stalin tried to control how people thought in the Soviet Union.
- List communist changes to Soviet society.
- Outline Soviet foreign policy under Stalin.

Terms, People, and Places

command economy   russification
collectives   atheism
kulaks   Comintern
Gulag
socialist realism

Note Taking

Reading Strategy: Identify Main Ideas
Summarize the main points of the section in a chart like the one below.

The Soviet Union Under Stalin		
Five-Year Plans	Methods of Control	Daily Life

In January 1924, tens of thousands of people lined up in Moscow's historic Red Square. They had come to view the body of Lenin, who had died a few days earlier. Lenin's widow, Nadezhda Krupskaya, wanted to bury him simply next to his mother. Communist party officials—including Joseph Stalin—wanted to preserve Lenin's body and put it on permanent display. In the end, Lenin's body was displayed in Red Square for more than 65 years. By preserving Lenin's body, Stalin wanted to show that he would carry on the goals of the revolution. However, in the years that followed, he used ruthless measures to control the Soviet Union and its people.

A Totalitarian State

Karl Marx had predicted that under communism the state would eventually wither away. Under Stalin, the opposite occurred. He turned the Soviet Union into a totalitarian state controlled by a powerful and complex bureaucracy.

Stalin's Five-Year Plans Once in power, Stalin imposed government control over the Soviet Union's economy. In the past, said Stalin, Russia had suffered because of its economic backwardness. In 1928, he proposed the first of several "five-year plans" aimed at building heavy industry, improving transportation, and increasing farm output. He brought all economic activity under government control. The government owned all businesses and distributed all resources. The Soviet Union developed a **command economy,** in which government officials made all basic economic decisions. By contrast, in a capitalist system, the free market determine most economic decisions. Privately owned businesses compete to win the consumer's choice. This competition regulates the price and quality of goods.

Mixed Results in Industry Stalin's five-year plans set high production goals, especially for heavy industry and transportation. The government pushed workers and managers to meet these goals by giving bonuses to those who succeeded—and by punishing those who did not. Between 1928 and 1939, large factories, hydroelectric power stations, and huge industrial complexes rose across the Soviet Union. Oil, coal, and steel production grew. Mining expanded, and new railroads were built.

Despite the impressive progress in some areas, Soviet workers had little to show for their efforts. Some former peasants did become skilled factory workers or managers. Overall, though, the standard of living remained low. Central planning was often inefficient, causing shortages in some areas and surpluses in others. Many managers, concerned only with meeting production quotas, turned out large quantities of low-quality goods. Consumer products such as clothing, cars, and refrigerators were scarce. Wages were low and workers were forbidden to strike. The party restricted workers' movements.

Forced Collectivization in Agriculture Stalin also brought agriculture under government control, but at a horrendous cost. The government wanted farmers to produce more grain to feed workers in the cities. It also hoped to sell grain abroad to earn money.

As you have read, under Lenin's New Economic Plan (NEP), peasants had held on to small plots of land. Many had prospered. Stalin saw that system as being inefficient and a threat to state power. Stalin wanted all peasants to farm on either state-owned farms or **collectives,** large farms owned and operated by peasants as a group. On collectives, the government would provide tractors, fertilizers, and better seed, and peasants would learn modern farm methods. Peasants would be permitted to keep their houses and personal belongings, but all farm animals and implements were to be turned over to the collective. The state set all prices and controlled access to farm supplies.

Some peasants did not want to give up their land and sell their crops at the state's low prices. They resisted collectivization by killing farm animals, destroying tools, and burning crops. Stalin was furious. He believed that **kulaks,** or wealthy farmers, were behind the resistance. He responded with brutal force. In 1929, Stalin declared his intention to "liquidate the kulaks as a class." To this end, the government confiscated kulaks' land and sent them to labor camps. Thousands were killed or died from overwork.

Even after the "de-kulakization," angry peasants resisted by growing just enough to feed themselves. In response, the government seized all of their grain to meet industrial goals, purposely leaving the peasants to starve. In 1932, this ruthless policy, combined with poor harvests, led to a terrible

Effects of the Five-Year Plans on Soviet Industry

SOURCE: B.R. Mitchell, *European Historical Statistics, 1750–1970*

"Industrialism is the Path to Socialism"
As this 1928 poster proclaims, Stalin's government saw rapid industrialization as the key to the success of the Soviet Union. *Using the line graph, describe the effect of the Five-Year Plans on steel and brown coal output.*

famine. Later called the Terror Famine, it caused between five and eight million people to die of starvation in the Ukraine alone.

Although collectivization increased Stalin's control of the peasantry, it did not improve farm output. During the 1930s, grain production inched upward, but meat, vegetables, and fruits remained in short supply. Feeding the population would remain a major problem in the Soviet Union.

✔ **Checkpoint** How did Stalin take control of the Soviet Union's economic life?

Stalin's Terror Tactics

In addition to tactics like the Terror Famine, Stalin's Communist party used secret police, torture, and violent purges to ensure obedience. Stalin tightened his grasp on every aspect of Soviet life, even stamping out any signs of dissent within the Communist elites.

Terror as a Weapon Stalin ruthlessly used terror as a weapon against his own people. He perpetrated crimes against humanity and systematically violated his people's individual rights. Police spies did not hesitate to open private letters or plant listening devices. Nothing appeared in print without official approval. There was no free press, and no safe method of voicing protest. Grumblers or critics were rounded up and sent to the **Gulag,** a system of brutal labor camps, where many died.

The Great Purge Even though Stalin's power was absolute, he still feared that rival party leaders were plotting against him. In 1934, he launched the Great Purge. During this reign of terror, Stalin and his secret police cracked down especially on Old Bolsheviks, or party activists from the early days of the revolution. His net soon widened to target army heroes, industrial managers, writers, and ordinary citizens. They were charged with a wide range of crimes, from counterrevolutionary plots to failure to meet production quotas.

Between 1936 and 1938, Stalin staged a series of spectacular public "show trials" in Moscow. Former Communist leaders confessed to all kinds of crimes after officials tortured them or threatened their families or friends. Many of the purged party members were never tried but were sent straight to the Gulag. Secret police files reveal that at least four million people were purged during the Stalin years. Some historians estimate the toll to be much greater.

Results of the Purge The purges increased Stalin's power. All Soviet citizens were now well aware of the consequences of disloyalty. However, Stalin's government also paid a price. Among the purged were experts in industry, economics, and engineering, and many of the Soviet Union's most talented

Food as a Weapon
In 1932, when peasants failed to meet unrealistic crop quotas, Stalin retaliated by seizing all of their grain to sell on the market, leaving millions to starve. Below, a woman and her son search for food during the famine. *Describe the effect of Stalin's ruthless policies on the production of oats, wheat, and potatoes.*

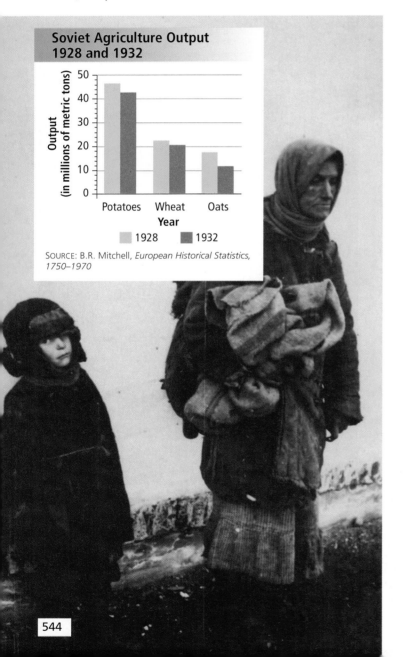

Soviet Agriculture Output 1928 and 1932

Output (in millions of metric tons)

■ 1928 ■ 1932

SOURCE: B.R. Mitchell, *European Historical Statistics, 1750–1970*

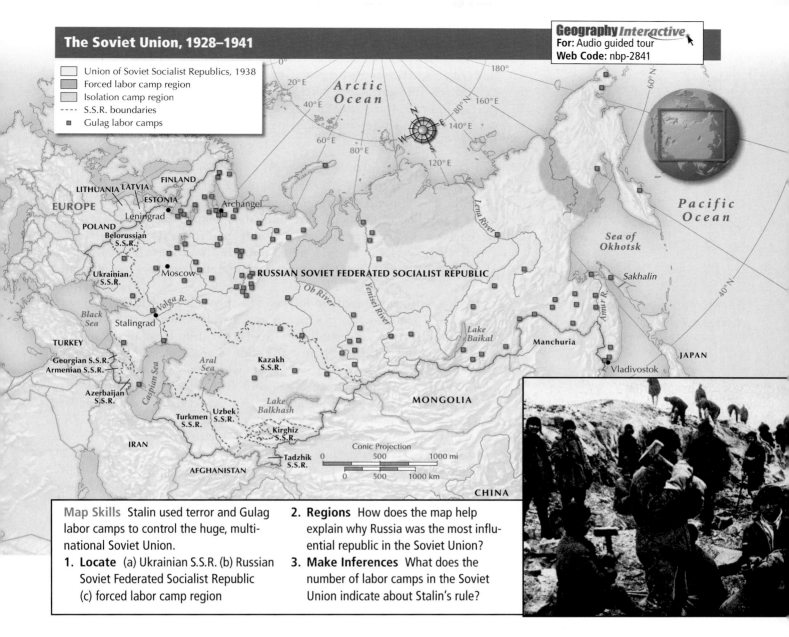

The Soviet Union, 1928–1941

Legend:
- Union of Soviet Socialist Republics, 1938
- Forced labor camp region
- Isolation camp region
- ---- S.S.R. boundaries
- ■ Gulag labor camps

Map Skills Stalin used terror and Gulag labor camps to control the huge, multinational Soviet Union.

1. **Locate** (a) Ukrainian S.S.R. (b) Russian Soviet Federated Socialist Republic (c) forced labor camp region

2. **Regions** How does the map help explain why Russia was the most influential republic in the Soviet Union?

3. **Make Inferences** What does the number of labor camps in the Soviet Union indicate about Stalin's rule?

A Gulag labor camp in 1934

writers and thinkers. The victims included most of the nation's military leaders and about half of its military officers, a loss that would weigh heavily on Stalin in 1941, when Germany invaded the Soviet Union.

✔ **Checkpoint** In what ways did Stalin's terror tactics harm the Soviet Union?

Communist Attempts to Control Thought

At the same time that he was purging any elements of resistance in Soviet society, Stalin also sought to control the hearts and minds of Soviet citizens. He tried to do this by tirelessly distributing propaganda, censoring opposing ideas, imposing Russian culture on minorities, and replacing religion with communist ideology.

Propaganda Stalin tried to boost morale and faith in the communist system by making himself a godlike figure. He used propaganda as a tool to build up a "cult of personality" around himself. Using modern technology, the party bombarded the public with relentless propaganda. Radios and loudspeakers blared into factories and villages. In movies, theaters, and schools, citizens heard about communist successes and the evils of capitalism. Billboards and posters urged workers to meet or exceed production quotas. Headlines in the Communist party newspaper *Pravda,* or "Truth," linked enemies at home to foreign agents seeking to overthrow the Communist regime.

Censorship and the Arts At first, the Bolshevik Revolution had meant greater freedom for Soviet artists and writers. Under Stalin, however, the heavy hand of state control also gripped the arts. The government controlled what books were published, what music was heard, and which works of art were displayed. Stalin required artists and writers to create their works in a style called **socialist realism.** Its goal was to show Soviet life in a positive light and promote hope in the communist future.

In theory, socialist realism followed in the footstep of Russian greats Tolstoy and Chekhov; in practice it was rarely allowed to be realistic. Socialist realist novels usually featured a positive hero, often an engineer or scientist, battling against the odds to accomplish a goal. Popular themes for socialist-realist visual artists were peasants, workers, heroes of the revolution, and—of course—Stalin.

If they refused to <u>conform</u> to government expectations, writers, artists, and composers faced government persecution. The Jewish poet Osip Mandelstam, for example, was imprisoned, tortured, and exiled for composing a satirical verse that was critical of Stalin. Out of fear for his wife's safety, Mandelstam finally submitted to threats and wrote an "Ode to Stalin." Boris Pasternak, who would later win fame for his novel *Doctor Zhivago,* was afraid to publish anything at all during the Stalin years. Rather than write in the favored style of socialist realism, he translated foreign literary works instead.

Despite restrictions, some Soviet writers produced magnificent works. Yevgeny Zamyatin's classic anti-Utopian novel *We* became well known outside of the Soviet Union, but was not published in his home country until 1989. The novel depicts a nightmare future in which people go by numbers, not names, and the "One State" controls people's thoughts. *And Quiet Flows the Don,* by Mikhail Sholokhov, passed the censor. The novel tells the story of a man who spends years fighting in World War I, the Russian Revolution, and the civil war. Sholokhov later won the Nobel Prize for literature.

Russification Yet another way Stalin controlled the cultural life of the Soviet Union was by promoting a policy of **russification,** or making a nationality's culture more Russian. By 1936, the U.S.S.R. was made up of 11 Soviet Socialist Republics. The Russian Soviet Federated Socialist Republic consisted of the old Russian heartland and was the largest and dominant republic. The other

Soviet Art
In this Socialist Realist sculpture, a factory worker and a collective farmer raise the hammer and sickle together.

Anna Akhmatova (ahk MAH tuh vuh), one of Russia's greatest poets, could not publish her works because she had violated state guidelines. Still, she wrote secretly. In this passage from "Requiem," she describes the ordeal of trying to visit her 20-year-old son, imprisoned during the Stalinist terrors:

Primary Source

❝ For seventeen long months my pleas,
My cries have called you home.
I've begged the hangman on my knees,
My son, my dread, my own.
My mind's mixed up for good, and I'm
No longer even clear
Who's man, who's beast, nor how much time
Before the end draws near. ❞
—Anna Akhmatova, "Requiem"
(tr. Robin Kemball)   🔊 AUDIO

SSRs, such as Uzbek and the Ukraine, were the homelands of other nationalities and had their own languages, historical traditions, and cultures. At first, Stalin encouraged the autonomy, or independence, of these cultures. However, in the late 1920s, Stalin turned this policy on its head and systematically tried to make the cultures of the non-Russian SSRs more Russian. He appointed Russians to high-ranking positions in non-Russian SSRs and required the Russian language to be used in schools and businesses.

War on Religion The Communist party also tried to strengthen its hold on the minds of the people by destroying their religious faith. In accordance with the ideas of Marx, atheism, or the belief that there is no god, became an official state policy. Early on, the Communists targeted the Russian Orthodox Church, which had strongly supported the tsars. Many priests and other religious leaders were among those killed in the purges or sent to die in prison camps. Other religions were persecuted as well. At one show trial, 15 Roman Catholic priests were charged with teaching religion to the young, a counterrevolutionary activity. The state seized Jewish synagogues and banned the use of Hebrew. Islam was also officially discouraged.

The Communists tried to replace religion with their own ideology. Like a religion, communist ideology had its own "sacred" texts—the writings of Marx and Lenin—and its own shrines, such as the tomb of Lenin. Portraits of Stalin replaced religious icons in Russian homes. However, millions of Soviets continued to worship, in private and sometimes in public, in defiance of the government's prohibitions.

The Party Versus the Church
To weaken the power of the Russian Orthodox Church, the party seized church property and converted churches into offices and museums. Here, Red Army soldiers carry off religious relics from a Russian church. *How might the policy of destroying churches in such a public way have backfired on the party?*

 Checkpoint How did Stalin use censorship and propaganda to support his rule?

Soviet Society Under Stalin

The terror and cultural coercion of Stalin's rule made a mockery of the original theories and promises of communism. The lives of most Russians did change. But, while the changes had some benefits, they were often outweighed by continuous shortages and restricted freedoms.

The New Elite Takes Control The Communists destroyed the old social order of landowning nobles at the top and peasants at the bottom. But instead of creating a society of equals as they promised, they created a society where a few elite groups emerged as a new ruling class. At the head of society were members of the Communist party. Only a small fraction of Soviet citizens could join the party. Many who did so were motivated by a desire to get ahead, rather than a belief in communism.

The Soviet elite also included industrial managers, military leaders, scientists, and some artists and writers. The elite enjoyed benefits denied to most people. They lived in the best apartments in the cities and rested at the best vacation homes in the country. They could shop at special stores for scarce consumer goods. On the other hand, Stalin's purges often fell on the elite.

Benefits and Drawbacks Although excluded from party membership, most people did enjoy several new benefits. The party required all children to attend free Communist-built schools. The state supported technical schools and universities as well. Schools served many important goals. Educated workers were needed to build a modern industrial state. The Communist party also set up programs for students outside school. These programs included sports, cultural activities, and political classes to train teenagers for party membership. However, in addition to important basic skills, schools also taught communist values, such as atheism, the glory of collective farming, and love of Stalin.

The state also provided free medical care, day care for children, inexpensive housing, and public recreation. While these benefits were real, many people still lacked vital necessities. Although the state built massive apartment complexes, housing was scarce. Entire families might be packed into a single room. Bread was plentiful, but meat, fresh fruit, and other foods remained in short supply.

Women in the Soviet Union Long before 1917, women such as Nadezhda Krupskaya and Alexandra Kollontai worked for the revolution, spreading radical ideas among peasants and workers. Under the Communists, women won equality under the law. They gained <u>access</u> to education and a wide range of jobs. By the 1930s, many Soviet women were working in medicine, engineering, or the sciences. By their labor, women contributed to Soviet economic growth. They worked in factories, in construction, and on collectives. Within the family, their wages were needed because men and women earned the same low salaries.

✓ **Checkpoint**   How did Communist schools benefit the state and the Communist party?

Vocabulary Builder

<u>access</u>—(AK ses) *n.* the ability to get and use

Crowded Lives
At the start of the first Five-Year Plan, millions of Soviets moved from the country to cities to take jobs in new industrial plants. This influx led to extremely crowded living conditions. These men gather in close quarters in a Soviet hostel in the early 1930s. *How does this photograph reflect the drawbacks of a centrally planned command economy?*

Soviet Foreign Policy

Between 1917 and 1939, the Soviet Union pursued two very different goals in foreign policy. As Communists, both Lenin and Stalin wanted to bring about the worldwide revolution that Marx had predicted. But as Soviets, they wanted to guarantee their nation's security by winning the support of other countries. The result of pursuing these two different goals was a contradictory and generally unsuccessful foreign policy.

In 1919, Lenin formed the Communist International, or **Comintern.** The purpose of the Comintern was to encourage world-wide revolution. To this end, it aided revolutionary groups around the world and urged colonial peoples to rise up against imperialist powers.

The Comintern's support of revolutionary groups outside the Soviet Union and its propaganda against capitalism made Western powers highly suspicious of the Soviet Union. In the United States, fear of Bolshevik plots led to the "Red Scare" in the early 1920s. Britain broke off relations with the Soviet Union when evidence revealed Soviet schemes to turn a 1926 strike into a revolution. Even so, the Soviet Union slowly won recognition from Western powers and increased trade with capitalist countries. It also joined the League of Nations. However, mistrust still poisoned relations, especially after the Great Purge.

 Checkpoint How did the Soviet Union's foreign policy goals contradict one another?

Looking Ahead

By the time Stalin died in 1953, the Soviet Union had become a military superpower and a world leader in heavy industry. Yet Stalin's efforts exacted a brutal toll. The Soviet people were dominated by a totalitarian system based on terror. The reality of communism fell far short of Lenin's promises. Most people in the Soviet Union lived meager lives compared with people in the West.

SECTION 4 Assessment

Progress Monitoring *Online*
For: Self-quiz with vocabulary practice
Web Code: nba-2841

Terms, People, and Places

1. What do many of the key terms listed at the beginning of the section have in common? Explain.

Note Taking

2. **Reading Skill: Identify Main Ideas** Use your completed chart to answer the section Focus Question: How did Stalin transform the Soviet Union into a totalitarian state?

Comprehension and Critical Thinking

3. **Identify Effects** What were the goals and results of Stalin's five-year plans? How did the effects differ between industry and agriculture?

4. **Contrast** How did the command economy under Stalin differ from a capitalist economy?

5. **Synthesize Information** What methods did Stalin use to create a totalitarian state?

6. **Synthesize Information** One historian has said that socialist realism was "communism with a smiling face." What do you think he meant?

7. **Compare** Compare life under Stalin's rule with life under the Russian tsars.

● **Writing About History**

Quick Write: Choose an Organization Compare-and-contrast essays are often organized either point by point or by block. The first organization involves a discussion of one idea first, followed by the discussion of another, and emphasizes the two ideas. The second discusses all of the similarities, followed by all the differences, and emphasizes the comparison or contrast itself. Write an outline for each type for an essay comparing and contrasting the results of the Five-Year Plans in industry and agriculture.

Adolf Hitler with a member of a Nazi youth organization

WITNESS HISTORY 🔊 AUDIO

The Nazis in Control of Germany

In the 1930s, Adolf Hitler and the Nazi party brought hope to Germans suffering from the Great Depression. On the dark side of Hitler's promises was a message of hate, aimed particularly at Jews. A German Jewish woman recalls an attack on her family during *Kristallnacht*, a night in early November 1938 when Nazi mobs attacked Jewish homes and businesses.

66 They broke our windowpanes, and the house became very cold. . . . We were standing there, outside in the cold, still in our night clothes, with only a coat thrown over. . . . Then they made everyone lie face down on the ground . . . 'Now, they will shoot us,' we thought. We were very afraid. 99

Focus Question How did Hitler and the Nazi party establish and maintain a totalitarian government in Germany?

Hitler and the Rise of Nazi Germany

Objectives

- Analyze the problems faced by the Weimar Republic.
- Describe the Nazi party's political, social, economic, and cultural policies.
- Summarize the rise of authoritarian rule in Eastern Europe in the 1920s and 1930s.

Terms, People, and Places

chancellor	Gestapo
Ruhr Valley	Nuremberg Laws
Third Reich	

Note Taking

Reading Skill: Identify Main Ideas As you read, summarize the section's main ideas in a flowchart like the one below.

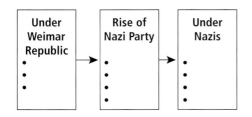

Under Weimar Republic	Rise of Nazi Party	Under Nazis
•	•	•
•	•	•
•	•	•

In November 1923, a German army veteran and leader of an extremist party, Adolf Hitler, tried to follow Mussolini's example by staging a small-scale coup in Munich. The coup failed, and Hitler was soon behind bars. But Hitler proved to be a force that could not be ignored. Within a decade, he made a new bid for power. This time, he succeeded by legal means.

Hitler's rise to power raises disturbing questions that we still debate today. Why did Germany, which had a democratic government in the 1920s, become a totalitarian state in the 1930s? How could a ruthless, hate-filled dictator gain the enthusiastic support of many Germans?

The Weimar Republic's Rise and Fall

As World War I drew to a close, Germany tottered on the brink of chaos. Under the threat of a socialist revolution, the kaiser abdicated. Moderate leaders signed the armistice and later, under protest, the Versailles treaty.

In 1919, German leaders drafted a constitution in the city of Weimar (VY mahr). It created a democratic government known as the Weimar Republic. The constitution set up a parliamentary system led by a **chancellor,** or prime minister. It gave women the vote and included a bill of rights.

Political Struggles The republic faced severe problems from the start. Politically, it was weak because Germany, like France, had many small parties. The chancellor had to form coalitions that easily fell apart.

The government, led by moderate democratic socialists, came under constant fire from both the left and right. Communists demanded radical changes like those Lenin had brought to Russia. Conservatives—including the old Junker nobility, military officers, and wealthy bourgeoisie—attacked the government as too liberal and weak. They longed for another strong leader like Bismarck. Germans of all classes blamed the Weimar Republic for the hated Versailles treaty. Bitter, they looked for scapegoats. Many blamed German Jews for economic and political problems.

Runaway Inflation Economic disaster fed unrest. In 1923, when Germany fell behind in reparations payments, France occupied the coal-rich **Ruhr Valley** (roor). Germans workers in the Ruhr protested using <u>passive</u> resistance and refused to work. To support the workers, the government continued to pay them, and printed huge quantities of paper money to do so. Inflation soon spiraled out of control, spreading misery and despair. The German mark became almost worthless. An item that cost 100 marks in July 1922 cost 944,000 marks by August 1923. Salaries rose by billions of marks, but they still could not keep up with skyrocketing prices. Many middle-class families saw their savings wiped out.

Vocabulary Builder

<u>passive</u>—(PAS iv) *adj.* not active, nonviolent

Recovery and Collapse With help from the Western powers, the government did bring inflation under control. In 1924, the United States gained British and French approval for a plan to reduce German reparations payments. Under the Dawes Plan, France withdrew its forces from the Ruhr, and American loans helped the German economy recover. Germany began to prosper. Then, the Great Depression hit, reviving memories of the miseries of 1923. Germans turned to an energetic leader, Adolf Hitler, who promised to solve the economic crisis and restore Germany's former greatness.

Inflation Rocks Germany
A man uses German marks to paper his wall because it costs less than buying wallpaper. At the height of the inflation, it would have taken 84,000 fifty-million mark notes like the one below, to equal a single American dollar. *Why would inflation hit middle class people with modest savings hard?*

Weimar Culture Culture flourished in the Weimar Republic even as the government struggled through crisis after crisis. The tumultuous times helped to stimulate new cultural movements, such as dadaist art and Bauhaus architecture. Berlin attracted writers and artists from around the world, just as Paris did. The German playwright Bertolt Brecht sharply criticized middle-class values with *The Three-Penny Opera*. The artist George Grosz, through scathing drawings and paintings, blasted the failings of the Weimar Republic. However, many believed that this modern culture and the Weimar Republic itself were not in keeping with Germany's illustrious past.

✓ **Checkpoint** What political and economic problems did the Weimar Republic face?

The Nazi Party's Rise to Power

Adolf Hitler was born in Austria in 1889. When he was 18, he went to Vienna, then the capital of the multinational Hapsburg empire. German Austrians

Adolf Hitler

As a boy, Adolf Hitler (1889–1945) became obsessed with Germany's 1871 victory in the Franco–Prussian War. "The great historic struggle would become my greatest spiritual experience," he later wrote. "I became more and more enthusiastic about everything . . . connected with war."

In school, young Hitler was known as a ringleader. One of his teachers recalled, "He demanded of his fellow pupils their unqualified obedience." He failed to finish high school and was later crushed when he was rejected by art school.

After Hitler came to power, he used his elite guard of storm troopers to terrorize his opponents. But when he felt his power threatened, Hitler had leaders of the storm troopers murdered during the "Night of the Long Knives" on June 30, 1934. **Why do you think historians study Hitler's upbringing?**

made up just one of many ethnic groups in Vienna. Yet they felt superior to Jews, Serbs, Poles, and other groups. While living in Vienna, Hitler developed the fanatical anti-Semitism, or prejudice against Jewish people, that would later play a major role in his rise to power.

Hitler went to Germany and fought in the German army during World War I. In 1919, he joined a small group of right-wing extremists. Like many ex-soldiers, he despised the Weimar government, which he saw as weak. Within a year, he was the unquestioned leader of the National Socialist German Workers, or Nazi, party. Like Mussolini, Hitler organized his supporters into fighting squads. Nazi "storm troopers" fought in the streets against their political enemies.

Hitler's Manifesto In 1923, as you have read, Hitler made a failed attempt to seize power in Munich. He was arrested and found guilty of treason. While in prison, Hitler wrote *Mein Kampf ("My Struggle")*. It would later become the basic book of Nazi goals and ideology.

Mein Kampf reflected Hitler's obsessions—extreme nationalism, racism, and anti-Semitism. Germans, he said, belonged to a superior "master race" of Aryans, or light-skinned Europeans, whose greatest enemies were the Jews. Hitler's ideas were rooted in a long tradition of anti-Semitism. In the Middle Ages, Christians persecuted Jews because of their different beliefs. The rise of nationalism in the 1800s caused people to identify Jews as ethnic outsiders. Hitler viewed Jews not as members of a religion but as a separate race. (He defined a Jew as anyone with one Jewish grandparent.) Echoing a familiar right-wing theme, he blamed Germany's defeat in World War I on a conspiracy of Marxists, Jews, corrupt politicians, and business leaders.

In his recipe for revival, Hitler urged Germans everywhere to unite into one great nation. Germany must expand, he said, to gain *Lebensraum* (LAY buns rowm), or living space, for its people. Slavs and other inferior races must bow to Aryan needs. To achieve its greatness, Germany needed a strong leader, or Führer (FYOO rur). Hitler was determined to become that leader.

Hitler Comes to Power After less than a year, Hitler was released from prison. He soon renewed his table-thumping speeches. The Great Depression played into Hitler's hands. As unemployment rose, Nazi membership grew to almost a million. Hitler's program appealed to veterans, workers, the lower middle classes, small-town Germans, and business people alike. He promised to end reparations, create jobs, and defy the Versailles treaty by rearming Germany.

With the government paralyzed by divisions, both Nazis and Communists won more seats in the Reichstag, or lower house of the legislature. Fearing the growth of communist political power, conservative politicians turned to Hitler. Although they despised him, they believed they could control him. Thus, with conservative support, Hitler was appointed chancellor in 1933 through legal means under the Weimar constitution.

Within a year, Hitler was dictator of Germany. He and his supporters suspended civil rights, destroyed the socialists and Communists, and disbanded other political parties. Germany became a one-party state. Like Stalin in Russia, Hitler purged his own party, brutally executing Nazis he felt were disloyal. Nazis learned that Hitler demanded unquestioning obedience.

✔ **Checkpoint** Describe the Nazi party's ideology and Hitler's plans for ruling Germany.

The Third Reich Controls Germany

Once in power, Hitler and the Nazis moved to build a new Germany. Like Mussolini, Hitler appealed to nationalism by recalling past glories. Germany's First Reich, or empire, was the medieval Holy Roman Empire. The Second Reich was the empire forged by Bismarck in 1871. Under Hitler's new **Third Reich,** he boasted, the German master race would dominate Europe for a thousand years.

To combat the Great Depression, Hitler launched large public works programs (as did Britain and the United States). Tens of thousands of people were put to work building highways and housing or replanting forests. Hitler also began a crash program to rearm Germany and schemed to unite Germany and Austria. Both measures were a strong repudiation, or rejection, of the hated Versailles treaty.

Germany Becomes a Totalitarian State To achieve his goals, Hitler organized an efficient but brutal system of totalitarian rule. Nazis controlled all areas of German life—from government to religion to education. Elite, black-uniformed troops, called the SS, enforced the Führer's will. His secret police, the **Gestapo** (guh STAH poh), rooted out opposition. The masses, relieved by belief in the Nazis' promises, cheered Hitler's accomplishments in ending unemployment and reviving German power. Those who worried about Hitler's terror apparatus quickly became its victims or were cowed into silence in fear for their own safety.

The Campaign Against the Jews Begins In his fanatical anti-Semitism, Hitler set out to drive Jews from Germany. In 1935, the Nazis passed the **Nuremberg Laws,** which deprived Jews of German citizenship and placed severe restrictions on them. They were prohibited from marrying non-Jews, attending or teaching at German schools or universities, holding government jobs, practicing law or medicine, or publishing

"Night of Broken Glass"
On the night of November 9, 1938, and into the next day, German mobs smashed the windows of Jewish homes and businesses, looted Jewish shops, and burned synagogues. Many Jewish people were dragged from their homes and beaten in the streets. Not only did the Nazi government authorize these attacks, it made the Jewish victims pay for the damage.

books. Nazis beat and robbed Jews and roused mobs to do the same. Many German Jews fled, seeking refuge in other countries.

Night of Broken Glass On November 7, 1938, a young Jew whose parents had been mistreated in Germany shot and wounded a German diplomat in Paris. Hitler used the incident as an excuse to stage an attack on all Jews. *Kristallnacht* (krih STAHL nahkt), or the "Night of Broken Glass," took place on November 9 and 10. Nazi-led mobs attacked Jewish communities all over Germany, Austria, and the annexed portions of Czechoslovakia. Before long, Hitler and his henchmen were making even more sinister plans for what they called the "Final Solution"—the extermination of all Jews.

Nazi Youth To build for the future, the Nazis indoctrinated young people with their ideology. In passionate speeches, the Führer spewed his message of racism. He urged young Germans to destroy their so-called enemies without mercy. On hikes and in camps, the "Hitler Youth" pledged absolute loyalty to Germany and undertook physical fitness programs to prepare for war. School courses and textbooks were rewritten to reflect Nazi racial views.

Like Fascists in Italy, Nazis sought to limit women's roles. Women were dismissed from upper-level jobs and turned away from universities. To raise the birthrate, Nazis offered "pure-blooded Aryan" women rewards for having more children. Still, Hitler's goal to keep women in the home and out of the workforce applied mainly to the privileged. As German industry expanded, women factory workers were needed.

Purging German Culture The Nazis also sought to purge, or purify, German culture. They denounced modern art, saying that it was corrupted by Jewish influences. They condemned jazz because of its African roots. Instead, the Nazis glorified old German myths such as those re-created in the operas of Richard Wagner (VAHG nur).

Hitler despised Christianity as "weak" and "flabby." He sought to replace religion with his racial creed. To control the churches, the Nazis combined all Protestant sects into a single state church. They closed Catholic schools and muzzled the Catholic clergy. Although many clergy either supported the new regime or remained silent, some courageously spoke out against Hitler.

✓ **Checkpoint** How did the Nazi party maintain its control of Germany?

Authoritarian Rule in Eastern Europe

Like Germany, most new nations in Eastern Europe slid from democratic to authoritarian rule in the postwar era. In 1919, a dozen countries were carved out of the old Russian, Austro-Hungarian, Ottoman and German empires. Although they differed from one another in important ways, they faced some common problems. They were small countries whose rural agricultural economies lacked capital to develop industry. Social and economic inequalities separated

Vocabulary Builder

regime—(ruh ZHEEM) *n.* a government in power

Nazi Book Burnings
Nazis burned books of which they disapproved, such as *All Quiet on the Western Front,* in huge, organized public bonfires. The Nazis viewed Remarque's novel as an insult to the German military.

poor peasants from wealthy landlords. None had much experience with the democratic process. Further complicating the situation, tensions leftover from World War I hindered economic cooperation between countries. Each country in the region tried to be independent of its neighbors, which hurt all of them. The region was hit hard by the Great Depression.

Ethnic Conflict Old rivalries between ethnic and religious groups created severe tensions. In Czechoslovakia, Czechs and Slovaks were unwilling partners. Serbs dominated the new state of Yugoslavia, but restless Slovenes and Croats living there pressed for independence. In Poland, Hungary, and Romania, conflict flared among various ethnic groups.

Democracy Retreats Economic problems and ethnic tensions contributed to instability, which in turn helped fascist rulers gain power. In Hungary, military strongman Nicholas Horthy (HAWR tay) overthrew a Communist-led government in 1919. By 1926, the military hero Joseph Pilsudski (peel SOOT skee) had taken control over Poland. Eventually, right-wing dictators emerged in every Eastern European country except Czechoslovakia and Finland. Like Hitler, these dictators promised order and won the backing of the military and wealthy. They also turned to anti-Semitism, using Jewish people as scapegoats for many national problems. Meanwhile, strong, aggressive neighbors eyed these small, weak states of Eastern Europe as tempting targets.

✔ **Checkpoint** Why did authoritarian states rise in Eastern Europe after World War I?

Notable Jewish Figures of Europe, Early 1900s

Person	Achievements
Marc Chagall	Forerunner of Surrealism
Gustav Mahler	Composed symphonies and conducted many major orchestras
Arnold Schoenberg	Pioneered new styles of music
Franz Kafka	Influential style of surrealist writing
Albert Einstein	Important scientist
Sigmund Freud	Founder of psychoanalysis
Edmund Husserl	Founder of phenomenology movement
Rudolph Lipschitz	Worked on number theory and potential theory

The table above lists a few of the notable Jewish people whose exceptional talents flew in the face of Hitler's claims of Aryan superiority. Some of these people fled Europe in the face of the Nazi regime. **Chart Skills** *Describe how losing some of its leading thinkers might have hurt Nazi Germany.*

SECTION 5 Assessment

Progress Monitoring *Online*
For: Self-quiz with vocabulary practice
Web Code: nba-2851

Terms, People, and Places

1. Place each of the terms listed at the beginning of the section into one of the following categories: politics, culture, or economy. Write a sentence explaining your choice.

Note Taking

2. **Reading Skill: Identify Main Ideas** Use your completed flowchart to answer the section Focus Question: How did Hitler and the Nazi Party establish and maintain a totalitarian government in Germany?

Comprehension and Critical Thinking

3. **Express Problems Clearly** List three problems faced by the Weimar Republic.

4. **Recognize Ideologies** What racial and nationalistic ideas did Nazis promote?

5. **Summarize** What were some of the restrictions that Hitler placed on German Jews?

6. **Demonstrate Reasoned Judgment** Do you think that there are any reasons why a government would be justified in banning books or censoring ideas? Explain.

7. **Identify Effects** Why did dictators gain power in much of Eastern Europe?

8. **Draw Conclusions** Both Stalin and Hitler instituted ruthless campaigns against supposed enemies of the state. Why do you think dictators need to find scapegoats for their nation's ills?

● **Writing About History**

Quick Write: Use Compare-and-Contrast Transitions Use strong transitions to help readers navigate your compare-and-contrast essays. Words such as *however, but, nevertheless, yet, likewise, similarly,* and *instead* signal comparison-and-contrast relationships. Add one of these words to the statements below to clarify their meanings.

- Hitler's rise was based on hate. He was a popular leader.
- Germany became a fascist state. Many of the countries of Eastern Europe became fascist states.

Quick Study Guide

Progress Monitoring *Online*
For: Self-test with vocabulary practice
Web Code: nba-2861

■ Causes and Effects of the Great Depression

Cause and Effect	
Long-Term Causes	**Immediate Causes**
• Worldwide interrelationship of governments and economies • Gold standard • Overproduction of goods • Agricultural slump • Uneven distribution of wealth	• Falling demand • Financial crisis kicked off by New York stock market crash • Banks demand repayment of loans • American loans to other countries dry up • Without capital, businesses and factories fail

↓

Worldwide Economic Depression	

↓

Immediate Effects	Long-Term Effects
• Vast unemployment and misery • Protective tariffs imposed • Countries abandon gold standard • Loss of faith in capitalism and democracy • Authoritarian leaders emerge	• Rise of fascism and Nazism • Governments experiment with social programs • People blame scapegoats • World War II begins

■ Three Totalitarian States: Italy, the Soviet Union, and Germany

Country	Dictator in Power	Ideology	Example of Terror Tactics
Italy	Benito Mussolini in power in 1922	Fascist; Fanatic nationalism	Black Shirts suppressed dissent.
Soviet Union	Joseph Stalin in power in 1924	Communist	Stalin sent millions to Gulag labor camps.
Germany	Adolf Hitler in power in 1933	Fascist; Racial policies of hatred, aimed particularly at Jews	Nazis began to restrict and terrorize German Jews.

■ Some Cultural Figures of the Post World War I Era

Literature
Ernest Hemingway
Virginia Woolf
Langston Hughes
Mikhail Sholokhov

Music and Theater
Louis Armstrong
Bertolt Brecht

Visual Arts
Pablo Picasso
Jean Arp
Salvador Dali
Frank Lloyd Wright
George Grosz
Vasily Kandinsky

■ Key Events in Europe and the United States, 1919–1939

Britain, France, and the United States
Germany, Italy, and the Soviet Union

1919–1920
Red Scare sweeps the United States.

1925
Seven European nations sign the Locarno treaties, raising hopes for world peace.

1926
More than three million workers in several different industries strike in Britain.

1920

1925

1919
The Weimar Republic is established in Germany.

1922
Benito Mussolini comes to power after the March on Rome.

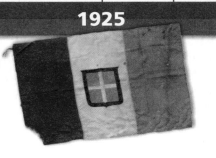

Concept | Connector

■ Cumulative Review

Record the answers to the questions below on your Concept Connector worksheets. In addition, record information from this chapter about the following concept:

• Dictatorship: Mussolini and Hitler

1. **Dictatorship** Stalin was by no means the first ruler to attempt to maintain absolute control over Russia. Compare and contrast Stalin with the following leaders:
   • Ivan the Terrible
   • Peter the Great
   • Catherine the Great
   • Nicholas II

2. **Political Systems** Mussolini, Hitler, and Stalin all ruled over totalitarian states. In a totalitarian state, the government tries to control all aspects of its people's lives. In direct contrast, the people control democratic governments. Read more about Enlightenment ideas about democracy, and then make a table contrasting those ideas with the ideas of totalitarianism. Consider the following:
   • Sources of power
   • Role of government in the economy
   • Role of leaders

3. **Science** Einstein's theories of relativity changed the way many people looked at the universe. His theories challenged Newton's theories, which developed during the Scientific Revolution in the late 1600s. Learn more about the theories of Newton. Then write a brief paragraph contrasting Newton's theories with Einstein's theories.

■ Connections To Today

1. **Dictatorship: North Korea's Kim Jong Il** Dictatorship as a form of government still exists today. Kim Jong Il (below), head of a communist totalitarian regime in North Korea, is considered among the most dangerous of the present-day dictators. In fact, Kim has been described as "Stalinist." Kim took over as dictator from his father, Kim Il-Sung, in 1994. Since then, he has violated the civil liberties of his own people, and he has destabilized international relations in the region with claims that North Korea possesses nuclear weapons. Research Kim Jong Il's record in North Korea and write two paragraphs comparing his regime to Stalin's in Russia.

2. **Political Systems: The Former Soviet Union** The Soviet Union came to an end in 1991. Its collapse produced 14 new republics, besides the Russian Federation, as each of the former SSRs became independent. The transition was not easy. Choose one of the following countries and then research and write a brief report on its transition from SSR to independent republic: Armenia, Azerbaijan, Belarus, Estonia, Georgia, Kazakhstan, Kyrgyzstan, Latvia, Lithuania, Moldova, Tajikistan, Turkmenistan, Ukraine, Uzbekistan.

1929
The Great Depression begins in the United States.

1930
Construction on the Maginot Line begins on the border of France and Germany.

1933
Prohibition is repealed in the United States.

History *Interactive*
For: Interactive timeline
Web Code: nbp-2862

1930

1935

1928
Joseph Stalin launches the first of his Five-Year Plans in the Soviet Union.

1932
Stalin's ruthless policies, combined with failed crops, cause mass starvation in the Soviet Union.

1933
Adolf Hitler becomes chancellor of Germany.

1935
The Nazi Party in Germany passes the Nuremberg Laws, limiting the rights of Jews.

Chapter Assessment

Terms, People, and Places

Match the following terms with the definitions below.

flapper
Harlem Renaissance
Franklin Delano Roosevelt
disarmament
totalitarian state

Benito Mussolini
command economy
Gulag
Ruhr Valley
Third Reich

1. rebellious young woman of the 1920s
2. leader of the first modern fascist state
3. reduction of armed forces and weapons
4. government in which a one-party dictatorship regulates every aspect of citizens' lives
5. president of the United States who established the New Deal to help Americans during the Great Depression
6. African American cultural movement in the 1920s and 1930s
7. coal-rich industrial region of Germany

Main Ideas

Section 1 (pp. 522–527)
8. How did Western culture and society change in reaction to World War I?

Section 2 (pp. 529–535)
9. Describe the search for peace in the 1920s and its results.
10. What were the effects of the Great Depression?

Section 3 (pp. 536–540)
11. What is fascism?
12. How did Mussolini's fascist regime rule Italy?

Section 4 (pp. 542–549)
13. Summarize conditions in the Soviet Union under Stalin.

Section 5 (pp. 550–555)
14. How did Hitler establish a totalitarian state in Germany?

Chapter Focus Question
15. What political and economic challenges did the Western world face in the 1920s and 1930s, and how did various countries react to these challenges?

Critical Thinking

16. **Synthesize Information** How did the literature and art of the 1920s reflect the influence of World War I?
17. **Identify Causes** What imbalances helped cause the Great Depression of the 1930s?
18. **Recognize Ideologies** Why did the ideology of fascism appeal to many Italians?
19. **Compare Points of View** Describe the similarities and differences between fascism and communism.
20. **Recognize Propaganda** Why was propaganda an important tool of totalitarian dictators?
21. **Recognize Points of View** "England can only be saved by direct action. When it's saved, we can begin to think about Parliament again." Based on what you have read, which of the three competing postwar ideologies does this statement express—democracy, fascism, or communism? Explain.

● Writing About History

Writing a Compare-and-Contrast Essay The period between World War I and World War II was a time of rapid change with some serious crises of its own. Write a compare-and-contrast essay on one of the following pairs of ideas: society before and after World War I, solutions to alleviate the Great Depression in the United States and in Germany, fascism compared to democracy in the 1920s and 1930s, or a topic of your own choosing.

Prewriting
• Choose a valid topic for your essay by choosing two things that are neither too similar nor wildly different.
• Choose categories in which the two items could be compared and contrasted.

• Use a Venn diagram to gather and record details for your essay.

Drafting
• Develop a thesis that introduces the items you are comparing and the point you intend to make by the comparison.
• Outline how you will organize your arguments and the details that will support them.
• Write an introduction explaining what you are comparing and contrasting, a body, and a conclusion that restates your main points.

Revising
• Use the guidelines for revising your essay on page SH12 of the Writing Handbook.

Document-Based Assessment

Hitler's Rise to Power

In 1919, Hitler joined the National Socialist German Workers Party, later known as the Nazi party. It was a marginal party that only received one million votes in 1924. By 1932, however, the Nazi party, with Hitler at its helm, was Germany's largest party. Many factors contributed to Hitler's surprising rise to power, as the documents below illustrate.

Document A

This poster, displayed in Berlin in 1932, tells voters: "We want work and bread! Elect Hitler!"

Document B

"The National Socialist movement must strive to eliminate the disproportion between our population and our area—viewing this latter as a source of food as well as a basis for power politics. . . . We must hold unflinchingly to our aim . . . to secure for the German people the land and soil to which they are entitled. . . ."

—From ***Mein Kampf*** by Adolf Hitler

Document C

" . . . [T]hough the Fuehrer's anti-Semitic programme furnished the National Socialist party in the first instance with a nucleus and a rallying-cry, it was swept into office by two things with which the "Jewish Problem" did not have the slightest connexion. On the one side was economic distress and the revulsion against Versailles; on the other, chicanery and intrigue. . . . Hitler and his party had promised the unhappy Germans a new heaven and a new earth, coupled with the persecution of the Jews. Unfortunately, a new heaven and earth cannot be manufactured to order. But a persecution of the Jews can. . . ."

—From ***The Jewish Problem*** by Louis Golding, 1939

Document D

"The Versailles settlement was seen as a means by which Germany's enemies aimed to keep the Reich prostrate forever and had to be overturned not merely to restore the status quo ante, but to allow Germany to expand and seize the "living space" that it allegedly needed in the east. And violence was viewed as the means by which to achieve a Third Reich and a German-dominated Europe—by smashing the democratic Weimar "system," destroying Marxism, solving the "Jewish question," breaking the "chains of Versailles," and building up the armed forces so that Germany again could go to war."

—From ***Nazism and War*** by historian Richard Bessel

Analyzing Documents

Use your knowledge of the rise of Nazism in Germany and Documents A, B, C, and D to answer questions 1–4.

1. Document A focuses on which factor that aided Hitler's rise to power?
   A anger over World War I
   B social considerations
   C the economy
   D racial and religious prejudice

2. According to Document C, the Nazis persecuted the Jews, because
   A most Germans hated them.
   B they wanted to keep attention from other problems.
   C they had already achieved their other goals.
   D their opponents were all Jews.

3. According to Document D, the Nazis' main goal was to
   A dominate Europe.
   B get revenge for the Treaty of Versailles.
   C stop communism.
   D end democracy.

4. Explain why Germany was fertile soil for the Nazis following World War I. Give your reasons, using these documents and information from the chapter.

A City Lies in Ruins

March 6, 1944—The Allies' mission to bomb Berlin, Germany, includes 810 bombers plus 800 fighter escorts. The stream of aircraft stretches a mile wide and a half-mile deep and takes more than half an hour to pass over any given point. Approaching the city, the bombers press on through flak—anti-aircraft fire from the ground—"so thick you can walk on it." Then, bomb bay doors open, and their payloads rain down on the city.

Listen to the Witness History audio to hear more about the Allied bombing efforts.

◀ **Cologne, Germany, in ruins, 1944**

Japanese pilot's goggles recovered from Pearl Harbor

"Cricket" noisemakers used by Allied paratroopers to locate each other after landing

An advertisement praising the benefits of penicillin

Chapter Preview

Chapter Focus Question How did aggressive world powers emerge, and what did it take to defeat them during World War II?

Note Taking Study Guide *Online*
For: Note Taking and Concept Connector worksheets
Web Code: nbd-2901

A Desperate Peace

British Prime Minister Neville Chamberlain spoke to a jubilant crowd upon returning to London from a conference with Adolf Hitler in Munich, Germany, in September 1938:

❝ For the second time in our history, a British Prime Minister has returned from Germany bringing peace with honor. I believe it is peace for our time . . . Go home and get a nice quiet sleep. **❞**

Focus Question What events unfolded between Chamberlain's declaration of "peace for our time" and the outbreak of a world war?

Neville Chamberlain and headlines announcing the Munich Pact

From Appeasement to War

Objectives

- Analyze the threat to world peace posed by dictators in the 1930s and how the Western democracies responded.
- Describe how the Spanish Civil War was a "dress rehearsal" for World War II.
- Summarize the ways in which continuing Nazi aggression led Europe to war.

Terms, People, and Places

appeasement	Francisco Franco
pacifism	Anschluss
Neutrality Acts	Sudetenland
Axis powers	Nazi-Soviet Pact

N̲o̲te Taking

Reading Skill: Recognize Sequence As you read, keep track of the sequence of events that led to the outbreak of World War II by completing a table like the one below.

Acts of Aggression	
Japan	
Italy	
Germany	
Spain	

After the horrors of World War I, Western democracies desperately tried to preserve peace during the 1930s while ignoring signs that the rulers of Germany, Italy, and Japan were preparing to build new empires. Despite the best efforts of Neville Chamberlain and other Western leaders, the world was headed to war again.

Aggression Goes Unchecked

Throughout the 1930s, challenges to peace followed a pattern. Dictators took aggressive action but met only verbal protests and pleas for peace from the democracies. Mussolini, Hitler, and the leaders of Japan viewed that desire for peace as weakness and responded with new acts of aggression. With hindsight, we can see the shortcomings of the democracies' policies. These policies, however, were the product of long and careful deliberation. At the time, some people believed they would work.

Japan Overruns Manchuria and Eastern China One of the earliest tests had been posed by Japan. Japanese military leaders and ultranationalists thought that Japan should have an empire equal to those of the Western powers. In pursuit of this goal, Japan seized Manchuria in 1931. When the League of Nations condemned the aggression, Japan simply withdrew from the organization. Japan's easy success strengthened the militarist faction in Japan. In 1937, Japanese armies overran much of eastern China, starting the Second Sino-Japanese War. Once again, Western protests did not stop Japan.

Hitler Remilitarizes Germany
Hitler rebuilt the German military during the 1930s in defiance of the Treaty of Versailles. The government's investment in armaments also helped pull Germany out of the Great Depression. Here, German police march in goose step as Hitler salutes in the background. *How did rearmament affect the rest of Germany?*

Italy Invades Ethiopia In Italy, Mussolini decided to act on his own imperialist ambitions. Italy's defeat by the Ethiopians at the battle of Adowa in 1896 still rankled. In 1935, Italy invaded Ethiopia, located in northeastern Africa. Although the Ethiopians resisted bravely, their outdated weapons were no match for Mussolini's tanks, machine guns, poison gas, and airplanes. The Ethiopian king Haile Selassie (HY luh suh lah SEE) appealed to the League of Nations for help. The League voted <u>sanctions</u> against Italy for violating international law. But the League had no power to enforce the sanctions, and by early 1936, Italy had conquered Ethiopia.

Vocabulary Builder
<u>sanctions</u>—(SANGK shunz) *n.* penalties

Hitler Goes Against the Treaty of Versailles By then, Hitler, too, had tested the will of the Western democracies and found it weak. First, he built up the German military in defiance of the treaty that had ended World War I. Then, in 1936, he sent troops into the "demilitarized" Rhineland bordering France—another treaty violation.

Germans hated the Versailles treaty, and Hitler's successful challenge made him more popular at home. The Western democracies denounced his moves but took no real action. Instead, they adopted a policy of **appeasement,** or giving in to the demands of an aggressor in order to keep the peace.

Keeping the Peace The Western policy of appeasement developed for a number of reasons. France was demoralized, suffering from political divisions at home. It could not take on Hitler without British support. The British, however, had no desire to confront the German dictator. Some even thought that Hitler's actions constituted a justifiable response to the terms of the Treaty of Versailles, which they believed had been too harsh on Germany.

In both Britain and France, many saw Hitler and fascism as a defense against a worse evil—the spread of Soviet communism. Additionally, the Great Depression sapped the energies of the Western democracies. Finally, widespread **pacifism,** or opposition to all war, and disgust with the destruction from the previous war pushed many governments to seek peace at any price.

Three leaders in Europe and one in Japan launched ambitious plans to increase their power.

● Benito Mussolini—Italy

● Adolf Hitler—Germany

● Tojo Hideki—Japan

● Francisco Franco—Spain

As war clouds gathered in Europe in the mid-1930s, the United States Congress passed a series of **Neutrality Acts.** One law forbade the sale of arms to any nation at war. Others outlawed loans to warring nations and prohibited Americans from traveling on ships of warring powers. The fundamental goal of American policy, however, was to avoid involvement in a European war, not to prevent such a conflict.

Rome-Berlin-Tokyo Axis In the face of the apparent weakness of Britain, France, and the United States, Germany, Italy, and Japan formed what became known as the Rome-Berlin-Tokyo Axis. Known as the **Axis powers,** the three nations agreed to fight Soviet communism. They also agreed not to interfere with one another's plans for territorial expansion. The agreement cleared the way for these anti-democratic, aggressor powers to take even bolder steps.

✓ **Checkpoint**   Describe the German, Italian, and Japanese drives for empire.

Spain Collapses Into Civil War

In 1936, a local struggle in Spain polarized public opinion throughout Europe. Trouble in Spain started in 1931, when popular unrest against the old order forced the king to leave Spain. A republic was set up with a new, more liberal constitution. The government passed a series of controversial reforms, taking land and privileges away from the Church and old ruling classes. Still, leftists demanded more radical reforms. Conservatives, backed by the military, rejected change.

In 1936, a conservative general named **Francisco Franco** led a revolt that touched off a bloody civil war. Fascists and supporters of right-wing policies, called Nationalists, rallied to back Franco. Supporters of the republic, known as Loyalists, included Communists, Socialists, and those who wanted democracy.

People from other nations soon jumped in to support both sides. Hitler and Mussolini sent arms and forces to help Franco. The Soviet Union sent soldiers to fight against fascism alongside the Spanish Loyalists. Although the governments of Britain, France, and the United States remained neutral, individuals from those countries, as well as other countries, also fought with the Loyalists. Anti-Nazi Germans and anti-Fascist Italians joined the Loyalist cause as well.

Both sides committed horrible atrocities. The ruinous struggle took more than 500,000 lives. One of the worst horrors was a German air raid on Guernica, a small Spanish market town, in April 1937. German planes dropped their load of bombs, and then swooped low to machine-gun anyone who had survived the bombs. Nearly 1,000 innocent civilians were killed. To Nazi leaders, the attack on Guernica was an experiment to identify what their new planes could do. To the rest of the world, it was a grim warning of the destructive power of modern warfare.

By 1939, Franco had triumphed. Once in power, he created a fascist dictatorship similar to the dictatorships of Hitler and Mussolini. He rolled back earlier reforms, killed or jailed enemies, and used terror to promote order.

✓ **Checkpoint**   How did the Spanish Civil War involve combatants from other countries?

German Aggression Continues

In the meantime, Hitler pursued his goal of bringing all German-speaking people into the Third Reich. He also took steps to gain "living space" for Germans in Eastern Europe. Hitler, who believed in the superiority of the German people, or "Aryan race," thought that Germany had a right to conquer the inferior Slavs to the east. "Nature is cruel," he claimed, "therefore we, too, may be cruel . . . I have the right to remove millions of an inferior race that breeds like vermin."

Austria Annexed From the beginning, Nazi propaganda had found fertile ground in Austria. By 1938, Hitler was ready to engineer the **Anschluss** (AHN shloos), or union of Austria and Germany. Early that year, he forced the Austrian chancellor to appoint Nazis to key cabinet posts. When the Austrian leader balked at other demands in March, Hitler sent in the German army to "preserve order." To indicate his new role as ruler of Austria, Hitler made a speech from the Hofburg Palace, the former residence of the Hapsburg emperors.

The Anschluss violated the Versailles treaty and created a brief war scare. Some Austrians favored annexation. Hitler quickly silenced any Austrians who opposed it. And since the Western democracies took no action, Hitler easily had his way.

The Czech Crisis Germany turned next to Czechoslovakia. At first, Hitler insisted that the three million Germans in the **Sudetenland** (soo DAY tun land)—a region of western Czechoslovakia—be given autonomy. Czechoslovakia was one of only two remaining democracies in Eastern Europe. (Finland was the other.) Still, Britain and France were not willing to go to war to save it. As British and French leaders searched for a peaceful solution, Hitler increased his demands. The Sudetenland, he said, must be annexed to Germany.

Note Taking

Reading Skill: Recognize Sequence
Complete this timetable of German aggression as you read.

German Aggression	
March 1938	
September 1938	
March 1939	
September 1939	

Germany in Czechoslovakia
A Sudeten woman grieves while dutifully saluting Hitler's troops (below). German tanks roll through Wenceslas Square in Prague (left).

At the Munich Conference in September 1938, British and French leaders again chose appeasement. They caved in to Hitler's demands and then persuaded the Czechs to surrender the Sudetenland without a fight. In exchange, Hitler assured Britain and France that he had no further plans to expand his territory.

"Peace for Our Time" Returning from Munich, British Prime Minister Neville Chamberlain told cheering crowds that he had achieved "peace for our time." He told Parliament that the Munich Pact had "saved Czechoslovakia from destruction and Europe from Armageddon." French leader Edouard Daladier (dah lahd yay) reacted differently to the joyous crowds that greeted him in Paris. "The fools, why are they cheering?" he asked. British politician Winston Churchill, who had long warned of the Nazi threat, judged the diplomats harshly: "They had to choose between war and dishonor. They chose dishonor; they will have war."

✓ **Checkpoint** Why did Hitler feel justified in taking over Austria and the Sudetenland?

Geography *Interactive*
For: Audio guided tour
Web Code: nbp-2911

Aggression in Europe and Africa to September, 1939

Map Skills Between 1936 and 1939, Germany and Italy repeatedly threatened peace in Europe.

1. Locate (a) Austria (b) Rhineland (c) Poland

2. Regions The strip of land between East Prussia and the rest of Germany is called the Polish Corridor. Why is that an appropriate name for the region?

3. Predict Consequences Which countries in 1939 were probably the most likely targets for future acts of German or Italian aggression? Explain.

Germany, 1935
Occupied by Germany, 1936
Occupied by Germany, 1938–1939
Italy and Italian territories, 1935
Occupied by Italy, 1935–1939

Europe Plunges Toward War

Just as Churchill predicted, Europe plunged rapidly toward war. In March 1939, Hitler broke his promises and gobbled up the rest of Czechoslovakia. The democracies finally accepted the fact that appeasement had failed. At last thoroughly alarmed, they promised to protect Poland, most likely the next target of Hitler's expansion.

Nazi-Soviet Pact In August 1939, Hitler stunned the world by announcing a nonaggression pact with his great enemy—Joseph Stalin, the Soviet dictator. Publicly, the Nazi-Soviet Pact bound Hitler and Stalin to peaceful relations. Secretly, the two agreed not to fight if the other went to war and to divide up Poland and other parts of Eastern Europe between them.

The pact was based not on friendship or respect but on mutual need. Hitler feared communism as Stalin feared fascism. But Hitler wanted a free hand in Poland. Also, he did not want to fight a war with the Western democracies and the Soviet Union at the same time. For his part, Stalin had sought allies among the Western democracies against the Nazi menace. Mutual suspicions, however, kept them apart. By joining with Hitler, Stalin tried to protect the Soviet Union from the threat of war with Germany and grabbed a chance to gain land in Eastern Europe.

Invasion of Poland On September 1, 1939, a week after the Nazi-Soviet Pact, German forces invaded Poland. Two days later, Britain and France declared war on Germany. World War II had begun.

The devastation of World War I and the awareness of the destructive power of modern <u>technology</u> made the idea of more fighting unbearable. Unfortunately, the war proved to be even more horrendous than anyone had imagined.

✔ **Checkpoint** What convinced Britain and France to end their policy of appeasement? Why?

Why the West Appeased Hitler

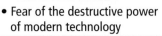

- Fear of the destructive power of modern technology
- Widespread pacifism following World War I
- Hitler's actions seen as a justifiable response to the harsh Treaty of Versailles
- Widespread economic depression
- Hitler's fascism seen as a defense against Soviet communism
- Faith in diplomacy and compromise
- Misreading of Hitler's intentions

Chart Skills Agree or disagree with the following statement: "World War II was in large part a continuation of World War I." Provide evidence from the chart and your knowledge of history to support your view.

Vocabulary Builder

<u>technology</u>—(tek NAHL uh jee) *n.* scientific advances applied to practical purposes

---

Progress Monitoring *Online*
For: Self-quiz with vocabulary practice
Web Code: nba-2911

SECTION **1** Assessment

Terms, People, and Places

1. For each term, person, or place listed at the beginning of the section, write a sentence explaining its significance.

Note Taking

2. **Reading Skill: Recognize Sequence** Use your completed tables to answer the Focus Question: What events unfolded between Chamberlain's declaration of "peace for our time" and the outbreak of a world war?

Comprehension and Critical Thinking

3. **Identify Central Issues** How did the Western democracies respond to the aggression of the Axis powers during the 1930s?
4. **Synthesize Information** Why did Germany and Italy become involved in the Spanish Civil War?
5. **Recognize Cause and Effect** How was the Munich Conference a turning point in the road toward world war?
6. **Analyze Information** Why do you think some historians call the period between 1919 and 1939 the 20-year truce?

● Writing About History

Quick Write: Explore a Topic Choose one specific event from this section and write a series of questions that you could use to direct research on the topic. For example, on the formation of the Rome-Berlin-Tokyo Axis you could ask

- How did the Axis benefit each of the member countries?
- How did the Axis clear the way for the members to take even bolder aggressive actions?

German fighter plane

Janina Sulkowska in the early 1930s

WITNESS HISTORY ◀ AUDIO

Janina's War Story

66 It was 10:30 in the morning and I was helping my mother and a servant girl with bags and baskets as they set out for the market. . . . Suddenly the high-pitch scream of diving planes caused everyone to freeze. . . . Countless explosions shook our house followed by the *rat-tat-tat* of strafing machine guns. We could only stare at each other in horror. Later reports would confirm that several German Stukas had screamed out of a blue sky and . . . dropped several bombs along the main street— and then returned to strafe the market. The carnage was terrible. 99

—Janina Sulkowska, Krzemieniec, Poland, September 12, 1939

Focus Question Which regions were attacked and occupied by the Axis powers, and what was life like under their occupation?

The Axis Advances

Objectives

- Describe how the Axis powers came to control much of Europe, but failed to conquer Britain.
- Summarize Germany's invasion of the Soviet Union.
- Understand the horror of the genocide the Nazis committed.
- Describe the role of the United States before and after joining World War II.

Terms, People, and Places

blitzkrieg
Luftwaffe
Dunkirk
Vichy

General Erwin Rommel
concentration camps
Holocaust
Lend-Lease Act

Note Taking

Reading Skill: Recognize Sequence Sequence events as you read in a flowchart.

September 1939: Germany invades Poland.

Diplomacy and compromise had not satisfied the Axis powers' hunger for empire. Western democracies had hoped that appeasement would help establish a peaceful world order. But Nazi Germany, Fascist Italy, and imperial Japan plunged ahead with their plans for conquest.

The Axis Attacks

On September 1, 1939, Nazi forces stormed into Poland, revealing the enormous power of Hitler's **blitzkrieg,** or "lightning war." The blitzkrieg utilized improved tank and airpower technology to strike a devastating blow against the enemy. First, the **Luftwaffe,** or German air force, bombed airfields, factories, towns, and cities, and screaming dive bombers fired on troops and civilians. Then, fast-moving tanks and troop transports pushed their way into the defending Polish army, encircling whole divisions of troops and forcing them to surrender.

While Germany attacked from the west, Stalin's forces invaded from the east, grabbing lands promised to them under the Nazi-Soviet Pact. Within a month, Poland ceased to exist. Because of Poland's location and the speed of the attacks, Britain and France could do nothing to help beyond declaring war on Germany.

Hitler passed the winter without much further action. Stalin's armies, however, forced the Baltic states of Estonia, Latvia, and

Lithuania to agree to host bases for the Soviet military. Soviet forces also seized part of Finland, which put up stiff but unsuccessful resistance.

The Miracle of Dunkirk During that first winter, the French hunkered down behind the Maginot Line. Britain sent troops to wait with them. Some reporters referred to this quiet time as the "phony war." Then, in April 1940, Hitler launched a blitzkrieg against Norway and Denmark, both of which soon fell. Next, his forces slammed into the Netherlands and Belgium.

In May, German forces surprised the French and British by attacking through the Ardennes Forest in Belgium, an area that was considered invasion proof. Bypassing the Maginot Line, German troops poured into France. Retreating British forces were soon trapped between the Nazi army and the English Channel. In a desperate gamble, the British sent all <u>available</u> naval vessels, merchant ships, and even fishing and pleasure boats across the channel to pluck stranded troops off the beach of **Dunkirk.** Despite German air attacks, the improvised armada ferried more than 300,000 troops to safety in Britain. This heroic rescue raised British morale.

Vocabulary Builder

<u>available</u>—(uh VAYL uh bul) *adj.* ready for use; at hand

France Falls Meanwhile, German forces headed south toward Paris. Italy declared war on France and attacked from the south. Overrun and demoralized, France surrendered. On June 22, 1940, Hitler forced the French to sign the surrender documents in the same railroad car in which Germany had signed the armistice ending World War I. Following the surrender, Germany occupied northern France. In the south, the Germans set up a "puppet state," with its capital at **Vichy** (VEE shee).

Some French officers escaped to England and set up a government-in-exile. Led by Charles de Gaulle, these "free French" worked to liberate their homeland. Within France, resistance fighters used guerrilla tactics against German forces.

Operation Sea Lion With the fall of France, Britain stood alone in Western Europe. Hitler was sure that the British would sue for peace. But Winston Churchill, who had replaced Neville Chamberlain as prime minister, had other plans. Faced with this defiance, Hitler made plans for Operation Sea Lion—the invasion of Britain. In preparation for the invasion, he launched massive air strikes against the island nation.

Beginning in August 1940, German bombers began a daily bombardment of England's southern coast. For a month, Britain's Royal Air Force valiantly battled the Luftwaffe. Then, the Germans changed their tactics. Instead of bombing military targets in the south, they began to bomb London and other cities.

YOUR COURAGE
YOUR CHEERFULNESS
YOUR RESOLUTION
**WILL BRING
US VICTORY**

Winston Churchill's defiance gave voice to the determination of the British. *How did Churchill give weight to his speech?*

Primary Source

66 We shall defend our island, whatever the cost may be, we shall fight on the beaches, we shall fight on the landing grounds, we shall fight in the fields and in the streets, we shall fight in the hills; we shall never surrender. 99
—*Winston Churchill, June 4, 1940*   AUDIO

Germany Launches the Blitz German bombers first appeared over London late on September 7, 1940. All through the night, relays of aircraft showered high explosives and firebombs on the sprawling capital. The bombing continued for 57 nights in a row and then sporadically until the next May. These bombing attacks are known as "the blitz." Much of London was destroyed, and thousands of people lost their lives.

SURVIVING THE BLITZ

From 1940 to 1941, Germany tried to pummel Britain into submission during a months-long bombing campaign known as "the blitz." From September through May, German pilots targeted London with night after night of bombing, but other cities such as Liverpool, Glasgow, and Belfast became targets, too. These nighttime raids sent ordinary civilians scrambling for safety—in crowded public shelters, in homemade shelters, or even in the London Underground. During the blitz, German bombers killed more than 40,000 British civilians and damaged millions of homes. AUDIO 🔊

◀ Fearing poisonous gas attacks, the British government issued gas masks to its citizens. However, gas was never used against British civilians.

Small gestures of kindness helped Londoners deal with the effects of bombing raids. ▼

MOTHERS
Send them
out of
London

▲ Nearly three million people were evacuated from Britain's cities to the safer countryside.

London did not break under the blitz. Defiantly, Parliament continued to meet. Citizens carried on their daily lives, seeking protection in shelters and then emerging to resume their routines when the all-clear sounded. Even the British king and queen chose to support Londoners by joining them in bomb shelters rather than fleeing to the countryside.

Hitler Fails to Take Britain German planes continued to bomb London and other cities off and on until May 1941. But contrary to Hitler's hopes, the Luftwaffe could not gain air superiority over Britain, and British morale was not destroyed. In fact, the bombing only made the British more determined to turn back the enemy. Operation Sea Lion was a failure.

Africa and the Balkans Axis armies also pushed into North Africa and the Balkans. In September 1940, Mussolini ordered forces from Italy's North African colony of Libya into Egypt. When the British army repulsed these invaders, Hitler sent one of his most brilliant commanders, **General Erwin Rommel,** to North Africa. The "Desert Fox," as he was called, chalked up a string of successes in 1941 and 1942. He pushed the British back across the desert toward Cairo, Egypt.

In October 1940, Italian forces invaded Greece. They encountered stiff resistance, and in 1941 German troops once again provided reinforcements. Both Greece and Yugoslavia were added to the growing Axis empire. Even after the Axis triumph, however, Greek and Yugoslav

Thinking Critically
1. **Draw Conclusions** What lessons might the British have learned from their experience of the blitz?
2. **Make Inferences** Why do you think that the blitz failed to break the morale of the British people?

During air raids, some 60,000 Londoners sought shelter in the Underground, or subway, each night. Thousands of others slept in church crypts, basements, and other underground shelters.

guerrillas plagued the occupying forces. Meanwhile, both Bulgaria and Hungary had joined the Axis alliance. By 1941, the Axis powers or their allies controlled most of Europe.

 Checkpoint Which regions fell under Axis rule between 1939 and 1941?

Germany Invades the Soviet Union

After the failure in Britain, Hitler turned his military might to a new target—the Soviet Union. The decision to invade the Soviet Union helped relieve Britain. It also proved to be one of Hitler's costliest mistakes.

An Unstoppable German Army Stalls In June 1941, Hitler nullified the Nazi-Soviet Pact by invading the Soviet Union in Operation Barbarossa, a plan which took its name from the medieval Germanic leader, Frederick Barbarossa. Hitler made his motives clear. "If I had the Ural Mountains with their incalculable store of treasures in raw materials," he declared, "Siberia with its vast forests, and the Ukraine with its tremendous wheat fields, Germany under National Socialist leadership would swim in plenty." He also wanted to crush communism in Europe and defeat his powerful rival, Stalin.

Hitler unleashed a new blitzkrieg in the Soviet Union. About three million German soldiers invaded. The Germans caught Stalin unprepared.

Vocabulary Builder

nullified—(NUL uh fyd) *vt.* made invalid

The Holocaust

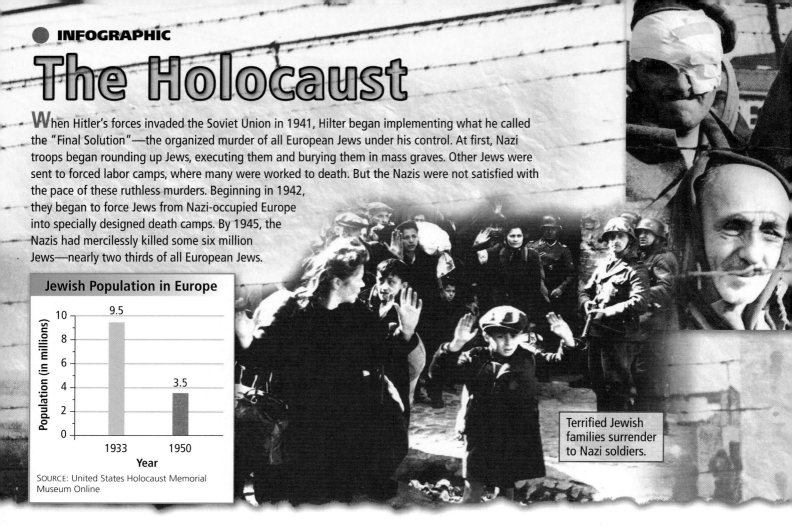

When Hitler's forces invaded the Soviet Union in 1941, Hilter began implementing what he called the "Final Solution"—the organized murder of all European Jews under his control. At first, Nazi troops began rounding up Jews, executing them and burying them in mass graves. Other Jews were sent to forced labor camps, where many were worked to death. But the Nazis were not satisfied with the pace of these ruthless murders. Beginning in 1942, they began to force Jews from Nazi-occupied Europe into specially designed death camps. By 1945, the Nazis had mercilessly killed some six million Jews—nearly two thirds of all European Jews.

Jewish Population in Europe

Population (in millions) vs Year:
- 1933: 9.5
- 1950: 3.5

SOURCE: United States Holocaust Memorial Museum Online

Terrified Jewish families surrender to Nazi soldiers.

His army was still suffering from the purges that had wiped out many of its top officers.

The Soviets lost two and a half million soldiers trying to fend off the invaders. As they were forced back, Soviet troops destroyed factories and farm equipment and burned crops to keep them out of enemy hands. But they could not stop the German war machine. By autumn, the Nazis had smashed deep into the Soviet Union and were poised to take Moscow and Leningrad (present-day St. Petersburg).

There, however, the German advance stalled. Like Napoleon's Grand Army in 1812, Hitler's forces were not prepared for the fury of "General Winter." By early December, temperatures plunged to −40°F (−4°C). Thousands of German soldiers froze to death.

Germany's Siege of Leningrad The Soviets, meanwhile, suffered appalling hardships. In September 1941, the two-and-a-half-year siege of Leningrad began. Food was rationed to two pieces of bread a day. Desperate Leningraders ate almost anything. For example, they boiled wallpaper scraped off walls because its paste was said to contain potato flour.

Although more than a million Leningraders died during the siege, the city did not fall to the Germans. Hoping to gain some relief for his exhausted people, Stalin urged Britain to open a second front in Western Europe. Although Churchill could not offer much real help, the two powers did agree to work together.

✓ **Checkpoint** What caused Hitler's invasion of the Soviet Union to stall?

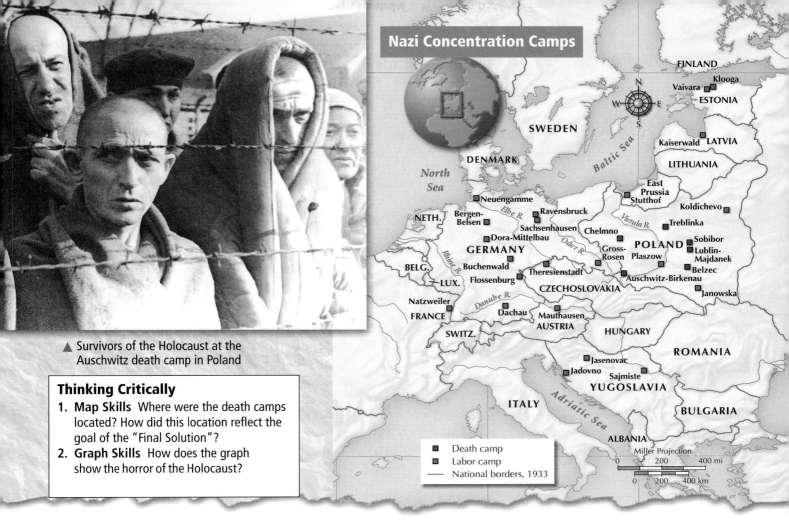

Nazi Concentration Camps

FINLAND
Klooga
Vaivara
ESTONIA
SWEDEN
Kaiserwald LATVIA
Baltic Sea
LITHUANIA
DENMARK
North Sea
East Prussia
Stutthof
Koldichevo
Neuengamme
Ravensbruck
Treblinka
NETH.
Bergen-Belsen
Sachsenhausen
Chelmno
Sobibor
Dora-Mittelbau
GERMANY
Gross-Rosen
POLAND
Lublin-Majdanek
BELG.
Buchenwald
Plaszow
Belzec
LUX.
Flossenburg
Theresienstadt
Auschwitz-Birkenau
Janowska
Natzweiler
CZECHOSLOVAKIA
FRANCE
Dachau
Mauthausen
SWITZ.
AUSTRIA
HUNGARY
ROMANIA
Jasenovac
Jadovno
Sajmiste
YUGOSLAVIA
ITALY
BULGARIA
ALBANIA

■ Death camp
■ Labor camp
— National borders, 1933

Miller Projection
0   200   400 mi
0   200   400 km

▲ Survivors of the Holocaust at the Auschwitz death camp in Poland

Thinking Critically
1. **Map Skills** Where were the death camps located? How did this location reflect the goal of the "Final Solution"?
2. **Graph Skills** How does the graph show the horror of the Holocaust?

Life Under Nazi and Japanese Occupation

While Nazi forces rampaged across Europe, the Japanese military conquered an empire in Asia and the Pacific. Each set out to build a "new order" in the occupied lands.

Hitler's "New Order" Hitler's new order grew out of his racial obsessions. As his forces conquered most of Europe, Hitler set up puppet governments in Western European countries that were peopled by Aryans, or light-skinned Europeans, whom Hitler and his followers believed to be a "master race." The Slavs of Eastern Europe were considered to be an inferior "race." They were shoved aside to provide more "living space" for Germans, the strongest of the Aryans.

To the Nazis, occupied lands were an economic resource to be plundered and looted. The Nazis systematically stripped conquered nations of their works of art, factories, and other resources. To counter resistance movements that emerged in occupied countries, the Nazis took savage revenge, shooting hostages and torturing prisoners.

But the Nazis' most sinister plans centered on the people of the occupied countries. During the 1930s, the Nazis had sent thousands of Jewish people and political opponents to **concentration camps**, detention centers for civilians considered enemies of the state. Over the course of the war, the Nazis forced these people, along with millions of Polish and Soviet Slavs and people from other parts of Europe, to work as slave laborers. Prisoners were poorly fed and often worked to death.

Note Taking

Reading Skill: Identify Supporting Details In a concept web like the one below, fill in details about how the Nazis and Japanese military treated people under their power during World War II. Add circles as necessary.

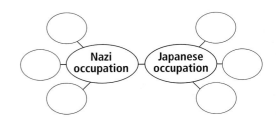

Nazi occupation — Japanese occupation

The Nazis Commit Genocide At the same time, Hitler pursued a vicious program to kill all people he judged "racially inferior," particularly Europe's Jews. The Nazis also targeted other groups who did not meet the Aryan racial ideal, including Slavs, Romas (Gypsies), homosexuals, and the disabled. Political and religious leaders who spoke out against Nazism also suffered abuse. Starting in 1939, the Nazis forced Jews in Poland and other countries to live in ghettos, or sections of cities where Jewish people were confined. Many died from starvation, disease, overwork, and the harsh elements. By 1941, however, German leaders had devised plans for the "Final Solution of the Jewish problem"—the genocide of all European Jews.

To accomplish this goal, Hitler had six special "death camps" built in Poland. The Nazis shipped "undesirables" from all over occupied Europe to the camps. There, Nazi engineers designed the most efficient means of killing millions of men, women, and children.

As the prisoners reached the camps, they were stripped of their clothes and valuables. Their heads were shaved. Guards separated men from women and children from their parents. The young, elderly, and sick were targeted for immediate killing. Within a few days, they were herded into "shower rooms" and gassed. The Nazis worked others to death or used them for perverse "medical" experiments. By 1945, the Nazis had massacred some six million Jews in what became known as the **Holocaust.** Nearly six million other people were killed as well.

Jewish people resisted the Nazis even though they knew their efforts could not succeed. In July 1942, the Nazis began sending Polish Jews from the Warsaw ghetto to the Treblinka death camp at a rate of about 5,000 per day. In the spring of 1943, knowing that their situation was hopeless, the Jews took over the ghetto and used a small collection of guns and homemade bombs to damage the Nazi forces as much as possible. On May 16, the Nazis regained control of the ghetto and eliminated the remaining Warsaw Jews. Still, their courage has inspired many over the years.

In some cases, friends, neighbors, or strangers protected Jews. Italian peasants hid Jews in their villages. Denmark and Bulgaria saved almost

The Japanese in China
Since 1937, the Japanese had been trying to expand into Asia by taking over China. Although the Japanese occupied much of Eastern China, the Chinese refused to surrender. The occupying Japanese treated the Chinese brutally. Below, Japanese soldiers load Chinese civilians onto trucks to take them to an execution ground during the sacking of Nanjing in 1937.

all their Jewish populations. Many people, however, pretended not to notice what was happening. Some even became collaborators and cooperated with the Nazis. In France, the Vichy government helped ship thousands of Jewish people to their deaths. Strict immigration policies in many Western countries as well as conscious efforts to block Jewish immigration prevented many Jews from gaining refuge elsewhere.

The scale and savagery of the Holocaust are unequaled in history. The Nazis deliberately set out to destroy the Jews for no reason other than their religious and ethnic heritage. Today, the record of that slaughter is a vivid reminder of the monstrous results of racism and intolerance.

Japan's Brutal Conquest Japanese forces took control across Asia and the Pacific. Their self-proclaimed mission was to help Asians escape Western colonial rule. In fact, the real goal was a Japanese empire in Asia. The Japanese invaders treated the Chinese, Filipinos, Malaysians, and other conquered people with great brutality, killing and torturing civilians throughout East and Southeast Asia. The occupiers seized food crops, destroyed cities and towns, and made local people into slave laborers. Whatever welcome the Japanese had first met as "liberators" was soon turned to hatred. In the Philippines, Indochina, and elsewhere, nationalist groups waged guerrilla warfare against the Japanese invaders.

✓ **Checkpoint** How did Hitler's views about race lead to the murder of six million Jewish people and millions of Slavs, Gypsies, and others?

Japan Attacks the United States

When the war began in 1939, the United States declared its neutrality. Still, although isolationist feeling remained strong, many Americans sympathized with those who battled the Axis powers. As one of those sympathizers, President Franklin Delano Roosevelt (FDR) looked for ways around the Neutrality Acts to provide warships and other aid to Britain as it stood alone against Hitler.

American Involvement Grows In March 1941, FDR persuaded Congress to pass the **Lend-Lease Act.** It allowed him to sell or lend war materials to "any country whose defense the President deems vital to the defense of the United States." The United States, said Roosevelt, would not be drawn into the war, but it would become "the arsenal of democracy," supplying arms to those who were fighting for freedom.

To show further support, Roosevelt met secretly with Churchill on a warship in the Atlantic in August 1941. The two leaders issued the Atlantic Charter, which set goals for the war—"the final destruction of the Nazi tyranny"—and for the postwar world. They pledged to support "the right of all peoples to choose the form of government under which they will live" and called for a "permanent system of general security."

Japan and the United States Face Off When war broke out in Europe in 1939, the Japanese saw a chance to grab European possessions in Southeast Asia. The rich resources of the region, including oil, rubber, and tin, would be of immense value in fighting its war against the Chinese.

In 1940, Japan advanced into French Indochina and the Dutch East Indies. To stop Japanese aggression, the United States banned the sale of war materials, such as iron, steel, and oil to Japan. Japanese leaders saw this move as an attempt to interfere in Japan's sphere of influence.

Meeting at Sea
President Roosevelt and Prime Minister Churchill issued the Atlantic Charter in August 1941.

Damage at Pearl Harbor	
U.S. ships sunk or damaged	19
U.S. aircraft destroyed	188
Americans killed	2,348
Americans injured	1,109

SOURCE: *Columbia Encyclopedia, Sixth Edition*

December 7, 1941
On the sleepy Sunday morning of December 7, 1941, the military complex at Pearl Harbor was suddenly jolted awake by a surprise attack. Planes screamed down from the sky, dropping bombs and torpedoes. Americans were shocked and horrified by the attacks. *How did Pearl Harbor change the isolationist policies of the United States?*

Japan and the United States held talks to ease the growing tension. But extreme militarists, such as General Tojo Hideki, hoped to expand Japan's empire, and the United States was interfering with their plans.

Attack on Pearl Harbor With talks at a standstill, General Tojo ordered a surprise attack. Early on December 7, 1941, Japanese airplanes bombed the American fleet at Pearl Harbor in Hawaii. The attack took the lives of about 2,400 people and destroyed battleships and aircraft. The next day, a grim-faced President Roosevelt told the nation that December 7 was "a date which will live in infamy." He asked Congress to declare war on Japan. On December 11, Germany and Italy, as Japan's allies, declared war on the United States.

Japanese Victories In the long run, the Japanese attack on Pearl Harbor would be as serious a mistake as Hitler's invasion of the Soviet Union. But in the months after Pearl Harbor, possessions in the Pacific fell to the Japanese one by one. The Japanese captured the Philippines and other islands held by the United States. They overran the British colonies of Hong Kong, Burma, and Malaya, and advanced deeper into the Dutch East Indies and French Indochina. By 1942, the Japanese empire stretched from Southeast Asia to the western Pacific Ocean.

✔ **Checkpoint** Why did Japanese leaders view the United States as an enemy?

SECTION 2 **Assessment**

Progress Monitoring *Online*
For: Self-quiz with vocabulary practice
Web Code: nba-2921

Terms, People, and Places

1. For each term, person, or place listed at the beginning of the section, write a sentence explaining its significance.

Note Taking

2. **Reading Skill: Recognize Sequence** Use your completed flowchart and concept web to answer the Focus Question: Which regions were attacked and occupied by the Axis powers, and what was life like under their occupation?

Comprehension and Critical Thinking

3. **Summarize** Describe Hitler's blitzkrieg tactics.

4. **Recognize Effects** Referring to the Battle of Britain in 1940, Winston Churchill said "Never in the field of human conflict was so much owed by so many to so few." What did he mean?

5. **Recognize Ideologies** Hitler translated his hatred into a program of genocide. How do ethnic, racial, and religious hatreds weaken society?

● **Writing About History**

Quick Write: Gather Information Use the library and reliable Internet sources to find information about Pearl Harbor. Create a source card for each book or Web site you use. Then create note cards to record and organize at least three pieces of information.

British poster encouraging women to work in factories to increase production

American medal awarded for supporting the war

WITNESS HISTORY 🔊 AUDIO

Support the War!

For the Allies to succeed against the relentless Axis war machine, everyone—on the home front as well as on the battlefield—had to work tirelessly. Ships needed to be built in a matter of days, not months. Airplanes, tanks, and ammunition had to be mass-produced. As factories converted to war production, the production of consumer goods such as automobiles ceased. All efforts were focused on the massive production of the materials of war.

Focus Question How did the Allies begin to push back the Axis powers?

SECTION 3

The Allies Turn the Tide

Objectives

- Understand how nations devoted all of their resources to fighting World War II.
- Explain how Allied victories began to push back the Axis powers.
- Describe D-Day and the Allied advance toward Germany.

Terms, People, and Places

Rosie the Riveter	Stalingrad
aircraft carrier	D-Day
Dwight Eisenhower	Yalta Conference

Note Taking

Recognize Sequence In a flowchart like the one below, sequence the events that turned the tide of the war towards the Allies.

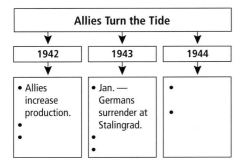

Allies Turn the Tide		
1942	1943	1944
• Allies increase production. • •	• Jan. — Germans surrender at Stalingrad. • •	• •

As 1942 began, the Allies were in trouble. German bombers flew unrelenting raids over Britain, and the German army advanced deep into the Soviet Union. In the Pacific, the Japanese onslaught seemed unstoppable. But helped by extraordinary efforts on the home front and a series of military victories, the tide was about to turn.

All-Out War

To defeat the Axis war machine, the Allies had to commit themselves to total war. Total war means nations devote all of their resources to the war effort.

Governments Increase Power To achieve maximum war production, democratic governments in the United States and Great Britain increased their political power. They directed economic resources into the war effort, ordering factories to stop making cars or refrigerators and to turn out airplanes or tanks instead. Governments implemented programs to ration or control the amount of food and other vital goods consumers could buy. They raised money by holding war bond drives, in which citizens lent their government certain sums of money that would be returned with interest later. Prices and wages were also regulated. While the war brought some shortages and hardships, the increase in production ended the unemployment of the depression era.

Under the pressures of war, even democratic governments limited the rights of citizens, censored the press, and used propaganda to win public support for the war. In the United States and Canada, many citizens of Japanese descent lost their jobs, property, and civil rights. Many Japanese Americans and Japanese Canadians were even interned in camps after their governments decided that they were a security risk. The British took similar action against German refugees. Some 40 years later, both the United States and Canada provided former internees with reparations, or payment for damages, but for many the compensation came too late.

Women Help Win the War As men joined the military, millions of women around the world replaced them in essential war industry jobs. Women, symbolized by the character **"Rosie the Riveter"** in the United States, built ships and planes and produced munitions.

British and American women served in the armed forces in many auxiliary roles—driving ambulances, delivering airplanes, and decoding messages. In occupied Europe, women fought in the resistance. Marie Fourcade, a French woman, helped downed Allied pilots escape to safety. Soviet women served in combat roles. Soviet pilot Lily Litvak, for example, shot down 12 German planes before she herself was killed.

✔ **Checkpoint** How did the Allies mobilize all of their resources for the war effort?

The Allies Forge Ahead

The years 1942–1943 marked the turning point of the war. The Allies won victories on four fronts—the Pacific, North Africa and Italy, the Soviet Union, and France—to push back the Axis tide.

Japanese Navy Battered In the Pacific, the Japanese suffered their first serious setback at the Battle of the Coral Sea. The battle lasted for five days in May 1942. For the first time in naval history, the enemy ships never even saw each other. Attacks were carried out by planes launched from **aircraft carriers,** or ships that transport aircraft and accommodate the take-off and landing of airplanes. The Japanese were prevented from seizing several important islands. More importantly, the Americans sank one Japanese aircraft carrier and several cruisers and destroyers.

This Allied victory was followed by an even more impressive win at the Battle of Midway in June 1942, which was also fought entirely from the air. The Americans destroyed four Japanese carriers and more than 250 planes. The battle was a devastating blow to the Japanese. After Midway, Japan was unable to launch any more offensive operations.

The Big Three Plot Their Strategy After the United States entered the war, the Allied leaders met periodically to hammer out their strategy.

Air War in the Pacific
Allied forces won decisive victories in the Coral Sea and at Midway Island. The Japanese pilots below may have taken part in these battles, which were fought from planes launched from aircraft carriers. *How do you think aircraft carriers changed naval warfare?*

Technology That Helped Win the War

Deadlier bombs, machines that broke secret codes, dive-bombers—all of these technologies gave those who used them a military advantage. Scientists and engineers on both sides of World War II created and improved technologies at a fast and furious pace in a desperate effort to win the war.

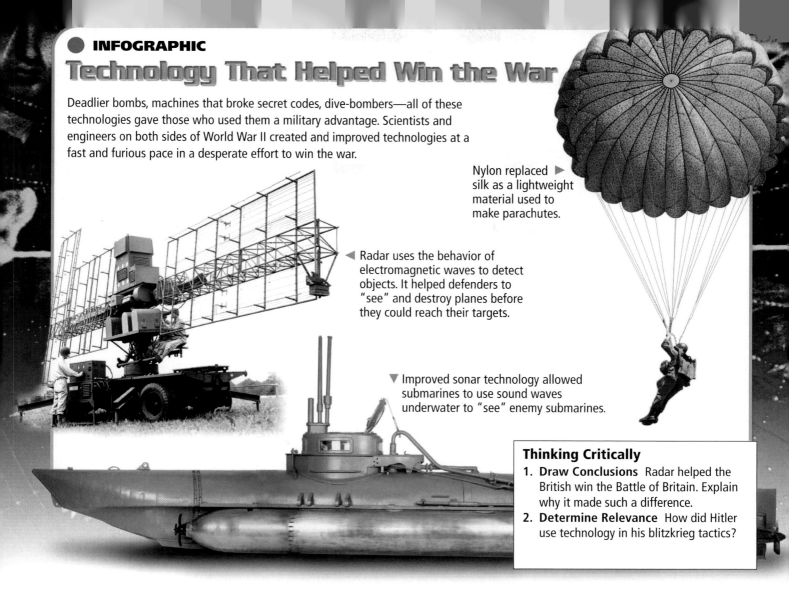

Nylon replaced ▶ silk as a lightweight material used to make parachutes.

◀ Radar uses the behavior of electromagnetic waves to detect objects. It helped defenders to "see" and destroy planes before they could reach their targets.

▼ Improved sonar technology allowed submarines to use sound waves underwater to "see" enemy submarines.

Thinking Critically
1. **Draw Conclusions** Radar helped the British win the Battle of Britain. Explain why it made such a difference.
2. **Determine Relevance** How did Hitler use technology in his blitzkrieg tactics?

In 1942, the "Big Three"—Roosevelt, Churchill, and Stalin—agreed to focus on finishing the war in Europe before trying to end the war in Asia.

From the outset, the Allies distrusted one another. Churchill and Roosevelt feared that Stalin wanted to dominate Europe. Stalin believed the West wanted to destroy communism. None of the new Allies wanted to risk a breakdown in their alliance, however. At a conference in Tehran, Iran, in late 1943, Churchill and Roosevelt yielded to Stalin by agreeing to let the borders outlined in the Nazi-Soviet Pact stand, against the wishes of Poland's government-in-exile. However, Stalin also wanted Roosevelt and Churchill to open a second front against Germany in Western Europe to relieve the pressure on the Soviet Union. Roosevelt and Churchill replied that they did not yet have the resources. Stalin saw the delay as a deliberate policy to weaken the Soviet Union.

Allied Victory in North Africa In North Africa, the British led by General Bernard Montgomery fought Rommel. After the fierce Battle of El Alamein in November 1942, the Allies finally halted the Desert Fox's advance. Allied tanks drove the Axis back across Libya into Tunisia.

Later in 1942, American General **Dwight Eisenhower** took command of a joint British and American force in Morocco and Algeria. Advancing on Tunisia from the west, the Allies trapped Rommel's army, which surrendered in May 1943.

The Pain of Defeat
German prisoners are marched through the snowy streets of Stalingrad after their defeat by the Soviet army.

Allies Advance Through Italy
With North Africa under their control, the Allies were able to cross the Mediterranean into Italy. In July 1943, a combined British and American army landed first in Sicily and then in southern Italy. They defeated the Italian forces there in about a month.

After the defeats, the Italians overthrew Mussolini and signed an armistice, but fighting did not end. Hitler sent German troops to rescue Mussolini and stiffen the will of Italians fighting in the north. For the next 18 months, the Allies pushed slowly up the Italian peninsula, suffering heavy losses against strong German resistance. Still, the Italian invasion was a decisive event for the Allies because it weakened Hitler by forcing him to fight on another front.

Germans Defeated at Stalingrad A major turning point occurred in the Soviet Union. After their lightning advance in 1941, the Germans were stalled outside Moscow and Leningrad. In 1942, Hitler launched a new offensive. This time, he aimed for the rich oil fields of the south. His troops, however, got only as far as **Stalingrad.**

The Battle of Stalingrad was one of the costliest of the war. Hitler was determined to capture Stalin's namesake city, and Stalin was equally determined to defend it. The battle began when the Germans surrounded the city. As winter closed in, a bitter street-by-street, house-by-house struggle raged. A German officer wrote that soldiers fought for two weeks for a single building. Corpses "are strewn in the cellars, on the landings and the staircases," he said. In November, the Soviets encircled their attackers. Trapped, without food or ammunition and with no hope of rescue, the German commander finally surrendered in January 1943.

After the Battle of Stalingrad, the Red Army took the offensive and drove the invaders out of the Soviet Union entirely. Hitler's forces suffered irreplaceable losses of both troops and equipment. By early 1944, Soviet troops were advancing into Eastern Europe.

✓ **Checkpoint** How did the Allies push back the Axis powers on four fronts?

The Allies Push Toward Germany

By 1944, the Western Allies were at last ready to open a second front in Europe by invading France. Allied leaders under Eisenhower faced the enormous task of planning the operation and assembling troops and supplies. To prepare the way for the invasion, Allied bombers flew constant missions over Germany. They targeted factories and destroyed aircraft that might be used against the invasion force. They also bombed railroads and bridges in France.

The D-Day Assault The Allies chose June 6, 1944—known as **D-Day**—for the invasion of France. Just before midnight on June 5, Allied planes dropped paratroopers behind enemy lines. Then, at dawn, thousands of ships ferried 156,000 Allied troops across the English Channel. The troops

World War II in Europe and North Africa, 1942–1945

Map Skills Axis power reached its height in Europe in 1942. Then the tide began to turn.

1. **Locate** (a) Vichy France (b) Soviet Union (c) El Alamein (d) Normandy (e) Berlin

2. **Place** Describe the extent of Axis control in 1942.

3. **Make Inferences** How did geography both help and hinder Allied advances?

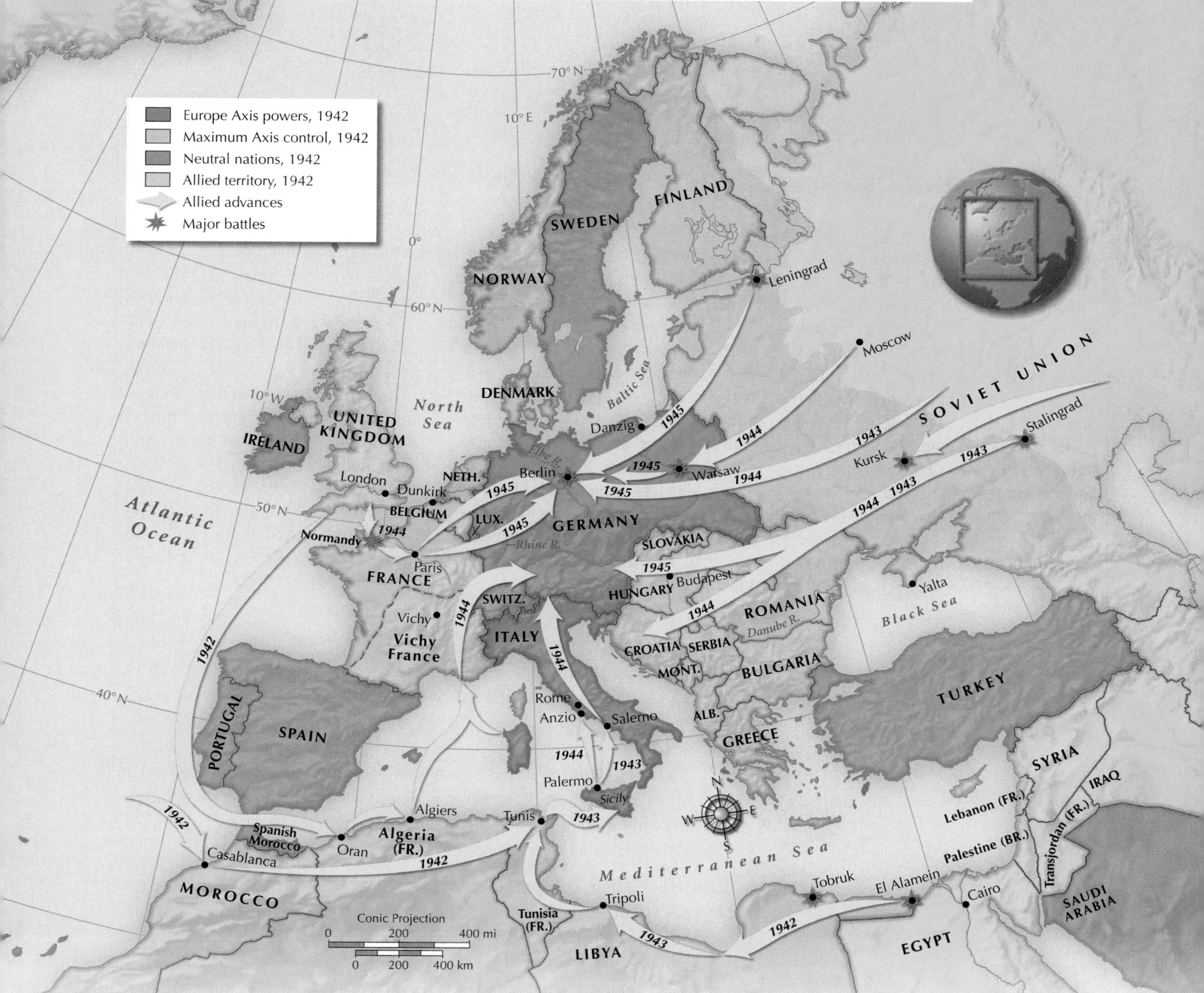

Legend
- Europe Axis powers, 1942
- Maximum Axis control, 1942
- Neutral nations, 1942
- Allied territory, 1942
- Allied advances
- Major battles

Timeline

Jan 1943 — Germans surrender at Stalingrad
Jul 1943 — Allied forces land in Sicily
Jan 1945 — Soviets enter Warsaw
May 7, 1945 — Germany surrenders

1942   1943   1944   1945   1946

Nov 1942 — British defeat Germans at El Alamein
Sep 1943 — Italians surrender to Allies
Jun 6, 1944 — D-Day invasion at Normandy
Mar 1945 — British and American forces cross Rhine

Churchill

Winston Churchill (1874–1965) was a staunch antisocialist and defender of the British Empire. As a member of Parliament, he loudly warned the British of the threat posed by Nazi Germany. After Neville Chamberlain's government failed to defend Norway from Hitler, Churchill replaced him as prime minister on May 10, 1940. Within seven weeks, France had surrendered, and Nazi forces threatened Britain. Churchill's courage and defiance steeled British resolve in the darkest days of the war when Britain stood alone against the Nazis. **How did Churchill inspire the British people?**

Roosevelt

In 1933, Franklin Delano Roosevelt (1882–1945) started his first term as president, promising to bring the United States out of the Great Depression. During his second term, FDR lent, and then gave, millions of dollars in war supplies to the struggling British. Japan's attack on Pearl Harbor quickly brought the United States into the war. From the start of American involvement, Roosevelt took the lead in establishing alliances among all countries fighting the Axis powers—including the Soviet Union. **How did Roosevelt influence World War II before Pearl Harbor?**

Stalin

Joseph Stalin (1879–1953) was born Joseph Dzhugashvili (joo gush VYEE lyee). He changed his name to Stalin, meaning "man of steel," after he joined the Bolshevik underground in the early 1900s. Stalin emerged as the sole ruler of the Soviet Union in the 1920s, and he maintained an iron grasp on the nation until his death in 1953. When Hitler's army invaded the Soviet Union and threatened Moscow in 1941, Stalin refused to leave the capital city. He eventually forced the Germans into retreat. **Why would Churchill and Roosevelt have distrusted Stalin?**

WITNESS HISTORY VIDEO

Watch *Triumph at Normandy* on the **Witness History Discovery School**™ video program to experience the planning and execution of the D-Day invasion.

Vocabulary Builder

incessant—(in SES unt) *adj.*
uninterrupted, ceaseless

fought their way to shore amid underwater mines and raking machine-gun fire. As one soldier who landed in the first wave of D-Day assault recalled,

Primary Source

66 It all seemed unreal, a sort of dreaming while awake, men were screaming and dying all around me. . . I honestly could have walked the full length of the beach without touching the ground, they were that thickly strewn about.99
—Melvin B. Farrell, *War Memories*

Still, the Allied troops clawed their way inland through the tangled hedges of Normandy. In early August, a massive armored division under American General George S. Patton helped the joint British and American forces break through German defenses and advance toward Paris. Meanwhile, other Allied forces sailed from Italy to land in southern France. In Paris, French resistance forces rose up against the occupying Germans. Under pressure from all sides, the Germans retreated. On August 25, the Allies entered Paris. Within a month, all of France was free.

Allies Continue to Advance By this time, Germany was reeling under <u>incessant</u>, round-the-clock bombing. For two years, Allied bombers had hammered military bases, factories, railroads, oil depots, and cities.

The goal of this kind of bombing was to cripple Germany's industries and destroy the morale of its civilians. In one 10-day period, bombing almost erased the huge industrial city of Hamburg, killing 40,000 civilians and forcing one million to flee their homes. In February 1945, Allied raids on Dresden, not an industrial target, but considered one of the most beautiful cities in Europe, killed as many as 135,000 people.

After freeing France, Allied forces battled toward Germany. As their armies advanced into Belgium in December, Germany launched a massive counterattack. At the bloody Battle of the Bulge, which lasted more than a month, both sides took terrible losses. The Germans were unable to break through. The battle delayed the Allied advance from the west, but only for six weeks. Meanwhile, the Soviet army battled through Germany and advanced on Berlin from the east. Hitler's support within Germany was declining, and he had already survived one assassination attempt by senior officers in the German military. By early 1945, the defeat of Germany seemed <u>inevitable</u>.

Uneasy Agreement at Yalta In February 1945, Roosevelt, Churchill, and Stalin met again at Yalta, in the southern Soviet Union. Once again, the Big Three planned strategy in an atmosphere of distrust. Stalin insisted that the Soviet Union needed to maintain control of Eastern Europe to be able to protect itself from future aggression. Churchill and Roosevelt favored self-determination for Eastern Europe, which would give people the right to choose their own form of government. However, Churchill and Roosevelt needed Stalin's help to win the war.

At the **Yalta Conference,** the three leaders agreed that the Soviet Union would enter the war against Japan within three months of Germany's surrender. In return, Churchill and Roosevelt promised Stalin that the Soviets would take possession of southern Sakhalin Island, the Kuril Islands, and an occupation zone in Korea. They also agreed that Germany would be temporarily divided into four zones, to be governed by American, French, British, and Soviet forces. Stalin agreed to hold free elections in Eastern Europe. However, as you will read later, growing mistrust would later cause a split between the Allies.

✔ **Checkpoint** What agreements did Churchill, Roosevelt, and Stalin come to at Yalta?

Vocabulary Builder
<u>inevitable</u>—(in EV ih tuh bul) *adj.* unavoidable, inescapable

SECTION 3 **Assessment**

Progress Monitoring *Online*
For: Self-quiz with vocabulary practice
Web Code: nba-2931

Terms, People, and Places

1. For each term, person, or place listed at the beginning of the section, write a sentence explaining its significance.

Note Taking

2. **Reading Skill: Recognize Sequence** Use your completed timeline to answer the Focus Question: How did the Allies begin to push back the Axis powers?

Comprehension and Critical Thinking

3. **Analyze Information** How did democratic governments mobilize their economies for war?

4. **Determine Relevance** Explain why the battles of Midway, El Alamein, and Stalingrad were important turning points in the war.

5. **Predict Consequences** Why didn't the Yalta Conference lead to lasting unity among the Big Three leaders?

● **Writing About History**

Quick Write: Develop a Thesis A thesis statement summarizes the main idea of your research paper. The thesis statement should express an idea that can be defended or refuted. It should also be narrow enough to be addressed clearly in your writing.

Based on what you have read, write a thesis statement for an essay explaining the importance of the Battle of Stalingrad.

D-DAY

In the earliest hours of June 6, 1944, the Allies launched a surprise invasion of Normandy in France—the largest amphibious, or land and water, invasion in history. More than 156,000 Allied troops crossed the English Channel. Thousands of these troops landed on the beaches, fighting and clawing their way up the steep cliffs under heavy German fire. Paratroopers dropped from the sky. By the end of the day, about 2,500 men had given their lives. But by August, the Allies had made their way to Paris and freed it from German control.

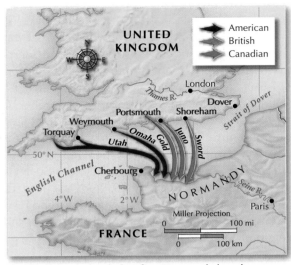

▲ Allied troops landed at five Normandy beaches, code-named Utah, Omaha, Gold, Juno, and Sword.

Overcoming Hitler's Defenses at Normandy

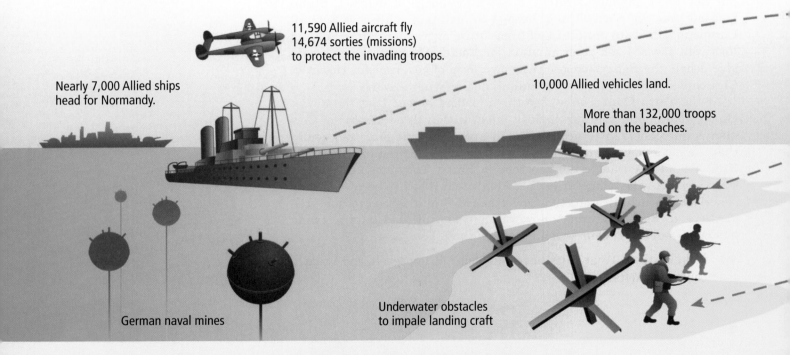

11,590 Allied aircraft fly 14,674 sorties (missions) to protect the invading troops.

Nearly 7,000 Allied ships head for Normandy.

10,000 Allied vehicles land.

More than 132,000 troops land on the beaches.

German naval mines

Underwater obstacles to impale landing craft

Allied troops faced daunting obstacles on D-Day. Naval mines threatened ships trying to land. Steel obstacles on the beaches could rip the bottoms out of landing craft at high tide. The Germans waited atop the steep cliffs.

▼ British special forces storm the beach.

Wounded Allied soldiers after the battle ▲

Allied Troop Strengths and Casualties on D-Day		
Country	Troops	Estimated Casualties*
United States	73,000	6,603
Britain	61,715	2,700
Canada	21,400	946
Allied Total	156,115	10,249

*includes those killed, wounded, missing, and captured
SOURCE: The D-Day Museum Online

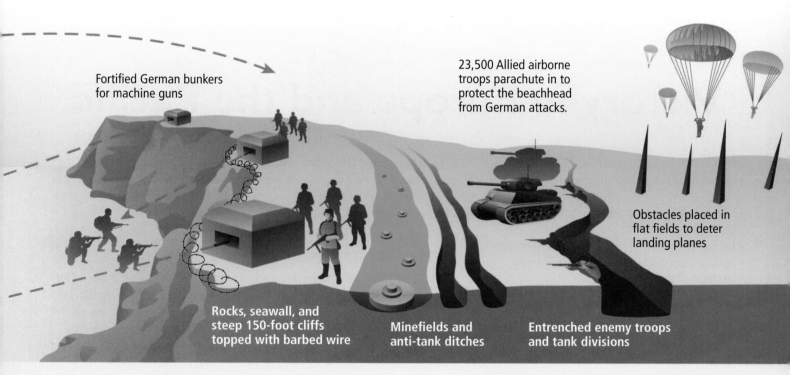

Fortified German bunkers for machine guns

23,500 Allied airborne troops parachute in to protect the beachhead from German attacks.

Obstacles placed in flat fields to deter landing planes

Rocks, seawall, and steep 150-foot cliffs topped with barbed wire

Minefields and anti-tank ditches

Entrenched enemy troops and tank divisions

▼ Omaha Beach at the end of D-Day

Thinking Critically

1. **Chart Skills** Which of the Allies suffered the greatest losses on D-Day?
2. **Draw Conclusions** Why do you think the D-Day landings were made on beaches instead of at established harbors?
3. **Diagram Skills** What do you think was the greatest obstacle the Allies had to overcome on D-Day? Explain.

History Interactive

For: interactive map, audio, and more
Visit: PHSchool.com
Web Code: nbp-2932

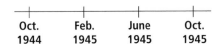

Allied soldier
in the Pacific

WITNESS HISTORY 🔊 AUDIO

A Soldier Remembers

A defeated General Douglas MacArthur left the Philippines in 1942. As he departed, he pledged his determination to free the islands with the words "I shall return." In October 1944, that pledge became a reality when MacArthur landed on the Philippine island of Leyte. As one soldier recalled,

66 When I heard that he had returned, I finally had the feeling that I might have a chance of living through the war. . . . [O]nce they landed in Leyte, I knew it was only a question of hanging on for a few more months and I would be able to live through it.99
—Edwin Ramsey

Focus Question How did the Allies finally defeat the Axis powers?

Victory in Europe and the Pacific

Objectives
- Describe the reasons for the final defeat of the Nazis.
- Summarize how the Allies began to push back the Japanese in the Pacific.
- Explain the American strategy for ending the war against Japan and the consequences of that strategy.

Terms, People, and Places

V-E Day	kamikaze
Bataan Death March	Manhattan Project
Douglas MacArthur	Hiroshima
island-hopping	Nagasaki

Note Taking

Reading Skill: Recognize Sequence Use a timeline like the one below to sequence the events that led to the defeat of the Axis powers.

Oct. 1944	Feb. 1945	June 1945	Oct. 1945

By early spring 1945, the war in Europe was nearing its end, and the Allies turned their attention to winning the war in the Pacific. There remained a series of bloody battles ahead, as well as an agonizing decision for American President Harry Truman.

Nazis Defeated

By March 1945, the Allies had crossed the Rhine into western Germany. From the east, Soviet troops closed in on Berlin. In late April, American and Russian soldiers met and shook hands at the Elbe River. All over Europe, Axis armies began to surrender.

In Italy, guerrillas captured and executed Mussolini. As Soviet troops fought their way into Berlin, Hitler committed suicide in his underground bunker. On May 7, Germany surrendered. Officially, the war in Europe ended the next day, May 8, 1945, which was proclaimed **V-E Day** (Victory in Europe). After just 12 years, Hitler's "thousand-year Reich" was bomb-ravaged and in ruins.

The Allies were able to defeat the Axis powers in Europe for a number of reasons. Because of the location of Germany and its allies, they had to fight on several fronts simultaneously. Hitler, who took almost complete control over military decisions, made some poor ones. He underestimated the ability of the Soviet Union to fight his armies.

The enormous productive capacity of the United States was another factor. By 1944, the United States was producing twice as much as all of the Axis powers combined. Meanwhile, Allied bombing hindered German production. Oil became so scarce because of

World War II in the Pacific, 1941–1945

Map Skills After the Battle of Midway, the Allies took the offensive in the Pacific. They gradually worked their way north towards Japan itself.

1. **Locate** (a) Japan (b) Pearl Harbor (c) Iwo Jima (d) Okinawa (e) Hiroshima (f) Manila
2. **Regions** Describe the extent of Japanese control in 1942.
3. **Draw Conclusions** How did geography make it difficult for Japan to maintain control of its empire?

Geography *Interactive*
For: Audio guided tour
Web Code: nbp-2941

SOVIET UNION

Aleutian Islands   150° W

MONGOLIA   Manchuria (Manzhouguo)
Kuril Islands
Beijing   Korea   JAPAN
CHINA   Tokyo
Hiroshima
Chongqing   Shanghai   Nagasaki
Midway Island (June 1942)
Hawaiian Islands   30° N
Okinawa (April–June 1945)
India   Iwo Jima (Feb.–March 1945)
Formosa   Pearl Harbor (Dec. 1941)
Burma   Hong Kong   Wake Island (Dec. 1941)
Bataan   Philippine Sea   Mariana   Saipan (June–July 1944)
(Jan.–April 1942)   (June 1944)   Islands
French   Manila
Indochina   Leyte Gulf   Guam   Pacific
THAILAND   (Oct. 1944)   (July–Aug. 1944)   Ocean
Malaya   Marshall Islands
Singapore   Tarawa (Nov. 1943)
Borneo   Solomon   Gilbert Islands   0°
Celebes   Islands
Java Sea (Feb. 1942)   Dutch East Indies   New Britain (Dec. 1944)
Indian   New   Guadalcanal (Aug. 1942–Feb. 1943)
Ocean   Guinea   Eastern Solomons (Aug. 1942)
Santa Cruz (Oct. 1942)
Coral Sea (May 1942)
AUSTRALIA   Coral Sea
Miller Projection
0   1000   2000 mi
0   1000   2000 km
60° E   90° E   120° E   180°

Japanese-controlled area, 1942
Maximum extent of Japanese control, 1942
Allied advances
Major battles
Atomic bomb targets

General Douglas MacArthur

bombing that the Luftwaffe was almost grounded by the time of the D-Day invasion. With victory in Europe achieved, the Allies now had to triumph over Japan in the Pacific.

✔ **Checkpoint** How did the Allied forces finally defeat the Germans?

Struggle for the Pacific

Until mid-1942, the Japanese had won an uninterrupted series of victories. They controlled much of Southeast Asia and many Pacific islands. By May 1942, the Japanese had gained control of the Philippines, killing several hundred American soldiers and as many as 10,000 Filipino soldiers during the 65-mile **Bataan Death March.** One survivor described the ordeal as "a macabre litany of heat, dust, starvation, thirst, flies, filth, stench, murder, torture, corpses, and wholesale brutality that numbs the memory." Many Filipino civilians risked—and sometimes lost—their lives to give food and water to captives on the march.

After the battles of Midway and the Coral Sea, however, the United States took the offensive. That summer, United States Marines landed at Guadalcanal in the Solomon Islands. Victory at Guadalcanal marked the

Vocabulary Builder
objective—(ub JEK tiv) *n.* something worked toward; a goal

beginning of an "island-hopping" campaign. The goal of the campaign was to recapture some Japanese-held islands while bypassing others. The captured islands served as steppingstones to the next objective. In this way, American forces, led by General **Douglas MacArthur,** gradually moved north towards Japan. By 1944, the United States Navy, commanded by Admiral Chester Nimitz, was blockading Japan, and American bombers pounded Japanese cities and industries. In October 1944, MacArthur began the fight to retake the Philippines. The British, meanwhile, were pushing Japanese forces back into the jungles of Burma and Malaya.

✔ **Checkpoint** What strategy did General MacArthur use to fight the Japanese in the Pacific?

Defeat for Japan

With war won in Europe, the Allies poured their resources into defeating Japan. By mid-1945, most of the Japanese navy and air force had been destroyed. Yet the Japanese still had an army of two million men. The road to victory, it appeared, would be long and costly.

Invasion or the Bomb? In bloody battles on the islands of Iwo Jima from February to March 1945 and Okinawa from April to July 1945, the Japanese had shown that they would fight to the death rather than surrender. Beginning in 1944, some young Japanese men chose to become **kamikaze** (kah muh KAH zee) pilots who undertook suicide missions, crashing their explosive-laden airplanes into American warships.

While Allied military leaders planned for invasion, scientists offered another way to end the war. Scientists understood that by splitting the atom, they could create an explosion far more powerful than any yet known. Allied scientists, some of them German and Italian refugees, conducted research, code-named the **Manhattan Project,** racing to harness the atom. In July 1945, they successfully tested the first atomic bomb at Alamogordo, New Mexico.

News of this test was brought to the new American president, Harry Truman. Truman had taken office after Franklin Roosevelt died unexpectedly on April 12. He realized that the atomic bomb was a terrible new force for destruction. Still, after consulting with his advisors, and

Nuclear Blast
The world's first nuclear explosion instantly vaporized the tower from which it was launched. Seconds later an enormous blast sent searing heat across the desert and knocked observers to the ground. Shown here is an atomic bomb's characteristic mushroom cloud. *Why might the scientists who created the bomb have counseled leaders not to use it?*

determining that it would save American lives, he decided to use the new weapon against Japan.

At the time, Truman was meeting with other Allied leaders in the city of Potsdam, Germany. They issued a warning to Japan to surrender or face "complete destruction" and "utter devastation." When the Japanese ignored the warning, the United States took action.

Utter Devastation On August 6, 1945, an American plane dropped an atomic bomb over the city of **Hiroshima.** The bomb flattened four square miles and instantly killed more than 70,000 people. In the months that followed, many more would die from radiation sickness, a deadly after-effect of exposure to radioactive materials.

On August 8, the Soviet Union declared war on Japan and invaded Manchuria. Again, Japanese leaders did not respond. The next day, the United States dropped a second atomic bomb, this time on the city of **Nagasaki.** More than 40,000 people were killed in this second explosion.

Finally, on August 10, Emperor Hirohito intervened, an action unheard of for a Japanese emperor, and forced the government to surrender. On September 2, 1945, the formal peace treaty was signed on board the American battleship *Missouri,* anchored in Tokyo Bay.

✔ **Checkpoint** What strategies did the Allies use to end the war with Japan?

Hiroshima in Ruins
The atomic bomb reduced the center of Hiroshima to smoldering ruins (top left), but the full effect of the bomb would take years to materialize. A woman (above) pays respects to the victims of the atomic bomb at the Memorial Cenotaph in Peace Memorial Park in Hiroshima. A cenotaph is a monument that honors people who are buried elsewhere.

SECTION 4
Assessment

Progress Monitoring *Online*
For: Self-quiz with vocabulary practice
Web Code: nba-2941

Terms, People, and Places
1. For each term, person, or place listed at the beginning of the section, write a sentence explaining its significance.

Note Taking

2. **Reading Skill: Recognize Sequence** Use your completed flowchart to answer the Focus Question: How did the Allies finally defeat the Axis powers?

Comprehension and Critical Thinking
3. **Determine Relevance** How did the location of the Axis powers in Europe contribute to their defeat?
4. **Draw Inferences** What factors besides ending the war in the Pacific might have contributed to President Harry Truman's decision to drop the atomic bomb?

● **Writing About History**

Quick Write: Make an Outline Once you have a thesis and have gathered research on your topics, you must choose an organization. Some choices are compare and contrast, order of importance, chronological, and cause and effect. Using one of these organizations, create an outline for the following thesis statement: The atomic bomb was a decisive weapon in World War II.

Newspaper headline on the day the Japanese surrendered

A sailor embraces a nurse when the end of the war is announced.

WITNESS HISTORY ◀)) AUDIO

The War Is Over!

American President Harry Truman made these remarks on the day the Japanese surrendered:

66 Our first thoughts, of course—thoughts of gratefulness and deep obligation—go out to those of our loved ones who have been killed or maimed in this terrible war. On land and sea and in the air, American men and women have given their lives so that this day of ultimate victory might come and assure the survival of a civilized world . . . 99

Focus Question What issues arose in the aftermath of World War II and how did new tensions develop?

The End of World War II

Objectives
- Describe the issues faced by the Allies after World War II ended.
- Summarize the organization of the United Nations.
- Analyze how new conflicts developed among the former Allies after World War II.

Terms, People, and Places

Nuremberg
United Nations (UN)
Cold War
Truman Doctrine

Marshall Plan
North Atlantic Treaty
    Organization (NATO)
Warsaw Pact

Note Taking

Reading Skill: Recognize Sequence Sequence the events following World War II by creating an outline of this section. Use the outline below as a starting point.

> I. The War's Aftermath
>   A. Devastation
>   1. As many as 50 million dead
>   2.

Even as the Allies celebrated victory, the appalling costs of the war began to emerge. The war had killed as many as 50 million people around the world. In Europe alone, over 30 million people had lost their lives, more than half of them civilians. The Soviet Union suffered the worst casualties, with over 20 million dead. As they had after World War I, the Allies faced difficult decisions about the future.

The War's Aftermath

"Give me ten years and you will not be able to recognize Germany," said Hitler in 1933. Indeed, Germany in 1945 was an unrecognizable ruin. Parts of Poland, the Soviet Union, Japan, China, and other countries also lay in ruins. Total war had gutted cities, factories, harbors, bridges, railroads, farms, and homes. Over twenty million refugees wandered Europe. Amid the devastation, hunger, disease, and mental illness took their toll for years after the fighting ended. As they had after World War I, the Allies faced difficult decisions about the future.

Horrors of the Holocaust Numbers alone did not tell the story of the Nazi nightmare in Europe or the Japanese brutality in Asia. During the war, the Allies were aware of the existence of Nazi concentration camps and death camps. But only at war's end did they learn the full extent of the inhumanity of the Holocaust. American General Dwight Eisenhower, who visited the camps, was stunned to come "face to face with indisputable evidence of Nazi brutality and ruthless disregard of every sense of decency."

War Crimes Trials At wartime meetings, the Allies had agreed that Axis leaders should be tried for "crimes against humanity." In Germany, the Allies held war crimes trials in **Nuremberg,** where Hitler had staged mass rallies in the 1930s. Nearly 200 Germans and Austrians were tried, and most were found guilty. A handful of top Nazis received death sentences. Others were imprisoned. Similar war crimes trials were held in Japan. Many of those accused of war crimes were never captured or brought to trial. However, the trials showed that political and military leaders could be held accountable for actions in wartime.

Occupying Allies The war crimes trials further discredited the totalitarian ideologies that had led to the war. Yet disturbing questions remained. Why had ordinary people in Germany, Poland, France, and elsewhere accepted—and even collaborated in—Hitler's "Final Solution"?

The United States felt that strengthening democracy would ensure tolerance and peace. The Western Allies built new governments in occupied Germany and Japan with democratic constitutions to protect the rights of all citizens. In Japan, the occupying forces under General MacArthur helped Japanese politicians to create a new constitution that gave power to the Japanese people, rather than the emperor.

✔ **Checkpoint** Why did the Allies hold war crimes trials for Axis leaders?

Establishing the United Nations

In April 1945, delegates from 50 nations <u>convened</u> in San Francisco to draft a charter for the **United Nations (UN).** The UN would play a greater role in world affairs than did its predecessor, the League of Nations.

Under the UN Charter, each of the member nations has one vote in the General Assembly. A much smaller body called the Security Council has greater power. Each of its five permanent members—the United States, the Soviet Union (today Russia), Britain, France, and China—has the right to veto any council decision. The goal was to give these great powers the authority to ensure the peace. The Security Council has the power to apply economic sanctions or send a peace-keeping military force to try to resolve disputes. Differences among the nations on the Security Council, most notably the United States and the Soviet Union, have often kept the UN from taking action. Since the fall of the Soviet Union in 1991, more peacekeeping delegations have been approved.

The UN's work would go far beyond peacekeeping. The organization would take on many world problems—from preventing the outbreak of disease and improving education to protecting refugees and helping nations to develop economically. UN agencies like the World Health Organization and the Food and Agricultural Organization have provided aid for millions of people around the world.

✔ **Checkpoint** Compare and contrast the United Nations and the League of Nations.

Casualties of World War II

	Military Dead*	Military Wounded*	Civilian Dead*
Allies			
Britain	264,000	277,000	93,000
France	213,000	400,000	350,000
China	1,310,000	1,753,000	1,000,000
Soviet Union	7,500,000	14,012,000	15,000,000
United States	292,000	672,000	6,000
Axis Powers			
Germany	3,500,000	5,000,000	780,000
Italy	242,000	66,000	153,000
Japan	1,300,000	4,000,000	672,000

World War II resulted in enormous casualties and disruption. Afterwards, millions of displaced Europeans, like the Germans above, searched for relatives they had been separated from during the war. **Chart Skills** *Which nation suffered the greatest number of both civilian and military casualties?*

* All figures are estimates.

SOURCE: *Encyclopædia Britannica; The Harper Encyclopedia of Military History,* R. Ernest Dupuy and Trevor N. Dupuy

Vocabulary Builder

<u>convened</u>—(kun VEEND) *vi.* met; assembled

The Alliance Breaks Apart

Amid the rubble of war, a new power structure emerged. In Europe, Germany was defeated. France and Britain were exhausted. Two other powers, the United States and the Soviet Union, emerged as the new world leaders. The United States abandoned its traditional policy of isolationism to counter what President Truman saw as the communist threat.

Differences Grow Between the Allies During the war, the Soviet Union and the nations of the West had cooperated to defeat Nazi Germany. After the war's end, the Allies set up councils made up of foreign ministers from Britain, France, China, the United States, and the Soviet Union to iron out the peace agreements discussed at various conferences during the war. The councils concluded peace agreements with several Axis nations in 1947. However, reparations in Germany and the nature of the governments of Eastern Europe caused divisions to deepen between the former Allies. Conflicting ideologies and mutual distrust soon led to the conflict known as the Cold War. The Cold War was a state of tension and hostility between nations aligned with the United States on one side and the Soviet Union on the other, without armed conflict between the major rivals.

The Cold War Begins Stalin had two goals in Eastern Europe. First, he wanted to spread communism in the area. Second, he wanted to create a buffer zone of friendly governments as a defense against Germany, which had invaded Russia during World War I and again in 1941.

As the Red Army had pushed German forces out of Eastern Europe, it had left behind occupying forces. At wartime conferences, Stalin tried to persuade the West to accept Soviet influence in Eastern Europe. The Soviet dictator pointed out that the United States was not consulting the Soviet Union about peace terms for Italy or Japan, both of which were defeated and occupied by American and British troops. In the same way, the Soviet Union would determine the fate of the Eastern European lands that it occupied.

Roosevelt and Churchill rejected Stalin's view, making him promise "free elections" in Eastern Europe. Stalin ignored that pledge. Most Eastern European countries had existing Communist parties, many of which had actively resisted the Nazis during the war. Backed by the Red Army, these local Communists in Poland, Czechoslovakia, and elsewhere destroyed rival political parties and even assassinated democratic leaders. By 1948, pro-Soviet communist governments were in place throughout Eastern Europe.

✔ **Checkpoint**   What post-war issues caused the Western Allies and the Soviet Union to disagree?

New Conflicts Develop

Stalin soon showed his aggressive intentions outside of Eastern Europe. In Greece, Stalin backed communist rebels who were fighting to overturn a right-wing monarchy supported by Britain. By 1947, however, Britain could no longer afford to defend Greece. Stalin was also menacing Turkey in the Dardanelles.

A Widening Gulf
Although Stalin and Truman were friendly at the Potsdam Conference (above), this Soviet propaganda poster from 1949 shows that relations between the two nations were becoming strained. The poster urges support "For a stable peace! Against those who would ignite a new war." The small caricatures of Churchill and Uncle Sam in the lower corner indicate who "those" people are.

The Truman Doctrine Truman took action. On March 12, 1947, Truman outlined a new policy to Congress: "I believe that it must be the policy of the United States to support free peoples who are resisting attempted subjugation by armed minorities or by outside pressures." This policy, known as the **Truman Doctrine,** was rooted in the idea of containment, limiting communism to the areas already under Soviet control.

The Truman Doctrine would guide the United States for decades. It made clear that Americans would resist Soviet expansion in Europe or elsewhere in the world. Truman soon sent military and economic aid and advisors to Greece and Turkey so that they could withstand the communist threat.

The Marshall Plan Postwar hunger and poverty made Western European lands fertile ground for communist ideas. To strengthen democratic governments, the United States offered a massive aid package, called the **Marshall Plan.** Under it, the United States funneled food and economic assistance to Europe to help countries rebuild. Billions of dollars in American aid helped war-shattered Europe recover rapidly.

President Truman also offered aid to the Soviet Union and its satellites, or dependent states, in Eastern Europe. However, Stalin declined and forbade Eastern European countries to accept American aid. Instead, he promised help from the Soviet Union in its place.

Germany Stays Divided Defeated Germany became another focus of the Cold War. The Soviet Union took reparations for its massive war losses by dismantling and moving factories and other resources in its occupation zone to help rebuild the Soviet Union. France, Britain, and the United States also took some reparations out of their portions of Germany. However, Western leaders wanted the German economy to recover in order to restore political stability to the region. The Western Allies decided to unite their zones of occupation. Then, they extended the Marshall Plan to western Germany. The Soviets were furious at Western moves to rebuild the German economy and deny them further reparations. They strengthened their hold on eastern Germany.

The Berlin Airlift
After World War II, Germany, and Berlin within it, was divided into communist and noncommunist zones. In the photo below, children in West Berlin greet a plane delivering supplies during the Berlin Airlift.

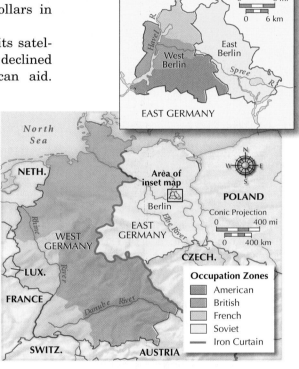

The Red Menace
Films like *The Red Menace* (1949) dramatized the threat of communism in the United States and formed a vital part of the propaganda war.

Vocabulary Builder
invoked—(in VOKED) *vt.* resorted to; called upon

Germany thus became a divided nation. In West Germany, the democratic nations allowed the people to write their own constitution and regain self-government. In East Germany, the Soviet Union installed a socialist dictatorship under Stalin's control.

The Berlin Airlift Stalin's resentment at Western moves to rebuild Germany triggered a crisis over Berlin. Even though it lay deep within the Soviet zone, the former German capital was occupied by all four victorious Allies. In June 1948, Stalin tried to force the Western Allies out of Berlin by sealing off every railroad and highway into the Western sectors of the city. The Western powers responded to the blockade by mounting a round-the-clock airlift. For more than a year, cargo planes supplied West Berliners with food and fuel. Their success forced the Soviets to end the blockade. Although the West had won, the crisis deepened.

Opposing Alliances Tensions continued to grow. In 1949, the United States, Canada, and ten other countries formed a new military alliance called the **North Atlantic Treaty Organization (NATO).** Members pledged to help one another if any one of them were attacked.

In 1955, the Soviet Union responded by forming its own military alliance, the **Warsaw Pact.** It included the Soviet Union and seven satellites in Eastern Europe. Unlike NATO, however, the Warsaw Pact was often <u>invoked</u> by the Soviets to keep its satellites in order. The Warsaw Pact cemented the division of Europe into "eastern" and "western" blocs. In the East were the Soviet-dominated countries of Eastern Europe. These countries were communist in name but dictatorships in practice, like the Soviet Union itself. In the West were the Western democracies, led by the United States.

The Propaganda War Both sides participated in a propaganda war. The United States spoke of defending capitalism and democracy against communism and totalitarianism. The Soviet Union claimed the moral high ground in the struggle against Western imperialism. Yet linked to those stands, both sides sought world power.

 Checkpoint What foreign policy pattern did the United States establish with the Truman Doctrine?

SECTION **5** Assessment

Progress Monitoring *Online*
For: Self-quiz with vocabulary practice
Web Code: nba-2951

Terms, People, and Places

1. What do many of the key terms listed at the beginning of the section have in common? Explain.

Note Taking

2. **Reading Skill: Recognize Sequence** Use your completed outline to answer the Focus Question: What issues arose in the aftermath of World War II and how did new tensions develop?

Comprehension and Critical Thinking

3. **Compare and Contrast** How did the peace made after World War II differ from that made after World War I?

4. **Identify Central Issues** What was the main purpose of the UN when it was founded?

5. **Recognize Causes** List two causes of the Cold War.

6. **Draw Conclusions** Why is it important to remember the inhumanity of the Holocaust?

● **Writing About History**
Quick Write: Credit Sources When you use quotes or ideas from your sources in your paper, you must give proper credit. One way to do this is to list the author and page number of the material you have used in parentheses following the statement. Then, include a bibliography at the end of your paper. Research a topic from this section and write a paragraph using two sources. Credit the sources where appropriate and list them at the end.

Genocide

▲ Jewish survivor of Ebensee concentration camp

What factors have led groups of people or governments to commit genocide?

After learning the extent of the Jewish Holocaust in World War II, British Prime Minster Winston Churchill called genocide "a crime that has no name." As a result of the Nuremberg trials in which Nazi officials were tried for "crimes against humanity," the United Nations drew up a treaty defining and criminalizing genocide. Genocide is any act committed with the idea of destroying an entire national, ethnic, racial or religious group. The Holocaust is perhaps the most well-known case of genocide, but consider these other examples from the twentieth century:

▲ Skulls of victims of the Cambodian Khmer Rouge

Armenia

In 1915, as World War I raged, the government of the Ottoman empire ordered the systematic extermination of most of the male Armenian population and the forced deportation of Armenian women, children, and elderly. By the end of the brutal deportation, up to 1.5 million Ottoman Armenians had been exterminated.

Several German military leaders who later became Nazis were stationed in the Ottoman empire during World War I, and may have applied what they observed there to their persecution of Jewish people during World War II.

Cambodia

In 1975, after years of civil war, Pol Pot, leader of the Khmer Rouge, came to power in Cambodia, a Southeast Asian country. Pol Pot attempted to transform Cambodia into a communist agricultural society by exterminating the country's professional and educated middle class. Over the course of four years of Khmer Rouge rule, between one and two million people were massacred or worked to death through forced labor.

► Jean Paul Akayesu, a local government official, being tried by a UN court for ordering mass killings in Rwanda.

Rwanda

In the African nation of Rwanda, the Tutsi and Hutu groups share the same language and other cultural characteristics. But social, political, and economic factors divide them. In 1994, the Hutu-led government called on military personnel to eliminate members of the Tutsi political opposition. The hatred and violence spread quickly. Soon Hutu civilians were murdering their Tutsi neighbors. In 100 days, more than 800,000 Tutsis were slaughtered.

Armenian Genocide in the Ottoman Empire

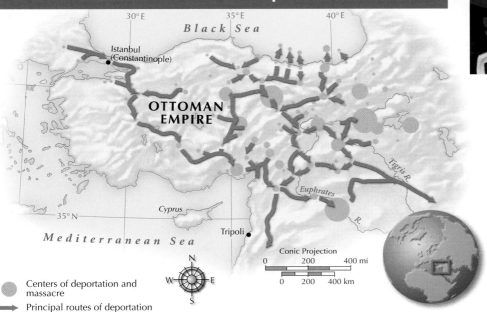

Black Sea

Istanbul (Constantinople)

OTTOMAN EMPIRE

Cyprus

35°N

Mediterranean Sea

Tripoli

Tigris R.

Euphrates

R.

30°E 35°E 40°E

Conic Projection
0   200   400 mi
0   200   400 km

● Centers of deportation and massacre

➡ Principal routes of deportation

Thinking Critically

1. How was the role of government similar in the Holocaust and in the genocides described above?
2. Conduct research at your school or local library to find out more about these and other examples of genocide. Write a brief essay about what happened and why.

Quick Study Guide

Progress Monitoring *Online*
For: Self-test with vocabulary practice
Web Code: nba-2961

Key Causes of World War II

- Failure of World War I peace settlement, Treaty of Versailles
- Global economic depression
- Fascism, militarism, and imperialism in Germany, Italy, and Japan
- Weakness of the League of Nations
- British and French appeasement

The Allies vs. the Axis

As the map below shows, many countries joined the major Axis and Allied powers in fighting the war.

Allies, July 1943
Axis Powers, July 1943
Neutral Countries, July 1943

Key Political Leaders

Allies
Franklin Delano Roosevelt, *U.S. president*
Harry S Truman, *U.S. president*
Neville Chamberlain, *British prime minister*
Winston Churchill, *British prime minister*
Joseph Stalin, *Soviet dictator*
Charles de Gaulle, *leader of Free French*

Axis Powers
Adolf Hitler, *German dictator*
Benito Mussolini, *Italian dictator*
Hirohito, *Japanese emperor*
Tojo Hideki, *Japanese prime minister*

Reasons for Allied Victory

Location of Germany—surrounded by enemies
Location of Japan—dependent on imported goods
Poor military decisions by Axis leaders
Huge productive capability of the United States
Better technology developed and used by Allies

Key Events of World War II

Europe and Africa
The Pacific

1939 **1940** **1941**

Sept. 1939
Germany invades Poland. France and Britain declare war on Germany.

June–July 1940
France falls to Germany. Germany begins Battle of Britain.

June 1941
Germany invades the Soviet Union.

Sept. 1940
Japan signs Tripartite Pact with Germany and Italy.

Dec. 1941
Japan attacks Pearl Harbor.

Concept Connector

■ Cumulative Review

Record the answers to the questions below on your Concept Connector worksheets. In addition, record information from this chapter about the following concepts:

- Cooperation: United Nations
- Conflict: World War II
- Technology: Nuclear Power

1. **Democracy** During World War II, the United States government interned Japanese Americans in camps, citing security concerns. This was a curtailment of American citizens' individual rights. Do you think such actions are ever justified by a democratic government? Why or why not?

2. **Genocide** What was the Holocaust? Compare the Holocaust to the Armenian genocide carried out by the Ottoman Turks. How were they similar and different? Consider:
   - nation-building and nationalism
   - murder of minority leaders
   - large-scale deportations
   - systematic torture and murder
   - use of concentration camps

3. **Science** Several advances in science improved the survival rates of injured soldiers during World War II. Do research to learn more about one of the following medical advances during World War II and then compare it to Louis Pasteur's advances. Which do you think was more significant?
   - blood plasma
   - sulfanilamide or sulfa powder
   - widespread use of penicillin

■ Connections to Today

1. **Conflict: The Arab-Israeli Conflict** Partly in response to the horrors of the Holocaust, the United Nations created a plan to divide Palestine into two states—one Arab and one Jewish. Jews accepted the plan, but Arabs rejected it. When the Jewish state of Israel was born in 1948, the surrounding Arab countries invaded Israel. Between 1956 and 1973, three more wars erupted between Israel and Arab states. Conflict between Arabs and Israelis continued into the early 2000s despite many attempts at peace. What historical reasons did the United Nations have for creating a Jewish state in Palestine?

Jewish Migration to Israel

Year	Immigrants
1948	120,000
1949	240,000
1950	170,000

SOURCE: United States Holocaust Memorial Museum Online

2. **Cooperation: The United Nations Is Established** Fifty nations met in April 1945 to draft a charter for the United Nations. Today, the UN's work goes far beyond peacekeeping to include economic development, disease prevention, and refugee protection. Conduct research and write two paragraphs about a program sponsored by the UN in the last five years.

History Interactive
For: Interactive timeline
Web Code: nbp-2962

Nov. 1942
The Allies push Rommel back in North Africa.

Jan. 1943
Germans surrender at Stalingrad.

June 1944
D-Day invasion of Normandy

May 1945
Germany surrenders.

1942   1943   1944   1945

June 1942
Japan defeated at Battle of Midway.

Feb. 1943
Japan defeated at Guadalcanal.

Oct. 1944
Japan defeated at Battle of Leyte Gulf.

Aug–Sept. 1945
U.S. drops atomic bombs on Hiroshima and Nagasaki, Japan. Japan surrenders.

Chapter Assessment

Terms, People, and Places

1. Define **appeasement** and **Anschluss**. How was Hitler's Anschluss an example of British and French appeasement?
2. Define **blitzkrieg.** What were the advantages of this war tactic?
3. Where did the **D-Day** invasion take place? What was its significance?
4. What happened at the **Yalta Conference**? How did it foreshadow later events?
5. What technological advantage did the **Manhattan Project** give the Allies? How was it used?
6. Describe how the **Marshall Plan** was part of the **Truman Doctrine**.

Main Ideas

Section 1 (pp. 562–567)
7. Summarize the steps that Axis powers took to achieve world power prior to World War II.

Section 2 (pp. 568–576)
8. How did the people of Britain fend off a German invasion?
9. How did Germany and Japan rule the people they conquered? How did this contribute to their hold on power?

Section 3 (pp. 577–583)
10. How did government control of economic production help defeat Germany and Japan?
11. Summarize how the Allies defeated Germany.

Section 4 (pp. 586–589)
12. What strategy did the Allies use to defeat Japan?

Section 5 (pp. 590–594)
13. What conflicts emerged between the former Allies after the end of World War II?

Chapter Focus Question
14. How did aggressive world powers emerge, and what did it take to defeat them during World War II?

Critical Thinking

15. **Recognize Cause and Effect** How did the World War I peace settlement help cause World War II?
16. **Analyze Information** What lessons does the Holocaust have for people today?

17. **Analyzing Cartoons** How does this cartoon reflect the cause of Hitler's defeat?
18. **Predict Consequences** The Atlantic Charter called for the establishment of a "permanent system of general security." What form did this "system" take when it was established following the war?
19. **Synthesize Information** Was participation by the United States crucial to winning the war? Explain.
20. **Draw Conclusions** Which battle was most important in the war in Europe? In the war in the Pacific? Explain.

● Writing About History

Writing a Research Report The history of World War II includes many stories of great courage and personal sacrifice. Write a research report on one of the following topics in which you describe the actions of the person or group: the Kindertransport, Oskar Schindler, Miep Gies, Raoul Wallenberg, Dietrich Bonhoeffer. Consult pages SH13–SH15 of the Writing Handbook for additional help.

Prewriting
• Do some preliminary research on each of the topics listed above.
  • Choose the topic that interests you most and take notes about the people involved and the personal risks they took.

• Create a set of questions about the topic and gather additional resources.

Drafting
• Develop a working thesis and choose information to support the thesis.
• Make an outline organizing the report.
• Write an introduction in which you explain why the topic is interesting, a body, and a conclusion.

Revising
• Use the guidelines for revising your report on page SH15 of the Writing Handbook.

Document-Based Assessment

The Decision to Use the Atomic Bomb

Perhaps no decision in American history has been more hotly debated than Harry S. Truman's decision to drop atomic bombs on Hiroshima and Nagasaki, Japan, in August 1945. Documents A and B are two historians' views on Truman's decision.

Document A

"It was believed with deep apprehension that many thousands, probably tens of thousands, of lives of Allied combatants would have been spent in the continuation of our air and sea bombardment and blockade. . . . But the people who would have suffered most, had the war gone on much longer and their country invaded, were the Japanese. One American incendiary air raid on the Tokyo area in March 1945 did more damage and killed and injured more Japanese than the bomb on Hiroshima."

—From ***The Atomic Bomb and the End of World War II*** by Herbert Feis

Document B

"Even without the use of the atomic bombs, the war would probably have ended before an American invasion of Kyushu [one of the four main islands of Japan] became necessary. Conditions in Japan were steadily deteriorating . . . The destruction of cities from B-29 raids, diminishing food supplies, [and] decreased public morale fostered enough discontent to worry the emperor and his advisors. . . . Even without the atomic attacks, it seems likely that the emperor at some point would have acted in the same way that he did in the aftermath of Hiroshima to end the war."

—From ***Prompt and Utter Destruction: Truman and the Use of Atomic Bombs Against Japan*** by J. Samuel Walker

Document C

In the spring of 1945, the Allies' island-hopping campaign in the Pacific brought them closer to the heart of Japan. When American troops invaded first the island of Iwo Jima, then the island of Okinawa, the Japanese fought fiercely, but unsuccessfully, to keep them from gaining control. They knew that the Allies planned to use the islands as a base for an invasion of Japan itself.

Troops Killed at Iwo Jima and Okinawa, 1945		
Battle	Japanese troops killed	American troops killed
Iwo Jima	21,000	6,800
Okinawa	100,000	12,000

SOURCE: Encyclopaedia Brittannica

Document D

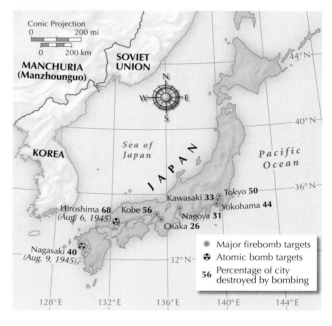

Analyzing Documents

Use your knowledge of World War II and Documents A, B, C, and D to answer questions 1–4.

1. Which of the following cities experienced the most damage from the American bombing raids?
   A Tokyo
   B Yokohama
   C Hiroshima
   D Osaka

2. Which of the following statements BEST summarizes Herbert Feis's explanation for Truman's use of the atomic bomb?
   A Use of the atomic bombs would cause more destruction.
   B Use of the atomic bombs would save lives.
   C Use of the atomic bombs would ensure surrender.
   D Use of the atomic bombs would make it more difficult for Japan to rebuild its military.

3. J. Samuel Walker's main argument against the use of atomic bombs is that
   A atomic bombs were more destructive than conventional bombs.
   B an American invasion would not have been as destructive as the bombs.
   C the war would have ended anyway.
   D the Japanese emperor opposed the use of atomic bombs.

4. **Writing Task** Which of the historians quoted in Documents A and B do you agree with most strongly? Why? Use your knowledge of World War II and specific evidence from the documents to support your opinion.

THE **WORLD** TODAY

Greenland (Denmark)

Arctic Ocean

ICELAND

NETHERLANDS ❶
BELGIUM ❷
GERMANY ❸
SWITZERLAND ❹
ITALY ❺
SLOVENIA ❻
AUSTRIA ❼
CZECH REPUBLIC ❽
SLOVAKIA ❾
HUNGARY ❿
CROATIA ⓫
BOSNIA & HERZEGOVINA ⓬
SERBIA & MONTENEGRO ⓭
ALBANIA ⓮
MACEDONIA ⓯
BULGARIA ⓰
ROMANIA ⓱
MOLDOVA ⓲
ARMENIA ⓳
AZERBAIJAN ⓴

Alaska (U.S.)

CANADA

NORTH AMERICA

UNITED STATES

New York

Los Angeles

MEXICO
Mexico City

Hawaii (U.S.)

Pacific Ocean

BAHAMAS
HONDURAS
CUBA   HAITI   DOMINICAN REPUBLIC
BELIZE   JAMAICA   Puerto Rico (U.S.)
GUATEMALA
EL SALVADOR   PANAMA
NICARAGUA   VENEZUELA   GUYANA
COSTA RICA   SURINAME
COLOMBIA   French Guiana (France)
ECUADOR

French Polynesia (France)

SOUTH AMERICA   BRAZIL
Lima   PERU
BOLIVIA   São Paulo
PARAGUAY

CHILE   URUGUAY
ARGENTINA   Buenos Aires

Falkland Islands (U.K.)

Atlantic Ocean

NORWAY   SWEDEN   FINLAND

ESTONIA
DENMARK   LATVIA   Moscow
LITHUANIA
UNITED KINGDOM
IRELAND   ❶   Berlin   POLAND   BELARUS
London   ❷   EUROPE   UKRAINE
Paris   ❸❾
❹   ❿   ⓲
FRANCE   ❺   ⓫   ⓭   ⓱   GEORGIA
⓮   ⓯   ⓰   ⓴
PORTUGAL   Madrid   Rome   Istanbul   ⓳
SPAIN   ❻   GREECE   TURKEY
MOROCCO   TUNISIA   CYPRUS   SYRIA
LEBANON   IRAQ
ISRAEL   KUWAIT
ALGERIA   LIBYA   Cairo   JORDAN   SAUDI
EGYPT   ARABIA

MAURITANIA   SUDAN
SENEGAL   MALI   NIGER   CHAD   ERITREA   YEMEN
Dakar   BURKINA   DJIBOUTI
GAMBIA   FASO   NIGERIA   AFRICA   ETHIOPIA
GUINEA-BISSAU   GUINEA   CENTRAL   SOMALIA
SIERRA LEONE   Lagos   AFRICAN
LIBERIA   CAMEROON   REP.   UGANDA   KENYA
CÔTE D'IVOIRE   BENIN   RWANDA
GHANA   TOGO   CONGO   DEM. REP.   BURUNDI
EQUATORIAL GUINEA   OF CONGO   TANZANIA
GABON   MALAWI
ANGOLA   ZAMBIA
MOZAMBIQUE
NAMIBIA   ZIMBABWE
BOTSWANA
Johannesburg   SWAZILAND   MADAGASCAR
SOUTH   LESOTHO
AFRICA

N
W   E
S

Geography *Interactive*
For: Audio guided tour
Web Code: nbp-7000

18

The Cold War
1945–1991

Berlin Is Walled In

On August 13, 1961, the first morning after the Berlin Wall was built, thousands of East Berliners arrived at the main border crossing hoping to travel to West Berlin. Transportation Police, or Trapos, blocked the way. Robert Lochner recalls, "A timid old woman . . . asked one of the Trapos when the next train would go to West Berlin. Sneeringly he answered: 'None of that anymore, grandma. You are all now caught in a mousetrap.'" Listen to the Witness History audio to hear more about the Berlin Wall.

◀ **East German guards watch the newly built Berlin Wall.**

U.S. President Ronald Reagan

Chapter Preview

Chapter Focus Question How did the Cold War develop, how did it shape political and economic life in individual nations, and how did it end?

Pin promoting the Soviet reforms that helped to end the Cold War

U.S. military helicopter over Vietnam

Note Taking Study Guide *Online*
For: Note Taking and Concept Connector worksheets
Web Code: nbd-3001

Nuclear fallout shelter sign

Winston Churchill

WITNESS HISTORY 🔊 AUDIO

An Iron Curtain

In 1946, Winston Churchill, former prime minister of Britain, spoke of an "iron curtain" sealing off the countries in Eastern Europe that the Soviet Union had occupied at the end of World War II:

66 [A]n iron curtain has descended [fallen] across the Continent. Behind that line lie all the capitals of the ancient states of Central and Eastern Europe. . . . [A]ll these famous cities . . . lie in what I must call the Soviet sphere, and are all subject . . . to a very high . . . measure of control from Moscow. 99

Focus Question What were the military and political consequences of the Cold War in the Soviet Union, Europe, and the United States?

The Cold War Unfolds

Objectives

- Understand how two sides faced off in Europe during the Cold War.
- Learn how nuclear weapons threatened the world.
- Understand how the Cold War spread globally.
- Compare and contrast the Soviet Union and the United States in the Cold War.

Terms, People, and Places

superpowers
anti-ballistic missiles (ABMs)
Ronald Reagan
détente
Fidel Castro

John F. Kennedy
ideology
Nikita Khrushchev
Leonid Brezhnev
containment

Note Taking

Reading Skill: Summarize Sum up the consequences of the Cold War in the United States, Europe, and the Soviet Union in a chart like the one below.

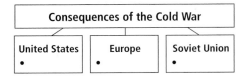

Consequences of the Cold War		
United States •	**Europe** •	**Soviet Union** •

After World War II devastated Europe and Japan, two great powers remained: the United States and the Soviet Union. These two nations were known as **superpowers,** or nations stronger than other powerful nations. The Cold War between these superpowers cast a shadow over the world for more than 40 years.

Two Sides Face Off in Europe

Cold War confrontation began in Europe, where the two superpowers' armies confronted each other after World War II. Each superpower formed a European military alliance made up of the nations that it occupied or protected. The United States led the North Atlantic Treaty Organization, or NATO, in Western Europe. The Soviet Union led the Warsaw Pact in Eastern Europe. The two alliances in Europe faced each other along the Iron Curtain, the tense line between the democratic West and the communist East.

A Wall Divides Berlin Berlin was a key focus of Cold War tensions. The city was split into democratic West Berlin and communist East Berlin. In the 1950s, West Berlin became a showcase for West German prosperity. A massive exodus of low-paid East Germans, unhappy with communism, fled into West Berlin. To stop the flight, East Germany built a wall in 1961 that sealed off West Berlin. When completed, the Berlin Wall was a massive concrete barrier, topped with barbed wire and patrolled by guards. The wall showed that workers, far from enjoying a communist paradise, had to be forcibly kept from fleeing.

Eastern Europe Resists Other explosions of Cold War tension included revolts against Soviet domination in East Germany, Poland, Hungary, and Czechoslovakia. One of the earliest revolts occurred in East Berlin. In 1953, some 50,000 workers confronted the Soviet army in the streets of the German capital. The uprising spread to other East German cities, but the demonstrators could not stand up to Russian tanks.

In 1956, Eastern Europeans challenged Soviet authority in the name of economic reform in both Poland and Hungary. Poles were responding in part to Soviet-backed mass arrests of noncommunist leaders and government seizures of private lands and industry. Hungarian leader Imre Nagy (nahj) went furthest, ending one-party rule and seeking to pull his country out of the Warsaw Pact. In response, Soviet troops launched a massive assault that overwhelmed resistance. Nagy was later executed.

In early 1968, Czechoslovak leader Alexander Dubček introduced greater freedom of expression and limited democracy. This blossoming of freedom came to be known as the "Prague Spring." Soviet leaders feared that democracy would threaten communist power and Soviet domination. Warsaw Pact troops launched a massive invasion of Czechoslovakia in August of that year to put an end to these freedoms.

✔ **Checkpoint** How was Europe divided, and what were three consequences of its division?

Nuclear Weapons Threaten the World

One of the most terrifying aspects of the Cold War was the arms race that began right after World War II. At first, the United States was the only nuclear power. By 1949, however, the Soviet Union had also developed nuclear weapons. By 1953, both sides had developed hydrogen bombs, which are much more destructive than atomic bombs.

Critics argued that a nuclear war would destroy both sides. Yet each superpower wanted to be able to deter the other from launching its nuclear weapons. Both sides engaged in a race to match each other's new weapons. The result was a "balance of terror." Mutually assured destruction—in which each side knew that the other side would itself be

Soviet Nuclear Missiles
Every year on May 1, the Soviet Union demonstrated its military strength, including nuclear weaponry, in a parade through Moscow's Red Square. *Why might the Soviet Union have wanted to show off its nuclear might?*

Arms Control Agreements

Date	Agreement	Effect
1963	Nuclear Test Ban Treaty	Banned testing of nuclear weapons in the atmosphere
1972	SALT I Interim Agreement	Froze existing number of weapons held by each side
1972	SALT I Anti-Ballistic Missile Treaty	Set strict limits on missiles that could shoot down missiles from the other side
1979	SALT II Treaty	Set absolute limit on number of weapons each side could hold
1991	START Treaty	Required both sides to reduce the number of weapons each held

Chart Skills Compare the Nuclear Test Ban Treaty, the SALT II Treaty, and the START Treaty. *How did each of the later treaties advance beyond the treaty that came before it?*

SOURCE: *Encyclopaedia Britannica*

destroyed if it launched its weapons—discouraged nuclear war. Still, the world's people lived in constant fear of nuclear doom.

Limiting Nuclear Weapons To reduce the threat of nuclear war, the two sides met at disarmament talks. Although mutual distrust slowed progress, the rival powers did reach some agreements. In 1969, the United States and the Soviet Union began Strategic Arms Limitation Talks (SALT) to limit the number of nuclear weapons held by each side. In 1972 and 1979, both sides signed agreements setting these limits.

One of these agreements limited **anti-ballistic missiles (ABMs),** or missiles that could shoot down other missiles from hostile countries. ABMs were seen as a particular threat to the balance of terror because, by giving one side some protection against the other, they might encourage the protected side to attack. They were also seen as a technology that could provoke a renewed arms race. During the 1980s, U.S. President **Ronald Reagan** launched a program to build a "Star Wars" missile defense against nuclear attack. Critics objected that this program would violate the ABM treaty. Nonetheless, the two sides signed the Strategic Arms Reduction Treaty (START) in 1991.

Building Détente American and Soviet arms control agreements led to an era of **détente** (day TAHNT), or relaxation of tensions, during the 1970s. The American strategy under détente was to restrain the Soviet Union through diplomatic agreements rather than by military means. The era of détente ended in 1979, when the Soviet Union invaded Afghanistan.

Stopping the Spread of Nuclear Weapons By the late 1960s, Britain, France, and China had developed their own nuclear weapons. However, many world leaders worked to keep the arms race from spreading any further. In 1968, many nations signed the Nuclear Non-Proliferation Treaty (NPT). These nations agreed not to develop nuclear weapons or to stop the proliferation, or spread, of nuclear weapons.

✓ **Checkpoint** What factors discouraged the use of nuclear weapons during the Cold War?

The Cold War Goes Global

Although the Cold War began in Central Europe, it quickly spread around the world. When World War II ended, the Soviets were assisting communist forces in China and Korea. American leaders saw that the United States faced a conflict as global as the two world wars that had preceded it. They therefore developed policies to respond to challenges anywhere in the world.

Building Alliances and Bases As part of its strategy to contain Soviet power, the United States reached out to the rest of the world both diplomatically and militarily. The NATO alliance with Europe's democracies was only one of several regional alliances.

Geography *Interactive*
For: Interactive map
Web Code: nbp-3011

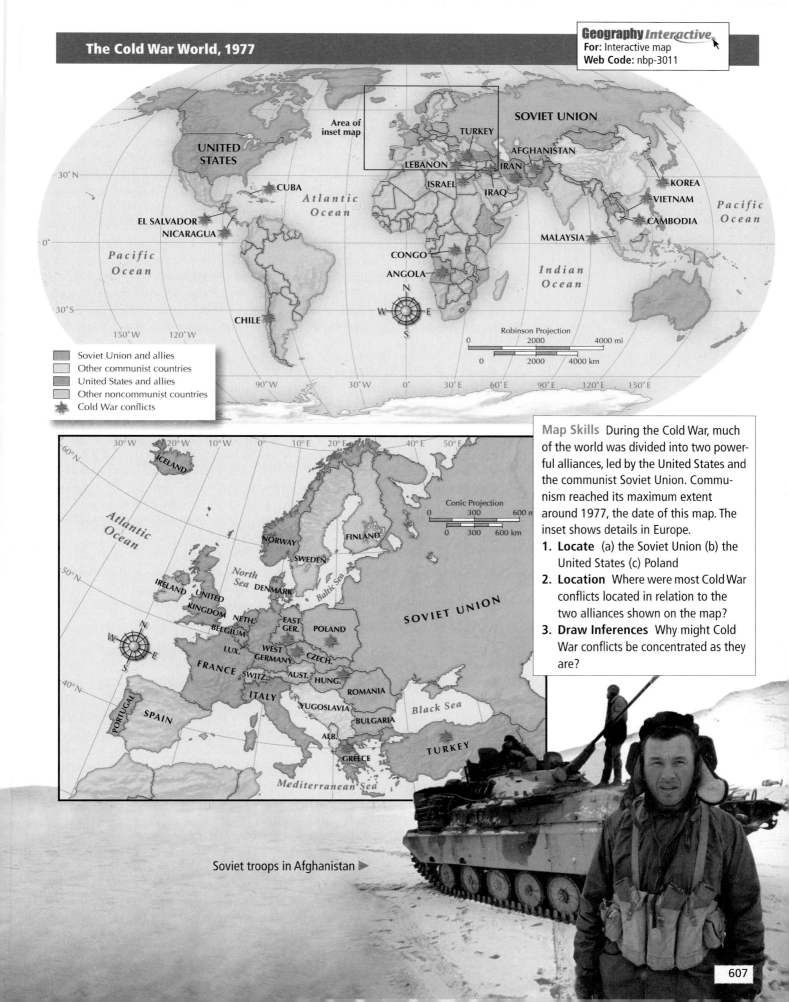

Legend:
- Soviet Union and allies
- Other communist countries
- United States and allies
- Other noncommunist countries
- ✴ Cold War conflicts

Robinson Projection

Conic Projection

Map Skills During the Cold War, much of the world was divided into two powerful alliances, led by the United States and the communist Soviet Union. Communism reached its maximum extent around 1977, the date of this map. The inset shows details in Europe.

1. **Locate** (a) the Soviet Union (b) the United States (c) Poland
2. **Location** Where were most Cold War conflicts located in relation to the two alliances shown on the map?
3. **Draw Inferences** Why might Cold War conflicts be concentrated as they are?

Soviet troops in Afghanistan ▶

607

In 1955, the United States and its allies formed another alliance, the Southeast-Asia Treaty Organization (SEATO). SEATO included the United States, Britain, France, Australia, Pakistan, Thailand, New Zealand, and the Philippines. The Central Treaty Organization (CENTO) comprised Britain, Turkey, Iran, and Pakistan. The United States also formed military alliances with individual nations, such as Japan and South Korea.

Meanwhile, the Soviet Union formed its own alliances. In addition to the Warsaw Pact in Europe, the Soviet Union formed alliances with governments in Africa and Asia. A Soviet alliance with the government of Communist China lasted from 1949 to 1960. The Soviet Union and its allies were often known as the Soviet bloc.

Unlike the Soviets, the Americans established army, navy, and air force bases around the globe. By the end of the Cold War, the Soviets faced the military nightmare of encirclement by an enemy. American army camps, naval stations, and air bases spread across Europe, Asia, North America, and the Pacific islands, while American fleets patrolled the world's oceans.

Where the Cold War Got Hot Because both superpowers had a global reach, local conflicts in many places played into the Cold War. Often, the United States and its allies supported one side, and the Soviet bloc supported the other. Through such struggles, the superpowers could confront each other indirectly rather than head to head. Political shifts around the world added to Cold War tensions. When communist forces won control of mainland China in 1949, the United States feared that a tide of communism would sweep around the world. During this period, European colonies in Africa and Asia demanded independence. As colonies battled for independence, liberation leaders and guerrillas frequently sought help from one or the other Cold War power.

On occasion, the Cold War erupted into "shooting wars," especially in Asia. Both Korea and Vietnam were torn by brutal conflicts in which the United States, the Soviet Union, and China played crucial roles. More commonly, however, the superpowers provided weapons, training, or other aid to opposing forces in Asia, Africa, or Latin America.

Cuba Goes Communist The most serious Cold War conflict in the Western Hemisphere involved the Latin American island nation of Cuba, just 90 miles off the coast of Florida. In the 1950s, Fidel Castro organized an armed rebellion against the corrupt dictator who then ruled Cuba. By 1959, Castro had led his guerrilla army to victory and set about transforming the country. This transformation is known as the Cuban Revolution. Castro sought the support of the Soviet Union. He nationalized businesses and put most land under government control. In addition, Castro severely restricted Cubans' political freedom. Critics of the new regime were jailed or silenced, and hundreds of thousands fled to Florida.

The United States attempted to bring down the communist regime next door. In 1961, President John F. Kennedy supported an invasion attempt by U.S.-trained Cuban exiles. The Bay of Pigs Invasion, known for the bay where the invaders came ashore in Cuba, quickly ended in failure when Castro's forces captured the invaders. The United States imposed a trade embargo on Cuba that remains in effect today.

Cuban Missiles Spark a Crisis In 1962, the Soviet Union sent nuclear missiles to Cuba. President Kennedy responded by imposing a naval blockade that prevented further Soviet shipments. Kennedy demanded that the Soviet Union remove its nuclear missiles from Cuba, and for a few tense days, the world faced a risk of nuclear war over the issue. Finally, however, Soviet Premier Nikita Khrushchev agreed to remove the Soviet missiles, and war was averted.

✓ **Checkpoint** How did the U.S. and the Soviet Union confront each other around the world during the Cold War?

WITNESS HISTORY VIDEO

Watch *Showdown: The Cuban Missile Crisis* on the **Witness History Discovery School**™ video program to experience the dramatic showdown between the Soviet Union and the United States.

Discovery
SCHOOL

● **INFOGRAPHIC**
THE CUBAN MISSILE *CRISIS*

In the summer of 1962, the United States learned that the Soviet Union was shipping nuclear missiles to Cuba, less than 100 miles off the coast of Florida. President John F. Kennedy demanded that the Soviet Union remove the missiles from Cuba. In October 1962, the United States imposed a naval blockade on Cuba. For one week, a tense confrontation brought the world to the brink of nuclear war. Finally, on October 28, Khrushchev agreed to remove the Soviet missiles. 🔊 AUDIO

▲ Soviet Premier Nikita Khrushchev

◄ U.S. President John F. Kennedy

During the U.S. naval blockade, the U.S. Navy surrounded Cuba with ships. (See the map below). In this photo, the USS *Barry* inspects the cargo of a Soviet freighter returning from Cuba.

▲ This aerial photo shows Soviet missiles being unloaded at a Cuban port.

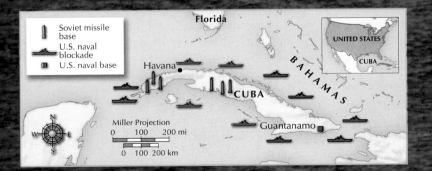

Thinking Critically
1. **Map Skills** Considering Cuba's location on the map, why did Soviet nuclear missiles on the island pose a threat to the United States?
2. **Draw Conclusions** Why might Khrushchev have agreed to withdraw the missiles from Cuba?

Contrasting Systems

Communist Countries	Democratic Capitalist Countries
The Communist Party makes all political decisions.	The people and their elected representatives make decisions.
Command economy (The government makes most economic decisions and owns most property.)	Market economy (Private consumers and producers make most economic decisions and own most property.)
The political leadership values obedience, discipline, and economic security.	The political leadership values freedom and prosperity.

Chart Skills The communist system often offered few choices for consumers, such as for the Russian woman above. By contrast, capitalist societies provided a wealth of choices for consumers, such as for the American girl at the right. *What facts in the chart above help to explain the different experiences of consumers under these contrasting systems?*

The Soviet Union in the Cold War

Victory in World War II brought few rewards to the Soviet people. Stalin continued his ruthless policies. He filled labor camps with "enemies of the state" and seemed ready to launch new purges when he died in 1953.

Soviet Communism In the Soviet Union, the government controlled most aspects of public life. Communists valued obedience, discipline, and economic security. They sought to spread their communist **ideology,** or value system and beliefs, around the globe. The Soviet Union also aimed to spread its communist command economy to other countries. In command economies, government bureaus make most economic decisions. They often make decisions for political reasons that do not make much economic sense. The government owns most property.

Stalin's Successors Hold the Line After Stalin's death in 1953, **Nikita Khrushchev** (KROOSH chawf) emerged as the new Soviet leader. In 1956, he shocked top Communist Party members when he publicly denounced Stalin's abuse of power. Khrushchev maintained the Communist Party's political control, but he closed prison camps and eased censorship. He called for a "peaceful coexistence" with the West.

Khrushchev's successor, **Leonid Brezhnev** (BREZH nef) held power from the mid-1960s until he died in 1982. Under Brezhnev, critics faced arrest and imprisonment.

Some Soviets Bravely Resist Despite the risk of punishment, some courageous people dared to criticize the government. Andrey Sakharov (SAH kuh rawf), a distinguished Soviet scientist, spoke out for civil liberties. Brezhnev's government silenced him. As a Soviet soldier during World War II, Aleksandr Solzhenitsyn (sohl zhuh NEET sin) wrote a letter to a friend criticizing Stalin. He was sent to a prison camp. Under Khrushchev, he was released and wrote fiction that drew on his experience as a prisoner. His writing was banned in the Soviet Union, and in 1974 he was exiled. Despite the government's actions, Sakharov and Solzhenitsyn inspired others to resist communist policies.

✓ **Checkpoint** How did the Soviet government handle critics of its policies?

The United States in the Cold War

The Cold War was not just a military rivalry. It was also a competition between two contrasting economic and political value systems. Unlike the communist countries, the democratic, capitalist countries, led by the United States, gave citizens the freedom to make economic and political choices. These nations valued freedom and prosperity.

Free Markets While communist countries had command economies, capitalist countries had market economies. In market economies, producers and consumers make economic decisions. Prices are based on supply and demand in a free market. Property is privately owned. Producers compete to offer the best products for the lowest prices. By deciding what to buy, consumers ultimately decide which products are produced. Producers who win consumers' business make profits and grow.

The United States economy is basically a market economy. However, the United States and Western Europe have what can be called mixed economies, because their governments have an economic role.

Containing the Soviet Union America's basic policy toward communist countries was known as **containment.** This was a strategy of containing communism, or keeping it within its existing boundaries and preventing further expansion. This strategy meant supporting any government facing invasion or internal rebellion by communists.

Living With Nuclear Dangers The nuclear threat led many people in the United States and other countries to build fallout shelters. Fallout shelters

Preparing for a Nuclear Attack
"Duck and cover" air-raid drills were common during the Cold War, even though it is doubtful that ducking and covering would offer much protection in an actual nuclear attack. *What does this photo suggest about Americans' fears during the Cold War?*

Red Scare Culture
Pop culture during the "red scare" of the 1940s and 1950s reflected the fears of the times. "I Was a Communist for the FBI" thrilled movie-goers in 1951.

were structures, often underground, designed to protect people from fallout, or radioactive particles from a nuclear explosion. In 1961, the U.S. government launched a community fallout shelter program to create fallout shelters in public and commercial buildings, stocked with a two-week supply of food for the surrounding population. The fear of nuclear attack reached a peak in the United States during the Cuban missile crisis of 1962. Thousands of Americans built private fallout shelters underneath their backyards.

From the 1950s into the 1970s, American schools conducted air-raid drills in anticipation of a nuclear attack. These drills were nearly as common as fire drills. Children were trained to duck underneath desks and crouch with their hands over their heads. Although this would not have protected them from an actual nuclear explosion, the drills reflected the widespread fear of nuclear war.

Seeking Enemies Within Cold War fears led to a "red scare" within the United States. During the late 1940s and early 1950s, many Americans feared that communists inside the United States might try to undermine the U.S. government. Around 1950, Senator Joseph McCarthy led a hunt for suspected American communists. McCarthy became notorious for unproven charges. Accusing innocent people of communism, and the fear that this created, became known as McCarthyism. McCarthy's influence, however, faded after he attacked the patriotism of the United States Army.

During the same period, the House Un-American Activities Committee (HUAC) led a similar campaign to identify supposed communist sympathizers. HUAC was made up of members of the U.S. House of Representatives. In 1947, the Committee sought to expose communist sympathizers in Hollywood's movie industry. People who had flirted with communist ideas in their youth and later rejected them were labeled as communists. Many who were labeled in this way were no longer able to get decent jobs.

✓ **Checkpoint** How did America respond to the threat of communism at home and overseas?

Assessment

Progress Monitoring Online
For: Self-quiz with vocabulary practice
Web Code: nba-3011

Terms, People, and Places

1. For each term, person, or place listed at the beginning of the section, write a sentence explaining its significance.

Note Taking

2. **Reading Skill: Summarize** Use your completed chart to answer the Focus Question: What were the military and political consequences of the Cold War in the Soviet Union, Europe, and the United States?

Comprehension and Critical Thinking

3. **Make Generalizations** What kinds of conflicts resulted from the global confrontation between the two superpowers?

4. **Draw Inferences** How did the buildup of nuclear weapons discourage their use?

5. **Make Comparisons** Identify similarities and differences between the Soviet Union and the United States during the Cold War.

● **Writing About History**

Quick Write: Understand the Purpose To write a problem-solution essay, you first need to understand the purpose of this type of essay. In this section, you learned that the superpowers' possession of nuclear weapons posed a risk of nuclear war. Write sentences answering each of the following questions: What makes this issue a problem? What benefit comes from solving this problem?

Cooperation

These soldiers, from five different nations, were all part of a NATO-led peacekeeping force in Bosnia in 1999.

In what ways have groups or countries cooperated over time?

Throughout history, people have worked together to achieve their goals, knowing that there is "strength in numbers." For example, prehistoric humans cooperated in hunting for food. Later, countries worked together as allies to defend themselves from threats or to attack other countries. Today, military alliances still exist, but countries also cooperate to improve trade and to resolve problems that affect the entire world. Consider the following examples of cooperation:

Military

After World War II, facing the threat of attack by the Soviet Union, 12 nations from North America and Europe formed a defensive alliance called the North Atlantic Treaty Organization (NATO). Led by the United States, NATO played a vital role in winning the Cold War. Today, 26 NATO members contribute to the group's collective security.

Economic

The goal of expanding trade has continued to lead to international alliances. The European Union (EU), established in 1993, focuses on economic cooperation among its 25 members. Another regional trading group, the North American Free Trade Agreement (NAFTA), started in 1994. NAFTA's free trade zone includes the United States, Canada, and Mexico.

World Issues

Today, the issue of climate change has led to cooperation among nations and the people of the world. In 2005, the Kyoto Accords went into effect. This treaty is an attempt to limit the global emissions of greenhouse gases, such as carbon dioxide. Many scientists believe that these gases contribute to climate change, which could damage the environment.

The European Union

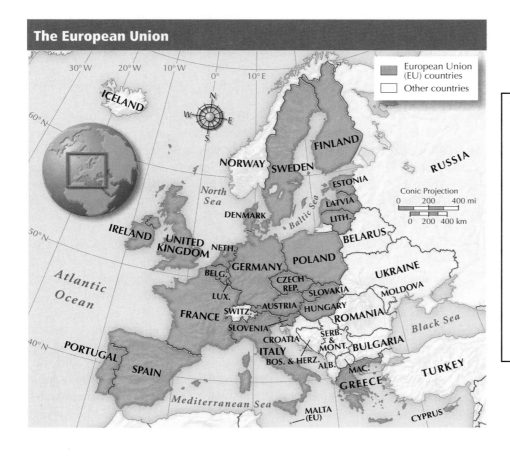

Thinking Critically

1. Markets are often limited to a single country because of legal barriers and fees collected at borders. When nations join the European Union (EU), barriers and fees no longer limit trade across borders. Based on the map, how has the EU changed the physical extent of markets in member countries?

2. **Connections to Today** Research these or other examples of international cooperation to find out more about them. Write an editorial supporting or opposing economic or military agreements among nations.

Marshall Plan poster

Marshall Plan food aid being distributed in France

WITNESS HISTORY 🔊 AUDIO

The Marshall Plan

In a speech at Harvard University in June 1947, U.S. Secretary of State George Marshall made the case for the Marshall Plan, a United States assistance program for Western Europe.

❝ Our policy is directed not against any country or doctrine but against hunger, poverty, desperation, and chaos. Its purpose should be the revival of a working economy in the world so as to permit the emergence of . . . conditions in which free institutions can exist. ❞

Focus Question How did the United States, Western Europe, and Japan achieve economic prosperity and strengthen democracy during the Cold War years?

The Industrialized Democracies

Objectives
- Understand how the United States prospered and expanded opportunities.
- Explain how Western Europe rebuilt its economy after World War II.
- Describe how Japan was transformed.

Terms, People, and Places

recession	Konrad Adenauer
suburbanization	welfare state
segregation	European Community
discrimination	gross domestic product
Dr. Martin Luther King, Jr.	(GDP)

Note Taking

Reading Skill: Categorize Keep track of changes in the industrialized democracies with a chart like the one below.

Economic and Political Changes in the Industrialized Democracies		
United States	**Western Europe**	**Japan**
•	•	•
•	•	•
•	•	•

The industrialized democracies of North America, Western Europe, and Japan grew in prosperity and went through social change during the Cold War. Throughout this period, the United States was the world's wealthiest and most powerful country. By the end of the Cold War, however, Western Europe and Japan rivaled the United States economically.

America Prospers and Changes

In the postwar decades, American businesses expanded into markets around the globe. The dollar was the world's strongest currency. Foreigners flocked to invest in American industry and to buy U.S. government bonds. America's wealth was a model for other democracies and a challenge to the stagnant economies of the communist world.

America Plays a Central Role During the Cold War, the United States was a global political leader. The headquarters of the League of Nations had been symbolically located in neutral Switzerland. The headquarters of the newly formed United Nations was built in New York City.

The United States also played a leading economic role. America had emerged untouched from the horrendous destruction of the Second World War. Other nations needed American goods and services, and foreign trade helped the United States achieve a long postwar boom. The long postwar peace among democratic nations helped to spread this boom worldwide. The World Bank, an international agency that finances world economic development, was headquartered in Washington, D.C. The International Monetary Fund (IMF), which oversees the finances of the world's nations, was based there as well.

The Postwar American Boom America's economic strength transformed life in the United States itself. During the 1950s and 1960s, boom times prevailed. **Recessions,** or periods when the economy shrinks, were brief and mild. Although segments of the population were left behind, many Americans prospered in the world's wealthiest economy. As Americans grew more affluent, many moved from the cities to the suburbs. The movement to communities outside an urban core is known as **suburbanization.** Suburbanites typically lived in single-family houses with lawns and access to good schools. Suburban highways allowed residents to commute to work by car.

During the postwar decades, many Americans also moved to the Sunbelt, or the states in the South and Southwest of the United States. Jobs in these states were becoming more plentiful than in the industrialized North, and the warmer climate was an added bonus. The growing availability of air conditioning and water for irrigation in states such as Arizona helped make the movement to the Sunbelt possible.

The wide popularity of American culture abroad vividly illustrated the global influence of the United States. The world embraced twentieth-century art forms such as American movies, television, and rock-and-roll music. American originals such as Elvis Presley, musical comedies, Hollywood romances, and action movies had a worldwide following.

The federal government contributed to the economic boom. Under President Truman, Congress created programs that helped veterans, the elderly, and the poor. Truman's successor, Dwight Eisenhower, approved government funding to build a vast interstate highway system. Government programs also made it easier for people to buy homes.

Moving to the Suburbs
This cartoon from the 1950s shows a family moving from the city to the suburbs. The photo below shows a suburb in New York in 1954. *Why might suburbs such as this attract families from cities?*

The Oil Shock of the 1970s
In 1973 and 1974, a reduction in the supply of oil led to shortages and higher prices for gasoline. In the photos above, motorists wait on line to fill up with scarce gasoline.

An Oil Shock Brings Recession However, America's growing dependence on the world economy brought problems. In the early 1970s, a political crisis in the Middle East led to decreased oil exports. Oil prices soared worldwide. Waiting in long lines for scarce and expensive gasoline, Americans became aware of their dependence on imported oil and on global economic forces.

In America and in the other industrialized democracies, which were even more dependent on imported oil, higher prices for oil left businesses and consumers with less to spend on other products. The decades of postwar prosperity ended with a serious recession in 1974. During the 1970s and 1980s, the world's economies suffered a series of recessions alternating with years of renewed prosperity.

✔ **Checkpoint** How was the U.S. economy linked to the broader global economy during the Cold War?

Democracy Expands Opportunities

Although America prospered after World War II, the American promise of equality and opportunity had not yet been fulfilled for ethnic minorities and women. In the postwar decades, these groups demanded equality. In American politics, liberals and conservatives offered contrasting programs to increase opportunities for the American people.

Segregation and Discrimination The prosperity of the postwar years failed to benefit all Americans equally. Although slavery had been abolished a century before, many states denied equality to African Americans and other minority groups. These groups faced legal **segregation,** or forced separation, in education and housing. Minorities also suffered **discrimination**—unequal treatment or barriers—in jobs and voting. After World War II, President Harry Truman desegregated the armed forces. Then, in 1954, the U.S. Supreme Court made a landmark ruling, *Brown* v. *Board of Education of Topeka,* declaring that segregated schools were unconstitutional.

Americans Demand Civil Rights By 1956, a gifted preacher, Dr. Martin Luther King, Jr., had emerged as a leader of the civil rights movement. This movement aimed to extend equal rights to all Americans, and particularly African Americans. King organized boycotts and led peaceful marches to end segregation in the United States. In 1963, King made a stirring speech. "I have a dream," he proclaimed, "that one day this nation will rise up and live out the true meaning of its creed: 'We hold these truths to be self-evident, that all men are created equal.'"

Americans of all races joined the civil rights movement. Their courage in the face of sometimes brutal attacks stirred the nation's conscience. Asians, Latinos, Native Americans, and other groups joined African Americans in demanding equality. The U.S. Congress outlawed public segregation, protected voting rights, and required equal access to housing and jobs. Poverty, unemployment, and discrimination still plagued many African Americans. However, some were elected to political office or gained top jobs in business and the military.

Women Demand Equality Women too faced discrimination in employment and other areas. Inspired by the civil rights movement, women fought gender-based discrimination during the 1960s and 1970s. The women's rights movement won laws banning discrimination against women. More women also gained higher salaries and positions in politics and business.

The Government's Role Grows During the 1960s, the government further expanded social programs to help the poor and disadvantaged. Under Presidents John F. Kennedy and Lyndon Johnson, both Democrats,

BIOGRAPHY

MARTIN LUTHER KING, Jr.
Dr. Martin Luther King, Jr. (1929–1968) was born in Atlanta, Georgia, and grew up in the segregated American South. He earned a doctorate in divinity in 1955 and became a minister at a church in Montgomery, Alabama. Beginning that year, King helped lead the Montgomery Bus Boycott to protest segregation on the city's buses. In the years that followed, King emerged as the most respected leader of the American civil rights movement. He was repeatedly attacked and jailed for his beliefs. He helped organize the massive March on Washington, D.C., for civil rights in 1963. He gave his famous "I Have a Dream" speech at this event. King lived to see the passage of the Civil Rights Act of 1965 that outlawed segregation. However, he was killed in 1968 by an assassin. **How did King's actions show courage?**

Congress funded Medicare, providing health care for the elderly. Other programs offered housing for the poor.

Republicans Respond In the 1980s, President Reagan and the Republican Party called for cutbacks in taxes and government spending. They argued that cutting taxes was the best way to improve opportunities for Americans. Congress ended some social programs, reduced government regulation of the economy, and cut taxes. At the same time, however, military spending increased.

The combination of increased spending and tax cuts greatly increased the national budget deficit, or the shortfall between what the government spends and what it receives in taxes and other income. To deal with the deficit, Republicans pushed for deeper cuts in social and economic programs, including education, welfare, and environmental protection.

✔ **Checkpoint** Over time, how did the U.S. government expand opportunities for Americans?

Western Europe Rebuilds

Americans arriving in Europe as liberators or occupiers in 1945 were astonished at the damage that the war had inflicted. Germany in particular lay in ruins. Many Europeans had suffered grievously. However, Western Europe recovered economically more rapidly than anyone had expected—and then moved on to even higher standards of living.

Germany Divided and Reunited At the end of World War II, the United States, Britain, and France—all democracies—occupied the western portion of Germany. The Soviet Union occupied eastern Germany. The goal had been to hold elections throughout Germany for a single German government, but disputes between the Soviet Union and the Western powers led to Germany's division into two separate countries by 1949. West Germany became a member of NATO, while East Germany became a member of the Warsaw Pact. For 40 years, differences between the two Germanys widened.

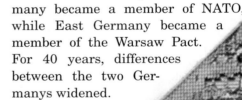

Wartime Destruction in Germany
Many German cities suffered serious wartime damage. In this photo, civilians walk through the rubble left by wartime bombing in Nuremberg, Germany, in 1945. *What challenges would residents of a city face after such heavy destruction?*

While West Germany had a democratic government, East Germany was a communist state. While West Germany enjoyed an economic boom, East Germany's command economy stagnated. Before the Berlin Wall was built, millions of East Germans fled to the freedom and prosperity of West Germany. After the wall was built, some East Germans still managed to escape, but others were shot as they tried to cross the border.

In 1989, as Soviet communism declined, Germany moved toward reunification. Without Soviet backing, East German communist leaders were unable to maintain control. They were forced to reopen their western borders. Quickly, East Germans demanded reunification with the West. In 1990, German voters approved reunification.

West Germany's "Economic Miracle"

Early in the Cold War, the United States rushed aid to its former enemy through the Marshall Plan and other programs. It wanted to strengthen West Germany against communist Eastern Europe. From 1949 to 1963, **Konrad Adenauer** (AHD uh now ur) was West Germany's chancellor, or prime minister. He guided the rebuilding of cities, factories, and trade. Because many of its old factories had been destroyed, Germany built a modern and highly productive industrial base. Despite high taxes to pay for the recovery, West Germans created a booming industrial economy.

Britain's Narrowed Horizons

Britain's economy was slow to recover after the war. Despite U.S. assistance through the Marshall Plan, Britain could no longer afford a large military presence overseas. Therefore, Britain abandoned its colonial empire in the face of demands for independence. After several years of economic hardship, however, Britain's economy recovered during the 1950s and 1960s. Although Britain did not enjoy a boom like Germany's, its living standard did improve.

Other European Nations Prosper

Most European nations emerged from World War II greatly weakened. Like Britain, European colonial powers such as Belgium and the Netherlands gave in to demands for independence from former colonies. France was forced to abandon its

The Iron Curtain Divides Germany
While the Berlin Wall divided the city of Berlin, a much longer series of concrete walls, barbed wire, and watchtowers ran along the border between East and West Germany, forming part of the Iron Curtain. *Why might East Germany have built a fortified border such as this?*

empire after bloody colonial wars in Vietnam and Algeria drained and demoralized the country.

Most Western European countries had suffered serious wartime damage. Like West Germany, they received U.S. assistance through the Marshall Plan. As in West Germany, this helped them to build more modern and productive facilities. During the 1950s and 1960s, most of Europe enjoyed an economic boom. Living standards improved greatly for most Dutch, Belgians, French, and Italians. Poorer European countries, such as Spain and Ireland, were able to attract outside investment that led to economic growth.

Building the Welfare State In the postwar decades, Europeans worked to secure their economic prosperity. From the 1950s through the 1970s, European nations expanded social benefits to their citizens. During this time, many European nations also moved toward greater economic cooperation.

Many European political parties, and particularly those representing workers, wanted to extend the **welfare state.** A welfare state is a country with a market economy but with increased government responsibility for the social and economic needs of its people. The welfare state had its roots in the late 1800s. During that period, Germany, Britain, and other nations had set up basic old-age pensions and unemployment insurance.

After 1945, European governments expanded these social programs. Both the middle class and the poor enjoyed increased benefits from national healthcare, unemployment insurance, and old-age pensions. Other programs gave aid to the poor and created an economic cushion to help people get through difficult times.

However, the welfare state brought high taxes and greater government regulation of private enterprise. In Britain, France, and elsewhere, governments took over basic industries such as railroads, airlines, and steel. Conservatives, or people who favor free markets and a limited role for government, condemned this drift from the free enterprise system toward socialism.

Limiting the Welfare State In 1979, British voters turned to the Conservative Party, which denounced the welfare state as costly and inefficient. The Conservatives were led by Margaret Thatcher. Thatcher's government reduced social welfare programs and returned government-owned industries to private control. Faced with soaring costs, other European nations also moved to limit social welfare benefits and to privatize state-owned businesses during the 1980s and 1990s.

Toward European Unity Greater economic cooperation helped fuel Europe's economic boom during the 1950s and 1960s. In 1952, six nations—West Germany, the Netherlands, Belgium, Luxembourg, France, and Italy—set up the European Coal and Steel Community. This agency established free trade in coal and steel among member states by eliminating tariffs, or fees, and other barriers that limited trade. This small start spurred economic growth across Western Europe and led to further regional cooperation.

In 1957, the same six European nations signed a treaty to form the European Economic Community, later known simply as the **European Community.** This was an organization dedicated to establishing free trade among member nations for all products. The European Community

Building Britain's Welfare State
Britain's Labour Party won support after World War II by expanding social programs and the government's role in the economy.

gradually ended tariffs and allowed workers and capital to move freely across national borders. In later years, the European Community expanded to include Britain and other European countries.

✓ **Checkpoint** What were some advantages and disadvantages of the welfare state in Europe?

Japan Is Transformed

In 1945, Japan, like Germany, lay in ruins. It had suffered perhaps the most devastating damage of any nation involved in World War II. Tens of thousands of Japanese were homeless and hungry.

American Occupiers Bring Changes Under General Douglas MacArthur, the Japanese emperor lost all political power. Japan's new constitution established a parliamentary democracy. Occupation forces also introduced social reforms. They opened the education system to all people, with legal equality for women. A sweeping land-reform program bought out large landowners and gave land to landless farmers.

In 1952, the United States ended the occupation and signed a peace treaty with Japan. Still, the two nations kept close ties. American military forces maintained bases in Japan, which in turn was protected by American nuclear weapons. The two countries were also trading partners, eventually competing with each other in the global economy.

Japan Develops a Democracy Over the years, democracy took root in Japan. The Liberal Democratic Party (LDP) dominated the government from the 1950s to the 1990s. The LDP, however, differs from political parties in the United States. The LDP is a coalition, or alliance, of factions that compete for government positions.

Peace Comes to Japan
A 1945 poster printed by a Japanese bank encourages people to "make a bright future for Japan."

Land Reform Benefits Japanese Farmers
Japan's postwar land reform redistributed land from wealthy landlords to small farmers such as the ones in this photo. *How would ownership of land benefit farmers?*

An Economic Miracle Relies on Exports Like Western Europe, Japan achieved an economic miracle between 1950 and 1970. Its **gross domestic product (GDP)** soared year after year. GDP is the total value of all goods and services produced in a nation within a particular year.

Japan's success was built on producing goods for export. At first, Japan sold textiles. Later, it shifted to selling steel and machinery. By the 1970s, Japanese cars, cameras, and televisions found eager buyers on the world market. Soon, a wide range of Japanese electronic goods were competing with Western, and especially American, products.

How did Japan enjoy such success? After World War II, Japan, like Germany, had to rebuild from scratch. Also like Germany, it had successfully industrialized in the past, so it quickly built efficient, modern factories that outproduced older industries in the West. With American military protection, Japan spent little money on its own military and could invest more in its economy. In addition, Japan benefited from an educated and skilled workforce. Finally, the government protected home industries by imposing tariffs and regulations that limited imports.

These policies, along with the high quality of Japanese exports, resulted in a trade surplus for Japan. That is, Japan sold more goods overseas than it bought from other countries. By the 1980s, United States manufacturers were angered by what they saw as unfair competition, and the United States pushed Japan to open its economy to more imports. However, Japan's trade surplus persisted.

Japan's Economic Miracle
By the 1970s and 1980s, Japan prospered by manufacturing products to be sold overseas, such as the televisions being assembled in this photo.

✓ **Checkpoint** What factors explain Japan's economic success in the decades after World War II?

Progress Monitoring *Online*
For: Self-quiz with vocabulary practice
Web Code: nba-3021

Terms, People, and Places

1. Place each of the key terms at the beginning of the section into one of the following categories: politics, culture, or the economy. Write a sentence for each term explaining your choice.

Note Taking

2. **Reading Skill: Categorize** Use your completed chart to answer the Focus Question: How did the United States, Western Europe, and Japan achieve economic prosperity and strengthen democracy during the Cold War years?

Comprehension and Critical Thinking

3. **Compare Points of View** How did Democrats and Republicans differ on the best ways to improve opportunity for Americans?

4. **Make Comparisons** How was the economic development of Western Europe during the Cold War years similar to or different from that of Japan?

5. **Make Generalizations** How was trade important to the economic development of Western Europe, the United States, and Japan during the postwar decades?

 Writing About History

Quick Write: Brainstorm Possible Solutions To write a problem-solution essay, you first need to brainstorm possible solutions to a problem you have defined. In this section, you learned that European welfare states offered social benefits but that these benefits were very costly. List possible solutions to this problem, and explain the advantages and disadvantages of each.

Chinese Communist soldier marching into Beijing, 1949

The "little red book" of quotations from Mao Zedong

WITNESS HISTORY 🔊 AUDIO

Communist Victory in China

On September 21, 1949, at a rally in the Chinese capital, Beijing, the victorious Communist leader Mao Zedong said:

❝ We have closed our ranks and defeated both domestic and foreign oppressors through the People's War of Liberation and the great people's revolution, and now we are proclaiming the founding of the People's Republic of China. ❞

Focus Question What did the Communist victory mean for China and the rest of East Asia?

Communism Spreads in East Asia

Objectives

- Analyze China's communist revolution.
- Describe China's role as a "wild card" in the Cold War.
- Explain how war came to Korea and how the two Koreas followed different paths.

Terms, People, and Places

collectivization	Kim Il Sung
Great Leap Forward	Syngman Rhee
Cultural Revolution	Pusan Perimeter
38th parallel	demilitarized zone

Note Taking

Reading Skill: Summarize Complete this chart to summarize the effects of the Communist Revolution on China and the impact of the Cold War on China and Korea.

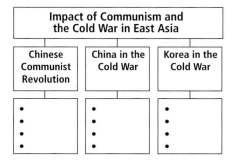

Impact of Communism and the Cold War in East Asia		
Chinese Communist Revolution	China in the Cold War	Korea in the Cold War
• • • •	• • • •	• • • •

In the late 1940s, communism made advances in East Asia. With their victory in China in 1949, the Communists gained control of one fifth of the world's people.

China's Communist Revolution

By the end of World War II, the Chinese Communists had gained control of much of northern China. After Japan's defeat, Communist forces led by Mao Zedong (Mao Tse-tung) fought a civil war against Nationalists headed by Jiang Jieshi (jahng jeh shur). Battles raged until Mao's forces swept to victory and set up the People's Republic of China. The defeated Nationalists fled to the island of Taiwan, off the Chinese coast. After decades of struggle, China was finally under Communist control.

How the Communists Won Mao's Communists triumphed for several reasons. Mao had won the support of China's huge peasant population. Peasants had long suffered from brutal landlords and crushing taxes. The Communists redistributed land to poor peasants and ended oppression by landlords.

While support for the Communists grew, the Nationalists lost popularity. Nationalist policies had led to widespread economic hardship. Many Chinese people also resented corruption in Jiang's government and the government's reliance on support from Western "imperialist" powers. They hoped that the Communists would build a new China and end foreign domination.

Widespread support for the Communists in the countryside helped them to capture rail lines and surround Nationalist-held cities. One after another, these cities fell, and Mao's People's Liberation Army

BIOGRAPHY

Vocabulary Builder

communes—(KAHM yoonz) *n.* commonly owned and operated farms or communities

emerged victorious. After their victory against the Nationalists, the Communists conquered Tibet in 1950. In 1959, Tibet's most revered religious leader, the Dalai Lama, was forced to flee the country.

Changing Chinese Society Mao Zedong built a Communist one-party totalitarian state in the People's Republic of China. Communist ideology guided the government's efforts to reshape the economy and society that China had inherited from the dynastic period. The Communist government discouraged the practice of Buddhism, Confucianism, and other traditional Chinese beliefs. Meanwhile, the government seized the property of rural landlords and urban business owners throughout China.

Opponents of the Communists were put down as "counterrevolutionaries." Many thousands of people who had belonged to the propertied middle class, or "bourgeoisie," were accused of counterrevolutionary beliefs. They were then beaten, sent to labor camps, or killed.

With Soviet help, the Chinese built dams and factories. To boost agriculture, Mao at first distributed land to peasants. Soon, however, he called for **collectivization,** or the forced pooling of peasant land and labor, in an attempt to increase productivity.

The Great Leap Forward Fails From 1958 to 1960, Mao led a program known as the **Great Leap Forward.** He urged people to make a superhuman effort to increase farm and industrial output. In an attempt to make agriculture more efficient, he created communes. A typical commune brought together several villages, thousands of acres of land, and up to 25,000 people. Rural communes set up small-scale "backyard" industries to produce steel and other products.

The Great Leap Forward, however, proved to be a dismal failure. Backyard industries turned out low-quality, useless goods. The commune system cut food output partly by removing incentives for individual farmers and families, leading to neglect of farmland and food shortages. Bad weather added to the problems and led to a terrible famine. Between 1959 and 1961, as many as 55 million Chinese are thought to have starved to death.

The Cultural Revolution Disrupts Life China slowly recovered from the Great Leap Forward by reducing the size of communes and taking a more practical approach to the economy. However, in 1966, Mao launched the Great Proletarian **Cultural Revolution.** Its goal was to purge China of "bourgeois" tendencies. He urged young Chinese to experience revolution firsthand, as his generation had.

In response, teenagers formed bands of Red Guards. Waving copies of the "little red book," *Quotations From Chairman Mao Tse-tung* [Zedong], Red Guards attacked those they considered bourgeois. The accused were publicly humiliated or beaten, and sometimes even killed. Skilled workers and managers were forced to leave their jobs and do manual labor on rural farms or in forced labor camps. Schools and factories closed. The economy slowed, and civil war threatened. Finally, Mao had the army restore order.

✔️ **Checkpoint** What were the main successes and failures of the Chinese Communist Revolution?

China, the Cold War's "Wild Card"

In 1949, the triumph of the Communists in China had seemed like a gain for the Soviet Union and a loss for the United States and its democratic allies. The number of people under communist rule had more than tripled. China's role in the Cold War, however, proved to be more complex than a simple expansion of communist power.

Split With the Soviet Union The People's Republic of China and the Soviet Union were uneasy allies in the 1950s. Stalin sent economic aid and technical experts to help China modernize, but distrust between the two countries created tensions. Some of these tensions dated back to territorial disputes between tsarist Russia and dynastic China. By 1960, border clashes and disputes over ideology led the Soviets to withdraw all aid and advisors from China. Western fears of a strong alliance between the Soviet Union and China had proved unfounded.

Promoting the Cultural Revolution
The Cultural Revolution poster above shows soldiers holding "little red books" and urges them to "destroy all enemies." The photo to the left shows Chinese soldiers waving their "little red books" during this same period. *What do these images suggest about freedom of speech and freedom of thought during the Cultural Revolution in China?*

Washington Plays the China Card Relations between China and the United States were even more complex. After Jiang Jieshi (Chiang Kai-shek) fled to Taiwan, the United States supported his Nationalist government as the rightful representative of China. Washington refused diplomatic recognition of the mainland People's Republic of China, which American leaders saw as a communist threat to all of Asia.

As the Cold War dragged on, however, the United States took a second look at the People's Republic. From the American point of view, there were strategic advantages to improving relations with Communist China after its split with the Soviet Union. By "playing the China card," as this strategy was sometimes called, the United States might isolate the Soviets between NATO in the west and a hostile China in the east.

The United States allowed the People's Republic to replace Taiwan in the United Nations in 1971. A year later, U.S. President Richard Nixon visited Mao in Beijing. Finally, in 1979, the United States set up formal diplomatic relations with China.

Taiwan and the Nationalists Jiang Jieshi's government continued to rule Taiwan under martial law as a one-party dictatorship. Not until the late 1980s did Taiwan's government end martial law and allow opposition

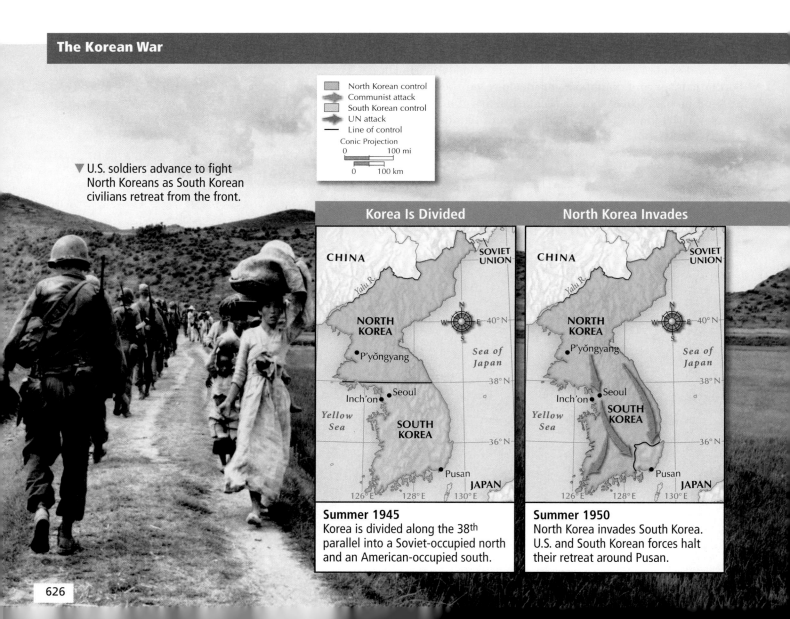

The Korean War

North Korean control
Communist attack
South Korean control
UN attack
Line of control
Conic Projection
0   100 mi
0   100 km

▼ U.S. soldiers advance to fight North Koreans as South Korean civilians retreat from the front.

Korea Is Divided

CHINA

SOVIET UNION

Yalu R.

NORTH KOREA

•P'yŏngyang

Sea of Japan

40° N

38° N

•Seoul
Inch'on•

Yellow Sea

SOUTH KOREA

36° N

•Pusan

JAPAN

126° E   128° E   130° E

Summer 1945
Korea is divided along the 38th parallel into a Soviet-occupied north and an American-occupied south.

North Korea Invades

CHINA

SOVIET UNION

Yalu R.

NORTH KOREA

•P'yŏngyang

Sea of Japan

40° N

38° N

•Seoul
Inch'on•

Yellow Sea

SOUTH KOREA

36° N

•Pusan

JAPAN

126° E   128° E   130° E

Summer 1950
North Korea invades South Korea. U.S. and South Korean forces halt their retreat around Pusan.

parties. Mainland China saw Taiwan as a breakaway province and threatened military action when Taiwanese politicians proposed declaring the island's formal independence. In the long term, the mainland government insisted that Taiwan be rejoined with China. Taiwan's government resisted such pressure.

✓ **Checkpoint** How did China's relationships with the Soviet Union and the United States change during the Cold War?

War Comes to Korea

The nation of Korea occupies a peninsula on China's northeastern border. Like East and West Germany, Korea was split in two by rival forces after World War II. And like other divided lands, the two Koreas found themselves on opposite sides in the Cold War.

A Divided Nation Korea was an independent kingdom until Japan conquered it in the early twentieth century. After Japan's defeat in World War II, Soviet and American forces agreed to divide Korea temporarily along the **38ᵗʰ parallel** of latitude. However, North Korea, ruled by the

---

Map Skills In June 1950, North Korea invaded South Korea. U.S. troops made up the bulk of the UN force that aided South Korea. When UN troops neared the Chinese border, Communist China sent troops to aid North Korea.

1. **Locate** (a) the 38ᵗʰ parallel (b) Pusan (c) Inch'on (d) Yalu River
2. **Movement** Which nation gained new territory by the end of the war?
3. **Draw Conclusions** How might UN forces have avoided war with China?

Geography *Interactive*
For: Audio guided tour
Web Code: nbp-3031

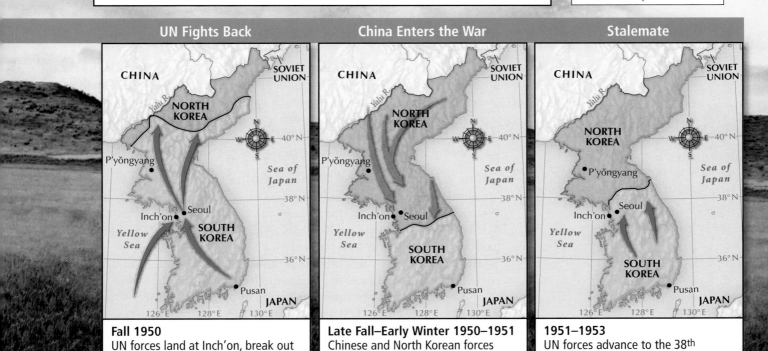

UN Fights Back

Fall 1950
UN forces land at Inch'on, break out of the Pusan Perimeter, and advance to the Yalu River.

China Enters the War

Late Fall–Early Winter 1950–1951
Chinese and North Korean forces push UN forces back to the 37th parallel.

Stalemate

1951–1953
UN forces advance to the 38th parallel in January 1951. A ceasefire in June 1953 ends a long stalemate.

Winter Battle Scene in Korea
U.S. soldiers rest after winning a battle for a snowy hill in Korea, February 1951. *Based on the photograph, what advantage did these soldiers gain by winning control of this hill?*

dictator **Kim Il Sung,** became a communist ally of the Soviet Union. In South Korea, the United States backed the dictatorial—but noncommunist—leader, **Syngman Rhee.**

North Korean Attack Brings a United Nations Response

Both leaders wanted to rule the entire country. In early 1950, Kim Il Sung called for a "heroic struggle" to reunite Korea. North Korean troops attacked in June of that year and soon overran most of the south. The United Nations Security Council condemned the invasion. The United States then organized a United Nations force to help South Korea.

United Nations forces were made up mostly of Americans and South Koreans. Although U.S. troops arrived in early July, North Korean troops continued to advance until United Nations forces stopped them in August along a line known as the **Pusan Perimeter.** This perimeter was centered on the port city of Pusan, in the southeastern corner of the Korean peninsula.

In September 1950, United Nations troops landed on the beaches around the port of Inch'on, behind enemy lines. These U.S.-led troops quickly captured Korea's north-south rail lines and cut off North Korean troops from their supply of food and ammunition. North Korean forces in the south soon surrendered. By November, United Nations forces had advanced north to the Yalu River, along the border of China.

China Reverses United Nations Gains

The success of the U.S.-led forces alarmed China. In late November, Mao Zedong sent hundreds of thousands of Chinese troops to help the North Koreans. In tough winter fighting, the Chinese and North Koreans forced United Nations troops back to the south of the 38th parallel.

The Korean War turned into a stalemate. Finally, in 1953, both sides signed an armistice, or end to fighting. Nearly two million North Korean and South Korean troops remained dug in on either side of the **demilitarized zone** (DMZ), an area with no military forces, near the 38th parallel. The armistice held for the rest of the Cold War, but no peace treaty was ever negotiated.

✔ **Checkpoint** Explain when and why China became involved in the Korean War.

Two Koreas

Like the two Germanys, North and South Korea developed separately after the armistice—North Korea as a communist command economy, South Korea as a capitalist market economy. As in Germany, the capitalist portion of the country had an economic boom and rising standards of living, while the communist zone went through economic stagnation and decline. Also as in Germany, the United States gave economic and military aid to capitalist South Korea, while the Soviets helped the communist north.

Unlike democratic West Germany, however, South Korea was governed by a series of dictators and military rulers during much of the Cold War. Unlike East Germany, where a series of officials led the communist government, a single dictator controlled North Korea throughout the Cold War. Whereas Germany was reunited at the end of the Cold War, Korea remained divided.

South Korea Recovers After the war, South Korea slowly rebuilt its economy. By the mid-1960s, South Korea's economy had leapt ahead. After decades of dictatorship and military rule, a prosperous middle class and fierce student protests pushed the government to hold direct elections in 1987. These elections began a successful transition to democracy. Despite the bloody Korean War, most South Koreans during the Cold War years wanted to see their ancient nation reunited, as did many North Koreans. All Koreans shared the same history, language, and traditions. For many, this meant more than Cold War differences.

North Korea Digs In Under Kim Il Sung, the command economy increased output for a time in North Korea. However, in the late 1960s, economic growth slowed. Kim's emphasis on self-reliance kept North Korea isolated and poor. The government built a personality cult around Kim, who was constantly glorified as the "Great Leader" in propaganda. Even after its Soviet and Chinese allies undertook economic reforms in the 1980s, North Korea clung to hard-line communism.

 Checkpoint How did North Korea's economic performance compare to South Korea's?

Progress Monitoring *Online*
For: Self-quiz with vocabulary practice
Web Code: nba-3031

Terms, People, and Places

1. For each term, person, or place listed at the beginning of the section, write a sentence explaining its significance.

Note Taking

2. **Reading Skill: Summarize** Use your completed chart to answer the Focus Question: What did the Communist victory mean for China and the rest of East Asia?

Comprehension and Critical Thinking

3. **Recognize Ideologies** What ideologies did Mao's programs to transform China reflect?

4. **Draw Inferences** How did the United States use the changing relationship between China and the Soviet Union to its own advantage?

5. **Predict Consequences** How might the history of Korea have been different if United Nations forces had not stepped in to oppose the North Korean invasion in 1950?

● **Writing About History**
Quick Write: Write a Thesis Statement
To write a problem-solution essay, you need to choose the best solution to a problem. In this section, you learned that both North and South Koreans wanted to reunify their country, but that Cold War differences got in the way. List possible solutions to Korea's Cold War division and write a thesis statement arguing for the best solution.

U.S. military helicopter in Vietnam

A family watches President Kennedy speak on television.

WITNESS HISTORY 🔊 AUDIO

America's Role in Vietnam

In a television interview on September 2, 1963, U.S. President John F. Kennedy referred to U.S. support for the noncommunist government of South Vietnam. He did not foresee that five years later, more than 500,000 Americans would be fighting a bloody and divisive war there.

❝ I don't think that unless a greater effort is made by the Government to win popular support that the war can be won out there. . . . We can help them, we can give them equipment, we can send our men out there as advisors, but they have to win it, the people of Viet-nam, against the Communists. ❞

Focus Question What were the causes and effects of war in Southeast Asia, and what was the American role in this region?

War in Southeast Asia

Objectives

- Describe events in Indochina after World War II.
- Learn how America entered the Vietnam War.
- Understand how the Vietnam War ended.
- Analyze Southeast Asia after the war.

Terms, People, and Places

guerrillas	Viet Cong
Ho Chi Minh	Tet Offensive
Dienbienphu	Khmer Rouge
domino theory	Pol Pot

Note Taking

Reading Skill: Summarize Complete a chart like the one below to summarize the events connected to the wars in Southeast Asia.

War in Southeast Asia		
Indochina After World War II	Vietnam War	Aftereffects of War
•	•	•

Southeast Asia's wars were, for many local participants, nationalist struggles against foreign domination. Like Korea, however, Southeast Asia eventually played a part in the global Cold War.

Indochina After World War II

In mainland Southeast Asia after World War II, an agonizing liberation struggle tore apart the region once known as French Indochina. The nearly 30-year conflict had two major phases. First was the war against the French, dating from 1946 to 1954. Second was the Cold War conflict that involved the United States and raged from 1955 to 1975.

Indochina Under Foreign Rule The eastern part of mainland Southeast Asia, or Indochina, was conquered by the French during the 1800s. The Japanese overran Indochina during World War II, but faced fierce resistance, especially in Vietnam, from local **guerrillas** (guh RIL uz), or small groups of loosely organized soldiers making surprise raids. The guerrillas, determined to be free of all foreign rule, turned their guns on the European colonialists who returned after the war. The guerrillas were strongly influenced by communist opposition to European colonial powers.

Ho Chi Minh Fights the French After the Japanese were defeated, the French set out in 1946 to re-establish their authority in Indochina. In Vietnam, they faced guerrilla forces led by

Ho Chi Minh (hoh chee min). Ho was a nationalist and communist who had fought the Japanese. He then fought the French in what is known as the First Indochina War. An unexpected Vietnamese victory at the bloody battle of Dienbienphu (dyen byen foo) in 1954 convinced the French to leave Vietnam. Cambodia and Laos had meanwhile gained their independence separately.

Vietnam Is Divided After 1954, however, the struggle for Vietnam became part of the Cold War. At an international conference that year, Western and communist powers agreed to a temporary division of Vietnam. Ho's communists controlled North Vietnam. A noncommunist government led by Ngo Dinh Diem (ngoh din dee EM), supported by the United States, ruled South Vietnam. The agreement called for elections to reunite the two Vietnams. These elections were never held, largely because the Americans and Ngo Dinh Diem feared that the Communists would win.

Some South Vietnamese preferred Ho Chi Minh, a national hero, to the South Vietnamese government backed by the United States, a foreign power. But Ho's communist rule in the North alienated some Vietnamese. Many Catholic and pro-French Vietnamese fled to the south.

The United States supported Ngo Dinh Diem's regime against what American leaders saw as the communist threat from North Vietnam. Meanwhile, Ngo Dinh Diem's dictatorial regime alienated many Vietnamese with its corruption and brutal tactics against political opponents.

By the early 1960s, communist guerrilla fighters had appeared in the jungles of South Vietnam. Many of them were South Vietnamese, but they received strong support from the north. Many saw their fight as a nationalist struggle to liberate Vietnam from foreign domination.

✔ Checkpoint Why did Vietnamese guerrillas fight the French in Indochina?

Ho Chi Minh

Ho Chi Minh (1890–1969) was born in central Vietnam at a time when Vietnam was under French colonial control. Ho discovered communism while working abroad and quickly adapted it to his struggle against French rule back in Vietnam. While Soviet Communism gave a leading role to urban workers, Ho saw rural peasants as the driving force behind a successful revolution. Ho was more interested in national liberation than following a Soviet communist model. As president of North Vietnam, he led his people first against French control and later against the U.S-backed South Vietnamese government. **How did Ho Chi Minh's approach to communism differ from the Soviet model?**

America Enters the Vietnam War

American foreign policy planners saw the situation in Vietnam as part of the global Cold War. They developed the **domino theory**—the view that a communist victory in South Vietnam would cause noncommunist governments across Southeast Asia to fall to communism, like a row of dominoes. America's leaders wanted to prevent this from happening.

The War Intensifies Ho Chi Minh remained determined to unite Vietnam under communist rule. He continued to aid the National Liberation Front, or **Viet Cong,** the communist rebels trying to overthrow South Vietnam's government. At first, the United States sent only supplies and military advisors to South Vietnam. Later, it sent thousands of troops, turning a local struggle into a major Cold War conflict.

THE VIETNAM WAR

The Vietnam War thrust American soldiers into an alien and dangerous environment of jungles and swamps. The Viet Cong guerrillas were often local villagers, so it was hard for American soldiers to tell friend from foe. Local guerrillas' knowledge of the land allowed them to hide behind vegetation or behind the earthen banks of canals before a surprise ambush. The map at the right shows how North Vietnam delivered supplies to the Viet Cong in South Vietnam along the Ho Chi Minh Trail. These supply lines and the Viet Cong's knowledge of the land made the Viet Cong a deadly foe, even against the better-equipped American forces.

🔊)) AUDIO

Viet Cong guerrillas train in a ditch for combat against American soldiers.

An American soldier sits on the bank of a canal during a skirmish with Viet Cong snipers. Vietnamese children are clinging to their mothers nearby, trying to stay low to avoid gunfire.

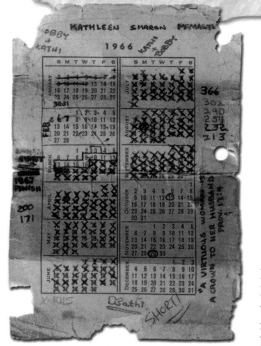

▲ This 1966 calendar may have belonged to one of the 58,000 American soldiers killed in the Vietnam War. It was left at the Vietnam Veterans Memorial in Washington, D.C., by a visitor.

On August 1, 1964, South Vietnamese commandos conducted raids on North Vietnamese islands in the Gulf of Tonkin. The following day, the North Vietnamese attacked a nearby U.S. Navy destroyer, the *Maddox,* which they mistakenly believed had assisted the South Vietnamese raids. Three days later, sailors on the *Maddox* thought that they had been attacked a second time, although it seems likely that their sonar and radar equipment were malfunctioning due to heavy seas.

U.S. President Johnson reported the attacks to Congress without mentioning the South Vietnamese raids or the doubts about the second attack. Believing that the attacks had been unprovoked, Congress passed the Gulf of Tonkin Resolution on August 7, 1964. The resolution authorized the President to take all necessary measures to prevent further aggression in Southeast Asia.

After the resolution passed, the United States began bombing targets in North Vietnam. Eventually, more than 500,000 American troops were committed to the war. At the same time, both the Soviet Union and China sent aid—but no troops—to help North Vietnam.

The Vietnam War, 1968–1975

CHINA

NORTH VIETNAM
- Dien Bien Phu
- Hanoi
- Haiphong

LAOS

Gulf of Tonkin

Hainan

20° N

- Vientiane

Mekong R.

Hué

Danang

15° N

Tet Offensive, 1968
North Vietnam's final offensive, 1975
Ho Chi Minh Trail
American bases

THAILAND

CAMBODIA

Gulf of Thailand

- Phnom Penh

SOUTH VIETNAM

- Saigon

Mekong Delta

10° N

Miller Projection
0   100   200 mi
0   100   200 km

100° E   105° E   110° E

South China Sea

▲ This American soldier is patrolling a swamp in the Mekong Delta in the summer of 1969.

Thinking Critically
1. **Map Skills** Based on the map and the accompanying text, why might the United States have wanted to attack targets in Cambodia?
2. **Draw Conclusions** How did Vietnam's geography and landscape create disadvantages for U.S. forces?

During the Vietnam era, young American men were required to register for the military draft. Men were then selected for the draft in a random lottery. Many saw fighting for their country as their patriotic duty. However, to avoid being drafted, some military-age American men left the country and sought refuge in other nations not involved in the war.

Guerrilla War Like the French in Vietnam, America faced a guerrilla war. The rebels in South Vietnam tended to be local peasants. They thus knew the countryside much better than their American enemies. They also knew the local people. Villagers frequently offered them safe haven against foreign troops. The close connections between guerrilla fighters and the villagers turned the Vietnamese villages themselves into military targets. Supplies for the guerrillas came from the north, following trails that wound through the jungles of neighboring Cambodia and Laos. In response, American aircraft and ground troops crossed the borders of these nations, drawing them into the war.

The Tet Offensive Despite massive American support, South Vietnam failed to defeat the communist guerrillas and their North Vietnamese allies. In 1968, guerrilla forces came out of the jungles and attacked American and South Vietnamese forces in cities all across the south. The assault was unexpected because it took place during Tet, the Vietnamese New Year. The communists lost many of their best troops and did not hold any cities against American counterattacks. Nevertheless, the bloody **Tet Offensive** marked a turning point in public opinion in the United States.

 Checkpoint How did the domino theory lead the United States to send troops to Vietnam?

The Vietnam War Ends

As the fighting continued, civilian deaths caused by the bombing of North Vietnam and growing American casualties inflamed antiwar opinion in the United States. Growing numbers of American troops were prisoners of war (POWs) or missing in action (MIAs). Some Americans began to think that the Vietnam War was a quagmire, or swamp, in which the United States was becoming more and more bogged down.

More Americans Oppose the War As the war continued, the nation became deeply and bitterly divided over the ongoing struggle. Many Americans of all ages continued to support the war effort in Vietnam. Others wanted to end the loss of lives. More and more young people turned out for massive street demonstrations, all part of a growing antiwar movement. It was clear that an increasing number of Americans wanted no more "body bags" coming back or television footage of burned Vietnamese villages. At the same time, many agreed with a housewife who said, "I want to get out, but I don't want to give up."

America Withdraws In the end, American leaders decided that they had to get out of Vietnam. Faced with conflict at home and abroad, President Lyndon Johnson, who had presided over the massive expansion of the war in the 1960s, decided not to run for a second term. Johnson also opened peace talks with North Vietnam in Paris.

Although American troops had seldom lost a battle in the long struggle, they had not destroyed the Vietnamese Communists' determination to keep fighting. Johnson's successor, President Nixon, came under increasing pressure to <u>terminate</u> American involvement. Nixon finally negotiated the Paris Peace Accord in January 1973. This agreement established a cease-fire, or a halt in fighting. The United States agreed to withdraw its troops, and North Vietnam agreed not to send any more troops into the South. The accord left South Vietnam to determine its own future and set a goal of peaceful reunification with the North.

North Vietnam Wins the War Two years after American troops had withdrawn from the country, the North Vietnamese conquered South Vietnam. The South Vietnamese capital, Saigon, was renamed Ho Chi Minh City in 1976 in honor of the late leader. The North Vietnamese capital, Hanoi, became the capital of the reunited nation.

 Checkpoint Why did the United States withdraw its troops from Vietnam?

Southeast Asia After the War

After the American withdrawal from Vietnam, some dominos did fall. Both Cambodia and Laos ended up with governments dominated by Communist Vietnam. However, the falling dominoes stopped at the

Peace Necklace
The peace sign on this necklace was a popular symbol of protest against the Vietnam War.

Vocabulary Builder
<u>terminate</u>—(TUR mih nayt) *vt.* finish, bring to an end

former borders of French Indochina. Other parts of Southeast Asia remained thoroughly capitalist, if less than democratic.

Tragedy in Cambodia During the Vietnam War, fighting had spilled over into neighboring Cambodia. In 1970, the United States bombed North Vietnamese supply routes in Cambodia and then briefly invaded the country. Afterwards, the **Khmer Rouge** (kuh MEHR roozh), a force of Cambodian communist guerrillas, gained ground in Cambodia. Finally, in 1975, the Khmer Rouge overthrew the Cambodian government.

Led by the brutal dictator **Pol Pot,** the Khmer Rouge unleashed a reign of terror. To destroy all Western influences, they drove people from the cities and forced them to work in the fields. They slaughtered, starved, or worked to death more than a million Cambodians, about a third of the population.

In the end, it took a Vietnamese invasion to drive Pol Pot and his Khmer Rouge back into the jungle. Vietnam imposed an authoritarian government on Cambodia, but they at least ended the genocide.

Vietnam Under the Communists In the newly reunited Vietnam, the communist victors imposed a harsh rule of their own on the south. Hundreds of thousands of Vietnamese fled their country, most in small boats. Many of these "boat people" drowned. Survivors landed in refugee camps in neighboring countries. Eventually, some settled in the United States. Meanwhile, Vietnam had to rebuild a land destroyed by war. Recovery was slow due to a lack of resources and an American-led embargo, or blockage of trade. For years, the country remained mired in poverty.

✔ **Checkpoint** How did communist Vietnam dominate parts of Southeast Asia after the Vietnam War?

Fleeing Communist Control
These South Vietnamese refugees are fleeing their country after communist forces took control in April 1975. Refugees who fled in small boats like this one were known as "boat people." *Why might people choose to flee across the open ocean in a small boat like this one?*

SECTION 4 **Assessment**

Progress Monitoring *Online*
For: Self-quiz with vocabulary practice
Web Code: nba-3041

Terms, People, and Places
1. For each term, person, or place listed at the beginning of the section, write a sentence explaining its significance.

Note Taking
2. **Reading Skill: Summarize** Use your completed chart to answer the Focus Question: What were the causes and effects of war in Southeast Asia, and what was the American role in this region?

Comprehension and Critical Thinking
3. **Draw Conclusions** Why did the French withdraw from Indochina in the 1950s?
4. **Summarize** How did a local struggle in Vietnam become a major Cold War conflict?
5. **Compare Points of View** What different opinions did Americans have about U.S. involvement in the Vietnam War?
6. **Synthesize Information** When the text states that "dominos fell" after the Vietnam War, what does this mean?

● **Writing About History**

Quick Write: Write a Supporting Paragraph To write a problem-solution essay, you need to provide arguments to support a proposed solution to a problem. In this section, an American was quoted as wanting to "get out" of South Vietnam without giving up on it. Write a thesis statement proposing a way to do this. Based on the text or your own ideas, write a paragraph with arguments supporting your thesis statement.

THE FALL OF THE SOVIET UNION

Soviet president Mikhail Gorbachev was due to sign a treaty that would reduce the power of the Soviet government. On August 18, 1991, two days before the signing, a committee of Communist hardliners detained Gorbachev at his summer home. The next day, the committee announced to the nation that Gorbachev had resigned and that they were taking control of the government. The committee sent columns of tanks and troops to take control of the capital, Moscow. (See photo at the right.) However, Boris Yeltsin, the president of Russia, the largest Soviet republic, defied the hardliners. Yeltsin called on thousands of Russians to resist the unlawful takeover. Finally, on August 21, the hardliners gave up their takeover and ordered Soviet troops to retreat from Moscow. Yeltsin's defeat of the hardliners led a few months later to the breakup of the Soviet Union.

◄ Soviet president Mikhail Gorbachev

Soviet Union, 1991

Arctic Ocean

EUROPE

Baltic Sea

N
W E
S

SOVIET UNION

Pacific Ocean

Black Sea

Caspian Sea

ASIA

Conic Projection
0   500   1000 mi

0   500 1000 km

History *Interactive*

For: Interactive timeline, audio, and more
Visit: www.PHSchool.com
Web Code: nbp-3041

▲ Russian president Boris Yeltsin, holding a sheet of paper at left, stands atop a Soviet tank on August 19, 1991, and calls on Russians to resist the attempted takeover of the Soviet Union by hardliners. Behind him, a supporter holds a Russian flag. Yeltsin's success in defying the takeover broke the power of the central Soviet government and led to the independence of Russia and the other Soviet republics.

◄ Stanislav Shushkevich (left), president of Belarus; Boris Yeltsin (center), president of Russia; and Leonid Kravchuk (right), president of Ukraine, agreed on December 8, 1991, to dissolve the Soviet Union, effective at the end of 1991.

Thinking Critically

1. **Analyze Images** Why is it significant that Russian President Yeltsin is standing on top of a Soviet tank in the photo at the top of the page?
2. **Synthesize Information** How did the events of August 1991 cause the Soviet government to lose power to Russia?
3. **Map Skills** Based on the maps, why would Russia's wish for independence lead to the Soviet Union's breakup?

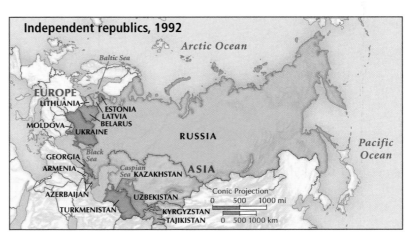

Independent republics, 1992

637

Soviet pin promoting "openness, democracy, and restructuring"

WITNESS HISTORY ◀》 AUDIO

A Democratic Transformation

On November 4, 1989, hundreds of thousands of people demonstrated for democracy in the streets of East Berlin. Never before had so many dared to speak out. Speaking to the crowd, author Stefan Heym captured the mood:

   66 Dear friends, fellow citizens, it is as if someone had thrown open the window after all the years of stagnation. . . . What a transformation! **99**

Ultimately, the transformation in Eastern Europe led to the end of the Cold War.

Focus Question What were the causes and effects of the end of the Cold War?

Demonstrators in East Berlin, November 4, 1989

The End of the Cold War

Objectives

- Understand how the Soviet Union declined.
- Analyze the changes that transformed Eastern Europe.
- Explain how communism declined worldwide and the United States became the sole superpower.

Terms, People, and Places

mujahedin	Lech Walesa
Mikhail Gorbachev	Solidarity
glasnost	Václav Havel
perestroika	Nicolae Ceausescu

N͟ote Taking

Reading Skill: Categorize Complete a flowchart like the one below to categorize each event connected to the end of the Cold War.

End of the Cold War		
Soviet Union •	Eastern Europe •	Rest of the World •

The global Cold War between two armed camps led by the United States and the Soviet Union lasted almost half a century. In the years around 1990, however, the struggle finally ended. The much-feared nuclear confrontation between the two superpowers never came about, but the end was as clear as any military victory.

The Soviet Union Declines

Western fears of growing Soviet power did not come true. In fact, Soviet communism was doomed. Signs of the weakness of the Soviet system had in fact been visible from the beginning.

A Hollow Victory Stalin's Soviet Union emerged from World War II as a superpower with an Eastern European sphere of influence stretching from the Baltic to the Balkans. Victory, however, brought few rewards to the Soviet people. Stalin continued to fill forced labor camps with "enemies of the state."

Reforms Give Way to Repression Under Stalin's successor, Nikita Khrushchev, Soviets enjoyed greater freedom of speech. Some government critics were freed from prisons and labor camps. Khrushchev oversaw a shift in economic priorities away from heavy industry and toward the production of consumer goods. But Khrushchev remained firmly committed to a command economy.

    The thaw in Moscow inspired some East Europeans to move toward greater independence. However, Khrushchev himself remained a determined cold warrior. When Hungarians tried to break free of Soviet control in 1956, Khrushchev sent tanks in to enforce obedience, and his successor, Leonid Brezhnev, did the same thing when Czechs challenged the Soviets in the "Prague spring" of 1968.

The Command Economy Stagnates The Soviet Union rebuilt its shattered industries after World War II, using equipment stripped from Germany. The government poured resources into science and technology, launching *Sputnik I,* the first artificial satellite, in 1957.

Yet the Soviet economy faced severe problems. Collectivized agriculture remained so unproductive that Russia, a grain exporter in tsarist times, had to import grain to feed its people. The Soviet command economy could not match Western market economies in producing consumer goods. Soviet shoes and television sets were far inferior, while such luxuries as clothes washers or automobiles remained rare.

Central economic planning led to inefficiency and waste. A huge bureaucracy decided what and how much to produce. Government planners in Moscow, however, knew little about local needs. They chose to produce many unneeded goods. Consumers' needs often were not met. Although workers were paid low wages, lifetime job security gave them little <u>incentive</u> to produce better-quality goods.

Unlike the economies of Western Europe and the United States, which experienced booms during the Cold War, the economies of Eastern Europe and the Soviet Union stagnated. People saw little improvement in their standards of living and envied the prosperity of the West. Soviet economic inferiority made it impossible for the Soviet Union to keep up with the United States in the arms race and in military preparedness.

Cracking Under the Burden of Military Commitments As you have read, Soviet-American relations swung between confrontation and détente during the Cold War. Meanwhile, both sides maintained large military budgets and built expensive nuclear weapons.

Vocabulary Builder

<u>incentive</u>—(in SENT iv) *n.* something that encourages a person to take action or work harder

Soviet Tanks Bring Repression
A boy watches Soviet tanks in the Hungarian capital, Budapest, in 1956. The Soviet Union sent tanks to stop Hungary's attempt to take an independent course. *What does this suggest about the independence of Eastern European countries such as Hungary during the Cold War?*

The arms race put a particular strain on the inefficient Soviet command economy. And when U.S. President Ronald Reagan launched a new round of missile development, it was clear that the Soviet economy could not afford to match it.

Soviets Have Their Own "Vietnam" in Afghanistan In 1979, the Soviet Union became involved in a long war in Afghanistan, an Islamic country just south of the Soviet Union. A Soviet-supported Afghan government had tried to modernize the nation. Its policies included social reforms and land redistribution that would reduce the power of regional landlords. Afghan landlords—who commanded armed men as warlords—and Muslim conservatives charged that both policies threatened Islamic tradition. When these warlords took up arms against the government, Soviet troops moved in.

Battling **mujahedin** (moo jah heh DEEN), or Muslim religious warriors, in the mountains of Afghanistan, however, proved as difficult as fighting guerrillas in the jungles of Vietnam had been for Americans. By the mid-1980s, the American government began to smuggle modern weaponry to the mujahedin. The Soviets had years of heavy casualties, high costs, and few successes. Like America's Vietnam War, the struggle in Afghanistan provoked a crisis in morale for the Soviets at home.

Gorbachev Tries Reform In 1985, an energetic new leader, **Mikhail Gorbachev** (GAWR buh chawf), came to power in the Soviet Union. With the economy in bad shape and the war dragging on in Afghanistan, Gorbachev was eager to bring about reforms. The changes he urged, however, soon spiraled out of control.

Gorbachev sought to avoid Cold-War confrontations. He signed arms control treaties with the United States and pulled Soviet troops out of Afghanistan.

At home, he called for **glasnost,** or openness. He ended censorship and encouraged people to discuss the country's problems openly. He also urged **perestroika** (pehr uh STROY kuh), or restructuring, of the government and economy. To improve efficiency, he reduced the size of the bureaucracy and backed limited private enterprise. His reforms made factory managers rather than central planners responsible for decisions. They also allowed farmers to sell produce on the free market.

Analyzing Political Cartoons

The Crumbling Soviet Union This cartoon shows Soviet leader Mikhail Gorbachev with an egg-shaped head sitting on a wall marked with the national symbol of the Soviet Union. The cartoon draws on the nursery rhyme *Humpty Dumpty.*
1. What does the cartoon suggest about the state of the Soviet Union under Gorbachev?
2. What does it imply about Gorbachev's future?
3. How does this cartoon communicate ideas without using any words?

An Empire Crumbles Gorbachev's reforms, however, brought economic turmoil. Shortages grew worse and prices soared. Factories that could not survive without government help closed, leading to high unemployment. Those whose jobs were threatened denounced the reforms. Other critics demanded even more radical changes.

Gorbachev's policies also fed unrest across the Soviet empire. Eastern European countries from Poland to Bulgaria broke out of the Soviet orbit beginning in 1989. The Baltic States—Estonia, Latvia, and Lithuania—which the Soviet Union had seized in 1940, regained full independence in 1991. Russia's postwar empire seemed to many to be collapsing. Soviet hard-liners tried to overthrow Gorbachev that year and restore the old order. Their attempted coup failed, but it further weakened Gorbachev, who soon resigned as president.

At the end of 1991, the remaining Soviet republics separated to form 12 independent nations, in addition to the three Baltic States. The largest of these was Russia, which had most of the population and territory of the former Soviet Union. The next largest were Kazakhstan and Ukraine. Maps of Europe and Asia had to be redrawn to reflect the new political boundaries. After 69 years, the Soviet Union had ceased to exist.

✔ **Checkpoint** How did Gorbachev's policies lead to a new map of Europe and Asia?

Defending Lithuania's Independence
This woman, holding a Lithuanian flag, is guarding Lithuania's parliament building and TV tower from Soviet troops that tried and failed to regain control after Lithuania declared independence in January 1991.

Changes Transform Eastern Europe

The Soviet Union had maintained control over its Eastern European satellites by force. When Gorbachev introduced glasnost and perestroika in the Soviet Union, Eastern Europeans began to seek greater freedom in their own countries. As the Soviet Union crumbled, Eastern Europeans demanded an end to Soviet domination. This time they got it.

Demands for Freedom Increase As you have read, unrest had long simmered across the Soviet bloc. Many Eastern Europeans opposed communist rule. Nationalists resented Russian domination. Revolts had erupted in Poland, Hungary, Czechoslovakia, and elsewhere in the 1950s and 1960s. In the 1980s, demands for change mounted once again.

Hungary Quietly Reforms In 1968, when Czechoslovakia's defiance of Soviet control led to a Soviet invasion, Hungary quietly introduced modest economic reforms. Because Hungary remained loyal to the Warsaw Pact and maintained communist political control, it was allowed to go ahead with these reforms, which included elements of a market economy. During the 1970s, Hungary expanded its market economy. During the late 1980s, under the spirit of glasnost, Hungarians began to criticize the communist government more openly. Economic troubles led to greater discontent. Finally, in 1988 and 1989, under public pressure, the communist government allowed greater freedoms. New political parties were allowed to form, and the western border with Austria was opened.

Poland Embraces Solidarity Poland led the way in the new surge of resistance that shattered the Soviet satellite empire. In 1980, economic hardships ignited strikes by shipyard workers. Led by **Lech Walesa** (lek vah WEN suh), they organized **Solidarity,** an independent labor union. It won millions of members and demanded political as well as economic change.

Lech Walesa and Solidarity

Lech Walesa, at the left, speaks at a shipyard workers' strike in August 1980. The following month, he helped found the Polish national union known as Solidarity (Solidarnosc in Polish). At the right, Poles defy the government by holding a banner for the outlawed Solidarity union in 1983. *Why would a Communist government ban a labor union?*

Under pressure from the Soviet Union, the Polish government outlawed the union and arrested its leaders, including Walesa. Still, unrest continued. Walesa became a national hero, and the Polish government eventually released him from prison. Pope John Paul II visited Poland, met with Solidarity leaders, and criticized communist policies. The pope was the former Karol Wojtyla, archbishop of the Polish city of Cracow.

East Germans Demand Change Unlike Poland or Hungary, East Germany resisted Gorbachev's calls for change. In 1988, the rigidly communist East German government banned Soviet publications, because it considered glasnost subversive. East Germany's communists blocked moves toward a market economy or greater political freedom. However, East Germans could watch television broadcasts from West Germany. They were thus intensely aware how much more prosperity and political freedom existed on the other side of the Berlin Wall. When Hungary opened its border with Austria in 1989, thousands of East Germans fled through Hungary and Austria to West Germany. Thousands more held demonstrations across East Germany demanding change.

Communist Governments Fall In the late 1980s, Gorbachev declared that he would not interfere with Eastern European reforms. Poland legalized Solidarity and, in 1989, held the first free elections in 50 years. A year later, Lech Walesa was elected president of Poland. The new government began a difficult, but peaceful, transition from a command economy to a market economy.

A flowering of opposition and reform movements spread across the Eastern European countries. By late 1989, a powerful democracy movement was sweeping throughout the region. Everywhere, people took to the streets, demanding reform. One by one, communist governments fell. In Czechoslovakia, **Václav Havel** (VAHTS lahv HAH vul), a dissident writer and human rights activist, was elected president. In East Germany, the gates of the Berlin Wall were opened, and the country started down the road to reunification with West Germany. Most changes came peacefully, but when Nicolae Ceausescu (chow SHES koo), Romania's longtime dictator, refused to step down, he was overthrown and executed.

For the first time since 1939, Eastern European countries were free. They dissolved the Warsaw Pact in 1991 and requested that Russian troops leave. By then, the Soviet Union itself had crumbled.

Czechoslovakia Splits Czechoslovakia was a relatively new nation, formed in 1918 at the breakup of the Austro-Hungarian Empire. Before 1918, the country's Czech and Slovak ethnic groups—each with its own language and traditions—had lived separately. After Czechoslovakia's founding, Czechs dominated the country's government. During World War II, Czechoslovakia was conquered and partitioned, or divided, by Nazi Germany. Czechoslovakia was reunified under communist control after the war. When the Communists lost power in 1989, some Slovaks began to call for independence. In 1992, the Slovaks and Czechs peacefully agreed to divide Czechoslovakia into the new nations of Slovakia and the Czech Republic.

✔ **Checkpoint** How did glasnost in the Soviet Union lead to the end of communism in Eastern Europe?

Communism Declines Around the World

The defeat of communism in the Soviet bloc affected communist countries from China to Castro's Cuba. Many were already suffering economic decline by the 1980s as their command economies stagnated. Some took a second look at free-market economics. Few, however, made many concessions to democracy.

China Builds on Deng's Reforms Gorbachev had urged the leaders of other communist states to consider both political and economic changes. Leaders of the People's Republic of China accelerated the compromises with capitalism that Deng Xiaoping had introduced in the 1980s. The result was an amazing economic boom, including double-digit growth rates for more than a decade.

China's Communist Party, however, undertook no political reforms. Watching communist power unravel in Eastern Europe, China's leaders worked to preserve one-party Communist rule—and their own power.

Vietnam and North Korea Differ Communist Vietnam opened itself to the world in the 1990s and established diplomatic relations with the United States. Vietnam also began to find its way economically, appealing to tourists and becoming a leading exporter of coffee to the world.

North Korea, on the other hand, hunkered down in grim isolation and refused to reform its economy or political

Capitalism Comes to China
Chinese consumers shop for mobile phones in this recent photo. *Do the activities in this photo reflect a command economy or a market economy? Explain why.*

system. Its rigidly totalitarian government often proved unable even to feed its people. Hundreds of thousands of North Koreans died of starvation or malnutrition during the 1990s.

Cuba Declines In Cuba, communism seemed to many to be living on borrowed time. Deprived of Soviet support but still crippled by America sanctions, the Cuban economy deteriorated. Many felt that communism in Cuba would not long outlive its founder, the aging Fidel Castro.

 Checkpoint How did communist countries react differently to the collapse of the Soviet bloc?

The United States as Sole Superpower

With the collapse of its great rival, the United States was widely recognized as the only remaining superpower. After years of thin budgets, Russia's armed forces seemed weak and ineffective. Only the United States could project its power around the world.

The United States thus emerged as the world's leading military power. From time to time, the United States exercised this power. Beginning in the 1990s, the United States staged several military missions around the world. You will learn more about these in upcoming chapters.

Americans seemed unsure of their proper role in the world. Some objected to the risk and expense of being "the world's policeman." Others, however, believed that the United States should play an even more aggressive part in world affairs.

America's unrivaled power produced mixed reactions around the world. When the Soviet threat had loomed, American power had been seen as a valuable counterweight. Some continued to see the United States as a protector of freedom. With no rival threat in sight, however, people in many parts of the world were less pleased to see any single nation as powerful as the United States had become.

 Checkpoint Why did America's position as the sole superpower produce mixed reactions?

SECTION 5 Assessment

Progress Monitoring *Online*
For: Self-quiz with vocabulary practice
Web Code: nba-3051

Terms, People, and Places

1. For each term, person, or place listed at the beginning of the section, write a sentence explaining its significance.

Note Taking

2. **Reading Skill: Categorize** Use your completed chart to answer the Focus Question: What were the causes and effects of the end of the Cold War?

Comprehension and Critical Thinking

3. **Draw Conclusions** Why was the Soviet Union unable to keep up with the market economies of the West?

4. **Summarize** How did Gorbachev's reforms lead to the breakup of the Soviet empire?

5. **Recognize Cause and Effect** Why were Eastern Europeans able to break free of Communist governments and Soviet domination in the late 1980s?

6. **Draw Inferences** How did the collapse of the Soviet Union affect the power of other countries around the world?

● **Writing About History**

Quick Write: Gather Evidence To write a problem-solution essay, you need to gather evidence to support a proposed solution to a problem. In this section, you learned that rigidly communist countries faced isolation and economic decline after the fall of the Soviet Union. Identify a solution to this problem and gather evidence to support your solution. Then write a paragraph with a thesis statement proposing a solution. Include the evidence you have gathered in support of your thesis statement.

Václav Havel: *New Year's Address*

Václav Havel was a leading dissident and human rights activist in communist Czechoslovakia. When the "democracy movement" swept through Eastern Europe in 1989, Havel was elected president. In the following speech delivered on January 1, 1990, Havel asks the citizens of Czechoslovakia to accept responsibility for their past and to move forward in building a democracy. Havel calls on Czechs and Slovaks to be active participants in their new democracy.

Václav Havel

Our country is not flourishing. The enormous creative and spiritual potential of our nations is not being used sensibly. Entire branches of industry are producing goods that are of no interest to anyone.... [W]e have today the most contaminated environment in Europe....

But all this is still not the main problem. The worst thing is that we live in a contaminated moral environment. We fell morally ill because we became used to saying something different from what we thought. We learned not to believe in anything, to ignore each other, to care only about ourselves. Concepts such as love, friendship, compassion, humility, or forgiveness lost their depth and dimensions.... Only a few of us were able to cry out loud that the powers that be should not be all-powerful....

We had all become used to the totalitarian system and accepted it as an unchangeable fact and thus helped to perpetuate it. In other words, we are all ... responsible for the operation of the totalitarian machinery....

Why do I say this? It would be very unreasonable to understand the sad legacy of the last forty years as something alien, which some distant relative bequeathed to us. On the contrary, we have to accept this legacy as a sin we committed against ourselves. If we accept it as such, we will understand that it is up to us all, and up to us only, to do something about it. We cannot blame the previous rulers for everything, not only because it would be untrue but also because it could blunt the duty that each of us faces today, namely, the obligation to act independently, freely, reasonably, and quickly. Let us not be mistaken: the best government in the world, the best parliament and the best president, cannot achieve much on their own. And it would also be wrong to expect a general remedy from them only. Freedom and democracy include participation and therefore responsibility from us all.

Czechoslovak democracy demonstrators

Thinking Critically

1. **Identify Point of View** Who does Havel hold responsible for Czechoslovakia's totalitarian past?
2. **Draw Conclusions** What does Havel see as the solution to his country's problems?

Quick Study Guide

Progress Monitoring *Online*
For: Self-test with vocabulary practice
Web Code: nba-3061

■ Cold War Contrasts

Communist Countries	Industrialized Democracies
Compete in arms race to maintain "balance of terror."	Compete in arms race to maintain "balance of terror."
Form Warsaw Pact. China follows separate path.	Form NATO and SEATO.
Seek to spread communism.	Seek to contain communism.
Command economies	Market economies
Economic stagnation, low standards of living	Economic "miracles," prosperity with scattered recessions
Repression of dissent, labor camps	Free expression, but fears lead to an episode of McCarthyism
Power is closely held by communist parties.	Democracy is established in Japan, civil rights movement extends democracy in the United States.
Lost arms race.	Won arms race.

■ Cold War Hot Spots

Korea	Vietnam
Divided into communist north and noncommunist, U.S.-supported south.	Divided into communist north and noncommunist, U.S.-supported south.
China provided troops to support North Korea.	China and the Soviet Union provided economic and military aid, but not troops, to North Vietnam.
The United States led United Nations troops supporting South Korea.	The United States and some allies provided troops to support South Vietnam.
Warfare mainly involved regular troops.	Viet Cong fighting in the south were mainly guerrillas.
United States troops remained in South Korea after war.	United States troops withdrew before the war ended.
Korean War ended in a stalemate between the two sides and a ceasefire.	Vietnam War ended when North Vietnam defeated South Vietnam and reunited the country.

■ Steps in the Collapse of the Soviet Empire

- The command economy could not create wealth or raise living standards as quickly as market economies.
- The Soviet Union could not afford the expense of maintaining a "balance of terror" in the arms race.
- East Europeans resisted communism and Soviet control.
- Soviet military failure in Afghanistan led to calls for change.
- Reforms in Russia included glasnost, or freedom of expression, and perestroika, or market reforms.

- East Germans forced their government to open the Berlin Wall.
- Eastern European nations rejected Soviet control and adopted market economies and democracy.
- Glasnost led to drive for independence by Soviet ethnic minorities and the breakup of the Soviet Union.
- Soviet Union was divided into 15 independent nations.
- The Warsaw Pact was dissolved.

■ Key Events of the Cold War

Americas, Europe, and Soviet Union

East and Southeast Asia

| 1945 World War II ends in Europe. | 1949 Germany is divided. | 1959 Fidel Castro leads communist revolution in Cuba. |

1945 ———— 1955

1945 — World War II ends in Asia.

1949 — Mao Zedong leads communists to victory in China.

1950–1953 — Korean War

毛主席语录
QUOTATIONS FROM CHAIRMAN MAO TSE-TUNG

Concept Connector

Cumulative Review

Record the answers to the questions below on your Concept Connector worksheets. In addition, record information from this chapter about the following concept:

• **Cooperation: European Community**

1. **Empires** The Soviet Union could be described as an empire, since it incorporated many different countries and ethnic groups. How was the Soviet Union similar to or different from other empires that you have studied, such as the Spanish Empire in the Age of Discovery or the British Empire? Consider the following:
   • geography and distance
   • the role of ideology
   • economic ties

2. **Dictatorship** Many Communist rulers could be described as dictators, such as Mao Zedong or Pol Pot. Compare these Communist dictators to other dictators you have studied, such as Adolf Hitler, Benito Mussolini, or Ivan the Terrible. Think about how their rule involved these factors:
   • nationalism
   • genocide
   • military power

3. **Genocide** Pol Pot's regime was responsible for the deaths of millions in Cambodia. How did this genocide compare with earlier genocides you have learned about, such as the Jewish Holocaust or the Armenian genocide? Consider the role of:
   • ideology
   • racial, religious, or ethnic prejudice

Connections to Today

1. **Conflict: India and Pakistan** The Cold War was a tense standoff between the United States and the Soviet Union, with only brief outbreaks of actual fighting. Since India and Pakistan gained independence in 1947, the two countries have engaged in a similar conflict. This conflict involves occasional fighting, often involving guerrillas in the disputed Kashmir region. Since 1998, both India and Pakistan have had nuclear weapons. Using recent news articles and the Internet, research the current state of this conflict. How is it similar to the Cold War? How is it different?

Kashmir Sweater

2. **Democracy: The Global Spread of Democracy** This chapter describes the spread of democracy to West Germany and Japan and later to Eastern Europe. Using an encyclopedia, research the move to democracy in an Eastern European country. Then research a move to democracy in a country in Latin America, East Asia, or Africa. How was the transition to democracy similar or different in these two countries?

1961
Berlin Wall is built.

1989
Eastern Europeans overthrow communist rulers.

1991
The Soviet Union breaks up and the Cold War ends.

1965   **1975**   **1985**   **1995**

1964
U.S. enters the Vietnam War.

1975
Vietnam War ends with North Vietnamese victory.

1976
Mao Zedong dies.

History Interactive
For: Interactive timeline
Web Code: nbp-3061

Chapter Assessment

Terms, People, and Places

Choose the italicized term in parentheses that best completes each sentence.

1. The United States aimed to prevent the spread of communism through a policy of (*containment/glasnost*).
2. (*Ngo Dinh Diem/Ho Chi Minh*) was the leader of North Vietnam.
3. European nations eliminated barriers to trade by establishing the (*welfare state/European Community*).
4. At the end of the Korean War, a cease-fire line was established near the (*38th parallel/Pusan Perimeter*).
5. A period of economic decline is a (*budget deficit/recession*).
6. During the 1970s, the United States and the Soviet Union had a period of reduced Cold War tensions known as (*collectivization/détente*).

Main Ideas

Section 1 (pp. 604–612)
7. How did the Cold War develop in the Soviet Union, Europe, and the United States?
8. What were the main features of the nuclear arms race?

Section 2 (pp. 614–622)
9. How did political and economic life change during the Cold War years in the United States?
10. What was the relationship between economic growth and trade in Western Europe and Japan?

Section 3 (pp. 623–629)
11. How did the Korean War influence U.S. relations with Communist China? How did those relations change as a result of hostility between China and the Soviet Union?

Section 4 (pp. 630–635)
12. Why did the United States enter the Vietnam War?

Section 5 (pp. 638–644)
13. How did Gorbachev's reforms lead to the breakup of the Soviet Union?
14. What events marked the end of the Cold War?

Chapter Focus Question
15. How did the Cold War develop, how did it shape political and economic life in individual nations, and how did it end?

Critical Thinking

16. **Analyze Visuals** Turn to the photo of the Berlin Wall on the first page of this chapter. How do you think that the Berliners in this photo felt about the wall that had been built through their city?
17. **Make Comparisons** What factors contributed to economic booms after World War II in Western Europe, the United States and Japan? Why was the economic performance of Eastern Europe and the Soviet Union different?
18. **Draw Inferences** You have read that the leaders of the Soviet Union retained power in Poland and elsewhere in Eastern Europe for over forty years. How were they able to do so despite lacking the consent of the governed?
19. **Predict Consequences** During the Cold War, many nations formed alliances with one superpower for protection against the other. After the Cold War, the United States emerged as the sole superpower. How might this change the nature of alliances?
20. **Recognize Cause and Effect** Which factors allowed North Vietnam to achieve victory over South Vietnam? What were some consequences of North Vietnam's victory in Vietnam and other parts of Southeast Asia?

● Writing About History

Writing a Problem-Solution Essay Write a problem-solution essay on one of the Cold War problems listed below. Research the problem, choose a solution, and write a short essay outlining the problem and your proposed solution. Problems to address include the military standoff on the Iron Curtain, the arms race, and the division of Germany, Korea, or Vietnam. Consult page SH10 of the Writing Handbook for additional help.

Prewriting
- Go online or do library research to find evidence on each of the problems listed above.
- Choose the problem that interests you most and take notes about the evidence you find.

- Decide on the best solution to this problem and gather the evidence that supports your solution.

Drafting
- Write a first paragraph stating the problem and explaining why it is important.
- Write a thesis statement arguing for your solution to the problem.
- Write a second paragraph beginning with your thesis statement, followed by sentences providing evidence to support your thesis.

Revising
- Use the guidelines for revising your report on page SH12 of the Writing Handbook.

Document-Based Assessment

Cold War Chills

The United States and the Soviet Union confronted each other in the Cold War—a global conflict that included a nuclear arms race. In Document A, Nikita Khrushchev discusses the border fortifications that prevented East Germans from entering West Germany. In Document B, U.S. Vice President Richard Nixon warns Khrushchev about restricting western access to Berlin.

Document A

"Seeing that their government had reasserted control over its own frontiers, the East Germans were heartened by the solidification and fortification of their state. . . .I know there are people who claim that the East Germans are imprisoned in paradise and that the gates of the Socialist paradise are guarded by armed troops. I'm aware that a defect exists, but I believe it's a necessary and only temporary defect."

—From ***Khrushchev Remembers*** by Nikita Khrushchev

Document B

". . . I hope the Prime Minister has understood all the implications of what I said," Nixon went on, with an oblique [indirect] reference to Berlin. "What I mean is that the moment we place either one of these powerful nations, through an ultimatum, in a position where it has no choice but to accept dictation or fight, then you are playing with the most destructive force in the world."

Khrushchev: (flushed, wagging a finger near Nixon's face): We too are giants. If you want to threaten, we will answer threat with threat.

Nixon: We never engage in threats.

Khrushchev: You wanted indirectly to threaten me. But we have means at our disposal that can have very bad consequences.

Nixon: We have too.

—From ***Time***, August 3, 1959

Document C

Document D

Fortifications that kept East Germans from crossing into West Germany

Analyzing Documents

Use your knowledge of the Cold War and Documents A, B, C, and D to answer questions 1–4.

1. The author's purpose in Document A was to
   A explain East German discipline.
   B offer a balanced perspective on the Cold War.
   C argue for a fortified barrier between East and West Germany.
   D explain the role of the Soviet Union in East Germany.

2. The tone of the exchange in Document B is
   A friendly and joking.
   B tense and hostile.
   C cautious.
   D businesslike.

3. Document C shows that
   A West Berlin was located inside West Germany.
   B the border between East and West Germany passed through Berlin.
   C East Germany surrounded West Germany.
   D two East German borders separated West Berlin from West Germany.

4. **Writing Task** How was the Cold War fought? Use what you have read in the chapter, along with these documents, to write a response.

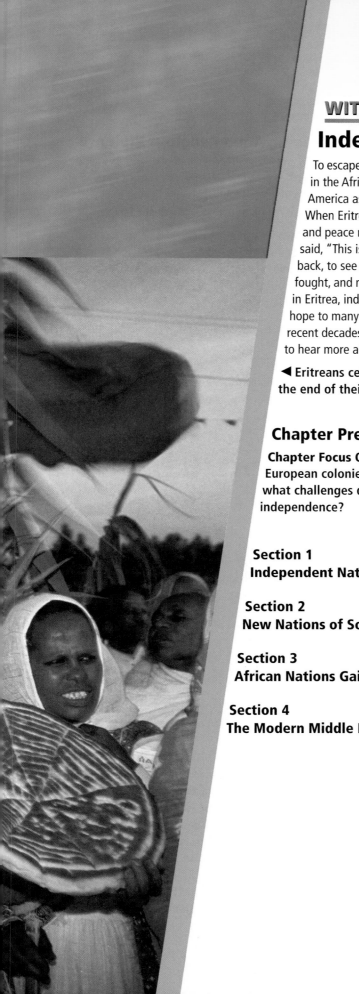

Independence in Eritrea

To escape the dangers of the war for independence in the African nation of Eritrea, Almaz Isaac fled to America as a refugee when she was a teenager. When Eritrea won its independence ten years later and peace returned, Almaz returned to Eritrea. She said, "This is the first time I've been able to come back, to see my family. We waited, our people fought, and now this is it. We have our freedom." As in Eritrea, independence brought a new sense of hope to many countries in Africa and elsewhere in recent decades. Listen to the Witness History audio to hear more about independence in Africa.

◄ Eritreans celebrate independence in 1993 at the end of their long war for freedom.

Monument showing the sandals worn by soldiers in Eritrea's war for independence

Chapter Preview

Chapter Focus Question How did former European colonies gain independence, and what challenges did they face after independence?

Section 1
Independent Nations of South Asia

Section 2
New Nations of Southeast Asia

Section 3
African Nations Gain Independence

Section 4
The Modern Middle East

Flag of the Southeast Asian nation of Malaysia

Hat worn by border guards in India

Note Taking Study Guide *Online*
For: Note Taking and Concept Connector worksheets
Web Code: nbd-3101

Hat worn by Indian border guards along the border with Pakistan

A family of refugees fleeing religious violence after India and Pakistan gained independence

WITNESS HISTORY 🔊 AUDIO

Fleeing Amid Religious Violence

India and Pakistan gained independence in a time of terrible religious violence. Damyanti Sahgal, a Hindu, describes her experience fleeing from a Muslim region at the time of independence:

66 When we came close to Amritsar, we found that they had started stopping trains, killing people in them, but we were lucky. Everyone said put your windows up, they are cutting down people. 99

While many South Asians greeted independence, they had to live with the bitter aftermath of the violence and distrust that accompanied it.

Focus Question What were the consequences of independence in South Asia for the region and for the world?

Independent Nations of South Asia

Objectives

- Understand why independence brought partition to South Asia.
- Describe how Indian leaders built a new nation.
- Summarize how Pakistan and Bangladesh grew apart.
- Explain how India and Pakistan pursued independence from the superpowers in their foreign relations.

Terms, People, and Places

partition	Indira Gandhi
Sikhs	Punjab
Kashmir	Golden Temple
Jawaharlal Nehru	Bangladesh
dalits	nonalignment

Note Taking

Reading Skill: Identify Causes and Effects Fill in a concept web like this one to keep track of causes and effects of events in South Asia. Add ovals as needed for additional concepts.

At the same time that the Cold War was unfolding, a global independence movement was reshaping the world. Among the first new nations to win independence were the former British colonies of South Asia.

Independence Brings Partition

Local activists in British India had demanded self-rule since the late 1800s. As independence neared, however, a long-simmering issue surfaced. What would happen to the Muslim minority in a Hindu-dominated India?

Two New Nations Emerge Like Mohandas Gandhi, most of the leaders and members of the Congress Party were Hindus. However, the party wanted a unified India that would include both Muslims and Hindus. The Muslim League, led by Muhammad Ali Jinnah, had a different view of liberation. The Muslim League feared discrimination against the Muslim minority in a unified India. Therefore, the Muslim League demanded the creation of a separate nation, called Pakistan, that would include the parts of British India where Muslims formed a majority. In the 1940s, tensions between Muslims and the Hindu majority in British India led to increasing violence.

As violence between these two groups threatened to spiral out of control, Britain decided that the only solution was a **partition,** or division, of the subcontinent into a Muslim-majority Pakistan and a Hindu-majority India. The new nations of Pakistan and India gained independence on August 15, 1947.

Refugees Flee Amid Violence However, Hindus and Muslims still lived side by side in many cities and rural areas. As soon as the new borders became known, millions of Hindus on the Pakistani side of the borders packed up their belongings and fled to the new India. At the same time, millions of Muslims fled into newly created Pakistan. An estimated 10 million people fled their homes, most of them on foot.

Muslims fleeing along the crowded roads into Pakistan were slaughtered by Hindus and **Sikhs** (seeks), members of an Indian religious minority. Muslims massacred Hindu and Sikh neighbors. Around one million people died in these massacres. Others died of starvation and exposure on the road.

Struggles Over Kashmir Following independence, India and Pakistan fought a war over **Kashmir,** a state in the Himalayas with Muslim and Hindu populations. Its Hindu ruler sought to join India even though much of the state's Muslim majority wanted to be part of Pakistan. In 1949, India and Pakistan agreed to stop fighting.

The peace between the two nations was short-lived. In 1965, Pakistan and India fought another war over Kashmir and have had several brief clashes since then. Over the years, Muslim Kashmiri separatists, supported by militants from neighboring Pakistan, have fought Indian troops. Indian forces, in turn, have attacked Muslim Kashmiris.

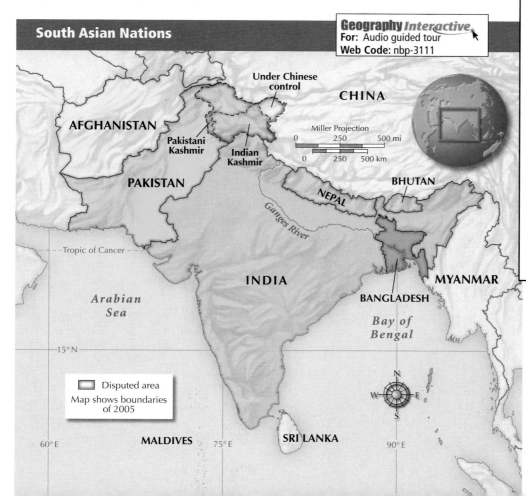

South Asian Nations

Geography *Interactive*
For: Audio guided tour
Web Code: nbp-3111

Map Skills The former British colony of India had become the independent nations of Pakistan, India, and Bangladesh by 1971. The region's other nations had also achieved independence by that date. The status of Kashmir, however, remained in dispute.

1. **Locate** (a) Bangladesh (b) Pakistani Kashmir (c) Indian Kashmir
2. **Regions** Which other nation also has a stake in the Kashmir conflict?
3. **Make Inferences** Bangladesh was once part of Pakistan. How might its location have contributed to its people's desire for independence?

A Nuclear Arms Race In the 1970s, India launched a program to develop nuclear weapons, carrying out its first test explosion in 1974. These actions prompted Pakistan to launch its own nuclear weapons program. In 1998, India tested its first actual nuclear weapons. Pakistan responded that same year with its own tests. The emergence of these two new and hostile nuclear powers in South Asia alarmed other nations in Asia and around the world.

Conflict Divides Sri Lanka The British colony of Ceylon, an island just south of India, gained independence in 1948. It changed its name to Sri Lanka (sree LAHNG kuh) in 1972. A majority of Sri Lankans are Buddhists who speak Sinhalese. However, a large Tamil-speaking Hindu minority lives in the north and east. Sri Lanka adopted policies that favored the Sinhalese majority. These policies angered many Tamils. In the late 1970s, Tamil rebels began a military struggle for a separate Tamil nation. After years of fighting, Sri Lanka's government and the Tamil rebels signed a peace agreement in 2002. The rebels agreed to stop fighting, and the government agreed to give the Tamil region some freedoms. However, it was uncertain whether this agreement would hold.

✓ **Checkpoint** Why have India and Pakistan fought several wars over Kashmir?

Building a Nation in India

Independent India faced many challenges. Ethnic and religious tensions continued to threaten India's unity. Hundreds of millions of Indians struggled daily for adequate food and shelter.

Nehru Confronts Social Problems From 1947 to 1964, **Jawaharlal Nehru** led India as its first prime minister. One of his first priorities was to strengthen India's economy. However, rapid population growth hurt Nehru's efforts to improve living conditions. While food output rose, so did India's population. The government encouraged family planning to reduce the birthrate. However, many Indians, especially in rural areas, saw children as an economic resource. Children were expected to work the land and to care for parents in old age.

In modern India, discrimination based on caste, or inherited status, continued. In the 1930s, Mohandas Gandhi had campaigned to end the inhumane treatment of **dalits,** or outcastes. In 1947, India's new constitution banned discrimination against dalits. Nehru's government also set aside jobs and places in universities for them. Still, higher-caste Hindus generally got better schooling and jobs.

Indira Gandhi
Prime Minister Indira Gandhi led India from 1966 to 1977 and again from 1980 to 1984.

A Woman Leads India Nehru died in office in 1964. Two years later, the Congress Party elected his daughter, **Indira Gandhi,** as prime minister. In India, as in many other countries, women had traditionally faced discrimination. Indira Gandhi's rise to power marked a great advance for Indian women. Gandhi's leadership proved to the world that women could hold powerful positions.

Sikhs Rebel Some Indian Sikhs wanted independence for the prosperous and largely Sikh state of **Punjab.** In 1984, armed Sikh separatists took dramatic action. They occupied the **Golden Temple,** the Sikh religion's holiest shrine. When talks failed to oust them, Indira Gandhi sent troops. Thousands of Sikhs died in the fighting, and the Golden Temple was damaged. A few months later, Gandhi's Sikh bodyguards assassinated her, igniting more religious violence.

Religious Unrest Threatens India India faced a real challenge in building the national unity necessary for stability. When India gained independence, its people spoke more than 100 languages and dialects. A majority of Indians were Hindu, but millions were Muslim, Sikh, Christian, or Buddhist. At times, India's religious divisions led to violence.

By the late 1980s, the Congress Party faced strong competition from the Hindu nationalist Bharatiya Janata Party (BJP). While the Congress Party had separated religion and government, the BJP called for a government built on Hindu principles.

The BJP supported destroying one of India's most important mosques, in the city of Ayodhya (uh YOHD yuh). Hindu nationalists claimed that Muslims had torn down a sacred Hindu temple centuries before to build the mosque. When BJP-backed rioters destroyed the mosque in 1992, Indians feared more religious unrest. Although there have been occasional outbreaks of violence in the years since, India has avoided all-out religious conflict. It remains the world's largest democracy.

Religions of India

Religion	Population (millions)	Percentage	Regional Concentration
Hinduism	828	80.5	Throughout India
Islam	138	13.4	Kashmir, Northern India, Southwest Coast
Christianity	24	2.3	Northeastern India, Southwest Coast
Sikhism	19	1.9	Northwestern India
Buddhism	8	0.8	Northeastern India, West Coast
Others	11	1.0	Throughout India

Chart Skills What is India's largest minority religion? Where do most of its followers live?

SOURCE: Census of India 2001

✔ **Checkpoint** How did Nehru's government address discrimination against lower castes?

Pakistan and Bangladesh Take Different Paths

Pakistan gained independence in 1947, at the same time as India. However, Pakistan was a divided country. West Pakistan occupied the northwestern portion of British India, including the western part of the divided province of Punjab. One thousand miles to the east was East Pakistan, later renamed Bangladesh. Between the two regions was the new India. In the bitterness that followed partition, India made trade and travel between the two Pakistans difficult.

The Two Pakistans Grow Apart From the beginning, West Pakistan tended to dominate the nation's government, even though East Pakistan had a larger population. The government concentrated most economic development programs in West Pakistan, while East Pakistan remained mired in poverty. Most people in East Pakistan were Bengalis, while West Pakistanis came from other ethnic groups. Many Bengalis resented the central government's neglect of their region.

Bangladesh Breaks Away In 1971, Bengalis declared independence for East Pakistan under the new name of **Bangladesh,** or "Bengali Nation." Pakistan's military ruler ordered the army to crush the rebels. India supported the rebels by attacking and defeating the Pakistani army in Bangladesh. Pakistan was eventually <u>compelled</u> to recognize the independence of Bangladesh.

WITNESS HISTORY VIDEO

Watch *Pakistan: Improving Education* on the **Witness History Discovery School**™ video program to see how teachers are being trained in Pakistan's countryside.

Vocabulary Builder
<u>compelled</u>—(kum PELD) *v.* made to or forced

Pakistan's Shaky Government Pakistan has lacked political stability for most of its history. In addition to the tensions between East and West Pakistan, resentments also divided the main ethnic groups of West Pakistan. These resentments continued after Bangladesh broke away. In addition, there were sharp disagreements between Islamic fundamentalists—people who believe that society and government should strictly follow Islamic principles—and those who wanted greater separation between religion and state. Repeatedly, Pakistan's rulers, often backed by the military, dismissed elected governments. Sometimes, the military simply seized power.

Islamic Fundamentalism Grows During the 1980s, the war in Afghanistan after the Soviet invasion drove over a million Afghan refugees into Pakistan. Many of these Afghan refugees turned to Islamic fundamentalism because of their anger at the non-Muslim Soviet invaders. Many young men from these communities joined the mujahedin rebels fighting Soviet forces. Pakistan's Islamic fundamentalists gained power by forming ties with Afghan refugees. After the Soviets withdrew from Afghanistan, these fundamentalists turned against the United States because they resented U.S. influence in the Middle East and in Pakistan. During the 1990s, Pakistan backed Afghanistan's fundamentalist Taliban regime, which supported the terrorist group Al Qaeda. However, when the United States launched a military campaign against Al Qaeda and the Taliban in 2001, Pakistan's government supported the United States.

Floods Ravage Bangladesh
Devastating floods often occur in Bangladesh after the summer rains. In this photo, relief workers are delivering supplies to a family trapped on their roof. *How might frequent floods make it more difficult to improve the economy of Bangladesh?*

Bangladesh Struggles After Bangladesh won its independence in 1971, the country faced many challenges. Bangladesh is one of the world's poorest and most crowded countries. Its population, more than half as large as that of the United States, lives in an area the size of Alabama. The flat Ganges Delta, just a few feet above sea level, covers much of the country. Bangladesh has suffered from devastating and deadly tropical storms and floods. During the 1970s and 1980s, the government controlled much of Bangladesh's economy. In 1990, Bangladesh moved from military to democratic rule.

✓ **Checkpoint** What geographic factors pose challenges for Bangladesh?

Finding an Independent Path

India and Pakistan were among the first of more than 90 new nations to emerge after World War II. By the 1930s, nationalist movements had taken root in European colonies across Africa, Asia, and the Middle East. After World War II, nationalist leaders such as Gandhi and Nehru insisted on independence. When India and Pakistan gained independence, nationalist leaders in Africa and other regions demanded the same for their countries.

In 1955, India and Pakistan helped organize a conference of newly independent states in Bandung, Indonesia. These nations gathered to condemn colonialism and Cold War expansion, both by Western powers and by the Soviet Union. This conference marked the birth of the doctrine of **nonalignment,** or political and diplomatic independence from both Cold War superpowers. The Nonaligned Movement had its first formal meeting in 1961 in Yugoslavia. India was one of the leaders of this movement, most of whose members were Asian, African, and Latin American nations. Because they rejected both the Western allies, or the First World, and the Soviet alliance, or the Second World, the Nonaligned Movement was seen as the voice of a "Third World" of countries belonging to neither Cold War alliance.

✓ **Checkpoint** How did India and Pakistan play a global leadership role?

SECTION 1

Assessment

Progress Monitoring *Online*
For: Self-quiz with vocabulary practice
Web Code: nba-3111

Terms, People, and Places

1. For each term, person, or place in the beginning of the section, write a sentence explaining its significance.

Note Taking

2. **Reading Skill: Identify Causes and Effects** Use your completed concept web to answer the Focus Question: What were the consequences of independence in South Asia for the region and for the world?

Comprehension and Critical Thinking

3. **Recognize Cause and Effect** Why did the partition of British India cause refugees to flee?

4. **Express Problems Clearly** What problems did India's religious diversity pose?

5. **Summarize** Why did Bangladesh separate from Pakistan?

6. **Draw Conclusions** How did the doctrine of nonalignment influence the relations of India and Pakistan with the Cold War superpowers?

● **Writing About History**

Quick Write: Outline Your Topic To write a compare-and-contrast essay, you need to consider two subjects and find similarities and differences between them. In this section, you learned that India and Pakistan share a common history but were separated at independence. Write features of each country's history in three lists: a list of features specific to India, a list of features specific to Pakistan, and a list of features shared by both countries.

Indonesia's flag

WITNESS HISTORY 🔊 AUDIO

All for All

Almost every Southeast Asian nation has a rich variety of peoples and religions. Indonesia's independence leader, Sukarno, stressed the importance of unity for all Indonesians:

66 [W]e are establishing an Indonesian state which all of us must support. All for all. Not the Christians for Indonesia, not the Islamic group for Indonesia . . . but the Indonesians for Indonesia—all for all! 99

Religious diversity was only one of many challenges that Indonesia would face in the decades after independence.

Focus Question What challenges did Southeast Asian nations face after winning independence?

Sukarno, Indonesia's first president

New Nations of Southeast Asia

Objectives

- Explain the political and economic contrasts in mainland Southeast Asia.
- Understand how Indonesia's size posed challenges.
- Summarize how the Philippines sought democracy.

Terms, People, and Places

autocratic	East Timor
Aung San Suu Kyi	Ferdinand Marcos
Sukarno	Benigno Aquino
Suharto	Corazon Aquino

Note Taking

Reading Skills: Understand Effects Fill in a concept web like the one below to keep track of the effects of recent historical processes in Southeast Asia. Add to it as needed for additional concepts in the section.

Malaysian diversity and prosperity
Wealth distributed among ethnic groups
Profitable industries
New Nations of Southeast Asia

Southeast Asia includes a portion of the Asian mainland and thousands of islands. By World War II, European nations and the United States had colonized much of Southeast Asia. During World War II, the Japanese occupation broke the power of the Europeans. This spurred local rebels to fight against foreign occupation. After World War II, these rebels demanded independence.

Mainland Contrasts

Mainland Southeast Asia is a region of contrasts. Thailand and Malaysia have prospered as market economies. However, their neighbor Myanmar, or Burma, has suffered under a brutal government that is **autocratic.** That is, the government has unlimited power.

Malaysia Prospers British colonies on the Malay Peninsula and the island of Borneo gained independence in the 1950s and joined to form the nation of Malaysia. The oil-rich monarchy of Brunei, on Borneo, and the prosperous city-state of Singapore gained independence as separate nations.

Malaysia has a very diverse population. People of Chinese and Indian descent have long dominated business. They have made the nation a Southeast Asian leader in profitable industries such as rubber and electronics. The government, however, has tried to include the Malay majority in the country's prosperity. The result has been a more equal distribution of wealth in Malaysia than in most countries in the region.

Myanmar Suffers Britain granted independence to its former colony of Burma in 1948. Burma was renamed Myanmar (MYAHN mahr) in 1989. Ethnic tensions have plagued Myanmar. The majority, Burmans, have dominated other ethnic groups. The military government has limited foreign trade, and living standards remain low.

Under mounting foreign pressure, elections were held in 1990. A party opposed to military rule won. It was led by **Aung San Suu Kyi** (awn sahn soo chee), whose father had helped Burma win independence. The military rejected the election results and jailed, killed, or exiled many opponents. Suu Kyi was held under house arrest. In 1995, Suu Kyi won the Nobel Peace Prize for her "nonviolent struggle for democracy and human rights," but she remained a prisoner in her own country.

✔ **Checkpoint** How did Malaysia's approach to ethnic diversity differ from Myanmar's?

Indonesia's Size Poses Challenges

After World War II, the Netherlands attempted to regain power in Indonesia, formerly the Dutch East Indies. The Dutch, however, were forced to give up their possessions when the Indonesian government declared independence in 1949 after the Japanese defeat.

Geography and diversity posed an obstacle to unity in Indonesia. Indonesia includes more than 13,000 islands, many very small but some as large as European nations. Javanese make up almost half of the population, but there are hundreds of other ethnic groups. About 90 percent of Indonesians are Muslims, but the population includes substantial Christian, Buddhist, and Hindu minorities.

Democracy Falters In the first years after independence, Indonesia formed a democratic, parliamentary government under its first president, **Sukarno.** In 1965, a group of army officers attempted to seize power. An army general, **Suharto,** blocked them, but by the following year had himself seized power from Sukarno. Suharto claimed that Communists had been behind the officers' failed attempt to seize power. Based on Suharto's charges, hundreds of thousands of Communists and suspected Communists were slaughtered. Suharto ruled the next three decades as a dictator.

In 1997, an Asian financial crisis shook Indonesia to its roots. Rioters protested massive government corruption. President Suharto was forced to resign in 1998 after 32 years in power. A series of democratically elected governments worked to restore economic and political stability. However, Islamic extremists have terrorized foreigners and non-Muslims and caused instability in some regions.

East Timor Fights for Freedom Indonesia seized **East Timor,** a former Portuguese colony, from Portugal in 1975. However, most East Timorese wanted independence. For years, the government battled the mostly Catholic East Timorese. East Timor finally won independence from Indonesia in 2002. This very poor new nation struggled to meet its people's need for jobs and decent living standards.

Ethnic Conflicts and Natural Disasters Religious and ethnic conflicts fueled violence in parts of Indonesia. In the Moluccas, a group of eastern islands, fighting between Muslims and Christians

Southeast Asia's Oil Wealth
Oil and gas reserves have been an important source of wealth for Indonesia and its neighbors. This oil well is in the oil-rich monarchy of Brunei (broo NY). Brunei is on the island of Borneo, which is divided among Brunei, Malaysia, and Indonesia.

RELIGIOUS DIVERSITY IN SOUTHEAST ASIA

Southeast Asia is one of the worlds most religiously diverse regions. This diversity is a result of its history as a crossroads between South and East Asia. In some countries, such as Indonesia and the Philippines, religious differences have played a part in civil conflicts. In others, such as Malaysia and Singapore, people of different religions live together in peace.

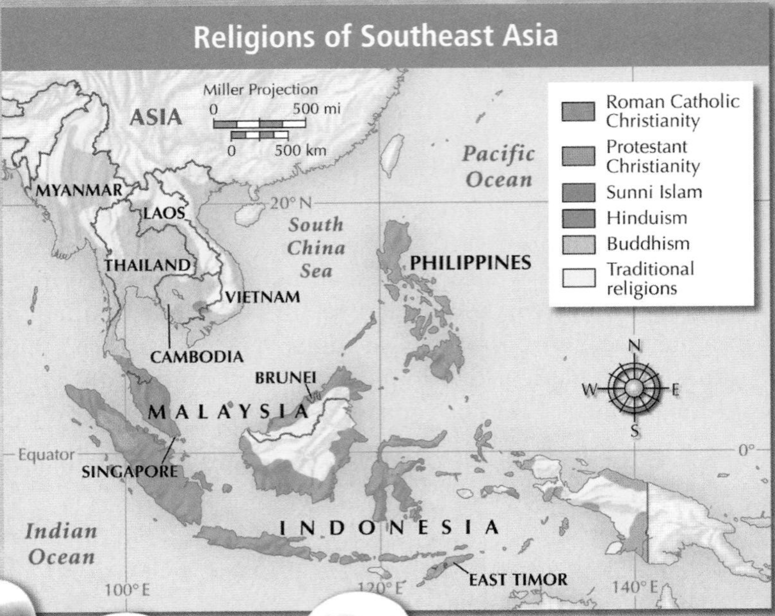

Islam links many Southeast Asians to other parts of the Muslim world. The Indonesian Muslim woman to the left is attending a prayer service for peace in the Middle East.

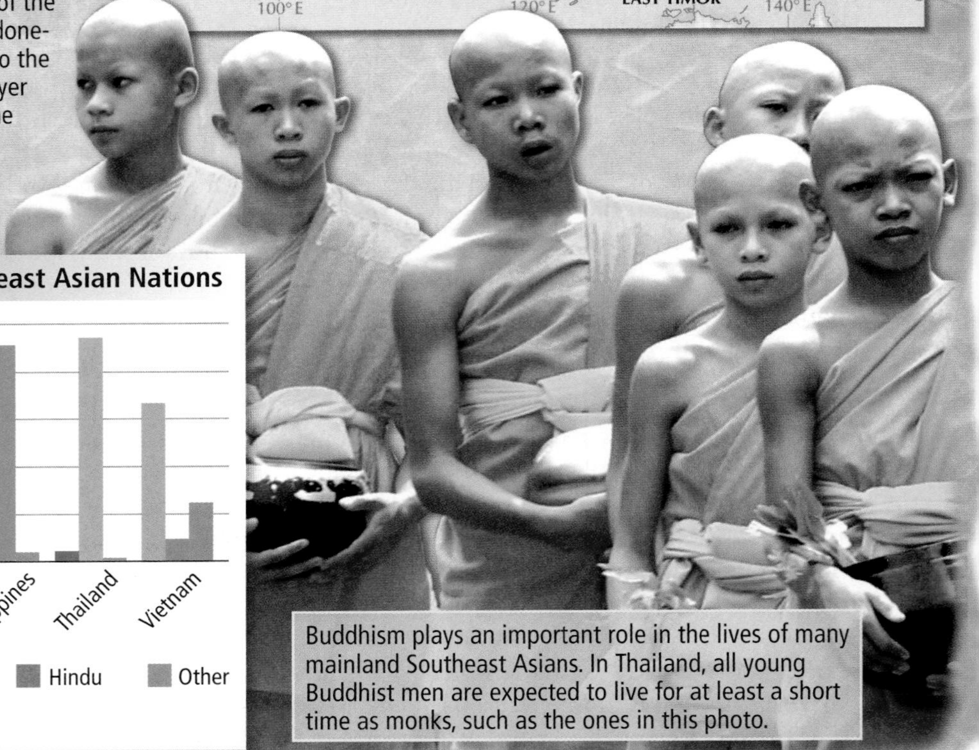

Religions of Southeast Asia

Roman Catholic Christianity
Protestant Christianity
Sunni Islam
Hinduism
Buddhism
Traditional religions

Religious Composition of Major Southeast Asian Nations

Percent

Indonesia   Malaysia   Myanmar   Philippines   Thailand   Vietnam

■ Muslim   ■ Buddhist   ■ Christian   ■ Hindu   ■ Other

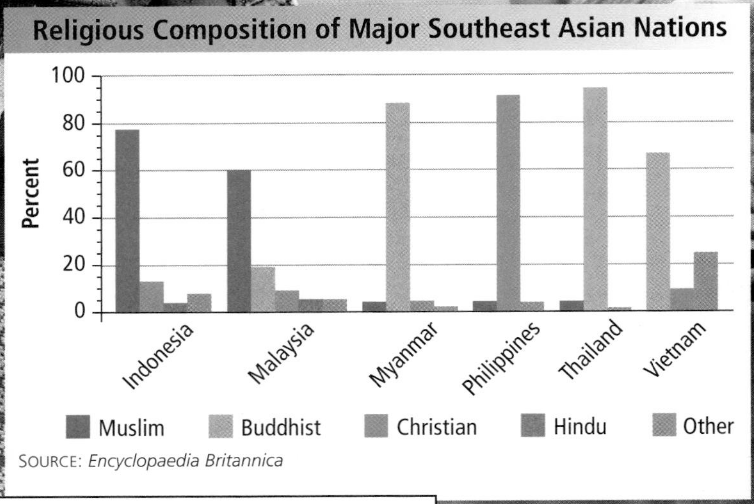

SOURCE: *Encyclopaedia Britannica*

Buddhism plays an important role in the lives of many mainland Southeast Asians. In Thailand, all young Buddhist men are expected to live for at least a short time as monks, such as the ones in this photo.

Thinking Critically

1. **Graph Skills** Based on the graph, are the people in the two photos members of their country's majority or minority religion?
2. **Map Skills** Notice that some religious groups shown on the graph for Malaysia do not have distinct areas on the map. What might explain this?

claimed thousands of lives. Discrimination against Chinese on the island of Java led to vicious attacks on their businesses. Rebels in Papua, on the island of New Guinea at the eastern end of Indonesia, sought independence from Indonesia, as did conservative Muslim rebels in Aceh (AH chay), at the northwestern end of Indonesia.

Natural disasters have added to Indonesia's troubles. In 2004, an earthquake caused a tsunami (tsoo NAH mee), or giant wave, that devastated the coast of Aceh and left over 100,000 dead. Related tsunamis ravaged Thailand, Sri Lanka, and other countries around the Indian Ocean.

✓ **Checkpoint** How was Indonesia's democracy affected when Suharto gained power?

The Philippines Seeks Democracy

Like Indonesia, the Philippines is a group of islands with a diversity of ethnic groups. Catholics are the <u>predominant</u> religious group, but there is a Muslim minority in the south. In 1946, the Philippines gained freedom peacefully after almost 50 years of American rule. The United States, however, continued to influence the country through military and economic aid.

Marcos Becomes a Dictator Although the Filipino constitution set up a democratic government, a wealthy elite controlled politics and the economy. The peasant majority was poor. For a time, the government battled Huks (hooks), local Communists with strong peasant support. **Ferdinand Marcos,** elected president in 1965, abandoned democracy. He became a dictator and cracked down on basic freedoms. He even had **Benigno Aquino** (beh NEE nyoh ah KEE noh), a popular rival, murdered.

Filipinos Demand Democracy When Marcos finally held elections in 1986, voters elected **Corazon Aquino** (kawr ah SOHN), widow of the slain Benigno. Marcos tried to deny the results, but the people of Manila held demonstrations that forced him to resign during the "people power" revolution. Under Aquino and her successors, this fragile democracy struggled to survive. The economy grew during the 1990s but then slowed. Poverty persisted. Another corrupt president, Joseph Estrada, tried to cling to power. Once again, in 2001, popular protests forced him from office. As urbanization increased, unrest grew in crowded slum neighborhoods.

Clashes With Rebels Drag On Rebel guerrillas have fought across the Philippines for decades, taking many lives. Some rebels are Communists. Others belong to Muslim separatist groups in the south. Some Muslim rebels have ties to international terrorism. As part of its war on terrorism, the United States has aided the Filipino government in its fight against Muslim rebels.

 Checkpoint How were corrupt rulers forced from office in the Philippines?

Vocabulary Builder

<u>predominant</u>—(pree DAHM uh nunt) *adj.* most common or numerous

SECTION 2 Assessment

Progress Monitoring *Online*
For: Self-quiz with vocabulary practice
Web Code: nba-3121

Terms, People, and Places

1. For each term, person, or place listed at the beginning of the section, write a sentence explaining its significance.

Note Taking

2. **Reading Skill: Understand Effects** Use your completed concept web to answer the Focus Question: What challenges did Southeast Asian nations face after winning independence?

Comprehension and Critical Thinking

3. **Make Comparisons** Why did policies toward ethnic diversity lead to prosperity in Malaysia but to conflict in other parts of Southeast Asia?

4. **Synthesize Information** How have religious and ethnic diversity affected the recent history of Indonesia?

5. **Draw Inferences** What conclusions might separatist movements in Indonesia draw from East Timor's successful independence struggle?

6. **Recognize Cause and Effect** What causes explain the overthrow of Ferdinand Marcos?

● **Writing About History**

Quick Write: Evaluate Your Topic To write a compare-and-contrast essay, you can organize your ideas in a point-by-point comparison. In this section, you learned that Malaysia and Indonesia are both ethnically diverse. Draft two sentences for an essay. In each sentence, compare or contrast an aspect of ethnic diversity in one of these countries with a related aspect of ethnic diversity in the other.

The Union Jack, the flag of the United Kingdom, flew over many African countries before independence.

Britain's Prince Philip and Queen Elizabeth II congratulate Jomo Kenyatta as his nation, Kenya, gains independence in 1963.

WITNESS HISTORY ◄)) AUDIO

Kenya Achieves Independence

A scene from a novel by Ngugi wa Thiong'o describes the moment of independence in Nairobi, Kenya's capital:

> ❝ A minute before midnight, lights were put out. . . . In the dark, the Union Jack [British flag] was quickly lowered. When next the lights came on the new Kenya flag was . . . waving in the air. ❞
> —Ngugi wa Thiong'o, *A Grain of Wheat*

Kenya was one of more than 40 African nations that gained independence from European colonial powers in the decades after World War II.

Focus Question What challenges did new African nations face?

African Nations Gain Independence

Objectives
- Describe how Africa's colonies gained independence.
- Explain how Africans built new nations.
- Analyze the recent histories of five African nations.

Terms, People, and Places

savannas	Mobutu Sese Seko
Kwame Nkrumah	Islamist
Jomo Kenyatta	Katanga
coup d'état	Biafra

N**ote** **Taking**

Reading Skill: Identify Causes and Effects Fill in a concept web like this one to keep track of the causes and effects of independence in Africa.

In Nairobi, in villages throughout Kenya, and in other new African nations, bands played new national anthems, and crowds cheered the good news. However, as Africans celebrated their newfound freedom, they also faced many challenges.

Africa's Colonies Gain Independence

After World War II, European colonial powers were forced to withdraw from former colonies such as India and Vietnam. During the decade after the war, Africans, too, increasingly demanded independence.

A Geographically Diverse Continent Africa is the world's second-largest continent, more than three times the size of the United States. Tropical rain forests cover central Africa's Congo Basin and coastal West Africa. Vast **savannas,** or grasslands with scattered trees, make up interior West Africa, East Africa, and much of central and southern Africa. Africa has the world's largest desert—the Sahara—in the north and the smaller Kalahari Desert in the south, as well as fertile coastal strips in North and South Africa.

Africa's people are concentrated in the most fertile areas, such as the savanna and forest regions of Nigeria and the moist highlands of East Africa. These regions produce enough food to support large populations. Africa's people, however, have been moving from the countryside to the constantly growing cities.

Africa has rich deposits of minerals such as gold ore, copper ore, and diamonds. The continent produces valuable cash crops, including coffee and cacao—used to make chocolate. Africa also has large petroleum reserves. European colonial powers did not want to lose control of these valuable resources.

Colonies Demand Independence More and more Africans, however, demanded freedom. Skilled speakers and organizers such as **Kwame Nkrumah** (KWAH may un KROO muh) in the Gold Coast (later Ghana), **Jomo Kenyatta** in Kenya, and **Léopold Senghor** (lay oh POHLD sahn GAWR) in Senegal led independence movements in their countries.

Sometimes such political pressure was enough to win independence. This was the case in the British colonies that became Nigeria and Ghana and in France's many West African colonies. The liberation struggle turned violent, however, in colonies where large numbers of European colonists had settled, such as in Kenya and Algeria.

 Checkpoint Why did European powers resist independence for their African colonies?

Africans Build New Nations

Some new African nations enjoyed peace and democracy. Others were plunged into crisis by civil war, military rule, or corrupt dictators. In recent years, however, there has been a hopeful trend toward greater democracy in many African nations.

Confronting Ethnic Divisions European colonial powers had drawn boundaries between their colonies without regard for the territories of the continent's hundreds of ethnic groups. Most African nations gained independence as a patchwork of peoples with diverse languages and religions. Once freedom was won, many Africans felt their first loyalty was to their own ethnic group, not to a faceless national government. As a result, ethnic and regional conflict plagued many nations.

Dictators Seize Power Many early leaders established one-party political systems. Multiparty systems, these leaders declared, encouraged disunity. Many one-party states became dictatorships. Dictators often used their positions to enrich themselves and a privileged few.

When bad government policies led to unrest, the military often seized power. More than half of all African nations suffered military coups (kooz). A coup, or **coup d'état** (koo day TAH), is the forcible overthrow of a government. Some military rulers were brutal tyrants. Others sought to improve conditions. Military leaders usually promised to restore civilian rule once they had cleaned up the government. In many cases, however, they gave up power only when they were toppled by other military coups.

Moving Toward Democracy More and more Africans demanded an end to strong-man rule and a move to greater democracy. Meanwhile, Western governments and the World Bank required democratic reforms as a condition for loans. In response to these pressures, some governments made changes. They legalized opposition parties and allowed freedom of speech.

Africa's Mineral Wealth
A miner in the West African country of Sierra Leone rinses and sifts gravel from a pit in an effort to find rough diamonds. Rich mineral deposits are important to the economies of many African nations.

In nations such as Tanzania, Nigeria, and Benin, multiparty elections were held, removing long-ruling leaders from office.

Foreigners Jostle for Influence Although African nations gained political independence, colonial powers often retained control of businesses in their former colonies. Many new nations thus remained dependent economically on their former colonizers.

During the Cold War, the Soviet Union and the United States competed for military and strategic advantage through alliances with several African countries. For example, the United States supported **Mobutu Seso Seko,** the dictator of Zaire (now known as the Democratic Republic of the Congo), to counter Soviet support for the government of neighboring Angola. Likewise, during the 1970s, the United States had an alliance with the government of Somalia, while the Soviet Union supported neighboring Ethiopia. These countries attracted superpower interest because they controlled access to the Red Sea, a vital shipping route connecting Asia, Europe, and Africa. Each superpower wanted to make sure that the other did not gain an advantage.

 Checkpoint Why have African countries moved toward democracy in recent years?

Market Women in Ghana
In West African countries such as Ghana, many of the businesspeople are women. The woman in this photo runs a grocery stand in a local market. *Why might West African political candidates seek to win the favor of local market women?*

The Stories of Five African Nations

While the new nations of Africa faced many of the same challenges, each nation had a unique history. To gain a better understanding of the process of nation-building in Africa, we will examine the recent histories of five important nations.

Ghana The first African nation south of the Sahara to win freedom was the British colony of Gold Coast. During the 1940s, Kwame Nkrumah organized a movement for independence from Britain. In 1957, Gold Coast finally won independence. The nation took the name *Ghana,* after the ancient West African kingdom. The name linked the new nation with an African past.

As president, Nkrumah advocated socialism and nationalized, or placed under government ownership, many businesses. His government built a massive dam for electric power that created Lake Volta, the world's largest artificial lake, but left Ghana with massive debts. Gradually, his government became more dictatorial and corrupt. In 1966, he was overthrown by the first of several military coups in Ghana.

Ghana's last coup, in 1981, was led by a young military officer named Jerry Rawlings. Rawlings took steps to strengthen Ghana's economy, which is based largely on overseas sales of cocoa and gold.

Independence in Africa

Map Skills From the late 1800s until the 1950s and 1960s, most African countries were colonies of European powers, which drew their borders. Most African nations gained independence during the 1950s and 1960s.

1. **Locate** (a) Kenya (b) Democratic Republic of the Congo (c) Angola (d) Ghana

2. **Regions** Which was the last of the Democratic Republic of the Congo's neighbors to gain independence?

3. **Draw Conclusions** When must the Cold War conflict involving independent Angola have taken place?

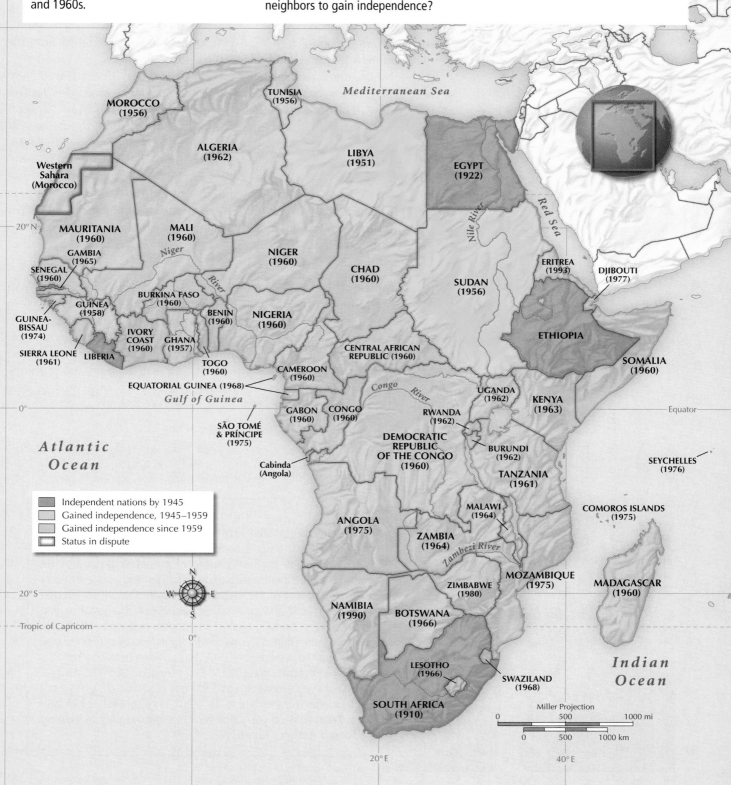

MOROCCO (1956)

TUNISIA (1956)

Mediterranean Sea

ALGERIA (1962)

LIBYA (1951)

EGYPT (1922)

Western Sahara (Morocco)

Nile River

Red Sea

20°N

MAURITANIA (1960)

MALI (1960)

Niger

NIGER (1960)

CHAD (1960)

SUDAN (1956)

ERITREA (1993)

DJIBOUTI (1977)

GAMBIA (1965)

SENEGAL (1960)

River

BURKINA FASO (1960)

GUINEA (1958)

GUINEA-BISSAU (1974)

BENIN (1960)

NIGERIA (1960)

IVORY COAST (1960)

GHANA (1957)

ETHIOPIA

SIERRA LEONE (1961)

LIBERIA

TOGO (1960)

CENTRAL AFRICAN REPUBLIC (1960)

SOMALIA (1960)

CAMEROON (1960)

EQUATORIAL GUINEA (1968)

Gulf of Guinea

Congo River

UGANDA (1962)

KENYA (1963)

GABON (1960)

CONGO (1960)

RWANDA (1962)

Equator

SÃO TOMÉ & PRÍNCIPE (1975)

DEMOCRATIC REPUBLIC OF THE CONGO (1960)

BURUNDI (1962)

Atlantic Ocean

Cabinda (Angola)

TANZANIA (1961)

SEYCHELLES (1976)

Independent nations by 1945
Gained independence, 1945–1959
Gained independence since 1959
Status in dispute

MALAWI (1964)

COMOROS ISLANDS (1975)

ANGOLA (1975)

ZAMBIA (1964)

Zambezi River

MOZAMBIQUE (1975)

MADAGASCAR (1960)

20°S

ZIMBABWE (1980)

NAMIBIA (1990)

BOTSWANA (1966)

Indian Ocean

Tropic of Capricorn

0°

LESOTHO (1966)

SWAZILAND (1968)

SOUTH AFRICA (1910)

Miller Projection

0   500   1000 mi

0   500   1000 km

20°E

40°E

Rawlings also restored democracy to Ghana, bringing political stability to the country. He won a free election in 1992, and then peacefully handed over power in 2001 after losing an election to an opponent.

Kenya In Kenya, freedom came only after armed struggle. White settlers had taken over land in the fertile highlands, where they displaced African farmers. Most of these farmers were Kikuyu (kee KOO yoo), Kenya's largest ethnic group. White settlers saw Kenya as their homeland and had passed laws to <u>ensure</u> their own domination. "The land is ours," declared Jomo Kenyatta, a leading spokesman for the Kikuyu. "When Europeans came, they kept us back and took our land." Kenyatta supported nonviolent methods to end the oppressive laws.

In the 1950s, more radical leaders turned to guerrilla warfare. They burned farms and attacked settlers and Africans who worked with the colonial rulers. The British called the guerrillas the Mau Mau. To stop the violence, the British arrested Kenyatta and killed thousands of Kikuyu. The rebels were crushed, but the movement lived on. In 1963, Kenyatta, whose imprisonment had made him a national hero, became the first leader of an independent Kenya.

As president, Kenyatta jailed opponents and outlawed opposition parties. Kenya's ruling party resisted free elections until violent demonstrations and foreign lenders forced it to move toward democracy during the 1990s. Finally, in 2002, Kenya's first fair election removed the ruling party from office.

Algeria In the 1800s, France had conquered Algeria after a brutal struggle. A million French people settled there over time. They were determined to keep the Algerian people from winning independence.

Algerian nationalists set up the National Liberation Front. In 1954, this group turned to guerrilla warfare to win freedom. France, which had just lost its Asian colony of Vietnam, sent half a million troops to maintain its possession of Algeria. France was especially reluctant to lose Algeria after oil and natural gas were discovered there in the 1950s.

Vocabulary Builder

<u>ensure</u>—(en SHOOR) *v.* make sure or certain, guarantee

BIOGRAPHY

Jomo Kenyatta

Jomo Kenyatta (c. 1894–1978) was born in a small Kikuyu village and educated at a Christian mission. Moving to Nairobi, he was quickly drawn to the first stirrings of the nationalist cause. He became a prominent anticolonial organizer and was eventually elected president of the Kenya Africa Union. The British arrested Kenyatta in 1952 and convicted him in 1953 on charges of inciting the Mau Mau uprising against the British. Released in 1961, he resumed leadership of the movement for independence, which was finally granted in December 1963. When Kenya became a republic in 1964, Kenyatta was elected its first president. Under his 15-year rule, Kenya enjoyed political stability and economic advances. Each year, October 20, the date of his arrest, is celebrated as Kenyatta Day. **What role do you think national heroes play in helping to form a nation's identity?**

An Election Celebration
Citizens of Mauritania, in West Africa, celebrate the reelection of the country's president in 2003. *What signs of democracy do you see in this photograph?*

A long and costly war raged in Algeria. Hundreds of thousands of Algerians were killed. Eventually, public opinion in France turned against the war. Finally, in 1962, Algeria celebrated its freedom.

A coup in 1965 began a long period of military rule. During the late 1960s and 1970s, Algeria nationalized foreign firms and created a command economy based on oil and gas exports. Since the 1980s, the country has returned to a market economy. When the government allowed free elections in 1992, an **Islamist** party won the most votes. Islamists are people who want government policies to be based on the teachings of Islam. The military rejected the election results. Seven years of civil war between the Islamists and the military left 100,000 Algerians dead. Since 1999, the government has largely stopped the fighting, but the country remains tense. Critics have accused the government of rigging elections.

Democratic Republic of the Congo The Democratic Republic of the Congo (or the Congo), formerly a Belgian colony, covers a vast region of central Africa, a million square miles of rain forest and savanna centered in the Congo River basin. The huge country contains valuable natural resources, including diamonds and the copper of **Katanga** province. Belgium sought to maintain control of these resources. In 1960, therefore, it rushed to declare the colony independent, though the Congolese were not prepared for self-government. This enabled Belgian mining companies, working with politicians in Katanga, to retain effective control of the province and its valuable minerals.

The Belgian-backed province rebelled against the Congo shortly after independence. The country's first prime minister, Patrice Lumumba, appealed for Soviet help to fight the rebels. Seeing the appeal to the Soviets as a Cold War challenge, the United States supported Lumumba's rival, Colonel Joseph Mobutu, later known as Mobutu Sese Seko. Mobutu captured Lumumba, and Lumumba was executed shortly thereafter.

The United Nations ended the Katanga rebellion in 1963. In 1965, Mobutu overthrew Congo's government and ruled as a military dictator.

Mobutu's harsh and corrupt rule let Congo's poverty and instability fester. He was finally driven into exile in 1997 by a rebellion based in the eastern part of the country. Civil war ravaged the country for six years, as regional military forces based on ethnic loyalties fought over the country's mineral wealth. In 2003, a ceasefire brought an uneasy peace, but the country remained divided among regional factions.

Nigeria Nigeria stretches from the dry grasslands of the north to the moist rain forests of the south. It has the largest population in Africa. Its people belong to hundreds of ethnic groups, but three groups dominate. The mainly Christian Ibo (EE boh) and Yoruba (YOH roo buh) people live in the south, and the mainly Muslim Hausa (HOW suh) people dominate the north. After World War II, the British gradually gave in to growing demands for independence. Nigeria won independence peacefully in 1960. The discovery of oil in the southeast in 1961 raised hopes for the new nation's economic future.

Unfortunately, regional, ethnic, and religious differences soon led to conflict. In 1966, Nigeria suffered the first of several military coups. A second coup later that year by northern Muslim officers led to a rebellion in the oil-rich southeast by the Ibo people, who declared independence as the Republic of **Biafra.** A three-year war ensued that left hundreds of thousands dead. In the end, Nigeria's military defeated the Biafran rebels and ended Biafra's independence.

During the 1970s and 1980s, a series of military rulers violently suppressed opposition and diverted much of the country's oil earnings for their own enrichment. Opposition to military rule increased during the 1990s. Finally, in 1999, a military government allowed free elections. After the return to democracy, however, Nigeria's people faced an increase in crime. Meanwhile, ethnic and religious divisions gave rise to renewed violence.

✓ **Checkpoint** How did Biafra and Katanga reflect the challenges to unity that the new African nations faced?

Nigeria's Oil Industry

Nigeria's economy relies heavily on revenues from its oil industry. This oil worker is operating a drill to create an oil well in southeastern Nigeria.

Progress Monitoring *Online*
For: Self-quiz with vocabulary practice
Web Code: nba-3131

Terms, People, and Places

1. Place each of the key terms at the beginning of the section into one of the following categories: politics, economy, or geography. Write a sentence for each term explaining your choice.

Note Taking

2. **Reading Skill: Identify Causes and Effects** Use your completed concept web to answer the Focus Question: What challenges did new African nations face?

Comprehension and Critical Thinking

3. **Make Comparisons** Why did some countries gain independence peacefully, while others faced violent struggles?

4. **Identify Central Issues** Why did the Cold War superpowers seek alliances with African nations?

5. **Express Problems Clearly** Based on the history of Algeria, what were some problems caused by military rule?

6. **Draw Conclusions** How have religious and ethnic divisions affected Nigeria's history?

● Writing About History

Quick Write: Provide Elaboration To write a compare-and-contrast essay, you need to provide examples that support the main point of the essay. Suppose that the point of your essay is to compare and contrast challenges faced by Algeria and Nigeria since independence. Draft two sentences for an essay. In each sentence, give examples that compare or contrast a challenge faced by these countries.

Kwame Nkrumah: *Autobiography*

Kwame Nkrumah led the people of Gold Coast in their quest for independence from Britain. After succeeding in 1957, Nkrumah became the first prime minister and renamed the country Ghana. In this excerpt from his *Autobiography,* Nkrumah speaks of the need to establish economic independence as a means of maintaining political independence. Nkrumah describes the difficult work of building an independent economy.

▲ Prime Minister Kwame Nkrumah of Ghana

Independence for the Gold Coast was my aim. It was a colony, and I have always regarded colonialism as the policy by which a foreign power binds territories to herself by political ties with the primary object of promoting her own economic advantage. No one need be surprised if this system has led to disturbances and political tension in many territories. There are few people who would not rid themselves of such domination if they could. . . .

I saw that the whole solution to [our] problem lay in political freedom for our people, for it is only when a people are politically free that other races can give them the respect that is due to them. It is impossible to talk of equality of races in any other terms. No people without a government of their own can expect to be treated on the same level as peoples of independent sovereign[1] states. It is far better to be free to govern or misgovern yourself than to be governed by anybody else. . . .

Once this freedom is gained, a greater task comes into view. All dependent[2] territories are backward in education, in science, in agriculture, and in industry. The economic independence that should follow and maintain political independence demands every effort from the people, a total mobilization of brain and manpower resources. What other countries have taken three hundred years or more to achieve, a once dependent territory must try to accomplish in a generation if it is to survive. . . .

▲ Ghana's leaders—including Kwame Nkrumah, at center—celebrate Ghana's independence in 1957.

Thinking Critically
1. **Identify Point of View** What does Nkrumah think the people of a dependent territory must do before they can achieve economic independence?
2. **Draw Inferences** Based on Nkrumah's remarks, what makes economic independence difficult for newly independent nations to achieve?

1. sovereign (SAHV run) *adj.* not subject to any other power
2. dependent (dee PEN dunt) *adj.* subject to the power of another

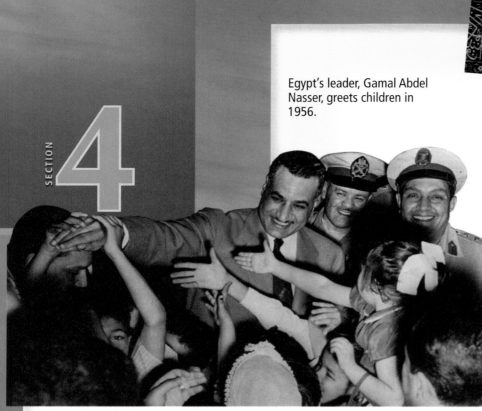

Egypt's leader, Gamal Abdel Nasser, greets children in 1956.

Islamic ornamental writing from a mosque in Iran

WITNESS HISTORY ◀» AUDIO

Remembering Nasser

As a young boy in Syria, Nasser Rabbat recalls seeing the Arab leader, Gamal Abdel Nasser.

❝One of my earliest memories dates back to the winter of 1960 when I was almost four years old. I remember . . . screaming with the crowd around us 'Nasser, Nasser.' . . . I had been taught . . . to be proud of . . . Nasser, 'the unifier of the Arabs' and 'the leader of our new renaissance.'❞
—Nasser Rabbat, "On being named Nasser"

Gamal Abdel Nasser's Arab nationalism and other forms of nationalism were among the most important forces to shape the Middle East in the decades after World War II.

Focus Question What are the main similarities and differences among Middle Eastern nations?

The Modern Middle East

Objectives

• Analyze the diversity of the Middle East and the political challenges it has faced.

• Explain the region's conflicts over resources and religion.

• Outline the history of nation-building in three Middle Eastern nations.

Terms, People, and Places

kibbutz
secular
hejab
Suez Canal
Gamal Abdel Nasser

Anwar Sadat
Mohammad Mosaddeq
Ruhollah Khomeini
theocracy

Note Taking

Reading Skill: Identify Causes and Effects Fill in a concept web like this one to keep track of events in the Middle East since 1945.

Leaders of Nasser's generation tried to build strong nations across the Middle East. Despite rich reserves of oil and natural gas in some parts of the region, however, internal divisions and autocratic governments hindered progress throughout the Middle East.

Diversity Brings Challenges

The Middle East, as we use the term in this chapter, is the region stretching from Egypt in the west to Iran in the east and from Turkey in the north to the Arabian Peninsula in the south. Though most people in the region today are Muslims, there are also Christian communities and the predominantly Jewish nation of Israel. Most countries have large ethnic or religious minorities.

Kurds Seek Freedom An ethnic group called the Kurds lives in the northern Middle East. Borders drawn by Europeans and others divided their homeland among Iran, Iraq, Syria, and Turkey. In each country, the Kurds are a minority and have faced discrimination, particularly in Iraq and Turkey.

During the decades after World War II, the Turkish government harshly ruled the Kurdish minority in the east. For example, it became illegal for Kurds to speak their language in public. Beginning in the 1970s, Kurdish rebels fought Turkish forces. During the 1980s and 1990s, thousands of Kurds died in the fighting.

In 1991, however, Turkey legalized the use of the Kurdish language, and in 1999 the main Kurdish rebel force gave up the use of violence, though tensions continue. Kurds also faced brutal treatment in Iraq. After Iraq's defeat in the 1991 Gulf War, Kurds in northern Iraq rebelled and set up their own governments with British and American military support.

Israel Is Founded As you have learned, Britain supported a Jewish national homeland in part of its mandate of Palestine. The horrific experience of Jews in the Holocaust added to worldwide support for a Jewish homeland. Jews, including many Holocaust survivors, migrated to Palestine in large numbers after World War II. In 1947, the UN drew up a plan to divide Palestine into an Arab and a Jewish state. Jews accepted the plan, but Arabs rejected it. They felt that all of Palestine should belong to them.

After Britain withdrew from Palestine in 1948, Jews proclaimed the independent State of Israel, and within a year David Ben-Gurion became prime minister. Arab states launched the first of several wars against Israel but were defeated. Israel developed rapidly. A skilled and educated work force built businesses. Kibbutzim produced crops for export. A **kibbutz** (kih BOOTS) is a collective farm. Israel attracted Jews from Europe, the United States, the Soviet Union, and Africa as well as Jews expelled from other Middle Eastern lands.

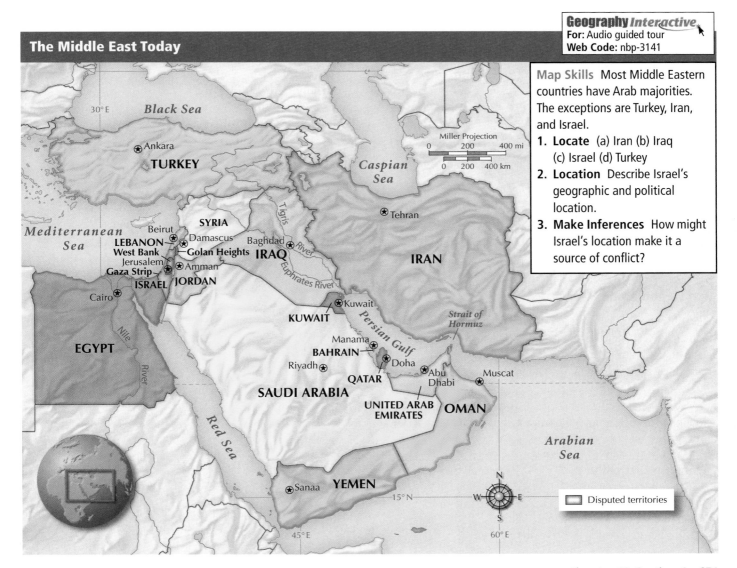

Geography *Interactive*
For: Audio guided tour
Web Code: nbp-3141

The Middle East Today

Map Skills Most Middle Eastern countries have Arab majorities. The exceptions are Turkey, Iran, and Israel.
1. **Locate** (a) Iran (b) Iraq (c) Israel (d) Turkey
2. **Location** Describe Israel's geographic and political location.
3. **Make Inferences** How might Israel's location make it a source of conflict?

The conflicts of 1948 created enormous refugee problems. As a result of the war, hundreds of thousands of Palestinian Arabs fled their homes in Israeli territory. The UN set up camps in neighboring areas to house them. Hundreds of thousands of Jews from Arab lands were also driven from their homes. Both sides feel embittered by the displacements.

Political Systems Limit Freedom Most Middle Eastern nations have had autocratic governments. In some countries, nationalist military leaders seized power. In other countries, such as Jordan and Saudi Arabia, hereditary monarchs remained in power. Only Israel and Turkey had stable multiparty democratic systems by 2005.

✓ **Checkpoint** Why did many people around the world support a Jewish homeland in Palestine?

Conflicts Over Resources and Religion

Parts of the Middle East sit atop the world's largest oil and gas reserves. Oil-rich nations have prospered, but other Middle Eastern nations have struggled economically. Meanwhile, Muslim Middle Easterners have disagreed over the role of Islam in a modern economy.

Supplying the World With Oil Because the Middle East commands vital oil resources, it has strategic importance to the United States and other powers. Nations with large oil reserves are Saudi Arabia, Iran, Iraq, Kuwait, and the United Arab Emirates (U.A.E.). These nations are all members of the Organization of the Petroleum Exporting Countries (OPEC), founded in 1960. In 1973, OPEC's Arab members blocked oil shipments to the United States to protest U.S. support for Israel. This oil embargo

● **INFOGRAPHIC**

Islam and the Modern World

Like other religions, Islam faces the challenge of adapting its traditions to a changing modern world. While religious traditions remain important to Muslims, Western culture has gained influence. Traditionally, in Islamic countries, women were not expected to read or write. Today, Muslim women are pursuing educations and new career opportunities. While Islamists call for a return to tradition, many Muslims embrace a mixture of traditional and modern ways.

The Iraqi artist ▲ Hassan Massoudy combines the Islamic tradition of calligraphy, or ornamental writing, with abstract Western styles.

◀ The basic principles of Islam, such as pilgrimage and prayer, remain important to modern Muslims, such as the Iraqi pilgrim to the left.

Thinking Critically
1. **Graph Skills** Which has risen faster since 1990 in Turkey and Saudi Arabia, men's literacy or women's literacy?
2. **Analyze Visuals** How do these photos and art reflect a mix of Islamic tradition and Western styles?

contributed to a worldwide recession. Since the 1970s, OPEC has focused on regulating the price of oil rather than on taking political stands.

Islam Confronts Modernization Some Middle Eastern nations adopted Western forms of **secular,** or nonreligious, government and law, keeping religion and government separate. Many Middle Eastern leaders also adopted Western economic models in a quest for progress. In the growing cities, people wore Western-style clothing, watched American television programs, and bought foreign products. Yet life improved very little for many people.

By the 1970s, some Muslim leaders were calling for a return to Sharia, or Islamic law. These conservative reformers, often called Islamists, blame social and economic ills on the following of Western models. Islamists argue that a renewed commitment to Islamic <u>doctrine</u> is the only way to solve the region's problems. The Islamist movement appeals to many Muslims. Some have used violence to pursue their goals. However, many Muslims oppose the extremism of the Islamists.

Vocabulary Builder
<u>doctrine</u>—(DAHK trin) *n.* teachings, principles, or beliefs

Women's Options Vary Conditions for women vary greatly from country to country in the modern Middle East. Women in most countries have won equality before the law. Some women have entered professions such as law and medicine. In Turkey, Syria, and Egypt, many urban women gave up the tradition of **hejab,** or wearing the traditional Muslim headscarves and loose-fitting, ankle-length garments meant to conceal.

On the other hand, religiously conservative Saudi Arabia and Iran require women to wear hejab. In Saudi Arabia, women are not allowed to drive. In many Islamic countries, girls are less likely to attend school than boys. This is because of a traditional belief that girls do not need an education for their expected role as wives and mothers. Muslim women have begun to challenge this belief.

✓ **Checkpoint** Why are Islamists opposed to secular government in Islamic countries?

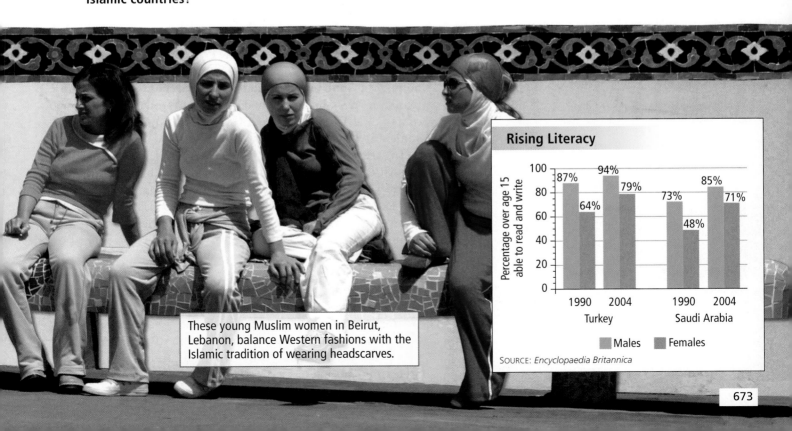

These young Muslim women in Beirut, Lebanon, balance Western fashions with the Islamic tradition of wearing headscarves.

Rising Literacy

Percentage over age 15 able to read and write

Turkey
- 1990: Males 87%, Females 64%
- 2004: Males 94%, Females 79%

Saudi Arabia
- 1990: Males 73%, Females 48%
- 2004: Males 85%, Females 71%

■ Males ■ Females

SOURCE: *Encyclopaedia Britannica*

Building Nations in the Middle East

Across the Middle East, leaders sought to build strong and prosperous nations. However, in the years since World War II, each nation has faced different challenges.

Egypt, a Leader in the Arab World Egypt has the largest population of the Arab nations. While most of Egypt is desert, its large population is crammed into the narrow Nile River valley. Egypt's location is strategically important, because it shares a long border with Israel and controls the **Suez Canal,** which links Europe with Asia and East Africa.

In 1952, **Gamal Abdel Nasser** seized power in Egypt. Determined to modernize Egypt and stop Western domination, Nasser nationalized the Suez Canal in 1956, ending British and French control. Although Britain and France responded militarily, the United States and the Soviet Union forced them to withdraw. Nasser's Arab nationalism made him popular throughout the Arab world. Nasser led two unsuccessful wars against Israel. To counter U.S. support for Israel, Egypt relied on Soviet aid. Egypt's foreign relations thus took on Cold War significance.

In 1979, Nasser's successor, **Anwar Sadat,** became the first Arab leader to make peace with Israel. Sadat also weakened ties with the Soviet Union and sought U.S. aid. However, Islamists denounced the undemocratic government's failure to end corruption and poverty. In 1981, Muslim fundamentalists assassinated Sadat. Under Sadat's appointed successor, Hosni Mubarak, extremists turned to terrorist attacks, and harsh government crackdowns tended to increase support for Islamists.

Iran's Islamic Revolution Because of its vast oil fields, Iran attracted British, Soviet, and American interest. In 1945, Iran's monarch, Shah Mohammad Reza Pahlavi, had Western backing but faced nationalist opponents at home, led by **Mohammad Mosaddeq** (MAW sah dek). When Mosaddeq was elected prime minister in 1951, he nationalized the Western-owned oil industry. In 1953, the United States helped the shah oust Mosaddeq, a move that outraged many Iranians. The shah returned Iran's oil industry to Western control. For the next 25 years, American support helped the shah stay in power.

To strengthen Iran and to quiet unrest, the shah used oil wealth to build industries. He also redistributed land from wealthy landlords and religious institutions to peasants and extended new rights to women. Opposition to the shah came from landowners, merchants, students, and the Islamic clergy. The shah's secret police terrorized critics driving many into exile.

In the 1970s, the shah's foes rallied behind one of these exiles, Ayatollah **Ruhollah Khomeini** (ROO hoh lah koh MAY nee). The ayatollah, a religious leader, condemned Western influences and accused the shah of violating Islamic law. In 1979, massive protests finally drove the shah into exile. Khomeini returned to Iran, and his supporters proclaimed an Islamic republic.

An Islamist Government
Iran's political leaders, who are Muslim clergymen, gather in 2003 to commemorate the death of Ayatollah Khomeini, a religious leader and the founder of Iran's Islamist government. The leaders are seated beneath a giant portrait of Khomeini. *How does promoting the memory of Khomeini help to justify rule by religious leaders?*

The new government was a **theocracy,** or government ruled by religious leaders. They replaced secular courts with religious ones and abolished women's rights. They also brutalized opponents, just as the shah had. The government allowed Islamists to seize the American embassy in 1979 and hold 52 hostages for more than a year. In the early 2000s, concern grew that Iran might try to develop nuclear weapons.

Oil, Religion, and Threats to Stability Saudi Arabia, a vast desert land, has the world's largest oil reserves. It also includes Islam's holy land. Since the 1920s, kings from the Sa'ud (sah OOD) family have ruled Saudi Arabia. They justify their rule by their commitment to the strict Wahhabi sect of Sunni Islam.

However, Saudi Arabia's economic development after World War II depended on massive oil exports to the Western world. In return, Saudi leaders relied on the military support of the United States. Although Saudi Arabia joined the OPEC oil embargo in 1973, the nation's rulers quickly returned to their cooperative relationship with the West.

To build support within the country, the royal family backed fundamentalist religious leaders. However, some of these leaders and their followers criticized the kingdom's close ties to the West. They also charged that Western influence in the kingdom violated Islamic principles.

Increasingly, opponents of the kingdom's Western ties adopted violent or terrorist tactics. Attacks on western targets included an attack on a U.S. military compound in 1996 and another on a U.S. consulate in 2004. These attacks threatened to disrupt the Saudi oil industry, which depends on Western expertise. Some feared that growing unrest could threaten the country's ability to supply oil vital to the world's economy.

Other oil-rich monarchies along the Persian Gulf, such as Kuwait, Bahrain, Qatar, and the United Arab Emirates, face similar threats. In Kuwait, Qatar, and the U.A.E., foreign citizens are a majority of the population. In Bahrain, there has been growing opposition among the majority of the people, who follow Shiite Islam, toward Bahrain's royal family, who follow the Sunni branch of Islam.

✓ Checkpoint What were Ayatollah Khomeini's reasons for opposing the shah?

SECTION 4 **Assessment**

Progress Monitoring *Online*
For: Self-quiz with vocabulary practice
Web Code: nba-3141

Terms, People, and Places

1. For each term, person, or place listed in the beginning of the section, write a sentence explaining its significance.

Note Taking

2. **Reading Skill: Identify Causes and Effects** Use your completed concept web to answer the Focus Question: What are the main similarities and differences among Middle Eastern nations?

Comprehension and Critical Thinking

3. **Summarize** How was the Holocaust connected to the birth of Israel?
4. **Identify Central Issues** What changes in government policies did the Islamists seek?
5. **Draw Conclusions** Why did Egypt attract the interest of the superpowers during the Cold War?
6. **Synthesize Information** How has the Saudi royal family's support for fundamentalism made their kingdom more unstable in recent years?

● **Writing About History**

Quick Write: Revise Your Writing When you write a compare-and-contrast essay, combining short sentences can improve your writing. Write a short sentence that states a fact about a Middle Eastern country. Write a second sentence stating a similar or different fact about another Middle Eastern country. Revise your sentences by joining them into a single sentence that compares or contrasts these facts, using conjunctions such as *while, whereas, yet, both, and,* or *also.*

Quick Study Guide

Common Themes in New Nations

- Borders drawn by European colonial powers left nations with diverse religions and ethnic groups.
- Ethnic and religious conflicts brought instability.
- Military coups, one-party systems, and dictatorships kept some countries from achieving democracy.
- Citizens and foreign lenders have forced former dictatorships to hold elections and transition to democracy.
- Natural resources such as oil have been a source of wealth for some nations but have fueled conflicts in Africa.
- During the Cold War, the United States and Soviet Union competed for influence, particularly in regions with natural resources such as oil, or locations near strategic waterways.

Leaders of New Nations

- Jawaharlal Nehru, *first prime minister of India*
- Indira Gandhi, *first female prime minister of India*
- Aung San Suu Kyi, *leader of Myanmar democracy movement*
- Sukarno, *founder and first president of Indonesia*
- Suharto, *military dictator of Indonesia*
- Corazon Aquino, *democratic president of the Philippines*
- Kwame Nkrumah, *founder and first president of Ghana*
- Jomo Kenyatta, *founder and first president of Kenya*
- David Ben-Gurion, *first prime minister of Israel*
- Gamal Abdel Nasser, *an Arab nationalist and first president of Egypt*
- Mohammad Reza Pahlavi, *shah of Iran*
- Ruhollah Khomeini, *leader of the religious government of Iran*

New Nations Emerge

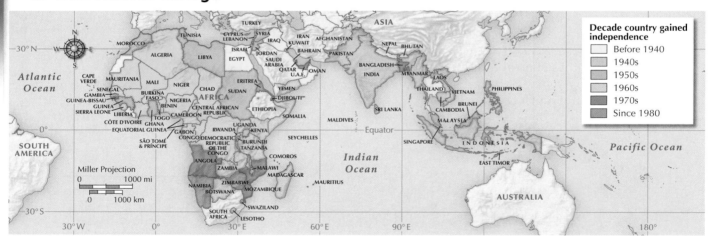

Key Events in the Emergence of New Nations

Africa and the Middle East
South and Southeast Asia

1946 Syria and Jordan gain independence.

1948 Israel is founded.

1956–1966 More than 30 African nations win independence.

1945

1955

1965

1947 India and Pakistan win independence after partition.

1966 Suharto establishes military dictatorship in Indonesia.

Concept | Connector

■ Cumulative Review

Record the answers to the questions below on your Concept Connector worksheets.

1. **Revolution** Between 1946 and 1970, European colonies around the world won independence. Compare this process with the American Revolution, which brought independence to the United States in the late 1700s. Consider the following:
   - the presence or the absence of military conflict
   - the challenge of forming stable governments after independence

2. **Nationalism** Although India has large religious minorities, the Bharatiya Janata Party (BJP) promoted Hindu nationalism, or the idea that India should favor the Hindu majority and the Hindu religion. Given India's history of religious violence, do you think that the BJP's stand contributed to peace and stability in India? Why or why not?

3. **Dictatorship** After gaining independence in the mid-twentieth century, many African nations fell under the rule of dictators. Compare the rule of Mobutu Sese Seko, the dictator of the Democratic Republic of the Congo (formerly Zaire) with the rule of earlier dictators such as Mussolini, Hitler, and Stalin. Think about the following:
   - whether the dictatorship brought order or disorder
   - the relationship of the dictatorship to foreign powers

4. **Geography's Impact** Middle Eastern nations possess the world's largest reserves of oil, a very valuable resource. Saudi Arabia has the world's greatest oil exports. In the first half of the twentieth century, the United States was the world's leading oil exporter. Today, the United States is the world's leading oil importer. How has oil affected the history of these two countries during the past 100 years?

■ Connections To Today

1. **Conflict: Struggles for Independence** Former European colonies such as Algeria had to fight deadly wars to win their independence. Today, in different parts of the world, people continue to fight for independence. Examples include Chechnya, which has rebelled against Russia, and Kosovo, which has fought for independence from Serbia and Montenegro. Research one of these regions. Explain why that region is fighting for independence.

2. **Economic Systems: Market Economies** During the 1980s and 1990s, many African nations shifted from command economies to market economies. China shifted toward a market economy during this same period and has seen growing prosperity. Research an African country that has made this shift, such as Ghana, Algeria, or Tanzania. Explore why a market economy has or has not brought prosperity to that country.

| 1973 OPEC oil embargo | 1979 Iranian revolution | 1990–2002 African nations move toward democracy. | **History** *Interactive*
For: Interactive timeline
Web Code: nbp-3151 |

1975   **1985**   **1995**   **2005**

1971 Bangladesh wins independence.

1986 "People power" revolution in the Philippines

1998 Indonesia returns to democracy.

Chapter Assessment

Terms, People, and Places

Match the following definitions with the terms listed below.

Indira Gandhi	coup d'état
nonalignment	theocracy
Corazon Aquino	kibbutz

1. rule by religious leaders
2. a political leader in the Philippines
3. the first female prime minister of India
4. a collective farm
5. political and diplomatic independence
6. the forcible overthrow of a government

Main Ideas

Section 1 (pp. 650–655)

7. Why was British India divided into India and Pakistan?
8. How did religious and ethnic diversity pose challenges for South Asian nations after independence?

Section 2 (pp. 656–659)

9. Compare the nations of Southeast Asia in the progress that they have made toward democracy.

Section 3 (pp. 660–667)

10. How did African nations win their independence? How did this differ among nations?
11. What obstacles slowed progress toward democracy for some African nations?

Section 4 (pp. 668–673)

12. How has the Islamist movement affected politics in the Middle East?

Chapter Focus Question

13. How did former European colonies gain independence, and what challenges did they face after independence?

Critical Thinking

14. **Draw Conclusions** How did the Philippines and Indonesia achieve democracy?
15. **Synthesize Information** How has religion influenced the recent history of the Middle East?
16. **Analyzing Visuals** The photograph below shows refugees from the partition of India and Pakistan. What does it suggest about conditions for these refugees?

17. **Make Comparisons** Compare the impact of ethnic and religious diversity on the histories of India and Pakistan.
18. **Analyze Information** How have the natural resources of the Middle East affected its recent history?
19. **Draw Conclusions** How were African nations affected by military rule and dictatorships? Support your conclusions with examples.
20. **Recognize Cause and Effect** What have been some lasting effects of colonial rule on African nations?

● Writing About History

Writing a Compare-Contrast Essay Write a compare-contrast essay on the post-independence histories of two countries covered in different sections of this chapter. Possible features to compare and contrast include the effects of ethnic and religious diversity or progress toward democracy. Discuss similarities and differences in the histories of the two countries. Consult page SH10 of the Writing Handbook for additional help.

Prewriting

• Go online or do library research to find information about the post-independence histories of countries covered in this chapter.

• Choose two countries that interest you and take notes about the challenges these countries faced.
• Gather evidence that supports comparisons and contrasts between these countries.

Drafting

• Write a first paragraph with a thesis statement and details about similarities between the two countries.
• Write a second paragraph with a topic sentence and details about differences between the two countries.

Revising

• Use the guidelines for revising your report on page SH12 of the Writing Handbook.

Document-Based Assessment

The Kashmir Question

In 1947, British India was partitioned into Hindu-majority India and Muslim-majority Pakistan. Kashmir is claimed by both India and Pakistan and has been a battleground between the two countries. The documents below help to show why the "Kashmir problem" remains worrisome today.

Document A

Hum kya chahtey? Azaadi! (What do we want? Freedom!)

—Slogan in Kashmir Valley

Document B

"Mr. Jinnah and his colleagues in the Muslim League, the creators of Pakistan, had always considered that the Vale of Kashmir at least would form part of the new Islamic State . . . When in 1933 Choudhri Rahmat Ali coined the word Pakistan as a suitable name for the State, he intended the letter K in 'Pak' to stand for Kashmir. The geographical and historical links between the Panjab and the Vale of Kashmir were so close that it was inevitable that the two regions should find themselves combined in the thoughts of the protagonists of a separate Islamic State."

—From ***Crisis in Kashmir, 1947–1966*** by Alastair Lamb

Document C

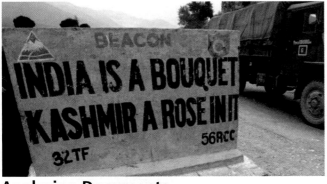

Document D

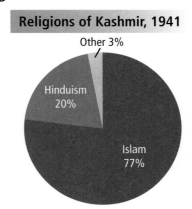

Religions of Kashmir, 1941

Other 3%
Hinduism 20%
Islam 77%

SOURCE: *Census of India, 1941*

Document E

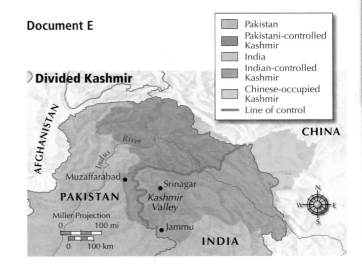

Divided Kashmir

Legend:
- Pakistan
- Pakistani-controlled Kashmir
- India
- Indian-controlled Kashmir
- Chinese-occupied Kashmir
- Line of control

Analyzing Documents

Use your knowledge of World War II and Documents A, B, C, D, and E to answer questions 1–4.

1. According to Document B, Kashmir and Pakistan share
   A the same heroes and poets.
   B a similar history and geography.
   C the same language and literature.
   D similar architecture and art.

2. What argument does the billboard in Document C support?
   A India is a diverse country, and the region of Kashmir is an important part of it.
   B India will never let go of Kashmir.
   C Kashmir is more beautiful than other parts of India.
   D Indians are tired of dealing with Kashmir and its thorny problems.

3. According to Document D, Kashmir's population
   A is evenly balanced among its different religions.
   B is about one-half Hindu and "Other."
   C only has two religious affiliations.
   D is more than three-quarters Muslim.

4. **Writing Task** Why has Kashmir continued to be a volatile spot for so long? What are the main causes of the conflict there? Use information from these documents along with information from the chapter to write your response.

Life in a War Zone

For more than a year, hostile troops surrounded the city of Sarajevo in Bosnia and fired down on it from the hills above. Zlatko Dizdarevic, a journalist in Sarajevo, wrote this journal entry during the conflict: "It's been a relentless morning. Shells are falling close by us, perhaps closer than ever before. The official alert remains in force; so does our private and personal alert. We evaluate our chances, run risks, and keep hoping." Listen to the Witness History audio to hear more about the war in Bosnia.

◀ **A boy dodging sniper fire to get water,** Sarajevo, Bosnia, 1993

Chapter Preview

Chapter Focus Question Why have deadly conflicts plagued some regions of the world?

Section 1
Conflicts Divide Nations

Section 2
Struggles in Africa

Section 3
Conflicts in the Middle East

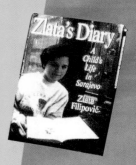

Zlata's Diary, a teenage girl's account of the conflict in Bosnia

Nelson Mandela, who led a struggle against racial discrimination and became president of South Africa

A fallen statue of Saddam Hussein, the dictator of Iraq, who was overthrown by American troops

Note Taking Study Guide *Online*
For: Note Taking and Concept Connector worksheets
Web Code: nbd-3201

Zlata Filipovic in 1994

WITNESS HISTORY 🔊 AUDIO

A Young Girl in Wartime

Zlata Filipovic (fee LEEP uh vich) was 11 years old in 1992 when she began a diary about her life in war-torn Sarajevo, the capital of Bosnia. Here is an excerpt:

66 Today a shell fell on the park in front of my house, the park where I used to play and sit with my girl-friends. A lot of people were hurt . . . AND NINA IS DEAD . . . She was such a sweet, nice little girl. 99
—Zlata Filipovic, *Zlata's Diary*

Bosnia is just one of the nations that have faced ethnic, religious, or national conflicts in recent decades.

Focus Question Why have ethnic and religious conflicts divided some nations?

Conflicts Divide Nations

Objectives
- Explain the complex causes of ethnic and religious conflicts.
- Describe how war ravaged Chechnya.
- Understand how Yugoslavia broke apart.

Terms, People, and Places

Northern Ireland	ethnic cleansing
Good Friday Agreement	Kosovo
Chechnya	Slobodan Milosevic
multiethnic	

Note Taking

Reading Skill: Recognize Sequence Fill in a flowchart like the one below to keep track of the sequence of events in the conflicts in Northern Ireland, Chechnya, and Yugoslavia.

Sequence of Conflicts		
Northern Ireland	**Chechnya**	**Yugoslavia**
• **1922**: Six Irish counties vote to remain in the United Kingdom.	•	•
•	•	•

Many wars and conflicts in recent decades have arisen over ethnic or religious differences. Such differences have led to civil wars within nations. Regional rivalries have also resulted in wars between nations.

Ethnic and Religious Conflicts

Ethnic and religious conflicts have often had more than one cause. The root of the conflict is often a cultural difference between two groups based on ethnicity, religion, or both. However, it takes more than cultural differences to create conflict. Malaysia and Singapore, for example, have great ethnic and religious diversity, but little internal conflict. Both countries enjoy peace because they have tried to distribute economic resources and political power fairly among their ethnic and religious groups.

War in Sri Lanka Conflicts occur when members of one ethnic or religious group feel that they face unfair treatment, or discrimination, by members of another group. For example, in Sri Lanka, where Sinhalese Buddhists are the majority, Sinhalese nationalists made Sinhalese the only official language. They ended the official use of the Tamil language. They also created government support for the Buddhist religion. Sinhalese nationalists excluded the Hindu Tamils from power. This led to the bloody civil war described in the previous chapter. The Tamil rebels agreed to a ceasefire in 2002 only when the government agreed to negotiations over a separate Tamil regional government.

Avoiding War in Canada In some countries, however, ethnic conflicts have found peaceful resolutions. For example, Canada has an English-speaking majority. In the past, many French-speaking people in the province of Quebec felt that Canada's government treated them unfairly. Some wanted Quebec to become independent. Meanwhile, others used democratic means to increase government support for French language and culture in Quebec. In 1995, Quebec's people voted to remain in Canada. In Canada, a democratic form of government has helped to prevent violent conflict.

Northern Ireland's Troubles Northern Ireland's difficulties began when Ireland won independence in 1922. Six northern counties, which had a Protestant majority, voted to remain part of Britain as **Northern Ireland.** Minority Catholics in Northern Ireland faced economic and political discrimination. Many Catholics demanded civil rights and unification with the rest of Ireland, which had a Catholic majority.

Beginning in the 1960s, extremists on both sides turned to violence and terrorism. The Irish Republican Army (IRA) attacked Protestants, and armed Protestant militias targeted Catholics.

Peace talks dragged on for years. Finally, in 1998, Protestants and Catholics signed a peace accord, known as the **Good Friday Agreement.** However, lasting peace was threatened by distrust on both sides, occasional acts of violence, and the IRA's reluctance to turn over weapons.

✔ **Checkpoint** Why did conflict break out in Northern Ireland?

Contrasting Ethnic Relations

Nation	Political System	Ethnic Conflict
Sri Lanka	Limits rights of minority groups	Has led to violence
Canada	Protects minority groups	Resolved democratically

Chart Skills Based on the chart and the information in this section, explain why the response of the ethnic minority to discrimination in Sri Lanka differed from that in Canada.

War Ravages Chechnya

Ethnic and religious minorities in several former Soviet republics fought for freedom from domination by the republics' majorities. In Azerbaijan, ethnic Armenians declared independence for the region of Nagorno-Karabakh, where they are the majority. Fighting between Azerbaijani forces and the Armenians left thousands dead.

Probably the fiercest conflict in the former Soviet Union has been the struggle of Muslim Chechen nationalists to free their homeland, **Chechnya,** from the control of Russia. Russia brutally crushed a Chechen revolt in the mid-1990s, killing huge numbers of civilians. Both sides committed war crimes such as torture. A 1997 peace treaty failed, and embittered Chechen separatists took their battle into other parts of Russia.

In 1999, new fighting erupted. Russian troops won control of Grozny, the capital of Chechnya, in 2000. However, rebels fought on in Chechnya's southern mountains. Some Chechens turned to terrorist attacks elsewhere in Russia. Russia charged that Chechen rebels were linked to Muslim terrorists in other parts of the world.

Grozny in Ruins
Grozny, the capital of Chechnya, lay in ruins in 2000 after Russian troops won a battle for control of the city.

✔ **Checkpoint** How has the war in Chechnya affected neighboring regions of Russia?

Yugoslavia Breaks Apart

Ethnic, nationalist, and religious tensions tore Yugoslavia apart during the 1990s. Before 1991, Yugoslavia was **multiethnic,** or made up of several ethnic groups. These groups included Serbs, Montenegrins, and Macedonians, who were Orthodox Christians; Croats and Slovenes, who were Roman Catholics; and the mostly Muslim Bosniaks and Albanians. A majority of Yugoslavians—including the Serbs, Montenegrins, Croats, and Bosniaks—all spoke the same language, Serbo-Croatian, but these groups had different religions. Albanians, Slovenes, and Macedonians spoke minority languages.

Yugoslavia was made up of six republics, similar to states in the United States. These were Slovenia, Croatia, Serbia, Bosnia and Herzegovina (often known as Bosnia for short), Montenegro, and Macedonia. Each republic had a dominant ethnic group but also was home to ethnic minorities. Serbs formed the majority in Serbia but were an important ethnic minority in several of the other republics. Serbs <u>dominated</u> Yugoslavia, which was held together and controlled by its Communist Party.

Vocabulary Builder

<u>dominate</u>—(DAHM uh nayt) *v.* to control or have power over

Republics Break Away The fall of communism led to nationalist unrest. The Serbs tried in vain to keep control over Yugoslavia. Slovenia and Croatia were the first to declare independence from Yugoslavia in 1991. When Croatia declared independence, however, fighting broke out between ethnic Croats and Serbs, who formed a minority within Croatia. Macedonia and Bosnia soon declared independence from Yugoslavia as well. By 1992, Yugoslavia was left with the republics of Montenegro and Serbia. Finally, in 2003, what remained of Yugoslavia was renamed *Serbia and Montenegro.*

Civil War Devastates Bosnia Fighting between Serbs and Croats in Croatia spread to neighboring Bosnia when Bosnia declared independence in 1992. Bosnian Serbs fought to set up their own separate government in Bosnia. They received money and arms from Yugoslavia, then dominated by Serbia. Muslim Bosniaks, the largest group in Bosnia, lived scattered throughout the country. They did not want Bosnia divided into ethnic regions.

During the war, all sides committed atrocities. Serbs in Bosnia conducted a vicious campaign of what they called **ethnic cleansing.** This meant killing people from other ethnic groups or forcibly removing them from their homes to create ethnically "pure" areas, in this case for Serbs. Thousands of Bosniaks and Croats were killed, sometimes in mass executions. Croatian and Bosniak fighters took revenge. Croats launched an ethnic cleansing campaign to drive ethnic Serbs from parts of Croatia. To many, ethnic cleansing recalled the horrors of the Holocaust during World War II.

Finally, NATO air strikes against the Bosnian Serb military forced the warring parties to negotiate. Guided by the United States, they signed the

Former Yugoslavia in 2005

Geography *Interactive.*
For: Audio guided tour
Web Code: nbp-3211

Yugoslavia, 1990
Provincial border
Republic border

Conic Projection
0   50   100 mi
0   50   100 km

Map Skills The former nation of Yugoslavia had broken apart into five new nations by 1992. During the early 2000s, the regions of Montenegro and Kosovo moved toward greater independence from Serbia within the nation of Serbia and Montenegro.

1. **Locate** (a) Sarajevo (b) Serbia (c) Kosovo
2. **Location** Which new nation does not share a border with Serbia on any side?
3. **Make Inferences** How did the location of Bosnia and Herzegovina put it at risk of becoming involved in conflicts between Serbians and Croatians?

Dayton Accords, ending the war in 1995. An international force helped maintain a fragile peace in Bosnia.

The Fight for Kosovo As Bosnia reached a tense peace, a crisis broke out in the Serbian province of Kosovo. Ethnic Albanians made up about 90 percent of Kosovo's population. The rest of the population was mostly Serbian.

In 1989, Serbian president Slobodan Milosevic (mih LOH shuh vich), an extreme Serbian nationalist, had begun oppressing Kosovar Albanians. Peaceful protests led to more repression. In the mid-1990s, a small guerrilla army of ethic Albanians began to respond with armed attacks on Serbian targets. Milosevic, however, rejected international peace efforts. In 1999, NATO launched air strikes against Serbia. Yugoslav forces attempted ethnic cleansing of Albanian civilians.

However, NATO air strikes eventually forced Yugoslavia to withdraw its forces from Kosovo. UN and NATO forces restored peace. As Kosovo rebuilt, tensions remained high between ethnic Albanians and Serbs living there. Although Kosovo remained part of Serbia in theory, the region was under UN control after 1999. The majority ethnic Albanians sought independence, while ethnic Serbs wanted to remain part of Serbia.

Albanian Guerrillas in Kosovo
These ethnic Albanian guerrillas were moving into an area after Serbian-dominated Yugoslav forces withdrew in 1999. *What does this photograph suggest about relations between ethnic Albanians and Serbians in Kosovo?*

✓ **Checkpoint** How did the breakup of Yugoslavia lead to ethnic cleansing in Bosnia and Herzegovina?

SECTION 1
Assessment

Progress Monitoring *Online*
For: Self-quiz with vocabulary practice
Web Code: nba-3211

Terms, People, and Places
1. What do many of the terms, people, and places listed at the beginning of the section have in common? Explain.

Note Taking
2. **Reading Skill: Recognize Sequence** Use your completed flowchart to answer the Focus Question: Why have ethnic and religious conflicts divided some nations?

Comprehension and Critical Thinking
3. **Synthesize Information** Based on the peaceful example of Malaysia, what might bring lasting peace to Northern Ireland?
4. **Predict Consequences** Based on your knowledge of the causes of ethnic conflict, how effective do you think Russia's methods will be in resolving the conflict in Chechnya?
5. **Draw Conclusions** Why did the breakup of Yugoslavia lead to increased ethnic conflict?

● **Writing About History**
Quick Write: Explore a Topic To write a research report, you first need to frame questions that will help you to explore your topic. Choose one of the conflicts in this section and write a series of questions that you could try to answer through research. For example, if you choose the Northern Ireland conflict, you might ask why the IRA has been reluctant to turn over weapons, or who has been responsible for recent attacks in Northern Ireland.

Since 1994, peace has returned to Rwanda. This recent photo shows Rwandan boys running home after school.

WITNESS HISTORY 🔊 AUDIO

Recovering From Genocide

Although other African nations suffered brutal ethnic conflicts and civil wars, Rwanda's 1994 genocide was one of the most deadly. However, as UN Secretary General Kofi Annan points out, Rwanda's recovery in the years since offers hope that the continent's conflicts can be resolved.

❞ Rwanda has much to show the world about confronting the legacy of the past and is demonstrating that it is possible to reach beyond tragedy and re-kindle hope. ❞
— Tribute by Kofi Annan on the tenth anniversary of genocide in Rwanda

This section explores the problems that have led to conflicts in Rwanda and in other African countries.

Focus Question Why have conflicts plagued some African countries?

Struggles in Africa

Objectives
- Understand South Africa's struggle for freedom.
- Describe how struggles for independence and Cold War rivalries brought decades of conflict to South Africa's neighbors.
- Analyze how ethnic conflicts killed millions in Rwanda and Sudan.

Terms, People, and Places

apartheid	Desmond Tutu
African National	F.W. de Klerk
Congress (ANC)	Hutus
Sharpeville	Tutsis
Nelson Mandela	Darfur

Note Taking

Reading Skill: Recognize Sequence Keep track of the sequence of events in the conflicts in South Africa and its neighbors. Add boxes as needed.

> **1910:** White minority controls government of independent South Africa.
>
> ↓　　　　↓　　　　↓
>
> **1948:**

In the 1950s and 1960s, many new nations won independence in Africa. National unity, however, was hard to achieve. Most African nations were home to diverse ethnic groups. Often, people did not even share a common language. They spoke dozens of local languages. Religious differences and longstanding rivalries further divided people within a nation.

After independence, a single ethnic group often dominated a nation's government and economy at the expense of other groups. The Cold War further complicated matters, as you have read. As a result, several African nations suffered internal conflicts and civil war.

South Africa Struggles for Freedom

In South Africa, the struggle for freedom was different from that elsewhere in Africa. In 1910, South Africa achieved self-rule from Britain. Freedom, however, was limited to white settlers. The black majority was denied the right to vote. Whites made up less than 20 percent of the population but controlled the government and the economy. The white-minority government passed racial laws that severely restricted the black majority.

Apartheid Divides South Africa After 1948, the government expanded the existing system of racial segregation, creating what was known as **apartheid,** or the separation of the races. Under apartheid, all South Africans were registered by race: Black,

White, Colored (people of mixed ancestry), and Asian. Apartheid's supporters claimed that it would allow each race to develop its own culture. In fact, it was designed to protect white control over South Africa.

Under apartheid, nonwhites faced many restrictions. Blacks were treated like foreigners in their own land. Under the pass laws, they had to get permission to travel. Other laws banned marriages between the races and <u>stipulated</u> segregated restaurants, beaches, and schools. Black workers were paid less than whites for the same job. Blacks could not own land in most areas. Low wages and inferior schooling condemned most blacks to poverty.

Fighting for Majority Rule

The **African National Congress (ANC)** was the main organization that opposed apartheid and led the struggle for majority rule. In the 1950s, as the government established apartheid, the ANC organized marches, boycotts, and strikes. In 1960, police gunned down 69 men, women, and children during a peaceful demonstration in **Sharpeville,** a black township. The government then outlawed the ANC and cracked down on groups that opposed apartheid.

The Sharpeville massacre and crackdown pushed the ANC to shift from nonviolent protest to armed struggle. Some, like **Nelson Mandela,** went underground. As an ANC leader, Mandela had first mobilized young South Africans to peacefully resist apartheid laws. As government violence grew, Mandela joined ANC militants who called for armed struggle against the white-minority government. In the early 1960s, Mandela was arrested, tried, and condemned to life in prison for treason against apartheid. Even while Mandela was in prison, he remained a popular leader and powerful symbol of the struggle for freedom.

In the 1980s, demands for an end to apartheid and for Mandela's release increased. Many countries, including the United States, imposed economic sanctions on South Africa. In 1984, black South African bishop **Desmond Tutu** won the Nobel Peace Prize for his nonviolent opposition to apartheid.

Overcoming Apartheid

Outside pressure and protests at home finally convinced South African president **F. W. de Klerk** to end apartheid. In 1990, he lifted the ban on the ANC and freed Mandela. In 1994, South Africans of every race were allowed to vote for the first time.

Vocabulary Builder

stipulated—(STIP yoo layt ed)
 v. required, specified

WITNESS HISTORY VIDEO

Watch *Nelson Mandela and the End of Apartheid* on the **Witness History Discovery School**™ video program to learn about the struggle against apartheid.

The Sharpeville Massacre
When South African police opened fire on peaceful demonstrators at Sharpeville in 1960, many demonstrators ran for their lives. *How might this police action lead anti-apartheid activists to give up on peaceful methods?*

Apartheid's Impact

For more than 40 years, apartheid shaped the lives of the black majority and of whites and other minorities in South Africa. Whites made up less than one fifth of South Africa's population, as you can see in the graph at the right. However, apartheid gave whites not only political power, but also control of South Africa's best lands and economic resources. This hurt blacks, Asians, and people of mixed backgrounds economically and socially. *Based on the information in the graph and elsewhere in this section, about what percentage of South Africa's population suffered from apartheid?*

South Africa's Population by Race

Colored (mixed race) 8.6%

Asian (Indian) 2.6%

White 13.6%

Black 75.2%

SOURCE: *CIA World Factbook*, 2005

Graph Skills This graph shows South Africa's population by race. The percentages have changed little since the years of apartheid. Which racial group is the majority in South Africa?

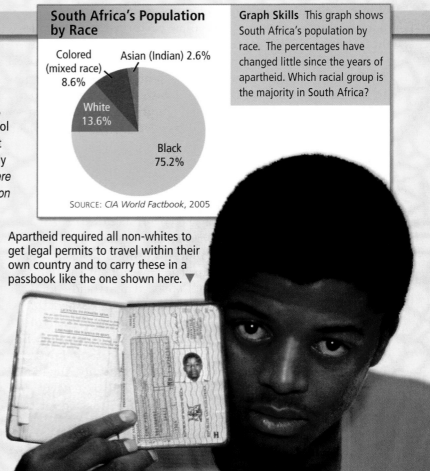

Apartheid required all non-whites to get legal permits to travel within their own country and to carry these in a passbook like the one shown here. ▼

▲ Apartheid gave many white South Africans a life of privilege.

Deprived of opportunities, many black South Africans lived in poverty.

They elected Nelson Mandela the first president of a truly democratic South Africa. Mandela helped to heal the country's wounds when he welcomed old political foes into his government, including whites who had supported apartheid. "Let us build together," he declared.

After 1994, South Africa faced huge challenges. With majority rule, black South Africans expected a better life. Although South Africa was a rich, industrial country, it could afford only a limited amount of spending for housing, education, and other programs. The gap between blacks and whites remained large. Whites owned more than three fourths of the land. Black poverty and unemployment remained high. The crime rate soared in the cities and nearby shantytowns. South Africa's government struggled to address these problems.

✔ **Checkpoint** What factors finally brought an end to apartheid in South Africa?

South Africa's Neighbors Face Long Conflicts

Most African nations achieved independence through peaceful means during the 1950s and 1960s. In southern Africa, however, the road to freedom was longer and more violent. For many years, the apartheid government of South Africa supported white minority rule in neighboring Namibia and Zimbabwe.

Meanwhile, as Britain and France gave up their African possessions, Portugal clung fiercely to its colonies in Angola and Mozambique. In response, nationalist movements turned to guerrilla warfare. Fighting dragged on for 15 years, until Portugal agreed to withdraw from Africa. In 1975, Angola and Mozambique celebrated independence.

Independence did not end the fighting, however. Bitter civil wars, fueled by Cold War rivalries, raged for years. South Africa and the United States saw the new nations as threats because some liberation leaders had ties to the Soviet Union or the ANC. The United States and South Africa aided a rebel group fighting the new government of Angola. South Africa aided a rebel group in Mozambique.

The fighting did not stop until 1992 in Mozambique and 2002 in Angola, where tensions remained even after a ceasefire. Decades of war had ravaged both countries. Slowly, however, they have begun to rebuild.

✔ **Checkpoint** Why did fighting continue after Angola and Mozambique achieved independence?

Ethnic Conflicts Kill Millions

After independence, ethnic conflicts plagued several African nations. The causes were complex. Historic resentments divided ethnically diverse nations. Unjust governments and regional rivalries fed ethnic violence.

Rwanda and Burundi Face Deadly Divisions The small nation of Rwanda, in Central Africa, faced one of Africa's deadliest civil wars. The Rwandan people included two main groups. **Hutus** were the majority group, but the minority **Tutsis** had long dominated Rwanda. Both groups spoke the same language, but they had different traditions. After independence, tensions between these two groups simmered.

Tensions worsened in the early 1990s. In 1994, extremist Hutu officials urged civilians to kill their Tutsi and moderate Hutu neighbors. Around 800,000 Tutsis and moderate Hutus were slaughtered. Another 3 million of Rwanda's 8 million people lost their homes to destructive mobs. As the death toll rose, the international community failed to act. After several months, France sent in troops to stop the killing.

With UN assistance, Rwanda set about rebuilding and recovering from the horrors of genocide. Those accused of genocide faced trials in an international court. Hutus and Tutsis had to find ways to live peacefully. World leaders pledged to stop any future genocide wherever it might occur. Their readiness to do this, however, was limited.

The neighboring nation of Burundi has a similar population and history. As in Rwanda, tensions between Tutsis and Hutus led to civil war during the 1990s. While the fighting did not lead to a genocide like that in Rwanda, guerrilla groups fought for much longer in Burundi. Although several guerrilla groups signed a peace treaty in 2000, fighting continued in the years that followed.

Sudan's Ethnic Strife After independence, Sudan's Arab Muslim north dominated the non-Muslim, non-Arab south. Arab-led governments enacted laws and policies that discriminated against non-Muslims and against other ethnic groups. For example, the government tried to impose Islamic law even in non-Muslim areas. For decades, rebel groups in the south battled northern domination. War, drought, and famine caused millions of deaths and forced many more to flee their homes.

Note Taking

Reading Skill: Identify Causes and Effects Fill in a concept web like the one below to keep track of the causes and effects of the conflicts in Rwanda and Sudan.

Arab Militia in Darfur
Arab militias in Sudan's Darfur region, such as the one shown here, are known as *janjaweed* or "bandits." During 2004 and 2005, these militias carried out murder and ethnic cleansing against the non-Arab villagers of Darfur. *How might an attack by this militia affect unarmed villagers?*

However, in 2004, southern rebels signed a peace agreement with Sudan's government. The southern rebels agreed to stop fighting, and the government agreed to give the south limited self-government, power in Sudan's national government, and freedom from Islamic law.

However, by 2004, ethnic conflict had also spread to Sudan's western region of **Darfur.** This conflict raised fears of a new genocide. Arab militias, backed by the government, unleashed terror on the non-Arab Muslim people of Darfur. They burned villages and drove hundreds of thousands of farmers off the land that fed them and into refugee camps, where they faced the threat of starvation. The UN, the United States, and other nations organized a huge aid effort to help refugees.

✓ **Checkpoint** How did the conflict in Darfur differ from the conflict in southern Sudan?

SECTION **2 Assessment**

Progress Monitoring *Online*
For: Self-quiz with vocabulary practice
Web Code: nba-3221

Terms, People, and Places

1. For each term, person, or place listed at the beginning of the section, write a sentence explaining its significance.

Note Taking

2. **Reading Skill: Recognize Sequence** Use your completed flowchart to answer the Focus Question: Why have conflicts plagued some African countries?

Comprehension and Critical Thinking

3. **Analyze Information** Was apartheid a product of a democratic system of government? Explain.

4. **Summarize** What was South Africa's role in the conflicts that plagued its neighbors from the 1960s to the 1990s?

5. **Make Comparisons** How was the ethnic conflict in Burundi similar to or different from the conflict in Rwanda?

6. **Synthesize Information** A newspaper headline read, "Looking at Darfur, Seeing Rwanda." Explain what that headline meant. How did the world community respond to genocide after the events in Rwanda?

● **Writing About History**

Quick Write: Gather Information To write a research report, you need to gather information about your topic. Choose one of the conflicts in this section and gather facts about the topic from the library or reliable sources online. Make a list of facts about your topic.

Nelson Mandela: *Glory and Hope*

Nelson Mandela delivered this speech after having been elected president in South Africa's first multiracial election in 1994. Knowing that the injustices of apartheid would be hard to overcome, Mandela asked the people to work together for peace and justice.

Students in South Africa after the end of apartheid

Today, all of us do, by our presence here, and by our celebrations . . . confer glory and hope to newborn liberty.

Out of the experience of an extraordinary human disaster that lasted too long must be born a society of which all humanity will be proud.

Our daily deeds as ordinary South Africans must produce an actual South African reality that will reinforce humanity's belief in justice, strengthen its confidence in the nobility of the human soul and sustain all our hopes for a glorious life for all. . . .

The time for the healing of the wounds has come. . . .

The time to build is upon us.

We have, at last, achieved our political emancipation.[1] We pledge ourselves to liberate all our people from the continuing bondage of poverty, deprivation, suffering, gender and other discrimination. . . .

We have triumphed in the effort to implant hope in the breasts of the millions of our people. We enter into a covenant[2] that we shall build the society in which all South Africans, both black and white, will be able to walk tall, without any fear in their hearts, assured of their inalienable right to human dignity—a rainbow nation at peace with itself and the world. . . .

We understand it still that there is no easy road to freedom.

We know it well that none of us acting alone can achieve success.

We must therefore act together as a united people, for national reconciliation,[3] for nation building, for the birth of a new world.

Let there be justice for all. Let there be peace for all. Let there be work, bread, water, and salt for all. . . . The sun shall never set on so glorious a human achievement!

---

1. emancipation (ee man suh PAY shun) *n.* the gaining of freedom from bondage or control by others

2. covenant (KUV uh nunt) *n.* a binding and solemn pledge to do something

3. reconciliation (rek un sil ee AY shun) *n.* a settling of differences that results in harmony

Thinking Critically

1. **Identify Alternatives** When apartheid ended, there was a danger of a backlash by blacks against whites who supported apartheid. How does Mandela's speech respond to that danger?
2. **Draw Inferences** In addition to political freedom, what further freedoms does Mandela call for in his speech?

Nelson Mandela with supporters in 1994

An Israeli soldier and a Palestinian Arab pass each other in the street.

Two Peoples Claim the Same Land

Many Jewish Israelis believe that the quotation from the Bible, below, promises Israel to the Jewish people as descendents of Abraham (Abram). Many Muslims also believe that they are the spiritual heirs to Abraham, as stated in the Quran. They too feel entitled to the land as part of Abraham's legacy. Representatives of both peoples have lived in the land for centuries.

❝ On that day the LORD made a covenant with Abram, saying, 'To your descendants I give this land. . . .'❞

—Genesis 15:18

❝ He [Allah] has chosen you and has placed no hardship on you in practicing your religion—the religion of your father Abraham. ❞

—Quran 22:78

Focus Question What are the causes of conflict in the Middle East?

Conflicts in the Middle East

Objectives
- Understand why Arabs and Israelis fought over land.
- Explain why civil war ravaged Lebanon.
- Outline Iraq's long history of conflict.

Terms, People, and Places

occupied territories	Saddam Hussein
Yasir Arafat	no-fly zone
intifada	weapons of mass
Yitzhak Rabin	destruction (WMDs)
Jerusalem	insurgent
militia	

N<u>o</u>te Taking

Reading Skill: Recognize Sequence Keep track of the sequence of events in the conflicts in the Middle East with a flowchart like the one below.

Middle Eastern Conflicts		
Arab-Israeli Conflict	**Lebanon**	**Iraq**
• **1948**: Israel is founded •	• •	• •

For decades, the Middle East has been the focus of conflicts that have had a global impact. The Middle East commands vast oil resources and key waterways such as the Persian Gulf. During the Cold War, both the United States and the Soviet Union wanted access to the oil and the waterways. Since the end of the Cold War, Western nations have acted to prevent regional powers from interfering with the region's oil supply. Meanwhile, the persistent dispute between Israelis and Palestinian Arabs has added to tensions.

Arabs and Israelis Fight Over Land

Modern Israel was established in 1948 in accordance with the United Nations Partition Plan. The Palestinian Arabs regarded the UN action as illegitimate and rejected the state offered to them. Conflicting claims to this land led to repeated violence. After the 1948 war that followed Israel's founding, Israel and its Arab neighbors fought three more wars, in 1956, 1967, and 1973. In these wars, Israel defeated Arab forces and gained more land. Between the wars, Israel faced guerrilla and terrorist attacks. Repeatedly, the United States tried to bring about peace.

Israel Controls the Occupied Territories In the 1967 war, in response to hostility by its neighbors, Israeli forces took control of territories occupied by Jordan and Egypt since 1948, including the West Bank, East Jerusalem, and the Gaza Strip. They also took control of the Sinai Peninsula from Egypt and the Golan Heights from Syria. In 1973, these nations attacked Israel on Yom Kippur, one of the holiest days of the Jewish year.

In the 1973 war, Arabs failed to regain the regions they had lost to Israel, called by Palestinians the **occupied territories.** Israel's government later helped Jewish settlers build homes in settlements in these territories, causing more bitterness among the Palestinians.

Palestinian Attacks Bring Israeli Response By the 1960s, the Palestine Liberation Organization (PLO) was leading the Palestinian struggle against Israel. It was headed by **Yasir Arafat.** It had deep support among Palestinians who fled or had been forced off their lands during the various wars. The PLO called for the destruction of Israel.

For years, the PLO launched attacks against Israelis at home and abroad. Airplane hijackings and the killing of Israeli athletes at the 1972 Olympic games brought PLO demands to the attention of the world.

Palestinians also opposed Israel in the occupied territories by mounting **intifadas,** or uprisings. Demanding an end to the Israeli occupation, young Palestinians stoned Israeli troops. Armed Palestinians fired on Israeli soldiers and civilians. Suicide bombers blew up buses, stores, and clubs inside Israel, killing many civilians.

Israel responded forcefully. Over the years, Israeli troops sealed off Palestinian towns, destroyed the homes of suicide bombers and their families, and targeted terrorist leaders, killing many Palestinians.

Seeking Peace Despite the violence, the United States, the UN, and others pushed for peace and made some progress. Golda Meir, Israel's first female prime minister, was trying to arrange a negotiated peace when Arab nations attacked Israel in the 1973 war. As you have learned, Israel and Egypt signed a peace accord in 1979. Israel then returned the Sinai Peninsula to Egypt. In 1994, Jordan's King Hussein made peace with Israel. However, talks between Israel and Syria failed over issues of security, recognition of Israel, and control of the Golan Heights.

A City Sacred to Many
Jerusalem is dotted with many places that are sacred to the Jewish people, Christians, and Muslims. This photograph shows the Western Wall, a Jewish holy place. In the background is the Dome of the Rock, an important Islamic shrine. *How might Jerusalem's sacred status make it harder to resolve competing Israeli and Palestinian Arab claims to the city?*

The Israeli-Palestinian Conflict

Legend:
- Israel, 1949
- Occupied by Israel after 1967

LEBANON
SYRIA
Golan Heights
Haifa
Sea of Galilee
Mediterranean Sea
Jordan River
Tel Aviv
West Bank
Ramallah
Jerusalem
Jericho
Bethlehem
Hebron
Dead Sea
Gaza
Gaza Strip
ISRAEL
JORDAN
EGYPT
Elat

Conflict has dragged on for years in the region. Palestinian Arabs resent the Israeli occupation. Some have responded with suicide bombings targeting Israeli civilians. Israeli forces have responded with attacks on Palestinian militants that have also killed some civilians. Hopes for peace in the region center on ending this cycle of violence and retaliation.

◀ Palestinian suicide bombers have set off deadly explosions in public places that have killed Israeli civilians. The bus in this photo was torn apart by a bomb carried by a Palestinian terrorist.

Another breakthrough occurred after Israel and the PLO began direct talks. In 1993, Yasir Arafat and Israeli Prime Minister **Yitzhak Rabin** (rah BEEN) signed the Oslo Accord. It outlined a plan to give Palestinians in Gaza and the West Bank limited self-rule under a Palestinian Authority. The PLO recognized Israel's right to exist, and the Palestinian Authority pledged to stop terrorism against Israel. Arafat assumed leadership of the Palestinian Authority.

Facing Setbacks However, years of talks brought few results, and violence continued. In 2000, radical Palestinian groups such as Hamas stepped up terrorist attacks, vowing to destroy Israel. Israeli prime minister Ariel Sharon demanded Arafat's removal as head of the Palestinian Authority for failing to prevent these attacks. Palestinian suicide bombings and Israeli reprisals brought fear and bitterness on both sides.

Overcoming Obstacles to Peace Beyond the distrust and bitterness, many obstacles to peace remain. One obstacle is land claims. Many Palestinians want a right to settle anywhere in Israel, under a "Right of Return." This policy would bring a large number of Palestinians into Israel, which could undermine the Jewish state and spark further violence. A second obstacle is the future of Israeli settlements in the occupied territories. Israeli settlers have been determined to remain. Palestinians have insisted that they must leave.

Jerusalem is a third stumbling block. As you have read, Israel occupied East Jerusalem during the 1967 war. Until 1967, Jordan had denied Jews access to their holy sites. Later, Israel declared that area part of Israel, while giving other religions control over their holy sites. Palestinians, however, want East Jerusalem to be the capital of a future Palestinian state. A final obstacle is that many Arabs are unwilling to recognize Israel's right to exist.

Israeli counterattacks in the occupied territories have killed Palestinians, including some civilians. Some 20,000 people attended this funeral for Palestinians killed in an Israeli attack.

History Interactive
For: Interactive map
Web Code: nbp-3231

Some Israelis and Palestinians, such as the men in this photograph, have chosen peaceful dialogue rather than violence as a way to bridge their differences. Dialogue between the two sides offers the best hope for ending this regional conflict. ▼

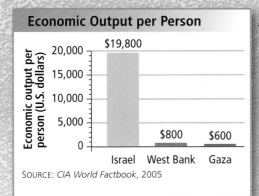

Economic Output per Person

Economic output per person (U.S. dollars)

Israel	West Bank	Gaza
$19,800	$800	$600

SOURCE: *CIA World Factbook*, 2005

Lack of development, years of conflict, and corruption have crippled the economy of the West Bank and Gaza. Meanwhile, Palestinian attacks have forced Israel to limit Palestinians' access to jobs in Israel. Poverty in the West Bank and Gaza Strip has led to desperation among Palestinians.

During the early 2000s, new steps toward peace offered some hope. The United States devised a new plan, called the "road map" to peace. It called for two states, Israel and a democratic Palestine, to exist side by side. In 2004, Israeli prime minister Sharon launched a plan to withdraw Israeli settlements from Gaza. The plan angered some Israelis and did not satisfy Palestinians, who wanted Israeli settlements removed from the West Bank as well. Still, the plan was a step toward peace.

Further progress followed the death in 2004 of Yasir Arafat, whom the Israelis distrusted. His democratically elected successor, Mahmoud Abbas (ah BAHS), pledged to stop Palestinian terrorist attacks on Israel. Israel responded in 2005 by releasing hundreds of Palestinian prisoners. While these events brought new hopes for peace, serious obstacles remain.

✓ **Checkpoint** **What obstacles have prevented peace between Israel and the Palestinians?**

Civil War Ravages Lebanon

Lebanon is home to <u>diverse</u> ethnic and religious groups. Until the mid-1900s, had been a thriving center of commerce. By the 1970s, however, the Arab-Israeli conflict was contributing to problems in neighboring Lebanon.

Tension Grows The government depended on a delicate balance among Arab Christians, Sunni Muslims, Shiite Muslims, and Druze (people with a religion related to Islam). Christians held the most power, because they had been the largest group when Lebanon gained independence. After mostly Muslim Palestinians fled into Lebanon from areas that became Israel in 1948, Muslims outnumbered Christians in Lebanon. This upset Lebanon's delicate religious balance. Muslim Lebanese demanded a greater share of power.

Thinking Critically
1. **Graph Skills** How does economic output in the West Bank and Gaza Strip compare with that in Israel?
2. **Draw Conclusions** How might violence by both sides tend to prolong the Palestinian-Israeli conflict?

Vocabulary Builder
<u>diverse</u>—(dih VURS) *adj.* multiple, varied, different

Civil War and Its Aftermath In 1975, religious tensions plunged Lebanon into a civil war. Christian and Muslim **militias,** or armed groups of citizen soldiers, battled each other. In 1982, Israel invaded southern Lebanon to stop cross-border attacks, and Syria occupied eastern Lebanon to secure its borders.

In 1990, the civil war finally ended. Beirut, the ruined capital, was slowly rebuilt and again became a center of commerce. Despite economic growth, divisions remained among Lebanon's diverse population. Although Israel withdrew its forces in 2000, it remains alert to attacks across its northern border. Syrian troops remained until 2005, when popular protests led to their withdrawal. Lebanon's fate seemed tied to the prospects for peace among its neighbors.

✓ **Checkpoint** How did an influx of Palestinians contribute to ethnic conflict in Lebanon?

Saddam Hussein's Dictatorship
Saddam Hussein, shown here in a propaganda poster in 1982, turned Iraq into a brutal police state, in which critics were tortured and killed.

Iraq's Long History of Conflict

Iraq has had a long history of internal and external conflicts. These conflicts have been due partly to its oil wealth and ethnic diversity. During the Cold War, the United States and Soviet Union competed for influence in oil-rich Iraq. After World War II, Iraq's monarchy had close ties to the United States, but the monarchy was overthrown in 1958. In the years that followed, Iraq's rulers developed closer ties with the Soviet Union.

For centuries, Iraq's Sunni Arab minority had dominated the country. The Kurdish minority and the Shiite Arab majority had little power. During the 1970s, Kurds took up arms to fight for power over their homeland in northern Iraq. Iraq's government responded brutally.

The Iran-Iraq War Costs Many Lives In 1979, **Saddam Hussein** seized power in Iraq and ruled as a dictator. In 1980, after the Islamic revolution in Iran, Saddam Hussein tried to take advantage of the turmoil there by seizing a disputed border region. His action triggered a prolonged war.

During the 1980s, the war began to reflect Cold War rivalries. Iran was bitterly opposed to the United States. This helped Iraq to win U.S. support. The war dragged on until 1988, and took a heavy toll on both Iran and Iraq.

During the war, Saddam Hussein unleashed chemical weapons on Kurdish civilians. Chemical weapons killed several thousand Kurds in an attack on one Kurdish village. Some charged him with genocide against the Kurds.

The Gulf War Brings Defeat In 1990, Iraq invaded Kuwait to control its vast oil fields and gain greater access to the Persian Gulf. For the United States, Saddam Hussein's move was not only illegal, but also a threat to the oil resources of the Persian Gulf region. President George H.W. Bush formed a coalition of Western and Middle Eastern nations to drive Iraq out of Kuwait. Coalition forces launched a counterattack against Iraqi forces in Kuwait in 1991. In the 1991 Gulf War, the U.S.-led coalition operated under the UN banner. It quickly liberated Kuwait and crushed Iraqi forces.

Despite defeat, Saddam Hussein remained in power. He brutally crushed revolts by the majority Shiite Muslims in the south and the minority Kurds in the north. Throughout Iraq, he used torture, terror, and execution to impose his will.

Saddam Hussein Defies Restrictions To protect the Kurds and Shiites, the United States, France, and Britain set up **no-fly zones,** areas where Iraqi aircraft were forbidden to fly. The UN worked to keep Saddam Hussein from using oil profits to build **weapons of mass destruction (WMDs),** or biological, nuclear, and chemical weapons. It imposed economic sanctions limiting how much oil Iraq could sell and how it could spend its money. Iraq repeatedly violated the no-fly zones. It also failed to cooperate fully with UN weapons inspectors who were sent to find WMDs.

U.S. Forces Defeat Saddam Hussein In 2002, the United States and Britain charged that Saddam Hussein still had WMDs. American President George W. Bush accused the Iraqi president of supporting terrorists. The United States and Britain then joined together in a coalition to invade Iraq.

Coalition forces toppled Saddam Hussein and occupied the country in the 2003 Iraq War. They then set out to rebuild the war-ravaged country. Many Iraqis welcomed the end of Saddam Hussein's vicious regime. At the same time, many of them resented foreign occupation.

Iraq Tries to Rebuild Efforts to rebuild Iraq were hampered by guerrilla attacks and suicide bombings. **Insurgents,** or rebels, targeted foreigners and Iraqi citizens, especially those cooperating with foreign troops.

In 2005, national elections were held. For the first time in Iraq's history, the country's Shiite majority won control of the government. The new government, however, faced attacks from various insurgent groups, particularly Sunnis bitter about their loss of power.

Iraq faced other difficulties in trying to build a democratic government. Ethnic and religious divisions posed serious obstacles. Iraq's new government needed to find a way to bring Iraq's Shiites, Sunnis, Kurds, and other minorities together.

Iraq Has an Election
Iraqis line up to vote in the election of January 2005, the country's first free election in more than 35 years. The barbed wire in the foreground is a sign of security concerns. There was widespread concern about possible attacks by Sunni Arabs, many of whom boycotted the election.

✔ **Checkpoint** Why has conflict persisted in Iraq since the defeat of Saddam Hussein?

SECTION 3 Assessment

Terms, People, and Places

1. What do each of the terms, people, and places listed at the beginning of the section have in common? Explain.

Note Taking

2. **Reading Skill: Recognize Sequence**
Use your finished flowchart to answer the Focus Question: What are the causes of conflict in the Middle East?

Comprehension and Critical Thinking

3. **Draw Conclusions** Why has the Arab-Israeli conflict been so persistent?
4. **Summarize** How has Jerusalem been an obstacle to resolving the conflict?
5. **Identify Central Issues** What were the causes of Lebanon's civil war?
6. **Synthesize Information** Why did the UN impose economic sanctions in Iraq after the 1991 Gulf War?

● **Writing About History**

Quick Write: Make an Outline To write a research report, you need to make an outline that organizes information that you have gathered. Suppose that you are writing a research report on the Arab-Israeli conflict. Make an outline that organizes the information in this section about that conflict.

Quick Study Guide

Progress Monitoring *Online*
For: Self-test with vocabulary practice
Web Code: nba-3241

■ Conflicts in Iraq

Conflict	Duration	Main Events
Iran-Iraq War	1980–1988	Saddam Hussein tried to seize an Iranian border region. Saddam used chemical weapons against Kurds
Gulf War	1990–1991	Saddam Hussein invaded Kuwait. Coalition led by United States defeated Saddam's army and freed Kuwait.
Iraq War	2003	Coalition led by the United States defeated Saddam Hussein's forces and occupied Iraq. Fighting with insurgents continued after Saddam's defeat in 2003.

■ Conflicts in Former Yugoslavia

Area of Conflict	Duration	Main Events
Croatia	1991–1995	Croatian forces fought with ethnic Serbs and the Yugoslav army over ethnic Serb areas. Serbs faced ethnic cleansing.
Bosnia	1992–1995	Ethnic Serbs, Croats, and Muslim Bosniaks fought each other. Muslims faced ethnic cleansing by Serbs.
Kosovo	1996–1999	Ethnic Albanians clashed with the Yugoslav army. Yugoslav forces attempted ethnic cleansing of Albanians.

■ Locations of Regional Conflicts

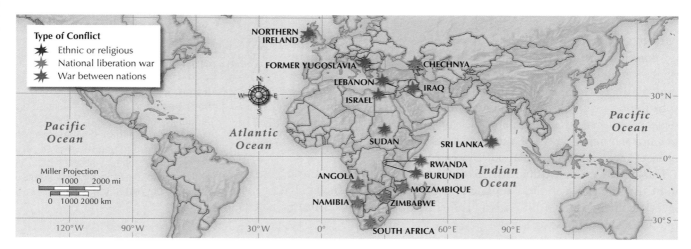

Type of Conflict
★ Ethnic or religious
★ National liberation war
★ War between nations

NORTHERN IRELAND
FORMER YUGOSLAVIA
CHECHNYA
LEBANON
IRAQ
ISRAEL
SUDAN
SRI LANKA
RWANDA
BURUNDI
ANGOLA
MOZAMBIQUE
NAMIBIA
ZIMBABWE
SOUTH AFRICA

Pacific Ocean
Atlantic Ocean
Pacific Ocean
Indian Ocean

Miller Projection
0   1000   2000 mi
0   1000 2000 km

120°W   90°W   30°W   0°   60°E   90°E
30°N   0°   30°S

■ Key Events of Regional Conflicts

Africa and Europe
Middle East

1945   **1955**   **1965**

1948
South Africa expands apartheid system.

1960
Sharpeville massacre marks violent turn in anti-apartheid struggle.

Late 1960s
Religious conflict in Northern Ireland turns violent.

1948
Israel's founding brings attack by Arab neighbors.

1967
Israel gains territory in the 1967 war and Palestinians increase attacks on Israel.

Concept Connector

■ Cumulative Review

Record the answers to the questions below on your Concept Connector worksheets.

1. **Dictatorship** Like earlier dictators, such as Mussolini and Hitler, Saddam Hussein adopted an aggressive policy of seizing lands outside his borders. He also used brutal methods against his own population. How did Saddam Hussein's dictatorship compare with earlier dictatorships? Consider
   - his internal policies.
   - his policies toward neighboring nations.

2. **Genocide** Compare the genocide in Rwanda with at least one earlier example of genocide, such as those in Cambodia, Nazi Germany, or the Ottoman empire. Think about
   - the role of ethnic hatred.
   - the response of the international community.

3. **Conflict** During the century following the Reformation in Europe, religious differences sparked a series of wars. How does the recent conflict in Northern Ireland compare with those earlier religious conflicts? Consider
   - whether the conflicts involved more than one nation.
   - the importance of social and economic inequalities.

4. **Empire** Like earlier empires, Russia controls numerous regions and ethnic groups. The conflict in Chechnya can be seen as an effort by one ethnic group to break away. How does this conflict compare to earlier efforts to break away from an empire, such as the Vietnamese and Algerian wars for independence from the French empire?

■ Connections to Today

1. **Democracy** In this chapter, you read that Canada's democracy has allowed ethnic differences to be resolved peacefully, rather than through violent conflict. Through democratic means, the French-speaking majority in Quebec has secured rights for their language in Canada, even though French speakers are a minority in Canada (see the graphs below). Use the library and online research to identify another country where a democratic system has recently helped bring a peaceful resolution to ethnic differences. Compare your country's ethnic politics to those in Canada.

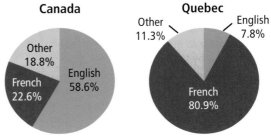

SOURCE: Statistics Canada, 2001 Census

2. **Cooperation** In this chapter, you learned that members of the NATO military alliance cooperated to end ethnic cleansing and warfare in Kosovo in 1999. Use the library and online research to identify a more recent case in which cooperation among concerned nations has helped to bring peace to a country involved in a violent conflict. How does this recent case compare to what you learned about Kosovo?

History Interactive
For: Interactive timeline
Web Code: nbp-3241

| 1992 Ethnic conflict erupts in Bosnia. | 1994 Conflict in Rwanda leads to genocide. | 1994 Open elections bring end of apartheid in South Africa. | 1999 Brutal ethnic conflict in Kosovo brings NATO intervention. |

1975   **1985**   **1995**   **2005**

1975
Lebanon plunges into civil war.

1991
U.S.-led coalition defeats Iraq in Gulf War.

2003
U.S.-led coalition defeats Saddam Hussein and occupies Iraq.

Chapter Assessment

Terms, People, and Places

Choose the italicized term in parentheses that best completes each sentence.

1. Muslim nationalists in (*Kosovo/Chechnya*) have fought to free their homeland from Russian control.
2. There were hopes that (*the Good Friday Agreement/ethnic cleansing*) would provide for a peaceful resolution of the conflict in Northern Ireland.
3. (*Desmond Tutu/Nelson Mandela*) led the struggle against apartheid even when he was imprisoned for his role in the African National Congress.
4. In Rwanda, extremist (*Hutus/Tutsis*), the country's ethnic majority, slaughtered members of the country's ethnic minority in 1994.
5. Both Israel and the Palestinians claim (*the occupied territories/Jerusalem*) as their capital.
6. The Palestine Liberation Organization was headed by (*Yasir Arafat/Yitzhak Rabin*).
7. Efforts to rebuild Iraq after Saddam Hussein's overthrow were slowed by (*intifada/insurgent*) attacks.

Main Ideas

Section 1 (pp. 682–685)
8. Why does ethnic diversity lead to violent conflicts in some places but not in others?
9. How did Yugoslavia's breakup lead to ethnic conflicts?

Section 2 (pp. 686–690)
10. How did South Africa overcome apartheid?
11. What factors contributed to Africa's deadly ethnic conflicts?

Section 3 (pp. 692–697)
12. Explain the basic causes of the Israeli-Palestinian conflict.
13. What obstacles did Iraq face in its effort to rebuild after years of war?

Chapter Focus Question
14. Why have deadly conflicts plagued some regions of the world?

Critical Thinking

15. **Predict Consequences** Identify possible solutions to the ethnic conflicts in Bosnia and Kosovo and predict the consequences of these solutions.
16. **Draw Conclusions** Why was the idea of majority rule so important to people in South Africa and in neighboring African countries?
17. **Express Problems Clearly** What are the main problems that have stood in the way of a peace settlement between Palestinians and Israelis?
18. **Recognize Cause and Effect** How did Saddam Hussein's policies cause suffering for Iraqis?
19. **Analyzing Visuals** What is the main message of the cartoon below? How might violence have been prevented in these countries?

● Writing About History

Writing a Research Report This chapter discusses several ethnic and regional conflicts. Choose one of the conflicts covered or find another conflict that interests you. Write a research report on the causes of the conflict, how the conflict unfolded, and how it was resolved or might be resolved. Consult page SH13 of the Writing Handbook for additional help.

Prewriting
- Do online or library research to read background materials about your conflict.
- Take notes on relevant details, events, and the people involved in the conflict.
- Create a set of questions about your conflict and gather additional resources.

Drafting
- Develop a working thesis about the cause of this conflict—for example, is the main issue control of land, government policies, or some other issue?
- Make an outline to organize a report that supports your thesis. Find information from your research that supports each part of your outline.
- Write an introduction explaining your thesis, a body, and a conclusion.

Revising
- Use the guidelines for revising your report on page SH15 of the Writing Handbook.

Document-Based Assessment

The Palestinian Question

In 1947, the United Nations drew up a plan dividing Palestine into two states, Jewish and Arab, which the Arabs rejected. The next year, Israel was established as an independent nation according to the United Nations guidelines. As a result of the 1967 war, Israel gained control of the West Bank and Gaza. Gaza was unilaterally given to the Palestinians in 2005. Palestinians still do not have an independent state of their own. Despite ongoing conflict between Israelis and Palestinians, many on both sides still hope for peace.

Document A

UN Partition Plan, 1947

Document B

Israel and Occupied Territories, 2006

Document C

"As I have said, we came to Palestine to do away with the helplessness of the Jewish people through our own endeavors. Therefore, you will realize what it meant for us to watch from here millions of Jews being slaughtered during these years of war. . . . We Jews only want that which is given naturally to all peoples of the world to be masters of our own fate . . . . We are certain that given an opportunity of bringing in large masses of Jews into this country, of opening the doors of Palestine to all Jews who wish to come here, we can . . . create a free Jewish society built on the basis of cooperation, equality, and mutual aid."

—From **"The Zionist Case"** by Golda Meir (speech given March 25, 1946)

Document D

"Late at night when everything is quiet I think about how I will ever forgive the Israelis for what they did to me. I don't mean stealing my homeland, killing my people, turning me into a refugee, or depriving me from having a Palestinian state. I'm talking about myself—what they did to my personality.

I wish I had a normal life: no tension, no rage, no hatred, no hard feelings toward anybody. Even if they leave my country and give me back my rights, how will I overcome these feelings inside me?"

—From **"Children of a Tenth-Class God?"** by Nihaya Qawasmi (1998)

Analyzing Documents

Use your knowledge of the Palestinian-Israeli conflict and Documents A, B, C, and D to answer questions 1–4.

1. According to Documents A and B, what is the present status of the area outlined in the UN Partition Plan?
   A It is divided between Israel and neighboring countries.
   B Palestine is now an independent nation.
   C Part of it is the State of Israel, part is occupied by Israel, and part is ruled by the Palestinians.
   D It is divided among three independent nations.

2. In Document C, "helplessness" refers to
   A Israel's inability to help the Palestinians.
   B the inability of Jews in Palestine to help Jews in Nazi territory.
   C the inability of Palestinians to change their attitude toward Israel.
   D the inability of the Allies to do anything about Nazi atrocities.

3. Which words best describe the feelings of the author of Document D toward Israel?
   A acceptance and understanding
   B discouragement and fear
   C anger and resentment
   D trust and hope

4. **Writing Task** What are the prospects for a peaceful settlement of the Palestinian question? Use the documents on this page along with information from the chapter to write a short essay on this topic.

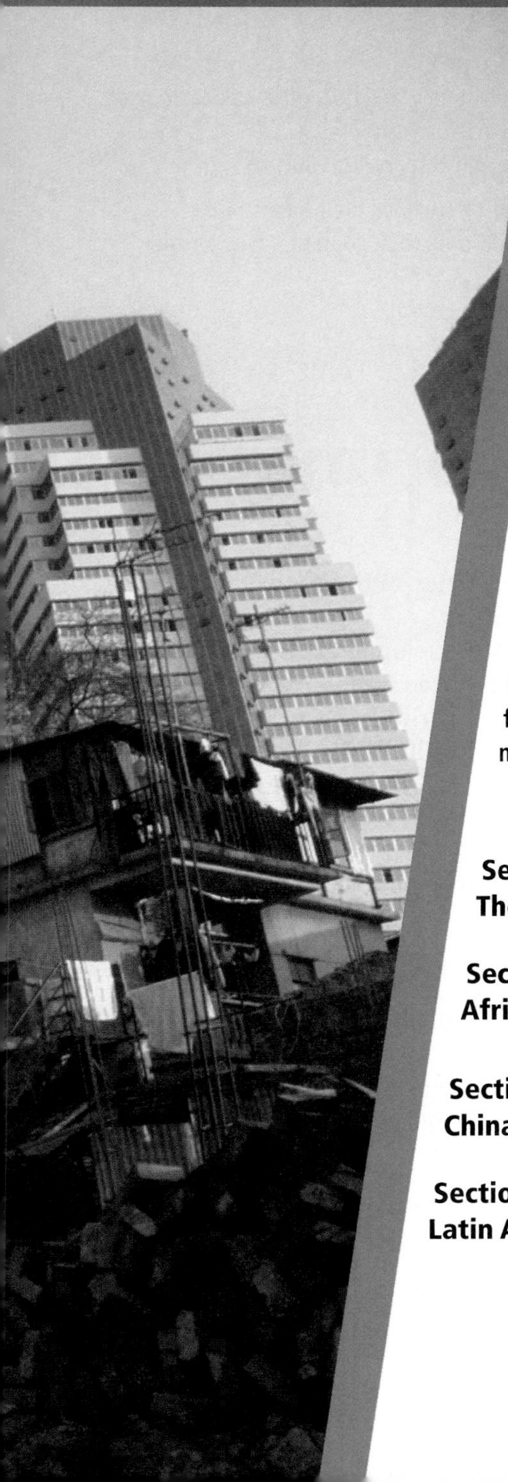

WITNESS HISTORY AUDIO

A Sleeping Giant Awakes

In the past few decades, many nations in the developing world have experienced rapid social and economic change. One such nation is China. Fifty years ago, China was recovering from civil war and just starting to modernize. Today, China is an economic powerhouse. Robert Broadfoot, managing director of Hong Kong's Political and Economic Risk Consultancy, said,

> "... I have never seen so much hope in China. The Chinese will produce much cheaper items and export them. I think that will shape the course of commerce in the coming century."

Listen to the Witness History audio to hear more about China's economic development.

◀ China's rapid development is reflected in the city of Shenzhen, where modern glass buildings tower above old, shabby houses.

Exports like toys have fueled China's economy.

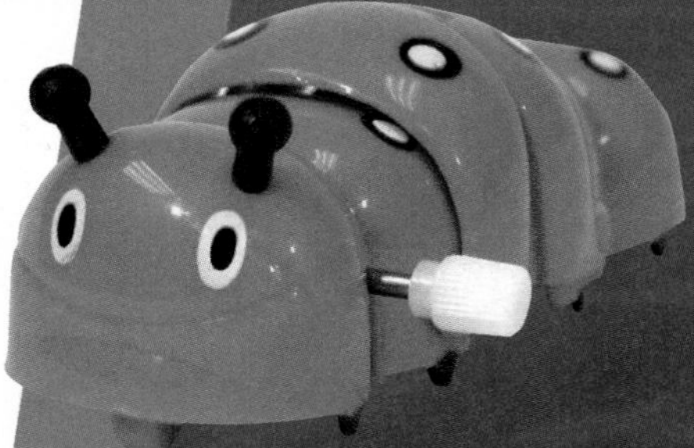

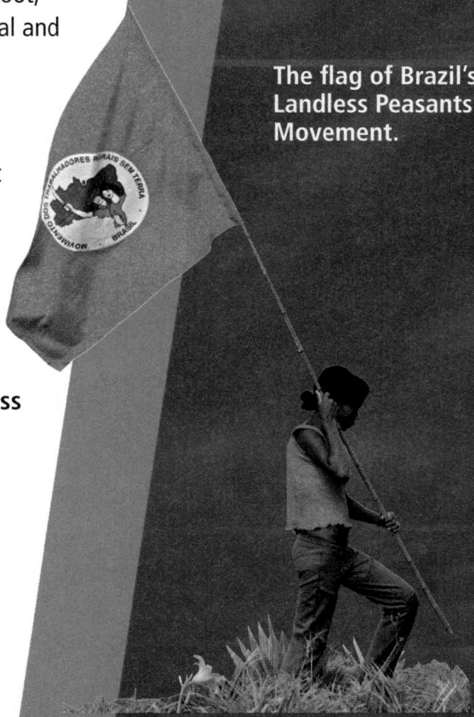

The flag of Brazil's Landless Peasants' Movement.

Chapter Preview

Chapter Focus Question **What challenges have nations of the developing world faced, and what steps have they taken to meet those challenges?**

Section 1
The Challenges of Development

Section 2
Africa Seeks a Better Future

Section 3
China and India: Two Giants of Asia

Section 4
Latin America Builds Democracy

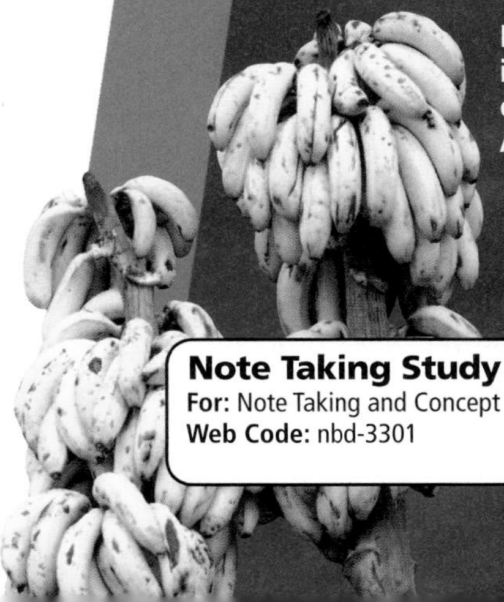

Bananas are an important cash crop in many Latin American nations.

Note Taking Study Guide *Online*
For: Note Taking and Concept Connector worksheets
Web Code: nbd-3301

A loan recipient poses with the cows she bought to help generate income.

Bangladesh's currency, the taka

WITNESS HISTORY 🔊 AUDIO

Building a Better Life

Bangladeshi Laily Begum used to sleep in a cow shed and spend her days begging. Then she got a loan for $119 from Grameen Bank, a Bangladesh-based organization that lends money to the poor. She bought a cow and began to build her own business selling milk. Today she and her husband own several shops and a restaurant.

❝ People now come to me for help . . . I can feed myself and my family, and now other people look at me and they treat me with respect. ❞
—Laily Begum, February 12, 1998

Focus Question How have the nations of the developing world tried to build better lives for their people?

The Challenges of Development

Objectives
- Understand the paths that nations in Asia, Africa, and Latin America have taken in developing strong economies.
- Describe some obstacles to development in the global South.
- Explain how development is changing patterns of life in the developing world.

Terms, People, and Places

development
developing world
literacy
traditional economies

Green Revolution
fundamentalists
shantytowns

N̲ote T̲aking

Reading Skill: Identify Supporting Details
Expand this chart to record details about development as you read.

Development		
Economic Change	Obstacles	Changes in Patterns of Life
•	•	•
•	•	•

Dozens of new nations emerged in Africa and Asia in the decades after World War II. A central goal in these regions, as well as in Latin America, was **development.** Development is the process of building a stronger and more advanced economy and creating higher living standards. The nations working toward development in Africa, Asia, and Latin America are known collectively as the **developing world.** The developing world is also known as the global South because it is mostly south of the Tropic of Cancer. Since most industrialized nations are north of the Tropic of Cancer, they are sometimes known as the global North.

Developing Strong Economies

Leaders in the developing nations aimed to improve agriculture and industry. They built railroads, highways, and huge dams to produce electricity. Since a strong economy requires well-trained workers, developing nations built schools to increase **literacy,** or the ability to read and write.

Transforming Economies For centuries, most people in Asia, Latin America, and Africa had lived and worked in **traditional economies.** These are economies that rely on habit, custom, or tradition and tend not to change over time. In traditional economies, property is often owned in common by a family or a tribe.

Traditions, or customs—rather than a central government—limit freedom of enterprise, or the freedom producers have to make business decisions. Traditions also limit competition and the range of choices for consumers. In traditional economies, most people are farmers or craftspeople who make or grow only enough to meet local needs, using simple methods passed down from earlier generations.

European colonists had introduced market economies to these regions to promote the sale of European products. After independence, some political leaders tried to speed development by replacing market and traditional economies with government-led command economies. This meant that governments owned businesses and controlled farming.

To pay for development, many countries <u>procured</u> large loans from banks and governments in the global North. They then had trouble paying off their loans. Since the 1980s, lenders from the global North have required many countries to sell off government businesses and to pursue development as market economies. Lenders have required developing countries to make these changes so that they could pay off their loans.

After developing countries shifted to market economies, companies and individuals from the global North invested in industries in developing countries. When people invest money, they put their money into something that will produce income for them. These investors have financed industries in developing nations that export consumer goods to the industrialized world.

Vocabulary Builder

procure—(proh KYOOR) *v.* obtain, make an effort to get

The Global North and Global South

Geography *Interactive*
For: Audio guided tour
Web Code: nbp-3311

Map Skills The developed countries are also known as the global North, while the developing countries are known as the global South.

1. **Locate** (a) Brazil (b) India (c) Japan
2. **Regions** Which continents lie partly within both the global North and the global South?

3. **Make Comparisons** Based on the graph, how does the standard of living of nations in the global North compare with that in the global South?

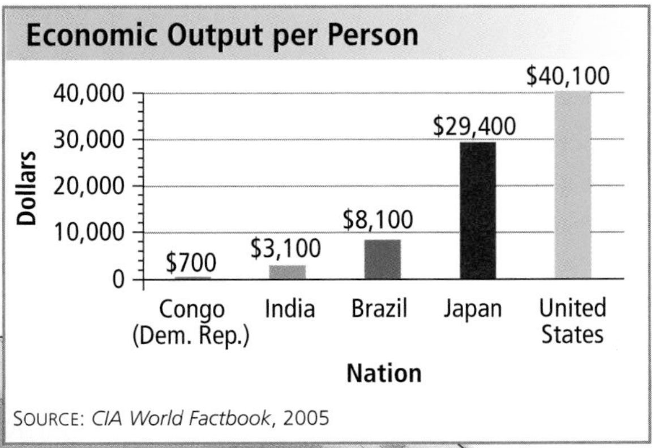

Economic Output per Person

SOURCE: *CIA World Factbook*, 2005

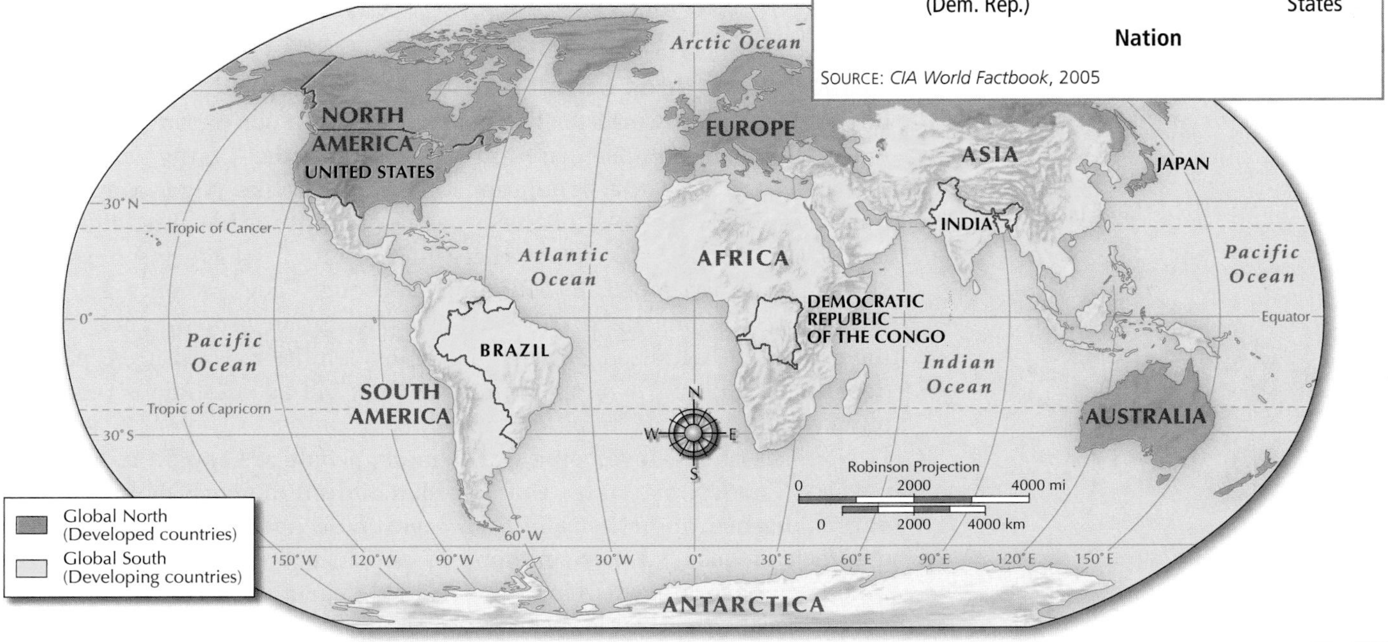

Global North (Developed countries)
Global South (Developing countries)

The Green Revolution Beginning in the 1950s, commercially improved seeds, pesticides, and mechanical equipment such as tractors were introduced in many parts of the developing world. These new products involved new farming methods. Together these products and methods are known as the **Green Revolution.** The Green Revolution increased agricultural production in countries such as India and Brazil, feeding many more people. However, only the big landowners could afford these new tools and methods. Because they farmed more land, they could also grow crops more cheaply than those who still farmed on small plots in traditional ways. As a result, prices for crops dropped below what smaller farmers needed to be paid to make a living. Many were forced to sell their farms to big landowners and move to cities.

✔ **Checkpoint** Why did foreign lenders push developing nations to adopt market economies?

Obstacles to Development

Despite loans from the developed world and improvements brought by the Green Revolution, most nations in the global South have faced many challenges to development. Most have found it difficult to escape poverty and the problems associated with it.

Rising Populations Strain Resources Population has grown rapidly in the developing world for the past 100 years. Poor parents often have many children because children can provide the family with added income. Each year the populations of countries like Nigeria and India increase by millions. All of these people need food, housing, education, jobs, and healthcare. Meeting these needs puts a staggering burden on governments strapped for funding. Although governments in many developing nations have tried to slow population growth, their efforts have met with limited success. In many traditional cultures, parents depend on children to support them in their old age. Religious teachings often encourage large families as well.

Now, across the developing world, many people are caught in a cycle of poverty. The UN estimates that 35,000 children die each day from starvation, disease, and other effects of poverty. Because of malnutrition and the lack of good schools, millions of people are prone to disease and unable to earn a good living. They and their children remain poor and cannot escape this tragic cycle.

Depending on Child Labor In traditional farming societies, families depend on children to work on the farm. When people are forced off their farms, they often move to the cities and take low-paying manufacturing jobs. Because they do not make enough money in these jobs to buy what they need, parents must also depend on their children's wages to survive. In India today, around 44 million children work for pay. In Pakistan, children make up 10 percent of the workforce.

Economic Dependence Despite their efforts to build industry, many developing nations continue to rely on their former colonial rulers or other industrialized nations for technology and manufactured goods. Also, some developing nations produce only one main export crop or commodity, such as sugar, cocoa, or copper. Their economies depend on global prices for that one product. If prices drop, these economies suffer.

Because they are poor, developing nations also rely on the wealth of industrialized nations for investment. For example, a developing nation with oil deposits might not have enough money to build its own oil wells and pipelines. So it might turn to a foreign oil company to build these things. In return, the foreign oil company would get some of the income from that oil.

✔ **Checkpoint** What factors trap people in the developing world in a cycle of poverty?

Patterns of Life Change

Economic development has unleashed great changes across the developing world. Just as the Industrial Revolution disrupted traditional ways of life in Europe and North America, economic development is now transforming life in the global South.

Women's Roles Evolve Across the developing world, the move away from traditional ways of life has brought new opportunities for women. New constitutions have spelled out equality for women, at least on paper. In some countries, women like Sri Lanka's president Chandrika Kumaratunga (chahn DREE kuh koo mahr uh TOON guh) have become political leaders. Although women are still less likely than men to have a good education, the gap has narrowed. Women are entering the workforce in growing numbers and contributing their skills to their nations' wealth.

Different Kinds of Labor
A combine harvester cuts rice stalks in Suriname, while women in Senegal prepare the fields by hand for the coming rain. *Which group of farmers is likely to get the highest yield on its crops?*

Religion Influences Societies In recent times, religious revivals have swept many developing regions. Some religious leaders are called **fundamentalists** because they call for a return to what they see as the fundamental, or basic, values of their faiths. Many have sought political power to oppose changes that they think are undermining their valued religious traditions.

Cities Rapidly Grow In African, Asian, and Latin American nations, people have flooded into cities such as São Paulo, Brazil, and Mumbai, India, to find jobs and escape rural poverty. Besides economic opportunities, cities offer attractions such as stores, concerts, and sports. However, with no money and few jobs, newcomers must often settle in **shantytowns.** These slums of flimsy shacks are as crowded and dangerous as the slums of Europe and North America were in the 1800s and early 1900s. They lack basic services, such as running water, electricity, or sewers. Drugs and crime are constant threats.

✓ **Checkpoint** Why have people moving to cities had to settle in shantytowns?

Mumbai: A Divided City
In Mumbai, India, a poor slum contrasts sharply with an affluent suburb. *Why might slums be a particular problem for large, developing cities?*

Progress Monitoring *Online*
For: Self-quiz with vocabulary practice
Web Code: nba-3311

SECTION 1 Assessment

Terms, People, and Places

1. For each term, person, or place listed at the beginning of the section, write a sentence explaining its significance.

Note Taking

2. **Reading Skill: Identify Supporting Details** Use your completed chart to answer the Focus Question: How have the nations of the developing world tried to build better lives for their people?

Comprehension and Critical Thinking

3. **Summarize** In general, what are the economic goals of developing nations?
4. **Categorize** What are the differences between the global North and the global South?
5. **Identify Central Issues** Why do developing countries remain dependent on former colonial powers or other industrialized countries?
6. **Predict Consequences** How might modern products and technologies weaken traditional cultures?

● **Writing About History**

Quick Write: Explore a Topic Choose one challenge facing developing nations and write a series of questions you could use to direct research on the topic. For example, on the topic of industrialization in developing nations you could ask:
- Which five developing nations have the highest level of industrialization today?
- What industries do these nations engage in?

Democracy

How has the practice of democracy developed over time?

The American Revolution led to the establishment of a nation based on the principle of democracy, or rule by the people. Later democratic revolutions in Latin America, Africa, and Asia looked back to the birth of the United States for inspiration. Even today, developing nations around the world seeking a model for democratic government often turn to the Constitution of the United States. Yet democracy developed before 1776 and before the Enlightenment ideals that so deeply influenced the American framers. Much of that early development took place in England, although history's first democracies developed in the city-states of ancient Greece.

▲ Ancient Greek orator Demosthenes gives a speech to a crowd of Athenians.

Athenian Democracy

Athens had a direct democracy. That is, all citizens—a male minority that excluded women, people not from Athens, and slaves—could take part in ruling the city-state. This new form of government was partly a reaction to earlier rule by tyrants. The men of Athens rejected submitting to a powerful central authority. Athenian democracy upheld the ideals of liberty and equality. The citizens of Athens safeguarded free speech. They believed that all citizens must be equal before the law.

▼ In the annual open-air assembly in Appenzell, Switzerland, citizens vote directly on major issues.

Magna Carta

During the Middle Ages in Europe, democracy did not exist. However, in England the king was forced to accept limits on his rule. He agreed to consult the most powerful groups in the realm before making important decisions, such as raising taxes. The Magna Carta was one of the first documents to set limits on a king's power. This agreement between King John of England and his barons, crafted in 1215, established the rights of barons. It also emphasized that the law applied to everyone, including the king.

English Bill of Rights

In 1689, one year after England's Glorious Revolution, Parliament passed a Bill of Rights. This bill restated existing laws and made it clear that the monarch must follow them. It declared that the ruler had to seek the consent of Parliament, which represented propertied English males, before taking certain actions. It also affirmed several rights of the people, including the right to petition the monarch, freedom of speech in Parliament, and freedom from excessive bail, excessive fines, and cruel punishments.

Thinking Critically

1. What motivated people in the examples above to seek democracy?
2. **Connections to Today** Using reliable online or library sources, research a recent struggle for democracy in a country such as Ukraine or Myanmar. How do recent events compare to the ones mentioned on this page?

A Nigerian child stands in front of the massive trunk of a felled ironwood tree.

WITNESS HISTORY 🔊 AUDIO

Plundering Forests at Gunpoint

In Ivory Coast, also known as Côte d'Ivoire (koht dee VWAHR), civil war has allowed armed gangs to log trees that have taken hundreds of years to grow. This is having a devastating effect on local economies. Village chief Kouadio Yao (KWAH dyoh yow) told a United Nations worker of watching a nearby grove of valuable teak trees being completely destroyed. He was helpless to save it.

66 If someone came with a gun, would you be able to stop them and demand that they pay for the trees? What I do know is that because of the conflict, we have lost everything.**99**
—Integrated Regional Information Networks (IRIN), December 23, 2004

Focus Question What challenges have African nations faced in their effort to develop their economies?

Africa Seeks a Better Future

Objectives

- Describe the choices African nations had to make as they began to develop their economies.
- Understand obstacles that African nations faced in their search for well-being.
- Analyze the challenges faced by a developing nation by taking a closer look at Tanzania.

Terms, People, and Places

socialism
desertification
urbanization

endangered species
Wangari Maathai
sustainable development

Note Taking

Reading Skill: Identify Main Ideas As you read, use a concept web to record the main ideas in this section and to note details that support those main ideas.

After World War II, the emerging nations of Africa faced many challenges. A few achieved social stability and strong economic development. However, as part of the developing world, all African nations faced challenges to the economic and social welfare of their citizens, as many still do today.

Making Economic Choices

Development means building productive economies and raising standards of living. To achieve these goals, African nations had to establish industries, build transportation systems, develop resources, increase literacy, and solve problems of rural poverty. Many had little capital to invest in such projects. As a result, they had to make difficult choices about how to run their countries.

Socialism or Capitalism Many newly independent nations chose **socialism,** a system in which the government controls parts of the economy. They hoped to end foreign influence on their economies as well as the inequalities between rich and poor. But to regulate the economy, socialist governments created large bureaucracies, which generally were inefficient.

Other nations relied on capitalism, or market economies with private ownership of property, as a path to development. These countries often had more efficient economies, but they allowed more profit to be taken out of the country by foreign owners.

Cash Crops or Food In the early years, governments sought to increase earnings that could fund development by growing cash crops for export, such as coffee or cotton. But land used for export crops could not be used to produce food crops. As a result, countries that had once been able to feed their own people now had to import food. This was costly. Also, many nations became dependent on a single crop, such as coffee, which put their economies at the mercy of abrupt changes in the market.

Meanwhile, many governments kept food prices artificially low to prevent unrest among the urban poor. Low prices, however, discouraged local farmers from growing food crops. Governments then had to <u>subsidize</u> part of the cost of importing food from overseas.

✓ **Checkpoint** Why did governments promote the growth of cash crops?

Vocabulary Builder
<u>subsidize</u>—(SUB suh dyz) *v.* support with government spending

Facing Obstacles to Well-Being

Developing African nations faced many challenges to well-being. These included rapid population growth, disease, the migration of people from rural areas to cities, and damage to the environment and wildlife.

Drought Brings Starvation In the late 1900s, long droughts contributed to famine in parts of Africa. Livestock died, and farmland turned to dust. The Sahel, a semi-desert region just south of the Sahara, was especially hard hit. There, overgrazing and farming removed topsoil and sped up **desertification,** or a change from fertile land to desert. The loss of so much farmland and pasture led to famine. Food shortages continued despite huge international relief efforts.

Displaced by Drought
A Sudanese mother and children escape famine caused by years of drought. *How can geography affect migration patterns?*

AIDS Kills Millions Since the 1980s, the devastating disease AIDS (Acquired Immune Deficiency Syndrome) has taken a heavy toll on Africa's people. AIDS is caused by a deadly virus commonly called HIV. HIV damages the body's ability to fight off infections.

AIDS spread rapidly across Africa. In nations such as South Africa and Botswana, up to one third of adults were infected with HIV. In the early 2000s, the UN estimated that more than 2 million Africans died of the disease each year. Their deaths left millions of orphaned children. The loss of so many skilled and productive workers also damaged many countries' economies.

People Move to Cities Africa is the most rural continent, but it has a very high rate of **urbanization,** or movement of people from rural areas to cities. This shift has meant hardship for many. However, in much of West Africa, the growth of cities has benefited women. Historically, West African women dominated urban markets as traders. The growth of urban markets increased opportunities for these women. Urbanization also brought people from different ethnic groups together in cities and helped to replace ethnic loyalties with a larger national identity. However, modern urban lifestyles weakened traditional cultures and undermined ethnic and kinship ties. Many educated Africans took pride in those traditions. Yet young urban dwellers often scorned traditional ways.

711

ENDANGERED SPECIES

The threats to Africa's endangered species include a loss of habitats and poaching, or illegal hunting. The map below shows that most of Africa's forests have been disturbed or cut down. However, Africans have taken steps to save their rich wildlife. Earnings from tourism have given local people a stake in saving these animals' lives.

► Elephants have been killed for their valuable tusks.

▲ Foreign demand for leopard skins has encouraged illegal killing of leopards.

▲ Africa's wildlife draw foreign tourists, who provide a steady income to local guides and tour operators. This gives Africans a stake in preventing poaching.

◄ African nations have set aside preserves to protect endangered species such as these mountain gorillas in Rwanda.

Undisturbed forest
Disturbed forest
Formerly forested land

Miller Projection

0   1000 mi
0   1000 km

N
W   E
S

Thinking Critically

1. **Draw Conclusions** Based on the map at the right, how have changes in Africa's forest cover affected its forest species?
2. **Synthesize Information** How might wildlife tourism discourage poaching in Africa?

Facing Environmental Threats Urbanization, farming, and logging have devoured nearly 70 percent of Africa's animal habitats. Destroyed habitats have caused many kinds of animals to become **endangered species,** or species threatened with extinction. Other animals are being killed off. Foreign demand for elephant tusks to make ivory, for example, or for rare pelts, or furs, has encouraged impoverished Africans to kill endangered animals, even when laws make this illegal.

In Kenya, an environmental activist named **Wangari Maathai** (mah THY) challenged government policy by starting the Green Belt Movement. She worked with local women on projects of **sustainable development.** This is economic development that aims to provide lasting well-being for future generations rather than short-term gains.

✓ **Checkpoint** What are some advantages and disadvantages of urbanization in Africa?

Tanzania: A Closer Look

Tanzania has been very poor since it gained independence in the early 1960s. Fifty percent of its population lives below the poverty line. This means that half of Tanzanians do not make enough money to meet their basic needs. In 2003, the per capita income was estimated at $290 per year.

When the country gained independence, most Tanzanians were farmers or herders. To improve life, the new government embraced what was called "African socialism." This was based on African village traditions of cooperation and shared responsibility. The government took over banks and businesses. Farmers were encouraged to move to large villages and farm the land collectively. The goal was to increase output and sell surplus crops to towns or for export.

The government's experiment failed, partly because farmers refused to leave their land. Farm output did not rise. This experiment also resulted in a huge and inefficient government bureaucracy. The expense of this huge bureaucracy and high oil prices plunged Tanzania into debt. In 1985, new leaders introduced economic reforms, including cutting the size of government, promoting a market economy, and encouraging foreign investment.

Today, Tanzania remains overwhelmingly agricultural. About nine tenths of Tanzanian workers work in agriculture. Over half of Tanzania's GDP comes from agriculture. The government continues to make attempts to develop a more profitable, mixed economy. However, the country has had to rely on loans from international lenders to avoid economic crisis.

Although Tanzania remains poor, its economy also received a boost in the early 2000s from the opening of a huge new gold mine. The government planned to use profits from gold, along with foreign aid, to reduce poverty and improve services such as clean water, schools, and healthcare.

✓ **Checkpoint** What economic experiments did Tanzania try after independence, and why?

BIOGRAPHY

Wangari Maathai

While working with a women's rights group, Kenyan activist Wangari Maathai (born in 1940) came up with the idea of getting ordinary women involved in tree-planting projects. In 1977, she launched the Green Belt Movement (GBM). This grassroots organization promotes reforestation and controlled wood cutting to ensure a sustainable supply of wood fuel. The group also sought jobs for women in Kenya, Tanzania, and other East African countries. In 2004, Maathai became the first African woman to be awarded the Nobel Peace Prize. Today, Maathai continues to work with the GBM. She is also a member of Kenya's government. **In what ways might planting trees help improve women's lives?**

SECTION 2 Assessment

Terms, People, and Places

1. For each term or person listed at the beginning of the section, write a sentence explaining its significance.

Note Taking

2. **Reading Skill: Identify Main Ideas** Use your completed concept web to answer the Focus Question: What challenges have African nations faced in their effort to develop their economies?

Comprehension and Critical Thinking

3. **Summarize** What obstacles kept many African nations from developing strong economies?

4. **Synthesize Information** Why have African nations had trouble feeding their people?

5. **Draw Inferences** Urbanization is a problem for many developing nations. Why do you think this is?

6. **Summarize** Why did Tanzania's economic reforms fail?

● Writing About History

Quick Write: Gather Information Review the material in this section on social issues in Africa. For each problem, list the causes, the effects, and any actions that have been taken to solve that problem.

A man tries to stop a line of tanks heading into the crowd of protesters in Tiananmen Square (top). Protesters erect a statue of the goddess of democracy in front of a poster of Mao (right).

WITNESS HISTORY ◀)) AUDIO

A Violent Crackdown

By the late 1980s, many Chinese citizens were protesting for more political freedom. Cheng Zhen, a student at the time, describes what she saw in Beijing's Tiananmen (tyen ahn mun) Square on the night of June 4, 1989.

66 [A]t about 2 A.M. we . . . could see that the troops were already in the square, and we quickly ran to the other side. . . . While I was running, I noticed a young man ahead of me. He picked up a bottle on the ground, and was about to throw it at the troops, angry because they were holding up their guns and firing. Suddenly, he fell to the ground. . . . He was shot. . . . 99
—BBC News Online, June 2, 2004

Focus Question How do China and India compare in building strong economies and democratic governments?

China and India: Two Giants of Asia

Objectives

- Analyze how China has reformed its economy but limited freedom.
- Describe the continuing challenges that China faces.
- Understand how India has faced poverty but built a stronger economy.
- Explain important Indian social reforms.

Terms, People, and Places

Deng Xiaoping	Mumbai
Tiananmen Square	Mother Teresa
one-child policy	dalits
Kolkata	

Note Taking

Reading Skill: Identify Main Ideas As you read, make a table like this one to record the main ideas.

Reform and Change in China and India		
Type	China	India
Economic	• Free market •	
Political		

China and India are home to two-fifths of the world's people. These two giant nations dominate Asia economically, too. Today, China is a major industrial nation. While India's economy is smaller, it is a leading power in Asia and in the world. In the last 60 years, both nations have faced challenges to economic development. They have addressed some of these, while others remain unresolved.

China Reforms Its Economy But Limits Freedom

As you have read, Chinese leader Mao Zedong died in 1976. After Mao's death, more moderate leaders took control of China. By 1981, **Deng Xiaoping** (dung show ping) had set China on a new path. Deng was a practical reformer, more interested in improving the economy than in political purity. "I don't care if a cat is black or white," he declared, "as long as it catches mice."

Modernizing the Economy Deng's program, the Four Modernizations, emphasized agriculture, industry, science, and defense. The plan allowed some features of a free market, such as some private ownership of property. Communes, or collectively owned farms, were also dismantled, and peasant families were allotted plots of farmland in what was called the "responsibility system." Farmers still did not own the land, and the government took a share of their crops. However, farmers could sell any surplus produce and keep their profits. Chinese entrepreneurs were allowed to set up businesses, too. Managers of state-run factories were given more freedom, but were expected to make their plants more efficient. Deng also welcomed foreign capital and technology. Investors from Japan, Hong Kong, Taiwan, and Western nations invested heavily in Chinese firms.

These economic reforms brought a surge of growth. In coastal cities, foreign investment created an economic boom. Some Chinese enjoyed an improved standard of living. They bought televisions, refrigerators, and cars. On the other hand, crime and corruption grew, and a growing economic and regional gap developed between poor rural farmers—mainly in China's interior—and wealthy city dwellers.

Vocabulary Builder
disperse—(dih SPURS) *v.* break up and scatter

Communists Crack Down Economic reforms and more contact with the West led some Chinese to demand greater political freedom. In the late 1980s Chinese students, workers, and others supported a democracy movement like those that were then sweeping Eastern Europe. However, Deng and other Communist leaders refused to allow democratic reforms.

In May of 1989, thousands of demonstrators, many of them students, occupied **Tiananmen Square** (tyen ahn mun skwehr), a huge public plaza at the center of China's capital, Beijing. They raised banners calling for democracy. The demonstrators refused to <u>disperse</u>, and after several days the government sent in troops and tanks. Thousands of demonstrators were killed or wounded in what became known as the Tiananmen Square Massacre. Many others were arrested and tortured. The crackdown showed that China's Communist leaders were afraid of losing control. To them, order was more important than political freedom.

✔ **Checkpoint** Which group did the economic reforms in China benefit most?

China Faces Continuing Challenges

Almost 30 years of economic reforms helped quadruple China's economic output. By some measures, as of the mid-2000s its economy was the world's second largest after that of the United States. However, even as China's economy strengthened, the nation faced many internal challenges.

Limiting a Huge Population China's population, now more than 1.3 billion, is the largest in the world. In the 1980s, the government's **one-child policy,** which limited urban families to a single child, aimed to keep population growth from hurting economic development. Rural families were allowed two children. However, these measures worked better in urban areas than in rural areas. Rural families who wanted more than two children to help on the farm often just paid fines. Even so, population growth slowed overall after 1980.

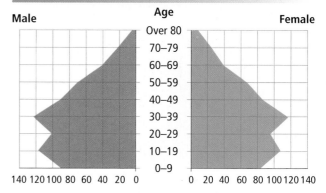

China, Estimated Population by Age and Gender, 2005

Male	Age	Female
	Over 80	
	70–79	
	60–69	
	50–59	
	40–49	
	30–39	
	20–29	
	10–19	
	0–9	

140 120 100 80 60 40 20 0   0 20 40 60 80 100 120 140

Population (in millions)

Graph Skills China's population growth has slowed in recent years due to government efforts like the one-child policy, encouraged in the billboard below. *According to the graph, in what age groups is most of China's population concentrated? What might this mean for China's future?*

SOURCE: U.S. Census Bureau, International Data Base

一对夫妇只生一个孩子

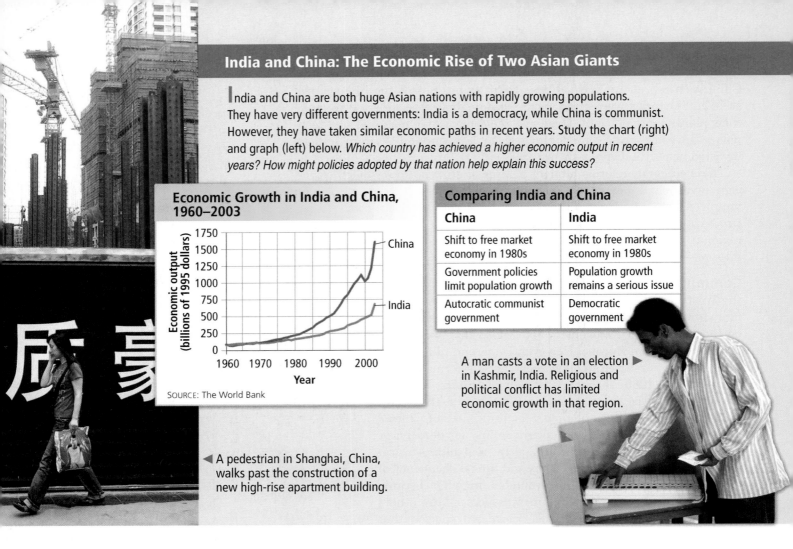

India and China: The Economic Rise of Two Asian Giants

India and China are both huge Asian nations with rapidly growing populations. They have very different governments: India is a democracy, while China is communist. However, they have taken similar economic paths in recent years. Study the chart (right) and graph (left) below. *Which country has achieved a higher economic output in recent years? How might policies adopted by that nation help explain this success?*

Economic Growth in India and China, 1960–2003

SOURCE: The World Bank

Comparing India and China

China	India
Shift to free market economy in 1980s	Shift to free market economy in 1980s
Government policies limit population growth	Population growth remains a serious issue
Autocratic communist government	Democratic government

A man casts a vote in an election in Kashmir, India. Religious and political conflict has limited economic growth in that region. ▶

◀ A pedestrian in Shanghai, China, walks past the construction of a new high-rise apartment building.

Economic Growth Brings New Problems Many state-run industries in China were unprofitable. While it sold off some of these industries, the government hesitated to do away with others, fearing high unemployment. Rapid urbanization occurred as millions of rural workers flocked to the cities. Urban newcomers lived in poverty and strained limited resources, while government officials favored wealthy people with connections. Finally, economic growth led to severely polluted air and water, causing illness and death. Growing travel and trade helped to spread AIDS across China, and it became a serious new health problem.

Human Rights Suffer Despite economic reforms, the Communist Party continued to jail critics and reject calls for political reform. Human-rights activists inside and outside China focused on many abuses, especially as China prepared to host the 2008 Olympics. They pointed to issues like the lack of free speech and the use of prison labor to produce cheap export goods. Critics denounced China's suppression of Tibet's ancient Buddhist culture. China's trading partners pressured China to end these kinds of abuses. Party leaders responded that outsiders had no right to try to impose "Western-style" ideas of human rights on the non-Western cultures of China or Tibet.

✔ **Checkpoint** How did the Chinese government respond to political criticism?

India Builds Its Economy

Like China, upon its independence in 1947 India was a large, poor nation embarking on a path of economic development. With a population of around 1.1 billion, India is the world's largest democracy.

Agriculture and Industry Expand Like other developing nations, India set out to use modern technology to expand agriculture and industry. The government adopted elements of a command economy, using five-year plans to set economic goals and manage resources. Development, however, was uneven. While it developed some industries, India lacked oil and natural gas, key resources for economic growth. Instead, it had to rely on costly imported oil.

Seeking to increase food production, Nehru promoted the Green Revolution in the late 1960s. New seeds, chemical fertilizers, and irrigation methods improved crop output. Still, only farmers with enough land and money could afford these things. Most farmers continued to use traditional methods, relying on the seasonal rains for water. They produced barely enough to survive.

Beginning in the 1980s, India shifted toward more of a free-market system. It privatized some industries and eased some restrictions on foreign investment. By the 1990s, Indian textiles, technology, and other industries were expanding rapidly. Meanwhile, Indian companies began to sell publishing, computer, and customer-support services to the rest of the world.

Combating Population Growth and Poverty As in other poor countries, India's population growth hurt efforts to improve living conditions. While food output has risen, so has demand. More than one-third of Indians live below the poverty line, unable to meet their basic needs for food, clothing, and shelter. Growing populations put added pressure on India's healthcare system, which faced additional challenges after 1990 from the spread of AIDS.

India's population boom and the labor-saving methods of the Green Revolution resulted in millions of rural families migrating to cities. But

Bangalore: A Customer Support Center
Workers in Bangalore, India, serve as customer service operators for American and European companies. To make callers feel more comfortable, the operators are trained in English and American slang. *How do you expect the customer service industry to change as more countries develop?*

Combating Poverty
Mother Teresa worked with the poor in Calcutta, India.

overcrowded cities like **Kolkata** (or Calcutta) and **Mumbai** (or Bombay) could not provide jobs and basic services for everyone. To help the urban poor, **Mother Teresa,** a Roman Catholic nun, founded the Missionaries of Charity in Calcutta. This group provides food and medical care to thousands. Still, millions more remain in desperate need.

The Indian government backed family planning, but did not adopt the harsh policies that China did. Efforts to slow population growth had limited success. Poorer Indians, especially in rural areas, still see children as an economic resource who help work the land and care for parents in old age.

 Checkpoint How did the Green Revolution affect India's economic growth?

Reforming Indian Society

In India, as elsewhere, the spread of education and the growth of a modern economy undermined traditional patterns of life. These changes have brought improvements for India's lowest social castes and for women. Yet most Indians still live in villages and followed traditional ways.

Confronting Caste Discrimination India's constitution banned discrimination against people in the lowest caste, or **dalits.** The government set aside jobs and places in universities for them. However, prejudice and discrimination persist. Higher-caste Hindus generally receive better schooling and jobs. They also sometimes block government plans to open more jobs to dalits.

Women Make Progress Under the constitution, Indian women were granted equal rights. In the cities, well-to-do girls are educated. Some educated women have entered professions or, like Indira Gandhi, won political office. On the other hand, girls from poor families often receive little or no education. In rural areas, women are expected to do unpaid—but valuable—work in household industries or farms. However, Indian women have begun taking political action and setting up self-help organizations to improve their lives.

 Checkpoint How did the Indian government try to improve the status of dalits?

Progress Monitoring *Online*
For: Self-quiz with vocabulary practice
Web Code: nba-3331

Terms, People, and Places

1. For each term, person, or place listed at the beginning of the section, write a sentence explaining its significance.

Note Taking

2. **Reading Skill: Identify Main Ideas** Use your completed table to answer the Focus Question: How do China and India compare in building strong economies and democratic governments?

Comprehension and Critical Thinking

3. **Identify Central Issues** What obstacles to economic development does China still face?
4. **Draw Inferences** How did the Green Revolution contribute to urbanization in India?
5. **Summarize** What economic goals has the Indian government pursued and how has it met these goals?
6. **Predict Consequences** Do you think that China can continue to develop economically without making political reforms? Explain.

● **Writing About History**

Quick Write: Write a Conclusion Choose one subheading from this section—for example "Reforming Indian Society." After rereading the text under that subheading, write a conclusion that summarizes the information.

Brotherhood by Octavio Paz

▲ Octavio Paz

Mexican poet, essayist, and critic Octavio Paz (1914–1998) was one of Latin America's great modern writers. Besides enjoying enormous success as an author, he was also a diplomat. Paz held diplomatic positions in France and India, where he was exposed to different schools of literature. In France, he explored surrealism. This literary movement encouraged the expression of the irrational and freed Paz to write beyond the limits of literal meaning. In India, Paz studied Buddhism, which also influenced his work. However, even as he contributed to the global culture, Paz maintained his national identity. He thought and wrote much about Mexico, its past, and its place in the modern world. In 1990, Paz became the first Mexican writer to receive the Nobel Prize for Literature. The poem below is dedicated to the Greek scientist and geographer Ptolemy (TAHL uh mee), who wrote one of the most influential astronomy texts of the ancient world.

Brotherhood	Hermandad
Homage to Claudius Ptolemy	*Homenaje a Claudio Ptolomeo*
I am a man: little do I last	Soy hombre: duro poco
and the night is enormous.	y es enorme la noche.
But I look up:	Pero miro hacia arriba:
the stars write.	las estrellas escriben.
Unknowing I understand:	Sin entender comprendo:
I too am written,	también soy escritura
and at this very moment	y en este mismo instante
someone spells me out.	alguien me deletrea.

Thinking Critically

1. **Analyze Literature** What do you think is the meaning of the lines "I am a man: little do I last / and the night is enormous"?
2. **Draw Conclusions** Why do you think Paz chose the title "Brotherhood" for this poem?

A woman at a municipal dump in Mexico collects garbage to sell.

WITNESS HISTORY 🔊 AUDIO

A Daily Struggle

Carolina Maria de Jesus (day zhay ZOOS) faced a life of hardship in the slums of São Paulo (sow POW loh), Brazil. Like millions of other poor, rural people, she came to the city hoping to improve her life. Instead, to buy food, she spent her days combing through garbage for paper, cans, and other scraps to sell. In her diary, de Jesus described her daily struggle against poverty:

> 66 July 16 . . . I went to Senhor Manuel, carrying some cans to sell. . . . He gave me 13 [coins]. I kept thinking that I had to buy bread, soap, and milk. . . . The 13 [coins] wouldn't make it. I returned . . . to my shack, nervous and exhausted. I thought of the worrisome life that I led. Carrying paper, washing clothes for children, staying in the street all day long. 99
> —Carolina Maria de Jesus, *Child of the Dark*

Focus Question What challenges have Latin American nations faced in recent decades in their struggle for democracy and prosperity?

Latin America Builds Democracy

Objectives
- Analyze how Latin America grappled with poverty.
- Describe Latin America's difficult road to democracy.
- Understand the struggle for democracy in Argentina.

Terms, People, and Places

import substitution	Sandinista
agribusiness	contra
liberation theology	indigenous
Organization of	Juan Perón
American States	Mothers of the
(OAS)	Plaza de Mayo

Note Taking

Reading Skill: Identify Main Ideas and Supporting Details As you read this section, make an outline like the one below.

> I. Economic and Social Forces
>   A. Society
>   1.
>   2.

Latin America comprises Mexico, Central America, the Caribbean, and South America. It includes 33 independent nations, ranging from small islands, such as Grenada, to giant Brazil.

For decades, Latin American nations have faced political, economic, and social challenges similar to those of other developing nations—rapid population growth, poverty, illiteracy, political instability, and authoritarian governments.

Latin America Grapples With Poverty

From the 1950s to the 1980s, economic development failed to change deep-rooted inequalities in many Latin American countries. Due to inequality and growing populations, most countries saw little improvement in living standards.

Promoting Industry and Agriculture In Latin America, as in other developing regions, nations often relied heavily on a single cash crop or commodity to earn money for needed imports. If harvests failed or if world demand fell, their economies were hard hit.

To reduce their dependence on imported goods, many Latin American governments adopted a policy of **import substitution,** or manufacturing goods locally to replace imports. This policy, pursued mainly in the 1950s and 1960s, was a mixed success. Many of the new industries needed government help or foreign capital to survive.

Geography *Interactive*
For: Interactive map
Web Code: nbp-3341

Map Skills Latin American nations have been diversifying their economies in recent decades.

1. **Locate** **(a)** Venezuela **(b)** Nicaragua **(c)** Brazil **(d)** Haiti

2. **Region** Which region is the least diversified? What factors might explain this?

3. **Synthesize Information** Locate the areas on the map with manufacturing and trade. Are those areas likely to be near cities or countryside? Explain.

▲ Mexican men harvest tangerines, carrying baskets weighing up to 200 pounds.

UNITED STATES

Atlantic Ocean

Gulf of Mexico

BAHAMAS

Tropic of Cancer

MEXICO

CUBA

DOMINICAN REPUBLIC

U.S. Virgin Islands (U.S.)

British Virgin Islands (U.K.)

ST. KITTS AND NEVIS

ANTIGUA AND BARBUDA

20° N

HAITI

JAMAICA

BELIZE

Puerto Rico (U.S.)

Guadeloupe (Fr.)

GUATEMALA HONDURAS

Caribbean Sea

Martinique (Fr.)

DOMINICA

BARBADOS

EL SALVADOR

NICARAGUA

ST. LUCIA

ST. VINCENT & THE GRENADINES

GRENADA

COSTA RICA PANAMA

VENEZUELA

TRINIDAD AND TOBAGO

GUYANA SURINAME

French Guiana (Fr.)

COLOMBIA

ECUADOR

Equator 0°

PERU

BRAZIL

▲ A man works at an off-shore oil rig in Venezuela. Like many oil companies in Venezuela, the company he works for is foreign-owned.

Pacific Ocean

BOLIVIA

20° S

PARAGUAY

Tropic of Capricorn

CHILE

	Forestry
	Livestock raising
	Mainly commercial farming
	Mainly subsistence farming
	Manufacturing and trade
	Little or no activity
⚒	Petroleum (oil)

URUGUAY

Atlantic Ocean

ARGENTINA

Equal Area Projection

0   500   1000 mi

0   500   1000 km

40° S

120° W   100° W   80° W   60° W

Falkland Islands (U.K.)

40° W   20° W

721

FIGHTING POVERTY IN BRAZIL

More than a quarter of Brazil's population lives on less than two dollars a day. A minority controls most of the country's wealth and income. In recent years, though, better jobs and education have provided more opportunities for many Brazilians. The country's steady economic growth, shown in the graph at right, has helped make these improvements possible.

◄ In Brazil's countryside, most land is owned by a wealthy few. In this photo, members of the Landless Peasants' Movement occupy a large privately owned ranch.

To escape rural poverty, many ► Brazilians seek better-paying urban employment, such as the factory job shown here.

Latin American governments gradually gave up promoting import substitution because of its high cost. In recent decades, they have tried to generate income by promoting exports. Specifically, they have encouraged a variety of cash crops and industries that they hope will produce goods for export.

Governments have also backed efforts to open more land to farming through irrigation and the clearing of forests. Much of the best farmland belongs to **agribusinesses,** or giant commercial farms, often owned by multinational corporations. In Central America and Brazil, developers have cleared tropical rain forests for farmland. However, this practice has had environmental costs, as you will read in the next chapter.

A Gap Between the Rich and the Poor Grows A key feature of Latin America has been the uneven distribution of wealth. In many countries, a tiny elite has controlled the land, businesses, and factories. These powerful few have opposed reforms that might undermine their position. As a result, the gap between the rich and the poor has widened.

Poverty Threatens Livelihoods Latin America, like other developing regions, experienced a population explosion that contributed to poverty. Although population growth slowed in some countries during the 1990s, economies were hard pressed to keep pace with growing populations. The populations of countries like Mexico and Brazil quadrupled between 1930 and 1980. Overall, the population of Latin America surpassed 400 million in 2000.

In rural areas, population pressures made life even more difficult for farmers. Even though a family might own a small plot for growing food, most farmers worked on the estates of large landowners for low wages so that they could buy tools, building supplies, clothing, and the food that they could not grow themselves.

A shortage of land drove millions of peasants to the cities. Today, more than half of Latin Americans live in cities. Some newcomers have found jobs in factories, offices, or stores. Many more, like Carolina de Jesus, survive by odd jobs. They fill the shantytowns on the edges of Latin

WITNESS HISTORY VIDEO

Watch *Making a Living in Peru* on the **Witness History Discovery School**™ video program to learn how economic challenges affect ordinary Latin Americans.

DISCOVERY
SCHOOL

Brazilians have also escaped from poverty through education, such as this adult literacy class. ▼

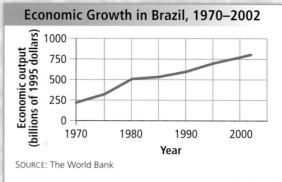

Economic Growth in Brazil, 1970–2002

SOURCE: The World Bank

Thinking Critically
1. **Make Generalizations** How did Brazil's economic output change from 1970 to 2002?
2. **Synthesize Information** How did this change help Brazilians to move out of poverty?

American cities, such as Mexico City and São Paulo. The shantytowns in those cities have become among the largest in the world.

Religions Reach Out to the Poor The Catholic Church remained a powerful force across Latin America. Although it was often tied to the ruling class, some church leaders spoke up for the poor. During the 1960s and 1970s, many priests, nuns, and church workers crusaded for social justice and an end to poverty. This movement, known as **liberation theology,** urged the church to become a force for reform. Meanwhile, evangelical Protestant groups won converts among the poor in many countries.

 Checkpoint How have Latin American governments tried to improve their economies?

The Difficult Road to Democracy

Democracy was difficult to achieve in Latin American nations plagued by poverty and inequality. From the 1950s on, many groups pressed for reforms. They included liberals, socialists, urban workers, peasants, and Catholic priests and nuns. Although they differed over how to achieve their goals, all wanted to improve conditions for the poor. Conservatives, however, resisted reforms. Conflict between conservatives and reformers contributed to political unrest in many nations.

Military Rulers Seize Power Between the 1950s and 1970s, as social unrest grew, military leaders in Argentina, Brazil, Chile, and other nations seized power. Claiming the need for order, they imposed harsh, autocratic regimes. These military rulers outlawed political parties, censored the press, and closed universities. They also imprisoned and executed thousands. "Death squads" linked to the government murdered many more. Many Latin American writers, such as Pablo Neruda of Chile and Gabriel García Márquez (gahr SEE ah MAHR kes) of Colombia, went into exile after having spoken out against autocratic regimes or social inequality.

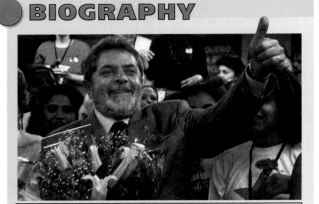

Lula da Silva

Luiz Inácio Lula da Silva is a true self-made person. He was born in 1945 into a poor family, the seventh of eight children. As a small boy, Lula attended school, but by the age of seven he was already working part-time as a street vendor to help his parents provide for the family. At age 14, Lula left school for good and took a full-time factory job. Ambitious and intelligent, Lula took courses to improve his skills, qualifying him for better jobs. As he worked his way up in the company, Lula also became involved in workers' rights issues. In 1980, he and others started the Workers' Party, which became a major political force in Brazil. The party included workers, intellectuals, social activists, and religious leaders. As democracy came to Brazil, Lula was elected to various posts, including federal deputy of the state of São Paulo. He then ran for president three times. In 2002, in a fourth campaign, the former penniless street child's perseverance paid off when he was finally elected president of South America's largest nation. **How does Lula's life illustrate both the problems and successes of development in Brazil?**

Threatening Revolution During this time, guerrillas and urban terrorists battled repressive governments across much of Latin America. Some were responding to the call to revolution by Cuba's Fidel Castro. They believed that only communism could end inequalities. Other rebels were nationalists who opposed economic and cultural domination by the United States.

Cold War fears about the spread of Marxism complicated moderate reform efforts. Many conservatives saw any call for reform as a communist threat. Conservative groups were often supported by the United States, which often put them, or kept them, in power.

Links With the United States Politically, a fact of life for Latin Americans has been the looming presence of the United States. An economic and military giant, it has dominated the **Organization of American States (OAS),** a group formed in 1948 to promote democracy, economic cooperation, and human rights in the region. United States influence also remained powerful within individual Latin American states. Today, Latin America and the United States are still closely linked. The United States is the region's most important investor and trading partner.

Despite these links, the United States and its Latin American neighbors view each other very differently. The United States sees itself as the defender of democracy and free markets in the region and a provider of much-needed aid. Meanwhile, many people in Latin America both admire the wealth of the United States and resent what they see as its military, economic, and cultural domination.

In 1977, the United States signed treaties agreeing to turn over control of the Panama Canal to Panama in 2000. While the turnover raised concerns in the United States, Latin American countries welcomed it as a sign of respect for Panama's independence.

The United States Intervenes Militarily During the Cold War, the United States backed anti-communist dictators in Latin America. On occasion, it intervened militarily—sending military equipment, supplies, and trainers—to stop the spread of communism.

In 1954, the United States helped to overthrow Guatemala's democratically elected, but Communist-influenced government. In 1961, President John F. Kennedy's administration supported the Bay of Pigs invasion against Castro, and ever since, the United States has imposed economic sanctions on Cuba. In 1973, the United States secretly backed the military coup that toppled Chile's newly elected socialist president, Salvador Allende (ah YEN day), putting military dictator Augusto Pinochet (pee noh SHAY) in power.

In 1979, Nicaragua's **Sandinistas,** a movement of socialist rebels, toppled the ruling Somoza family. The Sandinistas introduced land reform and tried to redistribute wealth to the country's poor. Claiming that Nicaragua could become "another Cuba," United States President Ronald Reagan backed the **contras,** guerrillas who fought the Sandinistas. Fighting raged on until a 1990 compromise brought peace and multiparty elections to the country.

Waging War on Drugs Cold War concerns were not the only reason for U.S. military interventions. As illegal drug use grew in the United States, the U.S. government declared a "war on drugs" in the 1980s. In 1989, U.S. forces invaded Panama and arrested its president, Manuel Noriega (mahn WAYL noh ree AY guh), for drug trafficking. Later, he was tried and convicted.

The United States also tried to stop illegal drugs from being smuggled north from Colombia, Peru, Bolivia, and elsewhere. The United States pressed Latin American governments to destroy drug crops and crush the drug cartels, or criminal gangs that smuggled drugs. Governments cooperated, but critics in Latin America <u>alleged</u> that the main problem was the demand for illegal drugs in the United States. Despite efforts to stop the drug trade, drug lords bribed government officials. They also hired assassins to kill judges, journalists, and others who worked against them.

Vocabulary Builder

<u>allege</u>—(uh LEJ)
v. assert, charge, claim

Civil Wars Shake Central America In Central America, revolutionaries battled authoritarian governments in several civil wars. From the 1960s into the 1990s, rebels in Guatemala fought a series of military regimes. Guatemala's military responded savagely. They especially targeted Guatemala's **indigenous,** or native, population, slaughtering tens of thousands of Native Americans.

In the 1970s and 1980s, reformers and revolutionaries challenged El Salvador's landowning and military elite. One reformer, Archbishop Oscar Romero, preached liberation theology until he was assassinated in 1980. A brutal civil war shook El Salvador until the rebels and military agreed to a UN-brokered peace in 1991. With massive aid from outside, El Salvador's fragile democracy survived.

Latin America Moves Toward Democracy

By the 1990s, pressure from democracy activists and foreign lenders had led most military rulers to restore democracy. Argentina, Brazil, Chile, and other countries held free elections. The United States used economic pressure and the threat of military action to restore Haiti's elected president to office.

A Vote for Democracy
Vicente Fox, standing with his daughter, is inaugurated as president in 2000 (bottom). A boy stands next to an anti-PRI sign in Chiapas, Mexico (top). *What effect might Fox's election have on the participation of young people in Mexican politics?*

In Mexico, which had escaped military rule, pressure grew for political reform. There, a single party—the Institutional Revolutionary Party (PRI)—had dominated the government since the 1920s. It claimed to represent all groups in Mexican society. In reality, however, PRI bosses moved forcefully against any serious opposition.

Under pressure, the PRI made some reforms in the 1990s. Stung by corruption, drug scandals, and internal splits, it lost much support. In 2000, an opposition candidate, Vicente Fox, was elected president, ending the PRI's long grip on power. Fox pushed to end corruption, reduce poverty, and spur economic growth. He also worked to protect the rights of indigenous people.

✓ **Checkpoint** What obstacles have stood in the way of democracy in Latin America?

Struggling for Democracy in Argentina

In the early 1900s, Argentina had a stable government run by a wealthy elite. It enjoyed a robust economy, based on exports of beef and grain. As the most prosperous country in Latin America, it attracted millions of immigrants. Then in the 1930s the Great Depression struck, followed by 50 years of political and economic upheavals.

Protesting the Military
The Mothers of the Plaza de Mayo protest government policies in 1985 (right) and 2002 (below).

Between 1946 and 1955, nationalist president **Juan Perón** (pay ROHN) enjoyed great support from workers. He increased the government's economic role. He raised wages and backed labor unions. However, Perón's government suppressed opposition. Many educated people fled the country. His policies led to economic troubles, and Perón was ousted in a military coup in 1955. The military was in and out of power for the next 20 years. Perón was again elected president in 1973.

When he died a year later, however, a new wave of political unrest plunged Argentina into political chaos. The military again seized control in 1976. Opposed by leftist guerrillas, the military waged a "dirty war" of torture and murder against its own citizens. As many as 20,000 people were kidnapped by the government and disappeared. Week after week, in the Plaza de Mayo, a central plaza in Buenos Aires, the Argentine capital, women marched silently holding pictures of their missing sons and daughters. These women became known as the **Mothers of the Plaza de Mayo.**

By 1983, failed policies and a lost war with Britain over the Falkland Islands forced the military to restore civilian rule and allow elections. A financial crisis in 2001 devastated Argentina's economy and brought widespread poverty. However, Argentina's democracy survived this crisis, and its economy recovered rapidly after 2003.

✓ **Checkpoint** What role did Argentina's military play in the struggle for democracy?

SECTION 4 Assessment

Progress Monitoring *Online*
For: Self-quiz with vocabulary practice
Web Code: nba-3341

Terms, People, and Places

1. For each term or person listed at the beginning of the section, write a sentence explaining its significance.

Note Taking

2. Reading Skill: Identify Main Ideas and Supporting Details Use your completed outline to answer the Focus Question: What challenges have Latin American nations faced in recent decades in their struggle for democracy and prosperity?

Comprehension and Critical Thinking

3. Draw Conclusions How has U.S. involvement in Latin America both helped and hurt the region?

4. Analyze Information Explain the impact of social inequality on politics in Argentina.

5. Make Inferences What do you think was the appeal of liberation theology to people in Latin American nations?

● Writing About History

Quick Write: Develop a Working Thesis and Choose Supporting Information Reread the information in this section or review your outline. Then develop a thesis statement that expresses what you think is the main idea of this section. Locate details within the text that support your thesis statement. Evaluate your thesis to be sure that the details support it, and if not, revise it accordingly.

Mario Vargas Llosa:
Latin America—The Democratic Option

In this speech delivered in 1987, Peruvian novelist, playwright, and journalist Mario Vargas Llosa (BAHR gahs YOH sah) (born 1936) discussed the state of democracy in Latin America. He also described the changes that he believed were needed to maintain and extend that democracy.

The democratization of Latin America, even though it has today an unprecedented[1] popular base, is very fragile. To maintain and extend this popular base, governments will have to prove to their citizens that democracy means not only the end of political brutality but progress—concrete benefits in areas such as labor, health, and education, where so much remains to be done. But, given Latin America's current economic crisis, when the prices of its exports are hitting record lows and the weight of its foreign debt is crushing, those governments have virtually no alternative but to demand that their citizens—especially the poor—make even greater sacrifices than they've already made. . . .

A realistic and ethically sound approach that our creditors could take would be to demand that each debtor nation pay what it can without placing its stability in jeopardy. . . .

If we want democracy to take hold in our countries, our most urgent task is to broaden it, give it substance and truth. Democracy is fragile in so many countries because it is superficial[2], a mere framework within which institutions and political parties go about their business in their traditionally arbitrary, bullying way. . . .

Perhaps the hardest struggle we Latin Americans will have will be against ourselves. Centuries of intolerance, of absolute truths, of despotic governments, weigh us down—and it won't be easy to shake that burden off. The tradition of absolute power that began with our pre-Columbian empires, and the tradition that might makes right that the Spanish and Portuguese explorers practiced, were perpetuated in the nineteenth century, after our independence, by our *caudillos*[3] and our oligarchies[4], often with the blessing or direct intervention of foreign powers.

▲ Mario Vargas Llosa in 1997

1. **unprecedented** (un PRES uh den tid) *adj.* new; never having happened before
2. **superficial** (soo pur FISH ul) *adj.* shallow; on the surface
3. *caudillos* (kow THEE yohs) *n. pl.* military dictators
4. **oligarchies** (AHL ih gahr keez) *n. pl.* governments run by a few powerful individuals or families

Thinking Critically
1. **Synthesize Information** According to Vargas Llosa, what currently threatens democracy in Latin America?
2. **Recognize Cause and Effect** How has Latin America's past led to the region's difficulty in maintaining democracy?

Quick Study Guide

Progress Monitoring Online
For: Self-test with vocabulary practice
Web Code: nba-3351

■ Key Problems Facing Developing Nations

- rapid population growth
- urbanization
- widespread poverty
- food shortages
- economic dependence on foreign lenders and on exports
- repressive, authoritarian governments
- diseases
- environmental damage
- poor education

■ Economic Output for Selected Developing Nations

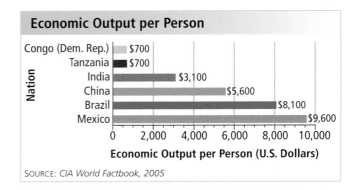

Economic Output per Person

Nation	Economic Output per Person (U.S. Dollars)
Congo (Dem. Rep.)	$700
Tanzania	$700
India	$3,100
China	$5,600
Brazil	$8,100
Mexico	$9,600

SOURCE: *CIA World Factbook, 2005*

■ Global North and Global South

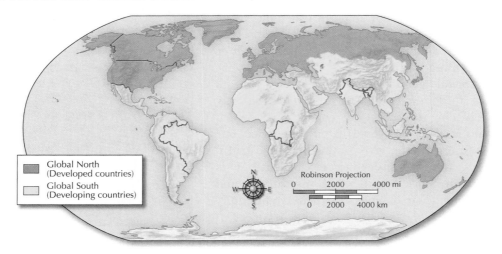

Global North
(Developed countries)

Global South
(Developing countries)

Robinson Projection

0   2000   4000 mi

0   2000   4000 km

■ Key Events in the Developing World

1950s–1960s
Green Revolution transforms agriculture.

Africa and Asia
Latin America

1945	1955	1965

1946
Juan Perón is elected president of Argentina.

1950s–1960s
Latin American countries pursue policy of import substitution.

Concept Connector

■ Cumulative Review

Use your Concept Connector worksheets and the text to help answer these questions.

1. **Economic Systems** In the early 1900s, the Soviet Union shifted from a market economy to develop as a command economy. However, in the late 1900s, the Soviet Union's command economy failed. In this chapter, you read that many developing nations attempted to develop as command economies in the middle 1900s but that this attempt largely failed. How does the experience with command economies in developing countries compare with that in the Soviet Union? Consider the role of debt and the question of efficiency.

2. **Dictatorship** Compare the events that surrounded the seizure of power by Latin American dictators to the rise of earlier dictators such as Franco, Hitler, or Mussolini. Think about the following:
   - the economic situation at the time
   - the consequences of the dictators' seizure of power

3. **Revolution** During the French Revolution, the poor and the middle classes rebelled against privileged monarchs and aristocrats. During the Russian Revolution, the Communists mobilized working people to overthrow the privileged rulers of Russia. How do recent rebellions in Latin America, for example in Guatemala or Nicaragua, compare with earlier revolutions? Consider social and economic inequalities and ideologies or belief systems.

4. **Technology** In the 1800s, nations in Europe and North America poured resources into building coal mines, factories, and railroads. Today, African nations are working to increase the number of hydroelectric plants. How do these two efforts compare? Why do you think there is such a push today for increasing the production of electricity?

■ Connections to Today

1. **Cooperation** In this chapter, you read about cooperation between the United States and the nations of Latin America. In recent years, cooperation among Latin American nations and between the United States and Latin America has spread to include economic development. Mercosur is a trade alliance among South American nations. Meanwhile, the United States has proposed trade alliances with Chile and Central American nations. Refer to online news services or other sources to learn about Latin American trade alliances today. Investigate whether cooperation in the area of trade has spread in recent years within Latin America and between Latin America and the United States.

2. **Nationalism** In this chapter, you learned that during the 1950s and 1960s many developing nations tried to decrease their economic dependence on foreign investors by developing their own industries. Then, in the 1980s and 1990s, many of these nations put more emphasis on foreign trade and investment, often under pressure from foreign lenders. However, the pendulum has begun to swing back toward economic independence. After 2000, China, Argentina, and other nations put the economic concerns of their own people ahead of those of foreign investors. Why might a nation choose a course of economic independence? Consult news sources to find out how countries that resisted foreign economic pressure have fared in recent years.

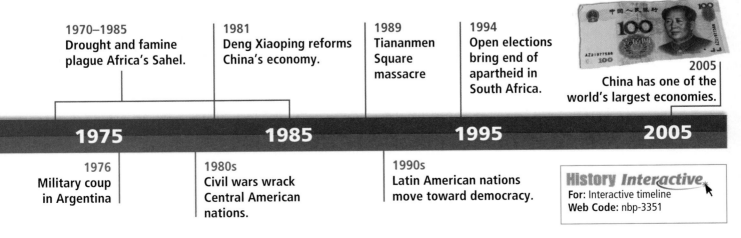

1970–1985
Drought and famine plague Africa's Sahel.

1981
Deng Xiaoping reforms China's economy.

1989
Tiananmen Square massacre

1994
Open elections bring end of apartheid in South Africa.

2005
China has one of the world's largest economies.

1975   **1985**   **1995**   **2005**

1976
Military coup in Argentina

1980s
Civil wars wrack Central American nations.

1990s
Latin American nations move toward democracy.

History Interactive,
For: Interactive timeline
Web Code: nbp-3351

Chapter Assessment

Terms, People, and Places

Complete each sentence by choosing the correct answer from the list of terms below. You will not use all the terms.

desertification
developing world
Green Revolution
liberation theology

sustainable development
Tiananmen Square
urbanization
Mumbai

1. In parts of Africa, drought and over-farming have brought about the _____ of land that was previously farmable.
2. Many Catholic clergy were part of a movement known as _____ that called for social justice and an end to poverty.
3. New nations attempting to improve their economies and achieve higher living standards are known as the _____.
4. Many poorer nations have seen rapid _____, or the movement of rural people to the cities.
5. In 1989, troops had a deadly encounter with protesters in _____.
6. The use of new technologies in the mid-1900s for improving crop production was known as the _____.

Main Ideas

Section 1 (pp. 704–708)
7. Summarize the challenges faced by most developing nations.
8. Compare and contrast the global North with the global South.

Section 2 (pp. 710–713)
9. How successful were new African nations that tried to develop by creating command economies?
10. Who is Wangari Maathai and what was her role in sustainable development efforts in Africa?

Section 3 (pp. 714–718)
11. After Mao's death, what reforms did China's government make and what reforms did they block?
12. What were the main challenges to economic growth in India?

Section 4 (pp. 720–726)
13. What role did the military play in the governments of Latin America?
14. Describe the democratic progress that was made in Mexico in 2000.

Chapter Focus Question
15. What challenges have nations of the developing world faced and what steps have they taken to meet those challenges?

Critical Thinking

16. **Synthesize Information** How has rapid population growth affected developing nations?
17. **Draw Conclusions** Which problem facing developing nations do you think is the most important one to solve? Explain your answer.
18. **Analyze Images** How does the photo of Mumbai at the end of section 1 reflect some of the challenges facing developing nations? Explain your answer.
19. **Make Inferences** Many developing nations are ruled by dictators or by one party, as in China. Does autocratic rule help or hurt economic progress? Explain.
20. **Cause and Effect** How did the Cold War affect the United States' relations with Latin American nations?

● Writing About History

Writing a Research Report As governments in the developing world struggle to grow their economies and improve the well being of their citizens, they may set policies that cause damage to the environment and threaten local plant and animal species. Write a research report in which you discuss how one developing nation you read about in this chapter is balancing economic development with environmental concerns. Consult page SH13 of the Writing Handbook for additional help.

Prewriting
• Do online or library research to read background materials about developing nations.
• Choose a developing nation and take notes on relevant details, events, and the people.

• Create a set of questions about your developing nation and gather additional resources.

Drafting
• Develop a working thesis about this nation's economic status—for example, is it succeeding or failing?
• Make an outline to organize the report. Then choose information from your research that supports each part of your outline.
• Write an introduction explaining your thesis, a body, and a conclusion.

Revising
• Use the guidelines for revising your report on page SH15 of the Writing Handbook.

Document-Based Assessment

China's Economy

China has one of the fastest-growing economies in the world. Many who once thought of China as backward now see the country as a lively economic giant. Though China's economic gains are impressive, China's critics see a dark underside, as Documents C and D illustrate.

Document A

"China's annual GDP [gross domestic product, or economic output] growth has averaged more than 8 percent in the past 25 years, and in 2003, its GDP grew by a record-breaking 9.1 percent. . . . Noting these economic achievements as well as the complete success of China's first manned space flight in 2003, Premier Wen Jiabao in his annual address to the NPC [National People's Congress] in March 2004 pointed to a national strength that has reached new heights. . . ."

—From **China Internet Information Center**, May 4, 2005

Document B

Chinese workers assemble electronic parts.

Document C

". . . China has not changed in non-economic matters . . . [T]he leadership remains deaf to democracy and human rights. Religion is on a tight leash. . . . Basic legal safeguards are non-existent in the judicial system, and prison conditions are harsh. Privacy rights are routinely violated, and the government maintains tight restrictions on freedom of speech and the press. Increased control and monitoring of the Internet has led to arrest of dissidents, and most "Netizens" practice self-censorship, or face the long arm of the law. Freedom of association and assembly are virtually non-existent. . . ."

—From **"Only China's Economy Has Changed"** in *Taipei Times*, April 29, 2005, by Robert Bedeski

Document D

"China's grim 19th century style mines—many of them little more than holes in the ground—claimed yet more lives this week. A gas explosion ripped through the Sunjiawan coal mine in the northeastern province of Liaoning on Monday, killing at least 210. . . . They were just the latest casualties in a familiar story of mining accidents, which routinely claim the lives of dozens of young miners every month. . . . Many of those who die belong to China's growing underclass. They are desperately impoverished boys and men from rural villages."

—From **The Wall Street Journal**, February 18, 2005, by Sara Davis and Mickey Spiegel

Analyzing Documents

Use your knowledge of China's economic reforms and Documents A, B, C, and D to answer questions 1–4.

1. The author of Document A is best described as a
   A harsh critic of China's economic inequality.
   B strong supporter of China's economic policies.
   C shrewd observer of China's social system.
   D half-hearted supporter of the socialist market economy.

2. What is the main point of Document C?
   A China's social progress is equal to the country's economic gains.
   B China's human rights record is poor, despite economic progress.
   C China's economic progress outweighs any human rights problems.
   D China's economic success has led a commitment to human rights.

3. Some critics of China say that China's new wealth has not been evenly shared. According to Document D, one of the groups that has been left out is
   A people from the large cities.
   B young people.
   C women.
   D males from rural villages.

4. Do the current leaders of China deserve praise or criticism? Give your opinions based on the documents on this page and information from the chapter.

A Changing World

In 2001, Mongolia's prime minister declared that "in order to survive we have to stop being nomads." His words—and his plans to settle 90% of Mongolia's people in cities by the year 2030—came as a shock to a people who have been nomadic herders for centuries. At the same time, his idea seemed inevitable. Listen to the Witness History audio to hear more about how Mongolians are struggling to modernize without losing their traditions.

◄ **A Mongolian nomadic family uses a satellite dish on their tent to feed their solar-powered television.**

Chapter Preview

Chapter Focus Question What are the major issues facing the world today?

Section 1
Industrialized Nations After the Cold War

Section 2
Globalization

Section 3
Social and Environmental Challenges

Section 4
Security in a Dangerous World

Section 5
Advances in Science and Technology

Logo for the international aid organization CARE

Euro coin

NASA seal

Note Taking Study Guide *Online*
For: Note Taking and Concept Connector worksheets
Web Code: nbd-3401

A euro coin

Turkish people hold red and blue balloons, symbolizing Europe and Turkey, to celebrate Turkey's decision to apply to the EU.

WITNESS HISTORY 🔊 AUDIO

The Nations of Europe Unite

❝Resolved to mark a new stage in the process of European integration . . . Recalling the historic importance of the ending of the division of the European continent and the need to create firm bases for the construction of the future Europe . . . Desiring to deepen the solidarity between their peoples while respecting their history, their culture, and their traditions . . . [We] have decided to establish a European Union . . .❞
—The Maastricht Treaty on the European Union, 1992

Focus Question How did the end of the Cold War affect industrialized nations and regions around the world?

Industrialized Nations After the Cold War

Objectives

- Examine social, political, and economic trends in Europe after the Cold War.
- Analyze how the United States' and Russia's shifting roles have affected the balance of global power.
- Understand how important economic changes have affected Asia since the end of the Cold War.

Terms, People, and Places

European Union	surplus
euro	deficit
default	Pacific Rim
Vladimir Putin	

Note Taking

Reading Skill: Compare and Contrast Create a chart to compare and contrast developments in industrialized nations after the Cold War.

Europe	Russia/ United States	Asia
• 1991 Germany reunified	•	•
•	•	•

The end of the Cold War saw old empires crumble and new nations emerge. It also marked the beginning of a new global economy—an economy in which economic ties among nations and international trade would become driving forces in shaping global patterns.

The New Face of Europe

With the collapse of the Soviet Union and the end of the Cold War, the division between communist Eastern Europe and democratic Western Europe crumbled. Trade, business, travel, and communications across the region became easier. At the same time, new challenges emerged. Many European nations faced common problems such as large-scale immigration from the developing world, a rise in anti-foreign discrimination, and rising unemployment, especially among the young. As a region, Europe had to forge a new path in bringing its eastern and western sides closer together.

Germany Reunifies In 1990, East and West Germany were reunited after more than 45 years of division. Unification brought great national pride and excitement—but it also brought challenges. East Germany's economy and infrastructure were weak and had to be modernized. Unemployment rose in the former East Germany with the closing of communist-era factories, which were outdated and inefficient. In 2004, U.S. President George W. Bush announced that he would withdraw tens of thousands of American troops from Germany—stationed there since World War II—prompting fears of weakening the economy.

Reunification brought social problems as well. Racist groups such as neo-Nazis, a hate group that models itself after the Nazi party, blamed immigrants for the hard times and viciously attacked foreign workers. The vast majority of Germans condemned such actions, however. At the turn of the millenium, Germany still faced economic and social challenges but remained a strong European leader.

The European Union Takes Shape Like NATO, the European Economic Community expanded over the years to add the nations of Eastern Europe. In the 1990s, the group became the **European Union** and agreed on policies to promote a freer flow of capital, labor, and goods among European nations. By the early 2000s, more than a dozen countries had joined the EU, with an increasing number of applicants coming from Eastern Europe and former Soviet republics. In 2002, the **euro** became the common currency for most of Western Europe. By then, EU passports had replaced national passports. The expanded EU allowed Europe to compete with economic superpowers like the United States and Japan.

Yet some Europeans have had mixed feelings about the changing economic and social makeup of the EU. Most of the EU's Eastern European members have weaker economies than their Western European neighbors, the result of years of communist control. Older members of the EU fear that these nations will weaken the EU's economy overall. Other Europeans worry about the changing religious demographics of the EU. Many Eastern European nations have large Muslim populations—especially Turkey, currently a candidate nation. Some Europeans are concerned that if the EU changes too much too quickly, it will be less stable.

NATO Evolves With the end of the Cold War, the Warsaw Pact dissolved. As the nations of Eastern Europe made the transition to democratic, capitalist states, most wanted to join NATO. Poland, Hungary, and the Czech Republic joined in 1999, soon followed by other countries. In 2002, a NATO-Russia Council was set up.

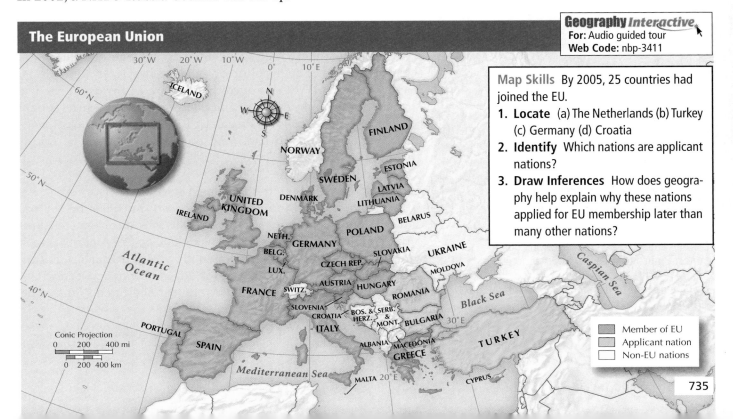

The European Union

Geography *Interactive*
For: Audio guided tour
Web Code: nbp-3411

Map Skills By 2005, 25 countries had joined the EU.

1. **Locate** (a) The Netherlands (b) Turkey (c) Germany (d) Croatia
2. **Identify** Which nations are applicant nations?
3. **Draw Inferences** How does geography help explain why these nations applied for EU membership later than many other nations?

Conic Projection

0   200   400 mi

0   200   400 km

Member of EU
Applicant nation
Non-EU nations

With a changing Europe, NATO has had to reassess its purpose. Many NATO policymakers have come to believe that NATO's primary goal should be that of peacekeeper and protector of human rights. During the early 1990s, NATO sent peacekeepers to Bosnia and Kosovo. More recently, terrorist attacks in Europe and elsewhere have forced NATO to examine its role in the global war on terrorism.

✓ **Checkpoint**   What challenges has Germany faced since reunification?

Global Power Shifts

When the Cold War ended and the Soviet Union collapsed, the balance of global power shifted. With the Soviet Union gone, the United States emerged as the world's sole superpower.

Russia Is Remade   After the breakup of the Soviet Union, Russia struggled to change to a market economy. President Boris Yeltsin privatized many industries and collective farms, but unemployment and prices still soared. Criminals flourished, and ruthless gangs preyed on owners of new businesses. Meanwhile, Russia's government—known for its widespread corruption—did little to stop the criminal activity. In 1998, Russia barely avoided financial collapse. It **defaulted,** or failed to make payments, on much of its foreign debt. High inflation and the collapse of the ruble, Russia's currency, forced many banks and businesses to close. People lost their savings and jobs.

In 2000, **Vladimir Putin** was elected president in Russia's second free election. Putin projected toughness and competence, promising to end corruption and build Russia into a strong market economy. He also secured Russia a consulting status with NATO. However, Putin repeatedly came under fire for increasing the power of the central government at the expense of people's civil liberties. The international community began to question his policies, concerned that he was becoming more autocratic than democratic.

The United States Becomes the Sole Superpower   As the world's only superpower, the United States had a great deal of global influence, both politically and militarily. In 1991, President George H.W. Bush waged the Persian Gulf War, driving Iraq from Kuwait and jump-starting peace talks between Israel and Palestine. His successor, President Bill Clinton, initiated peacekeeping operations in Haiti and the former Yugoslavia. And as you read, President George W. Bush took the U.S. back to war in the Middle East in the 2000s.

After the Cold War, the growing American economy supported the global economy. An economic boom in the 1990s helped produce a budget **surplus,** or money left over after expenditures. But from the late 1990s to the early 2000s, the American economy swung up and down. Slow economic growth and soaring military expenses led to huge budget deficits. A **deficit** is the gap between what a government spends and what it takes in through taxes and other resources.

✓ **Checkpoint**   How did the collapse of the Soviet Union affect the United States?

Protesting Putin
Demonstrators gather in Moscow in 2004 to protest Putin's policies. *What point do you think the protesters were making by holding up photos likening Putin to Adolf Hitler?*

Changes in Asia

As the Cold War ended, Asia experienced the successes and downturns of being part of the global economy.

The Pacific Rim A rising force in the global economy is the Pacific Rim, the vast region of nations that border the Pacific Ocean. The Pacific Ocean first became a highway for world trade in the 1500s. By the mid-1900s, links across the Pacific had grown dramatically. By the 1990s, the volume of trade across the Pacific was greater than that across the Atlantic. Some analysts have predicted that the 2000s will be the "Pacific century" because of this region's potential for further growth.

The Asian Tigers and Japan For decades, Japan dominated the Asian Pacific Rim. This small island nation rebuilt itself after World War II to become an economic powerhouse, modernizing and excelling at Western economics while at the same time preserving its own traditions. By the 1990s, however, Japan began to suffer from a long economic downturn.

In the meantime, Japan's neighbors—including Taiwan, Hong Kong, Singapore, and South Korea—surged ahead. Although they differ in terms of culture and history, all had quickly modernized and industrialized by the 1980s. All four were influenced to some degree by China and its Confucian traditions of education, loyalty, and consensus. Each stressed education as a means to increase worker productivity.

Because of their economic success, they earned nicknames such as the "Asian tigers" or the "four tigers." The Asian tigers first focused on light industries such as textiles. As their economies grew, the tigers concentrated on making higher-priced exports, such as electronics, for developed nations. Their extraordinary growth was due in part to low wages, long hours, and other worker sacrifices.

✓ **Checkpoint** What are the Asian Tigers?

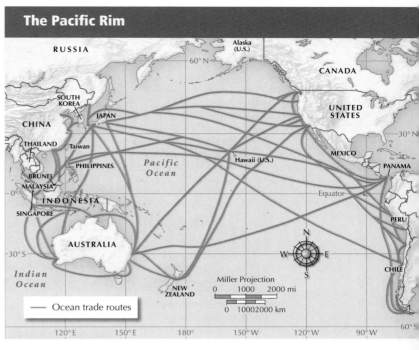

The Pacific Rim

Pacific Powerhouse
The countries of the Pacific Rim have geographic, cultural, and economic ties. The region is a major center of ocean trade routes, shown on the map above.

Assessment

Progress Monitoring Online
For: Self-quiz with vocabulary practice
Web Code: nba-3411

Terms, People, and Places

1. For each term, person, or place listed at the beginning of the section, write a sentence explaining its significance.

Note Taking

2. **Reading Skill: Compare and Contrast** Use your completed chart to answer the Focus Question: How did the end of the Cold War affect industrialized nations and regions around the world?

Comprehension and Critical Thinking

3. **Determine Relevance** How did the collapse of the Soviet Union affect organizations such as NATO and the EU?

4. **Draw Conclusions** Do you think an American investor would choose to invest large sums of money in Russia? Why or why not?

5. **Analyze Information** Why is the Pacific Rim seen as an important link in the global economy?

● Writing About History

Quick Write: Write a Thesis Statement
To persuade someone in an essay, you must have a strong opinion on a subject and express it clearly in a thesis statement. Write a single sentence that expresses the main point you want to make about developments in the industrialized world after the Cold War.

Russian immigrants sell caviar at a kiosk in Brooklyn, New York.

WITNESS HISTORY 🔊 AUDIO

A Connected World

❝Few topics are as controversial as globalization. That is hardly surprising. It is the defining feature of our time. Bringing distant markets and people across the world together is a huge change that affects everyone, whether they are peasants in India, students in London, or bankers in New York.❞
—Mike Moore, director-general of the WTO, 2000

Focus Question How is globalization affecting economies and societies around the world?

Globalization

Objectives

- Describe the ways in which countries around the world are interdependent.
- Understand how international treaties and organizations make global trade possible.
- Analyze the costs and benefits of global trade.

Terms, People, and Places

globalization	World Trade Organization
interdependence	(WTO)
outsourcing	protectionism
multinational	bloc
corporation	sustainability

Note Taking

Reading Skill: Compare and Contrast As you read, use the Venn diagram to track how globalization has affected developed and developing nations.

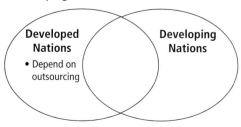

Globalization defines the world of the post-Cold War. **Globalization** refers to the process by which national economies, politics, cultures, and societies become integrated with those of other nations around the world. Globalization began on a small scale 500 years ago, with the European Age of Exploration. By the 1990s, globalization was occurring at a dramatic, unprecedented pace.

An Interdependent World

One major effect of globalization is economic interdependence. **Interdependence** is the dependence of countries on each other for goods, resources, knowledge, and labor from other parts of the world. Improvements in transportation and communication, the spread of democratic systems, and the rise of free trade—the buying and selling of goods by private individuals and corporations in a free market—have made the world increasingly interdependent. The spread of goods and ideas has even led to the development of a global culture. All of these links, from economic to cultural, have created both challenges and opportunities.

Doing the World's Work The world's rich and poor nations are linked. The nations of the developed world control much of the world's capital, trade, and technology. Yet they increasingly depend on largely low-paid workers in developing countries to produce manufactured goods cheaply. Companies in industrial nations also choose to outsource jobs. **Outsourcing** is the practice of sending work to the developing world in order to save money or increase efficiency. Many technological jobs have been outsourced to India, Russia, China, and the Philippines.

Multinational Corporations Grow Globalization has encouraged the rise of huge **multinational corporations.** These corporations have branches and <u>assets</u> in many countries and sell their goods and services throughout the world. Proponents of multinatinal corporations point out that they invest in the developing world, bring new technology to industries, provide jobs and technical assistance, and improve infrastructure. Critics feel that multinational corporations have too large an influence on the prices of goods, take large profits out of developing countries, and pay workers low wages, thus lowering their standard of living.

Financial Crises Affect Everyone One aspect of economic interdependence is financial interdependence in the world's markets. This means that an economic crisis in a country or a region can have a global impact. An example of this is the Asian financial crisis that affected the Asian tigers in the late 1990s. In 1997, a financial crisis struck Thailand and quickly spread to other Asian countries from Singapore to South Korea. The Asian financial crisis worsened Russia's economic woes and contributed to a recession in Japan, Asia's economic powerhouse. The fallout continued to spread around the globe as affected countries were unable to repay loans.

Oil: A Volatile Natural Resource In an interdependent world, natural resources—especially energy resources—play a huge role. All nations, for example, need oil for transportation and for products ranging from plastics to fertilizers. Any change to the global oil supply can have a major impact on economies and lives around the world.

For example, in 1973 OPEC limited oil exports and raised oil prices, sending economic shock waves around the world. Since then, whenever oil prices have risen sharply, people have faced economic uncertainties. Although people have invested in developing alternative fuels or conserving energy, the world has remained largely dependent on oil.

Vocabulary Builder

<u>asset</u>—(AS et) *n.* any property that has exchange value

Geography *Interactive*

For: Audio guided tour
Web Code: nbp-3421

World Oil Resources and Consumption

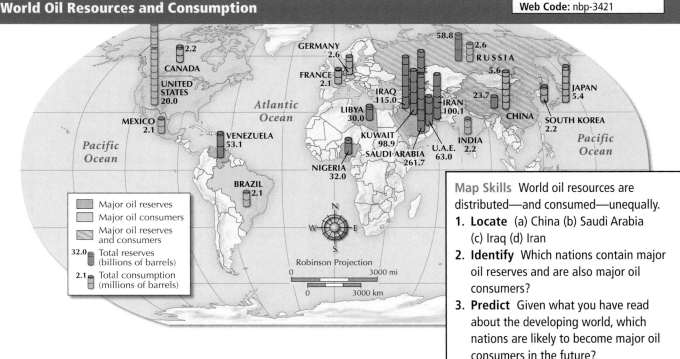

Major oil reserves
Major oil consumers
Major oil reserves and consumers
32.0 Total reserves (billions of barrels)
2.1 Total consumption (millions of barrels)

CANADA 2.2
UNITED STATES 20.0
MEXICO 2.1
Atlantic Ocean
Pacific Ocean
VENEZUELA 53.1
BRAZIL 2.1
GERMANY 2.6
FRANCE 2.1
LIBYA 30.0
NIGERIA 32.0
IRAQ 115.0
KUWAIT 98.9
SAUDI ARABIA 261.7
IRAN 100.1
U.A.E. 63.0
INDIA 2.2
58.8
2.6
RUSSIA 5.6
23.7
CHINA
JAPAN 5.4
SOUTH KOREA 2.2
Pacific Ocean

Robinson Projection
0   3000 mi
0   3000 km

Map Skills World oil resources are distributed—and consumed—unequally.
1. **Locate** (a) China (b) Saudi Arabia (c) Iraq (d) Iran
2. **Identify** Which nations contain major oil reserves and are also major oil consumers?
3. **Predict** Given what you have read about the developing world, which nations are likely to become major oil consumers in the future?

The Far-Reaching Effects of Debt In the 1980s, bank interest rates rose while the world economy slowed. Developing nations that had borrowed capital to modernize were hard hit. As demand for their goods fell, poor nations could not repay their debts or even the interest on their loans. Their economies stalled as they spent their income from exports on payments to foreign creditors.

The debt crisis hurt rich nations, too, as banks were stuck with billions of dollars of bad debts. To ease the crisis, lenders lowered interest rates, gave some nations more time to repay loans, or even canceled debts. In return, they required debtor nations to adopt reforms such as privatizing state-run industries. They argued that more efficient private enterprises would bring prosperity in the long run.

✓ **Checkpoint** What effect can a reduction in oil production in one country have on other countries around the world?

Global Trade Organizations and Treaties

Many international organizations and treaties link people and nations around the world. They have various goals, including encouraging development, settling economic issues, and promoting free trade. Free trade is a key part of global trade today.

International Organizations Expand The United Nations is an international organization whose responsibilities, along with its membership, have expanded greatly since 1945. The UN has acted in a peacekeeping role from Cambodia to Congo to the Balkans. In addition, it deals with political, social, economic, and cultural issues. Other international organizations deal specifically with economic issues. The World Bank, for example, offers loans and advice to developing nations. The International Monetary Fund (IMF) was established after World War II.

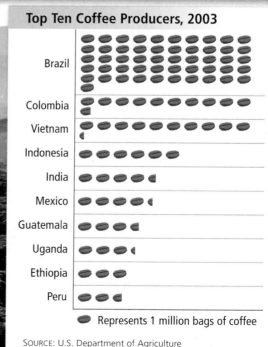

INFOGRAPHIC

COFFEE: From Shrub to Cup

Coffee is the most popular drink in the world today, other than water. Each year, people consume over 500 billion cups of coffee. Coffee is believed to have originated in the Kaffa region of Ethiopia, which gave the drink its name. Demand for coffee slowly spread from Africa to the Middle East and then to Europe. Eventually it reached Asia and the Americas. Coffee has had a tremendous cultural impact, shaping diets and social customs. Coffee has also dramatically influenced the global economy. After crude oil, it is the world's most actively traded commodity.

Top Ten Coffee Producers, 2003

Brazil
Colombia
Vietnam
Indonesia
India
Mexico
Guatemala
Uganda
Ethiopia
Peru

🫘 Represents 1 million bags of coffee

SOURCE: U.S. Department of Agriculture

Its goal is to promote international monetary cooperation and encourage global economic growth. It also monitors economic development and provides advice to developing nations. Other organizations include non-governmental organizations (NGOs). NGOs, which are usually not affiliated with governments, perform a variety of functions including monitoring human rights, disaster relief, and economic development.

Treaties Guide Global Trade The General Agreement on Tariffs and Trade (GATT) was signed in 1947 to expand world trade and reduce tariffs. In 1995, more than 100 nations joined to form the **World Trade Organization (WTO)** to strengthen GATT. Its goal was to set up global rules to ensure that trade flows as smoothly and freely as possible. One of the WTO's basic policies is its opposition to **protectionism,** or the use of tariffs and other restrictions that protect a country's home industries against competition. The Group of Eight (G-8) is an international organization of industrialized nations that meets yearly to discuss a wide range of economic and other issues. The G-8 consists of Great Britain, Canada, France, Germany, Italy, Japan, the United States, and Russia.

Regional Trade Blocs Promote Trade Many nations have formed regional **blocs,** or groups, to promote trade and meet common needs. Among the largest is the EU. NAFTA (North American Free Trade Association) is a regional trade bloc that went into effect in 1994 to facilitate trade among the United States, Canada, and Mexico. APEC (Asia-Pacific Economic Cooperation) promotes trade among Pacific Rim nations. OPEC, representing oil-producing countries, regulates the production of oil to stabilize the market. Organizations like these work to lower trade barriers among countries in their regions and promote the free exchange of goods and services. Some deal with both economic and political issues.

✓ **Checkpoint** Why was the IMF established?

The Fair Trade Movement ▶
The fair trade movement seeks to ensure that coffee growers receive fair prices for their crops and have decent living and working conditions. Coffee that has met these conditions is stamped with the fair trade logo.

Growing Coffee
A worker in Thailand picks raw coffee beans from a shrub. Less than 10 percent of the money made from coffee actually goes to the grower.

Drinking Coffee
By the time coffee beans are turned into cups of coffee in the developed world, they have passed through the hands of many middlemen and have been re-sold a number of times. The coffee crop that a small farmer earned $8,000 for growing is worth nearly a million dollars to the people who sell it.

Thinking Critically
1. **Chart Skills** What regions are the top 5 coffee producers located in?
2. **Draw Inferences** Why does a crop of coffee become more expensive each time it is sold by middlemen?

Costs and Benefits of Global Trade

With advanced communications and increased economic ties, globalization is expected only to increase in the years ahead. Yet people still debate the effect of globalization on people around the world.

Benefits of Trade Global trade has many benefits. Most obviously, it brings consumers great variety in the types of goods and services that are available to them. And because many people compete to provide those goods and services, it ensures that prices are generally kept low. Globalization exposes people to new ideas, technology, and communications.

Global trade also encourages growth in technology and communications, benefitting people's daily lives. Success in trade earns money that can be used to improve infrastructure, raise standards of living, and provide better services. Nations involved in free trade have often become more democratic. And most economists believe that trade works best when nations have an informed citizenry that is free to participate in economic processes.

The Anti-Globalization Movement A vocal movement opposes globalization. Generally, anti-globalizers focus attention on poverty. Many claim that rich countries exploit poor countries by raising their debt and lowering their standard of living. They also argue that nations that try to meet the demands of international trade are put at risk by specialization, or focusing their economies on one or two high-value commodities.

The anti-globalization movement often targets the World Bank and the IMF. Both of these organizations work to ease economic problems, but critics oppose the tough changes they often require nations to make. Anti-globalizers also often target the United States, which as the world's superpower is seen as the force behind policies they oppose.

Some people believe that globalization hurts indigenous peoples by taking their lands and disrupting their culture. Others say its emphasis on profits encourages too-rapid development, dangering sustainability. Sustainability is the ability to meet the needs of the present—for food, resources, shelter, and so on—without harming future generations.

✓ **Checkpoint** What benefits do global trade have on people's everyday life?

Anti-Globalization in Action
1999, an anti-globalization demonstration led to rioting when thousands of protesters disrupted WTO meetings in Seattle, Washington.

SECTION 2 Assessment

Progress Monitoring *Online*
For: Self-quiz with vocabulary practice
Web Code: nba-3421

Terms, People, and Places

1. What do each of the key terms listed at the beginning of the section have in common? Explain.

Note Taking

2. **Reading Skill: Compare and Contrast** Use your completed Venn diagram to answer the Focus Question: How is globalization affecting economies and societies around the world?

Comprehension and Critical Thinking

3. **Make Comparisons** Which countries benefit more from economic interdependence—developed or developing countries? Explain.

4. **Draw Inferences** Many Americans opposed the passage of NAFTA in 1994. Given what you have read in this section, what do you think their objections were?

5. **Demonstrate Reasoned Judgment** Do you think that increased globalization is inevitable? Explain.

● **Writing About History**

Quick Write: Generate Arguments One of the most effective ways to persuade is to address both sides of the topic you are covering. Create a chart to record facts about globalization. In one column, record the facts that support your position on globalization. In the second column, note arguments that could be used to attack your position.

People and the Environment

▲ A Haitian man burns trees to clear land for farming. Haiti, once heavily forested, has only about 1% forest cover today.

What impact have people had on the environment?

People have been changing the environment from the time they first made stone axes. As populations grew, so did their environmental impact. With the inventions of the Industrial Revolution, people's ability to alter the environment increased dramatically. Technological improvements in one field boosted improvements in other fields, increasing the overall impact of all technologies on the environment. This pattern continues today. Consider the human impact on land, water, and air through the following examples:

Land

Small populations of prehistoric hunter-gatherers had little long-term impact on their environment. The gradual shift to agriculture, however, put new stresses on the land. The more stable food supply supported higher populations, which required more food. Slash-and-burn techniques of clearing land eliminated forests in some areas. Waters from irrigation deposited salt on the soil, destroying soil fertility. In modern times overfarming, overgrazing, and other agricultural practices have encouraged large-scale soil erosion, in which winds carry valuable topsoil away. Today, wind erosion in China and West Africa is expanding deserts and stealing soils needed for food production.

Water

Through the ages, people have used rivers not just for drinking water and transportation but also as sewers. Waste creates unsanitary conditions for people downriver and eventually pollutes the ocean. People have also dammed rivers for flood control, hydropower, and irrigation. Farmers in Central Asia have taken so much water out of two rivers that they have turned a huge inland sea into a salty lake. The Aral Sea, once the fourth-largest body of inland water in the world, has shrunk by more than half in the last 50 years. With less river water draining into the sea, the region's wetlands are drying up, deserts are forming, and plant and animal life are disappearing.

Air

Air pollution is nothing new. In 1661, an English writer complained about the filthy smoke "belching forth" from coal fires. He said that the inhabitants of London "breathe nothing but an impure and thick Mist." Later, the popularity of coal-fired steam engines brought still more air pollution. By the mid-1900s, however, automobile exhaust had replaced coal smoke as the leading source of air pollution in many cities. London, Tokyo, Los Angeles, and Mexico City experienced a new phenomenon: poisonous smog. Today, government-imposed pollution standards have begun to clean the air in many cities, but few city dwellers anywhere would describe their air as fresh or pure.

Thinking Critically

1. Are negative impacts on the environment inevitable as countries industrialize? Explain your answer.

2. **Connections to Today** Research a developing country—such as Brazil, China, or Thailand—that is struggling with environmental issues. Explain the issues and their impact as well as how the country is meeting its environmental challenges.

◀ Bangladeshi children wade through unsanitary flood waters to access clean water from a pump.

A family in Indonesia tries to make their way to shelter after tsunamis destroyed their village in 2004. Aid organizations like CARE (logo above) worked to bring relief to the devastated region.

WITNESS HISTORY ◀)) AUDIO

Giant Waves Arrive

On December 26, 2004, an Indonesian man named Harmi went to the beach with hundreds of other people. An earthquake had hit his village, and people gathered to watch the sea recede from the beach.

❝ Suddenly . . . oh my God . . . there was a thundering sound from the sea. I saw the rolls of the waves ten meters (33 feet) high . . . the waves came three times. The worst was the second one, which swallowed thousands of houses in our village.**❞**

Harmi's village was completely destroyed.

Focus Question How do poverty, disease, and environmental challenges affect people around the world today?

Social and Environmental Challenges

Objectives
- Explain the causes and effects of global poverty, disasters, and disease.
- Analyze whether the basic human rights of people around the world are being upheld.
- Discuss the environmental challenges that have resulted from industrial development.

Terms, People, and Places

tsunami	acid rain
epidemic	deforestation
famine	erosion
refugee	global warming

Note Taking

Reading Skill: Compare Use a chart like this one to compare aspects of globalization.

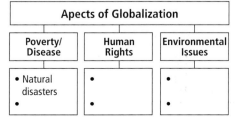

Apects of Globalization		
Poverty/ Disease	Human Rights	Environmental Issues
• Natural disasters	•	•
•		

Globalization involves much more than economic links and the spread of technology. It has brought all kinds of social and environmental issues to the world's attention. Poverty, disease, environmental threats, and human rights may originate in countries or regions. But they have global dimensions that often require global solutions.

Global Poverty, Disasters, and Disease

Half of the world's population, or almost 3 billion people, live on less than $2 a day. Almost 1 billion people cannot read or write. About 790 million people in the developing world suffer from hunger—many from extreme hunger. Millions of people suffer from life-threatening diseases. Although these are problems mainly of the developing world, they affect the nations of the developed world as well.

Causes of Poverty Experts cannot agree on the exact number of people living in poverty worldwide, in part because there are many ways to measure poverty. Experts do agree about some trends, however. First, the gap between rich and poor nations is huge and growing. Second, some progress has been made toward reducing poverty, but it has been uneven. India and China, for example, have enjoyed economic growth, which has meant fewer people overall living in poverty there, but extreme poverty still persists.

Poverty is a complex issue with many causes. Many poor nations owe billions in debt and have no extra money to spend to improve living conditions. Political upheavals, civil war, corruption, and poor planning also inhibit efforts to reduce poverty worldwide. Rapid population growth—especially in India, China, and the nations of Africa and Latin America—has made it harder for countries to provide basic services.

Organizations like the World Bank believe that erasing poverty is essential to global security and peace. In this spirit, they call on poor nations to limit population growth. They also encourage rich nations to forgive the debt of poor nations, making more funds available for education, healthcare, and other services.

Natural Disasters Affect Millions In 2004, a huge underwater earthquake in the Indian Ocean triggered a massive tidal wave, or **tsunami** (tsoo NAH mee). It swept over islands and the coasts of 11 countries ringing the Indian Ocean. More than 160,000 people were killed, mainly in Indonesia, Thailand, Sri Lanka, and India. Millions were left homeless or lost their livelihood.

Natural disasters range from earthquakes, floods, and avalanches to droughts, fires, hurricanes, and volcanic eruptions. They strike all over the world all the time. They cause death, destruction, and unsanitary

Vocabulary Builder
inhibit—(in HIB it) *v.* to hold back or keep from some action

MALARIA: WHEN A MOSQUITO STRIKES

Malaria is a disease that kills more than a million people a year worldwide, mostly children. Malaria is a parasite that is usually found in unsanitary conditions, especially stagnant water, in warm climates. Mosquitoes who breed on water pick up the parasite and then pass it to humans when they bite them. Forty percent of the world's population is at risk for contracting malaria, especially in developing countries. *Why do you think malaria is a risk mainly in developing countries?*

Global Malaria Risk
Significant
Low
None

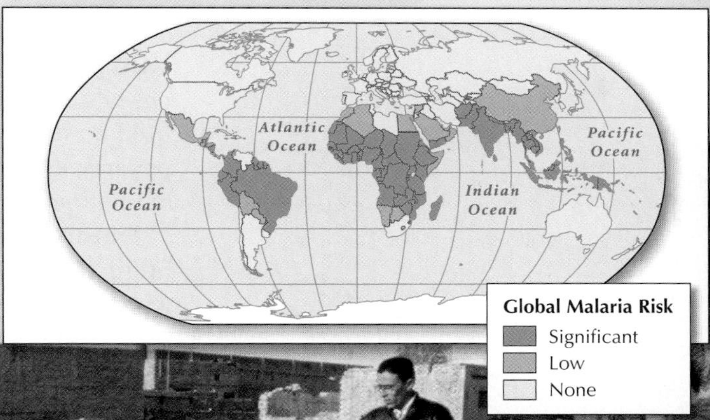

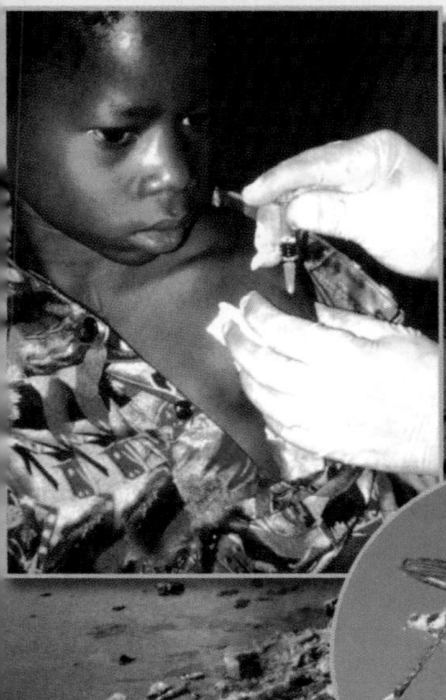

An African child receives a malaria vaccination.

Workers plan a new sewage project in Pakistan.

conditions that often lead to disease. They can destroy local economies, which can have a ripple effect on the global economy. One benefit of globalization is that news of natural disasters spreads instantly. In the past, the world only learned of such disasters after days, weeks, or months had passed. Today, the news triggers instant efforts to bring aid.

Global Disease Spreads Rapidly With millions of people on the move every day, disease can spread rapidly. In 2002 and 2003, plane travelers spread SARS (severe acute respiratory syndrome), a respiratory disease, from China to more than two dozen countries around the world. Other diseases such as avian flu (bird flu), mad cow disease, West Nile fever, and influenza have also raised concerns about the global spread of disease. Often diseases spread before health officials know they exist. Still, globalization has meant that health experts around the world, working together, can quickly identify and contain outbreaks of disease.

Some diseases have proved difficult to stop. When a disease spreads rapidly, it is called an **epidemic.** As you read, HIV/AIDS is an epidemic that began in the 1980s. HIV/AIDS has taken a huge economic and human toll around the world, especially in Africa and Southeast Asia. An estimated 20 million people have died of HIV/AIDS, and today nearly 40 million people are infected with it. By the early 2000s, treatment and prevention of AIDS had become a global priority. Some African nations like Uganda managed to lower rates of infection. Government and medical officials focused on educating people about how the HIV virus is transmitted and how people can prevent its transmission. Yet HIV/AIDS continues to spread, especially in Asia and Eastern Europe.

Hunger and Famine Threaten For tens of millions of people, hunger poses a daily threat. A major problem is that food does not get distributed to the people who need it most—especially in countries racked by poverty and civil strife. Hunger escalates into **famine** when large numbers of people in a region or country face death by starvation.

Natural disasters can cause famine. Human activity can also cause famine. War disrupts food distribution. During the 1970s and 1980s, civil wars raging in Ethiopia and Sudan intensified the effects of drought, leading to famine. Each side in the conflict tried to keep relief supplies from reaching the other. In many instances, only the efforts of international aid groups have saved millions of people from starvation.

Millions Migrate Globalization has led to a vast movement of people around the world. Some people choose to migrate because they see a chance for better opportunities. But others are **refugees,** people who are forced to move because of poverty, war, natural disasters, or persecution.

Many migrants do create better lives, but many others fail to find jobs or homes and sometimes meet hostility and discrimination. Many people in developed countries do not welcome immigrants, who they claim take away jobs and services from natural-born citizens.

Millions of migrants, both legal and illegal, continually head to Europe, Asia, and North America. Each year, the United States alone receives about a million legal immigrants and 300,000 or more illegal immigrants. By the

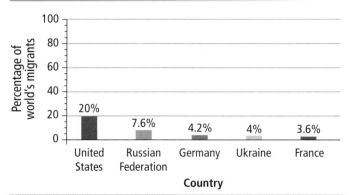

Top Five Destination Countries for International Migrants

Chart Skills In 2000, eleven nations in the developed world received over 40% of the world's total migrants. *What characteristics of the top five destination nations might attract migrants?*

SOURCE: *United Nations, Trends in Total Migrant Stock,* 2002

early 2000s, people from Latin America made up the largest immigrant group in the United States. Europe has been a destination for immigration since World War II. In the 1950s, Germany began welcoming large numbers of Turkish, Italian, and Russian immigrants to make up for the part of its labor force that was lost in the two world wars. France has a large North African population, largely from its former colony Algeria.

✓ **Checkpoint** What are some of the causes of famine and migration?

Human Rights

In 1948, UN members approved the Universal Declaration of Human Rights. It stated that all people are entitled to basic rights "... without distinction of any kind, such as race, colour, sex, language, religion, political or other opinion, national or social origin, property, birth or other status." In 1975, nations signing the Helsinki Accords guaranteed such basic rights as freedom of speech, religion, and the press as well as the rights to a fair trial, to earn a living, and to live in safety. Despite such agreements, human rights abuses—ranging from arbitrary arrest to torture and slavery—occur daily around the world.

The Role of the World Community Human rights abuses are not new, but globalization has brought them to the attention of the world in a new way. And the spread of democracy has forced people to question how human rights abuses can still happen in a modern world. In response, the world community has pressed countries to end abuses. In the 1980s, for example, economic pressure was used against South Africa to end apartheid, its system of legalized segregation.

Sometimes there is no stable government to pressure, or direct pressure does not work. Still, the UN, the United States, and human rights groups monitor and report on human rights violations, from Afghanistan, to Bosnia, to Congo. They even monitor human rights in nations that are part of the developed world, such as Russia.

Women Work for Rights For decades, a global women's movement has focused attention on the needs of women worldwide. The UN Charter supported "equal rights for men and women." By 1950, women had won the right to vote in most European nations, as well as in Japan, China, Brazil, and other countries. In most African nations, both women and men won the vote when their countries gained independence. Women have headed governments in Britain, Israel, India, Pakistan, the Philippines, and elsewhere.

Still, a report to the UN noted that while women represent half of the world's people, "they perform nearly two thirds of all working hours, receive only one tenth of the world's income, and own less than one percent of world property." The UN and other groups thus carefully monitor the human rights of women. They also condemn violence and discrimination against women. More than 165 countries have ratified a new women's human rights treaty.

Women in the Developed and Developing Worlds In the developed world, more and more women now work outside their homes.

An Illegal Crossing
Each year tens of thousands of illegal immigrants, like this family, risk their lives to cross the border between Mexico and the United States. *What factors lead people to risk their lives in illegal border crossings?*

They have gained high-profile jobs as business owners and executives, scientists, and technicians. Yet women often receive less pay for the same job that men do, and many must balance demanding jobs with child-rearing and housework. Still, many women do not have the option of not working, because many families need two incomes just to maintain a decent standard of living. Poor families need two incomes just to survive.

The education gap has been narrowing in developing nations, and women from the middle and elite classes have entered the workforce in growing numbers. Still, women often shoulder a heavy burden of work. In rural areas, especially in Africa where many men have migrated to cities to work, women do much of the farm work in addition to household tasks. In other regions, such as Southeast Asia, young women often leave home in search of work to support the family or to pay for their brothers' education. In many places, cultural traditions still confine women to the home or segregate men and women in the workplace.

Protecting Children Worldwide, children suffer terrible abuses. A 2005 UN report showed that half of the world's children suffer the effects of extreme poverty, armed conflict, and AIDS. Children are also the targets of human rights violations. In some nations, children are forced to serve as soldiers or even slaves. The resulting abuses not only damage children but also hurt a country's hope for the future. In 1989, the UN General Assembly approved the Convention on the Rights of the Child. This human rights treaty sets standards for basic rights for children, including the right to life, liberty, education, and healthcare. But ensuring these rights has proved difficult or even impossible.

In developing countries, tens of millions of children between the ages of 5 and 14 do not attend school. Instead, they work full time. Often, these child laborers work long hours in dangerous, unhealthy conditions for little pay. Many are physically abused by their employers and live in conditions of near slavery. Still, their families need the income the children earn. In some cases, children must work to pay off a family's debt. Human rights groups, the UN, and developed nations have focused a spotlight on child labor in order to end such practices.

Indigenous Peoples Face Challenges Indigenous peoples—including Native Americans, Aborigines in Australia, and Maoris in New Zealand—face discrimination and other abuses. Often, their lands have been forcibly taken. In South America, for example, developers have pushed into once-isolated areas, threatening the ways of life of indigenous peoples. Many Indians have died of diseases carried by the newcomers. During Guatemala's long civil war, the government targeted Mayan villagers, killing tens of thousands. The UN has worked to set standards to protect the rights of indigenous peoples.

✔ **Checkpoint** How are the human rights of children around the world violated?

Development and the Environment

Since earliest times, people have taken what they wanted from the environment. In the past, damage was limited because the world's population was small and technology was simple. Industrialization and the world population explosion have increased the damage done to the environment.

Ending Child Labor
RUGMARK, an organization that works to end child labor, sponsors the education of South Asian students like this girl. The RUGMARK label on her sleeve also appears on carpets and rugs that were made without child labor. *What effect might labels like this one have on people's buying habits?*

Health of the World Today

In the year 2000, the world population stood at just over 6 billion people. In 2050, it is projected to reach over 9 billion. The world's population in 2000 was sharply divided in terms of health and access to resources. Despite improvements in agriculture, medicine, and technology, huge numbers of people around the world lacked adequate food and access to safe water. Disease threatened some regions more than others. And in certain areas, poverty-stricken people made up the majority of the population.

Global HIV/AIDS Mortality

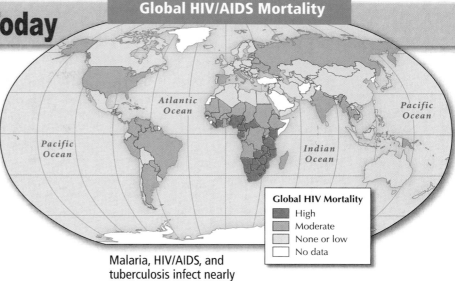

Global HIV Mortality
- High
- Moderate
- None or low
- No data

Malaria, HIV/AIDS, and tuberculosis infect nearly 50% of the world's population.

Access to Safe Water

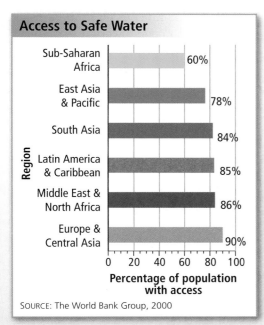

Region	Percentage of population with access
Sub-Saharan Africa	60%
East Asia & Pacific	78%
South Asia	84%
Latin America & Caribbean	85%
Middle East & North Africa	86%
Europe & Central Asia	90%

SOURCE: The World Bank Group, 2000

Many people around the world have no access to safe water. Drinking and using unsafe water spreads unsanitary conditions and disease.

World Per Capita GDP

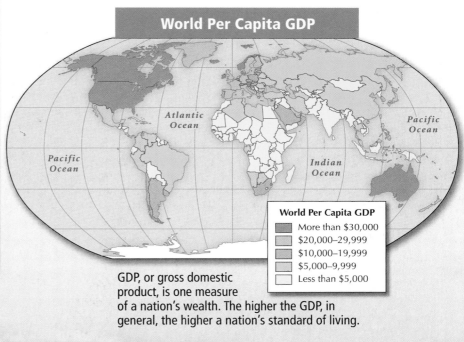

World Per Capita GDP
- More than $30,000
- $20,000–29,999
- $10,000–19,999
- $5,000–9,999
- Less than $5,000

GDP, or gross domestic product, is one measure of a nation's wealth. The higher the GDP, in general, the higher a nation's standard of living.

African farmers work with a member of a Japanese agricultural exchange program. These kinds of programs can help countries increase their GDP. ▶

History Interactive

For: Interactive world health statistics
Web Code: nbp-3431

Thinking Critically

1. **Map Skills** Which regions have high rates of disease and low percentages of their population with access to safe water?
2. **Compare** Compare the HIV/AIDS map and the chart with the map of global GDP. What can a nations GDP suggest about the health of its people?

As you have read, development improves lives and strengthens economies—but at a price. One of the great challenges of the twenty-first century is how to achieve necessary development without causing permanent damage to the environment.

Pollution Threatens the Environment Since the 1970s, environmentalists have warned about threats to the environment. Strip mining provides ores for industry but destroys land. Chemical pesticides and fertilizers produce larger food crops but harm the soil and water and may cause certain cancers. Oil spills pollute waterways and kill marine life. Gases from power plants and factories produce **acid rain,** a form of pollution in which toxic chemicals in the air fall back to Earth as rain, snow, or hail. Acid rain has damaged forests, lakes, and farmland.

Pollution from nuclear plants is another concern. In 1986, an accident at the Chernobyl nuclear power plant in the Soviet Union exposed people, crops, and animals to deadly radiation over a wide area. A similar accident occurred in 1978 at the Three Mile Island nuclear plant in Pennsylvania. Although the fallout was limited and no people were killed, the accident sparked a great debate about the benefits and hazards of nuclear power. Such accidents have caused industries and governments to develop better safety measures.

Growing Deserts, Shrinking Forests As you have read, desertification is a major problem, especially in the Sahel region of Africa. Another threat—especially in Africa, Latin America, and Asia—is **deforestation,** or the cutting of trees without replacing them. People cut trees for firewood or shelter, or to sell in markets abroad. Some burn down forests to make way for farms and cattle ranches, or for industry. In the Amazon basin region of Brazil, the world's largest rain forest, forests are also cleared in order to tap into rich mineral resources.

BIOGRAPHY

Edward O. Wilson

As a child in Alabama, Edward O. Wilson (1929–) developed a love for nature. His poor eyesight and limited physical strength encouraged him to focus on ants—small creatures that he could hold and look at closely. Wilson never grew out of his "bug period," becoming a renowned professor of biology at Harvard. In recent years, Wilson has increasingly focused his attention on environmental issues. In his 2002 book *The Future of Life,* he writes about how Earth's growing human population is affecting the planet and its resources. Calling the 2000s the "Century of the Environment," he appeals to "science and technology, combined with foresight and moral courage," to meet modern environmental challenges. *Why does Wilson believe that "foresight and moral courage" are needed to preserve the environment?*

Once forests are cleared, rains wash nutrients from the soil, destroying its fertility. Deforestation also causes **erosion,** or the wearing away of land, which encourages flooding. The deforestation of rain forests is particularly worrisome. Rain forests like the Amazon play a key role in absorbing poisonous carbon dioxide from the air and releasing essential oxygen. They are also home to millions of animal and plant species, many of which have become extinct because of deforestation.

Global Warming Another environmental challenge—one that is hotly debated—is **global warming.** Global warming refers to the rise of Earth's surface temperature over time. A rise in Earth's temperature could bring about changes such as the following: a rise in sea level, changes in weather patterns, increased desertification in some areas, and an increase in precipitation in others. Because climates in some areas could become colder, many scientists prefer to call the trend "climate change."

Scientists agree that Earth's temperature has risen slightly over the past century. Many scientists think that this warming comes from gases released into the atmosphere by human activity such as the burning of fossil fuels. These "greenhouse" gases trap warmth in Earth's atmosphere. Some scientists, however, and many policymakers, argue that global warming is due to natural fluctuations in Earth's climate.

The debate over a treaty called the Kyoto Protocol points to a central challenge facing world leaders: Does economic development have to conflict with protecting the environment? The treaty, signed by 140 countries, with the major exceptions of the United States and Australia, went into effect in 2005. Its purpose is to lower the emissions of carbon dioxide and other "greenhouse" gases that contribute to global warming. Many developing nations refuse to sign because they say they must exploit their resources in order to develop fully. The United States has not signed the Kyoto Protocol because it believes the treaty could strain economic growth. Nations that have signed the treaty, however, argue that developed nations must lead the way in slowing emissions.

Vocabulary Builder
fluctuation—(fluk choo AY shun) *n.* swing; rising and falling of something

✓ **Checkpoint**   What kinds of environmental issues do people face today?

SECTION 3 Assessment

Progress Monitoring *Online*
For: Self-quiz with vocabulary practice
Web Code: nba-3431

Terms, People, and Places
1. Place each of the key terms at the beginning of the section into one of the following categories: politics, culture, government, economy, or environment. Write a sentence for each term explaining your choice.

Note Taking

2. **Reading Skill: Compare** Use your completed chart to answer the Focus Question: How do poverty, disease, and environmental challenges affect people around the world today?

Comprehension and Critical Thinking
3. **Synthesize Information** How are global poverty, disease, disasters, and migration linked to each other? How might they be linked to globalization?
4. **Identify Central Issues** Why is protecting human rights not a central issue for many developing countries?
5. **Identify Assumptions** What assumptions can you make about the lack of participation on the part of some nations in the Kyoto Protocol?

● **Writing About History**
Quick Write: Decide on an Organizational Strategy Make a draft of a persuasive essay about social and environmental challenges. Your draft should include a thesis statement, begin with your second-strongest argument, and conclude with your strongest argument. To organize most efficiently, rank your remaining arguments from weakest to strongest.

Aung San Suu Kyi: *Freedom From Fear*

Aung San Suu Kyi, leader of Myanmar's National League for Democracy and winner of the Nobel Peace Prize, has worked courageously for human rights and democracy in her country. Because of her opposition to Myanmar's ruling military junta, she was held under house arrest from 1989 to 1995 and severely restricted thereafter. In this essay, Aung San Suu Kyi describes the need for courage when living under an oppressive government.

▲ Aung San Suu Kyi

Fearlessness may be a gift but perhaps more precious is the courage acquired through endeavor, courage that comes from cultivating the habit of refusing to let fear dictate one's actions, courage that could be described as 'grace under pressure'—grace which is renewed repeatedly in the face of harsh, unremitting[1] pressure.

Within a system which denies the existence of basic human rights, fear tends to be the order of the day. Fear of imprisonment, fear of torture, fear of death, fear of losing friends, family, property or means of livelihood, fear of poverty, fear of isolation, fear of failure. A most insidious[2] form of fear is that which masquerades as common sense or even wisdom, condemning as foolish, reckless, insignificant or futile the small, daily acts of courage which help to preserve man's self-respect and inherent[3] human dignity. It is not easy for a people conditioned by fear under the iron rule of the principle that might is right to free themselves from the enervating[4] miasma[5] of fear. Yet even under the most crushing state machinery courage rises up again and again, for fear is not the natural state of civilized man.

The wellspring[6] of courage and endurance in the face of unbridled power is generally a firm belief in the sanctity of ethical principles combined with a historical sense that despite all setbacks the condition of man is set on an ultimate course for both spiritual and material advancement. . . . It is man's vision of a world fit for rational, civilized humanity which leads him to dare and to suffer to build societies free from want and fear. Concepts such as truth, justice and compassion cannot be dismissed as trite[7] when these are often the only bulwarks[8] which stand against ruthless power.

▲ Burmese children living in Bangladesh protested for the release of Aung San Suu Kyi on the occasion of the Burmese foreign minister's visit to Bangladesh.

1. **unremitting** (un rih MIT ing) *adj.* not letting up
2. **insidious** (in SID ee us) *adj.* meant to harm
3. **inherent** (in HIHR unt) *adj.* part of one's basic nature
4. **enervating** (EN ur vayt ing) *adj.* weakening or destroying
5. **miasma** (my AZ muh) *n.* harmful atmosphere or influence
6. **wellspring** (WEL spring) *n.* source
7. **trite** (tryt) *adj.* overused; uninteresting
8. **bulwark** (BOOL wurk) *n.* serving as a defense

Thinking Critically

1. **Identify Main Ideas** Why does the author believe that even in harsh, cruel societies courage will rise up again and again?
2. **Apply Information** Give one example of a person refusing to let fear dictate his or her actions.

Taking a Stand

In the fall of 2002, United States President George W. Bush delivered a speech on international security before the United Nations in New York:

❝ We must choose between a world of fear and a world of progress. We cannot stand by and do nothing while dangers gather. We must stand up for our security and for the permanent rights and for the hopes of mankind.❞
—George W. Bush, Remarks at the United Nations General Assembly, September 12, 2002

Focus Question What kinds of threats to national and global security do nations face today?

President Bush emphasizes the importance of national security in a speech to U.S. Coast Guard members in 2003.

Security in a Dangerous World

Objectives

- Explain why nuclear, biological, and chemical weapons threaten global security.
- Analyze the various terrorist groups and why they are becoming more and more dangerous.
- Describe the various ways in which the United States and other nations have responded to terrorism.

Terms, People, and Places

proliferate   Afghanistan
terrorism   Taliban
Al Qaeda

Note Taking

Reading Skill: Compare and Contrast Use the chart to compare threats to global security.

Threats to Security	
Nuclear Weapons	Nuclear weapons unsecured in former Soviet Union

The end of the Cold War had promised an end to global conflict and the threat of nuclear war. Just a decade later, people and nations around the world once again worried about attack—from different, unpredictable sources.

The Power of Modern Weapons

In the latter half of the twentieth century, Russia and the United States built up arsenals of nuclear weapons. When the Cold War ended, those weapons still existed. At the same time, chemical and biological weapons threatened global security.

The Nuclear Nonproliferation Treaty In 1968, the Nuclear Nonproliferation Treaty (NPT) was signed by Russia, the United States, and 60 other countries. The purpose of the treaty was to ensure that nuclear weapons did not **proliferate,** or rapidly spread, to nations that had no nuclear weapons. By 2000, 187 nations in total had signed the treaty.

Today, the NPT is the most globally accepted arms control agreement. Yet it does not in itself guarantee that nuclear weapons won't be used. Four nations have not signed the treaty—India, Pakistan, Israel, and Cuba. Some nations that have signed it get around it by buying or selling nuclear technology or materials rather than actual weapons. And some nations—including Iran and North Korea—are suspected of buying or selling nuclear weapons even though they are treaty members. The International Atomic Energy Agency (IAEA) monitors nations regularly to check that they comply with the treaty.

The Problem of Russia When the Soviet Union collapsed, stockpiles of nuclear weapons and materials remained throughout its former territory. Unfortunately, preventing those materials from being mishandled has proven difficult. The unstable Russian government has not had the funds or the means to dismantle or secure the materials properly. At the same time, it is feared that those who worked in nuclear facilities, or those who have access to them, including smugglers, may be tempted to sell materials or knowledge to interested buyers.

In recent years, the United States and Europe have increased funding to help Russia to secure its nuclear weapons. In the 1990s, Russia and the United States also signed several treaties meant to assure that both countries reduce their arsenals of nuclear and other weapons. However, both countries have backed off from their commitment to these treaties in recent years, citing national security issues.

A Risky Situation
Vials of the bacteria that cause plague were left improperly secured in Kazakhstan by Soviet scientists.

Weapons of Mass Destruction As you have read, weapons of mass destruction (WMDs) include nuclear, biological, and chemical weapons. Nuclear weapons include the atom bomb, first used by the United States in World War II. Biological weapons refer to disease-carrying organisms, such as smallpox, or toxins that can be released into the air or into water supplies. Chemical weapons refer to chemical toxins, such as nerve gas and mustard gas, which was first used in World War I.

WMDs were used in warfare for much of the 1900s. However, in the 2000s they took on a new danger. Terrorist groups began to use them for their own purposes. And "rogue states"—nations that ignore international law and are seen as a threat to their neighbors and the world—saw them as a way to both defend themselves and increase their power. Often, rogue states are dictatorships that brutally mistreat their own citizens or attack their neighbors.

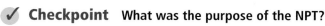 **Checkpoint** What was the purpose of the NPT?

Terrorism Threatens Global Security

The use of violence, especially against civilians, by groups of extremists—sometimes sponsored by governments that protect and fund them—to achieve political goals is called **terrorism.** Terrorists' goals range from releasing political prisoners to gaining territory. In the last two centuries, terrorists have launched repeated assaults on society. They have bombed buildings, slaughtered civilians, police, and soldiers, and assassinated political leaders. Terrorists generally have not been able to achieve their greater goals with violence. However, they have succeeded in inflicting terrible damage and generating widespread fear.

Terrorist groups use headline-grabbing tactics to draw attention to their demands. They might attack railway stations in Italy, release nerve gas in the subways of Tokyo, or blow themselves up as "suicide bombers" to kill Israeli civilians. Despite government efforts to prevent attacks, terrorists successfully set off a number of bombs in London in July 2005.

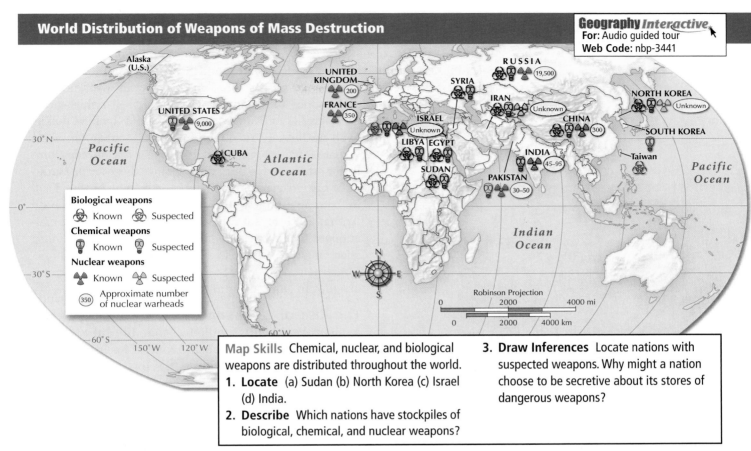

World Distribution of Weapons of Mass Destruction

Geography *Interactive*
For: Audio guided tour
Web Code: nbp-3441

Biological weapons
Known   Suspected
Chemical weapons
Known   Suspected
Nuclear weapons
Known   Suspected
(350) Approximate number of nuclear warheads

Robinson Projection

Map Skills Chemical, nuclear, and biological weapons are distributed throughout the world.
1. **Locate** (a) Sudan (b) North Korea (c) Israel (d) India.
2. **Describe** Which nations have stockpiles of biological, chemical, and nuclear weapons?
3. **Draw Inferences** Locate nations with suspected weapons. Why might a nation choose to be secretive about its stores of dangerous weapons?

Regional Terrorist Groups Particular regional terrorist groups have operated for decades. Several of them are located in the developed world, for example, in Europe. From the 1970s to the 1990s, the Irish Republican Army (IRA) used terrorist tactics to force Britain to give up Northern Ireland. The ETA, a Basque terrorist group, seeks to compel the Spanish government to allow the Basque region in the Pyrenees to secede. These and other groups committed bombings, shootings, and kidnappings to force their governments to change their policies.

Terrorist groups operate in many other regions. The Tamil Tigers in the island republic of Sri Lanka combine guerrilla warfare with terrorist bombings to achieve their goal of founding a separate state. In Latin America, groups like the Shining Path in Peru have used violence and killings to overthrow the government and set up their own regimes.

Terrorism and the Middle East Increasingly, the Middle East has become a training ground and source for terrorism. One historical reason for this has been Western colonial domination in the region. In addition, the establishment of the State of Israel in 1948 sparked anger among many Arabs. In 1964, a group of Arabs founded the Palestine Liberation Organization (PLO), with the goal of creating an independent Palestinian state. Although the PLO officially renounced terrorism in 1988, other Palestinian groups, such as Hamas, Islamic Jihad, and the Al-Aqsa Martyrs Brigade, practice terror to achieve their ends.

The Lebanese group Hezbollah formed after Israel invaded Lebanon. Originally, its goal was to oust Israel from Lebanon. Another stated goal is the destruction of Israel. Although it is a strong political party in Lebanon today, Hezbollah has been designated a terrorist organization by the United States and other countries.

Islamic Fundamentalism Islamic fundamentalism refers to the religious belief that society should be governed by Islamic law. A historical precedent for it was the Arab nationalism that helped nations in the Middle East come together after a history of European colonialism. This nationalism was strengthened by the creation of Israel as well as by a backlash against the presence of foreign powers in the oil-rich region. Socially, Islamic fundamentalism was encouraged by a lack of basic resources in many Arab nations. Islamic fundamentalists made Israel or Western nations scapegoats for their problems. In the past few decades, terrorist attacks have increased against these scapegoats.

Many governments have been heavily influenced by Islamic fundamentalism, including Iran and Saudi Arabia. Both of these nations have provided financial support for terrorist organizations. In other nations, such as Libya, Algeria, Egypt, and Turkey, Islamic fundamentalist groups have used violence in an attempt to gain power and take over the government.

The Rise of al Qaeda One powerful Islamic fundamentalist group is called **al Qaeda** (ahl KY duh), which means "the Base" in Arabic. The leader of al Qaeda is Osama bin Laden, the son of a rich Saudi Arabian family. Bin Laden had helped the warlords of Afghanistan drive the Soviets out of their country in the 1980s. In the 1990s, he mobilized al Qaeda to expel American business interests, political influence, and military power from Saudi Arabia. By the new millennium, he was providing aid, training, and money to scattered terrorist groups from Morocco to Indonesia. His goals had expanded to include aid for Palestinian terrorists fighting Israel and the expulsion of American power from the entire Middle East.

Early al Qaeda attacks on American interests occurred in Asia and Africa. Terrorists blew up two American embassies in East Africa in 1998 and damaged an American naval vessel in a port on the Arabian peninsula in 2000. But the major blow came when al Qaeda terrorists struck inside the United States itself.

On the morning of September 11, 2001, teams of terrorists hijacked four airplanes on the East Coast. Passengers challenged the hijackers on one flight, which crashed on the way to its target. But one plane plunged into the Pentagon in Virginia, and two others slammed into the twin towers of the World Trade Center in New York. More than 2,500 people were killed in the attacks.

A Dangerous Leader
New York City police stand near a "Wanted" poster in 2001. An Arab man holds up a poster supporting bin Laden. *How do views like the one this man expresses threaten the United States' security?*

✔️ **Checkpoint** What is al Qaeda?

The War on Terrorism

Al Qaeda's attack on the United States triggered a startling global shake-up. Governments around the world questioned their allies, their enemies, and even their own abilities to keep their citizens safe. Fighting terrorism became a central focus of national policies and international

WITNESS HISTORY VIDEO

Watch *The Taliban in Afghanistan* on the **Witness History Discovery School**™ video program to learn about Islamic fundamentalism in Afghanistan.

relations. In the United States, President George W. Bush declared war against terrorism in general and against al Qaeda in particular.

Wars in Afghanistan and Iraq Osama bin Laden and other al Qaeda leaders were living in **Afghanistan** in 2001. The government of that country, an Islamic fundamentalist group called the **Taliban,** refused to surrender the terrorists. The United States responded by attacking Afghanistan. With the help of Afghani warlords who opposed the Taliban and the use of military bases in neighboring Pakistan, American forces quickly overthrew the Taliban and drove the al Qaeda operatives into hiding or flight. Bin Laden, however, remained at large.

Two years after the war in Afghanistan, President Bush asked Congress to declare war on Iraq, arguing that Saddam was secretly producing WMDs. Because no WMDs were found, the war was bitterly debated among Americans and around the world. However, most in the global community welcomed the holding of free democratic elections in Iraq in early 2005, hoping that a democratic Iraq might positively influence the largely authoritarian Middle East.

New Security Measures Take Shape Over the years that followed September 11, the United States made increasing security a top <u>priority</u>. It strengthened and reorganized its intelligence services. The government created a new Department of Homeland Security and instituted more rigorous security measures at airports and public buildings. A long-term effort was launched to find out how terrorist groups were funded, with the goal of cutting off terrorists' money supply and thus limiting terrorist activity.

The United States also stepped up pressure on other countries not to develop WMDs that might fall into terrorist hands. American diplomats worked with European colleagues to dissuade Iran and North Korea from developing nuclear weapons. At the same time, President Bush urged the spread of democracy, which he declared was the best deterrent to terrorism and regional unrest. He also encouraged allies such as Russia to re-examine their commitment to democracy.

✔ **Checkpoint**   Why did the United States invade Afghanistan?

A New Future for a Historic Site
The World Trade Center was reduced to rubble in the 2001 terrorist attack (inset). Proposed designs for rebuilding the site (like the one above) include a memorial to the people who died there.

Vocabulary Builder

priority—(pry AWR uh tee) *n.* something deemed of greater importance than other things

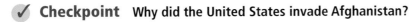

SECTION 4 Assessment

Progress Monitoring Online
For: Self-quiz with vocabulary practice
Web Code: nba-3441

Terms, People, and Places
1. For each term, person, or place listed at the beginning of the section, write a sentence explaining its significance.

Note Taking
2. **Reading Skill: Compare and Contrast** Use your completed chart to answer the Focus Question: What kinds of threats to national and global security do nations face today?

Comprehension and Critical Thinking
3. **Draw Inferences** Why might the United States and Russia be reluctant to fully commit to nuclear disarmament?
4. **Predict Consequences** How might nations around the world react should Middle Eastern nations democratically elect Islamic fundamentalist governments?
5. **Demonstrate Reasoned Judgment** Do you think that "preemptive" wars, or wars waged to prevent other wars or attacks, are sometimes necessary? Explain your answer.

● **Writing About History**
Quick Write: Draft the Opening Paragraph The paragraph that opens your essay is the place to grab the reader's interest. Remember that if the reader loses interest after reading the first paragraph, he or she is unlikely to continue reading. Draft an opening paragraph about threats to global security, using specific details to grab the reader's interest. An opening such as "There are many threats to global security" is much less compelling than a description of a specific threat.

A logo of the National Aeronautic and Space Administration (NASA)

Buzz Aldrin walks on the moon in 1969. The space capsule that he traveled in is reflected on his visor.

SECTION 5

WITNESS HISTORY ◄)) AUDIO

A Giant Leap for Mankind

On July 20, 1969, American astronauts Neil Armstrong and Edwin Aldrin landed on the moon after a four-day trip in the spacecraft *Apollo 11*. Stepping out onto the powdery surface, Armstrong—the first person ever to have walked on the moon—said, "That's one small step for man, one giant leap for mankind." Those words electrified a nation and defined a new era of world history.

Focus Question How have advances in science and technology shaped the modern world?

Advances in Science and Technology

Objectives

- Describe the exploration of space and the practical applications that resulted from it.
- Analyze the development and impact of the computer revolution.
- Explain how advances in medicine and biotechnology have shaped life today.

Terms, People, and Places

artificial satellite
International Space
   Station (ISS)
personal computer (PC)
Internet

biotechnology
laser
genetics
genetic engineering

Note Taking

Reading Skill: Compare Use the chart to compare the impacts of modern science and technology.

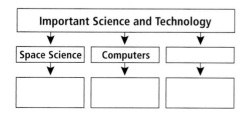

Important Science and Technology		
Space Science	Computers	

People in the past half century have used various terms to describe the age they live in, including "the atomic age," the "electronic age," and the "automobile age." All of these labels have one thing in common: their connection to modern science and technology. Since 1945, scientific research and technological development have had a transforming effect on human history. Startling new inventions, the computer revolution, and advances in the life sciences have redefined the world we live in and the lives we lead.

Exploring and Making Use of Space

By the second half of the twentieth century, there were few places on Earth that people had not begun to explore. Space was seen as the "final frontier"—an unknown world filled with opportunity. Within a few short decades, people had traveled to this frontier and had used its resources to help develop practical applications that transformed their lives.

The Space Race Begins Rockets are projectiles or vehicles propelled by the ejection of burning gasses from the rear of the rocket. In the early twentieth century, pioneers in rocketry like the American physicist Robert Goddard probed the potential of liquid-fueled rockets. From the beginning, Goddard believed that a rocket could carry people to the moon. At first people met his ideas with disbelief. Increasingly, German scientists took interest in Goddard's work, prompting him to work with great secrecy.

Nevertheless, during World War II German scientists, led by Wernher von Braun, developed Germany's "secret weapon," the V-2 rockets that flew across the English Channel to rain down on London.

During the Cold War, the United States and the Soviet Union competed with each other to build both rocket-propelled weapons and rocketry for the purpose of space exploration. Von Braun, who moved to the United States after World War II, became a leader in the American missiles and space program. In 1957, the space age began when the Soviet Union launched into orbit *Sputnik*, the first **artificial satellite,** or man-made object that orbits a larger body. In 1969, the United States Apollo program landed the first man on the moon. Both superpowers also explored the military uses of space and sent spy satellites to orbit Earth. Since the end of the Cold War, the United States and Russia have cooperated in joint space ventures.

Space Science Develops In the decades since *Sputnik* and *Apollo*, rockets have been launched to other planets and beyond. Robotic space vehicles have penetrated the mists of Venus and the rings of Saturn, landed on Mars, and circled the moons of Jupiter. Rocket missions have various goals. They can take scientific measurements, release permanent satellites or telescopes, and if they are manned, conduct medical or biological experiments. They can also provide information about the composition and formation of the universe itself.

Increasingly, nations have worked together to explore space. For example, Russia, the United States, Canada, Japan, and several countries in Europe are developing the **International Space Station (ISS).**

WITNESS HISTORY VIDEO

Watch *The Space Race* on the **Witness History Discovery School**™ video program to experience the superpowers struggle to win the space race.

Traveler's Tales

EYEWITNESS ACCOUNT

An Astronaut Views Earth From Space

Alan Bean is an American astronaut who participated in the United States' Apollo 12 moon-landing project. In 1969, Bean became the fourth person to walk on the moon. Deeply moved by his experience, he began taking art lessons upon his return to Earth to express visually what he had seen. He resigned from NASA in 1981 to devote himself to painting. The excerpt below, taken from a book about the Apollo mission that he wrote and illustrated, describes the view from the moon.

❝It was incredible to stand on the moon… and take a moment to reflect on all the dedicated people it took to get us there for America. We were the lucky ones. The stars were not visible because the sunlight reflecting from the bright lunar surface caused the irises of our eyes to contract, just as they do on earth at night when standing on a brightly lit patio. As we looked up, the sky was a deep, shiny black. I guessed that deep, shiny black was the color one sees looking into infinity . . . . I thought: Can all the people we know, all the people we love, who we've seen on TV, or read about in the newspapers, all be up there on that tiny blue-and-white marble? Earth—small but so lovely—was easily the most beautiful object we could see from the moon. It was a wondrous moment.❞

—Alan Bean,
from ***Apollo***, 1998

Thinking Critically
1. **Draw Inferences** Why does Bean call the astronauts the "lucky ones"?
2. **Analyze Information** How does Bean contrast his view of Earth with that of the lunar sky? What point does he make by contrasting these two views?

759

Construction on the ISS began in 1998. When it is completed in 2010, it will serve as a space laboratory, allowing scientists from many different countries to observe space, conduct research, and develop new space-related technologies.

The Impact of Artificial Satellites The thousands of artificial satellites that orbit Earth have a number of very specific applications. These applications can be divided into three groups—communications, observation, and navigation. Communications satellites relay information that is used in advanced communications, including television, telephone, and high-speed data transmission. Observation satellites observe Earth, providing data to scientists, weather forecasters, and military planners. Navigation satellites beam precise locations to ship captains and others who need to navigate Earth's surface.

By 2000, artificial satellites had revolutionized global communications. Maintaining stationary orbits over specific points on Earth's surface, artificial satellites can transmit phone messages or television pictures anywhere on Earth. Linked to cell phones or computers, they allow people separated by thousands of miles to communicate instantly.

✓ **Checkpoint** What is the International Space Station and what is its significance?

The Computer Revolution

The invention of the computer in the twentieth century caused an unprecedented information revolution. Very few aspects of modern life remain untouched by computers. Computers run businesses and power plants, help scientists conduct advanced research, and when connected to satellites, make global communications possible. The development of computer technology has given rise to the term "Information Age."

○ **INFOGRAPHIC**

Twentieth Century Scientific Milestones

Developing Nuclear Energy

During World War II, the United States was determined to create an atomic bomb that could be used against the Axis Powers. Scientists including Albert Einstein, J. Robert Oppenheimer, Enrico Fermi, and Edward Teller participated in the Manhattan Project, as it was called. The project achieved success in 1945 with the explosion of a test bomb in New Mexico.

◄ Einstein and Oppenheimer in 1947

Early Computers A computer is a device for making mathematical calculations and for storing, processing, and rapidly manipulating data. Computers have made it possible to preserve vast amounts of data. And when linked up in a vast network, they have brought written communication over enormous distances instantaneously.

The first electronic computers, built in the 1940s, were huge, slow machines. Later, thanks to inventions like the silicon chip, the computer was reduced in size. **Personal computers,** or **PCs,** became widely available in the 1970s for individual users, both at work and at home. By inserting basic programs into the machine, the user could perform complex and difficult tasks quickly and easily.

Over the next few decades, PCs replaced typewriters and account books in homes and businesses worldwide. At the same time, computer technology spread into many different fields. Computerized robots operate in factories. Computers remotely control satellites and probes in space and students use them in school classrooms. And computers increasingly aid scientists and architects in developing models to predict disasters, understand environmental changes, and plan urban development.

The Internet In the 1970s, various branches of the U.S. government along with groups in several American universities led efforts to link computer systems together via cables and satellites. By the 1990s, the "Internet" or "World Wide Web" was well established, again revolutionizing information technology. Using the **Internet,** a person can instantly communicate with other users around the world. The same person can also instantly access vast storehouses of information of all sorts.

By 2000, the Internet had grown to a gigantic network, linking individuals, governments, and businesses around the world. E-commerce, or buying and selling on the Internet, contributed to economic growth. The Internet also began to shape life in developing nations.

Breakthroughs in Medicine

Twentieth-century discoveries in medicine had a major impact on people around the world. For example, in 1952 researcher Jonas Salk (left) developed a vaccine for polio. Polio is a virus that spreads rapidly among people, especially children, causing paralysis. Before Salk's discovery, around 20,000 people in the United States contracted polio each year. Because of Salk's vaccine, the disease is extremely rare in the world today.

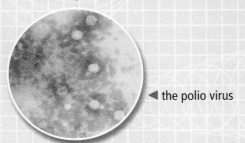

◀ the polio virus

DNA ▶ sequencer

Expanding the Science of Genetics

The study of genes was not new to the twentieth century. The work of James Watson and Francis Crick, (right) however, dramatically transformed the science of genetics. In 1953, the two men discovered the basic structure of DNA—the material in the chromosomes of all cells that determines how every organism functions. This discovery revolutionized the study of heredity and paved the way for genetic engineering.

Thinking Critically

1. **Draw Inferences** Why did Albert Einstein later regret his work on the Manhattan Project?
2. **Cause and Effect** How did the discovery of DNA affect the field of genetics? ◀)) AUDIO

A GLOBAL FOOD EVOLVES

What we now know as corn originally grew as a wild grass in the Americas. Thousands of years ago, ancient peoples began experimenting with this grass, carefully selecting good seeds and nurturing plants. About 7,000 years ago, Native Americans near present-day Mexico City developed small ears of corn, calling them *maize*. Indians throughout the Americas, and then European settlers, constantly experimented with corn to produce bigger and better ears. The experimentation still continues today.

▲ Eventually, Native Americans produced maize, a plant with ears of plump, soft kernels like today's corn. Maize became a staple crop for many Native American groups. They also developed multi-colored ears of corn, like those above, using them for food and in religious activities.

◄ Ancient wild corn was called *teosinte* (tee oh *SIN* tee). Teosinte kernels, hard and nut-like, grew on thick grassy stalks. Over thousands of years Native Americans domesticated teosinte, carefully preserving the seeds of the plants that produced the best ears.

▲ A biotechnology worker cuts into an ear of corn to extract a section of DNA, or genetic material, that will be used to improve the next corn crop. By selecting only specific DNA, scientists can transfer only the genes that will result in desirable crop traits, such as hardiness or resistance to insects.

At the beginning of the twenty-first century, about 6 percent of the world's population can access the Internet. By 2010, it is estimated that about 50 percent of the world's population will have access to the Internet—connecting them to a new world of ideas and information.

✓ **Checkpoint** What impact have personal computers had on people's lives?

Advances in Medicine and Biotechnology

Science and technology have revolutionized our understanding and our control of both human life and other forms of life on this planet. Developments in medicine and **biotechnology,** the application of biological research to industry, engineering and technology, have resulted in new ways to combat and prevent disease.

Breakthroughs Transform Medicine In the postwar era, pioneers in the life sciences such as Dr. Jonas Salk became household names. Before the Salk vaccine, the paralyzing disease polio had crippled thousands of children and adults—including President Franklin D. Roosevelt. Other medical researchers developed vaccines to help prevent the spread of smallpox and other diseases.

Breakthroughs in surgery also transformed the field of medicine. In the 1970s, surgeons learned to transplant organs, including the human heart, to save lives. **Lasers** made many types of surgery safer and more precise. Lasers are high-energy light beams that surgeons use to cut or repair tissues and organs. Scientists also had success in treating some cancers, a disease that affects the global population. In recent decades, computers and other technologies have become partners with doctors in diagnosing and treating disease. They have also made it easier for people to share information, thus making diseases easier to treat.

Biotechnology and Genetic Engineering In the past couple of decades, the field of biotechnology has exploded. Biotechnology companies make products including vaccinations, medicines, and industrial bacteria that can be used to treat waste or clean up toxic spills.

Biotechnology is closely related to the fields of genetics and genetic engineering, which have also made dramatic advances in recent years. Genetics is the study of genes and heredity, while genetic engineering is the <u>manipulation</u> of genetic material to produce specific results. Beginning in the 1950s, genetic researchers, spearheaded by Rosalind Franklin, J. D. Watson, and F.H.C. Crick, examined the chemical code carried by all living things. Their research established the central role of DNA—deoxyribonucleic acid—in the chromosomes that determine human heredity. Their work revealed the "double helix," spiral-shaped DNA that carries hereditary traits from parents to children.

Ongoing genetic research has produced new drug therapies to fight human diseases. Research has also created new strains of fruits and vegetables that are intended to resist disease or thrive in conditions that usually inhibit growth. Genetic cloning, or the process of creating identical organisms from the cell of a host organism, has many practical applications in raising livestock and in biological research.

Biotechnology and genetic engineering have brought benefits, but also debate. Some people believe that genetically modified foods are unnatural and potentially dangerous. The possibility of cloning genetically identical mammals—including human beings—has also raised ethical questions about the role of science in creating and changing life.

Standards of Living Rise As you have read, science and technology have often had a direct and powerful impact on human life. Advances in diagnosing and treating disease and increased agricultural output have raised life expectancies worldwide, as well as standards of living. Yet great challenges still remain, from overpopulation to disasters to corrupt governments. In the decades ahead, people will continue to look for ways to solve global problems, using whatever tools they have.

✓ **Checkpoint** How have scientific advances affected people's standard of living?

Vocabulary Builder

<u>manipulation</u>—(muh nip yoo LAY shun) *n.* the skillful handling of something with the purpose of achieving a specific result

---

SECTION 5 Assessment

Progress Monitoring *Online*
For: Self-quiz with vocabulary practice
Web Code: nba-3451

Terms, People, and Places

1. What do each of the key terms listed at the beginning of the section have in common? Explain.

Note Taking

2. **Reading Skill: Compare** Use your completed chart to answer the Focus Question: How have advances in science and technology shaped the modern world?

Comprehension and Critical Thinking

3. **Synthesize Information** Considering the history of the Cold War, explain why the United States and Russia competed against each other to achieve dominance in the space race.

4. **Recognize Cause and Effect** What impact has the computer revolution had on globalization?

5. **Express Problems Clearly** Biotechnology has provided many benefits, but many people worry about its long-term effects. Explain why this is so.

● **Writing About History**

Quick Write: Write a Conclusion Write a conclusion that restates your thesis, sums up the supporting details, and leaves readers with a final impression. This final impression can be a memorable statement or even a call to action. As you write a conclusion about science and technology in the modern world, consider what basic impression you want the reader to remember about the topic, even if he or she takes nothing else away from the essay.

Quick Study Guide

■ Key Components of Globalization

- Interdependence: dependence of countries on goods, resources, knowledge, and labor from other parts of the world
- Advances in communications and transportation
- Rise of huge multinational corporations
- Far-reaching effects of financial crisis, shortages of natural resources, and debt
- Rise of global economy with many global organizations and treaties

■ Influential Technology of the Twentieth Century

Technology	Description	Uses
Artificial satellite	Man-made object that orbits a larger body	Space exploration; spying and other military purposes; scientific research; navigation; communications
Computer	Device for storing, processing, and rapidly manipulating data	Creating and preserving data; making businesses and homes run more efficiently; controlling satellites and factories
Internet	Network of world computer systems linked by cables and satellites	Instant communication with users around world; instant data retrieval; means of commerce
Biotechnology	Application of biological research to industry	Vaccinations and medicines; industrial bacteria; genetic engineering

■ Major Challenges to Society Today

- Global poverty, disasters, and disease
- Ensuring human rights for all, including women, children, and indigenous peoples
- Environmental problems including pollution, deforestation, desertification, and climate change
- Threat of misuse of nuclear technology and weapons of mass destruction
- Terrorism

■ Important Industrialized Regions

Region	Description	Role in Global Economy
The United States	World's only superpower	Important world leader; largest trading country in world
The European Union	Union of 25 European nations with distinct governments but common economic, political, and cultural institutions	Currently includes over half of European nations and is growing; world's largest trading region
The Pacific Rim	Geographical region that includes the countries that border the Pacific Ocean	With many countries and huge populations, potential to be major player in global economy

■ Recent World Events

- 1986 Nuclear accident occurs in Chernobyl.
- 1988 Osama bin Laden forms al Qaeda.
- 1990 Germany is reunited.
- 1993 The European Union forms.
- 1994 NAFTA is created.
- 1995 The WTO forms.

1985 — 1990 — 1995

Concept Connector

■ Cumulative Review

Record the answers below on your Concept Connector worksheets. In addition, record information from this chapter about the following concepts:

- Trade: United States trade in the twentieth century
- Economic systems in the twentieth century

1. **Technology** Compare the development of computer technology and its effect on modern life with the invention of the telephone and its effect on life during the Industrial Revolution. Consider the impact of each on peopleŠdaily lives, business and trade, and communications.

2. **Trade** In the late 1900s, Japan became one of the world's economic powerhouses, prompting fears among some Americans that it would eventually dominate the United States' economy. How did this situation compare to that of European fears of Portuguese dominance in the 1500s?

3. **Cooperation** Is the work of NGOs essential in the 21st century? Think about the work that organizations like the International Red Cross do. Are there situations in which an NGO would be better suited to provide relief than a government or an organization like the United Nations? Why might groups of people in some situations be more likely to welcome aid from an NGO than from a government?

4. **Trade** Compare modern economic free trade policies—characterized by regional trade blocs and organizations like the WTO—with the economic policies of European nations toward their American colonies in the 1600s and 1700s. Think about
   - the goal of each set of policies
   - who the policies were meant to benefit
   - what effect the policies had both on ordinary people and on globalization in general

■ Connections To Today

1. **Advances in Science: Medical Procedures** In 1954, American doctor Joseph Murray performed the first organ transplant, successfully transplanting a kidney from a man into his twin brother. In 2004, nearly 30,000 organ transplants were performed. Think about the issues that people grappled with decades ago as they considered the ethics of organ transplantation. Then choose a medical procedure that is being debated today. (Possibilities might include stem cell research, genetic cloning, or the use of surrogate mothers.) Research your topic and then write two paragraphs: one that supports the procedure and one that opposes it.

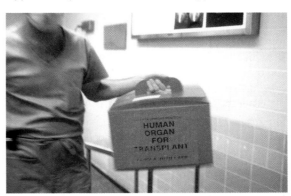

2. **Cultural Diffusion: Spread of Popular Culture** During the 20th century, American popular culture—especially American movies, music, and clothing—influenced people around the world. Consider the factors necessary for cultural diffusion. Why is popular culture from the United States widely influential? Predict which countries' popular culture will become widely influential in the early 21st century.

History Interactive
For: Interactive timeline
Web Code: nbp-3461

| 1997 **The Asian financial crisis hits.** | Sept. 11, 2001 **Al Qaeda attacks the United States.** |

2000   2005

| 2000 **Vladimir Putin is elected president of Russia.** | October 2001 **The United States begins war on the Taliban in Afghanistan.** | Dec. 26, 2004 **Tsunami devastates Southeast Asia.** |

Chapter Assessment

Terms, People, and Places

Choose the italicized term in parentheses that best completes each sentence.

1. A *(deficit/default)* is the gap between what a government spends and what it takes in through taxes and other resources.
2. One of the WTO's basic policies is its opposition to *(outsourcing/protectionism)*.
3. *(Famine/Acid rain)* is a particular concern in areas where there has been a natural disaster.
4. The belief that society should be governed by Islamic law is known as *(Islamic fundamentalism/terrorism)*.
5. *(Genetics/Artificial satellites)* have revolutionized communications.

Main Ideas

Section 1 (pp. 734–737)
6. Describe the status of Russia and the United States after the end of the Cold War.
7. How has economic power in Asia shifted over the past couple of decades?

Section 2 (pp. 738–742)
8. What are the main characteristics of economic interdependence?
9. Summarize the benefits and costs of globalization.

Section 3 (pp. 744–751)
10. What are the main causes of poverty?
11. Describe some of the environmental challenges of the 21st century.

Section 4 (pp. 753–757)
12. Why are nuclear weapons a particular problem in Russia?
13. What is Al Qaeda, and why is it such a threat?

Section 5 (pp. 758–763)
14. Summarize the impact of science and technology on modern life.

Chapter Focus Question
15. What are the major issues facing the world today?

Critical Thinking

16. **Analyze Information** Which region do you think will be the most important economically during the next half-century: the EU, the Pacific Rim, or the United States? Explain your answer.
17. **Predict Consequences** What might be the global impact if terrorists cut off supplies of natural gas or another important resource to a large American city?
18. **Geography and History** Consider the space race of the late 1900s. Why have nations throughout history found it important to explore frontiers?
19. **Recognize Cause and Effect** In this chapter you have read about how economic and technological changes have had an impact on people around the world. How might these changes also affect people's values and beliefs?

"Nothing's labeled. How are we supposed to know which fruit has been genetically engineered?"

20. **Analyze Visuals** What point is the cartoonist making about genetically modified foods in the cartoon above?
21. **Recognize Cause and Effect** How does outsourcing jobs affect both the home country and the country where the jobs are outsourced?
22. **Draw Inferences** How can globalization bring about a stronger commitment to human rights? How can it encourage human rights abuses, such as child labor?

● Writing About History

Write a Persuasive Essay People strongly debate many of the issues that face the world today. Choose a topic that interests you—and that you have a strong opinion about—and then write a persuasive essay. You may choose your own topic or select from the following: free trade, global warming, the war on terrorism, WMDs, or HIV/AIDS. Consult page SH16 of the Writing Handbook for additional help.

Prewriting
- Do library or Internet research to read about each of the topics listed above.
- Choose the topic that interests you most or another of your own.

- List questions about the topic and gather additional sources.

Drafting
- Develop your thesis and select persuasive arguments that support it.
- Organize and write the essay, using your second best argument in the introduction and your best argument in the conclusion.
- Be sure to include a personal appeal or an example that many people can relate to.

Revising
- Use the guidelines for revising your report on page SH17 of the Writing Handbook.

Document-Based Assessment

The Use of Alternative Energy

For many scientists, politicians, and citizens, energy consumption is a troubling issue. Most people agree that the world is too dependent on fossil fuels, which are not renewable. However, intense debate surrounds the questions of which alternate energy sources we should focus on and how quickly we need to have them developed.

Document A

U. S. Energy Consumption by Energy Source, 2003

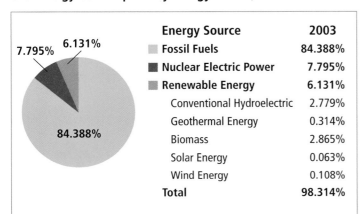

Energy Source	2003
Fossil Fuels	84.388%
Nuclear Electric Power	7.795%
Renewable Energy	6.131%
Conventional Hydroelectric	2.779%
Geothermal Energy	0.314%
Biomass	2.865%
Solar Energy	0.063%
Wind Energy	0.108%
Total	98.314%

SOURCE: *Energy Information Administration (EIA), Monthly Energy Review, April 2004, Department of Energy*

Note: Percentages may not equal 100 due to rounding.

Document B

"As we approach the end of the twentieth century there is no single thing we can do that will have as large an impact on the people of the world during the new century than the development of solar power satellites. They will bring prosperity, an opportunity for the poor nations of the earth to achieve true freedom from want, healing of our environment, and open the vast new frontier of space to all of us.

. . . With the development of solar power satellites we will tap directly into the power of the sun and save the world from impending chaos. There will be hope for the future as we enter the twenty-first century."

—From ***Sun Power*** by Ralph Nansen

Document C

"Renewables are not without their drawbacks. Solar and wind farms cannot generate much electricity on cloudy or still days. As intermittent energy sources, they require vast systems to store the energy they produce, or must rely on the rest of the electrical system for backup. And despite federal subsidies to spur technological innovation, renewable sources have not become economical enough to seriously challenge fossil fuels in an open market."

—From ***CQ Researcher,*** November 7, 1997

Analyzing Documents

Use your knowledge of global issues and Documents A, B, and C to answer questions 1–4.

1. Which document is supported by the actual U.S. energy consumption data shown in Document A?
   A Document B
   B Document C
   C both Documents B and C
   D neither Document B nor C

2. Which statement best describes the viewpoint of the author of Document B?
   A Biomass generators are a better alternative to fossil fuel than solar powered satellites.
   B Solar powered satellites are the most promising alternative to fossil fuel.
   C Solar powered satellites are not realistic or cost effective as an alternative to fossil fuel.
   D More research must be carried out to determine whether solar powered satellites are a realistic alternative to fossil fuel.

3. According to Document C, all are drawbacks of renewables except which of the following?
   A They are intermittent energy sources.
   B They are not cost-efficient.
   C They rely on traditional electricity sources.
   D They are worse for the environment.

4. **Writing Task** What does our energy future hold? Make some predictions for 50 years in the future. Use information from these documents along with information from the chapter to support your predictions.

Concept Connector Handbooks

Contents

Spanish doubloons

The Concept Connector Handbooks provide you with reference information that will make it easier for you to compare key concepts and events across time and place.

Lithuanian woman, 1991

Great Wall of China

Ancient Egypt

Egypt

Mediterranean Sea

Nile Delta

Giza
Memphis

Libyan
Desert

Nile River

Thebes

Red Sea

Miller Projection
0   200 mi

0   200 km

Nubian
Desert

Detail of the Bayeux Tapestry

ENTO PLENIS VE=
INTE RRA:
OONIS
MITIS

Atlas and Geography

What Is Geography?

Geography is the study of Earth's features, including its people, their surroundings, and the resources available to them. By describing the human environment in different times and places, geographers have added to our knowledge of world history. Often those geographers must draw conclusions from limited evidence. For example, studies might turn up common artistic styles or religious rituals in two widely separated groups of people. A geographer might conclude that the groups traded with each other and, in the process, developed shared cultural traits. Geographers use their favorite tool, the map, to show the results of their observations.

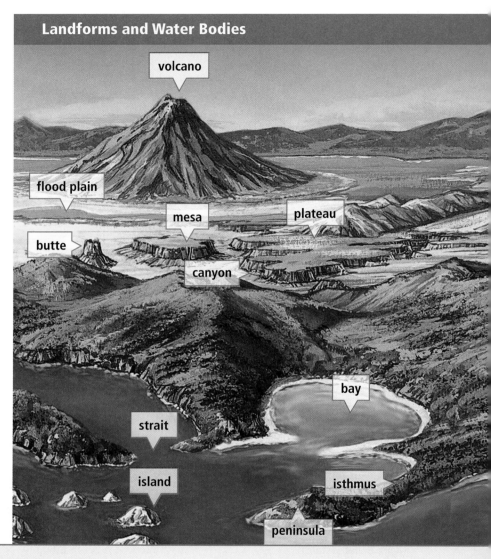

Landforms and Water Bodies

Glossary of Geographic Terms

basin
an area that is lower than surrounding land areas; some basins are filled with water

bay
a part of a larger body of water that extends into the land

butte
a small, high, flat-topped landform with cliff-like sides

canyon
a deep, narrow valley with steep sides; often has a stream flowing through it

cataract
a large waterfall or steep rapids

delta
a plain at the mouth of a river, often triangular in shape, formed when sediment is deposited by flowing water

flood plain
a broad plain on either side of a river, formed when sediment settles during floods

glacier
a huge, slow-moving mass of snow and ice

hill
an area that rises above surrounding land and has a rounded top; lower and usually less steep than a mountain

island
an area of land completely surrounded by water

isthmus
a narrow strip of land that connects two larger areas of land

mesa
a high, flat-topped landform with cliff-like sides; larger than a butte

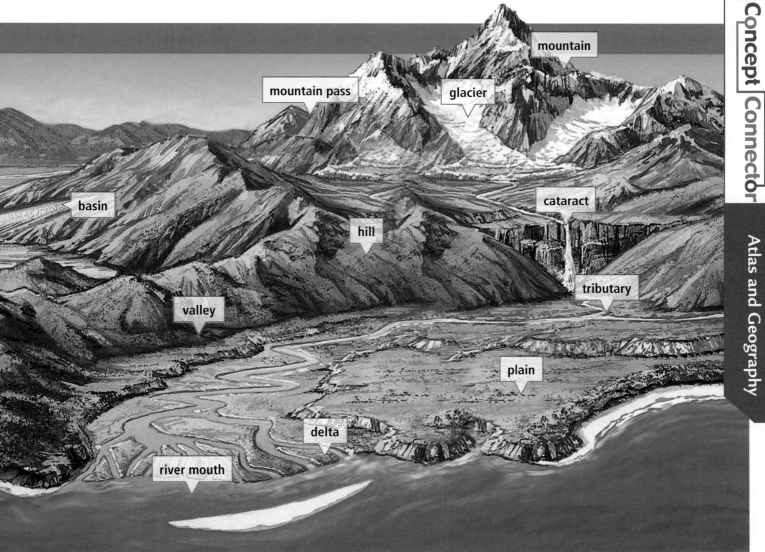

Labels on image: mountain, mountain pass, glacier, basin, cataract, hill, tributary, valley, plain, delta, river mouth

mountain
  a landform that rises steeply at least 2,000 feet (610 m) above surrounding land; usually wide at the bottom and rising to a narrow peak or ridge

mountain pass
  a gap between mountains

peninsula
  an area of land almost completely surrounded by water and connected to the mainland by an isthmus

plain
  a large area of flat or gently rolling land

plateau
  a large, flat area that rises above the surrounding land; at least one side has a steep slope

river mouth
  the point where a river enters a lake or sea

strait
  a narrow stretch of water that connects two larger bodies of water

tributary
  a river or stream that flows into a larger river

valley
  a low stretch of land between mountains or hills; land that is drained by a river

volcano
  an opening in the Earth's surface through which molten rock, ashes, and gases from the Earth's interior escape

Atlas and Geography

The World: Political

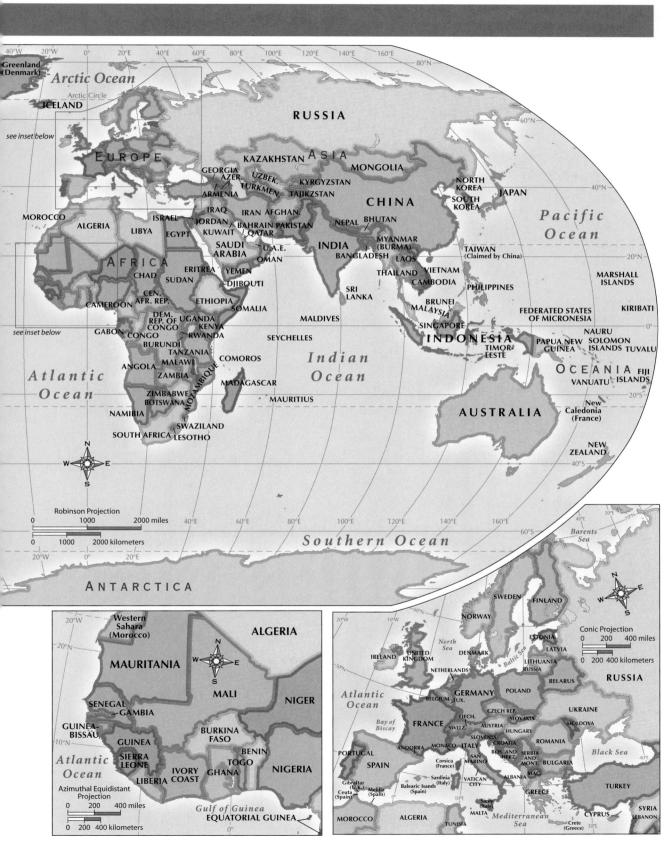

Robinson Projection

0   1000   2000 miles

0   1000   2000 kilometers

Azimuthal Equidistant Projection

0   200   400 miles

0   200   400 kilometers

Conic Projection

0   200   400 miles

0   200   400 kilometers

Atlas and Geography

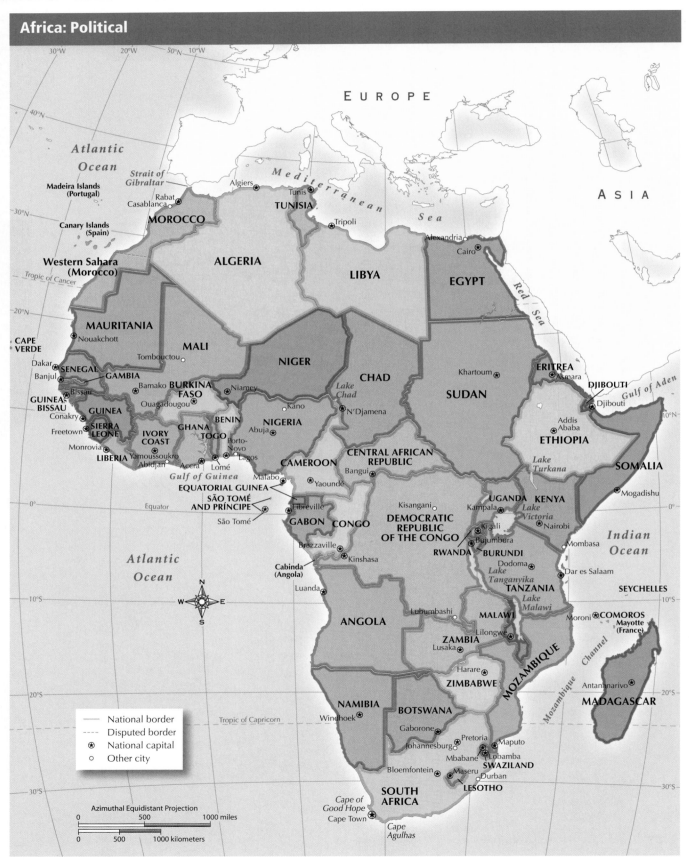

EUROPE

ASIA

Atlantic Ocean

Madeira Islands (Portugal)

Strait of Gibraltar

Algiers

Tunis

Mediterranean Sea

Tripoli

Alexandria

Cairo

Canary Islands (Spain)

Casablanca
Rabat

MOROCCO

TUNISIA

Western Sahara (Morocco)

Tropic of Cancer

ALGERIA

LIBYA

EGYPT

Red Sea

MAURITANIA

Nouakchott

MALI

Tombouctou

NIGER

CHAD

Khartoum

SUDAN

ERITREA

Asmara

DJIBOUTI

Djibouti

Gulf of Aden

CAPE VERDE

Dakar
SENEGAL
Banjul **GAMBIA**

Bamako
BURKINA FASO
Ouagadougou

Niamey

Kano

Lake Chad

N'Djamena

Addis Ababa

ETHIOPIA

GUINEA-BISSAU
Bissau
Conakry
SIERRA LEONE
Freetown
Monrovia
LIBERIA

GUINEA

GHANA
IVORY COAST
Yamoussoukro
Abidjan

BENIN
TOGO
Abuja
Porto-Novo
Accra Lomé Lagos

NIGERIA

CENTRAL AFRICAN REPUBLIC

Bangui

Lake Turkana

SOMALIA

Mogadishu

Gulf of Guinea

Malabo

CAMEROON

Yaoundé

EQUATORIAL GUINEA
SÃO TOMÉ AND PRÍNCIPE
São Tomé

Libreville

GABON **CONGO**

DEMOCRATIC REPUBLIC OF THE CONGO

Kisangani

Kampala

UGANDA **KENYA**

Lake Victoria
Kigali
Nairobi

Equator

Brazzaville
Kinshasa

RWANDA **BURUNDI**
Bujumbura
Dodoma
Mombasa

Indian Ocean

Cabinda (Angola)

Atlantic Ocean

Luanda

Lubumbashi

TANZANIA

Lake Tanganyika

Dar es Salaam

Lake Malawi

SEYCHELLES

N
W E
S

ANGOLA

MALAWI
Lilongwe

ZAMBIA
Lusaka

Moroni **COMOROS**
Mayotte (France)

Mozambique Channel

Harare

ZIMBABWE

MOZAMBIQUE

Antananarivo

MADAGASCAR

Tropic of Capricorn

NAMIBIA

Windhoek

BOTSWANA

Gaborone

Pretoria
Maputo
Johannesburg

Mbabane
Lobamba
SWAZILAND

Bloemfontein
Maseru
Durban

LESOTHO

Cape of Good Hope
Cape Town

SOUTH AFRICA

Cape Agulhas

——	National border
----	Disputed border
⊛	National capital
○	Other city

Azimuthal Equidistant Projection

0   500   1000 miles

0   500   1000 kilometers

Africa: Physical

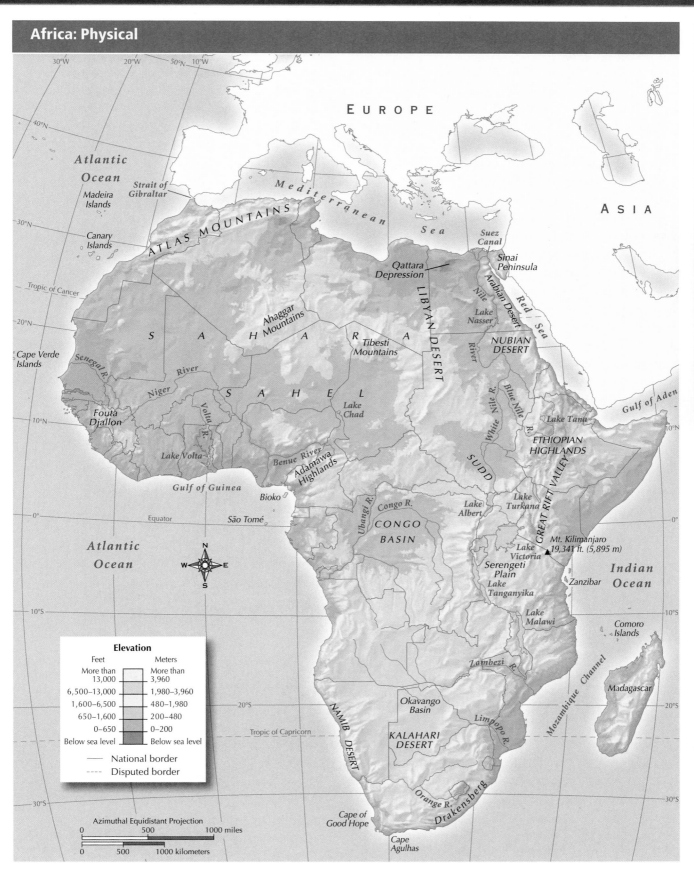

EUROPE

ASIA

Atlantic Ocean

Madeira Islands

Strait of Gibraltar

Mediterranean Sea

Canary Islands

Tropic of Cancer

Cape Verde Islands

Senegal R.

Niger River

Fouta Djallon

Volta R.

Lake Volta

Gulf of Guinea

Bioko

São Tomé

Equator

Atlantic Ocean

ATLAS MOUNTAINS

S   A   H   A   R   A

Ahaggar Mountains

Tibesti Mountains

S   A   H   E   L

Lake Chad

Benue River

Adamawa Highlands

Ubangi R.

Congo R.

CONGO BASIN

Qattara Depression

LIBYAN DESERT

Suez Canal

Sinai Peninsula

Nile River

Lake Nasser

Arabian Desert

Red Sea

NUBIAN DESERT

Gulf of Aden

White Nile R.

Blue Nile R.

Lake Tana

ETHIOPIAN HIGHLANDS

SUDD

Lake Albert

Lake Turkana

GREAT RIFT VALLEY

Mt. Kilimanjaro 19,341 ft. (5,895 m)

Lake Victoria

Serengeti Plain

Lake Tanganyika

Zanzibar

Indian Ocean

Lake Malawi

Comoro Islands

Zambezi R.

Mozambique Channel

Madagascar

Okavango Basin

Limpopo R.

NAMIB DESERT

KALAHARI DESERT

Tropic of Capricorn

Orange R.

Drakensberg

Cape of Good Hope

Cape Agulhas

N W E S

Elevation

Feet	Meters
More than 13,000	More than 3,960
6,500–13,000	1,980–3,960
1,600–6,500	480–1,980
650–1,600	200–480
0–650	0–200
Below sea level	Below sea level

—— National border

- - - - Disputed border

Azimuthal Equidistant Projection

0   500   1000 miles

0   500   1000 kilometers

30°W   20°W   10°W   0°   50°N   40°N   30°N   20°N   10°N   0°   10°S   20°S   30°S

Atlas and Geography

Asia: Political

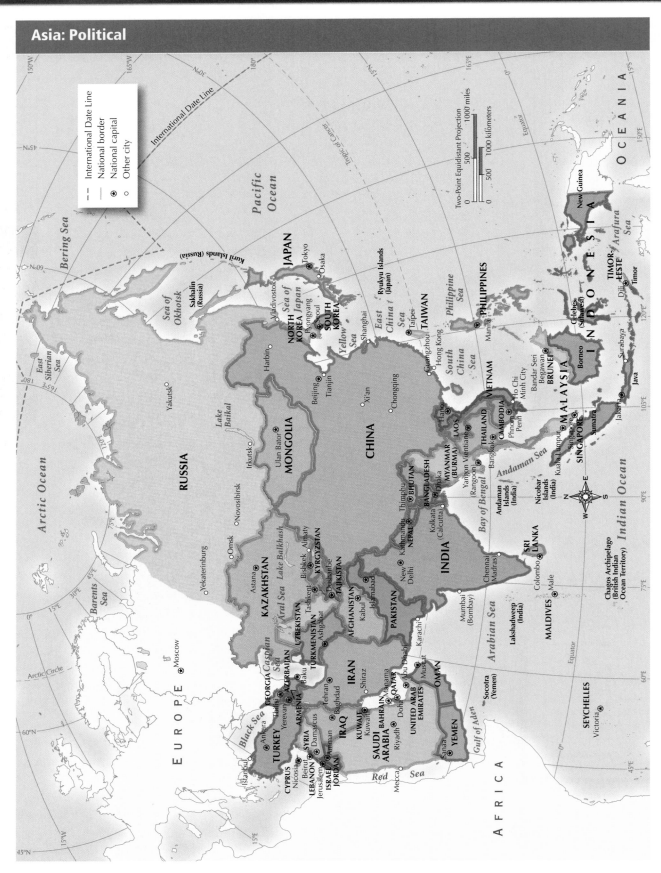

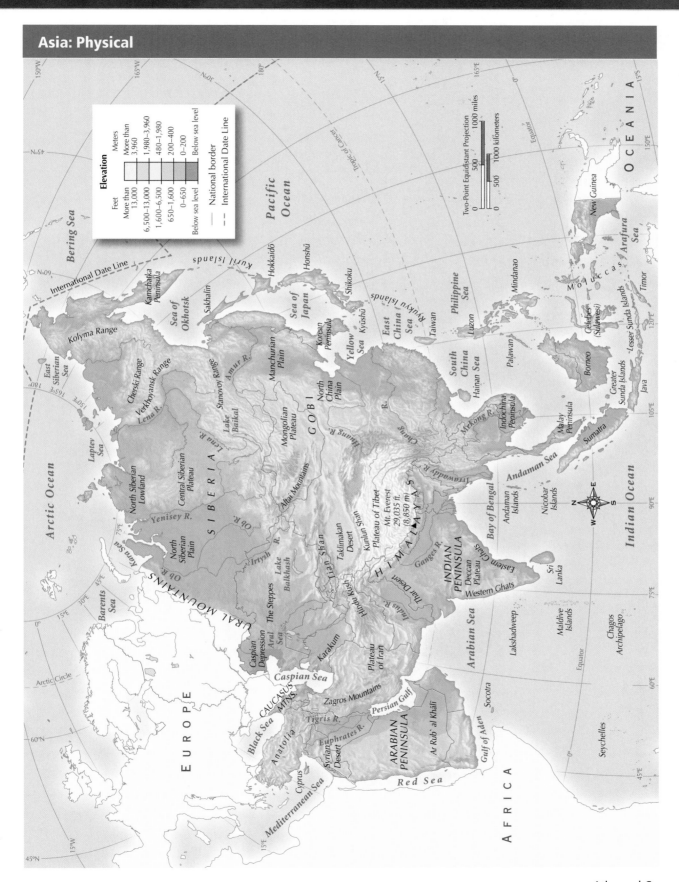

Asia: Physical

Elevation

Feet	Meters
More than 13,000	More than 3,960
6,500–13,000	1,980–3,960
1,600–6,500	480–1,980
650–1,600	200–400
0–650	0–200
Below sea level	Below sea level

—— National border
- - - International Date Line

Two-Point Equidistant Projection

0   500   1000 miles
0   500   1000 kilometers

Arctic Ocean

Bering Sea

East Siberian Sea

Laptev Sea

Kara Sea

Barents Sea

Black Sea

Mediterranean Sea

Red Sea

Gulf of Aden

Arabian Sea

Bay of Bengal

Andaman Sea

Indian Ocean

Pacific Ocean

Sea of Okhotsk

Sea of Japan

Yellow Sea

East China Sea

South China Sea

Philippine Sea

Arafura Sea

Caspian Sea

Aral Sea

EUROPE

AFRICA

OCEANIA

SIBERIA

Kolyma Range

Cherski Range

Verkhoyansk Range

Stanovoy Range

Kamchatka Peninsula

Sakhalin

Kuril Islands

Hokkaidō

Honshū

Shikoku

Kyūshū

Korean Peninsula

Ryukyu Islands

Taiwan

Luzon

Mindanao

Palawan

Borneo

Celebes (Sulawesi)

Moluccas

New Guinea

Timor

Lesser Sunda Islands

Greater Sunda Islands

Java

Sumatra

Malay Peninsula

Indochina Peninsula

Hainan

Amur R.

Lake Baikal

Lena R.

Yenisey R.

Ob R.

Irtysh

Lake Balkhash

North Siberian Lowland

North Siberian Plain

Central Siberian Plateau

Mongolian Plateau

Manchurian Plain

North China Plain

GOBI

Huang He R.

Chang R.

Mekong R.

Irrawaddy R.

Altai Mountains

Tian Shan

Taklimakan Desert

Kunlun Shan

Plateau of Tibet

Mt. Everest 29,035 ft. (8,850 m)

HIMALAYAS

Hindu Kush

Ganges R.

Indus R.

Thar Desert

INDIAN PENINSULA

Deccan Plateau

Western Ghats

Eastern Ghats

Sri Lanka

Andaman Islands

Nicobar Islands

Maldive Islands

Lakshadweep

Chagos Archipelago

Seychelles

Socotra

URAL MOUNTAINS

The Steppes

Karakum

Caspian Depression

Plateau of Iran

Zagros Mountains

Persian Gulf

CAUCASUS MTNS.

Anatolia

Cyprus

Tigris R.

Euphrates R.

Syrian Desert

ARABIAN PENINSULA

Ar Rub' al Khali

International Date Line

Arctic Circle

Tropic of Cancer

Equator

45°N

60°N

45°N

150°W

165°W

180°

165°E

150°E

135°E

120°E

105°E

90°E

75°E

60°E

45°E

15°W

0°

15°E

30°E

75°E

45°W

30°W

180°

165°

150°

135°

Atlas and Geography

Europe: Political

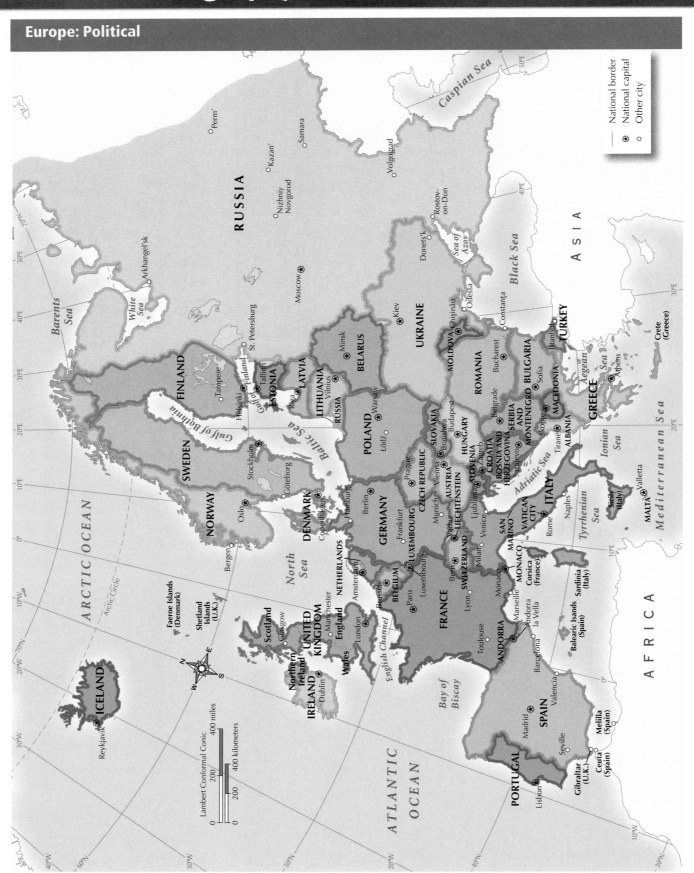

Legend:
— National border
⊛ National capital
○ Other city

Lambert Conformal Conic

0 200 400 miles
0 200 400 kilometers

ARCTIC OCEAN

Arctic Circle

ATLANTIC OCEAN

RUSSIA

Perm'

Kazan'

Samara

Nizhniy Novgorod

Volgograd

Arkhangel'sk

Barents Sea

White Sea

Moscow ⊛

St. Petersburg

Rostov-on-Don

Donets'k

Sea of Azov

Caspian Sea

Black Sea

ASIA

FINLAND
Tampere
Helsinki
Gulf of Finland

SWEDEN
Stockholm
Göteborg

NORWAY
Oslo
Bergen

Tallinn
ESTONIA
Riga
LATVIA
LITHUANIA
Vilnius

Minsk
BELARUS

Kiev
UKRAINE

Chişinău
MOLDOVA

Odesa
Constanţa

ROMANIA
Bucharest

BULGARIA
Sofia

Belgrade
SERBIA AND MONTENEGRO

MACEDONIA
Skopje

TURKEY
Istanbul

Crete (Greece)

Athens
GREECE

Aegean Sea

RUSSIA

POLAND
Warsaw
Łódź

Baltic Sea

Gulf of Bothnia

DENMARK
Copenhagen

GERMANY
Berlin
Hamburg
Frankfurt
Munich

Prague
CZECH REPUBLIC

SLOVAKIA
Bratislava
Vienna
AUSTRIA

Budapest
HUNGARY

SLOVENIA
Ljubljana
Zagreb
CROATIA

BOSNIA AND HERZEGOVINA
Sarajevo

Tiranë
ALBANIA

Ionian Sea

Adriatic Sea

ITALY
Rome ⊛
Naples
Venice
Milan

VATICAN CITY
SAN MARINO

Sicily (Italy)

MALTA
Valletta

Tyrrhenian Sea

Mediterranean Sea

NETHERLANDS
Amsterdam

BELGIUM
Brussels

LUXEMBOURG
Luxembourg

Paris
FRANCE
Lyon
Marseille
Toulouse

LIECHTENSTEIN
SWITZERLAND
Bern
Bordeaux

MONACO
Monaco

Corsica (France)

Sardinia (Italy)

ANDORRA
Andorra la Vella

Barcelona
Valencia
SPAIN
Madrid
Seville

Balearic Isands (Spain)

ANDORRA

PORTUGAL
Lisbon

Gibraltar (U.K.)
Ceuta (Spain)
Melilla (Spain)

Bay of Biscay

North Sea

UNITED KINGDOM
Scotland
Glasgow
Manchester
England
London
Wales

Shetland Islands (U.K.)
Faeroe Islands (Denmark)

NORTHERN IRELAND
IRELAND
Dublin

English Channel

ICELAND
Reykjavík

AFRICA

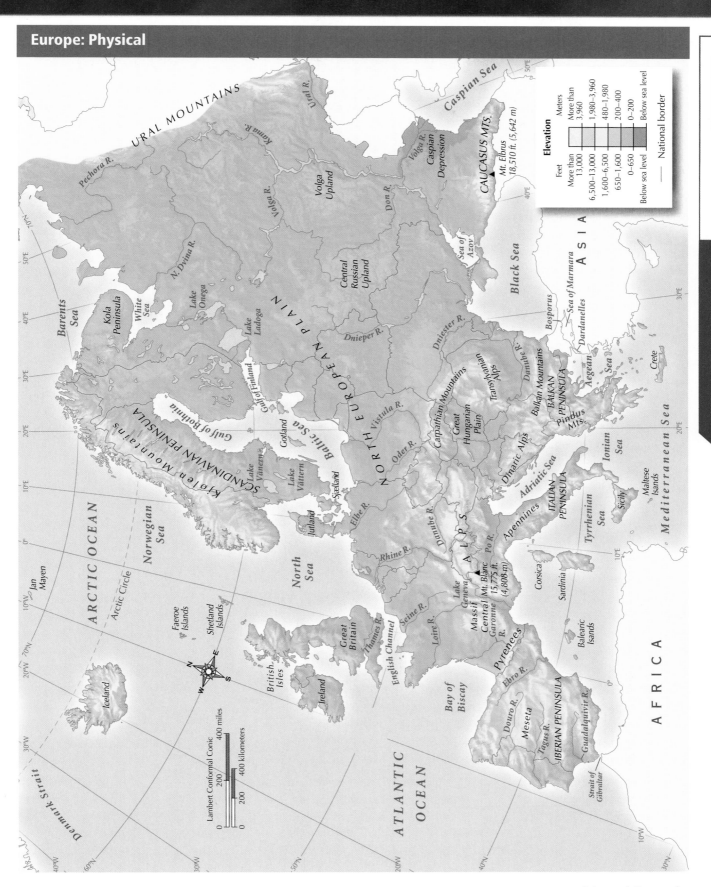

Concept Connector
Atlas and Geography

Elevation

Feet	Meters
More than 13,000	More than 3,960
6,500–13,000	1,980–3,960
1,600–6,500	480–1,980
650–1,600	200–400
0–650	0–200
Below sea level	Below sea level

— National border

Atlas and Geography

North and South America: Political

International Date Line

Bering Strait

Bering Sea

Beaufort Sea

Greenland (Denmark)

Baffin Bay

Nuuk

Davis Strait

Arctic Circle

60°N

Alaska (United States)

Gulf of Alaska

Great Bear Lake

Great Slave Lake

Hudson Bay

Labrador Sea

45°N

CANADA

Lake Winnipeg

Great Lakes

Vancouver

Ottawa

Toronto

Chicago

New York

Washington, D.C.

Atlantic Ocean

30°N

UNITED STATES

Los Angeles

Houston

Tropic of Cancer

MEXICO

Gulf of Mexico

Nassau

Havana

BAHAMAS

DOMINICAN REPUBLIC

CUBA

HAITI

Puerto Rico (United States)

Mexico City

JAMAICA

Port-au-Prince

Santo Domingo

U.S. Virgin Islands (United States)

Guadeloupe (France)

15°N

Belmopan

BELIZE

Kingston

Martinique (France)

Guatemala City

HONDURAS

Tegucigalpa

Caribbean Sea

DOMINICA

BARBADOS

GUATEMALA

San Salvador

NICARAGUA

TRINIDAD AND TOBAGO

EL SALVADOR

Managua

Caracas

GUYANA

San José

Panama

COSTA RICA

Georgetown

Paramaribo

PANAMA

VENEZUELA

French Guiana (France)

Bogotá

Cayenne

COLOMBIA

SURINAME

Equator

Quito

0°

Galápagos Islands (Ecuador)

ECUADOR

Pacific Ocean

PERU

BRAZIL

Lima

Lake Titicaca

La Paz

Brasília

15°S

BOLIVIA

Sucre

Tropic of Capricorn

PARAGUAY

Rio de Janiero

Asunción

São Paulo

CHILE

ARGENTINA

URUGUAY

Santiago

Buenos Aires

Montevideo

30°S

Río de la Plata

Atlantic Ocean

Falkland Islands (U.K.)

N W E S

— National border

- - - International Date Line

⊛ National capital

○ Other city

Lambert Azimuthal Equal-Area Projection

0   1000   2000 miles

0   1000   2000 kilometers

180° 165°W 150°W 135°W 120°W 105°W 90°W 75°W 60°W 45°W 30°W 15°W 0°

45°N 30°N 15°N 0° 15°S 30°S 45°S

North and South America: Physical

Elevation

Feet	Meters
More than 13,000	More than 3,960
6,500–13,000	1,980–3,960
1,600–6,500	480–1,980
650–1,600	200–400
0–650	0–200
Below sea level	Below sea level

—— National border

- - - International Date Line

Lambert Azimuthal Equal-Area Projection

0   1000   2000 miles

0   1000   2000 kilometers

Atlas and Geography

Australia, New Zealand, and Oceania: Political-Physical

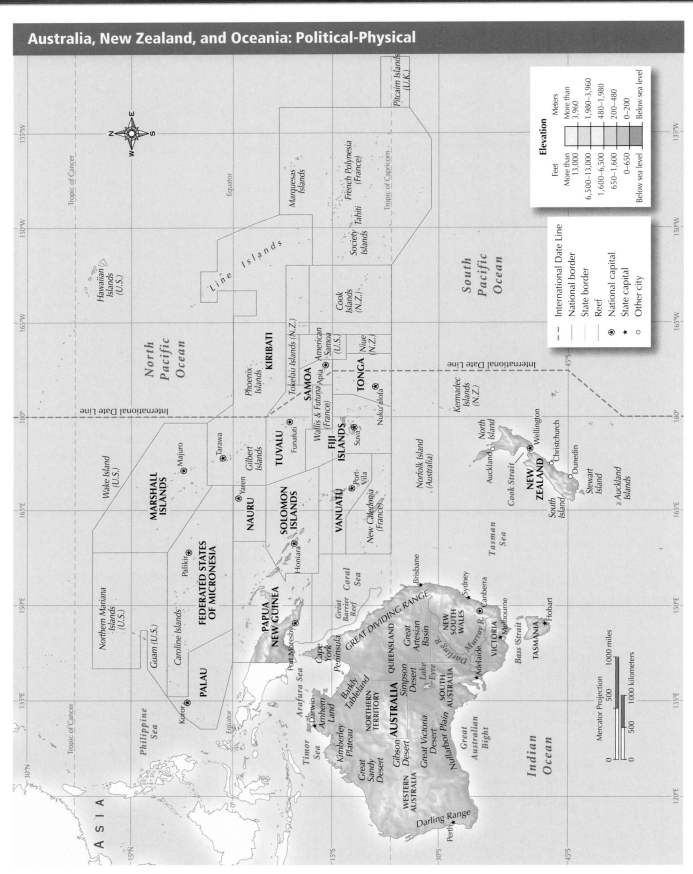

Elevation

Feet	Meters
More than 13,000	More than 3,960
6,500–13,000	1,980–3,960
1,600–6,500	480–1,980
650–1,600	200–480
0–650	0–200
Below sea level	Below sea level

- – – International Date Line
- ——— National border
- ——— State border
- Reef
- ⊛ National capital
- ★ State capital
- ○ Other city

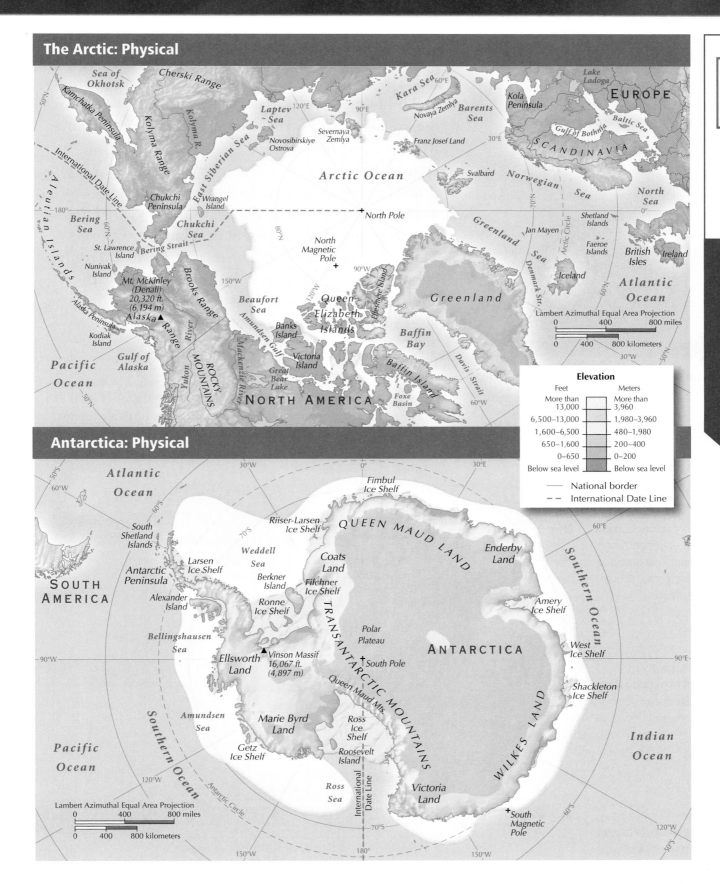

The Arctic: Physical

Sea of Okhotsk · Cherski Range · Kamchatka Peninsula · Kolyma Range · Kolyma R. · Laptev Sea · Kara Sea · 60°E · Novaya Zemlya · Barents Sea · Kola Peninsula · Lake Ladoga · EUROPE · Gulf of Bothnia · Baltic Sea · SCANDINAVIA · 120°E · 90°E · 30°E · Severnaya Zemlya · Franz Josef Land · Novosibirskiye Ostrova · International Date Line · East Siberian Sea · Arctic Ocean · Svalbard · Norwegian Sea · North Sea · 0° · 180° · Chukchi Peninsula · Wrangel Island · North Pole · Greenland Sea · Jan Mayen · Shetland Islands · Arctic Circle · Aleutian Islands · Bering Sea · Chukchi Sea · 80°N · North Magnetic Pole · Faeroe Islands · British Isles · Ireland · St. Lawrence Island · Bering Strait · 90°W · Iceland · Atlantic Ocean · Nunivak Island · 150°W · Queen Elizabeth Islands · Ellesmere Island · Denmark Str. · Mt. McKinley (Denali) 20,320 ft. (6,194 m) Alaska ▲ · Brooks Range · Beaufort Sea · 120°W · Greenland · Alaska Peninsula · Range · Yukon River · Amundsen Gulf · Banks Island · Baffin Bay · Kodiak Island · ROCKY MOUNTAINS · Mackenzie River · Victoria Island · Baffin Island · Pacific Ocean · Gulf of Alaska · Great Bear Lake · 60°W · 50°N · Foxe Basin · NORTH AMERICA · Davis Strait · 30°W

Lambert Azimuthal Equal Area Projection
0   400   800 miles
0   400   800 kilometers

Antarctica: Physical

Atlantic Ocean · 30°W · 0° · 30°E · Fimbul Ice Shelf · 60°W · Riiser-Larsen Ice Shelf · QUEEN MAUD LAND · 60°E · 70°S · Weddell Sea · Coats Land · Enderby Land · South Shetland Islands · Larsen Ice Shelf · Southern Ocean · Antarctic Peninsula · Berkner Island · Filchner Ice Shelf · Amery Ice Shelf · Alexander Island · Ronne Ice Shelf · TRANSANTARCTIC MOUNTAINS · SOUTH AMERICA · Bellingshausen Sea · Polar Plateau · ANTARCTICA · West Ice Shelf · 90°W · Ellsworth Land · Vinson Massif 16,067 ft. (4,897 m) ▲ · South Pole · 90°E · Amundsen Sea · Marie Byrd Land · Queen Maud Mts. · Ross Ice Shelf · WILKES LAND · Shackleton Ice Shelf · Getz Ice Shelf · Roosevelt Island · Pacific Ocean · 120°W · Ross Sea · International Date Line · Victoria Land · Indian Ocean · Antarctic Circle · South Magnetic Pole · 60°E · 150°W · 180° · 150°E · 70°S · 50°S · 120°E

Lambert Azimuthal Equal Area Projection
0   400   800 miles
0   400   800 kilometers

Elevation

Feet		Meters
More than 13,000		More than 3,960
6,500–13,000		1,980–3,960
1,600–6,500		480–1,980
650–1,600		200–400
0–650		0–200
Below sea level		Below sea level

—— National border
– – – International Date Line

History and Prehistory

You might think of history as everything that has ever happened. For historians, however, history began around 5,000 years ago with the appearance of writing in two civilizations—Sumer and Egypt. Everything before that is prehistory.

Prehistory ← 3000 B.C. → **History**

Writing systems appear in Sumer (above) and in Egypt *c.* 3000 B.C.*

* The *c.* before the date is Latin for *circa*, meaning "around" or "approximately."

Historians study how people lived in the past. They might examine their tools, weapons, jewelry, and building sites, but they rely mainly on written records. For this reason, we say that history began when writing began.

History is a changing story. A historian living at the time of an event may write what seems like a valid description, but a historian writing 100 years later may describe the same event another way entirely. This is because different generations have different perspectives on, or ways of looking at, history. In addition, as time passes, new evidence may appear to alter the interpretation of an event.

Major Eras in World History

Historians attempt to make sense of vast stretches of history by dividing them into periods. This periodization makes it easier to discuss a group of events by relating them to a broader theme.

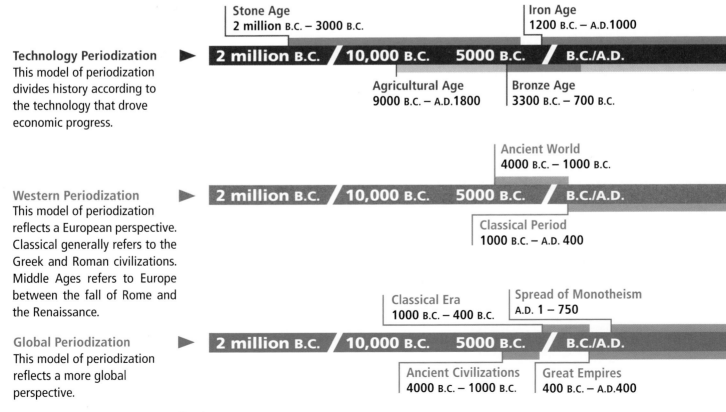

Technology Periodization
This model of periodization divides history according to the technology that drove economic progress.

Stone Age
2 million B.C. – 3000 B.C.

Iron Age
1200 B.C. – A.D.1000

2 million B.C. / 10,000 B.C. 5000 B.C. / B.C./A.D.

Agricultural Age
9000 B.C. – A.D.1800

Bronze Age
3300 B.C. – 700 B.C.

Western Periodization
This model of periodization reflects a European perspective. Classical generally refers to the Greek and Roman civilizations. Middle Ages refers to Europe between the fall of Rome and the Renaissance.

Ancient World
4000 B.C. – 1000 B.C.

2 million B.C. / 10,000 B.C. 5000 B.C. / B.C./A.D.

Classical Period
1000 B.C. – A.D. 400

Global Periodization
This model of periodization reflects a more global perspective.

Classical Era
1000 B.C. – 400 B.C.

Spread of Monotheism
A.D. 1 – 750

2 million B.C. / 10,000 B.C. 5000 B.C. / B.C./A.D.

Ancient Civilizations
4000 B.C. – 1000 B.C.

Great Empires
400 B.C. – A.D.400

Your textbook is divided this way, into units. Each unit deals with a period, or era, in world history. There are endless ways to categorize the past, depending on one's point of view. The time-lines below show three different examples of periodization.

Decades, Centuries, and Millenniums

Most nations today use a standard calendar that dates events from the believed birth of Jesus. For dates preceding his birth, this calendar uses the abbreviation b.c. ("before Christ"). For dates after his birth, it uses A.D. (anno Domini, Latin for "in the year of our Lord"). An alternative version of this calendar uses the abbreviations B.C.E. and C.E. meaning "Before the Common Era" and "Common Era."

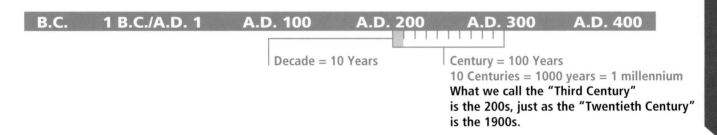

| B.C. | 1 B.C./A.D. 1 | A.D. 100 | A.D. 200 | A.D. 300 | A.D. 400 |

Decade = 10 Years

Century = 100 Years
10 Centuries = 1000 years = 1 millennium
**What we call the "Third Century"
is the 200s, just as the "Twentieth Century"
is the 1900s.**

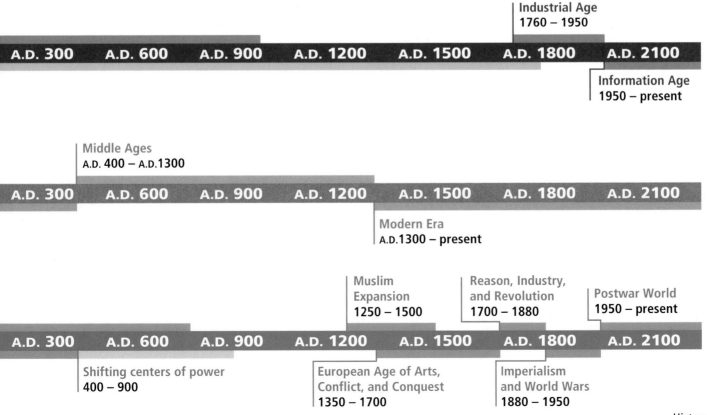

**Industrial Age
1760 – 1950**

| A.D. 300 | A.D. 600 | A.D. 900 | A.D. 1200 | A.D. 1500 | A.D. 1800 | A.D. 2100 |

**Information Age
1950 – present**

Middle Ages
A.D. **400 –** A.D.**1300**

| A.D. 300 | A.D. 600 | A.D. 900 | A.D. 1200 | A.D. 1500 | A.D. 1800 | A.D. 2100 |

Modern Era
A.D.**1300 – present**

**Muslim Expansion
1250 – 1500**

**Reason, Industry, and Revolution
1700 – 1880**

**Postwar World
1950 – present**

| A.D. 300 | A.D. 600 | A.D. 900 | A.D. 1200 | A.D. 1500 | A.D. 1800 | A.D. 2100 |

**Shifting centers of power
400 – 900**

**European Age of Arts, Conflict, and Conquest
1350 – 1700**

**Imperialism and World Wars
1880 – 1950**

History

World Regional Timelines

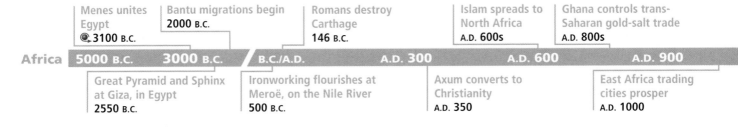

Africa

Menes unites Egypt	Bantu migrations begin		Romans destroy Carthage		Islam spreads to North Africa	Ghana controls trans-Saharan gold-salt trade

Menes unites Egypt
🔍 3100 B.C.

Bantu migrations begin
2000 B.C.

Romans destroy Carthage
146 B.C.

Islam spreads to North Africa
A.D. 600s

Ghana controls trans-Saharan gold-salt trade
A.D. 800s

Africa 5000 B.C. — 3000 B.C. — B.C./A.D. — A.D. 300 — A.D. 600 — A.D. 900

Great Pyramid and Sphinx at Giza, in Egypt
2550 B.C.

Ironworking flourishes at Meroë, on the Nile River
500 B.C.

Axum converts to Christianity
A.D. 350

East Africa trading cities prosper
A.D. 1000

Europe

Rise of Greek city-states
700s B.C.

Europe 5000 B.C. — 3000 B.C. — B.C./A.D. — A.D. 300 — A.D. 600 — A.D. 900

Western Roman empire falls
🔍 A.D. 476

Asia

Sumerian city-states thrive
3200 B.C.

Persian empire created
539 B.C.

Buddhism introduced to Japan
🔍 500s

Asia 5000 B.C. — 3000 B.C. — B.C./A.D. — A.D. 300 — A.D. 600 — A.D. 900

Indus Valley civilization develops
🔍 2500 B.C.

Gupta Golden Age begins in India
A.D. 320

Muhammad's Hijira from Mecca to Medina
🔍 622

The Americas

Cultivation of maize and cotton
3200 B.C.

Hopewell culture flourishes
A.D. 200s

Mississippian civilization thrives
800s

The Americas 5000 B.C. — 3000 B.C. — B.C./A.D. — A.D. 300 — A.D. 600 — A.D. 900

Rise of Olmec civilization
🔍 1400 B.C.

Height of Maya civilization
500s

🔍 **Turning point:** a decisive moment in world history that triggers a major social, political, economic, or cultural transformation.

World Population Growth

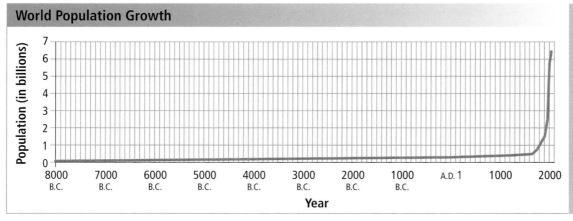

Population (in billions) vs Year

| 8000 B.C. | 7000 B.C. | 6000 B.C. | 5000 B.C. | 4000 B.C. | 3000 B.C. | 2000 B.C. | 1000 B.C. | A.D. 1 | 1000 | 2000 |

Graph Skills As the graph shows, the world's population gradually rose over many centuries, until it shot up suddenly, starting in the 1700s. Improvements in agriculture, greater control of disease, and the shift from manual labor to machines all helped to increase the population.

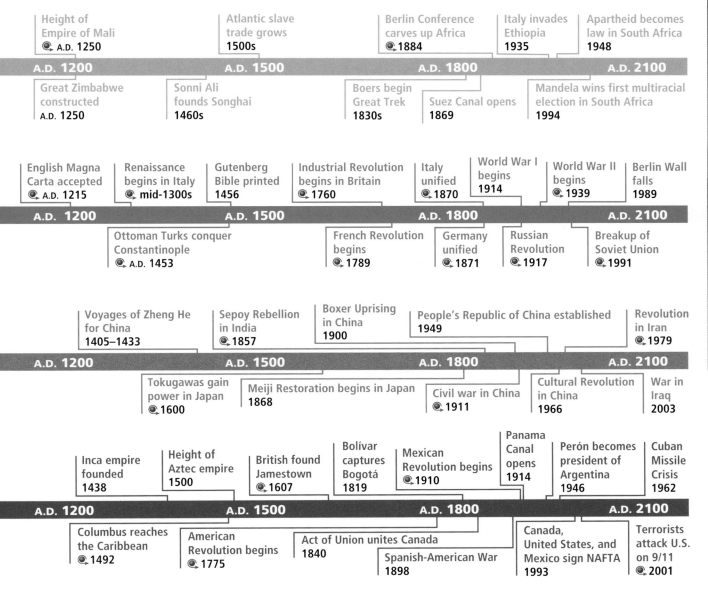

| Height of Empire of Mali ⊕ A.D. 1250 | | Atlantic slave trade grows 1500s | | | Berlin Conference carves up Africa 1884 | Italy invades Ethiopia 1935 | Apartheid becomes law in South Africa 1948 |

A.D. 1200 — **A.D. 1500** — **A.D. 1800** — **A.D. 2100**

| Great Zimbabwe constructed A.D. 1250 | Sonni Ali founds Songhai 1460s | | Boers begin Great Trek 1830s | Suez Canal opens 1869 | Mandela wins first multiracial election in South Africa 1994 |

| English Magna Carta accepted ⊕ A.D. 1215 | Renaissance begins in Italy ⊕ mid-1300s | Gutenberg Bible printed 1456 | Industrial Revolution begins in Britain ⊕ 1760 | Italy unified ⊕ 1870 | World War I begins 1914 | World War II begins ⊕ 1939 | Berlin Wall falls 1989 |

A.D. 1200 — **A.D. 1500** — **A.D. 1800** — **A.D. 2100**

| Ottoman Turks conquer Constantinople ⊕ A.D. 1453 | French Revolution begins ⊕ 1789 | Germany unified ⊕ 1871 | Russian Revolution ⊕ 1917 | Breakup of Soviet Union ⊕ 1991 |

| Voyages of Zheng He for China 1405–1433 | Sepoy Rebellion in India ⊕ 1857 | Boxer Uprising in China 1900 | People's Republic of China established 1949 | Revolution in Iran ⊕ 1979 |

A.D. 1200 — **A.D. 1500** — **A.D. 1800** — **A.D. 2100**

| Tokugawas gain power in Japan ⊕ 1600 | Meiji Restoration begins in Japan 1868 | Civil war in China ⊕ 1911 | Cultural Revolution in China 1966 | War in Iraq 2003 |

| Inca empire founded 1438 | Height of Aztec empire 1500 | British found Jamestown ⊕ 1607 | Bolívar captures Bogotá 1819 | Mexican Revolution begins ⊕ 1910 | Panama Canal opens 1914 | Perón becomes president of Argentina 1946 | Cuban Missile Crisis 1962 |

A.D. 1200 — **A.D. 1500** — **A.D. 1800** — **A.D. 2100**

| Columbus reaches the Caribbean ⊕ 1492 | American Revolution begins ⊕ 1775 | Act of Union unites Canada 1840 | Spanish-American War 1898 | Canada, United States, and Mexico sign NAFTA 1993 | Terrorists attack U.S. on 9/11 ⊕ 2001 |

The Parthenon, Athens, Greece

History

Flag of Giovine
Italia, 1833

UNIONE FORZA
E LIBERTA !!

Imperialism, Colonialism, Nationalism, and Revolution

Imperialism
A policy of pursuing, often through conquest, the economic and political domination of another state.

Colonialism
A policy of politically dominating a dependent territory or people.

Nationalism
A strong feeling of pride in, or devotion to, one's nation.

Revolution
The overthrow of a government from within.

Conquest and Empire

An empire is a group of states or territories controlled by one ruler. Empires often form in a haphazard way. For example, a small state with a strong army successfully defends itself against one neighboring state after another and incorporates their lands. Or at some point, an able ruler aggressively seeks more territory. Over time, the state expands into an empire. A strong military and able leadership are two factors that go into creating an empire. However, successful empires also must develop a government system that can maintain control of conquered peoples.

Selected Empires in World History

Conquests	Time Span	Location
Roman	509 B.C.–A.D. 180	Mediterranean region, Western Europe, Britain
Arab Muslim	A.D. 624–750	Southwest Asia, North Africa, Spain
Mongol	1206–1294	China, Central Asia, Eastern Europe
Ottoman	1299–1566	Southwest Asia, North Africa, Balkans, Eastern Europe
Spanish	1492–1560	Mexico, Central America, South America, Cuba, Florida

First Landing of Columbus by Frederick Kemmelmeyer

Major Conflicts in World History

This table shows selected major wars and conquests. Hundreds of other conflicts, large and small, have occurred throughout history. The cause of a conflict may be as simple as "I want what you have." For example, the basic need for food—and the land to grow it on—has been a prime cause of war. But most of the time, the reasons for wars are more complex. They can involve intertwining economic, political, religious, and cultural forces.

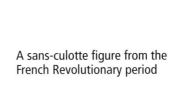

A sans-culotte figure from the French Revolutionary period

Selected Conflicts in World History

Conflict	Time Span	Location	Combatants
Persian Wars	499–448 B.C.	Greece	Greeks vs. Persians
Peloponnesian War	431–404 B.C.	Greece	Athens vs. Sparta
Punic Wars	264–146 B.C.	Mediterranean region	Rome vs. Carthage
Crusades	A.D. 1096–1291	Southwest Asia	Christians vs. Muslims
Hundred Years' War	1337–1443	France	England vs. France
Wars of King Philip II	1571–1588	Europe	Spain vs. Dutch Netherlands; Spain vs. England
Thirty Years' War	1618–1648	Central Europe (German states)	Holy Roman Empire, Spain, Poland, and others vs. Netherlands, Sweden, France, and others
English Civil War	1642–1649	England	Parliament (Roundheads) vs. Charles I and supporters (Cavaliers)
Seven Years' War (includes French and Indian War)	1756–1763	Europe; North America; India	Austria, Russia, and France vs. Prussia and Britain; Britain and its American colonies vs. France and its Native American allies; Britain vs. France
American Revolution	1775–1783	North America	Britain vs. its American colonies
French Revolution	1789–1799	France	Reformers (mainly middle class and peasants) vs. Louis XVI and supporters (mainly nobles and clergy)
Napoleonic Wars (end of the French Revolution)	1799–1815	Europe	France vs. combined European powers
Latin American Wars of Independence	1802–1824	Latin America	Colonies in Latin America vs. France and Spain
American Civil War	1860–1865	United States	North (Unionists) vs. South (Secessionists)
World War I	1914–1918	Europe (mainly France and Russia)	Allied powers vs. Central powers
World War II	1939–1945	North Africa, Europe, East Asia, Pacific Islands	Allies vs. Axis powers
Korean War	1950–1953	Korea	North Korea and China vs. South Korea and United States
Vietnam War	1959–1975	Vietnam	North Vietnam vs. South Vietnam and the United States

Regional Organizations

Through treaties, nations with common regional interests often work together to improve themselves politically, economically, and socially.

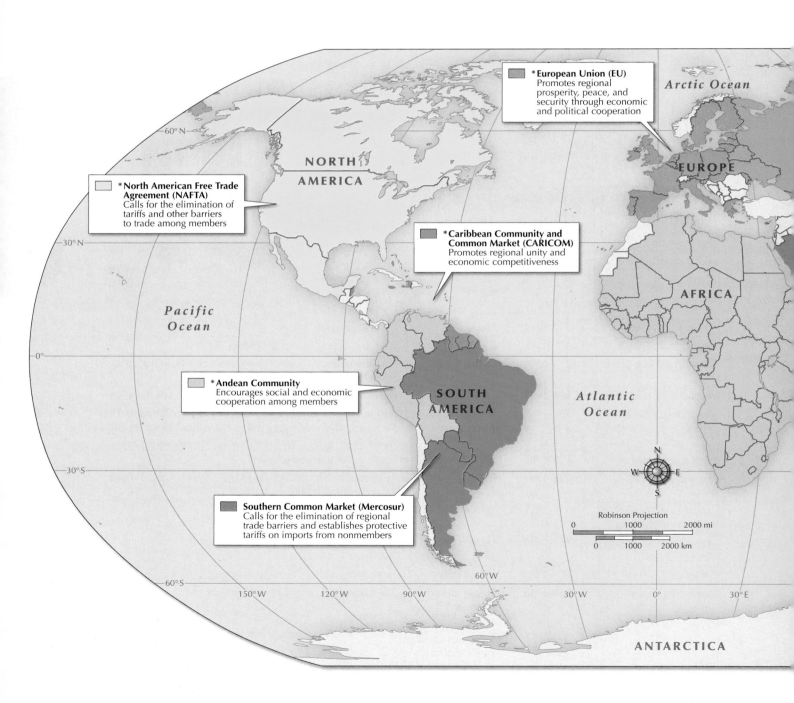

*European Union (EU)
Promotes regional prosperity, peace, and security through economic and political cooperation

*North American Free Trade Agreement (NAFTA)
Calls for the elimination of tariffs and other barriers to trade among members

*Caribbean Community and Common Market (CARICOM)
Promotes regional unity and economic competitiveness

*Andean Community
Encourages social and economic cooperation among members

Southern Common Market (Mercosur)
Calls for the elimination of regional trade barriers and establishes protective tariffs on imports from nonmembers

Robinson Projection

0   1000   2000 mi
0   1000   2000 km

International Organizations

These organizations promote cooperation across regions:

- Arab League
- International Monetary Fund (IMF)
- North Atlantic Treaty Organization (NATO)
- Organization for Economic Cooperation and Development (OECD)
- Organization of American States (OAS)
- Organization of Petroleum Exporting Countries (OPEC)
- United Nations (UN)
- World Trade Organization (WTO)

The United Nations

Of all the organizations in the world, the UN stands out as the main coordinator of international activities. With the support of its 191 member nations, the UN plays a vital, ongoing role in keeping the peace, fighting disease, promoting economic development, and providing humanitarian aid.

International aid poured into Indonesia following the December 2004 tsunami. Here an American navy pilot delivers supplies from the United States Agency for International Development (USAID), an independent federal agency.

Commonwealth of Independent States (CIS)
Encourages regional economic cooperation and the coordination of foreign and immigration policies

ASIA

*South Asian Association for Regional Cooperation (SAARC)
Provides a platform for working together to accelerate economic and social development

Gulf Cooperation Council (GCC)
Promotes regional unity through coordination of economic and defense policies

Pacific Ocean

Indian Ocean

AUSTRALIA

African Union (formerly Organization of African Unity)
Promotes unity, democracy, and economic development among member states

*Association of Southeast Asian Nations (ASEAN)
Seeks to advance economic cooperation, trade, and joint research and to promote peace and security in the region

60° E   90° E   120° E   150° E

*Free trade zone

Economics

Three Key Economic Questions		
What goods and services should be produced?	**How should goods and services be produced?**	**Who consumes the goods and services?**
How much of our resources should we devote to national defense, education, public health, or consumer goods? Which consumer goods should we produce?	Should we produce food on large corporate farms or on small family farms? Should we produce electricity with oil, nuclear power, coal, or solar power?	How do goods and services get distributed? The question of who gets to consume which goods and services lies at the very heart of the differences between economic systems. Each society answers the question of distribution based on its combination of social values and goals.

In 1923, due to the collapse of German currency, it was cheaper to paper a wall with Deutsche marks than it was to buy wallpaper.

In every society throughout history, people have had access to resources, such as water, fertile land, and human labor. Yet everywhere in the world, people's resources are limited. Economics is the study of how people choose to use their limited resources to meet their wants and needs.

Until modern times, people focused largely on resources related to agriculture. They farmed the land to produce food, mainly for their own consumption. This traditional way of meeting basic needs still defines some economies today. However, modern societies have also developed other economic systems to deal with the complexities of expanding trade and industrialization. An economic system is the method used by a society to produce and distribute goods and services.

Basic Economic Questions

Through its economic system, society answers three key questions. How a society answers these questions depends on how much it values different economic goals. Four different economic systems have developed in response to these three questions.

Economic Goals	
Economic efficiency	Making the most of resources
Economic freedom	Freedom from government intervention in the production and distribution of goods and services
Economic security and predictability	Assurance that goods and services will be available, payments will be made on time, and a safety net will protect individuals in times of economic disaster
Economic equity	Fair distribution of wealth
Economic growth and innovation	Innovation leads to economic growth, and economic growth leads to a higher standard of living.
Other goals	Societies pursue additional goals, such as environmental protection.

Major Trade Organizations

This map shows the major regional trade associations in the world today. In addition, 147 countries belong to the World Trade Organization (WTO). The WTO works to encourage trade by reducing tariffs, promoting international agreements, and mediating trade disputes among member nations.

A Grameen Bank officer meets with loan recipients in India.

Modern Economic Systems

	Description	Origin	Location Today
Traditional	People make economic decisions based on custom or habit. They produce what they have always produced and just as much as they need, using long-established methods.	Accompanied the rise of agriculture and home crafts	Mainly in rural areas within developing nations
Market (Capitalist, Free-Enterprise)	Economic decisions are made in the marketplace through interactions between buyers and sellers according to the laws of supply and demand. Individual capitalists own the means of production. Government regulates some economic activities and provides such "public goods" as education.	Capitalism has existed since the earliest buying and selling of goods in a market. The market economic system developed in response to Adam Smith's ideas and the shift from agriculture to industry in the 1800s.	Canada, Germany, Japan, United States, and a handful of other nations
Centrally Planned (Command, Socialist, Communist)	Central government planners make most economic decisions for the people. In theory, the workers own the means of production. In practice, the government does. Some private enterprise, but government dominates.	In the 1800s, criticism of capitalism by Karl Marx and others led to calls for distributing wealth according to need. After the 1917 Russian Revolution, the Soviet Union developed the first command economy.	Communist countries, including China, Cuba, North Korea, and Vietnam
Mixed (Social Democratic, Liberal Socialist)	A mix of socialism and free enterprise in which the government plays a significant role in making economic decisions.	The Great Depression of the 1930s ended laissez-faire capitalism in most countries. People insisted that government take a stronger role in fixing economic problems. The fall of communism in Eastern Europe in the 1990s ended central planning in most countries. People insisted on freer markets.	Most nations, including Brazil, France, India, Italy, Poland, Russia, Sweden, and the United Kingdom

Economics

Major Trade Organizations

This map shows the major regional trade associations in the world today. In addition, 147 countries belong to the World Trade Organization (WTO). The WTO works to encourage trade by reducing tariffs, promoting international agreements, and mediating trade disputes among member nations.

This illustration represents the cooperation among nations involved in NAFTA.

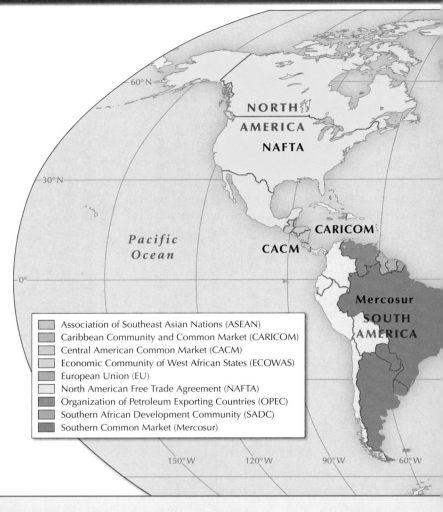

Association of Southeast Asian Nations (ASEAN)
Caribbean Community and Common Market (CARICOM)
Central American Common Market (CACM)
Economic Community of West African States (ECOWAS)
European Union (EU)
North American Free Trade Agreement (NAFTA)
Organization of Petroleum Exporting Countries (OPEC)
Southern African Development Community (SADC)
Southern Common Market (Mercosur)

Glossary of Economic Terms

barter
the direct exchange of one set of goods or services for another

budget
a plan for income and spending

capital
any human-made resource that is used to create other goods or services

communism
a political system characterized by a centrally planned economy with all economic and political power resting in the hands of the central government

currency
coins and paper bills used as money

depression
a recession that is especially long and severe

developed nation
industrialized country with a higher average level of material well-being

developing nation
country with limited industrialization and a lower average level of material well-being

economic system
the method used by a society to produce and distribute goods and services

entrepreneur
ambitious leader who combines land, labor, and capital to create and market new goods or services

export
a good that is sent to another country for sale

free enterprise
an economic system that permits the conduct of business with minimal government intervention

goods
physical objects such as clothes or shoes

import
a good that is brought in from another country for sale

industrialization
the extensive organization of an economy for the purpose of manufacturing

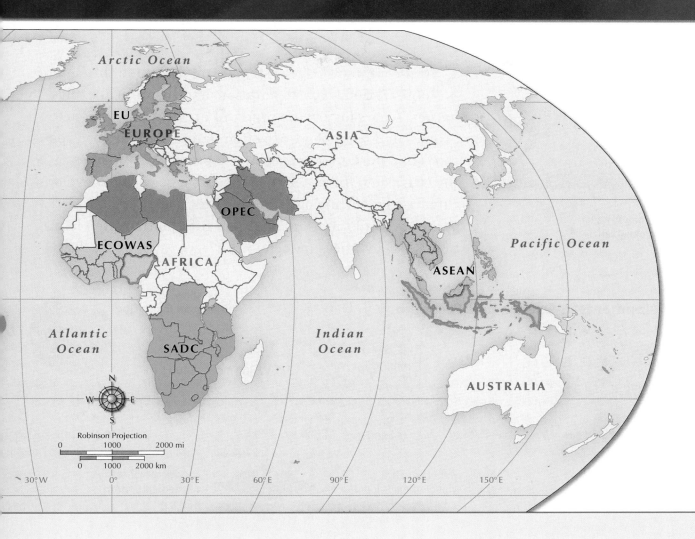

inflation
a general increase in prices

law of demand
economic law that states that consumers buy more of a good when its price decreases and less when its price increases

law of supply
tendency of suppliers to offer more of a good at a higher price

market
an arrangement that allows buyers and sellers to exchange things

market economy
economic system in which decisions on production and consumption of goods and services are based on voluntary exchange in markets

mixed economy
economic system that combines tradition and the free market with limited government involvement

opportunity cost
the most desirable alternative given up as the result of a decision

recession
a prolonged economic contraction

scarcity
limited quantities of resources to meet unlimited wants

socialism
a social and political philosophy based on the belief that democratic means should be used to evenly distribute wealth throughout a society.

tariff
a tax on imported goods

tax
a required payment to a government

traditional economy
economic system that relies on habit, custom, or ritual to decide questions of production and consumption of goods and services

welfare
government aid to the poor

Science and Technology

Egyptian A-frame and plumb line ▲

Science is knowledge systematically acquired through observation, experimentation, and theoretical explanation. Technology is the practical application of science. Science and technology are often paired, and for good reason. They work together, each one promoting progress in the other field. Inventors use the latest science to develop cutting-edge technology that, in turn, helps scientists gather new information. That new information often leads to further advances in technology.

Coin showing
Alexander the Great ▶

■ Key Developments in Science and Technology

Science and Technology

Copper tools and ornaments **10,000** B.C.	Light wooden plow **4000** B.C.	Kiln-fired bricks, pots **3500** B.C.	Irrigation **2400** B.C.	Iron weapons **1400** B.C.

10,000 B.C.　　　　　　　　　**5000** B.C.　　　　　　　　　B.C. │ A.D.

Widespread domestication of plants and animals **9000–6000** B.C.	Bronze objects **4500** B.C.	Dam **4000** B.C.	Pyramids **2800** B.C.	Plumbing, water pipes, sewer drains **2700** B.C.	Coins **600** B.C.

Medicine

Greek symbol of peace, now a symbol of medicine ▶

Hippocrates, father of medicine, born **460** B.C.

10,000 B.C.　　　　　　　　　**5000** B.C.　　　　　　　　　B.C. │ A.D.

Greek physician Galen born A.D. **130**

Communication

Egyptian cursive writing on papyrus ▼

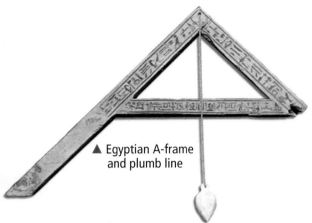

Pictographs **3500** B.C.	Writing **3200** B.C.	Alphabet **1700** B.C.	Paper A.D. **105**

10,000 B.C.　　　　　　　　　**5000** B.C.　　　　　　　　　B.C. │ A.D.

Papyrus **2800** B.C.

Transportation

Ancient dugout canoe *c.* **6000** B.C.	Wheeled cart from Sumer *c.* **3500** B.C.	Roman chariot *c.* A.D. **1**

10,000 B.C.　　　　　　　　　**5000** B.C.　　　　　　　　　B.C. │ A.D.

Portuguese square-sailed ship ▶

Square-sailed ships **3000** B.C.

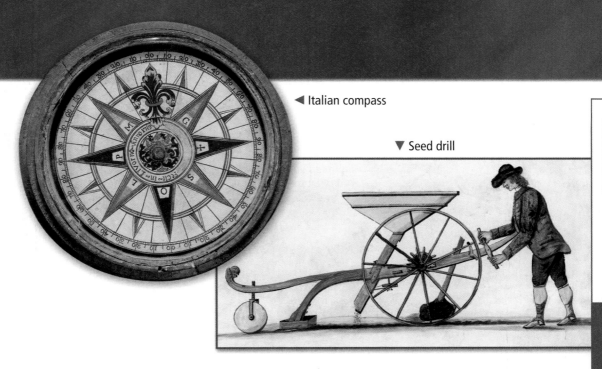

◀ Italian compass

▼ Seed drill

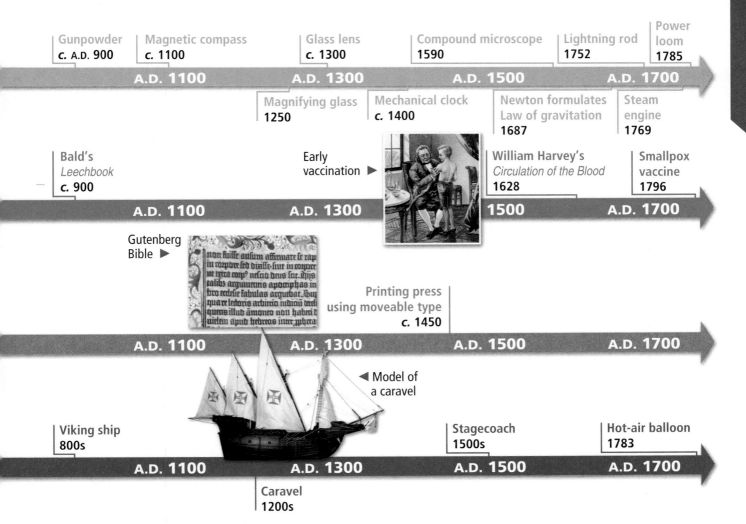

Gunpowder *c.* A.D. **900**	Magnetic compass *c.* **1100**		Glass lens *c.* **1300**		Compound microscope **1590**		Lightning rod **1752**	Power loom **1785**

A.D. 1100   **A.D. 1300**   **A.D. 1500**   **A.D. 1700**

	Magnifying glass **1250**	Mechanical clock *c.* **1400**	Newton formulates Law of gravitation **1687**	Steam engine **1769**

Bald's *Leechbook* *c.* **900**		Early vaccination ▶	William Harvey's *Circulation of the Blood* **1628**	Smallpox vaccine **1796**

A.D. 1100   **A.D. 1300**   **1500**   **A.D. 1700**

Gutenberg
Bible ▶

Printing press
using moveable type
c. **1450**

A.D. 1100   **A.D. 1300**   **A.D. 1500**   **A.D. 1700**

◀ Model of
a caravel

Viking ship **800s**			Stagecoach **1500s**	Hot-air balloon **1783**

A.D. 1100   **A.D. 1300**   **A.D. 1500**   **A.D. 1700**

Caravel
1200s

Science and Technology

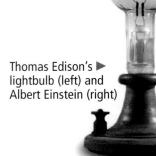

Thomas Edison's ▶
lightbulb (left) and
Albert Einstein (right)

Science and Technology

Electric motor 1821	Theory of evolution 1849	Incandescent lamp 1879	Quantum theory 1900	Frozen food 1924	

A.D. 1800　　　　　　　　　**A.D. 1850**　　　　　　　　　**A.D. 1900**

Canning of food 1809　　　Mechanical reaper 1843　　　Special Theory of Relativity 1905　　Plastics 1909　　Liquid fuel rocket 1926

Medicine

Anesthesia 1842　　Pasteurization of milk 1865　　Antiseptic surgery 1867　　Diphtheria antitoxin 1891　　Typhus vaccine 1909

A.D. 1800　　　　　　　　　**A.D. 1850**　　　　　　　　　**A.D. 1900**

Government focus on improving hygiene and public sanitation 1850–1950　　Genetics; laws of heredity 1866　　Rabies vaccine 1885　　X-ray 1895　　Penicillin, first antibiotic 1928

Communication

Telegraph 1837　　　　　　　　　　　　　Radio 1895

A.D. 1800　　　　　　　　　**A.D. 1850**　　　　　　　　　**A.D. 1900**

Telephone 1846　　　◀ Early telephone　　　Electronic television 1927

Transportation

Steam locomotive 1825　　　　　　　　　　Biplane 1903

A.D. 1800　　　　　　　　　**A.D.1850**　　　　　　　　　**A.D. 1900**

Steamboat 1807　　　Automobile c. 1860–1890

Daimler motor car ▶

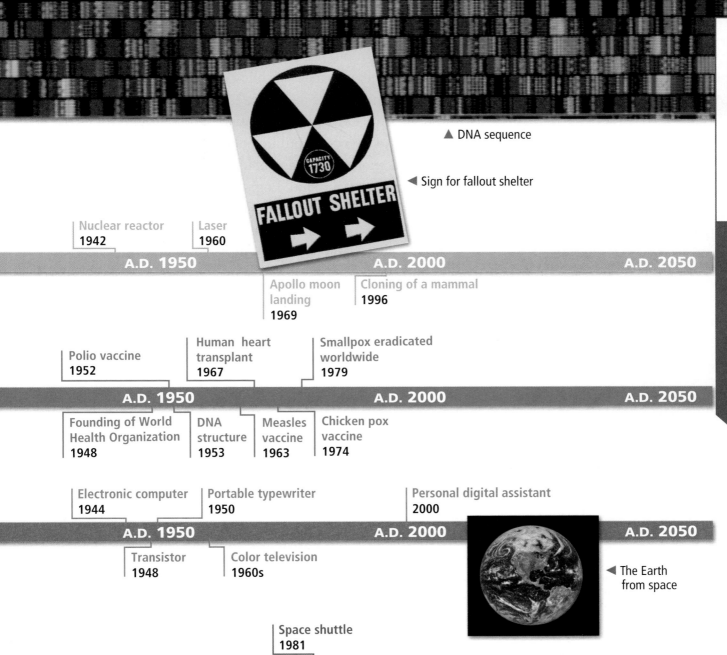

▲ DNA sequence

◄ Sign for fallout shelter

Nuclear reactor
1942

Laser
1960

A.D. 1950

A.D. 2000

A.D. 2050

Apollo moon
landing
1969

Cloning of a mammal
1996

Polio vaccine
1952

Human heart
transplant
1967

Smallpox eradicated
worldwide
1979

A.D. 1950

A.D. 2000

A.D. 2050

Founding of World
Health Organization
1948

DNA
structure
1953

Measles
vaccine
1963

Chicken pox
vaccine
1974

Electronic computer
1944

Portable typewriter
1950

Personal digital assistant
2000

A.D. 1950

A.D. 2000

A.D. 2050

Transistor
1948

Color television
1960s

◄ The Earth
from space

Space shuttle
1981

A.D. 1950

A.D. 2000

A.D. 2050

First commercial jet airliner
1949

Queen Mary 2 ocean liner
2005

◄ Jet airplanes

Government and Civics

Presidential elections in Ukraine, 2004

The main purpose of government is to create and enforce a society's public policies. Public policies cover such matters as defense, crime, taxation, and much more. Governments must have power in order to make and carry out public policies. Every government has and exercises three basic kinds of power: legislative, executive, and judicial. Legislative refers to the power to make laws. Executive refers to the power to enforce laws. Judicial refers to the power to interpret laws. These powers of government are often outlined in a nation's constitution, or body of fundamental laws. Different forms of government exercise their powers in different ways.

Forms of Government

Political scientists classify governments in order to help them describe, compare, and analyze different forms. Three particularly helpful classifications involve determining (1) the geographic distribution of governmental power within the state, (2) the relationship between the legislative and executive branches of the government, and (3) who can participate in the government. As the chart shows, modern forms of government vary widely.

Forms of Government

Country	Where is the power?		What is the relationship between the legislative and executive branches?		Who can participate?	
	Unitary: All powers held by the government belong to a single, central agency.	**Federal**: The powers of government are divided between a central government and several regional governments.	**Parliamentary**: The executive branch is made up of the prime minister, or premier, and that official's cabinet. The prime minister and cabinet are members of the legislative branch, or parliament.	**Presidential**: The executive and legislative branches of government are separate, independent of each other, and coequal.	**Democracy**: Supreme political authority rests with the people, who choose a small group of individuals to act as their representatives to carry out the day-to-day conduct of government.	**Dictatorship**: The government is not accountable to the people for its policies or for how they are carried out. Those who rule do not represent or consider the will of the people.
Botswana	✓		✓		✓	
Brazil		✓		✓	✓	
Costa Rica	✓		✓		✓	
Cuba	✓		✓			✓
France	✓			✓	✓	
India		✓	✓		✓	
Syria	✓			✓		✓
United States		✓		✓	✓	

Federal vs. Unitary Government

Today, about two dozen nations, including the United States, have a federal system of government. In this kind of system, two levels of government—central and state—divide power between them. In the unitary system, which is more common by far, all powers belong to the central government. One disadvantage of a federal system is its inefficiency. People must obey two sets of laws, which may overlap or even conflict. In a unitary system, one government governs all the people directly, even though it may yield certain powers to the states. On the other hand, a federal system allows for checks on the power of the central government and for some diversity of laws in regions with a distinctive culture, history, or language.

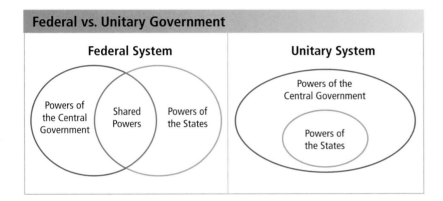

Federal vs. Unitary Government

Federal System

Powers of the Central Government | Shared Powers | Powers of the States

Unitary System

Powers of the Central Government

Powers of the States

Presidential and Parliamentary Governments

The Presidential Relationship Voters elect the legislature and the chief executive, who is part of the executive branch. The legislative and executive branches are independent and coequal.

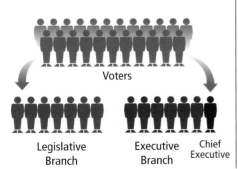

Voters

Legislative Branch

Executive Branch

Chief Executive

The Parliamentary Relationship Voters elect the legislature. The chief executive is drawn from the legislature.

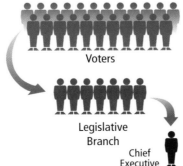

Voters

Legislative Branch

Chief Executive

Basic Concepts of Democracy

1. A recognition of the fundamental worth and dignity of every person. At various times, the welfare of one or a few individuals is subordinate to the interests of the many in a democracy. For example, a democratic society may force people to pay a tax or obey traffic signals.

2. A respect for the equality of all persons. The democratic concept of equality insists that all people are entitled to equality of opportunity and equality before the law—not necessarily equal distribution of wealth.

3. A faith in the majority rule and an insistence upon minority rights. In a democracy, the will of the people and not the dictate of the ruling few determine public policy. Unchecked, however, a majority could destroy its opposition and, in the process, destroy democracy. Thus, democracy insists upon majority rule restrained by minority rights.

4. An acceptance of the necessity of compromise. In a democracy, public decision making must be largely a matter of give-and-take among the various competing interests. People must compromise to find the position most acceptable to the largest number. Compromise is the process of blending and adjusting competing views and interests.

5. An insistence upon the widest possible degree of individual freedom. In a democracy, each individual must be as free to do as he or she pleases as far as the freedom of all will allow. Oliver Wendell Holmes once had this to say about the relative nature of each individual's rights: "The right to swing my fist ends where the other man's nose begins."

Catherine the Great of Russia

Forms of Dictatorship

Typically militaristic in character, an authoritarian or dictatorial regime usually acquires political power by force and may turn to foreign aggression to enhance its military strength and prestige. Authoritarianism has taken several related forms throughout history.

Absolutism A system in which the ruler holds complete authority over the government and the lives of the people. Some absolute monarchs ruled according to the principle of divine right. Modern forms of absolutism include military dictatorships that try to control every element of people's lives (see Totalitarianism).

Despotism Absolute rule with no constitutional restraints. The term *despot* was an honorable title in ancient times. Later, absolute monarchs who favored reforms became known as enlightened despots. Today, despot refers to a brutal and oppressive ruler.

Autocracy The concentration of power in one individual or group that uses force to maintain absolute control and smother any political opposition.

Louis XIV of France

Mehmed II of the Ottoman Empire

Glossary of Political Terms

bureaucracy
a large, complex administrative structure that handles the everyday business of government

citizen
a member of a state or nation who is entitled to full civil rights

civil service
those civilian employees who perform the administrative work of government

compromise
an adjustment of opposing principles or systems by modifying some aspect of each

constitution
the body of fundamental laws setting out the principles, structures, and processes of a government

foreign policy
everything a nation's government says and does in world affairs

immigrant
a person legally admitted as a permanent resident of a country

jury
a legally chosen group of persons who hear evidence and decide questions of fact in a court case

nation
a group of people who share the same way of life and live in the same area and under the same central government

Totalitarianism A form of absolutism in which the government sweeps away existing political institutions and exerts complete control over nearly every aspect of the society. In this system, a supreme leader often becomes the sole source of society's rules.

Communism An ideology that, in theory, calls for ownership of all land and other productive property by the workers. In practice, a system of repressive, single-party government that completely controls its citizens' lives and stifles all opposition.

Fascism A form of government that seeks to renew society by demanding citizens' complete devotion to the state. Often led by a dictator who strictly controls industry and labor, denies freedom and individual rights, and uses police and the military to silence opposition.

Adolf Hitler of Germany

Mural of Saddam Hussein

Mao Zedong's
Little Red Book

politics
   the activities of those who run or seek to run a government

rule of law
   idea that all citizens, including government officials, are subject to the law

sovereign
   having supreme power within its own territory

state
   a group of people living in a defined territory who have a government with the power to make and enforce law without the consent of any higher authority

suffrage
   the right to vote

tax
   a charge levied by government on persons or property to meet public needs

treaty
   a formal agreement between two or more sovereign states

Culture

Culture is a way of life, or a set of values and behaviors, that people in a society learn, share, and pass on from generation to generation. Culture mainly involves what people think, what they do, and what they create. It consists of such elements as language, religion, art, social organization, and technology. Cultures can change over time. Some elements are forgotten, and others are improved or replaced. Still others are picked up from outside cultures. This spread of ideas, customs, and technologies from one culture to another is known as cultural diffusion. Historically, cultures have spread mainly through trade, migration, and conquest.

World Languages

Language is a part of culture. Yet it is also the main tool by which people transmit their culture. Many thousands of languages have arisen since humans first began to communicate. Some 6,800 of those languages still survive. Related languages can be grouped into language families.

Principal Languages of the World	
Language	Speakers* (in millions)
Mandarin (Chinese)	873
Spanish	322
English	309
Hindi	180
Portuguese	177
Bengali	171
Russian	145
Japanese	122
German	95
Wu (Chinese)	77

* estimated number for whom this is their first language

Sign in a Native American language and English (above); fragment of a Dead Sea scroll, written in ancient Hebrew (below)

Major Belief Systems

Most of the world's major belief systems have existed for more than 2,000 years. Today, if the world included only 1,000 people, 330 of them would be Christian, 215 would be Muslim, 149 would be Hindu, 140 would follow no religion, 59 would be Buddhist, 37 would follow Chinese traditional religions, and 41 would hold primal-indigenous beliefs.

Major World Religions/Belief Systems

	Leading Figure; Dates	Key Beliefs	Writings	Number of Followers
Buddhism	Siddhartha Gautama (the Buddha); late sixth to fourth century B.C.	No gods, but buddhas, or "enlightened ones" exist; reincarnation (cycle of birth, death, and rebirth); the Four Noble Truths: (1) suffering is a part of life; (2) selfish desire leads to suffering; (3) desire can be overcome; (4) the Eightfold Path leads away from desire, toward release from the cycle of birth, death, and rebirth	*Tripitaka (The Three Baskets)*; the sutras; the tantras	373 million
Chinese Traditional Religions (blend of Buddhism, Confucianism, and Daoism)	Blending began in the A.D. 900s	Reincarnation (from Buddhism); virtuous way of life (from Confucianism); acting in harmony with nature and avoiding aggressive action (from Daoism)	*Dao de Jing (The Way of Power)*; *Zhuangzi* (named after the greatest interpreter of Daoism); (see also Buddhism and Confucianism)	398 million
Christianity	Jesus of Nazareth; early first century A.D.	One God; to save humans, God sent Jesus, who suffered, died, and rose from the dead; the Trinity: three figures (God the Father, God the Son, and God the Holy Spirit) united as one; love God above all else	The Bible: the Old Testament (Hebrew Bible) and the New Testament; various creeds and statements of faith	2.07 billion
Confucianism	Confucius; around 500 B.C.	No gods; not an organized religion, but a system of moral conduct based on the teachings of Confucius; kindness, love, and respect lead to a virtuous way of life	The *Lun yü (Analects)*; the *Wu-ching (Five Classics)*; the *Ssu Shu (Four Books)*	6.43 million (mainly in Korea)
Hinduism	No founder or central institution; around 1500 B.C.	Brahman, the ultimate God, is the source of all existence; many lesser gods, the main ones being Vishnu and Siva; reincarnation; law of karma (actions in one life affect next life); ahimsa (principle of noninjury or nonviolence)	The Vedas, sutras, epics, and puranas	837 million
Islam	Muhammad; early A.D. 600s	One God, Allah; Five Pillars, or duties: (1) profession of faith; (2) prayer; (3) charity; (4) fasting; (5) pilgrimage to Mecca in Saudi Arabia	Quran	1.25 billion
Judaism	Abraham; around 2000 B.C.	One God; God made a covenant, or pact, with Abraham and the Jewish people that if they obey God's commands, God will make Israel a great nation; actions are more important than beliefs	The Torah (the "Law"), the Nevi'im (the "Prophets"), and the Ketuvim (the "Writings"); oral tradition, written as the Talmud	14.6 million
primal-indigenous (includes tribal religions, animism, shamanism, and paganism)	Such religions have existed since prehistoric times	May be a high god; nature spirits (powerful life forces inhabiting the elements of nature); communication with spirits through prayers and offerings ensures the support of the spirits	none	238 million
Shinto	No founder; well established by the A.D. 500s	Many gods; Kami (superior, mystical, or divine powers) are the sources of human life; main deity is sun goddess Amaterasu O-mikami; each person is worthy of respect; truthfulness and purification (physical and spiritual) bring the blessings of the kami	No central sacred scripture; chief books: *Kojiki (Records of Ancient Matters)* and *Nihon shoki (Chronicles of Japan)*	2.68 million
Sikhism (combines elements of Hinduism and Islam)	Nanak; around A.D. 1500	One God; reincarnation; meditation can release one from the cycle of reincarnation; law of karma; all humans are equal	*Adi Granth (First Book)*	24.3 million

Concept Connector

Culture

Culture

The Arts

The arts tell much about a culture. Ancient civilizations produced artists only after they were capable of generating an agricultural surplus. Some people could then be spared from the fields to devote themselves to other pursuits, including the arts. Works of art, from paintings and sculptures to music, dance, and writing, reflect the culture in which the artist lived. Notice the variations among the arts presented in these pictures. Think about what each picture says about the culture that produced it.

▲ Neoclassical bust of Napoleon by Antonio Canova, *c.* 1802

Romantic poet, writer, and artist William Blake's *Songs of Innocence*, 1789 ▼

Major Art Movements

classicism
Greek and Roman art; emphasis on harmony, proportion, balance, and simplicity

byzantine
500s–1400s, Europe, Russia

Romanesque
late eleventh century, Europe

Gothic
1100s–1400s, Europe; cathedral architecture and religious art

Renaissance
c. 1400–1600, Europe; Leonardo, Michelangelo, Raphael

mannerism
c. 1520–1600, Europe; Parmigianino

baroque
seventeenth and early eighteenth centuries, Europe; Bernini, Caravaggio, Rubens

rococo
eighteenth century, Europe; Fragonard

neoclassicism
late eighteenth and early nineteenth centuries, Europe; revival of ancient Greek and Roman art; David, Canova

romanticism
late eighteenth to mid-nineteenth century, Europe, United States; Delacroix, Géricault, Turner, Blake, Hudson River school

Barbizon School
c. 1840–1870, France; landscapes; Rousseau, Corot, Millet

realism
nineteenth century, Europe and United States; Daumier, Courbet, Eakins

impressionism
late nineteenth century, France and United States; Monet, Renoir, Cassatt

pointillism
1880s, France; Seurat, Signac

Costume from Georg Friedrich Handel's baroque opera *Agrippina*, 1709 (right) ▶

Pointillist painting by Georges Seurat, *Porte-en-Bessin*, 1888 (far right) ▶

Bronze sculpture by Italian futurist Umberto Boccioni, *Unique Forms of Continuity in Space*, 1913

▲ Self-portrait by German expressionist Käthe Kollwitz, 1920

Poster for ► Émile Zola's realist novel *La Terre*, 1887

postimpressionism
late nineteenth century, France; Cézanne, Van Gogh, Gauguin

art nouveau
late nineteenth century, Europe; decorative arts

cubism
early twentieth century, Europe; Picasso, Braque

fauvism
c. 1905–1908, France; pure, bold colors applied in a spontaneous manner; Matisse

expressionism
c. 1905–1925, northern Europe; Rouault, Kokoschka, Schiele

futurism
c. 1909–1919, Italy; Boccioni

constructivism
c. 1915, Russia; abstract style using non-traditional materials; Rodchenko, Tatlin, Gabo, Pevsner

dadaism
c. 1915–1923, France; rejected accepted aesthetic standards; Duchamp

surrealism
1920s–1930s, Europe; Magritte, Dalí, Miró, Ernst, de Chirico

art deco
1920s–1930s; decorative arts characterized by sleek lines and slender forms

abstract expressionism
1940s, New York City; Pollock, de Kooning, Motherwell, Kline

minimalism
late 1950s, United States; Judd, Martin, Kelly

color field painting
1950s, United States; Newman, Rothko, Frankenthaler

pop art
1950s, United States; Warhol, Lichtenstein, Oldenburg

conceptual art
1960s and 1970s, international; questioned the definition of "art"

Sculpture for a park in Minneapolis by pop artist Claes Oldenburg, *Spoonbridge and Cherry*, 1988 ▼

A

abdicate to give up or step down from power (p. 236)

abdicar renunciar de un puesto de poder

abolition movement the campaign against slavery and the slave trade (p. 365)

movimiento por la abolición campaña contra la esclavitud y contra el tráfico de esclavos

absentee landlord one who owns a large estate but does not live there (p. 367)

dueño ausente dueño de una gran propiedad que no vive en ella

absolute monarch ruler with complete authority over the government and lives of the people he or she governs (p. 144)

monarca absoluto gobernante que tiene autoridad absoluta sobre la administración y la vida de los que están bajo su mando

abstract style of art composed of lines, colors, and shapes, sometimes with no recognizable subject matter at all (p. 527)

abstracto estilo de arte compuesto de líneas, colores y formas, y que a veces no tiene un tema reconocible

acid rain a form of pollution in which toxic chemicals in the air come back to Earth in the form of rain, snow, or hail (p. 750)

lluvia ácida forma de polución en la que los productos químicos tóxicos que se encuentran en el aire vuelven a la tierra en la lluvia, nieve o granizo

acropolis highest and most fortified point within a Greek city-state (p. 16)

acrópolis el punto más alto y fortificado de una ciudad-estado griega

Afghanistan an Islamic country in Central Asia; invaded by the Soviet Union in 1979; later home to the radical Islamist Taliban and the terrorist al Qaeda (pp. 170, 757)

Afganistán país islámico en Asia Central; invadido por la Unión Soviética en 1979; más tarde hogar de los radicales islamistas Talibán y de los terroristas de al Qaeda

African National Congress (ANC) the main organization that opposed apartheid and pushed for majority rule in South Africa; later a political party (p. 687)

Congreso Nacional Africano (ANC, por sus siglas en inglés) principal organización que se opuso al apartheid y que abogó por el gobierno de la mayoría de Sudáfrica; posteriormente, partido político

agribusinesses giant commercial farms, often owned by multinational corporations (p. 722)

industria agropecuaria inmensas granjas comerciales, generalmente administradas por corporaciones multinacionales

ahimsa Hindu belief in nonviolence and reverence for all life (p. 504)

ahimsa creencia hindú en la no violencia y en el respeto a todas las formas de vida

aircraft carriers ships that accommodate the taking off and landing of airplanes, and transport aircraft (p. 578)

portaaviones buque dotado de las instalaciones necesarias para el transporte, despegue y aterrizaje de aparatos de aviación

al Qaeda a fundamentalist Islamic terrorist organization led by Saudi Arabian Osama bin Laden (p. 756)

al Qaeda organización fundamentalista islámica terrorista liderada por el saudí Osama bin Laden

alliance formal agreement between two or more nations or powers to cooperate and come to one another's defense (p. 111)

alianza acuerdo formal de cooperación y defensa mutua entre dos o más naciones o potencias

Alsace and Lorraine provinces on the border of Germany and France, lost by France to Germany in 1871; regained by France after World War I (p. 456)

Alsacia y Lorena provincias en la frontera entre Alemania y Francia, que Alemania arrebató a Francia en 1871, y que Francia recuperó después de la Primera Guerra Mundial

Amritsar massacre an incident in 1919 in which British troops fired on an unarmed crowd of Indians (p. 503)

masacre de Amritsar incidente en 1919 en el que las tropas británicas dispararon contra un grupo de indios indefensos

anarchist someone who wants to abolish all government (p. 342)

anarquista persona que quiere abolir toda forma de gobierno

ancien régime old order; system of government in pre-revolution France (p. 210)

ancien regime antiguo orden; sistema de gobierno en la Francia prerevolucionaria

anesthetic drug that prevents pain during surgery (p. 247)

anestesia fármaco que suprime el dolor durante la cirugía

annex add a territory to an existing state or country (pp. 232, 332)

anexar agregar un territorio a un estado o país existente

Anschluss union of Austria and Germany (p. 565)

Anschluss unión de Austria y Alemania

anti-ballistic missiles (ABMs) missiles that can shoot down other missiles (p. 606)

misiles anti-balísticos (ABM, por sus siglas) misiles que pueden derribar otros misiles

apartheid a policy of rigid segregation of non-white people in the Republic of South Africa (pp. 497, 686)

apartheid política de estricta separación racial en Sudáfrica que fue abolida en 1989

appeasement policy of giving in to an aggressor's demands in order to keep the peace (p. 563)

contemporización política de aceptación de las exigencias de un agresor para mantener la paz

aristocracy government headed by a privileged minority or upper class (p. 16)

aristocracia gobierno encabezado por una minoría privilegiada o de clase alta

armada fleet of ships (p. 145)

armada flota de barcos

armistice agreement to end fighting in a war (p. 471)

armisticio acuerdo para dejar de luchar en una guerra

artificial satellite man-made object that orbits a larger body in space (p. 759)

satélite artificial objeto artificial que gira en el espacio alrededor de un cuerpo más grande

artisan a skilled craftsperson (p. 5)

artesano trabajador cualificado que hace objetos a mano

Asante kingdom kingdom that emerged in the 1700s in present-day Ghana and was active in the slave trade (p. 92)

reino Asante reino que surgió en el siglo XVIII en el actual Ghana y que tenía comercio de esclavos

Asia Minor the Turkish peninsula between the Black Sea and the Mediterranean Sea (p. 499)

Asia Menor la península turca entre el Mar Negro y el Mar Mediterráneo

assembly line production method that breaks down a complex job into a series of smaller tasks (p. 301)

cadena de montaje método de producción que divide un trabajo complejo en una serie de tareas menores

atheism belief that there is no god (p. 547)

ateísmo creencia de que no existen dioses

atrocity horrible act committed against innocent people (p. 468)

atrocidad acto brutal cometido en contra de inocentes

autocratic having unlimited power (pp. 169, 658)

autocrático que tiene poder ilimitado

autonomy self-rule (p. 274)

autonomía autogobierno

Axis powers group of countries led by Germany, Italy, and Japan that fought the Allies in World War II (p. 564)

Potencias del Eje grupo de países liderado por Alemania, Italia y Japón que luchó contra los Aliados durante la Segunda Guerra Mundial

B

balance of power distribution of military and economic power that prevents any one nation from becoming too strong (p. 152)

equilibrio de poder distribución del poder military y económico que evita que una nación se vuelva demasiado fuerte

balance of trade difference between how much a country imports and how much it exports (p. 411)

balance commercial diferencia entre lo que importa y exporta un país

Balfour Declaration statement issued by the British government in 1917 supporting the establishment of a homeland for Jews in Palestine (p. 502)

Declaración Balfour declaración hecha por el gobierno británico en 1917 en la que apoyaba la constitución de un estado judío en Palestina

Bangladesh literally "Bengali nation," nation east of India that was formerly part of Pakistan (p. 655)

Bangladesh literalmente significa "nación bengalí"; país al este de India que antiguamente formaba parte de Pakistán

baroque ornate style of art and architecture popular in the 1600s and 1700s (p. 189)

barroco estilo artístico y arquitectónico elaborado que se dio en los siglos XVII y XVIII

Bastille fortress in Paris used as a prison; French Revolution began when Parisians stormed it in 1789 (p. 215)

Bastilla fortificación en París usada como prisión; la Revolución Francesa empezó cuando los parisinos la asaltaron en 1789

Bataan Death March during World War II, the forced march of Filipino and American prisoners of war under brutal conditions by the Japanese military (p. 587)

Jornada de la Muerte desde Bataan episodio acaecido durante la Segunda Guerra Mundial, en el que prisioneros de guerra filipinos y estadounidenses fueron obligado a marchar bajo condiciones brutales por parte de militares japoneses

Biafra region of southeastern Nigeria that launched a failed bid for independence from Nigeria in 1966, launching a bloody war (p. 668)

Biafra región del sudeste de Nigeria que lanzó un fallido intento de independizarse de Nigeria en 1966, y por el que se desató una cruenta guerra

biotechnology the application of biological research to industry, engineering and technology (p. 762)

biotecnología la aplicación de investigaciones biológicas en la industria, la ingeniería y la tecnología

Black Shirt any member of the militant combat squads of Italian Fascists set up under Mussolini (p. 537)

Camisa Negra cualquier miembro de las escuadras militantes de combate de los fascistas italianos que estableció Mussolini

blitzkrieg lightning war (p. 568)

blitzkrieg guerra relámpago o guerra intensa y muy breve

bloc a group of nations acting together in support of one another (p. 741)

bloque grupo de naciones que actúan conjuntamente en apoyo mutuo

Boer War (1899–1902) a war in which Great Britain defeated the Boers of South Africa (p. 396)

Guerra Boer (1899–1902) guerra en la que Gran Bretaña venció a los Boer de Sudáfrica

Boers Dutch people who settled in Cape Town, Africa, and eventually migrated inland (p. 93)

Boers holandeses establecidos en Ciudad del Cabo, África, que con el tiempo emigraron hacia el interior

bourgeoisie the middle class (p. 211)

burguesía clase media

Boxer Uprising anti-foreign movement in China from 1898–1900 (p. 414)

Rebelión Bóxer movimiento en contra de los extranjeros ocurrido en China de 1898 a 1900

boyar landowning noble in Russia under the tsars (p. 169)

boyar noble ruso que poseía tierras en la época de los zares (p. 169)

boycott refuse to buy (p. 504)

boicot negarse a comprar

brahman in the belief system established in Aryan India, the single spiritual power that resides in all things (p. 8)

brahman en el sistema de creencias establecido en la India aria, el único poder espiritual que reside en todas las cosas

cabinet parliamentary advisors to the king who originally met in a small room, or "cabinet" (p. 160)

gabinete miembros del parlamento consejeros del rey que originalmente se reunían en un pequeño cuarto o "gabinete"

cahier notebook used during the French Revolution to record grievances (p. 214)

memorándum cuaderno usado durante la Revolución Francesa para anotar los agravios

calculus a branch of mathematics in which calculations are made using special symbolic notations; developed by Isaac Newton (p. 76)

cálculo rama de las matemáticas en la que los cálculos se hacen con notaciones simbólicas especiales; fue desarrollado por Isaac Newton

caliph successor to Muhammad as political and religious leader of the Muslims (p. 32)

califa sucesor de Mahoma como líder religioso político de los musulmanes

canonize recognize a person as a saint (p. 67)

canonizar reconocer a una persona como santo

Cape Town seaport city and legislative capital of South Africa; was the first Dutch colony in Africa (p. 93)

Ciudad del Cabo ciudad portuaria y capital legislativa de Sudáfrica; fue la primera colonia holandesa en África

capital money or wealth used to invest in business or enterprise (p. 251)

capital dinero o bienes que se usan para invertir en negocios o empresas

capital offense crime punishable by death (p. 365)

ofensa capital crimen que puede castigarse con la muerte

capitalism economic system in which the means of production are privately owned and operated for profit (p. 131)

capitalismo sistema económico por el que los medios de producción son propiedad privada y se administran para obtener beneficios

cartel a group of companies that join together to control the production and price of a product (p. 304)

cartel asociación de grandes corporaciones formada para controlar la producción y el precio de un producto

cartographer mapmaker (p. 85)

cartógrafo persona que hace mapas

caste in traditional Indian society, an unchangeable social group into which a person is born (p. 8)

casta grupo social en la sociedad tradicional de India, en el que una persona nace y del que no se puede cambiar

caudillo military dictator in Latin America (p. 440)

caudillo dictador militar en América Latina

censorship restriction on access to ideas and information (p. 189)

censura restricción en el acceso a ideas o información

chancellor the highest official of a monarch, prime minister (pp. 331, 550)

canciller oficial con más rango dentro de una monarquía, primer ministro

Chechnya a republic within Russia where rebels have fought for independence from Russia (p. 683)

Chechenia república dentro del territorio ruso en la que grupos rebeldes luchan por su independencia de Rusia

Cheka early Soviet secret police force (p. 482)

Cheka una de las primeras fuerzas policiales secretas soviética

chivalry a code of conduct for knights during the Middle Ages (p. 26)

caballería código de conducta para los caballeros durante la Edad Media

circumnavigate to travel completely around the world (p. 89)

circunnavegar viajar alrededor del mundo

city-state a political unit that includes a city and its surrounding lands and villages (p. 6)

ciudad estado unidad política compuesta por una ciudad y las tierras y aldeas que la rodean

civil disobedience the refusal to obey unjust laws (p. 504)

desobediencia civil negarse a obedecer leyes injustas

civil war war fought between two groups of people in the same nation (p. 113)

guerra civil guerra en la que luchan dos grupos de personas de una misma nación

coalition temporary alliance of various political parties (p. 374)

coalición alianza temporal de varios partidos políticos

Cold War state of tension and hostility between nations aligned with the United States on one side and the Soviet Union on the other that rarely led to direct armed conflict (p. 592)

Guerra Fría estado de tensión y hostilidad entre las naciones alineadas con Estados Unidos, por una parte, y con la Unión Soviética, por la otra, que salvo raras excepciones desembocó en un conflicto armado

collective large farm owned and operated by peasants as a group (p. 543)

granja colectiva granja grande que pertenece a campesinos que la administran en grupo

collective security system in which a group of nations acts as one to preserve the peace of all (p. 474)

seguridad colectiva sistema por el que un grupo de naciones actúa como una para preservar la paz común

collectivization the forced joining together of workers and property into collectives, such as rural collectives that absorb peasants and their land (p. 624)

colectivización unión forzada de trabajadores y propiedad en colectivos, como colectivos rurales que absorben a campesinos y sus tierras

colossus giant (p. 348)

coloso gigante

Columbian Exchange the global exchange of goods, ideas, plants and animals, and disease that began with Columbus' exploration of the Americas (p. 129)

Intercambio colombino intercambio global de bienes, ideas, plantas, animales y enfermedades que comenzaron con la exploración de las Américas por parte de Colón

Comintern Communist International, international association of communist parties led by the Soviet Union for the purpose of encouraging worldwide communist revolution (p. 549)

Comintern Internacional Comunista, asociación internacional de partidos comunistas liderada por la Unión Soviética con el propósito de extender por el mundo una revolución comunista

command economy system in which government officials make all basic economic decisions (p. 543)

economía controlada sistema en el que los funcionarios del gobierno toman todas las decisiones económicas básicas

commissar Communist party officials assigned to the army to teach party principles and ensure party loyalty during the Russian Revolution (p. 482)

comisario funcionario del partido comunista asignado al ejército para enseñar los principios del partido y para asegurar la lealtad al mismo durante la revolución rusa

communism form of socialism advocated by Karl Marx; according to Marx, class struggle was inevitable and would lead to the creation of a classless society in which all wealth and property would be owned by the community as a whole (p. 263)

comunismo forma de socialismo defendido por Karl Marx; según Marx, la lucha de clases era inevitable y llevaría a la creación de una sociedad sin clases en la que toda la riqueza y la propiedad pertenecería a la comunidad como un todo

compact an agreement among people (p. 122)

pacto acuerdo

compromise an agreement in which each side makes concessions; an acceptable middle ground (p. 68)

compromiso acuerdo en el que cada parte hace concesiones; un término medio aceptable

concentration camp detention center for civilians considered enemies of the state (p. 573)

campo de concentración centro de detención de los civiles que se considera enemigos del estado

Concert of Europe a system in which Austria, Russia, Prussia, and Great Britain met periodically to discuss any problems affecting the peace in Europe; resulted from the post-Napoleon era Quadruple Alliance (p. 600)

Concierto de Europa sistema por el cual Austria, Rusia, Prusia y Gran Bretaña se reunían periódicamente para discutir cualquier problema que afectara a la paz en Europa; resultado de la Cuádruple Alianza de la era postnapoleónica

concession special economic rights given to a foreign power (p. 404)

concesión derechos económicos especiales que se dan a un poder extranjero

confederation unification (p. 435)

confederación unificación

Congress of Vienna assembly of European leaders that met after the Napoleonic era to piece Europe back together; met from September 1814 to June 1815 (p. 237)

Congreso de Viena asamblea de líderes europeos que se reunió después de la era napoleónica para reconstruir Europa; se reunieron desde septiembre de 1814 a junio de 1815

conquistador Spanish explorers who claimed lands in the Americas for Spain in the 1500s and 1600s (p. 110)

conquistador los exploradores españoles que apropiaron tierras en América para España en los siglos XVI y XVII

conscription "the draft," which required all young men to be ready for military or other service (p. 467)

conscripción llamado a filas que exigía que todos los hombres jóvenes estuvieran listos para el servicio militar u otro servicio

constitutional government government whose power is defined and limited by law (p. 160)

gobierno constitucional gobierno cuyo poder está definido y limitado por las leyes

containment the U.S. strategy of keeping communism within its existing boundaries and preventing its further expansion (p. 611)

contención estrategia de Estados Unidos de mantener el comunismo dentro de sus fronteras existentes y de prevenir su expansión

Continental System blockade designed by Napoleon to hurt Britain economically by closing European ports to British goods; ultimately unsuccessful (p. 232)

sistema continental bloqueo diseñado por Napoleón para dañar a Gran Bretaña económicamente que consistía en cerrar los puertos europeos a los productos británicos; con el tiempo no tuvo éxito

contraband during wartime, military supplies and raw materials needed to make military supplies that may legally be confiscated by any belligerent (p. 468)

contrabando durante el tiempo de guerra, provisiones militares y materias primas necesarios para fabricar artículos militares, y que pueden ser confiscados legalmente por cualquiera de las partes beligerantes

contras guerrillas who fought the Sandinistas in Nicaragua (p. 724)

contras grupo guerrillero que luchó contra los sandinistas en Nicaragua

convoy group of merchant ships protected by warships (p. 463)

convoy grupo de barcos mercantes protegidos por barcos de guerra

corporation business owned by many investors who buy shares of stock and risk only the amount of their investment (p. 303)

corporación empresa propiedad de muchos inversores que compran acciones y que sólo arriesgan el monto de su inversión

Council of Trent a group of Catholic leaders that met between 1545 and 1563 to respond to Protestant challenges and direct the future of the Catholic Church (p. 69)

Concilio de Trento grupo de líderes católicos que se reunieron entre 1545 y 1563 para tratar los retos protestantes y liderar el futuro de la Iglesia Católica

coup d'état the forcible overthrow of a government (p. 663)

golpe de estado derrocamiento por la fuerza de un gobierno

creole person in Spain's colonies in the Americas who was an American-born descendent of Spanish settlers (pp. 118, 283)

criollo descendiente de colonos españolas nacido en las colonias españolas de América

Crimean War war fought mainly on the Crimean Peninsula between the Russians and the British, French, and Turks from 1853–1856 (p. 349)

Guerra de Crimea guerra librada principalmente en la península de Crimea entre los rusos y los británicos, franceses y turcos entre 1853 y 1856

Crusades a series of wars from the 1000s through the 1200s in which European Christians tried to win control of the Holy Land from Muslims (p. 29)

Cruzadas serie de guerras entre el siglo XI y el siglo XIII en las que los cristianos europeos intentaron ganar el control sobre los musulmanes de la Tierra Santa

cult of domesticity idealization of women and the home (p. 313)

culto a lo doméstico idealización de las mujeres y del hogar

cultural diffusion the spread of ideas, customs, and technologies from one people to another (p. 6)

difusión cultural divulgación de ideas, costumbres y tecnología de un pueblo a otro

cultural nationalism pride in one's country's culture (p. 494)

nacionalismo cultural orgullo de la cultura del país propio

Cultural Revolution a Chinese Communist program in the late 1960s to purge China of non-revolutionary tendencies that caused economic and social damage (p. 624)

Revolución Cultural programa de la China comunista a finales de la década de 1960 que pretendía eliminar de China todas las tendencias no revolucionarias y que causó daños económicos y sociales

cuneiform in the ancient Middle East, a system of writing that used wedge-shaped marks (p. 7)

cuneiforme en el antiguo Oriente Medio, sistema de escritura cuyos caracteres tenían forma de cuña

D

dada artistic movement in which artists rejected tradition and produced works that often shocked their viewers (p. 527)

dadaísmo movimiento artístico en el que los artistas rechazaban la tradición y producían obras que a menudo sorprendían a su público

daimyo warrior lord directly below the shogun in feudal Japan (p. 36)

daimio señor de la Guerra que en el Japón feudal estaba directamente abajo del shogun

dalits outcastes or members of India's lowest caste (pp. 654, 718)

dalits (o intocables) los marginados o miembros de las castas más bajas de India

Dardanelles vital strait connecting the Black Sea and the Mediterranean Sea in present-day Turkey (p. 464)

Dardanelos estrecho de vital importancia que conecta el Mar Negro y el Mar Mediterráneo en la actual Turquía

Darfur a region in western Sudan where ethnic conflict threatened to lead to genocide (p. 690)

Darfur región occidental de Sudán donde un conflicto étnico amenaza con provocar un genocidio

D-Day code name for the day that Allied forces invaded France during World War II, June 6, 1944 (p. 582)

Día D nombre en clave del día en que las fuerzas aliadas invadieron Francia durante la Segunda Guerra Mundial (6 de junio de 1944)

default fail to make payments (p. 736)

cese de pagos imposibilidad de realizar pagos

deficit gap between what a government spends and what it takes in through taxes and other sources (p. 736)

déficit diferencia entre los gastos de un gobierno y las recaudaciones por impuestos y otras fuentes de ingresos

deficit spending situation in which a government spends more money than it takes in (p. 213)

> **gasto deficitario** situación en la que un gobierno gasta más de lo que recauda

deforestation the destruction of forest land (pp. 408, 750)

> **deforestación** destrucción de tierras forestales

demilitarized zone a thin band of territory across the Korean peninsula separating North Korean forces from South Korean forces; established by the armistice of 1953 (p. 628)

> **zona desmilitarizada** estrecha franja de tierra que cruza la península de Corea y que separa las fuerzas de Corea del Norte y las fuerzas de Corea del Sur; establecida por el armisticio de 1953

democracy government in which the people hold ruling power (p. 17)

> **democracia** forma de gobierno en el que la soberanía reside en el pueblo

depopulation reduction in the number of people in an area (p. 165)

> **despoblación** reducción del número de la población en una zona

desertification process by which fertile or semi-desert land becomes desert (p. 711)

> **desertización** proceso por el que la tierra fértil o semifértil se convierte en desierto

détente the relaxation of Cold War tensions during the 1970s (p. 606)

> **distensión** relajamiento de las tensiones de la Guerra Fría en los años 70

developing world nations working toward development in Africa, Asia, and Latin America (p. 704)

> **mundo en desarrollo** países en vías de desarrollo de á frica, Asia y Latinoamérica

development the process of building a stronger and more advanced economy and creating higher living standards (p. 704)

> **desarrollo** proceso de creación de una economía más sólida y avanzada y un nivel de vida más alto

Diaspora the spreading of the Jews beyond their historic homeland (p. 7)

> **Diáspora** diseminación de los judíos más allá de su patria histórica

Dienbienphu small town and former French army base in northern Vietnam; site of the battle that ended in a Vietnamese victory, the French withdrawal from Vietnam, and the securing of North Vietnam's independence (p. 631)

Dienbienphu pequeño pueblo y antigua base del ejército francés en el norte de Vietnam; lugar de la batalla que terminó con la victoria vietnamita, la expulsión de los franceses de Vietnam y la obtención de la independencia de Vietnam del Norte

diet assembly or legislature (pp. 63, 425)

> **dieta** asamblea o cuerpo legislativo

direct democracy system of government in which citizens participate directly in the day-to-day affairs of government rather than through elected representatives (p. 17)

> **democracia directa** sistema de gobierno en el que los ciudadanos participan directamente en lugar de hacerlo a través de representantes electos en los asuntos diarios del gobierno

disarmament reduction of armed forces and weapons (p. 531)

> **desarme** reducción del ejército y del armamento

discrimination unequal treatment or barriers (p. 616)

> **discriminación** tratamiento desigual o barreras

dissenter Protestant whose views and opinions differed from those of the Church of England (p. 155)

> **disidente** protestante cuyos puntos de vista y opiniones diferían de los de la Iglesia de Inglaterra

divine right belief that a ruler's authority comes directly from God (p. 144)

> **derecho divino** creencia de que la autoridad de un gobernante proviene directamente de Dios

dominion self-governing nation (p. 435)

> **dominio** nación que se gobierna a sí misma

domino theory the belief that a communist victory in South Vietnam would cause noncommunist governments across Southeast Asia to fall to communism, like a row of dominoes (p. 631)

> **teoría del dominó** creencia de que una victoria comunista en Vietnam del Sur podría causar que los gobiernos no comunistas del sudeste de Asia cayeran bajo dominio del comunismo, como una fila de fichas de dominó

Dreyfus affair a political scandal that caused deep divisions in France between Royalists and liberals and republicans; centered on the 1894 wrongful conviction of Alfred Dreyfus, a Jewish officer in the French army (p. 375)

Caso Dreyfus escándalo político que causó divisiones profundas en Francia entre los realistas, liberales y republicanos; basado en la in justa condena en 1894 de Alfred Dreyfus, un oficial judío del ejérci to francés

Dual Monarchy the monarchy of Austria-Hungary (p. 344)

monarquía dual monarquía de Austria-Hungría

Duma elected national legislature in Russia (p. 353)

Duma en Rusia, asamblea legislative nacional electa

Dunkirk port in France from which 300,000 Allied troops were evacuated when their retreat by land was cut off by the German advance in 1940 (p. 569)

Dunkirk puerto de Francia desde donde fueron evacuadas 300,000 tropas aliadas en 1940 al ser bloqueada su retirada terrestre por el avance del ejército alemán

Dutch East India Company a trading company established by the Netherlands in 1602 to protect and expand its trade in Asia (p. 96)

Compañía Holandesa de las Indias Orientales compañía de comercio establecida por Holanda en 1602 para proteger y aumentar su comercio con Asia

dynamo a machine used to generate electricity (p. 301)

dínamo máquina que se usa para generar electricidad

dynastic cycle rise and fall of Chinese dynasties according to the Mandate of Heaven (p. 9)

ciclo dinástico florecimiento y caída de las dinastías chinas de acuerdo con el Mandato del Cielo

dynasty ruling family (p. 9)

dinastía familia gobernante

E

East Timor a former Portuguese colony, seized by Indonesia, that gained independence in 2002 (p. 659)

Timor Oriental antigua colonia portuguesa, ocupada por Indonesia, que obtuvo su independencia en 2002

economic nationalism an emphasis on domestic control and protection of the economy (p. 493)

nacionalismo económico énfasis en el control nacional y en la protección de la economía

Edict of Nantes law issued by French king Henry IV in 1598 giving more religious freedom to French Protestants (p. 148)

Edicto de Nantes ley promulgada por el rey francés Enrique IV en 1598 por la que se concedía mayor libertad religiosa a los protestantes frances (p. 148)

elector one of seven German princes who would choose the Holy Roman emperor (p. 163)

elector uno de los siete príncipes germanos que elegían al emperador del Sacro Romano

electorate body of people allowed to vote (p. 361)

electorado conjunto de personas a quienes se permite votar

elite upper class (p. 398)

élite clase alta

emancipation granting of freedom to serfs or slaves (p. 349)

emancipación concesión de libertad a esclavos o siervos

emigration movement away from one's homeland (p. 342)

emigración trasladarse de su propio país a otro

émigré person who flees his or her country for political reasons (p. 220)

exiliado persona que deja su país por razones políticas

empire a group of states or territories controlled by one ruler (p. 5)

imperio grupo de estados o territorios controlados por un gobernante

enclosure the process of taking over and consolidating land formerly shared by peasant farmers (p. 248)

cercamiento proceso de consolidar y apropiarse de una tierra que anteriormente compartían campesinos

encomienda right the Spanish government granted to its American colonists to demand labor or tribute from Native Americans (p. 116)

encomienda derecho a exigir tributo o trabajo a los natives americanos, que el gobierno español otorgó a sus colonos en América

endangered species species threatened with extinction (p. 712)

especies en vías de extinción especies amenazadas de extinción, es decir, de desaparición

English Bill of Rights series of acts passed by the English Parliament in 1689 that limited the rights of the monarchy and ensured the superiority of Parliament (p. 159)

engraving art form in which an artist etches a design on a metal plate with acid and then uses the plate to make multiple prints (p. 57)

grabado forma de arte en la que un artista graba un diseño con ácido en una placa de metal y después la usa para producir múltiples impresiones

enlightened despot absolute ruler who used his or her power to bring about political and social change (p. 191)

déspota ilustrado gobernante absoluto que usa su poder para precipitar cambios políticos y sociales

entente nonbinding agreement to follow common policies (p. 455)

entendimiento acuerdo no vinculante de seguir normas comunes

enterprise a business organization in such areas as shipping, mining, railroads, or factories (p. 251)

empresa entidad empresarial en áreas como transportes, minería, ferrocariles o fábricas

entrepreneur person who assumes financial risk in the hope of making a profit (pp. 131, 251)

empresario persona que asume riesgos financieros con la esperanza de obtener beneficios

epidemic outbreak of a rapidly spreading disease (p. 746)

epidemia brote de una enfermedad que se extiende rápidamente

erosion the wearing away of land (p. 751)

erosión el desgaste paulatino de la tierra

estate social class (p. 210)

estado clase social

Estates-General legislative body made up of representatives of the three estates in pre-revolutionary France

Estados Generales cuerpo legislativo formado por representantes de los tres estados en la Francia prerevolucionaria

ethnic cleansing the killing or forcible removal of people of different ethnicities from an area by aggressors so that only the ethnic group of the aggressors remains (p. 684)

limpieza étnica la matanza o expulsión forzosa de personas de diferentes grupos étnicos de una zona, llevadas a cabo por agresores para que su grupo étnico tenga permanencia exclusiva

ethnic group large group of people who share the same language and cultural heritage (p. 31)

étnico grupo grande de personas que comparten el idioma y la herencia cultural

euro common currency used by member nations of the European Union (p. 735)

euro moneda común usada por las naciones que pertenecen a la Unión Europea

European Community an international organization dedicated to establishing free trade among its European member nations (p. 620)

Comunidad Europea organización internacional dedicada a establecer un comercio libre entre sus naciones europeas miembros de todos los productos

European Union an international organization made up of over two dozen European nations, with a common currency and common policies and laws (p. 735)

Unión Europea organización internacional compuesta por más de dos docenas de países, con una misma moneda, y políticas y leyes en común

excommunication exclusion from the Roman Catholic Church as a penalty for refusing to obey Church law (p. 28)

excomunión exclusión de la Iglesia Católica Romana como castigo por rehusar obedecer la ley de la Iglesia

expansionism policy of increasing the amount of territory a government holds (p. 377)

expansionismo política de aumentar el territorio que posee un gobierno

extraterritoriality right of foreigners to be protected by the laws of their own nation (p. 412)

extraterritorialidad derecho de los extranjeros a recibir protección de las leyes de su propio país

F

faction dissenting group of people (p. 217)

facción grupo de disidentes

famine a severe shortage of food in which large numbers of people starve (p. 746)

hambruna escasez severa de alimentos por la que perece gran número de personas

fascism any centralized, authoritarian government system that is not communist whose policies glorify the state over the individual and are destructive to basic human rights (p. 539)

fascismo cualquier sistema de gobierno autoritario centralizado no comunista cuya política glorifica al estado o encima del individuo y que destruye los derecho humanos fundamentales

federal republic government in which power is divided between the national, or federal, government and the states (p. 201)

república federal gobierno en el que el poder se divide entre el gobierno nacional o federal y los estados

Federal Reserve central banking system of the United States, which regulates banks (p. 533)

Reserva Federal sistema central de banca de Estados Unidos que regula los bancos

feudalism loosely organized system of government in which local lords governed their own lands but owed military service and other support to a greater lord (p. 26)

feudalismo sistema de gobierno poco organizado en el que los señores gobierna han sus propias tierras, pero debían servicio militar y otras formas de apoyo a un superior

fief in medieval Europe, an estate granted by a lord to a vassal in exchange for service and loyalty (p. 26)

estado feudal durante la Edad Media, terreno que un señor cedía a un vasallo a cambio de servicio y lealtad

filial piety respect for parents (p. 15)

piedad filial respeto hacia los padres

finance the management of money matters including the circulation of money, loans, investments, and banking (p. 533)

finanzas o gestión de los asuntos monetarios incluyendo la circulación de dinero, préstamos, inversiones y banca

First Sino-Japanese War conflict between China and Japan in 1894–1895 over control of Korea (p. 427)

Primera guerra sino-japonesa conflicto entre China y Japón de 1894 a 1895 por el control de Corea

Flanders a region that included parts of present-day northern France, Belgium, and the Netherlands; was an important industrial and financial center of northern Europe during the Middle Ages and Renaissance (p. 57)

Flandes región que incluye partes de los actuales norte de Francia, Bélgica y Holanda; fue un importante centro industrial y financiero del norte de Europa durante la Edad Media y el Renacimiento

flapper in the United States and Europe in the 1920s, a rebellious young woman (p. 523)

flapper mujer joven y rebelde en los años 20 en Estados Unidos y Europa

Florence a city in the Tuscany region of northern Italy that was the center of the Italian Renaissance (p. 50)

Florencia ciudad de la región de Toscana en el norte de Italia que fue el centro del Renacimiento italiano

Fourteen Points list of terms for resolving World War I and future wars outlined by American President Woodrow Wilson in January 1918 (p. 471)

Catorce puntos lista de condiciones para resolver la Primera Guerra Mundial y futuras guerras, esbozada por el presidente estadounidense Woodrow Wilson en enero de 1918

free trade trade between countries without quotas, tariffs, or other restrictions (p. 364)

libre comercio comercio entre países, sin cuotas, tasas u otras restricciones

French and Indian War war between Britain and France in the Americas that happened from 1754 to 1763; it was part of a global war called the Seven Years' War (p. 124)

Guerra franco-india guerra entre Gran Bretaña y Francia en América, que duró desde 1754 a 1763; fue parte de una guerra global que se conoció como la Guerra de los Siete Años

French Indochina Western name for the colonial holdings of France on mainland Southeast Asia—present-day Vietnam, Laos, and Cambodia (p. 430)

Indochina francesa nombre occidental para las colonias de Francia en el sudeste asiático continental

fundamentalists religious leaders who call for a return to what they see as the fundamental, or basic, values of their faiths (p. 708)

fundamentalistas líderes religiosos que abogan por el retorno de lo que consideran ser los valores fundamentales, o básicos, de sus creencias

G

general strike strike by workers in many different industries at the same time (p. 532)

huelga general huelga de trabajadores de muchas industrias diferentes al mismo tiempo

genetic engineering manipulation of living organisms' chemical code in order to produce specific results (p. 763)

ingeniería genética alteración del código genético que portan todas las formas de vida con el fin de producir resultados específicos

genetics a branch of biology dealing with heredity and variations among plants and animals (p. 763)

genética rama de la biología que trata sobre la herencia y las variaciones entre sí de los animales y las plantas

Geneva Swiss city-state which became a Calvinist theocracy in the 1500s; today a major city in Switzerland (p. 65)

Ginebra ciudad estado suiza que se convirtió en una teocracia calvinista en el siglo XVI; en la actualidad es una de las principales ciudades de Suiza

genocide deliberate attempt to destroy an entire religious or ethnic group (p. 402)

genocidio intento deliberado de destruir la totalidad de un grupo religioso o étnico

germ theory the theory that infectious diseases are caused by certain microbes (p. 305)

teoría de los gérmenes teoría de que las enfermedades infecciosas son causadas por ciertos microbios

Gestapo secret police in Nazi Germany (p. 553)

Gestapo policía secreta de la Alemania nazi

ghetto separate section of a city where members of a minority group are forced to live (p. 71)

gueto área separada de una ciudad donde se fuerza a vivir a los miembros de una minoría

glasnost "openness" in Russian; a Soviet policy of greater freedom of expression introduced by Mikhail Gorbachev in the late 1980s (p. 640)

glasnost "apertura" en ruso; política soviética de mayor libertad de expresión introducida por Mikhail Gorbachev a finales de la década de 1980

global warming the rise of Earth's surface temperature over time (p. 751)

calentamiento global el aumento de la temperatura de la superficie terrestre a través del tiempo

globalization the process by which national economies, politics, cultures, and societies become integrated with those of other nations around the world (p. 738)

globalización proceso mediante el cual las economías nacionales, la política, la cultura y la sociedades se integran con las de otros países del mundo

Goa a state in western India; formerly a coastal city that was made the base of Portugal's Indian trade (p. 95)

Goa estado en el oeste de India; antiguamente una ciudad costera que se convirtió en la base del comercio en la India de Portugal

Golden Temple the Sikh religion's holiest shrine (p. 655)

Templo Dorado santuario de mayor peso sagrado de la religión sikh

Good Friday Agreement an agreement to end the conflict in Northern Ireland signed in 1998 by Protestants and Catholics (p. 683)

Acuerdo del Viernes Santo acuerdo firmado por protestantes y católicos en 1998 para poner fin al conflicto en Irlanda del Norte

Good Neighbor Policy policy in which American President Franklin Roosevelt promised that the United States would interfere less in Latin American affairs (p. 494)

Política del Buen Vecino politica con la que el presidente estadounidense Franklin Roosevelt prometio que Estados Unidos interferiria menos en los asuntos de America Latina

gravity force that pulls objects in Earth's sphere to the center of Earth (p. 76)

gravedad fuerza que atrae los objetos dentro de la esfera terrestre al centro de la Tierra

Great Depression a painful time of global economic collapse, starting in 1929 and lasting until about 1939 (p. 533)

Gran Depresión período nefasto de colapso de la economía mundial que empezó en 1929 y duró hasta 1939

Great Leap Forward a Chinese Communist program from 1958 to 1960 to boost farm and industrial output that failed miserably (p. 624)

Gran Salto hacia Adelante programa de la China comunista de 1958 a 1960 para aumentar la producción agrícola e industrial que fracasó miserablemente

Green Revolution the improved seeds, pesticides, mechanical equipment, and farming methods introduced in the developing world beginning in the 1950s (p. 706)

revolución verde la introducción, en los países en vías de desarrollo durante la década de 1950, de semillas, pesticidas, equipo mecánico y métodos de agricultura perfeccionados

griot professional storyteller in early West Africa (p. 35)

griot antiguo narrador de historias profesional en África occidental

gross domestic product (GDP) the total value of all goods and services produced in a nation within a particular year (p. 622)

producto interior bruto (PIB) valor total de todos los productos y servicios producidos en una nación en un determinado año

Guangzhou a coastal city in southeastern China, also known as Canton (p. 100)

Guangzhou ciudad costera del sudeste de China, también conocida como Cantón

guerrilla a soldier in a loosely organized force making surprise raids (p. 631)

guerrilla pequeños grupos de soldados pertenecientes a una fuerza poco organizada que despliega ataques por sorpresa

guerrilla warfare fighting carried on through hit-and-run raids (p. 235)

guerra de guerrillas lucha que se caracteriza por rápidos ataques y retiradas

guild in the Middle Ages, an association of merchants or artisans who cooperated to uphold standards of their trade and to protect their economic interests (p. 27)

gremio en la Edad Media, asociación de mercaderes o artesanos que cooperaban para mantener los valores de sus oficios y para proteger sus intereses económicos

guillotine device used during the Reign of Terror to execute thousands by beheading (p. 226)

guillotina aparato usado durante el Reinado del Terror para decapitar a miles de personas

Gulag in the Soviet Union, a system of forced labor camps in which millions of criminals and political prisoners were held under Stalin (p. 544)

Gulag en la Unión Soviética, un sistema de campos de trabajo forzado donde millones de criminales y prisioneros políticos fueron detenidos durante el gobierno de Stalin

Guomindang Nationalist party; active in China 1912 to 1949 (p. 508)

Guomindang partido nacionalista, activo en China entre 1912 y 1949

H

hacienda a large plantation (p. 490)
hacienda plantación grande

hajj one of the Five Pillars of Islam, the pilgrimage to Mecca that all Muslims are expected to make at least once in their lifetime (p. 32)

hayyi uno de los Cinco Pilares del Islam, la peregrinación a la Meca que se espera hagan todos los musulmanes por lo menos una vez en la vida

Hapsburg empire Central European empire that lasted from the 1400s to the 1900s and at its height included the lands of the Holy Roman Empire and the Netherlands (p. 142)

Imperio Habsburgo imperio centroeuropeo que duró desde el siglo XV hasta el siglo XX, y que en su plenitud abarcó los territorios del Sacro Imperio Romano y Holanda

Harlem Renaissance an African American cultural movement in the 1920s and 1930s, centered in Harlem (p. 525)

Renacimiento de Harlem movimiento cultural afroamericano durante las décadas de 1920 y 1930, que estaba centrado en Harlem

hejab headscarves and loose-fitting, ankle-length garments meant to conceal the body (p. 673)

hejab velos, pañuelos y prendas de vestir amplias y hasta los tobillos cuya finalidad es ocultar el cuerpo

heliocentric based on the belief that the sun is the center of the universe (p. 72)

heliocéntrico sistema basado en la creencia de que el Sol es el centro del universo

hierarchy system of ranking groups (p. 6)

jerarquía sistema que clasifica a las personas de una sociedad

Hiroshima mid-sized city in Japan where the first atomic bomb was dropped in August, 1945 (p. 589)

Hiroshima ciudad de tamaño medio de Japón donde fue lanzada la primera bomba atómica en agosto de 1945

Holocaust the systematic genocide of about six million European Jews by the Nazis during World War II (p. 574)

Holocausto el genocidio sistemático por parte de los nazis de alrededor de seis millones de judíos europeos durante la Segunda Guerra Mundial

home rule local self-government (p. 369)
autogobierno autogobierno local

homogeneous society society that has a common culture and language (p. 426)

sociedad homogénea sociedad que tiene un lenguaje y una cultura común

Huguenots French Protestants of the 1500s and 1600s (p. 148)

Hugonotes protestantes franceses de los siglos XVI y XVII

humanism an intellectual movement at the heart of the Renaissance that focused on education and the classics (p. 49)

humanismo movimiento intelectual durante el auge del Renacimiento que se centraba en la educación y los clásicos

humanities study of subjects such as grammar, rhetoric, poetry, and history, that were taught in ancient Greece and Rome (p. 49)

humanidades estudio de asignaturas como la gramática, la retórica, poesía e historia que se enseñaban en las antiguas Grecia y Roma

Hutus the group that forms the majority in Rwanda and Burundi (p. 689)

Hutus grupo mayoritario de Ruanda y Burundi

hypothesis an unproved theory accepted for the purposes of explaining certain facts or to provide a basis for further investigation (p. 74)

hipótesis teoría sin probar aceptada con el propósito de explicar determinados hechos o de proveer una base para una investigación posterior más profunda

I

ideology system of thought and belief (pp. 272, 610)

ideología sistema de pensamiento y creencias

immunity natural protection, resistance (p. 111)

imperialism domination by one country of the political, economic, or cultural life of another country or region (p. 388)

imperialismo dominio por parte de un país de la vida política, económica o cultural de otro país o región

import substitution manufacturing goods locally to replace imports (p. 720)

sustitución de importaciones la producción local de bienes para reemplazar su importación

impressionism school of painting of the late 1800s and early 1900s that tried to capture fleeting visual impressions (p. 322)

impresionismo escuela de pintura de finales del siglo XIX y principios del siglo XX que trataba de captar impresiones visuales fugaces

indemnity payment for losses in war (p. 412)

indemnización compensación como pago por pérdidas de guerra

indigenous original or native to a country or region (pp. 436, 725)

indígena originario o nativo de un país o región

indulgence in the Roman Catholic Church, pardon for sins committed during a person's lifetime (p. 62)

indulgencia perdón por los pecados cometidos en vida concedido por la Iglesia Católica Romana

inflation economic cycle that involves a rapid rise in prices linked to a sharp increase in the amount of money available (p. 130)

inflación ciclo económico caracterizado por un rápida subida de los precios ligada a un aumento rápido del dinero disponible

insurgents rebel forces (p. 697)

insurgentes fuerzas rebeldes

intendant official appointed by French king Louis XIV to govern the provinces, collect taxes, and recruit soldiers (p. 150)

intendente oficial publico nombrado por el rey francés Luis XIV para gobernar las provincias, recaudar impuestos y reclutar soldados

interchangeable parts identical components that can be used in place of one another in manufacturing (p. 301)

repuestos intercambiables componentes idénticos que pueden usarse unos en lugar de otros en el proceso de producción

interdependence mutual dependence of countries on goods, resources, labor, and knowledge from other parts of the world (p. 738)

interdependencia dependencia mutua de los países con los de otras partes del mundo en cuanto a productos, recursos, mano de obra y conocimientos

International Space Station (ISS) an artificial structure built and maintained by a coalition of nations with the purpose of research (p. 759)

Estación Espacial Internacional (ISS, por sus siglas en inglés) estructura artificial construida y mantenida por una coalición de naciones con el fin de llevar a cabo investigaciones

Internet a huge international computer network linking millions of users around the world (p. 761)

Internet inmensa red internacional de computadoras que une a millones de ususarios en todo el mundo

intifada Palestinian Arab uprisings against the Israeli occupation (p. 693)

intifadas levantamientos de árabes palestinos en contra de la ocupación israelí

Islamist a person who wants government policies to be based on the teachings of Islam (p. 667)

islamista persona que desea que las políticas del gobierno tengan su fundamento en las enseñanzas del Islam

island-hopping during World War II, Allied strategy of recapturing some Japanese-held islands while bypassing others (p. 588)

salto entre islas estrategia aliada durante la Segunda Guerra Mundial de retomar algunas de las islas ocupadas por los japoneses e ignorar y pasar de largo de otras

J

Jacobin member of a radical political club during the French Revolution (p. 221)

jacobino miembro de un club político radical durante la Revolución Francesa

Jerusalem capital of the Jewish state of Judea in ancient times; city sacred to Jews, Muslims, and Christians, parts of which are claimed by both Israel and the Palestinian Arabs (p. 694)

Jerusalén capital del estado judío de Judea en tiempos antiguos; ciudad sagrada para los judíos, musulmanes y cristianos, en la que parte de su territorio está reclamado tanto por Israel como por los árabes palestinos

jury group of people sworn to make a decision in a legal case (p. 28)

jurado grupo de personas que han prestado juramento par tomar una decisión en un caso legal

K

kaiser emperor of Germany (p. 333)

kaiser emperador de Alemania

kamikaze Japanese pilot who undertook a suicide mission (p. 588)

kamikaze piloto japonés que emprendía una misión suicida

Kashmir a former princely state in the Himalayas, claimed by both India and Pakistan, which have fought wars over its control (p. 653)

Cachemira antiguo estado principesco de los Himalayas, reclamado tanto por India como Pakistán, y por cuyo control han librado varias guerras

Katanga a province of the Democratic Republic of the Congo with rich copper and diamond deposits that tried to gain independence from Congo in 1960 (p. 667)

Katanga provincia de la República Democrática del Congo con ricos depósitos de cobre y diamantes, que intentó independizarse del Congo en 1960

Kellogg-Briand Pact an international agreement, signed by almost every nation in 1928, to stop using war as a method of national policy (p. 531)

Pacto de Kellogg-Briand acuerdo internacional firmado por casi todas las naciones en 1928 para erradicar el uso de la guerra como un metodo de politica nacional

Khmer Rouge a political movement and a force of Cambodian communist guerrillas that gained power in Cambodia in 1975 (p. 635)

Khmer Rouge movimiento político y fuerza guerrillera comunista de Camboya que llegó al poder en ese país en 1975

kibbutz a collective farm in Israel (p. 671)

kibbutz en Israel, granja comunitaria

kiva large underground chamber that the Anasazi used for religious ceremonies and political meetings (p. 21)

kiva gran sala subterránea que usaban los anazasi para ceremonias religiosas y reuniones políticas

knight a European noble who served as a mounted warrior (p. 26)

caballero noble europeo que servía como guerrero montado

Knossos an ancient Minoan city on the island of Crete

Cnosos antigua ciudad minoica en la isla de Creta

Kolkata a large city in India, also known as Calcutta (p. 718)

Kolkata ciudad grande de India, conocida también como Calcuta

Kosovo a province of Serbia with an Albanian ethnic majority that was the site of an ethnic conflict during the 1990s (p. 685)

Kosovo provincia de Serbia de mayoría étnica albanesa que sufrió un conflicto étnico durante la década de 1990

kulak wealthy peasant in the Soviet Union in the 1930s (p. 543)

campesino adinerado de la Unión Soviética en la década de 1930

Kulturkampf Bismarck's "battle for civilization," in which his goal was to make Catholics put loyalty to the state above their allegiance to the Church (p. 336)

Kulturkampf "batalla por civilización" de Bismarck, cuyo objetivo era que los católicos pusieran la lealtod al estado por encima de la lealtad a la Iglesia

L

La Reforma an era of liberal reform in Mexico from 1855 to 1876 (p. 441)

La Reforma era de reforma liberal en México desde 1855 a 1876

labor union workers' organization (p. 256)

sindicato organización de trabajadores

laissez faire policy allowing business to operate with little or no government interference (p. 186)

laissez faire política que permite a los negocios y empresas operar con poca o ninguna interferencia del gobierno

laser a high-energy light beam that can be used for many purposes including surgery, engineering, and scientific research (p. 762)

láser haz luminoso de alta energía que puede ser usado para muchos fines, entre ellos la cirugía, la ingeniería y la investigación científica

legitimacy principle by which monarchies that had been unseated by the French Revolution or Napoleon were restored (p. 238)

legitimidad principio por el que las monarquías que habían sido derrocadas por la Revolución Francesa o por Napoleón fueron restituidas

Lend-Lease Act act passed by the United States Congress in 1941 that allowed the president (FDR) to sell or lend war supplies to any country whose defense was considered vital to the United States (p. 575)

Ley de Préstamo y Arriendo decreto aprobado por el Congreso de Estados Unidos en 1941 que permitió al presidente (FDR) vender o arrendar materiales de guerra a cualquier país cuya defensa fuese considerada de vital importancia para Estados Unidos

levée morning ritual during which nobles would wait upon French king Louis XIV (p. 150)

recepción matutina ritual de la mañana en el que los nobles atendían al rey Luis XIV

libel knowing publication of false and damaging statements (p. 375)

libelo publicación intencional de declaraciones falsas que perjudican a alguien

liberation theology movement within the Catholic Church that urged the church to become a force for reform, social justice, and put an end to poverty (p. 723)

teología de la liberación movimiento dentro de la Iglesia Católica que urgía a la iglesia a liderar un llamamiento por la reforma, la justicia social el fin de la pobreza

limited monarchy government in which a constitution or legislative body limits the monarch's powers (p. 160)

monarquía limitada gobierno en el que la constitución o el cuerpo legislativo limitan los poderes de la monarquía

Line of Demarcation line set by the Treaty of Tordesillas dividing the non-European world into two zones, one controlled by Spain and the other by Portugal (p. 88)

Línea de demarcación línea establecida por el Tratado de Tordesillas que dividía el mundo fuera de Europa en dos zonas: una controlada por España y otra por Portugal

literacy the ability to read and write (p. 704)

alfabetismo capacidad de leer y escribir

Liverpool city and one of the largest ports in England; first major rail line linked Liverpool to Manchester in 1830 (p. 253)

Liverpool ciudad y uno de los puertos más grandes de Inglaterra; línea importante de ferrocarril unió Liverpool con Manchester en 1830

Long March epic march in which a group of Chinese Communists retreated from Guomindang forces by marching over 6,000 miles (p. 509)

Gran Marcha marcha épica en la que un grupo de comunistas chinos marcharon en retirada de las fuerzas del Guomindang por más de 6,000 millas

Louisiana Purchase territory purchased by Thomas Jefferson from France in 1803 (p. 377)

Compra de Luisiana territorio que Thomas Jefferson compró a Francia en 1803

Luftwaffe German air force (p. 568)

Luftwaffe fuerza aérea alemana

Lusitania British liner torpedoed by a German submarine in May 1915 (p. 468)

Lusitania crucero británico torpedeado por un submarino alemán en mayo de 1915

M

Macao region of southeastern China made up of a peninsula and two islands, a Portuguese territory from the mid-1800s to 1999 (p. 100)

Macao región al sudeste de China formada por una península y dos islas; fue territorio portugués desde mediados del siglo XIX a 1999

Maginot Line massive fortifications built by the French along the French border with Germany in the 1930s to protect against future invasions (p. 531)

Línea Maginot fortificaciones masivas construídas por los franceses a lo largo de la frontera france sa con Alemania en la década de 1930 para protegerse contra invasiones futuras

Mahdi a Muslim savior of the faith (p. 400)

Malacca a state and coastal city in southwestern Malaysia, was an early center of the spice trade (p. 95)

Malacca estado y ciudad costera en el sudoeste de Malasia; fue uno de los primeros centros del comercio de especias

Malindi a coastal town in southeastern Kenya (p. 90)

Malindi pueblo costero al sudeste de Kenia

Manchester city in England; one of the leading industrial areas; example of an Industrial Revolution city; first major rail line linked Manchester to Liverpool in 1830 (p. 253)

Manchester ciudad de Inglaterra; una de las principales áreas industriales; ejemplo de ciudad de la Revolución Industrial; la primera línea importante de ferrocarril unió Manchester con Liverpool en 1830

Manchuria historic province in northeastern China; rich in natural resources (p. 514)

Manchuria provincia histórica en el noreste de China; rica en recursos naturales

Manchus people originally from Manchuria, north of China, who conquered the Ming dynasty and ruled China as the Qing dynasty from the mid-1600s to the early 1900s (p. 101)

manchus personas originalmente de Manchuria, al norte de China, que derrotaron a la dinastía Ming y gobernaron como la dinastía Chin desde mediados del siglo XVII a principios del siglo XX

mandate after World War I, a territory administered by a Western power (p. 476)

mandato territorio administrado por un poder occidental después de la Primera Guerra Mundial

Manhattan Project code name for the project to build the first atomic bomb during World War II (p. 588)

Proyecto Manhattan nombre en clave del proyecto para la fabricación de la primera bomba atómica durante la Segunda Guerra Mundial

Manifest Destiny American idea that the United States should stretch across the entire North American continent (p. 377)

Destino Manifiesto idea estadounidense de que Estados Unidos debería extenderse hasta ocupar todo el continente norteamericano

manor during the Middle Ages in Europe, a lord's estate which included one or more villages and the surrounding lands (p. 26)

señorío durante la Edad Media en Europa, propiedad de un señor que incluía uno o más pueblos y sus terrenos adyacentes

Maori indigenous people of New Zealand (p. 438)

maorie pueblo indígena de Nueva Zelanda

March on Rome planned march of thousands of Fascist supporters to take control of Rome; in response Mussolini was given the legal right to control Italy (p. 537)

Marcha sobre Roma marcha planeada de miles de simpatizantes fascistas sobre Roma para tomar su control; en respuesta a ella a Mussolini se le concedió el derecho legal del control de Italia

Marseilles French port city; troops marched to a patriotic song as they marched from this city, the song eventually became the French national anthem (p. 228)

Marsella ciudad portuaria francesa; las tropas que marcharon al ritmo de una canción patrió-

tica desde esta ciudad inspiraron el himno nacional francés

Marshall Plan massive aid package offered by the United States to Europe to help countries rebuild after World War II (p. 593)

Plan Marshall paquete de ayuda a gran escala ofrecido por Estados Unidos a Europa para apoyar la reconstrucción de los países después de la Segunda Guerra Mundial

May Fourth Movement cultural movement in China that sought to reform China and make it stronger (p. 508)

Movimiento del Cuatro de Mayo movimiento cultural de China que se centró en reformar China y hacerla más fuerte

means of production farms, factories, railways, and other large businesses that produce and distribute goods (p. 263)

medios de producción granjas, fábricas, ferrocarriles y otros grandes negocios que producen y distribuyen mercancías

Meiji Restoration in Japan, the reign of emperor Meiji from 1868 to 1912 which was marked by rapid modernization and industrialization (p. 424)

restauración de Meiji en Japón, reino del emperador Meiji desde 1868 a 1912 que fue marcado por la rápida modernización e industrialización

mercantilism policy by which a nation sought to export more than it imported in order to build its supply of gold and silver (p. 132)

mercantilismo política por la que una nación trataba de exportar más de lo que importaba para aumentar sus reservas de o ro y plata

mercenary soldier serving in a foreign army for pay (p. 165)

mercenario soldado que sirve en un ejército extranjero a cambio de dinero

messiah savior sent by God (p. 19)

mésias salvador enviado por Dios

mestizo person in Spain's colonies in the Americas who was of Native American and European descent (pp. 118, 283)

mestizo persona de las colonias españolas de América descendiente de nativos y europeos

métis people of mixed Native American and French Canadian descent (p. 436)

métis pueblo de descendientes con mezcla de indígenas americanos y franceses canadienses

Middle Passage the leg of the triangular trade route on which slaves were transported from Africa to the Americas (p. 125)

Travesía Intermedia parte de la ruta del comercio triangular en la que los esclavos eran transportados desde África a las Américas

militarism glorification of the military (p. 456)

militarismo glorificación de las fuerzas armadas

militias armed groups of citizen soldiers (p. 696)

milicias grupos armados de soldados-ciudadanos

missionary someone sent to do religious work in a territory or foreign country (p. 91)

misioneros personas enviadas para hacer trabajos religiosos en un territorio u otro país

mobilize prepare military forces for war (p. 458)

mobilizar preparar las fuerzas militares para la guerra

Moluccas a group of islands in eastern Indonesia; was the center of the spice trade in the 1500s and 1600s (p. 84)

Molucas grupo de islas en el este de Indonesia; fue el centro del comercio de especias en los siglos XVI y XVII

Mombasa a city in southeastern Kenya, located on a small coastal island (p. 90)

Mombasa ciudad al sudeste de Kenia, localizada en una pequeña isla costera

monarchy government in which a king or queen exercises central power (p. 16)

monarquía gobierno en el que el poder reside en el rey o la reina

monopoly complete control of a product or business by one person or group (p. 92)

monopolio control total de un producto o negocio por una persona o grupo

monotheistic believing that there was only one god (p. 7)

monoteísta creencia en un solo dios

Monroe Doctrine American policy of discouraging European intervention in the Western Hemisphere (p. 443)

Doctrina Monroe política estadounidense de rechazo a la intervención europea en el hemisferio occidental

mosque Muslim house of worship (p. 33)

mezquita templo musulmán

Mothers of the Plaza de Mayo a movement of women who protested weekly in a central plaza in the capital of Argentina against the disappearance or killing of relatives (p. 726)

Madres de la Plaza de Mayo asociación de mujeres que se reunían semanalmente en una céntrica plaza de la capital de Argentina para protest por la desaparición o asesinato de sus familiares

Mughal empire Muslim empire that ruled most of northern India from the mid-1500s to the mid-1700s; also known as the Mogul or Mongol empire (p. 95)

imperio Mughal imperio musulmán que gobernó la mayor parte del norte de India desde mediados del siglo XVI a mediados del siglo XVIII; también se conoce como imperio Mogul o Mongol

mujahedin Muslim religious warriors (p. 640)

mujaedin guerreros religiosos musulmanes

mulatto in Spain's colonies in the Americas, person who was of African and European descent (pp. 118, 283)

mulato en las colonias españolas de América descendiente de africanos y europeos

multiethnic made up of several ethnic groups (p. 684)

multiétnico compuesto de varios grupos étnicos

multinational corporation company with branches in many countries (p. 739)

corporación multinacional empresa con sucursales en muchos países

Mumbai a large city in India, also known as Bombay (p. 718)

Mumbai ciudad grande de India, conocida también como Bombay

mutiny revolt, especially of soldiers or sailors against their officers (p. 128)

motín revuelta, especialmente de soldados y marineros contra sus oficiales

mutual-aid societies self-help groups to aid sick or injured workers (p. 308)

sociedades de ayuda mutua grupos de apoyo establecidos para ayudar a los trabajadores enfermos o heridos en accidentes laborales

mystic person who devotes his or her life to seeking direct communion with divine forces (p. 8)

místico persona que dedica su vida a buscar la comunión directa con las fuerzas divinas

N

Nagasaki a coastal city in southern Japan on the island of Kyushu; city in Japan where the second atomic bomb was dropped in August, 1945 (pp. 103, 589)

Nagasaki ciudad costera en el sur de Japón en la isla de Kyushu; ciudad de Japón donde fue lanzada la segunda bomba atómica en agosto de 1945

Napoleonic Code body of French civil laws introduced in 1804; served as model for many nations' civil codes (p. 231)

Código Napoleónico cuerpo de las leyes civiles francesas presentadas en 1804, que sirvieron como modelo para los códigos civiles de muchos países

nationalism a strong feeling of pride in and devotion to one's country (p. 228)

nacionalismo fuerte sentimiento de orgullo y devoción hacia el país propio

nationalization takeover of property or resources by the government (p. 492)

nacionalización apropiación de propiedades o recursos por parte del gobierno

natural law rules of conduct discoverable by reason (p. 182)

leyes naturales normas de conducta que se pueden descubrir mediante la razón

natural right right that belongs to all humans from birth, such as life, liberty, and property (p. 183)

derecho natural derecho que pertenece a todos los humanos desde el nacimiento: vida, libertad y propiedad

Nazi-Soviet Pact agreement between Germany and the Soviet Union in 1939 in which the two nations promised not to fight each other and to divide up land in Eastern Europe (p. 567)

Pacto nazi-soviético acuerdo en 1939 entre Alemania y la Unión Soviética mediante el cual las dos naciones prometen no atacarse mutuamente y dividirse entre sí territorio de Europa del Este

négritude movement movement in which writers and artists of African descent expressed pride in their African heritage (p. 498)

movimiento de la negritud movimiento en el que los escritores y artistas descendientes de africanos expresabansu orgullo por la herencia africana

neutrality policy of supporting neither side in a war (p. 458)

neutralidad política de mantenerse al margen en una guerra

Neutrality Acts a series of acts passed by the United States Congress from 1935 to 1939 that aimed to keep the United States from becoming involved in World War II (p. 564)

Leyes de Neutralidad serie de decretos aprobados por el Congreso de Estados Unidos de 1935 a 1939 con el fin de evitar la implicación del país en la Segunda Guerra Mundial

New Deal a massive package of economic and social programs established by FDR to help Americans during the Great Depression (p. 535)

Nuevo Tratado paquete masivo de programas económicos y sociales establecidos por FDR para ayudar a los estadounidenses durante la Gran Depresión

New France French possessions in present-day Canada from the 1500s to 1763 (p. 120)

Nueva Francia posesiones francesas en el actual Canadá desde el siglo XVI a 1763

nirvana in Buddhist belief, union with the universe and release from the cycle of rebirth (p. 14)

nirvana en el budismo, unión con el universo y liberación del ciclo de la reencarnación

no-fly zones in Iraq, areas where the United States and its allies banned flights by Iraqi aircraft after the 1991 Gulf War (p. 697)

zonas de exclusión del espacio aéreo zonas de Iraq en las que Estados Unidos y sus aliados prohibieron el vuelo a la aviación iraquí después de la Guerra del Golfo en 1991

nomad a person who moves from place to place in search of food (p. 4)

nómada persona que se traslada de un lugar a otro en busca de alimentos

nonalignment political and diplomatic independence from both Cold War powers (p. 656)

no alineación independencia política y diplomática de ambas potencias de la guerra fría

North Atlantic Treaty Organization (NATO) a military alliance between several North Atlantic states to safeguard them from the presumed threat of the Soviet Union's communist bloc; countries from other regions later joined the alliance (p. 594)

Organización del Tratado del Atlántico Norte (OTAN) alianza militar entre varios estados del Atlántico norte para salvaguardarlos de la supuesta amenaza del bloque comunista liderado por la Unión Soviética; más tarde se incorporarían a la alianza países de otras regiones

Northern Ireland the northern portion of the island of Ireland, a part of the United Kingdom that has had a long religious conflict (p. 683)

Irlanda del Norte parte norte de la isla de Irlanda y territorio del Reino Unido, que ha sufrido un conflicto religioso durante mucho tiempo

nuclear family family unit consisting of parents and children (p. 35)

familia nuclear unidad familiar que consta de los padres y sus hijos

Nuremberg a city in southern Germany where Hitler staged Nazi rallies in the 1930s, and

ENGLISH/SPANISH GLOSSARY

where Nazi war crimes trials were held after World War II (p. 591)

Nuremberg ciudad del sur de Alemania donde Hitler escenificó manifestaciones nazis durante la década de 1930, y donde se celebraron los juicios por crímenes de guerra nazis después de la Segunda Guerra Mundial

Nuremberg Laws laws approved by the Nazi Party in 1935, depriving Jews of German citizenship and taking some rights away from them (p. 553)

Leyes de Nuremberg leyes aprobadas por el partido nazi en 1935, que eliminaba algunos de los derechos de los judíos en Alemania

O

occupied territories areas controlled by a nation that are part of another entity; Palestinians use this term for certain lands Israel gained after the 1967 war. (p. 693)

territorios ocupados zonas controladas por una nación que forman parte de otra entidad. Los palestinos usan esta palabra para referirse a los territorios ocupados por Israel después de la guerra de 1967

oligarchy government in which ruling power belongs to a few people (pp. 16, 161)

oligarquía gobierno en el que el poder está en manos de unas pocas personas

one-child policy a Chinese government policy limiting urban families to a single child (p. 715)

política de un sólo hijo medida del gobierno chino que limita a las familias urbanas a tener únicamente un hijo

Open Door Policy American approach to China around 1900, favoring open trade relations between China and other nations (p. 414)

Política de puertas abiertas política estadounidense con respecto a China a principios del siglo XX, que abogaba por las libres relaciones comerciales entre China y otras naciones

Opium War war fought between Great Britain and China over restrictions to foreign trade (p. 412)

Guerra del opio guerra librada entre Gran Bretaña y China por las restricciones sobre el comercio exterior

Organization of American States (OAS) a group formed in 1948 to promote democracy, economic cooperation, and human rights in the Americas (p. 724)

Organización de los Estados Americanos grupo formado en 1948 con el fin de promover la democracia, la cooperación económica y los derechos humanos en las Américas

outpost a distant military station or a remote settlement (p. 96)

fuerte fronterizo estación militar distante o asentamiento lejano

outsourcing the practice of sending work to companies in the developing world in order to save money or increase efficiency (p. 738)

subcontratación práctica empresarial de enviar trabajo a compañías de países en vías de desarrollo con el fin de ahorrar dinero o aumentar el rendimiento

overproduction condition in which production of goods exceeds the demand for them (p. 533)

superproducción condición en la que la producción de mercancías excede la demanda

Oyo empire Yoruba empire that arose in the 1600s in present-day Nigeria and dominated its neighbors for a hundred years (p. 92)

imperio Oyo el imperio Yoruba que surgió en el siglo XVII en la actual Nigeria y dominó a sus vecinos durante cien años

P

Pacific Rim vast region of nations, including countries in Southeast Asia, East Asia, and the Americas, that border the Pacific Ocean (p. 737)

Cuenca del Pacífico vasta región de naciones, que incluye los países del sureste y este asiático y de las Américas, que limitan con el océano Pacífico

pacifism opposition to all war (p. 563)

pacifismo oposición a las guerras

Pan-Africanism movement which began in the 1920s that emphasized the unity and strength of Africans and people of African descent around the world (p. 497)

Panafricanismo movimiento que empezó en la década de 1920 que se centraba en la unidad y fuerza de los africanos y personas con ascendencia africana en todo el mundo

Panama Canal man-made waterway connecting the Atlantic and Pacific oceans (p. 445)

Canal de Panamá canal artificial que conecta los océanos Atlántico y Pacífico

Pan-Arabism movement in which Arabs sought to unite all Arabs into one state (p. 500)

Panarabismo movimiento en el que los árabes pretendían unir a todos los árabes en un sólo estado

pandemic spread of a disease across a large area, country, continent, or the entire world (p. 472)

pandemia propagación de una enfermedad a una gran área, país, continente o al mundo entero

parliamentary democracy a form of government in which the executive leaders (usually a prime minister and cabinet) are chosen by and responsible to the legislature (parliament), are also members of it (p. 362)

democracia parlamentaria forma de gobierno en la que la dirección ejecutiva (normalmente un primer ministro y un gabinete) es elegida por la asamblea legislativa (parlamento) y controlada por la misma, además de formar parte de ella

partition a division into pieces (pp. 173, 189, 653)

partición división en partes

pasha provincial ruler in the Ottoman empire (p. 401)

bajá gobernante provincial del imperio otomano

paternalistic the system of governing a country as a father would a child (p. 394)

paternalista sistema de gobernar un país como un padre lo hace con su hijo

patrician in ancient Rome, member of the land-holding upper class (p. 18)

patricio miembro de la clase alta terrateniente en la antigua Roma

patron a person who provides financial support for the arts (p. 50)

mecenas persona que proporciona apoyo financiero a la cultura y las artes

Peace of Westphalia series of treaties that ended the Thirty Years' War (p. 165)

Paz de Westfalia serie de tratados por los que se puso fin a la Guerra de los Treinta Años

penal colony place where people convicted of crimes are sent (pp. 365, 437)

colonia penal lugar al que se manda a los condenados por crímenes

peninsulare member of the highest class in Spain's colonies in the Americas (pp. 118, 283)

peninsular miembro de la clase más alta en las colonias españolas de América

peon worker forced to labor for a landlord in order to pay off a debt (p. 116)

peón trabajador forzado a trabajar para un terrateniente para pagar una deuda

peonage system by which workers owe labor to pay their debts (p. 442)

peonaje sistema en el que los trabajadores deben trabajo como pago por sus deudas

perestroika "restructuring" in Russian; a Soviet policy of democratic and free-market reforms introduced by Mikhail Gorbachev in the late 1980s (p. 640)

perestroika "reestructuración" en ruso; política soviética de reformas democráticas y de libre mercado que introdujo Mikhail Gorbachev a finales de la década de 1980

personal computer (PC) a small computer meant to be used by individuals or small businesses (p. 761)

computadora personal (PC, por sus siglas en inglés) pequeña computadora diseñada para uso individual o por parte de pequeñas empresas

perspective artistic technique used to give paintings and drawings a three-dimensional effect (p. 50)

perspectiva técnica artística usada para lograr el efecto de tercera dimensión en dibujos y pinturas

pharaoh title of the rulers of ancient Egypt (p. 6)

faraón título de los gobernantes del antiguo Egipto

Philippines a country in southeastern Asia made up of several thousand islands (p. 97)

Filipinas país al sudeste de Asia formado por varios miles de islas

philosophe French for "philosopher"; French thinker who desired reform in society during the Enlightenment (p. 184)

philosophe palabra francesa que significa "filósofo"; pensador francés que abogaba por reformas en la sociedad durante la Ilustración

pictograph a simple drawing that looks like the object it represents (p. 5)

pictografía dibujo sencillo que se parece al objeto que representa

Pilgrims English Protestants who rejected the Church of England (p. 122)

peregrinos protestantes ingleses que rechazaron la Iglesia de Inglaterra

plantation large estate run by an owner or overseer and worked by laborers who live there (p. 91)

plantación gran propiedad administrada por un dueño o capataz y cultivada por trabajadores que viven en ella

plebian in ancient Rome, member of the lower class, including farmers, merchants, artisans, and traders (p. 18)

plebeyo en la antigua Roma, miembro de clase baja, que incluía granjeros, mercaderes, artesanos y comerciantes

plebiscite ballot in which voters have a direct say on an issue (p. 231)

plebiscito votación en la que los votantes expresan su opinión sobre un tema en particular

pogrom violent attack on a Jewish community (p. 351)

pogrom ataque violento de una multitud hacia una comunidad judía

polis city-state in ancient Greece (p. 16)

polis ciudad-estado de la antigua Grecia

polytheistic believing in many gods (p. 9)

politeísta creencia en muchos dioses

popular sovereignty basic principle of the American system of government which asserts that the people are the source of any and all governmental power, and government can exist only with the consent of the governed (p. 198)

soberanía popular principio básico del sistema de gobierno estadounidense en el que se determina que el pueblo es la fuente de todo poder gubernamental, y que el gobierno sólo puede existir con el consentimiento de los gobernados

predestination Calvinist belief that God long ago determined who would gain salvation (p. 65)

predestinación creencia calvinista de que Dios decidió hace mucho tiempo quién conseguiría la salvación

premier prime minister (p. 374)

premier primer ministro

price revolution period in European history when inflation rose rapidly (p. 130)

revolución del precio período en la historia de Europa en que la inflación aumentó rápidamente

privateer privately owned ship commissioned by a government to attack and capture enemy ships, especially merchant's ships (p. 119)

corsario barco privado comisionado por un gobierno para atacar y capturar barcos enemigos, especialmentelos barcos mercantes

Prohibition a ban on the manufacture and sale of alcoholic beverages in the United States from 1920 to 1933 (p. 523)

Prohibición restricción de la fabricación y venta de bebidas alcohólicas en Estados Unidos desde 1920 a 1933

proletariat working class (pp. 263, 478)

proletariado clase trabajadora (p. 263)

proliferate to multiply rapidly (p. 753)

proliferar multiplicarse rápidamente

propaganda spreading of ideas to promote a cause or to damage an opposing cause (p. 468)

propaganda divulgación de ideas para promover cierta causa o para perjudicar una causa opuesta

prophet spiritual leader who interprets God's will (p. 7)

profeta líder espiritual a quien se le atribuye la interpretación de la voluntad de Dios

protectionism the use of tariffs and other restrictions to protect a country's home industries against competition (p. 741)

proteccionismo el uso de aranceles y otras medidas restrictivas para proteger a las empresas de un país de la competencia

protectorate country with its own government but under the control of an outside power (p. 391)

protectorado país con su propio gobierno pero que está bajo el control de una potencia exterior

provisional temporary (p. 373)

provisional temporal

Prussia a strong military state in central Europe that emerged in the late 1600s (p. 166)

Prusia estado centroeuropeo militarmente poderoso que emergió a finales del siglo XVII

psychoanalysis a method of studying how the mind works and treating mental disorders (p. 526)

psicoanálisis método que estudia el funcionamiento de la mente y trata los trastornos mentales

Punjab state in northwestern India with a largely Sikh population (p. 654)

Punjab estado del noroeste de India de población mayoritariamente sikh

purdah isolation of women in separate quarters (p. 408)

purdah aislamiento de las mujeres en recintos separadas

Pusan Perimeter a defensive line around the city of Pusan, in the southeast corner of Korea, held by South Korean and United Nations forces in 1950 during the Korean War; marks the farthest advance of North Korean forces (p. 628)

Perímetro de Pusan línea defensiva alrededor de la ciudad de Pusan, en el sudeste de Corea, custodiada por Corea del Sur y las fuerzas de las Naciones Unidas en 1950 durante la Guerra de Corea; marca el mayor avance de las fuerzas de Corea del Norte

putting-out system a system developed in the eighteenth century in which tasks were distributed to individuals who completed the work in their own homes; also known as cottage industry (p. 252)

sistema de trabajo a domicilio sistema desarrolla do en el siglo XVIII en el que las tareas se distribúan a individuos quienes completaban el trabajo en sus hogares; tambien se conoce como industria familiar

Q

Qing dynasty dynasty established by the Manchus in the mid 1600s and lasted until the early 1900s; China's last dynasty (p. 101)

dinastía Chin dinastía establecida por los manchus a mediados del siglo XVII que duró hasta principios del siglo XX; fue la última dinastía china

R

racism belief that one racial group is superior to another (p. 318)

racismo creencia de que un grupo racial es superior a otro

radicals those who favor extreme changes (pp. 276, 473)

radicales persona que quiere hacer cambios extremos

realism nineteenth-century artistic movement whose aim was to represent the world as it is (p. 320)

realismo movimiento artístico del siglo XIX cuyo objetivo era representar el mundo tal como es

Realpolitik realistic politics based on the needs of the state (p. 332)

Realpolitik política realista basada en las necesidades del estado

recession period of reduced economic activity (pp. 278, 615)

recesión periodo de reducción de la actividad económica

refugee a person who flees from home or country to seek refuge elsewhere, often because of political upheaval or famine (pp. 351, 746)

refugiado persona que abandona su hogar o país en busca de refugio en otro lugar, a menudo como consecuencia de inestabilidad política o hambruna

regionalism loyalty to a local area (p. 440)

regionalismo lealtad a un área local

Reich German empire (p. 333)

Reich imperio alemán

Reign of Terror time period during the French Revolution from September 1793 to July 1794 when people in France were arrested for not sup-

porting the revolution and many were executed (p. 225)

Reinado del terror período durante la Revolución Francesa desde septiembre de 1793 a julio de 1794, en el que la gente en Francia era arresta da por no apoyar la revolución; mucha gente fue ejecutada

reincarnation in Hindu belief, the rebirth of the soul in another bodily form (p. 14)

reencarnación según la creencia hindú, renacimiento del alma en otra forma corporal

reparation payment for war damage, or damage caused by imprisonment (p. 472)

indemnización pago por daños causados por guerra o encarcelamiento

repeal cancel (p. 365)

revocar cancelar

republic system of government in which officials are chosen by the people (pp. 18, 221)

república sistema de gobierno en el que los gobernantes son elegidos por el pueblo

revenue money taken in through taxes (p. 121)

rentas públicas dinero que se recauda por impuestos

rococo personal, elegant style of art and architecture made popular during the mid-1700s that featured designs with the shapes of leaves, shells, and flowers (p. 189)

rococó estilo de arte y arquitectura elegante y personal que se hizo popular a mediados del siglo XVIII y que incluía diseños con formas de hojas, conchas y flores

romanticism nineteenth-century artistic movement that appealed to emotion rather than reason (p. 319)

romanticismo movimiento artístico del siglo XIX que apelaba a la emoción más que a la razón

Rosie the Riveter popular name for women who worked in war industries during World War II (p. 578)

Rosita la Remachadora nombre popularmente dado a las mujeres que trabajaban en las fábricas de armamento durante la Segunda Guerra Mundial

rotten borough rural town in England that sent members to Parliament despite having few or no voters (p. 360)

"distrito podrido" en Inglaterra, ciudad rural que enviaba miembros al parlamento a pesar de no tener o tener pocos votantes

Ruhr Valley coal-rich industrial region of Germany (p. 551)

Valle del Ruhr región industrial alemana rica en carbón

russification making a nationality's culture more ethnically Russian (p. 546)

rusificación hacer la cultura nacionalista más étnicamente rusa

Russo-Japanese War conflict between Russia and Japan in 1904–1905 over control of Korea and Manchuria (p. 428)

Guerra ruso-japonesa conflicto entre Rusia y Japón de 1904 a 1905 por el control de Corea y Manchuria

S

sacraments sacred ritual of the Roman Catholic Church (p. 29)

sacramento ritual sagrado de la Iglesia Católica Romana

salon informal social gathering at which writers, artists, *philosophes,* and others exchanged ideas (p. 189)

salón reuniones sociales informales en las que escritores, artistas, filósofos y otros intercambiaban ideas

samurai member of the warrior class in Japanese feudal society (p. 36)

samurai miembro de la clase guerrera en la sociedad japonesa feudal

Sandinistas a socialist political movement and party that held power in Nicaragua during the 1980s (p. 724)

sandinistas partido y movimiento político socialista que gobernó Nicaragua durante la década de 1980

sans-culotte working-class man or woman who made the French Revolution more radical; called such because he or she wore long trousers instead of the fancy knee breeches that the upper class wore (p. 221)

sans-culotte hombre o mujer de la clase obrera que hicieron la Revolución Francesa más radical; llamados así porque llevaban pantalones largos a la rodilla como los que llevaba en vez de los pantalones ajustados la clase altas a la rodilla como los que llevaba la clase alta

sati Hindu custom that called for a widow to join her husband in death by throwing herself on his funeral pyre (p. 406)

sati costumbre hindú que requería que la esposa se uniera a su marido en la muerte arrojándose a su pira funeraria

savanna grassy plain with irregular patterns of rainfall (p. 662)

sabana planicie con pastizales cuyo régimen de lluvias es irregular

schism permanent division in a church (p. 30)

cisma división permanente de una iglesia

scientific method careful, step-by-step process used to confirm findings and to prove or disprove a hypothesis (p. 74)

método científico proceso cuidadoso y de varios pasos que se usa para confirmar descubrimientos y para aprobar o desaprobar una hipótesis

scorched-earth policy military tactic in which soldiers destroy everything in their path to hurt the enemy (p. 235)

política de tierra quemada táctica militar en la que los soldados destruyen todo lo que tienen a su paso para perjudicar al enemigo

scribe in ancient civilizations, a person specially trained to read, write, and keep records (p. 7)

escriba en las civilizaciones antiguas, persona especialmente educada para leer, escribir y mantener registros

secede withdraw (p. 379)

separar retirarse

secret ballot votes cast without announcing them publicly (p. 361)

voto secreto votos que se dan sin hacerlos públicos

sect a subgroup of a major religious group (p. 19)

secta subgrupo de un grupo religioso importante

secular having to do with worldly, rather than religious, matters; nonreligious (pp. 27, 673)

secular que tiene que ver más con asuntos mundanos que religiosos; no religioso

segregation forced separation by race, sex, religion, or ethnicity (pp. 379, 616)

segregación separación forzada por razón de raza, sexo, religión o etnia

self-determination right of people to choose their own form of government (p. 471)

autodeterminación derecho de los pueblos a elegir su propia forma de gobierno

sepoy Indian soldier who served in an army set up by the French or English trading companies (pp. 98, 406)

sepoy soldado indio que sirvió en un ejército establecido por las compañías de comercio francesas o inglesas

serf in medieval Europe, a peasant bound to the lord's land (p. 26)

siervo en la Europa medieval, campesino vinculado a las tierras del señor

shantytowns slums of flimsy shacks (p. 708)
　barrio de chabolas barrios muy pobres de casuchas endebles

Sharpeville a black township in South Africa where the government killed anti-apartheid demonstrators in 1960 (p. 687)
　Sharpeville municipio sudafricano habitado por personas de raza negra donde el gobierno mató a decenas de manifestantes antiapartheid en 1960

shogun in Japanese feudal society, supreme military commander, who held more power than the emperor (p. 37)
　shogún en la sociedad feudal japonesa, jefe militar supremo con más poder que el emperador

Sino-Japanese War war between China and Japan in which Japan gained Taiwan (p. 414)
　Guerra Sinojaponesa guerra entre China y Japón por la que Japón obtuvo el control de Taiwán

smelt melt in order to get the pure metal away from its waste matter (p. 249)
　refinar fundir mineral para separar el mineral puro de las impurezas

social contract an agreement by which people gave up their freedom to a powerful government in order to avoid chaos (p. 183)
　contrato social acuerdo mediante el cual el pueblo cede sus libertades a un gobierno poderoso para evitar el caos

social democracy political ideology in which there is a gradual transition from capitalism to socialism instead of a sudden violent overthrow of the system (p. 264)
　democracia social ideología política en la que hay una transición gradual del capitalismo al socialismo en vez de un derrocamiento violento del sistema

social gospel movement of the 1800s that urged Christians to do social service (p. 318)
　evangelio social movimiento del siglo XIX que urgía a los cristianos a que hicieran servicios sociales

social welfare programs to help certain groups of people (p. 337)
　bienestar social programas para ayudar a ciertos grupos de personas

socialism system in which the people as a whole rather than private individuals own all property and operate all businesses (pp. 263, 710)

socialismo sistema en el que el pueblo como un todo, en vez de los individuos, son dueños de todas la propiedades y manejan todos los negocios

socialist realism artistic style whose goal was to promote socialism by showing Soviet life in a positive light (p. 546)
　realismo socialista estilo artístico cuyo objetivo era promover el socialismo mostrando la vida en la Union Sovietica desde un perspectiva postiva

Solidarity a Polish labor union and democracy movement (p. 641)
　Solidaridad sindicato laboral y movimiento democrático polaco

sovereign having full, independent power (p. 96)
　soberano tener poder pleno e independiente

soviet council of workers and soldiers set up by Russian revolutionaries in 1917 (p. 478)
　soviet consejo de trabajadores y soldados establecido por los revolucionarios rusos en 1917

Spanish-American War conflict between the United States and Spain in 1898 over Cuban independence (p. 431)
　Guerra entre Estados Unidos y España (Guerra hispano-estadounidense) conflicto entre Estados Unidos y España en 1898 por la independencia de Cuba

speakeasies illegal bars (p. 523)
　speakeasies bares ilegales

sphere of influence area in which an outside power claims exclusive investment or trading privileges (p. 391)
　esfera de influencia área sobre la que un poder exterior se reserva privilegios comerciales o la exclusividad de realizar inversiones

St. Petersburg capital city and major port that Peter the Great established in 1703 (p. 170)
　San Petersburgo ciudad y capital con un puerto importante, establecida en 1703 por Pedro el Grande

stalemate deadlock in which neither side is able to defeat the other (p. 460)
　estancamiento punto muerto en una confrontación, en el que ninguna de las partes puede vencer a la otra

Stalingrad now Volgograd, a city in southwestern Russia that was the site of a fierce battle during World War II (p. 580)
　Stalingrado actual Volgogrado; ciudad del sudoeste de Rusia donde se libró una encarnizada batalla durante la Segunda Guerra Mundial

Stamp Act law passed in 1765 by the British Parliament that imposed taxes on items such as newspapers and pamphlets in the American colonies; repealed in 1766 (p. 197)

Ley del Timbre ley promulgada en 1765 por el Parlamento Británico que imponía gravá menes a artículos como diarios y panfletos en las colonias americanas; revocada en 1766

standard of living measures the quality and availability of necessities and comforts in a society (p. 309)

estándar de vida medida de la calidad y disponibilidad de las necesidades básicas y de los lujos en una sociedad

stock shares in a company (p. 303)

acciones títulos o valores de una compañía

suburbanization the movement to built-up areas outside of central cities (p. 615)

suburbanización proceso de construcción en áreas fuera del centro de la ciudad

Sudetenland a region of western Czechoslovakia (p. 565)

Sudetenland región occidental de la antigua Checoslovaquia

Suez Canal a canal linking the Red Sea and Indian Ocean to the Mediterranean Sea, which also links Europe to Asia and East Africa (pp. 372, 674)

Canal de Suez canal que une el Mar Rojo y el Océano índico con el Mar Mediterráneo, que a la vez une Europa con Asia y África Oriental

suffrage right to vote (p. 224)

sufragio derecho al voto

sultan Muslim ruler (pp. 33, 402)

sultán gobernante musulmán

superpower a nation stronger than other powerful nations (p. 604)

superpotencia nación suficientemente poderosa para influir en los actos y políticas de otras naciones poderosas

surplus an amount that is more than needed, excess (p. 736)

excedente cantidad de algo superior a lo que se necesita; exceso

surrealism artistic movement that attempts to portray the workings of the unconscious mind (p. 527)

surrealismo movimiento artístico que trata de mostrar el funcionamiento del inconsciente

sustainability the ability to meet the needs of the present without compromising the needs of future generations (p. 742)

sostenibilidad capacidad de satisfacer las necesidades actuales sin poner en peligro las necesidades de generaciones futuras

sustainable development economic development that aims to provide lasting well-being for future generations rather than short-term gains (p. 712)

desarrollo sostenible desarrollo económico que tiene como objetivo proporcionar el bienestar de generaciones futuras en vez de ganancias a corto plazo

T

Taiping Rebellion peasant revolt in China (p. 413)

Rebelión Taiping revuelta campesina en China

Taliban Islamic fundamentalist faction that ruled Afghanistan for nearly ten years until ousted by the United States in 2002 (p. 757)

Talibán facción islámica fundamentalista que gobernó Afganistán durante casi diez años hasta que fue expulsada por Estados Unidos en 2002

tariff tax on imported goods (p. 133)

tasa impuesto a mercancías importadas

temperance movement campaign to limit or ban the use of alcoholic beverages (p. 314)

campaña de moderación campaña para limitar o prohibir el uso de bebidas alcohólicas

tenement multistory building divided into crowded apartments (p. 256)

apartamento de vecindad edificio de varios pisos dividido en apartamentos donde vive mucha gente

Tennis Court Oath famous oath made on a tennis court by members of the Third Estate in France (p. 214)

Juramento del juego de pelota famoso juramento hecho en una cancha de frontón por los miembros del Tercer Estado en Francia

Tenochtitlán capital city of the Aztec empire, on which modern-day Mexico City was built (p. 111)

Tenochtitlán capital del imperio azteca, sobre la cual se construyó la actual Ciudad de México

terrorism deliberate use of random violence, especially against civilians, to achieve political goals (p. 754)

terrorismo uso deliberado de la violencia indiscriminada, especialmente en contra de civiles, para lograr fines políticos

Tet Offensive a massive and bloody offensive by communist guerrillas against South Vietnamese and American forces on Tet, the Vietnamese New Year, 1968; helped turn American public opinion against military involvement in Vietnam (p. 634)

Ofensiva Tet ofensiva masiva y sangrienta de las guerrillas comunistas contra los sudvietnamitas y las fuerzas estadounidenses durante el Tet, el Nuevo Año vietnamita, en 1968; ayudó a que la opinión pública estadouniden se se volviera en contra de la ocupación militar en Vietnam

theocracy government run by religious leaders

teocracia gobierno administrado por líderes religiosos (pp. 65, 675)

Third Reich official name of the Nazi party for its regime in Germany, held power from 1933 to 1945 (p. 553)

Tercer Reich nombre oficial del partido nazi durante su mandato en Alemania; mantuvo el poder desde 1933 a 1945

38th parallel an imaginary line marking 38 degrees of latitude, particularly the line at 38 degrees of latitude north across the Korean Peninsula, dividing Soviet forces to the north and American forces to the South after World War II (p. 627)

paralelo 38 línea imaginaria que marca los 38 grados de latitud, en particular la línea a 38 grados de latitud norte que cruza la península coreana, que dividía las fuerzas soviéticas al norte y las fuerzas estadounindenses al sur después de la Segunda Guerra Mundial

Tiananmen Square a huge public plaza at the center of China's capital, Beijing (p. 715)

Plaza de Tiananmen inmensa plaza pública en el centro de Beijing, la capital de China

Tokyo capital of Japan, on the eastern coast of Japan (p. 424)

Tokio capital de Japón, ubicada en la costa este de Japón

total war channeling of a nation's entire resources into a war effort (p. 467)

estado de guerra canalización de todos los recursos de una nación hacia la guerra

totalitarian state government in which a one-party dictatorship regulates every aspect of citizens' lives (p. 539)

estado totalitario gobierno en el que una dictadura de partido único regula todos los aspectos de la vida de los ciudadanos

trade deficit situation in which a country imports more than it exports (p. 411)

déficit comercial situación en la que un país importa más de lo que exporta

trade surplus situation in which a country exports more than it imports (p. 411)

excedente commercial situación en la que un país exporta más de lo que importa

traditional economies economies that rely on habit, custom, or ritual and tend not to change over time (p. 704)

economía de subsistencia economía basada en hábitos, costumbres o rituales y que no suele cambiar con el paso del tiempo

Treaty of Paris treaty of 1763 that ended the Seven Years' War and resulted in British dominance of the Americas (p. 124)

Tratado de París en 1763, tratado que terminó con la Guerra de los Siete Años y resultó en el dominio británico de las Américas

Treaty of Paris peace treaty made final in 1783 that ended the American Revolution (p. 200)

Tratado de París tratado de paz de 1783 que dio final a la Revolución Americana

Treaty of Tordesillas treaty signed between Spain and Portugal in 1494 which divided the non-European world between them (p. 88)

Tratado de Tordesillas tratado firmado por España y Portugal en 1494 por el que se dividían entre ellos el mundo fuera de Europa

triangular trade colonial trade routes among Europe and its colonies, the West Indies, and Africa in which goods were exchanged for slaves (p. 125)

comercio triangular ruta colonial de comercio entre Europa y sus colonias en las Indias Occidentales y África, en donde las mercancías se cambiaban por esclavos

tributary state independent state that has to acknowledge the supremacy of another state and pay tribute to its ruler (p. 36)

estado tributario estado independiente que debe reconocer la supremacía de otro estado y pagar tributo a su gobernante

tribute payment that conquered peoples may be forced to pay their conquerors (p. 20)

tributo pago que los conquistadores podían obligar a pagar a los pueblos conquistados

Truman Doctrine United States policy, established in 1947, of trying to contain the spread of communism (p. 593)

Doctrina Truman estrategia política establecida en 1947 con el propósito de contener la expansión del comunismo

tsar title of the rule of the Russian empire (p. 31)

zar título del regente del imperio ruso

tsunami very large, damaging wave caused by an earthquake or very strong wind (p. 745)

tsunami ola enorme y destructiva causada por un terremoto o vientos muy fuertes

turnpike private road built by entrepreneurs who charged a toll, or fee, to travelers who used it (p. 252)

autopista de peaje carretera construida con capital privado; el dueño de la carretera cobra una tarifa a los viajeros por usarla

Tutsis the main minority group in Rwanda and Burundi (p. 689)

Tutsis principal minoría de Ruanda y Burundi

Twenty-One Demands list of demands given to China by Japan in 1915 that, if agreed to, would have made China a protectorate of Japan (p. 508)

Veintiuna Exigencias lista de exigencias dadas por Japón a China en 1915 por las que, si hubiera estado de acuerdo, China se habría convertido en un protectorado de Japón

U

U-boat German submarine (p. 463)

U-Boat submarino alemán

ultimatum final set of demands (p. 457)

ultimátum serie final de exigencias

ultranationalist extreme nationalist (p. 514)

ultranacionalista nacionalista radical

United Nations (UN) international organization established after World War II with the goal of maintaining peace and cooperation in the international community (p. 591)

Naciones Unidas (ONU) organización internacional establecida después de la Segunda Guerra Mundial con el propósito de preservar la paz y la cooperación en la comunidad internacional

universal manhood suffrage right of all adult men to vote (p. 273)

sufragio universal masculino derecho de todos los hombres adultos a votar

untouchable in India, a member of the lowest caste (p. 504)

intocable en India, miembro de la casta más baja

urban renewal the process of fixing up the poor areas of a city (p. 306)

renovación urbana reconstrucción de las áreas pobres de una ciudad

urbanization movement of people from rural areas to cities (pp. 254, 711)

urbanización movimiento de personas de las áreas rurales a las ciudades

utilitarianism idea that the goal of society should be to bring about the greatest happiness for the greatest number of people (p. 261)

utilitarismo idea de que el objetivo de la sociedad debería ser lograr la mayor felicidad para el mayor número de personas

utopian idealistic or visionary, usually used to describe a perfect society (p. 58)

utópico idealista o visionario, normalmente se usa para describir una sociedad perfecta

V

V-E Day Victory in Europe Day, May 8, 1945, the day the Allies won World War II in Europe (p. 586)

Día de la Victoria en Europa (Día del Armisticio) (8 de mayo de 1945) día en que los aliados vencieron en Europa durante la Segunda Guerra Mundial

vanguard group of elite leaders (p. 508)

vanguardia grupo de líderes de la élite

vassal in medieval Europe, a lord who was granted land in exchange for service and loyalty to a greater lord, (p. 26)

vasallo durante la Edad Media, señor a quien se le cedía un terreno a cambio de servicio y lealtad al señor más importante

vernacular everyday language of ordinary people (p. 29)

vernáculo lenguaje diario de la gente corriente

Versailles royal French residence and seat of government established by King Louis XIV (p. 150)

Versalles residencia de la realeza francesa y sede de gobierno establecidos por el rey Luis XIV

viceroy representative who ruled one of Spain's provinces in the Americas in the king's name; one who governed in India in the name of the British monarch (pp. 115, 407)

virrey representante que regía una de las provincias de España en las Américas en nombre del rey; quien gobernaba en India en nombre del monarca británico

Vichy city in central France where a puppet state governed unoccupied France and the French colonies (p. 569)

Vichy ciudad en el centro de Francia desde donde un gobierno títere dirigió la Francia no ocupada y las colonias francesas

Viet Cong communist rebels in South Vietnam who sought to overthrow South Vietnam's government; received assistance from North Vietnam (p. 631)

Vietcong rebeldes comunistas en Vietnam del Sur que buscaban derrotar el gobierno de Vietnam del Sur; recibieron ayuda de Vietnam del Norte

W

War of the Austrian Succession series of wars in which various European nations competed for power in Central Europe after the death of Hapsburg emperor Charles VI (p. 166)

Guerra de Sucesión Austriaca serie de guerras en las que diversos países europeos lucharon por la hegemonía en centroeuropa después de la muerte de Carlos IV, emperador Habsburgo

warm-water port port that is free of ice year-round (p. 170)

puerto de aguas templadas puerto en el que sus aguas nunca se congelan a lo largo del año

Warsaw Pact mutual-defense alliance between the Soviet Union and seven satellites in Eastern Europe set up in 1955 (p. 594)

Pacto de Varsovia alianza de defensa mutua establecida en 1955 entre la Unión Soviética y siete países de Europa del Este pertenecientes a su esfera de influencia

weapons of mass destruction (WMDs) biological, nuclear, or chemical weapons (p. 697)

armas de destrucción masiva (ADM) armas biológicas, nucleares o químicas

welfare state a country with a market economy but with increased government responsibility for the social and economic needs of its people (p. 620)

estado de bienestar país con una economía de Mercado, pero con un gobierno con mayor responsabilidad sobre las nece sidades económicas de su pueblo

westernization adoption of western ideas, technology, and culture (p. 169)

occidentalización adopción de ideas, tecnología y cultura occidentales

Wittenberg a city in northern Germany, where Luther drew up his 95 theses (p. 63)

Wittenberg ciudad al norte de Alemania donde Lutero redactó sus 95 tesis

women's suffrage right of women to vote (p. 314)

sufragio femenino derecho de las mujeres a votar

World Trade Organization (WTO) international organization set up to facilitate global trade (p. 741)

Organización Mundial del Comercio (OMC) organización internacional constituida para facilitar el comercio en el ámbito mundial

Y

Yalta Conference meeting between Churchill, Roosevelt, and Stalin in February 1945 where the three leaders made agreements regarding the end of World War II (p. 583)

Conferencia de Yalta reunión mantenida en febrero de 1945 entre Churchill, Roosevelt y Stalin en la que los tres mandatarios alcanzaron un acuerdo con respecto a la finalización de la Segunda Guerra Mundial

Yorktown, Virginia location where the British army surrendered in the American Revolution (p. 200)

Yorktown, Virginia lugar donde el ejército británico se rindió en la Revolución Americana

Z

zaibatsu since the late 1800s, powerful banking and industrial families in Japan (p. 426)

zaibatsu familias japonesas de banqueros e industriales poderosos desde finales del siglo XIX

zemstvos local elected assembly set up in Russia under Alexander II (p. 349)

zemstvos asambla local electa que se estableció en Rusia en la época de Alejandro II

zeppelin large gas-filled balloon (p. 463)

zepelín dirigible, globo grande lleno de gas

ziggurat in ancient Mesopotamia, a large, stepped platform thought to have been topped by a temple dedicated to a city's chief god or goddess (p. 6)

zigurat templo piramidal de la antigua Mesopotamia dedicado al dios o diosa principal de una ciudad

Zionism a movement devoted to rebuilding a Jewish state in Palestine (p. 375)

zionismo movimiento dedicado a la reconstrucción del estado judío en Palestina

Italicized letters after page numbers refer to the following: *c* = chart; *g* = graph; *m* = map; *p* = picture; *q* = primary source

A

INDEX

INDEX

G

INDEX

INDEX

Staff Credits

The people who make up the **World History © 07** team—representing design services, editorial, editorial services, educational technology, marketing, market research, photo research and art development, production services, publishing processes, and rights & permissions—are listed below. Bold type denotes core team members.

Marla Abramson, Leann Davis Alspaugh, Stephanie Bradley, **Peter Brooks,** Kerry Lyn Buckley, Kerry Cashman, Todd Christy, Lori-Anne Cohen, Laura Edgerton Riser, Tom Ferreira, Lara Fox, Ellen Welch Granter, **Diane Grossman, Mary Ann Gundersen,** Mary Hanisco, Salena Hastings, Lance Hatch, **Katharine Ingram,** Tim Jones, Judie Jozokos, Lynne Kalkanajian, Courtney Lane, **Grace Massey, Constance J. McCarty,** Mark O'Malley, **Deborah Nicholls,** Jen Paley, Jonathan Penyack, **Gabriela Perez-Fiato,** Judi Pinkham, Marcy Rose, Rashid Ross, Robyn Salbo, **Colleen Searson,** Greg Slook, Laurel Smith, **Lisa Smith-Ruvalcaba,** Kara Stokes, **Sarah Yezzi**

Additional Credits

Paul Astwood, Gaylord Brynolfson, Sandra M. Graff, Lynette Haggard, John Judge, Kevin Keane, Beth Kun, Susan Nimmo, Kim Schmidt, Jan Shapiro, Ted Smykal, Erin Sunderland, Paula Wehde

Vendor

Pronk & Associates Inc.

Maps

XNR Productions, Inc.: SH25, SH27, SH28, SH29, 5, 7, 9, 15, 17, 31, 33, 35, 37, 39, 44–45, 51, 70, 81, 85, 92, 100–101, 113, 123, 127, 134–135, 136, 143, 164, 170, 173, 178–179, 192, 196, 203, 233, 237, 251, 278, 285, 287, 294–295, 299, 316–317, 331, 339, 341, 345, 354, 373, 380, 395, 403, 407, 412, 416, 431, 435, 437, 442, 444, 450–451, 459, 465, 468, 479, 490, 491, 498, 501, 510, 514, 517, 530, 545, 566, 572, 578, 581, 584, 587, 593, 595, 596, 599, 600–601, 607, 609, 613, 626, 627, 633, 636, 637, 649, 653, 660, 665, 671, 676, 679, 684, 689, 694, 698, 701, 705, 712, 721, 735, 737, 739, 745, 749, 755, 769, 772–773, 774, 775, 776, 777, 778, 779, 780, 781, 782, 783, 790–791, 794–795

Illustrations

Kenneth Batelman 567, 584–585; Kerry Cashman SH13, SH26, SH39, 2–3, 12–13, 24–25, 52–53, 58–59, 68–69, 74, 75, 78–79, 86–87, 100–101, 104–105, 112–113, 118, 126–127, 134–135, 136–137, 144, 147, 151, 156–157, 172, 174–175, 190, 196, 200, 202–203, 204–205, 212, 219, 226–227, 240–241, 252, 262, 266–267, 278–279, 287, 290–291, 304, 312–313, 315, 321, 324–325, 341, 350–351, 354–355, 362–363, 368, 372–373, 378, 382–383, 403, 406–407, 412–413, 416–417, 424–425, 432, 444, 446–447, 466–467, 477, 484–485, 490–491, 491, 498–499, 516–517, 524–525, 532–533, 538–539, 556–557, 570–571, 572–573, 579, 584–585, 596–597, 607, 609, 626–627, 632–633, 646–647, 676–677, 688, 692–693, 698–699, 716, 728–729, 740–741, 745, 749, 759, 760–761, 762, 764–765, 770–771, 784, 784–785, 785, 786–787, 796–797, 798–799, 801, 806–807; Ellen Welch Granter SH2, SH3, SH4, SH9, SH10, SH12, SH13, SH15, SH16, SH17, SH21, SH30, SH41; Kevin Jones Associates 220, 252, 273, 302, 350; Jen Paley SH5, SH20, SH23, SH37, 48, 56, 61, 64, 66, 72, 78, 84, 90, 95, 99, 104, 110, 115, 118, 120, 125, 129, 131, 134, 135, 136, 142, 144, 148, 154, 160, 163, 168, 172, 182, 188, 192, 193, 195, 201, 204, 210, 216, 223, 230, 240, 246, 247, 250, 254, 255, 260, 266, 272, 275, 276, 280, 283, 290, 298, 300, 305, 308, 312, 313, 319, 324, 327, 330, 334, 338, 343, 348, 354, 360, 364, 368, 371, 377, 382, 382, 388, 392, 400, 405, 410, 411, 416, 417, 422, 426, 429, 434, 439, 442, 444, 446, 447, 462, 464, 466, 471, 476, 477, 478, 481, 490, 491, 492, 493, 496, 503, 507, 508, 512, 516, 522, 524, 529, 533, 535, 536, 539, 542, 543, 544, 550, 555, 556, 562, 565, 567, 568, 572, 573, 576, 577, 585, 586, 590, 591, 596, 597, 599, 606, 610, 614, 623, 630, 638, 646, 652, 655, 658, 660, 662, 670, 673, 679, 682, 683, 686, 688, 689, 692, 695, 698, 699, 704, 705, 710, 714, 715, 716, 720, 723, 728, 734, 738, 740, 744, 746, 749, 753, 758, 764, 767, 786, 788, 789, 792, 793, 800, 801, 804, 805; Ted Smykal SH4, SH6, SH7, SH8, SH9, SH10, SH11, SH14, SH15, SH16, SH17, SH18, SH19, SH21, 131, 192, 316, 636, 660, 672, 727

Cover and Title Page

Ann Ronan Picture Library/HIP/The ImageWorks

Table of Contents

v, Kenneth Garrett/National Geographic Image Collection; **vi,** T, Photograph by Frank Khoury National Museum of African Art Smithsonian Institution; B, © Erich Lessing/Art Resource; **vii,** Michael Holford; **viii,** T, Joe Sohm/Chromosohm/VOA; B, Science Museum/SSPL; **ix,** © Christie's Images/CORBIS; **x,** Inset, The Granger Collection, New York; **x–xi,** © Bettmann/CORBIS; **xii,** photolibrary; **xiii,** Ron Giling/Das Fotoarchiv; **xvii,** Robertstock;**xviii,** Bildarchiv Preussischer Kulturbesitz/Art Resource, NY; **x,** L, Frank Nowikowski; **xiv,** L, © Wanda Beaver; R, © Photos by Eric L. Johnson/Courtesy of the Museum of World War II, Natick MA; Background, Time Life Pictures/Getty Images

Skills Handbook

SH1, © Jose Luis Pelaez, Inc./CORBIS; **SH2,** © IT Stock Free/AGE Fotostock; **SH3,** © Ed Bock/CORBIS; **SH6,** © Bananastock/PictureQuest; **SH13,** Public Record Office/HIP/The Image Works; **SH22,** Arthur Tilley/Getty Images; **SH24,** © Roger Wood/CORBIS; **SH31,** Keystone/Getty Images; **SH32,** North Wind Picture Archives; **SH33,** © Arcadio/Cartoonists & Writers Syndicate; **SH35,** The Science Museum/Science & Society Picture Library; **SH38,** Bettman/CORBIS; The Granger Collection, New York; **SH40,** © Charles Gupton/CORBIS

Review Unit

0, TL, Archivo Iconografico, S;A/Corbis; BL, © Archivo Iconografico, S.A./CORBIS; **0–1,** B, © ArtWolfe/Getty Images; **1,** TR, Réunion des Musées Nationaux/Art Resource, NY; BR, © Dirk Bakker; **2,** TR, Werner Forman/Art Resource, NY; TL, © Archivo Iconografico, S.A./CORBIS; BL, © Robert Frerck/Odyssey Productions, Inc.; **3,** T, The Art Archive/Museum of Mankind; B, Copyright of Christie's Images Inc., 2004; **4,** Erich Lessing/Art Resource, NY; **6,** © Archivo Iconografico, S.A./CORBIS; **8,** The Metropolitan Museum of Art, Gift of R. H. Ellsworth Ltd., in honor of Susan Dilon, 1987 (1987.80.1); Photograph by Bruch White; Photograph

© 1994 The Metropolitan Museum of Art; **9,** CM Dixon/HIP/The Image Works; **11,** TL, IML Image Group Ltd/Alamy; TR, The Art Archive/British Library; B, The National Trust Photolibrary/Alamy; **12,** T, Ronald Sheridan/Ancient Art & Architecture Collection Ltd; B, © Danny Lehman/CORBIS; **13,** MR, The Metropolitan Museum of Art, Purchase, Elaine Rosenberg Gift and funds from various donors, 1998. (1998.37); Photograph © 2001 The Metropolitan Museum of Art; T, John Bigelow Taylor/Art Resource, NY; M, By permission of the British Library; Or.8212/480–484 paper fragments from Loulan; M, The Trustees of The British Museum; B, © Richard A; Cooke/CORBIS; **14,** Photri Microstock; **16,** Réunion des Musées Nationaux/Art Resource, NY; **18,** Réunion des Musées Nationaux/Art Resource, NY; **19,** Erich Lessing/Art Resource, NY; **20,** akg-images/Francois Guénet; **21,** George H. Huey/CORBIS; **23,** T, Bildarchiv Preussischer Kulturbesitz/Art Resource, NY; B, The Art Archive/British Library; **24,** TL, Los Angeles County Museum of Art, The Nasli M.; TR, Werner Forman/Art Resource, NY; M, ArkReligion.com; B, © Gianni Dagli Orti/CORBIS; **25,** T, The Granger Collection, New York; M, The Art Archive/Archaeological Museum Lima/Mireille Vautie; BL, Time Life Pictures/Getty Images; R, Prisma/ANCIENT ART & ARCHITECTURE COLLECTION LTD; **26,** Bridgeman Art Library; **27,** T, Kunsthistorisches Museum, Vienna, Austria/Bridgeman Art Library; B, Archivo Iconografico, S.A./CORBIS; **28,** L, akg-images; R, Giraudon/Art Resource, NY; **29,** The Art Archive/San Francesco Assisi/Dagli Orti; **30,** San Vitale, Ravenna, Italy/Bridgeman Art Library; **32,** Topkapi Palace Museum, Istanbul, Turkey/Bridgeman Art Library; **34,** © Dirk Bakker; **36,** The Art Archive/British Library; **36–37,** Panorama Stock; **39,** © SAUSSIER-VAN DER STOCKT/GAMMA; **41,** L, REUTERS/Kimimasa Mayama; R, Getty Images; **43,** T, © Jeremy Horner/CORBIS; B, Jack Kurtz/The Image Works

Chapter One

46–47, © Vittoriano Rastelli/CORBIS; **47,** T, Arte & Immagini srl/Corbis; M, The Pierpont Morgan Library/Art Resource, NY; B, HIP/Art Resource, NY; **48,** L, Scala/Art Resource, NY; R, Ashley Simmons/Alamy Images; **49,** The Bridgeman Art Library/Getty Images; **50,** Bibliotheque Nationale, Paris; **52,** M, Dorling Kindersley; R, Private Collection/Bridgeman Art Library; L,

Scala/Art Resource, NY; **52–53,** The Image Bank/Getty Images; **53,** R, Mary Evans Picture Library; L, Dorling Kindersley; **54,** Mary Evans Picture Library; **55,** Archivo Iconografico, S;A/ Corbis; **56,** L, Mary Evans Picture Library; R, The Pierpont Morgan Library/Art Resource, NY; **57,** Archivo Iconografico, S.A./Corbis; **58,** Scala/ Art Resource, NY; **59,** TR, Dorling Kindersley; M, Erich Lessing/Art Resource, NY; L, Erich Lessing/Art Resource, NY; BR, Susannah Price/Dorling Kindersley; **60,** T, Mary Evans Picture Library; B, Andrea Pistolesi/Getty Images, Inc.; M, Dorling Kindersley; **61,** L, AAAC/Topham/The Image Works; R, London College of Printing/ Dorling Kindersley; **62,** Bildarchiv Preussischer Kulturbesitz/Art Resource, NY; **63,** © The Corcoran Gallery of Art/ CORBIS; **65,** Erich Lessing/Art Resource, NY; **66,** L, National Trust Photographic Library/Derrick E; Witty/ The Image Works; R, HIP/Art Resource, NY; **67,** Fine Art Photographic Library/ Corbis; **68,** Inset, The Granger Collection; **68–69,** Background, © Michael Busselle/CORBIS; **69,** L, Mary Evans Picture Library; R, The Granger Collection; **71,** Erich Lessing/Art Resource, NY; **72,** L, The Granger Collection, New York; R, Gustavo Tomsich/Corbis; **73,** L, The Granger Collection; R, © Reuters/CORBIS; **74,** R, Maximilian Stock Ltd;/Photo Researchers, Inc.; TL, Kevin Fleming/Corbis; BL, Royalty-Free/Corbis; **75,** R, AAAC/Topham/The Image Works; L, Glasgow University Library, Scotland/Bridgeman Art Library; **77,** TR, Victoria & Albert Museum, London/Art Resource, NY; MR, SciMAT/Photo Researchers, Inc.; BR, Mary Evans Picture Library/Photo Researchers, Inc.; BL, Sam Forencich/ NBAE via Getty Images; TL, Victoria & Albert Museum, London/Art Resource, NY; **78,** Scala/Art Resource, NY; **79,** T, FRANK & EARNEST, © Thaves/Dist. by Newspaper Enterprise Association, Inc.; The Pierpont Morgan Library/Art Resource, NY; The Granger Collection; **80,** T, Scala/Art Resource, NY; B, © Vittoriano Rastelli/CORBIS

Chapter Two

82–83, Instituto Portugues de Museus; **83,** T, V & A Museum/Art Resource; B, © Christie's Images/COR-BIS; **84,** R, Bridgeman Art Library; L, Ann Ronan Picture Library/The Image Works; **86,** L, The Granger Collection; R, National Maritime Museum; **86–87,** Museu de Marinha, The Granger Collection; **87,** TL, Antiquarian Images; TR, Michael Holford; M, HIP/

Scala/Art Resource; **88,** Preussischer Kulturbesitz/Art Resource, NY; **90,** L, Topham/The Image Works; R, Museum of African Art/Smithsonian Institution; **91,** Michael Holford; **93,** Werner Forman/Art Resource; **94,** B, The Art Archive/Museo de Arte Antiga; T, Metropolitan Museum of Art, Gift of Ernest Anspach, 1999 (199;295;4) Photograph (c) 2002 Metropolitan Museum of Art; **95,** R, Rainer Daehnhardt/Portuguese Academy of Antique Arms; L, British Library; **96,** R, Maritime Museum of Rotterdam; L, Royal Collection (c) 2005, Her Majesty Queen Elizabeth II; **97,** Rijksmuseum Amsterdam; **98,** British Library; **99,** L, The Ricci Institute, University of San Francisco; R, Vatican Library; **100,** The British Museum/The Image Works; **101,** M, © Christie's Images/CORBIS; L, The Granger Collection; R, British Museum/HIP/The Image Works; **102,** Cleveland Musuem of Art; **103,** Michael Holford; **104,** L, The British Museum/The Image Works; R, HIP/ Scala/Art Resource, NY; **105,** Cleveland Musuem of Art; **106,** T, The Granger Collection; B, Instituto Portugues de Museus; **107,** T, Giraudon/Art Resource; B, Granger Collection

Chapter Three

108–109, Schalkwijk/Art Resource, NY; **109,** T, Erich Lessing/Art Resource, NY; Musee Departemental des Antiquites, Rouen, France/Bridgeman Art Library; B, © Canadian Museum of Civilization, catalogue no. D-1511, image no. S90–1861; **110,** Biblioteca Medicea-Laurenziana/Florence Bridgeman Art Library; **111,** T, The Granger Collection; B, Biblioteque Nationale de France; **112,** Inset, akg-images; **112–113,** Background, Corbis; **113,** Frank Nowikowski; **114,** Ira Block; **115,** Hispanic Society of New York; **116,** Divisao de Documentacao Fotografica-Instituto Portugues De Museus; **117,** Dan Lehmann/Corbis; **118,** Joseph Martin/AKG Images; **119,** Musee Departemental des Antiquites, Rouen, France/Bridgeman Art Library; **120,** R, © Lee Snider/Photo Images/CORBIS; L, (c) Canadian Museum of Civilization, catalogue # 989.56.1, photo Merle Toole, #S90–640; **121,** Corbis; **122,** Michael Schwarz/Image Works; **123,** TR, National Museum of Natural History/Smithsonian Institution; BL, The Newark Museum/Art Resource, NY; TL, Victoria & Albert Museum, London/Art Resource, NY; BR, New York Historical Society; **124,** Gunter Marx; **125,** L, Royal Albert Museum/Bridgeman Art Library; R, Chicago Historical

Society; **126,** B, Ariadne Van Zandbergen/Lonely Planet Images; T, Corbis; **126–127,** Background, Corbis; T, © Royalty-Free/Corbis; **127,** T, British Library; B, British Library; **128,** Bettmann/Corbis; **129,** R, The Art Archive; L, (c) Canadian Museum of Civilization, catalogue no. D-1511, image no. S90–1861; **130,** R, Francis C. Mayer/ Corbis; L, Bancroft Library/UC-Berkeley; **131,** Background, © Darrell Gulin/CORBIS; R, RF/Corbis; M, Corbis; **132,** R, Robert Harding Image Library; L, Journal-Courier/Steve Warmowski/The Image Works; **133,** Erich Lessing/Art Resource, NY; **134,** M, Julie Habel/Corbis; BL, © Ed Quinn/ CORBIS; R, © PoodlesRock/CORBIS; TL, © Carlos Goldin/CORBIS; **135,** BL, Kim Blaxland/Getty Images; MR, Ira Block; TL, Corbis; BR, Ron Giling/Peter Arnold Inc.; TR, © Liba Taylor/CORBIS; **136,** © Steve Vidler/eStock Photo; **137,** TR, Levine/Roberts; BR, Lisa Knouse Braiman/Business Week; L, Stock Montage; **138,** R, National Gallery of Art; L, Schalkwijk/Art Resource, NY; **139,** Mary Evans Picture Library

Chapter Four

140–141, Erich Lessing/Art Resource, NY; **141,** B, Museums On Line; M, Dorling Kindersley; T, Erich Lessing/Art Resource; **142,** L, Bettmann/Corbis; Background, L, Bettmann/Corbis; R, Archivo Iconographica, S.A./Corbis; **144,** L, Bridgeman Art Library; MR, British Library/Bridgeman Art Library; Background, The National Maritime Museum; TR, Archivo Iconographica, S.A./Corbis; TL, Archivo Iconographica, S.A./Corbis; **145,** Bridgeman Art Library; **146,** Bridgeman Art Library; **147,** T, Art Resource, NY; B, Mary Evans Picture Library; **148,** L, Versailles, châteaux de Versailles et de Trianon/RMN/Art Resource; R, Bata Shoe Museum; **149,** © National Gallery Collection; By kind permission of the Trustees of the National Gallery, London/CORBIS; **151,** Background, T, Superstock; Background, B, Reunion des Musees Nationaux/Art Resource; TL, Scala/Art Resource, NY; BR, Topham/The Image Works; MR, Victoria & Albert Museum/Art Resource, NY; **153,** TR, Historical Picture Archive/Corbis; TL, Prisma/Ancient Art and Architecture Collection; B, Bettmann/Corbis; **154,** Art Resource, NY; **155,** Archivo Iconographico S.A./Corbis; **156,** TR, The Granger Collection; BR, British Museum/HIP/The Image Works; L, Fine Art Photographic Library/Corbis; **157,** TR, Bridgeman Art Library; L, Mary Evans Picture Library;

B, The Granger Collection; **158,** Background, HIP/The Image Works; Inset, Dorling Kindersley; **159,** B, The Granger Collection; T, Atwater Kent Museum/Bridgeman Art Library; **162,** B, The Parliamentary Archives; T, Corbis; **163,** L, Erich Lessing/Art Resource, NY; R, Royal Armouries; **166,** Archivo Iconographica, S.A./Corbis; **167,** Mary Evans Picture Library; **168,** R, Corbis; L, Corbis; **169,** The Granger Collection; **171,** Corbis; **172,** BL, The Granger Collection; Inset, C, Museums On Line; Background, B, Sovfoto; TR, akg-images; **174,** R, Mary Evans Picture Library; L, Royal Armouries; **175,** T, The Granger Collection; B, Bata Shoe Museum; **176,** Archivo Iconographica, S.A./Corbis; **177,** Bridgeman Art Library

Chapter Five

180–181, Réunion des Musées Nationaux/Art Resource, NY; **181,** T, Réunion des Musées Nationaux/Art Resource, NY; M, Bridgeman Art Library; B, The Granger Collection; **182,** Background, © Archivo Iconografico, S.A./Corbis; Inset, Musée Marmottan/Dorling Kindersley; **183,** The Granger Collection; **184,** R, Chateau de Versailles, France, Lauros/ Giraudon/Bridgeman Art Library; L, Réunion des Musées Nationaux/Art Resource, NY; **185,** L, The Granger Collection; R, Royalty-Free/Corbis; **186,** © Archivo Iconografico, S.A./ Corbis; **187,** T, The Granger Collection; B, © Archivo Iconografico, S.A./Corbis; **188,** Inset, Bettmann/Corbis; Background, Bildarchiv der Osterreichische Nationalbibliothek; **189,** The Granger Collection; **190,** L, Victoria & Albert Museum/Art Resource; **190–191,** Bridgeman Art Library; Background, T, Russ Lappa; Background, B, Russ Lappa; **191,** Inset, L, John Heseltine/ Corbis; Inset, M, Francis G. Mayer/Corbis; R, Dorling Kindersley; **192,** L, Kurpfalzisches Museum, Heidelberg, Germany/The Bridgeman Art Library; R, Museum of Tropinin and His Contemporaries, Moscow, Russia/Bridgeman Art Library; M, © Archivo Iconografico, S.A./Corbis; **194,** Background, © Archivo Iconografico, S.A./ Corbis; TL, Zuma/Corbis; BL, Reuters/ Corbis; **195,** L, The Granger Collection; R, The Granger Collection; **196,** Joe Sohm/Chromosohm/VOA; **197,** SuperStock, Inc.; **198,** L, National Portrait Gallery, Smithsonian Institution/ Art Resource, NY; M, Reunion des Musees Nationaux/Art Resource; R, © The Corcoran Gallery of Art/CORBIS; **199,** Bridgeman Art Library; **200,**

Background, The Granger Collection; **202,** Inset, Bettmann/Corbis; **202–203,** Bettmann/Corbis; **203,** Inset, L, Bettmann/Corbis; Inset, R, Hulton/Getty Images, Inc.; Background, T, Library of Congress; **204,** The Granger Collection; **205,** T, Steve Artley; B, British Library, London, UK/Bridgeman Art Library; **206,** R, Christie's Images/Corbis; L, The Granger Collection; **207,** Corbis

Chapter Six
208–209, Giraudon/Art Resource, NY; **209,** T, Musee de L'Histoire Vivante, Montreuil, France, Archives Charmet/Bridgeman Art Library; M, Erich Lessing/Art Resource, NY; B, Scala/Art Resource, NY; **210,** T, Erich Lessing/Art Resource, NY; B, The Granger Collection, NY; **211,** Snark/Art Resource, NY; **212,** TR, Giraudon/Art Resource, NY; B, Musee de la Ville de Paris, Musee Carnavalet, Paris, France, Archives Charmet/Bridgeman Art Library; TL, Musee du Ranquet, Clermont-Ferrand, France/Giraudon/Bridgeman Art Library; **213,** Musee Carnavalet, Paris, France, Lauros/Giraudon/Bridgeman Art Library; **214,** Background, Chateau de Versailles, France/Bridgeman Art Library; Inset, Giraudon/Art Resource, NY; **215,** RÈunion des MusÈes Nationaux/Art Resource; **216,** Réunion des Musées Nationaux/Art Resource, NY; **217,** (c) Judith Miller/Dorling Kindersley/Bill & Myrtle Aquilino; **218,** Background, Chateau de Versailles, France, Giraudon/Bridgeman Art Library; Inset, AKG Images; **221,** Giraudon/Art Resource, NY; **222,** Musee de la Ville de Paris, Musee Carnavalet, Paris, France, Giraudon/Bridgeman Art Library; **223,** The Art Archive/Bibliothèque des Arts Décoratifs Paris/Dagli Orti; **224,** Leonard de Selva/CORBIS; **225,** Giraudon/Art Resource, NY; **226,** L, Musee de la Ville de Paris, Musee Carnavalet, Paris, France, Giraudon/Bridgeman Art Library; R, The Art Archive/Musée Carnavalet Paris/Dagli Orti; M, Hulton Archive/Getty Images; **227,** TL, Hulton-Deutsch Collection/Corbis; BL, Musee de la Revolution Francaise, Vizille, France/Bridgeman Art Library; R, Max Alexander/Dorling Kindersley Media Library; **228,** T, British Library, London, UK/Bridgeman Art Library; B, Erich Lessing/Art Resource, NY; **229,** T, Réunion des Musées Nationaux/Art Resource, NY; B, Erich Lessing/Art Resource, NY; **230,** T, Scala/Art Resource, NY; B, Private Collection/Bridgeman Art Library; **231,** Giraudon/

Art Resource, NY; **233,** Scala/Art Resource, NY; **234,** Musee des Beaux-Arts, Rouen, France Lauros/Giraudon/Bridgeman Art Library; **235,** Giraudon/Art Resource, NY; **236,** Bibliotheque Nationale, Paris, France, Archives Charmet/Bridgeman Art Library; **238,** Giraudon/Art Resource, NY; **239,** B, Anders Blomqvist/Lonely Planet Images; TL, Christie's Images/CORBIS; TR, © Sovfoto/Eastfoto; **240,** Cleveland Musuem of Art; **241,** B, Private Collection/Bridgeman Art Library; T, © Riyadh Biji/Reuters/Corbis; **242,** R, The Fotomas Index; L, Giraudon/Art Resource, NY; **243,** Giraudon/Art Resource, NY

Chapter Seven
244–245, © NRM/Pictorial Collection/SSPL/The Image Works; **245,** T, National Railway Museum/Science and Society Picture Library; M, Bettman/CORBIS; B, Austrian Archives/CORBIS; **246,** NRM/SSPL/The Image Works; **247,** Time Life Pictures/Getty Images; **248,** Inset, Bettmann/CORBIS; B, The Granger Collection, New York; **249,** photolibrary; **250,** L, Fine Art Photographic Library, London/Art Resource, NY; R, National Railway Museum/Science and Society Picture Library; **251,** Science Museum/SSPL; **254,** Mary Evans Picture Library; **255,** Hulton Archive/Getty Images; **257,** T, Mary Evans Picture Library; B, Manchester Archives and Local Studies; **258,** Museum of London; **259,** Hulton-Deutsch Collection/CORBIS; **260,** Hulton-Deutsch Collection/CORBIS; **261,** B, The Granger Collection, New York; T, Fine Art Photographic Library/Art Resource, NY; **262,** L, Topham/The Image Works; R, The Stapleton Collection/Bridgeman Art Library; **264,** B, Austrian Archives/CORBIS; T, The Granger Collection, New York; **265,** T, J. Halaska/Photo Researchers, Inc. B, Courtesy Judi Pinkham; **266,** L, akg-images; R, Mary Evans Picture Library; **267,** T, Peter Titmuss/Alamy; B, The Art Archive/Museo Historico Nacional Buenos Aires/Dagli Orti; **268,** NRM/Pictorial Collection/SSPL/The Image Works; **269,** Image Select/Art Resource, NY

Chapter Eight
270–271, The Art Archive/Simon Bolivar Amphitheatre Mexico/Dagli Orti; **271,** T, Coleccion Museo Nacional de Columbia, Bogota; M, Musee des Tissus de Lyon/Pierre Verrier/Museum-Images 2003; BR, The Granger Collection, New York; **272,** Hadtorteneti

Muzeum, Budapest, Hungary/Archives Charmet/Bridgeman Art Library International; **274,** R, Igor Ursic/Chancery of HRH Crown Prince Alexander/The Royal Palace in Belgrade; L, Igor Ursic/Chancery of HRH Crown Prince Alexander/The Royal Palace in Belgrade; **276,** R, Musée des Tissus de Lyon/Pierre Verrier/Museum-Images 2003; L, North Wind Picture Archive; **277,** Musee de la Ville de Paris, Musee Carnavalet, Paris, France, Lauros/Giraudon/Bridgeman Art Library; **278,** ullstein bild/The Granger Collection, New York; **279,** L, Private Collection, Archives Charmet/Bridgeman Art Library; M, ullstein bild/The Granger Collection, New York; R, Louvre, Paris, France/Bridgeman Art Library International; Background, ullstein bild/The Granger Collection, New York; **280,** Scala/Art Resource, NY; **281,** The Granger Collection, New York; **282,** B, HIP/Art Resource, NY; T, Musee du Petit Palais, Paris, France/Bridgeman Art Library International; **283,** L, The Art Archive/Museo Nacional Bogota/Dagli Orti; R, Coleccion Museo Nacional de Columbia, Bogota; **284,** Chateau de Versailles, France/Bridgeman Art Library International; **285,** Bettmann/CORBIS; **287,** TM, Bettmann/CORBIS; TL, The Granger Collection, New York; B, The Granger Collection, New York; TR, The Art Archive/Archaeological and Ethnological Museum Quito Ecuador/Dagli Orti; **288,** The Art Archive/Miramare Museum Trieste/Dagli Orti (A); **289,** North Wind Picture Archives; **290,** North Wind Picture Archives; **291,** T, Reuters/Corbis; M, The Art Archive/Bibliothéque des Art Décoratifs Paris/Marc Charmet; B, Popular Book Co. Ltd.; **292,** T, age fotostock/SuperStock; B, The Art Archive/Simon Bolivar; **293,** akg-images

Chapter Nine
296–297, Photo by Lewis W. Hine/George Eastman House/Getty Images; **297,** MR, Mary Evans/The Women's Library; BR, © SSPL/The Image Works; TR, © Jacqui Hurst/CORBIS; **299,** Mary Evans Picture Library; Lewis B Hine/AKG Images; **300,** SSPL/The Image Works; **301,** B, Mary Evans Picture Library; T, SSPL/The Image Works; **302,** L, © SSPL/The Image Works; MR, The Art Archive/Dagli Orti; TR, © Michael Holford; BR, © ScienceMuseum,London/HIP/The Image Works; **303,** Hulton-Deutsch Collection/Corbis; **304,** Library of Congress; **305,** Background, Topham/The Image

Works; Inset, Bettmann/Corbis; **306,** Bettmann/Corbis; **307,** Hulton-Deutsch Collection/Corbis; **309,** The Art Archive/Musée de l'Affiche Paris/Dagli Orti; **310,** Inset, The Advertising Archives; R, Leland J. Prater/Corbis; **310–311,** © SSPL/The Image Works; **311,** TL, © Scala/Art Resource, NY; B, Siri Schwartzman/Prentice Hall; TR, © Michael Nicholson/CORBIS; M, Science Museum/Science & Society Picture Library; **312,** L, Underwood & Underwood/Corbis; R, Mary Evans/The Women's Library; **313,** B, Corbis; T, Museum of London/Topham-HIP/The Image Works; Background, Philip de Bay/Corbis; Inset, Museum of London, UK/Bridgeman Art Library; **314,** Hulton Archive Photos/Getty Images Inc.; **315,** Topham/The Image Works; **316,** TL, Tui De Roy/Minden Pictures; BL, Renee Lynn/Photo Researchers, Inc.; TR, Kevin Schafer/Corbis; BR, Oriol Alamany/Corbis; **317,** BR, The Granger Collection, New York; TR, Michael Nicholson/Corbis; TL, Mary Evans Picture Library; Inset, ML, Kevin Schafer/CORBIS; Inset, BL, © Tony Arruza/CORBIS; Inset, TL, © Tom Brakefield/Superstock; **318,** Underwood & Underwood/Corbis; **319,** Albert Bierstadt (American, 1830–1902) Hetch Hetchy Canyon Oil on canvas, 1875 Gift of Mrs. E. H. Sawyer and Mrs. A. L. Williston; Mount Holyoke College Art Museum, South Hadley, Massachusetts; **320,** Archivo Iconografico, S.A./Corbis; **321,** TR, Erich Lessing/Art Resource, NY; BR, Bettmann/Corbis; BL, Private Collection, Archives Charmet/Bridgeman Art Library; TL, Thomas Jefferson University; **322,** Erich Lessing/Art Resource, NY; **323,** BL, Art Resource; T, Art Resource; BR, © Superstock Inc./Superstock; **324,** Dave King (c) Dorling Kindersley, Courtesy of The Science Museum, London; **325,** Private Collection/The Bridgeman Art Library; **326,** R, © Christie's Images/SuperStock; L, © Jacqui Hurst/CORBIS; **327,** Copyright © North Wind Picture Archives/North Wind Picture Archives—All rights reserved

Chapter Ten
328–329, AKG Images; **329,** T, Judith Miller Archive/Dorling Kindersley; M, Istituto Mazziniano/Museo Risorgimento, Genova; B, Andy Crawford/Dorling Kindersley; **330,** L, Index Stock Imagery, Inc.; R, Judith Miller Archive/Dorling Kindersley; **331,** Deutsches Historiches Museum; **332,** Background, AKG Images; Inset,

Deutsches Historiches Museum; **334,** L, PPP/Popperfoto/Retrofile; R, Alison Harris/Dorling Kindersley; **335,** The Granger Collection, New York; **336,** Mary Evans Picture Library/WEIMAR ARCHIVE; **337,** AKG Images; **338,** L, Alinari/Art Resource, NY; R, Istituto Mazziniano/Museo Risorgimento, Genova; **339,** L, © Istituto per la Storia del Risorgimento Italiano; R, © Istituto per la Storia del Risorgimento Italiano; **340,** TM, Private Collection, Ken Welsh/Bridgeman Art Library; TR, Alinari/Art Resource, NY; TL, Private Collection, Alinari/Bridgeman Art Library; B, The Granger Collection, NY; **341,** Alinari/Art Resource, NY; **342,** L, Private Collection, Archives Charmet/ Bridgeman Art Library; **343,** R, Karl Shone/Dorling Kindersley; **346,** Mary Evans Picture Library; **347,** B, Central Press/Getty Images; T, ANJA NIEDRINGHAUS/AFP/Getty Images; **348,** (c) 1999 North Wind Picture; **349,** B, Private Collection/Bridgeman Art Library; T, Andy Crawford/Dorling Kindersley; **350,** HIP/Art Resource, NY; **351,** The Granger Collection, New York; **352,** B, Snark/Art Resource, NY; T, Mary Evans Picture Library; **354,** Bettmann/Corbis; **355,** B, Granger Collection, NY; T, Musée Carnavalet Paris/Dagli Orti/The Art Archive; **356,** T, Giraudon/Art Resource, NY; B, AKG Images; **357,** Greater London Council, UK/Bridgeman Art Library

Chapter Eleven

358–359, Blackburn Museum and Art Gallery, Lancashire, UK/Bridgeman Art Library; **359,** T, AKG Images; M, By permission of People's History Museum; B, © Bettmann/CORBIS; **360,** L, Hulton Archive/Getty Images; R, Victoria & Albert Museum, London/ Art Resource, NY; **361,** (C) THE BRIDGEMAN ART LIBRARY; **362,** R, AKG Images; MR, Palace of Westminster, London, UK,/Bridgeman Art Library; L, Corbis; ML, AKG Images; **363,** L, Private Collection/Bridgeman Art Library; M, Mary Evans Picture Library; R, PA/EMPICS; **364,** Bettmann/Corbis; **365,** Anti-Slavery International; **366,** Mary Evans Picture Library; **367,** T, By permission of People's History Museum; B, TUC Library Collections, London Metropolitan University; **368,** MR, The Illustrated London News Picture Library, London, UK/ Bridgeman Art Library; TR, Holt Studios Int./Photo Researchers, Inc.; Background, L, Miki Duisterhof/Getty Images, Inc.; BR, Trustees of the Watts Gallery, Compton, Surrey, UK/Bridge-

man Art Library; L, Sean Sexton Collection/Corbis; **370,** B, Bradford Art Galleries and Museums, West Yorkshire, UK/Bridgeman Art Library; T, AP/ Wide World Photos; **371,** R, Erich Lessing/Art Resource, NY; L, Hulton Archive/Getty Images; **372,** Inset, Hulton Archive/Getty Images; **372–373,** Background, Hulton Archive/Getty Images; **373,** BR, Musee de la Poste, Paris, France, Archives Charmet/ BridgemanArt Library; TR, The Granger Collection, NY; **374,** Dave G. Houser/ Corbis; **375,** AKG Images; **376,** Musee National de l'Education, Rouen, France, Archives Charmet/ Bridgeman Art Library; **377,** Stockbyte/Getty Images, Inc.; **378,** BR, Smithsonian Institution/Office of Imaging, Printing, and Photographic Services; BL, American Philosophical Society; Background, American Philosophical Society; T, Kevin R. Morris/ Bohemian Nomad Picturemakers/Corbis; **379,** New-York Historical Society/ Bridgeman Art Library; **380,** L, Pajaro Valley Historical Association; M, Oakland Museum of California; R, Benjamin Franklin Reinhart, An Evening Halt-Emigrants Moving to the West in 1840, 1867, Oil on canvas, 40 x 70 in., Corcoran Gallery of Art, Washington, D.C., Gift of Mr. and Mrs. Lansdell K. Christie, 59.21; **382,** Mary Evans Picture Library; **383,** Mary Evans Picture Library/The Women's Library; **384,** T, The Granger Collection, NY; B, AKG Images; **385,** Musee de la Ville de Paris, Musee Carnavalet, Paris, France, Archives Charmet/Bridgeman Art Library

Chapter Twelve

386–387, © Hulton-Deutsch Collection/CORBIS; **387,** M, Private Collection/Bridgeman Art Library; B, Ashmolean Museum, University of Oxford, Bridgeman Art Library; T, British Library; **388,** L, Mary Evans Picture Library; R, AKG-Images; **389,** National Archives UK; **390,** Roger Viollet/ Topham/The Image Works; **391,** Hulton Archive/Getty Images, Inc.; **392,** © AKG Images; **393,** The Royal Collection (c) 2005, Her Majesty Queen Elizabeth II; **394,** T, Mary Evans Picture Library; B, AKG Images; **396,** ML, The Granger Collection; **397,** Mary Evans Picture Library; **398,** Popperfoto/Robertstock; **399,** © Mansell/Time & Life Pictures/Getty Images; **400,** L, © Corbis; All Rights Reserved; R, Ashmolean Museum, University of Oxford, Bridgeman Art Library; **401,** AKG Images; **403,** Background, Public Record

Office/HIP/The Image Works; Inset, The Granger Collection; **404,** Hulton/Getty Images; **405,** R, British Library; L, Hulton Archive/Getty Images, Inc.; **406,** Inset, R, British Library/HIP/The Image Works; L, Mary Evans Picture Library; Inset, L, Royal Armories; **406–407,** Inset T, Royal Armouries; Background T, The Art Archive/Company of Girdlers/Eileen Tweedy; **407,** R, Mary Evans Picture Library; **408,** Inset, T, AFP/Getty Images, Inc.; Inset, B, Paul A. Souders/Corbis; Background, Colin Garatt/Corbis; **410,** B, Jeff Greenberg/ The Image Works; T, Chris Sorensen Photography; **411,** R, Bridgeman Art Library; L, Popular Book Co. Ltd.; **412,** L, British Museum/HIP/The Image Works; **413,** R, Harvard-Yenching Library, Harvard University; L, Panorama Stock; **414,** Corbis; **415,** Time-Life Pictures/Getty Images, Inc.; **416,** L, Bridgeman Art Library; R, British Library/HIP/The Image Works; **417,** Topham/The Image Works; **418,** T, The Granger Collection, New York; B, Time-Life Pictures/Getty Images, Inc

Chapter Thirteen

420–421, Peter Harholdt/CORBIS; **421,** T, The Granger Collection, New York; M, photolibrary;co/Index Stock Imagery; B, SSPL/The Image Works; **422,** L, Topham/The Image Works; R, Andy Crawford (c) Dorling Kindersley; **423,** B, The Art Archive/British Museum; **424–425,** Réunion des Musées Nationaux/Art Resource, NY; **425,** R, From the website of the National Diet Library (http,// www.ndl.go.jp/); L, trove;net/Index Stock Imagery; **426,** T, Old Japan Picture Library; **427,** B, Rykoff Collection/ CORBIS; **428,** Mary Evans Picture Library; **429,** B, Crown Agents; T, Mary Evans Picture Library; **430,** R, Courtesy National Archives, photo no; 350-P-AD-3-3; L, Bettman/CORBIS; **432,** TR, Getty Images; TM, Roy Miles Fine Paintings/Bridgeman Art Library International; TL, © Horace Bristol/CORBIS; BR, Ray Moller/Dorling Kindersley © Royal Pavilion Museum and Art Galleries, Brighton; Background, Crown Agents; BL, Prentice Hall; **434,** TL, Art Gallery of Ontario, Toronto, Canada/ Bridgeman Art Library; TR, © Royalty-Free/Corbis; **436,** T, photolibrary.co/ Index Stock Imagery; B, Mary Evans Picture Library; **438,** Inset, Auckland Art Gallery Toi o Tamaki, Gift of Mr H E Partridge, 1915; Background, Historical Picture Archive/CORBIS; **439,** L, Robert Frerck/Odyssey/Chicago © Banco de Mexico Diego Rivera

Museum Trust; R, © Royalty-Free/Corbis; **440,** The Art Archive/National History Museum Mexico City/Dagli Orti; **441,** R, Private Collection/Bridgeman Art Library International; L, The Art Archive/National History Museum Mexico City/Dagli Orti; **443,** Bettman/ CORBIS; **444,** BL, Image courtesy Smithsonian Institution; T, Image courtesy Smithsonian Institution; BR, SSPL/ The Image Works; Background, Corbis; **446,** T, Dorling Kindersley; B, © Werner Forman/CORBIS; **447,** © Royalty-Free/Corbis; **448,** B, The Art Archive/National History Museum Mexico City/Dagli Orti; T, © Asian Art & Archaeology, Inc./CORBIS

Chapter Fourteen

452–453, The Art Archive/Imperial War Museum; **453,** T, © C Squared Studios/Getty Images; M, Andy Crawford/Dorling Kindersley; B, SSPL/The Image Works; **454,** L, © Bettmann/ CORBIS; R, ULLSTEIN - Ullstein Bild; **456–457,** © CORBIS; **457,** The Granger Collection, New York; **458,** John McCutchson/The Chicago Tribune, 1914 Photo, Ken Karp; **459,** Jacques Moreau/Archives Larousse, Paris, France/Bridgman Art Library; **460,** L, © Hulton-Deutsch Collection/ CORBIS; R, Imperial War Museum, London/Dorling Kindersley; **461,** Snark/Art Resource, NY; **462,** R, © ULLSTEIN-Zennig; L, © SSPL/The Image Works; **462–463,** Foto Marburg/Art Resource, NY; **463,** TR, ENA/ Popperfoto/Robertstock/Retrofile; BR, © The Tank Museum; **465,** © Bettmann/CORBIS; **466,** Mary Evans Picture Library; **467,** L, © CORBIS; R, The Granger Collection, New York; **468,** B, Snark/Art Resource, NY; T, © David Pollack/CORBIS; **469,** © Hulton-Deutsch Collection/CORBIS; **470,** B, The Granger Collection, New York; T, © A. R. Coster/Hulton Archive/Getty Images; **471,** © CORBIS; **472,** R, SSPL/The Image Works; L, © Bettmann/CORBIS; **473,** B, © CORBIS; T, © Bettmann/ CORBIS; **476,** SSPL/The Image Works; **477,** L, Andy Crawford/Dorling Kindersley; R, akg-images; **478,** L, C.Walker/ Topham/The Image Works; R, AP Photo/Wonders Exhibit; **479,** © Hulton Archive/Getty Images; **480,** Inset, Christie's Images, London, UK/The Bridgeman Art Library; Background, akg-images; **481,** L, Novosti/The Bridgeman Art Library; R, Topham/The Image Works; **483,** © Topical Press Agency/Hulton Archive/Getty Images; **484,** L, © Bettmann/CORBIS; M, Snark/Art Resource, NY; R, Imperial War

Museum, London/Dorling Kindersley; **485,** L, The Granger Collection, New York; R, © Bettmann/CORBIS; **486,** T, The Imperial War Museum, London; B, C.Walker/Topham/The Image Works

Chapter Fifteen
488–489, Corbis; **489,** T, Frank Nowikowski; M, Bridgeman Art Library; B, Martin Plomer (c) Dorling Kindersley; **490,** R, Courtesy Susan Frost; L, Fernando Bueno/Getty Images; **491,** TL, Bettmann/Corbis; Center L, Bettmann/Corbis; Center, R, Bettmann/Corbis; BR, Bettmann/Corbis; BL Grouping, Center, Bettmann/Corbis; BL Groupling, L', Bettmann/Corbis; TR, Bettmann/Corbis; BL Grouping, R, Bettmann/Corbis; **492,** Bettmann/Corbis; **493,** Library of Congress; **494,** Frank Nowikowski; **495,** B, (detail) photograph © The Detroit Institute of Arts, 1995; Palacio Nacional stairway, Mexico City © Dirk Bakker, photographer; T, Time Life Pictures/Getty Images Inc.; **496,** R, Jackson Davis Collection/University of Virginia Library; L, Image courtesy of The Advertising Archives; **497,** National Library of South Africa; **498,** T, Bartko-Reher-GbR; B, Dept of Historical Papers/William Cullen Library; **498–499,** World-Sat International Inc.; **499,** B, Dept of Historical Papers/William Cullen Library; R, Corbis; **500,** The Granger Collection; **502,** Library of Congress; **503,** Corbis; **506,** Bettmann/Corbis; **507,** T, Corbis; B, Panorama Stock; **508,** The Granger Collection; **509,** Bettmann/CORBIS; **510,** Sovfoto; **512,** Time Life Pictures/Getty Images; **513,** B, Mansell Collection/Getty Images, Inc.; T, Random House Publishing Group; **514,** DAP/The Image Works; **515,** Hulton/Getty Images, Inc.; **516,** L, Bettmann/Corbis; R, The Granger Collection; **517,** B, The Granger Collection; T, Library of Congress; **518,** T, Center for American History/University of Texas; B, Bettmann/Corbis; **519,** DPA/The Image Works

Chapter Sixteen
520–521, Time-Life Getty Images, Inc. **521,** T, Prentice Hall; M, Library of Congress; B, David King Collection; **522,** © Bettmann/Corbis; **523,** R, Culver Pictures, Inc.; L, Drug Enforcement Administration; **524,** L, Underwood & Underwood/Corbis; Inset, Library of Congress; **524–525,** Corbis; **525,** Inset, Topham/The Image Works; R, Corbis; **526,** Robertstock; **527,** Tate Gallery/Art Resource; **528,** BM, Fogg Art Museum/Harvard University/

Bridgeman Art Library; BL, Scala/Art Resource, NY; BR, Art Resource, NY; Background, Roger Viollet/Topham/The Image Works; **529,** L, Corbis; R, Dorling Kindersley; **530,** Bettmann/Corbis; **531,** The Granger Collection; **532,** L, Detroit News; R, AkG Images; **532–533,** M, Collection of the Museum of American Finance; **533,** L, © Bettmann/CORBIS; R, Mary Evans Picture Library; **534,** Inset, The Granger Collection; Background, Roger-Viollet/Topham/The Image Works; **536,** T, Mary Evans Picture Library; B, Dorling Kindersley; **537,** Time-Life/Getty Images, Inc.; **538,** L, Museum of the Revolution, Moscow/Dorling Kindersley; R, Imperial War Museum, London/Dorling Kindersley; Inset R, David King Collection; Inset L, Stefano Bianchetti/Corbis; **538–539,** Bettmann/Corbis; **539,** Bettmann/Corbis; **540,** From the Fry Collection of Italian History and Culture; By courtesy of the Department of Special Collections, General Library System, University of Wisconsin-Madison; **541,** TR, The Granger Collection; TL, Corbis; B, Time-Life/Getty Images, Inc.**542,** David King Collection; **543,** David King Collection; **544,** London Express/Getty Images; **545,** David King Colllection; **546,** Andy Crawford/Dorling Kindersley; **547,** David King Collection; **548,** David King Collection; **550,** © Corbis; **551,** Inset, Corbis; Background, Corbis; **552,** Mary Evans Picture Library; **553,** D.O.W./US Holocaust Memorial Museum; **554,** Feltz/Topham/The Image Works; **556,** L, Andy Crawford/Dorling Kindersley; R, Dorling Kindersley; **557,** T, A/P Wide World Photos; B, Drug Enforcement Administration; **558,** Corbis

Chapter Seventeen
560–561, Time Life Pictures/Getty Images; **561,** T, © Photos by Eric L. Johnson/Courtesy of the Museum of World War II, Natick MA; M, © Photos by Eric L. Johnson/Courtesy of the Museum of World War II, Natick MA; B, The Advertising Archive; **562,** R, Getty Images; L, Photo by London Express/Getty Images; **563,** R, © Photos by Eric L. Johnson/Courtesy of the Museum of World War II, Natick MA; L, Getty Images; **564,** T, © Bettmann/CORBIS; TM, © Corbis; BM, © Corbis; B, © Corbis; **565,** R, Time Life Pictures/Getty Images; L, Getty Images; **568,** L, © Wanda Beaver; R, © Museum of Flight/CORBIS; **569,** © Photos by Eric L. Johnson/Courtesy of the Museum of World War II, Natick

MA; **570,** TR, © Photos by Eric L. Johnson/Courtesy of the Museum of World War II, Natick MA; L, © Photos by Eric L. Johnson/Courtesy of the Museum of World War II, Natick MA; BR, © CORBIS; **571,** © Bettmann/CORBIS; **572,** B, © Copyright 2000 Corbis; **572–573,** Inset, © Topham/The Image Works; Background, USHMM, courtesy of Mark Chrzanowski; **574,** Panorama Stock; **575,** AP/Wide World; **576,** AP/Wide World Photos; **577,** TL, The Granger Collection, New York; TR, © Ellen Granter; **578,** R, © Corbis; All Rights Reserved; L, © Bettmann/CORBIS; **579,** L, Hulton|Archive by Getty Images; R, Hulton Archive/Getty Images; B, Geoff Dann (c) Dorling Kindersley, Courtesy of the Imperial War Museum, London; Background, © Corbis; **580,** © Corbis; All Rights Reserved; **582,** © Bettmann/CORBIS; **584,** © Topham/The Image Works; **585,** T, © CORBIS; B, © Corbis; All Rights Reserved; **586,** R, Photo courtesy of the Military & Historical Image Bank; L, AP/Wide World Photos; **587,** AP/Wide World Photos; **588,** AP/Wide World Photos; **589,** T, Time Life Pictures/Getty Images; B, Richard Klune/Corbis; **590,** R, Alfred Eisenstaedt/Time-Life Pictures/Getty Images; L, Dorling Kindersley; **591,** T, (c) Dorling Kindersley, Courtesy of Andrew L Chernack; B, Hulton Deutsch/Corbis; **592,** T, Corbis; B, Library of Congress; **593,** © Bettmann/CORBIS; **594,** The Michael Barson Collection; **595,** TL, © Peter Guttman/CORBIS; TR, © Bettmann/CORBIS; B, AP/Wide World Photos; **596,** L, © Corbis; R, © Photos by Eric L. Johnson/Courtesy of the Museum of World War II, Natick MA; M, © Photos by Eric L. Johnson/Courtesy of the Museum of World War II, Natick MA; **597,** R, Hiroshima Peace Memorial Museum; L, © Photos by Eric L. Johnson/Courtesy of the Museum of World War II, Natick MA; **598,** T, © Photos by Eric L. Johnson/Courtesy of the Museum of World War II, Natick MA; B, Time Life Pictures/Getty Images

Chapter Eighteen
602–603, © Photos12;com/Polaris Images; **603,** T, © Jacques M. Chenet/CORBIS; M, Russ Lappa; B, © Bettmann/CORBIS; **604,** L, © Photos12;com/Polaris; R, Getty Images; **605,** Alamy Images; **606,** © Bettmann/CORBIS; **607,** © PATRICK ROBERT/CORBIS SYGMA; **609,** TL, © KEYSTONE/GAMMA; TR, © Bettmann/CORBIS; Background, © Bettmann/

CORBIS; BR, © AP/Wide World Photos; **610,** L, © Peter Turnley/CORBIS; R, © Bob Rowan; Progressive Image/CORBIS; **611,** © AP/Wide World Photos; **612,** Copyright © Courtesy Everett Collection/Everett Collection; **613,** © Reuters/Corbis; **614,** B, © David Seymour/Magnum Photos; T, Library of Congress; **615,** T, Reprinted from Electrical Merchandising, July 1957; Courtesy The State Museum of Pennsylvania; B, © Bettmann/CORBIS; **616,** L, © Corbis; R, © AP/Wide World Photos; **617,** © Bob Adelman/Magnum Photos; **618,** © Photos12; com/Polaris; **619,** © Brian Rose; **620,** © Topham/The Image Works; **621,** B, © Horace Bristol/CORBIS; TR, Imatake Shichiro/Prentice Hall; **622,** © Charles Gupton/Getty Images; **623,** L, © Baldwin H. Ward & Kathryn C. Ward/CORBIS; R, © Dave Bartruff/CORBIS; **624,** © Bettmann/CORBIS; **625,** R, Collection of the International Institute of Social History, Amsterdam; L, © GAMMA; **626–627,** BR, © Bettmann/CORBIS; **628,** © CORBIS; **630,** L, © Hulton/Getty; R, © Bettmann/CORBIS; **631,** © Time Life Pictures/Getty Images; **632,** BR, © AP/Wide World Photos; TR, © AP/Wide World Photos; BL, © Nathan Benn/CORBIS; TL, © Prentice Hall School Division; **632–633,** Background, © Bettmann/CORBIS; **634,** Russ Lappa/Prentice Hall; **635,** © Dirck Halstead/Getty Images; **636,** L, © ANTICOLI LIVIO/GAMMA; R, © AP/Wide World Photo; **637,** T, AP Photo; B, © HIRES CHIP/GAMMA; **638,** L, © AP/Wide World Photo; R, Russ Lappa; **639,** © Bettmann/CORBIS; **640,** Punch; **641,** © Pascal Le Segretain/CORBIS SYGMA; **642,** R, Time Life Pictures/Getty Images; L, © POLOGNE GDANSK 0880/GAMMA; **643,** Ricky Wong/Bloomberg News;/Landov; **645,** T, © Liba Taylor/CORBIS; B, © Jacques Langevin/CORBIS SYGMA; **646,** © Dave Bartruff/CORBIS; **647,** TR, TOLES © 2002 The Buffalo News; Reprinted with permission of UNIVERSAL PRESS SYNDICATE; All rights reserved; BR, © ANTICOLI LIVIO/GAMMA; L, © Bettmann/CORBIS; **648,** © Photos12;com/Polaris Images; **649,** © Martyn Goddard/CORBIS

Chapter Nineteen
650–651, Alexis Orand/Gamma; **651,** M, PhotoDisc/Getty Images; T, Andrew England/AP/Wide World Photo; B, AP/Wide World Photos; **652,** L, Henri Cartier-Bresson/Magnum Photos; R, AP/Wide World Photos; **654,**

Bettmann/Corbis; **655,** Phoenix Art Museum, Arizona, Gift of George P; Bickford/Bridgeman Art Library; **656,** Mike Goldwater/Network Photographers; **658,** L, Howard Sochurek//Time Life Pictures/Getty Images; R, Bernard Napthine/Lonely Planet Images; **659,** Christopher Furlong/Getty Images; **660,** L, EPA/Empics; R, AP Photo/Sakchai Lalit; **662,** R, Corbis; L, M & E Bernheim/Woodfin Camp & Associates; **663,** Fredrik Naumann/Panos Pictures; **664,** Christian Sappa/Network Photographers; **666,** Keystone/Getty Images; **667,** Ben Curtis/AP/Wide World Photos; **668,** Eric Miller/Panos Pictures; **669,** T, © Bettmann/CORBIS; B, Mark Kauffman/Time Life Pictures/Getty Images; **670,** L, Bettmann/Corbis; R, Patrick Ben Luke Syder/Lonely Planet Images; **672,** LANGE JACQUES/PARIS MATCH/GAMMA; B, Marco Di Lauro/Getty Images; T, Hassan Massoudy/ARS/Banque d'Images, ADAGP/Art Resource, NY; **674,** AP/Wide World Photos; **676,** R, Bettmann/Corbis; BL, Corbis; TL, Corbis; **677,** T, Mindaugas Kulbis/AP/Wide World Photos; BL, Christopher Furlong/Getty Images; BR, AP/Wide World Photos; **678,** T, Henri Cartier-Bresson/Magnum Photos; B, EPA/Empics; **679,** EPA/Empics

Chapter Twenty
680–681, © SAZY LAURENT/GAMMA; **681,** T, Prentice Hall; M, © Graeme Williams/South Photographs; B, Corbis; **682,** Les Stone/Corbis Sygma; **683,** TURESSON/PRESSENS BILD/GAMMA; **685,** OTHoNIEL/GAMMA; **686,** Dieter Telemans/Panos Pictures; **687,** Ian Berry/Magnum Photos; **688,** TL, David Turnley/Corbis; BL, Frankenfeld/SOUTH LIGHT/GAMMA; R, UN Photo Library; **690,** Espen Rasmussen/AFP/Getty Images; **691,** B, David Turnley/Corbis; T, Owen Franken/Corbis; **692,** Nasser Shiyoukhi/Ap/Wide World Photos; **693,** Ziv Koren/Polaris Images; **694,** Ap/Wide World Photos; **695,** R, AP Photo/Jacqueline Arzt; L, QUIDU NOEL/GAMMA; **696,** Peter Jordan/Network; **697,** ERIK DE CASTRO/Reuters/Corbis; **698,** Ian Berry/Magnum Photos; **699,** MICHAEL EVSTAFIEV/AFP/Getty Images; **700,** R, Carlson © 2004 Milwaukee Journal Sentinel/UPI; L, © SAZY LAURENT/GAMMA

Chapter Twenty-One
702–703, Tischler Fotografen/Peter Arnold, Inc.; **703,** B, © Corbis; T, Prentice Hall; M, EVARISTO SA/AFP/Getty Images; **704,** L, Zed Nelson/

Panos Pictures; R, © Prentice Hall; **706,** Ron Giling/Peter Arnold, Inc.; **707,** Clive Shirley/Panos Pictures; **708,** Mark Henley/Panos Pictures; **709,** T, Granger Collecton, NY; B, Neil Ray/Art Directors & Trip Photo Library; **710,** Mark Edwards/Peter Arnold, Inc.; **711,** Liba Taylor/Panos Pictures; **712,** L, Fiona Teede-UNEP/Peter Arnold, Inc.; M, ABPL/Nigel Dennis/Animals Animals-Earth Scenes; Background, Cyril Ruoso/Minden Pictures; R, Betty Press/Panos Pictures; **713,** William Campbell/Corbis; **714,** B, Peter Turnley/Corbis; T, Jeff Widener/AP/Wide World Photos; **715,** Barry Lewis/Network; **716,** L, Eugene Hoshiko/AP/Wide World Photos; R, © Findlay Kember/Polaris; **717,** Christopher Brown/Polaris; **718,** Kapoor Baldev/Sygma/Corbis; **719,** Barriopedro, EFE/AP/Wide World Photos; **720,** Janet Jarman/Corbis; **721,** R, Russell Gordon/Das Fotoarchiv/Peter Arnold, Inc.; L, David Rochkind/Polaris; **722,** L, Paulo Santos-Interfoto/AP/Wide World Photos; R, Paulo Santos/AP Wide World Photos; **723,** Anders Gunnartz/Peter Arnold, Inc.; **724,** Dado Galdieri/AP/Wide World Photos; **725,** B, Jose Luis Magana/AP/Wide World Photos; T, © Reuters/CORBIS; **726,** T, Rafael Wollmann/Gamma; B, ALI BURAFI/AFP/Getty Images; **727,** Inset, Steve Northup/Timepix/Time Life Pictures/Getty Images; Background, Corbis; **728,** R, Image Port/Index Stock Imagery, Inc.; L, © Bettmann/CORBIS; **729,** © Dennis Galante/Corbis; **730,** Jorgen Schytte/Peter Arnold, Inc.; **731,** China Photos/Reuters/Corbis

Chapter Twenty-Two
732–733, Gordon Wiltsie; **733,** M, © Matthias Kulka/CORBIS; B, NASA; T, CARE; **734,** L, AFP/Gettty Images; R, © Matthias Kulka/CORBIS; **736,** AFP/Getty Images, Inc. **738,** David Grossman/The Image Works; **740,** B, Russell Gordon/Das Fotoarchiv/Peter Arnold; T, Corel Corporation; **741,** BL, Mike Yamashita, Inc.; BR, Bananastock/Picturequest; T, Transfair USA; **742,** Paul A. Souders/Corbis; **743,** T, AFP/Getty Images, Inc.; B, © RAFIQUR RAHMAN/Reuters/Corbis; **744,** L, Getty Images, Inc.; R, CARE; **745,** Inset B, Noah Poritz/Photo Researchers, Inc.; Inset T, Photo Researchers, Inc.; Background, Caroline Penn/Corbis; **747,** T, Phil Huber/Black Star; B, Michael Newman/PhotoEdit; **748,** RUGMARK; **749,** Ron Giling/Das Fotoarchiv; **750,** AP/Wide World Photos; **752,** T, Alison Wright/The Image Works; B, Shawkat

Khan/AFP/Getty Images, Inc.; **753,** Larry Downing/Reuters/Corbis; **754,** Lynn Johnson/Aurora; **756,** T, Russell Boyce/Reuters/Corbis; B, Corbis; **758,** L, Photo Researchers; R, NASA; **759,** T, ESA/Corbis; B, Corbis; **760,** Background, Los Alamos National Laboratory/Photo Researchers, Inc.; L, Alfred Eisenstaedt/Time & Life Pictures/Getty Images; R, Bettmann/Corbis; **761,** R, Photo Researchers, Inc.; M, Photo Researchers, Inc.; L, Phototake; **762,** M, John Doebly/University of Wisconsin; R, Grant Heilman Photography; L, Jim Richardson/Corbis; **764,** Russell Boyce/Reuters/Corbis; **765,** T, Custom Medical Stock Photo, Inc.; B, CARE; **766,** T, Cartoon Stock; B, AFP/Getty Images, Inc.

Concept Connector Handbooks
768, T, Archivo Iconographica, S.A./Corbis; BL, © Pascal Le Segretain/CORBIS SYGMA; **768–769,** Musee de la Tapisserie, Bayeux, France/www.bridgeman.co.uk; **769,** Free Agents Limited/CORBIS; **784,** © Robert Frerck/Odyssey Productions, Inc.; **787,** Anders Blomqvist/Lonely Planet Images; **788,** B, National Gallery of Art; **789,** Giraudon/Art Resource, NY; **791,** AP/Wide World Photos; **792,** Corbis; **793,** Rafiqur Rahman/Reuters America LLC; **794,** Lisa Knouse Braiman/Business Week; **796,** TL, The Granger Collection, New York; TR, A. Eaton/Ancient Art & Architecture Collection; MR, Comstock/SuperStock; ML, © Michael Holford; B, V & A Museum/Art Resource; **797,** TL, National Maritime Museum; TR, Time Life Pictures/Getty Images; MR, Mary Evans Picture Library/Photo Researchers, Inc.; ML, The Pierpont Morgan Library/Art Resource, NY; B, Museu de Marinha; **798,** TL, © Michael Holford; TR, Alfred Eisenstaedt/Time & Life Pictures/Getty Images; M, The Art Archive/Dagli Orti; B, © ScienceMuseum,London/HIP/The Image Works; **799,** T, Photo Researchers, Inc.; M, Getty Images; BR, ESA/Corbis; BL, Chris Sorensen Photography; **800,** © James Hill; **802,** TL, Versailles, châteaux de Versailles et de Trianon/RMN/Art Resource, NY; R, Museum of Tropinin and His Contemporaries, Moscow, Russia/Bridgeman Art Library; **803,** TR, © Corbis; BR, Peter Jordan/Network; L, © Dave Bartruff/CORBIS; **804,** T, Gunter Marx; B, The Granger Collection, New York; **806,** TL, Scala/Art Resource, NY; TR, © Fitzwilliam Museum, University of Cambridge, UK; BL, © Archivo Iconografico, S.A./COR-

BIS; BR, Erich Lessing/Art Resource, NY; **807,** TL, Art Resource/The Museum of Modern Art; TM, Copyright ARS, NY;/Art Resource, NY; TR, © Historical Picture Archive/CORBIS; B, © Jeff Greenberg/eStockPhoto

Text
Grateful acknowledgment is made to the following for copyrighted material:

ACT, Inc.
Excerpt from "Writing Test Scores" from *www.act.org.* Copyright © 2005 by Act, Inc. All rights reserved. Reproduced by permission.

Ardis Publishing, A Division of The Overlook Press
Excerpt from "Requiem" by Anna Akhmatova, translated by Robin Kemball from *Anna Akhmatova, Selected Poems* edited by Walter Arndt. Copyright 1974 by Robin Kemball.

Cambridge University
Excerpt from "Chapter XVI, Passive Resistance" from *Hind Swaraj And Other Writings* by Mohandas K. Gandhi, edited by Anthony J. Parel, ed. © in the editorial matter, Anthony J. Parel, 1997. Reprinted by permission.

The Clarendon Press
Excerpts from "The Republic" by Plato from *Greek Philosophy: Thales To Aristotle, Second Edition, Revised and Expanded* edited by Reginald E. Allen. Copyright © 1966, 1985 by Reginald E. Allen. All rights reserved.

The College Board
Excerpt from "The SAT Scoring Guide" from *www.collegeboard.com.* Reproduced by permission. Copyright © 2005 collegeboard.com. All rights reserved.

Farrar, Straus and Giroux, LLC.
Excerpt from "Book Twenty: The Ranging of Powers" from *The Iliad* by Homer, translated by Robert Fitzgerald. Copyright © 1974 by Robert Fitzgerald. All rights reserved under International and Pan-American Copyright Conventions.

Heinemann Educational Books Ltd., A division of Reed Elsevier Inc.
Excerpt from "Attempt to Stop Invaders with Words" from *On Trial For My Country* by Stanlake Samkange. © Stanlake Samkange, 1966. All rights reserved.

ACKNOWLEDGMENTS

Houghton Mifflin Company
Poems: "Proudly stands the city of Mexico-Tenochtitlan..." from *Stolen Continents* by Ronald Wright. Copyright © 1992 by Ronald Wright. Reprinted by permission of Houghton Mifflin Company. All rights reserved.

Indiana University Press
Song: "Our homes and humble dwellings..." from *The Mexican Corrido as a Source for Interpretive Study of Modern Mexico (1870–1950)* by Merle E. Simmons. Copyright © 1957 by Merle E. Simmons.

New Directions Publishing Corporation
"Hermandad" by Octavio Paz and "Brotherhood" translated by Eliot Weinberger from *The Collected Poems of Octavio Paz: 1957–1987* copyright © 1986 by Octavio Paz and Eliot Weinberger. Reprinted by permission of New Directions Publishing Corp. All rights reserved.

Oxford University Press, Inc.
Poem: "This is the common good, for the polis and the whole demos..." by Tyrtaeus of Sparta from *Ancient Greece: A Political, Social, And Cultural History* edited by Sarah B. Pomeroy, Stanley Burstein, Walter Donlan, and Jennifer T. Roberts. Copyright © 1999 by Oxford University Press, Inc. All rights reserved.

The Estate of Paulette Goddard Remarque c/o Richard Kay/Pryor, Cashamn, Sherman & Flynn
Excerpt from *All Quiet on the Western Front* by Erich Maria Remarque. "Im Western Nichts Neues," copyright 1928 by Ullstein A.G.; Copyright renewed © 1956 by Erich Maria Remarque. "All Quiet On The Western Front," copyright 1929, 1930 by Little, Brown and Company; copyright renewed 1957, 1958 by Erich Maria Remarque. Reprinted by permission. All rights reserved.

The University of Chicago Press
Excerpt from "Antigone" by Sophocles, E. Wyckoff, Trans., in *The Complete Tragedies*, D. Grene & R. Lattimore, eds. Copyright © 1954 by The University of Chicago Press. Reprinted by permission. All rights reserved.

University of California Press, Inc.
Excerpt from "The Bronze Horseman" by Alexander Pushkin, translated by Waclaw Lednicki from *Waclaw Lednicki, Pushkin's Bronze Horseman* (Berkeley, CA: University of California Press, 1955).

The University of Oklahoma Press
"There was then no sickness; . . ." from *The Book of Chilam Balam of Chumayel,* by Ralph L. Roys. Copyright © 1967 by The University of Oklahoma Press. Reprinted by permission. All rights reserved.

Vintage Books, A Division of Random House, Inc.
Excerpt from "New Year's Address" from *Open Letters: Selected Writings, 1965–1990* by Václav Havel, selected and edited by Paul Wilson. Preface and translations copyright © 1985, 1988, 1991 by Paul Wilson. Czech originals copyright by Václav Havel. All rights reserved under International and Pan-American Copyright Conventions.

Warner/Chappell Music, Inc., A Division of Warner Brothers Music
Excerpt from "Brother Can You Spare a Dime?" lyrics by E.Y. Harburg & Jay Gorney. Copyright Warner Bros., Inc

W. W. Norton & Company, Inc.
Excerpt from "On Cruelty and Clemency: Whether It Is Better to Be Loved or Feared" by Niccolo Machiavelli from *The Prince: A Norton Critical Edition, Second Edition* translated by Robert M. Adams. Translation copyright © 1992, 1977 by W.W. Norton & Company, Inc.

Note: Every effort has been made to locate the copyright owner of material reprinted in this book. Omissions brought to our attention will be corrected in subsequent editions.

ACKNOWLEDGMENTS